McGRAW-HILL DICTIONARY OF ART

McGRAW-HILL

● McGRAW-HILL BOOK COMPANY   NEW YORK

DICTIONARY OF ART

Edited by
BERNARD S. MYERS
Consulting Editor, *Encyclopedia of World Art*
Editor, *Encyclopedia of Painting*
Formerly New York University, Rutgers University,
University of Texas, The City University of New York

Assistant Editor
SHIRLEY D. MYERS
Assistant Editor, *Encyclopedia of Painting*

Volume 3   GREECE — MASTER F.V.B.

TORONTO   LONDON   SYDNEY   JOHANNESBURG

Library of Congress Catalog Card Number: 68-26314
International Standard Book Number: 07-079724-2
Printed in Italy by Arnoldo Mondadori, Officine Grafiche - Verona
Illustration credits are listed in Volume 5.

ADVISORY COMMITTEE

Harry Bober, *Institute of Fine Arts, New York University*
Otto Brendel, *Columbia University*
W. G. Constable, *formerly Curator of Paintings, Boston Museum of Fine Arts*
Henry-Russell Hitchcock *Institute of Fine Arts, New York University*
† Robert Treat Paine, Jr., *Curator of Oriental Art, Boston Museum of Fine Arts*
J. W. Pope-Hennessy, *Director, Victoria and Albert Museum, London*

McGRAW-HILL STAFF

Executive Editor: David I. Eggenberger
Director of Design and Production: Gerard G. Mayer
Associate Editor: Beatrice Carson
Editing Managers: Tobia L. Worth; Margaret Lamb
Research Editor: Donald Goddard
Proof Editor: Gordon L. Gidley
Administrative Editor: M. Barat Kerr Sparks
Bibliographers: Sally Evans; Donald Goddard; Marian Williams
Editorial Assistant: Ethel M. Jacobson
Copy Editors and Proofreaders: Monica Bayley; Olive Collen; Beatrice Eckes
Art and Design: David Ross-Robertson; Edward Fox; Ann Bonardi

ART AND DESIGN STAFF

Picture Editor: Giorgio Marcolungo

Art Director: Fiorenzo Giorgi

Assistants: Massimo Bucchi
Raffaele Curiel
Isabella Piombo
Adolfo Segattini
Maurizio Turazzi

Line Drawings Prepared by: 5 Lines Studio - Rome
Design Italiana - Milan

G

GREECE. Greek art proper (as opposed to Mycenaean art, which was produced by people who were also ethnically Greeks) begins about 1000 B.C. with the first appearance of the style of vase painting that is called proto-Geometric. During the century in which this style flourished (1000–900 B.C.) a number of the features that were to characterize Greek art throughout its entire existence were already becoming apparent. First and foremost was the intense feeling for composition and structure. Whereas much of the decoration of Minoan and Mycenaean pottery had consisted of sprawling freehand designs, the makers of proto-Geometric pottery used rigid constructions of parallel dark and light bands scaled in size according to their position on the vase. The light ground bands were often filled with geometric patterns, especially concentric semicircles drawn with a compass. *See* AEGEAN ART.

The most important center for the production of proto-Geometric pottery was at Athens; the style also appears elsewhere in Greece and in Asia Minor. Until about 600 B.C. painted pottery is the only material of which there are sufficient remains on which to base a chronological framework for the development of Greek aesthetic sensibilities. Hence archaeologists have named the earliest periods after the prevalent styles of vase painting. *See* ATHENS: ANCIENT; VASE PAINTING, GREEK.

Geometric period (ca. 900–725 B.C.). The Geometric style of Greek vase painting grew naturally out of the proto-Geometric. Athens was once again the leader in the development of the style, although it appears in most other parts of Greece, the Aegean islands, and Asia Minor. The most characteristic monuments of the Geometric style are the large Dipylon vases (so called because the best examples have been found in the cemetery near the Dipylon gate in Athens). These were actually grave markers and were intended to receive offerings to the dead. In the decorated bands of these vases one sees almost all the characteristic motifs of Geometric pottery (meanders, zig-zags, triangles, and so on) and also rigidly geometricized figures of humans and animals. *See* DIPYLON VASE.

Miniature sculpture in bronze and terra cotta also appeared in the Geometric period. Most examples appear to date from the 8th century. Like the figures on painted vases, they display an insistence on the subordination of natural appearances to geometric form; the structure of individual parts is emphasized, and the relationship of these parts to the whole is carefully calculated.

Architecture in the Geometric period was crude compared to the preceding Mycenaean period. The most characteristic monuments are "megaron" structures, often with a hairpin-shaped plan, built with mud brick and thatched roofs upon stone foundations.

Orientalizing period (ca. 725–600 B.C.). Commercial expansion among the Greek cities in the 8th century led to the establishment of Greek trading centers on the east coast of the Mediterranean, especially in northern Syria. At the same time, or perhaps even earlier, Phoenician traders had begun to ply Greek waters. One result of these new connections was the absorption into Greek art of a new repertoire of traditionally Oriental motifs, such as the griffin, sphinx, siren, rosettes, and palmettes. In vase painting these motifs gradually usurped the place of geometric ornament and became a basic compositional element.

At the beginning of the Orientalizing period Corinth temporarily replaced Athens as the artistic leader of Greece, and the painted proto-Corinthian (ca. 725–650 B.C.) and Corinthian (ca. 650–550 B.C.) pottery is the most characteristic product of the period. The proto-Corinthian style was essentially a miniature style (used on small vases such as aryballoi and pyxides) and specialized in animal friezes and battle scenes (for example, the Macmillin vase in the British Museum in London; the Chigi vase in the Villa Giulia in Rome). Figures were usually painted in black against a light ground; details were added by incision and were sometimes painted over in red. In the ripe Corinthian style the compositions, as well as the vases employed, are larger and, except for the best examples, the quality of the draftsmanship is somewhat cruder. *See* CORINTH.

Greece. Doric column, Temple of Aphaia, Aegina.

In Athens in the first half of the 7th century a different style of vase painting, the proto-Attic style, was developed. It specialized in much larger compositions and made extensive use of outline drawing. A proto-Attic amphora from Eleusis (ca. 675 B.C.) is decorated with scenes showing Perseus pursued by Gorgons and Odysseus blinding the Cyclops—among the earliest illustrations of familiar Greek myths.

Sculpture in the early 7th century continued to be confined to statuettes in terra cotta and bronze of the style conventionally known as Daedalic. About 650 B.C., however, large-scale stone sculpture made its first appearance in the Aegean islands. The Greeks probably learned the technique for carving sculpture in stone through their contact with Egyptian sculpture at Naucratis. The statue dedicated by Nicandre at Delos is perhaps the earliest example known. *See* NAUCRATIS; NICANDRE.

The finest works of metal sculpture in the 7th century are the griffin protomes from bronze caldrons at Olympia and elsewhere. A rare example of statuary made from hammered metal sheets can be seen in statuettes from Dreros in Crete (ca. 650 B.C.). *See* OLYMPIA.

The 7th century also saw the development of characteristically Greek architectural orders and architectural sculpture. The early development of the Doric order can be traced in the Temple of Apollo at Thermon in Aetolia, while the first temples in the Ionic order can be seen in the eastern Aegean (Samos and Smyrna). Examples of relief sculpture used for architectural decoration also appeared at this time (from Prinias in Crete, Mycenae, and elsewhere). *See* DORIC ORDER; IONIC ORDER; SAMOS.

In this period one of the great minor arts of Greece—that of making stamped metal coinage—first appeared. The people of Miletus, under the influence of the neighboring Lydians who had invented coinage, were the first Greeks to produce coins (ca. 680 B.C.). At only a slightly later date the Aeginetans produced the first coinage on the mainland. Throughout the course of Greek history numismatic art faithfully followed the stylistic development of the major arts. *See* COINAGE, GREEK AND ROMAN; MILETUS.

Archaic period (ca. 600–480 B.C.). The transition from the Orientalizing to the archaic style of Greek art is simply one of terminology. There was no cultural break. The earlier period, which was one of assimilation, yielded naturally in the late 7th century to one in which the Greeks had finally arrived at the artistic repertoire that they would subsequently utilize.

In sculpture the kouros type was intensively developed, beginning with the monumental Sounion group (ca. 600 B.C.) and leading through the lean, aristocratic figures of the mid-6th century (the Melos and Tenea kouroi) to the brash, muscular figures of the second half of the century (the Anavysos kouros). Although simple naturalism was not the goal of archaic art, the sculptors and painters of the period were ever ready to incorporate the results of the observations of nature into their artistic schemes. The morphological changes traceable in the kouros figures can also be traced in other varieties of sculpture. *See* KOUROS TYPE.

The history of architectural sculpture in this period, from the pediments of the Temple of Artemis at Corfu (ca. 580 B.C.) to the pediments of the Temple of Aphaia

at Aegina (ca. 490–480 B.C.), reveals the progressive mastery of the compositional problems posed by this medium. *See* AEGINA.

In the late 7th century Athens regained her leadership in the production of painted pottery with the black-figured style. The great draftsmanship of the Athenian artists was already demonstrated in the Nessos amphora at the end of the 7th century, and it reached its peak in the work of Execias shortly after the middle of the 6th century. About 525 B.C. a new red-figured technique (figures left in the natural color of the clay while the background was painted black) was introduced. It permitted the artist to draw (rather than to incise) details of figures, and thus to keep pace with the accomplishments in foreshortening and naturalistic observation that were occurring in mural and easel painting. In both black-figured and red-figured ware a great variety of subjects, including scenes from everyday life as well as scenes from the great mythological repertoire of the Greeks, are represented. *See* BLACK-FIGURED VASE PAINTING; EXECIAS; RED-FIGURED VASE PAINTING.

By the beginning of the 6th century the Ionic and Doric orders of Greek architecture were fully developed and their subsequent stylistic development is primarily one of morphological variation. The so-called "Basilica" at Paestum is the best preserved of the archaic temples. *See* PAESTUM.

The chief building materials were sun-dried brick, wood, terra cotta, and stone. The first two were used in almost all earlier structures, but stone (limestone, conglomerate, and marble) replaced them for important structures before the classical period. The use of marble was determined by the importance of the building and the accessibility of quarries.

Early classical period (480–450 B.C.). Emerging victorious from their war with the Persians, the Greeks were inspired as never before to assert their cultural individuality and independence. In sculpture and painting, as in other aspects of the culture of the 5th century, a typically Greek view of the world was asserted, isolated from the artistic and intellectual traditions inherited from the other civilizations of the ancient world. The last of the schematized forms that the Greeks had inherited from the ancient East were discarded, and new forms, which emphasized the capacity for thought, action, and the moral consequences of action (human and divine), were created in response to the Greeks' new vision of heroic capability and universal order. *See* ARTEMISIUM ZEUS.

The new spirit is seen in earlier creations of classical sculpture such as the *Tyrannicides* of Critius and Nesiotes and the *Charioteer of Delphi*, and it came to perfection in the pediments of the Temple of Zeus at Olympia (462–457 B.C.). *See* CHARIOTEER OF DELPHI; CRITIUS AND NESIOTES; ZEUS, TEMPLE OF, OLYMPIA.

Greek painting in the early classical period was dominated by the works of Polygnotos and Mikon. The great paintings of the classical period have all disappeared. Because of its technical limitations the minor art of vase painting was unable to keep pace with stylistic developments of the great painters. An idea of the general appearance of early classical painting, however, may be derived from Etruscan tomb paintings, such as the Tomb of the Leopard, and vases, such as the Niobid crater in the Louvre. *See* ETRUSCAN ART; NIOBID PAINTER; POLYGNOTOS.

Ripe classical period (450–400 B.C.) and 4th century (400–323 B.C.). The individual personalities of Greek artists become more pronounced in the classical period. Myron and Pythagoras were the leaders in the formal development of Greek sculpture in the early classical period, and Pheidias and Polycleitus were the foremost sculptors of the ripe classical style. The various personal styles of the different artists were unified, however, by a tradition of professional criticism, in which ideas about formal, theoretical, and technical problems of sculpture—problems of proportion and composition, for example—were published and shared. *See* MYRON; PHEIDIAS; POLYCLEITUS; PYTHAGORAS.

The classical style, and perhaps Greek art as a whole, reached its climax in the Parthenon (447–432 B.C.). The temple itself is the subtlest and most refined creation of Greek architecture; its architectural decoration designed by Pheidias embodies the highest Greek cultural ideals and exhibits a unique balance of forms and design. With the Parthenon the notion of a classic art first became firmly established, and all later Greek art was influenced by its standards, as a model to be rebelled against or to be imitated. These standards implied an idealized conception of the human form and its proportions, as well as a serene and detached emotional approach. *See* PARTHENON, ATHENS.

In the 4th century B.C. Greek artists were preoccupied with elaborating on the stylistic legacy of the 5th century. The great sculptors of this period—Timotheus, Scopas, Praxiteles, and Lysippus—continued to develop the formal theoretical problems that the 5th-century sculptors had introduced into Greek art. Added to these were a new interest in the possibilities of emotional expression in sculpture—especially apparent in the art of Scopas and Timotheus—and an introspection and softness characteristic of the art of Praxiteles. Lysippus, in instituting new proportions, new compositional schemes, and a tendency toward realism, culminated 4th-century sculpture and laid the foundations of the Hellenistic style. *See* LYSIPPUS; PRAXITELES; SCOPAS; TIMOTHEUS.

In architecture the Corinthian order, which first appeared in the Temple of Apollo at Bassae in the late 5th century, appeared with increasing frequency, although the most important structures of the century were still in the Doric and Ionic orders. *See* CORINTHIAN ORDER.

The 4th century appears to have been the golden age of Greek painting. In the late 5th century the painter Apollodorus of Athens developed the technique of modeling through the use of light and shade, thus paving the way for the great painters of the 4th century, such as Zeuxis, Parrhasios, Euphranor, and Apelles. The achievement of these men is preserved, however, only by literary testimony. Vase painting, which was in the process of dying out in the 4th century, gives little information. Hellenistic and Roman painting give us some idea of the technique of the earlier masters but only the vaguest hint of the appearance of their actual works. *See* APELLES; APOLLODOROS; EUPHRANOR; PARRHASIOS; ZEUXIS.

The earliest figured mosaics in Greece date from the end of the 5th century B.C. (examples at Olynthus and Corinth) and are made from natural pebbles (as opposed to the cubic tesserae of many later Hellenistic mosaics). Exceptionally fine examples dating from the 4th century B.C. have recently been discovered at Pella in Macedonia. *See* OLYNTHUS.

The evolution of Greek aesthetic sensitivities can also be traced in the minor arts, such as engraved gems, engravings on metal (mirror cases, and so on), and even, to some extent, in furniture. *See* FURNITURE (GREECE); JEWELRY, HISTORY OF.

See also ARTISTS' SIGNATURES, GREEK AND ROMAN; EMBROIDERY; GREEK PAINTING; HELLENISTIC ART; THEATER; WEAVING, TEXTILE, GREEK AND ROMAN.

BIBLIOGRAPHY. M. H. Swindler, *Ancient Painting* . . ., New Haven, 1929; C. Picard, *Manuel d'archéologie grecque–La Sculpture*, Paris, 1935; W. B. Dinsmoor, *The Architecture of Ancient Greece*, 3d ed., London, 1950; G. Lippold, *Die griechische Plastik* (Handbuch der Archäologie im Rahmen des Handbuch der Altertumswissenschaft, pt. 6, vol. 3), Munich, 1950; E. Pfuhl, *Masterpieces of Greek Drawing and Painting*, tr. J. D. Beazley, New York, 1955; A. W. Lawrence, *Greek Architecture*, Baltimore, 1957; G. M. A. Richter, *The Sculpture and Sculptors of the Greeks*, rev. ed., New Haven, 1957; D. S. Robertson, *A Handbook of Greek and Roman Architecture*, 2d ed., Cambridge, Eng., 1959; M. Robertson, *Greek Painting*, Geneva, 1959; R. M. Cook, *Greek Painted Pottery*, London, 1960; C. T. Seltman, *Greek Coins*, rev. ed., London, 1960; G. M. A. Richter, *A Handbook of Greek Art*, 3d ed., London, 1963; J. Boardman, *Greek Art*, New York, 1964; D. E. Strong, *The Classical World*, New York, 1965.
JEROME J. POLLITT

GREECE: MUSEUMS OF. See under the names of the following cities:

Athens. Acropolis Museum; Agora Museum; Benaki Museum; Byzantine Museum; Kerameikos Museum; National Archaeological Museum.

Nauplion. Museum.

Olympia. Museum.

Rhodes. Archaeological Museum.

GREEK-BYZANTINE ARCHITECTURE, *see* PHOCIS: CHURCHES OF ST. LUKE OF STIRIS.

GREEK CANON, *see* CANON, GREEK.

GREEK COINS, *see* COINAGE, GREEK AND ROMAN.

GREEK KEY DESIGN, *see* FRET.

GREEK PAINTING. The history of Greek painting may be divided into several epochs on the basis of style. Its development may be studied further through the use of colors.

Chronology. The following periods of Greek painting, and the evidence on which the chronology is based, are generally accepted. (1) Late Bronze Age (1580–1200 B.C.): fragments of mural frescoes from Mycenae, Pylos, Tiryns, and elsewhere. (2) Proto-Geometric and Geometric periods (ca. 1000–725 B.C.): vase paintings exclusively. (3) Orientalizing and archaic periods (ca. 725–480 B.C.): vase paintings primarily; supplemented by painted terra-cotta slabs, early Etruscan tomb painting (which follows Greek stylistic development closely), and fragments of wall paintings from Gordion. (4) Early (480–450 B.C.) and ripe (450–400 B.C.) classical periods: vases; supplemented by literary descriptions (Pliny and Pausanias) of famous artists and their works and by Etruscan painting. (5) Fourth century B.C.: Etruscan painting, literary descriptions, engraved mirrors, cistae, and gems (vase painting declined). (6) Hellenistic period (323–31 B.C.): tomb paintings from Etruria, Alexandria, and southern Russia; painted stone grave steles from Alexandria and Pagasae; and mosaics. *See* ALEXANDRIA; ETRUSCAN ART; GORDION; HELLENISTIC ART; MYCENAE; VASE PAINTING, GREEK.

JEROME J. POLLITT

Use of colors. Greek monumental painting before the 5th century B.C. probably used no more than four basic colors—white, yellow, red, and black. Pliny the Elder calls them "white from Melos, Attic yellow, red from Sinope on the Black Sea, and the black called *atramentum*" (*Natural History*, XXXV, 50). As painters became less interested in sheer draftsmanship and more interested in color, however, these pigments were mixed to form many others. The 5th-century philosopher Democritus, in his treatises *On Color* and *On Painting*, lists some combinations: red, white, and a touch of yellow produce gold or bronze; red, black, and white in the proportion 3:1:2 produce purple; black and yellow produce indigo; yellow and purple produce green; and so on. Scholars have calculated that about 800 different shades could be created by mixing the four colors in this fashion.

Almost no evidence of ancient Greek monumental painting is available to aid the study of the Greek use of color. Vases, which reflect the subjects and style of monumental paintings, do not mirror the colors; extant Roman copies of Greek works may not reproduce the colors of the originals. Remains of architecture and sculpture, however, do provide information about the Greek sense of colors and their juxtaposition. Remains of the Typhon pediment (ca. 560 B.C.), from the old Temple of Athena or Hecatompedon on the Acropolis in Athens (Athens, Acropolis Museum), show strong, even violent, color contrast. One

Stephen Greene, *Edifice*. Whitney Museum of American Art. New York.

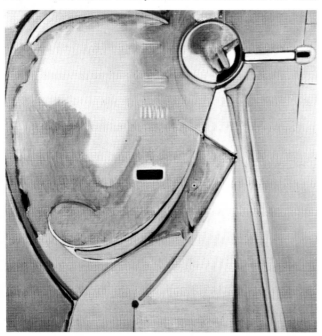

figure, a monster, has blue hair and beard, blue or greenish-blue irises, yellow eyeballs, red lips and cheeks, and black pupils and eyebrows. Much of his body is painted rose red, and his tail is decorated with red, blue, and yellow stripes. *See* HECATOMPEDON SCULPTURE.

Red and blue seem to predominate on most early statuary. Statues and architecture of the classical period were also lavishly colored. Little of the mellow, golden marble, which is admired today, was available to the ancients. Relief works were especially rich in color to make the figures stand out. Backgrounds were generally dark blue or red, though at least one 4th-century example of white exists. Figures in the round and architectural elements were also colored, with reds and blues predominating.

Hellenistic painting probably saw a more subtle use of a rich palette of colors. Artists had now become more interested in realism and illusionism; sensitive coloring and shading enhanced their new tastes.

BIBLIOGRAPHY. M. H. Swindler, *Ancient Painting...*, New Haven, 1929.

EVANTHIA SAPORITI

GREEK REVIVAL. Term referring to the revival of Greek decoration and architectural forms in the second half of the 18th century as part of the growing rationalism of that epoch. In 1762 the publication of Stuart and Revett's *Antiquities of Athens* set off the movement in England. It was continued by the many architects who visited Greece, and it reached a climax with the acquisition of the Elgin marbles. All these factors led to buildings in neo-Greek style in England and other countries. K. F. Schinkel, in Germany, and Ithiel Towne, in the United States, were among the leading practitioners of this style, which attained its height between 1820 and 1840. *See* SCHINKEL, KARL FRIEDRICH VON; TOWNE, ITHIEL.

The term Neo-Greek is also applied to a type of neoclassical painting in France during the Napoleonic period. In this approach, modern subjects or sentiments were rendered in the style of ancient Greek art or as the subjects of Greek history.

GREEN, VALENTINE. English engraver (b. Salford, near Evesham, 1739; d. London, 1813). Green made masterly engravings in mezzotint after the great English masters. The most famous are his female portraits after Reynolds and works after Romney and Benjamin West.

BIBLIOGRAPHY. W. G. Menzies, "Valentine Green and his Work," *The Connoisseur*, XIX, December, 1907.

GREEN, WILLIAM CURTIS. English architect (1875–1960). He was conservative but enlightened in his approach to traditionalism. His best-known work is the Dorchester Hotel, London (1931), and on a lesser scale, the workshops for Wolsey Motors (1923), characterized by a discriminating use of details. He was a water colorist of considerable ability.

GREENAWAY, KATE. English draftsman and painter (b. Hoxton, 1846; d. London, 1901). She created a new style of English children's book illustration by making a decorative unity of text and illustration. *Under the Window* (1879), which she wrote and illustrated, was her most successful work. Others include *Topo* (1878) and *Language of Flowers* (1884).

BIBLIOGRAPHY. M. H. Spielmann and G. A. Layard, *Kate Greenaway*, London, 1905.

GREENBAUM, DOROTHEA. American sculptor (1893–). Her two best-known works, both in marble and both in the collection of the Whitney Museum of American Art in New York, are *Drowned Girl* (1950) and *Girl with a Towel* (1943). Her style is naturalistic with impressionist overtones. Regardless of medium, Dorothea Greenbaum's sculpture reveals a personal application of modeling technique.

BIBLIOGRAPHY. W. H. Gerdts, *A Survey of American Sculpture*, Newark, N.J., 1962.

GREENE, BALCOMB. American abstract and figurative painter (1904–). He was born in Niagara Falls, N.Y. He was graduated from Syracuse University in 1926 and then studied psychology in Vienna. Greene first began to paint seriously in 1931 and is largely self-taught. He was first chairman of the American Abstract Artists in 1936. In 1939 he executed a mural for the New York World's Fair.

Greene had his first one-man show in 1947 and was given a retrospective exhibition in 1961 at the Whitney Museum of American Art, New York. Starkly geometric abstractions composed of clean-edged, tilting planes were abandoned in 1948 for studies of human figures, which appear transfixed and immobilized by some unnatural light that erodes and disintegrates their flesh.

BIBLIOGRAPHY. J. I. H. Baur, *Balcomb Greene*, New York, 1961.

GREENE, STEPHEN. American painter (1918–). Born in New York City, Greene began studying painting at the Art Students League (1936–37) and later attended the State University of Iowa, where he was a pupil of Phillip Guston. The first one-man exhibition of his work was held at Durlacher Brothers in New York in 1947, and subsequent shows were held there in 1949 and 1952; he was also given one-man shows at the Grace Borgenicht Gallery (1955, 1957, and 1958) and at the Staempfli Gallery (1961 and 1964). The last mentioned was the final stop of a retrospective exhibition which had originally opened at the Corcoran Gallery, in Washington, D.C., in 1963.

His work is in the Metropolitan Museum of Art and the Whitney Museum in New York, the Tate Gallery in London, and other museums. Greene's art is personal and expressionistic in its themes; it has evolved from a precise, linear figurative style to one of progressively free, symbolic abstraction.

BIBLIOGRAPHY. H. W. Janson, "Stephen Greene," *Magazine of Art*, XLI, 1948; H. Wohl, "Recent Paintings of Stephen Greene," *College Art Journal*, XVIII, no. 2, 1959; S. Greene, "Artist in America: A Case in Point," *Art in America*, XLIX, no. 1, 1961.

GREENE AND GREENE. American architectural firm. The domestic architecture of the brothers Charles S. Greene (1868–1957) and Henry M. Greene (1870–1954) spread from Pasadena to all of southern California. Characteristic features are a predilection for natural materials expressed in the use of heavy timbers in projecting rafters, extensive masonry walls, and the incorporation of a garden into the

Horatio Greenough, *Cupid Bound*. Marble. Museum of Fine Arts, Boston.

total design. The front sleeping porch of the David B. Gamble House (1908) in Pasadena sheltered a tile terrace below; the entry hall and stairwell were developed in mahogany and teak; and all joints were put together with wooden dowels. The sprawling Crowe House (1913) in Pasadena had an elongated U plan with a narrower interior gallery paralleling another gallery.

BIBLIOGRAPHY. E. McCoy, *Five California Architects*, New York, 1960.

GREENLAND, *see* ESKIMO ART; NORTH AMERICAN INDIAN ART (ESKIMO).

GREEN MOSQUE, *see* BRUSSA ARCHITECTURE.

GREENOUGH, HORATIO. American sculptor (1805–52). He was born in Boston. Coming from a well-to-do family,

Greenough was able to travel and study in Europe with little struggle. During 1824–26 he was influenced by Thorwaldsen and Bartolini, and his style took on a neoclassical manner. Greenough was an ardent admirer of Michelangelo, but few of the sounder principles of Michelangelo's art penetrated the veneer of latent classicism that prevailed in Greenough's work. *Cupid Bound* (Boston, Museum of Fine Arts), the *John Quincy Adams* bust (New York Historical Society), and the once controversial seated portrait of George Washington (Washington, D.C., Smithsonian Institution) typify his style. Greenough has in recent years become a hero to American designers of the "functionalist" aesthetic, especially since the recent paperback publication of his writings (which have been available since the 1850s), because of his early ideas of relating ornament to architecture. Despite this popularity, Greenough's chief claim to lasting recognition remains that *George Washington* was one of the very first public commissions awarded by the United States government to a native artist.

BIBLIOGRAPHY. H. Greenough, *The Travels, Observations, and Experience of a Yankee Stonecutter*, Boston, 1852; N. Wynne and B. Newhall, "Horatio Greenough, Herald of Functionalism," *Magazine of Art*, XXXII, 1934.

JOHN C. GALLOWAY

GREENSTED, CHURCH OF. Famous as the only surviving example of an Anglo-Saxon log church. It was probably built about 1013 and is slightly earlier than the earliest existing Norwegian stave churches. The construction involved the use of oak logs vertically halved and set upright in oak sills.

BIBLIOGRAPHY. N. Pevsner, *The Buildings of England*, vol. 11, Harmondsworth, 1954.

GREENWICH, QUEEN'S HOUSE. English house first designed in 1616 for the queen, Anne of Denmark. It was intended as a glorified bridge across a public road from the palace of Greenwich to the park. For this purpose the plans by Inigo Jones were devised in the shape of an H. They were only partly executed at the Queen's death in 1619 and were not taken up again until 1629, for Charles I. The building was completed in 1637. In 1662 John Webb filled in the spaces between the H shape, creating the square block seen today. It was described in 1619 as "some curious device" and was certainly "curious" to the majority in the advanced and uncompromising Palladianism of its elevations.

BIBLIOGRAPHY. J. N. Summerson, *Architecture in Britain, 1530–1830*, 4th rev. ed., Baltimore, 1963.

GREENWICH ROYAL HOSPITAL. The dating of this English building complex is complicated. The Charles II wing (1664–67) by John Webb was designed as a royal palace. The first hospital phase dates from 1694 to 1708, when the King Charles court base wing, King William's court, the interior west dormitory, and shells of Queen Anne's court buildings were erected. Next, from 1712 to 1721, King William's court was finished, and the north pavilions of Queen Anne's court were finished externally. Sir John Vanbrugh designed King William's block (ca. 1703) and the Great Hall. In 1716 Vanbrugh succeeded Sir Christopher Wren as Surveyor to the Hospital. In the third phase (1725–32), Queen Anne's buildings were finished. Finally, between 1735 and 1751, Queen Mary's court was completed.

Sir Christopher Wren was responsible for the main lines of the design, dictated by Webb's building; Nicholas Hawksmoor seems to have designed the west parts of King William's building. Ripley designed the east dormitory and William Newton internally reconstructed the chapel by 1789. The painted hall is Sir James Thornhill's great work, begun in 1708 and completed by 1727.

BIBLIOGRAPHY. J. H. V. Davies, "The Dating of the Buildings of the Royal Hospital at Greenwich," *The Archaeological Journal*, CXIII, 1956.

JOHN HARRIS

GREENWOOD, JOHN. American painter and engraver (b. Boston, Mass., 1727; d. Margate, England, 1792). He was apprenticed to Thomas Johnston, a painter and decorator. Greenwood became a successful, if stiff, portrait painter. In 1752 he went to Dutch Guiana, where he painted portraits until 1758, when he went to Holland. In 1762 he traveled to England, becoming an art dealer and remaining there until his death.

BIBLIOGRAPHY. A. Burroughs, *John Greenwood in America*, Andover, Mass., 1943.

GREGORIO DI CECCO DI LUCA. Italian painter (fl. 1389–1423). Late in life Gregorio was adopted by the Sienese painter Taddeo di Bartolo and worked with him on an altarpiece for S. Agostino, Siena, and other paintings. Gregorio's only known work is a *Madonna* in the Siena Cathedral Museum (1423), which has delicate but sharply drawn features and is one of the last paintings to have the traditional gold threading through the draperies.

GREGORY I, THE GREAT, ST. Pope and Doctor of the Church (ca. 540–604). He founded monasteries in Sicily and in Rome. St. Gregory was made one of seven deacons of Rome and was a papal representative in Constantinople. On his return to Rome he became abbot of St. Andrew's Benedictine monastery. As pope (590–604), he sent St. Augustine of Canterbury to convert England. St. Gregory developed the doctrine of Purgatory, fostered the veneration of relics, and is traditionally considered the author of the Gregorian Sacramentary and Gregorian chant. His attributes are the papal tiara and cross with triple bars and a dove. His feast is March 12.

See also SAINTS IN ART.

GREGORY OF NAZIANZUS, ST. Greek Church Father and Doctor and poet (329–389). Born in Arianzus, near Nazianzus, Cappadocia, he studied in Athens with St. Basil and Julian the Apostate. St. Gregory began his career as a monk, but the Church, after making him bishop of Sasima, assigned him to aid his father, who was then bishop of Nazianzus. In 379 St. Gregory was called to Constantinople, where his preaching was influential in reinstating the orthodox Nicene doctrine and won him tribute. He became known as "*theologus*" (the Theologian). The second ecumenical council (Constantinople I, 381) made him bishop of Constantinople, but he resigned from office during the council because of discord and retired first to Nazianzus, then to Arianzus, where he died. He is represented in Byzantine art in the Greek manner without

Greenwich Royal Hospital. A building complex begun in 1664 and periodically enlarged until 1751.

miter and often appears with SS. Athanasius, Basil, and John Chrysostom, the other Fathers of the Greek Church. St. Gregory does not appear in Western art. His feast is January 25 in the East and May 9 in the West.

See also SAINTS IN ART.

GREGORY OF NAZIANZUS, HOMILIES OF. Byzantine illuminated manuscript (ca. 880), in the National Library, Paris.

GRENOBLE. City in southeast France. Founded by the Romans and raised to the rank of a Roman city in the 4th century, Grenoble was the capital of Dauphiné from the 12th century until the province was ceded to France in 1349. The Carolingian crypt of the 11th-century Church of St-Laurent is the city's oldest monument. Also of considerable interest is the 15th-century Palais de Justice, now much restored, which was the palace of the Dauphins, as the lords of this province called themselves, and then of parliament. It consists of two wings, one flamboyant Gothic and the other Renaissance in style, within which are to be seen an early 16th-century chapel, handsome *boiseries* of the same period, a ceiling dating from 1600, and rooms decorated in the Louis XIV style. The 13th-century Church of St-André and the Cathedral of Notre-Dame, which dates in part from the 11th century, are also of interest. The art museum is one of the richest in France. *See* GRENOBLE: MUSEUM OF PAINTING AND SCULPTURE; SAINT-LAURENT.

Prehistoric and Gallo-Roman objects are displayed in the Dauphinois Museum, which is situated in an 18th-century chapel. Costumes, armor, and decorative arts of the region are also shown here.

The site of the city, nestled in an Alpine valley at the confluence of the Drac and Isère Rivers and girdled by mountains, is extraordinarily beautiful. Broad, tree-lined avenues give Grenoble an atmosphere of dignity and leisure that belies its industrial importance.

BIBLIOGRAPHY. G. Faure, *Au Pays de Stendhal*, Grenoble, 1920; P. David, *La Cathédrale de Grenoble*, Paris, 1939.

MADLYN KAHR

GRENOBLE: MUSEUM OF PAINTING AND SCULPTURE. French museum noted for its rich holdings of modern paintings from the school of Paris, including the following tendencies: impressionism (Monet, Renoir), postimpressionism (Gauguin, Vuillard, Bonnard, Roussel), Fauvism (Matisse, Marquet, Derain, Dufy, Vlaminck), cubism (Picasso, Braque, Gris), expressionism (Soutine, Chagall, Modigliani), and abstractionism (Magnelli, Bissière, Hartung, Vieira da Silva). The museum also displays old master canvases from Italy (Perugino, Veronese, Canaletto, Guardi), Flanders (Rubens), Spain (Zurbarán, Ribera), and France (Georges de La Tour, Philippe de Champaigne, Claude Lorraine).

In the museum's annex, in the Municipal Library, are manuscripts and incunabula, autographs, coins, wood engravings, and the famous ancient bronze *Venus of Grenoble*. There is also a Fantin-Latour museum in the same building.

BIBLIOGRAPHY. L. de Beylié, *Le Musée de Grenoble*, Paris, 1909; G. Kueny, *Le Musée de Peintures et de Sculptures*, Grenoble, 1962.

GREUZE, JEAN-BAPTISTE. French genre and portrait painter (b. Tournus, 1725; d. Paris, 1805). A pious Jansenist environment in his childhood partially contributed to the moralizing tenor of his art. Apprenticed about 1745 to C. Grandon in Lyons, Greuze was made to copy a master painting a day, which increased his suppleness but encouraged a superficial apperception of content that was ever after a deficiency in his art. About 1750 he enrolled at the Royal Academy in Paris under Natoire. He experienced difficulty in making his way until he won the protection of Louis Silvestre the Younger, the sculptor P. Pigalle, and the amateur La Live de Jully.

Greuze early declared opposition to the style of François Boucher. Like Chardin, he preferred the Dutch and Flemish genre style that was popular with collectors at this ascendant moment of morality. Formerly the aim of painting had been to please; now, under the influence of such men of letters as Lafont de Saint-Yenne, Rousseau, Diderot, Sédaine, and later, the Comte d'Angivillier, it was to instruct. Virtuous and heroic actions were represented in a continuation of the traditional academic vein, but they were heightened with emotionalism through a "return to nature," emulating the simple life of the humble. *The Father Reading the Bible to His Children* (1755; Paris, Louvre) was opportunely calculated for success, and gained Greuze admission as associate in the Academy.

A trip to Italy (1755–57) had little effect upon his confirmed instinct for genre. This is demonstrated in his painting *Broken Eggs* (signed and dated "Roma 1756"; New York, Metropolitan Museum), representing a forlorn and dishevelled adolescent girl, with a basket of broken eggs, and an old peasant woman blaming a sheepish youth for the damage. A small boy at the right looks both guilty and furtive. There can be no doubt of the studied innuendo here, which contributes a lecherous undertone to the scene. Though the picture is brilliantly painted, the composition is contrived. The emphasis on many detailed symbolic motifs attempts the moral content, but lacks the subtle humor, of the Dutch 17th-century Caspar Netscher prototype and the contemporary William Hogarth. Gestures and expressions are melodramatic, suggestive of the current novel. Such anecdotal genre became so elaborate with Greuze on occasion that he wrote, in the encyclopedic fashion of the time, detailed explanations to the Paris newspapers. His *Village Betrothal* (*L'Accordée de village*, 1761; Louvre), though only slightly less mawkish, received prodigious acclaim. Though this chatty morality proves provocative, it reasonably marks the paradox of this moment of transition in the 18th century from the spontaneous gallantry of Boucher to the earnest sobriety of the school of Jacques-Louis David.

In 1761 Greuze married the beautiful but vicious Gabrielle Balbuty. She posed as the coy soubrette in *The Broken Jug* (Louvre), which was bought by Madame du Barry. Greuze's wife all but consumed the rich profits of his art, which largely resulted from the popularity of engravings by Johann Georg Wille after his paintings. They separated in 1785 and were divorced in 1791. Much of Greuze's genre dwells upon domestic felicity, ironically underlining the conditions of his blighted home.

He was barred from exhibiting at the 1767 Salon until he submitted a reception piece to the Academy, a piece that had been due for thirteen years. He presented the *Emperor Septimius Severus Reproaching Caracalla* (Louvre), which was declared exemplary mediocrity. He was admitted as a genre painter and was therefore prohibited from aspiring to official rank in the Academy. He wrote furious protests to the newspapers to no avail, and resolved never again to exhibit at the Salon. Until 1800, instead, he showed his works privately, as did his friend Fragonard. The public flocked to his Louvre apartment, and he maintained

Jean-Baptiste Greuze, *Blond Child*. Municipal Museum, Montpellier.

his celebrity through the 1770s. With the increase of neoclassicism his vogue dwindled somewhat in the 1780s. He attempted to offset this by producing paintings of adolescent girls, semidraped and holding dead birds, faded flowers, cracked eggs, mirrors, and jugs; demurely toying with transparent fichus that barely concealed budding breasts; or modestly pouting with moist lips and lowered eyes. Such works were hypocritically entitled *Innocence* and *Flora* or, more aptly, *Love-Dreams* and *Desire*.

The strongest side of his art is portraiture, especially of children, where purity without sentimentality shines forth so refreshingly as to recall the work of his English contemporaries. Here the low but rich and glowing tonality is in marked contrast with the lavenders, roses, and nacreous whites of his "girl" paintings. He constrains the turgid color, the strong chiaroscuro, and the histrionics of his earlier genre pieces, such as *The Paralytic Tended by His Children* (1763; Leningrad, Hermitage) and *The Morning Prayer* (Montpellier, Fabre Museum). By the spontaneous dynamism of his drawing in any subject matter, however, where he models in large planes and forceful contours, in black and red chalk, he proves himself to be one of the best draftsmen of the 18th century in France. He had many Russian admirers, including Catherine the Great and Czar Paul I. The Austrian emperor, Joseph II, made him a baron. As the French Revolution approached, he was ruined. Though charitable portrait commissions were made by the new leaders, he had, like Fragonard, outlived his time and reputation. He had no David, however, to champion him, for his pupils were such lesser lights as J. S. Berthélemy, F. Dumont, and Mlle. J. P. Ledoux.

The largest collections of his works are in the Louvre, in the Wallace Collection in London, at Montpellier, and at Tournus. His works are also found in most of the provincial museums of France and in Baltimore, Berlin, Budapest, Dublin, Edinburgh, Glasgow, Leningrad, London (National Gallery), Minneapolis, Moscow, Munich, New York (Metropolitan Museum and Frick Collection), Rome, Rotterdam, Stockholm, Vienna, and York.

BIBLIOGRAPHY. C. Mauclair (pseud.), *Jean-Baptiste Greuze...*, Paris, 1905; E. L. and J. A. de Goncourt, *French XVIII Century Painters*, New York, 1948; J. Seznec and J. Adhémar, *Diderot Salons*, Oxford, Eng., vol. 1, 1957, vol. 2, 1960.
GEORGE V. GALLENKAMP

GRIEF (Claeu; Klaauw), JACQUES. Dutch still-life and flower painter (b. Dordrecht, ca. 1620; d. after 1676). Grief was one of the founders of the painters' guild in his native Dordrecht. He was also active in The Hague (1646–50), where, in 1649, he married the daughter of Jan van Goijen and thus also became the brother-in-law of Jan Steen.

BIBLIOGRAPHY. I. Bergström, *Dutch Still-Life Painting in the Seventeenth Century*, New York, 1956.

GRIEGO, DOMENICO, see GRECO, EL.

GRIEGO, EL, see ALVAREZ, MANUEL FRANCISCO.

GRIEN, HANS, see BALDUNG-GRIEN, HANS.

GRIER, SIR EDMUND WYLY. Canadian painter (b. Australia, 1862; d. Toronto, 1957). He lived in Toronto from 1876 and studied at the Slade School, London, and in Rome and Paris. A leading portrait painter, he became president of the Royal Canadian Academy and was knighted in 1935.

BIBLIOGRAPHY. Ottawa, National Gallery of Canada, *Catalogue of Paintings and Sculpture*, ed. R. H. Hubbard, vol. 3: *Canadian School*, Ottawa, 1960.

GRIFFIER, JAN. Dutch painter of landscapes and river views (b. Amsterdam, 1645? d. London, 1718). The date of Griffier's birth is not certain; some sources give 1652 or 1656. He was the pupil of Roelant Roghman in Amsterdam and of Jan Looten in London. In England Griffier worked on a boat on the Thames and painted many views of London. On his return voyage to Holland (1696) the ship, which he owned, was wrecked. He was then active in Rotterdam, and ten years later bought another ship and returned to England. He also painted views of the Mosel and Rhine rivers that recall the manner of Herman Saftleven. He collaborated with Willem van Mieris. Griffier's Italianate style suggests that he may have been to Italy.

BIBLIOGRAPHY. H. V. S. and M. S. Ogden, *English Taste in Landscape in the Seventeenth Century*, Ann Arbor, Mich., 1955.

GRILLANDAIO, DOMENICO, see GHIRLANDAJO, DOMENICO.

GRILO, SARAH, Argentinian painter (1920–   ). Born in Buenos Aires, Sarah Grilo was self-trained. She has had one-man exhibitions in Madrid (1949), Buenos Aires (since 1950), and the United States (1957). Her works are represented in European and American collections, as well as in private collections in Argentina. She is married to the artist José Antonio Fernández Muro. She paints geometric compositions in a cool harmony of color, influenced by Moholy-Nagy and the Bauhaus.

BIBLIOGRAPHY. S. L. Catlin, "New Vistas in Latin American Art," *Art in America*, XLVII, Fall, 1959; T. M. Messer, "Pan America: Contemporary Idioms," *Art in America*, XLIX, Fall, 1961; M. L. San Martín, *Pintura argentina contemporánea*, Buenos Aires, 1961.

GRIMALDI, FRANCESCO. Italian architect (b. Oppido Lucino, 1545; d. ca. 1630). A Theatine father, he was trained in Rome and was active in Naples, where he designed a number of churches in the classical style, including S. Andrea delle Dame (1585–90) and S. Paolo Maggiore (1591–1603).

GRIMALDI, GIOVANNI FRANCESCO (Il Bolognese). Italian painter, engraver, and architect (b. Bologna, 1606; d. Rome, 1680). He received his training in the Carracci school in Bologna and in 1626 moved to Rome, where he became a member of the Academy of St. Luke in 1636. While working on frescoes in the Doria Pamphili Palace, a building he had designed with Algardi, he was called to Paris (1649) and worked for the next two years in the Mazarin Palace, the Louvre, and for the Jesuits. After returning to Rome in 1651, he created frescoes for a number of churches and palaces, including the Borghese and Quirinale. Grimaldi was primarily a landscapist, in the Carracci tradition. He used this form both in frescoes with religious or mythological themes and in small cabinet paintings that proved to be so popular.

GRIMANI PALACE, VENICE. Italian palace built in the first half of the 16th century for the procurator Girolamo Grimani. The ground and first floors were the work of Michele Sanmicheli of Verona, and the second floor was added after 1561 by Gian Giacomo de' Grigi of Bergamo.

BIBLIOGRAPHY. G. Lorenzetti, *Venice and its Lagoon*, Rome, 1961.

GRIMM, LUDWIG EMIL. German painter and etcher (b. Hanau, 1790; d. Kassel, 1863). Grimm, who moved in the circles of Clemens Brentano and even Goethe, spent his youth traveling and his last forty-six years in Kassel. He is remembered chiefly for his etchings, such as *The Prussian from Schlüchtern*, although he also painted.

GRIMMER, ABEL. Flemish painter and architect (ca. 1573–before 1619). Abel was born in Antwerp. The son of Jacob Grimmer and a member of the Antwerp guild in 1592, he specialized in landscapes and small genre and religious subjects. His work has been confused at times with that of Frans Francken the Younger and Sebastiaen Vrancs.

BIBLIOGRAPHY. R. H. Wilenski, *Flemish Painters, 1430–1830*, 2 vols., New York, 1960.

GRIMMER, JACOB. Flemish landscape and history painter (b. Antwerp, ca. 1526; d. there, 1590). A student of Gabriel Bouwens (1639), Mathys Wellens de Cock, and C. van den Queborne, Jacob joined the Antwerp guild in 1547. His works are few and reminiscent of Pieter Brueghel the Elder.

BIBLIOGRAPHY. R. H. Wilenski, *Flemish Painters, 1430–1830*, 2 vols., New York, 1960.

GRIMOU (Grimoult), ALEXIS. French portrait painter (b. Argenteuil, 1678; d. Paris, 1735). He was a pupil of

Jean-François de Troy and a member of the Academy of St. Luke in Rome. He depicted many notables, including writers, somewhat ludicrously, in the guise of pilgrims, actors, and so forth. His art attempts to emulate that of Rembrandt, though at no time does he approach Rembrandt's stature as a draftsman.

BIBLIOGRAPHY. L. Dimier, *Les Peintres français du XVIIIe siècle...*, vol. 2, Paris, 1930.

GRIS, JUAN (Jose Victoriano Gonzalez). Spanish painter (b. Madrid, 1887; d. Paris, 1927). Working in France with Picasso, Braque, and others, Gris became one of the outstanding contributors to cubism. He studied in 1902 at the Madrid School of Arts and Crafts and in 1904 came under the influences of Art Nouveau and Jugendstil. The pseudonym "Juan Gris" was taken in that year. He studied briefly with the academic painter Carbonero in Madrid in 1906 and then went to Paris. Between 1906 and 1910 Gris worked for the journal *Le Charivari* and as a freelance illustrator and designer. He became a friend of Picasso, Max Jacob, André Salmon, Maurice Raynal, Daniel-Henry Kahnweiler, and Gertrude and Leo Stein.

Gris's first significant paintings appeared in 1910; but his assimilation and personalization of the cubist aesthetic was rapid and brilliant. From the time of his 1911 *The Book* and 1912 *Banjo and Glasses* (Paris, Galerie Louise Leiris) he proceeded to form a lucid and severe style even more programmatic than that of Picasso and Braque. He was one of the most inventive practitioners of *papiers collés* (*The Table*, 1915; Philadelphia Museum of Art). *See* PAPIERS COLLES.

Following his severely structured, quietly colored canvases of 1911–12 and the imaginatively textured works of 1913–15, he began an "architectural" phase about 1916. He composed with fewer fragmentations and overlappings of smaller units, broadening his sharp-edged planes into strongly vertical forms. *The Harlequin* (Chicago, private collection) and *The Guitar Player* (Paris, private collection) are typical of this style, which, with interesting variations, such as opposition of strongly geometric regularity by occasional free curves, obtained until Gris's death.

Gris was widely respected among Parisian artists and critics. In 1924 he lectured at the Sorbonne on his method, which, he insisted, began with the abstract and ended with the concrete, progressing, for example, from the idea of a cylinder to the image of a bottle. He remained throughout his brief life a bona fide cubist. He was represented in the major cubist exhibitions of 1912 and was given large retrospectives by Kahnweiler and Rosenberg. He also designed sets for many ballets and operas and was a prolific book illustrator.

BIBLIOGRAPHY. D.-H. Kahnweiler, *Juan Gris...*, Paris, 1946; Bern, Kunstmuseum, *Juan Gris*, 2d rev. ed., Bern, 1955; G. Schmidt, *Juan Gris und die Geschichte des Kubismus*, Baden-Baden, 1957; J. T. Soby, *Juan Gris*, New York, 1958.   JOHN C. GALLOWAY

GRISAILLE. Technique of carrying out an entire painting solely in shades of gray. This method has been used since the late Gothic period to create the illusion of relief sculpture. Grisailles have also been created as independent works of art, as models for engraving, and as the initial phase in the design of an oil painting. The method was especially

Juan Gris, *Le Tourangeau*, 1918. Museum of Modern Art, Paris.

Grisaille. Jean-Auguste-Dominique Ingres, *Odalisque*. Metropolitan Museum of Art, New York.

popular among 15th-century Flemish painters and in the latter half of the 18th century, when paintings were made to suggest classical reliefs. The outstanding example of 19th-century grisaille is the exquisitely toned *Odalisque* by Ingres (New York, Metropolitan Museum).

GRISELDA MASTER. Italian painter (fl. late 14th cent.). This name has been given to the author of three cassone panels in the National Gallery, London, illustrating scenes from the Griselda story in Boccaccio's *Decameron*. This and other works attributed to him mannerize the proportions and dancelike poses of Signorelli.

GROENINGEN, GERHARD VAN (Crispin Paludanus). Dutch engraver (fl. ca. 1560–90). His exact identity is not certain; he is probably the engraver known as Crispin Paludanus and possibly even Herder van Groeningen. His name is not mentioned in records. Plates signed "Ger. Gre.," "Ger. Groening.," or "Jnuen. faciebat." which are assigned to him, were done for the firm of Philipp Galle.

BIBLIOGRAPHY. G. K. Nagler, *Die Monogrammisten...*, Munich, 1876–78.

GROIN. Curved arris formed at the intersection of vaulting surfaces, as in the Roman Baths of Diocletian. A groin

Groin. Curved ridge marking the intersection of vaulting surfaces.

vault is one having such intersecting elements and is characteristic of Roman work. *See* ARRIS.

GROMAIRE, MARCEL. French painter (1892–   ). A native of Noyelles-sur-Sambre, Gromaire at the age of eleven decided to devote himself entirely to painting. Although he took courses in law, he soon abandoned them and began to frequent the different academies in Montparnasse (Colarossi, Ranson, La Palette). He met Matisse's pupils from the short-lived academy which had just been closed. An opponent of theories, Gromaire has remained outside all schools of painting, acknowledging only the influence of Matisse as draftsman.

Gromaire visited Belgium and Holland and spent some time in Germany and England. His principal artistic formation was derived from the French Gothic and Romanesque, the Flemish and French primitives, Brueghel, the impressionists, Cézanne, and Seurat. His art, however, has generally followed an expressionism far removed from the often pathological form of Scandinavian and German expressionism. After World War I his palette became more somber, his subject matter inspired by peasants and workers (*Les Musiciens mendiants*, 1919; *La Gare*, 1922; *La Loterie foraine*, 1923). Avoiding naturalistic expression, he achieved a great decorative quality.

In 1925 he exhibited his celebrated canvas *La Guerre* at the Salon des Indépendants. In this work he made his art conform to strict rules of composition. Excluding the picturesque and scorning the anecdotal, Gromaire envisioned a rigorously exalted, monumental universe. In 1933 an important exhibition of his work took place at the Kunsthalle, Basel. He was commissioned to decorate the façade of the Pavillon de Sèvres at the International Exposition of 1937. In 1939, together with Lurçat and Dubreuil, Gromaire initiated a movement in favor of a tapestry renaissance (*The Four Elements*; *The Four Seasons*). His colors, adapted to a necessary synthesis, are purposely sober, heavy, and dramatic, with predominating browns, grays, and greens. Gromaire has worked also in water color, lithography, and etching. He has done murals and has illustrated a number of books, including *Macbeth*.

Like Verhaeren, Gromaire exalts northern France, its rivers and trees, its roads and towns, as well as Brittany, the fantastic world of New York, and the glory of Paris in all its diversity. He has remained faithful to expressionism, deforming the objective world to create a vision of his own. Gromaire's work is included in many important museums and collections. He was awarded the Carnegie prize in 1952, the Guggenheim prize in 1956, and the Grand Prix National des Arts, Paris, in 1959. An important exhibition of Gromaire's work was held at the Maison de la Pensée Française, Paris, in 1957. In his recent work Gromaire seems to have freed himself from any traces of stylization and is taking new liberties with reality.

BIBLIOGRAPHY. J. Cassou, *Marcel Gromaire*, 2d ed., Paris, 1925; F. Gromaire, *Gromaire*, Paris, 1949; G. Dornand, *L'Eloge de Gromaire*, Paris, 1958.   ARNOLD ROSIN

GRONINGEN: PROVINCIAL AND MUNICIPAL ARCHAEOLOGICAL MUSEUM. Dutch collection specializing in art and artifacts of the prehistoric and Roman periods from the area of Groningen, as well as ecclesiastical and folk art of later periods. Chinese pottery and paintings

Marcel Gromaire, *La Guerre*, 1925. Musée du Petit-Palais, Paris.

by Rembrandt, Jordaens, Rubens, Fabritius, and later artists are also on exhibit.

GRONINGER, GERHARD. German sculptor and architect (b. Paderborn, 1582; d. Münster, 1652). Gröninger was active mainly in the churches of the bishop of Münster, where he executed sculptures in marble and alabaster all of which were polychromed. His major work was the *Lethmate Epitaph* (1625). He was influenced by the Netherlandish mannerists.

BIBLIOGRAPHY. G. Dehio, *Handbuch der deutschen Kunstdenkmäler*, vol. 5, Berlin, 1912.

GRONINGER, JOHANN MAURITZ. German sculptor (b. Paderborn? d. Münster, 1707). As sculptor to the court at Münster after 1674, Gröninger created the monument of Prince Bishop Christoph Bernhard van Galen and alabaster reliefs for the choir stalls in the Cathedral. Expressionistic naturalism characterizes his best work, such as the sculpture of the death of the Ewaldi brothers.

GRONINGER, JOHANN WILHELM. German sculptor (b. Münster, 1676). The tombs of Prince Bishop Friedrich Christian von Plettenberg (d. 1706) and Canon Ferdinand von Plettenberg (d. 1712), in the Münster Cathedral, are attributed to this son of Johann Mauritz Gröninger, whose expressionistic style he emulates and modifies.

GROOT, GUILLAUME DE. Belgian sculptor (b. Brussels, 1839; d. 1922). He received many commissions for monuments and architectural sculpture as well as portraits. In works for the Bibliothèque Royale, the Hôtel de Ville, the Maison du Roi, and the Banque Nationale, all in Brus-

Walter Gropius, Fagus Werke, 1910–11. Alfeld on the Leine, Germany.

sels, and other buildings, he adopted appropriate styles, moving with great facility from Gothic to Renaissance.

GROPIUS, MARTIN PHILIPP. German architect (1824–80). He worked in Berlin. His style, reflecting the influence of Schinkel, the antique, and the romantic classical style of the first half of the century, illustrates the stiffening of these trends into a purely academic tradition.

BIBLIOGRAPHY. H. Schliepmann, *Martin Gropius*, Berlin, 1892.

GROPIUS, WALTER. German-American architect, educator, and critic (1883–1969). Born in Berlin, Gropius, the son of an architect, studied architecture at Charlottenburg and Munich Universities during the first few years of this century. He traveled in Spain (1904–05), served in the Imperial Army (1905–06), became chief assistant to Peter Behrens (1907–10), and started private practice in Berlin (1910). He was director of the Weimar Art Academy and Weimar Arts and Crafts School, combining them, in 1919, into Das Staatliche Bauhaus Weimar. He moved the school to Dessau in 1925, and continued as director until 1928, when he resumed private practice in Berlin. From 1929 to 1957 he served as vice president of C.I.A.M. He was in private practice with E. Maxwell Fry in England (1934–37); became professor of architecture at Harvard (1937); and was chairman of the Department of Architecture in Harvard's Graduate School of Design (1938–52). He has since devoted his time to private practice (with The Architects' Collaborative, or TAC, which he formed in 1946), lecturing, and writing. *See* BAUHAUS; C.I.A.M.

Before World War I Gropius executed two of the key works of contemporary European architecture. In the Fagus Werke at Alfeld on the Leine (1910–11, with Adolf Meyer)

skeleton and skin are separated into the now familiar curtain wall formulation, aesthetically exploited here for the first time, even though the technique had been developed earlier in Chicago. In the Werkbund Exhibition at Cologne (1914; destroyed) he designed a model factory consisting of administration offices, garage, and work area. Flanking the administration offices were the famous cantilevered spiral stairs sheathed in glass cylinders, a breathtaking symbol of the technological basis of modern architecture.

Although the years from 1918 through 1928 were taken up almost exclusively with the development of the educational program of the Bauhaus, Gropius did execute some notable works at this time: the prescient project for the Chicago Tribune Competition (with Adolf Meyer, 1922), the classic Bauhaus building itself (Dessau, 1925–26), the unexecuted Total Theatre (1927), and prefabricated housing at the Weissenhof Exhibition, Stuttgart (1927). *See* WEISSENHOF EXHIBITION.

During the 1930s Gropius designed his own house at Lincoln, Mass. (1937), and the Chamberlain House at Sudbury, Mass. (1939), both with Marcel Breuer. These were among the first modern European buildings introduced to the United States and were greatly influential in subsequent American domestic architecture. Since World War II Gropius has executed one of his largest commissions (with TAC), the Harvard Graduate Center (1949), a complex of living, study, dining, and recreational facilities. The services of many artists of high calibre, such as Josef Albers, Joan Miró, Herbert Bayer, and Jean Arp, were used in the design of the Graduate Center. In the 1960s Gropius and TAC engaged in the design of the immense University of Baghdad, the culmination of his career.

From the beginning of his career Gropius established the theoretical format of his work, the social and technological basis of architecture. He then developed an architecture that is objective, teachable, and collaborative, thus differing fundamentally from the more subjective and expressive approach of Wright and Le Corbusier. Gropius's life, work, and writings remain a powerful living force among those who concern themselves with the design of our physical environment.

BIBLIOGRAPHY. W. Gropius, *The New Architecture and the Bauhaus*, New York, 1937; G. C. Argan, *Walter Gropius e la Bauhaus*, Turin, 1951; S. Giedion, *Walter Gropius: Work and Teamwork*, New York, 1954; J. M. Fitch, *Walter Gropius*, New York, 1960.

THEODORE M. BROWN

GROPPER, WILLIAM. American painter, cartoonist, and lithographer (1897–   ). Born in New York City, he studied with Henri, Bellows, and Giles. He is best known for his skillful political and social cartoons for radical periodicals. His paintings, of similar subjects, are expressionistic in style.

GROS, BARON ANTOINE-JEAN. French painter (b. Paris, 1771; d. Sèvres, 1835). He studied from 1786 to 1793 with J.-L. David, a friend of his painter father, Jean Gros. During a tumultuous seven-year period in Italy he painted many portraits, including some of Napoleon Bonaparte, whose wife Josephine befriended Gros. Back in Paris, he exhibited *Bonaparte at Arcole* in 1801 (painted 1796; Paris, Louvre). In 1804 his *Plaguehouse at Jaffa*, a painting showing Bonaparte consoling the afflicted in a lazaretto during the Egyptian campaign of 1799, established

Baron Antoine-Jean Gros, *The Plaguehouse at Jaffa*. Louvre, Paris. A scene from Napoleon's Egyptian campaign of 1799.

him among the foremost artists of his time. Scenes from other campaigns followed: *The Battle of Abukir* (1806; Versailles, Museum), with Murat as the central character; and *The Battle of Eylau* (1808; Louvre), in which Napoleon is apostrophized. Numerous fine portraits of the Emperor and his entourage ensued: King Jérôme Bonaparte of Westphalia and his Queen (1807, 1811; Versailles, Museum), several Napoleonic generals, and other celebrities.

After 1815, for the restored Bourbon family, he painted portraits of Louis XVIII and his niece the Duchesse d'Angoulême (1816; Versailles, Museum). She also figures in a huge work, *The Embarkment of the Duchesse d'Angoulême* (1817; Bordeaux, Museum of Fine Arts).

With David's exile in 1815, Gros became the head of his teacher's school, and in this capacity he continued to paint neoclassical scenes. In 1824 he terminated ten years' work on the cupola of the Panthéon in Paris, *The Apotheosis of Ste-Geneviève*, and in 1827 ceilings for the Charles X Museum in the Louvre. He continued to produce mythological subjects no longer in vogue.

A preromantic, Gros contributed to the developing romantic school. Géricault copied his work and, along with Delacroix, felt his influence. Gros's theme is the impetuous hero bravely engaged in the activity, mainly military, of his time. Gros's brushwork is energetic and free; his opulent colors are derived from the Venetians, to whom he was compared in his time.

BIBLIOGRAPHY. J.-B. Delestre, *Gros et sa vie et ses ouvrages...*, 2d ed., Paris, 1867; J. Tripier Le Franc, *Histoire de la vie et de la mort du baron Gros, le grand peintre...*, Paris, 1880; R. Escholier, *Gros, ses amis et ses élèves*, Paris, 1936.

NORMAN SCHLENOFF

GROSBOIS, CHATEAU OF. French château in the Department of Seine-et-Marne. Built shortly after 1600 for the financier Raoul Moreau, the Château of Grosbois is a characteristic example of the architecture of the reign of Henry IV. The appearance of the main façade, which is concave, is enhanced by the contrast of stone, brick, and plaster.

GROSS, CHAIM. American sculptor (1904–   ). Born in Austria-Hungary, Gross went to the United States in 1921. He has remained essentially independent of the various sculptural developments in American art since his arrival. Although his works are related in a general way to those of Zorach, De Creeft, and Lachaise, Gross imparts a playful rhythm to his figures, often working with superposed forms. He works principally in wood, as in *Acrobatic Dancers* (1942) and *Snake and Birds* (1954). An impressive earlier work is *Mother and Child* (1927; Newark Museum). A compact, semiabstract interpretation of the figure, usually with an attendant sense of offset balances, marks his typical sculptures.

BIBLIOGRAPHY. L. Goodrich and J. I. H. Baur, *American Art of Our Century*, New York, 1961.

GROSS CLINIC, THE. Oil painting by Eakins, in Jefferson Medical College, Philadelphia. *See* EAKINS, THOMAS COWPERTHWAITE.

GROSSMANN, RUDOLF. German painter, etcher, and lithographer (b. Freiburg im Breisgau, 1882; d. there, 1941). After sporadic training and extensive travel throughout Europe, Grossmann strove to create a stylistic synthesis of impressionism and expressionism. He is best known for his graphic work and book illustrations.

GROSSO, NICCOLO (Il Caparra). Italian ironsmith (fl. ca. 1500). The wrought-iron torch holders, banner brackets, and lanterns for the four corners of the Strozzi Palace in Florence (ca. 1500), which represent the high point of Italian Renaissance smithing, are the work of the Florentine called "Il Caparra." Vasari records that Caparra made andirons for Lorenzo de' Medici, and the lanterns on the Medici-Riccardi and Guadagni palaces in Florence (ca. 1503–06) are attributed to him on the basis of their similarity to those of the Strozzi Palace.

BIBLIOGRAPHY. H. Lüer and M. Creutz, *Geschichte der Metallkunst*, vol. 1, Stuttgart, 1904.

GROSZ, GEORGE. German-American painter and printmaker (1893–1959). Born in Berlin, he went to the United States in 1932. Grosz may be identified with three movements in modern art: Dada, Die Neue Sachlichkeit (New Objectivity), and American social realism of the 1930s and early 1940s. It may be more apt, however, simply to designate Grosz an expressionist with a strongly personal style, especially in his drawings and prints of the late 1910s and 1920s when his style was most incisive.

Grosz trained at the Dresden Academy of Fine Arts and the Berlin Arts and Crafts School and studied briefly in Paris. As a combat soldier in World War I and an observer of the postwar economic chaos in Germany, he was well acquainted with the cynical, often haunting incidents that led to the imagery of his pictures. His lithograph *Memories of New York* (1917), a sharp portrayal of the wartime metropolis, is a Dadaist document. The water color *Café Neptun* (1920; Art Institute of Chicago) and *Trench Warfare* (1923; now lost, formerly Dresden, State Art Collections), lampoon the civilian and the military aspects of world conflict. Another lithograph, *Christmas Eve* (1921), is typical of his satire of middle-class vapidity. Thought of, above all, as a draftsman, Grosz often worked tellingly in oils, as in the *Funeral of the Poet Panizza* (1917–18; Stuttgart, State Gallery), a consciously catastrophic-looking composition with surging human and architectural movement. His great series *Ecce Homo* (1923) was reissued in the 1960s.

With Otto Dix, Max Beckmann, and other Germans who tired of what in their view was the excessive romanticism of certain Die Brücke artists and the formalism of the Blue Rider, Grosz for a time in the mid-1920s arrived at a strongly realistic method, of which his *The Poet Max Hermann-Neisse* (1927; New York, Museum of Modern Art) is an example.

Grosz left Germany out of disgust with the political situation of the early 1930s, settling in New York in 1932. He was awarded a Guggenheim fellowship in 1937 and

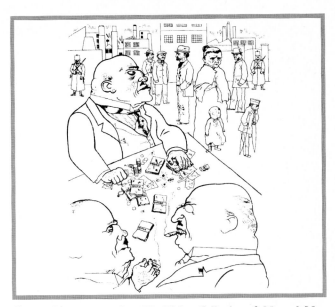

George Grosz, a page from *Die Räuber*. Collection of Mr. and Mrs. Bernard J. Reis, New York.

won the Carnegie International prize in 1945. For a time in the late 1930s Grosz painted New England landscapes and figure compositions with nudes; but he soon turned again for subjects to socially conscious, topical imagery, as in *The Pit* (1946; Wichita Art Museum), *Peace, II* (1946; New York, Whitney Museum) and *Waving the Flag* (1948). Grosz contributed significantly to the finer tradition of social realism of this century, and his graphic works in that genre are stylistically important to the general history of German expressionist drawing and printmaking.

BIBLIOGRAPHY. G. Grosz, *A Little Yes and a Big No: The Autobiography of George Grosz*, New York, 1946; J. I. H. Baur, *George Grosz*, New York, 1953; W. Haftmann et al., *German Art of the Twentieth Century*, New York, 1957.   JOHN C. GALLOWAY

GROTESQUE. Type of ornament motif consisting of arabesques which surround and entwine human figures, ani-

Grotesque. Roman ornamental forms revived in the Vatican Loggia.

mals, flowers, fruits, and sometimes even parts of architecture. The term comes from the Italian *grotteschi*, a word coined to describe that type of Roman ornament which was discovered during the Italian Renaissance in grottoes such as those in the Golden House of Nero. In his decoration of the Vatican Loggia, Raphael appears to have used the grotesque for the first time in modern history.

BIBLIOGRAPHY. A. Speltz, *Styles of Ornament*, rev. ed., New York, 1959.

GROTTO. Structure built in a garden or close to a terrace in imitation of a rocky natural setting. Grottoes were an important feature of Renaissance villas and spread from Italy to France and England. Built of heavy stone blocks, which bore rustication designed to suggest seaweed or moss, they were sometimes provided with a sheltering overhang and decorated with stalactites and statuary. Augmented by pools and fountains, they served as pleasant places for out-of-door entertainment.

BIBLIOGRAPHY. G. Masson, *Italian Villas and Palaces*, London, 1959.

GROUND. In etching, the acid-proof substance that is dabbed or applied on a zinc or copper plate before the line drawing is scratched with the etcher's needle. It may be composed of waxes, resins, and asphalts, in various combinations and states dependent on the tastes and habits of the particular printmaker.

GROUX, CHARLES DE. Belgian painter (b. Comines, 1825; d. Brussels, 1870). Groux was a student of Navez at the Brussels Academy. He is best known for his paintings depicting the life of the poor that he used to express his social philosophy, for example, *Le Bénédicité* (Brussels, Museum of Fine Arts). Stylistically he was a realist, strongly influenced by Courbet.

BIBLIOGRAPHY. M. Rooses, *Les Peintres belges du XIXᵉ siècle*, Paris, 1900.

GRUBER, FRANCIS. French painter (b. Nancy, 1912; d. Paris, 1948). Gruber studied under Bissière and Braque, and also under Friesz and Dufresne. His tragic expressionism and monumental conception (*Hommage à Le Nôtre*, 1936) have influenced young French painters, such as Bernard Buffet, who have remained faithful to reality. In 1947 Gruber was awarded the Prix National.

BIBLIOGRAPHY. B. Dorival, *Twentieth Century French Painters*, 2 vols., New York, 1958.

GRUE FAMILY. Family of potters and painters (fl. Castelli, near Naples, 1670-1750). Carlo Antonio, the outstanding and typical representative of the Castelli school, created dishes with landscape or mythological panels surrounded by tightly designed borders with *putti*, architectural motifs, and foliage. His sons, Francesco Antonio (1686-1746), Anastasio (1691-1743), Aurelio (1699-1744), and Liborio (1701-76), and a third generation carried on in the same style.

GRUEN, VICTOR. Austrian-American architect and planner (1903-   ). Born in Vienna, Gruen studied in Berlin under Peter Behrens and worked in Europe before going to the United States in 1938. Today his large office, with main headquarters in Los Angeles and Detroit, deals with such problems as suburban shopping centers and urban design, the best examples of which are Northland, near Detroit (1952), and the plan for Fort Worth, Tex.

BIBLIOGRAPHY. I. R. M. McCallum, *Architecture USA*, New York, 1959.

GRUNEWALD, ISAAC. Swedish painter (1889-1946). From 1908 to 1911 he studied with Matisse, and beginning in 1932 he taught in Stockholm. His influential work owes much to Matisse in its arbitrary color, sinuous line, and decorative rhythm. Grünewald produced portraits, figure compositions, landscapes and seascapes, murals, theater designs, and several publications, including a book on Matisse (1944).

BIBLIOGRAPHY. J. P. Hodin, *Isaac Grünewald*, Stockholm, 1949.

GRUNEWALD, MATHIAS (Mathis or Mathes Neithardt or Nithardt). German painter (b. Würzburg, ca. 1470-75; d. Halle, 1528). Grünewald is second only to Dürer as the greatest German painter of the 16th century.

In contrast to Dürer, about whom a great deal is known, Grünewald's life is a mystery which only some of the most intensive art-historical research of the past thirty years has begun to unravel. The name "Grünewald" is a completely fictitious one, invented for unknown reasons by Joachim von Sandrart, the 17-century artist and writer on art, in his *Teutschen Academie*. Grünewald's real name was Mathis (or Mathes) Neithardt, and this name is represented in works before 1519 by the initials M. N. In 1519 he signed his *Maria-Schnee Altar* with the initials M. N. G. (with the G inside the M and the N above). This stands for Mathis Neithardt Gothardt, which he created by adding the name of his wife to his own. It is generally agreed that Würzburg was his birthplace. The dating of his birth is supported by the similarity between Grünewald's style and that of the generation of German artists such as Altdorfer, Jerg Ratgeb, and Hans Leinberger, who were born about 1480.

Knowledge of Grünewald's early years and artistic training is nonexistent. Stylistic comparisons with other artists have been the only recourse of modern scholarship in the attempt to determine Grünewald's artistic origin. The results tend to point to the circle of the late Gothic painter Hans Holbein the Elder, although a strong similarity exists between the early Grünewald and the style of Martin Schongauer.

About 1500 Grünewald appeared in Seligenstadt, where he is recorded as a master, and began a rather active workshop, judging from the numerous entries in local tax records. Documents indicate that he was in the service of the archbishop-elector of Mainz, Uriel von Gemmingen. He is not mentioned as being a court painter, but instead as reputedly "Baumeister" (architect) for the rebuilding of the Schloss at Aschaffenburg. Under Gemmingen's famous successor, Albrecht von Brandenburg, Grünewald worked on the decoration of the Stiftskirche in Halle (1520-23). He painted at least two of his paintings at this time, the *Dead Christ* in Aschaffenburg and the *Meeting of SS. Erasmus and Maurice* in Munich.

The discovery of a list of Grünewald's possessions after his death, among them a group of Lutheran and Anabaptist

Mathias Grünewald, *Crucifixion*. National Gallery, Washington, D.C. (Samuel H. Kress Foundation, 1961).

writings, has materially supported the belief that the artist was involved in the futile Peasants' War of 1525. This would explain his sudden disappearance from the service of the archbishop and his appearance in Frankfurt in 1526. Grünewald remained in Frankfurt until the early summer of 1527, at which time he traveled to Halle, where he died a poor man.

Modern research concerning Grünewald's life has only served to strengthen the concept, already held by Sandrart in the 17th century, that Grünewald was a unique and completely unparalleled artistic personality. The many and varied sources that Dürer drew upon for his artistic development did not and could not have existed for Grünewald. That he knew the new Italian Renaissance developments is evident from the occasional use of Renaissance ornament; but it was of little use to him in achieving his great artistic goal, the expression of a deep, highly personal religious feeling. For this his native German tradition was source and inspiration enough.

The earliest work by Grünewald which is accepted without controversy is the *Mocking of Christ* (Munich, Bavarian State Picture Gallery, Old Pinacothek). A recent inscription, which reflects an earlier and possibly original one, gives the date 1503. The style of this panel, which is the least developed in the use of color, supports this date. Close to it in date is the small *Crucifixion with the Three Marys and St. John and Longinus* (Basel, Public Art Collections). It possesses a freedom of drawing similar to that of the *Mocking of Christ*. Between these two works, or after the Basel *Crucifixion*, depending on how the stylistic evolution is read, stand the four grisaille panels *SS. Lawrence and Cyriacus* (Frankfurt am Main, Städel Art Institute) and *St. Elisabeth and St. Lucy* (Donaueschingen, Fürstenbergische Gemäldegalerie). Both are works of the utmost sensitivity.

Around 1513 Grünewald began his masterpiece, the *Isenheim Altar* (Colmar, Unterlinden Museum). The work is large, consisting of nine panels: the *Crucifixion, Entombment*, and *SS. Sebastian and Anthony* form the first stage; the *Nativity, Annunciation*, and *Resurrection* are the second stage; and the *Meeting of St. Anthony and St. Paul in the Wilderness* and *Temptation of St. Anthony*, which flank a central shrine with carved wood figures by Nikolaus von Hagenau, form the third and last stage. It was probably finished about 1515, the date found on the jar of the Magdalen in the *Crucifixion* panel. The iconography is in many ways unique with Grünewald. He selected and treated his subjects to express a truly mystical interpretation of Christianity. Indeed, research has discovered many sources for the iconography in the writings of St. Bridget of Sweden. For instance, the figure of St. John the Baptist, which is pointing to Christ, is a remarkable graphic rendering of the words of St. Bridget: "You are the Lamb that John has pointed to with his finger." The *Nativity* is even richer in mystical symbolism.

In its freedom of painting, the panel *Crucifixion with St. John, the Virgin, and Mary Magdalen* (Washington, D.C., National Gallery) is close to the *Isenheim Altar*, yet the evident mannerism of the elongated figures and faces relates it to the later *Maria-Schnee Altar*. The last work consists of two panels, *The Virgin in the Garden* (Stuppach, parish church) and the *Miracle of the Snow* (Freiburg im

Breisgau, Municipal Collections). It was made for the Collegiate Church of Aschaffenburg, where the original frame exists with the date 1519.

The works of Grünewald's late period are the *Dead Christ*, or *Pietà* (ca. 1523; Aschaffenburg Collegiate Church), *Meeting of SS. Erasmus and Maurice* (ca. 1526; Munich, Old Pinacothek), and the so-called *Tauberbischofsheimer Altar* (ca. 1527; Karlsruhe, State Art Gallery). In these works religious expressionism becomes progressively more manneristic. The colors are darker and more sullen, and in the *Tauberbischofsheimer Altar* the facial expressions are almost demonic.

BIBLIOGRAPHY. H. A. Schmid, *Die Gemälde und Zeichnungen von Matthias Grünewald*, Strasbourg, 1911; H. Feurstein, *Matthias Grünewald*, Bonn, 1930; W. K. Zülch, *Der historische Grünewald*, Munich, 1938; J. K. Huysmans and E. Ruhmer, *Grünewald: The Paintings*, New York, 1958; N. Pevsner and M. Meier, *Grünewald*, New York, 1958.

DONALD L. EHRESMANN

GRUPELLO, GABRIEL. Flemish sculptor (b. Grammont, 1644; d. Kerkrade, 1730). After studying with Artus Quelninus II, Grupello became a master in Brussels in 1674. One of his most famous works is the Neptune Fountain (1675), now in the Museum of Fine Arts in Brussels. His statues *Diana* and *Narcissus* are also there. His sculpture before his departure for the Netherlands shows an 18th-century suaveness.

BIBLIOGRAPHY. H. Gerson and E. H. ter Kuile, *Art and Architecture in Belgium, 1600–1800*, Baltimore, 1960.

GRUSSAU (Krzeszow), ABBEY CHURCH OF. Silesian church, formerly in Germany and since 1945 in western Poland. Built between 1728 and 1735, it is stylistically related to the contemporary baroque architecture of Prague and has therefore been attributed to Kilian Ignaz Dientzenhofer.

BIBLIOGRAPHY. H. Popp, *Die Architektur der Barock- und Rokokozeit in Deutschland und der Schweiz*, Stuttgart, 1913.

Guadalajara, Mexico, Cathedral.

GRUUTHUUSE, HOTEL, BRUGES. Flemish Gothic structure, built between 1420 and 1470 as a residence for Louis of Bruges. It has been completely restored since it became the property of the city in 1873 and it now houses a museum of archaeology and industrial arts.

GUADALAJARA, MEXICO. Capital of the state of Jalisco and the second largest city in Mexico. It was founded in 1531 and became the seat of the bishopric of western Mexico in 1549. Laid out in a grid pattern, the city has its center at the Plaza Mayor, which is flanked by the great Cathedral (1571–1618) and the 17th-century Palacio del Gobierno. Nearby, an 18th-century seminary building now houses the museum collection of colonial and Pre-Columbian art. Among the many baroque churches are S. Francisco, the Oratorio of S. Felipe Neri, S. Monica, and Nuestra Señora de Guadalupe.

Notable neoclassical buildings of the 19th century are the Hospicio Cabañas and the Teatro Degollado. Many of Orozco's finest murals are to be found in this, his native city, including those in the Hospicio Cabañas, the university, and the Palacio del Gobierno. His former studio is now a museum. *See* GUADALAJARA, MEXICO: CATHEDRAL.

BIBLIOGRAPHY. A. Cháves Hayhoe, *Guadalajara de ayer*, Guadalajara, 1956.

GUADALAJARA, MEXICO: CATHEDRAL. Mexican church begun in 1571. The interior of the building shows the influence of Diego de Siloe's Gothic-Renaissance combination, in which Roman orders serve a Gothic purpose. Clusters of engaged Doric columns with gilded capitals support stilted entablatures. The interior is similar to the Cathedral of Granada, where, however, the Corinthian order was used. A uniform roof level is retained in all aisles, and the rib vaulting springs from the aisles. The choir was removed early in the 19th century, giving an uninterrupted view of the interior. The façade and towers were demolished by earthquakes in 1750 and 1818, and the current dome was erected in 1948. The Cathedral houses Murillo's *Assumption of the Virgin*.

BIBLIOGRAPHY. T. E. Sanford, *The Story of Architecture in Mexico*, New York, 1947.

GUADALAJARA, SPAIN. Provincial capital on the Henares River in Spain, about 35 miles east of Madrid. The Moorish Wadi al-Hadjara, Guadalajara was reconquered in 1085 and centuries later badly damaged during the Civil War (1936–39). It was important as the seat of the wealthy dukes of Infantado of the Mendoza family and early patrons of Renaissance art in Spain.

Here Iñigo López de Mendoza, the second duke, built the fantastic Gothic-Mudejar Infantado Palace. This building, despite its archaic details the first great central-court Renaissance palace in Spain, was begun about 1478, replacing a late-14th-century structure. The façade (1480) and the two-story arcuate patio, finished in 1483, are by Juan Guas and Enriques Egas. The asymmetric composition, spiral columns, mixtilinear arches, and strong heraldic emphasis are of late Gothic origin, but the large areas of flat pattern and some of the decorative motifs are of Toledan Mudejar inspiration, as were the magnificent wooden ceilings, one formed entirely of gilded *muqarnas*, or honeycomb vaulting, designed about 1495 by Lorenzo de

Trillo and burned about 1936. The fifth duke destroyed the unity of the design with numerous High Renaissance alterations (1570–80) but added frescoes by the Italian Romulo Cincinnatus.

Near Guadalajara, at Cegolludo, Lorenzo Vázquez built a palace for the first duke of Medinaceli, Luis de la Cerda y Mendoza, about 1490. The symmetrical façade with its careful rustication and horizontal cornice marks the first full acceptance of Renaissance forms in Spain. Only the windows are Gothic, but even these correspond to a design by Filarete for the Medici Bank in Milan, which Vázquez may have seen. In 1508 Vázquez completed S. Antonio at Mondejar near Guadalajara, a Franciscan church whose ruins show an elegant mixture of Renaissance ornament and Gothic structure. In Guadalajara itself Vázquez had completed by 1507 a palace for Antonio de Mendoza, whose surviving portal presents a composition in a very pure northern Italian Renaissance vocabulary. In the patio Renaissance columns support by means of transverse wooden "shoes" the heavy beams of a second story, a traditional Spanish solution given antique details.

A second phase of Renaissance style is introduced in the portal of the Church of La Piedad begun by Alonso de Covarrubias in 1526 and very like the north portal of the Cathedral of Como. The chapel of Juan de Zúñiga in the Church of Santiago of 1530 has been attributed to Covarrubias, and the tombs of Pedro González de Mendoza and his wife in the Church of S. Ginés, now much damaged, show his influence. Covarrubias may also have influenced the fine early-16th-century patio of the Hieronymite monastery of Lupiano near Guadalajara, whose vertical succession of semicircular, segmental, and trabeated galleries is fully Renaissance in ornamental detail.

BIBLIOGRAPHY. F. Layna Serrano, *El Palacio del Infantado en Guadalajara*, Madrid, 1941; F. Layna Serrano, *Historia de Guadalajara y sus Mendozas en los siglos XV y XVI*, 4 vols., Madrid, 1942.

JOHN D. HOAG

GUADALCANAL, *see* OCEANIC ART (MELANESIA: SOLOMON ISLANDS).

GUADALUPE, MONASTERY OF. Spanish monastery situated in Estremadura. Dedicated in the 14th century to the miraculous image of the Virgin found here and later widely venerated in Spanish America, the Franciscan (formerly Jeronymite) monastery of Guadalupe is a treasure-house of Spanish art. Besides its great 14th-century Gothic cloister, it has a gracious Mudejar cloister of the 16th century, a sacristy virtually unchanged since it was built in the 17th century, complete with eight large canvases by Zurbarán, and a baroque *camarín* painted by Luca Giordano. The treasure of the Virgin and collections of embroideries and textiles and illuminated choir books are among its riches.

BIBLIOGRAPHY. E. Tormo y Monzó, *The Monastery of Guadalupe*, Barcelona [1915?].

GUADALUPE HIDALGO, SHRINE OF. Chapel at Villa Madero, Mexico City, on the preconquest site of the Sanctuary of Tonantzin, mother of the gods, perhaps the most important Christian site in the republic of Mexico and one of the most important in the Western Hemisphere. This shrine was built to commemorate the Virgin's alleged appearance to a humble native, Juan Diego, in the winter of 1531. The story was officially recognized by the Pope, and the Virgin of Guadalupe (named after Our Lady of Guadalupe in Spain) became the patron saint of Mexico. The first hermitage was built of wattle and adobe shortly after the miraculous appearance. This church was rebuilt in 1567, and in 1622 a new and more important chapel was consecrated. The present building was opened for the cultus in 1709 and enlarged for the ever-increasing crowds of pilgrims in 1895. The collegiate church now houses the miraculous picture of the Virgin which is said to have appeared in Diego's mantle in place of the roses he plucked.

BIBLIOGRAPHY. T. E. Sanford, *The Story of Architecture in Mexico*, New York, 1947.

GUALTIERI DI GIOVANNI DA PISA. Pisan painter (fl. ca. 1389–1445). He appeared on the list of the Siena painters' guild as early as 1389. He worked from 1409 to 1411 in the sacristy of the Cathedral of Siena, where along with Niccolò di Naldo he painted the wooden ceiling and the vaults of three chapels. The last documentary reference to him was in 1445. According to Berenson he was one of the painters of frescoes in the Chapel of the Virgin in Siena Cathedral (ca. 1410) and also painted panels now in the Opera del Duomo.

BIBLIOGRAPHY. B. Berenson, "A Reconstruction of Gualtieri di Giovanni," *International Studio*, December, 1930.

GUANAJUATO, MONASTERY CHURCH OF. Mexican church, begun in 1747. The Jesuits, arriving in Guanajuato in 1732, built the church from a plan by Bethlehemite monk Fray José de la Cruz. Later phases of construction—especially the façades—proceeded under Felipe Ureña. The building was dedicated in 1765, but the Jesuits were expelled from Spanish dominions in 1767; the complex of buildings was taken over by the Filippine order in 1785. The church, of rose-brown local stone, has a particularly fine decorated triple façade at the entrance, stylistically influenced by Lorenzo Rodríguez's work in Mexico City. The interior was renovated in the neoclassical style. The lofty neoclassical dome collapsed in 1808, and the present dome was built between 1869 and 1884. The Jesuit foundation in Guanajuato included a school, later becoming Filippine College, then Colegio del Estado, and, in 1945, the University of Guanajuato. At one side of the neoclassical patio of the university, adjacent to the church, are 18th-century church façades used as portals to the school area.

BIBLIOGRAPHY. *Rasgo breve de la grandeza Guanajuateña*, Mexico City, 1957 (reprint of 1767 edition).

JOSEPH A. BAIRD, JR.

GUARANA, JACOPO. Italian painter and etcher (b. Verona, 1727; d. Venice, 1808). Beginning as a student and follower of S. Ricci, Carlo Cignani, and G. B. Tiepolo, he became a successful fresco and oil painter of the Venetian school and a member of the Academies of Venice, Florence, and Bologna. He was also sought after by the Academy of Copenhagen and the Empress of Russia.

GUARANA, VINCENZO. Italian painter (b. Venice, 1753; d. there, 1815) He was the son, pupil, and collaborator of Jacopo Guarana. Most of his works, portraits, religious and historical paintings, and frescoes, were painted in Venice. A flaccid follower of Giovanni Battista Tiepolo, he moved in the direction of neoclassicism.

GUARDI, FRANCESCO. Italian painter (1712–93). He is generally recognized as the greatest of the Venetian view painters of the 18th century. Very little is known of his early career; he seems to have worked in the shop of his elder brother Gianantonio Guardi until the age of forty-eight, producing heavy and uninteresting figural paintings, such as the two allegories of *Virtue* (ca. 1747; Sarasota, Fla., Ringling Museum). Only after the death of his brother in 1760 did Francesco emerge as a distinct artistic personality; with very few exceptions, all his known work after this date lies in the realm of *vedute* (views).

While there has been some suggestion that Francesco began his career of view painting under the instruction of his contemporary Canaletto, the stylistic character of his works makes this highly unlikely. Paintings dating in the 1740s and 1750s, such as the *Ruins* (Washington, D.C., National Gallery) and *Country Landscape* (Leningrad, Hermitage), clearly show that prior to Gianantonio's death Francesco was experimenting with the *vedute* genre through a close study of the work of Marco Ricci in the 1720s; frequently, Francesco made direct copies of Ricci's compositions. Francesco's paintings from the early 1760s, such as the *View of the Piazza S. Marco* (London, National Gallery), reveal a dependence on the work of Canaletto, but they consistently reflect that master's early style of the 1720s and 1730s in emphasizing dramatic shadows, more prominent figures, and unusual perspectives. The suggestion, then, is that after his brother's death Francesco worked independently, receiving inspiration not through contact with contemporary view painters but rather through a study of the early romantic *vedute* of Ricci, Canaletto, and the more dramatic Michele Marieschi. Consequently, the style of Francesco's views prior to 1770 is characterized by a tendency to dramatize subjects through strong shadows, to arrange his compositions so that the city seems to spread out from the center of the painting (unlike the classically focused views of Canaletto's work during these years), and to suggest the internal activity of Venice by the use of bright flickering colors and rich textural surfaces.

By 1770 Francesco's style in *vedute* had matured, and in his work between that year and his death there are no traces of stylistic influences from earlier painting. Typical of this period are the views of S. Maria della Salute (London, National Gallery), in which the brilliant color and extremely loose brushwork tend to dissolve the geometric structure of the church into an atmospheric harmony of water, land, and air. In the *Caprice* (1782; New York, Metropolitan Museum) Francesco's feeling for infinite space and a lyric quality of lightness increases even further. The colors are pale but lack the coldness of Canaletto's contemporary work; rather they are saturated with light and are spread across the surface in a series of vibrant tonal transitions. In the same year Guardi also painted an interior scene, *Gala Concert* (Munich, Old Pinacothek), showing a concert given in honor of some Northern counts; unlike the usual journalistic record of a given occasion, the painting is a dance of color and light, the individual figures nearly indistinguishable in the flickering pattern of highlights on the surface.

Francesco Guardi, *The Canals of Brenta*. Uffizi, Florence. A characteristic work by the 18th-century Venetian view painter.

In his last works, such as the 1789 *Fire of S. Marco* (Milan, Granvilla Collection), the structure of the buildings is completely dematerialized in the loose impressionistic handling of the paint surface, and the luminous color seems to derive from the combustion of the city itself. In these works Francesco reveals an atmospheric style based on color and light handled with a virtuosity unequaled by any painter before the impressionists of the 19th century.

BIBLIOGRAPHY. G. Fiocco, *Francesco Guardi*, Florence, 1923; M. Goering, *Francesco Guardi*, Vienna, 1944; J. B. Shaw, *The Drawings of Francesco Guardi*, London, 1951; V. Moschini, *Francesco Guardi*, London 1957; P. Zampetti, *Mostra dei Guardi* (catalog), Venice, 1965.

PENELOPE C. MAYO

GUARDI, GIACOMO. Italian landscape and history painter (b. Venice, 1764; d. there, 1835). He was a pupil and imitator of his father, Francesco Guardi. Although Giacomo's works are generally weak, they are somehow often mistaken for Francesco's.

GUARDI, GIANANTONIO. Italian painter (1699–1760). He was the head of a large workshop in Venice in which his younger brothers Nicolò Guardi and the more famous Francesco Guardi also worked. Gianantonio's artistic personality is extremely obscure; only the *Death of S. Joseph* (Berlin, former State Museums) and the *St. John of Malta* (Pozziuno) can definitely be ascribed to his hand. In the latter work the style is free and atmospheric with an emphasis on evanescent light. On the basis of these qualities it has recently been generally conceded that Gianantonio is responsible for the brilliant series of panels depicting scenes from the story of Tobit that decorates the organ loft in the Church of the Arcangelo Raffaele in Venice. If the series is definitely by his hand, then Gianantonio emerges as one of the greatest painters of the Venetian rococo style, expressing a previously unencountered de-materialization of form through fluid color and an almost incandescent quality of light.

BIBLIOGRAPHY. W. Arslan, "Per la definizione dell'arte di Francesco, Giannantonio e Nicolò Guardi," *Emporium*, C, 1944; A. Morassi, "Conclusioni su Antonio e Francesco Guardi," *Emporium*, CXIV, 1951; F. de Maffei, *Gian Antonio Guardi pittore di figura*, Verona, 1951; A. Morassi, "A Signed Drawing by Antonio Guardi and the Problem of the Guardi Brothers," *The Burlington Magazine*, XCV, August, 1953; P. Zampetti, *Mostra dei Guardi* (catalog), Venice, 1965.

GUARIENTO. Italian painter (b. 1338; d. before 1370). He was a member of the school of Padua. While it cannot be demonstrated that Guariento was ever a student of Giotto, he was clearly influenced by the art of that master, which he could have seen in the Arena Chapel in Padua. Of Guariento's work, twenty-nine panels from the ceiling of the chapel in the Palazzo del Capitano, Padua, have been preserved; they reveal a combination of Giottesque influences and those of the Byzantinized artists of 14th-century Venice. His major work, the great fresco of the Coronation of the Virgin in the Ducal Palace, Venice, was covered by Tintoretto's 16th-century *Paradise* fresco and rediscovered only in this century. In the stiff postures of the figures and in the regular groups of angels and apostles on Gothic thrones, Guariento's style again reveals a merging of the hieratic Venetian style with Giottesque naturalism.

BIBLIOGRAPHY. R. van Marle, *The Development of the Italian Schools of Painting*, vol. 4, The Hague, 1924.

GUARINI, GUARINO. Italian architect of the Piedmontese school (1624–83). Guarini was born in Modena. In 1639 he entered the order of the Theatines and moved to Rome to study theology, philosophy, mathematics, and architecture. He was ordained in Modena in 1647 and was soon appointed lecturer in philosophy at the house of his order. In 1660 he settled in Messina as a teacher of philosophy and mathematics. There he designed his first

Guarino Guarini, grand staircase of the Palazzo Carignano, Turin, built 1679.

Treasury of Guarrazar. Gold crowns of the Visigothic kings, 7th century. Cluny Museum, Paris.

buildings, among them the SS. Annunziata (destroyed in 1908 but preserved in the plates of his *Architettura civile*), a three-tiered centralized building reverting to mannerist principles of form. In 1662 Guarini went to Paris, where he designed the Theatine church of Ste-Anne-la-Royale (completed in 1720; destroyed in 1823) with an undulating Borrominesque façade. The vaulting of the dome, however, was—as in Messina—highly original in its use of spanning ribs and in its complex integration of drum, dome, and lantern.

In 1660 Guarini was called to Turin by Carlo Emanuele II of Savoy. Before settling there he did some traveling and in Lisbon designed S. Maria da Divina Providência (destroyed by the earthquake of 1755). His important buildings in Turin are the Collegio dei Nobili (1678), the Palazzo Carignano (1679), and the two centralized churches: the Cappella della Sta Sindone (1667–90) and S. Lorenzo (1668–87). The two palaces follow the style of Borromini, particularly the oval salone and the undulating façade of the Palazzo Carignano. Both churches have fantastic and extravagantly complex cone-shaped domes. In the Sta Sindone the segmental arches, superimposed on the inner shell, diminish in span as they approach the twelve-ribbed underpinning of the lantern. A diaphanous and dizzying effect of height is produced by the light filtered through this grid and by the exaggerated perspective. In S. Lorenzo sixteen interlocking ribs springing in pairs from an octagon above the pendentive zone form an octagon in the center of the dome, whose outer rings are the base for a brilliantly lit drum and lantern.

The suspended, diaphanous form of Guarini's domes,

it has been suggested, may spring from his desire to find a symbolic form suggestive of infinity. Central European late baroque architects took over not only his dome but also his experiments with banded vaults and diagonal, forward-tilted or three-dimensional arches. His influence was carried throughout Europe by the publication in 1737 of his *Architettura civile*; the engravings from that work, however, had been known from 1668 on. Guarini also was the author of a mathematical treatise, *Placita philosophica*, published in 1665.

BIBLIOGRAPHY. P. Portoghesi, *Guarino Guarini*, Milan, 1956; R. Wittkower, *Art and Architecture in Italy, 1600–1750*, Baltimore, 1958.

HELLMUT WOHL

GUARRAZAR, TREASURY OF. Visigothic gold crowns in the Cluny Museum, Paris, and the National Archaeological Museum, Madrid. *See* VISIGOTHIC ART.

GUAS, JUAN. Spanish architect (fl. after ca. 1450; d. 1497). Guas was the most outstanding Spanish architect at the end of the 15th century. A Breton by birth, he was trained in Brussels and settled in Toledo about 1450. From 1459 to 1469 he worked on the Lion Gate at the Cathedral there, and beginning in 1483 he worked on the *trascoro*. In 1494 he was *maestro mayor*. He built S. Juan de los Reyes in Toledo (1479/80), which was first intended to be the burial church for the Catholic kings, the Infantado Palace in Guadalajara (1480–83), and the Chapel of S. Gregorio at Valladolid (1488). Guas developed the cryptolateral (blind-aisled) church plan and reconciled medieval form with Mudejar ornament and Italian space design.

BIBLIOGRAPHY. G. Kubler and M. Soria, *Art and Architecture in Spain and Portugal and Their American Dominions, 1500-1800*, Baltimore, 1959.

GUASPRE, LE, *see* DUGHET, GASPARD.

GUAYASAMIN CALERO, OSWALDO. Ecuadorian painter (1919–   ). Guayasamín studied in his native city of Quito. Work from his first show was circulated in the United States by the State Department. *Fatigue* (1952; Quito, Casa de la Cultura Ecuadoriana) exemplifies the socially oriented side of his art. Rooms were devoted to his work at the São Paulo Bienal of 1957 and at the second Inter-American Bienal in Mexico City in 1960.

BIBLIOGRAPHY. S. Catlin and T. Grieder, *Art of Latin America since Independence*, New Haven, 1966.

GUBBIO WARE. Majolica pottery decorated by Maestro Giorgio (Giorgio Andreoli) from about 1500 to 1530 and made in a factory he established with his brother in the town of Gubbio. Although Giorgio produced pottery of his own, he became famous throughout Italy for his golden and ruby-colored luster glazes. The lusters were made from gold and silver and were applied not only to the ware made in Gubbio but also to pieces sent from Urbino, Faenza, and Castel Durante.

BIBLIOGRAPHY. W. B. Honey, *European Ceramic Art from the End of the Middle Ages to about 1815*, 2 vols., London, 1949–52; G. Savage, *Pottery through the Ages*, Baltimore, 1959.

GUDE, HANS. Norwegian painter (b. Christiania, now Oslo, Norway, 1825; d. Berlin, 1903). He was, perhaps, most proficient at painting mountain landscapes. *Mountain Heights* (1857; Oslo, National Gallery) shows a heavy fog settling over the moors as an autumn evening approaches.

BIBLIOGRAPHY. C. Laurin, E. Hannover, and J. Thiis, *Scandinavian Art*, New York, 1922.

GUDEA, PORTRAIT STATUES OF. Gudea was the ruler of Lagash in southern Mesopotamia in the period after the fall of the Akkad dynasty. It is not definitely known whether he directly followed the Akkad kings and reigned while the Guti, who had invaded from the eastern mountains, were ruling northern Babylonia (ca. 2180–2125 B.C.) or whether he was somewhat later and contemporary with Urnammu, the first king of the 3d dynasty of Ur (ca. 2125 B.C.).

The extraordinary number of statues of Gudea come predominantly from Lagash and are mostly made of diorite, a stone which had to be imported into Babylonia from Magan, as eastern Arabia was then called. The greatest number of Gudea statues are now in the Louvre, since the excavations at Lagash were conducted by the French. The statues vary in pose but are otherwise remarkably similar in style. The usual costume is a long robe with tasseled or fleeced edge, wound around the body, over the left shoulder and under the right shoulder so that the right arm is left bare. The corner of the garment is tucked in over the right breast. Many of the figures also wear a wool cap or wig.

In both standing and seated statues the head is frequently large in proportion to the body, the chin is prominent and flattened, the eyes are oval with heavy lids, and a continuous eyebrow decorated with a chevron design runs over the eyes. The figure usually has an extremely abbreviated neck. The shoulders are broad and muscular, and the bare right arm is well modeled. Generally the hands

Portrait statues of Gudea. Example from Lagash. Louvre, Paris.

are humbly clasped together and nothing is held between them. The head, when no cap covers it, is bald; the ears are large and flat against the head. In the standing figures there is little or no articulation of the body under the drapery. In the seated figures there is simply a bend at the waist and knees. In both, the feet and ankles are cut out from the block and modeled. The seat is a small bench with inward-curving legs and a single horizontal bar on each side.

Nearly all the statues bear lengthy Sumerian inscriptions, listing Gudea's accomplishments and giving the name of the statue; the list serves as a prayer to the god or goddess for Gudea's life and health. The materials used other than diorite are alabaster, steatite, dolerite, and granite. The size of the statues varies from over life size to well under life size. One small standing Gudea in the Stoclet Collection, Brussels, is only 16 inches high.

Besides the simple seated or standing figures, there is one standing figure that holds a flowing vase and two seated statues that have architect's plans or writing materials on their laps.

See also TELLOH.

BIBLIOGRAPHY. A. Parrot, *Tello*, Paris, 1948.

PRUDENCE O. HARPER

GUDOHINUS GOSPELS. Merovingian illuminated manuscript, in the Municipal Library, Autun.

GUELPH TREASURE (Welfenschatz). Collection of medieval metal, enamel, and jewelry work assembled by the German house of Brunswick (Braunschweig) from the 11th through the 14th century. It remained in their hands until it was sold in 1929 by Duke Ernest Augustus of Brunswick-Lüneburg to various art dealers. The eighty-two pieces that the treasure comprised are in various museums throughout the world. Forty-four works (Byzantine, Italian, Rhenish, and northern German) are in the Museum of Arts and Crafts, Berlin, among them the Guelph Cross and the Eilbertus portable altar (both described below). Nine are in Cleveland. *See* CLEVELAND, OHIO: CLEVELAND MUSEUM OF ART.

The collection was started in 1038, when, upon the death of Liudolf, the first duke of Brunswick, his widow, Gertrude, donated a number of pieces to Brunswick Cathedral in his memory. In Gertrude's donation were, among other pieces, several gold crosses. One, the famous Guelph Cross, of enameled gold, gilded silver, gold filigree work, and precious stones, is an unparalleled example of early Romanesque metalwork. The recto of the cross has an enameled gold plaque of an evangelist symbol on each arm. The center of the cross, set with a large gem, is surrounded by small gems and delicate filigree work. Gertrude also donated an arm reliquary of St. Blasius made of gold, filigree work, and precious stones. These two works and a niello, cloisonné-enamel, gem-studded portable altar compose the earliest noteworthy pieces of the collection. The latter, called the Gertrudis Altar, is in the Cleveland Museum.

The next significant addition to the treasure was made by Henry the Lion. After a pilgrimage to Constantinople and Jerusalem in 1173 he returned home with relics—the arm bones of the apostles—for which he had made jeweled silver and gold arm reliquaries. He also donated a portable altar that bears the inscription "Eilbertus Coloniensis me fecit." This 12th-century work is of enameled copper with six figures, separated by a colonnade, on the main face. The top, which is especially unusual, is a series of miniatures on vellum depicting eight scenes from the life of Christ, the Twelve Apostles, and a large central miniature of Christ in Majesty. The entire surface is covered by a solid rock-crystal plaque. Another 12th-century Rhenish piece of unique importance is a large reliquary (4.6 by 4 centimeters) in the shape of a Byzantine dome. It is covered with enameled copper plaques and ivory figurines and rests upon metal feet sculptured in the form of griffins. The only other extant piece similar to this is in the Victoria and Albert Museum, London.

Duke Otto the Mild (d. 1344) added an illuminated Gospel book with a cover of silver decorated with miniatures on vellum set in rock crystal. The center of the cover contains a rock-crystal cross encasing fragments of the true cross, and the entire cover is embellished with gold filigree and precious stones. Engraved on the silver back of the cover are depictions of St. Blasius enthroned and flanked by Duke Otto and Duchess Agnes. The cover and manuscript are dated 1339.

STANLEY FERBER

GUEPIERE, PHILIPPE DE LA. German architect (1715–73). Guêpière worked mainly in Stuttgart and Karlsruhe. At first instructed by his father, he later studied with Jacques François Blondel and in Rome. His main work

Guelph Treasure. Cross base. Museum of Arts and Crafts, Berlin.

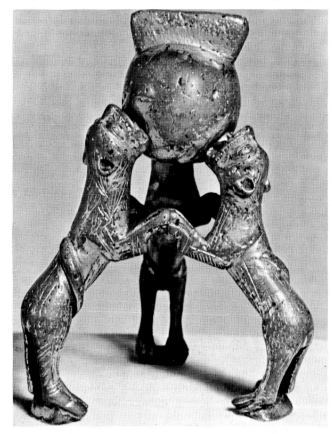

is at Stuttgart Castle, where he designed the left wing and interiors in the rococo style. His later work on Castle Monrepos tends toward new restraint and precision.

GUERCINO (Giovanni Francesco Barbieri). Italian painter (b. Cento, 1591; d. Bologna, 1666). He first studied with Gennari in Cento and the Zagnoni di Bastia in Modena, but received his stylistic education in Ferrara (1616), Bologna, where he studied with the Centesque painter Cremonino (1617), and Venice (1618). After a stay in Rome (1621–23), he returned to Cento when his patron, Pope Gregory XV, died and remained in that city except for a brief sojourn in Piacenza (1626–27) until 1642, when he transferred to Bologna.

Guercino's first style, nourished by his contact with Scarsellino in Ferrara, Lodovico Carracci in Bologna, and Titian in Venice, is amply demonstrated in his *Martyrdom of St. Peter* (1618; Modena, Civic Museum), one of a series of powerful altarpieces painted during the five years previous to his move to Rome. They all show his baroque predilections: a painterly technique in which light tends to dissolve forms, strong chiaroscuro, warm colors, forceful contrapposto poses, and sweeping compositional movement.

In this style he created his first Roman fresco, the illusionistic *Aurora*, on a ceiling in the Villa Ludovisi (1621). In Rome he entered the second phase of his stylistic development; under the influence of Agucchi's theories and Domenichino's paintings, Guercino moved toward classicism. This is already visible in his *Burial and Acceptance into Heaven of S. Petronilla* (1621; Rome, Capitoline Museum) which, for all its sense of immediacy, is far quieter in composition than his previous works. This solution may be compared, for example, with the one adopted in connection with a similar compositional problem posed by his *St. William Receiving the Habit* (1620; Bologna, National Picture Gallery).

He continued in this direction, subordinating *mouvementé* compositional organization to structural horizontals and verticals in the *Martyrdom of St. Lawrence* (1629; Ferrara, Cathedral). He comes close to duplicating the style of Guido Reni in the *Guardian Angel* (1641; Fano, Pinacoteca) and finally arrives at a staid and sterile classical formula in such works as *St. Thomas Aquinas* (1663; Bologna, S. Domenico). Guercino influenced the development of a baroque style in classically oriented Rome during the early 1620s; but he also showed the strength of the classical tradition, carried on into the 17th century by such artists as Reni, Sacchi, and Poussin.

BIBLIOGRAPHY. D. Mahon, *Studies in Seicento Art and Theory*, London, 1947; N. Grimaldi, *Il Guercino, Gian Francesco Barbieri, 1591-1666*, Bologna, 1957; R. Wittkower, *Art and Architecture in Italy, 1600-1750*, Baltimore, 1958.   STEPHEN E. OSTROW

GUERIN, GILLES. French sculptor (b. Paris, ca. 1609; d. there, 1678). A pupil of Charles Le Brun's father and perhaps of Simon Guillain, Guérin became a member of the Royal Academy of Painting and Sculpture in 1648. His works include *Louis XIV Trampling the Fronde* (Chantilly, Condé Museum) and many tombs, including those of C. de Vieuville (Paris, Louvre) and Henri de Bourbon

Guercino (Giovanni Francesco Barbieri), *Diana Bathing*. Carrara Academy, Bergamo, Italy.

Pierre-Narcisse Guérin, *Phaedra and Hippolytus*. Louvre, Paris. A work that won honorable mention in the Salon of 1802.

(Vallery). Guérin also engraved the Pavillon du Louvre after designs of Jacques Sarrazin. He worked in a vigorous 17th-century French style.

BIBLIOGRAPHY. L. Dussieux, ed., *Mémoires inédits sur la vie et les ouvrages des membres de l'académie royale de peinture et de sculpture*, vol. 1, Paris, 1854.

GUERIN, PIERRE-NARCISSE. French neoclassical painter (b. Paris, 1774; d. Rome, 1833). Guérin first entered the atelier of Brennet, then that of Regnault. He won the Prix de Rome in 1797 but was not able to take advantage of this honor because the program was suspended during Napoleon's Italian campaign. He received acclaim for his *Marcus Sextus Returned from Exile* (Paris, Louvre), which was shown at the Paris Salon of 1799. It was interpreted as symbolizing the return of *emigrés* forced to leave France because of the Revolution.

Guérin's painting followed the style and manner set forth by David, but it lacked the spare intensity of David's most orthodox neoclassical works. His art accepts the mode but not the dogma, and it lacks conviction. In the Salon of 1802, Guérin won an honorable mention for his *Phaedra and Hippolytus* (Louvre). In it he used far more complex and dramatic lighting than David. The head of Theseus suggests that of Brutus in David's 1789 painting *The Lictors Bringing the Bodies of His Sons to Brutus*. David patterned his conception after an ancient Roman bronze; Guérin, in following David's example, is a further step away from the original. He idealizes and elongates his figures. Unlike David, who wanted to reveal the steadfastness and patriotic zeal of noble ancients and to set forth an example to his contemporaries, he merely wished to tell a story in a charming manner.

Guérin finally went to Italy. Though he spent about five years there, his work was hardly affected. He returned to Paris in 1810 and exhibited three works at the Salon that year, including *Aurora and Cephalus* (Louvre). It reflects a trend away from David and toward the romantic. The lighting, which comes from above and slightly behind the figures, causes shadows to be dark. The effect would be dramatic if there were not a saccharine, sleek, somewhat erotic character to the stylized figures. It is as if there were some recall of the rococo. One of the other works done in 1810, *Bonaparte Pardoning the Rebels at Cairo*, is more in the manner of Gros. Guérin opened a studio in Paris and had around him a number of ardent romantics: Géricault, Scheffer, Orsel, and Léon Cogniet. He was made professor at the Ecole des Beaux-Arts in 1814 and a member of the Institute the following year. His most famous student was Delacroix. He refused the directorship of the French Academy in Rome in 1816 but relented and accepted it in 1822. He held the post for six years. He was made a baron in 1829.

BIBLIOGRAPHY. R. Escholier, *La Peinture française: XIXe siècle*, vol. 1: *De David à Géricault*, Paris, 1941.

ROBERT REIFF

GUERNICA. Oil painting by Picasso, in the Museum of Modern Art, New York. *See* PICASSO, PABLO.

GUERRERO, XAVIER. Mexican painter (1896–). Guerrero was born in San Pedro de las Colonias, Coahuila. He served as technical advisor to Roberto Montenegro (1922) and Rivera (1923) and was an early experimenter in encaustic and fresco. With Siqueiros he founded *El Machete*, literary organ of the mural movement, in 1924, and later, in the thirties, he was one of the founders of the League of Revolutionary Writers and Artists.

In collaboration with Rivera, Guerrero helped paint the Ministry of Education in Mexico City; with Siqueiros he participated in the commission to fresco the Escuela México in Chillán, Chile (1939). In the latter city Guerrero himself decorated a workers' club. His best independent murals were done in 1950 for the Benito Juárez House of Pensions in Mexico City.

BIBLIOGRAPHY. A. Reed, *The Mexican Muralists*, New York, 1960.

GUERRERO GALVAN, JESUS. Mexican painter (1910–). Guerrero Galván was born in Tonilá, Jalisco. He first studied art at the School of Plastic Arts in San Antonio, Tex., and in 1922 entered the studio of the academic painter José Vizcarra in Guadalajara. In 1924 he painted with a group of young artists in Guadalajara under Zuno and by 1925 he was living in Mexico City, where he did both easel and mural painting. He was an artist in residence at the University of New Mexico in 1942; he has also taught at governmental schools in Mexico. Frequent exhibitions in Mexico and the United States have placed Guerrero Galván's works in many public and private collections. Sensitive, even a trifle sweet, his paintings are quiet studies of men, women, and children of a distinctly Indian type, like the painter. Soft in color, large in form, the works are realist without being detailed.

BIBLIOGRAPHY. M. Helm, *Modern Mexican Painters*, New York, 1941; Instituto Nacional de Bellas Artes, *45 Autorretratos de pintores mexicanos*, Mexico City, 1947; B. S. Myers, *Mexican Painting in Our Time*, New York, 1956.

GUERRERO Y TORRES, FRANCISCO ANTONIO. Mexican architect (ca. 1749–92). Guerrero was the designer of the Valparaíso House in Mexico City (1769), the Pocito Chapel at Guadalupe (1779), and the Enseñanza Church in Mexico City (1772–78). These buildings are characterized by unconventional curvilinear plans, columnar portals, and linear ornament. They break away from the heavily ornamented baroque style of Lorenzo Rodríguez to a neoclassicism based on the style of the 17th century.

BIBLIOGRAPHY. G. Kubler and M. Soria, *Art and Architecture in Spain and Portugal and Their American Dominions, 1500–1800*, Baltimore, 1959.

GUERRINI, LORENZO. Italian sculptor (1914–). Born in Milan, Guerrini studied at the Academy in Rome, in Breslau and Berlin, and then in Paris. He has traveled extensively in central and eastern Europe and in Brazil. Since his first one-man show in Milan, he has been exhibiting internationally. He sculpts directly in stone and executes abstract pieces such as *Metamorphosis* (1957) and *Man Renews Himself* (1957).

GUGLIELMI, O. LOUIS. American painter (b. Cairo, Egypt, 1906; d. Amagansett, N.Y., 1956). He went to the United States in 1914 and studied at the National Academy of Design from 1920 to 1925. His early paintings were tightly rendered realistic studies of urban genre and social themes, such as *Wedding in South Street* (1936; New York, Museum of Modern Art). Guglielmi's exact depiction was also suitable for subjects with strong surrealistic connotations, as in *Terror in Brooklyn* (1941; New York, Whitney Museum), which places frightened figures under a glass enclosure on a city street. His later paintings of industrial and city scenes, abstracted and purified in form, are related to precisionism.

BIBLIOGRAPHY. Walker Art Center, *The Precisionist View in American Art*, Minneapolis, 1960.

GUGLIELMO, FRA. Italian sculptor (ca. 1238–1312). Of Pisan origin, Fra Guglielmo was one of the earliest Dominican artists. He was associated with the workshop of Nicola Pisano. The execution of the Arca of St. Dominic in S. Domenico Maggiore, for which Nicola had been commissioned in 1264, is often ascribed to Fra Guglielmo, but he was probably only one of several sculptors to participate in the carving. He did execute the pulpit in S. Giovanni Fuori Civitas, Pistoia (1270), in which he follows the classicism of Nicola, but in an old-fashioned and foursquare manner. It has also been conjectured that Fra Guglielmo may have taken part in the designing and building of S. Maria Novella in Florence.

BIBLIOGRAPHY. W. G. Waters, *Italian Sculptors*, 2d ed., London, 1926.

GUGLIELMO (Wiligelmus) DA MODENA. Northern Italian sculptor (fl. Modena, early 12th cent.). His earliest work is the decorative sculpture on the Cathedral at Modena (1099–1106), including the reliefs of the Creation on the south façade of the main portal and various ornamental friezes. The "Enoch-Elias" tablet there gives his name as Wiligelmus, probably indicating a Germanic origin. Also attributed to him are the bishop's throne of Bari (1098) and an archivolt with angel heads at Monopoli (1107). Wiligelmus is among the first of Italian sculptors to master narrative and monumental figural reliefs.

BIBLIOGRAPHY. T. Krautheimer-Hess, "Die figurale Plastik der Ostlombardei von 1100 bis 1178," *Marburger Jahrbuch für Kunstwissenschaft*, IV, 1928; F. Arcangeli, "Tracce di Wiligelmo a Cremona," *Paragone*, XXI, 1951.

Guglielmo da Modena, relief depicting the creation of Eve on the façade of Modena Cathedral.

GUGLIELMO DEL PIOMBO, FRA, *see* PORTA, GUGLIELMO DELLA.

GUHA, *see* SIKHARA.

GUIDI, VIRGILIO. Italian painter (1892–   ). He was born in Rome and studied at the academy there. He was associated with the Novecento group. In the 1930s Guidi painted impressionistic landscapes and classical figures. His work became more abstract after World War II, with formally simplified figures and rich color.

BIBLIOGRAPHY. A. Gatto, *Virgilio Guidi*, Milan, 1947.

GUIDO, ALFREDO. Argentine painter (1892–   ). Guido was born in Rosario. Cubistic structure characterizes his art after 1915, when he began studies in Europe. He had done murals and prints, but figurative subjects in oils and tempera are his major expression (for example, *Stevedores Resting*, 1938; New York, Museum of Modern Art).

BIBLIOGRAPHY. M. L. San Martín, *Pintura argentina contemporánea*, Buenos Aires, 1961.

GUIDO DA COMO, *see* COMO, GUIDO DA.

GUIDO DA SIENA. Sienese painter (fl. 13th cent.). Some critics consider Guido the founder of Sienese 13th-century painting, but his claim to the title hinges upon the genuineness of the date 1221 inscribed on the *Madonna Hodetria* (Siena, Palazzo Pubblico). Most of this signed work was repainted in the 14th century, and scholarly discussion has centered on the possible falsification of the date. The untouched *Christ with Angels* of the pinnacle shows Guido's indebtedness to and divergence from the Byzantine style. To him or to his circle have been attributed the *St. Dominic* (Cambridge, Mass., Fogg Art Museum), *Madonna and Four Saints*, and *St. Peter Enthroned* (both Siena, Academy). Guido succeeded in humanizing his subjects, but much of the hieratic majesty of Romanesque sculpture remains.

BIBLIOGRAPHY. G. H. Edgell, *A History of Sienese Painting*, New York, 1932.

GUIDO DI PALMERUCCIO. Italian painter (fl. 1313–49). Frescoes in S. Maria dei Laici and the Palazzo del Comune, both in Gubbio, have been ascribed to Guido on the basis of his documented activity in both buildings. Broad figures and modeling, sensitive expressions, and the sweeping compositional use of line indicate the influence of Pietro Lorenzetti and distinguish Guido as the leading artist of his period in Gubbio.

GUIDO PAGANINO, *see* MAZZONI, GUIDO.

GUILLAIN, SIMON. French sculptor (b. Paris, 1581; d. there, 1658). The son and pupil of Nicolas Guillain, Simon Guillain was one of the original twelve professors of the Royal Academy of Painting and Sculpture (1648). He became rector there in 1657. He did much religious sculpture, including the high altar for St-Eustache, Paris, and decorative statues for the interior and exterior of the Sorbonne. His most important work was the Pont-au-Change monument to Louis XIII (1647), fragments of which are preserved in the Louvre. Guillain worked in a vigorous French classic style.

BIBLIOGRAPHY. L. Dussieux, ed., *Mémoires inédits sur la vie et les ouvrages des membres de l'académie royale de peinture et de sculpture*, vol. 1, Paris, 1854; A. Michel, *Histoire de l'art*, vol. 6, pt. 2, Paris, 1922.

GUILLAUME, JEAN BAPTISTE CLAUDE EUGENE. French sculptor (b. Montbard, 1822; d. Rome, 1905). He studied in Dijon and with Pradier in Paris. Guillaume produced dignified portraits and figures in a powerful style based on Roman sculpture and was influential as a teacher and director of the Ecole des Beaux-Arts.

GUILLAUMIN, JEAN BAPTISTE ARMAND. French impressionist painter (b. Moulins, 1841; d. Paris, 1927). At sixteen he went to Paris to work in his uncle's shop, but he also attended the Académie Suisse, where he met Pissarro, who was to become a lifelong friend. Guillaumin was largely self-taught. In 1866 he left a position as a clerk to paint full time. Two years later he was so destitute that he and Pissarro were painting blinds to earn barely enough to survive. Guillaumin painted a picture of Pissarro at this task. In 1872 he took a position with the Department of Bridges and Causeways in order to support his aged grandparents and himself. He was to hold this position until he won 100,000 francs in a city lottery nearly twenty years later. At that time he left his job and painted full time again. He exhibited in the celebrated Salon des Réfusés in 1863 and had three landscapes in the first impressionist exhibition of 1874.

He exhibited with the impressionists regularly thereafter. His painting was included in the first public showing of impressionist art in the United States, at the American Art Galleries in New York City in 1886, under the sponsorship of the astute dealer Durand-Ruel. Guillaumin used to visit the favorite impressionist rendezvous, the Café Guerbois, and Cézanne made an etching of him.

Guillaumin considered himself an artistic revolutionary throughout his life. He was receptive to new ideas and did incorporate some of them in his painting, but he himself was not an innovator. Unlike other impressionists, he

Jean Baptiste Armand Guillaumin, *Pont Louis-Philippe, Paris.* **National Gallery, Washington, D.C.**

did not snub Van Gogh, Gauguin, or Seurat. He made friends with Signac and gave him advice in his painting. Père Tanguy, the dealer of the leading avant-garde painters around the turn of the century, also exhibited works by Guillaumin. Guillaumin was included in the 1891 exhibition organized by the "XX" in Brussels. He made a number of etchings, using Dr. Gachet's press, as did Cézanne, Van Gogh, and others. The doctor also owned works of Guillaumin.

All phases of the impressionist development appear in the art of Guillaumin, from still lifes in the manner of early Manet to the near-Fauve color harmonies of Monet's turn-of-the-century art. Compared with his more celebrated colleagues, his art lacks breadth of conception and invention. The *Pont Louis-Philippe, Paris* (1875; Washington, D.C., National Gallery) superficially resembles a Monet, but, despite the considerable skill of execution and the sincerity, the painting appears somewhat calculated and wanting Monet's freshness, spontaneity, and sparkle.

BIBLIOGRAPHY. E. des Courières, *Armand Guillaumin*, Paris, 1924.
ROBERT REIFF

GUILLOCHE. Pattern of braided, interlaced circles the centers of which are sometimes filled with rosettes. The torus molding in Greek architecture was often ornamented with the guilloche.

GUIMARD, HECTOR. French architect (1867–1942). He worked in Paris and is considered the most accomplished architect of the French Art Nouveau style. His first important work, Castel Béranger, is one of the first buildings in Art Nouveau style. Much of his work has now disappeared, but his well-known entrances to the Paris Métro stations, made of cast metal in freely patterned vegetable forms, still remain. (One of these archways now stands in the sculpture garden of the Museum of Modern Art, New York.)

He also designed furniture, textiles, and so on, and considered himself the initiator of a new art movement, which he called "Style Guimard." He formed a museum of his work, which was destroyed in World War II. After 1915

Guilloche. Ornamental motif of braided, interlaced circles often used in Greek architecture.

his work loses its vibrant, forceful quality and becomes symmetrical and classicizing.

BIBLIOGRAPHY. H. Guimard, "An Architect's Opinion of 'l'Art Nouveau'," *Architectural Record*, 1902.

GUJARAT TEMPLES. Gujarat, a state in western India, was an important trading center from the 11th to the 13th century, its prosperity stimulating the construction of numerous richly designed Brahmanical and Jain temples. The Gujarat temples are of the northern, or "Indo-Aryan," style and are distinguished by the organization of the elaborate decor into three horizontal bands and by clustered turrets on the śikharas. The temples were extensively damaged by the Muslim invasion of 1298 and by an earthquake in the 19th century. The most impressive example today is the Sūrya temple at Modhera, south of Patan. The relatively well-preserved Jain temples of Mount Abu in Rajasthan are in the Gujarat style. *See* MODHERA.

BIBLIOGRAPHY. H. Cousens, *The Architectural Antiquities of Western India*, London, 1926; P. Brown, *Indian Architecture*, vol. 1: *Buddhist and Hindu Periods*, 4th ed., Bombay, 1959.

GULBENKIAN, CALOUSTE, FOUNDATION, LISBON, *see* LISBON: MUSEUMS (CALOUSTE GULBENKIAN FOUNDATION).

GULBRANSSON, OLAF. Norwegian draftsman and painter (b. Oslo, 1873; d. Tegernsee, 1958). One of the most famous caricaturists of modern times, Gulbransson is closely identified with the early-20th-century tradition of Munich satire, in spite of his Norwegian birth and training. His caricatures were always masterfully rendered, with economy of line and with acute observation. Like his friend Wilhelm Busch, Gulbransson used his art in the pursuit of truth and equity, and only rarely with biting or cynical criticism.

Gulbransson studied at the Royal Norwegian Drawing School, then worked on his own for the comic paper *Tyrihans* and for *Transviksposten* and *Karikaturen*. In 1900 he went to Paris. After a brief association with F. Colarossie, he returned in 1901 to Oslo, where he produced an album of twenty-four caricatures of famous Norwegians.

In 1902 he went to Munich, a move which was profoundly formative in his development. Very quickly, particularly through his productive association with the magazine *Simplizissimus*, he was absorbed into the artistic circle that dominated Munich at the turn of the century. He made the acquaintance of such men as Wilhelm Busch, T. T. Heine, R. Wilke, and B. Paul, each a powerful political satirist. In 1929 he became professor at the Munich Academy.

His output of caricature was largely concentrated in *Simplizissimus* (his earliest contribution appears in vol. 7, no. 38). Most of his other drawings, which include noncaricature, appeared in folio form (*Famous Contemporaries*, Munich, 1905; *Out of my Drawer*, Munich, 1912) or as book illustrations (L. Thoma's *Tante Frieda*, 1907; A. Wohlmuth's *74 Fables*). He painted masks and sets for the theaters of Munich as well.

His work falls roughly into two periods. Before 1916 it was essentially ornamental and linear. He used few lines, but each one was extremely important and expressive and had a decorative tendency toward swing and arabesque. A great caricaturist, he could project an exaggerated reality with few lines. Most of his published work was done before 1916. After that time, his ornamental period was behind him; his work softened, and he used more modeling and some color.

BIBLIOGRAPHY. W. Schäfer, *Der andere Gulbransson*, Königsberg, 1939; Council of Europe, *Sources of the XXth Century*, Paris, 1960.
JULIA M. EHRESMANN

GUNBAD-I-KABUS, TOMB TOWER OF, GURGAN. The earliest of the fifty tomb towers still extant in Iran (built in 1006–07). It rises 167 feet above ground, and its underground part is about 35 feet deep. An interior dome is hidden by a conical roof. Ten right-angled flanges project from the circular body.

BIBLIOGRAPHY. A. U. Pope, *Persian Architecture*, New York, 1965.

GUNDELACH, MATTHAUS. German painter (b. Hessen or Kassel? ca. 1566; d. Augsburg, 1653). Shortly before 1609 he went to Prague, where he was court painter to Kaiser Rudolf II and a follower of Joseph Heintz. He moved to Augsburg in 1615. Paintings such as the *Adoration of the Magi* (Augsburg, Schloss Rosenberg) show the strong influence of the mannerists Hans von Aachen and Bartholomeus Spranger.

GUNDESTRUP SILVER CALDRON. Celtic metalwork of the 1st century B.C., in the State Museum of Fine Arts, Copenhagen.

GUNTHER, IGNAZ. German sculptor (b. Altmannstein, 1725; d. Munich, 1775). After seven years with Johann

Ignaz Günther, *Pietà*. Church of SS. Peter and Paul, Weyarn, Germany.

Baptist Straub in Munich (1743–50), Günther worked with Egell at Mannheim (1751–52) and at the Vienna Academy (1752–54), where he was awarded a first prize. Thus, most of his work was executed in collaboration with older sculptors until 1754, when he settled in Munich for the remainder of his life.

In the statue of Mary Magdalen in the Starnberg Museum (1755), the distinctive characteristics of his art are already evident: elongated proportions, oval face, attenuated neck, ecstatic expression, and angular and expectant movement of the body. The features conform to a simplified arrangement with the nose and mouth paralleling the downward angle of the prominent eyes. The multidirectional draperies and turns of the body create a radial effusiveness and openness of form, which surpass in complexity similar characteristics in the sculpture of Egid Quirin Asam, of whom Günther was a great admirer.

In the high altar and side altars of Rott am Inn (1760–62), where Günther worked with the architect Johann Michael Fischer and the painter Matthäus Günther in a typical 18th-century collaboration, this effluent rococo use of space is shown to greater advantage in an architectural setting. The high altar is arranged around the central void of a large painting. The supporting columns on either side create a perspective and third dimension in which the sculptures exist and link this world to the architecture of the church. Crowning the vertical movement are figures of the Trinity, angels, and *putti* placed high above the altar in a radiating nimbus. Four saints on the ground level form another perspective and establish the transition into the space of the church itself.

Following this Günther created the bronze doors at the Schloss Schleissheim (1763), the polychrome *Guardian Angel* in the Burgersaal, Munich (1763), and sculpture groups for the church at Weyarn (1763–65), including the *Pietà* and the *Annunciation*. Multidirectional movement vitalizes these elegant figures, creating an aura of energy. The massive form of the body of Christ is a complexity of facets rather than a unity in the Renaissance sense. Günther's colors, which are pastel variations of the primaries plus flesh tones, bridge the gap between ideality of form and palpable energy, between fantasy and reality.

Günther then went on to design high altars at Neustift bei Friesing (1765–66), Starnberg (1766–68), and Mallersdorf (1768–70). Figures are more monumental, gestures more sweeping, and compositions more unified. There is a more profound sense of space in that figures in different parts of the altar are compositionally linked, often over wide gaps of space. This is consonant with the three-dimensional complexities of contemporaneous architecture.

Late works, such as the reliefs of Joseph and St. Theresa in the Bavarian National Museum, Munich (1771), and the *Pietà* at the church of Nenningen (1774), are less playful. Sustained lines of gesture and drapery and cutting angles enhance the tragic expressions of the figures. Draperies now seem to reveal the inner tension of body and spirit rather than a dispersal of physical energy.

BIBLIOGRAPHY. A. Schoenberger, *Ignaz Günther*, Munich, 1954.
DONALD GODDARD

GUNTHER, MATTHAUS. German painter (b. Unterpeissenberg, 1705; d. Wessobrunn, 1788). He was chief master of the Augsburg rococo school of painting. Günther was the student of Asam; his style was strongly influenced by his master and indirectly by Tiepolo. His most important works were ceiling frescoes such as those for the cloister church in Wilten (1749) and the Schloss Süching.

BIBLIOGRAPHY. H. Gundersheimer, *Matthäus Günther*, Augsburg, 1930.

GUNUK, *see* XANTHUS.

GURK CATHEDRAL. Triple-nave and triple-apse Austrian basilica of severe Romanesque proportions, with a westwork, built from 1140 to 1200. An exterior of massive simplicity, decorated with arched corbel tables and blind arcades, encloses an austere interior enriched by 13th-century frescoes and late Gothic vaulting. The choir and apse are raised above a handsome groin-vaulted crypt, which is supported on a forest of columns with plain cubic capitals. The upper chapel of the westwork was completely frescoed in about 1220. This and fresco cycles of the late Gothic give Gurk its importance in the history of medieval painting.

BIBLIOGRAPHY. K. Ginhart and B. Grimschitz, *Der Dom zu Gurk*, Vienna, 1930.

GURO, *see* AFRICA, PRIMITIVE ART OF (WEST AFRICA: IVORY COAST).

GUSTAVIAN STYLE. Style of art and literature in Sweden from about 1780 to 1810 (corresponding to the neoclassical period in France and the rest of Europe). The Gustavian style marks the beginning of an indigenous

Philip Guston, *Martial Memory*. City Art Museum, St. Louis.

Swedish art after centuries of subservience to German culture.

BIBLIOGRAPHY. J. Roosval, *Swedish Art*, Princeton, 1932.

GUSTON, PHILIP. American painter (1912–   ). Born in Montreal, Canada, he now lives in New York. Guston studied at the Otis Art Institute in Los Angeles but is mainly self-taught. His works of the late 1930s and early 1940s were executed in the socially conscious style of mixed realism-surrealism then popular in the United States. *Martial Memory* (1941; St. Louis, City Art Museum) is typical, with its masked, enigmatic figures poignantly arranged in a slum setting.

After teaching at the State University of Iowa from 1941 to 1945, Guston took first prize at the Carnegie International, held a one-man show at the Midtown Galleries, and won a Guggenheim fellowship (1948), a Prix de Rome (1949), and an American Academy of Arts and Letters grant (1949). About 1950, a *White Painting* series signaled his development of a more abstract method, which matured in such canvases as *Dial* (1956), *The Clock* (1957), and *The Tale* (1961). Although Guston is sometimes called an abstract impressionist, his style clearly belongs to the tradition of abstract expressionism, or action painting.

BIBLIOGRAPHY. New York, Museum of Modern Art, *12 Americans*, New York, 1956; S. Hunter, *Modern American Painting and Sculpture*, New York, 1959; F. O'Hara, "Growth and Guston," *Art News*, LXI, 1962.

JOHN C. GALLOWAY

GUTIERREZ, FRANCISCO. Spanish sculptor (1723/24–82). Trained in Madrid under Luis Salvador Carmona, he won a scholarship to Rome in 1746 for his model entered in an academy competition on the theme of Abraham being stopped by an angel from sacrificing his son Isaac. An early work, the *Pietà* (Tarazona Cathedral), shows the influence of his teacher's late baroque style but is more serene. His goddess Cybele for the Cybele Fountain (with lions by French sculptor Robert Michel) in Madrid is an example of pure neoclassicism. His main occupation was carving architectural ornamentation.

BIBLIOGRAPHY. F. Abbad Rios, "Una obra inédita de Francisco Gutiérrez," *Archivo español de arte*, XVIII, Madrid, 1946.

GUTIERREZ, JOSE LUIS. Mexican painter and teacher (1900–68). Born in Miacatlán, Morelos, Gutiérrez was a pioneer in the application to painting of industrial compounds such as vinylite, silicones of nitrocellulose, and acrylics. After a decade of work in the United States during the 1930s, he returned to Mexico, where from 1945 on he taught his techniques at the National Polytechnic Institute of Mexico and at Mexico City College. His plastic materials have been widely used by mural painters in Mexico and elsewhere, for example, by Tamayo in the UNESCO building in Paris.

BIBLIOGRAPHY. A. Reed, *The Mexican Muralists*, New York, 1960; J. Gutiérrez and N. Roukes, *Painting with Acrylics*, New York, 1965.

GUTTAE. Small truncated cones or cylinders (from the Latin *gutta*, "drop") under the triglyphs and mutules of the Doric entablature, as in the Parthenon and the Theseum, Athens. Guttae are assumed to be the stone forms of wooden pegs used to fasten roof timbers.

GUTTENBERG, CARL GOTTLIEB. German engraver (b. Wöhrd, near Nürnberg, 1743; d. Nürnberg, 1790). Between 1780 and the French Revolution, Guttenberg lived in Paris, where he acquired the neat style of Johann Georg Wille. His principal plates are for *Voyage pittoresque du royaume de Naples* by the Abbé de Saint-Non.

BIBLIOGRAPHY. E. Bock, *Die deutschen Meister (Die Zeichnungen alter Meister im Kupferstichkabinett)*, 2 vols., Berlin, 1921.

GUTTER. Channel used to carry rain from roofs.

GUTTER, FLYING. Flared roof. Curved up at the eaves and projecting 2 feet and more to protect walls from rain, as in Flemish farmhouses, flying gutters were adopted in Dutch colonial architecture of the 17th century.

GUTTUSO, RENATO. Italian painter (1912–   ). He was born in Palermo. Shortly after his arrival in Rome in 1931 Guttuso became a member of the romantic Roman school. His subsequent associations, the Milan Corrente movement and the postwar Fronte Nuovo delle Arti, emphasize the strong social concerns that underlie Guttuso's painting. His earlier style was expressionistic and influenced by Picasso, for example, *Battle with Wounded Horses* (1942; Rome, National Gallery of Modern Art). Although he stresses realistic subjects, Guttuso's awareness of modern abstract design can be seen in *The Mafia* (1948; New York, Museum of Modern Art) as well as in a more recent series of cubistic landscapes.

BIBLIOGRAPHY. G. Marchioro, *Renato Guttuso*, Milan, 1952.

GUTWEIN, JOHANN BALTHASAR. German engraver (b. Augsburg, 1702; d. Würzburg, 1785). After studying with his father, Johann Caspar Gutwein, and working seven years in Italy, Gutwein was appointed court and university engraver in Würzburg. His works are mainly engraved layouts and views after architecture, particularly that of Johann Balthasar Neumann; copies of portraits and wall paintings; and dedicatory plates for Würzburg monuments (Hofkirche, 1745).

BIBLIOGRAPHY. F. Hirsch, *Das Sogenannte Skizzenbuch Balthasar Neumanns*, Heidelberg, 1912.

Renato Guttuso, *Man Reading a Newspaper*. Beldi Collection, Oleggio.

GUY, FRANCIS. American landscape painter (b. Lorton, England, 1760; d. Brooklyn, N.Y., 1826). In 1795 he moved to Brooklyn and opened a silk-dyeing plant. From 1798 to 1817 he lived in Philadelphia and Baltimore. He returned to Brooklyn, where he painted literal views of urban life in a meticulous but primitive and naïve manner.

BIBLIOGRAPHY. J. H. Pleasants, *Four Late Eighteenth Century Anglo-American Landscape Painters*, Worcester, Mass., 1943.

GUYOT DE BEAUGRAND, *see* BEAUGRAND, GUYOT DE.

GUYS, ERNEST ADOLPHE HYACINTHE CONSTANTIN. French illustrator and journalist (b. Flushing, Holland, 1805; d. Paris, 1892). Guys's family came from Grenoble; his father was an official in the French navy. When he was eighteen Guys joined Lord Byron in the Greek war of independence against the Turks. From this experience he came to know many Englishmen and acquired a knowledge of their language.

Just when he began to draw is not known, and he seems to have had no formal training as an artist. Guys went to England when he was about twenty-five and made his living teaching French. He began to sell drawings to magazines, and in the late 1840s he was employed by the *Illustrated London News* as a traveling war correspondent. He recorded scenes of the Revolution of 1848 in Paris, the Crimean War, and other conflicts. He also made trips to Spain, Italy, Germany, and Turkey to make drawings of tourist attractions. These drawings were reworked by artisans into wood engravings, the common form of reproduction then in use for popular magazines. Of course, much was lost in character and spontaneity in the process of conversion. Many original drawings have survived; Guys must have made thousands of them. He worked from memory for the most part, as did Daumier. He seems to have worked rapidly, at least so the drawings suggest. He used a pen or pencil and then added washes of water color, not for its color, but to lend atmosphere and give body to the line drawing.

Guys returned to Paris in the late 1850s. He assumed the pose of a dandy but at the same time was belligerent about preserving his anonymity. In fact, when Baudelaire began to write his celebrated articles about Guys in *Le Figaro* in 1863, Guys insisted that he not be named, that only his initials be used. He never exhibited publicly and never signed any of his work. It was in Paris that he made his best-known drawings: of the activity of the fancy gentlemen and their beribboned, crinoline-skirted, flirtatious ladies, their high-stepping horses, the breezy, dizzy spectacle of the passing crowd along the Bois de Boulogne and other fashionable boulevards of Paris. Guys does not particularize his subjects. His women all bear the same features, which are similar to those in fashion magazines of the time.

He was admired by the impressionist group, who knew him personally from his infrequent visits to the Café Guerbois, and Manet painted his portrait. Baudelaire's ex-

Constantin Guys, *Girl on a Green Background*. Carnavalet Museum, Paris. A typical example of the illustrator's technique.

tensive collection of Guys's drawings is now in the Carnavalet Museum in Paris.

BIBLIOGRAPHY. G. Geffroy, *Constantin Guys, l'historien du Second Empire*, Paris, 1920; C. P. Baudelaire, *Constantin Guys, le peintre de la vie moderne*, Geneva, 1943; C. P. Baudelaire, *Au temps de Baudelaire, Guys, et Nadar*, Paris, 1945; G. Besson, *Constantin Guys*, Paris, 1950; C. Guys, *Dessins de Constantin Guys* (catalog), by B. Streiff, Lausanne, 1957.

ROBERT REIFF

GUZANA, *see* TELL HALAF.

GUZMAN DE ROJAS, CECILIO. Bolivian painter (1900–   ). Born in Potosí, Guzman, after initial training in Cochabamba, traveled in Spain and France. He continued his studies in Madrid, Barcelona, and Paris and exhibited at the Barcelona Fair of 1929. After returning to Bolivia, he became the Inspector General of Fine Arts (1929) and the director of the National School of Fine Arts, La Paz (1931) and was the prime influence in the national movement toward modern art. His works, which include historical murals and paintings, portraits, and landscapes, often have a heavy, linear insistence and symbolic approach that recall the Art Nouveau movement of Austria.

BIBLIOGRAPHY. R. Villarroel Claure, *Arte contemporáneo*, La Paz, 1952.

GWALIOR. City and district in Madhya Pradesh, India. The city was once a princely municipality, and its major feature is a fortress set on a rocky height, overlooking the road from central India to the plains of the north. This fortress is first mentioned in writings dated A.D. 525. It has been ruled by various successive groups. In 1232 it was taken by the Muslims. Raja Man Singh built two of the palaces within the fort complex, which has six palaces, six temples, a mosque, and other buildings as well. The fortress wall is 1.75 miles in length and 300 to 900 yards broad. The massive red sandstone towers are fine examples of early Hindu architecture. The windows in the walls are setback slits which recede six times, rectangle within rectangle. The rock face of the fort is an outdoor book, covered with Hindu and Jain scriptural writings. The famous Bāgh caves, which contain fine examples of classical paintings, are also in Gwalior. *See* BAGH.

GWATHMEY, ROBERT. American painter and graphic artist (1903–   ). Born in Richmond, Va., he studied at the Maryland Institute of Design and at the Pennsylvania Academy of Fine Arts. Gwathmey's subjects are scenes of Southern life, particularly the life of the Negro. The vigorous element of social commentary, only implied in some paintings, for example, *Hoeing* (1943; Pittsburgh, Carnegie Institute), is obvious in others. While his subjects are realistic, his painting style involves the simplified forms of modern abstraction. Objects, figures, and parts of figures are formed of exact, dark outlines and flat areas of color and are composed with a strong awareness of two-dimensional design and pattern, as in *Sowing* (1949; New York, Whitney Museum).

BIBLIOGRAPHY. E. McCausland, "Robert Gwathmey," *Magazine of Art*, XXXIX, 1946.

GYMNASIUM. Place where physical exercises are performed; developed first as an architectural complex in ancient Greece. A Greek gymnasium might include an open race track (doromus), a xystus (covered, colonnaded race track), baths, and a palaestra with small rooms arranged around a peristyle. In the late 5th century B.C. gymnasiums became centers of learning, where young men received academic as well as physical training. A large niche, usually in the center of one of the interior walls, was used as a room for teaching (ephebeion). In Roman times larger and more sumptuous thermae generally took the place of gymnasiums. In modern central Europe the term gymnasium is used to designate the school just below the university level.

GYNAECEUM. Women's gallery in a church, as in Hagia Sophia, Constantinople. The term is also applied to women's quarters, as in the Palace of Diocletian, Split, where the gynaeceum occupied the large northwest wing.

GYOKUDO (Uragami Gyokudo). Japanese calligrapher and painter (1745–1820). Gyokudo was also a warrior, Confucian scholar, and poet. Resigning from the service in 1794, he became a wanderer. He had no formal learning in painting, and his landscapes, done either in ink alone or with light touches of colors, show a strong individual style. Seemingly nimble and careless brushstrokes create the strong poetic feeling that characterizes his works.

BIBLIOGRAPHY. J. E. H. Covell, *Japanese Landscape Painting*, New York, 1962.

GYSBRECHTS, CORNELIS NORBERTUS. Flemish painter of still life and trompe l'oeil. Very little is known of this attractive artist, except that he obtained his inscription as a master at the Antwerp Guild of St. Luke in 1659 or 1660 and that he was court painter in Copenhagen from about 1670 to 1672. The rare paintings by which Gysbrechts has come to our attention represent extensive paraphernalia, trompe l'oeil, and often pictures within pictures. He can be best studied in Denmark: at Castle Rosenborg in Copenhagen, at the National Museum in Frederiksborg, and at Castle Gaunø, an 18th-century château on an island in southern Sjælland, Denmark.

GYSELS, PIETER. Flemish painter of genre and still-life scenes as well as of landscapes (b. Antwerp, 1621; d. ca. 1690). He is best known for his landscapes done in close imitation of Jan Breughel the Elder, although the technique sometimes becomes careless, in keeping with late-17th-century procedures. His kermisses are reminiscent of David Vinckeboons.

BIBLIOGRAPHY F. J. van den Branden, *Geschiedenis der Antwerpsche Schilderschool*, Antwerp, 1883.

GYULAFEHERVAR (Karlsberg) CATHEDRAL. Hungarian cathedral in central Romania, founded in the 11th century and destroyed by the Mongols in 1241. The apse had been rebuilt by 1290. It is a cross-plan basilica with a square crossing and a square monks' choir preceding the choir and sanctuary.

BIBLIOGRAPHY. A. Hekler, *Ungarische Kunstgeschichte*, Berlin, 1937.

H

HAAGEN, JORIS VAN DER (Johann van der Hagen; Joris Verhagen). Dutch landscape painter (b. possibly Dordrecht or Arnhem, ca. 1615; d. The Hague, 1669). From 1640 Van der Haagen was active in The Hague Guild of St. Luke. In 1656 he was one of the founders of Pictura, a painters' confraternity in The Hague. Van der Haagen visited Amsterdam in 1650 and 1657 and collaborated there with Adriaen van de Velde and, most often, with Dirck Wijntrack.

BIBLIOGRAPHY. J. K. van der Haagen, *De Schilders van der Haagen en hun Werk*, Voorburg, 1932.

HAAN, JACOB MEYER DE, *see* MEYER DE HAAN, JACOB:

HAARLEM, CORNELIS CORNELISZ. VAN (Cornelisz. Haarlem). Dutch painter of history, mythology, religious subjects, and some portraits (b. Haarlem, 1562; d. there, 1638). Cornelis van Haarlem was first a pupil of the Haarlem portrait painter Pieter Pietersz., and then of Gillis Congnet in Antwerp. In 1579 he traveled through France and the southern Netherlands. In 1583 he was recorded back in his native Haarlem. With Karel van Mander and Hendrick Goltzius he founded the Haarlem Academy, which was strongly under the influence of Italian mannerist concepts of art and art theory.

It should be noted that of the three founders of the Haarlem Academy only Cornelis van Haarlem did not visit Italy. His visit to France, however, certainly exposed him to the work of the Italian-inspired school of Fontainebleau. It seems likely that he was also influenced by the more direct Italian contacts of his two Haarlem colleagues. His painting style is somewhat softer than that of Goltzius, although there are often compositional similarities. Van Haarlem continued to work in the mannerist tradition until the end of his life, although his work after about 1620 begins to show the impact of the baroque style introduced into the Netherlands by the school of Utrecht.

BIBLIOGRAPHY. W. Stechow, "Cornelis van Haarlem en de Hollandsche laat-maniëristische schilderkunst," *Elsevier's geïllustreerd maand-schrift*, XC, 1935; J. Bruyn, "Een keukenstuk van Cornelis Cornelisz. Van Haarlem," *Oud-Holland*, LXVI, 1951; J. Rosenberg, S. Slive, and E. H. ter Kuile, *Dutch Art and Architecture, 1600–1800*, Baltimore, 1966.

LEONARD J. SLATKES

HAARLEM. City in the province of North Holland, the Netherlands, and ancient capital of the Counts of Holland. It was a prosperous settlement by the middle of the 12th century; the Town Hall, originally a palace of the Counts, dates from that time, but was completely remodeled early in the 17th century.

The major extant monument that antedates the 17th century is the vast Church of St. Bavo, known as the Groote Kerk, which dates from the 15th century. Its lofty ribbed vault of cedarwood, 15th-century Gothic pulpit sounding board, early 16th-century carved choir stalls and screen, and fine 18th-century organ are the most interesting features of the interior. *See* ST. BAVO.

Fronting on the central market square, along with the Groote Kerk, are the Meat Market, built by the Ghent architect Lieven de Key in 1603, and the much-altered Gothic Town Hall. Of the old city gates, only the late-15th-century Amsterdam Gate survives. Also of interest are the old Weigh House (1597) and the 17th-century almshouses. *See* MEAT HALL.

Famous through the centuries for its cloth and its tulips, Haarlem is most renowned as an art center. Some notable painters were born there, while numerous others came there to live and work. The greatest of all Haarlem masters, Frans Hals, was brought to the city from his native Antwerp as a child, and spent the rest of his life painting and teaching in Haarlem. The Frans Hals Museum displays a number of his major canvases. *See* HAARLEM: FRANS HALS MUSEUM; HAARLEM SCHOOL.

Among the other famous Haarlem painters were Cornelis van Haarlem, Esaias van de Velde, Jan van Goyen, Jan van Scorel, Maerten van Heemskerk, Jacob van Ruisdael, and the pupils of Frans Hals, including Adriaen van Ostade, Pieter Saenredam, and Judith Leijster.

The Teyler Museum is an 18th-century building housing a collection of drawings by Rembrandt, Leonardo, Michel-

Cornelis van Haarlem, *Adam and Eve*. Art Gallery, Hamburg.

angelo, Raphael, and others, and prints, along with natural history collections.

BIBLIOGRAPHY. L. Dumont-Wilden, *Amsterdam et Haarlem*, Paris, 1913; A. Melchior, *De Haarlemsche Sint Bavo*, Haarlem, 1945; G. L. Burke, *The Making of Dutch Towns: A Study in Urban Development from the Tenth to the Seventeenth Centuries*, London, 1956.

MADLYN KAHR

HAARLEM: FRANS HALS MUSEUM. Dutch collection. The museum is located in the Old Men's Almshouse (Oldemannenhuys), which was designed by the city architect of Haarlem, Lieven de Key, in 1608. The museum complex went through various stages of restoration and reconstruction before it was opened to the public in 1913. The name of the museum is in a sense misleading, for although the collection is extremely rich in works by Frans Hals it is not limited to works by this master. The emphasis tends to be on artists connected with Haarlem, but this limitation is not strictly followed, and one therefore finds works by Gerard Ter Borch, Nicolaes Maes, Pieter Codde, and others. Since the collection is still in its original 17th-century building, it is particularly interesting to see the works in the setting for which they were created. In this aspect the museum is unusually sensitive to the requisites of the works of art and their display.

Of the artists represented, there can be no doubt that Frans Hals, through his various group and individual portraits, emerges best. Among his famous works is the 1616 *Banquet of the Officers of the Haarlem Militia Company of St. George*, one of the landmarks of 17th-century Dutch painting. Other works by Hals include the *Officers of the Militia Company of St. Hadrian* and two pendant portraits originally commissioned for the Old Men's Almshouse: the *Governors of the Old Men's Almshouse* and the *Lady Governors of the Old Men's Almshouse*, both from about 1664.

The museum is rich in works by painters of the 16th-century school of Haarlem, including such important ones as Cornelis Cornelisz. van Haarlem's 1599 group portrait of the *Banquet of the Officers of the St. George Militia Company* and his *Marriage of Peleus and Thetis* of 1593. Works by other members of the famous Haarlem Academy of the latter part of the 16th century include Karel van Mander's *Annunciation* and *Dance around the Golden Calf* and Hendrick Goltzius' *Mercury* and *Minerva*, pendants from 1611.

BIBLIOGRAPHY. H. P. Baard, *Frans Hals and the Group Portraits at Haarlem*, Haarlem, 1949; *Frans Halsmuseum der Gemeente Haarlem* (catalog), Haarlem, 1960.

LEONARD J. SLATKES

HAARLEM SCHOOL. This school began about 1600, when Karel van Mander established in Haarlem the first Dutch academy. In its early years, Hendrik Goltzius gave a classical form to its development; this soon gave way to a style based on the international mannerism represented by Bartholomeus Spranger. Cornelis Cornelisz. van Haarlem was the chief exponent of this Haarlem mannerism. The 17th century saw the flowering of the Haarlem school when Frans Hals was the chief master. He freed the school from foreign influences and established a truly national school of Dutch painting. Portraiture, still life, and especially landscape painting were highly developed in Haarlem by such painters as Jan Jansz., P.

Milijn, Isaak van Ostade, Salomon van Ruysdael, and Jacob van Ruisdael. *See* GOLTZIUS, HENDRICK; HAARLEM, CORNELIS CORNELISZ. VAN; HALS, FRANS FRANSZ.; MANDER, KAREL VAN; OSTADE, ISAAK VAN; RUISDAEL, JACOB ISAACKSZ. VAN; RUYSDAEL, SALOMON VAN; SPRANGER, BARTHOLOMEUS.

BIBLIOGRAPHY. W. von Bode, *Die Meister der holländischen und flämischen Malerschulen*, 6th ed., Leipzig, 1951; W. Martin, *Dutch Painting of the Great Period, 1650–97*, London, 1951.

HACHIBUSHU IN KOFUKUJI, NARA. Japanese lacquer sculpture (8th cent.). It represents a group of eight supernatural-looking creatures who were originally hostile to the Buddha's teachings but were later converted and became the guardians of the Shaka Buddha. These statues, made in the hollow dry-lacquer technique, once stood, together with a group of the Ten Great Disciples of the Shaka Buddha, in the Western Golden Hall of the Kōfukuji (734). They must have been made about this date. Some figures are shown with animal heads, some with multiple heads and arms. Despite their extraordinary appearance, details such as faces and hands are realistically rendered. They are probably the works of Shogun Mampuku and his collaborators, who made the statues to be housed in the Western Golden Hall. *See* TEN GREAT DISCIPLES IN KOFUKUJI, NARA.

BIBLIOGRAPHY. Tokyo National Museum, *Pageant of Japanese Art*, vol. 3: *Sculpture*, Tokyo, 1952; *Masterpieces of Japanese Sculpture*, introd., text, and comment. by J. E. Kidder, Jr., Rutland, Vt., 1961.

HACHT, TOBIAS VAN, see HAECHT, TOBIAS VAN.

HACKAERT, JAN JANSZ. Dutch landscape painter (b. Amsterdam, 1628/29; d. there? after 1685). He traveled in Switzerland and perhaps in Italy. In Amsterdam he was friendly with Adriaen van de Velde, who sometimes painted animals and figures for him. He also collaborated with Johannes Lingelbach and Claes Berchem. Hackaert was influenced by the work of Jan Both.

BIBLIOGRAPHY. S. Stelling-Michaud, *Unbekannte Schweizer Landschaften aus 17. Jahrhunderts*, Zurich, 1937.

HACKERT, JACOB PHILIPP. German landscape painter and engraver (b. Prenzlau, 1737; d. near Florence, 1807). Jacob first studied with his father, Philipp Hackert, then at the Royal Academy of Arts in Berlin with Le Sueur. He lived mostly in Italy but traveled to Sweden (1764) and France. Hackert worked for Catherine II of Russia and was official painter to King Ferdinand I of Naples. He painted many *vedute* (views) in the manner of Vanvitelli, but such varied influences as Hubert Robert's or Carlevarijs's are detectable in his prolific *oeuvre*.

BIBLIOGRAPHY. F. De Filippis and O. Morisani, *Pittori tedeschi a Napoli nel Settecento*, Naples, 1943.

HADDON HALL. The English dream castle of the Gothic North, located in Derbyshire County. The earliest parts are Norman, discernible about Peveril's Tower, along the south and west walls, and in the chapel. The main cross wing, from about 1370, consists of the hall, parlor, kitchen, and offices. The northwest gate tower is from about 1530, as are the apartments east of this, while those to the south toward the chapel are slightly earlier. The chapel chancel was added in 1427, and there were additions to the hall about 1550. The main rooms are the chapel (late

Sir Francis Haden, *Hampton Court*. Engraving. British Museum, London.

12th cent.), the hall (ca. 1370), the east gallery (ca. 1600), the kitchen (ca. 1370), parlor and solar (altered ca. 1500; rare paneling dated 1545), the Earl's apartments (ca. 1500), and the long gallery (early 17th cent.). The garden is a perfect Jacobean example.

BIBLIOGRAPHY. N. Pevsner, *The Buildings of England*, vol. 8, Harmondsworth, 1953.

HADEN, SIR FRANCIS SEYMOUR. English etcher (b. London, 1818; d. Alresford, 1910). Haden studied to be a surgeon in Paris and Grenoble. While a medical student in Paris, he attended a state art school, training his eye and hand for his profession and unconsciously developing an ability for his future avocation.

Haden first experimented with etching in 1843, when he transcribed six Italian architectural subjects from watercolor drawings he made during a holiday in Italy. He did not take up etching again until 1858; during the intervening time he was involved with medical duties. But at this time his interest was revived by seeing the work of Charles Jacques and by Charles Meryon's *Eaux-fortes sur Paris* set. He also studied Rembrandt's etchings, but the strongest impulse undoubtedly came from his association with Whistler, whose half-sister he married, and who was a constant house companion. Whistler had just published his so-called "French set" in 1858 and dedicated it to his brother-in-law. The rewarding friendship between these two men ended unhappily in 1867. At the start, however, they would take sketching trips, sometimes working together on a plate such as *Trees in the Park*. Haden preferred to transcribe nature directly. It is said that he carried a prepared copper plate with him, on which he drew the scene before him.

Haden developed a mastery for creating the mood of a serene landscape. Such plates as *Kensington Gardens* (1859), *Shere Mill Pond* (1860), and *Sunset in Ireland* (1863) show his particular fondness for sylvan settings. He was fortunate in having the service and friendship of the master printer Frederick Goulding, who printed his plates after 1867.

In 1880 Haden founded the Society of Painter-Etchers, which was later given royal patronage. He published a volume of notes, *About Etching* (1879), and a monograph on Rembrandt (1877). In 1894 he was knighted.

BIBLIOGRAPHY. M. C. Salaman, *The Etchings of Sir Francis Seymour Haden, P.R.E.*, London, 1923.

KNEELAND MC NULTY

HADRA VASES. Group of inscribed sepulchral vases of local Alexandrian manufacture, of which several are in the Metropolitan Museum, New York. They were named after the ancient cemetery (Hadra) east of Alexandria, Egypt, in which they were found in 1883–84. Their principal shape is that of a hydria. The vases present two distinct types of decoration, brownish glaze on a clay-colored ground and polychrome decoration on a white ground. The decoration consists of a floral frieze on the neck, shoulder, and handle zone of the hydria. Inscriptions with the name of the deceased and the year, month, and day of his death were written with ink or were incised on the front of the vase, beneath the floral decoration and separated from it by a thick zone of glaze. Some of the vases are securely dated on the basis of their inscriptions.

BIBLIOGRAPHY. B. F. Cook, *Inscribed Hadra Vases*, New York, 1966.

HADRIAN, MAUSOLEUM (Tomb) OF, *see* SANT'ANGELO, CASTEL, ROME.

HADRIAN, VILLA OF, TIVOLI, *see* TIVOLI.

HAECHT (Verhaecht; Hacht), TOBIAS VAN. Flemish painter (1561–1631). Van Haecht was born in Antwerp. He traveled in Italy until about 1590. The first master of Peter Paul Rubens, Van Haecht became well known for his large-size landscapes peopled with small figures, done in 16th-century style. On a minor artistic level, they vaguely recall the conceptions of Josse de Momper.

BIBLIOGRAPHY. F. J. van den Branden, *Geschiedenis der Antwerpsche Schilderschool*, Antwerp, 1883.

HAECHT, WILLEM VAN, II. Flemish painter (1593–1637). Willem was a disciple of his father, Tobias van Haecht. He traveled in France and Italy and became a master in his native Antwerp in 1626. He was known particularly as a painter of collectors' galleries, such as that of Cornelis van der Geest, in whose house he lived from 1626 to 1637.

BIBLIOGRAPHY. S. Speth-Holterhoff, *Les Peintres flamands de cabinets d'amateurs au XVIIe siècle*, Brussels, 1957.

HAEFLIGER, PAUL. Australian painter and critic (1912–). He was art critic of the Sydney *Morning Herald* for fifteen years. In this position of influence he revolutionized art standards as well as critical writing in Australia. He is married to Jean Belette, a neoclassic painter. Since 1950 they have lived in Majorca.

HAENSBERGEN (Haensbergh), JOHANN VAN. Dutch landscape and portrait painter (b. Gorinchem? 1642; d. The Hague, 1705). Haensbergen was a pupil of Cornelis van Poelenburgh in Utrecht. He was married at The Hague in 1665, but is mentioned at Utrecht a few years later. By 1669 he settled at The Hague. He was head (*hoofdman*) of the confraternity Pictura (1682–83; 1689–90) and a director of the academy. His landscapes recall his teacher, Poelenburgh, while his portraits are in the style of the late works of Nicolaes Maes and Constantijn Netscher. He was also an art dealer.

BIBLIOGRAPHY. A. Bredius, "Iets over oude copieën," *Oud-Holland*, XXIX, 1911.

HAE-WON, *see* SHIN YUN-BOK.

HAGEN, JOHANN VAN DER, *see* HAAGEN, JORIS VAN DER.

HAGENAU (Hagnower), NIKOLAUS (Niclas) VON. Alsatian sculptor, specializing in altars and cabinetry (b. ca. 1445; fl. Strasbourg until 1526). He often collaborated with his brothers Veit Hagenau and Paul Hagenau. The first work that is believed to be his own is the high altar of the Strasbourg Cathedral (1500–01), although it is known that in 1486 he had worked on the altar of the Mary Church and on the choir for Bishop Albrecht of Strasbourg. Hagenau also executed Bishop Albrecht's tomb. Vöge ascribes the sculptured figures of the *Isenheim Altar* to him as well. He worked in a strong late Gothic idiom.

BIBLIOGRAPHY. W. Vöge, *Niclas Hagnower*, Freiburg im Breisgau, 1931.

HAGENAUER, JOHANN BAPTIST. German sculptor (b. Strasbourg, 1732; d. Vienna, 1810). Hagenauer began his career as an ornamental sculptor working in the late rococo style. Later he adopted neoclassicism and created larger decorative works of sculpture. From 1774 he was a teacher at the Viennese Academy. His most important works are the garden figures for the Nymphenburg in Munich.

BIBLIOGRAPHY. A. Feulner, *Skulptur und Malerei des 18. Jahrhunderts in Deutschland*, Potsdam, 1929.

HAGIA IRENE, CONSTANTINOPLE. Byzantine church inaugurated by Constantine the Great. It formed a double church with the original Hagia Sophia. The original disposition of Hagia Irene is nearly impossible to determine, for the Constantinian church was destroyed in 532 and rebuilt by Justinian. Razed by fire and rebuilt in 564, the church was destroyed and rebuilt at least twice after that.

The church as it exists today is primarily of the 8th century (a rebuilding following an earthquake in 740), with portions from as late as the 14th century and subsequent Turkish additions. It is of a three-aisled basilican plan, with a single eastern apse and a narthex on the west. The most interesting feature of Hagia Irene is its vaulting. The nave is divided into two unequal bays. The eastern bay is a large square, vaulted by a high dome on a drum. This nave bay is separated from the aisles by the four large piers upon which the dome rests and by an arcade of four slender columns. The aisles are vaulted by lateral ribbed barrel vaults. The western bay is a lateral rectangle, separated from the aisles by piers and columns and

vaulted by a low elliptical dome. The narthex is groin-vaulted, while the gallery above the aisles and narthex is covered by lateral barrel vaults. The masonry, alternating bands of courses of hewn stone and brick, is typically Constantinopolitan.

Little decoration remains in the church. Iconoclastic and Turkish depredations have left the interior bare. Where the Turkish whitewash has been removed (in the conch of the apse), there is a thin mosaic cross against a gold field, typical of iconoclastic work.

The chief significance of Hagia Irene is that it represents one of the early major types of Justinianian building: the domed basilica. The origin and sources of this type of building have not been established, but a number of 6th-century ruins of Justinianian foundation furnish evidence of its widespread use and possible sources. One such ruin is the so-called Church B in Philippi, the excavated plan of which shows a relationship to Hagia Irene. Of the few remains of the building, the masonry and style of carving on capitals and archivolts indicate a mid- or late-6th-century Constantinopolitan origin. Another such example, not exactly the same but of similar type, is the 6th-century church of Kasr-ibn-Wardan in Syria. Here, too, the masonry shows Constantinopolitan workmanship or influence. *See* KASR-IBN-WARDAN.

The range of this type, as witnessed by the two examples cited, gives rise to the question of whether Hagia Irene was the model for the provincial buildings or vice versa. The answer to such a question may well offer a partial solution to the larger question of the sources of Justinianian architecture.

STANLEY FERBER

HAGIA SOPHIA, CONSTANTINOPLE. Great Byzantine church built between 532 and 537. It was the work of two Greek engineers, Isidorus of Miletus and Anthemius of Tralles. Here for the first time in Christian architecture, instead of the master builders of old, there appear men who were trained in the theories of statics, mathematics, geometrical projections, and physics. They could apply theoretical knowledge to the practical problems of building or engineering, draw plans and sections, and train assistants to carry them through. This approach produced the architectural-engineering wonder that is Hagia Sophia.

The masonry of the building is solid brick throughout, with the courses of mortar often as thick as or thicker than those of brick. Only the central cores of the massive piers are not brick, these being made of great blocks of hewn stone. The exterior of the church, as in most Byzantine building of the time, is plain, without decoration. The original disposition of exterior masses has been modified by Turkish additions to the four heavy external buttresses and by the provision of surrounding minarets. Perhaps as a result of the rapidity with which it was constructed or perhaps owing to earthquakes, parts of the central dome collapsed in 553 and again in 557. At the latter date, the dome was reconstructed slightly higher than it had been originally, but it still remained the flattest large-scale dome ever built.

Hagia Sophia has a square basilican plan, divided into a nave and two aisles. The nave culminates in a chancel and a semicircular apse. The basilican plan in a square

Palace of Hagia Triada. Excavations of the royal villa.

rather than a rectangular scheme sets the pattern for the remainder of the structural development. Although the church is basilican, the square plan gives the impression of a central-plan building. The central-plan aspect is emphasized by four massive piers, spanned by arches, subdividing the nave into a central area about 100 feet square. The piers rise straight to the arches, which are joined by pendentives to support an immense dome vaulting the central area. The aisles, of three bays each, are separated from the nave by a columnar screen between the piers and by conch-vaulted, niched arcades at the end bays. A full gallery, groin-vaulted, continues this plan on the second level.

The specific character of the church comes from the placement of the windows and openings and the combination of the resultant light-space rhythm with the complex vaulting system. The central dome is flanked on the east and west by half domes. At the east the half dome is buttressed by a barrel vault over the chancel and culminates in a half dome over the apse. The north and south walls rise straight between the piers to their spanning arches and are strengthened by four massive exterior buttresses. The effect of the central dome, pierced by windows around its entire base, is "as if the vault of heaven were suspended above one." This central source of light is supplemented by an intricate and subtle arrangement of windows and openings in the other parts of the building. The north and south walls have two rows of windows, the upper row of five and the lower of seven, above the gallery, which has a seven-arched screen arcade, while the aisles have a five-arched screen arcade. The openings in the conches (the four niched corner bays), going from upper to floor level, have a 7:5:3 relationship, while the apse has a 5:3:3 pattern of openings.

The total effect is that of light filtering down and losing itself among the columns of the aisles at floor and gallery levels. The brilliance of the light in the nave dissolves into semidarkness in the aisles. The rhythm of the light pattern combines with the structure to evoke a statement of spatial affirmation and denial, a response created by the opposition of curved to flat surfaces and of massive weight-bearing piers to thin nonstructural columns and by the apparent weightlessness of the mighty dome.

The effect is further enhanced by the light-scattering quality of the brilliant multicolored marble revetments on the piers, walls, and arch spandrels and by the marvelously planned coloristic unity of the whole. Green marble is used for the columns of the nave and gallery arcades. Dark porphyry is used for the columns of the conch and a light-colored marble for the columns and piers in the galleries. In all cases the color is used to create visual separations and relationships between the spatial units that comprise the whole. In still another way the light-dark contrasts are emphasized: the capitals and cornices are intricately and deeply carved so as to create their own patterns of light and shade. The sum total of all these elements creates a mystic, ever-changing light pattern on a series of subtly interrelated, rhythmically articulated spatial units.

The original mosaic decorations have for the most part disappeared because of the ravages of the iconoclasts and the Muslims, except for the relatively unimportant decorative work in and near the dome. However, many later mosaics of excellent quality, mostly from the 9th through the 13th century, still decorate Hagia Sophia. Perhaps the most imposing of these is a large 13th-century mosaic of the Deësis, whose subtle, delicate colors and humanistic outlook seem to presage the developments in the West a century and a half later. In the narthex there is a fine 9th-century mosaic of an emperor kneeling before Christ which shows the power and monumentality achieved by the Byzantines immediately after the period of iconoclasm. In the south vestibule there is an impressive 10th-century mosaic depicting the Virgin flanked by the emperors Constantine and Justinian. This mosaic indicates how quickly Byzantine art proceeded to a frontal, hieratic, and stylized approach to figural depictions. The full history of the successive mosaic additions to Hagia Sophia affords a picture of the development of later Byzantine pictorial art.

Despite the ravages of time, invasion, natural and manmade disasters, and sheer neglect, Hagia Sophia remains one of the architectural wonders of the world.

BIBLIOGRAPHY. W. P. Lethaby and H. Swainson, *The Church of Sancta Sophia, Constantinople*, London, 1894; T. Whittemore, *The Mosaics of St. Sophia at Istanbul*, 4 vols., Paris, 1933–52; E. H. Swift, *Hagia Sophia*, New York, 1940.   STANLEY FERBER

HAGIA TRIADA, PALACE OF. Royal villa in Hagia Triada, Crete, a town in the southern Mesara plain, near Phaistos. The building has been variously identified as a palace and as a royal villa. It lacks the essential characteristics of the major Minoan palaces and was perhaps used as a place of retreat for the royal family of Phaistos. Based on archaeological evidence, the palace seems to have been built just after the construction of the New Palace of Phaistos. It was destroyed sometime toward the end of the 16th century B.C., either simultaneously with the destruction of the other Cretan palaces or perhaps slightly later. It was excavated by the Italian School of Archaeology at the beginning of this century.

The palace lay in the center of an earlier settlement. The plan of the building does not conform to the general layout of the other palaces in Crete but forms an irregular L shape, with one side extending to the east and the other to the south. The side that runs to the east has a long portico with a row of alternating columns and pillars which screen eight storerooms that were originally two-storied. The main residential quarters lay at the angle of the two sides. They consisted of the men's quarters; the queen's hall; the archive, which was lined with alabaster; a corridor with storerooms where several large pithoi were found; and the servants' quarters. Two Late Minoan shrines were found near the servants' quarters. The palace also had an upper floor, as indicated by the remains of a stairway. Unlike the other Cretan palaces, it had no central court, and its façade lacked the recesses found in the western façades of the other palaces. The residential quarter was situated on an artificially leveled terrace at the northwest corner of the building. An L-shaped veranda similar to the veranda in the palace at Cnossus opened on a terrace. The men's quarters consisted of a long hall opening onto the terrace by a row of alternating piers and doors and of additional rooms separated from one another by a screen of piers and a light well.

The excavations in this palace have yielded valuable works of art, including the fresco depicting a cat stalking a bird, which was found in the queen's hall; the famous sarcophagus with offering scenes; and three steatite vases, the Chieftain's Cup, the so-called Harvesters' Vase, and a funnel-shaped rhyton with scenes of boxing and wrestling. In one of the storerooms was found an important bronze hoard, perhaps the greatest to have been discovered in a prehistoric site.

BIBLIOGRAPHY. S. Marinatos, *Crete and Mycenae*, New York, 1960; J. W. Graham, *The Palaces of Crete*, Princeton, 1962.

EVANTHIA SAPORITI

HAGIOGRAPHY, *see* SAINTS IN ART.

HAGIOS DIMITRIOS (St. Demetrius), THESSALONIKA.
Greek church founded at the end of the 5th century. It was rebuilt between 629 and 643 and again after a fire in 1917. In plan the building is a basilica with five aisles, crossed by a spacious transept flanked by an aisle. There are galleries around the whole building except for the apse. The beautiful capitals show a wide variety of late-antique, Early Christian, and Byzantine forms, and mosaics of the 7th century have been preserved on the piers of the nave arcade. These show the titular saint and other ecclesiastical and civil personages in frontal iconic poses; they are important documents from the period of the iconoclastic controversy.

BIBLIOGRAPHY. C. Diehl et al., *Les Monuments chrétiens de Salonique*, Paris, 1918; F. W. Volbach, *Early Christian Art*, New York, 1962.

HAGIOS PANTOCRATOR. Name of numerous Byzantine and Greek churches dedicated to Christ as World Ruler (Pantocrator). This dedication was made primarily to churches of the mid-Byzantine period—that is, domed churches on a cross-in-square plan. The central cupola almost always contained a mosaic or fresco of Christ Pantocrator.

BIBLIOGRAPHY. O. Demus, *Byzantine Mosaic Decoration*, London, 1948.

HAGNOWER, NICLAS, *see* HAGENAU, NIKOLAUS VON.

HAGUE, RAOUL. American sculptor (1905–   ). Born in Istanbul of Armenian parents, he went to America in 1921, first living in Iowa and then settling in New York, where he studied at the Art Students League. Typically, Hague's work is directly carved in wood or stone. *Ohio Wormy Butternut* (1948; New York, Museum of Modern Art) and *Sawkill Walnut* (1955; New York, Whitney Museum of American Art), despite their generally abstract appearance, divulge a basic adherence to the human figure. Hague's forms are fluid and sensitively finished in the chosen medium. His later development depends more upon purely abstract images.

BIBLIOGRAPHY. T. B. Hess, "Introducing the Sculpture of Raoul Hague," *Art News*, LIII, 1955; L. Goodrich and J. I. H. Baur, *American Art of Our Century*, New York, 1961.

HAGUE, THE. Capital city of the Netherlands and of the province of South Holland. Until the 13th century it was merely the site of a hunting lodge in a forest. The Binnenhof is a grandiose ensemble of buildings of various eras that constitutes the cultural and geographic heart of the city. The oldest edifice of this ensemble is the Palace of the Counts, built in about 1250 as the residence of Count William II of Holland, who moved his court from Haarlem to the Hague at that time. In about 1280 his son, Count Floris V, added the imposing Ridderzaal, the scene in modern times of the Speech from the Throne, which opens sessions of Parliament.

Around the medieval nucleus of the Binnenhof were built elegant Dutch Renaissance and baroque town houses during the 17th and 18th centuries. Many of these survive, contributing to the aristocratic tone of The Hague, although few remain private residences. Among the finest are those designed by the Parisian Huguenot Daniel Marot, who was chief architect to William III; an example is the Royal Library, which contains valuable collections of illuminated manuscripts, coins, and gems.

The classical Mauritshuis, built by Pieter Post for Count Johan Maurits van Nassau and located beside the Binnen-

Haida Indians. Silver bracelet carved to represent a raven, from Masset, Queen Charlotte Islands, British Columbia, Canada. Museum of the American Indian, New York.

hof in 1633–44 (after plans by Jacob van Campen), houses the famous picture gallery of The Hague. *See* HAGUE, THE: MUSEUMS.

Decorative arts, historical material related to The Hague, Oriental arts, and modern paintings, including excellent impressionist and postimpressionist canvases, are shown at the Municipal Museum. The Bredius Museum displays Dutch paintings and appropriate decorative arts in a handsome 17th-century residence.

BIBLIOGRAPHY. G. L. Burke, *The Making of Dutch Towns: A Study in Urban Development from the Tenth to the Seventeenth Centuries*, London, 1956.

MADLYN KAHR

HAGUE, THE: MUSEUMS.
Important public art collections in The Hague, Netherlands, are located in the museums listed below.

Mauritshuis Art Gallery. World-famous collection of paintings, located in a palacelike structure in classical style dating from 1633 to 1644. The building was erected for Prince Johan Maurits of Nassau Siegen by Pieter Post from plans by Jacob van Campen. The exterior, in its combination of brick and sandstone and in its lines inspired by antiquity, gives a picturesque effect that is enhanced by its location on a small lake. The building was last restored in 1909.

After the Napoleonic wars the Royal Picture Gallery was placed in the Mauritshuis. Besides numerous paintings of early members of the House of Orange, the collection is renowned for its outstanding works of the Flemish and Dutch schools, crowned by some of Rembrandt's most famous paintings. Among the most noteworthy works of the Flemish schools from the 15th to the 17th century are Rogier van der Weyden's *The Descent from the Cross* (ca. 1463), Hans Memling's expressive *Portrait of a Man*, Anthonis Mor's *Portrait of a Goldsmith* (1564), David Teniers's *Kitchen Interior* (1644), Van Dyck's *Portrait of the Artist Quinten Simons* (ca. 1630), and Rubens's *Adam and Eve in Paradise*, a small-size canvas he did in cooperation with Jan Breughel, who was so often responsible for the landscapes, flowers, and animals in Rubens's work.

Paintings of the Dutch school are mainly from the 17th century, the golden age of painting in Holland. Such artists as Frans Hals, Gerard Ter Borch, Frans van Mieris, Gerrit Dou, Jan Steen, Aert van der Neer, and Jacob van Ruisdael are represented by typical works. Paulus Potter's *The Young Bull* stands out for its tremendous size, unusual in Dutch painting of that period. Johannes Vermeer is represented by two of his most wonderful works: the *View of Delft* (ca. 1658), with its townscape silhouettes mirrored in the river in transparent nuances of light and atmosphere, and *The Girl with the Pearl* (ca. 1660), with its crystal-clear visual impression. The greatest treasures of the Mauritshuis are its Rembrandts. To mention only a few, there are *The Anatomy Lesson of Dr. Nicolaas Tulp* (1632), the earliest of his famous group portraits; *Saul and David* (1658), in which he gives the Biblical figures universal human significance; and three self-portraits, one from before 1630, another from 1635, and the third from the artist's last year (1669), each becoming progressively more introspective and timeless.

Among the German paintings are two portraits by Hans Holbein the Younger and works by Lucas Cranach the Elder and the Younger. An interesting aspect of the collection is the group of paintings by northern artists such as Hans Rottenhammer, Claes Berchem, Bartholomeus Breenberg, the landscapist Johannes Both, and the *Caravaggisti* Pieter Lastman and Gerrit van Honthorst who came under Italian influence. G. A. Pellegrini's painted decorations, made at the time of a renovation in 1718, are the only Italian works. The paintings of Chardin and Pater and the sculpture of Houdon and Falconet represent the French school.

BIBLIOGRAPHY. Royal Picture Gallery, *Abridged Catalogue of the Pictures and Sculptures*, The Hague, 1958.

LOTTE PULVERMACHER-EGERS

Municipal Museum (Gemeentemuseum). Housed in a building by H. P. Berlage (built 1919–34) and opened in 1935. The extensive ceramics collection includes Greek, Islamic, Chinese, Japanese, delft, and Hague wares, as well as Italian majolica. Its collection of 19th- and 20th-century painting includes works by Jongkind, Sisley, Monet, Boudin, Van Gogh, Signac, Toorop, Picasso, Léger, and Klee, and an important group by Mondrian.

HAHN, HERMANN.
German sculptor (b. Kloster Weilsdorf, 1868; d. Munich, 1942). Hahn studied at the Munich School of Arts and Crafts (1887–92) and then worked at the Academy with Rumann. He traveled extensively and returned to Munich to teach and work. Among his sculptures are the *Moltke Monument* and a fountain (1909) in Bremen, *Goethe* in Chicago (1914), and the *Chariot Driver* in Munich (1928–31). His work is in the classical tradition of Adolf Hildebrand.

HAHNEL, ERNST JULIUS.
German sculptor (b. Dresden, 1811; d. there, 1891). Hähnel studied architecture in Dresden and sculpture in Munich. Remaining within the neoclassic style, he also absorbed the manner of the High Renaissance, combining the two in decorative sculpture, portrait and figure statues, and reliefs.

HAIDA INDIANS.
The Haida Indians have occupied sites in the coastal and insular areas of British Columbia, especially in the Queen Charlotte Islands, since prehistoric times. They were referred to as early as 1771 as carvers of totem poles, one of their most spectacular art forms. The Haida had organized a society of specific ranks and clans well before the arrival of the white man. Aristocratic families of the Eagle and Raven groups were prominent among patrons of a wood art that produced mortuary figures and totem poles of monumental size and astonishing technical finish. Utilitarian articles such as spoons and bowls were imaginatively conceived in animal form. A more recent tradition is argillite or slate carving. Haida sculpture, both ancient and historic, is characterized by great technical mastery. *See also* BRITISH COLUMBIAN INDIANS; NORTH AMERICAN INDIAN ART (NORTHWEST COAST).

BIBLIOGRAPHY. J. R. Swanton, *Contributions to the Ethnology of the Haida* (American Museum of Natural History, Memoir 8, pt. 1), New York, 1905; M. Barbeau, *Totem Poles: A Recent Native Art of the Northwest Coast of America* (Smithsonian Institution, Annual Report for 1931), Washington, D.C., 1931.

HAINAUT.
Province in southwestern Belgium, formed out of the medieval county of the same name. Its chief centers are Tournai, Mons, Charleroi, and Jumet. Throughout the

Halberstadt Cathedral. The nave of the German Gothic edifice, built in stages between 1239 and 1491.

Middle Ages Hainaut was a major artistic area. In the 12th century it was the center of a distinctive school of Romanesque architecture and sculpture whose major creation was the Cathedral of Tournai. The golden ages of art in Hainaut occurred in the 14th and 15th centuries, when the province enjoyed considerable prosperity owing to its active communes and its fortuitous union with the Duchy of Burgundy. In the 14th century a more or less indigenous school of late Gothic architecture thrived in Hainaut, as seen in the churches of St-Jacques and St-Quentin in Tournai. In the 15th century the tapestry industry was of great importance, and Hainaut eventually replaced Arras as the chief center of that art. *See* TOURNAI.

BIBLIOGRAPHY. C. C. A. Dehaisnes, *Histoire de l'art dans la Flandre, l'Artois et le Hainaut avant le XVe siècle*, Lille, 1886; P. Clemen, ed., *Belgische Kunstdenkmäler*, 2 vols., Munich, 1923.

HAITIAN PAINTING. The native school of painting in Haiti began to flourish with the establishment of the Centre d'Art at Port-au-Prince in 1944. Prior to that time, most artists had worked only sporadically, and then at decorative jobs, painting the walls of houses, useful objects, and other products of everyday life. The Centre d'Art gave them a place to work with easel paintings and murals, as well as crafts, and to exhibit and sell their paintings.

The Centre d'Art was started by DeWitt Peters, an American painter and teacher, who managed to gain some small support from the governments of Haiti and the United States. He discovered and brought together a number of artists who, once they were able to devote most of their time to painting and to exhibit and sell their work, became widely known throughout the world. These included Hector Hyppolite, Philomé Obin, Rigaud Benoit, Wilson Bigaud, and many others. Obin started his own branch of the Centre d'Art in northern Haiti at Cap-Haitien. *See* BIGAUD, WILSON; BENOIT, RIGAUD; HYPPOLITE, HECTOR; OBIN, PHILOME.

A number of different trends developed. Most of the artists work in a primitivistic style to record historical events, religious rites, and scenes of Haitian life in a direct and legible manner. Flat planes of vivid, simplified colors and linear patterns are used to great advantage, and Peters went to great pains to encourage artists in this trend, which derives its vitality from native and, ultimately, African traditions. Religion and, particularly, voodoo beliefs play a central role in giving support to the symbolic strength of this work. Artists such as Antonio Joseph represent a more "sophisticated" side of Haitian painting at the Centre. They are more closely aligned with the traditions of Western art, but the work of the former group has been most widely admired, especially in France. *See* JOSEPH, ANTONIO.

BIBLIOGRAPHY. S. Rodman, *Renaissance in Haiti*, New York, 1948.
DONALD GODDARD

HAIZMANN, RICHARD. German sculptor and watercolorist (1895–   ). A former art dealer and a self-taught artist, he was influenced at first by the German expressionists. His highly finished abstract and figural sculptures, like those of Arp, emphasize organic form and smooth surfaces.

HAJDU, ETIENNE. Romanian sculptor (1907–   ). He was born in Turda and attended the Ecole des Arts Décoratifs, Paris, studying under Bourdelle. Although his early training was essentially academic, his mature style is abstract, expressed in deceptively simple volumes and arabesques. Marble, wood, and various metals were employed in his work. His sculpture has been exhibited at the Whitney Museum of American Art, New York (1955), at the Fugel Gallery, Basel (1956), and elsewhere in Europe and the United States.

HAK-BO, *see* YI SANG-JWA.

HAKONE: ART MUSEUM, *see* ATAMI: ART MUSEUM.

HALBERSTADT CATHEDRAL. German Gothic church, built between 1239 and 1491. The Cathedral, a three-aisled basilica, retains several parts of the Ottonian cathedral of 992, which had been restored several times. The earliest phase is represented in the twin-tower west façade, which was constructed so as to preserve the Ottonian westwork and the first three bays of the nave. The second building campaign, carried out in 14th-century High Gothic style, began at the east end with the beautiful Lady Chapel behind the high altar. In 1402 the choir was consecrated. The transept and the remainder of the nave were built in the second half of the 15th century in the late Gothic style. The Cathedral thus represents practically the entire span of Gothic building in addition to pre-Gothic construction.

Even more important is the sculpture, which ranges from the *Crucifixion* group (1220) above the choir screen to the many beautiful pier statues dating through to the very end of the Gothic style. That a number of these can be dated lends additional importance. Especially notable are three figures from an *Entombment* (ca. 1360), figures of the twelve Apostles (the St. Andrew is dated 1427) on the choir piers, and the St. George (1487) and St. Sebastian (1510) on the crossing piers. Most unusual is the standing figure of St. Jerome with his lion (ca. 1500) which, with its boldly modeled surfaces, suggests 20th-century German sculpture.

BIBLIOGRAPHY. O. Doering, ed., *Kreise Halberstadt, Land und Stadt,* Halle, 1902; H. Giesau, *Der Dom zu Halberstadt,* Burg bei Magdeburg, 1929.   EDWARD P. LAWSON

HALDENWANG, CHRISTIAN. German engraver (b. Durlach, 1770; d. Bad Rippoldsau, 1831). Despite hack training with C. von Mechel in Basel, Haldenwang developed considerable skill and grace in making engraved and aquatint landscapes. He was named to the court at Karlsruhe. He illustrated panorama guidebooks and left many known engravings after Ruisdael, Lorraine, Poussin, and Elsheimer.

HALF-LENGTH PORTRAIT. Type of painted portrait showing only the upper half of the figure. A standard form of portraiture since the late medieval period, it achieved its first widespread popularity in Flemish painting of the 15th century.

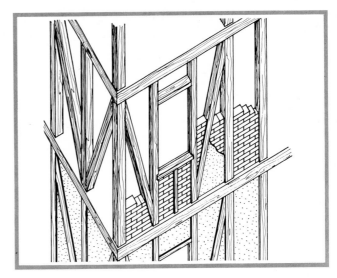

Half timber. A type of wood construction.

HALF TIMBER. Denoting a type of wood construction in which posts, girts, and other structural members are exposed, the interspaces being filled in with brick or with other materials, which were sometimes plastered. Half-timbered houses were built in colonial America, one method using brick nogging to fill spaces in the timber frame, the other using plaster to produce strong color contrasts known as black-and-white work.

HALF TONE. Type of photomechanical reproduction process used to print the intermediary gray tones of a photograph. A negative image is projected through a glass screen, which has a fine grid of horizontal and vertical lines, onto a photographically sensitive printing plate. The image is thus broken into minute dots whose concentration produces various tones of gray.

BIBLIOGRAPHY. L. R. McCabe, *The Beginnings of Half-tone,* Chicago, 1924.

HALF UNCIAL. Early medieval book script consisting almost entirely of minuscule letters, some of which were

Half uncial. Example from Cod. B 159, Ambrosian Library, Milan.

Peter Adolphus Hall, miniature. Jacquemart-André Museum, Paris.

derived from cursive, but most from the uncial script. The half uncial, the principal book hand from the 5th to the 8th century, may be seen in the manuscript of St. Hilary of Poitiers (6th cent.; Rome, Archives of St. Peter). *See* CURSIVE SCRIPT; MINUSCULE; UNCIAL.

BIBLIOGRAPHY. E. M. Thompson, *An Introduction to Greek and Latin Palaeography*, Oxford, 1912.

HALICARNASSUS, MAUSOLEUM OF, *see* MAUSOLEUM OF HALICARNASSUS.

HALL, PETER ADOLPHUS. Swedish miniature painter and pastelist (b. Borås, 1739; d. Liège, Belgium, 1793). He studied natural science in Sweden before going to Germany

Hypostyle hall. Temple of Amun at Karnak.

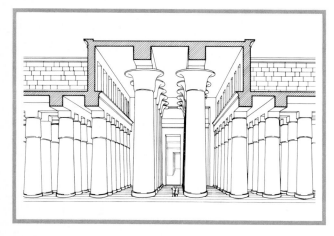

(Berlin, 1756; Hamburg, 1758), where he apparently learned miniature painting on ivory. Back in Stockholm, he became a pupil of P. H. L'Archevêque and of G. Lundberg. In 1766, while portraying the court, Hall was befriended by A.-C. Roslin, who urged him to go to Paris. There he was immediately successful; the *Mercure de France* styled him the "Van Dyck of miniature." In 1769 he became an associate of the Royal Academy, but he never gained membership, though he exhibited in the Salon of that year and subsequent years.

Under Louis XV Hall was appointed Painter of the Children of France. Under Louis XVI he became Painter to the King and worked in the Ministry of Foreign Affairs, for the *Bâtiments* and the *Menus Plaisirs*, executing miniature royal portraits that were used as diplomatic gifts. He became a member of the Stockholm Academy in 1773. In 1784 Gustavus III urged him to return to Sweden, but Hall, like Roslin, preferred to remain in Paris. At the onset of the French Revolution, however, he was unable to cope with the political ferment in France and sought, to no avail, the patronage of the King of Sweden. In 1791 he moved to Aix-la-Chapelle and portrayed members of the Prussian court.

Hall tried simultaneously to follow the styles of Hubert Robert, Fragonard, Greuze, Mme Vigée-Lebrun, and L. Tocqué, all of whom were his friends. Hall's work is often confused with that of Greuze, Roslin, and Tocqué. He occasionally intentionally reduced his works in scale for reproductive purposes. Hall's miniature portrait of Count Esterhazy (Narbonne) is after a lost original by Tocqué, engraved by G. F. Schmidt in 1759. L. Moreau the Younger frequently engraved portraits after Hall. His chief pupil was his daughter, Adélaïde-Victorine, marquise de la Grange, who followed her father's style weakly.

The chief repositories of his work are the Louvre, the National Museum in London, the National Museum in Stockholm, and the Wallace Collection in London. His minute landscapes possess the intimacy and freedom of execution of those larger ones by Hubert Robert and P.-A. Baudouin; his female portraits are sentimental, and occasionally provocative in the same sense as are those of Greuze.

BIBLIOGRAPHY. F. Villot, *Hall, célèbre miniaturiste du XVIIIᵉ siècle, sa vie, ses oeuvres, sa correspondance*, Paris, 1867; H. Bouchot, *La Miniature française (1750-1825)*, Paris, 1907.

GEORGE V. GALLENKAMP

HALL, HYPOSTYLE. Hall (from the Greek *hypostylos*, "resting on pillars") in which the roof rests on columns. The term is applied especially to the columned halls of ancient Egyptian temples. The Temple of Amun at Karnak has a huge hypostyle hall with a central avenue of taller columns that raise the roof above adjacent columns to create a clerestory admitting light to the interior.

HALL CHURCH. Type of church (German *Hallenkirche* or *dreischiffige Kirche*) associated especially with medieval architecture in which nave and aisles are of approximately the same height. Lacking triforium and clerestory, as found in churches whose aisles are lower than the nave, the hall church obtained its light from windows at the aisles. Germany produced many *Hallenkirchen*, among them St. Stephen (1257–1328) and St. Quentin (1450), Mainz; the

Frauenkirche, Nürnberg; and St. Elizabeth, Marburg. *See* MARBURG: CHURCH OF ST. ELIZABETH.

HALLER, HERMANN. Swiss sculptor (b. Bern, 1880; d. Zurich, 1950). He started as a student of architecture and painting in Munich and Stuttgart. After a trip to Rome with Paul Klee, and his residence there (1901–05), Haller emerged as a sculptor. His style, although it involved greater delicacy and simplification of form, is essentially in the tradition of 19th-century figure sculpture, as represented particularly by Rodin. Haller was virtually immune to the artistic ferment of Paris during his years there (1907–14). An ethereal quality evolved in his sensitive handling of portraits and slender female figures, particularly in the studies of young, ungainly girls. In 1934 he was awarded the gold medal of the Academy of Florence at the Venice Biennale and, in 1949, the Grand Prix de Zurich.

BIBLIOGRAPHY. M. Joray, *La Sculpture moderne en Suisse*, 2 vols., Neuchâtel, 1955-59.

HALLER VON HALLERSTEIN, CARL. German architect (1774–1817). He worked in Berlin and Nürnberg. He was a pupil of David Gilly and was strongly influenced by Gilly's son Friedrich. Haller traveled to Italy and Greece, where he studied the Temple of Aegina with Cockerell. His later projects are close to the designs of Gilly and Schinkel.

HALLES CENTRALES, PARIS, *see* BALTARD, VICTOR.

HALLMARK. Symbols stamped on silver and gold objects, showing that they contain no more than the legal amount of alloy according to an authorized assay office. A complete modern hallmark includes a town or assay office mark, a maker's mark, a date letter, a standard mark, and occasionally, additional special marks.

HALL OF A HUNDRED COLUMNS, *see* XERXES, APADANA OF.

HALLSTATT CIVILIZATION. European Iron Age civilization named for the cemetery and salt mine at Hallstatt, in the Austrian Alps. While the site has material from both the late Bronze Age and the early Iron Age, use of the term "Hallstatt" must be restricted to the period of the early Iron Age. Influences radiating from Italy, which brought the use of iron and some decorative as well as representational elements of Mediterranean art, inspired the rise of Hallstatt civilization in south-central Europe in the 8th century B.C. In the 7th and 6th centuries this civilization expanded into Yugoslavia and westward through southern Germany to the Rhineland, Switzerland, and France and extended even into northwestern Spain.

See also OPPIDA.

BIBLIOGRAPHY. F. Morton, *Hallstatt*, vol. 1: *Hallstatt und die Hallstattzeit*, Hallstatt, 1953; K. Kromer, *Das Gräberfeld von Hallstatt*, vol. 1, Florence, 1959.

HALO, *see* NIMBUS.

HALPERT, SAMUEL. American painter (b. Białystok, Poland, 1884; d. Detroit, 1930). He went to the United States at an early age and studied at the National Academy of Design in New York City. In 1902 he went to Paris, where he worked for a year under Bonnat at the Ecole des Beaux-Arts, then traveled in France, Spain, Portugal, and England. He returned to the United States in 1911.

Halpert was among the first American artists to be influenced by modern art in Europe. After a period of impressionistic work, he found the basis of his style in Cézanne and Fauvism. His *Still Life* (1913; New York, Ira Spanierman Collection) exhibited in the 1913 Armory Show, for example, was obviously derived from Cézanne, but the more Fauve *Brooklyn Bridge* (1913; New York, Whitney Museum of American Art) shows the broad color application and simplified forms that were characteristic of his work by 1920. In his later paintings the Cézannesque analytic approach to the formal structure of individual objects was transmuted into a strong compositional arrangement of the subject, as in the interior *Her First Book of Lessons* (1921; Detroit Institute of Arts).

BIBLIOGRAPHY. H. Comstock, "Samuel Halpert: Post-Impressionist," *International Studio*, LXXV, 1922.   JEROME VIOLA

HALS, CLAES (Nicolaes) FRANSZ. Dutch painter of landscape, genre, and possibly portraits (b. Haarlem, 1628; d. there, 1686). He was the son, and probably pupil, of Frans Hals. In 1655 Claes married at Haarlem, and the following

Hallstatt civilization. Funerary vases. Examples in the Landesmuseum, Württemberg (top), and the Karolinus Augustus Museum, Salzburg (bottom).

Dirck Hals, *The Garden Party*. Rijksmuseum, Amsterdam. A work showing the technical influence of the artist's brother, Frans.

year he entered the Haarlem Guild of St. Luke. His paintings are rare, possibly because he operated a tavern in Haarlem from 1664 on. However, he continued as a member of the painters' guild, and in 1682 he was an official of the organization. In 1672 he was recorded as a member of the Reformed church.

His few landscapes show the influence of Jacob van Ruisdael. He also painted views of Haarlem (Haarlem, Frans Hals Museum).

BIBLIOGRAPHY. W. Martin, *De Hollandsche schilderkunst in de zeventiende eeuw*, vol. 1, Amsterdam, 1935.

HALS, DIRCK. Dutch painter of genre and portraits (b. Haarlem, 1591; d. there, 1656). He was the younger brother and pupil of Frans Hals. Dirck seems to have spent most of his life at Haarlem, but he was recorded as living in Leyden in 1641/42 and 1648/49. His style is dependent primarily on that of his brother Frans, especially in Dirck's early portraits such as *Female Portrait* (1620; Rotterdam, Boymans–Van Beuningen Museum).

The technical influence of his brother is still apparent in such works as *The Garden Party* (Amsterdam, Rijksmuseum), but in subject matter and individual motifs the important influence is that of Willem Buijtenwegh. With Buijtenwegh, Dirck helped establish the "merry company" as one of the standard Dutch genre types (*Party of Young Men and Women at Table*, 1626; London, National Gallery). After about 1631 Dirck limited his compositions to one or two figures in an interior (*Woman Tearing up a Letter*, 1631; Mainz, Museum of Antiquities and Picture Gallery). In the 1640s he seems to have returned to the more crowded compositions for which he is best known.

BIBLIOGRAPHY. W. Bürger, "Dirk Hals et les fils de Frans," *Ga-zette des Beaux-Arts*, 1st series, XXV, 1868; N. Maclaren, *National Gallery Catalogues: The Dutch School*, London, 1960; J. Rosenberg, S. Slive, and E. H. ter Kuile, *Dutch Art and Architecture, 1600–1800*, Baltimore, 1966.   LEONARD J. SLATKES

HALS, FRANS FRANSZ. Dutch painter of portraits and genre (b. Antwerp? between 1581 and 1585; d. Haarlem, 1666). His family is first recorded at Haarlem in 1591, but it seems probable that they had immigrated from Flanders after the fall of Antwerp to the Spanish in 1585. Hals seems to have received his first training under the Haarlem painter and writer on art Karel van Mander, probably from about 1600 until Van Mander retired to write his famous book in 1603. In 1610 Hals became a member of the Haarlem Guild of St. Luke.

Much has been written about Hals's character, and it is often stated that he was a drunkard and a wife beater. This story was embroidered upon by later Dutch artists' biographers, and it is used in conjunction with the fact that from 1616 Hals was troubled by a long list of petty claims made by his various creditors. It is based on the mistaken assumption that he was the Frans Hals who in 1616 was brought before the Haarlem authorities for these offenses. In reality, the man charged with drunkenness and wife beating was a certain Frans Cornelisz. Hals, not Frans Fransz. Hals; the artist's first wife, in fact, had died in 1615.

Although Hals must have been between twenty-five and thirty years old in 1610, no works can be attributed to him until this date. The earliest work usually given to Hals is the problematic *Banquet in a Park*, generally dated about

Frans Hals, *Portrait of Nicolaes Hasselaer*. Rijksmuseum, Amsterdam.

1610 (formerly Berlin, State Museums; destroyed during World War II), which can be seen as developing out of Van Mander's style of about 1600. It is the only example of this genre can be given with any certainty to Hals. For the most part this particular type of painting was taken up by such painters as Willem Buijtenwegh, Esaias van de Velde, and Hals's brother Dirck. Since the documentation of this picture must always remain, as a result of its destruction, somewhat problematic, the first work that can be considered Hals's is the *Portrait of Jacobus Zaffius* (Haarlem, Frans Hals Museum), dated 1611 but not signed. The attribution, based on an engraving dated 1630 and inscribed "F. Hals pinxit," seems quite certain. The portrait appears to relate to the work of such late-16th-century portrait painters as Cornelis Ketel and Hendrick Goltzius.

Dating from the same time as the Zaffius portrait are the companion portraits *Portrait of a Man Holding a Skull* (Birmingham, Barber Institute of Fine Arts) and *Portrait of a Woman* (Chatsworth, Trustees of the Chatsworth Settlement). These early works indicate that Hals had a natural predilection for portrait painting. It should be noted that throughout his long career all his pictures, even those with religious and genre subjects, maintain a general portrait character. This is especially apparent in the rare religious works by Hals, for example, the recently discovered *St. Luke* and *St. Matthew* (Odessa, State Art Gallery).

In 1616 Hals painted his monumental civic guard portrait, the *Banquet of the Officers of the Haarlem Militia Company of St. George* (Frans Hals Museum). In every way this painting ushers in the golden age of Dutch painting. Hals had a distinct advantage in the execution of this large painting; from 1612 to 1615 he had been a member of the company and therefore knew the character and personality of the officers. While this painting can be related to the development of group portraiture by earlier Haarlem artists, there can be no doubt that Hals, while maintaining the general sense of decorum required in such works, introduced compositional elements that depart from the rigid solutions of placement found in works executed at the end of the 16th century.

In 1616 Hals became an associate of the Haarlem society of rhetoricians (De Wijngaertranken); he maintained this association until 1625. During the same year the first evidence of his financial difficulties was manifested. In 1617 Hals remarried at Spaarndam, near Haarlem. (The couple had eight children, several of whom became painters.) Between 1616 and 1664 Hals painted nine monumental group portraits, more than any other major artist of the period. Nevertheless, he was repeatedly in financial difficulties.

During the 1620s Hals perfected his virtuoso painting technique in such works as the so-called *Yonker Ramp and His Sweetheart* (1623; New York, Metropolitan Museum). This identification of the models, made during the late 18th century, is certainly a romantic one. It is possible that the painting represents, in reality, either a prodigal son or a pure genre rendering on the order of a "merry company." During this period Hals painted what has been termed one of the most brilliant of all baroque portraits, the so-called *Laughing Cavalier* (1624; London, Wallace Collection), which has abundant vitality and brilliant virtuosity of brushstroke. It seems possible that at this time Hals was influenced by the Utrecht followers of Caravaggio. The tonalities of the Wallace Collection picture suggest that Hals knew the works of Hendrick Terbrugghen. This Utrecht influence is supported by such works as the *Merry Drinker* (ca. 1628/30; Amsterdam, Rijksmuseum); however, the influence would be limited to such elements as pose and gesture and to broad concepts of tonality, certainly not to brushwork.

During the 1630s Hals received commissions for three large civic guard portraits. About 1633 he executed the *Officers of the Militia Company of St. Hadrian* and about 1639 he produced the *Officers of the Militia Company of St. George* (both, Frans Hals Museum). Hals's fame during the 1630s was not limited to Haarlem, and in 1633 he was given a commission for a civic guard group from Amsterdam. Considering that by 1633 both Rembrandt and Thomas de Keyser were active in Amsterdam, the commission must be seen as an exceptional tribute to his reputation and his skill as a painter. This work, popularly known as the *magere* ("poor") company painting and officially titled *The Company of Captain Reynier Reael and Lieutenant Cornelis Michielsz. Blaeuw* (completed in 1637; Rijksmuseum), follows the Amsterdam tradition of full-length figures (Haarlem groups were traditionally three-quarter-length portraits). Hals apparently made small oil sketches of the various officers and took them back to Haarlem, where he continued to work. When the portrait was not completed by 1636, however, it was sent to Amsterdam, where it was finished by Pieter Codde.

During the last decades of Hals's life he seems to have stopped painting genre subjects and devoted himself entirely to portrait painting. In 1649 he painted a portrait of his most famous sitter, *Descartes* (Copenhagen, State Museum of Fine Arts). In 1661 Hals was exempted from paying the annual dues of the Haarlem Guild of St. Luke because of his old age, and the following year he was given a lifetime subsidy by the burgomasters of Haarlem. About 1664, at more than eighty years of age, Hals painted his two last group portraits, the *Governors of the Old Men's Almshouse* and the *Lady Governors of the Old Men's Almshouse* (both, Frans Hals Museum). Even at this extreme age Hals's brush maintains its incomparable effectiveness. The simple black-and-white tonality of the *Lady Governors*, the personal shorthand character of the impressionistic brushwork, and the incisive characterization of the personalities make this one of the high points of Dutch portrait painting of the 17th century.

See also HAARLEM: FRANS HALS MUSEUM.

BIBLIOGRAPHY. W. Bode, *Frans Hals und seine Schule*, Leipzig, 1871; W. R. Valentiner, *Frans Hals* (Klassiker der Kunst, vol. 28), 2d ed., Stuttgart, 1923; F. Schmidt Degener, *Frans Hals*, Amsterdam, 1924; W. R. Valentiner, *Frans Hals Paintings in America*, Westport, Conn., 1936; F. Hals, *Frans Hals, the Civic Guard Portrait Groups*, foreword by H. P. Baard, Amsterdam, 1950; S. Slive, "Frans Hals Studies," *Oud-Holland*, LXXVI, 1961; Haarlem, Frans Hals Museum, *Frans Hals: Exhibition on the Occasion of the Centenary of the Municipal Museum at Haarlem*, Haarlem, 1962; J. Rosenberg, S. Slive, and E. H. ter Kuile, *Dutch Art and Architecture, 1600–1800*, Baltimore, 1966.

LEONARD J. SLATKES

HALS, HARMEN FRANSZ. Dutch painter of genre and portraits (b. Haarlem, 1611; d. there, 1669). He received his training from his father, Frans Hals. In 1642 Harmen was recorded at Vianen, and in 1657 and 1661 he was living at Gorinchem. Two years later he was at the nearby town of Noordeloos. The *Portrait of a Young Painter* (Art Institute of Chicago) by Frans Hals may be a portrait of Harmen. For the most part Harmen painted "merry company" groups and peasant scenes, such as *Peasant Company* (Haarlem, Frans Hals Museum), which recall the works of his father's pupil Jan Miense Molenaer as well as those of Adriaen Brouwer.

BIBLIOGRAPHY. W. Martin, *De Hollandsche schilderkunst in de zeventiende eeuw*, vol. 1, Amsterdam, 1935.

HALS, JAN (Johannes) FRANSZ. Dutch painter of genre and portraits (b. Haarlem, possibly between 1617 and 1632). He was the son of Frans Hals and his second wife. Jan seems to have received his training from his father. In 1640 he entered the Delft painters' guild as a foreigner. A certain Jan Hals married in Bloemendaal in 1648, and for a second time in Haarlem in 1649. It has been suggested that Frans Hals's son who was buried in the New Church, Haarlem, in 1674 may be Jan.

At times Jan's work can be deceptively close to that of his father, as can be seen in the 1648 *Portrait of a Man* (Frederiksstad, Kiaer Collection). At other times his work is related to the style of his older brother Harmen.

BIBLIOGRAPHY. S. Slive, "Frans Hals Studies," *Oud-Holland*, LXXVI, 1961; J. Rosenberg, S. Slive, and E. H. ter Kuile, *Dutch Art and Architecture, 1600–1800*, Baltimore, 1966.

HAMADAN, see ECBATANA.

HAMBIDGE, JAY, see DYNAMIC SYMMETRY.

HAMBURG. Port city on the Elbe and Alster Rivers, in northwestern Germany. Although Hamburg was a member of the medieval Hanseatic League, its period of greatest prosperity has been in modern times. Despite extreme damage in World War II, several important older monuments have been preserved, including the Jakobikirche (late 14th cent.), the Katharinenkirche (late 14th–early 15th cent.), and the Michaeliskirche (1750–62). Among noteworthy modern buildings are the Chilehaus, a landmark of expressionist architecture (architect Fritz Höger, 1922–23), the Church of the Trinity (architect Richard Riemerschmid, 1956), and the State Opera House (architects G. Weber, W. Lux, W. Gastreich, and H. Ebert, 1954–55). Museums include the Museum of Arts and Crafts, with sculpture and decorative arts, and the Art Gallery. *See* HAMBURG: MUSEUMS.

BIBLIOGRAPHY. K. Schellenberg, *Das alte Hamburg*, Leipzig, 1936; *Die Bau- und Kunstdenkmäler der Freien und Hansestadt Hamburg*, ed. G. Grundmann, vol. 1–   , Hamburg, 1953–   .

HAMBURG: MUSEUMS. Important public art collections in Hamburg, Germany, are located in the museums listed below.

Art Gallery. Founded in 1850 (the old gallery building dates from 1869, the new one from 1919), the Hamburg Kunsthalle is one of Germany's most outstanding and active museums, excelling in 19th- and 20th-century paintings. Works of the German schools range from the 14th century to the present; among the early ones the most noteworthy are Master Bertram's *Grabow Altar* (14th cent.) from St. Peter's Church, Hamburg, and Master Francke's *St. Thomas Altar* (1424). Works of the 15th and 16th centuries are represented by Cranach, Holbein, and others. The 17th- and 18th-century collection includes paintings by Chodowiecki, Elsheimer, Graff, Mengs, and J. H. W. Tischbein (19 paintings). Among the artists of the romantic school are C. D. Friedrich (11 works), P. O. Runge (self-portraits of 1802 and 1805; a portrait of his wife, 1804; and a portrait of his parents, 1806), and M. von Schwind.

The picture gallery stresses works from the second half of the 19th century through the present, by Böcklin (*Self-Portrait*, 1873), Feuerbach (*Judgment of Paris*, 1870), Klinger, Leibl, Lenbach, Menzel, Thoma (10 works), Trübner, and Uhde. Among the outstanding 20th-century masters, the ones best represented are Baumeister (7 paintings), Beckmann (among his 11 works is the well-known portrait of Professor Meyer), Dix, Feininger, Heckel, Hofer, Kandinsky, Kirchner, Klee, Kokoschka, Liebermann (35 works), O. Müller, Nolde, Schmidt-Rottluff (5 paintings), and Slevogt.

Italian paintings range from the 14th to the 20th century. There are some outstanding 18th-century works by Canaletto, Magnasco, Ricci, and Tiepolo. Paintings of the 20th century include De Chirico's *Melancholy of a Street* and Severini's *Train between Houses*, an example of the short-lived futurist movement.

Although there are some 15th- and 16th-century paintings (by Metsys, Mostaert, and others), Holland and Flanders are represented mainly by 17th-century works, such as *Simeon in the Temple* and *Portrait of M. Huygens* (1632) by Rembrandt, eight paintings by Jacob van Ruisdael, and paintings by Rubens, among others, the *Assumption of the Virgin*.

French paintings range from Philippe de Champaigne's *Marie Gives Crown and Scepter to Louis XIV* (1643) and Vernet's *Storm at the Seashore* (1782) to works by 19th- and 20th-century artists such as Bonnard, Cézanne, Corot, Courbet, Degas, Delacroix, Géricault, Manet (*Nana*), Monet, Pissarro, Renoir, Sisley, Toulouse-Lautrec, and Vlaminck.

In the collection of drawings, which includes all European schools from the Middle Ages through the present, the accent lies on works by German romantic artists, such as Runge and C. D. Friedrich, as well as on those by the 17th-century Dutch masters. There are approximately 60,000 items in the print collection, from works by Dürer and his contemporaries through modern times. The sculpture collection contains, for the most part, works from classicism to our time, that is, from Rauch and Schadow to Moore, Picasso, and Giacometti. A collection of coins and medals, from antiquity through today, forms another, smaller section.

BIBLIOGRAPHY. H. Jedding, *Keysers Führer durch Museen und Sammlungen*, Heidelberg, Munich, 1961.

LOTTE PULVERMACHER-EGERS

Barlach House. Founded in 1962, this museum is dedicated to the work of the expressionist sculptor Ernst Barlach (1870–1938). Originating from the private collection of the industrialist H. E. Reemtsma, who had promoted Barlach's work and had supported the artist during Nazi persecution, the gallery contains some of the master's principal works.

HAMEEL, ALART DU. Dutch architect, sculptor, and engraver (ca. 1449–1509). Hameel was a native of 's Hertogenbosch, where Jerome Bosch drew a portrait of him in 1504. Between 1478 and 1494 Hameel was active at the Cathedral of St. Jan in 's Hertogenbosch. He was also employed in Lieven and Antwerp, but settled permanently in his native town in 1502 and worked mainly as an engraver.

HAMEL, THEOPHILE. Canadian painter (1817–70). After serving an apprenticeship with Antoine Plamondon, Hamel studied in Rome and other European cities. He was principally a portrait painter, working in Quebec and Montreal. Many of his works show the influence of the romantic movement.

HAMELSCHENBURG. Castle near Hameln, Germany. One of the proudest monuments of the German Renaissance, the Hämelschenburg was built on the steep slopes of the Emmertal in 1588–89, probably by Cord Tönnis and Johann Hundertossen. Its interior was altered in the 19th century.

BIBLIOGRAPHY. E. Hempel, *Geschichte der deutschen Baukunst*, Munich, 1949.

HAMEN Y LEON, JUAN VAN DER. Spanish painter (b. Madrid, 1596; d. there, 1631). Hamen, the son and student of the Flemish painter Juan van der Hamen the Elder, was a still-life specialist, although he also painted portraits. Like Velázquez, Sanchez Cotán, and Zurbarán, he focuses on the textural and formal qualities of each

Hammer beam. Projecting support for a rafter.

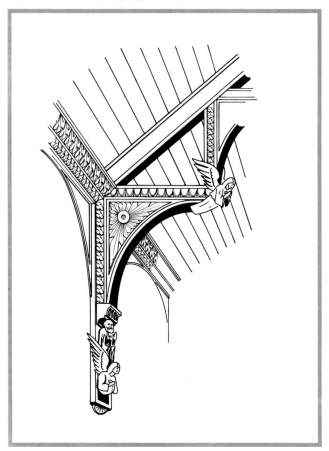

object in isolation. In his *Still Life* (1627; Washington, D.C., National Gallery) and *The Cook* (1630; Amsterdam, Rijksmuseum) the strange juxtapositions and predetermined scattering of shapes seem to represent a purification of earlier Netherlandish genre still lifes.

BIBLIOGRAPHY. Sociedad española de amigos del arte, Madrid, ... *Floreros y bodegones en la pintura española* (catalog), 1936-40.

HAMILTON, GAVIN. English painter (b. Murdieston House, Lanarkshire, 1723; d. Rome, 1798). He is not to be confused with the minor conversation-piece artist Gawen Hamilton (1697–1737).

Gavin Hamilton spent most of his life in Italy, but retained connections with the British gentry primarily through his activities as a connoisseur and dealer in antique art. His paintings are of considerable interest to the historian of neoclassic art, for the themes he used and even, to a less extent, his style of painting anticipate by twenty years the French neoclassicism of David. Prints after his paintings enjoyed wide circulation on the Continent during the 1760s and 1770s, and there seems little doubt that he was a significant, although minor, influence on David and his school.

BIBLIOGRAPHY. E. K. Waterhouse, *Painting in Britain, 1530–1790*, Baltimore, 1953.

HAMILTON, THOMAS. Scottish architect (1785–1858). Edinburgh High School (1825) is his major contribution to the "New Town" and one of the high points of the Scottish Greek revival. The Caton Hill Monument and the Burns Monument, Ayr, also illustrate his sensitive use of the classical style.

BIBLIOGRAPHY. J. N. Summerson, *Architecture in Britain, 1530–1830*, 4th rev. ed., Baltimore, 1963.

HAMLET AND HORATIO. Oil painting by Delacroix, in the Louvre Museum, Paris. *See* DELACROIX, EUGENE.

HAMMAN AS-SARAKH. Early Islamic bath–audience-hall complex in Syria. It was built on a plan very similar to that of Qusayr 'Amra and is vaulted in the same manner, but its ashlar masonry is better executed and its arches are more pointed, leading Creswell to date it within Ummayad times but later than Qusayr 'Amra. There were traces of extensive frescoes, but all have now vanished. *See* QUSAYR 'AMRA.

BIBLIOGRAPHY. K. A. C. Creswell, *A Short Account of Early Muslim Architecture*, Harmondsworth, 1958.

HAMMER BEAM. Short beam, similar to a cantilever, projecting from the wall of a building and resting on a concave strut. The hammer beam was used in British late medieval and Tudor roofs. It supported a rafter and was constructed in single or double tiers. The end of the beam was often decorated with a carved and painted angel, a grotesque head, or other device. An example of its use is the Great Hall of Edinburgh Castle. *See* CANTILEVER.

HAMMURABI, STELE OF. The stele of the Babylonian king Hammurabi (1792–1750 B.C.), in the Louvre, Paris, is inscribed with Hammurabi's famous code of laws. It was found at Susa, Iran, in 1901, by the French archaeological mission there. For many years it was the earliest law code known in the Near East. Others have now been found from as early as the Ur III period (2125 B.C.). Hammurabi's stele was taken as loot from Mesopotamia by the conquering Elamites, probably in the 13th century B.C., and brought to their capital at Susa. It may originally have been set up at Sippar, and copies undoubtedly existed in other major temples in Mesopotamia. The beautifully inscribed text is in Akkadian and covers most of the stele.

The monument is made of black basalt and is just over 7 feet high. The top is semicircular. The upper 2 feet bear, in high relief, the standing figure of Hammurabi and the seated sun god Shamash. The bearded King, clad in a long robe and a brimmed cap typical of the period, and wearing a necklace, approaches the god. The bearded god, seated on a niched throne, wears a collar of beads and a tiered and fringed garment. On his head is the multihorned crown that is symbolic of divinity. Since he is the sun god, he has flames coming from his shoulders, and his outstretched right hand extends the rod and ring, of uncertain symbolism, toward the King. With this gesture he charges the King to enforce the laws. Under the god's feet is the scale pattern that represents mountainous country, and over his head there was originally a sun disk.

Below this scene the laws are listed. First are those that refer to legal procedures concerning the courts, judges, witnesses, and prosecutors. The law itself, which follows these introductory clauses, deals with every conceivable relationship in daily life: the family, military service, agriculture, commerce, and a penal code. This code is famous for its doctrine of an eye for an eye and a tooth for a tooth, but it was applicable only among equals. Finally, there are laws concerned with the purchase and sale of slaves. The purpose of the law, as stated, is to give equal security to all and to ensure the righteous administration of justice. Both the form of the code itself and the type of law are based specifically on the earlier code of Lipit-Ishtar (1934 B.C.). The representation of Hammurabi on this stele is one of the few that exist.

BIBLIOGRAPHY. A. Parrot, *Archéologie mésopotamienne*, vol. 2, Paris, 1953; S. A. Pallis, *The Antiquity of Iraq*, Copenhagen, 1956.
PRUDENCE O. HARPER

HAMPTON COURT PALACE. English country house built by Cardinal Wolsey between 1514 and 1529, then given to Henry VIII. Wolsey's work is roughly the west front center, the Base Court, the Clock Court, and the plan of the chapel and cloisters west of this. Henry completed the chapel and added the Great Hall and wings to the west front and parts of the present Fountain Court. Wolsey's mason was John Pedman; Henry's was John Malton. William III's rebuilding commenced in 1689 to compromise plans by Sir Christopher Wren. He built the east and south fronts, the Fountain Court, and parts of the Clock Court. For George I and II William Kent rebuilt the Clock Court tower in Jacobean revival style and made internal alterations (ca. 1732–35). Work then ceased and in 1838 the state apartments were first opened to the public.

Anne Boleyn's Gateway from the Base Court has medallions by Giovanni da Maiano. Wren's Colonnade leads to the King's Staircase, with paintings by Verrio and ironwork by Tijou. The King's side extends along the south front, with paintings by Verrio and carvings by Gibbons.

Stele of Hammurabi, found at Susa in 1901. Louvre, Paris.

The Queen's side, along the east front, has the Queen's gallery with a chimney by John Nost, the Queen's bedroom with a ceiling by Sir James Thornhill, and the Queen's dining room with paintings by Verrio. At the northern end are the public dining room and the Prince of Wales's rooms, all by Kent.

Behind the King's Apartments is the Cartoon Gallery, fitted up originally for Raphael's cartoons (now London, Victoria and Albert). The Communication Gallery opens to the Queen's staircase with a ceiling by Kent; and the Queen's guard chamber and Queen's presence chamber are also by Kent. Behind the Communication Gallery is Wolsey's Cabinet with an early Renaissance ceiling. The Chapel Royal has a pendant ceiling of 1535–36 and a reredos carved by Gibbons.

The parks and gardens include Home Park and Bushey Park, laid out by London and Wise from 1689. Adjacent to the palace are the fountain garden, the flower gardens, the privy garden with Tijou's twelve great iron screens, the Elizabethan-revival knot garden, and the sunken garden with Wren's banqueting house. The Orangery contains Andrea Mantegna cartoons. Near Henry VIII's tennis court (1529) are the maze and the Lion Gates with the Diana Fountain on axis.

BIBLIOGRAPHY. N. Pevsner, *The Buildings of England*, vol. 3, Harmondsworth, 1951.

JOHN HARRIS

HAMSA. Buddhist and Hindu ornament. The *haṁsa* (goose or swan) is the mount of Brahmā. Because of the similarity in sound, *haṁsa*, the goose, symbolizes the sacred *auṁ*.

HANAK, ANTON. Austrian sculptor (b. Brunn, 1875; d. Vienna, 1934). In his youth Hanak learned cabinet-making before studying sculpture at the Vienna Academy. He joined the Viennese Secession in 1911. From 1924 he taught at the School of Arts and Crafts in Vienna and then at the Vienna Academy, where Wotruba and Leinfellner were among his pupils. Hanak's sculpture is neoclassical.

HAN ART, *see* CHINA: ARCHITECTURE, BRONZES, CALLIGRAPHY, JADE, LACQUER, PAINTING, PAPER, SCULPTURE.

HANDMANN, EMMANUEL JAKOB. Swiss painter (b. Basel, 1718; d. Bern, 1781). After studying with Schnetzler in Schaffhausen and Restout in Paris, Handmann traveled through France and Italy for several years, when he returned to Basel and then Bern. Working in pastels and oils, he was a landscapist as well as the most sought-after portraitist in Bern during the third quarter of the 18th century. His work, particularly in portraiture, has the clarity, simplicity, lightness, and momentary quality found particularly in the work of his countryman Liotard.

HAND OF GOD. Marble sculpture by Rodin, in the Metropolitan Museum of Art, New York. *See* RODIN, AUGUSTE.

HAND SCREEN. Printing process using a cloth screen through which thick inks are forced with a squeegee, dauber, rag, or stiff brush, to produce, for example, the silk screen print. Hand screening is distinguished from

Hampton Court Palace, south façade.

commercial processes by the manual and individual application of the ink.

HANG-CHOU (Hangchow). City in the coastal province of Chekiang, China. Set in the verdant hills surrounding the estuary of the Ch'ien-t'ang River, it is framed on one side by the beautiful Western Lake (Hsi-hu). Streams, canals, lakes, rolling hills, and a mild climate make Hangchou one of the most beautiful spots in China. The city reached its greatest glory when it served as the capital of the Southern Sung emperors, from 1127 to 1279. The city greatly impressed Marco Polo when he visited it in 1280, soon after Kublai Khan had moved his troops into the southern capital, and his account of what he called Quinsai is the most elaborate of all the places he visited in China. The Imperial Palaces, then located at the southern end of the city, partly served as the governor's quarters, and although a degree of disrepair was already visible to Marco Polo he still used superlatives in his description of the luxurious buildings and grounds.

Today little is to be seen of ancient buildings in Hangchou itself. But in the vicinity of the city and the Western Lake are a number of caves and rock sculptures that go back to the 10th century and the Sung period.

BIBLIOGRAPHY. A. C. Moule, *Quinsai: With Other Notes on Marco Polo*, Cambridge, 1957; A. C. H. Boyd, *Chinese Architecture and Town Planning, 1500 B.C.–A.D. 1911*, Chicago, 1962.

MARTIE W. YOUNG

HANGING GARDENS OF BABYLON. One of the seven wonders of the ancient world. The Hanging Gardens of Babylon were described in detail by Flavius Josephus, Diodorus, and Strabo as stepped terraces that were accessible by means of stairs, planted with large exotic trees and irrigated by hydraulic machines that worked continuously to raise water from the Euphrates. It is surmised that they were arranged over a series of seven massive vaults on either side of a corridor running north and south, surrounded by a passage and an outer line of rooms located in the northeast corner of the palace of Nebuchadnezzar II (604–562 B.C.). The thickness of the walls and vaults, the double well, the use of dressed stone, and the low level of the cellars excavated favor this identification.

BIBLIOGRAPHY. R. Koldewey, *Das wieder erstehende Babylon*, 4th ed., Leipzig, 1925; W. Otto, *Handbuch der Archäologie*, Munich, 1939–54.

HANIWA, *see* JAPAN: CERAMICS (HISTORICAL DEVELOPMENT: TOMB PERIOD); JAPAN: SCULPTURE.

HAN KAN. Chinese painter (fl. mid-8th cent.). He was famous for his paintings of horses. He was called to the court of Ming-huang during the T'ien-po era (742–756) of the T'ang dynasty for the express purpose of depicting the famous imperial steeds. According to one tradition, Han Kan started his career under the great poet-painter Wang Wei, and went on to gain a reputation for himself as a mural painter. Literary records indicate that several temples around the capital of Ch'ang-an contained wall decorations of Buddhist and Taoist subject matter by Han Kan, but there is no question that his lasting fame was due to his paintings of horses. *See* WANG WEI.

In contrast to so many of the great T'ang painters, whose feats must remain in the realm of the legendary, Han Kan's painting style can be studied in at least one painting that possibly could be original: the small painting in ink on paper in the collection of Sir Percival David, London. According to the inscription on this painting, the famous steed of Ming-huang called Shining Light of Night was depicted by Han Kan. The painting is complete with seals and inscriptions dating from the 10th century.

BIBLIOGRAPHY. H. Giles, *An Introduction to the History of Chinese Pictorial Art*, 2d rev. ed., Shanghai, 1918; O. Sirén, *Chinese Painting, Leading Masters and Principles*, vol. 1, New York, 1956.

MARTIE W. YOUNG

HANKAR, PAUL. Belgian architect (1861–1901). He worked near Brussels. A pupil of Beyaert, Hankar is falsely associated with the Art Nouveau style. Although he was an architectural innovator of his period, his productions, mainly domestic, are crude and uneven.

BIBLIOGRAPHY. C. Conrardy and R. Thibaut, *Paul Hankar*, Brussels, 1923; C. de Maeyer, *Paul Hankar*, Brussels, 1962.

HAN-LIN. Chinese academy of scholars and artists. Instituted during the reign of the T'ang emperor Ming-huang in 754, the Han-lin Academy was initially an organization of competent scholars responsible for preparing edicts and other court documents. Artists were also admitted in Ming-huang's time. This fact is significant for the light it throws on the government's patronage of contemporary art and artists. Sickman has characterized the Han-lin as "a nucleus for scholarship and a bulwark against pretense and incompetence." The academy had a long history during which its internal organization changed from century to century. It was burned, along with its collections of literary works, during the Boxer Rebellion of 1900.

BIBLIOGRAPHY. J. and A. H. Burling, *Chinese Art*, New York, 1953; L. Sickman and A. Soper, *The Art and Architecture of China*, Baltimore, 1956.

HANNBERG: PFARRKIRCHE. German parish church erected in the 15th century. It is one of the best-preserved examples of a completely fortified church. Three fortified walls form a square court much like those of castles.

BIBLIOGRAPHY. A. von Reitzenstein and H. Brunner, *Reclams Kunstführer*, vol. 1: *Bayern*, Stuttgart, 1964.

HANNEMAN, ADRIAEN. Dutch portrait, history, and genre painter and engraver (b. The Hague, ca. 1601; d. there, 1671). He was a pupil of Jan Anthonis van Ravesteijn and Daniel Mijtens. Hanneman was active in England for about sixteen years and was influenced by Anthony van Dyck and Cornelius Johnson. Hanneman was one of the organizers of the painters' confraternity Pictura, in The Hague, founded in 1656, and became its director. He was painter in residence to the court in The Hague and was friendly with Constantijn Huygens.

BIBLIOGRAPHY. A. Bredius and E. W. Moes, "Adriaen Hanneman," *Oud-Holland*, XIV, 1896.

HANNEQUART, JEHAN, *see* HENNECART, JAN.

HANNOT, JOHANNES. Dutch still-life painter (fl. Leyden, ca. 1650–1700). Little is known of his background. In 1650 he was reported as a member of the guild in Leyden. Hannot was probably an amateur, for he was also a wine merchant. His works show him to be a follower of Jan Davidsz. de Heem. Hannot was in Leyden in 1683.

BIBLIOGRAPHY. A. P. A. Vorenkamp, *Bijdrage tot de geschiedenis van het Hollandsch stilleven in de zeventiende eeuw*, Leyden, 1934.

HANNOVER: MUSEUMS. Important public art collections in Hannover, Germany, are in the museums listed.

Kestner Museum. Founded in 1889, the museum has a fine collection of antiquities and applied arts. Egyptian works from the Old Kingdom, especially the 5th dynasty, and from the New Kingdom, which reached its climax in the 18th dynasty, are of outstanding quality, as are works from the Near East (including bronzes from Luristan) and from Greece, Etruria, and Rome (Greek black- and red-figured vases; marble head of a youth, ca. 470 B.C.; highly expressive bust of Emperor Caracalla). The museum contains ecclesiastical objects (especially metalwork and textiles), furniture from the Renaissance, ceramics and glass from the 16th and 17th centuries, drawings from Germany, France, Italy, and the Netherlands, and manuscripts and miniatures from the 12th century on.

Lower Saxony Landesmuseum. Founded in 1853, the museum is rich in paintings and sculptures from early medieval to modern times. Among altarpieces from Lower Saxony, the *Death of the Virgin* (end of 13th cent.) and the *Passions Altar* (15th cent.) by the workshop of Master Bertram are outstanding. The so-called German Renaissance of the 16th century is represented by the works of Burgkmair, Cranach, and Holbein; the romantic school and the 19th century, by artists such as Böcklin, Feuerbach, Leibl, Lenbach, and Thoma. Most noteworthy are paintings by German expressionist, Brücke, and Bauhaus artists (Feininger, Corinth, Heckel, Hofer, Kirchner, Marc, O. Müller, Nolde, Schmidt-Rottluff, and Slevogt). The Landesmuseum also contains paintings from France (Poussin and Delacroix), Italy (Antonio Veneziano, Perugino, and Raphael), and Belgium and Holland (Rubens, Jordaens,

A. de Gelder, Rembrandt, and Honthorst). Among the sculptures, a *Madonna* and a *St. John the Baptist* by Riemenschneider deserve mention, as does the excellent collection of European 19th- and 20th-century masters (Archipenko, Barlach, Kolbe, Moore, and Rodin).

BIBLIOGRAPHY. H. Jedding, *Keysers Führer durch Museen und Sammlungen*, Heidelberg, Munich, 1961.

LOTTE PULVERMACHER-EGERS

HANSEN, CHRISTIAN FREDERIK. Danish architect (1756–1845). He worked in Copenhagen. He was a pupil of C. F. Harsdorff in Copenhagen. In 1782 Hansen went to Italy where he studied antiquities and the work of Palladio. In 1784 he went to Altona, then to Hamburg, and finally to Holstein, where he was made Inspector of Public Buildings. In 1804 he moved to Copenhagen, and he was appointed director of the Academy in 1811.

One of the most distinguished architects of his period, he is considered to have brought the classical style to northern Europe. His work, although consistently original, recalls the designs of Boullée and Ledoux, the etchings of Piranesi, and the buildings of Palladio and contains specific classical associations.

BIBLIOGRAPHY. W. Jakstein, *Landesbaumeister Christian Friederich Hansen, der Nordische Klassizist*, Neumünster in Holstein, 1937.

HANSEN, EMIL, *see* NOLDE, EMIL.

HANSEN, THEOPHIL VON. Austrian architect (1813–91). He worked in Vienna and Athens. Although his designs are mainly in the High Renaissance mode, his work in Athens initiated the Greek revival in that city, and his Vienna Parliament House is considered the last large monument of the Greek revival.

BIBLIOGRAPHY. G. Niemann and F. von Feldegg, *Theophilos Hansen und seine Werke*, Vienna, 1893.

HANS OF COLOGNE (Juan de Colonia). Spanish architect (b. ca. 1410; d. before 1481). He was active in Burgos beginning about 1440. In 1454 he is recorded as the supervising architect of the Cathedral there. He designed its towers, whose open tracery work resembles that of the Cathedral of Cologne. Hans also built the Carthusian church of Miraflores near Burgos (begun 1477) and the Chapel of the Concepción at the Cathedral of Burgos (begun 1477). His son Simon succeeded him in his post at Burgos and built the Chapel of the Purificación at the Cathedral, an example of late-Gothic ornamental style.

BIBLIOGRAPHY. L. Torres Balbás, *Ars Hispaniae*, vol. 7: *Arquitectura gótica*, Madrid, 1952.

HANS VON TUBINGEN. Austrian painter (fl. 1433–62). He headed a workshop in Wiener Neustadt and was the leading master in the area of Styria, Carinthia, and Krain (Carniola) during the middle years of the 15th century. The *Altarpiece of St. Lambert* (Graz, Landesmuseum Joanneum), depicting the triumph of King Ludwig of Hungary over his enemies, is his major work. Other paintings in the Museum of Art History, Vienna, private collections in Linz and Olberg, and elsewhere, formerly connected with the Master of the Abbey of St. Lambert, are now attributed to Hans. Stylistically, these works are conservative, drawing on the International Gothic traditions of northern Italy, Bohemia, and Flanders. They nonetheless

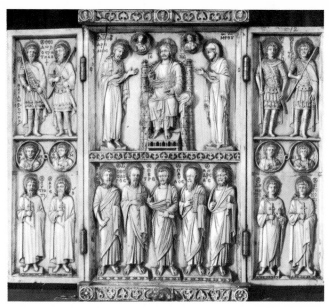

Harbaville Triptych. Ivory. Louvre, Paris.

maintain the colorful decorativeness and spiritual expressiveness of the earlier style.

BIBLIOGRAPHY. K. Oettinger, *Hans von Tübingen und seine Schule*, Berlin, 1938.

HAO. Chinese term that refers to one of the alternate names by which an artist may be known. The term is sometimes translated as "pen name" or "sobriquet." As distinguished from the *tzu*, the *hao* could be adopted by the individual whenever the will so moved him, or it could be conferred upon him by another. An artist could have a number of *hao*, taken at different times to mark significant occasions in his life. Occasionally a *hao* is connected with a special place such as the studio of the artist. A *hao*, therefore, can be composed of more than two characters normally encountered in the *tzu* and can have a variety of personal connotations. A typical example of a *hao* is that of the Yüan-dynasty painter Wu Chen, who took as his *hao* the phrase Mei-hua tao-jen (Taoist of the Plum Blossom). *See also* TZU.

HARAM AS-SHARIF, *see* DOME OF THE ROCK, JERUSALEM.

HARAPPA, *see* INDUS VALLEY CIVILIZATION.

HARBAVILLE TRIPTYCH. Tenth-century Byzantine ivory relief panels, in the Louvre Museum. Paris.

HARD-EDGE PAINTING, *see* ALBERS, JOSEF; GLARNER, FRITZ; KELLY, ELLSWORTH; NEWMAN, BARNETT; ROTHKO, MARK.

HARDING, CHESTER. American painter (b. Conway, Mass., 1792; d. Boston, 1866). After a varied career as soldier, cabinetmaker, and innkeeper, Harding met a portrait painter and decided to follow that profession. He traveled through Kentucky and Ohio, accepting commissions at twenty-five dollars each. He went to Philadelphia and enrolled at the Pennsylvania Academy of Fine Arts for a short time (his only real instruction in painting). He quickly became a popular portraitist, his homespun personality and possibly assumed rustic air only enhancing his reputation. His success continued during the four years he spent in England (1823–27) and on his subsequent return to the United States. Harding painted many notables, for example, *John Marshall* (1828; Cambridge, Mass., Fogg Art Museum). Among the best portraits in his uneven output are *Amos Lawrence* (ca. 1845; Washington, D.C., National Gallery) and *Anna Hardaway Bunker* (ca. 1857; Indianapolis, John Herron Art Institute).

BIBLIOGRAPHY. C. Harding, *Sketch of Chester Harding, Artist, Drawn by his own Hand*, ed. M. E. White, Boston, 1929.

HARDING, JAMES DUFFIELD. English water-colorist (1797–1863). His father, a pupil of Paul Sandby, apprenticed him to an engraver; he also received about a dozen lessons from Samuel Prout. Harding exhibited from 1818 at the Old Water-Colour Society and from 1811 to 1858 (in oils) at the Royal Academy of Arts. He also taught and published works on art.

Harding's style is competent but derivative, noticeable for the then new practice of using bright opaque colors with highlights in opaque white. He occasionally worked in oils and was an able lithographer. His lithographs reflect the influence of Bonington.

BIBLIOGRAPHY. J. D. Harding, *Lessons on Art*, London, 1849; J. Rothenstein, *An Introduction to English Painting*, London, 1933; R. and S. Redgrave, *A Century of British Painters*, repr., London, 1947.

HARDOUIN, JULES, *see* MANSART, JULES-HARDOUIN.

HARDWICK, PHILIP. English architect (1792–1870). He was the architect to various companies, hospitals, and estates. His style is eclectic, and he is best known for his essay in the Greek Doric on a monumental scale: the 1836 Euston Station Arch in London.

HARDWICK, PHILIP CHARLES. English architect (1822–92). The overspent Georgian influence of his father, Philip Hardwick, is preponderant, as seen in the neo-Greek Hall of Euston Station in London (1846), a late-classical masterpiece. His Great Western Hotel at Paddington in London (late 1850s) is in the French revival style.

BIBLIOGRAPHY. H. R. Hitchcock, *Architecture, Nineteenth and Twentieth Centuries*, Baltimore, 1958.

HARDWICK, THOMAS. English architect (1752–1829). He was a pupil of Sir William Chambers, whose style he followed. As well as being clerk of works at Hampton Court and Windsor Castle, Hardwick had an ecclesiastic practice and built the well-known St. Marylebone New Church in London (1813–17).

HARE, DAVID. American sculptor, writer, and photographer (1917–   ). He was born in New York City and went to school in New York, Arizona, and Colorado. He majored in analytical chemistry until 1936 and worked as a color photographer and commercial artist from 1939 to 1943. Influenced by Giacometti, Hare began sculpture in 1942. From 1942 he collaborated with Breton, Ernst, and Duchamp on the magazine *VVV*. Since 1951 Hare has

worked in welded metal and has had several shows at the Kootz Gallery. He made trips to Paris, notably in 1951–52. Until recently he was one of the most active surrealist sculptors in America. His *Sunrise* (1955) is in the Albright-Knox Art Gallery, Buffalo, and *Figure Waiting in the Cold* (1951) is in the Whitney Museum of American Art, New York. He did several architectural commissions, such as the Eternal Light and Menorah for Temple Beth El, Providence, R.I., and a large relief for the lobby of 750 Third Avenue, New York City. Hare made important contributions in the area of fantastic body imagery and personal interpretations of nature in metal sculpture.

BIBLIOGRAPHY. R. Goldwater, "David Hare," in *Three American Sculptors*, New York, 1959.   ALBERT ELSEN

HARE'S-FUR (Hare's-foot) GLAZE, *see* TEMMOKU.

HARI-HARA. Combination of the names of Vishnu and Siva, representing union of the two Hindu deities in one.

HARITI. Hindu goddess, the protectress of children. Hāritī is a reformed yakshī.

HARKAVY, MINNA R. Estonian-born American sculptor (1895–   ). The bronze *American Miner's Family* (1931; New York, Museum of Modern Art) marked this artist's style as "socially conscious." The forms were essentially naturalistic but marked by romantic simplifications, which, in some later works, border on stylization. The bronze

David Hare, *Juggler*, 1950–51. Steel. Whitney Museum of American Art, New York.

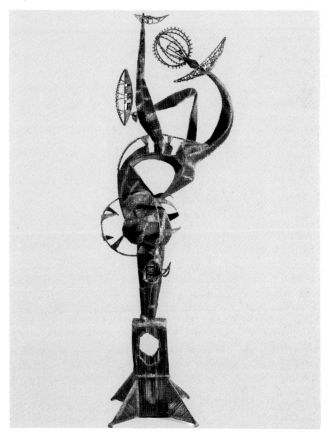

Harlech Castle. Welsh stronghold begun in 1283.

portrait of Leo Stein (1932) is, with its integration of specific likeness and sympathetic interpretation of character, one of Harkavy's finest works. Among later works, her bronze *The Last Prayer* (1949; New York, Whitney Museum of American Art) and *Martyr* (1954; New York, Museum of Modern Art) are thoughtful developments of her earlier expression. Harkavy combines an honest sentimentality with strong personal interpretation of subjects.

BIBLIOGRAPHY. New York, Museum of Modern Art, *Recent Sculpture U.S.A.*, New York, 1959.

HARLECH CASTLE. One of Edward I's Welsh castles, located north of Barmouth. It resembles Caerphilly Castle in Wales. Harlech Castle can be ascribed to the great military designer James of St. George. It was begun in 1283 on a concentric plan and finished about 1290. The outer wall was added between 1316 and 1320.

BIBLIOGRAPHY. S. Toy, *Castles, a Short History of Fortifications from 1600 B.C. to A.D. 1600*, London, 1939.

HARLOT'S PROGRESS. Engraving series by Hogarth. *See* HOGARTH, WILLIAM.

HARLOW, GEORGE HENRY. English portrait and history painter (b. London, 1787; d. there, 1819). He was a precocious boy and in 1802 was apprenticed to Sir Thomas Lawrence, on whose style he based his own. Harlow's most successful historical painting is *The Trial of Queen Catherine* (1817; England, private collection). He was in Rome in 1818.

HARMIKA. Square block atop the *aṇḍa* of a stūpa. The *harmikā* is a symbol of the square garment worn by the Buddha.

HARMODIUS AND ARISTOGEITON, *see* CRITIUS AND NESIOTES.

HARMON, ARTHUR LOOMIS, *see* SHREVE, LAMB, AND HARMON.

HARNETT, WILLIAM MICHAEL. American painter (b. Clonakilty, Ireland, 1848; d. New York City, 1892). His family settled in Philadelphia when Harnett was a child. From the age of seventeen he worked as an ornament engraver while occasionally studying at the Pennsylvania Academy of Fine Arts and at the National Academy of Design and Cooper Union in New York City. He began painting still lifes in 1874 and the next year started a painter's shop in New York. In 1876 he returned to Philadelphia, where he remained for four years.

During this period he produced a great many illusionistic still lifes, including what are probably the first paintings combining newspapers, mugs, and pipes. In these early works, for example, *Still Life with Bric-a-brac* (1878; Cambridge, Mass., Fogg Art Museum), Harnett concentrated on the rendition of the textures of common objects arranged on a tabletop in a pyramidal composition derived from the still lifes of Raphaelle Peale. He occasionally used a painted relief surface to intensify the visual reality of the depicted objects, but in his later works he avoided such a heavy-handed ancillary to trompe l'oeil effect. Probably during this time Harnett introduced the painting of paper money into American art. *Shinplaster* (1879; Philadelphia Museum of Art) shows the dirty, wrinkled bill that was his favorite subject in this genre.

In 1880 Harnett went to Europe, spending approximately six years in England, France, and Germany, including four years in Munich. During his European stay Harnett's paintings underwent changes in both style and subject. He began to paint on a much smaller scale with a generally freer brushstroke, although the overall impression remained detailed. The everyday objects of his earlier still lifes were replaced by a use of antiques and curios. These changes have been attributed to the influence of Meissonier and of the Munich school of painting.

The outstanding innovation of Harnett's late years was the portrayal of doors against which various things were suspended or hung in a shallow but entirely convincing space. One of the largest of these paintings is the 6-foot-high second version of *After the Hunt* (1885; San Francisco, Museum of the Legion of Honor); the best known is perhaps the musical *Old Models* (1892; Boston, Museum of Fine Arts). In these works his skill in the creation of subtle compositions, apparent also in the early texture pieces, overshadows even the verisimilitude of his technique.

Although famous in his lifetime, Harnett's pictures were scattered and embellished with other signatures after his death. Their recent return to authenticity and prominence is largely owing to the researches of Alfred Frankenstein.

BIBLIOGRAPHY. A. Frankenstein, *After the Hunt*, Berkeley, 1953.

JEROME VIOLA

HARPIGNIES, HENRI JOSEPH. French painter and graphic artist (b. Valenciennes, 1819; d. St-Privé, 1916). He studied with Achard and was in Rome from 1850 to 1852. Harpignies was friendly with Corot and accompanied him to Italy in 1860. Corot's tonality was a constant influence on Harpignies's landscapes, which he painted in several regions of France and Italy. His paintings are soberly composed and colored interpretations of nature, although the landscapes based upon Italian scenes tend to be brighter in color and higher in key. The stress on tones was perhaps part of his feeling for the importance of good drawing. He also did about thirty-eight engravings and drypoints of landscapes, sometimes with figures.

HARPY. Malevolent female creature, whose name, meaning "snatcher," is derived from ancient Greek mythology. Originally winged goddesses representing the capricious and dangerous storm winds that cause seamen to disappear, Harpies were later depicted as having human faces with birdlike bodies. Harpies stole or polluted the food of Phineus, until they were killed or driven off by his fellow Argonauts.

HARPY TOMB, *see* LYCIA.

HARRAN: GREAT MOSQUE. Ruined mosque in what is now southeastern Turkey. A masonry structure roughly 120 square yards, it was almost undoubtedly begun by Marwan II (r. 744–50), the last Umayyad caliph, who made Harran his capital. The sanctuary may, however, have been extended two bays to the south, and its façade was certainly reconstructed shortly before 1184 at the order of Saladin. The plan, with a four-aisled sanctuary open to the *sahn* (courtyard) by nineteen arches, recalls the Great Mosque of Damascus. The center arch was wider and higher, probably opening into a "transept" centered on a mihrab. Single-aisled *riwags* (arcades) lined the three remaining sides of the *sahn*, near the center of which there was (as at Damascus) a domed treasury raised on columns over an octagonal basin. The roofs were of timber and were gabled.

BIBLIOGRAPHY. K. A. C. Creswell, *A Short Account of Early Muslim Architecture*, Harmondsworth, 1958.

HARRIS, HARWELL HAMILTON. American architect and educator (1903–   ). Born in Redlands, Calif., he attended Pomona College and the Otis Art Institute. He collaborated with Richard Neutra (1930–33), was secretary of the American group of C.I.A.M. (1931–33), and established his own office in 1934. Harris has taught at several schools, including the University of Texas, Columbia, and Yale. His architecture is generally associated with the Bay Region Style developed in California. The influence of Frank Lloyd Wright may be seen in Harris's house for Ralph Johnson in Los Angeles (1951). *See* BAY REGION STYLE; C.I.A.M.

HARRIS, LAWREN STEWART. Canadian painter (1885–   ). He studied painting in Munich and Berlin, worked as an illustrator in the Near East and Minnesota, and was influenced by Scandinavian landscape painting. He was a "Group of Seven" member, and since 1912 has painted simplified landscapes in the Maritimes, the Arctic, Ontario, and the Rockies. He has lived in Toronto and Vancouver.

BIBLIOGRAPHY. Art Gallery of Toronto, *Lawren Harris, Paintings, 1910–48*, Toronto, 1948.

HARRIS, ROBERT. Canadian painter (b. Wales, 1849; d. Montreal, 1919). He spent his youth on Prince Edward

William Michael Harnett, *Old Models*. Museum of Fine Arts, Boston.

Island, and studied in Boston and in Europe under Alphonse Legros and Léon Bonnat. A well-known teacher, Harris became the president of the Royal Canadian Academy and exhibited internationally. He painted portraits, genre, historical subjects, and landscapes.

HARRIS, THOMAS. English architect (1829–1900). He believed that architecture should reflect industrial change. His Harrow flats (1860) were vigorous but mannered and exposed construction. With the Lisson Grove warehouse

(1874), his elevations are protomodernist in their straight-forward simplicity and expression of structure.

BIBLIOGRAPHY. D. Harbron, "Thomas Harris," *The Architectural Review*, XCII, 1942.

HARRISON, PETER. American architect (1716–75). Born in Yorkshire, England, Harrison went to the American colonies in 1740, working first as a merchant in Newport, R.I. Apparently self-taught, he became the first thorough-going Palladian architect in the colonies. He introduced classical elements, absorbing the lessons of Palladio, James Gibbs, and others into a unique style. His early Redwood Library (1749–58), Newport, was the first building to use a temple portico. The openness and lightness of his King's Chapel (1749–58), Boston, with its slender Corinthian coupled columns supporting a coved ceiling, follows the example of the churches of James Gibbs. Later works, the Touro Synagogue (1759-63) and the Brick Market (1761–72), both in Newport, drew on elements from the designs of Inigo Jones. *See* KING'S CHAPEL, BOSTON.

HARRISON, WALLACE KIRKMAN. American architect (1895–   ). Born in Worcester, Mass., he studied at the Ecole des Beaux-Arts, Paris, traveled on a Rotch Fellow-ship, and worked as a draftsman for McKim, Mead and White before forming partnerships with Helmle and Corbett (1927–29), Corbett and MacMurray (1929–35), Fouilhoux (1935–41), Fouilhoux and Abramovitz (1941–45), and Abramovitz (1945). Essentially an architectural coordinator, Harrison has been associated with such large-scale and influential works as Rockefeller Center (1931–37) and the United Nations complex (1952), both in New York City, designed by an international team he headed. *See* HARRISON AND ABRAMOVITZ; NEW YORK.

BIBLIOGRAPHY. New York, Museum of Modern Art, *Built in U.S.A., 1932–1944*, ed. E. Mock, New York, 1944.

HARRISON AND ABRAMOVITZ. American architectural firm of Wallace Kirkman Harrison (1895–   ) and Max Abramovitz (1908–   ) in New York City, established in 1945; one of the largest design firms in the country. Their funnel-shaped auditorium at Oberlin College (1953) in Ohio is embellished by an undulating sur-face at its entrance, expressive of the literary and musical activities within. The Alcoa Building (1952) in Pittsburgh, employing prefabricated curtain walls of pressed aluminum panels, incorporates several technical innovations. The firm has also executed the United States Embassy (1953) in Havana and the C.I.T. Building (1957) and Time and Life Building (1960), both in New York City. *See* HARRISON, WALLACE KIRKMAN.

HARROWING OF HELL. Better known as Christ in Limbo, it is the representation of Christ's descent into Hell after His resurrection for the purpose of releasing captured souls. Usually Christ is shown pulling Adam by the hand through doors that represent the Gates of Hell; often the Devil is seen crushed by the door upon which Christ has trampled. The source for the subject is the apocryphal Book of Nicodemus. The Harrowing of Hell is common in Byzantine art after the 7th century; it first appears in Western art about A.D. 1000 in illuminated manuscripts.

BIBLIOGRAPHY. O. Erich, *Die Darstellung des Teufels in der christlichen Kunst*, Berlin, 1931.

HART, GEORGE OVERBURY ("Pop" Hart). American painter and graphic artist (b. Cairo, Ill., 1868; d. New York City, 1933). His only formal artistic training occurred in brief periods spent at the Art Institute of Chicago and at the Académie Julian in Paris. A born wanderer, he supported himself in his travels by various odd jobs and always carried portfolios of drawings of the genre scenes that met his eye. These at first were done only for his own amusement and interest, and it was not until about 1921 that his art became paramount.

Hart preferred water color to oil because of the immediacy and spontaneity of its effects, but his search for freedom of expression often involved a mixture of media (for example, water color with pastel, charcoal, or pencil) that sometimes disturbed his critics. A similar technical experimentation can be seen in his etchings and lithographs, where he aimed at the painterly effects of his water colors.

BIBLIOGRAPHY. G. O. (Pop) Hart, *Twenty-four Selections from his Work*, ed. with an introd. by H. Cahill, New York, 1928.

HART, JAMES McDOUGAL. American landscape painter (b. Scotland, 1828; d. Brooklyn, N.Y., 1901). He was apprenticed at fifteen to a sign and banner painter in Albany. He worked in Munich and Düsseldorf in the 1850s. In Düsseldorf he developed the facile realism that characterizes his placid and sentimental landscapes of rural New York State.

HART, JOEL TANNER. American sculptor (b. Winchester, Ky., 1810; d. Florence, Italy, 1877). He had little formal training. Shobal Clevenger encouraged him to develop his talent for sculpture. A succession of classically derived portrait busts was favorably received, and a marble statue of Henry Clay, carved in Italy (Richmond, Va.), made Hart famous.

BIBLIOGRAPHY. A. T. Gardner, *Yankee Stonecutters*, New York, 1945.

HART, WILLIAM. American painter (b. Paisley, Scotland, 1823; d. Mt. Vernon, N.Y., 1894). He came to the United States in 1831. Hart worked in the spirit of the later

Wallace Kirkman Harrison, United Nations Building, New York.

Marsden Hartley, *Still Life No. 3*, 1923. Art Institute of Chicago. A work emulating Cézanne.

Hudson River school, painting peaceful landscapes of the northeastern states.

HARTFORD, CONN.: FIRST CHURCH.

Meeting-house of the Society of the First Church, built in the Greek revival style in 1806–07. The front of the rectangular building is preceded by a portico with four Ionic columns surmounted by a three-storied steeple.

BIBLIOGRAPHY. G. L. Walker, *History of the First Church in Hartford, 1633–1883*, Hartford, Conn., 1884.

HARTFORD, CONN.: WADSWORTH ATHENEUM.

American collection opened in 1844 by Daniel Wadsworth, whose collection of American paintings included a number of scenes of the American Revolution by John Trumbull and Hudson River paintings by Thomas Cole. The museum now also contains the J. P. Morgan Collection of classical bronzes, Italian Renaissance objects, 17th-century silver, and 18th-century porcelain; the Wallace Nutting Collection of early American furniture; Central and South American art; and period rooms, tapestries, and armor. The painting collection ranges from 1300 to the present day, including works by Piero di Cosimo, Rubens, Tintoretto, Cranach, Tiepolo, Picasso, Hopper, Miró, and Mondrian.

The museum owns *The Ecstasy of St. Francis*, one of the few paintings by Caravaggio in the United States. Also worthy of mention are Zurbarán's *St. Serapion* and two important 17th-century French paintings, Poussin's *Crucifixion* and Louis Le Nain's *Peasants in a Landscape*. In the modern field there are works by Arp, Calder, Dali, Gabo, and Pevsner, among others.

BIBLIOGRAPHY. S. L. Faison, Jr., *A Guide to the Art Museums of New England*, New York, 1958.

HARTIGAN, GRACE.

American painter (1922–   ). Born in Newark, N.J., she studied with Isaac Lane Muse in Newark and worked as a draftsman in the middle 1940s. In her earlier paintings she applied the technical means of the abstractionist New York school to the figure, for example, *River Bathers* (1953; New York, Museum of Modern Art) and *Masquerade* (1954; Art Institute of Chicago). In other paintings of the 1950s the urban environment is more insistent as subject matter but is still described in rich color and broad, loose strokes, as in *City Life* (1956; New York, Nelson A. Rockefeller Collection) and *Essex Market* (1956; New York, Mrs. John D. Rockefeller, III, Collection). Hartigan's recent works are more personally lyrical treatments of interiors, landscapes, and still lifes.

BIBLIOGRAPHY. B. H. Friedman, ed., *School of New York*, New York, 1959; New York, Museum of Modern Art, *The New American Painting...*, New York, 1959.

HARTLEY, MARSDEN (Edmund Marsden Hartley).

American painter and writer (b. Lewiston, Me., 1877; d. Ellsworth, Me., 1943). He studied in Cleveland, at the New York School of Art with F. Luis Mora, Frank V. Du Mond, and William Merritt Chase, and at the National Academy of Design. In his first exhibition, at Stieglitz's Photo-Secession Gallery in 1909, Hartley showed heavily painted mountain landscapes influenced by the style of Giovanni Segantini, whose works he had probably seen in reproduction.

Hartley went to Paris in 1912. He was in Germany in 1913 and 1914, where he met Kandinsky, Marc, and Klee and exhibited with the Blaue Reiter group in Munich and Berlin. During this period he painted strongly colored, expressionistic, abstract compositions based upon the ornamental paraphernalia of German militarism, for example,

Portrait of a German Officer (1914; New York, Metropolitan Museum). For a whlle, after his return to the United States, Hartley used a form of cubistic abstractions in which he arranged flat, mostly linear shapes, but in the beautifully poised *Movement No. 10* (1917; Art Institute of Chicago) a pear and two bananas betray the still-life source of the composition. In the early 1920s Hartley worked in Paris and in the south of France, painting still lifes and the Provençal landscape in emulation of Cézanne, for example, *Still Life No. 3* (1923; Art Institute of Chicago).

Hartley's mature style began to emerge on his Mexican journey of 1932; in intense, mystical landscapes (including Mt. Popocatepetl) the fructifying effect of his lifelong admiration for Ryder can clearly be seen. In 1936 Hartley revisited Gloucester, Mass., and painted landscapes with less simplified forms and strong, almost violent coloring.

By 1938 Hartley had settled in Maine, determined to become the painter of his native state. He painted the figure in a series of so-called "archaic portraits" of Nova Scotian fishermen done from memory, for example, *Fishermen's Last Supper* (1940–41; New York, Mr. and Mrs. Roy R. Neuberger Collection). His late landscapes and marines, such as the powerful *Evening Storm, Schoodic, Maine* (1942; New York, Museum of Modern Art), were the most personal and fully realized paintings of his career. The stylistic characteristics of these late works, rich coloring and an abstraction from carefully observed natural forms, can be seen in the stylized clouds, deep-blue mountains, and red forest of *Mount Katahdin, Autumn, No. 1* (1939–40; Lincoln, Sheldon Memorial Art Gallery).

BIBLIOGRAPHY. E. McCausland, *Marsden Hartley*, Minneapolis, 1952. JEROME VIOLA

Hans Hartung, *T 1963 - R 40*. Fine Arts Museum, Brussels.

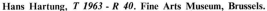

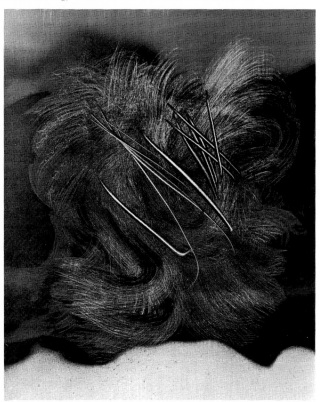

HARTUNG, HANS. French painter (1904–   ). Born in Leipzig, he began to paint when quite young and was influenced by Rembrandt, then by Kokoschka, Nolde, and Franz Marc. His early abstractions and water colors date from 1922. While attending classes at the Leipzig and Dresden academies (1924–28), he met Kandinsky (1925). Hartung was one of the first to reject all visible forms and all exterior representation; his painting became entirely abstract. He traveled in France, Italy, Holland, and Belgium. In 1935 he left Germany and settled in Paris. He became a French citizen in 1944. Hartung is one of the most famous exponents of French abstract art. His painting in black sprays and splashes is reminiscent of Japanese calligraphy, as in *T. 56–19* (1956).

BIBLIOGRAPHY. M. Rousseau et al., *Hans Hartung*, Stuttgart, 1949; M. Seuphor, *L'Art abstrait: Ses origines, ses premiers maîtres*, Paris, 1950; M. Seuphor, "Hans Hartung," *Art Digest*, XXIX, March, 1955; B. Dorival, *Twentieth Century French Painters*, 2 vols., New York, 1958.

HARTUNG, KARL. German sculptor (1908–   ). He was born in Hamburg and studied there with Bossert at the School for Arts and Crafts. From 1929 to 1933 he was in Paris and Italy, especially Florence. Among the stronger influences on his development were Maillol, Despiau, and Etruscan art. In 1936 he turned to a semiabstract mode. His works were not exhibited during the Nazi years in Germany, although he was in the armed services from 1941 to 1945. Since 1950 he has taught at the Academy of Fine Arts in Berlin and has been represented in major exhibitions in Germany, Paris, Amsterdam, London, Switzerland, and the United States. His recent style sometimes refers to the human figure with sharply reduced, fluid volumes and sometimes depends upon a geometric superposition of abstract forms.

BIBLIOGRAPHY. E. Trier, *Moderne Plastik*, Frankfurt am Main, 1955; M. Seuphor, *The Sculpture of This Century*, New York, 1960.

HARTWIG, CLEO. American sculptor (1911–   ). Born in Webberville, Mich., she studied at the Art Institute in Chicago and at the International School of Art in the United States and Europe. Since 1943 she has had several one-man shows, primarily in New York City, where she lives, and examples of her work are owned by museums throughout the United States. Most of Hartwig's works are human or animal figures in wood, clay, and stone, although she has also made excursions into abstraction. The influence of José de Creeft and John Flannagan is evident in the careful treatment of textures and in the enclosing of rounded forms within the block of material.

HARUNOBU (Suzuki Harunobu). Japanese Ukiyo-e printmaker (1725–70). He ranks among the greatest masters of this genre. He was a pupil of Shigenaga but was also influenced by Toyonobu. Harunobu's greatest contribution to the art of wood-block printing was the perfection of *nishiki-e* (brocade prints). These prints are stamped in many colors, sometimes twelve or more. In 1765 he and his collaborators introduced the technique, which revolutionized the art of printmaking. Harunobu is particularly well known for his portrayal of young, doll-like girls of good family, often buffeted by wind or rain that emphasizes their frailty. His color harmony is subtle and refined, and his lines flow smoothly and expressively, if never charged with power. His romantic and delicate moods of young love captured the public, and many artists imitated his style. *See* SHIGENAGA; TOYONOBU; UKIYO-E.

BIBLIOGRAPHY. L. V. Ledoux, *Japanese Prints by Harunobu and Shunshō in the Collection of Louis V. Ledoux*, New York, 1945; J. A. Michener, *Japanese Prints*, Rutland, Vt., 1959.

HARUSHIGE (Suzuki Harushige), *see* KOKAN.

HASAN KHAN SUR, TOMB OF, SASARAM. Indian tomb located in a town of Bihar State in eastern India. Completed in 1535, the tomb was the first of several erected for the Suri rulers by the master builder Aliwal Khan. Octagonal in plan, crowned by a dome above the central chamber and encircled by an octagonal corridor, the structure is of the type that was brought into being by the Lodi rulers at Delhi. The tomb is built of stone and sparsely ornamented; its effect is somber and severe.

BIBLIOGRAPHY. P. Brown, *Indian Architecture*, vol. 2: *Islamic Period*, 4th ed., Bombay, 1959.

HASEGAWA SCHOOL, *see* TOHAKU.

HASENAUER, KARL VON. Austrian architect (1833–94). A pupil of Van der Null and Siccardsburg, he is best known as the architectural partner of Gottfried Semper, with whom he designed many of the monumental buildings of Vienna in the seventies and eighties.

HASHIMOTO. GAHO. Japanese painter (1835–1908). Gahō Hashimoto was a member of the Kanō family. In 1887 he was appointed chairman of the Japanese painting department in the newly established Tokyo Fine Arts School (now Tokyo University of Fine Arts). Later, with Okakura Tenshin (the spiritual successor of Ernest Fenollosa), he founded the artists' organization Nihon Bijutsuin (Academy of Arts of Japan). *See* JAPAN: PAINTING (MODERN PERIOD).

BIBLIOGRAPHY. N. Ueno, ed., *Japanese Arts and Crafts in the Meiji Era* (Centenary Culture Council Series, Japanese Culture in the Meiji Era, vol. 8), Tokyo, 1958.

HASHIMOTO, KANSETSU. Japanese painter (1883–1945). He first studied with a Shijō master but later was more influenced by the traditional arts of China and Japan. His ink painting, reflecting the influences of various schools, can be seen on sixty screens in the Kenninji in Kyoto (1940). *See* SHIJO SCHOOL.

HASSAM, FREDERICK CHILDE. American painter, illustrator, and graphic artist (b. Dorchester, Mass., 1859; d. East Hampton, N.Y., 1935). Hassam attended the Boston Art School and worked as a wood engraver and illustrator before 1883, when he went to Paris and studied with Boulanger and Lefébvre. He was a member of The Ten, a group of impressionist artists formed in 1898.

From his first contacts with the works of Monet in Paris, Hassam painted in an impressionist manner, but, perhaps because of his early academic training, he rarely dissolved a scene completely in its light and managed to keep a relatively firm drawing beneath the strokes of pure, bright color. Unlike the personal dissection of light itself that is often found in Monet, the light in Hassam's paintings is inextricable from the objects and scenes it illumi-

Childe Hassam, *Against the Light*. Art Institute of Chicago.

nates. Many of his early paintings are of street scenes in New York, Boston, and Paris, for example, *Washington Arch, Spring* (1890; Washington, D.C., Phillips Collection), in which the fleeting impression of the movements of fashionable people is stressed, often with such technical complications as variations in weather or wet pavements. In these pictures the color is bright and the paint handling loose. He painted flag-filled street views during World War I.

Hassam was also concerned with the figure, especially that of women. He painted women either outdoors in full light, as in the painting of a woman leaning against rocks and reading, called *Summer Sunlight* (1892; New York, American Academy of Arts and Letters), or in variously lit interiors, such as the profile half-figure *Against the Light* (1910; Art Institute of Chicago). About 1915 Hassam began to work in lithography and etching. In the approximately 300 prints he produced, the same interest in the capture of light is evident as in the paintings, in spite of the limitations of the black-and-white media.

Hassam's later landscapes and shore scenes are the most broadly painted and perhaps, of all his work, come closest to true impressionism, as in the rough-surfaced *Montauk* (1922; American Academy of Arts and Letters). During his career Hassam's paintings won general popularity as well as the rewards of official recognition. He was elected a national academician in 1906.

BIBLIOGRAPHY. C. Hassam, ... *Childe Hassam*, comp. by N. Pousette-Dart, New York, 1922; A. Adams, *Childe Hassam*, New York, 1938.

JEROME VIOLA

HASTA. Sanskrit word meaning "hand." It is the hand position, or mudrā, applied to Hindu images.

Hatching. Method of representing light and shadow.

Haunch. Section of an arch.

HASTINGS, THOMAS, *see* CARRERE AND HASTINGS.

HATCHING. Method or technique used in drawing, engraving, painting, tapestry weaving, and so on, in which gradations of light and shadow are represented by series of fine parallel lines made close together. These may be straight or curved.

HATFIELD HOUSE. Seventeenth-century English mansion in Hertfordshire County. One of the great Jacobean mansions of England, it was built by Robert Cecil, Earl of Salisbury, between 1608 and 1612. In its totality it does not conform to the traditional pattern for houses of its period. The plan is a square U with symmetry observable only on the north and south fronts. The frontispiece to the south between the wings was completed by a carpenter, Robert Lyming. This façade with the cupola above is now thought to be a possible early design by Inigo Jones. The hall has a spectacular screen and opens out to the great staircase in the same lavish style. The gardens, a restored example of the Jacobean manner, were partly laid out by Salomon de Caus.

BIBLIOGRAPHY. N. Pevsner, *The Buildings of England*, vol. 7, Harmondsworth, 1953.

HATHORIC CAPITAL. Egyptian architectural type in which the head of Hathor, a cow goddess sometimes represented with a cow's ears, is used as a column capital. The Hathoric capital is found in the ancient Temple of Hathor, Dendera, and in Philae.

HATHORIC COLUMN. Type of Egyptian column imitating the handle of a sistrum rattle (as in the sistrum column), topped by a cubic block, two sides of which are carved in high relief with the face of Hathor surmounted by the façade of a shrine. As early as the New Kingdom four faces top a square pillar (Serabit el Khadem), the prototype of the late Hathoric capital on a cylindrical shaft (in the Saitic dynasty, the capital was one-third the total height). In the Ptolemaic period this capital is set on a composite column.

BIBLIOGRAPHY. G. Jéquier, *Manuel d'archéologie égyptienne*, vol. 1: *Les éléments de l'architecture*, Paris, 1924.

HATRA. Parthian fortress in Mesopotamia (3d cent. B.C.), designed on a circular plan. Hatra is the ancient name for modern Al Hadhr in northwest Iraq. Houses of Iranian-Parthian style are of hewn blocks of stone, adorned with sculptured motifs including masks. The temples have a square central room, and a staircase leads to the roof, where the altars on which the sacred fire burned were located.

BIBLIOGRAPHY. R. Ghirshman, *The Arts of Ancient Iran from Its Origins to the Time of Alexander the Great*, New York, 1964.

HATSHEPSUT, MORTUARY TEMPLE OF, DEIR EL BAHARI, *see* DEIR EL BAHARI.

HATTUSAS, *see* BOGHAZKEUY.

HAUNCH. Section of an arch between the springing and the crown.

HAUSMANN, RAOUL. Austrian sculptor (1886–   ). Born in Vienna, Hausmann was cofounder with Huelsenbeck of the Berlin Dada movement (1919) and in this period carved Dada sculptures and reliefs. He now lives in France and is best known for his photomontages.

BIBLIOGRAPHY. M. Seuphor, *The Sculpture of This Century*, New York, 1960.

HAUSSMANN, GEORGES EUGENE. French city planner (1809–91). Appointed prefect of the Seine Department by Napoleon III, Haussmann was responsible for the extensive replanning and shaping of Paris between 1853 and 1869. He brought a new monumentality to traditional French rationalistic plans, creating long, wide boulevards that connect circular plazas in straight lines. This plan provided a clear arterial system and a city of magnificent vistas punctuated by such monuments as the Arc de Triomphe de l'Etoile and the Opéra. Many major European and Latin American cities later emulated the urban style set by Haussmann.

BIBLIOGRAPHY. D. H. Pinkney, *Napoleon III and the Rebuilding of Paris*, Princeton, 1958.

HAVANA: NATIONAL MUSEUM. Cuban collections, including the museums of History and Fine Arts. It houses a group of Cuban paintings of the colonial and modern periods in addition to works by Murillo, Zurbarán, and other Spanish painters.

HAVELL, WILLIAM. English painter (b. Reading, 1782; d. 1857). He was the son of a drawing master. His work is principally associated with the Thames—with vistas of river and lush foliage. He also painted in Wales and in 1816 went to China with Lord Amherst. He traveled to India in 1817 and also visited Italy. Havell was one of the first members of the Old Water-Colour Society.

HAVILAND, JOHN. American architect (1792–1852). Born in England, Haviland studied with James Elmes in London and emigrated to the United States in 1816. Working primarily in Philadelphia, he designed a number of churches and other buildings in a variety of vigorously conceived revival styles with their strongly handled masses. He is best known, however, for his radial prison designs, which were to have a great impact both in Europe and the United States. The best example is the Eastern State Penitentiary in Philadelphia (1823–35), which has cell blocks radiating from the center and makes use of elements from medieval castle architecture. Haviland also designed the

prison in New York City known as the Tombs (1836–38), which has details from Egyptian architecture.

HAWAII, *see* OCEANIC ART (POLYNESIA).

HAWKSMOOR, NICHOLAS. English architect (1661–1736). His early associaton with Sir Christopher Wren exposed him to the traditional late Stuart style. At Greenwich Hospital, where he was clerk of works in 1698, Hawksmoor met Wren's baroque style, which was to influence him particularly in Castle Howard, which he built with Sir John Vanbrugh. The Vanbrugh-Hawksmoor partnership is difficult to analyze, but Hawksmoor's contribution can be summarized as ornament and movement. As surveyor for the building of fifty new churches, he was able to express his individual genius.

His six churches are perhaps the most inspired buildings of their period. His activity at Oxford illustrates the Roman and medieval elements of his style. He also designed the gable and towers of the west front at Westminster Abbey (ca. 1734). The mausoleum at Castle Howard (1729–36) may be the greatest building of the English renaissance. *See* HOWARD, CASTLE; WESTMINSTER ABBEY, LONDON.

BIBLIOGRAPHY. K. Downes, *Nicholas Hawksmoor*, London, 1960.

HAWTHORN DESIGN. Earlier Western designation for the popular plum-branch decoration found on many large Chinese vases, particularly blue-and-white and *famille-noire* and *famille-verte* pieces. Presumably the term was used because of the resemblance of the hawthorn branch to the *Prunus* design. The term is still occasionally encountered in auction catalogs and among collectors.

HAYDON, BENJAMIN ROBERT. English history painter (b. Plymouth, 1786; d. London, 1846). He went to London in 1804 to study at the Royal Academy of Arts schools. From the first, his overpowering ambition was to become a history painter such as England had not yet seen. Raphael and Michelangelo were constantly before him as

Nicholas Hawksmoor, the Mausoleum of Castle Howard, Yorkshire.

Benjamin Robert Haydon, *Punch or May Day*. Tate Gallery, London.

exemplars, and he planned compositions that were on the grandest scale and beyond his capacity. His enthusiasm and powers of concentration were nonetheless very remarkable, and he impressed contemporary opinion. Had he been a less violent and less self-absorbed personality, he could have had a more successful career. His early patrons included Thomas Hope, Lord Mulgrave, and Sir George Beaumont.

His main works are *The Death of Dentatus* (1809; Marquess of Normandy Collection), *The Judgment of Solomon* (1814; lost), a great popular success, *The Entry into Jerusalem* (1820; Norwood, Ohio, St. Mary's Seminary), and *The Raising of Lazarus* (1823; London, Tate). All are on a very large scale. In some smaller scenes of contemporary life, such as *Punch or May Day* (1829; Tate), he shows unexpected observation and humor, and some of his portraits, such as *Wordsworth* (1842; London, National Portrait Gallery), are original and powerful.

Haydon wrote and spoke eloquently in favor of the acquisition of the Elgin marbles for the nation and of the encouragement of public and governmental support for the arts. His *Lectures on Painting and Design* were published in 1846.

BIBLIOGRAPHY. T. Taylor, ed., *Autobiography and Memoirs of Benjamin Robert Haydon*, 3 vols., London, 1853; E. George, *The Life and Death of Benjamin Robert Haydon*, London, 1948.

KENNETH J. GARLICK

HAYE, CORNEILLE DE LA, *see* CORNEILLE DE LYON.

HAYEZ, FRANCESCO. Italian painter (b. Venice, 1791; d. Milan, 1882). He studied in Rome, where he was influenced by the classicism of Canova. After 1821 Hayez joined the romantics, and in his last period he turned to painting realistic historical paintings.

BIBLIOGRAPHY. G. Nicodemi, *Dipinti di Francesco Hayez*, Milan, 1934.

HAYMAN, FRANCIS. English painter (b. Exeter, 1708; d. London, 1776). Little is known about the details of Hayman's life, but evidence suggests that he was highly esteemed by his contemporaries. He was for a time president of the Society of Artists; he was also a founder-member and, later, librarian of the Royal Academy of Arts. His active career as a painter seems to have been confined to about fifteen years, from 1740 to 1755.

Hayman is a minor artist, but he occupies a central position in a number of mid-18th-century artistic developments. He is probably best known in the conversation-piece style of portraiture, a facet of his work well represented by the so-called *Gascoigne Family* in the Henry E. Huntington Library and Art Gallery, San Marino, Calif. He has an easily recognizable manner that is not particularly prepossessing, but he nevertheless managed to infuse into the conversation piece a little of the French curvilinear grace and elegance of grouping. In these qualities he prepares the way for the early works of Gainsborough, who was certainly in close contact with Hayman for a while during the 1740s. The French component in Hayman's style is probably due to his association with the engraver Gravelot, with whom he collaborated in designing and engraving the illustrations for *Hanmer's Shakespeare* (1744).

Hayman was also active as a decorator, notably in a series of large-scale pictures executed for Vauxhall, the pleasure garden of mid-18th-century London. The themes he touched on in these decorations were extraordinarily varied, ranging from Shakespearian scenes to genre episodes representing everyday games and pastimes. In both types of subject Hayman was among the British innovators, and both subsequently became very popular with English artists. Two paintings from this series, *Sliding on the Ice* and *The Dance of the Milkmaids on Mayday*, are in the Victoria and Albert Museum, London.

Hayman's artistic personality is still not fully defined. Some of his paintings and many of his drawings are frequently attributed to other men. However, enough is now known of his work to indicate that he was one of the most versatile and adventuresome British painters of the 1740s.

BIBLIOGRAPHY. E. K. Waterhouse, *Painting in Britain, 1530–1750*, Baltimore, 1953.

ROBERT R. WARK

HAYSTACKS. Oil painting in a series of that name by Monet, in the Metropolitan Museum of Art, New York. *See* MONET, CLAUDE-OSCAR.

HAYTER, STANLEY WILLIAM. English painter and printmaker (1901–   ). Born in London, he graduated with honors in organic chemistry and geology from Kings College in 1921, after which he worked for the World Nickel Company and then the Anglo-Iranian Oil Company, traveling in the Near and Middle East. In 1926 he returned from Persia and settled in Paris to devote himself entirely to art. From the age of fourteen he had painted; he had also been interested in the graphic arts for many years and was aware that graphic art, especially the intaglio mediums of engraving and etching, had possibilities that had been either overlooked or undeveloped for generations. The engraved work of Joseph Hecht and Jacques Villon stimulated his interest. At this time he began to teach printmaking techniques. In 1933 he moved to 17 rue Campagne-Première, from which the name "Atelier 17" derived. Atelier 17 was to become the most influential print workshop of the 20th century.

In 1940 Hayter went to the United States to teach at the California School of Fine Arts in San Francisco. Later the same year he set up an Atelier 17 in New York City and taught at the New School for Social Research. An Atelier 17 exhibition was held at the Museum of Modern Art in 1944 (earlier exhibitions of the group had been held in Paris and London in 1934). In 1948 Hayter taught painting and theory at the California School of Fine Arts and then taught printmaking at the Art Institute of Chicago until 1949. During this year he published *New Ways of Gravure*, in which he discussed his theories and experiments in printmaking. He became professor of fine arts at Brooklyn College, New York. In 1950 he returned to Paris to reestablish Atelier 17 there, leaving the New York studio under the direction of his pupils. In 1951 Hayter was decorated with the Legion of Honor, and in 1959 he was awarded the Order of the British Empire. In 1960 Hayter again taught printmaking at the California School of Fine Arts.

Francis Hayman, *The Gascoigne Family*. Henry E. Huntington Library and Art Gallery, San Marino, Calif.

Despite his preoccupation with the teaching of techniques, Hayter has said that "Technique is a process which sets the imagination free and makes its action visible; it has no other function." His own work, such as *Tarantelle* and *Cronos* in mixed intaglio media, shows a freedom of line commensurate with this creed.

The many artists who have worked at Atelier 17 under the inspired guidance of Hayter have set the style of printmaking for this century. They include Picasso, Miró, Lasansky, and Peterdi.

BIBLIOGRAPHY. M. Conil-Lacoste, "L'Atelier 17," *L'Oeil*, LIII, 1959; University of Kentucky Art Gallery, *Graphics '60. 3 Masters of Intaglio: Hayter, Lasansky, Peterdi*, 1960.
KNEELAND MC NULTY

HAY WAIN, THE. Oil painting by Constable, in the National Gallery, London. *See* CONSTABLE, JOHN.

HAZOR (Tell El Qedah). Large mound in Upper Galilee, with ruins on various levels dating from the Middle Bronze Age to the Hellenistic period. A strategic and commercial center, Hazor was influenced by many cultures. Cobbled and paved streets and drainage canals were unearthed, and on the lowest level, a large two-storied building was found, its large hall divided by square stone monoliths, the mud floors paved with stone slabs.

Rock-cut tombs, temples with animal orthostats, palaces with basalt columns and capitals, shrines, sacrificial altars, bronze axes, incense stands, and alabaster offertory vessels were discovered. There were also quantities of pottery, among them Cypro-Phoenician and Mycenaean examples. Among the other finds were metal implements, carved or incised bone and ivory objects, coins, cylinder seals, scarabs, human and animal figurines, weapons, and jewelry as well as eight Hebrew inscriptions and one Akkadian inscription incised in cuneiform, the earliest of its type discovered in Palestine.

BIBLIOGRAPHY. J. Garstang, "The Site of Hazor," *Annals of Archaeology and Anthropology*, XIV, March, 1927; Y. Yadin et al., *The James A. De Rothschild Expedition at Hazor*, 3 vols., Jerusalem, 1958–61.

HEALY, GEORGE PETER ALEXANDER. American portrait painter (b. Boston, 1813; d. Chicago, 1894). He first opened a portrait studio in Boston and later studied painting with Gros and Couture in Paris. Healy's portraits of notables at home and abroad were painted in a photographically hard and realistic manner.

BIBLIOGRAPHY. M. de Mare, *G. P. A. Healy, American Artist*, New York, 1954.

HEARNE, THOMAS. English painter (b. near Malmesbury, Wiltshire, 1744; d. 1817). He studied in London and exhibited his water colors there from 1765 to 1806. In 1771 he visited the Leeward Islands as draftsman to the governor and remained three years. His drawings are often monochromatic, but nevertheless manage to convey a great sense of light and warmth. Many of them were engraved.

HEAVEN, ALTAR OF, *see* PEKING. *See also* HEAVEN, TEMPLE OF, PEKING.

HEAVEN, TEMPLE OF, PEKING. Chinese temple begun in the 15th century by the Ming emperors. It lies off the axis to the east in the Outer (or Chinese) City of Peking. However, the main axis of the circular temple itself, which has a circular triple marble balustraded base, runs north

Temple of Heaven, Peking. Originally built in 1420, burned in 1889, and restored in 1890.

and south. The Temple of Heaven is one of the loveliest temples in China with its magnificent sweep of curved eaves and its beautiful roof made of blue tiles. The temple has had a turbulent history: it was originally built in 1420, was repaired in 1751, burned in 1889, and was restored in 1890. The courtyard containing the temple is flanked by two very fine rectangular halls.

Featured in the interior, which consists of a circular chamber about 50 feet high, is a circular lantern in a roof. The roof stands on a double ring of twelve outer columns, in the center of which are placed four columns in the form of a square. Four horizontal beams connect these

columns to carry over curved beams in the form of a circle. These in turn carry two intermediate posts, thus forming a circular lantern. In the interior the decoration is unusually rich, and the columns are gigantic.

The three roofs of the temple are covered with blue glazed tiles, and the exterior of the building is highly colored with red columns and with panels and brackets of red, blue, green, and gold. The central slope of the staired balustrade is carved with intricate dragon designs. There was a "spirit" stair, not to be used by ordinary mortals. The emperor may have been carried over this incline in his sedan.

Before the temple is an impressive gateway with three arched openings; the central one, being slightly larger, beautifully frames the temple for the approaching visitor. The gateway forms part of a circular wall surrounding the temple.

A subtle balance is struck between the temple and the neighboring Altar of Heaven. Both are surrounded by a walled wooden enclosure of a rectangular shape, the two northern corners being rounded. The enclosure is just under 1 mile from north to south and just over 1 mile from east to west. The ensemble, which is known collectively as the Altar of Heaven, is approached by a ramp leading up to the raised causeway, which joins the temple at the north end with the altar proper at the south end.

See also PEKING.

BIBLIOGRAPHY. D. G. Mirams, *A Brief History of Chinese Architecture*, Shanghai, 1940; A. C. H. Boyd, *Chinese Architecture and Town Planning, 1500 B.C.–A.D. 1911*, Chicago, 1962.

ABRAHAM A. DAVIDSON

HEBALD, MILTON. American sculptor (1917–   ). Born in New York City, Hebald has produced figures that often suggest an almost manneristic svelteness, as may be seen in the bronze *Three Graces* (1961) and the over-life-size seated statue of James Joyce placed over the writer's grave in Zurich (1966).

HEBERT, ANTOINE AUGUSTE ERNEST. French painter (b. La Tronche, 1817; d. there, 1908). He was a student of David d'Angers and Delaroche. Hébert was an academic painter of genre and historical and religious subjects, but some of his portraits show an unusual interest in personality.

HEBERT, LOUIS-PHILIPPE. Canadian sculptor (1850–1917). Hébert was born in Sainte Sophie d'Halifax, Quebec. He received a prize for his wood carving at an early age and later became one of Canada's leading academic monumental sculptors. Among his many public monuments are figures for the Quebec Legislature (ca. 1880) and the Queen Victoria Monument in Ottawa (1901). Hébert lived in Paris for some time and exhibited there (1893–1913).

HEBREW ART. The seminomadic Hebrew tribes, during their wanderings in the ancient Near East, do not seem to have produced noteworthy works of art. Their simple worship of Yahweh was closely linked to a tent and an Ark. Although the Book of Exodus describes elaborate artistic appurtenances as belonging to the tent-sanctuary in the desert, these descriptions are probably insertions into the account by later writers who wanted to give Mosaic sanction to the established Temple cult and to glorify the venerated past. In view of the rigid aniconic attitude toward art that generations of scholars have persistently attributed to the ancient Hebrews, it must be stressed with what high esteem craftsmen working for Yahweh were regarded in ancient Israel. Tradition went so far as to endow the craftsman Bezalel with skills surpassing even those of the greatest artists in antiquity (Exodus 31:3–11).

Only with the settlement in the land of Canaan, the gradual unification of the tribes, and the establishment of commercial and diplomatic alliances, especially under the monarchy of Solomon in the 10th century B.C., did art begin to assume an important place in ancient Israel. Emulating other Near Eastern monarchs, Solomon embarked on an extensive building program including palaces and a Temple. Because he lacked skilled native workmen, Solomon imported Hiram of Tyre (I Kings 7:13–51) from neighboring Phoenicia to help carry out his ambitious projects. The resultant Phoenician influence on Solomon's Temple is evident from a comparison of it with a 9th-century B.C. royal chapel of a Phoenician king excavated at Tell Tainat, Syria. This chapel has the same tripartite division of porch (*ulam*), holy place (*hekal*), and Holy of Holies (*debir*) as does the Temple described in I Kings 6. The *cherubim* spreading their wings above the desert Ark in the Holy of Holies (I Kings 8:7) may have been hybrid creatures with a human head, the body of a lion or bull, and eagle's wings, also familiar from Phoenician art. Similarly, the well-known volute proto-Aeolian capitals used in Phoenicia were probably employed in the construction of Solomon's Temple. *See* SOLOMON'S TEMPLE, JERUSALEM.

The transition from a seminomadic to an agricultural-urban life also led the Hebrews to adopt and fashion fertility idols. Excavated pottery figurines and plaques of nude female figures, many of Astarte holding her breasts with her hands or carrying lotus flowers, testify to the prevalence of this practice.

Luxuries indulged in by the privileged classes in the 8th-century B.C. Northern Kingdom of Israel, which included "houses of ivory" (Amos 3:15) and "beds of ivory" (Amos 6:4), were denounced by the prophet Amos. Examples of such ivory decoration, used primarily as inlays in furniture, have been found in excavations of that period from Samaria, the capital of the Northern Kingdom.

Hebrew art. "Tomb of Absalom," near Jerusalem.

They are executed in the eclectic Phoenician style. (Note also the prophet Isaiah's denunciations of luxuries in 8th-century Judah, in Isaiah 3:16–24.)

By and large, ancient Hebrew art was restricted to the service of the Temple cult and the privileged classes at court. Particularly during the period of the first Temple, this art was most heavily influenced by the styles emanating from Phoenicia. For later periods, *see* JEWISH ART.

BIBLIOGRAPHY. W. F. Albright, *The Archaeology of Palestine*, Harmondsworth, 1949; A. Reifenberg, *Ancient Hebrew Arts*, New York, 1950; J. B. Pritchard, *The Ancient Near East in Pictures Relating to the Old Testament*, Princeton, 1954.

JOSEPH GUTMANN

HECATOMPEDON. Building measuring 100 feet (from the Greek *hekatompedos*, "100 feet long"). The term was applied by the Greeks to a temple of Athena in Athens and was interpreted to mean the Parthenon, whose naos is said to measure 100 Attic feet or whose façade at the upper step approximates a hecatompedon. However, other evidence points to a lost *tristyle-in-antis* hecatompedon of Athena situated on the Acropolis that may have been directly beneath the Parthenon which inherited the name.

HECATOMPEDON SCULPTURE. Fragments of limestone sculpture (560–550 B.C.) in the Acropolis Museum, Athens. They were from the first hecatompedon (Temple of Athena) on the Acropolis. The fragments, which formed the pedimental decoration of the temple, represent Hercules struggling with the Triton in the presence of the three-headed monster Typhon (known also as Bluebeard). Another limestone group, representing two lions attacking a bull, is considered to have come from the same temple. Traces of the original polychromy, blue, red, and green, are still preserved on these fragments. These are perhaps the earliest remains of color used in sculpture. The three faces of Typhon show great liveliness. The corners of the pediment were filled with the snakelike tails of the two monsters. *See* HECATOMPEDON.

BIBLIOGRAPHY. E. Lapalus, *Le Fronton sculpté*, Paris, 1947; G. M. A. Richter, *A Handbook of Greek Art*, London, 1959.

HECKE, JAN VAN DEN. Flemish painter (1620–84). Born in Quaremonde, he was active in Antwerp. He painted still lifes in the manner of Jan Fyt; flowers, in which he emulated Daniel Seghers; landscapes; and kermis scenes, in which he showed himself under the influence of David Teniers the Younger.

BIBLIOGRAPHY. F. J. van den Branden, *Geschiedenis der Antwerpsche Schilderschool*, Antwerp, 1883.

HECKEL, ERICH. German expressionist painter (1883–1970). He was born at Döbeln, near Chemnitz, and after 1955 lived at Hemmenhofen. Heckel studied architecture at the Technische Hochschule, Dresden, where he began his first paintings, wood sculptures, and woodcuts. As an artist he is largely self-taught. He met Kirchner in 1905 and together with Schmidt-Rottluff and Bleyl founded Die Brücke. After living in Dresden and Oldenburg and visiting Rome, Heckel moved to Berlin in 1911. In 1912 he and Kirchner painted murals on hemp in a chapel at the International Exhibition at Düsseldorf, which was organized by a group of local artists called the Sonderbund. During World War I Heckel was a member of the medical corps in Flanders.

After the war he made his home in Berlin. He was active in the social program of the Arbeitsrat für Kunst (Workers' Council for Art), and he traveled throughout the Continent. In the early 1920s he painted several decorative frescoes for the Erfurt Museum. He was forced to move to Carinthia after his art was denounced by the Nazis as "degenerate." During World War II several of his works were lost when his studio was bombed. In 1949 he settled at Lake Constance and the same year went to Karlsruhe Academy, where he taught until 1955.

Heckel seems restrained compared to his colleagues in the expressionist movement. He admired such disparate artists as Poussin and Vermeer for their bright color in broad areas, Munch, and Van Gogh, and particularly liked South Seas sculpture. Like his fellow expressionists, he rejected the finish and detail of academic art in search for the *Urform*, or the initial impulse of creation. His landscapes appear as masses of shattered crystals with paths shooting off to the horizon and spiky trees pointing to a sky heavy with clouds that billow, heave, and subside. His color is naturalistic but heightened for effect. His skies, for instance, are blue, but a blue that is frequently unusually sharp, raw, and acid. His world is a shaken and disturbed one, as if in the wake of cataclysmic forces.

His best-known pictures are of gaunt, tortured women, self-enclosed, withdrawn, and ascetic, as if inhibited or suffering from loneliness or extremes of despair. He made several fine woodcuts, some of which he exhibited at the 1910 Brücke show in Dresden. After World War I his painting underwent a reversal in mood and some loss of power. His portraits reveal a growing concern for a clear, accurate image, while his landscapes express optimism. He favored sunlit scenes and sweeping vistas, and his beach scenes show bathers who sport and appear to enjoy their surroundings.

BIBLIOGRAPHY. H. Köhn, *Erich Heckel*, Berlin, 1948.

ROBERT REIFF

HECKENDORF, FRANZ. German painter and graphic artist (1888–1962). He was born in Berlin and studied there. His early paintings are impressionistic. The intense color and exciting drawing of his mature style, in landscapes, figures, and still lifes, indicate the general influence of Kirchner.

BIBLIOGRAPHY. J. Kirchner, *Franz Heckendorf* (Junge-Kunst, vol. 6), Leipzig, 1919.

HEDA, GERRIT WILLEMSZ. Dutch still-life painter (fl. 1642–before 1702). Born in Haarlem, he was a pupil of his father, the still-life painter Willem Heda, in 1642. Gerrit is noted as dead on a list of painters made by Vincent van der Vinne, who died in July, 1702. There are dated works by Gerrit from 1642 to 1667. It is possible that he collaborated with his father on still-life paintings, and there are a number of works signed "Heda" without initials. For the most part his independent works are close, if not somewhat weaker, imitations of his father's style, such as *Still Life* (1642; Amsterdam, Rijksmuseum), signed "Jonge Heda" (Young Heda).

BIBLIOGRAPHY. N. R. A. Vroom, *De Schilders van het monochrome banketje*, Amsterdam, 1945; I. Bergström, *Dutch Still-Life Painting in the Seventeenth Century*, New York, 1956.

Erich Heckel, *Glassy Day*, 1913. Marcus Cruss Collection, Berlin.

Willem Claesz. Heda, *Still Life with a Metal Tumbler*. Fine Arts Museum, Besançon.

HEDA, WILLEM CLAESZ. Dutch still-life painter (b. Haarlem, 1594; d. there, 1680/82). Although Heda's teacher is not known, his earliest work, a *Vanitas Still Life with a Skull* (1621; The Hague, Bredius Museum), suggests that Floris van Dijck had a role in his development. In 1631 Heda was listed in the records of the Haarlem Guild of St. Luke, and he was later an official of the guild as well as dean. In 1642 his son Gerrit Heda was listed as his pupil.

Heda was responsible, along with Peter Claesz., for the popularization of the breakfast-piece type of still life in Holland. Heda's work in the 1630s presents a refined, almost classically conceived arrangement supported by a rich use of tonal painting (*Still Life*, 1637; Paris, Louvre). About 1640 his still-life paintings became larger, richer, and considerably more decorative, and at this time he also began to abandon the traditional horizontal format in favor of the vertical (*Still Life*, 1648; Leningrad, Hermitage).

BIBLIOGRAPHY. H. E. van Gelder, *W. C. Heda, A. van Beyeren, W. Kalf*, Amsterdam, 1941; I. Bergström, *Dutch Still-Life Painting in the Seventeenth Century*, New York, 1956; J. Rosenberg, S. Slive, and E. H. ter Kuile, *Dutch Art and Architecture, 1600–1800*, Baltimore, 1966.

HEDINGHAM CASTLE. One of the best preserved and most impressive Norman keeps in England, located in Essex. It was begun by the powerful De Vere family about 1140. Remaining are the inner bailey and part of the outer bailey, which now encircles a Georgian house of 1719. Two of the four corner turrets, rising nearly 100 feet, survive. The inner bailey has three stories and a magnificent broad arch that leads to the main hall in the second story.

HEEM, CORNELIS DE. Flemish painter (1631–95). Born in Leyden, De Heem was active in Antwerp. He painted still lifes in the manner of his father, Jan de Heem, and almost reached equal heights in his best works. By comparison, however, he is generally lacking in balance of composition and can be recognized by a cooler color scheme and harder execution.

BIBLIOGRAPHY. W. Bernt, *Die niederländischen Maler des 17. Jahrhunderts...*, vol. 2, Munich, 1948.

HEEM, JAN DAVIDSZ. DE. Dutch painter of still lifes and portraits (b. Utrecht, 1606; d. Antwerp, 1683/84). He seems to have been a pupil of his father, David de Heem, at Utrecht, and also studied with Balthasar van der Ast at Utrecht. De Heem was active in Leyden from 1626 to 1632 and studied with David Bailly there. In 1636 De Heem was listed as a member of the Antwerp Guild of St. Luke, and he remained in Antwerp until 1647. He returned to his native Utrecht after 1669 and was a member of the Painters' College. With the French invasion of 1672, he fled to Antwerp, where he remained for the rest of his life.

De Heem's earliest works are clearly related to the styles of his various masters. His *Still Life with Fruit* (1624; Arnhem, formerly Braams Collection) is close to Van der Ast, and his *Still Life with Books* (1628; The Hague, Mauritshuis Art Gallery) is more in the manner of Bailly. About this time he seems also to have come under the influence of the young Rembrandt in Leyden, and he is known to have collaborated with Rembrandt's friend and associate Jan Lievens.

While he was active in Antwerp De Heem reflected something of the sumptuous and opulent aspects of the Flemish baroque in his large still-life paintings of the 1640s (*Still Life*, 1640; Paris, Louvre). In Antwerp he was also influenced more directly by the work of Daniel Seghers. De Heem's portrait *Prince William of Orange* (Lyons, Palais St-Pierre) utilizes a painted floral framework that must ultimately have derived from that of Seghers. De Heem's sons Cornelis and Jan painted in their father's manner. He had many pupils, including Maria von Oosterwijck and Abraham Mignon.

BIBLIOGRAPHY. W. Martin, "Figuurstukken van Jan Davidszoon de Heem," *Oud-Holland*, XLII, 1925; A. P. A. Vorenkamp, *Bijdrage tot de Geschiedenis van het hollandsche stilleven in de zeventiende eeuw*, Leyden, 1934; R. van Luttervelt, *Schilders van het stilleven*, Naarden, 1947; I. Bergström, *Dutch Still-Life Painting in the Seventeenth Century*, New York, 1956.

LEONARD J. SLATKES

HEEMSKERCK, EGBERT VAN. Dutch painter of genre and history (b. Haarlem, 1634/35; d. London, 1704). He was the pupil of Pieter de Grebber in Haarlem. In 1663 Heemskerck was reported in The Hague, and two years later he was living in Amsterdam. Exactly when Heemskerck went to England is not known; however, a painting of a *Quaker Meeting* (Munich, Höck sale, 1892) was signed and dated "London, 1690." While in England he was patronized by Lord Rochester.

Heemskerck painted numerous scenes of peasant life that seem to have been influenced by the style of Adriaen Brouwer (for example, *Two Peasants*, Leyden, Stedelijk Museum). Among Heemskerck's best works is the *Peasant*

Dance in an Inn (Copenhagen, State Museum of Fine Arts). Some of his works seem to indicate a knowledge of the style of Jan Molenaer, but the nature of this influence has not been defined. Heemskerck's son Egbert van Heemskerck the Younger was also a painter.

BIBLIOGRAPHY. A. Welcker, "Die Zeichnungen von Egbert van Heemskerck Sr. und Jr.," *Die Graphischen Künste*, III, 1938; F. Saxl, "The Quaker's Meeting," *Journal of the Warburg and Courtauld Institutes*, VI, 1943.

HEEMSKERCK (Veen), MAERTEN VAN. Dutch painter, draftsman, and engraver (b. Heemskerck, 1498; d. Haarlem, 1574). He studied with Cornelis Willemsz. and Jan van Scorel in Haarlem and in 1532 went to Italy to study directly from the antique. Heemskerck stayed for the most part in Rome, and filled two copious notebooks with perceptive drawings and sketches of antique and Early Christian ruins (Berlin, former State Museums, Print Cabinet). Aside from their intrinsic value, the sketchbooks have been extremely important to archaeologists in determining the appearance of many medieval churches prior to or during their remodeling in the Renaissance, for example, St. Peter's, Rome. Heemskerck returned to Haarlem from Italy in 1535, and remained there until his death. He was a highly successful and skillful practitioner of the Italianate manner, with a deep understanding of the antique.

BIBLIOGRAPHY. G. J. Hoogewerff, *De noord-nederlandsche Schilderkunst*, vol. 4, The Hague, 1943.

HEERE, LUCAS DE. Flemish painter (b. Ghent, 1534; d. Paris? 1584). A student of Frans Floris and a teacher of Karel van Mander, De Heere worked primarily in Ghent, France, and England. His dependence on Floris may be noted in *The Liberal Arts in Time of War* (ca. 1567; Turin, Municipal Museum of Ancient Art), for which a signed drawing exists in the State Collection of Graphic Arts, Munich.

BIBLIOGRAPHY. Amsterdam, Rijksmuseum, *Le Triomphe du maniérisme européen...* (exposition catalog), Amsterdam, 1955.

HEEREMANS, THOMAS. Dutch painter of landscapes, beach scenes, and villages (b. ca. 1641; d. after 1699). He was reported at Haarlem in 1663, and became a member of the Guild of St. Luke the following year. His work shows the influence of Claes Molenaer, and his river land-

Jan Davidsz. de Heem, *Still Life with Books*. Mauritshuis, The Hague.

Stele of Hegeso. Attic grave relief in the Kerameikos, Athens.

scapes follow the pattern of Jacob van Ruisdael. Heeremans specialized in winter landscapes.

BIBLIOGRAPHY. C. Hofstede de Groot, "Der Maler T. Heeremans," *Repertorium für Kunstwissenschaft*, XIV, 1891.

HEERSCHOP, HENDRIK. Dutch genre painter and etcher (b. Haarlem, 1620/21; d. there? after 1672). He was a pupil of Willem Heda in Haarlem and probably a pupil of Rembrandt in Amsterdam. Heerschop was reported as a member of the Haarlem Guild of St. Luke in 1648 and 1661. Some of his paintings show the influence of the Haarlem painter Thomas Wijck.

BIBLIOGRAPHY. W. Bernt, *Die niederländischen Maler des 17. Jahrhunderts...*, vol. 2, Munich, 1948.

HEES, GERRIT VAN. Dutch painter of landscapes, cityscapes, and village scenes (d. Haarlem, 1670). Van Hees was active in Haarlem, where he was documented in 1660 and 1663. A *View of a Village* (1650; Haarlem, Frans Hals Museum) by Van Hees is fully signed and dated. He was a follower of Jacob van Ruisdael and Meindert Hobbema.

BIBLIOGRAPHY. A. Bredius, "De schilder Gerrit van Hees," *Oud-Holland*, XXXI, 1913.

HEGESO, STELE OF. Celebrated Attic grave relief (early 4th cent. B.C.) in the Kerameikos, Athens. It represents the deceased, Hegeso, seated on a chair and receiving a box of jewelry from her maid. The figure recalls the seated goddesses on the Parthenon frieze and is a noteworthy example of post-Parthenon art.

BIBLIOGRAPHY. M. Bieber, *The Sculpture of the Hellenistic Age*, New York, 1955.

HEIAN PERIOD, *see* JAPAN (HEIAN PERIOD).

HEIDELBERG: PALATINATE MUSEUM. German museum founded as the City Collections (Städtische Sammlungen) in 1879. It is housed in the former town palace of Philipp Morass (built 1712). Besides owning extensive collections on the history of the Palatinate, the city, and the University of Heidelberg, the museum is especially rich in German paintings from the 15th to the 20th century as well as in German sculpture. The latter group includes Tilmann Riemenschneider's *Windsheimer Altar of the Twelve Apostles* (before 1509).

BIBLIOGRAPHY. H. Jedding, *Keysers Führer durch Museen und Sammlungen*, Heidelberg, Munich, 1961.

HEIDELBERG CASTLE. Partially ruined German castle in the university city of Heidelberg. This was the fortified residence of four electors palatine, who gradually replaced a medieval castle with a Renaissance palace.

Frederick II (r. 1544–56) built the Gläserne Saalbau ("building with the mirrored hall"), using Italianate arcading on three stories of the exterior. At right angles to it, linking it to a medieval block, Otto Henry (r. 1556–59) built the Ottheinrichsbau, the first true example of German Renaissance palace architecture. Stylistically a synthesis of Italian and Netherlandish elements, it is richly ornamented with statues symbolizing heroes, emperors, virtues, and planets, and a statue of Otto Henry. On the other side of the Gläserne Saalbau is the Friedrichsbau (1601–07), erected by Frederick IV (r. 1592–1610). This is in a more classical manner, with the sides overlooking the town and facing the court treated as independent façades. Figures in niches represent Frederick's ancestors from Charlemagne on. The Englischer Bau (1614) was named after Elizabeth of England, wife of the "Winter King," Frederick V (r. 1610–23). What remains of it suggests the influence of contemporary north Italian architecture and is thus an illustration of the Palladianism discernible in much north European architecture of about this time. Salomon de Caus created the once-famous garden, the Hortus Palatinus, east of the castle for Frederick V.

Explosions in 1689 and 1693 damaged the buildings, and they have remained in ruins ever since. Only the Friedrichsbau was restored (1879–1903).

BIBLIOGRAPHY. K. Rossmann, *The Otto Henry Building of the Castle of Heidelberg and His* [sic] *Builder*, Heidelberg, 1949.

NORBERT LYNTON

HEIDER, HANS. German sculptor (fl. Upper Bavaria, ca. 1400). He is mentioned in 1406 as the creator of the tomb of the count palatine Aribo in the monastery church of Seeon. Other works by Heider, such as the gravestone of E. von Laiming (ca. 1406), are in the monastery cloister. His art was influential on sepulchral sculpture in Salzburg.

BIBLIOGRAPHY. P. M. Halm, "Hans Heider und die Salzburger Marmorplastik in der ersten Hälfte des 15. Jahrhunderts," *Kunst und Kunsthandwerk*, XVI, 1913.

HEIJDEN (Heijde; Heyden), JAN VAN DER. Dutch painter of cityscapes, architecture, landscapes, and still lifes and etcher (b. Gorinchem, 1637; d. Amsterdam, 1712). Houbraken tells us that Van der Heijden was a pupil of a glass painter. He traveled in Holland, Flanders, and the Rhineland. Houbraken's statement that he made a paint-

ing of the London Royal Exchange has not been confirmed.

Van der Heijden is best known for his delightful views of Amsterdam streets and canals, painted mostly in the 1660s. They were the first such paintings to be done in Amsterdam and had an important influence on 18th-century Dutch architectural painting. Typical views of Amsterdam, The Hague, Cologne, and other cities, as well as imaginary landscapes, are to be found in most European and many American museums.

He was also a mechanical engineer and inventor. In 1690 he published a book on fire pumps with his own illustrations.

BIBLIOGRAPHY. C. Hofstede de Groot, *Beschreibendes und kritisches Verzeichnis der Werke der hervorragendsten holländischen Maler des 17. Jahrhunderts*, vol. 8, Esslingen, 1923.

HEIJI WAR SCROLLS. Japanese *emaki* (late 13th cent.). The set of three scrolls is now divided between the Museum of Fine Arts in Boston, the National Museum of Tokyo, and the Seikadō Foundation in Tokyo. The scrolls describe the coup d'état of 1159, which started the long struggle between the Taira and Minamoto families. The Boston scroll, the *Burning of the Sanjō Palace*, is perhaps the best of the three. The excitements and horrors of wars are depicted uncompromisingly by a realistically minded artist. The rhythmic arrangement of figures full of action and the dramatic contrast in color between the burning

Heidelberg Castle. Ottheinrichsbau, the first example of German Renaissance palace architecture.

Heiji War Scrolls. Detail representing the raiding of the Imperial Palace. National Museum, Tokyo.

flames and the warriors' costumes create an epic beauty rarely surpassed in other battle pictures of Japan.

BIBLIOGRAPHY. R. T. Paine and A. Soper, *The Art and Architecture of Japan*, Baltimore, 1955; H. Okudaira, *Emaki (Japanese Picture Scrolls)*, Rutland, Vt., 1962.

HEIKE SUTRAS. Japanese illuminated sūtras (1164–67). The set of thirty-three scrolls was donated by Kiyomori (known also as Heike), the head of the Taira clan, to the Itsukushima Shrine, where they are still kept. The paper of the sūtras is decorated with gold and silver dust, and the introductory pictures illustrate various themes, most of which are taken from the Lotus Sūtra. The rollers of the scrolls are sumptuously decorated with crystal, gold, silver, and lacquer inlaid with shells. The paintings are small and reflect the luxurious and sophisticated tastes of the court of the time. *See* LOTUS SUTRA.

BIBLIOGRAPHY. Tokyo National Museum, *Pageant of Japanese Art*, vol. 1, *Painting*, pt. 1, Tokyo, 1952.

HEIL, DANIEL VAN. Flemish painter (ca. 1604–62). Heil, a native of Brussels, was a landscape painter of the Brussels school, whose archaic style is redolent of 16th-century concepts. Greater freedom is attained in works depicting conflagrations at night and in winter scenes that sometimes successfully rival those of Jacques d'Arthois.

BIBLIOGRAPHY. H. Fierens-Gevaert, *Catalogue de l'exposition rétrospective du paysage flamand*, Brussels, 1926.

HEILBRONN: ST. KILIAN CHURCH TOWER. A topping structure was added (1513–29) to the old tower of the German Church of St. Kilian, which was built in the second half of the 13th century and enlarged in the 15th. Hans Schweiner completed the single west tower

(late 13th–early 16th cent.) with an openwork top. A large arcaded octagon with a balustrade forms the base for smaller octagons, and the whole is topped by the standing figure of a knight holding a banner of the city. The fantastic architecture combines Gothic and Renaissance-like motifs in a type of mannerism that preceded the introduction of the true Renaissance into Germany. The church was heavily damaged in 1944–45 but has been restored.

BIBLIOGRAPHY. R. Hootz, ed., *Deutsche Kunstdenkmäler*, vol. 3: *Baden-Württemberg*, Munich, 1959.

HEILBRONN, HANS VON, *see* SEYFER, HANS.

HEILIGENKREUZ. Oldest Cistercian cloister in Lower Austria. It was founded by Margrave Leopold III and consecrated in 1187. In spite of extensive baroque rebuilding, the cloister remains one of the most important late Romanesque-early Gothic monastic structures in Austria. The most notable building of the complex is the Stiftskirche, which has a Romanesque nave and Gothic choir and side aisles with the earliest cross-ribbed vaulting in Austria.

BIBLIOGRAPHY. E. Hempel, *Geschichte der deutschen Baukunst*, Munich, 1949.

HEILIGER, BERNHARD. German sculptor (1915–   ). Born in Stettin, he was trained there in stone carving and then studied in Berlin at the Academy of Fine Arts until 1938. A visit to Paris followed. He was influenced by Maillol. Heiliger's art was banned by the Nazi regime. Following World War II he was appointed to a professorship at the Berlin School of Fine Arts. Since 1950 he has exhibited widely abroad; his work has been represented at São Paulo, the Venice Biennale, and the Brussels International Exposition of 1958. His style, which is related to that of Viani in Italy and Hartung in Germany, reveals a thoughtful adherence to the rhythms of the human figure at the same time that it is generally abstract in concept. His *Seraph* (1950) in cast stone is characteristic.

BIBLIOGRAPHY. H. Schaefer-Simmern, *Sculpture in Europe Today*, Berkeley, 1955; M. Seuphor, *The Sculpture of This Century*, New York, 1960.

HEIMBACH, WOLFGANG. German painter (b. Ovelgönne? ca. 1610–20; d. after 1678). Known as a portrait painter, he worked in northern Germany and in Denmark. A most typical work is the family portrait of Anton von Oldenburg (1667; Hamburg, private collection). Frans Hals exerted a strong influence on his art.

HEINE, THOMAS THEODOR. German painter and graphic artist (b. Leipzig, 1867; d. Stockholm, 1948). A prominent personality in the German Jugendstil innovations in book design and illustration, Heine was also a master of caricature and satirical drawing. After training in Düsseldorf, Munich, and Diessen am Ammersee, he took up book illustration. He began contributing to the avant-garde illustrated weekly *Simplizissimus* in 1896 and became its best-known associate. In 1933 Heine emigrated, first to Prague, then to Brno, to Oslo, and in 1942 to Stockholm. He developed a powerful outline style, which can be seen in his graphic portfolios, *Bilder aus dem Familienleben* and *Torheiten*. An autobiographical novel appeared in 1945 under the title *Ich warte auf das Wunder*.

BIBLIOGRAPHY. K. H. Salzman, "In Memoriam Thomas Theodore Heine," *Aufbau*, VI, pt. 1, 1948.

HEINTZ, JOSEPH. Swiss painter (b. Basel, 1564; d. Prague, 1609). Heavily influenced by his studies in Rome with Hans von Aachen (1584–87), Heintz worked in the international mannerist style of the late 16th century. In 1581 he was called to the court of Rudolf II in Prague, where he painted scenes from mythology and the Bible and portraits. An example is *Satyrs with Nymphs* (1599; Munich, Old Pinacothek).

BIBLIOGRAPHY. W. Dorst, *Barockmalerei in dem germanischen Ländern*, Wildpark-Potsdam, 1926; E. Gradmann and A. M. Cetto, *Schweizer Malerei und Zeichnung im 17. und 18. Jahrhundert*, Basel, 1944.

HELENA, ST. Roman empress (ca. 250–ca. 330). She was the wife of Constantius I and the mother of Constantine the Great. She was converted to Christianity about 313. According to tradition, St. Helena discovered the true cross in Jerusalem and the nails of the Crucifixion; she is represented in many legends of the true cross. In art she is shown as an empress, with crown and imperial mantle, and usually with the cross and the Crucifixion nails. The crown of thorns is sometimes included. Her feast is August 18. *See also* SAINTS IN ART.

HELIKER, JOHN. American painter (1909–   ). Born in Yonkers, N.Y., he studied in 1928–29 at the Art Students League with Kenneth Hayes Miller, Boardman Robinson, and Kimon Nicolaides. From his early representational work (in which he especially concentrated on drawing) Heliker brought to abstraction a strong feeling for nature.

Behind or within the geometric subdivisions of such a painting as *Scava* (1950; New York, American Academy of Arts and Letters) can be seen many allusions to natural processes or forms. Subsequently, Heliker's geometry loosened and his debt to landscape became, quietly, more obvious, as in *Of Maine* (1953; New York, Whitney Museum of American Art).

BIBLIOGRAPHY. A. C. Ritchie, *Abstract Painting and Sculpture in America*, New York, 1951; Whitney Museum of American Art, *Nature in Abstraction...*, New York, 1958.

HELION, JEAN. French painter (1904–   ). He was born in Couterne, Orne, and now lives in Paris. He studied engineering and architecture in Lille and worked as a draftsman for an architect. Since 1922 he has devoted himself to painting. He never had formal training. In 1926 Torres García introduced Hélion to cubism. His interest in abstract painting led him to Mondrian, and in 1927 Hélion exhibited at the Salon des Indépendants. In 1931 he came to know Theo van Doesburg and helped him edit his publication, *L'Art Concret*. Hélion was active in the Abstraction-Création group at this time. During World War II he escaped from a German prison camp and wrote a book about his adventures, *They Shall Not Have Me*. He has had over 20 one-man shows, and his work is in the Museum of Modern Art in New York, Philadelphia Museum of Art, Museum of Fine Arts in Boston, Art Institute of Chicago, and museums in Beauvais, Lille, and Laon.

Hélion's early work is cubist in character. Prior to 1931 the mark of Mondrian's influence is evident, but thereafter Hélion developed a style very much his own. With pastel color he combined monumental shapes, recalling machined surfaces, which were mostly flat, but some gently curved and with a slight sheen. These were frequently arranged in sequences against a ground to suggest depth. Hélion favored a vertically accented, upright canvas at this time.

After the war his style changed radically. He went through a surrealist phase and later a somewhat mannered realism. In 1953 he exhibited a number of large still-life paintings in this style. Since then his brushstrokes have become broader and less descriptive. He has a limited palette, favoring browns and blues. He paints a variety of

Jean Hélion, *Composition*. Philadelphia Museum of Art.

subjects: portraits (mostly of his friends), landscapes, roof tops, and the sea around Belle-Isle-en-Mer. He admires the art of Hals, Velázquez, Manet, and Chardin.

BIBLIOGRAPHY. J. Ashbery, "Hélion Paints a Series of Portraits," *Art News*, LVIII, 1960.   ROBERT REIFF

HELIOPOLIS. Greek name (meaning city of the sun) of the city Iwnw ("On" of the Bible), dedicated to the sun god Re' and located northwest of Cairo, Egypt. The predynastic capital of Egypt, Heliopolis remained its cultural center and was still visited by later Greek philosophers. There is an early circular structure of brick with concentric rings and doorways forming five ambulatories.

Djeser built at Heliopolis and, after him, several other Pharaohs. Amenemhat I (12th dynasty) built a temple to Re'-Harakhte and Atum on the site of an earlier one. His son, Sesostris I (Senusert I), erected two obelisks in front of it, one of which is still standing. Two other obelisks, erected by Thutmosis III, are now in New York and London. Akhenaten and Rameses II also built at Heliopolis.

Concerning the layout of the temple "Horus-of-the-eastern-horizon-Re'-Harakhte," we know that it had three courts, the rearmost of which contained an altar surrounded by cells and a sacred upright stone, or benben, inside a hypaethral chapel. The benben monument may possibly have been the prototype of the obelisk. A fragmentary paw of a colossal hawk in sandstone found there measures almost 4 feet in width for three toes (Turin, Municipal Museum of Ancient Art). *See* HYPAETHROS.

ALEXANDER M. BADAWY

HELIOPOLIS, LEBANON, *see* BAALBEK.

HELIOS. In Greek mythology, the sun-god; also the god of herds and clocks. Helios is represented as a strong and beautiful youth with a crown of rays, driving a quadriga. Called Hyperion by Homer, he is the son of the Titan Hyperion and the Titaness Theia. Selene and Eos are his blood relations. By Clymene, Helios begat Phaëthon, who almost destroyed the universe with fire. The nymph Rhodos bore him seven sons (the Heliades) and a daughter. These

Heliopolis. Obelisk erected by Sesostris I (12th dynasty).

sons ruled the island of Rhodes, and his descendants built the colossus showing his image. Rhodes was dedicated to Helios, and he was also worshiped on the island of Sicily in ancient times. *See* COLOSSUS.

BIBLIOGRAPHY. R. Graves, *The Greek Myths*, New York, 1957.

HELIX. Greek term applied to the volute in Ionic and Corinthian capitals. The helix is found also in anthemion ornament, as in the Erechtheum, Athens.

HELL. The abode of the dead or of the damned after death. In Christian art, the imagery of hell (based on the New Testament concept of hell as a place for the damned) began to develop toward its characteristic form in the Romanesque art of the 11th and 12th centuries. In scenes of the Last Judgment the eternally damned are shown being tormented by demons and cast into the open jaws of the leviathan. In the Gothic and Renaissance periods the depiction of hell became increasingly complex with greater attention paid to the varieties of sin and its punishments in the fiery underworld.

HELLADIC ART. Art of the people living on the Greek mainland during the third and second millenniums B.C., the Bronze Age of Greece. The early, middle, and late periods of Helladic art established by scholars correspond generally to the periods for both Minoan and Cycladic art.

Typical of the early period (ca. 2500–1950 B.C.) were small fortified cities such as Lerna in Argolis. Princely palaces and circular tombs were also built. Pottery of the period seems to imitate metalware in its emphasis on glazed surfaces.

In the middle period (ca. 1950–1600 B.C.) cities were rebuilt after the coming of a wave of Indo-Europeans. Megaron structures were favored and the more sophisticated Minyan ware with its varied colors and shapes developed. In the late Helladic period (ca. 1600–1100 B.C.), generally known as the Mycenaean age, art and culture were under strong Minoan influence.

See also AEGEAN ART.

HELLEMONT, MATTHEUS VAN, *see* HELMONT, MATTHEUS VAN.

HELLENIC ART, *see* GREECE.

HELLENISTIC ART. The art of the Hellenistic age (ca. 323–31 B.C.), in contrast to Greek art of the classical period, must be understood in terms of the new social and political conditions created by the conquests of Alexander the Great and the establishment of new kingdoms by his successors. The creation of vast kingdoms in Asia and Egypt, ruled by a Greek-speaking upper class but inheriting many political and religious traditions of the ancient Near East, marked the end of the Greek city-state as an important political unit. Although preserving and cherishing the forms and principles of the art of classical Greece, Hellenistic artists no longer felt bound by the artistic programs and tastes of the small classical communities. The importance of Greece itself, in fact, as a center of artistic production began to diminish as new intellectual and artistic centers grew up in Alexandria, Antioch, and Pergamon. *See* ALEXANDRIA; ANTIOCH; PERGAMON.

The social conditions of the Hellenistic age were responsible for two distinguishing characteristics of its art: the existence of widely separated regional centers and the adaptation of art to fulfill the needs of individuals rather than of communities. These characteristics were not unknown in classical Greece, which had had both regional centers (Athens and Argos, for example) and private art (grave monuments), but the degree of their emphasis was vastly increased in the Hellenistic period. Moreover, the sharp distinction between public and private art that existed in the classical period was obliterated in the Hellenistic age, since public monuments such as the great Altar of Zeus at Pergamon were conceived and commissioned by individual monarchs. Many of the great monuments of Hellenistic art, in fact, fall under the heading of royal art—the art by which a monarch represents himself and his achievements to his subjects and the rest of the world.

The general stylistic trends of Hellenistic art as a whole and also the development of its different regional centers are best studied through the medium of sculpture. Hellenistic architecture, although often grandiose, was largely conservative; as in the case of classical painting, no major specimen of Hellenistic painting has been preserved, and even vase painting, which provides such invaluable evidence for the development of classical painting, is rare in the Hellenistic period.

Hellenistic Art. *Dying Gaul and His Wife*. National Museum, Rome.

Sculpture. During the first seventy years of the Hellenistic period, from the death of Alexander in 323 to about 250 B.C., the development of Hellenistic sculpture was dominated by the schools of artists who were trained in the traditions of 4th-century Greek sculpture. The most original and influential of these was Lysippus of Sicyon, who was, during part of his career, the court sculptor for Alexander the Great. The heroic portraits that Lysippus made of Alexander were renowned in antiquity and led to the creation of a new genre, the heroic ruler portrait. Some notion of the quality of Lysippus's portraits can be derived from the Azara herm in Paris (Louvre), a badly damaged Roman copy. The stylistic innovations in the work of Lysippus, which left a lasting mark on almost all Hellenistic sculpture, are best seen in his *Apoxyomenos*, of which a Roman copy exists in Rome (Vatican Museums). The most influential of these innovations was the introduction of a high degree of torsion into the sculptured form, with the result that a viewer could only successfully comprehend the figures by moving around them and viewing them from several angles. A new realism in portraiture also seems to have arisen in the school of Lysippus, perhaps as a result of a growing sensitivity toward the role that social position (prince, poet, athlete, peasant) played in distinguishing human types. *See* LYSIPPUS.

Among the most famous works of the Lysippean school in the early 3d century B.C. are the *Tyche* (Fortune) of Antioch by Eutychides (ca. 296–293 B.C.; Roman copy in the Vatican), the *Anzio Girl* by Phanis (Roman copy in the Terme, Rome), and the *Crouching Aphrodite* of Doidalsas (ca. 250–240 B.C.; many copies). *See* DOIDALSAS; EUTYCHIDES.

While the school of Lysippus was spreading its new, progressive style throughout the Hellenistic world, a more traditional group of sculptors upheld the classical style at Athens. The products of this Athenian school varied from correct but uninspired works such as the *Themis* of Chairestratus to the profound portrait of Demosthenes by Polyeuctus (ca. 280 B.C.). *See* POLYEUCTUS.

The middle Hellenistic period (ca. 250–150 B.C.) was dominated by the school of Pergamon, whose sculptors assimilated stylistic features of both classical and early Hellenistic sculpture, and added to them an increased sense of drama and pathos, thus originating the style that is often called the Hellenistic baroque. The greatest works of the early period of the school's activity (ca. 250–200 B.C.) were two votive groups of freestanding sculpture commemorating the victory of Attalus I over the Gauls in 238 B.C. Many Roman copies of figures of Gauls, Amazons, and so on, most notably the *Dying Gaul and His Wife* in the National Museum of Rome, are thought to be based on these groups.

The masterpiece of the later Pergamene school (200–150 B.C.) is the relief sculpture from the great Altar of Zeus (Berlin, former State Museums). In this work the Hellenistic tendency toward emotional expressiveness in sculpture is fully developed.

Another great center for the production of Hellenistic art grew up between 300 and 150 B.C. in Alexandria. The finest extant works of this school are its portraits of Ptolemaic kings and queens. The small city of Priene in Asia

Minor was also an active center. *See* ALEXANDRIAN STYLE; PRIENE. *See also* APHRODISIAS.

The production of Hellenistic sculpture had been thriving on the island of Rhodes since the early Hellenistic period. (The famous Colossus of Rhodes was the work of Chares, a member of the school of Lysippus.) By 150 B.C. the Rhodian school had reached a high stage of development and produced some of the best works of the mid- and late 2d century B.C. Both the *Laocoön* group in the Vatican Museums and the *Nike of Samothrace* in the Louvre are associated with Rhodian sculptors, and they date from about the mid-2d century B.C. To the Rhodian school of the later 2d century belong a freestanding group of Muses, known in numerous Roman copies, and perhaps also the relief by Archelaos in London (British Museum; perhaps a Roman copy) commonly called the *Apotheosis of Homer*. The *Farnese Bull* group in Naples (National Archaeological Museum) is a heavily restored Roman copy of a Rhodian work dating perhaps from the early 1st century B.C. *See* COLOSSUS; LAOCOON; RHODES SCHOOL (SCULPTURE); VICTORY OF SAMOTHRACE.

The original vitality of Hellenistic sculpture began to wane after about 150 B.C., and it was near this time that a new classicistic movement began to develop, with its center at Athens. Athenian sculptors, returning to the great creations of the 5th century for inspiration, developed a style that is now generally called Neo-Attic. The most fruitful market for this classicistic sculpture was Rome, which also at this time began to develop a sculptural school of its own, specializing in portraiture. One of the consequences of the classicistic tradition in the late Hellenistic period was the perfection of the technique of copying statues. The result of this development was an increase in the demand for copies of 5th-century masterpieces and a consequent decline in the demand for original works. *See* APHRODITE OF MELOS; NEO-ATTIC STYLE.

Painting. The development of the art of painting in the Hellenistic age can only be sketched out in a general way from occasional finds of painted tombs, grave stelae, and special varieties of painted vases. The works of the outstanding masters of the period are all lost. A few Romano-Campanian wall paintings are probably based on these works, but there is no way of judging the accuracy of these copies.

Because of the scarcity of monuments a stylistic development of Hellenistic painting is difficult to trace. Painted grave stelae from Alexandria and Pagasae, however, appear to exhibit certain stylistic analogies, at least in the representation of human figures, to the stylistic development of sculpture: there is an Atticizing period in the late 4th and early 3d century, followed by a period in which proportions and composition suggest an analogy with Lysippean sculpture; and toward the end of the 3d century, a new interest in the importance of landscape and a diminishing of the importance of the human figure.

Important examples of Hellenistic mural painting have been preserved in tombs in Alexandria, Etruria, and Kazanlik, Bulgaria. The evidence they provide is supplemented by wall paintings on houses at Delos and on the painted stone vases from Centuripe, Sicily. The estimated dates for these monuments vary widely. *See* DELOS.

A few Roman paintings and mosaics are frequently taken to be copies of specific Hellenistic paintings. The *Alexander* mosaic in Naples, for example, is usually connected with a painting of Alexander and Darius in battle by Philoxenus of Eretria (late 4th or early 3d cent. B.C.). *See* PHILOXENUS.

The art of making tessellated mosaic (made from cut stones rather than natural pebbles) seems to have been invented in the Hellenistic period. Recent discoveries at Morgantina in central Sicily suggest that this island played a significant role in the development of this mosaic technique. Important series of Hellenistic mosaics have been discovered at Alexandria, Delos, and Pompeii. *See* POMPEII. *See also* GLASS.

Architecture. The most ambitious undertaking of Hellenistic architecture was the construction of large Ionic temples in Asia Minor, such as the temples of Apollo at Didyma (ca. 330 B.C.), Artemis at Sardis (ca. 325 B.C.), Dionysos at Teos (ca. 130 B.C.), and Artemis Leukophryene at Magnesia on the Meander (ca. 160 B.C.). In the Olympieion at Athens (ca. 165 B.C.) the Corinthian order, which had hitherto been used in combination with the older orders and, if used alone, was confined to small monuments, came into its own as a separate order. *See* OLYMPIEION, ATHENS.

Hellenistic architects did not create any drastically new forms. A survey, however, of the many buildings in such highly developed cities as Pergamon and Priene conveys an idea of the splendor of their achievement in both religious and secular architecture.

BIBLIOGRAPHY. W. B. Dinsmoor, *The Architecture of Ancient Greece*, 3d ed., London, 1950; B. R. Brown, *Ptolemaic Painting and Mosaics*, Cambridge, Mass., 1957; M. Robertson, *Greek Painting*, Geneva, 1959; W. W. Tarn, *Hellenistic Civilization*, 3d ed., rev., London, 1959; M. Bieber, *The Sculpture of the Hellenistic Age*, rev. ed., New York, 1961; G. M. A. Richter, *A Handbook of Greek Art*, 3d ed., London, 1963.

JEROME J. POLLITT

HELLMER, EDMUND. Austrian sculptor (1850–1935). He was born in Vienna and studied there before going to Rome in 1869. He executed several public monuments with complex figures and relationships recalling the baroque. His later works show a rococo-like fluidity of movement.

HELL SCROLL. Japanese *emaki* (12th cent.). This scroll, a work of more than one artist, is divided between the National Museum of Tokyo and the National Commission for the Protection of Cultural Properties. It illustrates the eight hells, each with sixteen subsidiary hells attached, and forms part of a group of picture scrolls that illustrate the Buddhist theology of the Six Roads of Reincarnation. The pictures are relatively small, but vividly express the merciless torments and terrors to which the damned are subjected.

BIBLIOGRAPHY. *Nihon emakimono zenshū (Japanese Scroll Paintings)*, vol. 6: *Jigoku zōshi, Gaki zōshi, Yamai zōshi*, Tokyo, 1960; H. Okudaira, *Emaki (Japanese Picture Scrolls)*, Rutland, Vt., 1962.

HELMARSHAUSEN, ABBEY OF. German abbey on the Weser River, famous in early Romanesque times for its goldsmith work. Mainly through the work of Roger von Helmarshausen and his followers, an impressive number of cut and engraved pieces of high quality was produced. Among these are Roger's silver altar (ca. 1100) in Paderborn (Cathedral Treasury) and a silver-plated nielloed crucifix (early 12th cent.) in Minden, which was probably a workshop product. *See* ROGER VON HELMARSHAUSEN.

HELMBREKER, THEODOOR. Dutch genre painter (b. Haarlem, 1633; d. Rome, 1696). He was a pupil of Pieter de Grebber in Haarlem. In 1652 Helmbreker was listed as a member of the Haarlem painters' guild, and the following year he left for Italy with Cornelis Bega, Guillem Dubois, and Vincent van der Vinne. Helmbreker is known to have worked for Doge Loredano in the Doge's Palace, Venice, for about four months. In 1654 he was in Rome working for Cardinal Carlo de' Medici, and he lived in the cardinal's palace on the Pincio. In Italy he was friendly with Jan Wils, and the two artists started back to Holland together; however, Helmbreker became ill at Lyons and remained there for almost two years. Once back in Holland he did not remain long, and by 1668 he was in Rome again.

In 1669 he became a member of the Jesuit Brotherhood of S. Maria in Camposanto. He traveled to Naples in 1672 and executed fresco decorations for the Orderhouse of the Jesuits over a period of two and one-half years. However, in 1677, he was recorded as marrying in Rome. Late in 1678 Helmbreker went to Paris, where he worked with Frederick de Moucheron. He then returned to Holland for a short time. On his return trip to Rome he visited Turin (1681), where he worked for the Duke of Savoy. In Italy he was well patronized and was made a member of the Academy of St. Luke as well as the Virtuosi al Pantheon.

Helmbreker is known primarily for his pastorals and crowded gypsy scenes in the tradition of Bamboccianti realism. Such paintings as are in the Balella and Busiri Vici collections in Rome have a brio and rhythmic density that anticipates the decorative verve of Venetian 18th-century painting. Helmbreker's religious paintings are more pretentious and less interesting.

BIBLIOGRAPHY. W. Martin, *De Hollandsche schilderkunst in de zeventiende eeuw*, vol. 2, Amsterdam, 1936.

LEONARD J. SLATKES

HELMONT, *see* GASSEL, LUCAS.

HELMONT (Hellemont), MATTHEUS VAN. Flemish painter (b. Antwerp, 1623; d. Brussels, after 1679). He painted genre scenes in the manner of Adriaen Brouwer and David Teniers the Younger and, occasionally, market scenes. His technique is rather crude, the palette is high in color, and the types themselves are often simple borrowings from Brouwer and Teniers.

BIBLIOGRAPHY. F. J. van den Branden, *Geschiedenis der Antwerp-sche Schilderschool*, Antwerp, 1883.

HELSINGOR (Elsinore): KRONBORG CASTLE. Danish castle in northeast Zealand on the Oresund, built (1574–84) largely for King Frederick II and restored between 1926 and 1929. It replaced a 15th-century castle and was designed by two architects from the Netherlands, Hans van Paeschen and Anthonis van Opbergen. The simple, enclosed perimeter of wings around a square central court has gables on its steep roofs and four towers of a distinctly Netherlandish style. The extremely spare interior has a long Knight's Hall and gallery, a chapel, and a King's

Apartment with a ceiling painting by Honthorst, among other rooms, that are particularly noteworthy.

HELSINKI CENTRAL STATION. Railroad station in Helsinki, Finland, designed by Eliel Saarinen. The design won in a competition in 1904, six years before construction began. Although completed in 1914, the building, one of Saarinen's best early works, was not put into use until after World War I.

The work is one of the finest and best known of a group of *fin de siècle* stations built throughout Europe in an Art Nouveau spirit. Anticlassical and antitraditional, Saarinen attempted to create new forms for the new century. With a conspicuous tower, an immense arch, and clean spaces bounded by simple, primly decorated surfaces, its forms are close to those of the Austrian Sezession architects Joseph Olbrich, Joseph Hoffmann, and Otto Wagner. This Germanic Art Nouveau approach can be readily contrasted with an eclectic attitude by comparing the Helsinki Station with the former Pennsylvania Station in New York, which was designed and built about the same time.

BIBLIOGRAPHY. C. L. V. Meeks, *The Railroad Station, an Architectural History*, New Haven, 1956.

HELST, BARTHOLOMEUS VAN DER. Dutch portrait painter (b. Haarlem, 1613; d. Amsterdam, 1670). Although it is not certain who his teacher was, Van der Helst's earliest dated work, the 1637 *Regents of the Walloon Orphanage* (Amsterdam, Walloon Orphanage), shows the influence of Nicolaes Eliasz. Pickenoij. Van der Helst arrived in Amsterdam about 1636; the 1637 *Regents* portrait appears to be his first important commission. From the mid-1640s on Van der Helst replaced Rembrandt as the most fashionable painter of portraits in Amsterdam. His portraits reflect the general change of style that took place in Dutch painting about 1640. The more courtly and elegant portrait manner of Flemish painting, specifically that of Anthony van Dyck, is apparent in such works as Van der Helst's *Portrait of the Painter Paulus Potter* (1654; The Hague, Mauritshuis Art Gallery).

Van der Helst is also noted for his beautifully rendered large group portraits of the Amsterdam civic guards. *The Company of Captain Roelof Bicker and Lieutenant Jan Blaeuw* (begun in 1639; finished in 1643; Amsterdam, Rijksmuseum, on loan from the city of Amsterdam) shows the influence of both Frans Hals and Rembrandt in individual motifs without being affected by either in the total fabric of the painting. In the 1650s Van der Helst continued to paint group portraits that reflect the change of style in Dutch painting in general toward the courtly and that also reflect the new taste in civic company portraits, which limit those portrayed to the governors of each company (*The Four Governors of the Handbow Archers' Guild of St. Sebastian*, signed and dated 1657; original date was 1653; Amsterdam, Rijksmuseum, on loan from the city of Amsterdam). Van der Helst's style was extremely influential, and a number of contemporary painters followed his lead in portraits (Ferdinand Bol and Govert Flinck). His son Lodewijk worked in his style.

BIBLIOGRAPHY. J. J. de Gelder, *Bartholomeus van der Helst*, Rotterdam, 1921; N. Maclaren, *National Gallery Catalogues: The Dutch School*, London, 1960; J. Rosenberg, S. Slive, and E. H. ter Kuile, *Dutch Art and Architecture, 1600–1800*, Baltimore, 1966.

LEONARD J. SLATKES

Bartholomeus van der Helst, *The Four Governors of the Handbow Archers' Guild of St. Sebastian.* Rijksmuseum, Amsterdam.

HELT-STOCADE, NICOLAES VAN. Dutch history and portrait painter (b. Nijmegen, 1614; d. Amsterdam, 1669). Perhaps a pupil of Marten Ryckaert at Antwerp, in 1646 Van Helt was a master in the Antwerp guild. In 1649 he was commissioned to decorate the hunting lodge of the Prince of Orange. In 1652 he became a citizen of Amsterdam and two years later helped found the painters' guild in that city. He visited Rome and Venice and also spent some time in France as court painter to Louis XII. In Rome he belonged to the Northern painters' organization, the Bentvueghels, where he was given the nickname "Stockade." He sometimes used this nickname as part of his signature. Van Helt was Jan Asselijn's brother-in-law.

BIBLIOGRAPHY. E. W. Moes, "Nicolaes van Helt Stocade," *Amsterdamsch Jaarboekje,* 1902.

HEMATITE. Seldom used reddish-brown pigment made from the iron oxide ore hematite. It was used mainly in ancient Egypt and by certain primitive peoples of Africa.

HEMESSEN, JAN SANDERS VAN. Flemish painter (fl. 1519?–56?). He was born in Hemessen, near Antwerp, and probably died in Antwerp, but we are almost entirely uninformed concerning the facts of his life and career. Neither his birth date nor his death date is documented. He is known to have been a student of Hendrick van

Cleve by 1519, however, and from this it may be inferred that he was born about 1500. He is listed as an independent master in Antwerp by 1524. Between 1519 and 1550 he seems to have been in Antwerp, although it has been proposed that he made an Italian journey during which he visited Florence. Karel van Mander speaks of Hemessen as a citizen of Haarlem, although no traces of his activity in that city have been discovered. Attempts to identify Hemessen as the Brunswick Monogrammist have not been convincing. No works are known from the first decade of Hemessen's activity as an independent master. His earliest dated painting is a *St. Jerome* of 1534 (formerly with a Vienna dealer). The latest is an *Expulsion of the Money Changers from the Temple* (1556; Nancy, Museum of Fine Arts).

Hemessen's compositions are usually filled with a few half-length or knee-length figures pressed close to the frontal plane with a strongly contrasted distant view in the background. The close-up figures are monumental in scale, intensely observed, strongly modeled in light and dark, and often foreshortened in an exaggerated manner. His works have been compared with those of Gossaert, Metsys, and Marinus van Reymerswaele. More than theirs, however, Hemessen's art exhibits those nearly irreconcilable traits of northern realism and Italian monumentality. These qual-

Jan Sanders van Hemessen, *Loose Company*. State Art Gallery, Karlsruhe. Typical tightly compressed composition with half-length figures.

ities are well illustrated in his so-called *Loose Company* (Karlsruhe, State Art Gallery). Also notable in this painting are certain anachronisms, such as the 15th-century head-dress of the male figure in the foreground. Anachronisms of this sort are a phenomenon of the period that still remains to be examined. The significance of Hemessen as a forerunner of Aertsen and Jordaens has often been recognized.

BIBLIOGRAPHY. M. J. Friedländer, *Die altniederländische Malerei*, vol. 12, Leyden, 1935.

NORMAN W. CANEDY

HEMICYCLE. Semicircular structure, as in arenas, orchestras, and theaters, such as that of the Greek theater of Epidaurus. The term also denotes a large semicircular recess.

HENDRICKJE STOFFELS. Oil painting by Rembrandt, in the former State Museums, Berlin. *See* REMBRANDT HARMENSZ. VAN RIJN.

HENDRICUS A RIJSSEL, *see* AERTS, HENDRIK.

HENNECART (Hennequart; Hannequart), JAN (Jehan). Flemish painter (fl. 1454–75). A court painter and *valet*

de chambre to Philip the Good and Charles the Bold of Burgundy, he is known to have been employed as a decorative artist and book illuminator. None of his works has survived. With his fellow artist from Brussels, Pierre Coustain, and others, he contributed to the decorations for the marriage of Charles the Bold at Bruges (1468).

HENNEKIN (Hennekyn), PAULUS. Dutch portrait and still-life painter (b. 1611/14; d. Amsterdam, 1672). He painted portraits in a style similar to that of Bartholomeus van der Helst, whom he may have known in Amsterdam. Hennekin's son David was also a painter.

BIBLIOGRAPHY. A. P. A. Vorenkamp, *Bijdrage tot de geschiedenis van het Hollandsch stilleven in de zeventiende eeuw*, Leyden, 1934.

HENNEQUART, JEHAN, *see* HENNECART, JAN.

HENNEQUIN, JAN (Jean Bandol or Bondol; Jean de Bruges). Franco-Flemish miniaturist (fl. Paris ca. 1368–81; d. after 1381). Bandol (the name by which he is usually known) restored to French miniature painting some of the vitality it had lost after the death of Jean Pucelle. His earliest known works are in the *Heures de Savoie* (Portsmouth, England), which were begun by Pucelle for Blanche of Burgundy and completed by Bandol. His mature masterwork is the *Bible historiale* (The Hague, Mauritshuis Art Gallery), done for Charles V in 1371. The miniatures are notable for their closeness to panel painting in the use of space, volume, and perspective. The painted frames of the miniatures also resemble the real frames of panel paintings rather than those of the contemporary illuminations.

BIBLIOGRAPHY. G. Bazin, *L'Ecole franco-flamande, XIV–Xᵤ siècles*, Geneva, 1941.

HENNER, JEAN-JACQUES. French painter (b. Bernweiler, Alsace, 1829; d. Paris, 1905). Henner's early training was in Strasbourg, at the school of Gilles Guérin, and after 1846 in Paris, at the Ecole des Beaux-Arts under Martin Drolling. From 1855 to 1857 he worked as a portrait painter in his native Bernweiler. Returning to Paris, Henner won the Prix de Rome for *Adam and Eve Find the Body of Abel*. He spent the next six years studying the old masters, particularly Correggio. *The Penitent Magdalen* (Colmar Museum) is strongly influenced by Venetian painting. After his debut in the Salon of 1863 with a portrait of Schnetz, director of the French Academy in Rome, he continued to exhibit in the Salon until 1903. In 1889 Henner succeeded Cabanel in the Institut de France, and he won a Grand Prix at the Paris International Exhibit of 1900. He is known for his sensuous nudes displayed in rich, Venetian landscapes (*Byblis Turned into a Spring*, 1867) and sensitive female portraits (*Mlle. Fouquier*, 1897).

BIBLIOGRAPHY. C. Grad, *Jean-Jacques Henner*, Nancy, 1887; L Loviot, *J. J. Henner et son oeuvre*, Paris, 1912.

HENOSTYLE. Having one column, as in Greek architecture. The primitive Aegean structure in Korakou, Corinth, is henostyle in antis in that it has a single column set between flanking walls or antae.

HENRARD, ROBERT ARNOLD. Belgian sculptor (b. Dinant, 1617; d. Liège, 1676). Henrard was in Rome under François Duquesnoy until 1642, when he returned to Liège and took Carthusian orders. Most of his major works were executed for the Carthusian Cloister at Liège, including statues of the order's saints and a *Madonna* in the portal tympanum modeled after Duquesnoy. His celebrated reliefs include a *Martyrdom of St. Lambert* (ca. 1659; Liège, St. Lambert's Church), but his Carthusian works have not survived. Henrard's style is a somewhat ponderous and awkward baroque; his most celebrated pupil was Jean Delcour.

BIBLIOGRAPHY. E. Marchal, *La Sculpture et les chefs-d'oeuvre de l'orfèvrerie belges*, Brussels, 1895.

HENRI, ROBERT. American painter and teacher (b. Cincinnati, Ohio, 1865; d. New York City, 1929). He studied at the Pennsylvania Academy of Fine Arts with Thomas P. Anschutz and in Paris with Bouguereau and Fleury and at the Ecole des Beaux-Arts. Henri's true teachers were the painterly masters of realism: Hals, Velázquez, Courbet, Manet, and, for a while, Whistler.

After traveling in Europe, Henri taught in Philadelphia, where he met Sloan, Glackens, Luks, and Shinn; these five artists were the nucleus of the future group The Eight. In 1901 he settled in New York, painting and exerting

Jan Hennequin, *The Apocalypse*, detail (tapestry woven by Nicolas Bataille, ca. 1381). Musée des Tapisseries, Angers.

enormous influence as a teacher, first in Chase's school, then independently, and at the Art Students League. His early works were street scenes, landscapes, portraits, and full-length studies of women, for example, *Young Woman in Black* (1902; Art Institute of Chicago). In the years before World War I, Henri was fascinated by the portrayal of various human types. Among the results of his wide travels were paintings of Negroes, such as *Willie Gee* (1904; Newark Museum), Irish peasants, such as *Himself* and *Herself* (both 1913; Art Institute of Chicago), and American Indians, such as *Diegito* (1916; Santa Fe, Museum of New Mexico). Most of his last works were portraits and paintings of children.

The basis of Henri's artistic style was the swift and fluent recording in paint of the immediately perceived facts of the subject. In this he was little different from his skillful academic contemporaries. His crucial place in American painting is justified by his teaching, the magnetic power of his personality, and his devotion to his principles. Beyond instruction in facile brushwork, he taught the importance of truth in life and art. For Henri there was no separation between the two; he stressed the painting of contemporary reality in the same breath as

Jean-Jacques Henner, *The Penitent Magdalen*. Colmar Museum.

he urged his students to read Whitman and Dostoievsky.

He constantly fought against aesthetic restrictions; the exhibition of The Eight was a protest against the narrowness of the National Academy, and Henri was active in other rebel groups and took part in the 1910 Independents' exhibition and the 1913 Armory Show. Although his works were conservative in technique and "modern" only in subject matter, Henri, through the vitality of his teaching and the directness of his painting, gave new life to the American tradition of realism.

BIBLIOGRAPHY. W. Yarrow and L. Bouché, *Robert Henri*, New York, 1921; R. Henri, *The Art Spirit*, Philadelphia and London, 1923; H. A. Read, *Robert Henri*, New York, 1931.

JEROME VIOLA

HENRI II STYLE FURNITURE, *see* FURNITURE (MANNERISM).

HENRY, EDWARD LAMSON. American painter (b. Charleston, S.C., 1841; d. New York City, 1919). He first studied at the Pennsylvania Academy of Fine Arts and later in Paris with Gleyre and Courbet. Henry painted themes from American history and from life on Long Island and in the Catskills. His style is hard and dry and reveals a universal homeliness and a pictorial factualism.

BIBLIOGRAPHY. E. McCausland, *The Life and Work of Edward Lamson Henry*, Albany, N.Y., 1945.

HENRY II AND KUNIGUNDE. Romanesque stone sculpture, at the Adam Portal, Cathedral of Bamberg, Germany.

HENRY VII CHAPEL, LONDON, *see* WESTMINSTER ABBEY, LONDON.

HENRY THE LION, MONUMENT OF. Romanesque bronze sculpture (1162), in Brunswick, Germany.

HENTRICH AND PETSCHNIGG. German architectural firm of Helmut Hentrich (1905–   ) and Hubert Petschnigg (1913–   ). Located in Düsseldorf, it is responsible for one of the most imaginative high-rise buildings erected in Europe in recent years. The structure, built in 1960, is the 22-story Phönix-Rheinrohr Building in Düsseldorf, composed of three metallic-sheathed slabs.

HEPHAESTEUM (Hephaisteion), *see* THESEUM.

HEPHAESTUS. Greek god of fire and metalworking. In Rome he was worshiped as Vulcan. Although Hephaestus was a son of Zeus and Hera, he was lame and ungainly and usually was represented in art as a bearded man dressed as a smith. On his forge, he created beautiful and ingenious objects, such as the armor of Achilles and the necklace of Harmonia. He was the husband of Aphrodite and suffered from her flagrant infidelities.

HEPPLEWHITE, GEORGE. English furniture designer and cabinetmaker (d. London, 1786). Aside from the fact that he was apprenticed to Gillow at Lancaster, little is known of Hepplewhite's early years. He moved to Redcross Street, Cripplegate, London, about 1775 and carried on an exten-

Robert Henri, *Herself.* Art Institute of Chicago.

sive business which was continued by his wife, Alice, after his death. No work from his shop has been conclusively identified, except through resemblance to designs published in *The Cabinet-Makers's and Upholsterer's Guide*, which Alice published first in 1788 and in numerous editions after that. Using the drawings of a number of designers, the *Guide* is essentially a compilation of the English neoclassical style of the time.

As seen in the *Guide*, and the similar designs attributed to him in *The Cabinet-Maker's London Book of Prices* (1788), the furniture associated with Hepplewhite is light in scale, with surface decoration often inlaid or painted. Unusual pale woods were often used in contrast to the ubiquitous mahogany in efforts to exploit surface ornament. Most often legs, either round or square in cross section, are tapered, and reeded or fluted, and the whole repertoire of neoclassical motifs is used on case pieces.

The end of the 18th century was a period of great variety of form, with many small tables, chests, and cabinets used. Perhaps most characteristic of Hepplewhite are the chairs with backs in the shield design which he is said to have originated. The Prince of Wales feather pattern so frequently found on shield-back chairs is probably not symbolic and possibly a Hepplewhite innovation.

BIBLIOGRAPHY. A. Hepplewhite and Co., *Hepplewhite Furniture Designs . . .*, pref. R. Edwards, London, 1947.

MARVIN D. SCHWARTZ

HEPTASTYLE (Septastyle). Having seven columns, as in classical temple porticoes. Heptastyle temples were unusual in ancient Greek architecture.

HEPWORTH, BARBARA. English sculptor and draftsman (1903–   ). She was born in Wakefield, Yorkshire, and had already begun to make clay portraits before attending Leeds Art School in 1920. From 1921 to 1924 she studied sculpture at the Royal Art College and during this time met Henry Moore. While in Italy (1924–26), she learned direct stone carving from Ardini. Her first show was in 1928. Meeting Arp and Brancusi in Paris in 1932 had a great influence on her style. Her first abstract works date from about 1934. She joined the Abstraction-Création group in 1933. Since 1936 she has lived in Cornwall, working in both wood and stone. Her *Cosden Head* (1949) is in the Birmingham Museum and Art Gallery. Several of her finest works are in her own collection. To a great sensitivity to sensuous closed and open form, Hepworth has wed a poetic consciousness. The Tate Gallery, London, held a retrospective of her work in 1968, and she was one of the two artists who represented Great Britain at the 1968 Venice Biennale.

BIBLIOGRAPHY. B. Hepworth, *Carvings and Drawings*, London, 1952.

HERA (Juno). Wife of Zeus and, thereby, Greek goddess of married women. Hera was worshiped as Juno in Rome, and she probably represents an older, pre-Hellenic earth-goddess of great power. She is depicted as a matronly woman, dressed in a flowing robe and wearing a diadem. Many myths deal with her jealous but often vain pursuit of her husband's numerous paramours. Her center of worship was Samos.

HERACLES, *see* HERCULES.

HERALDRY. Art of designing and authenticating armorial bearings. It originated in the 12th century, supposedly because it was necessary to identify, through a readily visible device, the various knights who took part in the Third Crusade. Hence shields were used to display heraldic symbols. In later times heraldry developed into an elaborate system of genealogical symbolism, far removed from its original function.

BIBLIOGRAPHY. C. Boutell, *Heraldry*, rev. ed., New York, 1954.

HERAT ACADEMY. Established by Baisunkur Mirza (d. 1433), a grandson of Tamerlane (Timur), at the Timurid capital of Herat in Afghanistan, the Herat Academy was devoted to the art of the book. Representing one of the major schools of Persian painting, it flourished between about 1415 and the destruction of Herat in 1507. The lively, detailed, and Chinese-influenced style of the school culminates in the work of Bihzad, the leading artist of the academy between 1468 and 1506. *See* ISLAMIC PAINTING (TIMURID PERIOD).

HERBAL, *see* DIOSCORIDES MANUSCRIPT.

HERBIG, OTTO. German painter and lithographer (1889–   ). Born in Dondorf, he studied in Jena, in Berlin with Lovis Corinth, and in Weimar. About 1917, Herbig met James Ensor and Erich Heckel in Ostend. This contact led Herbig toward an expressionist style based on

George Hepplewhite, mahogany card table, ca. 1785. Temple Newsam House, Leeds, England.

Die Brücke, consisting of loosely brushed and richly colored landscapes, flower subjects, and portraits.

HERCULANEUM. Ancient Italian city 4 miles east of Naples. It lay along the lower slopes of Vesuvius and faced toward the sea on one side. According to legend, its founder was Heracles (Hercules), which indicates the city's Greek origin. The first literary mention of the city

Barbara Hepworth, *Biolite*, 1949. Arnold Collection, London.

Herculaneum. *The Chiron Centaur and the Young Achilles*, fragment of a mural painting. National Museum, Naples.

under the name of Heracleion is found in Theophrastus (314 B.C.). Herculaneum's first inhabitants were the Oscans; they were followed by the Tyrrhenians and later by the Samnites. Like Pompeii, it was seriously damaged in the earthquake of A.D. 63 and completely destroyed by the eruption of Vesuvius in A.D. 79. During the eruption it was buried under mud lava, which was converted into tufa. Herculaneum was discovered by the Austrian prince d'Elboeuf in the 18th century. Several excavations have been undertaken there in the course of the years.

The area occupied by the city was about one-third that of Pompeii, and its population is estimated at one-quarter. The city had a regular ground plan that mirrored the Hippodamean layout of the Greek city. It was clearly divided into eight insulae (city blocks) and was crossed by a main artery (*decumanus maximus*) and by three smaller streets that ran parallel to the coastline from northwest to southeast. The houses on the side of the sea had terraces and verandas projecting over the shore, supported by heavy earth-filled walls.

The most important public buildings that have come to light are the theater, the thermae, and the palaestra. The theater was built on several stories of arcades. It has yielded important works of sculpture, which once adorned its niches, and some of the finest examples of ancient painting (*Heracles and Telephus, Chiron and Achilles, Marsyas and Olympus*). The thermae, erected during the early Augustan period (30–10 B.C.), were sumptuously decorated in Nero's time with frescoes, stucco bas-reliefs, and pavings of marble mosaics. They were divided into two sections for men's and

women's baths and had a large palaestra in the center. The palaestra was a municipal sports ground with colonnades and a swimming pool.

Some of the houses at Herculaneum are intact, with their ceilings and upper stories preserved. The average house consisted of terraces, porticoes, peristyles, and bays furnished with glass windows. Among the most important houses are the Samnite House, the House of the Stags, and the House of the Mosaic Atrium. The Samnite House, the oldest house in Herculaneum, has preserved its Samnite structure. It had a gallery with Ionic columns. The House of the Stags, of Nero's time, is so named because of the two groups of stags beset by hounds that decorated the great triclinium; they constitute the finest examples of sculpture in Herculaneum. It consisted of a small atrium, a small and a large triclinium, and ancillary quarters. The House of the Mosaic Atrium had chessboard mosaic decoration. It had a solarium with small bedrooms at both ends, a large triclinium, and a wide portico, in the middle of which were the garden, the fountains, and the pool (piscina).

See also PAPYRI, VILLA OF THE, HERCULANEUM.

BIBLIOGRAPHY. A. Maiuri, *Ercolano*, Rome, 1959; M. Brion, *Pompeii and Herculaneum*, New York, 1960.

EVANTHIA SAPORITI

HERCULES (Heracles). Greatest hero of classical mythology, called Heracles in Greece. He was depicted as a man of extraordinary strength, bearing a lionskin and a club. The son of Zeus and a mortal, Alcmene, he was obliged to perform twelve prodigious labors, which were concerned with the Nemean lion, Hydra, Erymanthean boar, Keryneian hind, Stymphalian birds, Augean stables, Cretan bull, mares of Diomedes, Amazon's girdle, Geryon, Cerebus in Hades, and the apples of the Hesperides.

HERE DE CORNY, EMMANUEL. French architect (1705–63). Héré de Corny worked in Nancy and was responsible for many edifices there. His chief work is the planning unit comprising the Place Royale (Place Stanislas), the Place de la Carrière, and the Place du Gouvernement. His style is notable for its beauty, imagination, high decorative quality, and sensitivity to architectural effects. *See* NANCY.

BIBLIOGRAPHY. L. Hautecoeur, *Histoire de l'architecture classique en France*, vol. 3, Paris, 1950.

HEREDIA, LUIS ALBERTO. Ecuadorian painter (1909–   ). Born in Quito, he lives and works in the small town of Pomasquí, where he has produced primitivistic votive paintings for the local church. In the early 1940s he executed a painting on commission from the Museum of Modern Art in New York City.

HEREFORD CASTLE. One of the few pre-Conquest English castles, built about 1048 with a motte and bailey. It was possibly related to Richard's Castle, also in Herefordshire.

BIBLIOGRAPHY. S. Toy, *Castles, a Short History of Fortifications from 1600 B.C.–A.D. 1600*, London, 1939.

HEREFORD CATHEDRAL. English cathedral whose choir belongs to the Norman rebuilding from 1079, dedicated in 1110. The nave followed in about 1145 and the retrochoir was begun about 1190. The Lady Chapel was not complete until 1225. To the 13th century belong the choir clerestory and vault, the north transept, the aisle walls by Hugh Mason, and the inner north porch. To the 14th century belong the central tower and the destroyed chapter house. The 15th century saw the construction of the south transept vault, cloisters, chantry chapels, and vicar's cloister. About 1520–30 the outer north porch and the bishop's cloisters were built. The west front and single west tower fell in 1786, were rebuilt by James Wyatt, and were again rebuilt by J. Oldrid Scott between 1902 and 1908.

BIBLIOGRAPHY. J. Harvey, *The English Cathedrals*, London, 1950.

HERHOLDT, JOHANN DANIEL. Danish architect (1818–1902). He worked in Copenhagen. Influenced by German architecture, he cultivated domestic materials, such as brick. His National Bank (1866–70) is considered one of the finest examples in Europe of the Tuscan Rundbogenstil, while German clarity is seen in his Neo-Gothic work.

BIBLIOGRAPHY. K. Millech, *Danske arkitekturstrømninger, 1850–1950*, Copenhagen, 1951.

HERING, LOY. German sculptor (b. Kaufbeuren, ca. 1485; d. Eichstätt, ca. 1554). Probably the son of the goldsmith Michael Hering, he was apprenticed to Hans Peuerlein of Augsburg and worked with him until 1513. In that city Hering was undoubtedly influenced by Renaissance currents from northern Italy. In 1513 he settled in Eichstätt and remained there for the rest of his life, working for the Italian-educated bishop Gabriel von Eyb and his successors as well as for churches in Bamberg, Würzburg, Vienna, and other cities. He created relatively few monumental statues, among them *St. Willibald* in Eichstätt and *Bishop Georg von Limburg* in Bamberg. Many of his religious relief compositions are drawn from engravings by Dürer, with whom he was one of the first to enthusiastically adopt Italian Renaissance forms. Although his work still adheres to Gothic linearity and generalizations of form, it contains impressively rounded figures with full draperies and Renaissance architectural settings.

BIBLIOGRAPHY. F. Mader, *Loy Hering*, Munich, 1905.

HERKOMER, SIR HUBERT VON. English painter, sculptor, and graphic artist (b. Waal, Bavaria, 1849; d. Budleigh Salterton, Devonshire, 1914). Much of his youth was divided between Southampton and Munich, with a trip to America in 1851. Herkomer studied at the South Kensington School, London, from 1866 to 1867. He painted sentimental genre and rural subjects, such as *The Guards' Cheer* (1898; Bristol, City Museum and Art Gallery), although he also began doing portraits after about 1880. About 1898 he started to experiment with enamel painting, in which he achieved remarkable effects, in modeling as well as in brilliancy, and he used this medium in both portrait and allegorical paintings.

BIBLIOGRAPHY. A. L. Baldry, *Hubert von Herkomer, R. A. . . .*, London, 1901; J. S. Mills, *Life and Letters of Sir Hubert Herkomer . . .*, London, 1923.

HERLIN, FRIEDRICH. German painter (b. Rothenburg? ca. 1435; d. Nördlingen, ca. 1500). The date and place of Herlin's birth as well as his early years and training are still open to speculation. He is traceable in Nördlingen

Friedrich Herlin, *The Group of Donors*, detail of the high altar for St. Georgkirche. Rathaus, Nördlingen.

after 1459 and is mentioned in the tax records of Nörd-lingen in 1469 and thereafter fairly consistently until 1499. In 1467 he is recorded as being a resident of Rothenburg, where he stayed for two years in order to gain the civic rights that entitled him to paint the high altar in the Church of St. Jakob. A painter, Hans Hörlin, traceable in Nördlingen from 1422 to 1476, has been thought by some scholars to be Herlin's father, but without precise knowledge of Hörlin's art this identification remains tenuous.

Strong stylistic influences from Netherlandish painters, evident in Herlin's works dating after the *Rothenburg Altar*, suggest that he traveled to Flanders about 1468. This Netherlandish trip, however, remains a controversial point, since even the earliest of Herlin's works show some degree of awareness of Netherlandish painters. Perhaps he made two trips to Flanders, one early in his career, about 1450, just after completing his apprenticeship, and another about 1468. This would explain the imitative and somewhat poorly understood use of elements from Rogier van der Weyden's style in the *Rothenburg Altar* and the more sophisticated understanding and incorporation of Rogierian elements in his later works, such as the high altar in St. Blasiuskirche in Bopfingen.

Herlin's two major works, the high altar of St. Blasiuskirche in Bopfingen and the high altar of St. Georgskirche in Nördlingen, are two of the most successful German paintings done under the influence of Netherlandish paintings. Both works show a remarkable understanding of the concepts of Netherlandish art incorporated into a purely German and personal style, not a mere adoption of motifs or slavish imitation of style that is so frequently found in the works of lesser masters of this period.

The St. Blasiuskirche high altar (ca. 1472) shows scenes from the life of Christ and St. Blasius. The panels abound with Rogierian elements, for example, the three-figured composition with the donor in the *Nativity* panel. Characteristic of Herlin are the intense, almost fierce facial expression and the dynamic movement of the figures, seen especially in the panel of the *Martyrdom of St. Blasius.*

A further development toward a freer composition and a more subtle expression of emotion is found in the high altar for St. Georgskirche (now in the Nördlingen Rathaus). It has been dated between 1477 and 1478 on the basis of the sculpture in the central shrine by Simon Leinberger. It shows some scenes from the life of Christ and St. George. The group of donors is noteworthy for its expressive portraiture.

Herlin's last work, a large panel depicting the Virgin with saints and donors, dated 1488, is now in the Nördlingen Rathaus.

BIBLIOGRAPHY. K. Martin, "Ein unbekannter Altar von Friedrich Herlin und seine Herkunft," *Münchner Jahrbuch der bildenden Kunst*, II, 1951; A. Stange, *Deutsche Malerei der Gotik*, vol. 8, Munich, 1957.

DONALD L. EHRESMANN

HERM. In Greek antiquity, a quadrangular stone pillar having a phallos partway up the front and surmounted by a head of Hermes, usually bearded. Hermae were set up in streets, at crossroads, in gymnasia, and on graves. They were probably related to the cults of Hermes as god of travel and of roads and to his association with fertility.

Herm. Head of Hermes, found at the Athens gymnasium, 1st or 2d century A.D. National Museum, Athens.

HERMES (Mercury). Greek god of commerce and travel. He was called Mercury in Rome. Originally represented as a bearded man with broad traveler's hat and herald's staff or caduceus, Hermes was later shown as a youth wearing winged sandals (*talaria*) and cap (*petasus*). His swiftness and diplomatic eloquence made him the messenger of the gods, who always forgave his shrewd and dishonest dealings. Stone pillars, topped by a human head, were erected for his worship at roadsides. *See* HERM.

HERMES AND DIONYSUS. Greek marble sculpture by Praxiteles, in the Olympia Museum. *See* PRAXITELES.

HERMITAGE MUSEUM, LENINGRAD, *see* LENINGRAD: HERMITAGE MUSEUM.

HERMOGENES. Greek architect from Priene (fl. 193–156 B.C.). He was a great proponent of the Ionic order and wrote books which codified its forms and proportions. These writings had a great influence on Vitruvius and, through him, on later European architecture. He was the architect of the temples of Dionysos at Teos and Artemis Leukophryne at Magnesia.

BIBLIOGRAPHY. W. B. Dinsmoor, *The Architecture of Ancient Greece*, 3d ed., London, 1950.

HERMOPOLIS WEST (Tuna el Gebel). Site in Middle Egypt on the desert plateau west of the Bahr Yusef, a canal flowing parallel to the Nile. Its unique importance is that it offers data about Hellenistic and Greco-Roman art in Egypt, compensating us for the loss of the capital, Alexandria, which is virtually out of reach below sea level.

Hermopolis West was the necropolis of the city's rich

Hermopolis West. Hand of Iknaton, limestone relief from Hermopolis. Norbert Schimmel Collection, New York.

class, and is located at some distance in the valley. It also had a huge temple of Thoth, identified by the Greeks with Hermes, and an immense complex of underground galleries containing innumerable mummies of baboons and ibises, animals sacred to Thoth. These galleries, cut in the gravel in the hallowed district north of the temple, have no regular plan. They consist of passages (ca. 13 ft. high) with doorways opening onto lateral chambers (ca. 13 by 33 ft.). The doorways were found blocked by masonry walls, and the chambers were filled to their ceilings with layers of jars, in pairs, plastered rim to rim, each containing an animal mummy or pseudo-mummy. More often than not, the bundle consists of some bones within linen wrappings. The small altars and stelae erected in the galleries and the statuettes of ibises are more valuable (to the Egyptologist) as offerings of the pilgrims than are the mummies. Two wide stairways with shallow risers descend to the entrances. A chamber with the characteristic mummification bed stands near the upper end of one staircase. One of the priests had himself buried in a stone sarcophagus in one of the rooms.

The Temple of Thoth, surrounded east and west by a balustrade of tall stone pillars, is oriented north toward the galleries. It consists of a forecourt with a papyriform portico and a second court (much ruined at the rear) with a hydraulic installation and a grove of palm trees. The fountain and plants were provided with water from a deep cylindrical well, which had a helical staircase within its shell of red brick and was connected to a second rectangular well. Some water machine, now restored as a sakia, raised the water. The grove was probably part of an installation for keeping sacred baboons and ibises. Such precincts for sacred animals are characteristic of late Egyptian temples.

Near the temple, to the east, begins the necropolis with its chapels. The larger ones, of an earlier date, are built of dressed stone with façades in the Ptolemaic style; and the smaller, of Roman date, are of plastered brickwork with simple façades. Earlier burials are set at the bottom of deep vertical shafts in anthropomorphic sarcophagi that are profusely inscribed. In the later chapels the burials are inside or on a sarcophagus built in the shape of a funerary bed (Greek *kline*), in an alcove flanked by engaged columns

or pilasters carrying a shell, a typical Hellenistic motif. The walls are usually painted with a dado imitating stone orthostates that is sometimes surmounted by murals representing scenes from Greek legends, such as Electra or the Trojan Horse, or panels with cupids and animals executed in the Hellenistic style. Wide brushstrokes of red, brown, pink, and green are distributed in a spirited design with accurate perspective and no ground line. Contrasting with this are the murals in one house (No. 21), which imitate, in a poor style, Egyptian paintings of funerary deities ministering to the deceased woman, a Greek who is once represented in the traditional Egyptian garb and on the opposite wall, in perspective, as a Greek.

The northernmost chapel is the largest, belonging to Petosiris, the high priest of Thoth (ca. 332 B.C.). It is a small temple with a squarish, pillared hall from which descends the shaft. At the front of the hall is a shallow, transverse pronaos with a façade of the open type, consisting of composite columns and an intercolumnar parapet wall similar to those in the large Ptolemaic temples. The scenes of daily life in low relief, in the rear hall, are of the traditional Egyptian repertory and style, but show a mixture of Greek and Egyptian methods of representation in the pronaos: three-quarter views; front and side views; perspective; and the use of light skin colors, buffs, blues, and red lines for the wrinkles.

Among the objects from the tombs, besides pottery, are beautiful plaster masks of mummies, a mine of information about ethnic types, hairdresses, jewelry, and styles. At Hermopolis West the process of juxtaposition of Greek and Egyptian arts in the Greco-Roman period can be studied adequately.

BIBLIOGRAPHY. G. Lefèbvre, *Le Tombeau de Petosiris*, 3 vols., Cairo, 1923–24; S. Gabra, *Rapport sur les fouilles d'Hermopolis ouest (Touna el-Gebel)*, Cairo, 1941; A. Badawy, "Le Grand temple Gréco-Romain à Hermoupolis ouest," *Chronique d'Egypte*, XXXI, No. 62, 1956; A. Badawy, "Au Grand temple d'Hermoupolis ouest, l'installation hydraulique," *Revue Archéologique*, XLVII, 1956; A. Badawy, "At the Cemetery of Hermupolis West, A Fortnight of Excavation," *Archaeology*, 1958.

ALEXANDER M. BADAWY

HERNANDEZ, ALEJO, *see* FERNANDEZ, ALEJO.

HERNANDEZ, GREGORIO, *see* FERNANDEZ, GREGORIO.

HERODES ATTICUS, ODEUM OF, ATHENS. Large music and lecture hall on the south slope of the Acropolis. Pausanias knew of it but did not see it, and it may be inferred that it was built shortly after his visit, probably about A.D. 170. Herodes Atticus (101–177) was a wealthy Athenian philanthropist, whose generosity supported many contemporary building projects.

The plan of the Odeum is based on that of a Roman theater. It has a semicircular orchestra; a deep cavea of seats divided into blocks by stairways and a diazoma; a raised stage 20 meters deep; and behind the stage a massive wall with a lower story of niches and two upper stories of arched windows. It was originally covered with a roof of cedarwood and seated about 5,000 people.

BIBLIOGRAPHY. M. Bieber, *The History of the Greek and Roman Theatre*, 2d ed., Princeton, 1961.

HERON, PATRICK. English painter (1920–   ). Heron studied at the Slade School in London and had his first one-man show in 1947 at the Redfern Gallery in London.

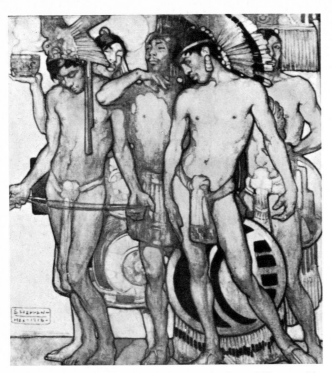

Saturnino Herrán, design detail of the uncompleted mural *Nuestros Dioses* for the National Theater, Mexico City.

Juan de Herrera, Cathedral of Valladolid, view of side aisle. The architect worked at Valladolid after 1585.

He was early influenced by Bonnard, Braque, and De Stael but has since developed a style of restrained and controlled abstraction often using carefully adjusted, rough-edged rectangular forms. Heron has also written widely on contemporary art.

HERP, WILLEM VAN. Flemish painter (b. Antwerp, 1614; d. there, 1677). He was a genre painter, and his style was influenced both by the school of Adriaen Brouwer and David Teniers the Younger and by that of Rubens and Jordaens. The mixture is pleasant and lends dignity as well as intensity to his works. He occasionally painted figures into the landscapes of Jacques d'Arthois.

BIBLIOGRAPHY. W. Bernt, *Die niederländischen Maler des 17. Jahrhunderts...*, vol. 2, Munich, 1948.

HERRADE OF LANDESBERG (Herrad von Landsperg). Abbess of the cloister Hohenburg in Alsace in the second half of the 12th century, she is also called St. Odilia. Herrade of Landesberg is important as the author, and possibly the illuminator, of the elaborately allegorical manuscript *Hortus deliciarum* (ca. 1175).

HERRAN, SATURNINO. Mexican painter (b. Aguascalientes, 1887; d. Mexico City, 1918). Trained at the Mexican Academy according to European traditions, Herrán was, nevertheless, one of the first to embrace "Mexicanism," that is, to substitute native for imported themes. Influenced by his Spanish contemporary Sorolla, Herrán created pictorial anecdotes—sentimental and typical—from the passing scene with a facile but academic technique. Through his art marches a parade of picturesque types: Creoles with shawls, guitar players, noble Indians, and so on. A shallow synthesis of present and past was sometimes his aim, as in *Nuestros Dioses* (a never-completed mural for the National Theater), in which the Aztec goddess Coatlicue is fused with a crucified Christ.

BIBLIOGRAPHY. J. Fernández, *Arte mexicano de sus orígenes a nuestros días*, 2d ed., Mexico City, 1961.

HERREGOUTS, HENDRIK (Le Romain). Flemish painter (b. Mechlin, 1633; d. Antwerp, 1704). A painter of religious works and portraits, he was trained by his father, David Herregouts, but developed his own style in Italy, where he lived for several years. After some time in Cologne, he returned to the Netherlands, becoming a member of the Guild of St. Luke in Antwerp in 1664 and in Mechlin in 1666. Paintings by Herregouts are to be found in several churches in Antwerp, Bruges, Mechlin, and Cologne.

HERRERA, FRANCISCO, THE ELDER. Spanish painter (b. Seville? ca. 1576; d. Madrid, 1656). During his years in Seville (1610–40), Herrera was at first influenced by the complex compositions of Roelas. When he worked on a series of paintings depicting the life of St. Bonaventure with Zurbarán, it was the latter who determined the style. Herrera's distinctive style emerges in the rich colors and brushwork and the noble, if ineptly grouped, figures of the *Temptation of St. Jerome* (1636; Rouen, Museum of Fine Arts) and *St. Basil Dictating His Rule* (1639; Paris, Louvre). A weakening of these qualities occurred after his move to Madrid in 1640.

BIBLIOGRAPHY. J. S. Thacher, "Paintings of Francisco de Herrera the Elder," *Art Bulletin*, XIX, 1937.

HERRERA, FRANCISCO, THE YOUNGER. Spanish painter and architect (b. Seville, 1622; d. Madrid, 1685). After studying architecture and painting in Rome and still-life painting with Recco in Naples, Herrera returned to

Seville in 1656, where he was made co-president, with Murillo, of the new academy. In 1672 he was appointed court painter at Madrid. The elegant airborne figures and piquant colors of his *Triumph of St. Hermengild* in the Prado, Madrid, and the *Triumph of St. Francis* in the Seville Cathedral (both 1660–70) reveal a narcissistic virtuosity. Herrera's career after 1677, when he was made master of the royal works by Charles II, was devoted almost entirely to architecture. His one work, the great Church of El Pilar in Saragossa, for which he refined the earlier plans of Felipe Sánchez, has been completely altered since. The huge symmetrical structure was to have had an enclosed nave, creating a dramatic focus for the choir and altar.

HERRERA, JUAN DE. Spanish architect (ca. 1530–97). On his graduation from Valladolid University, Herrera accompanied Philip II to Italy and Brussels (1547–51); between 1551 and 1559 he was in Italy again and at Yuste, Spain. By 1563 Herrera was Juan Bautista de Toledo's assistant at the Escorial. Gradually (after 1572) he completed the roofs and added a two-story section to the west façade of the great palace-monastery. Herrera's principal contributions later were reorganizing the workshops for more efficient construction, designing the church between 1574 and 1582, and building the infirmary. He also worked at Aranjuez (after 1567), at Seville (the Exchange, after 1582), and at the Cathedral of Valladolid (after 1585). His style was one of refined adjustment of structure and proportion, following 16th-century mathematical consonances; he reinterpreted traditional Spanish church and palace plans with great imagination in a way that was influential for later generations of designers.

BIBLIOGRAPHY. G. Kubler and M. Soria, *Art and Architecture in Spain and Portugal and Their American Dominions, 1500–1800*, Baltimore, 1959.

HERRINGBONE. Ornament resembling the spine of a herring. The pattern is formed by alternating layers of parallel sloping lines, one layer slanting in a direction different from that of the adjacent layer.

HERSFELD ABBEY. Former Benedictine abbey in Germany, now a "glorious ruin." It was originally founded in 769, with its first building program dating from 831; the present early Romanesque ruins date from 1037. The monumental and massive forms and the clearly defined spatial areas show this abbey to have been an important proto-Romanesque structure.

HERWIJCK, STEVEN VAN. Dutch medalist, sculptor, and painter (b. Utrecht, ca. 1530; d. London, 1565/67). Known as "Steven Hollandicus" and "Hollandus" to Horace Walpole, who misconstrued the writings of George Vertue, Herwijck trained in Italy before working in Utrecht, Antwerp, Warsaw, and London. Dated and signed works from 1558 to 1562 show Italianate influence in the group of portrait medals attributed to him.

BIBLIOGRAPHY. G. F. Hill, "Stephen H., Medallist and Painter," *Burlington Magazine*, XII, March, 1908; G. F. Hill, "Recent Acquisitions for Public Collections," *Burlington Magazine*, XXXIII, 1918.

HESDIN, JACQUEMART DE. Franco-Flemish manuscript illuminator (fl. ca. 1384–1410/11). Jacquemart was from Artois, then part of Flanders. He worked for Jean, duc de Berry, for whom he produced four magnificent illuminated manuscripts. Chronologically they are the *Petites heures du Duc de Berry* (Paris, National Library); the *Très belles heures de Notre-Dame*, or Turin-Milan Hours (Turin, Municipal Museum of Ancient Art); the *Très belles heures de Jehan de France*, or Brussels Hours (Brussels, Royal Library); and the *Grandes heures du Duc de Berry* (Paris, National Library). *See* TURIN-MILAN HOURS.

The manuscripts span the period from about 1385 to about 1402. They show an early indebtedness to the French master-illuminator Jean Pucelle, as well as strong Italianate influences. The style of Jacquemart, wherever it can be distinguished from that of his assistants, is marked by a delicate, idyllic sensitivity. One can also discern the emergence of space as a positive factor in the compositions of the illuminations. The group of manuscripts credited to Jacquemart and his workshop comprises a fitting prelude to the emergence of Flemish panel painting in the next generation.

HESIUS, WILHELM. Belgian architect (1601–90). He worked in Antwerp, and was also a Jesuit priest, scholar, and lecturer. His designs for ecclesiastical architecture are *retardataire*. His Jesuit church at Löwen rigidly adheres to traditional planning practices with the exception of the crossing dome, an innovation in local architecture.

BIBLIOGRAPHY. H. Gerson and E. H. ter Kuile, *Art and Architecture in Belgium, 1600–1800*, Baltimore, 1960.

Jacquemart de Hesdin, illumination from *Les Petites heures du Duc de Berry*. National Library, Paris.

HESSE, LUDWIG FERDINAND. German architect (1795–1876). He worked in Berlin. A painter as well as an architect, he was influenced by Schinkel's theories and style. He is best known for his work for Friedrich Wilhelm IV in Potsdam, and especially for his picturesque and eclectic work at Sans Souci Palace.

HESSELIUS, GUSTAVUS. American portrait, religious, and mythological painter (b. Falun, Sweden, 1682; d. Philadelphia, 1755). Trained in Europe in a late baroque manner, Hesselius went to America in 1712 and worked in Philadelphia, Maryland, and Delaware. He was the major painter in the middle colonies until about 1750; his importance rested especially on his few religious and mythological paintings, the earliest executed in colonial America. These include the *Last Supper* (1721–22; lost) and *Bacchus and Ariadne* (Detroit Institute of Arts) and *Bacchanalian Revel* (Philadelphia, Pennsylvania Academy of Fine Arts), both probably 1720–30. The most important collection of his paintings is that of the Historical Society of Pennsylvania, Philadelphia.

BIBLIOGRAPHY. Philadelphia Museum of Art, *Gustavus Hesselius*, Philadelphia, 1938; E. P. Richardson, "Gustavus Hesselius," *Art Quarterly*, XII, 1949.

HESSELIUS, JOHN. American portrait painter (b. Philadelphia or Prince George's Co., Md., 1728; d. Bellefield, Md., 1778). The son of Gustavus Hesselius, John worked in Maryland, Virginia, Delaware, and Philadelphia before settling permanently in Annapolis prior to 1762. His first portraits (in the early 1750s) reflect his father's style and perhaps that of Feke, but his mature work from the mid-1750s on represents more the rococo style of Wollaston. Characteristic of Hesselius's rococo manner are *Charles Calvert and His Slave* (1761; Baltimore, Museum of Art) and *Mrs. Richard Galloway, Jr.* (1764; New York, Metropolitan Museum).

BIBLIOGRAPHY. T. Bolton and G. Groce, "John Hesselius; An Account of His Life and First Catalogue of His Portraits," *Art Quarterly*, II, 1939; J. H. Pleasants, *Two Hundred and Fifty Years of Painting in Maryland*, Baltimore, 1945.

HEXASTYLE. Having six columns, as in the front portico of classical temples. The Doric Temple of the Cabiri in

Gustavus Hesselius, *Bacchus and Ariadne*. Detroit Institute of Arts.

Samothrace and the east front of the Erechtheum in Athens, with their freestanding porches of six columns, are prostyle hexastyle examples. With porches in front and rear, the Doric Temple of Apollo, Delos, is amphiprostyle hexastyle. With their encircling colonnades having six columns in front, the Heraeum in Olympia and the temples of Apollo, Zeus, and Athena in Syracuse are peripteral hexastyle.

HEXENFOOS. Symbols painted on Pennsylvania German barns to protect them from evil spirits, ward off lightning, and keep animals from being bewitched or *ferhexed*. The most popular *hexenfoos* were stars within circles, others being rosettes, whirls, quatrefoils, and polygons. Their use today is primarily decorative.

HEYDEN, JACOB VAN DER. German painter, engraver, and publisher (b. Strasbourg, 1573; d. Brussels, 1645). The son of Jan van der Heyden, Jacob studied with Raphael Coxie. Jacob executed a large number of engraved portraits, a series of fine, small-format scenes from the Bible, allegories, and landscapes. Among his most important pages are large portraits of officers of the Thirty Years' War.

HEYDEN, JAN VAN DER, see Heijden, Jan van der.

HEYDEN, PETER VAN DER (Petrus a Merica). Flemish engraver (b. Antwerp, ca. 1530). He made reproductive engravings exclusively, working from about 1551 to 1572 for the Antwerp publisher Hieronymus Cock. Heyden's exact translations into engraving of Peter Brueghel the Elder's drawings are his most famous works. Among these are the *Seven Vices*, the *Seven Virtues*, the *Battle of the Moneybags and Strongboxes*, *Spring*, and *Summer*.

HIBERNO-SAXON ART. The British Isles attained a high level of culture a century before Charlemagne's revival of learning on the Continent. This cultural efflorescence grew out of the fusion of Celtic (Irish) with Northumbrian art. The former, with its Germanic, Bronze Age, anticlassical base, contributed a rich linear and decorative vocabulary, and the latter contributed a humanistic, classical figure and narrative tradition. The genius of Hiberno-Saxon art is in the effective synthesis of these elements. Further, through the missionary zeal of Irish and Northumbrian monks, the Hiberno-Saxon cultural advances were spread throughout the Continent. Irish monks from Iona and Lindisfarne founded such major monasteries in Europe as St. Gall, Bobbio, and Echternach. It had long been thought that Celtic art was the basic factor in the emergence of Hiberno-Saxon art, but recent thought has tended to place greater emphasis on the role of the Northumbrian monasteries (such as Lindisfarne) in this development. *See* BOBBIO, ABBEY OF; CELTIC ART; ECHTERNACH SCHOOL; IONA; LINDISFARNE; NORTHUMBRIAN ART; ST. GALL: MONASTERY.

Examples of the exquisite metalwork of Hiberno-Saxon art are the Tara Brooch (ca. 800; Dublin, National Museum) and the cover of the Lindau Gospels (8th or 9th cent.; New York, Morgan Library), made at St. Gall. Both works have the complex, zoomorphic interlace designs, which twist and turn upon themselves to create a dynamic, tactile surface. These pieces are visually exciting and display a marvelous skill. The continuity of this tradition is evident as late as 1000, in the Shrine of the Gospels of St. Malaise, in Dublin. In these works, as throughout Hiberno-Saxon art, linear structure is the prevailing characteristic.

The earlier Irish works contributing to Hiberno-Saxon art show a broadness of treatment that contrasts with the delicate, metallic quality of Northumbrian art. The development of Hiberno-Saxon manuscript illumination is best illustrated by comparing the early, primarily Celtic, Book of Durrow (7th cent.) with the Hiberno-Saxon Book of Kells (8th cent.; both, Dublin, Trinity College Library). The former has thick interlacing bands, with large areas of the illuminated page bare of any decoration. The broad decorative motifs serve primarily as framing or filling devices; a distinction is always made between the page and the illumination. In the Book of Kells it is as if the motifs and decorative elements of Durrow had come to a baroque flowering. Field and figure are almost indistinguishable. Spirals and interlaces, lacertines and geometric ornament run riot across the page. The individual motifs are refined to the greatest conceivable delicacy, and then elaborated almost beyond recognition.

Perhaps the greatest contribution, however, was in the area of manuscript writing. As early as the Book of Durrow a cursive script was employed. This is combined with a regular hierarchy of letters that aids in ordering and organizing a page of script. These innovations reached their fruition in the great Carolingian scriptoria and the Caroline minuscule. *See* MANUSCRIPT WRITING; MINUSCULE.

The wide-ranging activities (and influence) of Hiberno-Saxon culture is evidenced in such manuscripts as the Echternach Gospels (ca. 690; Paris, National Library), the St. Gall Gospels (8th cent.; St. Gall, Library), and the Cuthbert Gospels (ca. 760–770; Vienna, National Library).

BIBLIOGRAPHY. A. K. Porter, *The Crosses and Culture of Ireland*, New Haven, 1931; N. Aberg, *Occident and Orient in Art of the Seventh Century*, pt. 1: *The British Isles*, Stockholm, 1943.

STANLEY FERBER

HICKS, EDWARD. American painter (b. Newtown, Pa., 1780; d. there, 1849). Trained by a coachmaker from the age of thirteen, Hicks went into the coachmaking and painting business at Milford, Pa., in 1801, and then established himself at Newtown in 1811 for the remainder of his life. As the head of a successful workshop his principal activity remained the painting of signs, clock faces, furniture, carriages, historical markers, and other practical items. Although his paintings were widely known in the East, he was more renowned as a leading Quaker preacher during his lifetime.

Hicks was the leading folk, or primitivist, American painter of the first half of the 19th century. His art reflects the practical nature of his occupation and his religious convictions. Although he sometimes painted from nature in farm scenes done for his neighbors, he usually relied on contemporary prints for motifs and entire pictures. His principal theme, of which he did more than fifty paintings, was *The Peaceable Kingdom* (versions in the Brooklyn Museum; Albright-Knox Art Gallery, Buf-

Hiberno-Saxon art. Book of Kells, 8th-century illuminated manuscript. Trinity College Library, Dublin.

falo; Worcester Art Museum; and elsewhere). Depicting the eleventh chapter of Isaiah, it usually shows the peacefully gathered animal kingdom in the foreground and the scene of William Penn's treaty with the Indians in the background, representing the Quaker fulfillment of the Biblical prophecy.

BIBLIOGRAPHY. A. Ford, *Edward Hicks, Painter of the Peaceable Kingdom*, Philadelphia, 1952.

HIDEYORI (Kano Hideyori). Japanese painter (d. 1557). Hideyori is believed to have been the second son of Motonobu, and he was one of the earliest Kanō masters to pioneer in portraying genre scenes. A pair of his screens, *Maple Viewing at Takao* (Tokyo, National Museum), successfully blends the Kanō and Tosa traditions and reflects a new interest in the life of the common man. *See* KANO SCHOOL; TOSA SCHOOL.

HIERAKONPOLIS (Kom el Ahmar). Greek name of Nekhen, probably the earliest capital of Upper Egypt. From the predynastic period (end of the 4th millennium B.C.) there remain the quadrangular podium of a shrine, surrounded by a stepped retaining wall of sandstone, and a tomb chamber with painted walls representing historical moments of the life of a local chief. The temples built by the Pharaohs Kha'sekhem and Kha'sekhemwy date from the Archaic period and have granite doorjambs carved with a scene from the foundation ceremony. A large double enclosure in brick, oriented with its corners toward the cardinal points of the compass, has a fortified entrance with a bent-axis approach in the western corner, protruding from the north façade. This was probably the royal residence. There are remains of houses ascribable to the 3d dynasty. Finds from Hierakonpolis include two maceheads: that of the Scorpion King (predynastic period; Oxford, Ashmolean Museum) and that of King Naʻrmer (1st dynasty; Cairo, Egyptian Museum) carved with scenes recording the wars of unification of Upper and Lower Egypt.

BIBLIOGRAPHY. J. E. Quibell, *Hierakonpolis*, London, 1900–02.

HIERATIC. Strictly speaking, the term "hieratic" (from the Greek *hieratikos*, sacerdotal) is used in art criticism to denote a style that has been subjected to strict rules sanctioned by religion. More generally, it implies qualities of monumentality and formal abstraction, a tendency toward dehumanization and rigidity, fixity and immutability. Not limited to any single style or period of art history, it can be applied to the greater part of Egyptian sculpture, to the portrait statues of Constantine, to a great deal of Byzantine art, and to the Madonnas of Duccio. With equal reason, it can be descriptive of certain works of primitive art, such

as African woodcarving, as well as some contemporary sculpture and painting.

HIEROGLYPH. Written symbol whose meaning is unknown. Derived from the Greek words for "priestly carving," the term was first applied to the pictorial script of ancient Egypt. After being deciphered the script was found to consist both of signs representing the names of objects and signs standing for phonetic sounds. The description "hieroglyphic" has been extended to undeciphered scripts such as ancient Mayan.

BIBLIOGRAPHY. A. H. Gardiner, *Egyptian Grammar*, 3d ed. rev., London, 1957.

HIERON (Temenos). Sacred place; a temple, but more usually the enclosure in which the temple was contained. Greek temples of importance were customarily surrounded by a wall to form the sacred precinct. Within this enclosure, called the hieron or temenos, the shrine and auxiliary structures were erected. Sacred precincts, such as those in Olympia and Delphi, contained the temple of the ruling deity as well as temples of lesser deities, treasures, stoae, altars, votive columns, groves, and exedrae. They were

Joseph Highmore, *Pamela in the Bedroom with Mrs. Jewkes and Mr. B.*, illustration for *Pamela*. Tate Gallery, London.

entered through a gateway or propylaeum, as in the temenos of the Temple of Athena Polias, Priene, and in the Acropolis in Athens.

HIGGINS, EUGENE. American painter (b. Kansas City, Mo., 1874; d. New York City, 1958). He studied in Paris from 1894 to 1904 under Laurens, Constant, and Gérôme. Influenced by Millet, Higgins painted the sufferings of workers, peasants, and the poor in an emotional, but academic, style.

HIGHBOY. American term, introduced in the 19th century, to describe the 17th- and 18th-century chest of drawers on tall legs. In two parts, the highboy consists of a lower section of two tiers of drawers and an upper part of four or five tiers of drawers in a frame that sets into the lower section. Originally called a tall or high chest, it was introduced in England after the Restoration and was out of fashion before 1750. American examples date from as early as 1690, or from the beginning of the William and Mary style, to the Chippendale style, which went out of fashion after the Revolution. From a base of six trumpet-turned legs joined by stretchers and a flat-topped case covered with rich walnut veneer, the design evolved to one of four carved cabriole legs and a case topped by a broken pediment with richly carved center drawers.
BIBLIOGRAPHY. H. Comstock, *American Furniture*, New York, 1962.

HIGHLIGHT. That part of an oil painting where the light effects are most intense. A highlight may be either a large area of the composition (such as that occupied by a saintly figure) or many small areas of light (such as those imitating the effect of natural light reflected off highly polished or wet objects).

HIGHMORE, JOSEPH. English painter (b. London, 1692; d. Canterbury, 1780). He was probably Hogarth's closest competitor during the middle years of the 18th century. Like Hogarth, Highmore was a representative of the rococo in England, and his paint application has the crisp, vigorous, decorative quality of that style. He is best known as a portraitist and for his illustrations for Samuel Richardson's *Pamela* (now divided between London, Tate Gallery; Cambridge, Fitzwilliam Museum; and the Melbourne Art Gallery). His narrative paintings lack the satiric element of Hogarth, but sometimes have more lightness and elegance. Highmore retired to Canterbury in 1762, and does not appear to have continued to paint after that date.
BIBLIOGRAPHY. E. K. Waterhouse, *Painting in Britain, 1530–1790*, Baltimore, 1953.

HIGH RELIEF, *see* ALTO-RELIEVO.

HIGH RENAISSANCE. Short-lived "classic" phase in Italian art (1495–1520). In painting (Leonardo da Vinci, *The Last Supper*, 1495–98; Milan, S. Maria delle Grazie) and in sculpture (Michelangelo, *David*, 1501–04; Florence, Academy) the figures are more ample, mature, and serene and betray a more pronounced *contrapposto* than the figures of the 15th century. Architecture, as exemplified by Bramante's Tempietto in the courtyard of S. Pietro in Montorio, Rome, shows modeling of the wall surface. The masters of the High Renaissance—Raphael, Michelangelo,

Titian—in their later work depart from this brief moment of equilibrium. *See also* RENAISSANCE.
BIBLIOGRAPHY. H. Wölfflin, *Classic Art*, 2d ed., London, 1953; S. J. Freedberg, *Painting of the High Renaissance in Rome and Florence*, 2 vols., Cambridge, Mass., 1961.

HILANI. Large hall used by Assyrian and Babylonian rulers as a court of judgment. The *hilani* is the forerunner of the Roman judgment hall, or basilica.

HILDEBRAND, ADOLF E. R. VON. German sculptor (b. Marburg, 1847; d. Munich, 1921). Hildebrand became a uniquely influential artist in Germany during his lifetime and has become internationally known for his essay, *Problem der Form in der bildenden Kunst*.

His early youth was spent in Switzerland, where his talent for drawing was first demonstrated. He was an outstanding pupil in art school in Nürnburg at the age of fifteen, working in both sculpture and painting. In his early twenties Hildebrand traveled to Rome and became a close friend of Conrad Fiedler, the lawyer and art patron, and Hans von Marées, the painter. Influences from both men were added to his own penetrating ideas.

In 1873 Hildebrand and Marées collaborated on a mural decoration, and Hildebrand's sculpture met with an enthusiastic reception in a Viennese exhibition. His work was now conditioned to some extent both by Marées's theory of harmonious form and by his own studies of 15th-century and classical arts in Rome and Florence. An exhibition of his figures and other works in Berlin in 1874 was also successful, and he became renowned throughout Germany. In 1889 he won first prize in the competition for a monument to Wilhelm I.

The Wittelsbach Fountain (1894–95; Munich) was the first of many large civic monuments of its genre. Its figures convey formal values that go beyond the general neoclassical expression of the time. Here they are used to symbolize both the beneficent and the destructive forces of water. He designed private and public fountains for Jena, Strasbourg (largely destroyed in 1919), Worms, Berlin, and Cologne. Hildebrand also planned most of the architectural settings for these compositions. After 1897 Hildebrand lived alternately in Florence and Munich.

It seems paradoxical that statues of so ostensibly a neoclassical, austere aesthetic as Hildebrand's were in fact based upon a credo of "pure form," which astonishingly resembles in tone and in various particulars the stated aims of several cubist, constructivist, and related masters of our time. He insisted upon a timeless, purified formalism devoid of sentimentality and mere pictorial attractiveness. He stressed absolute completeness of surface, clarity of underlying structure, and receptivity to three-dimensional viewing from near or far distances, particularly in the nude figures, which perhaps best project in actual material his complex hypotheses.

Hildebrand's portrait busts, however, were more specific and more nearly intimate in mode. Certain of his later compositions disclose an affinity for the richness of the Bavarian baroque. Nonetheless, even in the latter he directly refines qualities of a traditional style rather than taking the eclectic method of so many of his German and French contemporaries. Harmony and simplicity were constants for him. Hildebrand's figures reflect the period style of neoclassical aloofness. Nevertheless, they subtly combine and resolve aspects of Archaic, Polycleitan, and 4th-century Greek aesthetic with Hildebrand's own concept of modeling as successive, delicately turned planes in space.

His most significant sculptures include the Wittelsbach Fountain and a series of nude youths; busts of Bismarck, Conrad Fiedler, General von Baeyer, Wilhelm von Bode, and Arnold Böcklin; reliefs of mythological figures as well as relief portraits, including Wilhelm II; memorials to Brahms, Bismarck, and Schiller; and monuments on the graves of various noblemen. He also designed several buildings. Hildebrand's works are in galleries and museums in Berlin, Munich, Frankfurt, Breslau, Dresden, Mannheim, Weimar, and elsewhere.

BIBLIOGRAPHY. F. Haack, *Die Kunst des 19. Jahrhunderts*, Esslingen, 1918; A. von Hildebrand, *The Problem of Form*, New York, 1932.

JOHN C. GALLOWAY

HILDEBRANDT, JOHANN LUCAS VON. Austrian architect (1668–1745). Born in Genoa, he was a pupil of Carlo Fontana in Rome. In 1696 he settled in Vienna and was appointed court architect to the Emperor in 1700. Hildebrandt's first works were influenced by northern Italian and French architecture, as well as by local tradition. His best-known work is the Belvedere Castle, Vienna (1715–22), a country palace comparable to Versailles in scale and to Vaux-le-Vicomte in its mass. Both in this work and in the Mirabell Palace, Salzburg (ca. 1710), he achieved architectural emphasis through decorative patterns rather than through three-dimensional effects. He stands for consistency, logic, and simplification to achieve greater monumentality within the framework of baroque complexity and variation.

BIBLIOGRAPHY. B. Grimschitz, *Johann Lucas von Hildebrandt*, Vienna, 1959.

HILDEGARD OF BINGEN. Virgin mystic and prophetess, known also as Sibyl of the Rhine (b. Böckelheim/ Nahe, 1098; d. Rupertsberg, 1179). At an early age she went to the cloister of Rupertsberg near Bingen to become a nun. Later she was beset with compulsive visions and, being unable to write, dictated them to a monk. *Scivias* (*Know Thy Ways!*) and the *Book of Merits* are her principal writings. She appears to have encouraged manuscript illumination; her prayer book (Munich, Staatsbibliothek) is one of the masterpieces of Middle Rhenish illumination.

HILDESHEIM. City about 18 miles southeast of Hannover, Germany, at the foot of the Harz Mountains. Hildesheim rose to importance in 822, when Charlemagne made it the seat of a bishopric. The first cathedral, of which nothing remains, was dedicated in 872 and has since been rebuilt.

The city received its major impetus under Bishop Bernward (993–1022/23). He had the city walled (a sign of an already achieved wealth and prominence) and, especially, stimulated the growth of the metalworker's art, which had flourished there since the 9th century. During the 13th century Hildesheim received the rights of a free city within the Holy Roman Empire, and trade and commerce grew as it became a member of the Hanseatic League. *See* BERNWARD, BISHOP.

The modern city is divided into two parts by vestiges of the medieval walls and ramparts. The old section of the town contains many well-preserved examples of domestic architecture of the late Gothic period. These include houses with half-timbering, steeply pitched roofs, and upper stories that protrude beyond the lower ones. The principal secular building of the old town is the Rathaus, a particularly fine example of 15th-century German Flamboyant Gothic style. It is decorated with frescoes of the city's history. Other old architectural examples include the Tempelherrenhaus (late Gothic) and the former Guildhall of the Butchers (Knochenhaueramthaus), considered one of the finest examples of wooden building in Germany.

The old churches are numerous and important. Probably the most significant is St. Michael's, founded by Bishop Bernward and dedicated in 1015. It was an important progenitor of the Romanesque architectural style, and is renowned for its bronze doors (1007–15). The doors, with scenes from Genesis and the life of Christ, were executed by Hildesheim's bronze workshop, which was also responsible for the Easter column (reminiscent of the Column of Trajan) of 1015 in St. Michael's; two candelabra and an ornate gold cross that belonged to Bernward (Hildesheim, St. Magdalena); and the large bronze baptismal font of about 1225 (Hildesheim, Cathedral). The workshop was famous enough to make its influence felt as far away as Gnesen, Poland, where the Cathedral has bronze doors (12th cent.) in the manner of Hildesheim's. *See* ST. MICHAEL'S, HILDESHEIM.

St. Godehard, dedicated in 1172, and the rebuilt Cathedral, dedicated in 1061, stand as fine examples of the mature Romanesque style in Saxon Germany. They show a simple, weighty traditional approach to the problems of Romanesque style. Located in the suburb of Moritzberg is an abbey church of mid-11th-century foundation, the sole example of a purely columnar basilica in northern Germany. *See* ST. GODEHARD. *See also* HILDESHEIM TREASURE.

STANLEY FERBER

Johann Lucas von Hildebrandt, Belvedere Castle, Vienna.

HILDESHEIM TREASURE. Hoard of Roman silver objects of the Augustan age, found near Hildesheim, Germany, in 1868 (Hildesheim, Römer-Pelizaeus Museum). The collection includes plates, drinking vessels, and cooking utensils, most of them sumptuously ornamented. Among the finest pieces is a patera with a seated Athena in high relief. Other pieces are decorated with heads of Attis and Cybele, in masks and emblems.

BIBLIOGRAPHY. E. Pernice and F. Winter, *Die Hildesheimer Silberfund*, Berlin, 1901.

HILL, CARL FREDRIK. Swedish painter (1849–1911). From 1871 to 1873 he attended the Royal Academy Art School in Stockholm. For the next four years he painted in France, producing landscapes and seascapes, often in rich, broken color but differing from impressionism in their haunting mood. Then, late in 1877, he turned to violently expressive, pre-Van Gogh exaggerated forms and arbitrary color. Hill produced several thousand remarkable drawings, anticipating later art movements.

BIBLIOGRAPHY. E. Blomberg, *Carl Fredrik Hill, hans friska och sjuka konst*, Stockholm, 1949; A. Anderberg, *Carl Hill, hans liv och hans konst*, Malmö, Sweden, 1951.

HILL, JOHN. English-American graphic artist (b. London, ca. 1760; d. West Nyack, N.Y., 1850). Hill was employed in the London printshop of Rudolf Ackermann, making

Nicholas Hilliard, miniature of the Earl of Somerset. National Portrait Gallery, London.

aquatint plates after designs etched by such artists as Rowlandson. He emigrated to New York in 1816. He first made small plates, then turned to larger landscape prints, for example, *Hudson River* (New York, 1828), an aquatint portfolio after paintings by W. G. Wall.

BIBLIOGRAPHY. D. M. Stauffer, *American Engravers upon Copper and Steel*, 2 vols., New York, 1907.

HILLIARD, NICHOLAS. English miniaturist and goldsmith (ca. 1547–1619). He was the son of Richard Hilliard, a goldsmith in Exeter. Hilliard was first apprenticed to a goldsmith, but by 1560 he was already painting miniatures, basing his style on the miniatures of Hans Holbein the Younger. The first great English-born painter, he was appointed goldsmith and limner to Elizabeth I well before 1583. His first dated portrait of the Queen (1572; London, National Portrait Gallery) is clearly from life. An iconic portrait of her in robes of state probably dates from two or three years earlier. His career, including a visit of several years to France, has only recently been traced in documents, including the household accounts of the Duc d'Alençon, English public papers, the books of the Goldsmiths' Company, and records of legal transactions.

Hilliard's known work is all on a small scale; it is likely that he also worked in oils that were nearly life-size. The *Pelican*, *Armada*, and *Ermine* portraits of the Queen are often very reasonably ascribed to him. Although his sitters included many important figures of late-16th-century England, their identity has often been confused or lost. He composed (ca. 1600) the *Treatise Concerning the Art of Limning*. He designed and possibly executed in part one of the Royal Great Seals for Elizabeth and gold medals for her successor, James I. He also probably designed many of the elaborate enameled jeweled settings for his miniatures, for example, the *Armada Jewel* (London, Victoria and Albert), the *Drake Pendant*, and the *Lyte Jewel*. Hilliard was gradually outstripped by his pupil Isaac Oliver, and after 1600 his work declined in liveliness. However, James I confirmed the royal patronage in 1603 and again in 1617.

A certain flatness in modeling is due to Hilliard's preference for an even (and more flattering) light and to his avoidance of strong shadows as unsuited to painting "in small compass." His technique, though meticulous, shows broad handling and free calligraphic line. His understanding of water-color technique shows fugitive flesh tints and shading in transparent colors, when these have not been faded by exposure to light.

Many miniatures from Hilliard's hand, often with the date or sitter's age in his elegant calligraphy forming part of the design, are in the Royal collections, in private collections (especially of the Duke of Buccleuch and Duke of Portland), and in the main English public collections. Many now lack the original turned boxes or settings in which they were held in the hand or worn. There are also fine examples in the Metropolitan Museum of Art, New York.

BIBLIOGRAPHY. C. Winter, *Elizabethan Miniatures*, London, 1943; London, Victoria and Albert Museum, *Nicholas Hilliard and Isaac Oliver* (catalog), by G. Reynolds, London, 1947; J. Pope-Hennessy, *A Lecture on Nicholas Hilliard*, London, 1949; E. Auerbach, *Nicholas Hilliard*, London, 1961.

PATRICIA M. BUTLER

HILLIER, TRISTRAM PAUL. English painter (1905–   ). Born in Peking, he studied with Henry Tonks at the Slade School in London and with Lhote in Paris. Hillier became an associate of the Royal Academy in 1957. His landscapes are represented in the Tate Gallery, London, and in the national collections of Canada and Australia.

HILL JAR (Po-shan-lu). Chinese bronze or pottery vessel with a cover in the form of a hill or mountain. The shape was used extensively in the Han dynasty. In bronzes the bottom was usually in the form of a stem cup; in pottery the bottom unit was normally cylindrical and squat with small feet. The bronze vessels had holes in the cover to allow incense to be burned inside.

The characteristic conical cover represented a wave-encircled mountain with animals and riders; similar relief bands encircled the body. These hills possibly represented the Taoist Isles of the Blessed. Many hill jars were done in green-glazed terra cotta; a few, in inlaid bronze.

HIMATION. Outer cloak, made of wool or linen, worn by Greek men and women over an inner garment called a chiton or a peplos. The himation was worn in a variety of ways, sometimes covering the whole body, sometimes removed from one shoulder, and it offered a rich variety of compositional patterns to the Greek sculptors.

BIBLIOGRAPHY. M. Bieber, *Griechische Kleidung*, Berlin, 1928.

HIMEJI CASTLE. Japanese castle founded in the 14th century and enlarged and improved in 1608. The roofs and gables of its main donjon and three-cornered pavilions create a complex yet beautiful profile. It not only represents the perfected form of Japanese castle architecture, but is also the best preserved of the numerous castles that have suffered serious damage since their beginnings.

BIBLIOGRAPHY. Tokyo National Museum, *Pageant of Japanese Art*, vol. 6: *Architecture and Gardens*, Tokyo, 1952.

HINAYANA. Southern school of Buddhism practiced in Ceylon and much of Indochina. Hīnayāna (Lesser Vehicle) represents the original teachings of Buddha whereby enlightenment may be achieved. Each person is responsible for his own destiny; only the conscious mental and spiritual purification of the individual can lead to nirvāna. One who attains perfect purification is an arhat. *See* ARHAT; NIRVANA. *See also* MAHAYANA; VAJRAYANA.

HINDU ART, *see* INDIA.

HIPPODAMUS. Greek architect and town planner from Miletus (fl. ca. mid-5th cent. B.C.). He was famed for having introduced the gridiron system into town planning. The rebuilding of Miletus after the Persian Wars and the remodeling of Piraeus toward the middle of the 5th century were under his supervision. *See* MILETUS; PIRAEUS.

BIBLIOGRAPHY. R. E. Wycherley, *How the Greeks Built Cities*, 2d ed., London, 1962.

HIPPODROME. Course used by the Greeks for horse and chariot races, with tiers of seats for spectators, as in the hippodrome in Pessinus in Asia Minor. The Greek hippodrome was the prototype of the Roman circus. The Byzantine hippodrome was used for public spectacles, the crowning of emperors, and triumphal processions.

HIPPOLYTE, *see* AMAZONS.

HIRADO. Kiln area in Mikawachi, near Arita, where the finest-quality Japanese porcelain was produced from 1751 to 1843 under the patronage of the lords of Hirado. Most pieces were decorated with a pale underglaze of violet-blue. However, in the 19th century some very fine sculptural pieces with enamel decoration were produced. *See* JAPAN: CERAMICS.

BIBLIOGRAPHY. London, Oriental Ceramic Society, *Catalogue of an Exhibition of Japanese Porcelain* (cat. entries 41–49), London, 1956.

HIRAME (Hira maki-e). Japanese lacquer treatment combining *hira*, a flat relief, and *maki-e*, a simple decorative technique of painting a design in wet lacquer, sprinkling with metal dust, and polishing down with charcoal. In *hira maki-e*, a final relief effect is added to the metal-dust decoration by overpainting with lacquer where desired.

HIROSHIGE (Ando Hiroshige). Japanese Ukiyo-e printmaker (1797–1858). He studied with a Utagawa master and first specialized in portraits of women and actors. Greatly inspired by Hokusai's landscape series published in 1831, Hiroshige then became solely interested in this genre. In 1832 he made his first journey from Edo (present-day Tokyo) to Kyoto by way of the Tōkaidō Highway. The *Fifty-three Stations on the Tōkaidō Highway*

Hippodrome. Open-air stadium for horse and chariot racing and other public spectacles.

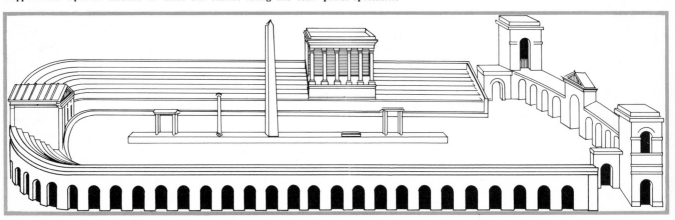

(1833), which overnight made him the foremost landscapist in wood-block prints, was based on sketches made during this trip. He saw his native land with a poetic eye and portrayed it in various moods under moonlight, drenching rain, and drifts of snow. Less inclined to be dramatic than Hokusai, he created restful and reflective landscapes. Two sons-in-law of Hiroshige, who were lesser artists, later used his name; this accounts for the uneven artistic quality in some of the prints bearing his name. *See* HOKUSAI; UKIYO-E; UTAGAWA SCHOOL.

BIBLIOGRAPHY. L. V. Ledoux, *Japanese Prints, Hokusai and Hiroshige in the Collection of Louis V. Ledoux*, Princeton, 1952; J. A. Michener, *Japanese Prints*, Rutland, Vt., 1959; H. Andō, *Hiroshige*, text by W. Exner, New York, 1960.

HIRSAU: ST. AURELIUS. German early Romanesque church, built between 1038 and 1071. A simple basilica with wooden roofing and clerestories, it adopted a twin-tower western-façade motif related in type to the early Cathedral of Strasbourg. Rebuilt about 1120, St. Aurelius adopted the plan of Cluny II.

HIRSAU: SS. PETER AND PAUL. German abbey church, built under Abbot William from 1082 to 1091. In appearance, it is strongly modeled after Cluny II. Along with St. Aurelius (as remodeled), it has given rise to the name "Hirsauer Schule," whose churches are characterized by heavy masonry and moldings and by simple decoration.

HIRSCH, JOSEPH. American painter and graphic artist (1910–   ). Born in Philadelphia, he studied at the Philadelphia Museum of Art, with Henry Hensche in Provincetown, and with George Luks in New York. From 1935 to 1936 Hirsch traveled in Europe, Egypt, and the Far East. He was an artist-correspondent during World War II. Hirsch's earlier paintings are socially oriented urban genre scenes, sometimes sympathetic, as in *Two Men* (1937; New York, Museum of Modern Art), sometimes satiric, as in *The Senator* (1941; New York, Whitney Museum of American Art). His more recent work is more concerned with subtle brushwork and nuanced color with which he creates vivid compositions of the human figure.

BIBLIOGRAPHY. New York, Museum of Modern Art, *Americans 1942...*, New York, 1942.

HIRSCH, STEFAN. American painter and graphic artist (b. Nürnberg, Germany, 1899; d. New York City, 1964). He studied at the University of Zurich and with Hamilton Easter Field after his arrival in the United States in 1919. Hirsch was a painter of figures, still lifes, and landscapes. In the 1920s his paintings were associated with the precisionist style, for example, *New York, Lower Manhattan* (1921; Washington, D.C., Phillips Collection), which depicts skyscrapers and ships on the river in severe and blocklike form. His later works, such as the landscape *Pic of Orizaba* (1932; New York, Whitney Museum of American Art), while more loosely treated, are still formally simplified.

HIRSCHFIELD, MORRIS. American "naïve" painter (b. Poland, 1872; d. New York City, 1946). Originally a suit manufacturer, he began painting after his retirement in

Hiroshige, *The God of Thunder under the Sumida Gawa Bridge.* Woodcut.

1937. His subjects are animals, figures, and nudes, with a stress on texture and line.

BIBLIOGRAPHY. S. Janis, *They Taught Themselves...*, New York, 1942.

HIRSCHVOGEL, AUGUSTIN. German etcher, glass painter, and maker of enamels (b. Nürnberg, 1503; d. there, 1553). The most important German etcher of the mid-16th century, he made some 150 plates, mainly between 1543

Augustin Hirschvogel, *The Creation of Eve.* Engraving.

Hittite Art. Ivory carving of animal combat from Nimrud. National Museum, Baghdad.

and 1549. Hirschvogel, Albrecht Altdorfer, and Hanns Sebald Lautensack made the earliest pure landscape etchings.
Hirschvogel's preferred subjects were hilly landscapes with
broad stretches of water, executed with delicacy and charm.
He traveled to Venice and later to Austria and Hungary.
His figures, aside from strict portraits, are as Italianate as
his landscapes are northern. *Cleopatra*, for example, is not
only a Venetian figure but is executed in the dotted technique of Giulio Campagnola. Hirschvogel made numerous
ornamental prints: designs of ewers, dagger sheaths, and
coats of arms. In 1543 he published in Nürnberg a book
called *Geometria* with thirty-nine etched plates of dia-
grams. He signed his plates with various monograms.

BIBLIOGRAPHY. G. K. Nagler, *Die Monogrammisten...*, vols. 1 and
3, Munich, 1858, 1863; K. Schwarz, *Augustin Hirschvogel, Ein deutscher Meister der Renaissance*, Berlin, 1917.

HISASHI, *see* SHISHINDEN.

HISATSUGU, *see* ZOAMI.

HISPANO-MORESQUE ARCHITECTURE, *see* ISLAMIC
ARCHITECTURE (HISPANO-MORESQUE PERIOD).

HISPANO-MORESQUE POTTERY, *see* CERAMICS; ISLAM
(POTTERY AND TILES: HISPANO-MORESQUE SCHOOL).

HISSARLIK, *see* TROY.

HISTORICAL PAINTING. Noblest type of painting possible for painters, according to 17th-century theories. In
line with this idea 18th-century artists, such as Benjamin
West in England, devoted themselves to the depiction of
scenes from ancient history, classical mythology, and Christian lore. The aim of their canvases was the teaching of
a moral lesson, a practice carried into the early 19th
century by David. *See* DAVID, JACQUES-LOUIS; WEST, BEN-
JAMIN.

BIBLIOGRAPHY. G. Evans, *Benjamin West and the Taste of His
Times*, Carbondale, Ill., 1959.

HITCHENS, IVON. English painter (1893–   ). Born
in London, he studied at the St. John's Wood and Royal
Academy schools. Since 1938 his work has been included
in every important British international exhibition, and he
was given a retrospective at the Venice Biennale in 1956.
His paintings are in the collections of the Tate Gallery
and the Victoria and Albert Museum and in other public
collections of Great Britain and the Commonwealth. In
the United States he is represented at the Toledo Museum
of Art and the Albright-Knox Art Gallery, Buffalo. His
canvases are free, calligraphic abstractions of landscape
in which planes of pure color create space and movement.

HITTITE ART. The Hittites, an ancient Indo-European
people, immigrated to Asia in the 3d millennium B.C. and
established a powerful empire in eastern central Anatolia.
They developed a great civilization that influenced for
many centuries the entire Middle and Near East. They
themselves, however, were influenced by Mesopotamian
civilization, adapting to their own needs many of its customs, arts, and languages and often borrowing motifs from
Hurrian art, as well as from that of Syria and Mesopotamia. As early as the second half of the 3d millennium B.C. the Hittite Old Empire was firmly established
and had begun its expansion to the south. Later, Hittite
tribes invaded Syria and Palestine and extended their fron-
tiers to the Aegean Sea.

In the 2d millennium, early in the Old Kingdom period
(1778–1450 B.C.), the Hittite king Hattusilis I made Hattusas his capital. Hattusas, near the modern Turkish village of Boghazkeuy south of the Halys River, was built
on a rocky height in central Anatolia and strongly fortified. Hattusilis led his forces through the Taurus Mountains and conquered Yamkad and Aleppo. About 1600
B.C. his successor, Mursilis, raided and sacked Babylon,
the supreme power of the Middle East. *See* ANATOLIA;
BOGHAZKEUY.

The influence of Hittite civilization and art was felt
throughout the neighboring lands. The most important art
development took place in the latter half of the 2d millennium on the Anatolian plateau, where the Hittites united

the cities of eastern Anatolia into a single state. In 1200 B.C. Hattusas was attacked and burned by warriors from the north, and Hittite power in Anatolia came to an end. Remnants of the Hittites fled into northern Syria and founded the Syro-Hittite states, which flourished through the next five centuries, though attacked from time to time by the Assyrians. Some Hittites survived also in Cilicia, whose capital was Adana and where the Hittite hieroglyphic was used along with the Phoenician script. The Phrygians and Urartians, who had supplanted the Hittites, also continued to use the Old Hittite hieroglyphic. Hittite architecture and arts continued to exert their influence, and the Hittite tradition persisted to the end of the 1st millennium B.C., influencing even Greek architecture.

Military art, war strategy, and tactics were highly developed among the Hittites, who put the element of surprise to very good use in their attacks. They developed horse breeding, and they invented the light horse-drawn chariot, which they used effectively in their raids against enemy territory. They also developed the art of defense, and their cities were protected by strong fortifications. Excavations at Boghazkeuy revealed massive double stone walls surrounding the old city. Over the outer walls was a superstructure of bricks, and projecting rectangular towers at regular intervals reinforced the walls. The wall gateways were also reinforced with huge blocks of masonry. At first, building foundations were unadorned. Then the use of large cut and polished orthostates came into use, and later the orthostates were carved in relief. Later still, gateways and gate towers began to be adorned with animals carved in relief and heads projecting in the round, and finally the entire building façade had carvings in relief. This tradition, which was adopted by the Assyrians, persisted to the middle of the 1st millennium, and examples of it have been unearthed in Carchemish, Malatya, Tell Halaf, Karatepe, and elsewhere. In the gates of Boghazkeuy and Alaca Hüyük and in Carchemish there are excellent examples of sculpture in the round—sphinxes and lions with the front parts emerging fully from the block, the heads very carefully executed. *See* ALACA HUYUK; CARCHEMISH; KARATEPE; TELL HALAF.

The treasures discovered in the famous cemetery of Alaca Hüyük, dating from the 2d millennium B.C., give further evidence of the development of Hittite art. The shaft graves of the cemetery had roofs of wood logs and contained male and female dead, sometimes both in the same grave. The men were buried with their weapons, the women with their ornaments. The tombs contained a great number of utensils, toilet articles, bulls and other animal figurines, cult objects in silver and bronze, metal ornaments, jugs and goblets of gold, rhytons in the form of animals, and many metal sun disks, some adorned with figures of stags, which were the symbols of a god. Artistically executed jewelry, gold pins, rings, and beads were also found in abundance. The Hittite land contained various metals, including copper, silver, and gold, and the Hittites became skilled metalworkers. They developed metalwork to a high degree, and they knew the technique of smelting, hammering, soldering, repoussé work, and the *cire-perdue* process of casting. At Carchemish finely cut cylinder seals were found, as well as a set of exquisite figures carved on steatite, or lapis lazuli, and set in gold

caissons. These figures were reproductions of the famous reliefs discovered in the Hittite rock sanctuary at Yazilikaya, near Boghazkeuy, showing running warriors wearing short skirts, high ribbed caps, and shoes with upturned toes, as well as a great number of deities and many symbolic religious scenes. *See* YAZILIKAYA.

Hittite pottery also shows a highly developed art, and fine polychrome pottery from the period of the Old Kingdom has been unearthed. It is in various shapes with geometric or stylized designs in black, red, and white paint. Later pottery from the Empire period is wheel-made, usually red, with graceful shapes.

The Hittites had many religious cults, and many monuments have been found, dedicated to various deities. Five temples have been discovered in Boghazkeuy, with many small rooms around a paved court. The cella of the temples, where the enthroned god stood, was approached indirectly through two small rooms on its left. Stone idols from Kültepe show the body in the form of a disk, covered with geometric designs, a long neck supporting the head. Sometimes, on the more primitive idols, there are two or even three heads, but with only one pair of eyes between them. *See* KULTEPE.

In writing, the Hittites used both hieroglyphic and cuneiform; Hittite hieroglyphics have been found carved on stone and rock. They were the first to use the art of writing for historical records, which was later adopted by the Assyrian king Shalmaneser I (ca. 1280 B.C.). At Carchemish two historical friezes still survive, one of which depicts the celebration of the rebuilding of a god's temple and the return of the god to its shrine.

Excavations in Boghazkeuy revealed thousands of Hittite clay tablets, most of them dating from the imperial age of the great king Suppiluliumas I (1380–1346 B.C.) and some from the earlier Old Hittite Kingdom (1778–1450 B.C.). Written in cuneiform characters, they relate much of the history of the Hittites, their customs and religious beliefs, their rituals, laws, royal decrees, and treaties with other nations. From these we learn of King Hattusilis III's treaty with Rameses II of Egypt, with whom Hattusilis, who rebuilt Hattusas in the early 13th century B.C., maintained a correspondence. Hattusilis was also in correspondence with the Kassite kings of Babylonia and was the writer of the first known autobiography. Public laws governed every phase of the life of the Hittites: morals, marriage, dowry, divorce, property, crime, religious life, and social and economic conditions.

Various peoples inhabited the land of the Hittites; although the ruling classes preferred the Hittite language, the mixed population also used their own languages, and tablets discovered in many sites are written in languages other than Hittite. Many unearthed law tablets are bilingual—Hittite and Akkadian or Sumerian. Cuneiform inscriptions discovered in Karatepe are also bilingual, and a Hittite tablet with cuneiform inscriptions was found in Tarsus, as well as a conical bulla with Hittite hieroglyphics. A great number of the Boghazkeuy tablets are now in the Istanbul museum; others are in the former State Museums in Berlin, the British Museum in London, and the Louvre in Paris. *See* TARSUS.

BIBLIOGRAPHY. E. Neufeld, *The Hittite Laws*, London, 1951; O. R.

Meindert Hobbema, *The Waterwheel.* Louvre, Paris. The artist was a pupil of Jacob van Ruisdael.

Gurney, *The Hittites*, 2d ed., Baltimore, 1961; S. Lloyd, *The Art of the Ancient Near East*, London, 1961; L. Woolley, *The Art of the Middle East*, New York, 1961; A. L. Oppenheim, *Ancient Mesopotamia*, Chicago, 1964.

LUCILLE VASSARDAKI

HITTORFF, JACQUES IGNACE. French architect (1793–1867). He worked in Paris. His early travels in Sicily, where he made controversial archaeological studies on polychromy in ancient architecture, predisposed him to revive external polychromy on contemporary buildings. Although the colored enameled plaques that he suggested for the exterior of his St-Vincent-de-Paul (1824–44) were not carried out, he achieved brilliant polychromy in such works as the Cirque des Champs Elysées and the Cirque d'Hiver. Hittorff's most famous building is the Gare du Nord (1861–65), also originally polychromatic on the interior. His interest in archaeological colorism led him to assist Ingres with the architectural backgrounds of many of his paintings.

BIBLIOGRAPHY. L. Hautecoeur, *Histoire de l'architecture classique en France*, vol. 6, Paris, 1955.

HITZIG, G. H. FRIEDRICH. German architect (1811–81). He worked in Berlin. After studying in Paris and working as an assistant of Schinkel, Hitzig designed buildings following the eclectic mode of the mid-century. Some of his work presages later neobaroque and academic modes.

BIBLIOGRAPHY. H. R. Hitchcock, *Architecture, Nineteenth and Twentieth Centuries*, Baltimore, 1958.

HIUNKAKU, KYOTO. Japanese Buddhist temple within the compound of the Nishi Honganji in Kyoto. Although definite proof is lacking, it is commonly thought that this building was constructed from materials that were moved, sometime between 1615 and 1623, from the Jurakudai Palace (1586–90) of Hideyoshi after the palace's demolition in 1592. The three-storied building was modeled after the Kinkakuji and the Ginkakuji. It faces a pond, and the asymmetrical layout of its curved and triangular gables creates a setting of unusual beauty. *See* GINKAKUJI; KINKAKUJI; NISHI HONGANJI, KYOTO.

BIBLIOGRAPHY. Tokyo National Museum, *Pageant of Japanese Art*, vol. 6: *Architecture and Gardens*, Tokyo, 1952; R. T. Paine and A. Soper, *The Art and Architecture of Japan*, Baltimore, 1955.

HIZEN. Province in northwestern Kyushu, Japan, that is the closest to Korea. Here the Korean influence was strong during the 16th and 17th centuries. The Karatsu kilns were located in Hizen, and early blue-and-white porcelains in the Korean manner are frequently called Hizen ware. *See* JAPAN: CERAMICS.

HOBAN, JAMES. American architect-builder (ca. 1762–1831). He was born in Ireland. He designed the Old South Carolina State House in the 1780s. His buildings in Washington, D.C., include the White House (1792), derived from Gibbsian models, and Blodget's Hotel (1797). He was associated with the construction of the Capitol (1793–1802) and was also active in Philadelphia. *See* WASHINGTON, D.C.

HOBBEMA, MEINDERT (Meyndert; Meijndert). Dutch landscape painter (b. Amsterdam, 1638; d. there, 1709). Hobbema was the son of Lubbert Meyn(d)ertsz. He seems to have been the first in his family to adopt the surname Hobbema, and apparently did so as a young man. He is known to have been a pupil of Jacob van Ruisdael, presumably after June, 1657, when Ruisdael settled in Amsterdam. The names of such artists as Salomon van Ruysdael, Cornelis Vroom, and even Anthonie van Borssum are mentioned in connection with the development of Hobbema's style, however, and it is possible that he had some contact with their work. Nevertheless, it is Ruisdael's style that is most important to the understanding of Hobbema's development and style. In 1668 Hobbema was appointed wine gauger of the Amsterdam tax office; it is often stated that he stopped painting after this appointment. While it is true that his production fell off in quantity after 1668, some of his most famous pictures date from these late years.

Hobbema's earliest dated work, *River Scene* (1658; Detroit, Institute of Arts), seems basically dependent on the manner of Salomon van Ruysdael for the composition and for the handling of details, such as the trees. However, the quality of brushwork as well as the use of color betray his basic indebtedness to Ruisdael. For the most part Hobbema's river views are early works. Until about 1662 Hobbema's development was still based on the style of his master. His *Forest Swamp* (1662; Melbourne, National Gallery of Victoria) is based on an early etching by Ruisdael. In 1663 Hobbema moved out on his own with such works as the *Landscape with Trees and a Causeway* (Blessington, Ireland, Sir Alfred Beit Collection). During the late 1660s Hobbema created a number of paintings that clearly place him, with Ruisdael, among the great landscape painters of Holland.

In 1669 Hobbema created the work that is rightly considered his masterpiece, *The Avenue, Middelharnis* (London, National Gallery). The general conception of the London picture is certainly based on similar spatial and pictorial ideas of Ruisdael (*Wheatfields*, New York, Metropolitan Museum), but the painting is far from an imitative work and builds on the concepts established by his teacher. In many ways *The Avenue, Middelharnis* is the last great landscape painting of the golden age of Dutch painting.

BIBLIOGRAPHY. E. Michel, *Hobbema et les paysagistes de son temps en Hollande*, Paris, 1890; J. Rosenberg, "Hobbema," *Jahrbuch der Preussischen Kunstsammlungen*, XLVIII, 1927; G. Broulhiet, *Meindert Hobbema (1638–1709)*, Paris, 1938; W. Stechow, "The Early Years of Hobbema," *Art Quarterly*, Spring, 1959; N. Maclaren, *National Gallery Catalogues: The Dutch School*, London, 1960; W. Stechow, *Dutch Landscape Painting of the Seventeenth Century*, London, 1966.   LEONARD J. SLATKES

HOCHST PORCELAIN. Höchst was the scene of extensive faïence and porcelain production, the latter beginning in 1746 and the former about 1751. It came under the protection of the Elector of Mainz from 1765 until 1796, when difficulties with the French forced its closing. Of a coarse-bodied opaque composition covered with soft milk-white glaze, the output of Höchst often resembled Frankenthal and followed the fashion in going from rococo to neoclassical design.

BIBLIOGRAPHY. K. Roeder and M. Oppenheim, *Das Höchster Porzellan...*, Mainz, 1930.

HO CH'U-PING, TOMB OF, HSIN-P'ING. Chinese tomb located in Shensi Province. It contains the only known large-scale example of stone sculpture that can be dated to the Earlier Han dynasty. The principal work at the site is the *Horse Trampling Barbarian*, a representation of a horse standing over a prone human figure. Ho Ch'ü-ping, who died in 117 B.C., was a celebrated general of the Han emperor Wu-ti, and the subject of the sculpture is a probable reference to the general's triumphs over the barbarian tribes of Kansu Province and central Asia. *See also* CHINA: SCULPTURE.

BIBLIOGRAPHY. V. Ségalen et al., *Mission archéologique en Chine*, 2 vols., Paris, 1923-24.

HODEGETRIA MADONNA. Byzantine type of Madonna and Child in which the Madonna holds the Christ on her left arm. Unlike the motherly Eleousa Madonna type, the Hodegetria Madonna is hieratic. The Child exhibits no awareness of His mother; He gazes out frontally, blesses with His right hand, and holds a scroll in His left. *See* ELEOUSA MADONNA.

BIBLIOGRAPHY. O. M. Dalton, *Byzantine Art and Archaeology*, Oxford, 1911.

HODGES, CHARLES HOWARD. English painter and engraver (b. England, 1764; d. Amsterdam, 1837). After studying with John Raphael Smith, Hodges left England for Holland in 1788. He was equally successful at painting and engraving portraits, but his best works are portrait plates done after 1800, many after Reynolds. He also engraved romantic genre scenes.

BIBLIOGRAPHY. C. J. Davenport, *Mezzotints*, London, 1904.

Hodegetria Madonna, Byzantine icon, 1342. National Museum, Sophia.

Feb. 1912 Selbstbild. F. Hodler

HODGKINS, FRANCES. British painter (b. Dunedin, New Zealand, 1870; d. Dorsetshire, 1947). She went to England in 1900. From 1902 to 1912 she lived in Paris, where she taught at the Académie Colarossi and at her own school. She was primarily a painter of water-color landscapes and still lifes.

BIBLIOGRAPHY. A. R. Howell, *Frances Hodgkins: Four Vital Years*, London, 1951.

HODLER, FERDINAND. Swiss painter (b. Bern, 1853; d. Geneva, 1918). He studied in Thun and in Geneva with Menn, a landscape painter, and visited Spain in 1878. Hodler's earlier work, linear and detailed in treatment and derived from Holbein and Millet, shows his native leaning toward philosophical attitude and dramatic figure composition, for example, *The Meditating Peasant* (1882) and *Le Guerrier furieux* (1884; both Geneva, Museum of Art and History). In *Night* (1890; Bern, Art Museum), a symbolic portrayal of sleep, nightmare, and death, Hodler attempted to use the firm outline and strong naturalism of his style to depict mystical or transcendental ideas and feelings. He was in Paris in 1891 for the exhibition of *Night* at the Salon and came in contact with the French symbolists and also with the paintings of Gauguin, both of which probably further deepened his already strongly idealistic orientation.

By the middle 1890s Hodler had developed his characteristic style, a fusion of the linear and the monumental. Details and expressive contours are greatly simplified, and the evocative effect is dependent on the rhythmic lines, spatial relationships, and grave, ritualistic gestures of the stylized figures, for example, the robed men of *Eurythmia* (1895) and the five seated female nudes of *Day* (1900; both Bern, Art Museum). More complicated groupings of heroicized figures are found in his historical subjects, for example, *The Retreat after the Battle of Marignano* (1900; Zurich, Schweizerisches Landsmuseum) and the mural *The Departure of the Jena Volunteers* (1908; Jena, Schiller University).

Despite their sculpturesque elements Hodler's paintings, including his panels, hold to the surface in a decorative flatness resulting from their pale coloration, the pattern of repeated shapes, emphasized silhouettes, and a composition that keeps all forms parallel to the picture plane and to each other. This formal device, which he called "parallelism," was an outgrowth of Hodler's pantheistic philosophy in which man and nature were linked by the same events and swept by the same rhythms. It is mostly in this rhythm of linear arabesques constantly repeated in both small details and larger units that Hodler is related to the Art Nouveau decorative style of his time. Parallelism and symmetry sometimes reached an extreme in his late landscapes, such as *Thunersee* (1905; Geneva, Museum of Art and History), but these paintings are also marked by warmer color and a more personal handling of paint.

BIBLIOGRAPHY. E. Bender and W. Y. Müller, *Die Kunst Ferdinand Hodlers*, 2 vols., Zurich, 1923–41; F. Hodler, *Hodler: Köpfe und Gestalten*, text by W. Ueberwasser, photographs by R. Spreng, Zurich, 1947; W. Hugelshofer, *Ferdinand Hodler*, Zurich, 1952.

JEROME VIOLA

Ferdinand Hodler, *Self-portrait*, 1912. Art Museum. Basel.

HOECKE, JAN VAN DEN. Flemish painter (1611–51). He was born in Antwerp. He is said to have studied under Rubens, and, in fact, Van den Hoecke's large-size religious and decorative canvases show that he was influenced by the master. In his later works he drew inspiration from Anthony van Dyck. He collaborated with Daniel Seghers and Paul de Vos.

BIBLIOGRAPHY. J. F. van den Branden, *Geschiedenis der Antwerpsche Schilderschool*, Antwerp, 1883.

HOECKE, ROBERT VAN DEN. Flemish painter (b. Antwerp, 1622; d. 1668). A half brother of Jan van den Hoecke, Robert is primarily known as the author of landscapes and winter scenes in the tradition of Jan Breughel I, which are animated with numerous delicately executed small figures. He also painted battles and encampments, and, more rarely, interiors in the manner of Cornelis Saftleven.

BIBLIOGRAPHY. J. F. van den Branden, *Geschiedenis der Antwerpsche Schilderschool*, Antwerp, 1883.

HOEFNAGEL, GEORG (Joris). Flemish miniature painter and engraver (b. Antwerp, 1542; d. Vienna, 1600). He was a student of Hans Bol. Hoefnagel traveled widely in Spain, England, Italy, and France. Much in demand for his naturalistic style, he worked at the court of Bavaria, in Prague and Vienna for Emperor Rudolf II, and for Archduke Ferdinand at Innsbruck. There he executed his masterpiece, a missal with 500 illuminations (Vienna, Austrian National Library).

BIBLIOGRAPHY. R. H. Wilenski, *Flemish Painters, 1430–1830*, 2 vols., New York, 1960.

HOET, GERARD. Dutch painter of genre, portraits, and history; also printmaker, miniaturist, and art dealer (b. Zaltbommel, 1648; d. The Hague, 1733). He was a pupil of his father, Moses Hoet, and of Warner van Rijsen. Hoet was active in The Hague, in Paris, and in Utrecht, where he settled and helped found an art academy in 1696. Hoet worked in The Hague from 1715 until his death. He also wrote on art.

HOETGER, BERNHARD. German sculptor and architect (b. Hörde, 1874; d. Interlaken, Switzerland, 1949). After serving as an apprentice for a stone carver in Detmold, he studied under Janssen at the Düsseldorf Academy (1898). Hoetger lived in Paris (1900–07) and exhibited in the Salon d'Automne (1905). From 1911 to 1919 he resided in Darmstadt, where he was the leader of a colony of artists. He left Germany in 1933 because of the Nazi regime and traveled through France, Switzerland, and the Iberian Peninsula.

His sculptural style went through an evolution from an initial influence of Rodin to the influence of archaic Greece before he finally arrived at his own expression of human tragedy, using old women and sickly children as subjects. In architecture he was also eclectic. He was influenced by romanticism in the reconstruction of Böttcherstrasse in Bremen and by Art Nouveau and cubism in building the Paula Modersohn-Becker House, also in Bremen, which now houses the Paula Modersohn-Becker Collection.

BIBLIOGRAPHY. C. E. Uphoff, *Bernhard Hoetger*, 2d ed., Leipzig, 1922; A Thiele, *Bernhard Hoetger*, Recklinghausen, 1960.

HOFBURG, VIENNA. Complex of buildings in Austria. This vast ensemble, which was the official residence of the emperor of Austria-Hungary, includes buildings of three periods: a Gothic nucleus around the Schweizerhof, a series of baroque wings known as "In der Berg," and a 19th-century group facing the Heldenplatz.

BIBLIOGRAPHY. M. Dreger, *Baugeschichte der K. K. Hofburg in Wien bis zum XIX Jahrhunderte*, Vienna, 1914.

HOFER, CARL. German painter (b. Karlsruhe, 1878; d. Berlin, 1955). He studied with Hans Thoma for two years at the academy in Karlsruhe. At that time he admired the romantic allegorical art of Böcklin. Hofer was in Rome from 1903 to 1908; there he saw the painting of Hans von Marées and was influenced by it. He lived for five years in Paris, where he came to know and was influenced by Cézanne. He became a member of the Neue Künstlervereinigung in 1909, the year of its inception, and was represented in its first exhibition in Munich. He traveled for a year in India before settling in Berlin, and had his first one-man show a year later. During World War I he was interned in France. In 1918 he was appointed a teacher in the Berlin Academy.

It was in the atmosphere of bitterness and disillusionment of postwar Berlin that Hofer evolved the style by which he came to be known. In 1930 he turned to abstract painting, to return a year later to his former style. In 1933 he was dismissed from his teaching position and his art was classified as "degenerate" by the Nazis. In 1934 he won second prize for painting at the Carnegie Institute International in Pittsburgh with *Pastorale* and, in 1938, first prize for *Wind* (both Pittsburgh, Carnegie Institute). In 1943 his studio was bombed and many pictures were destroyed. In 1945 he was appointed director of the Hochschule für bildende Künste in Berlin. He was given a large retrospective in 1946 in Berlin.

Prior to World War I Hofer painted full-size figures like those of Marées, but transposed in the manner of Cézanne. Though he exhibited with the expressionists, he insisted that he was not one of them. After the war his figures lost their warmth and earthiness and became lean and emaciated, with protruding bones and large, dark eyes full of questioning. He painted clowns, sleeping figures, card players, wan servant girls, and other figures, who, like Picasso's Blue Period creatures, live a marginal existence. Hofer's people look like wooden mannequins. He favored grays with accents of hard, bright color. Contours assume an unexpected and unnatural sharpness, and forms a rigid angularity. The same aura of melancholy and despair appears in the landscapes from Ticino and the stark, rather stiff still-life paintings. In 1950 his works assumed a new freedom of treatment and an increased heaviness of contour.

BIBLIOGRAPHY. A. Jannasch, *Carl Hofer*, Potsdam, 1948; C. Hofer, *Aus Leben und Kunst*, Berlin, 1952.

ROBERT REIFF

HOFF, ROBERT VAN'T. Dutch-English architect (1887–   ). Hoff was born in Rotterdam and studied architecture. Before World War I he visited the United States, where he was greatly impressed by the work of Frank Lloyd Wright. One of the original members of de Stijl, Hoff made his greatest contribution with two very

Carl Hofer, *The Green Banner*. Hofer Collection, Berlin.

Wrightian houses built in Huis ter Heide, near Utrecht, in 1916. He left the de Stijl movement in 1920. Since then he has lived in England.

BIBLIOGRAPHY. H. L. C. Jaffé, *De Stijl, 1917–1931*, Amsterdam, 1956.

HOFFLER, JOSEF. German sculptor (b. Kaiserslautern, 1879; d. Bergzabern, 1915). Trained in wood carving as a young man, Höffler traveled through Germany and Austria working in the furniture trade. He then received formal instruction in sculpture with Rümann at the Munich Academy. In 1907 Höffler exhibited with the Munich Sezession. His figures, portraits, reliefs, and animal sculptures show something of the simplification and emotional expressiveness of contemporary expressionism, and some have an austere and forbidding quality.

HOFFMAN, MALVINA. American sculptor (b. New York City, 1887; d. there, 1966). She studied painting with John White Alexander and sculpture with Herbert Adams and

Gutzon Borglum in New York and with Rodin in Paris.

She received numerous honors, both professional and academic. One of her earliest awards was accorded at the 1911 Salon in Paris. In 1917 and again in 1921 she received important American medals at National Academy of Design exhibitions. In later years she won a number of decorations from foreign governments, including the French Legion of Honor.

The Harvard University *Bacon Memorial*, dedicated to Harvard students who were killed in World War I, discloses Hoffman's capacity to personify specific, somber sentiment and to reinterpret with sensitivity settings belonging to traditional epochs of the history of sculpture (in this case, the English medieval reclining-knight type). *Russian Bacchanale* (Paris, Luxembourg Museum) and *Pavlova Gavotte* (Detroit Institute of Arts) testify to a certain deftness of interpretation of the figure in space, with a personally directed charm that helps to offset the eclectic approach. *Crusader* heads in the Art Institute of Chicago and the Metropolitan Museum of Art in New York denote Hoffman's considerable technical gifts, although these, like many of her smaller works, convey a graceful sentimentality deriving ultimately from the sterner tenderness of Rodin and much medieval sculpture. Her work is represented in the Brooklyn Institute of Arts and Science, the Norton Gallery in West Palm Beach, the National Academy of Design, the Stockholm Museum of Art, and the Academy in Rome, as well as in relief panels on various public buildings.

She was influential as a writer on sculptural methodology. Her best-known book is *Sculpture Inside and Out*, which is useful for its detailed treatment of professional handling of various media.

BIBLIOGRAPHY. M. Hoffman, *Sculpture Inside and Out*, New York, 1939.

JOHN C. GALLOWAY

HOFFMANN, JOSEPH. Austrian architect and designer (b. Pirnitz, 1870; d. Vienna, 1956). A student of Otto Wagner, Hoffmann was one of the leading European architects at the turn of the century. He founded the influential Wiener Werkstätte in 1903, a major focus of design activity running counter to Art Nouveau. His first important work was the Convalescent Home at Purkersdorf (1903–04), a simplified composition of white stucco walls penetrated by precisely incised window openings. Of more historical value is the Palais Stoclet in Brussels (1905–11). Asymmetrically composed of pure planar elements, it is prophetic of de Stijl.

BIBLIOGRAPHY. J. F. M. Hoffmann, *Josef Hoffmann*, ed. A. Weiser, Geneva, 1930; G. Veronesi, *Josef Hoffmann*, Milan, 1956.

HOFFMANN, LUDWIG. German architect (1851–1932). He worked in Berlin. Such a work as the Leipzig Imperial Law Courts indicates the conservative and traditional quality of Hoffmann's designs by its academic character. He was appointed Berlin city architect in 1896.

BIBLIOGRAPHY. F. Stahl, *Ludwig Hoffmann*, Berlin, 1914.

HOFLEHNER, RUDOLF. Austrian sculptor (1916–   ). Born in Linz, Hoflehner studied forging and welding at the School of Mechanical Engineering there before attending the Academy of Fine Arts in Vienna. His sculpture

was abstract until he visited Greece (1954); he has since turned to the figure, for example, *Doric Figure* (1958; Vienna, Künstlerhaus).

HOFMANN, HANS. German-American painter (b. Weissenberg, Germany, 1880; d. New York City, 1966). He settled in the United States in 1932. He was a leader of the abstract expressionist school in the United States and the teacher of many outstanding younger painters.

Hofmann studied in Munich from 1904 to 1907. From 1907 to 1914 he painted in Paris, where he met the cubist and Fauvist masters. His first one-man show was at the Paul Cassirer Gallery in Berlin in 1910. From 1915 until 1932 Hofmann directed his own school in Munich, where he attracted an international following. He visited the United States several times, teaching at the University of California (Berkeley) and elsewhere before opening his own school in New York in 1934.

Hofmann's style, not fully abstract until about 1939, was thoughtfully developed out of Fauvist and cubist principles and was to some extent conditioned by expressionism. He was always devoted to bold experimentation with color, remarking that painting means building with color.

He was given a one-man show at the California Palace of the Legion of Honor, San Francisco, in 1931. A major retrospective was shown at the Whitney Museum of American Art, New York, the San Francisco Museum of Art, the Walker Art Center, Minneapolis, and the Munson-Williams-Proctor Institute, Utica, in 1957. His works were shown at the Venice Biennale in 1960, and the Museum

Malvina Hoffman, *Pavlova Gavotte*. Detroit Institute of Arts.

Hofmann, *Clair de Lune Sonata*. Formerly Kootz Gallery, New York.

of Modern Art in New York gave him a retrospective in 1963.

Characteristic works by Hofmann are *The Window* (1950; New York, Metropolitan Museum), *Magenta and Blue* (1950; Whitney Museum of American Art), and *Sanctum Sanctorum* (1962). In 1964 he gave the University of California at Berkeley forty-five of his paintings, together with funds to construct the Hans and Maria Hofmann Memorial Galleries to house these works.

Hofmann typically worked with a notably liberated thrust of vibrant, often pure color, and in shapes that remotely suggest an origin in nature or man-made objects. Certain of his pieces after 1960, however, include with irregular patterns a nucleus of clean-edged rectangles, the result being a powerful synthesis of geometry and free-form abstraction. He was consistently one of the most vigorous of the action group. There is no question that abstract expressionism in America owes as much to Hofmann as to any individual artist. His painting and his teaching were of indispensable force.

BIBLIOGRAPHY. H. Hofmann, *Search for the Real and Other Essays*, Andover, Mass., 1948; A. C. Ritchie, *Abstract Painting and Sculpture in America*, New York, 1951; F. S. Wight, *Hans Hofmann*, Berkeley, 1957; C. Greenberg, *Hofmann*, Paris, 1961; W. C. Seitz, *Hans Hofmann* (catalog), New York, 1963.   JOHN C. GALLOWAY

HOGAI (Kano Hogai). Japanese painter (1828–88). Hōgai was trained in the Kanō tradition, and his talents were discovered by Ernest Fenollosa, an American scholar who directed the attention of the Japanese to their traditional art. Hōgai became a pioneer in the movement to reestablish this tradition in modern Japan. *See* KANO SCHOOL.

BIBLIOGRAPHY. N. Ueno, ed., *Japanese Arts and Crafts in the Meiji Era* (Centenary Culture Council Series, Japanese Culture in the Meiji Era, vol. 8), Tokyo, 1948.

HOGAN. Navaho hut built of mud daubed on a rough log frame, usually rectangular with a pyramidal roof.

HOGARTH, WILLIAM. English painter (b. London, 1697; d. there, 1764). Hogarth's initial training was as an engraver, and his printmaking activity was very important throughout his career. In the late 1720s, having practiced engraving for about a decade, he began to give more serious attention to painting. He had studied in Sir James Thornhill's art school and in 1729 married his master's daughter. To earn a living he turned to portrait painting and quickly perfected the small-scale portrait group, or conversation piece. His masterpiece in this form is *Children Playing "The Indian Emperor" Before an Audience* (ca. 1731; Earl of Ilchester Collection).

Hogarth soon found a more remunerative form of activity than painting conversation pieces: he began to compose series of narrative pictures that were designed to appeal to a large public and were disseminated through prints. The first series, *A Harlot's Progress*, was engraved in 1732. It consisted of a half-dozen pictures depicting the story of a country girl who comes to the city and falls into evil ways. In this first series it appears probable that the idea of a sequence grew more or less spontaneously while Hogarth was working. But the great popular success of the prints prompted him to work out other series, notably *The Rake's Progress* (engraved in 1735) and *Marriage à la Mode* (painted between 1743 and 1745; London, National Gallery). The latter is Hogarth's masterpiece. The paintings in the earlier series had been executed primarily with the engraver in mind, but Hogarth clearly intended the *Marriage à la Mode* series to exist in terms of both the original paintings and the engravings executed after them. The paintings themselves are among the most brilliant performances in the whole range of British art.

Ironically, in spite of his success, Hogarth had a lifelong aspiration to be a serious historical painter. He made numerous attempts in this vein throughout his career, but these works were coolly received in his own day and have since come to be regarded primarily as historical curiosities.

Hogarth's paintings stand as the most important manifestations of rococo influences in England. At his best he can take his place comfortably beside the finest of his French contemporaries. His paintings have the sparkle, vigor, and decorative interest of the Continental rococo, but there is an additional fresh forthright dimension in the social aspect of his subject matter that anticipates developments in the rest of Europe. In series after series of paintings and prints he relentlessly attacked the morals and manners of the British aristocracy and middle class—their social behavior, entertainments, law courts, and government. In this he was aided by a prodigious visual memory that enabled him to capture the comic character of individual poses, expressions, and habits as well as entire scenes, which he placed in theatrical settings, based in part on his own experience of the English theater. He is thus the great originator of the satiric tradition in English art.

He also made a contribution of importance to the history of art theory. In 1753 he published *The Analysis of Beauty*, a loosely organized and discursive book, but one containing many suggestive ideas. Possibly the most important of these involves observations concerning the expressive qualities of lines and shapes apart from the objects represented.

William Hogarth, *The Calais Gate*. National Gallery, London. The great originator of the satiric tradition in English art.

The principal groups of Hogarth's paintings are in London, in the National Gallery and Sir John Soane's Museum. His finest painting in America is probably *The Lady's Last Stake* (Buffalo, Albright-Knox Art Gallery). There are examples of his conversation pieces at the Philadelphia and Metropolitan Museums of Art. Single portraits are more widely scattered, with notable examples in the Frick Collection, New York; the Worcester Museum; and the Henry E. Huntington Library and Art Gallery, San Marino, Calif. His portraits, although unpopular, are straightforward and powerful delineations of character unusual for their time.

BIBLIOGRAPHY. A. Dobson, *William Hogarth*, London, 1907; A. P. Oppé, *The Drawings of Hogarth*, London, 1948; R. B. Beckett, *Hogarth*, London, 1949; W. Hogarth, *The Analysis of Beauty*, ed. J. Burke, Oxford, 1955; F. Antal, *Hogarth and His Place in European Art*, London, 1962; R. Paulson, *Hogarth's Graphic Works*, 2 vols., New Haven, 1965.

ROBERT R. WARK

HOGER, FRITZ. German architect (b. Beckenreihe, Holstein, 1877; d. Bad Segeberg, Holstein, 1949). He was a leading expressionist during the 1920s, comparable to Eric Mendelsohn. Höger's angular Chilehaus in Hamburg (1923) is one of the largest and most typical of the mode.

HOHENSTAUFEN ART. German and Italian art connected with the Swabian house of Hohenstaufen, which came to power with the election of Conrad III as German king in 1138. Succeeding Hohenstaufens—Frederick I (Barbarossa), Henry VI, Otto IV, and Frederick II—were also crowned Holy Roman emperors, ruling until 1250. Although much German art, and particularly castle architecture, was connected with the ruling family, their distinctive contribution was made during the reign of Frederick II (1215–50) in Apulia and Sicily. A network of castles, continuing the Norman tradition, was erected throughout, and north of, Apulia by the vigorous emperor, who may have had a hand in designing some of them. Most of them, like Castel del Monte, Lucera, and Lagopesole, are symmetrical, geometric masses with powerful masonry. Frederick also fostered a revival of classical forms, evident in architectural details and sculpture, which

Hokusai, *On the Road*. Woodcut. Part of his intense and passionate curiosity for all living things.

was to have a generative effect on the early development of the Renaissance in Italy. *See* MONTE, CASTEL DEL.

BIBLIOGRAPHY. O. E. Wulfing, *Burgen der Hohenstaufen*, 2 vols., Düsseldorf, 1958-60; C. A. Willemsen and D. Odenthal, *Apulia: Imperial Splendor in Southern Italy*, New York, 1959.

HOHOKAM INDIANS. A North American Indian culture centered in the Gila and Salt Rivers area of Arizona near present-day Phoenix. An important site is Snaketown. The Hohokam group flourished from the last few centuries B.C. until about A.D. 1400. Its origin remains unknown, although its roots undoubtedly extend much further back into prehistory. Primarily an agricultural people, the Hohokam are believed to be the first North American Indians to practice systematic irrigation of crops.

The Hohokam are best known for their pottery, though an important secondary tradition of small stone sculpture, including mosaic-inlaid plaques, also existed. Figures of terra cotta, usually quite small, and copper bells cast in the lost-wax technique were produced in the intermediate centuries. Both bowls and palettes of stone, many of them decorated with animal or amphibian forms, also appeared. Since shell ornaments of the Hohokam involved a Pacific Ocean material, it is apparent that trade was widespread.

During the late prehistoric, or classic, period prior to Spanish occupation, walled villages enclosing single-storied, contiguous dwellings were developed, possibly as a result of collaboration with an intrusive people sometimes called the Salado. Low mounds topped by temporary houses sometimes appeared within adobe-walled areas. Ball courts similar to those of the Mayas were present. There are remark-able differences in architecture, as well as in many general cultural traits, between the Hohokam and neighboring Pueblo tribes.

Among the several impressive types of pottery produced by the Hohokam are Sweetwater red-on-gray and Snaketown red-on-buff of the early periods; Santa Cruz red-on-buff, Kana-a black-on-white, and Lino black-on-gray, dating probably from about A.D. 500; and Sacaton red-on-buff and Casa Grande wares from later phases. Hohokam vessels compare favorably in the technical sense with those of the Pueblo peoples, though they are not as well known. Hohokam art is extensively represented in the Gila Pueblo Collection, now located at the University of Arizona, and in the Arizona State Museum.

As architects, the Hohokam are notable for their adaptation of communal dwelling units to their desert culture and for their priority in the development of canal irrigation. As potters and sculptors they are distinguished for their technical proficiency in the use of terra cotta and for their unique (in the Southwest) copper casting of ornaments.

See also NORTH AMERICAN INDIAN ART (SOUTHWEST).

BIBLIOGRAPHY. H. S. Gladwin et al., *Excavations at Snaketown...*, 4 vols., Globe, Ariz., 1937–48; E. W. Haury, *The Excavation of Los Muertos and Neighboring Ruins...*, Cambridge, Mass., 1945.

JOHN C. GALLOWAY

HOITSU (Sakai Hoitsu). Japanese painter (1761–1828). The younger brother of the lord of Himeji, Hōitsu studied under many painters of different schools. He particularly admired the art of Kōrin, which he revived. He was also indebted to the Shijō school for the handling of naturalistic details, which he combined with brilliant and strong colors in a decorative manner. See KORIN; SHIJO SCHOOL.

BIBLIOGRAPHY. T. Akiyama, *Japanese Painting* [Geneva?], 1961.

HOKKEDO. Japanese Buddhist temple within the compound of the Tōdaiji in Nara. It is also known as the Sangatsudō (Hall of the Month of March), since the Hokke (Lotus Sūtra) ceremony is held in this hall every March. It is one of the few original buildings of the Tōdaiji to survive a series of destructions. The original plan, dating from 733 or 746, was enlarged about 1196 by the addition of a large anteroom built across the south façade. At the same time the roof was relaid to cover both structures, creating an unusual profile. Excellent clay statues of the Nara period can be seen here. See TODAIJI, NARA.

BIBLIOGRAPHY. Tokyo National Museum, *Pageant of Japanese Art*, vol. 6: *Architecture and Gardens*, Tokyo, 1952; R. T. Paine and A. Soper, *The Art and Architecture of Japan*, Baltimore, 1955.

HOKUSAI (Katsushika Hokusai). Japanese Ukiyo-e printmaker (1760–1849). Hokusai studied with Shunshō and first made prints of actors and wrestlers in the Katsukawa style and of girls in the Kiyonaga manner. During his long career he studied many other styles of painting and prints, for he never tired of experimenting. He was a man of eccentric nature, changing his name more than thirty times and his residence more than ninety. His personality is vividly revealed in many of his dynamic, restless landscape scenes, in which he captured men in the most unusual relationship to nature. The proportions of men to landscape are often alarmingly exaggerated and distorted, with men dwarfed against a background of the terrifying force of nature. In 1807 he began illustrating many books by the novelist Bakin. Hokusai's *Manga Sketchbooks* are the fascinating record of an intense and passionate curiosity for all living things. See KATSUKAWA SCHOOL; KIYONAGA; SHUNSHO; UKIYO-E.

BIBLIOGRAPHY. L. V. Ledoux, *Japanese Prints, Hokusai and Hiroshige, in the Collection of Louis V. Ledoux*, Princeton, 1952; J. R. Hillier, *Hokusai*, New York, 1955; J. A. Michener, *Japanese Prints*, Rutland, Vt., 1959.

HOLABIRD, JOHN AUGUR, see HOLABIRD AND ROOT.

HOLABIRD, WILLIAM, see HOLABIRD AND ROCHE.

HOLABIRD AND ROCHE. American architectural firm of William Holabird (1854–1923) and Martin Roche (1855–1927). Their partnership was formed in 1883 and lasted until 1923. Best known for business structures, they pioneered the development of the skyscraper. Innovators in structural matters, they also exploited the steel frame to its full architectonic advantage. Their buildings are considered to be among the clearest statements of skeletal architecture of the period and are ranked as major achievements of the Chicago school. The Marquette Building (1894) was the first in a series that was remarkably consistent in style and treatment of the façade. Elements common to these structures include Chicago windows, continuous piers with recessed spandrels, and largely uniform exteriors. Their Tacoma Building (1887–89) is considered the first building whose exterior is completely supported by a skeleton frame.

BIBLIOGRAPHY. C. W. Condit, *The Rise of the Skyscraper*, Chicago, 1952.

HOLABIRD AND ROOT. American architectural firm, established in 1927 following the death of Martin Roche of the partnership of Holabird and Roche. Holabird's son, John Augur Holabird (1886–1945), and John W. Root (b. 1887) inherited or secured commissions for some of Chicago's best-known skyscrapers, notably the original Daily News Building, the Palmolive Building, and the Board of Trade Building. In 1935 the firm added a new wing to Richard Schmidt's Henrotin Hospital in Chicago. Holabird and Root also designed the eight-story addition (built in 1960–61) to the Carson, Pirie, Scott Co. Building, which extends the long west elevation by three bays. The façade below the lintel of the second floor, however, does not achieve the brilliance of the cast-iron ornament of Sullivan and Elmslie.

BIBLIOGRAPHY. C. W. Condit, *The Chicago School of Architecture*, Chicago, 1964.

HOLBEIN, AMBROSIUS. German painter and woodcut designer (b. Augsburg, 1494; d. ca. 1519–20). Ambrosius studied with his father, Hans Holbein the Elder. He later settled in Basel, where he produced religious paintings, portraits, woodcuts, and drawings. In style, he is very close to the elder Holbein.

HOLBEIN, HANS, THE ELDER. German painter and draftsman (b. Augsburg, ca. 1465; d. Isenheim, 1524). The father of the famous Hans Holbein the Younger, the elder Holbein began his career as a painter working in the style of the Netherlandish realists of the early 15th century. Later he adopted the Renaissance style, which was beginning to predominate in the Augsburg school, to which he belonged. He worked mainly in Augsburg with short periods in Ulm, Frankfurt, and lastly Isenheim. His most important works are the altar panel from the cloister church in Weingarten (1493; Augsburg, Cathedral), which is in the Netherlandish style; the *Passion Altar* (1501; Frankfurt am Main, Städel Art Institute); and the *St. Sebastian Altar* (1516; Munich, Old Pinacothek), a work typical of his Renaissance style. Frescoes by him have recently been discovered during repairs to St. Peter's Church at Lindau.

BIBLIOGRAPHY. N. Lieb and A. Stange, *Hans Holbein der Altere*, Munich, 1960.

HOLBEIN, HANS, THE YOUNGER. German painter and designer of woodcuts and of other minor arts (b. Augsburg, 1497/98; d. London, 1543). He was the son of the late Gothic painter Hans Holbein the Elder. There is no documentation of his early years in Augsburg, and it is only from a sketch dated 1511 by the elder Holbein of his sons Hans and Ambrosius that an approximation of Hans the Younger's birth date can be made; the sketch records Hans's age as fourteen. Nothing else is known of his youth, although it is certain that he received his early artistic training from his father.

In 1515 Holbein went with his elder brother Ambrosius to Basel. There they became apprenticed to the Swiss painter Hans Herbst. His apprenticeship with Herbst was essentially a continuation of the training Holbein had received in his father's workshop and was in the general stylistic climate of the Augsburg school, whose leading master was Hans Burgkmair. The Basel style was more "classic" than Dürer's, with some influence of Italian painting, especially

PARVVLE PATRISSA, PATRIÆ VIRTVTIS ET HÆRES
 ESTO, NIHIL MAIVS MAXIMVS ORBIS HABET.
GNATVM VIX POSSVNT COELVM ET NATVRA DEDISSE,
 HVIVS QVEM PATRIS, VICTVS HONORET HONOS.
ÆQVATO TANTVM, TANTI TV FACTA PARENTIS,
 VOTA HOMINVM, VIX QVO PROGREDIANTVR, HABENT
VINCITO, VICISTI. QVOT REGES PRISCVS ADORAT
 ORBIS, NEC TE QVI VINCERE POSSIT, ERIT.

in the abundant use of ornament, which later became one of Holbein's major contributions to the design of the minor arts. Within a short time after his arrival in Basel, Holbein began to attract the patronage of the wealthy burghers and of the Humanists. One of the latter, the eminent Erasmus of Rotterdam, was to become Holbein's close friend and greatest promoter.

In 1518 Holbein made a trip to northern Italy, possibly to Milan. His style was not noticeably influenced by the trip, probably because he was already acquainted with much Italian art through intermediary sources. Upon his return to Basel in 1519, Holbein was received into the painters' guild and established his workshop. Early in 1524 he traveled in France, from Lyons south to Avignon. It is assumed that this trip was made for the purpose of broadening his artistic experience by contact with the new Renaissance court art of France.

On the advice of his friend Erasmus, Holbein set out on his first trip to London in the autumn of 1526. He carried with him letters of introduction from Erasmus to the English Humanist Thomas More and to the court of Henry VIII. He traveled down the Rhine to the Low Countries, where he stopped for a short visit with the Flemish painter Quentin Metsys (Massys) in Antwerp. Holbein had hoped, and rightly, that he could be successful as a portrait painter in the art-conscious yet art-starved English capital. It appears that he was quite successful, for upon his return to Basel two years later he purchased two houses and became a prominent figure in the local government.

Securing a city pension for his wife and children, Holbein set out in 1532 on his second trip to England, destined never to return. His fame in London was by now widespread. He received countless numbers of commissions from the German merchants, who had their colony in the steel yard, and from the royal court. Holbein became court painter to Henry VIII and established his workshop in the gate tower of the Palace of Whitehall. He produced not only portraits but also many designs for all manner of decorative and minor arts such as festival decorations, court costumes, silverware, armor, seals, and bookbindings, to name but a few. He died of the plague which swept London in October, 1543.

Holbein's works fall naturally into four periods: the first Basel period (1515–26), which can be divided into an early and late period by the trip to Italy in 1518–19; the first London period (1526–28); the second Basel period (1528–32); and the second London period (1532–43). Holbein's artistic development is not characterized by sudden or even significant changes. Instead, it is a gradual evolution of a precise impersonal style, which in his mature works is the apex of realistic painting. In contrast to his famous contemporaries Dürer and Grünewald, Holbein strove to free his art of any personal involvement with the content. He desired an objectivity through which he could discover new beauties in nature. His objective approach found its greatest fulfillment in his work as a portraitist.

The major works of the earliest Basel period are the

Hans Holbein the Younger, *Edward VI as a Child*. National Gallery, Washington, D.C.

double portrait *Burgomaster Jakob Meyer zum Hasen and His Wife* (1516; Basel, Public Art Collections) and the wall paintings for the interior of the house of Burgomaster Hertenstein in Lucerne, begun in 1517 (now destroyed, but preserved in copies and in eight original sketches in the Public Art Collections, Basel). Stylistically they are part of the late Gothic tradition of Holbein the Elder, but already reveal a strong interest in realistic effects and a love of Renaissance ornament. Both qualities are considerably more developed in the works of the latter part of the first Basel period, for example, *Dead Christ* (1521; Basel, Public Art Collections), the *Solothurn Madonna* (1522; Solothurn, Museum); the first *Portrait of Erasmus* (1523; Basel, Public Art Collections) and the *Madonna with the Family of Burgomaster Meyer* (1525–26; Darmstadt, Hessian Landesmuseum). His first great woodcut series, the *Totentanz* (*Dance of Death*), was not published until 1538 in Lyons.

The works of the first London trip are difficult to separate from the works of the second sojourn, but most scholars agree that the *Portrait of Thomas More* (New York, Frick Collection) and the *Portrait of Niklaus Kratzer* (Paris, Louvre) date from the first London period.

Works from the second Basel period include the *Portrait of the Artist's Family* (1528/29; Basel, Public Art Collections), the *Portrait of Erasmus as an Old Man* (1531–32; Basel, Public Art Collections), the woodcut illustrations to the Old Testament (published in 1531), and possibly also the famous title page to the *Complete Works of Erasmus* (printed in 1541).

The second London period is the period of the great portraits. These include the *Portrait of George Gisze* (1532; Berlin, former State Museums) and the *Portrait of Hermann Wedigh* (1532; New York, Metropolitan Museum), from among the many commissions by the German merchant colony in London. From court commissions his most famous paintings are *The Ambassadors* (1533; London, National Gallery), *Portrait of Thomas Cromwell* (1534; Frick Collection), *Double Portrait of Henry VIII and Jane Seymour* (1536; Lugano-Castagnola, Thyssen-Bornemisza Museum, and The Hague, Mauritshuis), *Portrait of Princess Christine of Denmark* (1538; London, National Gallery); and the three-quarter-length *Portrait of Henry VIII* (1542; York, Castle Howard).

BIBLIOGRAPHY. P. Ganz, *Die Handzeichnungen Hans Holbein des Jüngeren*, 8 vols., Berlin, 1911–37; A. B. Chamberlain, *Hans Holbein the Younger*, 2 vols., London, 1913; H. A. Schmid, *Hans Holbein der Jüngere*, 3 vols., Basel, 1945–48; P. Ganz, *The Paintings of Hans Holbein*, London, 1950. DONALD L. EHRESMANN

HOLE, WILLIAM. English engraver (fl. ca. 1607–24). Hole was a little known and relatively undistinguished engraver whose work consists mainly of engraved portraits of authors, made for London publishers. Examples are a portrait of Michael Drayton prefixed to his *Works* and a frontispiece to Drayton's *Polyolbion*.

BIBLIOGRAPHY. H. Farquhar, "A Note on William Holle, Cuneator of the Mint," *Numismatic Chronicle*, VIII, 1908.

HOLGUIN, MELCHOR PEREZ. Spanish colonial painter in Bolivia (b. Cochabamba, ca. 1660; d. Potosí? after 1724). Melchor Pérez Holguín was probably influenced by the work of Bitti in Potosí, where Holguín spent his life. *Entry of the Viceroy into Potosí* (1716; Madrid, Museum of America) is an unusual subject. *Last Judgment*

(1708; Potosí, S. Lorenzo) is one of his many religious works in Potosí and Sucre churches.

BIBLIOGRAPHY. G. Kubler and M. Soria, *Art and Architecture of Spain and Portugal and Their American Dominions, 1500–1800*, Baltimore, 1959.

HOLL, ELIAS. German architect of the Swabian school (1573–1646). Holl was the founder of the Renaissance style of civic architecture in southern Germany. As a young man he went to Italy, and on his return to his native Augsburg he applied the principles of Palladian architecture to the prevailing traditions of urban design. His crowning achievement is the Town Hall at Augsburg (1615–20), the first German building wholly designed according to the symmetrical and proportional canons of the classical style.

BIBLIOGRAPHY. E. Hempel, *Baroque Art and Architecture in Central Europe*, Baltimore, 1965.

HOLL, FRANCIS (Frank) MONTAGUE. English painter and illustrator (b. 1845; d. London, 1888). His portraits were in great demand (he painted 198 from 1879 until his death), for his broad, emphatic manner was eminently suited to commemorate the strong features of the man of action and importance in government, church, or business. His lack of color and elegance made him less successful in representing women. His story-telling pictures, which he exhibited at the Royal Academy every year from 1864 until his death, are of a type that appealed to the Victorian sensibility but are now mainly of literary interest. They depict, in an eloquent manner, the miseries and sorrows of the poor. His personal sympathies toward his subject matter were genuine and deep, so that his work might be called pathetic, rather than sentimental. Many public and private English collections contain examples of his work. His illustrations may be seen in the *Graphic*, for the years 1874 to 1876.

BIBLIOGRAPHY. "The Death of Frank Holl, R. A., 1845–1888" [Obituary], *Portfolio*, XIX, 1888.

HOLLAND, HENRY. English architect (1745–1806). Holland developed a proto–Greco-Roman style. His Gallic sympathies were evidenced by the French craftsmen in his employ at Carlton House, London (1783–95, destroyed), where he created apartments in a chaste, learned neoclassicism. Of his country houses, Berrington Hall, Herefordshire (1778), is one of the best.

HOLLAND, JAMES. English water-colorist (1800–70). He belongs with the group of mid-19th-century water-colorists including Thomas Shotter Boys and William Callow. These men continue the virtuoso tendencies of Richard Parkes Bonington, but Holland was also considerably influenced by Turner's color. There is a good collection of his work in the Henry E. Huntington Library and Art Gallery, San Marino, Calif.

BIBLIOGRAPHY. T. S. R. Boase, *English Art 1800–1870*, Oxford, 1959.

HOLLAR, WENCESLAUS (Wenzel). Bohemian printmaker (b. Prague, 1607; d. England, 1677). A prolific etcher, he left a valuable topographical record of his travels and

Wenceslaus Hollar, *Marine Animals*. Copper engraving.

Holy Sepulchre, Jerusalem. Entrance to the aedicula in the Rotunda.

especially of his adopted city, London. Working in a delicate but unemphatic style, he also treated genre and historical subjects, and documented on copper the collection of the Earl of Arundel.

BIBLIOGRAPHY. G. F. C. Parthey, *Wenzel Hollar*, Berlin, 1853.

HOLY APOSTLES, CHURCH OF THE, see APOSTLES, CHURCH OF THE HOLY, CONSTANTINOPLE; THESSALONIKA.

HOLY SEPULCHRE, JERUSALEM. Buildings at and near the traditional site of Jesus' crucifixion and tomb. Helena, the mother of the emperor Constantine, explored the site about A.D. 326, and her imperial son ordered that a sumptuous church be built nearby. The architect Zenobius provided a five-aisled basilica of nearly square plan, lit by clerestories and furnished with a coffered and gilded ceiling. Presumably an open atrium court stood in front of the basilica. The nave of the basilica terminated in a cylindrical apse; beyond was the mound of Calvary. Still farther behind the church was the tomb; later in the 4th century it was surrounded and capped by a large domical structure of circular plan, the Rotunda of the Anastasis. This last, as the chief of all the martyr shrines of Christendom, greatly influenced Christian architecture of the East and West.

Constantine's basilica has all but disappeared, and on the site today there is a Crusader church of the 12th century. Similarly, the rotunda has undergone extensive changes, the present works largely dating from the 19th century. Here and there are fragments of the earlier paving, columns, mosaics, and walls, but the present Holy Sepulchre is an artistic patchwork of many periods.

BIBLIOGRAPHY. H. Vincent, *Jérusalem, Recherches de topographie, d'archéologie et d'histoire*, vol. 1, Paris, 1912; J. W. Crowfoot, *Early Churches in Palestine*, London, 1941; K. J. Conant, "The Original Buildings at the Holy Sepulchre in Jerusalem," *Speculum*, XXXI, 1956.

HOLZMANN, HANS, see HULSMAN, JAN.

HOMER, WINSLOW. American painter and graphic artist (b. Boston, 1836; d. Prout's Neck, Me., 1910). About 1855 Homer was apprenticed to the lithography firm of J. H. Bufford in Boston. He began free-lance magazine illustration in 1857, becoming a regular contributor to *Harper's Weekly*. In 1859 he moved to New York City, where he studied drawing in a Brooklyn school and painting, briefly, in 1861, with the French artist Frédéric Rondel. His journalistic works, primarily wood engravings, were characterized by formal simplification, clear outlines, animated groupings of figures, and tonal contrasts. These stylistic characteristics probably strongly influenced the development of his later art.

His first mature oil paintings, dating from about 1862, are of Civil War subjects. In these, he was plainly concerned with objectively recording the scene before him, with particular emphasis on light-and-shade effects, an interest which independently paralleled that of early French impressionism. Yet, paradoxically combined with this realistic intent is a strong tendency toward two-dimensional design, for example, *Prisoners from the Front* (1866; New

Winslow Homer, *Prisoners from the Front*, 1866. Metropolitan Museum of Art, New York.

York, Metropolitan Museum), one of Homer's rare explorations into the depiction of personality, in which the Union officer and the Confederate prisoners are arranged across the picture plane against a high landscape background. The same approach is evident in *Croquet Scene* (1866; Art Institute of Chicago), in which the playing lawn rises to the hedge and becomes a flat background against which the profile figures are posed. Foreshortening is avoided, and the depiction of illumination is used to provide a pattern of light and dark areas.

Homer was in France for most of 1867, but despite the occasional later parallels to Monet or Degas, there is little real evidence for any French influence on his style, especially as these parallels can logically be seen as developments of his own earlier tendencies. Only the higher keyed palette of *Bridle Path in the White Mountains* (1868; Williamstown, Mass., Clark Art Institute) is new; the flattened effect of brightly lit profile figures and space rendered more by scale than perspective had been used before. Even more advanced and original in composition are the fashionable women and beach scene of *Long Branch, New Jersey* (1869; Boston, Museum of Fine Arts) or the decorative *High Tide* (1870; New York, Metropolitan Museum), with its figures set in a triangle and poised against a tilted-up background.

In Homer's paintings of the 1870s the depiction of light and shadow becomes more important, as in the incipient impressionism of *New England Country Schoolhouse* (1871; St. Louis, City Art Museum) or *Snap the Whip* (1872; Youngstown, Ohio, Butler Institute of American Art). But Homer's impressionism, like that of later American artists, remained only incipient. The final step, the dissolution of form under the impact of light, was never taken. The solidity of the figures in *The Carnival* (1877; Metropolitan Museum), for example, is deemphasized more by the broad handling of paint than by any rendering of light or atmospheric effects. In 1881 and 1882, Homer spent considerable time on the coast of the North Sea at Tynemouth, England. There, mostly in drawings and water colors, he began the depiction of man working amid and against the forces of nature that was to be his most important contribution to American art, for example, *Fisherfolk in a Boat* (1881; Cambridge, Mass., Fogg Art Museum).

On his return to the United States, Homer settled in Prout's Neck, Me., which, except for frequent trips to Canada, Florida, the West Indies, and the Adirondacks, was his home for the rest of his life. The subjects of his mature works were chosen from these settings of sea and mountain and treated in strongly designed compositions with a depersonalized and fundamentally realistic vision. For the most part, figures exist as functions in their contexts, as in *Eight Bells* (1886; Andover, Mass., Philipps Academy, Addison Gallery of American Art) or *Huntsman and Dogs* (1891; Philadelphia Museum of Art). Homer's characteristic strong pictorial structure is perhaps best seen in his paintings of the sea and of animals, such as *High Cliff, Coast of Maine* (1894; Washington, D.C., Smithsonian Institution, National Collection of Fine Arts) and *The Fox Hunt* (1893; Philadelphia, Pennsylvania Academy of the Fine Arts), or the birds and sea of the water color *Right and Left* (1909; Washington, D.C., National Gallery). This

sense of structure, along with fresh color and a free, vigorous handling of the medium, was enormously influential in the history of the modern American water color.

BIBLIOGRAPHY. L. Goodrich, *Winslow Homer*, New York, 1944; A. T. E. Gardner, *Winslow Homer...*, New York, 1961.

JEROME VIOLA

HOMER, ILLUSTRATIONS OF. Scenes from the two great epic poems the *Iliad* and the *Odyssey* (9th/8th cent. B.C.), which represent respectively a few weeks in the tenth year of the Trojan War and the return voyage of Ulysses to Ithaca. They have been depicted in art since the 7th century B.C. In Greek art the earliest-known representation is an ivory comb from Sparta showing the judgment of Paris (Athens, National Museum). Although the epics are little known from sculpture, thousands of vase paintings, dating from the 7th to the 4th century B.C., illustrate scenes involving Achilles, Ajax, Ulysses, Hector, Patroklos, and other legendary heroes. Ancient authors describe wall paintings by Polygnotos, Apollodorus, Zeuxis, and others, but none are extant. Homeric themes remained popular among the Romans in painting, sculpture, mosaics, and metalwork. The most extensive treatment occurs in the famous *Odyssey Landscapes* (1st cent. B.C.; Rome, Vatican Museums).

After a lacuna in the early Middle Ages, interest in the Homeric legends revived in the 13th and 14th centuries, at the height of the chivalric tradition and cult of the hero. Great cycles were produced in fresco, tapestry, and manuscript illumination; Hector was particularly popular and was included as one of the nine worthies. With the Renaissance revival of classical culture, Homeric scenes were painted by many great Renaissance and baroque masters, especially Annibale Carracci, Rubens, Poussin, Claude Lorraine, and Tiepolo. During the later 18th century, in the romantic adulation of a golden age, enthusiasm for Homer reached its peak. Homeric scenes were depicted by most of the neoclassicists, particularly Angelica Kauffmann, John Flaxman, Berthel Thorwaldsen, and Benjamin West.

BIBLIOGRAPHY. M. R. Scherer, *The Legends of Troy in Art and Literature*, New York, 1963.

DONALD GODDARD

HOMER, PORTRAITS OF. The poet Homer was a popular subject of portraiture throughout the history of ancient art. In almost all cases, he is shown in a dignified Zeus-like form with a beard and long hair. Notable among the many types of portrait are the so-called 5th-century B.C. Epimenides type with regularized features and hair and closed eyes (Munich, State Antiquities Collection); the early 4th-century Modena type; the late 4th-century Apollonios of Tyana type with wide-open eyes (Rome, Capitoline Museum); and the Hellenistic blind type of the 2d century B.C. (London, British Museum), in which the face is given a look of exaggerated concentration.

BIBLIOGRAPHY. G. M. A. Richter, *The Portraits of the Greeks*, 3 vols., London, 1965.

HONAN WARE. Rather imprecise term adopted for several types of Chinese ceramic wares made in Honan Province that featured a black shiny glaze with a brownish cast. The kiln sites have never been established, however. The term "Honan ware" is confusing since some kinds of

Melchior d'Hondecoeter, *Fighting Cocks*. Academy, Venice.

Temmoku and black Ting ware feature the same kind of glaze characteristics. *See* TEMMOKU; TING WARE.

HONDECOETER, GIJSBERT GILLISZ. D'. Dutch painter of landscape and animals, mostly birds (b. Utrecht [or Amsterdam?], 1604; d. Utrecht, 1653). D'Hondecoeter was the son and pupil of the painter Gillis d'Hondecoeter. He was recorded as a member of the Guild of St. Luke in Utrecht between 1626 and 1632, and in 1632 was married there. In 1634 it is recorded that Hendrick Bloemaert painted a portrait of D'Hondecoeter and his wife.

D'Hondecoeter's early works suggest some knowledge of the manner of Roelant-Jacobsz. Savery, whom he could have known in Utrecht. D'Hondecoeter, however, is better known for his paintings of fowl (*Water Fowl*, 1652; Amsterdam, Rijksmuseum). Later landscapes suggest some contact with the works of Jan Both or perhaps Aelbert Cuijp. Melchior d'Hondecoeter was his son and pupil.

BIBLIOGRAPHY. A. Bredius, ed., *Künstler-Inventare*, vol. 4, The Hague, 1917; H. Gerson, *Ausbreitung und Nachwirkung der holländischen Malerei des 17en Jahrhunderts*, Haarlem, 1942; Centraal Museum, Utrecht, *Catalogus der Schilderijen*, Utrecht, 1952.

HONDECOETER, GILLIS CLAESZ. D'. Dutch painter of landscape and animals (d. Amsterdam, 1638). Born in Antwerp, D'Hondecoeter was a pupil of his father, Nicolaes Jansz. the Elder. In 1602 he was living in Utrecht. In 1610 he was reported in Amsterdam, and in 1638 he was an official of the Amsterdam painters' guild.

D'Hondecoeter is best known for his landscapes, often with animals, painted in a style that recalls the works of David Vinckeboons, Roelant-Jacobsz. Savery, and Gillis van Coninxloo. D'Hondecoeter's early *Orpheus with the Animals* (Stockholm, National Museum) shows the influence of Coninxloo, and it has been suggested that he might have studied with him. D'Hondecoeter also painted a *Village Landscape* (formerly Vienna, Figdor Collection), one of several of the same subject that recall the work of Esaias van de Velde. His son Gijsbert and grandson Melchior were both painters; Gijsbert was his pupil.

BIBLIOGRAPHY. A. Bredius, ed., *Künstler-Inventare*, vol. 4, The Hague, 1917; H. Gerson, *Ausbreitung und Nachwirkung der holländischen Malerei des 17en Jahrhunderts*, Haarlem, 1942; Centraal Museum, Utrecht, *Catalogus der Schilderijen*, Utrecht, 1952.

HONDECOETER, MELCHIOR D'. Dutch painter of animals, birds, and still lifes (b. Utrecht, 1636; d. Amsterdam, 1695). D'Hondecoeter was the grandson of the landscape painter Gillis D'Hondecoeter and the son and pupil of the landscape and bird painter Gijsbert d'Hondecoeter. He also seems to have studied with his uncle Jan Baptist Weenix and may have had some contact with Otto Marcellis van Schrieck, as indicated by the subject and handling of his *Birds, Butterflies, and a Frog* (London, National Gallery). D'Hondecoeter settled in The Hague in 1659, and in 1662 he was an official of the painters' confraternity. The following year he was in Amsterdam, where he spent the rest of his life.

D'Hondecoeter is best known for his paintings of bird fights (*Fight between a Cock and a Turkey*, Munich, Old Pinacothek) and birds in flight. He also painted a number of still-life subjects with dead birds and game. His *Still Life with Dead Birds* (Berlin, former State Museums) shows the influence of Weenix. Other works by D'Hondecoeter in this genre (Stockholm, National Museum) seem to indicate some contact with the works of Willem van Aelst.

BIBLIOGRAPHY. A. Bredius, "De Schilders Melchior de Hondecoeter en Johan le Ducq," *Archief voor Nederl. Kunstgeschiedenis*, V, 1882–83; N. Maclaren, *National Gallery Catalogues: The Dutch School*, London, 1960; J. Rosenberg, S. Slive, and E. H. ter Kuile, *Dutch Art and Architecture, 1600–1800*, Baltimore, 1966.

LEONARD J. SLATKES

HONNECOURT, VILLARD DE. French architect from Picardy (fl. ca. 1225–ca. 1250). His travels took him to Chartres, Laon, Reims, and elsewhere, where he sketched architecture and sculpture. He also went to Hungary about 1245, possibly as an architect. His sketches, preserved in the National Library in Paris, were made for his masons' lodge and include plans, parts of elevations, ornamental details, figure sculpture, and technical drawings, as well as figures drawn from life.

BIBLIOGRAPHY. H. Hahnloser, *Villard de Honnecourt*, Vienna, 1935.

HONORE, MASTER, *see* MASTER HONORE.

HONTHORST, GERRIT VAN. Dutch painter of genre, history, and portraits (b. Utrecht, 1590; d. there, 1656). Honthorst received his training in Utrecht from Abraham Bloemaert, probably about 1606. Between 1610 and 1612 he traveled to Italy, where he had as patrons Marchese Giustiniani, Cardinal Scipione Borghese, and the Grand Duke of Tuscany. In Rome Honthorst was strongly influenced by the work of Caravaggio and translated the strong dark-and-light patterns of the Italian artist into more con-

Gerrit van Honthorst, *Merry Violinist*, 1623. Rijksmuseum, Amsterdam.

crete representations with artificial illumination, usually candles (*Christ as a Child with St. Joseph*, Montecompatri, Convent of S. Silvestro). Honthorst was not totally dependent on Caravaggio while in Rome, however; such works as the *Madonna and Child with SS. Francis and Bonaventura and Princess Colonna-Gonzaga* (1618; Albano, Church of the Capuchins) would seem to indicate a knowledge of the Carracci and the more classicistic aspects of early baroque painting. In 1620 Honthorst was back in Utrecht, and two years later he was a master in the Utrecht Guild of St. Luke.

Honthorst's paintings after his return to Utrecht reflect his exposure to Italian art, but for the most part the influence of Caravaggio rather than that of the Carracci remains with him. This can be seen in his religious works (*Christ Crowned with Thorns*, Amsterdam, Pastorate of the Church of St. Dominic) as well as in his genre scenes (*The Dentist*, 1622; Dresden, State Art Collections). Honthorst's trademark, the lighted candle shaded with a hand, which had gained him the Italian nickname "Gerardo delle Notti," is present in both works. In 1622 Honthorst executed a *Musical Ceiling* (London, F. Stonor Collection), which is a rare Dutch blending of Italian ceiling painting concepts and Utrecht musical genre types. A somewhat modified version of this Italianate principle is applied to Honthorst's 1623 *Merry Violinist* (Amsterdam, Rijksmuseum).

After 1625 Honthorst's style begins to change; he lightens his palette and introduces more pastoral subject matter into his work (*Granida and Daifilo*, 1625; Utrecht, Centraal Museum). About this time the German painter and artists' biographer Joachim von Sandrart was in Honthorst's studio, first as a pupil and then as an assistant in the academy Honthorst founded. In 1627 Peter Paul Rubens visited Honthorst in Utrecht while on a journey. The following year Honthorst was in London, working at the court of Charles I, where he produced *Apollo and Diana* (1628; London, Hampton Court). In 1635 he executed several paintings for the court of Christian IV of Denmark. In his late works, however, Honthorst's powers had weakened, and the strength of his Caravaggio-based style was diluted with courtly influences. The courtly style of painting, which had such a strong influence on Dutch painting about 1640, was centered mainly in The Hague, where Honthorst lived from 1637 to 1652. He had numerous important foreign patrons during this period and painted many elegant portraits.

From 1649 until about 1651 he worked on the decorations of the Oranjezaal of the Huis ten Bos, near The Hague. In 1652 he returned to his native Utrecht. Honthorst, along with Hendrick Terbrugghen and Dirck van Baburen, were the founders of the Utrecht school and were responsible for the introduction of the baroque concepts and light effects of Caravaggio into the Netherlands.

BIBLIOGRAPHY. G. J. Hoogewerff, *Gherardo delle Notti...*, Rome, 1924; J. R. Judson, *Gerrit van Honthorst*, The Hague, 1959; J. Rosenberg, S. Slive, and E. H. ter Kuile, *Dutch Art and Architecture, 1600-1800*, Baltimore, 1966.

LEONARD J. SLATKES

HOOCH, PIETER DE, see HOOGH, PIETER DE.

HOOD, RAYMOND. American architect (1881–1934). He was born in Pawtucket, R.I. In association with John Mead Howells, Hood won the international competition for the Chicago Tribune Tower (erected 1923–25), with a rather medievalizing design. Hood's American Radiator Building (1924) in New York City shows a disturbing dependence upon past styles, but his McGraw-Hill Building (completed 1930) in New York City is the first of the new skyscrapers with a horizontal accent. The vertically stripped Daily News Building (1930) in New York City catches the eye with its clean precision. Other works are the Masonic Temple and the Scottish Rite Cathedral (1929) in Scranton, Pa., and the studios of the National Broadcasting Company (1927) in New York City. *See* CHICAGO TRIBUNE BUILDING, CHICAGO.

BIBLIOGRAPHY. R. M. Hood, *Raymond M. Hood* (foreword by A. T. North), New York, 1931.

HOOD AND HOWELLS. American architectural team of Raymond Hood (1881–1934) and John Mead Howells (1868–1959). They were associated on only three major building projects during their careers. Hood was the dominant figure on each occasion; he was primarily responsible for designing the winning entry in the Chicago Tribune Tower competition (1922, erected 1923–25), the apartment building at 3 East 84 Street, New York (1928), and the Daily News Building, New York (1930). In their first joint effort, Howells, who had been invited to submit designs, turned the work over to the then largely unknown Hood. At other times in their careers, however, the men practiced either alone or in partnership with different architects. It appears that little cross-pollination of ideas occurred, for each maintained a distinct style of design despite some collaborations. *See* CHICAGO TRIBUNE BUILDING, CHICAGO; HOOD, RAYMOND; HOWELLS, JOHN MEAD.

BIBLIOGRAPHY. R. M. Hood, *Raymond M. Hood* (foreword by A. T. North), New York, 1931.

HOODO OF BYODOIN. Japanese Buddhist temple in Uji, a suburb of Kyoto. The Byōdōin was originally built as a detached palace for Yorimichi, an important member

Hōōdō of Byōdōin. View of the eaves of the central block.

Pieter de Hoogh, *The Pantry*. Rijksmuseum, Amsterdam. A work suggesting knowledge of the perspective experiments of Fabritius.

of the Fujiwara family, but it was converted to a Buddhist temple in 1052. The Amida Hall, now commonly known as the Hōōdō (Phoenix Hall), was added in 1053, facing a pond. The name Phoenix Hall derives from the layout of the hall, which resembles a phoenix with its wings outspread, and from the roof decorated by acroteria of two bronze phoenixes. Wing structures of the hall are laid out in a clear symmetry, and they are connected to the central part by covered corridors, reminiscent of architectural settings depicted in Chinese paintings of the Amida's Paradise. The hall is a good example of *shinden*-style architecture. The interior of the central part of the hall is dec-

orated with paintings representing the descent of the Amida and his entourage. It also houses a statue of the Amida (1053), an aloofly impressive figure, by Jōchō; its effect is enhanced by an ornate aureole and canopy in *ajouré* (pierced) work: The temple also has relief sculptures of bodhisattvas on the walls. Architecture, garden, sculpture, and painting are brought together to re-create on earth the Amida's Paradise. *See* SHINDEN-ZUKURI.

BIBLIOGRAPHY. Tokyo National Museum, *Pageant of Japanese Art*, vol. 6: *Architecture and Gardens*, Tokyo, 1952; National Commission for the Protection of Cultural Properties, ed., *Kokuhō (National Treasures of Japan)*, 6 vols., Tokyo, 1963–

MIYEKO MURASE

HOOGH (Hooch), PIETER DE. Dutch genre painter (b. Rotterdam, 1629; d. after 1684). Dutch sources tell us that De Hoogh was a pupil of Claes Berchem at the same time as Jacob Ochterveldt, presumably at Haarlem. In 1653 (May and July) De Hoogh is mentioned as both servant and painter in the service of the Delft cloth merchant Justus de la Grange. He was recorded in Rotterdam the following year, and in 1655 he became a member of the Delft painters' guild. The exact date of De Hoogh's move to Amsterdam is not known, but he was probably living in that city by the middle of 1663. He seems to have remained in Amsterdam until at least 1677.

Although De Hoogh's earliest dated works are from the year 1658, several paintings can be placed earlier. Among these youthful works is the *Backgammon Players* (ca. 1653; Dublin, National Gallery of Ireland), which recalls the works of painters such as Pieter Codde and Willem Duijster. After his move to Delft De Hoogh came under the influence of the Delft school and such painters as Carel Fabritius and perhaps even Johannes Vermeer. The perspective of such works as *The Card Players* (1658; London, Buckingham Palace) and *The Pantry* (Amsterdam, Rijksmuseum) suggests some knowledge of the perspective experiments of Fabritius, as well as some acquaintance with the early works of Vermeer, in which a similar use of space and light is found. On the other hand, it should be noted that De Hoogh's works, in turn, must also have had an influence on the later works of Vermeer. De Hoogh's use of architectural units and space in *A Maid with a Child in a Court* (1658; London, National Gallery), for example, anticipated Vermeer's *A Street in Delft* (ca. 1660; Amsterdam, Rijksmuseum).

Such De Hoogh works as the *Mother beside a Cradle* (ca. 1659/60; Berlin, former State Museums) show some influence of the Rembrandt school. This influence seems to anticipate his move to Amsterdam, and his *Woman Peeling Apples* (London, Wallace Collection), probably painted in Amsterdam about 1663, seems to have been influenced by the works of such Rembrandt pupils as Nicolaes Maes. De Hoogh had a considerable following; such artists as Pieter Janssens Elinga, Jacob Vrel, Hendrick van der Burgh, and many others worked in his manner.

BIBLIOGRAPHY. C. H. C. Baker, *Pieter de Hooch*, London, 1925; W. R. Valentiner, "Pieter de Hooch," *Art in America*, XV, 1927; P. de Hooch, *Pieter de Hooch: The Master's Paintings in 180 Reproductions... with an intro. by W. R. Valentiner*, Stuttgart, 1930; F. van Thienen, *Pieter de Hooch*, Amsterdam, 1945.

LEONARD J. SLATKES

HOOGHE, ROMEYN DE. Dutch painter, draftsman, and etcher (b. The Hague, 1650; d. ca. 1720). He made more than 1,000 delicately drawn and highly detailed etchings of historical subjects, as single sheets and as book illustrations. These represent events in the Lowlands, France, England, and Spain; satires on political events; and splendid views of cities in Germany, Portugal, and the Lowlands.

HOOGSTRATEN, SAMUEL DIRCKSZ. VAN. Dutch painter of history, genre, and portraits; also art writer, poet, and playwright (b. Dordrecht, 1627; d. there, 1678). Hoogstraten received his first training from his father, Dirck van Hoogstraten, and then, in about 1642, studied with Rembrandt in Amsterdam. His fellow students in Rembrandt's workshop were probably Carel Fabritius and Abraham Funerius. By 1648 Hoogstraten was back in his native Dordrecht. He was active in Vienna in 1651 and received royal patronage in that city. The following year he was in Rome.

By 1653 he was back in Vienna, and the year after he was recorded in Dordrecht, where he appears to have remained until about 1662, when he was reported in London. He apparently remained in England until shortly after the great fire of September, 1666. He was listed in the books of Pictura, the painters' confraternity at The Hague, early in 1668. In 1673, however, he returned to Dordrecht, where he was appointed provost of the mint. During his last years he wrote his *Inleyding tot de Hooge Schoole de Schilderkonst*, which was published in 1678.

Hoogstraten's work in the 1640s is still close to Rembrandt's style of about the same period, as can be seen in Hoogstraten's *Self-Portrait with "Vanitas" Still Life* (1644; Rotterdam, Boymans–Van Beuningen Museum) and in his 1649 *Doubting Thomas* (Mainz, Museum of Antiquities and Picture Gallery). During the 1650s Hoogstraten abandoned the Rembrandtesque manner for a drier, more pedantic style (*Man at a Window*, 1653; Vienna, Museum of Art History), which recalls, in a general way, the works of Gabriel Metsu or Pieter de Hoogh. Hoogstraten was also interested in trompe l'oeil painting and perspective experiments. He made several perspective boxes, or peep shows (Detroit, Institute of Arts; London, National Gallery).

BIBLIOGRAPHY. J. O. Kronig, "Zwei Selbstbildnisse von Samuel van Hoogstraeten," *Kunstchronik*, XXV, 1914; W. R. Valentiner, "Rembrandt and Samuel van Hoogstraeten," *Art in America*, XVII, 1930; E. P. Richardson, "Samuel van Hoogstraeten and Carel Fabritius," *Art in America*, XXV, 1937; N. Maclaren, *National Gallery Catalogues: The Dutch School*, London, 1960.

LEONARD J. SLATKES

HOOKE, ROBERT. English scientist and architect (1635–1703). A colleague of Wren, he was concerned with the building of the City Churches in London. He is associated with the French style (Montagu House, London, 1675–

Samuel Dircksz. van Hoogstraten, *Self-Portrait with "Vanitas" Still Life*. Boymans–Van Beuningen Museum, Rotterdam.

79) and was an important country-house architect, as is shown by designs for Ragley Hall, Warwickshire (1679–83).

HOOKER, PHILIP. Provincial American architect (1766–1836). He began his career in 1790 in Albany, New York, and was the only architect in the vicinity. Hooker worked in Federal and Greek revival styles, producing many civic and domestic works in Albany, including the original State Capitol (1804–06; razed 1883).

BIBLIOGRAPHY. E. W. Root, *Philip Hooker*, New York, 1929.

HOPE, THOMAS. English connoisseur and amateur architect (b. Holland, ca. 1770; d. London, 1831). He was the acknowledged leader of the archaeological revival in decoration and furniture and an arbiter of taste. His *Household Furniture* (1807) gave designs for the interiors of his town house in London and of his country seat at Deepdene, Surrey.

HOPEWELL CULTURE. American Indian culture centered in Ohio; important sites also existed in Illinois, Indiana, Michigan, Tennessee, Wisconsin, and New York. The Hopewell Indians were the principal mound builders before the arrival of European settlers. Their remarkable earthworks were constructed for purposes of fortification, burial, or superposition of temples or residences. Mounds such as the Great Serpent in southern Ohio are designed in the shape of reptiles or animals. Many appear to date from the 10th to the 16th century.

The Hopewell Mound itself, located in Ross County, Ohio, yielded remarkably sophisticated examples of stone sculpture, most of which were fashioned as pipes. Ornaments of sheet mica and native copper were also discovered, both in animal form and shaped after the human hand.

See also MOUND BUILDERS; NORTH AMERICAN INDIAN ART (EASTERN UNITED STATES AND CANADA).

BIBLIOGRAPHY. C. C. Willoughby, "The Art of the Great Earthwork Builders of Ohio," *Holmes Anniversary Volume*, Washington,

Hopewell Culture. Great Serpent Mound, Serpent Mound State Park, Adams County, Ohio.

D.C., 1916; H. C. Shetrone and E. F. Greenman, "Explorations of the Seip Group of Prehistoric Earthworks," *Ohio Archaeological and Historical Quarterly*, XL, July, 1931.

HOPI INDIANS. A Pueblo people centered in northeastern Arizona. Some Hopi localities were probably occupied by A.D. 500. An outstandingly important Hopi town is Awatobi, developed from the 13th century until historic times. Spanish missionizing began about 1540.

In prehistoric times the Hopi designed planned villages that included cliff houses and multistoried dwellings. The kiva, a ceremonial chamber or men's clubhouse, was built on both rectangular and circular plans. The Hopi practiced a limited stone art, producing animal sculptures. In historic times they have been known for their colorful *kachina* figures made of painted wood, feathers, and cloth. Certain distinctive types of pottery were also produced in the Jeddito section. *See* KACHINA.

See also NORTH AMERICAN INDIAN ART (SOUTHWEST).

BIBLIOGRAPHY. P. E. Goddard, *Indians of the Southwest* (American Museum of Natural History, Handbook series, no. 2), New York, 1913; R. B. Woodbury, *Prehistoric Stone Implements of Northeastern Arizona*, Cambridge, Mass., 1954.

HOPPER, EDWARD. American painter (b. Nyack, N.Y., 1882; d. New York City, 1967). Hopper was first trained as an illustrator at a commercial school in New York City (1899–1900) and at the New York School of Art, where he was a student of painting under Robert Henri and Kenneth Hayes Miller until 1906. Between 1906 and 1910 Hopper made three trips to Europe, mostly to Paris and Spain. Painting scenes of the city and its inhabitants in Paris he was unaffected by the current developments of Fauvism and cubism, as he was to remain aloof from other avant-garde movements throughout his career. His attention was turned rather to the heroes of his teacher Henri—Velázquez, Goya, Manet, and Daumier—and to the impressionists.

Hopper's paintings were first exhibited, with those of other Henri students, at the Harmonie Club, New York, in 1908. Although one of his works was shown and sold at the Armory Show in 1913, he did not gain recognition until the 1920s. Working as an illustrator he painted little until 1920; the years between 1915 and 1923 were devoted primarily to etching. In 1923 he took up water-color painting, a medium well suited to his light-filled New England views, but his main output has been in oils.

With his roots in the teaching of Robert Henri, Hopper transformed the realism of the Ashcan school into a vehicle of poetic insight. Almost from the beginning he replaced the loosely painted, picturesque tableaux of the Ashcan artists with a more detached rendering of things as they are according to his own concentrated vision. He was concerned with the appearance of American life and landscape and drew his subjects from his surroundings, mostly in New York City and New England where he lived for part of each year from 1908. Long automobile trips through the United States also provided themes.

Concentrating on formal means, Hopper created compelling and unsentimentalized settings for strikingly solitary figures. Pictorial structure is achieved in terms of the architecture depicted: Victorian houses in New England

Edward Hopper, *Room in Brooklyn*, 1932. Museum of Fine Arts, Boston. A solitary figure and a city interior.

(*House by the Railroad*, New York, Museum of Modern Art), Cape Cod lighthouses (*Lighthouse at Two Lights*, 1929; New York, private collection), city interiors (*Room in Brooklyn*, 1932; Boston, Museum of Fine Arts) or street façades (*Nighthawks*, 1942; Art Institute of Chicago). The permanent geometry of horizontals and verticals is the framework for still figures, simple but subtle spatial patterns of architectural planes in depth, and planar contrasts of light and shade, atmosphere and mass.

The development of Hopper's style is one of purification rather than basic change. The figures and architecture of his later works are leaner and more monumental. In such paintings as *Second-Story Sunlight* (1960; New York, Whitney Museum) there is a greater clarity of light and a broader treatment of planes. The image is confronted more directly and uncompromisingly, as though to tear away the veil of isolation that characterized his earlier paintings.

Since the 1920s Hopper has been one of the most honored American painters. He was elected to the National Institute of Arts and Letters in 1945 and the American Academy of Arts and Letters in 1955, when he received the National Institute's gold medal for painting. Among his many exhibitions have been major retrospectives at the Museum of Modern Art in New York (1933) and the Whitney Museum of American Art in New York (1950 and 1964).

BIBLIOGRAPHY. M. W. Brown, "The Early Realism of Hopper and Burchfield," *College Art Journal*, VII, 1947; P. Tyler, "Edward Hopper: Alienation by Light," *Magazine of Art*, XLI, 1948; C. Zigrosser, "The Etchings of Edward Hopper," *Prints*, 1962; L. Goodrich, *Edward Hopper*, exhibition catalog, New York, 1964; *São Paulo 9: Edward Hopper and Environment U.S.A., 1957-1967*, essays by W. C. Seitz, foreword by L. Goodrich, Washington, D. C., 1968.
DONALD GODDARD

HOPPNER, JOHN. English painter of German extraction (ca. 1758–1810). He is one of the group of English por-

John Hoppner, *Jane Elizabeth, Countess of Oxford.* Tate Gallery, London.

traitists including Sir William Beechey, Sir Martin Archer, and (most notable) Sir Thomas Lawrence that follows the generation of the major late-18th-century portraitists, Reynolds, Gainsborough, and Romney. He attracted wealthy patrons whom he managed to retain throughout his life. He entered the Royal Academy school in 1775. In 1782 his *King Lear* received the highest award the Academy offered, the gold medal for history painting. His career, however, was to be in the more remunerative and less arduous field of portraiture. As a portraitist Hoppner was Lawrence's principal rival during the last years of the 18th century and during the first decade of the 19th century. He was elected associate of the Royal Academy in 1793 and full academician in 1795.

Hoppner, like the others in his group, shared in the great vogue for British portraits at the beginning of the 20th century. His reputation was at that time inflated, and it has suffered correspondingly in the inevitable reaction. At his best, he is a worthy follower of Reynolds. Unfortunately, he also shared with Reynolds an inclination to experiment with unstable pigments, and consequently many of his paintings are in poor condition. He is seldom able to sustain a large, full-length canvas. His most satisfying works are small, intimate portraits of women and children where his tendencies toward the sweet and charming are not misplaced.

Hoppner's portraits are widely scattered in public and private collections. Probably the major concentration of his works is in St. James's Palace, London.

BIBLIOGRAPHY. W. McKay and W. Roberts, *John Hoppner*, London, 1909.

ROBERT R. WARK

HORAE, *see* FATES.

HORD, DONAL. American sculptor (1902–   ). He was born in Prentice, Wis., and studied at the Santa Barbara School of Art and in Mexico. He was a Guggenheim Fellow. Hord's sculptures are frequently carved directly from hard stones in simple, compact, and figurative forms. His major works include the Balboa Park Fountain (San Diego, Calif.) and a monument for the American Battle Cemetery (Henri-Chapelle, Belgium).

BIBLIOGRAPHY. New York, Museum of Modern Art, *Americans, 1942...,* New York, 1942; O. W. Larkin, *Art and Life in America,* rev. ed., New York, 1960.

HOREAU, HECTOR. French architect (1801–72). He worked in Paris. His projected iron and glass designs for large spans on monumental buildings were too advanced to be practicable in his time. His designs for Les Halles in Paris and the 1851 London Exhibition building were two of those rejected.

BIBLIOGRAPHY. L. Hautecoeur, *Histoire de l'architecture classique en France,* vol. 7, Paris, 1957.

HOREHAM HALL. A fine and rare example of a pre-Reformation brick mansion, in Essex, England. Begun before 1520, it incorporates a mid-15th-century timber frame house, and includes a tower and brickwork of the later 16th century. The two-storied canted bay window is its most striking feature.

BIBLIOGRAPHY. N. Pevsner, *The Buildings of England,* vol. 11, Harmondsworth, 1954.

HORIZON. Horizontal line formed by passing a horizontal plane through the eye, or point of sight, to intersect a vertical plane (the picture plane) in perspective drawing.

HORNIG (Hornijk), LORENZ, *see* HORNUNG, LORENZ.

HORN OF PLENTY, *see* CORNUCOPIA.

HORNUNG (Hornig; Hornijk), LORENZ. German sculptor (b. Apolda, Thuringia; d. Pirna, 1624). Hörnung became a prominent citizen of Pirna, in Saxony, and was active in the area as a sculptor from 1600. Of his many works for the Von Bünau family, the major one is a family monument in the Bünau Chapel at the church of Lauenstein (1611).

HORNY, FRANZ. German painter (b. Weimar, 1797; d. Olevano, 1824). Horny began his artistic career at the Weimar Academy. There he attracted the attention of Baron von Rumohr who sent him to Italy in 1816 for further studies. After a short stay in northern Italy Horny settled in Rome, working first with Joseph Anton Koch and then with Peter Cornelius as a member of the Nazarenes. Horny worked with Cornelius on the frescoes of the Villa Massimi, executing rich floral decorations in the borders of Cornelius's Dante scenes. After Cornelius's departure for Germany, Horny remained in Rome and worked independently as a landscape painter. In 1821, together with Schnorr von Carolsfeld, he left Rome for Olevano where he spent the remaining years of his life.

The few extant works by Horny are mostly water colors, drawings, and a few portraits (*Portrait of the Painter Fohr,* 1817; Heidelberg, Palatinate Museum) and landscapes (*View of the Sabine Mountains*, Weimar, Staatliche Kunstsammlungen). Landscapes, his finest creations, constitute some of the most sensitive nature studies of the romantic period. Horny was influenced strongly by Schnorr von Carolsfeld and above all by his friend Karl Philipp Fohr.

BIBLIOGRAPHY. R. Hamann, *Die deutsche Malerei vom Rokoko bis zum Expressionismus*, Leipzig, 1925; E. L. Schellenberg, ed., *Der Maler Franz Horny*, Berlin, 1929.

DONALD L. EHRESMANN

HOROLOGIUM OF ANDRONICUS, ATHENS, *see* TOWER OF THE WINDS, ATHENS.

HORSESHOE ARCH, *see* ARCH.

HORTA, VICTOR. Belgian architect (1861–1947). He worked in Brussels. A pupil of the academician Alphonse Balat, he is best known as the initiator of the full-fledged Art Nouveau style in his Tassel House (1892–93), in which exposed metal structure is expressed as an organic form and glass is freely used. His other important works are the Maison du Peuple (1898–99) and the Innovation Department Store (1901). After 1906 his work loses importance, becoming academically dry and classicistic. Indeed, he turned his back on progressive architecture and was instrumental in voting down Le Corbusier's project for the League of Nations in 1927.

BIBLIOGRAPHY. S. T. Madsen, "Horta: Works and Style of Victor Horta before 1900," *Architectural Review*, CXVIII, 1955.

HORYUJI. Japanese Buddhist temple near Nara. The monastery was first dedicated in 607 to the Yakushi (Healing) Buddha in accordance with the will of Emperor Yōmei. The original monastery was apparently destroyed in a fire about 670, and the reconstruction was presumably carried out soon after, but at a site slightly northwest of the former location. Despite the reconstruction work, which lasted until 711, the oldest structures—namely, the pagoda, Golden Hall (Kondō), Middle Gate, and covered corridors—reflect architectural features of the Asuka period. They are considered the world's oldest existing wooden structures. Other buildings in the Hōryūji date from the Nara, Heian, and Kamakura periods.

Departing from tradition, the layout of the temple places the Golden Hall and pagoda in an east–west orientation, with the central axis left vacant. This architectural arrangement was probably chosen because two Buddha statues of the Yakushi and the Shaka were to be enshrined within the Golden Hall; the unique plan avoided giving either statue the primary position on the central axis. There are other examples of sculpture from the Nara and Kamakura periods in the Golden Hall, whose walls were decorated with paintings before a fire destroyed them in 1949. The pagoda houses four groups of clay sculptures (711) and was also decorated by wall paintings, which are now almost obliterated. *See* HORYUJI WALL PAINTINGS. *See also* JAPAN: LACQUERWARE (NARA PERIOD); TAMAMUSHI SHRINE; YUMEDONO.

BIBLIOGRAPHY. Tokyo National Museum, *Pageant of Japanese Art*, vol. 6: *Architecture and Gardens*, Tokyo, 1952; R. T. Paine and A. Soper, *The Art and Architecture of Japan*, Baltimore, 1955; J. Murata and T. Veno, *The Horyuji*, Tokyo, 1960; National Commission for the Protection of Cultural Properties, ed., *Kokuhō (National Treasures of Japan)*, vol. 1: *From the Earliest Time to the End of the Nara Period*, Tokyo, 1963.

MIYEKO MURASE

HORYUJI WALL PAINTINGS. Japanese wall paintings of the Asuka period (552–710). Before a tragic fire in 1949, the paintings decorating the walls of the Kondō (Golden Hall) of the Hōryūji near Nara were the oldest Buddhist wall paintings in Japan, and as such were regarded as among the finest examples in the Far East. They represented the easternmost flowering of the wall-painting tradition that started in the Ajaṇṭā Caves in India and was transformed in the hands of Central Asian and Chinese artists. The paintings were executed shortly after a fire of about 670 that destroyed the original building of the Hōryūji, and before 711, when the reconstruction of the temple was completed.

Four large walls showed the paradise of the four Buddhas: the Shaka (Historic Buddha), Yakushi (Healing Buddha), Miroku (Future Buddha), and Amida Buddha of the

Horizon. A feature of perspective drawing.

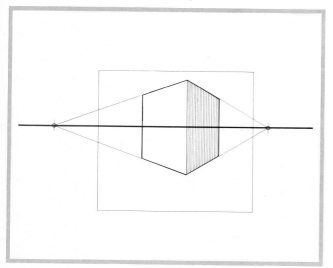

Hōryūji. Buddhist temple near Nara, Japan.

Western Paradise. Eight corner walls represented four pairs of standing or seated bodhisattvas, each pair acting as attendants to a paradise scene. Twenty small walls just under the ceiling, decorated with flying angels (Sanskrit, *apsara*), had fortunately been removed before the fire of 1949 and are now the sole survivors of the catastrophic accident.

The most beautiful of all the walls was that representing Amida's paradise. The Amida Buddha was seated in yoga fashion with his fingers forming a gesture of preaching the Law (Sanskrit, *dharmacakra mudrā*), and was flanked by two standing bodhisattvas. His strong, well-formed body was gently draped by soft, clinging clothes that accentuated the fleshy body underneath. Calmness and serenity marked his finely defined facial features. A sumptuously decorated baldachino surmounted the Buddha. At the far back there were small figures of men seated on lotus flowers symbolizing good men's souls reborn as bodhisattvas in the Amida's paradise of eternal bliss. The heavy jewelry worn by the bodhisattvas standing on either side of the Amida, and the languid grace of their bodies forming gentle S-curves, are strongly reminiscent of the Beautiful Bodhisattva in the Ajaṇṭā Caves of India. There was no direct Indian influence on Japanese painting, however. These paintings reflected an international style of Buddhist religious art that united India with the Far East.

The Hōryūji paintings were not done in a fresco technique; instead, a design was transferred to the dry wall by pouncing patterns. Outlines were then laid in red, giving the bodies a sense of volume and sensuous beauty. The "wire line" used in drawing was strong yet flexible, and the arbitrary shading along the drapery folds was used more for a decorative effect than to follow the logic of light and shade. The magnificence and grandeur of conception and the beauty of form and expression that marked these paintings make their loss a tragic event.

BIBLIOGRAPHY. T. Naitō, *The Wall-Paintings of Hōryūji* (American Council of Learned Societies, Studies in Chinese and Related Civilizations, no. 5), Baltimore, 1943; Nara, Hōryūji Monastery, *Wall Paintings in the Kondō*, reproductions with an introd. essay by I. Tanaka, 2 pts., Tokyo, 1951; T. Akiyama, *Japanese Painting* [Geneva?], 1961.   MIYEKO MURASE

HOSIOS LOUKOS.

Greek church of St. Luke of Stiris situated between Athens and Delphi. It is an 11th-century Byzantine structure renowned for its magnificent mosaics, which cover almost all of the upper walls and vaulting. In plan, it is a cross inscribed within a rectangle; the intersection of the arms of the cross is covered by a large dome. On the walls, arches, and lesser vaults 150 portraits of saints appear; in the major and higher positions are scenes from the life of Christ, archangels, the Virgin and Child, and the descent of the Holy Spirit. Throughout, the colors and compositions are superb, and the architectural spaces seem inhabited by the forms of the mosaic icons.

BIBLIOGRAPHY. R. W. Schultz and S. H. Barnsley, *The Monastery of Saint Luke of Stiris*, London, 1901; E. Diez and O. Demus, *Byzantine Mosaics in Greece*, Cambridge, Mass., 1931; O. Demus, *Byzantine Mosaic Decoration*, London, 1948.

HOSMER, HARRIET GOODHUE.

American sculptor (b. Watertown, Mass., 1830; d. there, 1908). She studied drawing and modeling in Boston and anatomy in St. Louis. Following this preparation she worked with John Gibson in Rome. Numerous marble figure groups, such as *Puck*, were popular; a bronze *Thomas Hart Benton* (St. Louis, City Art Museum) was the most ambitious of her works.

BIBLIOGRAPHY. A. T. Gardner, *Yankee Stonecutters*, New York, 1945; O. W. Larkin, *Art and Life in America*, rev. ed., New York, 1960.

HOSPICIO CABANAS, GUADALAJARA, MEXICO,

see OROZCO, JOSE CLEMENTE.

HOSPITAL OF THE INNOCENTS, FLORENCE.

Italian foundling hospital, planned by Filippo Brunelleschi in 1419 and built between 1421 and 1424. Florentine Renaissance architecture first took form in this building. The graceful colonnaded portico, consisting of nine semicircular arches (the two end arcades were added later) supported by Corinthian columns, has spandrels ornamented with the endlessly copied glazed terra-cotta medallions representing infants in swaddling clothes by Andrea della Robbia. The upper floor's pedimented rectangular windows correspond to the arches below. (The top floor is a modern addition.) While combined to totally new effect, these forms show Brunelleschi's dependence on Tuscan proto-Renaissance architecture of the 11th and 12th centuries, as Pevsner has pointed out. *The Adoration of the Magi,*

Hosios Loukos. Vault mosaic with four saints, 11th century.

Hōryūji wall paintings. Detail of a fresco decorating the walls of the Kondō (Golden Hall), end of 7th century.

Hospital of the Innocents, Florence, planned by Filippo Brunelleschi in 1419 and built between 1421 and 1424.

by Domenico Ghirlandajo, is the most noteworthy of the paintings shown in the gallery now housed here. *See* BRUNELLESCHI, FILIPPO.

BIBLIOGRAPHY. E. Carli, *Brunelleschi*, Milan, 1952.

HOTEL DE VILLE. French term designating a type of municipal building or town hall, similar to the *palazzo pubblico* in Italy and the *Rathaus* in Germany. It developed relatively late in France because of the slow development of town life. The most important examples were built between the 15th and 17th century; for instance, the 15th-century Hôtel de Ville in Bourges. The hôtel de ville is usually a long rectangular building, three-to-four stories high, with a steeply pitched roof. The main entrance is in the middle of one of the long sides. The Hôtel de Ville in Paris exemplifies this significant type of French Renaissance building.

BIBLIOGRAPHY. R. R. Blomfield, *A History of French Architecture, from the Reign of Charles VIII till the Death of Mazarin*, 2 vols., London, 1911.

HOUBRAKEN, ARNOLD. Dutch painter of history, genre, portraits, and landscape; also graphic artist and art writer (b. Dordrecht, 1660; d. Amsterdam, 1719). Houbraken first studied with Johan de Haen at the age of nine. In 1672 he was working with Willem van Drielenburg, and shortly afterward with Jacob Levecq. In 1674 Houbraken was a pupil of Samuel van Hoogstraten and remained with him until Hoogstraten's death in 1678. This was the period when Hoogstraten was writing his *Inleyding tot de Hooge Schoole de Schilderkonst* (published 1678), which must have later inspired Houbraken to undertake his three-volume work, *De groote Schouburgh der Nederlantsche Konstschilders en Schilderessen* (1718–21).

In 1678 Houbraken became a member of the Dordrecht Guild of St. Luke. He seems to have remained in his native city until 1709. In 1710 he became a citizen of Amsterdam, where he remained except for a nine-month interlude in England (1713/14).

As a painter Houbraken is somewhat dry and academic (*Romulus and Remus*, Amsterdam, Rijksmuseum). As a writer on art, however, he is one of the most important sources for Dutch 17th-century painting.

BIBLIOGRAPHY. C. Hofstede de Groot, *Arnold Houbraken und seine "Groote Schouburgh"* . . ., The Hague, 1893.

LEONARD J. SLATKES

HOUBRAKEN, JACOB. Dutch engraver (b. Dordrecht, 1698; d. Amsterdam, 1780). He was the best-known and perhaps the finest Dutch portrait engraver of the 18th century. Although the quality of Houbraken's work varies, Raphael Morghen could say of him: "No engraver has ever equaled and probably will not equal the Dutchman Jacob Houbraken in the manner of imitating the flesh and hair by means of the graver." The son of the painter Arnold Houbraken, Jacob turned to Nanteuil, Drevet, and Edelinck as models. During his career he did at least 400 single portraits, mostly after contemporary painters (for example, forty-nine after J. M. Quinkhard and twenty-four after Wandelaar). He also illustrated *Heads of Illustrious Persons of Great Britain* (London, 1743–52), a biographical dictionary written by Birch.

BIBLIOGRAPHY. L. Holman, "J. v. Houbraken," *American Art News*, II, 1921.

HOUCKGEEST, GERARD (Gerrit). Dutch architectural painter (b. The Hague, ca. 1600; d. Bergen op Zoom, 1661). Houckgeest was the nephew of the portrait painter Joachim Houckgeest. He may have studied with the architectural painter Bartholomeus van Bassen, for the only known etching by Houckgeest is after a Van Bassen painting. In 1625 Houckgeest was a member of the Guild of St. Luke at The Hague. He was living in Delft from 1635 and joined the painters' guild in that city in 1639. In

1652 he was at Steenbergen, and the following year he was living at Bergen op Zoom.

Houckgeest was almost exclusively a painter of church interiors. While living at Delft he was exposed to the growing interest in that city in perspective and interior representations of various types. His paintings show stylistic affinities to the works of Pieter de Hoogh and Johannes Vermeer. Houckgeest's favorite subject was the Old and New Church at Delft (*Interior of the New Church at Delft*, 1651; The Hague, Mauritshuis Art Gallery). With Emanuel de Witte and Hendrik van Vliet he is one of the most important innovators of the Delft school of architectural painters.

BIBLIOGRAPHY. H. Jantzen, *Das niederländische Architekturbild*, Leipzig, 1910; J. Rosenberg, S. Slive, and. E. H. ter Kuile, *Dutch Art and Architecture, 1600–1800*, Baltimore, 1966.

LEONARD J. SLATKES

HOUDON, JEAN ANTOINE. French sculptor (b. Versailles, 1741; d. Paris, 1828). A precociously talented youth, he entered the Ecole Royale de Sculpture at the age of twelve. There he studied with Jean-Baptiste Pigalle, Jean-Baptiste Lemoyne, and René-Michel Slodtz. In 1764 he began to study in Rome as a Prix de Rome winner. While in Rome he taught drawing and modeling in the Academy and immediately established his reputation as an important sculptor. Among sculptures of the Italian period are the well-known *Ecorché* and two statues, *St. John the Baptist* and *St. Bruno*, for the Church of S. Maria degli Angeli, Rome.

Houdon returned to France about 1768 and began his famous portraits of notable men and women of the era. Several busts, among them portraits of Catherine II, Prince Galitzin, and Denis Diderot received favorable mention in the 1773 Salon, while in the Salon of 1775 he was heralded as a major sculptor. Works included in the latter Salon were busts of A. R. J. Turgot and Christoph Gluck, and an *Iphigenia*.

His friendship with Benjamin Franklin, who sat for Houdon in 1778, led, in 1785, to a trip to the United States, where Houdon was commissioned to execute a life-size statue of Washington, which was eventually installed in the State Capitol at Richmond, Virginia. He also made portrait busts of Washington, Jefferson, John Paul Jones, and others.

After Houdon's return to France he was commissioned by the king of Prussia to execute a statue symbolic of winter, *La Frileuse*. Soon, the French Revolution interrupted further commissions, and the sculptor busied himself with various unfinished projects, among them *St. Scholastica*, for which he was denounced to the Convention.

During the reign of Napoleon, Houdon received few commissions, but he did undertake an ambitious project (never completed) for a column commemorating the Grand Army. He also made portrait sculptures of Napoleon, Josephine Bonaparte, and Marshal Ney. Napoleon awarded him the Legion of Honor in recognition of his contributions to France.

Perhaps the most famous of Houdon's sculptures is the statue of Voltaire (1781; Paris, Comédie Française). This work captures the individuality of the subject through lifelike modeling of the head, while the classically draped figure contributes to a sense of the universal and the time-

Arnold Houbraken, *Romulus and Remus*. Rijksmuseum, Amsterdam.

Jean Antoine Houdon, *Bust of Louise Brongniart*. Louvre, Paris.

less aspects of the man. Similarly, the statue *George Washington* (Richmond), in spite of the contemporary dress, portrays the individual character of Washington in terms of classical dignity.

The true greatness of Houdon was largely due to his ability to penetrate superficial appearances and bring forth the individual character of his subjects. He blended classical formality with psychological insight and produced a dynamic realism. Thus Houdon stands out as the great sculptor of the 18th century; during the several generations following his death his influence was immense among sculptors of the Western world.

BIBLIOGRAPHY. F. Novotny, *Painting and Sculpture in Europe, 1780–1880*, Baltimore, 1960.

BEN P. WATKINS

HOUGHTON, ARTHUR BOYD. English illustrator (b. 1836; d. South Hampstead, 1875). Houghton did much wood engraving in the 1860s. He produced a large number of drawings on wood blocks for Delziel's *Illustrated Arabian Nights' Entertainments*, and he also drew for *Fun, Graphic*, and other magazines. A number of his watercolors are in the British Museum.

BIBLIOGRAPHY. H. M. Cundall, *A History of British Water-Colour Painting*, London, 1908.

HOU-KANG, *see* AN-YANG.

HOURS OF MILAN, *see* TURIN-MILAN HOURS.

HOUSE OF CARDS. Oil painting by Chardin, in the National Gallery, Washington, D.C. *See* CHARDIN, JEAN-BAPTISTE-SIMEON.

HOUSES OF PARLIAMENT. Oil painting by Monet, in the National Gallery, Washington, D.C. *See* MONET, CLAUDE-OSCAR.

HOUSTON, RICHARD. Irish graphic artist and miniaturist (b. Ireland, 1721; d. London, 1775). Houston worked in mezzotint and etching, and made prints in the chalk manner. He produced a large number of portraits and other miscellaneous plates, but his work is uneven in quality. Many of his portraits are after Reynolds; Rembrandt was a favorite source for other plates.

BIBLIOGRAPHY. C. J. Davenport, *Mezzotints*, London, 1904.

HOUSTON, TEX.: MUSEUM OF FINE ARTS. Initiated in 1905, the museum was opened in its present building in 1924. The Cullinan Wing, by Mies van der Rohe, was recently added. The exhibitions include the Kress and Straus collections of European painting and sculpture.

Ancient art is represented by small collections of Egyptian, Greek, Roman, and Byzantine works. The sculpture on view, ranging from the medieval period through the 18th century, includes works by Luca della Robbia, Verrocchio, Pollaiuolo, Benedetto da Maiano, L'Antico, Riccio, Cellini, Giovanni Bologna, and Houdon.

Of interest among the Italian paintings are works by the Master of the Straus Madonna, Fra Angelico, Giovanni di Paolo, Domenico Veneziano, Giovanni Bellini, Lotto, Catena, Sebastiano del Piombo, Beccafumi, Vasari, Luini, Tintoretto, Cambiaso, Veronese, Pannini, Guardi,

Tiepolo, and Bellotto. Flemish and Dutch works of note are by Rogier van der Weyden, Memling, Joos van Cleve, Van Dyck, Rubens, and Hals. In French painting, Corneille de Lyon, Pater, Robert, Renoir, Cézanne, and Toulouse-Lautrec, among others, are represented. The Germans Holbein and Cranach, the Englishmen Reynolds and Raeburn, and the Spaniards Sánchez Coello, Murillo, and Goya are also represented.

The American collection ranges over the history of art in the United States; one of its notable features is a room devoted to the works of Frederic Remington. There is also a representative group of Latin American paintings.

BIBLIOGRAPHY. *Catalogue of the Edith A. and Percy S. Straus Collection*, Houston, 1945; *The Samuel H. Kress Collection at the Museum of Fine Arts of Houston*, Houston, 1953.

DONALD GODDARD

HOVANNES, JOHN. American sculptor (1900–   ). Born in Smyrna, Turkey, Hovannes studied in the United States at the Rhode Island School of Design, the Copley Society in Boston, and the Beaux-Arts Institute in New York City. In the 1930s and 1940s he exhibited stylized relieflike figure groups, often of working men.

HOVENDEN, THOMAS. American genre painter (b. Dunmanway, Ireland, 1840; d. Plymouth Meeting, Pa., 1895). He studied at the Cork School, attended the National Academy of Design, and received instruction from Cabanel in Paris. His colloquial themes of Breton peasants and Southern Negroes are painted in a sentimental and academically hard manner.

BIBLIOGRAPHY. E. P. Richardson, *Painting in America*, New York, 1956.

HOWARD, CHARLES. American painter, designer, and muralist (1899–   ). Born in Montclair, N.J., he studied in California. His early works are realistic paintings of social subjects. Later he painted Miró-influenced abstractions. He was associated with the London surrealists from 1936 to 1938.

HOWARD, JOHN GALEN. American architect (b. Chelmsford, Mass., 1864; d. San Francisco, 1931). Howard studied at the Massachusetts Institute of Technology and the Ecole des Beaux-Arts, Paris. He worked in the offices of H. H. Richardson in the 1880s and of McKim, Meade and White in the 1890s. He taught at the University of California, Berkeley, and designed its campus plan and several of its buildings, including Sather Tower.

HOWARD, CASTLE. Baroque house in Yorkshire, England, designed for the Earl of Carlisle from about 1699 by Sir John Vanbrugh and Nicholas Hawksmoor. It is the first essay by one of the most famous of architectural partnerships and was largely complete at Vanbrugh's death in 1726. The west wing was built only in 1753–59 by the Palladian Sir Thomas Robinson. The details and possibly the baroque movement of Castle Howard are Hawksmoor's contribution and lead directly to Blenheim Palace. The park is a notable classic landscape treated with architectural features: the Temple of the Four Winds (1724–26), by Vanbrugh, one of his best garden buildings; and the Mausoleum by Hawksmoor (begun 1728), a domed rotunda that is the architect's greatest work. *See* HAWKSMOOR, NICHOLAS; VANBRUGH, SIR JOHN.

BIBLIOGRAPHY. K. Downes, *Nicholas Hawksmoor*, London, 1960.

HOWE, GEORGE B. American architect (b. Worcester, Mass., 1886; d. Cambridge, Mass., 1955). Howe's major work, the Philadelphia Savings Fund Society Building, built with William Lescaze in 1931–32, presents a striking balance between the horizontals of the cantilevered floors and the vertical rhythms of the columns on the flank. The plan is T-shaped; the service areas are conveniently separated from the office spaces. Other works are his own house in Chestnut Hill, Pa. (1914–16); the Oshland School in Croton-on-Hudson, New York (1929), the first International style building on the east coast of the United States; the Thomas House on Soames Sound, Maine (1938–39), which has walls of wood and stone with cantilevers of reinforced concrete; and the Philadelphia Evening Bulletin Building (1954). *See* HOWE AND LESCAZE.

BIBLIOGRAPHY. T. F. Hamlin, *Forms and Functions of Twentieth-Century Architecture*, vols. 2, 4, New York, 1952.

HOWE AND LESCAZE. American architectural firm of George B. Howe and William Lescaze (1896–1969), active between 1929 and 1934. Among works designed by the firm were the Oak Lane County Day School in Philadelphia and the renowned Philadelphia Savings Fund Society Building (1931–32). This bank represents one of the first examples of the International style of architecture in an American skyscraper. It features a striking balance of horizontal and vertical masses. In the T-shaped plan, services are effectively separated from office spaces. The main banking room, originally in the form of a cube, conveys a certain severity; but the large floor area provides ample space for the customers. The monumental stairhall, however, may today seem overly dramatic. *See* HOWE, GEORGE B.

BIBLIOGRAPHY. F. Gutheim, "The Philadelphia Savings Fund Society Building: A Re-appraisal," *Architectural Record*, CVI, October, 1949.

HOWELLS, JOHN MEAD. American architect (b. Cambridge, Mass., 1868; d. 1959). After studying at the Ecole des Beaux-Arts, Paris, in the 1890s, Howells designed many commercial buildings in the United States, alone or in collaboration. He was competent in many styles, though a leading exponent of vertically styled skyscrapers. His best solo performance is the Beekman Towers in New York City (1928). *See also* HOOD AND HOWELLS.

HOYSALESVARA TEMPLE, HALEBID. Great double temple in the southern Deccan, Mysore State, India. The Hoysaleśvara was begun in 1235 by the last Hoysala king, Vīranarasiṁhadeva, at his residence at Halebīd, 10 miles east of Belūr. Its construction was terminated by the invasion of the Muslims in 1310; the tower and roof story were never completed, nor were parts of the upper walls. The temple, dedicated to the Hindu god Siva, is oriented eastward and stands upon a platform. It is made of stone that, soft when quarried, hardens on exposure. The exterior is literally covered with a rich profusion of sculpture, reaching the extreme limit of abundant plastic ornament. The subjects are scenes from the *Rāmāyaṇa*, celestial

beings, and animals. The temple has been likened to "a giant's jewel casket."

BIBLIOGRAPHY. A. K. Coomaraswamy, *History of Indian and Indonesian Art*, New York, 1927; H. R. Zimmer, *The Art of Indian Asia*, 2 vols., New York, 1955; P. Brown, *Indian Architecture*, 4th ed., 2 vols., Bombay, 1959.

HSIA CH'ANG. Chinese painter of bamboos (1388–1470). His *tzu* was Chung-chao. Born in K'un-shan in Kiangsu Province, he attained the rank of *chin-shih* in 1415 and held a high position in government. In his paintings he followed Wang Fu and became one of the most highly prized painters of the special subject of bamboos in his lifetime. The Art Institute of Chicago possesses the earliest dated bamboo paintings by Hsia Ch'ang (1441), and the William Rockhill Nelson Gallery, Kansas City, has the latest dated work (1464); thus American audiences have a somewhat unique opportunity in Chinese pictorial history to compare two fine paintings by a great master. *See* WANG FU.

BIBLIOGRAPHY. C. F. Kelley, "Bamboo Stream, Spring Rain Picture," *Chicago Art Institute Bulletin*, XLV, April, 1951.

HSIA KUEI. Chinese landscape painter (fl. early 13th cent.). He was active in the Painting Academy during the reign of the emperor Ning-tsung (1195–1224). As is the case with his celebrated contemporary Ma Yüan, with whom Hsia Kuei is so intimately linked, very little is known concerning the details of Hsia's life. He came from Ch'ien-t'ang near the capital of Hang-chou in Chekiang Province and eventually attained the highest rank in the Academy, gaining considerable praise from critics for his "glowing ink." He was dependent on Li T'ang for his style perhaps to a greater extent than Ma Yüan. Although he often employed the one-corner compositional device so characteristic of Ma Yüan, Hsia Kuei seems involved less with the creation of the visionary "idealized" world and more with the nuances of brush technique, as the critics indicate with their statements concerning his rich, lustrous ink tones. Hsia Kuei made less use of the single brush line than other members of the Academy, and the majority of extant Hsia Kuei paintings subordinate figures and architectural motifs. Hsia Kuei preferred to build in terms of graded ink washes, using overlapping brushstrokes to define a mass of foliage and varied washes of ink to depict mists, voids, or hard structures like trees and rocks. *See* LI T'ANG; MA YUAN.

Two distinctly different sides of Hsia Kuei can be seen in comparing the hand scroll in the National Palace Museum Collection, Sun Yat-sen Museum, in Formosa, with the often-reproduced *Landscape in a Rainstorm* formerly in the Kawasaki Collection, Japan. The long hand scroll (more than 30 ft.) is a magnificent work, bearing the title *Clear View of Streams and Mountains*. A similar hand scroll in the Sun Yat-sen collection (perhaps better known to Western students since it was exhibited in the London show of 1935) entitled *Ten Thousand Miles of Long River* is now generally thought to be a later copy. In *Clear View* the panoramic sweep of landscape echoes the great tradition of Northern Sung, with the element of time incorporated in the composition and developed on a remarkably sophisticated level. The brushwork is detailed, with a full vocabulary of strokes called forth by Hsia Kuei and

Hsia Kuei, *Twelve Views from a Thatched Hut*, detail. William Rockhill Nelson Gallery of Art, Kansas City.

combined throughout with large areas of mist, voids, and rock façades treated with the simple, bold ax stroke. The intricacies and complexities of this hand scroll contrast sharply with the handling seen in the modestly scaled *Landscape in a Rainstorm*. Here the brush is employed in sweeping strokes with greater elimination of detail and more numerous sharp tonal contrasts. The "wetness" of this painting seems appropriate for the subject (Hsia Kuei seemed fond of the idea of rainstorms), and the adulation given him by the Chinese for his handling of ink seems fully justified. *See also* Ts'UN.

Among paintings attributed to Hsia Kuei in American collections the hand scroll in the William Rockhill Nelson Gallery, Kansas City, entitled *Twelve Views from a Thatched Hut*, deserves particular notice. Although only four of the views remain in this fragment from a much longer work, something of Hsia Kuei's technical range can clearly be seen. The scroll effectively demonstrates why Hsia Kuei escaped some of the criticism leveled at Ma Yüan for his somewhat sentimentalized landscapes; the sense of discipline and the restraint that permeate Hsia Kuei's best works set him apart from other members of the Southern Sung Academy. *See also* MA-HSIA SCHOOL.

BIBLIOGRAPHY. O. Sirén, *Chinese Painting, Leading Masters and Principles*, vol. 2, New York, 1956; W. Willets, *Chinese Art*, vol. 2, Harmondsworth, 1958; Wang Shih-chien, ed., *Three Hundred Mas-**terpieces of Chinese Painting in the Palace Museum*, 6 vols., Taichung, 1959; S. E. Lee, *Chinese Landscape Painting*, 2d rev. ed., Cleveland, 1962.

MARTIE W. YOUNG

HSI-AN, *see* CH'ANG-AN.

HSIANG MO-LIN, *see* HSIANG YUAN-PIEN.

HSIANG SHENG-MO. Chinese painter of landscapes and of birds and flowers (1597–1658). Hsiang Sheng-mo was born in Chia-hsing, Chekiang Province; his *tzu* was K'ungchang and his *hao* I-an. The grandson of the famous Ming collector Hsiang Yüan-pien, he apparently had ample opportunity to acquaint himself with ancient masterpieces and drew praise from later critics such as Tung Ch'i-ch'ang for his studies of Sung and Yüan painters. The majority of Hsiang Sheng-mo's extant paintings are deceptively casual, simplified presentations of charming landscapes, executed with perception and sensitivity. *See* HSIANG YUAN-PIEN; TUNG CH'I-CH'ANG.

BIBLIOGRAPHY. O. Sirén, *Chinese Painting, Leading Masters and Principles*, vol. 5, New York, 1958.

HSIANG-T'ANG-SHAN. Mountain range in northern Honan and western Hopei provinces, China. In the early 20th century it was explored by Japanese scholars. Two series of cave temples called Northern and Southern Hsiang-t'ang-shan were found. They date mainly from the Northern Ch'i period (550–577). The sculpture from this site is marked by a great simplicity of handling and a sense of plastic volume indicative of the renewed contacts with India during this period. Several fine examples of Hsiang-t'ang-shan sculpture are in the University Museum, Philadelphia.

BIBLIOGRAPHY. S. Mizuno and T. Nagahiro, *Kyōdōzan sekkutsu*, Kyoto, 1937.

HSIANG YUAN-PIEN (Hsiang Mo-lin). Chinese collector and amateur painter (1525–90). He was widely known by his *hao* Mo-lin or *tzu* Tzu-ching. Hsiang was born in Chia-hsing, Chekiang Province, an area that had produced many famous painters. He came from a wealthy official family but declined to enter public service, preferring to devote his life to collecting and occasionally painting. The works of art owned by Hsiang probably formed the largest single private collection in China during late Ming times and included a wide range of objects in addition to paintings. Since he led a rather quiet life, not much is known of Hsiang Yüan-pien, but it is known that he was a patron of Ch'iu Ying among others. Hsiang's own paintings are of modest quality, devoted mostly to flowers, bamboos, and similar themes, generally executed on a small scale. *See* CH'IU YING.

BIBLIOGRAPHY. P. David, "Hsiang and his Album," *Transactions of the Oriental Ceramic Society*, XI, 1933–34.

HSIAO HSIU, TOMB OF. Chinese tomb of the Liang dynasty (502–557), located near Nanking. The seventh son of the emperor Wu-ti, Prince Hsiao Hsiu died in 518. On the path leading to his tomb is a pair of winged stone lions (sometimes confusingly called "chimeras" in the West), the earliest of the surviving lions of this local dynasty. The lions of Hsiao Hsiu are among the finest of the "Liang lions," powerfully expressive forms that fully justify their identification as guardian images or protectors.

BIBLIOGRAPHY. Chu Hsi-tsu et al., "Liu-ch'ao ling-mu t'iao-ch'a pao-kao" (Reports on the Investigations of the Tombs of the Six Dynasties), *Monumenta Sinica*, I, 1935.

HSIAO-T'UN, *see* AN-YANG.

HSIAO YUN-TSUNG. Chinese landscape painter (1596–1673). He was a native of Wu-hu in Anhui Province; his *tzu* was Ch'ih-mu and his *hao* Wu-men tao-jen. Although not well known to early Western students of Chinese painting, Hsiao Yün-tsung was a very prominent artist in his own day and was always highly regarded by Chinese connoisseurs. He was particularly influential as a designer of the wood blocks that illustrate many of the 17th-century manuals on painting. Several fine paintings in American collections (Los Angeles County Art Museum and Cleveland Museum of Art) show him as a painter of considerable imagination as well as technical dexterity.

BIBLIOGRAPHY. H. Trubner, "A Chinese Landscape by Hsiao Yün-ts'ung," *Oriental Art*, 1955; S. E. Lee, "Some Problems in Ming and Ch'ing Landscape Paintings," *Ars Orientalis*, II, 1957.

HSIA-T'ANG-SHAN. Mountain 25 miles southwest of Fei-ch'eng in Shantung Province, China. On it is located an offering shrine, the only such shrine that stands today in its original form. A date inscribed by a visitor in the year 129 places the shrine in the Han dynasty; the general unorganized composition and repetition of figures indicate a date much earlier. Some aspects of the style as well as the subject matter are closely related to the Shrine of Wu Liang. *See* WU LIANG TOMBS.

BIBLIOGRAPHY. E. Chavannes, *Mission archéologique dans la Chine septentrionale*, vol. 1, Paris, 1909.

HSIEH HO. Chinese painter (fl. late 5th cent. A.D.). Hsieh Ho attained some measure of recognition for his portraits during the Southern Ch'i dynasty (479–501) in Nanking. None of his paintings is extant, and little is known of the details concerning his life. Later critics were not unanimous in their praise of his paintings, and his real reputation stems from his authorship of the *Ku-hua p'in-lu* (Old Records of the Classification of Painters) in which Hsieh Ho enumerated the famous "six principles" of painting. In this short treatise the author may not necessarily have broken any new critical ground; he probably only codified and articulated the prevailing aesthetic theories of the late 5th century. In his classification of painters Hsieh Ho selected twenty-seven men and divided them into six classes, based on their merits relative to the six principles, but the importance of the *Ku-hua p'in-lu* lies less in any concrete information it transmits than in the influence it had on later writers and critics in supplying a model. *See* SIX PRINCIPLES OF CHINESE PAINTING.

BIBLIOGRAPHY. O. Sirén, *The Chinese on the Art of Painting*, Peking, 1936; W. R. B. Acker, ed. and tr., *Some T'ang and pre-T'ang Texts on Chinese Painting* (Sinica leidensia, vol. 8), Leyden, 1954.

HSIEN. Chinese term applied to a group of ancient bronze ritual vessels. The character *hsien* is found in old inscriptions on the bronzes themselves; a similar character, pronounced *yen*, is the one in current use by the Chinese, although *hsien* is the term most widely employed in Western literature. The vessel is a composite form and functions as a steamer. The lower half is a tripod like the *li* or

Hsien. An ancient bronze ritual vessel in composite form. Private collection, Paris.

ting. The top part, which fits into the mouth of the lower vessel, is bowl-shaped with a grill on the bottom. The two pieces may be separate or hinged. The shape appears throughout the early periods of bronze art in China, and the prototype for the bronze vessel can be found in late neolithic pottery. *See* TING.

BIBLIOGRAPHY. W. Willets, *Foundations of Chinese Art*, New York, 1965.

HSI-HU (Western Lake), *see* HANG-CHOU.

HSI KANG (Hsi Meng-ch'uan). Chinese painter (1746–ca. 1816). He was a native of Ch'ien-t'ang, Chekiang Province. A traditional painter-scholar, Hsi Kang was a prolific master whose surviving works are well represented in Japanese collections. He painted mostly landscapes, usually after the Yüan masters.

HSIN-AN, FOUR MASTERS OF, *see* ANHUI SCHOOL, FOUR MASTERS OF.

HSING WARE. Name given to a class of white Chinese porcelains. Supposedly produced in the late T'ang and Five Dynasties periods (9th and 10th cent.), they were named after the district of Hsing-chou in Hopei Province.

Hsü Pei-hung, *The Colt*. Ink on paper. Hsü Pei-hung Museum, Peking.

HSI-TA-TO, *see* SIDDHARTHA.

HSUAN-HO HUA-P'U (Sung Imperial Catalog). Catalog of paintings that were in the collection of the Chinese emperor Hui-tsung during the Hsüan-ho era (1119–25) of the Sung dynasty. It contains brief biographical notes on famous painters from the 3d century A.D. to the Sung period and gives a list of the titles of paintings attributed to each master in the imperial collection. Neither the compiler nor the precise date of the *Hsüan-ho hua-p'u* is known.

BIBLIOGRAPHY. Ting Fu-pao, *Ssu-pu tsung-lu i-shu pien*, 2 vols., Shanghai, 1957.

HSUAN-TE. Chinese emperor (r. 1426–35). The Ming emperor Hsüan-tsung, better known by his reign name Hsüan-te, was an emperor-painter of China, probably the best known outside of Hui-tsung of the Sung period. Like those of Hui-tsung, the paintings of Hsüan-te are devoted mainly to themes of animals, rendered with considerable skill and capturing some of the meticulous quality of the earlier Sung master. Most of the signed and dated paintings by the Ming emperor fall in the period between 1426 and 1429, covering the first four years of the reign. *See* HUI-TSUNG.

HSUEH-CH'UANG, *see* P'U-MING.

HSU HSI. Chinese painter (d. before 975). He was active at the court of the Li Yü of the Southern T'ang dynasty. Hsü Hsi, one of the triumvirate of great masters who pioneered the bird-and-flower category of paintings, was extolled at great length in early Chinese literary sources. His name in particular was associated with the *lo-mo* technique, whereby washes of ink or color flowed rather freely onto the surface of the painting after the outlines of the subject had been established. No authentic example of Hsü Hsi's painting style remains today, although a number of paintings with long-standing attributions to this master exist in Japan. Among these, the pair of paintings in the Chionin, Kyoto, depicting lotus flowers and birds is best known.

BIBLIOGRAPHY. B. Rowland, "Early Chinese Paintings in Japan: The Problem of Hsü Hsi," *Artibus Asiae*, XV, 1952; Teng Pai, *Hsü Hsi yü Huang Ch'uan* (Chung-kuo hua-chia ts'ung-shu, vol. 4), Shanghai, 1958.

HSU PEI-HUNG (Ju Peon). Chinese painter (b. I-hsing, Kiangsu Province, 1896; d. Peking, 1953). He moved to Shanghai at the age of nineteen. In 1917 he made a trip to Japan, and in 1919 he won a government scholarship to study in Paris, where he remained until 1928. Government support was withdrawn after four years in Paris, and Hsü Pei-hung's later years in the art capital of Europe were extremely difficult as he eked out an existence, which was to cost him his health. The years in Paris, however, were invaluable to him, and after his return to China he was to become one of the most influential Chinese teachers of the 20th century. He became a professor in the art department of National Central University in Nanking in 1928 and moved on to several other important academic posts. In 1932 he revisited Europe and organized major exhibitions of Chinese art in Paris, Berlin, and Milan. After World War II he became director of the Peking Academy of Art, having won recognition among both Europeans and Chinese as one of the greatest contemporary Chinese painters.

Among the paintings for which Hsü Pei-hung is best known are his powerful monochromatic ink sketches of galloping horses, subjects that he painted frequently from his early thirties. There are countless imitations of the distinctive style that Hsü Pei-hung evolved for depicting with impressionistic vigor the magnificent steeds so long favored by Chinese artists of the past. The sense of immediacy and penetrating presence that Hsü imparts in his horses puts him on the fringe of Western-style painting, but the fluid brushwork is still strongly Chinese in flavor.

BIBLIOGRAPHY. M. Sullivan, *Chinese Art in the 20th Century*, London, 1959; L. Hájek, A. Hoffmeister, and E. Rychterová, *Contemporary Chinese Painting*, London, 1961.

MARTIE W. YOUNG

HSU TAO-NING. Chinese painter (fl. early 11th cent.). Originally from Ho-chien in Hopei Province, he spent most of his life in Ch'ang-an. He apparently turned to painting as a profession rather late in life, but he did earn some contemporary esteem for his landscapes, which seem to carry on the great tradition of Li Ch'eng and of Fan K'uan. Hsü Tao-ning is best known in the United States for a striking hand scroll in the collection of the William Rockhill Nelson Gallery, Kansas City, that depicts a river valley with fishermen and a series of extraordinary mountains with an incessant sweeping rhythm. Something of the moving grandeur that characterizes the monumental style of landscape painting has been caught and transformed by Hsü Tao-ning to fit the demands of the hand scroll in this particular example. *See* FAN K'UAN; LI CH'ENG.

BIBLIOGRAPHY. O. Sirén, *Chinese Painting, Leading Masters and Principles*, vol. 1, New York, 1956.

HSU WEI. Chinese painter (1521–93). Born in Shan-yin, Chekiang Province, he led a colorful life that has been related in various chronicles in some detail. A child prodigy of sorts, Hsü Wei enjoyed early success with the help of an ambitious governor but suffered a series of reverses that eventually put him in jail. Always considered eccentric, he feigned madness and was finally released. He drank heavily and died in poverty. But such bare outlines hardly convey the career of this man, one of the real precursors of the great 17th-century individualists known as the Yang-chou eccentrics. His paintings are rather numerous, particularly in Japanese and European collections. Hsü Wei's best works are on a small scale and are restricted to themes such as bamboos, birds, or motifs of the four seasons. His explosive style mirrors his erratic temperament, and Hsü Wei's paintings appear almost like an ironic commentary on the literati painter's belief that the painting must reflect the temperament of the man. *See* YANG-CHOU, EIGHT ECCENTRICS OF.

BIBLIOGRAPHY. Ho Lo-chih, *Hsü Wei* (Chung-kuo hua-chia ts'ung-shu, vol. 15), Shanghai, 1958; Tseng Yu-ho, "A Study on Hsü Wei," *Ars Orientalis*, V, 1963.

HU. Chinese designation of a type of ancient bronze ritual vessel in the shape of a large vase or jar with a wide body, which narrows at the foot and at the shoulders. The character *hu* is an ancient one, but no pottery prototype for the bronze vessel has yet been found in the late neolithic cultures of China. The vessel exists in all the periods of bronze art, but it was an especially favored shape in the late Chou period, when the surface of the *hu* was often decorated with inscribed hunting scenes. In the Han dynasty the *hu* form was often duplicated in pottery.

HUAI STYLE. Scandinavian term for the Chinese decorative style of the Warring States (period, 480–221 B.C.; style, ca. 600–200 B.C.). It is based on bronzes found in the Huai River Basin of Anhui, in southeastern Honan, and in northeastern Shansi. Delicate reliefs or inlaid gold, silver, and other materials, create an animated dance of continuous spirals, volutes, and bird-and-animal parts. *See also* CHINA: BRONZES (CHOU DYNASTY).

Hu. Type of ancient bronze ritual vessel. Above: Chou dynasty. Velluz Collection, Paris. Below: Sung or Yüan dynasty. Private collection, Paris.

HUANG CH'UAN. Chinese bird-and-flower painter (fl. mid-10th cent.). Huang Ch'üan was an official at the Shu court in Szechwan in the Five Dynasties period and later held a high position in the new Sung court at K'ai-feng. His influence on the Sung Academy in the realm of bird-and-flower painting was indirect; both his sons, Huang Chü-tsai and Huang Chü-pao, reportedly carried on his style faithfully. Chinese critics traditionally have accorded Huang Ch'üan a high position in the history of painting, but nothing remains of this master today to reinforce the judgment of earlier historians.

The famous scroll in the Moore Collection of the Yale University Art Gallery, New Haven, Conn., entitled *Assembly of Birds on a Willow Bank*, has had a long-standing attribution to Huang Ch'üan that goes back to the 11th century. The painting has suffered from considerable retouching and preserves at best only Huang Ch'üan's composition. Huang Ch'üan's special technique, according to literary sources, consisted of precise and firm boundary lines filled with light washes of color.

BIBLIOGRAPHY. L. W. Hackney and Yau Chang-Foo, *A Study of Chinese Paintings in the Collection of Ada Small Moore*, New York, 1940; B. Rowland, "The Problem of Hui Tsung," *Archives of the Chinese Art Society of America*, V, 1951.

MARTIE W. YOUNG

HUANG KUNG-WANG. Chinese landscape painter (1269–1354). His *tzu* was Tzu-chiu. A native of Ch'ü-chou in Chekiang Province, he is traditionally counted among the "Four Great Masters" of the Yüan dynasty, the oldest of the four in age. He was a precocious child, well versed in history and philosophy; he served the Mongols briefly but retired to the hills of Fu-ch'un in his native province. His notes on landscape painting were collected under the title *Hsieh shan-hsiu chüeh* and edited by T'ao Tsung-i in his compendium *Cho keng lu* in 1366.

Judging by the accolades accorded him by later painters, Huang Kung-wang was the Yüan painter who had the most influence on the development of later landscape painting, but his extant paintings are so few that it is difficult to assess this master today. His only major extant work is the long hand scroll in the National Palace Museum Collection, Sun Yat-sen Museum, in Formosa, representing the Fu-ch'un mountains that the painter loved so dearly. From the evidence supplied by this one painting, *Dwelling in the Fu-ch'un Mountains*, it is possible to detect something of Huang Kung-wang's style. If we are to judge by literary sources, this particular work was the great masterpiece of the Yüan artist, often copied and studied. The painting was executed over a period of years in Huang Kung-wang's old age and can be seen as a summation of the painter's thoughts and attitude concerning landscape representation.

Painting to Huang Kung-wang was an intellectual exercise of the highest order, and the hand scroll seems to be a series of related constructions developed over a period of time, strokes added here and there in order to shift or darken a contour, to add texture to a rock. Thus strength was achieved without an ostentatious display of technical proficiency, and the literati ideal was maintained. According to Huang's inscription on the scroll, the painting took three years to consummate, once the outlines had been laid in; the painter added to the painting whenever he was spiritually moved, after wandering through his beloved

Huang Kung-wang, *Mountain Landscape*. British Museum, London.

hills. In every sense, then, Huang Kung-wang painted directly inspired by the visual world surrounding him, transforming the phenomena of earthly existence with a cool, deliberate manner in the best tradition of the restrained Chinese scholar.

BIBLIOGRAPHY. W. Speiser, "Die Yüan-Klassik der Landschafts-malerei," *Ostasiatische Zeitschrift*, n.s. VIII, 1931; S. Shimada and Y. Yonezawa, *Painting of the Sung and Yüan Dynasties*, Tokyo, 1952; Pan T'ien-shou and Wang Pai-min, *Huang Kung-wang* (Chung-kuo hua-chia ts'ung-shu, vol. 7), Shanghai, 1958.

MARTIE W. YOUNG

HUANG P'ING-HUNG. Chinese painter (1864–1955). Born in Hsi-hsien, Anhui Province, he moved to Shanghai in 1908 after having been thoroughly educated in art by his father. He became art editor for the famous Commercial Press and compiled a well-known anthology of writings on art that is still a classic source for modern scholars. In 1937 he went to Peking and was a teacher in the Academy of Art for eleven years. He was a friend and contemporary of the great Ch'i Pai-shih, and in many ways he was just as influential in shaping the direction of modern art in China. He lectured and traveled widely. *See* CH'I PAI-SHIH.

His own paintings showed a vigorous, individualistic style that belongs in the late *wen-jen* tradition of Jen Pai-nien and others, and because he has been considered a traditionalist, he, like other 19th- and 20th-century literati painters, has been largely overlooked in the West. Huang P'ing-hung was also a discriminating collector and student of all Chinese art. *See* JEN PAI-NIEN; WEN-JEN-HUA.

BIBLIOGRAPHY. M. Sullivan, *Chinese Art in the 20th Century*, London, 1959; L. Hájek, A. Hoffmeister, and E. Rychterová, *Contemporary Chinese Painting*, London, 1961.

HUA YEN. Chinese painter (b. Fukien Province, 1682; d. Hang-chou, 1765). Hua Yen moved his family to Hang-chou but spent the greater part of his life in Yang-chou, where he eventually earned his reputation as one of the "Eight Eccentrics of Yang-chou." He was known by his *hao* Hsin-lo shan-jen. Hua Yen was a prolific painter whose style is hard to characterize simply. His favored subjects, however, seem to be drawn from the world of animals and rendered with something of an impressionistic brush. He returned to Hang-chou late in his life. *See* YANG-CHOU, EIGHT ECCENTRICS OF.

HUA-YEN-SSU, TA-T'UNG. Chinese temple built in 1038. Located in Shansi Province, it dates to the period when the town of Ta-t'ung served as the capital for the Khitans and Jurchens (Liao and Kin, or Chin, dynasties, respectively). There are two separate and adjoining complexes; the northern precinct is referred to as "Upper" Hua-yen-ssu.

The Pao-chia-chiao-ts'ang-tien, a small library, is the chief feature of "Lower" Hua-yen-ssu. On the altar of this hall can be seen, in an excellent state of preservation, a group of Buddha images and attendant deities made of clay. The central group of three Buddhas, more than 15 feet high, is represented seated on large lotus thrones backed by wooden nimbuses. They and the numerous smaller flanking figures are among the finest examples of post-T'ang sculpture in China. The style is basically T'ang, but a new naturalism has modified the full-bodied late T'ang forms. According to an inscription on the beam, the Pao-

chia-chiao-ts'ang hall was built in 1038; it was extensively repaired after a fire in 1140, but most authorities now seem to agree with Japanese scholars that the impressive group of statues dates from the period before the reconstruction of the temple.

Upper Hua-yen-ssu was apparently added after 1062, the date when the Khitan emperors presented their imperial portraits to the temple. A large central hall, built under Kin patronage, is the main feature of the upper temple.

BIBLIOGRAPHY. L. Sickman and A. Soper, *The Art and Architecture of China*, Baltimore, 1956.

MARTIE W. YOUNG

HUBER, HERMANN. Swiss painter and graphic artist (1888–). He was born in Zurich and studied there, at the Düsseldorf Academy, and in Munich and Berlin. The influence of Renoir is seen in his early loosely brushed paintings of children and figures in landscapes. In the years around 1910, Huber painted symbolic themes and dramatic compositions related to Hodler. His later work, while still colorful, shows a firmer treatment of forms.

BIBLIOGRAPHY. H. Trog and C. Glaser, *Hermann Huber, Eine Monographie*, Potsdam, 1924.

HUBER, WOLF. Austrian painter and designer of woodcuts (b. Feldkirch in Vorarlberg, ca. 1490; d. Passau, 1553). Huber was apprenticed to Albrecht Altdorfer from 1510 to 1515. In 1515 he moved to Passau, where he became the court painter to the prince-bishop, a post he held until 1540. Together with Altdorfer, Huber is one of the chief representatives of the so-called Danubian school of painting. The influence of Altdorfer's style was strong, but Huber nonetheless developed an artistic personality of his own which enriched the Danubian school style with a new spontaneity.

Huber's major work is the *St. Anne Altar*, which he produced for the parish church of St. Nikolaus at Feldkirch. The center panel, the *Lamentation over the Dead Body of Christ*, is still in the church, but the outer and inner panels, consisting of four panels of scenes from the life of St. Anne, are in the Vienna Museum of Art History. This work is noted for the masterful integration of figure and landscape, and as such it is one of the greatest works of the Danubian style.

Earlier works by Huber are the *Epitaph of Bürgermeister Endl of Passau* (1517; Kremsmünster) and *Christ Taking Leave of His Mother* (1519; Vienna, Museum of Art History). Both show a close similarity to Altdorfer's work.

In his late period Huber's art changed. His composition became more daring, his figural treatment more expressive, his light values more mysterious. The most striking example of the change is the painting *Raising of the Cross* (Vienna Museum). Here the composition is remarkably close to that of Tintoretto. Other works of his late period are the *Crucifixion* (ca. 1535; Vienna Museum), the *Crowning of Thorns* (Sankt Florian, Monastic Collections), and the *Salvation of Mankind* (Vienna Museum). The style of Huber's late period is frequently called early baroque.

The woodcuts attributed to him are mainly from his early period. The most important ones are *Landsknechte*, *St. George*, and *St. Christopher*. His drawings, which are

Hudson River School. Thomas Cole, *The Oxbow (The Connecticut River near Northampton)*, 1846. Metropolitan Museum of Art, New York.

exceptional in their treatment of landscape, are found in Berlin, Munich, and Vienna.

BIBLIOGRAPHY. H. Voss, *Albrecht Altdorfer und Wolf Huber, Meister der Graphik*, Leipzig, 1910; P. Halm, "Die Landschafts- zeichnungen des Wolf Huber," *Münchner Jahrbuch der bildenden Kunst*, VII, 1930.

DONALD L. EHRESMANN

HUBERT, ST. Bishop (d. 727). He was the son of the Duke of Aquitaine. A 15th-century legend says that Hubert, like Eustace, was converted by seeing a stag dis- playing a crucifix between its antlers. Falling to the ground, Hubert was told to seek instruction from St. Lambert. He succeeded Lambert as bishop of Maastricht and Liège. He evangelized the forest of Ardennes, later becoming the patron saint of hunters and trappers. He died after a fishing accident in Meuse. His attribute is a stag with a crucifix between its antlers. His feast is November 3.

See also SAINTS IN ART.

HUBSCH, HEINRICH. German architect (1795–1863). Hübsch worked in Karlsruhe. A pupil of Weinbrenner, he succeeded him as state architect. Hübsch's writings, his archaeological studies of Early Christian and Roman- esque architecture, and his architectural style that tends to colorism and ornamentation, mark the trend away from classic to romantic architecture.

BIBLIOGRAPHY. A. Valdenaire, *Heinrich Hübsch; eine Studie zur Baukunst der Romantik*, Karlsruhe, 1926.

HUCHCHIMALLIGUDI TEMPLE, AIHOLE, *see* AIHOLE.

HU CHENG-YEN, *see* TEN-BAMBOO STUDIO, ALBUM OF.

Wolf Huber, *Christ Taking Leave of His Mother*, 1519. Museum of Art History, Vienna.

HUCHTENBURGH, JOHAN VAN. Dutch painter of battle and hunting scenes (b. Haarlem, 1647; d. Amster- dam, 1733). Van Huchtenburgh was the pupil of Thomas Wijck in Haarlem, and Wijck's son Jan was his friend. He traveled to Italy and was also active in Paris (1667) at the Gobelin factory under Adam Frans van der Meulen and Charles Le Brun. From 1676 to 1682 he traveled between Haarlem and Amsterdam. From 1708 to 1717 he worked for Prince Eugene of Savoy, for whom he painted ten large battle scenes.

BIBLIOGRAPHY. W. Bernt, *Die niederländischen Maler des 17. Jahrhunderts...*, vol. 2, Munich, 1948.

HUDSON, THOMAS. English painter (1701–79). Hudson is remembered primarily as the master of Reynolds. He is a competent minor portraitist, whose principal period of activity appears to have been during the 1740s and early 1750s. He spent the last twenty years of his life in retirement, leaving the stage to the more gifted younger generation.

BIBLIOGRAPHY. E. K. Waterhouse, *Painting in Britain, 1530–1790*, Baltimore, 1953.

HUDSON RIVER SCHOOL. Term applied to a group of American painters, active between 1825 and 1870, who specialized primarily in landscapes. Its most important members were Thomas Cole, John Kensett, George Inness, and Asher Brown Durand. Painters who worked in land- scape before 1825 are sometimes considered part of the school. These include Francis Guy, John Trumbull, and Washington Allston. All these men did not paint the Hud- son River, nor were they aware of being members of a school. The name was applied because some of the early members were drawn to the rich scenery of the Hudson

River Valley. All possessed a romantic attitude toward landscape. *See* ALLSTON, WASHINGTON; COLE, THOMAS; DURAND, ASHER BROWN; GUY, FRANCIS; INNESS, GEORGE; KENSETT, JOHN FREDERICK; TRUMBULL, JOHN.

BIBLIOGRAPHY. F. A. Sweet, *The Hudson River School and the Early American Landscape Tradition*, Chicago, 1945; C. E. Sears, *Highlights among the Hudson River Artists*, Boston, 1947.

HUE. General term meaning the color of an object; hue, however, frequently refers to a variation of a pure color. Yellow hue, for instance, implies not a pure yellow but a variation produced by the admixture of another color.

HUEJOTZINGO, MONASTERY CHURCH OF. Franciscan monastery church near Puebla, Mexico. Its site was chosen in 1524–29; the first church was built in 1529–39, probably under the direction of Fray Juan de Alameda. The present church was begun in 1544 and completed by 1571. Architecturally one of the most interesting Franciscan monasteries in Mexico, it has a vast rectangular atrium with corner chapels (*posas*) and a façade that combines ornamental influences of Gothic, Renaissance, and Mudejar origin. The monastic entrance features heavy, Romanesque-inspired arches with an arcaded cloister beyond. The ribbed-vaulted single-aisled church interior contains a well-preserved 16th-century retable that combines painting and sculpture. The fortified rear elevation suggests ornamentally the defensive character of early monastic settlements in Mexico.

BIBLIOGRAPHY. R. García Granados and L. Macgregor, *Huejotzingo, la ciudad y el convento franciscano*, Mexico, 1934; G. Kubler, *Mexican Architecture of the Sixteenth Century*, 2 vols., New Haven, 1948; J. A. Baird, Jr., *The Churches of Mexico, 1530–1810*, Berkeley, 1962.

HUERTA, JEAN (Jenaro) DE LA. Spanish sculptor (fl. mid-15th cent.; d. ca. 1457). Born in Daroca, Aragon, he probably was the pupil of the Burgundian Janin Lomme in the Spanish province of Navarre. In 1443 he began the tomb of the duke of Burgundy, John the Fearless, and his wife, Margaret of Bavaria, the conception of which he borrowed directly from Claus Sluter's tomb of Philip the Bold. Both tombs are in the Fine Arts Museum, Dijon.

BIBLIOGRAPHY. M. E. Gómez-Moreno, *Breve historia de la escultura española*, 2d ed., Madrid, 1951.

HUET, CHRISTOPHE. French painter and engraver (d. Paris, 1759). In the tradition of Audran and Berain, Huet was a student of Oudry. Christophe has been confused with his brother Nicholas who also studied with Oudry. Christophe is probably the Huet listed as a professor and member of the Academy of St. Luke in Paris who exhibited animal pictures and still lifes in the 1750s. The engravings of arabesques, *chinoiseries*, and *singeries* published by Huet represent the height of the rococo style. In the *singeries* and *chinoiseries* on the paneling of the château at Chantilly, dated 1735 and attributed to Huet, is found an extensive group of handsomely executed whimsical scenes that reveal as much a knowledge of classical tradition as a keen eye and alert wit. Huet's later work at the Hôtel de Rohan in Paris and the Château de Champs at Brie is equally fine.

BIBLIOGRAPHY. S. F. Kimball, *The Creation of the Rococo*, Philadelphia, 1943.

HUET, JEAN-BAPTISTE-MARIE. French animal and landscape painter and etcher (b. Paris, 1745; d. there, 1811). Huet concentrated on pastoral subjects, and his simple compositions were sought for reproduction in engraving, tapestry, porcelain, and furniture inlay. He created a vogue for monkeys in human guise (*singerie*). His textural depth in the downiness of fur and feathers is visually convincing, recalling Jan Fyt; his animation of animals recalls Jean-Baptiste Oudry's dog "portraits."

BIBLIOGRAPHY. C. Gabillot, *Les Hüet, Jean-Baptiste et ses trois fils*, Paris, 1892.

HUGHES, ARTHUR. English painter and illustrator (b. London, 1832; d. Kew Green, 1915). Hughes was an associate of the Pre-Raphaelites. He entered the Royal Academy of Arts schools in 1847 and won a medal there in 1849. By 1850 he had become interested in the graphic techniques of the Pre-Raphaelite painters through their periodical, *The Germ*. His paintings of the next ten years, which received the encouragement of his contemporaries William Holman Hunt and Dante Gabriel Rossetti, are characterized by their detail and bright palette. They include *Fair Rosamund* (1854; London, Tate Gallery), *Home from the Sea* (1856–63; Oxford, Ashmolean Museum), and *The Long Engagement* (1859; Birmingham Art Gallery), which have strong literary, if slightly sentimental, overtones. In 1858 Rossetti invited Hughes to participate in the mural decoration of the Oxford Union Debating Room with Burne-Jones and William Morris, but this work has since perished.

BIBLIOGRAPHY. R. Ironside and J. Gere, *Pre-Raphaelite Painters*, London, 1948.

HUGHES (Ball-Hughes), ROBERT BALL. American sculptor (b. London, 1806; d. Dorchester, Mass., 1868). Hughes went to the United States in 1829 and worked in New York City, Philadelphia, and Boston. He executed public monuments as well as portraits. Aside from the novelty of his late works—poker-burnt images in wood—Hughes's chief distinction is having made one of the very earliest works to be cast in bronze in the United States.

BIBLIOGRAPHY. E. Bolton, *American Wax Portraits*, Boston, 1929; E. D. Lovejoy, "Poker Drawings of Ball-Hughes," *Antiques*, L, 1946.

HUGO D'OIGNIES. Belgian goldsmith (fl. 1187–1228). A student of Nicolas de Verdun and a lay Augustine brother, he was first at Walcourt and then in the Cloister of St. Nicholas at Oignies near Namur. He was mentioned in a 17th-century chronicle as a famous goldsmith. Of the sixteen pieces attributed to him, three are inscribed. His richly ornamented early Gothic work is preserved in Namur, Brussels, Trier, and London.

BIBLIOGRAPHY. J. Labarte, *Histoire des arts industriels...*, 4 vols., Paris, 1864–66.

HUGUET, JAIME. Spanish painter (b. Valls? 1415/20; d. 1492). Huguet's early works—*St. George and the Princess* (Barcelona, Museum of Catalonian Art and Berlin former State Museums) and others ascribed to him—place him in Aragon from 1440 to 1447. Moving to Barcelona, where he operated a large studio and was closely connected with the court, he became the central figure in Catalan art. Most of his many commissions were executed with assistants, notably the members of the Vergós family who supplied wood carvings and goldwork, so that it is often difficult to distinguish Huguet's hand. Among the many retables of this period are those of *Vallmoll* (1447-50, Muntadas Collection), the *Epiphany* (1450-54; Vich Episcopal Museum of Archaeology and Art), *Sarria* (1450-60) and *S. Miguel* (1456-60; both Barcelona, Museum of Catalonian Art), *SS. Abdon and Senen* (1459-60; Tarrasa, S. Maria de Egara), *Constable Don Pedro of Portugal* (1464-65; Barcelona, Chapel of S. Agueda), the *Consecration of St. Augustine* (1466-70; Barcelona, Museum of Catalonian Art) and *St. Bernardine and the Guardian Angel* (1468-72, Barcelona Cathedral).

Huguet's style is at the opposite pole from the influence of Flemish naturalism that is evident in the paintings of Luis Dalmau. Huguet's art is instead characterized by its incisive, two-dimensional drawing, its elegant, elongated figures, and its decorative patterns of architectural setting and costume, which nonetheless involve the more naturalistic outlook of 15th-century art.

BIBLIOGRAPHY. J. Gudiol i Ricart and J. Ainaud de Lasarte, *Huguet*, Barcelona, 1948.   DONALD GODDARD

HUGUET OF BATALHA.

Portuguese architect (d. 1437/38). Huguet was the second architect in charge of the votive church of S. Maria da Vitória at Batalha. His contribution to the building is not known.

HUIJSUM (Huysum), JAN VAN.

Dutch painter of flower and fruit still lifes and some landscapes (b. Amsterdam, 1682; d. there, 1749). Van Huijsum was the son and pupil of the flower painter Justus van Huijsum the Elder. Jan van Huijsum's earliest dated work is a *Flower Still Life* (1706; Hamburg, Art Gallery). This picture, considering its late date in the history of Dutch painting, is surprisingly tight in its compositional arrangement and is almost symmetrical.

In his magnificent *Flower Still Life* of 1726 (London, Wallace Collection) the tight compositional arrangement has been replaced by a soft S-curve arrangement and a lighter, graceful quality. His *Flowers* (Amsterdam, Rijksmuseum) includes a text from Matthew 6:28-29 ("Consider the lilies of the field . . . Solomon in all his glory was not arrayed like one of these."), which indicates that he still worked in the moralizing tradition of earlier Dutch still-life painting.

Dutch sources tell us that Van Huijsum refused for the most part to have pupils; only one, Margareta Haverman, is known. Van Huijsum was the most acclaimed flower painter of his day, and his contemporaries called him "the phoenix of all flower painters." His younger brother Jacobus imitated his style.

BIBLIOGRAPHY. F. Schlie, "Sieben Briefe und eine Quittung von Jan van Huijsum," *Oud-Holland*, XVIII, 1900; M. H. Grant, *Jan van Huysum 1682-1749* . . ., Leigh-on-Sea, 1954; I. Bergström, *Dutch Still-Life Painting in the Seventeenth Century*, New York, 1956; C. White, *The Flower Drawings of Jan van Huysum*, Leigh-on-Sea, 1964.   LEONARD J. SLATKES

HUIJSUM (Huysum), JUSTUS VAN.

Dutch painter of genre, portraits, still lifes, and decorations (b. Amsterdam, 1659; d. there, 1716 [or 1723?]). Van Huijsum was a pupil of Claes Berchem in 1675. In 1681 he was married at Amsterdam, where apparently he was active his entire life.

He is the father of the still-life painter Jan van Huijsum, the battle painter Justus van Huijsum the Younger, and the painters Jacobus and Michiel van Huijsum.

Justus van Huijsum was mostly active as a flower painter, but he did do decorative pieces of various types (Utrecht, Centraal Museum). The inventory of works of art in his possession at the time of his death suggests that he was also active as an art dealer.

BIBLIOGRAPHY. W. Martin, *De Hollandsche schilderkunst in de zeventiende eeuw*, vol. 2, Amsterdam, 1936; Centraal Museum, Utrecht, *Catalogus der Schilderijen*, Utrecht, 1952.

HUI-TSUNG.

Eighth emperor of the Sung dynasty (r. 1101-26). Chao Chi (posthumous title Hui-tsung), the eleventh son of the emperor Shen-tsung, became an accomplished painter as well as a major patron of the arts, probably the most famous of all China's rulers in this respect. The political career of Hui-tsung was not a particularly distinguished one, however, for it was under his rule that the northern part of China fell to the Tatars. Most of his life seems to have been spent in developing his intellectual and aesthetic faculties, and by his lack of political understanding or interest he sealed his personal fate as well as that of his empire: in 1126 the Tatars sacked K'ai-feng and took Hui-tsung into captivity. He died in 1135 in distant Manchuria.

As a painter Hui-tsung personally led the way for his academy, and in the first year of his reign he issued a regulation that admonished painters to depict objects "true to color and form," in other words, strongly insisting on verisimilitude in all their works. Hui-tsung's own paintings became a standard: tightly conceived, meticulous in their handling, they reveal a painter interested in the literal recording of minute textures. Most of Hui-tsung's subjects were drawn from the world of "feathers and furs," a category that the Emperor made famous. In such examples as the *Five-colored Parakeet* (Boston, Museum of Fine Arts), or the *Quail and Narcissus* (Tokyo, Asano Collection), a heightened realism of effect is obtained by the most painstaking rendering of individual elements, so that feather by feather, leaf by leaf, a world is created that becomes superreal, the whole more than the simple sum of its parts. At the same time there is a very self-conscious aestheticism cultivated in these remarkable paintings of birds and flowers. The use of the asymmetrical composition (which leads ultimately to the famous one-corner composition of the Southern Sung style) is detectable, and in the very careful balance between bird, flowers, and empty space there is a timeless quality that transcends the limits of the momentary world of these small creatures. Nature is not duplicated in any photographic sense but becomes immortalized in these clear, lucid statements. Ideal perfection has been obtained.

In addition to his efforts as a painter, Hui-tsung also aggressively pursued his antiquarian interests. His collection of paintings, calligraphies, ceramics, bronzes, and other works of art was extensive. The *Hsüan-ho hua-p'u* records a part of his collection, listing more than 6,000 examples of painting alone. The greater part of these treasures was unfortunately destroyed in the capture of K'ai-feng by the Tatars. Presumably many of Hui-tsung's own paintings were lost at the same time. Of the few dozen works that

Hui-tsung, *Dove on a Flowering Peach Branch*. Inouye Collection, Tokyo. Asymmetrical composition with painstaking rendering of detail.

are attributed to him today, many are later imitations, most of them belonging to the bird-and-flower category. In addition to the examples cited above, the *Dove on a Flowering Peach Branch* (Tokyo, Inouye Collection) and the *Two Bullfinches* (New York, Crawford Collection), are works of high quality and deserve close attention. *See* HSUAN-HO HUA-P'U.

BIBLIOGRAPHY. B. Rowland, "The Problem of Hui Tsung," *Archives of the Chinese Art Society of America*, V, 1951; J. Cahill, *Chinese Paintings, 11th–14th Centuries*, New York, 1960.

MARTIE W. YOUNG

HULSDONCK, JACOB VAN. Flemish still-life painter (b. Antwerp, 1582; d. there, 1647). Hulsdonck first worked in Middelburg, then joined the Antwerp guild in 1609. He painted many fruit and flower pieces in a naïve but engaging manner.

BIBLIOGRAPHY. I. Bergström, *Dutch Still-Life Painting in the Seventeenth Century*, New York, 1956.

HULSMAN, JAN (Hans Holzmann). Flemish painter (b. Cologne, 1644). He was active in the southern Low Countries during the second part of the 17th century. The artist was a minor genre painter who specialized in the so-called Dutch manner.

BIBLIOGRAPHY. H. Gerson and E. H. ter Kuile, *Art and Architecture in Belgium, 1600–1800*, Baltimore, 1960.

HULST, FRANS DE. Dutch landscape and cityscape painter (b. Haarlem? ca. 1610; d. there, 1661). In 1630 De Hulst was listed as a member of the civil-guard group in Haarlem. The following year he became a member of the Guild of St. Luke there and lived in the house of Jan Miense Molenaer at Heemstede, near Haarlem. His early works recall Salomon van Ruysdael and Jan van Goijen. Later De Hulst worked in the manner of Roelof van Vries.

BIBLIOGRAPHY. L. Preston, *Sea and River Painters of the Netherlands in the Seventeenth Century*, London, 1937.

HULTZ, JOHANN. German architect (d. 1449). Hültz was a native of Cologne, but worked mainly in Strasbourg. After 1419 he was master of the works at the Cathedral there. He designed the turret of its tower (1420–39), a great example of the constructional fantasy of the Flamboyant Gothic style. *See* STRASBOURG: CATHEDRAL.

HUMANISM. Term denoting the Renaissance idea of man as the measure of all things. It implies an optimistic, rationalistic, and materialistic attitude toward the world as contrasted with medieval abstraction and spirituality. This attitude originated in and received constant stimulation from a lively interest in classical antiquity as it was expressed in literature and the arts. It led to an emphasis on experimentation and practical investigation. It was important for the fine arts in that it fostered the emergence of individual creative personalities as opposed to the anonymity that shrouded great artists of the Middle Ages.

HUMAYUN PERIOD, *see* MUGHAL PAINTING OF INDIA (HUMAYUN PERIOD).

HUMAYUN'S TOMB, DELHI. Indian mausoleum of Humayun, second emperor of Hindustan. Located to the southeast of the city, it is set within a spacious garden and approached through a monumental gateway. This great red and white marble mausoleum erected in 1556 set the style for later structures of the Mughal period. It is square in plan, with corner elements crowned by kiosks. An arched portal leads into the central chamber, which houses the white marble sarcophagus of the ruler, and above this chamber rises a dome of white marble.

BIBLIOGRAPHY. R. C. Arora, *Delhi: The Imperial City*, New Delhi, 1953.

HUMPHREY, JACK WELDON. Canadian painter (1901–). He studied in Boston and New York City and was associated with André Lhote and Hans Hofmann. Living in Saint John, he has painted landscapes of the region as well as figures in water color and oil. Recent oils show increasingly abstract tendencies.

BIBLIOGRAPHY. D. W. Buchanan, *The Growth of Canadian Painting*, London, 1950.

HUNDRED GUILDERS PRINT, *see* CHRIST HEALING THE SICK.

HUNDREISER, EMIL. German sculptor (b. Königsberg, 1846; d. Berlin, 1911). He studied with Leopold Rudolf Siemering at the Berlin Academy from 1865 to 1868. Hundreiser became a successful sculptor of monuments, executed, like the work of Siemering, in a sort of neo-baroque style.

HUNGARY, NATIONAL MUSEUM OF, *see* BUDAPEST: MUSEUM OF FINE ARTS.

HUNG-JEN. Chinese landscape painter (fl. 1st half of 17th cent.). His name was Chiang T'ao, his *tzu* Chien-chang, and his *hao* Mei-hua Ku-na. The appellation Hung-jen, by which he is best known, was his religious name, taken when he became a Buddhist monk soon after his mother died. Born in Hsieh-hsien in Anhui, he spent most of his life in his native province and was a rather quiet and retiring individual. He is considered the foremost painter of the Anhui school, and his landscapes are quite distinctive in style. They usually reflect a pensive mood, catching the quality of loneliness seen in the works of the Yüan painter Ni Tsan, whom Hung-jen greatly admired. The Ni Tsan style, however, has been transformed into something quite personal by Hung-jen, resulting in fragile, elegant landscapes constructed of thin lines and light washes, an ultimate refinement of Ni Tsan's cool, sparse world. *See* ANHUI SCHOOL, FOUR MASTERS OF; NI TSAN.

BIBLIOGRAPHY. O. Sirén, *Chinese Painters, Leading Masters and Principles*, vol. 5, New York, 1958.

HUNGRY DEMONS SCROLL. Japanese *emaki* (12th cent.). The scroll is divided between the National Museum of Tokyo and the National Commission for the Protection of Cultural Properties. It illustrates the World of Hungry Demons, situated between the World of Beasts and the World of Hell according to Buddhist theology. Pictures are executed with only light touches of color, allowing the carefully drawn lines to speak for the agonies of eternal hunger and thirst to which the ghosts are condemned.

BIBLIOGRAPHY. *Nihon emakimono zenshū (Japanese Scroll Paintings)*, vol. 6: *Jigoku zōshi, Gaki zōshi, Yamai zōshi*, Tokyo, 1960; H. Okudaira, *Emaki (Japanese Picture Scrolls)*, Rutland, Vt., 1962.

HUNT, RICHARD MORRIS. American architect (1827–1895). He was born in Brattleboro, Vt. The first American to study at the Ecole des Beaux-Arts, Paris, Hunt returned to the United States in 1855, less influenced, in general, by contemporary Parisian styles than by academic French tradition. He is known chiefly for his lavish town and country houses, in which he employed French Gothic and Renaissance motifs: his work includes "Biltmore" in North Carolina (1890–95), an American version of the Loire Valley châteaux, and the earlier W. K. Vanderbilt mansion in New York City (1881). Because of its height (260 feet), his mansarded Tribune Building, New York City (1873–75), is considered an early skyscraper. After 1888, Hunt designed expensive residences at Newport, R.I., which transformed the character of that resort community. The Breakers (1892–95) is among the best known. *See* BREAKERS, THE, NEWPORT, R.I.

HUNT, WILLIAM HENRY. English painter (b. London, 1790; d. there, 1864). He studied with John Varley and at the Royal Academy schools. His first exhibition was of three landscapes at the Royal Academy in 1807. He obtained early employment as a painter of country estates. Hunt painted portraits, humorous country genre scenes, and landscapes, but his popularity was mainly due to his still lifes, fruit, vegetables, and birds and their nests, executed with bright finish and great detail.

HUNT, WILLIAM HOLMAN. English painter (b. London, 1827; d. Kensington, 1910). He studied at the Royal Academy schools and there met John Everett Millais and Dante Gabriel Rossetti with whom he formed the Pre-Raphaelite Brotherhood in 1848. The characteristics of Hunt's paintings developed out of his religious convictions and out of his rather literal application of Pre-Raphaelite aesthetic theory, the one resulting in a strong moralizing approach, and the other, in a nearly endless accumulation of detail. Both characteristics are evident in *The Hireling Shepherd* (1851; Manchester, Whitworth Art Gallery) and *The Awakening Conscience* (1853; London, Collection of Sir Colin Anderson).

In 1854 Hunt made his first trip to the Near East with the intention of painting the life of Christ and Biblical scenes at their original sites. He returned again in 1869 and in 1873. His later religious paintings were filled with masses of personally symbolic details equaled in quantity only by the number of explanations Hunt wrote to accompany them.

BIBLIOGRAPHY. W. H. Hunt, *Pre-Raphaelitism and the Pre-Raphaelite Brotherhood...*, 2 vols., 2d ed., London, 1913; A. C. Gissing, *William Holman Hunt*, London, 1936.

JEROME VIOLA

HUNT, WILLIAM MORRIS. American painter (b. Brattleboro, Vt., 1824; d. Appledore, Isle of Shoals, Me., 1879). Hunt went to Europe in 1843 and studied sculpture in Rome and Paris. In 1846 he was in Düsseldorf but, dissatisfied with the tight and linear method of painting taught there, soon returned to Paris.

In Paris, Hunt studied painting with Couture from 1847 to 1852. He met Millet, whose influence on him was so strong that Hunt moved to Barbizon. Hunt bought many paintings by Millet and other Barbizon masters and brought his collection to the United States in 1855. In his own paintings of this period, many of the characteristics of Millet can be seen: a low horizon, the suggestion of monumentality, and a touch of the sentimental. But apart from these romantic elements, they also show a strong realism that, for a while, brought Hunt's work almost parallel with contemporary developments in France. The important portrait *Chief Justice Lemuel Shaw* (ca. 1860; Salem, Mass., Court House) is clearly painted and strongly designed with a characteristic stress on low-keyed tonality.

Later paintings, though similarly low-keyed, stress either an impressionistic immediacy of recording the visual experience (for example, *The Bathers*, 1877; New York, Metropolitan Museum), or a kind of atmospheric painting comparable to that of Boudin in France (as in *Gloucester Harbor*, 1877; Boston, Museum of Fine Arts). This was as far as Hunt's "impressionism" went. Like another American painter, Winslow Homer, Hunt was unwilling or unable to give up traditional strong, sculpturesque modeling in favor of the form-dissolving depiction of the given light. He retained, however, an interest in close arrangement of tones, as in *Miss Ida Mason* (middle 1870s; Boston, Museum of Fine Arts).

In 1878 Hunt was commissioned to paint two lunettes for the State Capitol in Albany, N.Y. Unfortunately, only the studies now exist; faults in architectural construction, speed of execution, and poor materials quickly ruined the paintings. Besides his artistic production, Hunt's importance for American art lies in the salutary influence he exerted as a teacher (especially on John La Farge) and in his crucial role in the development of late-19th-century American aesthetic taste.

BIBLIOGRAPHY. H. M. Knowlton, ed., *Art Talks by William Morris Hunt*, Boston, 1875 and 1876; H. M. Knowlton, *The Art-Life of William Morris Hunt*, Boston, 1899; M. A. S. Shannon, *Boston Days of William Morris Hunt*, Boston, 1923.

JEROME VIOLA

HUNTINGTON, ANNA VAUGHN HYATT. American sculptor (1876–   ). Born in Cambridge, Mass., Mrs. Huntington studied with Henry Hudson Kitson in Boston as well as with Herman MacNeil and Gutzon Borglum at the Art Students League in New York City. A resident of many years in France, she was made an honorary citizen of Blois in 1922. She developed a great facility with her sculptures of animals, working directly from models, in which the intense energy of physical action and reaction is forcefully expressed. Most of these figures are in violent movement and bear such titles as *Tiger Reaching* and *Colts in a Snow Storm*. Among her many monuments in the United States and Europe are the equestrian *Joan of*

Arc (1915) on Riverside Drive and the monument to El Cid at the Hispanic Society of America (1927–37), both in New York City.

BIBLIOGRAPHY. *Anna Hyatt Huntington* (American Sculptors Series, 3), New York, 1947; E. Schaub-Koch, *L'Oeuvre d'Anna Hyatt-Huntington*, Paris, 1949.

HUNTINGTON, DANIEL. American painter (b. New York City, 1816; d. there, 1906). He studied under Samuel F. B. Morse and Henry Inman. Huntington was a prolific painter of history, genre, and, especially, portraits of prominent people. He was president of the National Academy of Design from 1862 to 1870 and from 1877 to 1890.

HUNTINGTON (Henry E.) LIBRARY AND ART GALLERY, SAN MARINO, CALIF., *see* SAN MARINO, CALIF.: HENRY E. HUNTINGTON LIBRARY AND ART GALLERY.

HUNTSMEN IN THE SNOW. Oil painting by Brueghel the Elder, in the Museum of Art History, Vienna. *See* BRUEGHEL, PIETER, THE ELDER.

HUON-DONG-JA, *see* AN KYON.

HUON GULF–TAMI ISLAND, *see* OCEANIC ART (MELANESIA: NEW GUINEA).

William M. Hunt, *The Bathers*. Metropolitan Museum, New York.

HURD, PETER. American painter, illustrator, and lithographer (1904–   ). Born in Roswell, N.M., he was a pupil of N. C. Wyeth. His detailed tempera paintings are of figures and of Western landscapes and subjects, as well as portraits. He has also painted murals.

HURTADO, FRANCISCO (Francisco Hurtado Izquierdo y Fernandez). Spanish architect (b. Lucena, 1669; d. Priego, 1725). Hurtado was a major figure of early 18th-century Andalusia, with a large circle of followers. His earliest work may be an octagonal *camarín* (chamber for robing an image) in Malaga, with extraordinary foliated stucco enrichment.

His principal mature commissions were in Granada, where he worked on the Sagrario of the Carthusians from 1702 to 1720. The famous Sacristy is apparently based on a Hurtado plan (1713); some of its present character is due to later designers and craftsmen. Unfinished at his death (completed by others) was a complex group of rooms for the Carthusians at El Paular, Segovia. Other interior work (Santiago retable, Granada Cathedral, begun in 1707; *camarín* at Las Angustias, Granada) spread the implications of his style over southern Spain and ultimately to Mexico, through emigrant designers. A master ornamentalist and architectural-sculptural planner, Hurtado combined the late baroque traditions of Granada and Lucena with the man-

Francisco Hurtado, *camarín*, Las Angustias, Granada.

nerist-Mudejar traditions of Cordova; he introduced a number of significant changes in design that were influential for fifty years or more.

BIBLIOGRAPHY. R. Taylor, "Francisco Hurtado and His School," *Art Bulletin*, XXXII, March, 1950.

JOSEPH A. BAIRD, JR.

HUSLIJ, JACOB OTTEN. Dutch architect (1753–95). He worked in Amsterdam. At first working in the rococo style, he soon changed to the neoclassical mode. His chief concern was domestic architecture. Palladian reminiscences are seen in his surviving sketches.

HUVE, JEAN JACQUES MARIE. French architect (1783–1852). Huvé worked in Paris. A student of his father and of Percier, Huvé was connected with the Church of the Madeleine and completed work on it after Barthélemy Vignon's death. Supported by Louis XVIII, he also worked on hospitals, châteaux, and theaters. His style shows an elaboration on traditional classical vocabulary.

HUY: NOTRE-DAME. Late Gothic collegiate church in Belgium begun in 1311 and consecrated in 1377. It has a single-tower west façade and two towers flanking the choir. Its treasure of church furniture includes the chasses of St. Mengold and St. Domitien by Godfrey of Huy (ca. 1173).

HUYS, FRANS. Flemish engraver and publisher (1522–62). Born in Antwerp, Huys was exclusively a reproductive engraver and worked after the designs of Frans Floris, Hans Holbein (*Portrait of Erasmus*), and Pieter Brueghel (the famous set of eleven warships). These were all published by Hieronymus Cock. The addition of "exc." after his own name indicates that he was, in a few cases, his own publisher. In a set of twenty-five plates with busts in ovals, and thirteen with full-length figures, he portrayed 16th-century sovereigns and royal personages.

BIBLIOGRAPHY. A. M. Hind, *Engraving in England in the Sixteenth and Seventeenth Centuries*, pt. I: *The Tudor Period*, Cambridge, Eng., 1952.

HUYSMANS, CORNELIS (Huysmans of Mechlin). Flemish painter (1648–1727). Huysmans was active in his native Antwerp and in Mechlin. He painted landscapes, mainly woodland views, in the manner of his master, Jacques d'Arthois. The works were done in glowing colors with a broad brush. His conceptions are Italianate and related to Titian rather than to the classical discipline of Nicolas Poussin and Claude Lorraine.

BIBLIOGRAPHY. Y. Thiéry, *Le Paysage flamand au XVIIe siècle*, Brussels, 1953.

HUYSMANS, JAN-BAPTIST. Flemish painter (1654–1716). He was born in Antwerp and was the brother and pupil of Cornelis Huysmans. His canvases can be separated from his brother's only with some difficulty. On the whole, his palette appears less exuberant and his brushwork heavier. A *Landscape with Animals* (Brussels, Fine Arts Museum) is signed and dated 1697.

BIBLIOGRAPHY. Y. Thiéry, *Le Paysage flamand au XVIIe siècle*, Brussels, 1953.

HUYSMANS OF MECHLIN, see HUYSMANS, CORNELIS.

HUYSUM, see HUIJSUM.

HYDRA. Nine-headed serpent in Greek mythology. Its name was derived from the term for "water snake." The Hydra inhabited the marshes of Lerna and was capable of growing a new head as soon as one was removed. Its destruction constituted the first labor of Hercules, which he accomplished with the aid of his nephew Iolaus, who burned each stump as the heads were cut off by Hercules.

HYDRIA. Ancient Greek or Etruscan vessel for carrying water. Made of bronze or pottery, each hydria was equipped with three handles, with those on the sides serving as lifts and the third being used for pouring. In shape, the hydria is recognizable by its wide mouth with flaring rim, short neck, curved shoulder, and capacious body narrowing to a small foot. Hydriae of pottery bore painted mythological scenes and sometimes imitated bronze vessels in decorative details.

BIBLIOGRAPHY. G. M. A. Richter and M. J. Milne, *Shapes and Names of Athenian Vases*, New York, 1935.

HYPAETHROS. Structure open to the sky (from the Greek *hypaithros*, "under the sky"), as in the Egyptian Temple of Khonsu, Karnak, whose large open outer court is surrounded by a colonnade on three sides. Vitruvius uses the term to describe an opening in the middle of a Greek temple roof. Such roof openings, said to have originated in the Greek house, have been discerned in Greek temples.

HYPERBOLIC PARABOLOID. Warped surface generated by a straight line moving so as to touch two other straight

Hyperbolic paraboloid. A technique creating a warped surface.

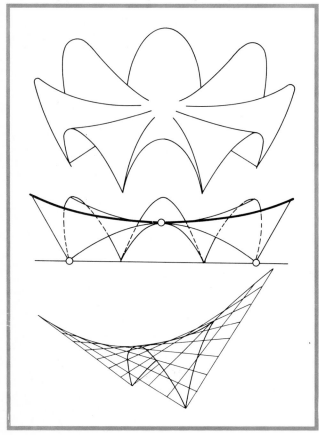

lines not in the same plane and remaining parallel to a plane director. Planes intersecting a hyperbolic paraboloid will form parabolas and hyperbolas as well as straight lines; this paraboloid is sometimes called a "warped quadrilateral" because it is the surface formed when the sides of a plane quadrilateral are skewed.

The hyperbolic paraboloid shares with other warped surfaces such as saddle-shaped hyperboloids of revolution, conoids, cylindroids, and helicoids the virtue of being composed of straight-line elements. This makes it possible to build large shells, having desirable structural and aesthetic qualities, with straight pieces of timber or steel or, in the case of reinforced concrete shells, with form lumber in straight boards. The hyperbolic paraboloid, together with other warped surfaces, represents a comparatively recent adventure in architectural form. Candela, in Mexico, and Le Corbusier, in his buildings for Philips at the Brussels Fair (1958), have contributed to a new idiom which in the United States has been adopted in reinforced concrete and wood construction. *See* CANDELA, FELIX; LE CORBUSIER.

MILTON F. KIRCHMAN

HYPOCAUST. Chamber used to distribute heat in ancient structures. In the Thermae of Caracalla, Rome, hypocausts under the floor sent heated air through flues distributed to various rooms.

HYPOGEUM. Underground structure. The term is applied to Egyptian rooms dug in cliffs, to underground galleries in ancient amphitheaters, and to other subterranean portions of buildings.

HYPOSCENIUM. Architectural element in the ancient Greek theater, assumed to be the low wall at the front of a raised stage.

HYPOTRACHELIUM. Architectural term derived from the Greek *hypotrachelion*, meaning "under the neck." It is the grooved section under the trachelium, or neck, between the shaft and capital of a column. The flutes of Greek Doric columns are usually continued into the flared section below the echinus. This flared necking is cut by a hypotrachelium of three grooves in archaic temples, later by one groove.

HYPPOLITE, HECTOR. Haitian painter (b. St. Marc, 1894; d. Port-au-Prince, 1948). As a young man Hyppolite traveled through America and Africa; he was probably subsequently influenced in his painting by the medieval Christian art he saw while in Ethiopia. For many years the only outlet for his art was in decorating houses and furniture. In 1944 he came into prominence, after being discovered by DeWitt Peters of the Centre d'Art in Port-au-Prince, and began to produce easel paintings on a regular basis. In them he evoked mysterious images from the voodoo rites, the religion that he practiced as a priest. His paintings are decorative in a two-dimensional style that provocatively parallels the styles of many contemporary European artists, particularly Henri Matisse. His work was enthusiastically received by Wifredo Lam and André Breton and was shown in surrealist exhibitions in Paris before his death.

BIBLIOGRAPHY. S. Rodman, *Renaissance in Haiti*, New York, 1948.

I

IACOPINO (Iacopo) DA TRADATE. Italian sculptor (fl. 1401–40). He was engaged in work on the Cathedral of Milan from 1401 to 1425; in 1440 he entered the service of Duke Giovanni Francesco Gonzaga at Mantua. Iacopino's statue of Pope Martin V, completed in 1421, in Milan Cathedral, with its realistic observation of detail and flowing drapery, marks the zenith of Lombard Gothic sculpture.

I AND MY VILLAGE. Oil painting by Chagall, in the Museum of Modern Art, New York. *See* CHAGALL, MARC.

I'ANSON, EDWARD. English architect and surveyor (1775–1853). He designed London warehouses, offices, and houses, and was surveyor to the commissioners of sewers for Surrey and Kent. He is best known for his system of draining South London by sewers and outlets, which became the model for other such projects.

IBARRA, JOSE DE. Mexican painter (b. Guadalajara, Spain, 1688; d. Mexico City, 1756). Ibarra, a disciple of Juan Correa, was the first significant Mexican painter of the 18th century. Industrious and prolific, he contributed pictures to many churches, including the Cathedrals of Mexico City and Puebla.
BIBLIOGRAPHY. M. Toussaint, *Arte colonial en México*, 2d ed., Mexico City, 1962.

IBBETSON, JULIUS CAESAR. English painter (1759–1817). He belongs to the tradition of genre and landscape painting that includes George Morland, Philippe-Jacques Loutherbourg, and certain phases of Francis Wheatley and Thomas Rowlandson. Ibbetson's landscapes are generally in the Dutch tradition as transmitted through early Gainsborough. His lively and neatly drawn figures resemble those of Loutherbourg and Wheatley. Ibbetson was a thoroughly competent practitioner in both oils and water colors, but was not an innovator in either medium. His works are widely scattered; many of them are still in private collections.
BIBLIOGRAPHY. R. M. Clay, *Julius Caesar Ibbetson*, London, 1948.

Ibn-Tulun Mosque, Cairo. The dome, crenellations, and minaret.

I BEAM. Standard rolled-steel beam resembling an I in section. (See illustration.)

IBIBIO, *see* AFRICA, PRIMITIVE ART OF (WEST AFRICA: NIGERIA).

IBN-TULUN MOSQUE, CAIRO. Abbasid mosque erected by Ahmad ibn-Tulun, governor of Egypt. When he found al-Fustat and al-'Askar outgrown, he ordered the establishment of a suburb in an area that later formed part of Cairo. There he erected a palace called al-Maydan and in 876 ordered construction begun on the Mosque of al-Maydan, which was later to bear his own name. Construction was completed in 879, and the existing mosque is essentially that building, although it has been repaired on many occasions. Entrance is from the north into a large open court. On the north, east, and west sides are open halls with two aisles, and on the mihrab side are five aisles in seventeen bays. Massive brick piers carry stilted, pointed arches. The soffits and edges of the arches are decorated in carved plaster with patterns deriving from the Samarra style. A detached, four-stage, cut-stone minaret adjoins the mosque.
BIBLIOGRAPHY. K. A. C. Creswell, *A Short Account of Early Muslim Architecture*, Harmondsworth, 1958.

IBO, *see* AFRICA, PRIMITIVE ART OF (WEST AFRICA: NIGERIA).

ICARUS. Son of the great inventor Daedalus of Athens. Icarus donned a flying device, as did his father, and both leaped from a cliff overlooking the sea in an attempt to escape from the Palace of Minos in Crete. When the youth flew too near the sun, the hot rays melted his waxen wings and he plunged to his death. A famous version of this Greek legend is the painting by Pieter Brueghel the Elder, *Fall of Icarus* (1558; Brussels, Fine Arts Museum).

ICHIJI KINRIN IN CHUSONJI, HIRAIZUMI. Japanese wood sculpture (13th cent.). Ichiji Kinrin is worshiped as the central icon in the Shingon (True Word) sect, in the ceremonies connected with solar and lunar eclipses. The

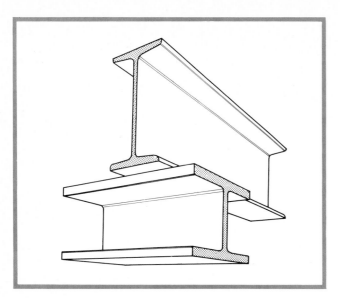

I beam. A horizontal member used in steel-frame construction.

back of the figure is entirely cut away, though it is not known whether it was originally so fashioned. The feminine beauty of its facial features and its sensuous white body with sloping shoulders contrast with the rather schematized sharp lines of the drapery folds. *See* SHINGON.

BIBLIOGRAPHY. R. T. Paine and A. Soper, *The Art and Architecture of Japan*, Baltimore, 1955.

ICON. Religious picture that portrays Christ, the Virgin Mary, angels, or individual saints. It is subject to great veneration within the Orthodox Church. Icons are always highly stylized representations in the Byzantine manner since they personify eternal truth. They are usually portable, and those made in Russia were often richly jeweled and luxuriously framed.

BIBLIOGRAPHY. D. T. Rice, *Russian Icons*, London, New York, 1947; D. T. Rice, *Byzantine Art*, rev. ed., London, Baltimore, 1954.

ICONOCLASM. Term, from the Greek, meaning "image-breaking." Iconoclasm attacks the use and veneration of the human image in religious art. Image-making is prohibited in Judaism, Islam, and other ancient religions, and is actively discouraged in some Protestant sects. It was an issue from the earliest years of the Christian church, but it was not until 726 that Emperor Leo III (r. 717–741) placed a ban on images and the iconoclastic controversy erupted. Leo and his successor, Constantine V (r. 741–775), were supported by Eastern bishops, particularly from Asia Minor, but generally opposed by the monastic communities, government bureaucracy, and the popes in Rome. Throughout the Byzantine Empire human representations of Christ and other figures were destroyed and replaced by symbols such as the cross or by abstract and floral ornamentation, influenced to some extent by Muslim art.

The ban was elaborated by the Council in Hiereia (754), which denounced idolatry and the idea of limiting Christ's nature to human representation. Its prosecution led to the repression of clergy and monasteries, as well as of political enemies, particularly under Constantine in the 760s. Under Empress Irene the Second Council of Nicaea (787) over-

threw the ban; Leo V (r. 813–820) renewed it. Images were finally restored (843) under the regents Theodora and Theoctistus during the minority of Michael III.

DONALD GODDARD

ICONOGRAPHY AND ICONOLOGY. In modern art history iconography is an auxiliary discipline concerned with the meaning of symbols and themes of works of art. The traditional discipline of iconography has expanded to include iconology; thus, while iconography proper deals mainly with the identification and classification of visual symbols, iconology seeks to discern the intrinsic meaning of these symbols and their broader interrelationships as themes. Iconology ultimately strives to understand a work of art in terms of a particular cultural environment.

Iconography was slow to develop an exact and systematic approach; in recent times, however, great impetus has been given to its growth. The beginnings of iconography were laid in the late 16th and the 17th century when a few theological scholars investigated the elementary Christian symbolism in art. One of the earliest investigations was *De picturis et imaginibus sacris* by Molanus (Jan Vermeulen), published in Louvain in 1570. The discovery of the Roman catacombs particularly interested these early iconographers because of the unusual and often cryptic symbolism they contained. Cesare Ripa's *Iconologia* (Rome, 1593) was an outgrowth of this interest. Concern with primitive Christianity persisted throughout the 17th and the early 18th century. Gottfried Arnold published his *Waare afbeelding der eerste christenen* (Amsterdam, 1700/01). Interest in the lives of the saints was also great during the same period. It led to the publication of the monumental *Acta sanctorum* (53 vols.) by a group of Belgian Bollandists between 1643 and 1794. *See* SAINTS IN ART.

The great classical archaeologists of the 18th century were not directly concerned with iconography, although J. J. Winckelmann, for instance, arranged works of art according to subject matter in his *Geschichte der Kunst des Altertums* (Dresden, 1764). His chief concern, however, was not with iconography but with the development of a more exact analysis of style. By the early 19th century iconography began to have a much more restricted meaning for archaeology: the study and classification of antique portraits. The general study of subject matter in art was called typology. Classical iconography developed considerably in the second half of the 19th century through new methods of comparative philology and textual criticism. The development was begun by J. Overbeck (*Griechische Kunstmythologie*, 3 vols., Leipzig, 1871–89) and was perfected by A. Fürtwängler (*Die antiken Gemmen*, Leipzig, Berlin, 1900).

The greatest progress in iconography during the 19th century was made by French scholars working chiefly on Christian art. Building upon the achievements of earlier iconographers, scholars such as A. N. Didron (*Iconographie chrétienne: Histoire de Dieu*, Paris, 1843) and A. Crosnier (*Iconographie chrétienne*, Caen, 1848) greatly expanded the knowledge of Christian symbolism and began to lay a foundation for the systematic classification of motifs. Great advances in the iconography of the saints were made by C. Cahier in his *Caractéristiques des saints* (Paris, 1867). The work was extended to include broader iconographical themes or programs by E. Mâle (*L'Art religieux du XIIIe siècle en France*, Paris, 1898 ff.) and G. Millet (*Recherches sur l'iconographies de l'évangile aux XIVe, XVe et XVIe siècles...*, Paris, 1916). Mâle made the first important study of a postmedieval period in his *L'Art religieux après le Concile de Trent* (Paris, 1932). The culmination of the French encyclopedic approach to Christian iconography was reached in *Dictionnaire d'archéologie chrétienne et de liturgie* by F. Cabrol and H. Leclercq (Paris, 1907–53).

German scholarship, on the heels of the French, soon introduced handbooks of Christian iconography, such as I. H. von Wessenberg's *Die christlichen Bilder* (Constance, 1827) and W. Menzel's *Christliche Symbolik* (Regensburg, 2d ed., 1854). The greatest German contributions to the development of iconography in the 19th century were made by A. Springer (*Ikonographische Studien*, Vienna, 1860) and F. X. Kraus (*Geschichte der christlichen Kunst*, 1896–1908).

Before the 20th century only isolated efforts were made to interpret the meaning of artistic subject matter beyond its purely didactic significance. In the early years of the 20th century, however, M. Dvořák and Julius von Schlosser began to see the necessity of viewing it as a reflection of religious and philosophical currents. Dvořák's idea that the history of art is the history of ideas developed to such an extent that old terminology was found to be restrictive. Aby Warburg adopted the term "iconology" to denote the study of the meaning of artistic subject matter; Erwin Panofsky gave form to the new study ("Zum Problem der Beschreibung und Inhaltsdeutung von Werken der bildenden Kunst," *Logos*, XXI, 1932). Panofsky stratified the subject matter into three levels: primary subject matter, secondary subject matter, and intrinsic meaning or content. The first level is simply the recognition of certain shapes and forms as representations of natural objects, such as human figures, animals, and plants. The second level is the significance of these objects as images or symbols. This is the area of iconography. The third level is concerned with the recognition of underlying principles in the work of art, which, when discerned, reveal the cultural climate in which it was produced. This is the realm of iconology.

Panofsky's approach to iconology requires of the scholar a thorough knowledge of the most varied aspects of the culture in which the work of art under study was produced. In order for an iconologer to distinguish the meanings that are intrinsic to a work at its creation, he must constantly check what he assumes are intrinsic meanings against knowledge gleaned from the literature, philosophy, and religion of the period. The danger of arbitrary iconological interpretation has led to much criticism of the method since its inception.

The most common criticism is that meanings may be found where none actually exist. The abundance of symbolism in medieval art, for example, has led some investigators to seek for symbolism in the religious art of later periods, where the existence of such symbolism is open to doubt. (For this criticism, see C. Gilbert, "On Subject and Not-Subject in Italian Renaissance Pictures," *Art Bulletin*, XXXIV, 1952.)

In the criticism voiced by O. Pächt ("Panofsky's 'Early Netherlandish Painting,'" *The Burlington Magazine*,

XCVIII, 1956), he objects to an approach to iconology that assumes that subject matter in art is controlled to the smallest detail by a consciously formulated program. This attitude, Pächt points out, is opposed to the idea that cultural history is a product of nonrational forces.

The most serious problem, which arises from extreme application of the iconological method, is the tendency to view a work of art as the embodiment of ideas rather than as a phenomenon of visual form, thus denying its *raison d'être* and its uniqueness. Most modern art historians strive to keep iconography and iconology in balance with the main concern of art history: the analysis and interpretation of style.

Along with the more spectacular achievements in the area of iconology, many extremely important advances in the systematization of iconography have recently been made. Among the most notable are the *Index of Christian Art*, begun by C. R. Morey at Princeton University; the *Iconographical Index of Dutch and Flemish Painting*, devised by H. van de Waal at The Hague; and the *Reallexikon zur deutschen Kunstgeschichte*, started by O. Schmitt in 1937.

BIBLIOGRAPHY. (For a complete bibliography of individual handbooks and studies see "Iconography and Iconology," *Encyclopedia of World Art*, vol. 7, New York, 1963); E. Cassirer, "Der Begriff der symbolischen Form im Aufbau der Geisteswissenschaften," *Vorträge der Bibliothek Warburg*, I, 1921–22; E. Panofsky, *Studies in Iconology*, New York, 1939; H. Ladendorf, "Fragen der Motivuntersuchung," *Wissenschaftliche Zeitung der Humboldt Universität Berlin: Geschichtliche und sprachwissenschaftliche Reihe*, V, 2, 1955; R. Wittkower, "Interpretations of Visual Symbols in Art," *Studies in Communication*, London, 1955.
DONALD L. EHRESMANN

ICONOSTASIS. In Eastern churches, a partition with icons used to separate the bema from the choir or apse. In Byzantine churches, the iconostasis with its customary three doors screened the sanctuary with its altar.

ICTINUS. Greek architect, probably an Athenian (fl. 2d half of 5th cent. B.C.). He was the architect of the Parthenon (with Callicrates), the Temple of Apollo Epikourios at Bassae, and one of the designers of the Periclean Telesterion at Eleusis, although, in the last case, his plans were never completely carried out. *See* BASSAE; ELEUSIS: HALL OF MYSTERIES; PARTHENON, ATHENS.

Ictinus brought the Doric tradition to its highest point of perfection (the Parthenon) and made fruitful innovations in the use of the other orders, especially at Bassae. As the cella of the Bassae temple and his designs for the Telesterion show, he was one of the first architects to be acutely interested in the problem of arranging interior space.

Like the great architects of an earlier period, such as Chersiphron and Theodorus, Ictinus wrote a book on his architecture (Vitruvius, VII, 12). *See* CHERSIPHRON; THEODORUS.

BIBLIOGRAPHY. W. B. Dinsmoor, *The Architecture of Ancient Greece*, 3d ed., London, 1950.

IDOLINO, THE. Greek sculpture of the classical period, in the Louvre Museum, Paris.

IFE, *see* AFRICA, PRIMITIVE ART OF (WEST AFRICA: NIGERIA).

IFFLEY, CHURCH OF. One of the best small Romanesque English churches, dated about 1170, with nave, square choir, and apse. The west end was vaulted in the 13th century. There is a rich west front with much beakhead and zigzag and an equally elaborately decorated interior.

BIBLIOGRAPHY. A. W. Clapham, *English Romanesque Architecture after the Conquest*, Oxford, 1934.

IGA. Reduction-fired Japanese stoneware of a medieval type, very similar to Shigaraki ware, but usually not included among the Six Ancient Kilns. Most recorded examples of Iga ware do not appear until the late 16th century. The bodies are extremely light pink.

BIBLIOGRAPHY. R. A. Miller, *Japanese Ceramics*, Rutland, Vt., 1960.

I. G. FARBEN ADMINISTRATION BUILDING, FRANKFURT AM MAIN. Administration complex built in 1930 by Poelzig. It is arranged as a series of tall, rectangular units connected by a thinner segmented circular corridor. The huge project demonstrates Poelzig's return to a strict and utilitarian monumentality similar to the early work of Behrens. The monumental ensemble, classical in feeling, is completely stripped of traditional ornament; the terraced landscape—stiff, symmetrical, and formal—harmonizes with the building. *See* POELZIG, HANS.

BIBLIOGRAPHY. H. J. Zechlin, "Das Verwaltungsgebäude der I. G. Farben in Frankfurt a. Main," *Wasmuths Monatshefte für Baukunst*, XV, 1931.

IGLOO. Eskimo hut built of snow blocks, usually laid in a continuous in-sloping spiral to form a dome. The inner surface of the igloo is usually lined with skins and furs. Ventilation is obtained through a small opening near the top of the dome.

IGNATIUS LOYOLA, ST. Founder of the Jesuits and Counter Reformation leader (1491–1556). Born in Guipuzcoa, Spain, St. Ignatius began writing his *Spiritual Exercises* after abandoning a military career for the holy life. He visited Rome and Jerusalem and studied in Spain

I-hsing. Teapot of unglazed reddish-brown stoneware. Victoria and Albert Museum, London.

and in Paris. In 1534, in Paris, he took vows of poverty and chastity with St. Francis Xavier and others. In 1540, Pope Paul III sanctioned the Society of Jesus, and St. Ignatius was elected general. He sought reform by encouraging education and frequent partaking of sacraments, preached the gospel to pagans, and fought heresy. He may be shown with Christ (who appeared to him), and often wearing IHS on his breast. His feast is July 31.

See also SAINTS IN ART.

IGOROT, *see* OCEANIC ART (INDONESIA: PHILIPPINES).

I-HSING (Yi-hsing). Town near Shanghai, in Kiangsu Province, China. It is the site of potteries that may have begun production as early as the 10th century and are still active. The potteries are famous in the West for the deep reddish-brown stoneware teapots of remarkably simple outline: pear-shaped or of flattened globular forms. The ware is not glazed and is not extensively decorated. The teapots became prized in Japan, and the I-hsing kilns flourished from the 16th century on. The teapots were also exported in great quantities to Europe with the first flush of tea consignments in the 17th century, and they were believed to be the best ware for brewing tea. They became widely imitated in Europe, by Jacobus Clauwe in Holland and Böttger in Meissen. Because of its similarity to a class of Spanish-American ware, I-hsing was sometimes called "boccaro" ware in Europe. In addition to teapots, the I-hsing potteries produced other ceramic shapes as well as pieces that imitated Chün ware in glaze and a ware that is closely related to Kuangtung ware. *See* CHUN WARE; KUANGTUNG WARE.

BIBLIOGRAPHY. G. Hedley, "Yi-hsing Ware," *Transactions of the Oriental Ceramic Society*, XIV, 1936–37.   MARTIE W. YOUNG

IJAW, *see* AFRICA, PRIMITIVE ART OF (WEST AFRICA: NIGERIA).

ILIAD, *see* HOMER, ILLUSTRATIONS OF.

ILICE, THE LADY OF, *see* ELCHE, THE LADY OF.

ILIUPERSIS (Sack of Troy). Famous painting by Polygnotos on the wall of the Lesche of the Cnidians at Delphi, which Pausanias described in detail. It consisted of a great number of figures identified by inscriptions and arranged in groups, "above," "below," and "in front of" one another, reflecting undoubtedly Polygnotos's development of a three-dimensional spatial setting for his scenes. *See* POLYGNOTOS.

BIBLIOGRAPHY. Pausanias, *Pausanias's Description of Greece*, book 10, tr. J. G. Frazer, London, 1898.

ILLUMINATIONS. Small painted scenes, patterns, and initial letters accompanying the text in manuscripts; also known as miniatures (which, however, can also mean small panel paintings). Illuminations are executed either in pen and ink or in opaque or transparent water colors. They are frequently heightened by the addition of gold leaf. *See* MINIATURES.

Illuminations appear in medieval manuscripts from the 5th century on. In the early Middle Ages the illumination of the Gospels and other books for religious use was done in the monasteries by monks. It became a major art form and developed a great variety of schools (Hiberno-Saxon,

Carolingian, Winchester School, and so forth). Gothic masters also illuminated secular books. *See* CAROLINGIAN ART AND ARCHITECTURE (MANUSCRIPT WRITING); GOSPELS, THE; GOTHIC ART (STAINED GLASS, PAINTING, AND MINOR ARTS); HIBERNO-SAXON ART; WINCHESTER SCHOOL.

In the International Style and later, during the 14th and 15th centuries, illumination underwent an extraordinary flowering in the hands of such French and Franco-Flemish masters as Jean Pucelle, the Limbourg Brothers, and Jean Fouquet. After the introduction of printed books in the late 15th century the art declined but continued to be practiced. *See* FOUQUET, JEAN; INTERNATIONAL GOTHIC PAINTING; LIMBOURG BROTHERS; PUCELLE, JEAN.

BIBLIOGRAPHY. E. Johnston, *Writing and Illuminating and Lettering*, 15th ed., London, 1927; D. Diringer, *The Illuminated Book: Its History and Production*, London, 1958.

ILLUMINATIONS, ON THE ART OF, *see* DE ARTE ILLUMINANDI.

ILLUSIONISM. Techniques of optical illusion by which artists create the semblance of reality. These include shading, foreshortening, perspective, and the representation of objects in so naturalistic a manner as to deceive the eye (trompe l'oeil). The term is also applied to methods of producing realistic effects in the art of late antiquity.

BIBLIOGRAPHY. California Palace of the Legion of Honor, *Illusionism & Trompe l'Oeil* (exhibition catalog), San Francisco, 1949; P. L. W. Lehmann, *Roman Wall Paintings from Boscoreale in the Metropolitan Museum of Art*, Cambridge, Mass., 1953.

IMAD MADONNA. Romanesque sculpture, in the Diocesan Museum, Paderborn, Germany.

IMAGINES. Painted waxen masks representing the ancestors of aristocratic Roman families. These masks were worn in the funeral processions of the nobility and also were displayed on certain ceremonial occasions. They were ordinarily kept in family shrines, each mask being mounted on a bust and accompanied by an inscription recording the life of the person represented.

BIBLIOGRAPHY. H. W. Johnston, *The Private Life of the Romans*, Chicago, 1903; A. N. Zadoks and J. Jitta, *Ancestral Portraiture in Rome...*, Amsterdam, 1932.

IMAM-RIZA, MESHED. The holiest site in Iran, founded in the 9th century. The Shrine of Imam-Riza commands the same devotion from Iranians as Mecca does from other Muslims. The wealth not only of the Iranians but also of Shi'ite communities in India and Central Asia has been lavished upon it. It consists of some thirty structures representing more than five centuries of building: mosques, oratories, colleges, libraries, sanctuaries, caravansaries—all connected by four huge courts, from 175 to 350 feet in length, which are surrounded by double-tiered arcades faced with enamel tile.

The interior structures are assembled around the sacred tomb chamber of Imam-Riza, which has been rebuilt and restored many times. A most impressive part of the complex, northeast of the tomb, is the domed Chamber of Allahvardi Khan of 1612. Its architect, Amir, is believed to have come from Isfahan. The structure has no façade, and the interior walls seem to dissolve mysteriously into arches, bays, and galleries. The dome of the sanctuary, 70 feet high and 36 feet in diameter, is filled with a mass of

Illuminations. Miniature from Jean Henry's *Lunettes de foi et de prudence celeste*, 15th century. Biblioteca Palatina, Parma.

stalactites and crowns the two stories of sumptuously modeled recesses. Just north of the tomb of Imam-Riza is the gold ivan (liwan) of Ali Shir Nawai; above, still heading north toward the periphery of the complex, is the tall and narrow blind ivan inscribed as the gift of Shah Abbas II and dated 1649. South of the tomb of Imam-Riza is the 15th-century Mosque of Gauhar Shad, which furnishes an impressive climax to the courts. Among the special oratories in a variety of styles is the faïence-faced Hall of Hospitality, just east of the Chamber of Allahvardi Khan, with its cascading stalactite vaults. The distance from the entrance on the west through the old court to the farther end of the lower esplanade on the east is well over 1,000 feet. *See* GAUHAR SHAD, MOSQUE OF, MESHED.

Everywhere the show of splendor is overwhelming. Reflected in pools are a golden dome and two golden minarets enriched with white inscriptions on ultramarine bands. The Chamber of Allahvardi Khan is decorated with a 5-foot dado of gold-toned marble, which sets off the deep blue tones of the revetments. The effect is further enriched by the turquoise tile floor.

The Shrine of Imam-Riza has been ravaged and almost destroyed many times since the 9th century, but inevitably reconstructions and additions have followed. Shah Abbas I entered Meshed in 1597 and began restoration in 1601.

BIBLIOGRAPHY. A. Pope, *Persian Architecture*, New York, 1965.

ABRAHAM A. DAVIDSON

IMARI, *see* JAPAN: CERAMICS.

IMBREX (Cover Tile). Roof tile used to cover joints between flat tiles or tegulae in classical architecture. Imbrices in Greek construction were of terra cotta or marble.

IMGUR BEL PALACE, BALAWAT, *see* BALAWAT: IM-GUR BEL PALACE.

IMHOTEP. Architect of King Djeser of the 3d dynasty. Imhotep was credited with the design and building of the King's famous Stepped Pyramid at Saqqara, the first great funerary monument built entirely of stone rather than of mud brick. Egyptians of the Late period worshiped him as a god of healing, and the Greeks, calling him Imouthes, identified him with their god Asklepios. *See* AESCULAPIUS.

IMMACULATE CONCEPTION, THE. Oil painting by Murillo, in the Prado Museum, Madrid. *See* MURILLO, BARTOLOME ESTEBAN.

IMMACULATISM, *see* CUBIST REALISM.

IMOLA, INNOCENZO DA (Innocenzo Francucci). Italian painter (b. Imola, 1490/94; d. Bologna, 1547/50). In his early years he assisted Francesco Francia in Bologna and, according to Vasari, was for several years in Florence with Albertinelli. Although Innocenzo worked for a time in Imola as an independent master, his main center of activity was Bologna, where he had settled by 1517. His earliest signed and dated work, marked "Innocentius Francutius J. F. 1515," is *The Madonna with SS. Sebastian, Roch, Cosmas, and Damian* (Bagnara di Romagna, SS. Giovanni Battista e Andrea). His most important frescoes, representing scenes from the life of the Virgin, are to be found in the Monastery of S. Michele in Bosco, Bologna (1517–22),

Innocenzo da Imola, *Portrait of a Woman.* Villa Borghese Gallery, Rome.

for which he also executed the main altarpiece (Bologna, National Picture Gallery). While both Florentine and Ferrarese influences may be noted in his painting, it is to Raphael's style that he is most deeply indebted. Of his students, Prospero Fontana and Primaticcio were the most important.

IMPASTO. Term, from the Italian, referring to the thickness of paint applied to canvas or panel. A thin and smooth impasto was the rule in painting through the Renaissance. Increasingly thick impastos, which show the evidence of the brushstroke and the palette knife in rough surfaces, have become common since the baroque period. Rembrandt used heavy layers of paint to capture light effects and the materiality of objects. Modern painters often apply raw pigment in a rough and direct manner to express the dynamics of the act and to stress the surface of the painting.

IMPERIAL BODYGUARDS SCROLL. Japanese portrait pictures of imperial bodyguards (ca. 1247; Tokyo, Okura Collection). Except for a few touches of color to the lips, the portraits are drawn in ink. The guards, who are individually named, their horses, and their costumes are portrayed with great care and with a keen eye for realistic details. Ink lines are carefully drawn, yet with a great sense of vigor and freedom. These characteristics are often associated with the art of Nobuzane, the great portraitist of the period. *See* NOBUZANE.

BIBLIOGRAPHY. Tokyo National Museum, *Pageant of Japanese Art*, vol. 1: *Painting*, pt. 1, Tokyo, 1952; National Commission for the Protection of Cultural Properties, ed., *Kokuhō (National Treasures of Japan)*, vol. 4: *The Kamakura Period*, Tokyo, 1966.

IMPERIAL SUMMER PALACE, PEKING. Palace complex set against the background of the Western Hills, about 6 miles northwest of the city walls of Peking, China. One of the most strikingly beautiful building and landscape ensembles constructed in China in the 19th century, the Imperial Summer Palace and its grounds (now the Summer Palace Park) extend over 823 acres, four-fifths of which is lake. The remainder consists of a composition of artificial hills, causeways, islands, and woods, with more than 100 buildings. The palace is situated on an almost peninsular piece of land overlooking the lake to the south.

The entrance to the site is from the east, where the imperial living quarters and the court buildings stood. From here all the way along the south shore runs a long, brightly colored covered way, which connects different parts of the composition. The span of each beam is decorated with scenes of the summer palace. At the center of the shore there rises to the top of the hill an ensemble of buildings and courts dominated by the octagonal tower, the Fo-hsiang-ko. The covered way passes along the shore beyond this point to the group at the west end. This contains the fantastic marble boat built by the empress dowager Tz'u-hsi, who was responsible for many of the buildings of the summer palace. On the north slope are ruins of an earlier summer palace of the Ch'ing dynasty, which was built in an eclectic European style and burned down in the expedition of 1860. The hill slopes down to a landscaped stream set with rocks and trees. The Jade Spring

Imperial Summer Palace, Peking. The palace is situated on an almost peninsular piece of land overlooking the lake.

Pagoda, set on one of the nearby hills, which existed before the summer palace was constructed, affords a striking vertical feature.

The lake is surrounded by an embankment and set with causeways and islands in a manner deliberately based on the Western Lake at Hang-chou. One of the principal islands, immediately opposite the Fo-hsiang-ko, is connected to the eastern shore of the lake by the famous Bridge of the Seventeen Arches. Protruding above the water are nearly elliptical arches increasing slightly in height toward the center of the bridge. Found on another part of the summer palace is a rare form of stone balustrade without intermediate parts.

The great lakes and the hill at the summer palace (although quite near the Western Hills) are artificial. The Western Hills seem to be too high to have been utilized effectively. The whole composition, however, is cleverly made to become part of the surrounding natural landscape. *See also* PORCELAIN PAGODA, PEKING.

BIBLIOGRAPHY. D. G. Mirams, *A Brief History of Chinese Architecture*, Shanghai, 1940; A. C. H. Boyd, *Chinese Architecture and Town Planning, 1500 B.C.–A.D. 1911*, Chicago, 1962.

ABRAHAM A. DAVIDSON

IMPLUVIUM. Shallow tank sunk in the floor of a Greek or Roman house to receive rain water. The impluvium was usually placed in the atrium, with an opening to the sky (compluvium) generally framed by the sloping roofs of a peristyle.

IMPOST. Member at the top of a pier or wall below the springing of an arch. A continuous impost is one in which arch moldings and impost are continuous; an impost block, or dosseret, is one constituting a separate member, as of moldings, entablature, or molded block. Examples of Roman imposts may be seen in the arches of Titus and Septimius Severus, Rome. An Early Christian impost block is in the basilican church of S. Clemente, Rome. *See* DOSSERET.

Impost. Member joining beginning of arch with top of pier or column.

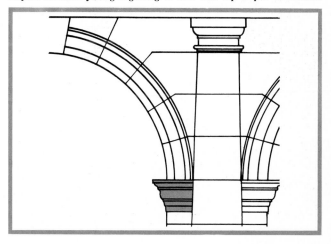

IMPRESSION. In the graphic arts, when one proves his plate, block, or stone by running a proof, he is said to have pulled an impression. Consequently, a damped sheet or handmade paper in direct contact with an inked plate, block, or stone will yield an impression.

IMPRESSIONISM. School of painting centered in France during the last quarter of the 19th century. With growing popularity, it became an international school. In its purest form it is an art that limits itself to the study of the properties of light and color. The favored subject is the landscape with water—a coastal region or a riverbank. In these scenes surfaces reflect light, and light from one object reflects, lightens, and colors a neighboring object. Clouds and haze are suffused or shot through with light. A boat pulled up on a shore is largely in shadow and thus rejects light. Light, therefore, is the featured element, and atmosphere is its medium.

The illusion of space is given primarily through the overlapping of planes and the use of atmospheric perspective. Composition is often quite informal, so much so that early critics of impressionism complained that pictures were incomplete, mere sketches that were fragmentary and even chaotic. In impressionist works, figures were frequently segmented and appeared marginal, or indifferent, to activity elsewhere in the picture. Unexpected angles of vision, plunging lines of sight, asymmetrical layouts, bold foreshortenings, and what appeared to be an almost accidental cropping of a view disturbed beholders. Color, too, seemed unnaturally bright. Earlier landscapists, particularly the popular Barbizon school painters, favored dark tones: browns, dark grays, and greens tempered with brown. Impressionists used the colors of the rainbow. They saw blue and purple in shadows. Frequently they would juxtapose colors and cause them to mingle and thus mix in the eye of the viewer.

With broken color and optical mixture, contours were softened and the illusion of mass and bulk was diminished. In its place the artists offered the impression of a fresh, initial view of nature, a view in which the momentary, the spontaneous, and the transient were fixed for all time. This effect was further heightened by reducing form elements to spots of color. While the artist was indifferent to sharp focus, he was concerned with the accuracy of tonal relationships and the precision of color choice. The shape of the spot had to correspond exactly to the object from which it was abstracted.

Monet has been called "the pacemaker of impressionism." There is nothing in the slightest haphazard about a Monet painting, especially one done during the "classical" period of impressionism, that is, in the 1870s. Monet and his fellow artists were not bound to any theories and depended largely on their aesthetic instincts to form their paintings. They were receptive only to the image of a light-filled vision before them and they responded with their sensibilities. The ideal of the impressionists lay within the concrete boundaries of visual sensation. *See* MONET, CLAUDE-OSCAR.

Monet spent his boyhood at the French channel town of Le Havre, where he met Boudin in 1856 and was influenced by him. Boudin painted pictures entirely out of doors, whereas most artists at that time made water-color sketches and completed the picture in the studio. Boudin painted the changing Normandy coast sky, one that would often have fair and stormy weather simultaneously. However, Boudin's painting lacked the breadth of Monet's. *See* BOUDIN, EUGENE LOUIS.

Monet went to Paris in 1859. In 1863 he saw the art of Manet, whose sensational *Déjeuner sur l'herbe* (Paris, Louvre) inspired him to paint his own version of the same theme (1865-66; Louvre). More important, Monet learned from Manet to reduce forms to areas of color and to realize the importance of the gradation of tones. Several other painters of about the same age were attracted to the art of Manet. They came to know each other and formed a group to exhibit their art. The first impressionist exhibition took place in April and May, 1874, in the studio of the photographer Nadar. Eight other impressionist exhibitions followed, the last in 1886. *See* MANET, EDOUARD.

Besides Monet, the leading impressionists are Renoir, Degas, Pissarro, Sisley, Berthe Morisot, and Bazille. By 1872 Manet was painting in the impressionist manner. The term "impressionist" was given to the group in 1874 in an article in *Le Charivari* by the journalist Louis Leroy, who used it derisively to describe what seemed to him a formlessness. Monet had a painting in the 1874 exhibition called *Impression, Sunrise*, and Leroy coined the term in describing that picture (Paris, Marmottan Museum). *See* BAZILLE, FREDERIC; DEGAS, HILAIRE GERMAIN EDGAR; MORISOT, BERTHE; PISSARRO, CAMILLE; RENOIR, PIERRE-AUGUSTE; SISLEY, ALFRED.

The impressionist group did not paint alike, nor did they limit themselves with respect to subject. They painted views of the boulevards and quays of Paris, nude peasant girls, city people on a holiday, ballet dancers, shopgirls, laundresses, race-track scenes, train stations, and even more formal subjects of a traditional character, such as portraits and still lifes. While Monet favored landscape, as did Pissarro and Sisley, Degas restricted himself largely to the human figure and to figures in an interior. Renoir painted both figures and landscapes. The group did not stay together very long, because they had organized originally not to forward any program but merely to find a place to exhibit and to exchange ideas and points of view.

In a broader use of the term, art that is impressionistic belongs to no special period, time, or place. Such diverse works as the Utrecht Psalter, some Chinese painting, and certain Pompeian murals are described as "impressionistic" because they give an impression of a certain scene rather than a sharp, detailed description.

BIBLIOGRAPHY. J. Leymarie, *Impressionism*, 2 vols., Geneva, 1955; J. Rewald, *The History of Impressionism*, rev. ed., New York, 1961; G. Bazin, *French Impressionist Paintings in the Louvre*, New York, 1966.

ROBERT REIFF

IMPRESSIONISM, SCIENTIFIC, *see* NEOIMPRESSIONISM.

IN ANTIS. Set between flanking walls or antae. The term is used to designate Greek temple types according to the number of columns *in antis*, for example, henostyle in an-

Impressionism. Claude Monet, *Rouen Cathedral*, 1894. Musée du Jeu de Paume, Paris.

tis, with one column between antae; distyle in antis, with two columns; and tristyle in antis, with three. *See* AMPHIDISTYLE IN ANTIS; DISTYLE IN ANTIS; HENOSTYLE; TRISTYLE IN ANTIS.

INCA ART. The Inca Empire was the culminating pre-Columbian Indian culture in western South America. Its capital was the Andean city of Cuzco, which was at its peak from about A.D. 1438 to 1533. Concentrated in the region of present-day Peru, the Incas produced very fine stone architecture and sponsored the continuance of a highly skilled production in weaving, ceramics, and metalwork. The ruling family of Incas, headed by The Inca (the divine emperor), had a mythological origin with Manco Capac about A.D. 1200, but real Inca expansion began with Pachacuti Inca Yupanqui, who ruled between 1438 and 1471, and ended with the Spanish execution of the Inca Atahualpa in 1533. *See* PERU.

All phases of Inca life were tightly organized into a socialistic state, which was, however, controlled by the absolute power of The Inca. A comparison with the Romans is suggested by the organization of the general population, the disciplined army, the engineering skills (indicated by the network of highways), the fortifications and other public works, the subordination of numerous foreign groups to central control, and the adaptation of cultural advances from previous peoples.

The greatest artistic contribution of the Incas was in architecture, ranging from such gigantic accomplishments as the Sacsahuamán fortress overlooking Cuzco to the hundreds of stone structures in Cuzco and elsewhere in which the stone fitting is so precise that mortar was not required and the thinnest of knife blades cannot be inserted between the stones. The technical skill of the Incas in metalwork, ceramics, and weaving was great, but most of the goldwork was destroyed by the Spaniards. Examples of weaving and ceramics indicate essentially just a large-scale extension of the basic advances of previous cultures. The Inca contribution in sculpture was minimal. There are no large pieces except symbolic and nonfigurative carvings such as the so-called Hitching Post of the Sun at Machu Picchu and the mysterious carvings at Kenko. Small zoomorphic forms are found on the surfaces of Cuzco buildings, and late wooden carvings survive.

The remains of Inca engineering skills in irrigation systems, agricultural terraces, temples, fortresses, and highways, many of which are still used, are dramatically illustrated by the most famous ruins, Machu Picchu. Perched on a rocky saddle 2,000 feet above the Urubamba River, Machu Picchu indicates in the magic of its setting an Inca aesthetic sensitivity that may not have had a sufficient opportunity to express itself in other arts in which earlier cultures had already set such a high standard. *See* MACHU PICCHU.

See also AMERICAS, ANCIENT, ART OF (PERU AND BOLIVIA).

BIBLIOGRAPHY. P. Kelemen, *Medieval American Art*, New York, 1943; W. C. Bennett, *Ancient Arts of the Andes*, New York, 1954; J. A. Mason, *The Ancient Civilizations of Peru*, Harmondsworth, 1957; W. C. Bennett and J. B. Bird, *Andean Culture History*, 2d and rev. ed. (Amer. Mus. of Natural History, Handbook Series, no. 15), New York, 1960.
LESTER C. WALKER, JR.

INCENSE BURNER. Any receptacle, usually of metal and with a perforated lid, made for the purpose of burning incense. In China, where they are called *acerra*, and in Japan, where they are known as *koro*, incense burners are among the most important works of the minor arts. In the Christian West the liturgical censer, or thurible, used to burn incense during the Mass is frequently a richly decorated work of goldsmithery.

BIBLIOGRAPHY. E. Atchley, *A History of the Use of Incense in Divine Worship*, London, 1909.

INCISING. Technique for creating designs by engraving their outline into the background. It is a type of intaglio similar to engraving and is most frequently used in metalwork. In general, any design or lettering that is cut into a material is called incised, for instance, the incised inscriptions on stone monuments.

INCRUSTATION. Technique of decoration in which a surface is inlaid with contrasting materials. True incrustation is restricted to the inlaying of stone with stone or stonelike materials, a technique popular in Byzantine architectural decoration. It played an extremely important role in early medieval Italian architecture, in which the incrusted materials were most often contrasting colors of marble (as in S. Miniato al Monte, Florence, 2d half of 11th cent.).

BIBLIOGRAPHY. C. Ricci, *Romanesque Architecture in Italy*, London, 1925.

INCUNABULA. Any works of art of an early epoch; specifically, books printed before 1500. Incunabula are relatively rare and are prized as much for their scarcity as for the exceptionally fine quality of their typography or illustration. An important incunabulum is Sebastian Brandt's

In antis. A type of temple with columns set between flanking walls.

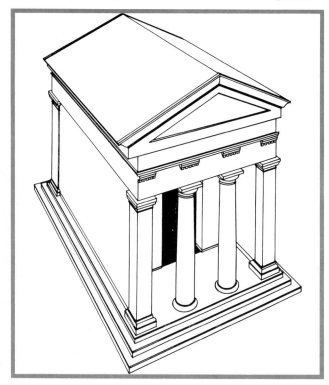

Inca art. View of fine stonework construction at the Inca site of Machu Picchu, high in the Andes.

Ship of Fools, printed by Bergmann von Olpe in 1494 at Basel. It contains woodcut illustrations by Dürer.

INDEPENDENCE HALL, PHILADELPHIA. Known also as the State House, it was erected from about 1730 to 1748, from designs furnished by Andrew Hamilton and Edmund Wooley, to house the provincial government. It was among the most ambitious civic projects of the period. The noteworthy features of this Revolutionary monument include a full, five-part Palladian plan, unique for its time in American governmental structures, and the Palladian window in the tower base.

BIBLIOGRAPHY. G. B. Tatum, *Penn's Great Town, 250 Years of Philadelphia Architecture*, Philadelphia, 1961.

INDIA. Some paleolithic and neolithic artifacts have been found in India, but the first culture in that region to produce objects of high artistic quality appeared in 3000 B.C. At that time a very advanced civilization existed in the Indus Valley around the cities of Mohenjo-daro and Harappā. The dates of this culture are still vague. Seals from the Indus Valley civilization have been found in the Near East in places dated in the middle of the 3d millennium B.C. Unquestionably these seals were produced by a culture that had already reached a well-advanced stage of development. But by about 1800 B.C., per-

haps because of a combination of disasters—drought, floods, and warfare—the civilization of the Indus River Valley came to an end.

The high state of that culture is evident in the remains of the city designed at Mohenjo-daro. The city was laid out on a basic grid pattern with main roads 60 feet wide, with drainage, and with multiple-storied buildings. The ruins yielded objects superb in design and execution, particularly seals (made of steatite) and sealings, painted ceramics, and some sculptures. The seals and their impressions, which were found by the hundreds, often are inscribed in a semipictographic script that has not yet been deciphered. Represented frequently on the seals are elephants, bulls, tigers, and rhinoceroses. Bulls shown feeding at a ceremonial trough may signify a lost ritual of a lost religion, as may other seals of a human figure, perhaps a divinity, in a tree. The human figure may be a prototype of the tree spirits known to have been worshiped in later Indian periods. Another example, a unique seal, depicts a three-headed deity seated cross-legged among animals, including a tiger and a bull, which later were to be identified iconographically with the god Siva. The figure may be a prototype of that Hindu deity.

The sculptures, all of miniature size, that is, rarely over 6 inches high, are in two different styles, indicating the coexistence of two traditions. One group, obviously related to Mesopotamia, consists of "priest" figures, which are basically cylindrical in form and modeled quite simply; they have striated hair held by a fillet and robes with trefoil designs. The other group, exemplified by a small sandstone male torso from Harappā and a copper figure of a dancing girl from Mohenjo-daro, is fully modeled with evident interest in organically moving form—a characteristic that remained basic to the aesthetic of most later Indian art.

The decline of the Indus Valley culture (ca. 1800 B.C.) coincided, and may be connected, with the invasion of the Aryans, whose ideas dominated India for more than a millennium. But practically nothing by these people has been found. A few clay and metal figurines of mother goddesses have been assigned to the period of Aryan rule, but these are probably folk arts of a primitive and aboriginal substructure of the imported Aryan civilization. *See* INDUS VALLEY CIVILIZATION.

MAURYAN ART

The first large body of Indian art known to us was produced in the 3d century B.C. Undoubtedly, in the 1,500 years between the end of the Indus Valley culture and the beginning of the Mauryan period (ca. 324–185 B.C.) art works had been created; presumably most were made of wood and did not survive the ravages of a tropical climate. The arts from the 3d century B.C. were mostly dedicated to Buddhism. To understand why, one must look back to the period roughly between 800 and 600 B.C., when the body of literature known as the Upanishads was being created. Among other things, the Upanishads demonstrate the incorporation of indigenous Indian thought into the Vedic thought of the Aryan conquerors. It was believed that when a man's body died his soul took another form and, according to his karma (his past acts), would move up or down the scale of life—up to a god or down to a reptile or insect—in an unending series of rebirths. The hope of the masses and the goal of the sage was to find a way to break this chain of life and achieve extinction of the soul. Gautama (Prince Siddhārtha, or Sākyamuni Buddha), the great religious teacher who lived probably in the 6th century B.C., proposed a method by which the individual through self-restraint and detachment from desire could break the chain of causation and attain nirvāṇa (a goal that is not defined, except as a state in which all individuality is lost). Although legend tells of converts flocking to Buddhism during Sākyamuni's life, it was Emperor Aśoka (r. ca. 273–236 B.C.) of the Mauryan dynasty who made Buddhism the dominant religion of India.

(For correlation of Chinese, Indian, and Japanese Buddhist terminology, *see* BUDDHIST TERMS, CORRELATION OF.)

The monuments of the Mauryan period are of three types: cave temples, monolithic pillars, and freestanding sculptures. The cave temples in the Barābar Hills near Gayā in Bihar were hollowed out of rock cliffs in the middle of the 3d century B.C. The most complicated of the Barābar temples is the Lomas Rishi, which is entered through a doorway carved in imitation of wood architecture. There is some doubt that the entrance is contemporaneous with the exterior, but it is not likely that it was carved much later than the rest of the cave. The entrance leads into the long side of a rectangular chamber, the end of which leads to a circular room with a dome-shaped ceiling. This second chamber represents a stūpa, a type of reliquary burial mound. The interior is plain, without any ornamentation, but the stone glistens as if polished; indeed the so-called "Mauryan polish" is a hallmark of sculptures from that period. *See* LOMAS RISHI CAVE.

Most typical of the Mauryan monuments are the "Aśoka pillars." These are polished sandstone monoliths, some almost 60 feet high, which are surmounted by finials of animals, for example, the elephant, the bull, and, particularly, the lion or a group of lions. Often these columns are inscribed with edicts of Emperor Aśoka urging that the moral precepts advocated by the Buddha be followed. Some pillars may have been erected by Aśoka's predecessors, but none probably are pre-Mauryan. The famous lion capital found at Sārnāth, near Benares (Sārnāth, Archaeological Museum), has a finial composed of four addorsed lions that originally were surmounted by a large wheel. The lions sit upon an abacus, around which, carved in relief, are a horse, bull, lion, and elephant, each separated by a wheel. The abacus itself rests on the capital, which is in the shape of an inverted lotus.

Each part of the capital is an aniconic and multiple Buddhist symbol. The wheel, deriving prestige from its resemblance to the traditionally worshiped solar disk, represents the Buddhist "wheel of life" (the sequence of death and life); it also symbolizes the teaching of the Buddha— "to put the wheel of the law in motion"—and, by extension, represents all Buddhist belief. The lions refer to the Buddha who was called the lion of the Sākya clan, and the animals on the abacus refer to the four directions. The column itself represents the axis of the universe. Nowhere does the image of the Buddha appear. In fact, this type of aniconic symbolism persisted at least to the end of the 1st century of the Christian era. *See* ASOKA COLUMNS; SARNATH.

Stylistically, the columns are more complex. Their general form derives from Near Eastern prototypes, possibly from Achaemenid Persia or even earlier sources. There is evidence that contact with Mesopotamia continued during the "lost" period between the end of the Indus Valley civilization and the founding of the Mauryan dynasty. During the Mauryan period ambassadors from as far as Greece were at Aśoka's court at Pāṭaliputra (modern Patna), where the Emperor's audience hall, as shown in the ruins, was a multicolumned building with a plan similar to the one erected by Darius at Persepolis. *See* PATALIPUTRA.

The lions with their stylized manes, rigidly sinewed legs, and heraldic grouping also attest to a Near Eastern derivation. Contrariwise, the horse, bull, and elephant on the abacus of the capital have the lithe movement and sensuous surface that characterized the Indus Valley seals. A few monumental figures of yakshas (gods of trees, rocks, and so on) also manifest a continuance of an indigenous tradition, as does a more than life-size torso in the Archaeological Museum, Patna. Despite differences in time and scale the Patna yaksha is related stylistically to the miniature torso from Harappā. The vitality of the Indus Valley manner again appears in a group of Mauryan terracotta figurines (found at Patna) to which have been added a very chic drapery and an air of courtly modishness.

This coexistence of two styles, one rigidly following formal conventions, the other free and fluid, persisted throughout the Mauryan period, and traces of the first, which came from the West, can be found even centuries later.

POST-MAURYAN STUPAS AND CAVE TEMPLES

The Mauryan empire disintegrated about 185 B.C., and its chief successor was the powerful dynasty of the Suṅgas, who, probably at the end of the 2d century B.C., erected the Great Stūpa at Bhārhut in central India (now Madhya Pradesh). The monumental stone railings of the stūpa (now mostly in the Indian Museum, Calcutta) were modeled after wood fencing with upright posts and crosspieces joined by tenon and groove. They were decorated in low and high relief with scenes from the Jātakas (tales from the Buddha's previous lives), figures of different deities, and floral motifs, many arranged in medallions. The deities carved on the rectangular posts, although relatively in high relief, are curiously flattened in a manner suggesting a persistence of Near Eastern influence. *See* BHARHUT.

At about the same time as the Bhārhut stūpa, cave temples were being carved from the rock cliffs at Bhājā and Kondāñe near Bombay. The chaitya halls in these early caves already follow the plan that was to become standard in many later sanctuaries; that is, they have a single long chamber with an entrance at the narrow end facing the stūpa at the far apsidal end. Again wood architecture is copied. For example, the stone columns slant inward as if to counteract the pull of the bentwood arches of their prototypes. At Bhājā both sides of the vihāra (monastery) doorway are decorated with monumental wall carvings, the first reliefs of such size known in India. One side appears to depict Sūrya, the sun god, in his chariot; the other, Indra riding on an elephant. Unlike the Bhārhut reliefs, those at Bhājā follow the same Indian tradition that was to be developed more fully at Sānchī about a century later. *See* BHAJA; KONDANE.

The Great Stūpa at Sānchī may have been originally dedicated by Aśoka, but the present structure and surrounding railings date from about the beginning of the Christian era. The toraṇas (gateways) are more elaborate and the ornamentation more intricately composed than the earlier railings from the Bhārhut stūpa. The Sānchī stūpa sculptures are among the most magnificent in India. They iquary and a symbol of Buddhism. Paradoxical are the Buddha, and innumerable animals, birds, and creatures presented in a creative symphony of shapes and forms. But religious symbols still are aniconic, thus maintaining the austere concept of the stūpa as both an idealized reliquary and a symbol of Buddhism. Paradoxical are the voluptuous yakshīs—small-waisted, large-hipped, and full-breasted, like mother goddesses—whose figures act as bracket supports on the toraṇas. Similarly contradictory are the royal donors in the vestibule of the chaitya hall at Kārle, which was excavated about the third quarter of the 1st century. These royal couples, heroic figures, exemplify the sensuous vitality that is essentially characteristic of most Indian art, whereas the simple stūpa within the hall expresses the Buddhist philosophy of abnegation. *See* KARLE; SANCHI.

BUDDHIST SCULPTURE

About the time the cave temples at Kārle were carved, the first anthropomorphic images of the Buddha appeared in two widely separated centers. One was Gandhāra, an area comprising part of present-day Afghanistan and northern Pakistan, near Peshawar. The other was Mathurā, about 90 miles south of Delhi. These first Buddha images were created for the Kushan rulers. The sudden transference from the symbol to the human figure may be explained by a transformation in Buddhist practice caused by the espousal of the Brahmanical concept of bhakti (adoration) as a form of devotion. For such worship the aniconic symbols, for example, the throne, footprint, and tree, were too coldly abstract. The figure of man was needed. At Gandhāra the artists drew upon the classic heritage of Greece and Rome, which had been known there since the conquest of the region in 327 B.C. by Alexander the Great. The Buddha was robed in a Roman toga, and his body was formed and posed like that of a Roman senator, and sometimes like that of Apollo. The Mathurā sculptures had a different model: the traditional yaksha. The two employed the same *lakṣaṇa* (distinguishing marks) of a Buddha: the *ushṇīsha* (a protuberance on the top of the head), the *ūrṇā* (a dot between the eyebrows), long-lobed ears, and so on. *See* GANDHARA; MATHURA.

With the appearance of the Buddha image came the concept of the Bodhisattva as a semidivinity, a concept that was to be important in the ideology of Mahāyāna Buddhism. The Bodhisattva in both Gandhāra and Mathurā is dressed in royal costume and is distinguished from a prince only by the addition of a halo. But the drapery was fashioned after the different traditional styles in each center, the Gandhāra being heavy and loose after Roman models, the Mathurā clinging. By the 4th to 5th century, however, both drapery types were synthesized, and the combination is called "wet drapery" to describe the concentric folds of a barely visible cloth over a seemingly naked body. This type became the model for most Buddha images throughout eastern Asia. *See* MAHAYANA.

Two other great religions, Jainism and Hinduism, coexisted and contended with Buddhism. While their arts, particularly their sculpture, have iconographic differences, they are otherwise essentially indistinguishable. Most of the architectural monuments that have survived from the pre-Christian and early Christian centuries are Buddhist and Jain, perhaps because these religions concentrated on hewing their sanctuaries from living rock, whereas the Hindus maintained the practice of building with wood, a more ephemeral material.

GUPTA AND CHALUKYAN ART

Although there is no lack of Hindu sculptures from the 1st and 2d centuries of our era, the earliest known Hindu sanctuaries are at Udayagiri, near Bhilsa, in the former state of Bhopāl in Madhya Pradesh (not to be confused with earlier Jain caves at Udayagiri and Khaṇḍagiri in Orissa). From an inscription with a date corresponding to A.D. 401, we know that these caves belong to the Gupta period (320–ca. 600) and that they were begun about 400. Udayagiri is best known for the colossal Varāha, boar avatar of Vishnu, carved in a shallow cave, hardly more than a niche. Varāha has a human body and a boar's head, and he is shown saving the earth goddess by raising her with his mouth from the flooding waters. The god's body is in the familiar form of the yaksha as developed in Mathurā at least three centuries earlier. He stands in profile, with one knee raised forward, and he is surrounded by devotees. This composition provided a formula for Varāha representations and was copied for centuries, even in the distant Deccan. *See* KHANDAGIRI AND UDAYAGIRI, ORISSA; UDAYAGIRI, BHOPAL.

During the centuries when the powerful Gupta kings ruled the north, most of the Deccan was under the rule of the Chālukyas, who were also munificent art patrons. The richest area of Chālukyan art, in the present states of Mysore and Maharashtra, encompasses the extensive temple sites of Bādāmi, Aihole, and Pattadakal, where we can observe the further development of Hindu (Brahmanical) cave architecture as well as the evolution of structural temples. The Hindu cave temples at Bādāmi were begun toward the end of the 6th century; one has a date of 578. In general, they carry on the type developed at Udayagiri a century or so earlier, but they are larger, more deeply cut into the rock, and more elaborately carved. The Bādāmi sanctuaries are entered through a narrow pillared veranda, which leads to a rectangular columned hall. The niches of the shrine are carved out of the back wall. Figures on the walls, ceilings, and brackets are in two styles, one deriving from the elegant elongated carvings of Amarāvatī to the south, the other from the heavier, northern Gupta tradition. At Aihole there are cave temples and the unique Lādh Khān temple (early 5th cent.), one of the earliest extant structures. *See* AIHOLE; AMARAVATI; BADAMI; MYSORE.

The evolution of the structural temple can be traced from the Vishnu temple at Deogarh, north of Jhansi in Madhya Pradesh, which consists of only a square, massively walled shrine with a doorway and false windows, each filled with a stone relief depicting a different avatar of Vishnu. Surmounting the entire shrine is a heavy tower, the śikhara. Such a building fulfills the basic requirements of the Brahmanical temple: it houses the god. As congregational ritual is not required, the area of the shrine where the cult image is placed, called the *garbhagriha* (womb chamber), is actually the only essential of the Hindu temple. By the time of the Guptas and Chālukyas, however, assembly halls (*maṇḍapa*), often entered through vestibules or porches, were placed in front of the shrines for the convenience of the worshiper, as at Aihole and Bādāmi. The Buddhists did the same, as can be seen at Sānchī. Typically, then, the temple consists of a solid-walled *garbhagriha*, a somewhat larger *maṇḍapa*, and a narrow open porch. Exterior decoration is usually confined to niches (false windows) containing a large image, reticulated stone screens in the true windows, and some floral motifs; on the back is a prominent carving of the deity to whom the temple was dedicated. The interior at first was generally undecorated.

The śikhara of the temple most frequently is of solid masonry. In the north, where it is sometimes labeled "Aryan," it is composed of many horizontal courses tapering toward the top and profusely adorned with carvings of chaitya windows and other motifs looking from a distance like geometric patterns. At the apex is an *āmalaka*, a single great stone shaped like a ribbed mushroom. Despite the fundamental horizontality of the decoration, the total effect of the tower is vertical and dazzling as the brilliant light strikes the outer surfaces of the carvings

and the shade deepens as we move into in the lower levels.

The temple tower of the south typically has fewer horizontal segments, usually only three or five, and they are emphasized by heavy cornice moldings. In place of the *āmalaka* they have a *stūpikā*, that is, a square or octagonal dome. The two kinds of śikhara are found together at Mahakut near Pattadakal, at Bādāmi, and at Aihole, each on a temple built about A.D. 600. No northern tower has been seen farther south, and only a few southern towers are extant in northern India.

Farther south, where the Pallava dynasty was dominant from the 6th to the 9th century, a great many monuments were built. Among them, at Māmallapuram, near Madras, is a group of seven temples, called rathas, each carved from a single huge boulder (ca. 640). Of these, two are like the standard southern temple with fully developed śikharas. One is apsidal like a Buddhist chaitya hall. Another is rectangular with a barrel vault and gabled ends. Still another has a thatched roof. It would seem from this curious rarity as if each ratha was meant to be executed according to a plan of a different type of temple current in southern India during the 7th century. Also at Māmallapuram, which was the seaport for the Pallavas' capital at nearby Kāñchīpuram (modern Conjeeveram), there are cave temples and a huge cliff covered with sculptures illustrating the Descent of the Ganges. *See* MAMALLAPURAM.

EVOLUTION OF TEMPLE AND CAVE ARCHITECTURE AND SCULPTURE

The next major step in the evolution of the Hindu temple was taken at the Kailāsanātha in Kāñchīpuram and in two Pattadakal temples, the Virūpāksha and the Pāpanātha, which were derived from the Pallava model. The main features of the change may be observed in the Virūpāksha (ca. 740). Here the *garbhagriha* was moved forward away from the back wall so that the worshiper could perform the rite of *pradakṣinā* (circumambulation) of the shrine. The devotee entered through a shallow porch adjacent to a dancing pavilion, which, though detached, functioned as part of the structure. The *maṇḍapa* was quite large but was only dimly lighted by windows screened by reticulated carvings and shaded by thick walls. Porches to the left and right gave some additional illumination. Pillars supporting the ceiling were richly carved with legendary scenes in the lively linear style of Amarāvatī. The worshiper traversed more than 40 feet of this dimly lighted hall before reaching the utter darkness of the main shrine. If he wished, he could pause along the way, for against the exterior walls, to the right and left of the shrine, were subsidiary shrines—one to Ganeśa, son of Siva and remover of obstacles, to whom worship was given in the hope that the prayer to Siva would reach the deity without hindrance. The interiors of these temples function brilliantly in relation to the Hindu concept. The worshiper leaves the brilliant light of the outside world and moves through the half-light of the *maṇḍapa* until he is confronted by the complete darkness of the shrine, the mysterious womb chamber. *See* KANCHIPURAM; PATTADAKAL.

With the construction of the Virūpāksha temple at Pattadakal, the Hindu architect solved the problems of the

India. *Buddha in Meditation*, ca. 10th century. High relief in sandstone. British Museum, London.

interior spaces of his building. In the larger temples, however, the awkward relationship between the śikhara and the mandapa remained unresolved until the end of the 9th century.

From the 6th through the 8th century cave architecture continued at an accelerated rate. The later sanctuaries in the Deccan, that is, Ajaṇṭā, Ellora, Aurangābād, and the great vihāra at Elephanta, were made within this time. In these caves are some of the greatest stone carvings and wall paintings ever produced in India. Until about A.D. 600 the subjects were mostly Buddhist, but during the 7th century Hindu themes predominated. Yet, whether the subject was Buddhist or Hindu, it was never the religion but the prevailing spirit of India itself that permeated the style of the arts. Thus the Vaishnavite sculptures on the Hindu temple at Deogarth expressed the same tranquillity as contemporaneous Buddhist carvings did at Ajaṇṭā, even though imperial patronage seems to have favored Buddhism. Also in the 7th century, when an outpouring of Hindu vitality produced the masterpieces at Elephanta, the most spirited carvings were made in the Buddhist caves at Ellora. And the Buddhist caves at Aurangābād in the Deccan have the same poised serenity as the Hindu temples of the same time, although Buddhism was then rapidly declining in the area. See AJANTA; AURANGABAD; ELEPHANTA; ELLORA.

The great art of hewing sanctuaries from live rock that had been developing for centuries came to a climax in the second half of the 8th century in the mammoth Kailāsa at Ellora. A full-size temple based on the Virūpāksha at Paṭṭadakal, the Kailāsa is as complete a building as if it had been constructed, although it was made by cutting away the stone of a high cliff in order to be able to display the rear and side exposures as well as the façade. The Kailāsa is more than an example of extraordinary technical virtuosity. The sculptures, made by master craftsmen impressed from distant areas, are unusually dramatic, and they express a nervous energy quite different from the repose reflected in the works of the previous century. See KAILASA TEMPLE, ELLORA.

The progress in structural building can be seen best at Bhuvaneśvara, Orissa, where a series of temples was erected from the 8th to the 12th century. The Mukteśvara temple (ca. 900) at Bhuvaneśvara was the first to have a square stepped dome over the roof of the assembly hall. In appearance this form interrupts the horizontal movement of the hall and creates a union with the vertical thrust of the tower. Another step was taken by the builders of the temples at Khajurāho in central India (10th–11th cent.) and those at Bhuvaneśvara (for example, the Liṅgarāja) dating from about the 12th century. They used not one but a series of two or three assembly halls and a porch that seems to extend away from the tower. Placed toward the rear, the tower marks the apex of a series of domes ascending from the first hall. Over this marvelously organic complex of rising shapes are countless sculptures that, though organized horizontally, seem to cascade downward from an elaborate śikhara. Each part seems to grow from another until transformed into a whole; the temple literally vibrates with movement. See BHUVANESVARA; KHAJURAHO.

The lavish proliferation of sculptures on the temples at Khajurāho and Bhuvaneśvara is also characteristic of the Jain temple complex at Mount Abu, in Rajasthan (11th–12th cent.), which is in the Gujarat style; in this group the local white marble was carved like lacework. Southward, at Somnāthpur, Belūr, and Halebīd, Mysore, the Hoyśalas (10th–13th cent.) impressed their own idiom on the style current at that time throughout India. Buddhist art in Bengal and Bihar accommodated itself to the general stylistic trend. The human figure lost its vital sensuousness in elaborately contrived posturings. Plastic forms gave way to graceful contours and significant design to overelaborate detail. See GUJARAT TEMPLES; HOYSALESVARA TEMPLE, HALEBID; SOMNATHPUR. See also GOMATESVARA, SRAVANA BELGOLA.

On some temples of the same period, particularly at Khajurāho and Konārak, what had been a robust delight in female voluptuousness became an overstated depiction of the sexual act with multiple elaborations and "perversions." The change may be attributed partly to a shift in Hindu thought away from the worship of Sakti (the female principle), caused by a fragmentation of the Sakti cult. Ultimately some of the subcults indulged in orgiastic ceremonies. Their erotic sculptures in a mannered style reflect a disturbed society. See KONARAK.

THE MUSLIM IMPACT

The deep-rooted weaknesses evident in Indian culture from the 10th century onward permitted the Muslims (who had begun to invade northern India during the 8th cent.) to spread through much of India by the beginning of the 11th century. Two centuries later the Muslims were established in northern India. The most important arts indigenous to India—temple building and sculpture—continued only in the south beyond the range of Muslim power. In the north, where the Muslims prevailed, the arts were confined to Muslim architecture and miniature painting. See also MUGHAL ARCHITECTURE OF INDIA.

Southern India from the 9th to the 11th century was dominated by the Cholas, who, apart from their stone sculpture, were great bronze makers in the traditions that had been instituted by the Pallavas two centuries earlier. The Chola bronzes, however, are more graceful and sensitive. Although they are elegant and mannerist, reminiscent of contemporaneous stone sculpture to the north, they rarely show evidence of the same stresses. Perhaps it was because the deep south was not under Muslim pressures.

Many of the bronze sculptures were made to be used on special holidays in ceremonies in which, as icons, they were taken out of their shrines and carried through the streets or into other buildings, often in symbolic celebration of nuptial rites. It was to accommodate such ceremonies that huge temple complexes developed in southern India. These were built over a period of centuries. Usually starting with a temple of the 8th or 10th century, these temples grew with the addition of other shrines, dance pavilions, and columned halls and were surrounded by a wall or a series of walls. By the 16th and 17th centuries the temple compound became, in fact, a miniature city. It contributed to Indian architecture such innovations as multicolumned halls, sometimes rightly called thousand-columned halls, and huge gateways (gopuras). The latter were placed at the center of each of the four walls surrounding the compound (or sections of the compound), and frequently they rose like towers 100 feet or more in the sky. The silhouettes of the gopuras are typical of southern India. The multicolumned halls engendered a new aesthetic within the temple precincts by the long corridors that were created by huge monolithic columns 15 or more feet high. The columns were carved meticulously; compared with earlier sculpture, they are metallic and lifeless in appearance (for example, the temples of Mīnākshī at Madura and Srīrangam at Trichinopoly and the small temple at Vellore). Less pretentious reliefs embellishing the halls have greater vitality. *See* MADURA; TRICHINOPOLY.

Early painting in India is known best from the murals at Ajaṇṭā and a few scattered examples elsewhere, particularly those (ca. A.D. 1000) at Tanjore, Madras, in the Great Temple. By the 13th century another form of painting—the miniature—was practiced in Bengal and Gujarat. In the 15th century the painting traditions that had been established centuries earlier underwent great stylization in hieratic icons of Jain manuscripts. *See* BENGAL; TANJORE. *See also* SADANGA.

The introduction of Persian painting in the 16th century by the Muslim invaders had an explosive effect on Indian painting. The interplay of this foreign art (often called Mughal, or Mogul, painting) with the indigenous Indian tradition (called Rajput) led to infinite variations: Rajput influenced by Mughal, Mughal influenced by Rajput, Mughal subjects by Rajput artists, and vice versa. *See* RAJPUT PAINTING OF INDIA.

In this welter of conflicting painting styles we find the Mughal tradition with its infinite detail of a true miniature style blending with the native Indian style, which is more of a mural tradition scaled to small size. Subjects include portraiture, illustrations of legendary tales, *rāgas* (paintings representing musical modes), and birds. The most notable bird painter was the Mughal artist Mansur (fl. early 17th cent.). By the 17th and 18th centuries local styles arose in various courts throughout Rajasthan and the Deccan; in the 18th century schools such as Kulu, Kangra, and Pahāri flourished in the Punjab hills. Work of high quality was continued in these areas well into the 19th century. *See* MANSUR; MUGHAL PAINTING OF INDIA.

About 1200 the victorious Muslim sultan of Delhi, Quṭb-ud-din Aibak (Quṭb ad-Din Aibeg), built his tower of victory, the Quṭb Minār in Delhi. This 238-foot structure firmly established Muslim architecture in India. From that time to the 20th century there was hardly any important building in northern India that did not follow Islamic modes. The stylistic prototypes came basically from Iraq, Persia, and Afghanistan. The Indian version of the Iraqi is exemplified by the tomb of Shams-ud-din Iltutmish (1235) in Delhi, whose domes are on squinches and whose walls are richly covered with Arabic script or abstract designs. The Quṭb Minār had its prototype in Afghanistan, but the Hindu craftsmen who carved the Arabic script in the same red sandstone used in Mathurā sculptures gave the surfaces, by some miracle of plasticity, a Hindu flavor. A century later (1325) the tomb of Ghiyas-ud-din Tughlak in Delhi, almost totally devoid of ornament, reflected in its austerity more of Afghan puritanism than traditional Indian warmth. *See* GHIYAS-UD-DIN TUGHLAK, TOMB OF, DELHI; QUṬB MINĀR.

Local Muslim styles arose throughout India. For example, carvings on 15th-century mosques at Ahmedabad in Gujarat are like stone translations of the traditional wood carvings of the area. The dignity of the buildings at Māṇḍū in the old Malwa area recalls the stern Afghan styles. The culmination of Muslim architecture came in the Delhi area. There the tomb of Humayun (begun 1564), although based on Persian models, included two new features: pairs of kiosks that abut the main chamber and an arcade that serves as a plinth and dramatizes the tomb and its setting. *See* AHMEDABAD; JAMI MASJID; DELHI; HUMAYUN'S TOMB, DELHI.

Humayun's grandson, Shah Jahan, built the Taj Mahal (1632–43) at Agra as a tomb for Mumtaz Mahal, his wife. The features introduced in Humayun's tomb were incorporated in the Taj Mahal but were rearranged far more gracefully. Red sandstone and white marble had been used for the earlier building, but the Taj was built entirely of white marble, embellished with semiprecious stones. The studied relationships of architectural forms and the perfection and interplay of various details make the Taj one of the world's masterpieces. When, a generation later (1678), the Taj was used as a model for a tomb erected in Aurangābād for the mother of Aurangzeb, an architectural caricature was created as the exquisite proportions of the original monument were lost in the meager constrictions of its imitation. *See* TAJ MAHAL, AGRA.

CONTEMPORARY TRENDS

With the fall of India and its complete subjection under British rule, all the arts waned. The art of architecture was resurrected with the advent of Le Corbusier's designs for the Punjab capital at Chandigarh, and painting and sculpture are now reviving. Of the older generation of contemporary painters, Jamini Roy, with his sophisticated rendering of Bengal folk subjects, is outstanding. Amrita Sher Gil's synthesis of European and Indian modes of painting forecast a new Indian tradition. The contemporary Indian artist now bases his work on European and American trends; and as Western influences become integrated with indigenous traditions a new definition of the Indian creative idiom is evolving. *See* CHANDIGARH.

See also BAGH; BEDSA; BODHGAYA; CHEZARLA; JAGANNATHA TEMPLE, PURI; KASHMIR; MANMODA; NALANDA; NASIK; ORISSA; PITALKHORA; RAJPUTANA TEMPLES; VIJAYANAGAR.

BIBLIOGRAPHY. B. Bhattacharya, *Indian Buddhist Iconography ...*, London, 1924; H. Cousens, *The Chālukyan Architecture of the Kanarese Districts* (Archaeological Survey of India, New Imperial Series, vol. 42), Calcutta, 1926; G. Yazdani, *Ajaṇṭā*, 4 vols., London, 1930–55; H. Cousens, *Medieval Temples of the Dakhani*, Calcutta, 1931; H. Cousens, *Somanatha and Other Medieval Temples of Kāthiāwāḍ*, Calcutta, 1931; J. H. Marshall, ed., *Mohenjo-Daro and the Indus Civilization*, 3 vols., London, 1931; B. Rowland, *The Wall-Paintings of India, Central Asia, and Ceylon*, Boston, 1938; J. N. Banerjea, *The Development of Hindu Iconography* (thesis), Calcutta, 1941; N. R. Ray, *Maurya and Sunga Art*, Calcutta, 1945; S. Kramrisch, *The Hindu Temple*, 2 vols., Calcutta, 1947; R. C. Majumdar, ed., *The History and Culture of the Indian People*, 10 vols., Bombay, 1951–65; H. R. Zimmer, *Philosophies of India*, New York, 1951; British Museum, Dept. of Oriental Antiquities, *Sculptures from Amārāvatī in the British Museum* by D. Barrett, London, 1954; S. Kramrisch, *The Art of India through the Ages*, London, 1954; H. R. Zimmer, *The Art of Indian Asia*, 2 vols., New York, 1955; H. Ingholt, *Gandhāran Art in Pakistan*, New York, 1957; P. Brown, *Indian Architecture*, vol. 1: *Buddhist and Hindu Periods*, 4th ed., Bombay, 1959; J. H. Marshall, *The Buddhist Art of Gandhāra*, Cambridge, Eng., 1960; P. Stern and M. Bénisti, *Evolution du style indien d'Amārāvatī*, Paris, 1961; R. S. Gupte and B. D. Mahajan, *Ajaṇṭā, Ellora and Aurangabad Caves*, Bombay, 1962.

J. LEROY DAVIDSON

INDIA: INDIAN MUSEUM, *see* CALCUTTA: INDIAN MUSEUM.

INDIANAPOLIS, IND.: JOHN HERRON ART INSTITUTE. Opened in 1906, the museum covers the history of art by showing a few important objects from each period rather than specializing in any particular one. One of its finest possessions is a pair of 12th-century Spanish frescoes, two of a group of six from the chapel of S. Baudelio. There is a small group of Sienese paintings. Included in the fine collection of 17th-century Dutch and Flemish paintings are Hobbema's *The Water Mill* and Van Dyck's *Triumphal Entry into Jerusalem*. There are seven canvases by Turner, including *The Fifth Plague of Egypt*, and a tray that he painted. There are also collections of Chinese pottery and bronzes, pre-Columbian pottery and sculpture, 19th-century French painting, and American art.

BIBLIOGRAPHY. E. Spaeth, *American Art Museums and Galleries*, New York, 1960.

INDIAN ART OF NORTH AMERICA, *see* NORTH AMERICAN INDIAN ART.

INDOCHINA, *see* CAMBODIA.

INDONESIA. Country in southeast Asia. More than 3,000 miles wide from east to west, it includes Sumatra, Java, Borneo, and Bali, as well as thousands of smaller islands and half of New Guinea.

For a discussion of primitive art, *see* OCEANIC ART (INDONESIA).

Into this vast expanse people began to come from southern China in the 3d millennium B.C. Later, Hinduism and Buddhism reached Indonesia. The areas that were first affected were those accessible to the travelers who came by sea from the nearer parts of southeast Asia or the more distant regions of India and Ceylon. After these initial contacts the influences were felt farther inland.

EVOLUTION OF ART FORMS

Early art styles have survived into modern times. This is perhaps best shown in textiles. The densely patterned banded forms, with rhomboids, key shapes, spirals, and human and animal figures repeated over entire surfaces in artistic regularity, are derived from patterns that developed under southeast Asian influence of the Dong-Son culture (which reached Indonesia between 700 and 300 B.C.). The symmetry of these forms combines with a fluidity and rhythm that came from Chinese influences of the late Chou period (ca. 600 B.C.–256 B.C.). The result is a blending of this fluidity and symmetry, one contained by the other, with the rigidity of a layered form and within it a more free-flowing, flowering linear grid aspect.

This double aspect of design is also seen in wood carving. For instance, in the main posts of houses, crisply carved vegetal forms seem to open up for diamondlike explosions of recessed mathematical sections. The ancient styles are perpetuated, too, in wooden statues.

Until about the 6th century A.D. the influence of Indian art was paramount in Java and Sumatra. During the 7th century artistic independence began to evolve. The mature Indonesian self-contained period may be dated from the 8th century onward.

Buddhism came to Indonesia in two waves. Hīnayāna Buddhism arrived first, from the 2d through the 6th century. In the early 7th century Mahāyāna Buddhism took a strong hold; it was capable of including elements of the already-present Hinduism and animism of the people. In the 8th and 9th centuries the Sailendra dynasty ruled Java, Sumatra, and eventually even Cambodia. Under the Sailendras the syncretized Buddhist-Hindu art developed. Artistic influences from India, because of the Sailendra dynasty's origins, were from Amarāvatī at first; later the Gupta and Pāla styles were important. Pilgrims made visits to India; since one of the major places visited was Nālandā, influences containing Vajrayāna elements came back to Indonesia. The great art of Indonesia is saturated with Tantric Vajrayāna Buddhist ideas. *See* AMARAVATI; HINAYANA; MAHAYANA; NALANDA; TANTRA; VAJRAYANA.

Between 750 and 850 impressive Hindu shrines were built in central Java. These were basically one-celled sanctuaries with high bases originally influenced by southern Indian prototypes, but they went beyond this style in an elaboration of curves everywhere but especially above the doorways. At Chandi Bima the shrine is still single-celled, but the use of enlarged heads upon the tower is distinctive and anticipates the large Cambodian faces centuries later, as well as the *kala* heads (masks of glory) at Chandi Djabung in the mid-14th century. These shrines are usually dedicated to Vishnu or to Siva, who can also be the protector of the state. In the 11th century we find the ruler Erlanga depicted as Vishnu; in this manifestation the King is acutely represented and the Boar of Vishnu that holds him up is vigorously treated in the Gupta style.

The greatest monument in Indonesia, both aesthetically and in size, is the imposing and impressive sanctuary at Barabudur. In spite of its stepped appearance, its general outline matches that of a dome. In this particular context the dome is understood as a stūpa. There are five square terraces, then three circular terraces, and, finally, a central platform. There once were 505 sculptured Buddha figures on the open terraces. Barabudur is a Mahāyāna Buddhist work of the 8th century, a great gesture of effort and belief. It was designed as a symbol of the universe, or mandala. The Gupta Indian elements have been made more supple and human here. The immense number of reliefs move with the rhythms of this art. This movement blends well with the actual walking-looking series of events. Originally Barabudur's sculptures were coated and colored. *See* BARABUDUR.

PUPPETS

The puppets of Indonesia are a distinctive art form. The puppet theater was well established in Java by the 9th century. The part that shadow puppets play in the artistic tradition of the islands is far more important than the role that puppets and marionettes may have had in a Western tradition. The Eastern puppets exerted influences upon both the sculptural and the painterly traditions and were by no means a minor or supplementary art. Usually made of leather, they are flat with major emphasis on contours of extreme twists, turns, and projections. In Java and Bali the leather becomes a fine parchment, light in shade and partially transparent. These flat forms are pierced with pins to make stencil-like holes in ornate patterns that reveal the characteristics of the person portrayed

Indonesia. The Great Temple, Besakih, Bali. 14th century. Large central temple dedicated to Siva.

within the outlines. Color is added, and gold foil is frequently used.

For symbolic reasons, everything is stylized for the subject; thus forms of face, hair, figure, clothing, and color do not necessarily correspond to any natural or local color. One puppet's face may be blue, another's black. The puppet is usually depicted with the face in profile and with a full frontal view of the shoulders. The shoulders are so exaggerated that they continue beyond the body and give the very long attached arms ample room to be manipulated. Running through the puppet is a long central brace by which it is held. The body is seen in a three-quarter view, with profiled legs. The feet usually do not agree with the seen angle of the legs, seemingly pointing to one side. The fixed stance of the legs is either wide-stepping for heroes or close together for heroines.

The Indonesian gamelan orchestra is a highly developed entity and accompanies the *wayang* plays. The puppets are called by many names, and these convey more than the word "puppet" denotes. There are the *wayang-purwa*, which means "shadow or ghost" or "first or oldest." The references here are wrapped up with ideas of ancestor worship and mystical ceremonies. These "ghosts" are connected with the people's oldest religious expressions, both in creation and in watchful meditation of performances. The *wayang-kulit* (shadow-ghost, leather-skin) performances are made before a screen. The *wayang-klitik* is a flat wooden figure with movable leather arms. The *wayang-golek* is a completely rounded wooden figure that was developed in Java; it is less powerful because more photographic. The

wayang-beber is a series of pictures on a scroll that rolls out in a continuous band. *See* JAVA.

BIBLIOGRAPHY. H. R. Zimmer, *The Art of Indian Asia*, 2 vols., New York, 1955; F. A. Wagner, *Indonesia, the Art of an Island Group*, tr. A. E. Keep, New York, 1959.

JOHN BRZOSTOSKI

INDRA. Hindu god, the personified atmosphere. In the ancient Vedas he is the chief of all the gods, but in the later mythology Indra has a secondary rank. His heaven is Swarga, and its capital Amarāvatī. His symbol is the thunderbolt. As regent of the eastern quarter of the compass he figures in the nativity of the Buddha. Indra also is called Sakra and is sometimes identified with the Buddhist Vajrapāṇi.

INDUSTRIAL DESIGN. The shaping of machine-made products for mass production. The industrial designer, like the craftsman of nonindustrial times, is responsible for the forms of the products his society uses. The need for industrial design grew out of the 19th-century Industrial Revolution when hand production evolved into machine production, but in the United States it was not until the Depression of the 1930s that industrial design became a powerful force.

One of the best-known precursors of modern design was Michael Thonet's bentwood chair, first perfected in 1856. As Drexler and Daniel (1959) point out, the bentwood process eliminated traditional hand-carved joints and led to the first mass production of standardized furniture. Some thirty-five years later, in Brussels and Paris,

Art Nouveau cleared the decks for what is thought of today as modern design. It became the first movement to break with the custom of imitating past styles, and although its characteristic whiplash curve disappeared in the austere, rectilinear styles that followed (the movement lasted only until 1910) something of its free, experimental spirit persisted. *See* ART NOUVEAU.

With the advent of World War I the Dutch de Stijl movement made an important contribution to industrial design. Led by the painter Piet Mondrian and the architect Gerrit Rietveld, de Stijl tried to reduce the elements of composition to independent rectangles and circles, to replace symmetry with freely asymmetrical balance, and to promote flat, primary colors. Such ideas were to have an important influence on Germany's Bauhaus, and many of them are still called upon as a basis for today's design. *See* DE STIJL.

The Bauhaus (established in Weimar in 1919 but closed by the Nazis in 1933) was the first school to teach industrial design. Director Walter Gropius had students develop designs that were actually manufactured by industry, and "Bauhaus" became a household word for modern design in Germany and later throughout the world. Characteristic of the Bauhaus style were functional designs expressed in severe geometric forms. Still associated with it are metal tube furniture, storage furniture, and the classic Barcelona chair, designed by Gropius's successor at the Bauhaus, Ludwig Mies van der Rohe. *See* BAUHAUS.

In the last twenty years both Scandinavia and Italy have made major contributions to design. Such figures as Hans Wegner and Sigvard Bernadotte, in Denmark, and Tapio Wirkkala and Kaj Franck, in Finland, have brought Scandinavian design to a high level of excellence. Among the most beautiful in the world, their designs are often so close to handcraft that they cannot be compared fairly to mass-production designs. *See* BERNADOTTE, SIGVARD; FRANCK, KAJ; WEGNER, HANS; WIRKKALA, TAPIO.

A burst of post-World War II energy sparked Italy's uniquely lyrical design movement. Characterized by sensuously sculptured products, it is well expressed in the "aerodynamic," teardrop forms of Pinin Farina's Ferrari sports cars, in the elegance of a Gio Ponti place setting or skyscraper, and in the sculptured lines of Marcello Nizzoli's Necchi sewing machine and Olivetti typewriter. *See* FARINA, PININ; NIZZOLI, MARCELLO; PONTI, GIO.

In the United States, the economic disaster of the 1930s led a number of desperate manufacturers to seek new product designs that would stimulate customers to buy. Among the first industrial designers to answer the call were Raymond Loewy, Walter Teague, Donald Deskey, Russel Wright, and Norman Bel Geddes. So striking—or at least novel—were some of their early designs that they sent sales charts skyrocketing. However, with the exception of such genuine innovators as Charles Eames and George Nelson, contemporary designers are less flashy and more sober. Indeed, the current conflict in American industrial design stems partly from this change. Since today's manufacturer may stake millions of dollars on a new product, he frequently asks the designer for an "acceptably" styled product rather than one featuring design innovations whose selling power has not been proved. At the same time, such American industrialists as Walter Paepcke of the

Container Corporation of America and Thomas J. Watson of International Business Machines have successfully set standards of design excellence in their various products. *See* DESKEY, DONALD; EAMES, CHARLES; LOEWY, RAYMOND; NELSON, GEORGE; TEAGUE, WALTER DORWIN; WRIGHT, RUSSEL.

BIBLIOGRAPHY. E. Kaufmann, *What is Modern Design?*, New York, 1950; M. R. Rogers, *Italy at Work: Her Renaissance in Design Today*, Rome, 1950; R. Loewy, *Never Leave Well Enough Alone*, New York, 1951; M. Bill, *Form: A Balance Sheet of Mid-Twentieth Century Trends in Design*, Basel, 1952; L. Mumford, *Art and Technics*, New York, 1952; H. Dreyfuss, *Designing for People*, New York, 1955; D. Wallance, *Shaping America's Products*, New York, 1956; A. Hald, *Swedish Design*, Stockholm, 1958; A. Drexler and G. Daniel, *Introduction to Twentieth Century Design from the Collection of the Museum of Modern Art*, New York, 1959; H. Read, *Art and Industry, the Principles of Industrial Design*, Bloomington, Ind., 1961; N. Pevsner, *Pioneers of Modern Design from William Morris to Walter Gropius*, rev. ed., Baltimore, 1964.

ANN FEREBEE

INDUS VALLEY CIVILIZATION.

Early Indian culture, so called because its chief sites, Mohenjo-daro, Harappā, and Chandhu-daro, are in the Indus River Valley. Since the original finds, which threw entirely new light on the history of Indian civilization, were made in the 1920s and 1930s, other sites have been found in western India. Although none of these so far is comparable in scope and richness to the original finds, there is no doubt that the civilization spread far beyond the Indus. One important site is being excavated near Udaipur in southern Rajasthan. *See* INDIA.

The excavations of the original two cities, Mohenjo-daro and Harappā, have never been completed, partly because

Industrial design. Charles Eames, side chair, 1946. Walnut plywood and metal.

of their size and partly because the subsoil water encroaches on the earliest levels. What remains shows a city of wide planned streets, multiple-storied buildings of kiln-baked bricks, and homes with built-in drainage systems. The artifacts give evidence of considerable sophistication. Seals made of steatite and sealings have been found by the hundreds. These bear inscriptions in an indecipherable script that had developed around the pictograph. Some of these seals have been found in Mesopotamia and in excavations near the Persian Gulf in sites that permit dating about 2500 B.C. The seals themselves depict various animals (rhinoceros, elephant, Brahman bull, and water buffalo) and mythical creatures. In addition, deities in trees, deities sitting in yoga positions, and bulls feeding at elaborate troughs indicate the religious character of these objects. One seal, depicting a three-faced deity surrounded by animals, including a tiger and a bull, may refer to a prototype of the later Hindu deity Siva.

Sculptures fall into two categories: one group, representing "priests," shows definite relationships with the Near East. The figures are basically cylindrical and have little modeling. The beard is simply striated and the hair tied with a circular fillet. The robe is decorated with a trefoil textile ornament, which, in common with the other features, is a Near Eastern characteristic. The other sculptures, exemplified by a male torso from Harappā in sandstone and a dancing girl from Mohenjo-daro in copper, have a sensuous surface quality that belies the almost Greek naturalism of their appearance. They have a fluid movement that was to remain basic to the main tradition of Indian art for the next 4,000 years.

Painted pottery relates both to the Near East and possibly to the neolithic pottery of China. The various stages of the Indus Valley civilization can best be observed through the variations in painted pottery until the final disappearance of the culture about 1800 B.C.

Among the minor artifacts is a series of conical stones and circular ring stones, which some authorities believe to be symbols of a phallic worship similar to that which developed in India much later. A considerable number of terra-cotta toys have been found, some quite complicated, such as a bullock cart with movable wheels and a highly ingenious clay animal whose loose head swung up and down against a balancing counterweight.

BIBLIOGRAPHY. J. H. Marshall, ed., *Mohenjo-Daro and the Indus Civilization*, 3 vols., London, 1931; *Cambridge History of India*, supplementary vol.: *The Indus Civilization* by R. E. M. Wheeler, 2d ed., Cambridge, Eng., 1960.

J. LEROY DAVIDSON

INEN, see SOTATSU.

INFANTADO PALACE, GUADALAJARA, SPAIN. The earliest of the large town palaces of the Spanish nobility and the first of Italian block-design outside Italy. Built by Juan Guas in 1480–83, the palace is notable for its arcaded courtyard. *See* GUADALAJARA, SPAIN.

BIBLIOGRAPHY. L. Torres Balbás, *Ars Hispaniae*, vol. 7: *Arquitectura gótica*, Madrid, 1952.

INFILLING. Stage in the execution of a painting following the sketch. Infilling takes place when the overall forms and colors are painted into the outlines of the sketch. The term is also used for the process of restoring a painting by filling up damaged paint areas.

INFRA-RED. Technically, that part of the invisible spectrum adjoining the red edge of the visible spectrum. Special photographic films, sensitive to infra-red rays, have been developed and are often employed in scientific investigations of paintings. The rays can reveal the forms of normally invisible layers of paint. Such layering can indicate preparatory stages of the painting; it may also indicate later restorations.

INGEGNO, L' (Andrea Alovigi, da Assisi, or di Aliogi). Italian painter (fl. 1484–1516). This follower of Perugino apparently assisted the master in executing frescoes at the Sistine Chapel, the Cambio in Perugia, and Orvieto Cathedral. According to Vasari, he became practically blind and was appointed by the popes to an administrative post in Assisi, in which he seems to have been active from 1501 to 1516. Although many works of the Umbrian school have been attributed to L'Ingegno, none can be authenticated. These reflect the lyricism of Perugino's landscapes, poses, and expressions and the unity of his spatial conceptions.

BIBLIOGRAPHY. A. Venturi, *Storia dell'arte italiana*, vol. 7, pt. 2, Milan, 1913; U. Gnoli, "Andrea da Assisi detto l'Ingegno," *Rassegna d'Arte*, XIX, 1919.

INGHAM, CHARLES CROMWELL. American portrait painter (b. Dublin, 1796; d. New York City, 1863). He studied at the Royal Dublin Society. Ingham settled in New York in 1817 and became a founder of the National Academy of Design. His figure pieces of women and children possess an enamellike finish, a graceful outline, and sentimental charm.

BIBLIOGRAPHY. A. T. Gardner, "Ingham in Manhattan," *Metropolitan Museum of Art Bulletin*, X, May, 1952.

INGRES, JEAN-AUGUSTE-DOMINIQUE. French painter and draftsman (b. Montauban, 1780; d. Paris, 1867). After an apprenticeship in Montauban with his artist father, Joseph Ingres, and in Toulouse with his father's colleagues, Ingres went to Paris in 1797 to study with Jacques-Louis David. Influenced by the new "Greek" doctrine of art championed in David's studio, Ingres painted his *Envoys of Agamemnon* (1801; Paris, Ecole des Beaux-Arts), for which he won the Prix de Rome (he did not go to Italy until 1806). In the next few years he painted several portraits: in 1804, his father, *Joseph Ingres*, his friend *Gilibert* (both Montauban, Ingres Museum), and a *Self-Portrait* (Chantilly, Condé Museum); in 1805, three famous portraits, *Monsieur Rivière*, *Madame Rivière*, and *Mademoiselle Rivière* (all Paris, Louvre); and in 1806, his friend the sculptor *Lorenzo Bartolini* (Aix-en-Provence, private collection), and *Napoleon on His Throne* (Paris, Les Invalides). During these years he executed, in the strikingly "primitive" style advocated by many young Davidians, *Venus Wounded by Diomedes* (Basel, Hirsh Collection).

In Rome from 1806 on, he continued to work on portraits: in 1807, *Madame Devauçay* (Bayonne, Bonnat Museum); his close friend *Granet* (Aix-en-Provence, Granet Museum), and a number of pencil sketches remarkable for their draftsmanship. Ingres's first attempt at a great historical painting was *Oedipus and the Sphinx* (1808; Louvre), a work he enlarged in 1827 to heighten its dramatic ef-

fect. Attracted to Greek themes, he painted *Jupiter and Thetis* (1811; Granet Museum), a huge Homeric work; his interest in distortion for pictorial effect can be observed in the neck of the goddess. The next year appeared *Romulus Vanquishing Acron* (Paris, Ecole des Beaux-Arts), an ambitious work ordered for Napoleon's Quirinal Palace in Rome. Among Ingres's Napoleonic portraits are *Monsieur de Norvins* (1811; London, National Gallery) and *Madame de Tournon* (1812; Philadelphia, McIlhenny Collection). Napoleonic allegories appeared in such works as *Vergil Reading His "Aeneid" before Augustus* (1812; Toulouse, Museum of the Augustines) and *The Dream of Ossian* (1813; Ingres Museum).

During the difficult years following the fall of Napoleon in 1814, Ingres drew some fine pencil portraits, including *The Stamaty Family* (1818) and *Paganini* (1819; both Bonnat Museum), and numerous sketches of his friends and of British tourists. In 1819 he worked on *Roger Freeing Angelica* (Louvre; later versions elsewhere) and *Paolo and Francesca* (Angers, Fine Arts Museum; Condé Museum; and elsewhere), and in 1820 he finished *Christ Giving the Keys to St. Peter* (Louvre). In 1818 he moved from Rome to Florence, where he produced the remarkable oil portraits of Monsieur and Madame Leblanc (1823; New York, Metropolitan Museum) and, in pencil, *The Lazzerini Family* (1822; Louvre).

In 1821 Ingres began work on an enormous painting, *The Vow of Louis XIII* (Cathedral of Montauban). At the Paris Salon of 1824 the heretofore-unsuccessful artist suddenly became famous with this work, influenced in many ways by Raphael. In 1825 Ingres was elected to the Institute of France and opened a studio for young painters. The next year he was awarded a commission for a ceiling in the Louvre, *The Apotheosis of Homer*, and four great voussoirs beneath it, which he exhibited in 1827 along with his fine portrait *Madame Marcotte de Ste-Marie* (Louvre). In 1834 the critics attacked his *Martyrdom of St. Symphorian* (Cathedral of Autun). Enraged, Ingres vowed to shun the Salon thereafter. He accepted the directorship of the Academy of France in Rome; there he painted from 1835 to 1840, inspiring a horde of Ingrists, who joined with his former students to spread his doctrine: emphasize drawing, the summit of art; use color as an adjunct of painting, not as an equal partner of drawing; follow the great masters and nature and add their lessons to your talent; preserve the naïveté of your vision; emphasize line always; learn to simplify; round out and fortify the contours; flatten the picture space.

During this period Ingres produced *Odalisque with Slave* (1839; Baltimore, Walters Art Gallery; other versions elsewhere), *Stratonice* (1840; Condé Museum; later versions elsewhere), and numerous pencil drawings offered to his disciples and admirers: Liszt, Gounod, Baltard.

In 1841 he was back again in Paris to undertake a major work, a large mural for the Duc de Luynes's Château de Dampierre: *The Age of Gold*, a paean to antiquity and to nude and innocent living in Arcadia under the rule of Justice. Ingres lived at the château until 1849, when his wife died and he abandoned the project. A small

Jean-Auguste-Dominique Ingres, *Madame Moitessier.* **National Gallery, Washington, D.C.**

final version of his theme exists at the Fogg Art Museum, Cambridge, Mass.

In the 1840s and 1850s Ingres produced a number of fine portraits, including *Madame Moitessier* (1851, Washington, D.C., National Gallery; 1856, London, National Gallery), the *Duc d'Orléans* (1842; Paris, Comte de Paris Collection; versions elsewhere), and *Madame d'Haussonville* (1845; New York, Frick Collection). In pencil, he portrayed the Gatteaux and Marcotte families and their circles. In 1852 his second wife, Delphine Ramel, posed for her portrait; a later oil painting of her appeared in 1859 (Winterthur, Reinhart Foundation). Most of her family also sat for Ingres.

In 1853 he was commissioned to decorate a ceiling of the Paris Hôtel de Ville with *The Apotheosis of Napoleon* (destroyed); in 1854 he portrayed himself as an equerry in *Jeanne d'Arc* (Louvre). In his old age he painted his famous *Turkish Bath* (1859–63; Louvre), originally a square composition but remade into an oval one. His last religious work, *Jesus among the Doctors* (completed 1862), now hangs in the Ingres Museum, to which he bequeathed many of his drawings.

In addition to the Ingrists, other painters admired and were influenced by Ingres: Degas in his early work and Renoir in his Ingrist period from 1880 on, Matisse, Picasso, and numerous contemporary artists.

See also MONTAUBAN: INGRES MUSEUM.

BIBLIOGRAPHY. J. Ingres, *24 Drawings*, New York, 1947 (biographical note by A. Mongan); J. Alazard, *Ingres et l'Ingrisme*, Paris, 1950; G. Wildenstein, *Ingres*, London, 1954; N. Schlenoff, *Ingres, ses sources littéraires*, Paris, 1956; H. Naef, *Rome vue par Ingres*, Lausanne, 1960.

NORMAN SCHLENOFF

INITIAL LETTER. First letter or group of letters on pages of illuminated manuscripts. The initial letter is set off from other letters by its larger size and, frequently, by its elaborate ornamentation. Some initial letters are illuminated; that is, the spaces encompassed by the letter contain paintings. Sometimes, as in the early Middle Ages, initial letters themselves are constructed of figures.

IN-JAE, see KANG HUI-AN.

INK. Deeply colored liquid applied with a pen or brush. It can be of any color; in the past, black and red were the most frequently employed. Ink drawings have been an important art form in the Orient since the 4th century of our era. In the West ink is used primarily for writing.

INK (China), see CHINA: INK.

INK, BROKEN, see P'O-MO.

INK, SPLASHED, see P'O-MO.

INK DRAWING. Descriptive term for any drawing made in ink, but not in general use as denoting a separate branch of the drawing disciplines, such as chalk drawing, wash drawing, and so on. Ink is used with both pen and brush to produce a pen, brush, or wash drawing. All the inks used in drawing are water-soluble solutions. The most common are Chinese (or India) ink, sepia, and bistre. Colored inks, outside the traditional browns and reds, are largely a modern product, and are also pigments in a water-base vehicle. Chinese ink is the earliest form of ink, said to have been invented about 2700 B.C. in China, and it has been in continual use to the present day. Essentially lamp-black baked with a glutinous substance, it is offered either in solution or in hard cakes intended for dilution. Sepia, which is dull brown, is obtained by extracting and diluting a secretion from the cuttlefish. Bistre is a reddish-brown ink derived from the soot of burned wood. In Chinese painting, which is actually brush drawing, inks are used almost exclusively as coloring matter. Inks are notable for their permanency.

BIBLIOGRAPHY. J. Taylor, *Learning to Look*, Chicago, 1957.

JULIA M. EHRESMANN

INLAY. Technique for producing decoration by sinking small pieces of material into a background that differs in color from them. In inlaid wood furniture, for example, these pieces may be of wood, metal, or mother-of-pearl. The pieces are precisely cut to fit certain hollows, and when the whole is given its final polish the joints are practically invisible. Intarsia is inlaid wood; tarsia, inlaid metal. *See* INTARSIA.

INMAN, HENRY. American painter (b. Utica, N.Y., 1801; d. New York City, 1846). He studied with J. W. Jarvis (1814–22), opened a studio in New York (1824), and went into partnership with his pupil, T. S. Cummings. Inman was a founder (1826) of the National Academy of Design and its first vice-president (1826–31). Between 1831 and 1834 he was a partner in the Philadelphia lithographic firm of Childs and Inman. He returned to New York in 1835 and painted portraits until a commission took him to England (1844–45).

Inman was a romantic realist whose artistic duality is seen in his photographically hard portraits, such as *Fanny Kemble Butler* (Brooklyn Museum), and in poetic, idyllic figure pieces, namely *Rip Van Winkle Awakening from His Dream*.

BIBLIOGRAPHY. T. Bolton, "Henry Inman, Portrait Painter," *Creative Art*, XII, February, 1933; T. Bolton, "Henry Inman, an Account of His Life and Works," *Art Quarterly*, III, 1940.

INNES, JAMES DICKSON. British landscape and figure painter (1887–1914). Born in Llanelly, he studied first in Wales and then at the Slade School of Fine Art in London from 1905 to 1908. Like Matthew Smith, Innes was particularly attracted to French landscape painters, and his work shows some influence of Gauguin and possibly the Fauves. He was a close friend of Augustus John and accompanied him on painting trips. Innes was a member of the New English Art Club and the Camden Town Group.

BIBLIOGRAPHY. J. Rothenstein, *Modern English Painters: Lewis to Moore*, London, 1956.

INNESS, GEORGE. American landscape painter (b. near Newburgh, N.Y., 1825; d. Bridge of Allan, Scotland, 1894). He was self-taught except for a very brief period of study with Regis Gignoux, a pupil of Delaroche, in New York City in 1846. Inness traveled in Europe in 1847, 1850, and 1854 and was in Italy and France from 1870 to 1874.

His early landscapes are in the spirit of the Hudson River school, particularly Cole and Durand, and were influenced by Ruisdael and Hobbema (both of whom he knew in engravings) in their detail and composition. Still in this style but slightly later is *The Old Mill* (1849; Art Institute of Chicago). In the 1850s and 1860s Inness moved away from his earlier literalism toward a more romantic generalization of solidly composed forms, as in *Summer in the Catskills* (1867) and the characteristically wide landscape of *Catskill Mountain* (1870; both Art Institute of Chicago). In Italy in the early 1870s he explored the Italian landscape as well as the landscapes of Claude Lorraine (*Twilight in Italy*, 1874; Art Institute of Chicago).

Throughout his career Inness was remarkable for the number of influences he was able to absorb into his own personal style, which stressed strong construction as well as an atmospheric approach: the Barbizon school, Poussin, Claude Lorraine, Constable, and Turner. A painting such as *Evening at Medfield* (1875; New York, Metropolitan Museum) shows the transition to the lyrical, more mood-filled, and technically delicate landscapes of his later years. In 1881 Inness turned from painting landscapes and briefly concentrated on the figure, which he had hitherto neglected. One of his few surviving figures, *Two Sisters in the Garden* (ca. 1881; Art Institute of Chicago), shows a broad brushwork and a tonal emphasis similar to that of his landscapes.

His late landscapes are emotional interpretations of nature, somewhat affected by his strong interest in the pantheistic philosophy of Swedenborg. Inness's use of a loose handling of paint and a deep scumbling of pigment and glaze produced evocative, virtually dematerialized scenes in which the concrete forms are almost lost in masses of color. A fine late example of his work is *The Home of the Heron* (1893; Art Institute of Chicago).

BIBLIOGRAPHY. G. Inness, *Fifty Paintings by George Inness*, introd. E. Daingerfield, New York, 1913; G. Inness, Jr., *Life, Art and Letters of George Inness*, New York, 1917; E. McCausland, *George Inness...*, Springfield, Mass, 1947.

JEROME VIOLA

INNSBRUCK: TYROLEAN LANDESMUSEUM (Tiroler Landesmuseum Ferdinandeum). Austrian museum founded in 1842. It occupies a building with a façade constructed to the drawings of Tommassi. Much of the collection is drawn from the area of the Tirol—from prehistoric sites, the medieval churches, the Goldenes Dachl in Innsbruck, and artists of all periods. Outstanding are paintings and sculpture by the 15th-century Tirolian artist Michael Pacher and his school. The museum also has German paintings by Strigel, Cranach, Baldung-Grien, Faistenberger, and Troger and Netherlandish works by Gossaert, the Master of Haarlem, Rembrandt, Dou, Ostade, Cuijp, Fabritius, and Van der Heijden.

INRO. Japanese term for a small receptacle for medicines. The *inrō* is usually divided into three or five compartments closely fitted on top of one another. It was originally used as a container for a signature seal and ink, but later its function was to hold medicine. In the mid-Edo period the *inrō* became an indispensable accessory for

George Inness, *Two Sisters in the Garden*. Art Institute of Chicago.

Inro. Three small receptacles for medicines.

samurai, who wore one hanging from a belt around his waist. Various materials, such as horn and metal, were used for *inrō*, and those made in lacquer, particularly in the *maki-e* technique (with gold or silver dust sprinkled over the lacquer), were popular. The finest examples of *inrō* date from the late 18th to the first half of the 19th century. Famous makers of *inrō* included Koma Kyūi (d.

Intarsia. Fra Domenico da Bergamo, intarsia decoration of the choir seats in S. Domenico, Bologna.

1663), Yamada Jōga (late 17th cent.), Kajikawa Kyūjirō (late 17th cent.), Iizuka Tōyō (late 18th cent.), Koma Koryū (late 18th cent.), Koma Kansai (1767–1835), and Hara Yōyūsai (1772–1845).

BIBLIOGRAPHY. W. Forman, *Japanese Netsuké*, London, 1960; F. M. Jonas, *Netsuké*, Rutland, Vt., 1960; R. Ueda, *The Netsuké Handbook*, Rutland, Vt., 1961.

INSTITUT, PALAIS DE L', PARIS, *see* QUATRE NATIONS, COLLEGE DES, PARIS.

INTAGLIO. Process in printmaking whereby an impression is made from a design that is incised in a plate; the image or design exists below the surface of the plate. The term is also used to describe a fine print made by a number of different techniques within this field, for example, etching, engraving, soft ground, and aquatint, in combination.

INTAGLIO ENGRAVING, *see* ENGRAVING.

INTARSIA. Decoration of furniture by inlaying pieces of wood, mother-of-pearl, tortoise shell, or ivory. Intarsia was known to antiquity and employed during the Renaissance, but it came into its own only in the 17th century. The later, rococo, phase of intarsia is called marquetry.

INTENSITY, COLOR. Quality of a color that gives brilliance or richness. One color may be more intense than another of the same hue because it lacks the admixture of graying colors. The impressionists tried to preserve intensity by mixing colors optically on the canvas rather than mechanically on the palette.

INTERAXIS. Space between two axes; also the distance center to center of columns, as distinguished from intercolumniation.

INTERCOLUMNIATION. Ratio of the space between columns and the diameter of the columns. The clear space between two columns in classical architecture was commonly measured in terms of the lower diameter of the shaft.

INTERLACE. Form of surface decoration made up of ribbon or threadlike elements intertwined in such a way as to produce an overall pattern. Barbarian ornament is usually an interlace of animal forms. Although the interlace is universal, it appears to be especially prevalent in the Near East.

INTERNATIONAL BUILDING EXHIBITION, *see* BERLIN.

INTERNATIONAL GOTHIC PAINTING. Term used to describe the style of painting (manuscript, panel, and fresco) prevalent in Europe, in varying degrees, from the last half of the 14th century through the first quarter of the 15th century.

The dates of the style, and the extent to which it flourished, varied throughout Europe, owing to differences in local artistic conditions and personalities. By and large, the International Gothic style might be described as a late manneristic development of the High Gothic. This meant an increased stylization and linearity in the treatment of figures, a flattening or elimination of space in the picture, and a strong reliance on surface, decorative qualities, highly sophisticated and artificial in concept. In view of these qualities, it may be considered a reaction to the full-blown classical naturalism of the High Gothic.

In Italy the revolution caused by the works of Giotto somewhat diminished the strength of the International style. Although it existed, and in some areas flourished, it was distinctly *retardataire* after Giotto. Nonetheless, Sienese painting of the time is of this style and *retardataire* in character. Painters such as Gentile da Fabriano also represent the conservative International style in Italy. *See* GENTILE DA FABRIANO.

See also LOMBARD SCHOOL.

The Burgundian court, Paris, and Flanders were the primary centers of the International style. Inasmuch as a revolution comparable to that of Giotto did not occur in the North until the time of the Van Eycks, the International style there must be considered not only a logical outgrowth of late medieval painting but the precursor of the Van Eycks' achievements.

In the *Très riches heures du Duc de Berry* by the Limbourg brothers (1413–16; Chantilly, Condé Museum) the minute observation devoted to the local scene and the attention to details that later characterize the works of Jan van Eyck already form a firmly established tradition. Another of the painters working within the general International style, but already experimenting in the realm of spatial development, was the Boucicaut Master. De-

Interlace. Fretted and inlaid window. Blue Mosque, Isfahan.

spite some innovations and the finesse of its technique, the International style, at best, remained pseudorealistic, for the realism of its observation was always modified and qualified by the highly artificial conventions of its courtly patrons. *See* BOUCICAUT MASTER; LIMBOURG BROTHERS.

In Germany the International style was more strongly

International Gothic painting. Giovanni di Paolo, *St. John in the Desert*. Art Institute of Chicago (Ryerson Collection).

entrenched, perhaps because there did not early appear an artist of the stature of Jan van Eyck. Hence, vestiges of this style lingered as late as the 1420s in the work of the Middle Rhenish Master of the Ortenberg Altar and in the slightly earlier *Helsinki Altar* of Master Francke. *See* MASTER FRANCKE.

Within this framework numerous creative and constructive personalities worked. Despite minor regional differences there are major stylistic affinities between such artists as Master Francke and the Boucicaut Master and between the Limbourg brothers and Pisanello. *See* PISANELLO, ANTONIO.

BIBLIOGRAPHY. G. Bazin, *L'Ecole franco-flamande, XIV–XV siècles,* Geneva, 1941.   STANLEY FERBER

INTERNATIONAL STYLE (Architecture). The major European architectural trend of the 1920s and 1930s, as formulated in France, Germany, and Holland. The term was suggested by Alfred Barr of the Museum of Modern Art in New York and first used as the title of an important book by Hitchcock and Johnson (1932), which appeared at the zenith of this European architectural achievement. With an emphasis on space instead of mass, typical International Style architecture is composed of rectilinear volumes defined by light, taut, undecorated planar and linear geometric components asymmetrically balanced by equivalent voids and solids that appear unaffected by gravity.

A description of International Style sources, formation, and influence is tantamount to a survey of the dominant Western architectural tendency of the second quarter of the 20th century; omitted from such a survey, however, are expressionist attitudes and works of the same period. General sources are worldwide: American skyscraper design of the 1890s in Chicago and New York; the early work of Frank Lloyd Wright; futurist projects of Sant'Elia; works by Peter Behrens, H. P. Berlage, Adolf Loos, Joseph Hoffmann, and other Europeans; the Dutch de Stijl movement; and the German Bauhaus. These coalesced after World War I into a widely accepted formal architectural discipline exhibiting the consistency and rigor of previous architectural syntaxes, such as Gothic and Renaissance.

Prophetic of the synthesis of the 1920s was the Fagus Works at Alfeld on the Leine (1910–11) by Gropius and Meyer. Dudok's Bavinck School and Municipal Baths at Hilversum (1921) and Mendelsohn's hat factory at Luckenwalde (1920–23) are quasi-International Style in their compositions of pristine geometric masses. One of the earliest space formulations was the tiny jewelry shop (1920–22) in Amsterdam designed by Rietveld, an assemblage of glazed, cubical volumes asymmetrically composed within a three-dimensional, rectilinear grid, linking inner and outer space. *See* DUDOK, WILLEM MARINUS; GROPIUS, WALTER; MENDELSOHN, ERIC; MEYER, ADOLF; RIETVELD, GERRIT THOMAS.

Also designed during the early 1920s were a number of unexecuted projects that contributed to the new architectural vision. Mies van der Rohe's revolutionary steel-framed, glazed skyscrapers (1919; 1920–21) were prophetic of his later Lake Shore Drive apartments in Chicago (1949–51), and his design for a reinforced concrete office building (1922), sheathed by a curtain wall, foreshadowed the classic Van Nelle Factory (1927–29) in Rotterdam designed by Brinkman and Van der Vlugt. Mies's project for a country house (1923), with its discontinuous planes, anticipated his Barcelona Pavilion of 1929. *See* BRINKMAN, J. A., AND VAN DER VLUGT, L. C.; MIES VAN DER ROHE, LUDWIG.

Le Corbusier's Citrohan houses (1919–22), extensions of his earlier Domino conception (1914–15), materialized in the architect's contribution to the 1927 Weissenhof Exhibition and embodied elements that recur in his work: open plan, usable roof area, and living spaces elevated on *pilotis.* Notable, too, was the Gropius and Meyer design for the *Chicago Tribune* competition of 1922, a lucid grid composition employing the structural skeleton as the dominant visual element, an architectural expression reminiscent of American skyscrapers of the late 19th century and prophetic of typical works of the 1950s and 1960s. Also important during these years were the pictorial house schemes by Van Doesburg and Van Eesteren, designed for the 1923 de Stijl exhibition in Paris. *See* DOESBURG, THEO VAN; EESTEREN, CORNELIS VAN; LE CORBUSIER; WEISSENHOF EXHIBITION.

After the prophetic stage of the early 1920s a period of realization began. Again Rietveld was early in projecting the spatial nature of the new architecture, as seen in his Schröder House of 1924, composed of discontinuous, colored, planar members hovering in a weightless state of equilibrium. Also realized in Holland during these years was Oud's housing block (1924–27) at Hook of Holland, a typical example of the period. The larger and more complex Bauhaus building (1925–26) is a classic, embodying the essentials of the International Style, and the Van Nelle Factory in Rotterdam gave definitive form to industrial building. *See* BAUHAUS; OUD, JACOBUS JOHANNES PIETER; SCHRODER HOUSE, UTRECHT.

At the end of the decade, Mies's Barcelona Pavilion, his Tugendhat House at Brno, Czechoslovakia (1930), and Le Corbusier's Villa Savoye at Poissy (1929–30) added to the list of seminal works of this fruitful era. Le Corbusier's Swiss Dormitory (1930–32) at the Cité Universitaire, Paris, though rooted in International Style principles, points toward the sculptural extensions of the style in mid-century. *See* SAVOYE HOUSE, POISSY-SUR-SEINE; TUGENDHAT HOUSE, BRNO.

The international character of the movement was decisively established by several major events. The Pan-European Weissenhof Exhibition (1927) and the foundation of the C.I.A.M. (1928) underscored the broad social, technological, and aesthetic basis of the International Style, and the literature of the period did much to propagate its attitudes and forms. As early as 1923 Le Corbusier published his prose poem *Vers une architecture,* the most influential architectural literary piece of a century prone to architectural verbalizing. Van Doesburg's doctrinaire "Tot een beeldende architectuur" (*De Stijl,* vol. 6, 1924) was an early articulation of the objectives of the period. Gropius's photo survey, *Internationale Architektur* (1925), emphasized in title as well as in content the breadth of the movement, and Ludwig Hilberseimer's *Internationale neue Baukunst* (1927) further promoted the movement. *Gli Ele-*

International Style. Eric Mendelsohn, stairwell of the Metalworkers' Union, Berlin, 1929.

menti dell'architettura funzionale (1932) by Alberto Sartoris was also influential. *See* C.I.A.M.

The most critically penetrating of the many works written about 1930 is Hitchcock and Johnson's brilliant essay, *The International Style: Architecture since 1922* (1932), written on the occasion of the first International Exhibition of Modern Architecture (Museum of Modern Art, 1932). They christened the movement and defined it as well.

After the high point of the early 1930s the International Style met with resistance in communist Russia and fascist Germany; yet it found its way to most other parts of the world: Scandinavia, North and South America, Japan, Spain, and England. The period was immensely significant, both in consolidating earlier international tendencies and in establishing the basis of a new architectural vocabulary, attitude, and practice. Despite constantly changing forms, the International Style continues to provide orientation to 20th-century architecture.

BIBLIOGRAPHY. H.-R. Hitchcock and P. Johnson, *The International Style: Architecture since 1922*, New York, 1932 (2d ed., 1966); H.-R. Hitchcock, "The 'International Style' Twenty Years After," *Architectural Record*, CX, August, 1952; H.-R. Hitchcock, *Architecture, Nineteenth and Twentieth Centuries*, Baltimore, 1958.

THEODORE M. BROWN

INTERNATIONAL STYLE (Painting), *see* INTERNATIONAL GOTHIC PAINTING.

INTERSECTING VAULT, *see* VAULT.

INTIMISM. Variety of late-19th-century painting associated with the Nabis, a Parisian group of symbolically inclined artists including Roussel, Vallotton, Sérusier, Maillol, Bonnard, and Vuillard. The last two represented the intimist branch of this movement. Essentially intimism was a form of impressionist technique applied to the depiction of everyday life in domestic interiors rather than to landscape, but it also stressed a sense of isolation.

Vuillard created interiors (*Two Women by Lamplight*; Paris, Georges Grannont Collection) in which he laid greater stress on the rendering of space and faithfully recorded the changes effected in colors by light, whether artificial or natural. Whereas Bonnard went gradually from a dark palette with predominating reds and yellows to brilliant colors, Vuillard extended the impressionist researches by using less brilliant colors, as in *Au lit* (1891; Paris, National Museum of Modern Art). Vuillard, who called himself derisively the "intimist," had a vision of rare subtlety, an innate sense of harmony and composition that made him an heir of Degas and Monet. His small decorations, or apartment frescoes (*Jardin de Paris*, executed for Alexandre Natanson, and *Intérieurs*, executed for Dr. Vaquez, in the Petit Palais, Paris), are typical of his intimism. His exquisite forms and enchanting precision recall the poets whom he admired: *La Chambre à coucher rouge* (Zurich, private collection), *Femme âgée examinant son ouvrage* (1893; Paris, private collection), and, above all, *Intérieur* (1898; Paris, private collection). *See* VUILLARD, EDOUARD.

Bonnard, the other great exponent of intimism, had a mixture of playfulness, humor, and tenderness in his pictures. His delicacy is expressed in the sense of mystery which he extracted from everyday scenes, as in *La Nappe à carreaux rouge* (Mme Marthe Bonnard and her dog

Dingo; Winterthur, Hahnloser Collection). Bonnard's later work, however, freed itself from the limitations of intimism with great emphasis on the nude figure, as in *Nu devant la cheminée* (1917; Saint-Tropez, Musée de l'Annonciade). *See* BONNARD, PIERRE.

With its poetical and mystical qualities, its warmth and universality, intimism occupies an important place in post-impressionist art.

BIBLIOGRAPHY. A. Armstrong-Wallis, "The Symbolist Painters of 1890," *Marsyas*, 1941; C. Roger-Marx, *Vuillard et son temps*, Paris, 1946; M. Raynal et al., *History of Modern Painting*, vol. 1: *From Baudelaire to Bonnard*, Geneva, 1949.   ARNOLD ROSIN

INTONACO. Final finishing coat of plaster preparatory to fresco painting. In true fresco, the colors are put directly on the moist intonaco so that the pigments adhere permanently to the ground.

INTRADOS. Soffit, or underside, of an arch or vault.

INUGSUK CULTURE, *see* ESKIMO ART.

INVALIDES, LES, PARIS. Home for disabled French soldiers, built between 1671 and 1676 to the designs of Libéral Bruant. The monumental church (Dôme) containing Napoleon's tomb, added to the south side of the buildings, was designed by Jules-Hardouin Mansart and built between 1680 and 1706. The institute itself is an austere composition of several wings forming internal courtyards, more strong than distinguished. The massiveness of the main (north) façade is eased by the relief *Louis XIV between Prudence and Justice* and by large statues of *Mars* and *Minerva*, all by Guillaume Coustou. The arched center bay leads to the Court of Honor, or Royal Court, a parade square flanked by arcaded buildings now housing the Museum of the Army. Beyond its south wing is the soldiers' church dedicated to St. Louis—a simple building, comprising nave, aisles, and a gallery, that Louis XIV soon considered too modest.

Mansart attached his church to the choir of Bruant's, but in effect it is a separate building and it ranks high among France's churches of all periods. Roughly square

Intrados. Underside of an arch.

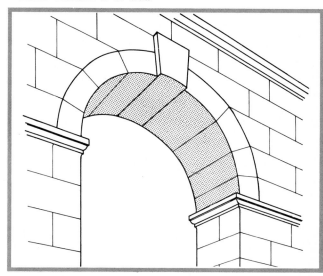

Les Invalides, Paris. The church (Dôme), designed by Jules-Hardouin Mansart, built 1680–1706.

in plan, except for the projecting choir, it is divided internally into four arms in the form of a Greek cross, with four chapels occupying the corners between them, and is crowned by a dome. This plan and the lower part of the façade owe a good deal to the works of the architect's granduncle, François Mansart, and the design of the drum and the dome derives in part from St. Peter's in Rome, but externally and internally J.-H. Mansart has fused classical elements with baroque qualities in an original way. The interior is dominated by eight tall freestanding Corinthian columns topped by a deep, curving entablature. The inner shell of the dome is cut horizontally to reveal a second shell, lit by hidden windows and painted by Charles de Lafosse (*St. Louis Returning His Sword to Christ*). The external dome is a third shell, of timber and lead, rising well above the internal shells and visible from afar, especially when the sunlight catches its gilt ornament.

The quality of the interior has been much impaired by the opening of the floor below the dome to make a well for the tomb of Napoleon, thus depriving the composition of its focal point. The tomb is the work of Visconti (1843), who also organized the transfer of Napoleon's ashes from St. Helena to the crypt. Other tombs in the church include those of Vauban, Turenne, and Napoleon II, king of Rome.

BIBLIOGRAPHY. L. Dimier, *L'Hôtel des Invalides*, 2d ed., Paris, 1928; A. Blunt, *Art and Architecture in France, 1500–1700*, Baltimore, 1954.

NORBERT LYNTON

INWOOD FAMILY. English architects, practicing between about 1800 and 1843. William and his eldest son, Henry William, were the most active members of the family. They are best known for their Greek revival buildings, notably St. Pancras New Church (1819–22) in London. Henry William also published two books on Greek antiquities and design.

IO. Oil painting by Correggio, in the Museum of Art a cloud, seduced. He then changed her into a white heifer to protect her from Hera's jealous anger. Hera, however, discovered Io's identity by deceit and sent a gadfly to persecute her. Io fled all over the world, crossing the Ionian Sea, which was named for her, and finally reaching Egypt. There she regained human form and bore Zeus a son, Epaphus.

IO. Oil painting by Correggio, in the Museum of Art History, Vienna. *See* CORREGGIO.

IONA. Island in the Inner Hebrides of Scotland. It was famous for the manuscripts and metalwork produced by its monastic scriptorium and workshops. Under St. Aidan (d. 651) and his successors, the Irish missionaries converted the local Anglo-Saxon tribes to Christianity and incorporated their indigenous decorative motifs into Christian works. One such example in metalwork is the 8th- or 9th-century back cover of the Lindau Gospels, in the Pierpont Morgan Library, New York. *See also* CELTIC ART.

IONIA, *see* GREECE.

IONIC ORDER. Style of architecture that evolved in the Ionian and eastern regions of ancient Greece. Like the other orders, Ionic had no fixed form but is distinguished primarily by its volute capital composed of spirals. The Ionic capital may have been a bracket type, originally made of wood, on which its spiral design was incised or painted.

Description. The Ionic shares with the Corinthian order a comparative richness and softness that sets it apart from the sense of geometric measure in the Doric. Its slender columns are generally fluted; early Ionic columns have shallow flutes meeting in sharp arrises, and later, more characteristic examples have their flutes separated by fillets. The Ionic base usually has an upper and a lower torus separated by a scotia. The Ionic entablature lacks the metopes and triglyphs of the Doric; it may or may not have dentils and a frieze.

In Roman Ionic, volutes generally project less than in Greek types. The Temple of Saturn, Rome (A.D. 284), a late example, has angle volutes, as at Pompeii, with the scroll showing on all four sides. *See* SATURN, TEMPLE OF, ROME.

MILTON F. KIRCHMAN

History. The Ionic order in Greek architecture is a product of the Orientalizing period of Greek art. Its roots are to be found in the architecture of the great eastern kingdoms—Egypt, Persia, Lydia, and so on—and its first manifestations in the Ionian Greek cities of Asia Minor.

The volute shape of the Ionic capital has been thought to be derived from a common Asiatic type of column in which the capital is formed from the overhanging leaves of a palmette. If this is so, the capitals (sometimes called

Ionic order. Temple of Athena Nike, Athens.

"Aeolic") from Neandria (late 7th cent. B.C.) and Larisa (early 6th cent. B.C.) may represent an intermediate stage between the Oriental and Greek types. On the other hand, the volute-shape Ionic capital may be directly derived from a similar type known on Hittite and Iranian reliefs.

The colossal dimensions and large number of columns employed in the great Ionic temples of Asia Minor suggest that they were inspired by the hypostyle halls of Egypt (Karnak, for example). The evolution of the Ionic temple can be traced most clearly in the sanctuary of Hera at Samos, where an altar to the goddess already existed in the Mycenaean period. In the early 8th century B.C. a building was constructed near the altar (perhaps to house votive offerings). It was on the site of this structure that, after a long series of rebuildings and expansions, the first great Ionic temple was built (ca. 570 B.C.) by the architects Theodorus and Rhoecus. This huge dipteral temple was burned and another, even larger, was constructed by the tyrant Polycrates (ca. 525 B.C.). This last Heraeum had 133 columns and was about 366 feet long, apparently the largest of all Greek temples. *See* SAMOS; THEODORUS.

The other great Ionic temple of the archaic period was the Temple of Artemis at Ephesus, built about 560 B.C. by the architects Chersiphron and Metagenes. It was burned in 356 B.C. and replaced by a Hellenistic temple. *See* CHERSIPHRON; EPHESUS.

Ionic structures in the western part of the Greek world are rare and usually demonstrate political connections with the east. Thus the Ionic treasuries at Delphi, such as the Siphnian Treasury (530 B.C.), were built by islanders; and the brilliant use of the order by Athenian architects of the 5th century B.C. in the Temple of Athena Nike (425) and in the Erechtheum (421–407) was probably stimulated by Athens's traditional connections with Ionia. The Ionic temple at Locri Epizephyrii (ca. 470 B.C. and later), a Greek city in southern Italy, is a rare example of the order in Magna Graecia. An archaic altar of Apollo at Amyklae (7th cent. B.C.) and the Philippeum at Olympia (ca. 338 B.C.) are examples of the Ionic order in the Peloponnesus. *See* ATHENS: ANCIENT; DELPHI; LOCRI EPIZEPHYRII.

In the Hellenistic period large Ionic temples were still erected in Asia Minor—for example, the temples of Artemis at Sardis (325 B.C.), Apollo Didymaeus at Miletus (330 B.C.), Artemis Leukophryene at Magnesia on the Maeander (130 B.C.), and Dionysos at Teos (130 B.C.). *See* APOLLO DIDYMAEUS, TEMPLE OF, MILETUS.

In the Roman period the Corinthian order was generally preferred to the Ionic, but a few purely Ionic buildings such as the little Temple of Fortuna Virilis in Rome (1st cent. B.C.) are known. *See* FORTUNA VIRILIS, TEMPLE OF, ROME.

BIBLIOGRAPHY. W. B. Dinsmoor, *The Architecture of Ancient Greece*, 3d ed., London, 1950; J. Boardman, "Chian and Early Ionic Architecture," *The Antiquaries Journal*, XXXIX, July–October, 1959; D. S. Robertson, *A Handbook of Greek and Roman Architecture*, 2d ed., Cambridge, Eng., 1959.
JEROME J. POLLITT

IPIUTAK CULTURE. Ancient Eskimo culture that flourished near Point Hope, Alaska, north of the Bering Strait, evidently during the first six centuries of the Christian era. Ipiutak art included curvilinear and animal patterns on ivory, as well as spiral, nonfigural, three-dimensional objects. The style relates to Old Bering Sea art. *See also* ESKIMO ART; NORTH AMERICAN INDIAN ART (ESKIMO).

BIBLIOGRAPHY. F. G. Rainey, "Ipiutak Culture at Point Hope, Alaska," *American Anthropologist*, XLIII, 1941.

IPPEN SCROLLS. Japanese *emaki* (1299). This set of twelve scrolls is in the Kankikōji, Kyoto. The scrolls, done on silk, depict the life of the priest Ippen (1239–89), who spent more than half a lifetime traveling through the country to popularize the Jishū teachings of Buddhism. Places that Ippen visited and the people with whom he came into contact are realistically portrayed with loving care by En-i. Our only knowledge of En-i comes from this *emaki*, which was made to commemorate the tenth anniversary of Ippen's death. The scrolls possess unusual charm in the expressive lyricism created by the small figures placed in a landscape seen through the different seasons. They describe towns and villages peopled with all types, including beggars and vagabonds. The rich, natural coloring that En-i used to capture the moods of seasons makes this *emaki* one of the most beautiful Japanese landscape paintings.

BIBLIOGRAPHY. *Nihon emakimono zenshū (Japanese Scroll Paintings)*, vol. 10: *Ippen hijiri-e*, Tokyo, 1960; H. Okudaira, *Emaki (Japanese Picture Scrolls)*, Rutland, Vt., 1962; National Commission for the Protection of Cultural Properties, ed., *Kokuhō (National Treasures of Japan)*, vol. 4: *The Kamakura Period*, Tokyo, 1966.

IRAN, ANCIENT, *see* PERSIA, ANCIENT.

IRAN, MUSEUMS OF, *see* TEHERAN: MUSEUMS (ARCHAEOLOGICAL MUSEUM; GOLESTAN PALACE).

IRANO-BUDDHIST STYLE, *see* ASIA, CENTRAL.

IRAQ, *see* MESOPOTAMIA.

IRELAND, MUSEUMS OF, *see* DUBLIN: MUSEUMS (MUNICIPAL ART GALLERY; NATIONAL GALLERY; NATIONAL MUSEUM; TRINITY COLLEGE LIBRARY).

IRIMOYA. Japanese roof combining hip and gable, the lower section a hipped roof leading to a gabled top, as in the Murōji temple near Nara.

Ippen Scrolls. Town scene from the *emaki* painted by En-i. National Museum, Tokyo.

IRIS. Marble sculpture from the Parthenon, Athens, now in the British Museum, London.

IRON, WROUGHT, *see* WROUGHT IRON, HISTORY OF.

IRON AGE. Term employed to cover culture periods with a technology based upon the use of iron. It is currently used for Near Eastern cultures of the early 1st millennium B.C. and for European ones of the middle and later 1st millennium B.C. Often, as in Greece, it is replaced by descriptive terms such as Geometric. *See also* HALLSTATT CIVILIZATION; LA TENE; VILLANOVANS.

IRON PAGODA, K'AI-FENG, *see* T'IEH-T'A, K'AI-FENG.

IRON STRUCTURES, *see* CONSTRUCTION, IRON.

IRONWORK, *see* WROUGHT IRON, HISTORY OF.

IROQUOIS INDIANS. In late pre-European and early historic times, the Iroquois formed an important confederation of tribes in New York, New England, and peripheral areas of Canada. Preceding cultures included the Lakoma, Frontenac, Laurentian, Hopewell of New York, and Owasco. The Iroquois were both farmers and hunters. *See* SENECA INDIANS.

Their most important prehistoric art was pottery, which disappeared during the 18th century, when pottery was replaced by European metal utensils. Historic Iroquois art includes ceremonial masks of cornhusks and wood, notable for their humorous distortion of human features, and the classical wooden war club with globular head. Other arts include beadwork and embroidered cloth. The characteristic Iroquois dwelling was the famous long house of gabled pole and bark. *See also* NORTH AMERICAN INDIAN ART (EASTERN UNITED STATES AND CANADA).

BIBLIOGRAPHY. L. H. Morgan, *League of the Ho-dé-no-sau-hee or Iroquois*, rev. ed., New York, 1922; W. A. Ritchie, *The Pre-Iroquoian Occupations of New York State*, Rochester, N.Y., 1944.

ISAAC MASTER. Italian painter of the Florentine school (fl. ca. 1300). The Isaac Master is an anonymous painter who has been proposed as the artist responsible for painting the first two bays nearest the entrance in the upper church of S. Francesco at Assisi. These frescoes are the *Pentecost* and the *Ascension* (entrance wall); the *Lamentation* and the fragmentary *Resurrection* (south wall, first bay); two scenes from the *Life of Joseph* (north wall, first bay); the *Four Doctors of the Church* (vault, first bay); and the two scenes from which the painter derives his name, *Jacob and Rebecca before Isaac* and *Esau Seeking Isaac's Bless-*

Iroquois Indians. Bone comb with two animals in combat. Museum of the American Indian, New York.

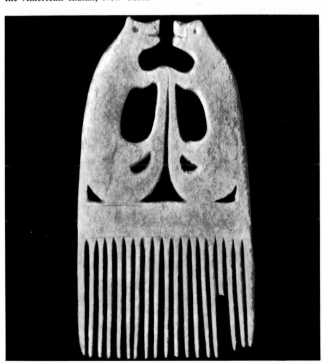

Pieter Fransz. Isaacsz., *The Company of Captain Gillis·Jansz.* Rijksmuseum, Amsterdam.

ing (north wall, second bay, on either side of the window). Some scholars have attributed these frescoes to Giotto, while others have seen in them the hands of several painters. The most recent opinion advocates that the two Isaac scenes and the design of the *Lamentation* are the work of the young Giotto and that the other compositions are by his assistants and followers. *See* GIOTTO DI BONDONE.

See also GADDI, GADDO.

BIBLIOGRAPHY. P. Toesca, *Gli affreschi del vecchio e del nuovo Testamento nella chiesa superiore del Santuario di Assisi*, Florence, 1948; C. Gnudi, *Giotto*, Milan, 1958; M. Meiss, *Giotto and Assisi*, New York, 1960; J. White, *Art and Architecture in Italy, 1250–1400*, Baltimore, 1966.

ISAACSZ., PIETER FRANSZ. Dutch-Danish painter of portraits and history (b. Helsingør, 1569; d. there, 1625). He was born in Denmark while his father, from Haarlem, was agent for the States-General there. In 1587 Isaacsz. was the pupil of Hans van Aachen and accompanied his master, as a servant, on a trip through Germany and Italy. He was also a student of Cornelius Ketel in Amsterdam. In 1607 Isaacsz. was still in Amsterdam, but appears to have returned to Denmark during that year.

From 1607 to 1610 he worked for King Christian IV, acquiring works of art for the King's castles. In 1610 Isaacsz. was back in Holland, but returned to Denmark in 1614. In 1616 he was tried on a political matter and was banished for three years. However, in 1617 he was back working as an agent of Christian IV. After his death it was discovered that he had been a spy in the Danish court for Sweden. He had numerous Danish students while living in Amsterdam.

BIBLIOGRAPHY. A. Riegl, *Das holländische Gruppenporträt*, 2 vols., Vienna, 1931.

ISABEY, JEAN BAPTISTE. French portrait painter, miniaturist, and lithographer (b. Nancy, 1767; d. Paris, 1855). He came to Paris about 1785 and studied in David's atelier. Isabey was an intimate friend of Napoleon and Josephine. He was put in charge of the production of official portraits of the Emperor and also organized the festivities at state occasions. He remained in favor with subsequent French monarchs. His portrait miniatures, executed in a personal technique related to water color, were detailed and brilliant and were very popular in the courts of Europe. One of the early group of artists to work in lithography, he produced a set of "Caricatures," contributed to Forbin's *Voyage dans le Levant* and Baron Taylor's *Voyage en Normandie*, and executed portraits. He was the father of Louis Gabriel Eugène Isabey.

BIBLIOGRAPHY. Mme de Basily-Callimaki, *J.-B. Isabey, sa vie, son temps*, 2 vols., Paris, 1909.

ISABEY, LOUIS GABRIEL EUGENE. French painter, water-colorist, and lithographer (b. Paris, 1803; d. there, 1886). He was the son and pupil of the miniaturist Jean Baptiste Isabey. Eugène made his Salon debut in 1824 with landscapes and seascapes, which remained his primary subject matter. In 1830 he accompanied an official expedition to Algeria as a draftsman. Isabey painted scenes of Brittany life, but his best-known paintings were his marines, dramatic and romantic treatments of the ocean. He was also an appreciated lithographer; he began to work in lithography about 1829, using subjects similar to those of his oil paintings and water colors.

BIBLIOGRAPHY. G. Hédiard, *Eugène Isabey*, Paris, 1906; A. Curtis, *Catalogue de l'oeuvre lithographié de Eugène Isabey*, Paris, 1939.

ISAIA DA PISA. Italian sculptor (fl. 15th cent.). He was active chiefly in Rome. He was employed in the Vatican in 1431; carved the monument of Cardinal Antonio Martinez Chaves (d. 1447) in St. John Lateran, which was commissioned of Filarete; and executed the monument of Pope Eugenius IV in S. Salvatore in Lauro (1450–55). In 1456–58 Isaia worked on the Triumphal Arch of the Castel Nuovo in Naples.

ISAIAH. Hebrew prophet of the 8th century B.C.; thought to be the author of the Book of Isaiah. In it, he is the principal prophet of the Messiah; the Messianic passages of his prophecy (especially Isa. 7:14; 9:6) have been used in art as prefigurations of Christ's birth. In Grünewald's *Isenheim Altar* (1517), for instance, Isaiah is shown in the *Annunciation* panel.

ISA KHAN, TOMB OF, DELHI. Indian mausoleum situated southeast of the city. This stone structure, erected about 1547, is of the type developed under the Lodi kings. The dome rises above a central octagon, which is surrounded by an open octagonal arcade crowned by a series of kiosks. As in similar monuments of this period and region, the profile is rather squat, with the dome quite low, and the ornament is sparse.

BIBLIOGRAPHY. P. Brown, *Indian Architecture*, vol. 2: *Islamic Period*, 4th ed., Bombay, 1959.

ISELIN, *see* YSELIN.

ISENBRANDT (Ysenbrand), ADRIAEN. Flemish painter active in Bruges (d. 1551). Isenbrandt is representative of the 16th-century Netherlandish artists who assimilated Italianate motifs and forms into their native Northern style. He became a free master at Bruges in 1510, after arriving in the city as a young man. Fairly substantial documentary evidence links Isenbrandt with the workshop of Gerard David; it is assumed, however, that he received earlier training elsewhere.

Although for motif, composition, and general style Isenbrandt depended on David, he also borrowed from most of the great 15th-century masters, Flemish and German; his work is generally *retardataire*. Most outstanding as a landscapist and as a colorist, he generally employed warm tones and rich contrasts of dark and light. Among his most noted works are *The Seven Sorrows of the Virgin* diptych (Bruges, Church of Notre-Dame, and Brussels, Fine Arts Museum) and a large triptych of the *Adoration of the Kings* (1518; Lübeck, Marienkirche) with the wings depicting a nude Adam and Eve, derived from the *Ghent Altarpiece*.

BIBLIOGRAPHY. M. J. Friedländer, *Die altniederländische Malerei*, vol. 11, Berlin, 1933.   STANLEY FERBER

ISENHEIM ALTAR. Oil panels by Grünewald, in the Unterlinden Museum, Colmar, France. *See* GRUNEWALD, MATHIAS.

ISE SHRINE. Japanese Shinto shrine. The present building dates from 1953; the date of the original structure is uncertain. The shrine has been duplicated faithfully since the end of the 7th century, and its heavy thatched roof, *chigi* (forked timbers), and *katsuogi* (billets placed over the roof ridge) reflect architectural features of the prehistoric period. Its inner shrine sanctifies the great goddess Amaterasu, who is believed to be one of the ancestors of the Japanese, and the outer shrine sanctifies the great god Toyuke.

BIBLIOGRAPHY. R. T. Paine and A. Soper, *The Art and Architecture of Japan*, Baltimore, 1955; Kokusai Bunka Shinkōkai, *Tradition of the Japanese Garden*, Tokyo, 1962.

ISFAHAN (Ispahan), ARCHITECTURE OF. The city of Isfahan is situated adjacent to the Zayandeh River in central Iran. The site was occupied as early as the Achaemenid period, and in the Parthian and Sassanian periods Isfahan was the capital of a province. Historians writing after the Islamic invasion of Iran described it as comprising two towns, Gai and Yahudiyeh, the latter settled by Jews. As they grew, these towns coalesced, and by the middle of the 11th century the city was surrounded by a massive wall. At this time it became the capital of the Saljuk dynasty, and several of these rulers erected important structures. It escaped the Mongol destruction and prospered mildly until the Safavid period, when, in 1598, Shah Ab-

bas chose it as the capital of Iran. In the 17th century it enjoyed a period of unrivaled prosperity and splendor, with a population of some 500,000 in Isfahan proper and in the Armenian colony of Julfa across the river.

Elements of a bridge and of a fire temple of the Sassanian period remain. The surviving structures of the Islamic centuries are numerous and well preserved. Outstanding is the Masjid-i-Jami, a vast, sprawling complex located at the northern end of the covered bazaar of Isfahan. Monuments of the Saljuk period include the minaret of the mosque in Barsian, the Chihil Dukhtaran minaret, the minaret in Gar, and the minaret and sections of the mosque in Sin. Dating from the later years of the Mongol Ilkhanid period are the shrine of Pir Bakran and the Mosque of Ashtarjan, both some distance west of the town; structures in Gaz, Garladan, Dashti, Kaj, and Eziran, all in the immediate vicinity of Isfahan; and the Imamzadeh Ja'far. Erected under the earlier rulers of the Safavid dynasty were the tomb of Harun Vilayet and the Masjid-i-'Ali. *See* MASJID-I-JAMI, ISFAHAN.

Under Shah Abbas and his successors a new imperial city emerged, provided with a profusion of public and private buildings. *See* ALI QAPU; CHIHIL SUTUN PALACE; LUTFULLAH MOSQUE; MADER-I-SHAH MADRASA; MAIDAN-I-SHAH; MASJID-I-SHAH.

Adriaen Isenbrandt, *Adoration of the Kings*, detail. Marienkirche, Lübeck.

Architecture of Isfahan. The Masjid-i-Shah, begun in 1612 by Shah Abbas the Great of Iran.

A stately avenue, the Chahar Bagh, leads to the bridge of Allah Verdi Khan, which spans the Zayandeh River and leads to Julfa, which was an Armenian colony. The Armenians were engaged in fine weaving and craftsmanship for the Safavid court, and they erected the Cathedral of All Saviours. The existing structure, dating from the mid-17th century, is an attractive mixture of Islamic and Christian styles of decoration.

BIBLIOGRAPHY. A. Godard, "Isfahan," *Athār-é Irān*, II, 1937; D. Wilber, *The Architecture of Islamic Iran: The Il Khānid Period*, Princeton, 1955; L. Lockhart, *Persian Cities*, London, 1960.
DONALD N. WILBER

ISHLALI. Town in central Mesopotamia on the Diyala River, marked by a large temple built in the Isin-Larsa period (2025–1763 B.C.) and dedicated to a mother-goddess, Ishtar Kitikum. The plan is a developed stage of an earlier type, located at the rear of two raised courtyards,

with a bent axis approach and a broad cella. *See* MESO-POTAMIA.

BIBLIOGRAPHY. H. Frankfort, *The Art and Architecture of the Ancient Orient*, Baltimore, 1954.

ISHTAR GATE, BABYLON. Triumphal arch in ancient Mesopotamia (now southern Iraq), dating from the time of Nebuchadnezzar II (604–561 B.C.) and dedicated to Ishtar, the goddess of love and war (reconstruction in Berlin, former State Museums; height ca. 77 ft.). Spanning Babylon's sacred way, between the outer and inner walls of the city, the Ishtar Gate was the starting point for the processions to the temple of the god Marduk, which stood on the summit of a seven-story ziggurat. The gate, a highly complex structure, was a double, arched gateway consisting of two separate gatehouses, each with an outer and an inner door, the gates united by short, connecting walls.

The gate was decorated with symbolic themes in polychrome reliefs.

Built entirely of baked brick and reinforced with gigantic pilasters, the gate, with its lofty towers, formed a splendid polychrome composition. It was decorated with the animal attributes of Marduk and Adad. The animals, dragons, lions, and bulls of glazed brick alternated on tiers superimposed on the façade of the gate. At the bottom, below the last tier, was a narrow frieze decorated with a band of white and yellow rosettes. Another frieze, corresponding to this one, with the same kinds of flowers but larger, decorated the top, above the first tier of animals. The figure of each animal stood out against a uniform background, which was tinted blue with powdered lapis lazuli. The dragons, sacred to Marduk, were white, with their horns, forked tongues, arched backs, and claws painted yellow. The bulls were brown, with green horns and hooves; the hair, which was distributed decoratively rather than in imitation of nature, and the tips of the tails were blue. The lions, of excellent proportions, were white, with yellow highlights on the manes, fangs, claws, and the tuft of hair at the end of the tails. The animals, represented in the act of walking, exhibit grace and dignity in their movements. These conventional heraldic figures of the time were undoubtedly products of Assyrian art. Each lion was modeled in sharp relief on a rectangular panel of clay, which was cut up into separate bricks while still soft. Then they were glazed, fired, and reassembled on the façade of the gate. The only material the architects had to work with was alluvial clay.

Architecture and ornamentation were skillfully adapted to each other. The animals were carved to scale and despite their large number were arranged in an orderly and harmonious fashion. There were 575 dragons and bulls and 120 lions in all. The play of light added brilliance to the deeply saturated color contrasts, which gave extraordinary splendor to the massive structure and dazzled and impressed visitors to the city. Crenelated battlements crowned the top of the gate.

BIBLIOGRAPHY. S. Lloyd, *The Art of the Ancient Near East*, London, 1961; A. Parrot, *The Arts of Assyria*, New York, 1961; L. Woolley, *The Art of the Middle East*, New York, 1961.

LUCILLE VASSARDAKI

ISIDORE OF MILETUS, *see* HAGIA SOPHIA, CONSTANTINOPLE.

ISIDORE OF SEVILLE, ST. Doctor of the Church and encyclopedist (ca. 560–636). Born at Seville of a noble, saintly family from Cartagena, St. Isidore succeeded his brother as archbishop of Seville. He strengthened the Spanish church by organizing councils (presiding over those at Seville and Toledo), establishing schools and religious houses, and helping turn the Visigoths from Arianism. He is famous for *Etymologies*, an encyclopedia encompassing all the secular knowledge of his time and Church doctrine, and for a history of the Goths. His attributes are a pen and book. His feast is April 4. *See also* SAINTS IN ART.

ISLAM. In the time of Muhammad the Arabs had little or no art of their own, but in their conquest of Syria, Mesopotamia, Egypt, and Iran they adopted the highly developed art of these countries.

EVOLUTION OF STYLE

In Syria the Arabs found kindred people who had migrated at an early date from southern Arabia. Some of them were descendants of the Nabataeans, who, about the middle of the 4th century B.C., had established an Arab kingdom around Petra. Later they moved farther north to Hauran or central Syria, where Nabataean architecture and decoration had a style of its own. Many typical Nabataean architectural and decorative elements have been found in Christian churches of Syria dating from the 4th to the 6th century of our era. It is known from literary sources that the Umayyad caliphs (661–750) requisitioned materials and artists from all the provinces for the construction of their new cities, palaces, and mosques. Byzantine and Syrian mosaicists were employed to decorate the Great Mosque of Damascus, for which an Iranian was chief architect. Coptic artists from Egypt worked for the Umayyads in Jerusalem, Damascus, and Mecca. The custom of requisitioning artists and materials from various provinces continued under the Abbasids (750–1258). *See* ISLAMIC ARCHITECTURE.

An Islamic style was evolved gradually and was derived chiefly from two artistic sources: the East Christian and the Sassanian art of Iran. In early Islamic monuments such as the mosaics of the Dome of the Rock in Jerusalem (691–92), the 8th-century stone façade from the palace at Mshatta, and the paintings of the desert palace at Kuseir 'Amra (Qusayr 'Amra; ca. 712) in Jordan, decorative motifs from East Christian and Sassanian art are found side by side. Sassanian art in Iran did not stop with the Arab conquest; it continued for several centuries.

Ishtar Gate, Babylon. Reconstruction. Former State Museums, Berlin.

The evolution of the Islamic style was to a certain extent also influenced by the arts and crafts of Iranian and Turkish nomads from eastern Iran and Central Asia. The contact between these nomads and the Arabs resulted in the introduction of many new features and techniques into Islamic art. Excavations at Kotcho, which was the capital of the Turkish Uighurs from the 7th to the 9th century, brought to light many interesting prototypes of Islamic art. The official religion of the Uighurs was Manichaeism, an Iranian religion founded by Mani. Manichaean miniature paintings of about the 9th century found at Kotcho show a striking resemblance to some 14th-century miniature paintings of the Mongol school. It is of interest to note that many Uighurs served as officials at the Mongol court of the Il-khans in Iran. Also, the art of rug knotting originated most probably in Central Asia, where fragments of knotted rugs came to light.

Islamic art had its beginnings in the mosque. The mihrab, or prayer niche, and the mimbar, or prayer pulpit, were the main objects, and were richly decorated. In the mosque we also find the sacred book of the Muslims, the Koran. The great contribution of the Arabs to the Islamic world is the Arabic script, which in early Korans shows angular or formal characters known as Kufic, from the town of Kufa in Mesopotamia. The earliest Korans in existence date from the 8th century and are written on parchment of natural color with black writing, but sometimes a blue or violet ground is used with gold. *See* ISLAMIC CALLIGRAPHY AND ILLUMINATION.

Already under the Umayyads we find the beginnings of a court art. The pleasure-loving rulers of that dynasty built magnificent palaces and hunting lodges richly decorated with wall paintings of elaborate figure compositions. The French archaeologist Schlumberger discovered in the ruins of an 8th-century Umayyad palace, Kasr (Qasr) al-Hair al-Gharbi, in Syria, two magnificent frescoes, one of which is based on the Hellenistic style, the other on the Sassanian. Although religious tenets (found in the Traditions of the Prophet) forbade Muslim artists to introduce human and animal figures into their work, such representations are commonly found in secular art, but not in mosques or in buildings for religious purposes. The rulers of many dynasties disregarded these tenets and lavishly decorated their palaces with figure subjects.

At an early period Islamic art developed a purely abstract style of decoration that is essentially Muslim. The most characteristic ornament that Islamic art gave to the world is the arabesque. Several misleading definitions of the arabesque are quite common. Properly, the arabesque is an ornament composed of gracefully curving scrolls, crossed or interlaced, bearing abstract motifs, suggesting leaves or blossoms, known as palmettes. There are full palmettes and half palmettes, which often merge with the stem. In spite of variations owing to locality and period, the arabesque always retains the same general characteristics. The evolution of the arabesque was gradual. It first appeared in the Umayyad and Abbasid periods during the 8th and 9th centuries, but not until the 12th century did the arabesque achieve its most elaborate form. Arabesque was popular in all periods of Islamic art. Arab, Persian, and Turkish artists created many varieties of decorative patterns in which arabesques were often combined with geometric designs of star-shaped forms and hexagons.

METALWORK

Every object, whether made for daily use or for ceremonial purposes, was lavishly ornamented. Such objects were made of metal, pottery, wood, ivory, and glass. In metalwork, early Islamic art followed the types developed by the Persians of the Sassanian era. In the province of Khurasan, in eastern Iran, we find the earliest school of inlay technique in which bronze objects were inlaid with red copper.

Saljuk period. The great period of Islamic metalwork began in the 11th century in Iran with the arrival of the Turkish Saljuks. The vessels of bronze and silver reveal new schemes of decoration and technique. Certain Saljuk objects, such as candlesticks and incense burners in the shape of animals, have a rich openwork decoration. One of the finest examples is a large incense burner (New York, Metropolitan Museum), inscribed with the name of the owner, Amir Saif ad-Dunya wad-Din Muhammad al-Mawardi, and made in A.H. 577 (A.D. 1181–82) by Ja'far ibn-Muhammad ibn-'Ali.

The art of inlaying objects of bronze and brass with copper and silver achieved its first artistic prominence in eastern Iran. The great centers of Saljuk metalwork were Herat (now in Afghanistan), Nishapur, Sistan, and Merv (Marv, now in Turkmen S.S.R.). The style created by Iranian craftsmen in these centers was soon adopted by all other Islamic provinces.

Mosul school. The most famous center of metalwork during the 13th century was Mosul, in northern Mesopotamia, which was ruled from 1127 to 1262 by the Saljuk atabegs of the Zangid dynasty who were great patrons of arts and crafts. Many known objects were made for Sultan Badr ad-Din Lulu, who ruled in Mosul from 1233 to 1259. In the work of the Mosul school every inch of the surface is inlaid with silver, and the whole background consists of a dense meander pattern.

Ayyubid and Mamluk periods. Fine metalwork inlaid with silver and gold was produced under the Ayyubids and Mamluks in Damascus, Aleppo, and Cairo. The height of Mamluk metalwork was reached under the sultan Nasir ad-din Muhammad ibn-Kalaun (r. 1293–94, 1308, 1309–40). A number of fine objects in various museums in the United States and Europe bear the name of this sultan and of his officials. Characteristic motifs appearing in the ornament are naturalistic leaves and blossoms of Chinese origin, which had been introduced into the Near East by the Mongols. Of great interest to students of Islamic civilization are bronze and brass vessels with Christian representation, occasionally inscribed with the names of Ayyubid sultans, some of whom, particularly those of Damascus, were tolerant toward Christians and at times were even allied with the kingdom of Jerusalem. A magnificent bronze basin (Washington, D.C., Freer Gallery) is richly inlaid with silver and shows scenes from the life of Christ as well as polo games. It is inscribed with the name of the Ayyubid sultan Salih Ayyub (r. 1240–49). Some of the metalwork was made in Cairo for the Rasulid sultans of Yemen, who were on friendly terms with the Mamluk sultans who ruled in Egypt.

At the end of the 14th century the art of inlaying in

Syria and Egypt was already in decline but was receiving increased attention in Europe. In the 15th century the Oriental trade established in Italy during the Crusades began to flourish. In Venice Muslim metalwork inspired native craftsmen, who developed a Venetian-Oriental school in which Muslim technique and ornament were adapted to Italian Renaissance taste. *See* ISLAMIC METALWORK.

POTTERY AND TILES

In the field of ceramic art the Muslims contributed many important technical processes and ornamental schemes. In the application of colored glazes to earthenware the Muslims were from an early period expert masters.

Baghdad school. The first great development of ceramic art was sponsored by the Abbasid rulers of Baghdad. Here, in the 8th and 9th centuries, artists from Egypt, Syria, Iran, and Mesopotamia were assembled. Excavations of the city of Samarra, which was the residence of the caliphs from 836 to 883, brought to light splendid examples of a new ceramic art. This new ceramic technique, which later spread all over the Islamic world and Europe, is known as luster painting. In this process the design is painted with metallic oxides on a white-enameled surface. In the second firing at a temperature of 500 to 800°F and through contact with smoke, the metallic oxides are reduced to a thin layer of gold or other colors, mostly brown or red.

Saljuk period. In Iran under the rule of the Saljuks and their successors, the shahs of Khwarizm, ceramic art reached its height. Iranian potters of the 12th and 13th centuries created magnificent ceramics that are generally classified among the finest ever produced. Techniques such as luster decoration, overglaze and underglaze painting, carving, and openwork were discriminately employed in various ceramic centers. Rayy, a flourishing Saljuk city near Teheran, was a ceramic center of great importance. Another celebrated center of the 13th and 14th centuries was Kashan. In 1301 a member of a famous family of Kashan potters, ibn-Abi Tahir, wrote a treatise on faïence techniques practiced in the 13th and 14th centuries.

Hispano-Moresque school. The luster technique was introduced into Spain from the Near East by the Arabs as early as the 9th century. A purely Moorish industry was established in the 14th century in Málaga and Granada. It was famous for ceramics with gold luster decoration, often in combination with blue. Another ceramic center of Spain which produced lusterware was Manises, near Valencia, where during the first half of the 15th century Gothic elements were gradually introduced.

Minai technique. Another elaborate ceramic method developed by Persian artists of the 12th century is the so-called Minai, or enamel, technique, in which the scenes or ornaments are painted with various pigments over a white or turquoise-blue glaze. The decoration of figure subjects shows court scenes, polo games, and episodes of the *Shah-nama*. A popular story frequently represented is that of the Sassanian king Bahram Gur and his mistress Azada. The technique of this ware, made in Rayy and Kashan, represents the true miniature style of 13th-century book illustrations, of which no examples survive.

Safavid period. In the 16th century the Safavid style of wall decoration in faïence rivaled the contemporary painting. The artists working in Isfahan for Shah Abbas I the Great created beautiful wall decorations with elaborate figure compositions. *See* ISLAMIC POTTERY AND TILES.

RUGS

The Islamic world gave us rugs and carpets. From representations of Oriental rugs in Italian paintings we know that they were imported to Europe by the end of the 13th century.

Turkish rugs. In 14th- and 15th-century paintings of the Italian and Dutch schools we find many representations of Oriental rugs of Turkish origin. The rugs are usually geometric in character and show a repeat pattern of squares and octagons, often combined with interlacings and arabesques. Some of them show a highly stylized animal decoration. Another type of Turkish rug, attributed to Ushak, in Asia Minor, is depicted in Italian and Dutch paintings of the 15th and 16th centuries. It shows an allover pattern of angular arabesques in yellow and blue on a red ground. These Turkish rugs influenced the color compositions of several 15th-century Italian painters.

Safavid period. The finest carpets in the world were made in Persia during the 16th and 17th centuries under the rule of the Safavids. The rulers of this great Persian dynasty established court looms in Tabriz, Kashan, Herat, and Isfahan. Under the Safavids the carpet was elevated to a work of art produced by master craftsmen, often from cartoons designed by famous illuminators and court painters like Mirak and Sultan Muhammad. Many types of Persian rugs are known, most of them made of wool; others, made of silk, are the most luxurious products of Kashan. Several dated 16th-century rugs are in existence. The earliest one is a hunting carpet in the Poldi-Pezzoli Museum, Milan, dated A.H. 929 (A.D. 1522–23). The magnificent medallion rugs, one in the Victoria and Albert Museum, London, and its companion piece, in the Paul Getty Collection of Los Angeles, were made to the order of Maksud of Kashan in A.H. 946 (A.D. 1539–40) as an offering for the shrine of Shaikh Safi at Ardebil.

Another type of Persian rug that was very popular is the animal rug. Related to the animal rugs are hunting carpets, of which only a few are in existence. The most famous of these is the silk hunting carpet in the Austrian Museum of Applied Art, Vienna, showing huntsmen attacking animals. In the border are representations of the Muslim paradise. Such carpets must have been designed by a great artist, and indeed the style recalls that of miniature paintings by Sultan Muhammad.

Shah Abbas period. Fine rugs were also made in the 17th century in the time of Shah Abbas I the Great (r. 1587–1628), who made Isfahan his capital. Here new court looms were established for the manufacture of rugs and silk fabrics. Other rug centers such as Kashan and Herat continued to produce fine carpets not only for the use of the court but also for export. In many 17th-century paintings by Italian and Dutch masters we see floral carpets that were made in the looms of Herat in the province of Khurasan.

The manufacture of silk rugs enriched with gold and silver threads continued in the 17th century at both Isfahan and Kashan. These rugs are sometimes referred to as "Polish" or "polonaise," because some of them bear coats of arms of noble Polish families for whom they were made in Persian court manufactories.

Mughal period. The technique of rug weaving was introduced into India from Persia. In the time of the Mughal emperor Akbar (r. 1556–1605) not only fine rugs were imported from Persia but also rug weavers, who settled in Agra, Fatehpur Sikri, and Lahore. The Mughal style was fully developed in the time of Shah Jahan (r. 1628–58), when Lahore became the main center of rug weaving. The Mughal artists developed a floral style that is typically Indian and Mughal. *See* Rugs, Near and Middle Eastern.

PAINTING

The Koran, unlike the Christian Gospels, was never illustrated. The artists concentrated on fine writing and rich but abstract illuminations. Islamic painting, that is, wall painting and miniature painting, was known since the 7th century. The art of the book was cultivated by the Muslims of Mesopotamia, Iran, Syria, and Egypt.

Saljuk period. Illustrated books on medicine, plants, mechanics, and fables were popular under the Saljuks and their followers. In the 13th century the Saljuk style of painting was fully developed in the Baghdad school. Three main artistic sources—the East Christian, the Persian, and the Turkish—contributed to the formation of the Islamic style of painting. The most popular books illustrated by painters of the Baghdad school were the *Makamat* (Assemblies) of Hariri and the *Kalila wa Dimna*, a collection of fables. The finest copy of the *Makamat* is in the National Library, Paris. It was completed in May, 1237, by Yahya ibn-Mahmud al-Wasiti, who was the calligrapher of the manuscript as well as the painter of the illustrations, which are masterpieces of early Islamic painting. In these illustrations the artist depicts the daily life of the 13th-century Arabs.

Mongol period. Of great importance in the development of Islamic painting was the Mongol invasion of the Middle East. The Mongols established the powerful Il-khan dynasty, which ruled from 1256 to 1353. In 1258 Hulagu captured Baghdad, which was destroyed and looted. It was soon rebuilt and again became a cultural and artistic center of the Muslim world. The Mongol school inaugurated one of the most important periods of Persian painting. Many paintings of that school show the influence of Chinese monochrome ink paintings of the Sung and Yüan dynasties. The Mongol rulers encouraged their court artists to illustrate the *Shah-nama* (Book of Kings), an epic poem by Firdausi. This great work, which served as an inspiration to Persian artists for centuries, is founded partly on history and partly on ancient legends of Iran.

Timurid period. The development of Persian miniature painting reached its height under Shah Rukh (r. 1404–47) of the Timurid dynasty. This ruler was a patron of the arts of the book and employed many artists in his famous library at Herat. His son Baisunkur Mirza was also a great patron of the arts and established in Herat an academy where forty painters, calligraphers, illuminators, and bookbinders, brought from western Iran, were employed. The Timurid school created a new, highly decorative style of painting, in which figures, landscape, and ornament form a two-dimensional pattern. The richness of color compositions is another characteristic of 15th-century Persian paintings.

The most famous painter of the end of the 15th century was Kamal ad-Din Bihzad, who was born about 1440 in Herat and was called "the Marvel of the Age." Only a few authentic works by him are extant. Bihzad freed himself from the stiffness and detailed work of the 15th-century school and revealed himself as a keen observer of nature. He was also a fine colorist, creating entirely new color combinations. His paintings are masterpieces of composition, full of action and realism. For the first time the figures of all ages show a definite individuality, which had been lacking in earlier paintings.

Safavid period. At the beginning of the 16th century, under the new Safavid dynasty, the center of Iranian painting shifted from Khurasan to Tabriz in western Iran, although Herat continued for some time as an important center of Persian painting. Manuscripts made for Shah Tahmasp are among the most sumptuous ever produced. In a copy of Nizami's *Khamsa* in the British Museum, London, the most celebrated court painters of Shah Tahmasp are represented. It contains works of Sultan Muhammad, Mirak, Muzaffer 'Ali, Mir Sayyid 'Ali, and Mirza 'Ali. Sultan Muhammad, a pupil of Mirak, was the chief painter and director of the school, and Shah Tahmasp himself took painting lessons from him.

The last great painter of Persia was Riza-i-Abbasi, who worked in Isfahan from 1598 to 1643. He is best known for his genre subjects, love scenes, and realistic portraits. He developed a free style of brushwork that has a certain calligraphic quality, and his style was widely imitated by many painters of the 17th and 18th centuries who lacked the originality of the master. Riza-i-Abbasi also influenced the style of contemporary wall painting, which survived in the palaces of Isfahan. *See* Islamic Painting.

See also Islamic Bookbinding; Islamic Glass and Crystal; Islamic Textiles; Seals: Stamp and Cylinder (Islamic Seals).

BIBLIOGRAPHY. T. Arnold, *The Legacy of Islam*, Oxford, 1931; A. J. Arberry, *The Legacy of Persia*, Oxford, 1953; M. S. Dimand, *A Handbook of Muhammadan Art*, 3d ed., New York, 1958; E. Kühnel, *Die Kunst des Islam*, Stuttgart, 1962.

MAURICE S. DIMAND

ISLAMIC ARCHITECTURE. The history of Islamic architecture is concerned with monuments that have a direct relationship to the Muslim religion, such as the mosque (*masjid*), the religious school or madrasa (*medrese*), the minaret (*minar* or *manara*), convents, shrines, and mausoleums, and with secular constructions, such as forts, palaces, houses, hospitals, bazaars, caravansaries, bridges, and fountains, that is, structures erected in lands controlled by rulers of the Islamic faith.

In the 7th century the Muslims moved out of Arabia and soon spread into Iran, Byzantium, Egypt, and Spain. The earlier monuments are found in these areas. At a somewhat later period monuments were erected in North Africa, Turkey, Afghanistan, and India, as well as in more remote places such as Albania, Indonesia, Russia, and Ceylon. The period of Islamic architecture has not come to an end; new structures are being built not only in the Muslim countries but even in the United States, England, and France.

Until recently Islamic architecture was considered a nonhistorical style, and the monuments were believed to

Islamic architecture. Samarra, Iraq, the minaret known as al-Malawiyyâh, 9th century.

be characterized by the bizarre, exotic, and disorganized. Islamic architecture, however, followed the historical development common to all styles of architecture: successive periods of (1) experimentation with plan forms and construction methods, (2) high style, and, finally, (3) concentration on technical and ornamental brilliance. In the Muslim world each of these periods was quite prolonged, and there was not an avid interest in trying new ways of building. For example, a few ways of setting the dome on a square chamber were worked out quite early and have been carried on almost unchanged.

The Muslim conquests spread into regions where older religions and cultures flourished, and many of the new structures borrowed from the old and were built by craftsmen of these localities. Thus, Christian churches, Sassanian palaces and fire temples, and Hindu temples all influenced early Muslim architecture. Materials in common usage as well as variations in climatic conditions also influenced the design of the monuments. For example, the mosques of Turkey reflected the tradition of dressed-stone masonry common to Armenian church architecture, but because of the cold climate the central court was often roofed over, rather than being open as in other Muslim lands. Decoration developed as geometric patterns and floral forms because of the prohibition against the representation of living beings.

The ritual requirements of Islam that had to be taken into account in religious structures were few in number, and this fact hastened the early standardization of the plan form of the mosque, the religious school, and the mausoleum. Thus, a mosque is readily recognizable as such, regardless of the time or place of its construction. The masjid, or place of prostration, required a central court where the believers literally prostrated themselves in prayer, a mihrab, or prayer niche, to indicate the direction of Mecca, a minaret, from which the call to prayer could be heard over a wide area, and a basin of clear water for ablutions before prayer. In time refinements were introduced: the sides of the court were lined with arcades that led into spacious rooms offering shelter from the sun of summer and the cold of winter; the area in front of the mihrab was treated as a sanctuary and crowned with a dome; and the mosque was approached through a lofty entrance portal. Finally, an ivan (liwan) was introduced at the midpoint of each side of the court. The ivan is a high, barrel-vaulted hall completely open to the court. The four-ivan plan was also employed in the religious schools, which frequently had rooms in two stories around the court. The mausoleums featured domes rising above square or octagonal chambers, with the burial usually in a basement crypt.

As would be expected, the finest monuments of Islam, those that survived because of their size and because of the care devoted to their construction, were ordered by the Muslim hierarchy. The caliphs—the men who wielded both spiritual authority and temporal power—were ardent builders. Rulers of many dynasties in many countries sought merit through the erection of religious monuments, and their courtiers followed the royal examples. However, haste was too frequently the order of the day, and mosques were raised upon inadequate foundations with walls of sun-dried brick rather than of baked brick or stone. Caliphs, sovereigns, and princes patronized secular architecture as well, ordering the construction of city walls, bridges, caravansaries, bazaars, and other urban amenities, as well as palaces. Historical accounts describe many splendid palaces in a wealth of detail; yet few of any real antiquity have survived: many were built of sun-dried brick; in addition, since Muslim rulers did not like to live in the palaces of their predecessors, palaces were quickly erected and almost as quickly abandoned. The ruins at Samarra illustrate palace construction in sun-dried brick on a monumental scale, the Alhambra and the Alcazar reflect the greater permanence of stone building, and Turkey and India offer palaces of later date that were occupied over relatively long periods.

Information about standing monuments derives from historical accounts and from the inscriptions on the structures themselves. Decorative inscriptions were prominent features of most Muslim structures and, as a rule, were executed in Arabic in various forms of Arabic script. Quotations from the Koran abound, but many inscriptions include the name of the patron and the date of building. Fairly frequently the names of the craftsmen are included, and sometimes the name of the architect is given. More frequently, however, the names are those of builders, masons, and decorators. There is little evidence to indicate that preliminary drawings were made, and it must be assumed that most of the monuments were erected by guild members who moved from one job to the next. It is probable that they carried sketchbooks and used a standard unit of measure, which seems to have varied from century to century. In cases where complicated vaults and stalactite ceilings were to be erected, it would seem that full-scale drawings were laid out on a smooth surface of white plaster.

The Islamic monuments are all of arcuated construction. In the earliest structures arches springing from piers or columns supported flat wooden roofs, but later vaults were erected over each bay. In variety, the vaults built over square and rectangular areas rival Gothic architecture. The dome was a highly developed feature of Muslim design, appearing over mosques, religious schools, tombs, and palaces. Direct influences on early domes were the rubble masonry domes of Sassanian Iran and the wooden domes of Christian Syria, but before long baked brick became the usual material, and the domes were frequently erected without the use of supporting centering. As these domes soared higher their interior height was out of scale with the chamber below, and the practice of inserting a lower, nonstructural dome was adopted. Such double domes were featured in Iran, Turkestan, and India and were distinguished by a bulbous profile. The domes were sheathed on the exterior with bright tiles, with brick or stone laid in patterns, or with sheets of lead; such coatings protected the fabric and gave excitement to the more distant vista.

In general, the structural fabric of Islamic monuments is not exposed but is concealed by decorative revetments. Brick was used extensively for fabric and ornament in the region from India to the area inland from the Mediterranean Sea, with the bricks square in shape and rather thin. Brick bonding patterns appeared in great variety, emphasizing the major planes and bearing surfaces of the buildings. Elaboration of this technique came with the use of bricks molded into special shapes and also with the use of thin strips of fired tile in interlacing patterns. On interior surfaces plaster coatings were incised with simulated bonding patterns. Exposed surfaces of finely dressed stone were characteristic of an area extending from the interior of Turkey along the Mediterranean through Egypt. Mihrabs, archivolts, and other features were executed in carved plaster in which floral forms predominated, but in later periods painted patterns were used upon dead-white plaster surfaces.

The extensive use of faïence is one of the most conspicuous features of Islamic architecture, with regional styles favoring different colors and designs. In India, Spain, and Turkey rather naturalistic floral patterns were used on interior surfaces; in Egypt and North Africa tones were more subdued and tilework was confined to limited areas. In Iran faïence was highly developed, and the entire exterior and interior surfaces of some monuments were covered with geometric or stylized floral designs. There were two distinctive manners of using faïence: one was that of square or octagonal tiles either glazed in solid colors or with a segment of a larger pattern fired on each tile in a number of colors; the other was that of faïence mosaic, in which the patterns were created by fitting together thousands of small pieces of faïence of several colors. *See* ISLAMIC POTTERY AND TILES.

Marble and alabaster were used, principally in the later periods, for decorative revetments. This technique was most brilliantly employed in India with such variations as the use of contrasting colors, carving in low relief, elaborate pierced screens, and *pietra dura*, in which patterns were created by inlays of colored marbles and of semiprecious stones.

In some of the earliest monuments wood beams and ceiling boards were elaborately carved and painted, but after vaulting came into use decorative woodwork was largely confined to mihrabs, to the mimbar, or pulpit, set alongside the mihrab in the mosque, to the *mushrabiya*, or open latticework screen, and to the portals of religious and secular structures. In all periods there was a close affinity between the decorative patterns used architecturally and those common to ceramics and illuminated manuscripts.

UMAYYAD PERIOD

The Umayyad caliphs (661–750) established residence in Syria and were soon engaged in devoting sums from the riches of conquest to construction, with the earliest structures featuring the pointed arch rather than the semicircular arch previously employed in this region. In 706 the Great Mosque of Damascus was begun as the conversion of an existing church; its arcades supported a flat roof. The mosque was much rebuilt in later periods, but the fine wall mosaics depicting towns and landscapes have been preserved. At Jerusalem, the Dome of the Rock (less properly called the Omar Mosque) was erected shortly before 700 on a site sacred first to Jews and Christians and then to Muslims, for this was the rock from which the prophet Muhammad was believed to have made his night journey to heaven. The octagonal structure is crowned by a wooden dome and provided with two concentric ambulatories; much of the interior surface is covered with splendid decorative mosaics, including Arabic inscriptions. Adjacent to the Dome of the Rock is the Aqsa (Aksa) Mosque, which was begun about 709 and reconstructed several times until it achieved its present form in the 11th century. It is rectangular in plan, as were most of the early mosques, and had a flat roof. A number of the original carved and painted roof beams and ceiling panels are preserved.

Many very large mosques were hastily built of mud brick to serve the needs of the Muslim armies and garrisons; few have survived and those only in very ruined condition. The Muslim hierarchy of this period descended from nomadic Arab tribesmen, and the caliphs returned to this kind of atmosphere when they erected fortified palaces along the limits of the desert east of Syria. The palaces of Mshatta, Qusayr 'Amra, Qasr al-Hair al-Gharbi, and Qasr at-Tuba are very well preserved, since they were constructed largely of dressed stone. The best known, Mshatta, was erected about 743. It measures some 470 feet along each of its exterior walls, the living quarters within culminating in a long basilical hall with a triple apse, a plan that featured borrowed pre-Islamic construction. Much of the entrance façade was decorated with carving in low relief.

Egypt was controlled by the Umayyads, and the 'Amr Mosque was erected as early as 641, at a settlement called al-Fustat, south of Cairo, by a general of that name.

It was doubled in size in 827 and subsequently rebuilt, but only traces of the original construction remain. The town of Fustat developed in size and commercial importance, and excavations into the mounds of debris at the site have brought to light many of the original houses—ivans facing on open rectangular courts containing pools. *See* UMAYYAD ARCHITECTURE.

Umayyads in Spain. By the early 8th century Muslim conquerors had taken over much of Spain and provided a haven for members of the Umayyad family when that caliphate was replaced by the Abbasid line. The prosperous Umayyad emirate of Cordova lasted until the 11th century, but surviving monuments are few in number; among these are parts of mosques that were later included within new churches. The Alcazar palace in Cordova was begun about 789, and the now-vanished Madinat az-Zahra, another great palace in Cordova, was erected after 936. *See* UMAYYAD ARCHITECTURE (SPAIN).

ABBASID PERIOD

Under the Abbasid caliphs (750–1258) the capital of Islam was moved from Damascus to Baghdad, and in 762 work was begun on a great circular city. Raqqa, a horseshoe-shaped town, the ruins of which have yielded quantities of fine ceramics, was laid out on the upper Euphrates River, and the greatest city of all, Samarra, was begun on the Tigris River north of Baghdad in 836. For nearly sixty years the site was developed with palaces, mosques, and other structures. Nearby, the octagonal, domed tomb called the Qubbat as-Sulaibiya has survived.

See also ISLAMIC PAINTING (UMAYYAD AND EARLY ABBASID PERIODS).

The fortified palace of Ukhaidir, south of Baghdad, is a fine structure of this period, but little remains in Baghdad itself. The influence of Samarra is evident in the ibn-Tulun Mosque in Cairo, which was begun in 876, especially in its plaster decoration and the spiraliform minaret. Long before the end of this period the early dependence upon plan types and features of pre-Islamic construction ended. *See* ABBASID ARCHITECTURE.

FATIMID PERIOD

Islamic architecture in Egypt found distinctive expression in the Fatimid period (969–1171) in Cairo (al-Qahira), which was founded in 969. A year later the al-Azhar Mosque was begun; it soon became the principal center of learning for the Muslim world. Between 990 and 1012 the ruler al-Hakim erected the mosque that bears his name; with its open court and sanctuary area five aisles wide and seventeen bays deep, it reflected earlier plans and structural features. The al-Guyushi Mosque of 1085 features a fine stucco mihrab. The tomb of Sayyida Ruqayya of 1132 had a carved wooden mihrab (Cairo, Museum of Islamic Art). The Mosque of al-Aqmar, erected in 1125, featured experiments with stalactites following models from Syria and farther east. During this period Cairo was enclosed by stone walls, and three of the monumental gateways, Bab an-Nasr, Bab al-Futuh, and Bab Zuweila, survive. *See* FATIMID ARCHITECTURE OF CAIRO.

AYYUBID PERIOD

Monuments of the succeeding Ayyubid period were constructed principally in Syria, notably a series of mosques and tombs in or near Damascus. In 1176, however,

Saladin ordered construction begun on a citadel crowning the Moqattam Hills of Cairo.

MAMLUK PERIOD

From 1252 until 1517 Egypt, Syria, and other regions were ruled by sultans of the Mamluk dynasties, and Cairo was embellished with monuments, many of which have survived to give a distinctive character to sections of the city. Sultan Bibars erected a four-ivan mosque in Cairo in 1266. The Zahiriya madrasa in Damascus, dated 1279, contains Bibars's tomb. The tomb of Sultan Qalaun (Kalaun) in Cairo, built in 1284, was one element in a complex that included a hospital and a mosque; this combination of other structures with a royal tomb was very typical of the period. The combined mosque-madrasa of Sultan Hasan, built between 1356 and 1363, is one of the most renowned monuments of Cairo. Within fortresslike walls, this structure features a square court faced by four finely proportioned ivans.

Palace architecture in Cairo is represented by the so-called Hall of Bibars, built in 1353. It is the sole surviving section of a much larger structure and features a pierced dome and stalactite corbels. The mosque-madrasa of Sultan Barquq, erected between 1388 and 1399, is reminiscent of that of Sultan Hasan, but the decoration is richer and more exuberant. Barquq's mausoleum, built after 1400, lies east of Cairo in an area called the Tombs of the Caliphs and includes the rooms of a madrasa and a monastery; the structure is one of the most representative of the period. The domes over the partially preserved mosque-madrasa of Sultan al-Muayyed, built between 1416 and 1422, and the tomb of Bars Bay, completed in the area of the Tombs of the Caliphs in 1432, display the culmination of elaborate interlace patterns in stone. The mausoleum of Kait Bay, completed at the Tombs of the Caliphs in 1474, includes a mosque, a madrasa, and a library; structural elements are attenuated and details highly refined.

In Syria, where the Mamluks took over Crusader castles and churches, they repaired and embellished existing mosques. Typical of this latter activity is the minaret built by Kait Bay at the Great Mosque of Damascus. Technical skill in construction and in the execution of details were features of the Mamluk period, with areas of plain masonry contrasting with richly decorated surfaces. *See* MAMLUK ARCHITECTURE (EGYPT AND SYRIA).

HISPANO-MORESQUE PERIOD

In Spain and Morocco the successive Almoravid and Almohad dynasties erected structures in the 12th and 13th centuries. In Seville the Great Mosque was greatly enlarged and, about 1200, provided with a towering minaret; now called the Giralda Tower, it is the sole surviving element of the mosque. In Morocco and western Algeria several important mosques were built or rebuilt. These included the mosque of Tlemcen (1136), the Qarawiyn Mosque in Fez (1135), the Koutoubiya (Kutubia) Mosque in Marrakesh (1150), and the Mosque of Hasan in Rabat. Characteristic of these structures were rather small courts, very extensive covered areas, and square stone minarets similar to the Giralda Tower. From the 16th through the early 18th century the construction of somewhat less monumental structures centered first in Marrakesh and later in Meknes. These mosques and madrasas displayed dec-

Islamic architecture. The Masjid-i-Jami in Isfahan.

oration in marble, carved plaster, and patterns of interlacing strips of wood and faïence.

See also MOORISH ARCHITECTURE (MOROCCO).

In Spain the Muslims lost more and more territory to the Christian rulers, and the palaces of the Alhambra and the Alcazar were among the last great monuments. The Alcazar, in Seville, was begun in the Almohad period and extensively altered in Mudejar style in the 14th century; the Alhambra, in Granada, was largely the product of the same century. Both palaces are noted for their charming patios and for decoration of extreme richness.

See also MOORISH ARCHITECTURE (SPAIN).

TURKISH ARCHITECTURE

In Turkey Muslim architecture developed under the Saljuk sultans of Anatolia between 1092 and 1308, notably in Konia. Most of the mosques and madrasas were of rather modest size, featuring cut-stone façades with elaborately carved portals, minarets of baked brick, and faïence-clad interior surfaces. Influence from Saljuk Iran was conspicuous in the opening decades of the period, and the octagonal towerlike tomb with a tent dome was widely used in Anatolia.

Under Sultan Kiliçarslan II work was begun on the Alauddin Mosque, in which stone columns supported a flat roof. By 1162 the Iplikçi Mosque displayed a more developed form, with stone piers supporting vaults and shallow domes. Characteristic of the stone-built roadside inns is the khan of Sultan Alauddin Keykubad I. Built in 1229, it has a large open court flanked by rooms and an extensive covered area designed for cold-weather living.

The Sirçali madrasa of 1243 in Konia set the plan type for this kind of structure: beyond an open court are three large rooms; the one on axis is an ivan, and the flanking ones carry domes. The type appears again in Konia in the Karatay madrasa of 1252 and in the Ince minareli madrasa of 1258. The latter structure well illustrates the so-called Turkish triangle, a filling element between the corners of a square chamber and the base of its dome. The Sahib Ata Mosque in Konia, also of 1258, displays an entrance façade of sandstone carved in high relief with a deep stalactite niche above the portal. *See* SALJUK ARCHITECTURE (KONIA).

Ottoman sultans ruled Turkey and other areas inland from the Mediterranean littoral from 1299 until 1923, and several distinctive periods of architecture were reflected in the monuments. In the Brussa period (1299–1501) construction centered in the town of Brussa (Bursa). Characteristic of this period and of the mosque plan that featured large domed chambers on the main axis flanked by smaller vaulted or domed rooms is the Green Mosque of 1421. *See* BRUSSA ARCHITECTURE.

In the classical period (1501–1703) building was concentrated in Istanbul, the imperial capital. As in these same centuries in India and Iran, the structural fabric was concealed by areas of fine marble and faïence tiles. In contrast to other Muslim lands, with the exception of India, the structures were freestanding on open sites and were designed by a series of chief architects to the sultans.

The renowned mosques in Istanbul feature an open forecourt flanked by minarets before the main structure, which is always crowned by a great dome. First in this series was the Mosque of Sultan Bayazid II (1501–06), with its dome flanked by half domes on either side of the main axis. Sinan, an architectural genius, worked with his associates in the construction of some 360 mosques, tombs, and other structures, including his masterpiece, the Sulaimaniye Mosque (1550–57) and still the most conspicuous of the Istanbul mosques. Another of his great monuments is the Sultan Selim II Mosque (1569–75) in Adrianople (Edirne), featuring a dome on circular pillars. One of the finest structures in Istanbul is the Ahmediye Mosque (1609–16), erected for Sultan Ahmad I. It is known as the Blue Mosque from the color of the interior faïence.

The Turkish baroque period (1730–1803) stressed elaborate decoration and the use of applied nonstructural elements, as in the Nuru Osmaniye Mosque (1755) in Istanbul. In the empire and cosmopolitan periods of the 19th century eclectic tastes predominated. In the neoclassical period of the early 20th century modern materials and methods of construction were employed.
See also OTTOMAN ARCHITECTURE.

IRANIAN ARCHITECTURE

Very few of the earliest Muslim monuments of Iran have survived, but the evidence indicates that architectural features of the preceding Sassanian period, including ivans facing on open courts, masonry domes on squinches, and panels of carved plaster, were carried over into the religious structures of Islam and that the elliptical arch was gradually replaced by the pointed one. In this and later periods, Iran included Turkestan and present-day Afghanistan.

Saljuk period. Saljuk rulers of Turkish stock held this area for 100 years from the middle of the 11th century. The Saljuk mosque and madrasa featured a rectangular open court with an ivan at the midpoint of each of its four sides and a dome rising over the sanctuary area. The same plan was used in the caravansaries and in religious schools. In addition, the square chamber crowned by a dome was used in freestanding tombs and shrines. Masonry was much less favored than construction in sun-dried or baked brick; exterior surfaces displayed elaborate brick bonding patterns; and a variety of types of vaults and domes were erected without supporting centering. Walls were thick, openings few, and the structures were massive and solid. *See* SALJUK ARCHITECTURE (IRAN).

The vast Masjid-i-Jami in Isfahan, many times rebuilt, contains elements of the Saljuk period, including two fine dome chambers of the end of the 11th century. The mosques in Ardistan and Qazvin had large courts with four ivans and great domes over the sanctuary areas. The largest of the freestanding dome chambers was the tomb of Sultan Sanjar in Marv, now in the Turkmen S.S.R. Tomb towers survive in Rayy, Damghan, Demavand, and Abarquh and, notably, in Maragha, Azerbaijan, where there are four towers of the 12th century. Near the end of the period painted plaster decoration came into vogue, mihrabs were of carved plaster, and trial efforts were made to introduce glazed tiles.

Mongol period. Early in the 13th century Mongol armies swept across the wide Iranian plateau. Soon the Mongol Il-khans, rulers of the conquered area, were converted to Islam and became ardent patrons of architecture. In a so-called golden age Ghazan Khan embellished Tabriz, his capital, with monuments that included his huge tomb, well illustrated in contemporary manuscripts but now a mass of debris. In the reign of his successor, Oljeitu (Uljaitu; r. 1305–16), the Masjid-i-'Ali Shah with its enormous ivan was erected in Tabriz, but the ruler devoted his attention to the building of a new capital in Sultanieh. Towering over this vanished city is the blue-tiled dome of his own mausoleum. In 1335 Abu Said built the impressive Masjid-i-Jami in Varamin with the standard four-ivan plan.

Many other structures of this period have survived, notably in the environs of Isfahan and in Yazd, where rather distinctive regional styles were developed. The change from Saljuk to Mongol style parallels that from Romanesque to Gothic; that is, walls were thinner, openings were larger, and massive walls and horizontal accents gave way to soaring, accentuated lines. Carved plaster continued in use in mihrabs; interiors featured blue patterns and inscriptions on white plaster; and faïence was used on both interior and exterior surfaces. *See* MONGOL ARCHITECTURE (IRAN AND TURKESTAN).

From the late 14th until the mid-15th century the great conqueror Timur and his descendants controlled Iran and Turkestan. Timur's own building is reflected in Samarqand in his domed tomb, the Gur-i-Mir, and in the mosque, madrasa, and tomb erected for Bibi Khanum, one of his wives. Gauhar Shad, wife of Timur's son, Shah Rukh, erected the mosque in Meshed within the shrine of Imam Riza as well as a complex of structures in Herat, with its lofty minarets. Brilliant faïence mosaic characterized these and many other monuments of the general period, and the use of marble and of papier-mâché decoration reflected the work of craftsmen brought from India and China. *See* TIMURID ARCHITECTURE (IRAN AND TURKESTAN).

Safavid period. Architecture in Iran reached a fine crescendo under the rulers of the Safavid line from about 1500 until well into the 18th century, especially under Shah Abbas (r. 1587–1628), who erected a royal city alongside ancient Isfahan. The Maidan-i-Shah, or Imperial Square, some 560 yards long and one-third as wide, was flanked with structures that are still in fine condition. To the south is the great Masjid-i-Shah, displaying the standard four-ivan plan and featuring a faïence-clad dome. To the east is the Lutfullah Mosque, a masterpiece in miniature with its single dome-crowned chamber, and to the west is the 'Ali Qapu, a six-story gateway giving access to the area of garden palaces. One of these palaces, the Chihil Sutun, has a noble open porch with twenty wood columns and royal reception halls. These monuments, as well as the Chahar Bagh avenue and the bridge of Allah Verdi Khan, show the splendor of the Safavid period. The structures in Isfahan and those in many other towns display interior and exterior surfaces completely covered in multicolored faïence mosaic or in square tiles decorated with bright patterns. *See* SAFAVID ARCHITECTURE.

INDIAN ARCHITECTURE

In India successive waves of invasion from the west, beginning about 1000, resulted in the establishment of Muslim states. Qutb ad-Din Aibeg (Qutb-ud-din Aibak; r. 1206–10) founded a dynasty in Delhi, erected a great mosque there, and started work on the red sandstone Qutb Minār. The plan form of the mosque came from Muslim practice in lands to the west, while long-established traditions of Hindu craftsmanship in stone were reflected in the structural elements and in the decorative carving.

The tomb of Ghiyas-ud-din Tughlak, founder of the Tughlak dynasty in Delhi, was completed in 1326 after his death and set the style of massive, somber mausoleums that prevailed for some centuries. In time, monuments hundreds of miles apart in western and eastern India displayed very similar characteristics. In the west the imposing Jami Masjid in Ahmedabad, completed in 1423, has a vast open court and a hypostyle hall with 300 pillars and countless domes; and in the east the Jami Masjid in Jaunpur, erected in 1470, has a large court and features towering arched portals. Both monuments are covered with a wealth of vigorous stone carving.

Mughal period. During the 16th and 17th centuries the Mughal empire controlled much of the Indian subcontinent, and such rulers as Humayun, Akbar, Shah Jahan, and Aurangzeb expended vast sums in the construction of mosques, palaces, fortresses, mausoleums, and entire new cities at Delhi, Agra, Lahore, Fatehpur Sikri, and other sites. Red sandstone replaced granite as the material used for the fabric of the structures, then the fabric was sheathed with marble, and at the height of the Mughal style the marble was enriched with inlaid patterns in semiprecious stones.

Humayun's tomb southeast of Delhi, erected in 1556, set the pattern for later mausoleums with its double dome and the bulbous form of the outer dome. In 1564 Akbar had work begun on the great fort in Agra, which contained hundreds of structures within a circuit of massive walls. In 1571 he started construction on his capital of Fatehpur Sikri, where the great Jami Masjid survives. His own tomb was in the form of a spreading pavilion, in contrast to the traditional use of a dome over a square chamber, and was followed by other similar structures in Agra.

Shah Jahan built structures of extreme decorative richness, the Diwan-i-Am, the Diwan-i-Khas, and the Rang Mahal, within the fort of Delhi between 1638 and 1648, and completed the Jami Masjid in Delhi in 1658. One of the largest mosques in the world, with an open court 400 feet on each side, the structure of red sandstone and white marble with its three domes of white marble is a model of fine proportions and carefully planned decoration. It was the direct inspiration for the Badshahi Mosque in Lahore, erected by Aurangzeb. Shah Jahan erected the world-famed mausoleum known as the Taj Mahal (1632–43) for his wife, Mumtaz Mahal. Set on the bank of the Jumna River in Agra, the dazzling structure of white marble is crowned by a 200-foot-high bulbous dome.

Under Aurangzeb the quality of architecture declined; proportions were less harmonious, and extravagantly rich decoration lost contact with structural forms. Typical of his period is the Badshahi Mosque in Lahore and the tomb of his empress in Aurangābād, which is an undistinguished copy of the Taj Mahal.

See also MUGHAL ARCHITECTURE OF INDIA.

BIBLIOGRAPHY. G. T. Rivoira, *Muslim Architecture*, Oxford, 1918; E. Diez, *Persien. Islamische Baukunst in Churasan*, Hagen, 1923; M. S. Briggs, *Muhammadan Architecture in Egypt and Palestine*, Oxford, 1924; C. Marçais, *Manuel d'art musulman*, Paris, 1926–27; E. T. Richmond, *Moslem Architecture*, London, 1926; J. Smolik, *Die timuridischen Baudenkmäler in Samarkand aus der Zeit Tamerlans*, Vienna, 1929; M. A. Charles, "Hagia Sophia and the Great Imperial Mosques," *Art Bulletin*, XII, 1930; E. Cohn-Wiener, *Turan; islamische Baukunst in Mittelasien*, Berlin, 1930; A. Gabriel, *Monuments turcs d'Anatolie*, 2 vols., Paris, 1931–34; R. Riefstahl and P. Wittek, *Turkish Architecture in South-western Anatolia*, Cambridge, Mass., 1931; L. Hautecoeur and G. Weit, *Les Mosquées du Caire*, 2 vols., Paris, 1932; E. Pauty, *Les Palais et les maisons d'époque musulmane, au Caire*, Cairo, 1932; J. Sauvaget, *Les Monuments historiques de Damas*, Beirut, 1932; F. Sarre, *Konia, seldschukische Baudenkmäler*, Berlin, 1936; A. Godard, "Isfahan," *Athār-é Irān*, II, 1937; M. A. Chaghatai, *Le Tadj Mahal d'Agra (Inde)*, 2 vols., Brussels, 1938; A. U. Pope, ed., *A Survey of Persian Art*, 6 vols. in 12, New York, 1938–39; E. Herzfeld, "Damascus: Studies in Architecture," *Ars Islamica*, IX–XIV, 1942–48; E. Herzfeld, *Geschichte der Stadt Sâmarrâ*, Berlin, 1948; R. W. Hamilton, *The Structural History of the Aqsa Mosque*, Jerusalem, 1949; K. A. C. Creswell, *The Muslim Architecture of Egypt*, 2 vols., Oxford, 1952–60; R. C. Arora, *Delhi: The Imperial City*, New Delhi, 1953; U. Vogt-Goknil, *Türkische Moskeen*, Zurich, 1953; K. A. C. Creswell, *A Bibliography of the Muslim Architecture of Egypt*, Cairo, 1955; J. Terry, *The Charm of Indo-Islamic Architecture*, London, 1955; D. N. Wilber, *The Architecture of Islamic Iran: The Il Khānid Period*, Princeton, 1955; L. A. Mayer, *Islamic Architects and Their Works*, Geneva, 1956; K. A. C. Creswell, *A Short Account of Early Muslim Architecture*, Harmondsworth, 1958; D. N. Wilber, *Iran: Past and Present*, 4th ed., Princeton, 1958; P. Brown, *Indian Architecture*, vol. 2: *Islamic Period*, 4th ed., Bombay, 1959; B. Unsal, *Turkish Islamic Architecture*, London, 1959; L. Lockhart, *Persian Cities*, London, 1960.

DONALD N. WILBER

ISLAMIC BOOKBINDING. The work of the calligrapher and the painter in the production of Islamic books was complemented by that of the binder, whose responsibility it was to protect the pages from injury and to give the exterior of the book an appearance worthy of its contents. Decoration was not confined to the exterior of the covers and the flap that closed over the front edge of the book. It was also lavished on the interior faces of the covers, and these *doublures*, or linings, are often elaborately ornamented. For bookbinding, leather is the ideal material, and various processes were employed in its decoration. The leather was tooled or stamped, with or without gold. Cutwork in gilded leather or paper over a colored ground was a more elaborate technique frequently used for the *doublures*.

The earliest known book covers of the Islamic period come from Egypt and may be dated from the 8th to the 11th century. Their decoration recalls the geometric ornament of certain Coptic bindings of the 8th and 9th centuries. Typical of the Egypto-Arabic bindings of the Mamluk period (13th–15th cent.), are the all-over patterns of geometric interlacings in blind tooling, enhanced by gold-tooled dots. Other Mamluk bindings show central medallions with arabesques of fine cut leather on colored backgrounds. The *doublures* of the Mamluk book covers usually show a stamped design of arabesques, sometimes with the addition of floral motifs. This style came into vogue in the beginning of the 14th century.

Persian bookbindings of the Timurid period (15th cent.) are among the finest ever produced. Technical skill and elaborate design characterize the bindings made at the Herat Academy, where the art of leather filigree was highly developed. The exteriors usually show a stamped decoration, and the *doublures* have cutout patterns against a blue background. Notable 15th-century bindings, decorated with typical realistic Timurid landscapes with deer and monkeys and also with Chinese motifs, are found on several manuscripts, some dated A.H. 841 and 849 (A.D. 1437 and 1445) in the Top Kapu Serai Library, Istanbul. The interiors usually have a cut-leather design in leather filigree against a blue background. The interior of the cover from a manuscript dated A.H. 850 (A.D. 1446) is very similar to one on the binding of a copy of Nizami's *Khamsa* dated A.H. 853 (A.D. 1449) in the Metropolitan Museum of Art, New York. The decoration consists of two Chinese phoenixes in combat placed against a background of Timurid floral scrolls inside a medallion.

In the 16th century, under the Safavid dynasty, book covers were elaborately ornamented, and gold was used more abundantly than in the 15th century. In some cases the decoration covered the entire surface; in others it was confined within medallions or other compartments. The exterior frequently shows stamped and gilded arabesques interlaced with delicate floral scrolls and Chinese cloud bands. On the interior the ornament consists of medallions and cartouches containing arabesques in delicate leather filigree on backgrounds of blue, pink, and green.

In another type of 16th-century Persian bookbinding the stamped and gilded decoration of the exteriors shows elaborate landscapes with birds and animals, reflecting the naturalistic style of Safavid painting. Decoration of Safavid bookbinding differed in technique from that of the Timurid era, which was hand-tooled and stamped. In the 16th century the decoration was pressed with large engraved matrices of copper or steel. The processes of pressing and gilding were usually combined, but sometimes the leather was gilded before being pressed with the hot matrix. The interiors of the book covers are usually decorated with gold paper filigree, which replaced the cut-leather work of the Timurid period. This paper filigree is placed in compartments of various colors such as red, blue, green, black, and lavender.

Painted and lacquered bookbindings came into vogue in the time of Shah Tahmasp. Although at first leather was used, the covers to be painted were usually of papier-mâché, which was covered with a coat of fine plaster or gesso and then with a thin layer of lacquer. Upon this background the design was painted in water colors. For protection the painting was covered with several layers of lacquer. The lacquer paintings consist of landscapes and hunting and garden scenes in the style of contemporary Safavid miniatures. According to the Turkish historian 'Ali, the famous painter Ustad Muhammadi was among the artists who painted lacquer book covers. A number of lacquered bookbindings of the 16th century with figure subjects are known. The finest examples are those in the Museum of Decorative Arts, Paris, the Royal Asiatic Society, London, and the British Museum, London.

The decoration of 17th- and 18th-century bookbindings follows the Safavid style of the 16th century, but the lacquer technique was used more frequently. The ornament usually consists of a naturalistic floral design with bouquets of flowers predominating.

Beautiful bookbindings were also made in Turkey; the craft followed stylistic developments similar to those in Persia. The leather is usually lighter in color, and the design is often more naturalistic.

BIBLIOGRAPHY. F. Sarre, *Islamic Bookbindings*, Berlin, 1923; M. Aga-Oglu, *Persian Bookbindings of the Fifteenth Century*, Ann Arbor, Mich., 1935.

MAURICE S. DIMAND

ISLAMIC CALLIGRAPHY AND ILLUMINATION.

The art of calligraphy, or beautiful writing, was cultivated by the Muhammadans from earliest times and was often more esteemed than that of painting. There are two principal styles of Arabic writing, a formal style known as Kufic (from the town of Kufa in Mesopotamia), with angular letters, and a cursive style, or Naskhi, with rounded letters. Both types of script were already known in the 7th century.

The earliest known Koran, written in Kufic and dated A.H. 168 (A.D. 784/785), is in the Egyptian Library, Cairo. Most of the early Abbasid Korans are written on parchment, either natural or colored blue, violet, or red, in black or gold ink. The Kufic writing shows thick and rounded letters with short verticals and exaggerated horizontals. This type of Kufic was used in Egypt, Syria, and Mesopotamia during the 9th century and part of the 10th. Some of these early Korans have illuminated pages of interlacings, foliate forms, and palmette scrolls, outlined in brown ink and painted in liquid gold, with touches of red, green, blue, and ocher. The highly decorative chapter headings of these early Korans show the title in Kufic within a rectangular panel and a background of arabesque scrolls from which a stylized tree or palmettes extend.

In the 11th century the use of Kufic script became less frequent in Korans. It was gradually replaced by Naskhi script, although it continued in use for chapter headings even at a much later date. Naskhi reached the height of its development in the first half of the 12th century.

Korans of the Mamluk period, of which there are magnificent examples in the Egyptian Library, show different types of rounded script written with great care and decorative sense. The large Korans are written in Thuluth or Tumar script, both varieties of the Naskhi script. There are some highly ornamental pages composed of Arabic writing and arabesques in gold on a blue ground.

In 12th-century Korans of Spain and North Africa we find a distinctive form of writing, known as Maghribi (Western). This script, occasionally called Andalusian or Cordovan, is characterized by the very round forms of its letters. It was developed in Spain after the center of the Maghrib had been shifted from Kairwan in North Africa to Andalusia. In Maghribi Korans of the 14th and 15th centuries, copied in Granada and Fez, the writing is less careful, but the polychrome decoration is often very rich.

In early Islamic Persia writing as well as methods of book illumination were adopted from the Arabs. Persian calligraphers developed early a variation of the Abbasid Kufic script in which the verticals were more emphasized than the horizontals. From this type of Kufic evolved another one, in which the letters are rendered more angularly. In Saljuk Korans of the 11th and 12th centuries the Persian type of Kufic is fully developed and the illumination is richer, as can be seen in a Koran in the British Museum, London, dated A.H. 427 (A.D. 1036). The illuminated pages with the interlacings and arabesque scrolls are typical of Saljuk art. In some of them the Kufic letters end in arabesque scrolls with palmettes (Kufic *fleuri*).

Several dated 12th-century Korans are in existence: one is in the National Library, Paris, written in Sistan in A.H. 505 (A.D. 1111); another is in the University of Pennsylvania Museum, Philadelphia, written in A.H. 559 (A.D. 1164); and a third is in the Chester Beatty Collection, Dublin, dated Jumada I, 584 (July, 1188). There are portions of other fine Saljuk Korans in the Chester Beatty Collection, the Teheran Museum, the shrine of Imam Riza, Meshed, and the Metropolitan Museum of Art, New York. Some of the leaves show highly decorative combinations of Kufic writing and arabesque scrolls with large palmettes.

Sometime during the 13th century a variation of Naskhi writing developed in Persia known as Talik, in which the characters show a tendency to slope downward from right to left, but the more rigid Naskhi continued in use for religious texts. Under the rule of the Mongol Il-khans (1256–1335) the art of calligraphy and illumination reached a new height. A number of fine Mongol Korans, some of them made at the order of the Il-khan ruler Uljaitu Khudabanda Muhammad, exist. The best-known ones are the Koran in the German Book Museum, Leipzig, written in Baghdad in A.H. 706 (A.D. 1306/07), and the Koran in the Egyptian Library, written in Hamadan by 'Abd Allah ibn-Muhammad in A.H. 713 (A.D. 1313). The latter has several fully illuminated pages that are masterpieces of abstract ornament. The field is divided into various geometric compartments containing arabesques or rosettes in gold and blue, occasionally with the addition of green. The geometric compositions are enhanced by the use of contrasting background colors, such as gold and blue, the favorite color combination of Iranian illuminators of all periods.

In the 15th century, under the rule of the Timurids, calligraphy attained the status of a great art. One of the

Islamic calligraphy. Page of a Koran. Ambrosian Library, Milan.

most famous masters of the 15th century was Mir 'Ali of Tabriz, who is credited with the invention (ca. 1429) of Nastalik script. A beautiful example of Mir 'Ali's early work is a copy of Khwaju Kirmani's love story, *Humay and Humayun*, dated A.H. 799 (A.D. 1396/97), in the British Museum.

One of the most celebrated calligraphers of the 15th century was Sultan 'Ali al-Mashhadi, a contemporary of the painter Bihzad, who worked in Herat at the court of Husain Mirza. Among his works is a copy of Mir 'Ali Shir Nawai's *Diwan*, dated A.H. 905 (A.D. 1499/1500). Other well-known calligraphers were Ja'far Baisunkuri of Tabriz, 'Abd al-Karim of Khwarizm, and Ibrahim Sultan, son of Shah Rukh. Ibrahim Sultan was a great patron of letters and was renowned for his ability to write in six different styles. A fine Koran written by him in A.H. 827 (A.D. 1424) is in the shrine of Imam Riza in Meshed.

Timurid illumination developed a distinctive style in which naturalistic plant ornament, derived from China, is combined with birds and animals. There are several types of Timurid illumination. In one the ornament is painted in gold and outlined in black; in another, the design is in gold alone, placed on a dark blue ground. Both types of illumination were most probably developed by the artists of the Shiraz school, best known from two manuscripts, the Gulbenkian Foundation's *Anthology* (Lisbon) and the British Museum's *Compendium* of A.H. 813 (A.D. 1410).

The richly illuminated title pages of several Timurid manuscripts, particularly those made for Shah Rukh and Baisunkur Mirza, are among the most sumptuous ever produced and represent the Herat style of illumination. One of the finest manuscripts of the Herat school is the *Shahnama* of 1429–30 in the Teheran Museum. It has elaborate illuminations in polychrome created by Herat court artists. The intricate interlaced arabesques and delicate floral scrolls of these illuminations show an astounding richness of detail and brilliancy of color comparable only to those found in enamels.

The arts of calligraphy and illumination developed by the Timurid artists continued to flourish in the 16th century under the Safavid rulers. A great calligrapher of the Safavid court at Tabriz was Sultan Muhammad Nur, who copied the fine Nizami of 1524–25 in the Metropolitan Museum of Art. Shah Mahmud an-Nishapuri, who did the famous *Khamsa* of 1539–43, in the British Museum, was a famous calligrapher of the time of Shah Isma'il and Shah Tahmasp.

Mir 'Imad, whose name even today is synonymous among the Persians with beautiful writing, was a celebrated calligrapher of the 17th century. In 1660 Mir 'Imad settled in Isfahan, where he copied many manuscripts for Shah Abbas.

The illuminations of Safavid 16th-century manuscripts are as rich as those of the Timurid era. The color scheme and the ornament of the Herat illuminations of the early 16th century differ only a little from those of the 15th century. The background is usually blue, although occasionally there are smaller compartments in gold or black, and the ornament is painted in white, yellow, pink, vermilion, red, blue, and green. An interesting innovation was the gold tooling.

Illumination in gold only was highly developed by Safavid artists. Several names of 16th-century illuminators or workers in gold (*muzahib*) are known. The well-known Bukhara painter Mahmud added to his signature the cognomen *muzahib*. Many manuscripts of the 16th century have page borders with floral scrolls, landscapes, animals, and human figures, painted in liquid gold, in shades of green and yellow. These borders are as fine as miniatures themselves. The style of illumination practiced at the court of Shah Tahmasp continued through the 16th and 17th centuries. In the 17th century the colors became more vivid, and large palmettes and lanceolate leaves were often used in the ornament.

Turkish calligraphy and illumination are best known to us from tughras, or calligraphic emblems, which form headings of imperial edicts of Turkish sultans. Those of Sulaiman the Magnificent (r. 1520–66) show a floral ornament in gold, blue, and black with the addition of other colors.

See also ISLAMIC BOOKBINDING.

BIBLIOGRAPHY. C. Huart, *Les Calligraphes et les miniaturistes de l'Orient musulman*, Paris, 1908; T. Arnold and A. Grohman, *The Islamic Book*, Paris, 1929.

MAURICE S. DIMAND

ISLAMIC GLASS AND CRYSTAL.

As early as the Roman period the Near East, particularly Syria and Egypt, was famous for beautiful glassware. In the Islamic period the various techniques of decorating glass known in antiquity continued to be used in all the provinces of the Muhammadan Near East.

EARLY ISLAMIC PERIOD

Early Islamic glass is known to us chiefly from finds in Egypt, Syria, and Mesopotamia. The 9th-century glass from Samarra shows a continuation of Sassanian forms found in Ctesiphon and Kish. Until recently, very little was known about Islamic glass of Persia. The material now available comes from various sites, such as Susa, Rayy, Nishapur, and Gurgan. The Persian glass shows forms and methods of decoration known from other provinces.

Early Islamic glass consists of bottles, flasks, vases, and cups for domestic use, many of them for oil and perfume,

in a great variety of styles and sizes. The majority, which date from the 8th and 9th centuries, are plain; others are decorated by various methods, usually with molded flutes, honeycomb patterns, or other designs, including inscriptions. Of the latter type are cups and pear-shaped jugs found in Egypt, Syria, Mesopotamia, and Persia.

Another group of early Islamic vessels has a stamped decoration, usually consisting of round medallions with disks, animals, or Kufic inscriptions. In some of these vessels the pattern is produced by double stamping or by a pinching iron, a method that seems to be an invention of the Muhammadan era. The design is usually geometric, although conventionalized birds appear.

Decorating glass vessels with applied threads or disks, a technique known in the Roman period, was particularly popular in Syria. The applied threads form zigzags, wavy bands, and disks or drops, either in the same color as the vessel or, more frequently, in blue. Some of the vessels with applied decoration are shaped in the form of camels that support baskets with containers. Vessels with applied disks are also either pre-Islamic or early Islamic, for example, a bowl in the former State Museums, Berlin, showing Kufic inscriptions as well as Sassanian motifs.

An interesting group of vessels such as flasks, cups, and bowls, mostly in purple manganese, has a decoration of applied white thread ornament that is marvered flush with the surface. These threads or rods were dragged, while still hot, with a comblike tool, a process that formed various designs: chevron, herringbone, or fern patterns. Often Islamic pieces of this type are wrongly regarded as Roman. The characteristic feature of the Islamic ones is the greater thickness of the vessel walls, the majority being of purple manganese, into which the white rods are not very deeply embedded.

Another survival of antiquity is the technique of engraving and cutting glass, either by hand or, more frequently, on the wheel. Some of the engraving on glass bottles and ewers from Egypt and Syria is rather simple, consisting of horizontal bands and wavy lines. Glass vessels of the 9th century found in Samarra and in Persia show an engraved decoration of high quality. Noteworthy among the pieces found in Nishapur by an expedition of the Metropolitan Museum of Art of New York is a portion of a blue dish with an engraved decoration of vine scrolls and a geometric design in compartments. Other glass objects from Nishapur of the 9th and 10th centuries are beakers, flasks, and jugs with cut decoration.

A large group of Islamic glass of the 8th and 9th centuries consists of small, thick perfume flasks, mostly prismatic, which by means of horizontal and vertical grooves and notches are cut into the shape of molar teeth. They are made of lead glass, either blue or green, and are found in all the Islamic provinces. Two such flasks in the Metropolitan Museum's collection came from excavations in Nishapur and are probably of Persian origin. Such perfume containers were also made in cut crystal.

In a number of early Islamic vessels, chiefly from Persia but also from Mesopotamia, the wheel-cut decoration consists of raised disks or of hollow medallions placed close together to form a honeycomb pattern. In some of the Persian pieces, such as globular vessels, the raised and hollow cuts are combined. Cut ornament of this type, which probably had its prototype in crystal, was particularly popular in the Sassanian era.

The wheel cutting of glass in the early Islamic era was not limited to the above-mentioned simple forms of decoration. From Egypt, Mesopotamia, and Persia, particularly Gurgan, come pieces decorated with floral and animal patterns in relief. An important group of 9th-century fragments of crystal-clear glass with low-relief decoration was found in Samarra. These fragments of the Abbasid period may be regarded, according to Lamm, as products of Mesopotamia, probably of Baghdad, which was famous for its cut glass.

FATIMID PERIOD

Under the Fatimids the glass industry of Egypt and, to some extent, that of Syria reached a high level of development. The main centers of the Egyptian industry were al-Fustat, Madinat al-Fayum, and Alexandria, which had been the chief center of the Roman industry. Al-Fustat seems to have been the chief center under the Fatimids, and here the various techniques used in the Tulunid period were perfected. Some of the finest and most luxurious glass was made for the Fatimid court, which was known for its luxury and splendor. The decoration of Fatimid glass either is based on earlier designs or shows the new style features developed by contemporary Arabic artists.

One of the great achievements of Fatimid glassmakers of Egypt and Syria was the decoration of glass by painting with luster or enamel-like colors. Unfortunately, this type of glass is now exemplified chiefly by fragments, although several more or less complete pieces are in the Museum of Islamic Art, Cairo, the British Museum, London, and the former State Museums, Berlin. These bowls and bottles are of greenish or manganese glass and have a decoration of scrollwork, geometric patterns, or Kufic writing, painted in brown luster and silver luster respectively. Also, other rich shades of luster—gold, copper, and various other shades employed in contemporary lustered ceramics—were used by Arabic glassmakers of the 10th through the 12th century. In some of the pieces luster colors are combined, and the decoration is painted on both sides. On others the decoration is painted with enamel-like colors together with gold and silver luster.

Rich effects were often produced by the use of glass pastes, usually in turquoise blue. Fragments of glass vessels of this type imitate earlier millefiori glass, which shows spots of red, green, yellow, and white as well as tiny pieces of gold leaf pressed into the surface. Gold painting was also known to Fatimid glassmakers. Most of the pieces found in al-Fustat are not decorated with gold leaf but are painted in liquid gold, the details being scratched out with a needle. A fragmentary bottle in the British Museum, decorated with dancers, trees, and birds painted in gold and rendered in the style of Fatimid art, probably dates from the 12th century. It has a Naskhi inscription, which, however, is not complete enough to make an attribution to a particular sultan possible, although Lamm has suggested 'Imad ad-Din Zangi II (r. 1171–97), atabeg of Sinjar and for a time of Aleppo.

The cut decoration of glass vessels was brought to perfection by Fatimid glassmakers. The style of cutting and the decoration are closely related to those of objects of rock crystal, which were greatly favored by the Fatimid

Islamic glass. Vase with applied decoration. Treasury of St. Mark's, Venice.

caliphs. The historian Makrizi's description of the destruction of the treasures of Caliph Mustansir in 1062 mentions a great number of both plain and decorated crystal vessels. Many fine pieces, of various sizes, came early into the possession of European courts and churches, often as reliquaries, and were regarded as great treasures. The most beautiful crystal vessels are in the Austrian Museum of Applied Art, Vienna, the treasury of St. Mark's, Venice, the Victoria and Albert Museum, London, the Pitti Palace, Florence, and the Louvre, Paris. Several of them bear the names of Fatimid caliphs; for instance, the pear-shaped ewer in St. Mark's bears the name al-'Aziz (r. 976–996). The St. Mark's ewer, which shows two seated lions separated by an arabesque tree, is of exquisite beauty and technical perfection. Animals and birds, singly or in groups, and arabesque devices were the most favored motifs in Fatimid crystals.

The cut-glass vessels contemporary with the Fatimid crystals were probably less costly substitutes for the latter. In their decoration they equal the crystals but in technique are often inferior to them. A special group is the so-called Hedwig glasses (some of them being associated with the wine miracle of St. Hedwig), consisting mostly of beakers, of which about thirteen exist today in various European collections and museums such as the German National Museum, Nürnberg, the Rijksmuseum, Amsterdam, the Silesian Museum, Wrocław (Breslau), and the treasury of the abbey of Oignies, near Namur. There is little doubt that this group of cut glass was made in Egypt in the 11th or 12th century.

AYYUBID AND MAMLUK PERIODS

The greatest era of Muhammadan glassmaking began at the end of the 12th century, reaching its climax in the 13th century and the first half of the 14th. The richly enameled and gilded decoration of this glassware is based on earlier, particularly Fatimid, traditions. The enameling technique was perfected by the glassmakers of Syria. Glass of Aleppo and Damascus, which became the leading centers of glass manufacture in the 13th and 14th centuries, must be classified among the finest ever produced. Al-Kazwini (ca. 1203–83), in describing Aleppo, which was an important art metropolis in the 13th century, mentions its glass bazaar and the magnificent ware it exported to foreign countries. A Persian geographer, Hafiz-i-Abru, speaks of the wonderful glass of Aleppo as being decorated with elegance and taste. Glass made in Damascus was also famous, especially in the time of the Mamluk sultans. Damascus draftsmen supplied the Cairo bazaars with luxurious products, and in European inventories of the 14th and 15th centuries gilded and enameled glassware is called Damascus glass.

Some of the earliest glass of this type was attributed to Raqqa, on the Euphrates, where enameled glass fragments were found. The most important pieces of the group are the beaker of Charles the Great in the Museum of Fine Arts, Chartres, and that of the eight priests of Douai, which can be assigned to the end of the 12th century. Characteristic of the Raqqa group are pearl motifs of blue and white enamel and heavy outlines. Whether these glasses of the Raqqa group were made there or were imported from northern Syria, they are closely connected with the development of enameled and gilded glass of Syria in the Ayyubid and Mamluk periods.

The richness of the decoration and the magnificent polychromy of the vessels were admired by early travelers, pilgrims, and Crusaders, who brought back many of the fine pieces now seen in various European church treasuries and museums. More numerous than the vessels are the lamps from Cairo mosques, made to order for the Mamluk sultans and their amirs, frequently bearing their names and badges. The Museum of Islamic Art in Cairo and the Metropolitan Museum possess important collections of lamps, basins, bottles, cups, trays, and several small beakers and flasks.

The technique of gilding and enameling consisted of several processes. The glassmakers first applied the gilded decoration, using a pen for the outlines and a brush for larger surfaces. After the first firing the design was outlined in red, and the enamel in various colors was applied thickly according to the design. The semiopaque enamels consisted of a flux containing much lead and colored with metallic oxides. Green was obtained from oxide of copper; red from oxide of iron; yellow from antimonic acid; and white, which was entirely opaque, from oxide of tin. The blue enamel, which plays such a prominent part in the decoration of this glass, was made from pulverized lapis lazuli mixed with colorless glass.

The style and decoration of the enameled and gilded glass vary according to the period. In 13th-century pieces, of both the Ayyubid and Mamluk periods, figure subjects, animals, arabesques, and Arabic inscriptions were the most popular motifs. The decoration is frequently arranged in horizontal zones of various widths, separated by narrow bands. Goblets of this period and jugs and bottles with figure subjects are among the most beautiful of Islamic glass. Some of the figure subjects are polo players, hunters, and court entertainers, not unlike those seen in silver-inlaid Saljuk and Ayyubid bronzes of Mesopotamia and Syria. On some of the glass, particularly beakers and jugs, figures are drawn on a large scale, occupying the main part of the vessels. Among the most famous examples of the former type of the Ayyubid period (1st half of 13th cent.) are the goblets in the State Museum, Kassel, and in the Louvre and an early Mamluk pilgrim bottle in St. Stephan's Cathedral, Vienna.

Under the Mamluks the Syrian glassmakers continued to manufacture fine gilded and enameled vessels. From 1260 on, in the time of Sultan Bibars, Damascus became the main center of glass production, although glass probably continued to be produced in Aleppo, Egypt, Mesopotamia, Asia Minor, and Persia. Even China imported fine glass vessels from Syria. Mamluk gilded and enameled glass can be divided into two groups: the early Mamluk (2d half of 13th cent.) and the late Mamluk (chiefly 14th cent.). Two most important early Mamluk pieces are the pilgrim bottle in the Museum of Art History, Vienna, and the cup in the Moore Collection of the Metropolitan Museum. The former is decorated with palmette scrolls and large figure subjects in medallions. The Moore cup is decorated with horizontal bands containing running animals, seated musicians, and drinkers. A noteworthy feature of this cup and of other early Mamluk pieces is the predominance of gilded decoration over enameled decoration, which is often confined to smaller surfaces than in the Ayyubid period.

The largest group of gilded and enameled glass of the Mamluk period consists of mosque lamps made to the order of the sultans and amirs as donations to Cairo mosques. Many of them are inscribed with the names of the sultans and their officials, permitting us to date them exactly. The mosque lamps date from the late 13th and the 14th century and reveal the changes of style brought about by Chinese influences introduced by the Mongols. The decoration of these lamps includes, besides large inscriptions and medallions with badges, arabesques and naturalistic floral motifs of Chinese origin, which gradually replaced the traditional abstract patterns. One of the earliest lamps in the Metropolitan Museum's collection was made for the mausoleum of the amir Aidakin al-Bundukdar (d. 1285), who was the commander of the arbalesters, as the badge showing two bows bound together indicates.

Two lamps in the Metropolitan Museum of the early 14th century are made of blue glass. One of them bears the name of the Mamluk sultan al-Muzaffar Rukn ad-Din Bibars II (r. 1308–09). The finely executed floral decoration of this lamp shows, besides the naturalistic lotus scrolls, a vine ornament that appears in a number of Mamluk lamps. Design and enameling of unusually high quality characterize the early period of Nasir Muhammad (1293–1340). Several lamps in the Metropolitan Museum represent this era. One of the finest, bearing the name of this sultan, was made for a hospice founded by Karim ad-Din and was found in the cemetery of al-Karafa near Cairo. Another, a few years later in date, was made for

Saif ad-Din Kusun, the cupbearer of Sultan Malik an-Nasir, whose badge, a red cup, appears in several medallions. It was probably made for his mosque, which was erected in 1329–30. This lamp is of special interest as it bears on the foot the name of the glassmaker, 'Ali ibn-Muhammad Amaki (or ar-Ramaki or az-Zamaki), who also made two other lamps, one now in the Museum of Islamic Art and the other in the Museum of Fine Arts in Boston. A lamp in the Metropolitan Museum, inscribed with the name of Sultan Nasir Muhammad and the badge of an anonymous cupbearer, shows a type of decoration that is quite different from the usual one. The name and title of the Sultan appear in three small medallions beneath the body, and the rest of the lamp has a naturalistic floral decoration of large rosettes and lotus palmettes placed between medallions with arabesques and badges.

Syrian glassmakers of the first half of the 14th century did not confine themselves to the manufacture of mosque lamps. Various vessels, such as vases, bottles, buckets, dishes, and cups of different sizes, were magnificently decorated. Their decoration is similar to that of the mosque lamps, but often representations of animals and human beings are added. A few of the vessels were made for the Rasulid sultans of Yemen, for instance, the Rothschild bottle in the Freer Gallery, Washington, D.C., inscribed with the name of Sultan Mujahid 'Ali (r. 1321–63).

A famous bottle, formerly in the Museum of Art History, Vienna, which came into the possession of the Hapsburgs in 1825, is now in the Metropolitan Museum. This large bottle may be considered one of the masterpieces of medieval Islamic glass. The gilded and enameled decoration covers almost the entire surface of the bottle. In the richness and brilliance of the enamel and in the perfection of the design, it surpasses most of the Mamluk glass. The main part of the body is decorated with a frieze of fighting warriors on horseback, armed with swords, lances, bows and arrows, and maces. The headgear of the warriors varies; some wear turbans and others wear Mongol caps and helmets. Of particular interest is the richness of color in the warrior frieze. The neck of the bottle has a broad band decorated with a Chinese phoenix, whose wings spread all around the neck. The narrow bands above and below contain scrolls or bird motifs. The Chinese influence and the naturalistic style of the landscape and figures indicate that the bottle dates from the beginning of the 14th century, probably about 1320.

The style of enameled lamps and vessels developed under Nasir Muhammad continued in the second half of the 14th century, but the numerous dated lamps show a gradual decline in both design and technique. The Museum of Islamic Art possesses a number of lamps inscribed with the name of Sultan Malik Nasir Hasan (r. 1347–60), some of which came from his madrasa, built in 1362. They are decorated in the traditional style or with an allover floral pattern that covers every inch of the glass.

LATE PERSIAN GLASSWARE

Under Shah Abbas I the Great (r. 1587–1628) a renaissance of glassmaking took place in Persia, most probably under European influence, chiefly Italian. From the *Travels* of Chardin, who visited Persia between 1664 and 1681, we learn that glass vessels were made at Shiraz and Isfahan, the former producing the best in the country. The supe-

riority of Shiraz glass is confirmed in the writings of other travelers. In the early 19th century, under the Kajar dynasty, glassmaking was still "... prosecuted with sufficient diligence and success," as we learn from the *Travels* (1817–20) of Sir Robert Ker Porter, who notes that window glass, bottles, and goblets made at Shiraz "... though not of the most elegant sort, are vendable all over the kingdom."

Persian glass, such as bottles, ewers, and dishes, continued to be made in the 18th and 19th centuries. The glass is white, amber, violet, green, or blue. Some pieces are decorated with painting and gilding; others have simple molded ornament. The painted and gilded decorations are coarsely executed as a rule, and the most attractive specimens are those that depend solely on the beauty of form and the color of the glass for their effect.

BIBLIOGRAPHY. G. Schmoranz, *Altorientalische Glassgefässe*, Vienna, 1898; G. Wiet, *Lampes et bouteilles en verre émaillé*, Cairo, 1929; C. J. Lamm, *Mittelalterliche Gläser und Steinschnittarbeiten aus dem Nahen Osten*, 2 vols., Berlin, 1929–30; A. U. Pope, *A Survey of Persian Art*, vols. 3, 6, New York, 1939.

MAURICE S. DIMAND

ISLAMIC METALWORK.

The continuation of the pre-Islamic Sassanian style of decoration is strongly apparent in early Islamic metalwork from Persia (7th–9th cent.), particularly in silver vessels, some of which are often wrongly assigned to the Sassanian era. Several silver dishes with hunting scenes and other purely Sassanian figure subjects in the Hermitage, Leningrad, belong to the early Islamic period. Some of them bear the names of their owners in Pahlavi, which permits a dating to the 8th century. Silver vessels with representations of animals and birds form an important group of post-Sassanian metalwork. Among the most popular animals of Sassanian art was the fantastic winged monster, *senmurv*, or hippocampus, part bird, part lion, and part dog. A silver dish in the British Museum, London, decorated with a *senmurv* is generally assigned to the 8th or 9th century. As in so many post-Sassanian silver vessels, the engraving plays a much more important role than the relief.

Two post-Sassanian silver jugs in the Hermitage with engraved decoration of birds and griffins within interlaced compartments are definitely of the Islamic era, since they bear Kufic inscriptions of about the 10th century. Both jugs may be examples of the little-known metalwork of the Samanids, who ruled in Khurasan and Transoxiana during the 10th century.

In the Gulistan Museum, Teheran, is a group of nine silver vessels, vases, ewers, and plates, found in Persia, decorated with bands of Kufic inscriptions in niello, giving the name of Amir Abu'l-Abbas Walkin ibn-Harun, who lived in Azerbaijan in 957.

Post-Sassanian bronze vessels can be divided into three groups: trays and plates, ewers, and aquamaniles in the shape of animals and birds. The decoration of early Islamic bronze plates and trays is engraved or in low relief, derived from Sassanian and East Hellenistic sources. A characteristic example of this type is a dish in the Hermitage with a plant decoration of vine trees and scrolls, stylized in a manner known from Umayyad and early Abbasid monuments and objects.

Early Islamic bronze ewers are either plain or have an engraved relief decoration, sometimes inlaid with copper. The shape of some of these ewers is Sassanian; others are

Islamic metalwork. Bronze jug, 7th century. Museum of Islamic Art, Cairo.

variations of this type or show new forms created by Persian artists of the 8th century. Of great importance is a small group of early Islamic bronze ewers in which the decoration, engraved and in relief, is enhanced by an inlay of red copper. Most of the ewers are in the Hermitage and were found in the Caucasus, in Daghestan. A ewer of this group with a decoration of pomegranate trees and palmette devices in low relief, partly inlaid with copper, is in the Walters Art Gallery, Baltimore. This group, which can be dated to the 8th century, represents the work of the earliest Islamic school of inlay technique, probably of the province of Khurasan.

Another type of early Islamic bronze vessel has a globular body and long tubular neck with a spout in the shape of birds. Six ewers of this type are extant: two in the Hermitage; two in the Museum of Islamic Art, Cairo, one of which is in the Harari Collection; one formerly in the collection of Countess Tortillia in Alexandria; and one in the Metropolitan Museum of Art, New York. Related to

these Persian ewers are bronze aquamaniles in the shape of animals and birds.

SALJUK PERIOD

With the arrival of the Saljuks in eastern Persia in 1037 a brilliant era in Islamic metalwork began. The vessels of gold, silver, and bronze reveal new ornament and schemes of decoration developed by the artists of the Saljuk period. The majority of Saljuk silver vessels, which date from the 11th to the 13th century, are in the Hermitage. The group consists of bowls, vases, and bottles with figure subjects, birds, animals, arabesques, interlacings, and Kufic inscriptions on a background of fine scrollwork.

The art of casting bronze objects such as mirrors, plaques, and animal figures with relief decoration was practiced under the Saljuks in both Persian and Mesopotamia. Two dated mirrors, one of A.H. 548 (A.D. 1153), the other of A.H. 675 (A.D. 1276), in the Harari Collection in the Museum of Islamic Art, are decorated with signs of the zodiac and a frieze of running animals. This type of decoration also appears on mirrors in the Louvre, Paris, and in the Metropolitan Museum. Other Saljuk mirrors show figure subjects, such as hunting scenes and the story of Bahram Gur and Azada.

Saljuk bronzes with engraved decoration, partly in low relief, include a great variety of objects for daily use such as ewers, kettles, mortars, candlesticks, lamps, incense burners, and boxes. These can be seen in various museums of Europe and the United States and are mostly of Persian origin. The decoration consists of birds, animals, arabesque scrolls, and inscriptions. Engraving combined with openwork was skillfully employed by Persian metalworkers for the decoration of candlesticks and incense burners, often in the shape of animals and birds. One of the largest and most important incense burners in the shape of a feline is in the Metropolitan Museum. It is 33 inches high and 31 inches long and was found in the ruins of Kariz near the modern town of Tayyabad, in the province of Khurasan, near the Afghanistan border. The rich openwork decoration consists of interlaced bands filled with double palmette leaves. In addition, there are arabesque scrolls and bands of Kufic inscriptions giving the name of the owner, the artist, and the date. The inscription reads: "Ordered by the Amir, the Just, the Wise Saif ad-Dunya wad-Din Muhammad al-Mawardi. The name of the artist is Ja'far ibn-Muhammad ibn-'Ali, who made this piece in the year A.H. 577 [A.D. 1181–82]." This 12th-century piece was undoubtedly a product of Khurasan, which in the time of the Saljuk was famous for its fine metalwork. Other well-known centers were Herat, Nishapur, Merv (Marv), and Sistan.

Saljuk metalworkers developed and perfected the technique of inlaying objects of bronze and brass with other metals such as copper and silver. There is conclusive evidence that the beginnings of this technique were in eastern Persia, particularly the province of Khurasan. Then it spread westward to the rest of Persia, to Mesopotamia, and to Syria. By the 13th century Mosul, in northern Mesopotamia, had become a famous center of Islamic inlay work.

As in the pre-Saljuk era, Persian metalwork of the 11th, 12th, and early 13th centuries was made of bronze (alloy of copper and tin) and not of brass (alloy of copper and zinc), as was usual in Mosul work and in later Persian work. Some of the vessels were inlaid in the traditional Persian manner, that is, with copper only; others were inlaid with copper and silver or with silver alone. A bronze vessel which is of the greatest importance in establishing the priority of Persia in the development of inlay technique is a kettle in the Hermitage, which is inscribed not only with the names of the makers but also with the place of manufacture. It was made in Herat by Muhammad ibn-al-Wahid and inlaid by Hajib Mas'ud ibn-Ahmad in A.H. 559 (A.D. 1163). The decoration, inlaid with copper and silver, consists of five horizontal bands, two with representations of warriors, hunters, and scenes depicting Saljuk festivities. Of particular interest are the animated inscriptions whose letters end in bodies or heads of humans or beasts. This type of writing was probably developed in the province of Khurasan and appears almost exclusively in Saljuk metalwork from Persia.

A group of candlesticks and related ewers with fluted or duodecagonal bodies forms an important part of Saljuk metalwork. A characteristic feature of these bronzes is the embossed decoration of birds and animals, mostly lions, in relief and in the round. The bodies of these candlesticks show rows of embossed hexagons with arabesques, lotus rosettes, and seven-disk rosettes inlaid with silver and copper. The ewers of this group, which is peculiar to Persia, show fluted or duodecagonal bodies, with straight necks and spouts turned upward. Several of them, inlaid with copper and silver, are of the 12th century. Some of the ewers (in the Harari Collection in the Museum of Islamic Art, in the Hermitage, and in the former State Museums, Berlin), in which the inlay of copper and silver is sparingly applied, can be dated to the 12th century. Others, in which the silver inlay is richer (two ewers in the British Museum, one in the Gulistan Museum, and one in the Louvre), should be dated to the beginning of the 13th century. Typical of the early-13th-century group is a ewer that was formerly in the J. P. Morgan Collection and is now in the Metropolitan Museum. The body has an allover pattern of interlacings, which end in heads of various animals and form twelve compartments containing signs of the zodiac and symbols of the planets. Ewers of this type and related candlesticks have been attributed for a long time to northern Persia or Armenia. All evidence known to us at the present time indicates, however, that they should be assigned to the province of Khurasan in Persia. The later Saljuk ewers, showing Mosul influence, were made most probably in western Persia.

Mosul school. The rich copper mines in Arghana Ma'adin (Engani Maden) and Ma'adin Khapur (Maden Khapur), both now in Turkey, supplied Mesopotamia and Syria with the ore for the manufacture of brass and bronze objects. The most important center of silver-inlaid metalwork during the 13th century in Mesopotamia was Mosul, which from 1127 to 1262 was in the hands of the Saljuk atabegs of the Zangid dynasty, great patrons of arts and crafts. There are about twenty-six pieces signed by Mosul artists, the earliest of which is a small box in the Benaki Museum, Athens, dated A.H. 617 (A.D. 1220). From a technical point of view, the Mosul school shows a definite advance in inlay technique. The engraved outlines so prominent in Persian metalwork gradually become subordinated to the

inlay. An outstanding piece of the Mosul school is a brass ewer in the British Museum, the work of Shuja ibn-Man'a of Mosul, made in Mosul in the month of Rajab, 629 (March, 1232). Every inch of the surface is inlaid with silver, and the whole background is covered by a meander pattern, which was greatly favored by Mosul metalworkers. The decoration consists of court scenes, hunting scenes, and a frieze of "animated" inscriptions.

Four brass objects with silver inlay bearing the name of Sultan Badr ad-Din Lulu (r. 1233–59) of Mosul are known. The outstanding pieces of this group are the basin in the Bavarian State Library, Munich, and a box and an astronomical table in the British Museum, dated A.H. 699 (A.D. 1241–42).

AYYUBID PERIOD
During the 13th century Mosul metalworkers frequently migrated to Syria and Egypt, working for the Ayyubid princes in Damascus, Aleppo, and Cairo. The style they took with them is that of the Mosul school, and it is often difficult to say where a piece was made unless the inscriptions indicate it. A brass ewer in the Louvre with the name of the Ayyubid sultan Malik Nasir Yusuf of Aleppo and Damascus (r. 1226–60), dated A.H. 657 (A.D. 1259), was made in Damascus by an artist from Mosul.

Of great interest to students of Islamic metalwork are vessels with Christian subjects, several of them inscribed with the names of Ayyubid sultans. Some of the Ayyubids, particularly those of Damascus, were tolerant toward Christians and at times were even allied with the kingdom of Jerusalem. A famous piece of this group is a basin from the Duke of Arenberg Collection, now in the Freer Gallery, Washington, D.C. It is inscribed with the name of the Ayyubid sultan Salih Ayyub of Egypt and Damascus (r. 1240–49). A unique bronze canteen, formerly in the Eumorfopoulos Collection and now in the Freer Gallery, is richly decorated with scenes from the life of Christ and figures of saints and fighting warriors, combined with the usual decoration found on other Islamic vessels of the period. Some of the warriors, shooting with European crossbows, probably represent Crusaders. The piece might have been made for a Christian prince, probably in Damascus about the middle of the 13th century.

MAMLUK PERIOD
Under the rule of the Mamluk sultans of Syria and Egypt fine metalwork was produced in Damascus, Aleppo, and Cairo, where the work was carried on by artists from Mosul and later by native craftsmen. The height of Mamluk metalwork was reached under the sultan Nasir ad-Din Muhammad ibn-Kalaun (r. 1293–94, 1308, and 1309–40). A number of pieces are known that bear the name of this Mamluk ruler or of his courtiers. A magnificent piece of this period is the kursi, or table, in the Museum of Islamic Art, dated A.H. 726 (A.D. 1327), richly decorated with silver and gold inlay.

Mamluk metalwork shows distinctive features that permit us to identify it as such. New decorative motifs have been added to the traditional arabesques. Most frequent among these are pairs of birds in compartments, which occasionally are arranged in a lozenge diaper. Other elements gradually invading the ornament are naturalistic motifs such as leaves and peonies, derived from Chinese art. This style came into the Near East in the second half of the 13th century with the Mongol conquest. Floral motifs of this kind as well as flying ducks often surround official blazons and medallions with the titles and the names of the early Mamluks and their courtiers. A typical example of this type is a basin in the British Museum, inscribed with the name of Nasir Muhammad. Another distinctive feature is the use of medallions with a Z meander, regarded as one of the characteristics of the Damascus school of inlay. The Damascus group shows an inlay technique of unusually high perfection. Brass objects such as writing cases, incense burners, and dishes are profusely inlaid with silver and gold, as can be seen in several fine pieces of this type in the Metropolitan Museum, the British Museum, and other collections.

Several brass bowls and basins of the late 13th and early 14th century, decorated with large figure compositions such as hunting scenes and combats, should also be assigned to Mamluk artists. The most famous piece of this group is the so-called Baptistery of St. Louis, in the Louvre, made by Muhammad ibn-al-Zain. The rich silver inlay of this basin and of other pieces of the group shows fine detail work in the rendering of the human figures and animals.

All through the 14th century the Mamluk metalwork made in Cairo and Syria was still of good quality. The style evolved in Nasir Muhammad's time was further developed. The naturalistic floral motifs became more evident in later work, as may be seen on a pen box in the Museum of Islamic Art, which is inscribed with the name of the sultan Mansur Salah ad-Din Muhammad (r. 1360–62).

After 1400 the quality of the metalwork produced in Egypt and Syria declined considerably. Makrizi, writing in 1420, makes the following comment: "The demand for inlaid ... copper [brass] work has fallen off in our time [in Cairo], and since many years the people have turned away from purchasing ... so that but a small remnant of the workers of inlay survive in this market." There are several objects known which bear the name of the Mamluk sultan Kait Bey (Kait Bay, r. 1468–96). A basin in the Top Kapu Serai, Istanbul, decorated with geometric interlacings, arabesques, and foliated scrolls was made for him.

RASULID PERIOD

Many silver-inlaid objects such as trays, braziers, and candlesticks were made in Cairo for the Rasulid sultans of Yemen, who were on friendly terms with the Mamluk sultans. A ewer in the Museum of Decorative Arts, Paris, inscribed with the name of al-Muzaffar Yusuf (r. 1250–95), was made in Cairo by 'Ali ibn-Husain ibn-Muhammad of Mosul in A.H. 674 (A.D. 1275). A rare and exceptionally fine brazier in the Metropolitan Museum bears the name of the same Rasulid sultan. It is richly decorated in Mamluk style with arabesques, Arabic inscriptions, and a frieze of animals. It has several five-petaled rosettes, which, as a badge of the Rasulids, occur on all the work made for these sultans.

MONGOL PERIOD

Persian metalwork of the Mongol period shows a decoration often similar to that of the Mosul school and of the Mamluk work of Syria and Egypt. There are, however, certain stylistic features peculiar to Persia. Some of the pieces bear inscriptions with the titles or, more rarely, the names of the Mongol rulers (Il-khans) of Persia. Definitely

Mongol are three bronze balls inlaid with silver and gold in the Harari Collection in the Museum of Islamic Art, Cairo, bearing the name of the sultan Uljaitu Khudabanda Muhammad (r. 1304–16) and showing a mixture of Syrian and Persian motifs.

In the second half of the 14th century the distinctive Persian features of Mongol metalwork are more strongly pronounced. Several dated pieces give us a basis for classifying this material. An important group of Mongol metalwork of the second half of the 14th century consists of bowls inlaid with silver and gold and decorated with figure subjects depicting court life, garden parties, and polo games, combined with naturalistic plants. The figures are conventionalized, often elongated, as in certain late Mongol miniature paintings. Most of the figures wear "sugar loaf" caps, which are shown in miniature paintings of Khwaju Kirmani's *Diwan* of 1396–97 in the British Museum.

SAFAVID PERIOD

The inlaying of brass objects with silver, which declined considerably in Persia during the 15th century, continued to be practiced in the 16th century under the Safavids. Copper vessels were often tinned to simulate silver, and iron and steel became popular. The decoration reflected the changing fashions of the time. The relief decoration consists mostly of arabesques, a pattern of animals and floral scrolls. The more luxurious type of Safavid metalwork is known to us from a very few bottles preserved in the Top Kapu Serai, Istanbul. They are of silver alloy, and in addition to an applied or inlaid gold decoration they are enriched with precious stones such as rubies, turquoises, and emeralds. According to tradition, the treasure in Istanbul was a part of the booty of Sultan Selim I in the war against the Persians under Shah Isma'il in 1514. Sixteenth-century Safavid brass candlesticks with engraved and relief decoration are pillar-shaped and sometimes are dated. The inscriptions on such candlesticks are usually taken from the Persian poem "The Moth and the Candle." The decoration consists of arabesques and floral scrolls, usually covering the whole surface but occasionally confined in compartments.

The Persian metalworkers of the 16th and 17th centuries achieved great skill in the handling of iron and steel and produced some excellent pieces that, technically, are not inferior to earlier work. Steel plaques, belts, arms, and armor show an openwork decoration or are damascened with gold. Persian metalworkers of the late 17th and 18th centuries continued the technique and conventional decorative schemes of the Safavid style of the 16th century, but the workmanship is inferior to that of earlier objects.

BIBLIOGRAPHY. F. Sarre and M. van Berchem, "Das Metallbecken des Atabeks Lulu von Mosul ...," *Münchener Jahrbuch der bildenden Kunst*, 1907; Y. I. Smirnov, *Argenterie Orientale*, St. Petersburg, 1909; M. S. Dimand, "Unpublished Metalwork of the Rasūlid Sultans of Yemen," *Metropolitan Museum Studies*, III, 1930–31; R. Harari, "Metalwork after the Early Islamic Period," in A. U. Pope, ed., *A Survey of Persian Art*, vols. 3, 6, New York, 1939; D. Barrett, *Islamic Metalwork in the British Museum*, London, 1949; D. S. Rice, *Le Baptistère de Saint-Louis*, Paris, 1951.

MAURICE S. DIMAND

ISLAMIC PAINTING. The early history of Islamic painting is still little known to us, but from the few monuments that have been discovered or unearthed in Syria, Mesopotamia, and Iran we can get at least some idea of the richness and splendor of wall decoration under the Umayyads and early Abbasids.

UMAYYAD AND EARLY ABBASID PERIODS

The earliest paintings that have been found thus far in Syria are preserved in Kuseir 'Amra (Qusayr 'Amra), a little desert lodge with a bath near Amman, Jordan, built by the Umayyad caliph Walid I about 712. The French archaeologist Schlumberger discovered in the ruins of Kasr (Qasr) al-Hair al-Gharbi, in Syria, an 8th-century palace with two magnificent frescoes, one Hellenistic, the other entirely Sassanian in style. *See* SASSANIAN ART.

Sixty miles north of Baghdad, in Mesopotamia, was the city of Samarra, founded in 836 by the caliph Mu'tasim as his new residence. The Abbasid caliphs resided in Samarra only fifty-six years, abandoning it in 892. The excavations in Samarra conducted by Sarre and Herzfeld have brought to light a city of great splendor and luxury. The walls of the principal rooms of the palace were adorned with wall paintings and carved stucco dadoes. The tradition of Sassanian art is quite evident in the wall paintings of the harem, which show dancing girls, musicians, animals, and birds, enclosed in floral scrolls. The dancers wear Persian garments and the typical Persian cap, or kulah. The frescoes of the throne room show male and female figures that are clearly of Sassanian origin.

A Persian school of painting contemporary with Samarra existed in Nishapur, a city in the eastern province of Khurasan, famous as the birthplace of Omar Khayyam. Excavations conducted by the Metropolitan Museum of Art, New York, unearthed buildings decorated with wall paintings of the 8th and 9th centuries in both monochrome and polychrome. One of the most interesting paintings, now in the Teheran Museum, done in black outline and wash, represents a mounted hunter, possibly a local prince of the Tahirid dynasty, wearing a rich costume, a helmet, two swords, and a round shield. He carries a hunting falcon, and attached to his saddle is the quarry, probably a deer. Also of importance for the history of Persian painting are several decorative panels found in a palace building at Nishapur. These panels, forming a dado about 4 feet high, were decorated with abstract compositions of huge palmette leaves, pomegranates, and pine cones painted in white, blue, red, and black. This ornament recalls the Abbasid ornament from Samarra stuccoes and paintings and also the lustered tiles of Kairwan, which were made in Baghdad.

Ghaznavid school. There is literary evidence that interest in the art of painting in eastern Iran existed at the courts of the Samanids and Ghaznavids. Sultan Mahmud of Ghazni (r. 998–1030) established an academy of painting under the direction of Abu Nasr. At his court resided the celebrated poet Firdausi, whose famous epic poem, the *Shah-nama* (Book of Kings), completed in 1010, inspired Persian painters through the ages. The walls of Firdausi's room at the palace were covered with paintings representing kings and heroes of Iran and Turan, with their horses, elephants, camels, and tigers.

Actual Ghaznavid paintings, dating from the early 11th century, were discovered by Schlumberger in a palace in Lashkari Bazar. The lower parts of the audience hall were covered with frescoes, while the upper part had cut-brick

decoration. The wall paintings show a continuous frieze of forty-four standing figures of the Turkish guard, the men represented in front view and dressed in long belted kaftans made of richly decorated fabrics.

SALJUK PERIOD

The conquest of Iran by the Turkish Saljuks in the 11th century inaugurated one of the most brilliant periods of Islamic art. In 1055 Tughril Beg entered Baghdad and was proclaimed sultan by the caliph. The Saljuks and their followers, the atabegs, were masters of Iran, Mesopotamia, Syria, and Asia Minor during the 11th, 12th, and 13th centuries. Their courts, in Marv, Rayy, Nishapur, Herat, Mosul, Baghdad, and Konia, became centers of Islamic art and culture. Here artists, working for their rulers, produced some of the finest works of art in ceramics, metalwork, weaving, and painting. In the 12th century the Saljuk style of painting was fully developed. The true miniature style of Saljuk painting in Persia survived in ceramics with lustered decoration and in a polychrome ware in which the decoration is painted over a white or sometimes a blue tin glaze. The polychrome, or Minai, ware is associated with two important Persian art centers, Rayy and Kashan. The rich decoration of this pottery consists of figure subjects such as court scenes, hunting scenes, and legendary episodes from the *Shah-nama*. The story of Bahram Gur and his mistress Azada is depicted on two fine bowls from the John Schiff Collection, now in the Metropolitan Museum; others are in the Freer Gallery, Washington, D.C. The styles of figures here and the conventionalized plants are related to some of the 13th-century miniature paintings of the Mesopotamian or Baghdad school. *See* ISLAMIC POTTERY AND TILES (SALJUK PERIOD).

Baghdad school. The center of the Mesopotamian school of painting was Baghdad. One of the earliest illustrated manuscripts of that school is the *Kitab al-baitara* (Book on Hippiatry), in the Egyptian Library, Cairo, completed in Baghdad at the end of March, 1209. It contains thirty-nine miniatures related in style to the paintings of the *Materia Medica* of 1224. Three main artistic sources, East Christian, Persian, and Turkish-Saljuk, contributed to the formation of the style, which is called Abbasid, Mesopotamian, or Baghdad. Under the Saljuks, Baghdad retained its importance as the cultural and artistic center of the Muslim world. But the artistic activities of Mesopotamia were not limited to Baghdad alone. Other local schools existed at the courts of Saljuk atabegs in Mosul, Diarbakr-Amida (now in Turkey), and other places.

The most popular books illustrated by painters of the 12th and 13th centuries were the *Makamat* (Assemblies) of al-Hariri; the *Kalila wa Dimna*, a collection of fables; and various books on plants, animals, and medicine, translated from the Syriac into Arabic. A manuscript of the *Materia Medica* (in the shrine at Meshed, in eastern Persia) was translated for the Ortukid prince Najim ad-Din Alfi (r. 1152–76) of Maridin (Mardin; now in southern Turkey). The few miniatures in which human figures are represented show the influence of Syriac painting. In 1181 Nur ad-Din Muhammad, the Ortukid sultan of Diarbakr, commissioned al-Jazari to write a treatise on his inventions, which included water clocks and various other automatic contrivances. The work, known as *Automata*, was completed in 1206. An illustrated copy, dated 1254, is in the

Islamic painting. Illustration from the *Khamsa* of Nizami, detail with the Mecca shown in aerial perspective. British Museum, London.

Top Kapu Serai Library, Istanbul. This work was particularly popular in the 14th century under the Mamluks of Egypt and Syria.

Several important 13th-century illustrated manuscripts are generally attributed to the Baghdad school of painting. Among them are about twenty miniatures from a manuscript of *Materia Medica*, an Arabic version of the Greek work by Dioscorides. These paintings, which are in various museums and collections of Europe and the United States, came originally from a manuscript dated 1224 and copied by 'Abd Allah ibn-al-Fazl. It is still preserved in the Top Kapu Serai Library. The miniatures illustrate the preparation of medicine, medical consultations, and operations. It is probable that ibn-al-Fazl was not only the calligrapher but also the painter of the illustrations. The style, derived from Syrian and Iranian sources, is simple but vigorous and is based on keen observation of Arabic life.

One of the most popular books of Arabic literature was the *Makamat*, written in the early 12th century by al-Hariri of Basra. In fifty recitals, or assemblies, the adventures of Abu Zaid, an Arab vagabond, are narrated by al-Harith ibn-Hammam. Written in prose and verse, the *Makamat* became a classic even during the author's lifetime. Soon after its appearance Arab artists began to illustrate the many stories of this book. Several illustrated copies are in existence, the best known being those in the National Library, Paris. The paintings of these manuscripts reveal the different styles that prevailed in Baghdad and the rest of Mesopotamia in the 12th and 13th centuries. In one copy, dated 1222/23, the figure subjects show the influence of Christian paintings found in Syriac manuscripts.

The most important copy of the *Makamat*, now in the National Library, Paris, was completed in May, 1237, by Yahya ibn-Mahmud al-Wasiti. Yahya from Wasit was not only the calligrapher of this manuscript but also the painter of the ninety-nine large illustrations, which are generally regarded as masterpieces of early Islamic painting. The fifty assemblies of the *Makamat* gave Yahya an unusual opportunity to depict the daily life of the 13th-century Arabs from birth to death. Yahya's style shows a synthesis of realism and stylization, with great freedom of drawing characterizing his work. Many of the faces, full of expression, are excellent character studies of 13th-century Arabs; and his horses, donkeys, and camels are full of life and animation. The compositions are frequently quite elaborate and show many artistic conventions that were adopted by Persian painters of the 14th and 15th centuries. In a number of paintings the artist grouped his figures closely together, thus giving the illusion of a great mass of people. Another feature of Yahya's style is the foreshortening of the figures of animals as seen from the rear, thus giving a suggestion of depth. His palette is rather rich but restrained in tone.

MONGOL PERIOD

Of great importance for the development of Persian painting was the Mongol invasion. Under the leadership of Chingiz (Genghis) Khan, the Mongols conquered many lands until their empire stretched from China to southern Russia. Before his death Chingiz Khan (r. 1206–27) divided the vast Mongol empire among his sons. Persia fell to the lot of Hulagu, who established the powerful Il-khan dynasty, which ruled successfully from 1256 to 1335. In 1258 Hulagu captured Baghdad, which was destroyed and looted.

In the beginning the Mongols were under the influence

of the Turkish Uighurs, who became their first teachers. Baghdad was rebuilt and again became an important cultural and artistic center. The Mongols began to assimilate the superior Persian culture and became enthusiastic patrons of art and learning. In Baghdad, Sultanieh, and Tabriz, the capital of the empire, the Il-khans established ateliers devoted to the various arts and crafts. They opened the doors of Persia to foreign influence, which came not only from the Far East but also from the Christian world. Buddhist priests, physicians, artists, and craftsmen came from China, bringing with them Chinese culture and art. Buddhist temples were built in Persia, as some of the Il-khans were adherents of Buddhism. The one built by Arghun (r. 1284–91) was decorated with frescoes representing Buddhist divinities and a portrait of the Emperor. In time, the Il-khans became Muhammadans and as such greatly encouraged Islamic art and literature. To their courts in Tabriz, Maragha, and Sultanieh came artists from all the provinces of the empire. Hulagu's library in Maragha contained manuscripts from all the conquered countries, including China.

The Mongol school of painting inaugurated one of the most important periods in the history of Persian painting. In the Mongol period (late 13th–14th cent.) several styles are discernible. These may be briefly characterized as Mesopotamian, Sino-Mongolian (a style in which Chinese and Central Asian elements are mixed), and Persian. Each of these styles played an important part in the gradual formation of a new Persian school of painting.

The earliest known manuscript of the Mongol period is the Persian copy of ibn-Bakhtishu's *Manafi al-Hayawan* (Description of Animals), in the Pierpont Morgan Library, New York. According to an inscription, this important manuscript was copied in Maragha at the order of the Il-khan ruler Ghazan Khan (r. 1295–1304). Its ninety-four illustrations show several styles. Twelve large animal pictures, among them a leopard, an elephant, and a rhinoceros, show the survival of the realistic style of the Mesopotamian school of the 13th century. To this group belongs the painting representing the first man and woman, depicted by the artist as Indians and probably derived from a fresco in one of the Buddhist temples built by the Il-khans. The second group of illustrations is stylistically in complete contrast to those of the polychrome Mesopotamian group. They are executed in a summary, impressionistic manner with little or no color, in imitation of ink paintings of the Chinese Sung and Yüan dynasties. Other illustrations show variations of the Chinese style with additions of Persian features.

The development of the Mongol school of Persian painting was greatly influenced by the historian Rashid ad-Din, the vizier of the emperors Ghazan and Uljaitu. He developed a new suburb in the vicinity of Tabriz called Rab-i-Rashidi, which had houses, shops, paper mills, caravansaries, hospitals, and a library of 60,000 volumes, including works on science and art in various languages. Artists and artisans of various nationalities were brought to Rab-i-Rashidi, and in the "streets of the savants" between 6,000 and 7,000 students and numerous professors were quartered. The arts of the book were especially favored by Rashid ad-Din. Various works, but mainly his own, were copied and illustrated by competent calligraphers and paint-ers. Of the copies of the *Jami at Tawarikh* made in his lifetime (he was executed in 1318), only a few fragmentary volumes have survived. The most important is a manuscript preserved in two parts: one, dated A.H. 707 (A.D. 1307), contains a history of the prophets, the early Persian kings, and the life of Muhammad and is in the library of Edinburgh University; the other, dated A.H. 714 (A.D. 1314), contains the history of India and part of the history of the Jews and is in the Royal Asiatic Society, London. The style of these paintings is entirely linear in the Chinese manner, in which color plays a subordinate role.

Although of foreign origin, the Il-khan dynasty encouraged its court painters to illustrate copies of the *Shah-nama* of Firdausi. This great work is based partly on history, partly on ancient legends of Persia. One of the earliest and most important Mongol copies, known as the Demotte *Shah-nama*, was probably begun about 1320 and was richly illustrated by several artists who worked at Tabriz for the Il-khan Abu Said (r. 1317–35).

The large illustrations of the Demotte *Shah-nama*, about fifty-five in all, now in various museums and private collections of Europe and the United States, are regarded as masterpieces of Persian painting. In some of the early illustrations, such as *The Funeral of Isfandiyar*, in the Metropolitan Museum, the linear Chinese style prevails; others painted later, perhaps about 1330, show a mixture of Chinese and Persian styles. The landscapes, painted in subdued colors, are Chinese in style; the figures, costumes, and architecture, rendered in rich colors, are Persian.

Another group of manuscripts of the Mongol period is of small size, their illustrations representing the true miniature style of Persia. Miniatures from at least three of these manuscripts are now in several collections in Europe and the United States. The largest number is in the Chester Beatty Collection in Dublin; others are in the Freer Gallery and in the Metropolitan Museum. They are painted on a gold ground in delicate colors, among which a turquoise blue is quite conspicuous. The style of these small paintings, which can be dated to about 1330, is based on traditions of the Saljuk school of miniature painting and recalls the Manichaean miniatures of Central Asia. One of the finest of the small manuscripts is a *Shah-nama*, formerly in the Schulz Collection, Leipzig, and now in the possession of Monroe Gutman of New York. The thirty-nine miniatures are of outstanding quality and are similar in style to some of the paintings in the Demotte *Shah-nama*. Although Mongol influence is apparent, the Persian character is predominant. Contemporary and similar in style are miniatures from a manuscript of the *Munis-al-ahrar*, an anthology by Muhammad Badr al-Jajarmi, dated Ramadan, 741 (February, 1341). The pages are decorated with bands of figures and animals, representing the moon and the signs of the zodiac.

JALAIRID SCHOOL

Toward the end of the 14th century a great change took place in Persian painting. The development of this new style has been generally attributed to the Shiraz school, but it is more probable that painters working for the Jalairids in Tabriz and Baghdad were responsible for the change. Their capital was Baghdad, and from 1359 they also controlled Tabriz. Sultan Uwais (r. 1356–74) was a patron of the arts, poet, calligrapher, and painter. The painter Shams ad-Din, a pupil of Ahmad Musa, worked in the time of Uwais and illustrated a *Shah-nama*. Ahmad (r. 1382–1410), son of Uwais, was also an enthusiastic patron of science, arts, and letters. 'Abd al-Hayy of Baghdad, a pupil of Shams ad-Din, instructed Sultan Ahmad in the art of painting. At his court we find a number of famous calligraphers, painters, and illuminators such as 'Abd al-Hayy, his favorite painter, Yunsaidh (a pupil of Shams ad-Din), Maruf, and Mir 'Ali. Another artist of Sultan Ahmad was Pir Ahmad, who according to Dust Muhammad was the "zenith of his time."

The four important manuscripts that should be assigned to the Jalairid school are: Qazwini's *Wonders of the World*, in the National Library, Paris, dated the first day of Rabi I, 791 (March 10, 1388); the poems of Khwaju Kirmani in the British Museum, copied in Baghdad by Mir 'Ali of Tabriz in A.H. 799 (A.D. 1396–97); a manuscript of miscellany in two parts, one in the British Museum, the other in the Chester Beatty Collection, dated A.H. 800 (A.D. 1397–98); and a manuscript of an anthology in the Museum of Turkish and Islamic Art, Istanbul, dated Muharram, 801 (September, 1398). The miniatures of these manuscripts are painted in a style that is essentially different from that of the earlier Mongol school. All the artistic conventions that are to be characteristic of Persian painting of the 15th and 16th centuries now appear. One of the miniatures in the manuscript of Khwaju Kirmani representing Humay and Humayun is signed by Jumaid, and it is probable that he was responsible for all the other miniatures of the manuscript. The realistic landscapes of the Mongol artists are replaced by purely decorative landscapes and gardens, which show definite outlines with minute details. Decorative landscapes created by artists of the Tabriz and Baghdad schools show characteristics that became standards of Persian painting, that is, plain gold or blue sky, spongy mountains, and numerous stylized trees and flowers.

TIMURID PERIOD

The birth of the new style of painting coincided with the arrival of another Mongol conqueror, Timur, or Tamerlane (r. 1370–1404). Like his Mongol ancestor Chingiz Khan, Timur first invaded Iran, capturing Tabriz in 1386. Under the Timurids, Samarqand and Bukhara grew in importance, and Herat, the capital, became a center of Muhammadan science, literature, and art. We know from literary sources that Timur took artists, among them 'Abd al-Hayy, back with him to his capital, Samarqand, which he embellished with magnificent buildings.

The development of Persian miniature painting reached its height under the rule of the Timurid princes Shah Rukh, Baisunkur Mirza, Ibrahim Sultan, and Iskandar. The artists working for the Timurids were responsible for the development of a true national style of Persian painting. Shah Rukh (r. 1404–47) was a patron of the arts of the book, employing many artists in the production of books for his famous library in Herat. Among the artists working for him were Khalil, regarded as one of the four marvels of the age and second only to Mani, and also Ghiyath ad-Din, who was a member of an embassy sent to China in 1419. Shah Rukh's son, Prince Baisunkur Mirza, was an even greater art patron than his father.

He founded a library and academy in Herat where forty painters, calligraphers, illuminators, and binders brought from western Persia (chiefly from Tabriz) were employed. At the head of his academy was the calligrapher Ja'far al-Tabrizi. A branch of the Timurid school flourished in Shiraz, which was the residence of Prince Ibrahim Sultan, another son of Shah Rukh.

Although the Timurid artists continued to illustrate such traditional works as the *Shah-nama*, the *Universal History* of Rashid ad-Din, and the fables of *Kalila wa Dimna*, they turned more toward the romantic and mystic poems of Nizami, Sa'di, and Jami. In these illustrations the Herat school developed a style expressive of the romantic and lyrical content of the poems. One of the greatest masterpieces of the Timurid school of painting is a *Shah-nama* in the Gulistan Museum, Teheran, copied by Ja'far Baisunkuri in A.H. 833 (A.D. 1429–30) for the library of Baisunkur. The twenty-two miniatures of this manuscript represent the height of the Herat school of painting. The miniatures show a certain formality in design as well as brilliant colors and a richness of detail that suggest contemporary illumination. Another masterpiece of the Timurid school is the magnificent copy of *Kalila wa Dimna* in the Gulistan Museum. The thirty-five exquisite miniatures are generally regarded as the finest examples of Persian animal and landscape painting in existence. The color compositions are greatly varied, and judging from the differences of style at least two painters were responsible for the illustrations.

After the death of Shah Rukh the Timurid style continued in Herat and other centers, particularly in Shiraz. At that time the Black Sheep and White Sheep Turkomans began to assert themselves in western Persia; the court of Uzun Hasan in Tabriz became a cultural and artistic center. The miniature paintings made for the Turkomans show a different style from that of Herat.

A new and brilliant period of Iranian painting was inaugurated in Herat under the patronage of Sultan Husain Mirza (r. 1468–1506) and his vizier Mir 'Ali Shir Nawai, a poet, musician, and painter. The most famous Iranian painter of this time was Kamal ad-Din Bihzad of Herat, called "the Marvel of the Age," who was born about 1440. Of Bihzad the Iranian historian Khwandamir (1475–1535 or 1537) wrote: "He sets before us marvelous forms and rarities of his art; his draftsmanship, which is like the brush of Mani, has caused the memorials of all the painters of the world to be obliterated, and his fingers endowed with miraculous qualities have wiped out the pictures of all the artists among the sons of Adam. A hair of his brush, through its mastery, has given life to the lifeless form." After the defeat of the Timurids by the Shaibanids in 1507, Bihzad remained in Herat working for the Uzbeg (Uzbek) sultan Shaibani Khan. About 1510, when Shah Isma'il (r. 1502–24) of the Safavid dynasty conquered Herat, Bihzard continued in favor. He moved to Tabriz, thus establishing in western Iran a school that influenced the further development of Persian painting. (See also Safavid period below.)

There are extant only a few authentic works bearing Bihzad's signature or showing the characteristics of his style. Some of the works that bear his name are copies, and some are contemporary works to which "signatures" were added later. Bihzad's style is best exemplified by the illustrations of two important manuscripts: the British Museum's *Khamsa* of A.H. 846 (A.D. 1442), with three miniatures which were painted in A.H. 898 (A.D. 1493), and a *Bustan* in the Egyptian Library, Cairo, dated A.H. 893 (A.D. 1488). In these paintings the artist reveals himself as a keen observer of nature. He is a fine colorist, using many new tonalities and creating entirely new color schemes with blue, gray, and green predominating. The miniatures of the Cairo *Bustan* represent Bihzad's style at its best. They are masterpieces of composition, full of action and realism, and the figures show a decided individuality of expression and gestures. Seven miniatures in a *Khamsa*, dated A.H. 899 (A.D. 1494–95), in the British Museum are signed by Kasim 'Ali, and several others may be attributed to Bihzad himself or to some other pupil.

SAFAVID PERIOD

At the beginning of the 16th century, under the new Safavid dynasty, the center of Iranian painting shifted from Khurasan to Tabriz, in western Iran, although Herat, a seat of the governors, continued as an art center for some time. Several early-16th-century manuscripts written in Herat and in other cities of Khurasan were most probably illustrated there. Bihzad's influence continued to be the dominating factor in both Herat and Tabriz. In Herat Bihzad's pupils followed the traditions of their great master, who may be regarded as the founder of the Safavid school of painting. In 1522 Shah Isma'il appointed Bihzad director of the royal library. Several miniatures are attributed to Bihzad's Tabriz period, but the most authentic seems to be a roundel with two figures. It is in a manuscript of specimens of calligraphy of the year 1524 and is now in a private collection in New York.

Several manuscripts from the period of Shah Isma'il and some single miniature paintings may be attributed to the Herat school. An interesting early-16th-century manuscript is a *Diwan* by Hafiz, formerly in the Cartier Collection, now in the Cary Welch Collection, Cambridge, Mass. It contains five important miniatures, one signed by Shaikh-zada and two by Sultan Muhammad. Shaikh-zada of Khurasan was a pupil of Bihzad and continued many of his conventions and characteristics. The paintings of Sultan Muhammad, which are discussed below, show a style totally different from that of Shaikh-zada. Related to the miniatures of the Cartier Hafiz are fifteen illustrations in a manuscript of Nizami's *Khamsa* in the Metropolitan Museum, which was copied in A.H. 931 (A.D. 1524–25) by Sultan Muhammad Nur, a poet and calligrapher.

There is a close resemblance between the miniatures in the Metropolitan Museum Nizami and those of a *Diwan* of Mir 'Ali Shir Nawai in the National Library, Paris, copied in Herat in A.H. 933 (A.D. 1526–27). As in the Nizami, one of the miniatures in the Paris *Diwan* is most probably by Sultan Muhammad. The majority of the illustrations of both manuscripts, as well as those of the Cartier *Diwan*, were most likely made in Herat and then brought partly unfinished to Tabriz for the library of Shah Tahmasp, where they were completed by Sultan Muhammad, who was the chief court painter and director of the academy of painting.

Manuscripts written and illustrated in Tabriz for Shah Tahmasp are among the most sumptuous ever produced. The developed style of his court artists is preserved in a copy of Nizami's *Khamsa* (1539–43) in the British Museum. It was written for Shah Tahmasp and contains two miniatures signed by Sultan Muhammad and others by Mirak, Muzaffer 'Ali, Mir Sayyid 'Ali (one of the founders of Mughal painting), and Mirza 'Ali. The style of these Safavid painters reflects the splendor of Shah Tahmasp's court.

A well-known painter of the second half of the 16th century was Ustad Muhammadi, a pupil of Sultan Muhammad. Several drawings and paintings bear the signature of this artist. The best known is a tinted drawing of a landscape in the Louvre, Paris, dated 1578, and a drawing of a rustic scene in the Cleveland Museum of Art. Several signed paintings of love scenes in the Museum of Fine Arts, Boston, show the individual style of Muhammadi. The figures are usually tall and slender with small, round faces.

During the last part of the 16th century the production of illustrated manuscripts continued, but the artists favored single figures of elegant men and women. The men wear large turbans often adorned with flowers and feathers. An artist who painted such single miniatures was Aka Riza, who was also responsible for the introduction of a calligraphic style in drawings. His work belongs to the early years of the reign of Shah Abbas I (1587–1628), who was a great patron of the arts. Shah Abbas made Isfahan his capital, where he built many fine palaces and mosques.

A famous painter, and the last great painter of Persia, was Riza-i-Abbasi, who worked at the court of Shah Abbas. This painter left a considerable number of signed paintings and drawings dating from 1598 to 1643. He is best known for his genre scenes, love scenes, and portraits characterized by a close observation of nature. The young and old men portrayed by Riza-i-Abbasi are likenesses of types seen in the streets of Isfahan or at the court. His drawings show a peculiar calligraphic style of undulating lines combined with short strokes. Riza-i-Abbasi's style was imitated by many painters of the 17th and 18th centuries, but all lacked the originality of the master.

TURKISH SCHOOL

The history of painting in Turkey is relatively little known, since many of the Turkish libraries are still inaccessible to foreign scholars. In 1479 Sultan Mehmet II (r. 1451–81) summoned the Italian painter Gentile Bellini and commissioned him to paint his portrait, which now hangs in the National Gallery, London. A portrait of an Oriental artist in the Isabella Stewart Gardner Museum, Boston, painted in the style of Islamic miniature paintings, is attributed to Bellini. At the same time, we find in the 15th century a more Turkish style exemplified by a portrait of Sultan Mehmet in the Top Kapu Serai Library, attributed to Sinan, in which the Sultan is depicted holding a rose in the right hand and a handkerchief in the left.

Among the Persian artists working in Istanbul were Shah Kuli, foremost painter at the court of Sulaiman the Magnificent (r. 1520–66), and Wali Jan of Tabriz, who arrived in Turkey in 1587. Shah Kuli is known as a painter of dragons and of large curving leaves, called *saz*. He was a great favorite of Sultan Sulaiman, who, according to the Turkish historian 'Ali, often visited him in his studio to admire his work. Wali Jan, a pupil of Siyawush, was praised by 'Ali for his "magic brush" and for the delicacy of his work. Examples of their work are preserved in European and American collections, particularly in the National Library, Paris, the Freer Gallery, and the Metropolitan Museum.

A Turkish school of painting, based partly on Persian prototypes, developed in the 16th century under Sulaiman the Magnificent. Among the famous artists of that era was Nigari (1494–1572), who has left a number of signed paintings. There are several portraits by this painter, one of Sulaiman, one of Admiral Barbaros Hayrattin, and others in the Top Kapu Serai. Another important painter of the 16th century was Osman, who was responsible for illustrations of several manuscripts in Istanbul such as the *Hunernama* (History of Turkish Sultans) and the *Surnama*, or Book on Circumcision Ceremonies of Prince Mehmet (under the reign of Murad III, 1574–95), containing 427 miniatures in a purely Turkish style of great decorative quality. Also by Osman are miniatures in a *Treatise on Astrology*, dated 1582, in the National Library, Paris. A large manuscript of *Sulaiman-nama*, dated A.H. 987 (A.D. 1579), in the Chester Beatty Collection belongs to this period. Hasan, a painter of the beginning of the 17th century, illustrated the manuscript of *Egri tarihi*, prepared for the occasion of the Egri campaign of Mehmet III (r. 1595–1603).

Islamic painting. A miniature illustrating the *Makamat* of al-Hariri of Basra. National Library, Paris.

During the 17th century Turkish artists continued to illustrate various historical works and painted portraits of sultans. Many such albums are in Istanbul, and some are in European collections. In the 18th century the painters continued the traditions of the earlier schools. An outstanding artist of the 18th century was Ressam Levni (1703–32). He was a prolific painter and left numerous portraits and book illustrations, all preserved in Turkish libraries. He was responsible for the 137 miniatures of the *Surnama* in the Top Kapu Serai Library. His portraits of sultans (Mustafa II and Ahmad III), of dancers, and of European gentlemen show a highly decorative quality and rich polychromy. Another known painter of the 18th century was Abdullah Bukhari, who left a number of paintings, many of Turkish women.

See also MUGHAL PAINTING OF INDIA.

BIBLIOGRAPHY. F. R. Martin, *The Miniature Painting and Painters of Persia, India, and Turkey from the 8th to the 18th Century*, 2 vols., London, 1912; P. W. Schulz, *Die persisch-islamische Miniaturmalerei*, 2 vols., Leipzig, 1914; E. Kühnel, *Miniaturmalerei im islamischen Orient*, Berlin, 1922; E. Herzfeld, *Die Malereien von Sâmarrâ*, Berlin, 1927; T. Arnold, *Painting in Islam* . . . , Oxford, 1928; A. K. Coomaraswamy, *Les Miniatures orientales de la Collection Goloubew au Museum of Fine Arts de Boston*, Brussels, 1929; A. Sakisian, *La Miniature persane du XIIᵉ au XVIIᵉ siècle*, Paris, Brussels, 1929; L. Binyon, J. V. S. Wilkinson, and B. Gray, *Persian Miniature Painting*. . ., London, 1933; I. Stchoukine, *La Peinture iranienne sous les derniers 'Abbâsides et les Il-khâns*, Bruges, 1936; N. Berk, *La Peinture turque*, Ankara, 1950; I. Stchoukine, *Les Peintures des manuscrits tîmurîdes*, Paris, 1954; M. S. Dimand, *Persian Miniature Painting*, Milan, 1956; M. S. Dimand, *A Handbook of Muhammadan Art*, 3d ed., New York, 1958; B. Gray, *Persian Painting*, New York, 1961; R. Ettinghausen, *Arab Painting*, London, 1962; E. Kühnel, *Die Kunst des Islam*, Stuttgart, 1962.

MAURICE S. DIMAND

ISLAMIC POTTERY AND TILES. The conquest of the Near East by the Arabs inaugurated a new era in the history of ceramic art. At first the Muhammadan potters of Egypt, Syria, Mesopotamia, and Persia followed local traditions, adopting the ceramic techniques of the conquered countries.

UMAYYAD AND ABBASID PERIODS

Early Muhammadan pottery of the 8th and 9th centuries varies a great deal in quality of design and technique. Muslim potters of the 8th to the 10th century knew various methods of decorating their pottery, and the great quantities of ceramics found in the Near East reveal an astounding richness of technique, pattern, and color scheme.

A popular type of early Islamic pottery had incised decoration, often applied to glazes, streaked or splashed with yellow-brown, green, and touches of purple manganese in imitation of Chinese T'ang ware, imported by the Abbasids. Great quantities of Persian pottery of this type, ranging in date from the end of the 8th century to the 10th, have come to light in sites throughout the Muhammadan East, for instance, in Samarra, Ctesiphon, Susa, Rayy, Nishapur, and Samarqand.

Excavations by the Metropolitan Museum of Art, New York, at Nishapur in eastern Persia have disclosed numerous varieties of Persian pottery with painted decoration, produced from the late 8th to the early 10th century. The patterns of the Nishapur ware, painted in monochrome or polychrome, are quite varied. We find single geometric designs, bands of Kufic writing, palmettes and arabesque scrolls, rosettes, birds, and human figures, often combined into elaborate allover patterns.

An interesting type of pottery peculiar to Nishapur shows a decoration of animals and birds, human figures, and Kufic writing painted in black only or in black combined with yellow, green, and other colors. Another group of Nishapur pottery of the 9th and 10th centuries is decorated with inscriptions in brownish or purplish black on a white ground. The inscriptions are placed either in the center of the bowl or across it or along the rim. Other bowls with inscriptions show slender letters similar to those appearing in a number of Samanid bowls found in Afrasiyab, a suburb of Samarqand.

Some of the types of painted pottery from Nishapur were known also in Samarqand. Ware common to both Nishapur and Samarqand has a decoration painted in purple manganese, olive green, and brick red on a white ground. The decoration consists of Arabic inscriptions and arabesque patterns. Other types of Nishapur pottery, known also in Samarqand, have a decoration painted in colored slips on backgrounds of various colors such as purple or brown manganese or brick red.

Ninth-century pottery of the Abbasid period has been found in Mesopotamian sites such as Samarra and Ctesiphon; in Persia, chiefly in Susa and Rayy; and also in the rubbish heaps of al-Fustat (Old Cairo) in Egypt. Abbasid pottery with luster decoration is justly regarded as among the finest products of Muhammadan ceramic art. The luster technique was a great invention of Muhammadan potters of the 8th or 9th century. This ware is usually made of fine yellowish clay covered with an opaque tin enamel upon which, after the first firing, the decoration was painted with metallic oxides. The objects were fired a second time slowly, at a lower temperature (about 500-800°F), and through contact with smoke the metallic oxides were reduced to a thin layer of metal. The color of the luster thus produced was either gold or one of various shades of brown or red. By the 9th century the potters had become masters of this ceramic process. Excavations at Samarra, north from Baghdad, brought to light some of the most magnificent examples of lusterware.

The lusterware found in Persia, chiefly in Rayy and Gurgan, can be divided into two classes, one showing a style typical of Persia, the other elements common to Persia and Mesopotamia. To the Persian group belong vessels with a decoration of animals, birds, human figures, and arabesques, with the addition of Kufic writing painted in gold luster.

Pottery with polychrome luster decoration has been found at Susa and Rayy in Persia and also in Egypt but is best known from excavations at Samarra, where the most beautiful pieces were discovered. The lusterware made for the use of the Abbasid caliphs between 836 and 883 surpasses in the beauty and brilliancy of its colors all Islamic lusterware made in later periods.

Of Mesopotamian origin are the magnificent tiles with lustered decoration in monochrome and polychrome of the mihrab in the Mosque of Sidi Okba in Kairwan, Tunisia. There are 139 square tiles arranged to form a frame for this mihrab. According to Arabic literary sources, they were imported from Baghdad at the beginning of the 9th century by one of the amirs of the Aghlabid dynasty. The Kairwan tiles, which are earlier than the Sa-marra ceramics, must have been the work of Baghdad potters.

FATIMID PERIOD

Under the rule of the Fatimids (10th-12th cent.) the ceramic art of Egypt reached an unusually high standard. It may be divided roughly into two groups, one with engraved decoration under monochrome glazes, the other with lustered decoration derived from Mesopotamia, chiefly from Baghdad. The former pieces are covered with various colored glazes such as green, blue, red brown, and purple. The Fatimid lusterware shows a body of varying fineness, covered with a white glaze upon which the decoration is painted in gold or brown luster. The rich decoration of this ware consists of figure subjects such as horsemen, dancers, animals, and birds on a background of arabesques. On the bottom of many of these pieces are the names of the makers, the most frequent being those of Sa'd and Muslim. Among the best-known pieces by Sa'd is a bowl in the Victoria and Albert Museum, London, representing a figure holding a mosque lamp or an incense burner.

SALJUK PERIOD

Under the Saljuks and their successors, the shahs of Khwarizm (12th-13th cent.), Persian potters created magnificent ceramic ware that must be classified among the most beautiful ever produced. Many patterns and ceramic techniques known in the pre-Saljuk era were perfected by the potters of the 12th and 13th centuries. Techniques such as luster decoration, overglaze and underglaze painting in monochrome and polychrome, engraving, and carving were discriminately employed in various ceramic centers. New methods of decoration such as openwork were used with great effect. Rayy, a flourishing Saljuk city near Teheran, was a ceramic center of great importance. Another important ceramic center of the 13th and 14th centuries was Kashan, where several prominent Persian potters, whose names are known, had their workshops.

One group of Saljuk pottery of the 11th and 12th centuries consists of white plates with a carved and incised decoration in low relief, painted with color glazes in cobalt blue, turquoise blue, yellow, and purple manganese. Most of this type of Saljuk ware of Persia, known sometimes as Lakabi ware, was found in Rayy and may be regarded as of local manufacture. The decoration of this ware consists of birds and animals with arabesque scrolls and, occasionally, of human figures.

Among the *graffiato* pottery of the Saljuk period are several interesting groups that come from Amol, Aghkand, and other sites. This pottery is often called Gabry (fire-worshiper) ware. Although the design is often highly decorative, this ware is of peasant manufacture. The best-known type of Gabry has been attributed to the kilns of the Garus region, particularly Yasukand. This pottery, which consists of ewers, tiles, and bowls of various sizes, is decorated with boldly drawn animals, birds, human figures, and Kufic writing combined with arabesque scrolls. The decoration either is incised or is formed by cutting away the slip around the pattern, which then stands out in relief. Although some of the pieces are very striking in design, the decoration is generally somewhat crudely drawn. The majority of this Gabry ware should be assigned to the 12th century.

The various types of 12th-century Saljuk pottery continued to be made in the 13th century. In general, however, decoration became more elaborate. Favored types of pottery were ewers in cobalt or turquoise blue decorated with huntsmen, dancing dervishes, and animals. To this group of pottery also belong large storage jars with monochrome glazes, showing an animal decoration, arabesque scrolls, and Kufic inscriptions.

In an interesting group of pottery, fragments of which were found at Rayy, the relief decoration is cut from a black slip and then covered with a blue glaze. The decoration consists of palmette scrolls, sphinxes, griffins, birds, and figure subjects rendered in an effective silhouette style. A group of Saljuk pottery, probably made in Kashan, with underglaze painting in black under a colorless or blue glaze, has a highly effective decoration of foliated scrolls, wreaths, plants, rosettes, birds, and fishes rendered in a sketchy, impressionistic manner. This type of pottery can be attributed with certainty to the beginning of the 13th century, as several dated pieces are known.

Openwork technique was developed by Saljuk potters of Persia. One of the great masterpieces of early-13th-century Persian ceramic art is a blue jug in the Metropolitan Museum. It shows over an inner wall an openwork decoration of animals, Harpies, and sphinxes against a background of arabesque pattern. The details of the decoration, as well as the leafy scrolls and plants, are painted black, and the arabesques are cobalt blue. The inscriptions contain verses from poems and the date A.H. 612 (A.D. 1215/16).

The Saljuk potters of the 12th century were responsible for the revival of the luster technique. The color of Persian lusterware of the Saljuk period varies from a pale greenish gold to a dark reddish brown. The vessels and tiles for wall decoration and prayer niches are richly embellished with various decorative motifs, among which are animals and birds, figure subjects, arabesques, and large inscriptions; the last-mentioned were used especially on tiles for prayer niches.

Saljuk lusterware was being produced in Persia by the 12th century. Several dated pieces are in existence: a fragmentary bottle in the British Museum, London, dated 1179, and a bowl in the Art Institute of Chicago, dated 1191. A number of other pieces in which the decoration is reserved in solid luster ground can be attributed to the late 12th century.

The 13th-century style of Persian lusterware is known to us from a great number of dated vessels and tiles, the earliest one being a star-shaped tile in the Museum of Islamic Art, Cairo, dated A.H. 600 (A.D. 1203). The patterns of the 13th-century pieces show firm outlines and an abundance of ornament on a small scale, with the addition of birds and animals covering the whole field.

That Kashan was an important ceramic center is evident from a treatise on Persian faïence technique written in 1301 by Abu'l Kasim 'Abd Allah ibn-'Ali ibn-Abi Tahir of Kashan. The author of this treatise was a member of a famous family of Kashan potters, producers of some of the most beautiful mihrabs known. The earliest works of this family are the three mihrabs of A.H. 612 (A.D. 1215/16) in the sanctuary of Imam Riza in Meshed. The fame of Kashan was so great that all tiles were often called Kashi or Kashani. Through the combination of writing and ornament in luster, turquoise blue, and cobalt blue, partly painted flat and partly in relief, Persian artists of Kashan created a new decorative scheme for tilework that was followed all through the 13th and 14th centuries.

The Persian potters of the 12th century invented a technique of painting with pigments of various colors, mostly over white but also over turquoise-blue or cobalt-blue glaze. There are several varieties of pottery with overglaze decoration dating from the late 12th and the 13th century. The treatise of 1301 on Kashan faïence technique mentions two types of overglaze decoration: one is decorated with gold leaf and painted with white, red, black, and yellow enamels; the other is painted with seven colors, although this method was no longer practiced in 1301. The process of decorating the ware with seven colors is the real Minai technique, closely related to miniature painting. The magnificent decoration of this polychrome pottery consists mostly of figure subjects such as horsemen, seated and standing figures, sphinxes, court scenes, hunting scenes, and legendary episodes from the *Shah-nama*.

A well-known type of Islamic pottery has long been associated with the town of Raqqa on the Euphrates. The majority of Raqqa ware dates from the 12th or 13th century and shows decorative elements that are characteristic of the era of the Saljuk atabegs of Syria and Mesopotamia. There are several varieties of Raqqa ware with both painted and lustered decoration. The lusterware consists of small and large vases, jugs, bowls, and *tazzas*. The decoration, painted in brown luster, shows arabesques, Arabic inscriptions, and, occasionally, highly stylized birds. Another well-known type of Raqqa pottery has a decoration painted in black under a turquoise-blue glaze. One of the masterpieces is a bowl in the Horace Havemeyer Collection in the Metropolitan Museum, with a design of two highly stylized peacocks. Polychrome Raqqa ware recalls some of the Persian ceramics of the 13th century. The decoration, painted in black, blue, green, and brown manganese, consists of sphinxes, warriors, hunters, animals, and arabesques.

The pottery found in Rusafa (the Christian Sergiopolis) in the Syrian Desert not far from Raqqa is related to Raqqa ware. The decoration is mostly identical with that of Raqqa pottery. There are two varieties of Rusafa ware, one with lustered decoration, the other with painted decoration.

MONGOL PERIOD

The conquest of Persia by the Mongols, who established the Il-khan dynasty in 1256, at first brought little change in the decoration of pottery and wall tiles. Among the techniques of the Mongol period are underglaze painting in black and blue, relief decoration, and overglaze painting with luster or with pigments and gold. The old ceramic centers, with the exception of Rayy, produced magnificent pottery and tiles that are seldom inferior to those of the Saljuk era. The dated pieces permit us to follow the evolution of style caused by the Mongol invasion. Chinese motifs and Chinese naturalism in the rendering of animals, birds, and landscapes gradually penetrated all branches of Islamic art, including ceramics.

The Mongol ceramic style was fully developed in the

early 14th century. The influence of Chinese art is evident in plants with peony and lotus blossoms, clouds, and phoenixes. The Mongol style is best exemplified by a group of pottery with painted decoration that is generally attributed to the Sultanabad (Anak) region. They show a mosaiclike pattern of small leaves that either form the sole decoration of bowls, vases, and tiles or are combined with flying birds, phoenixes, hares, deer, and human figures in Mongol costumes.

An important group of Mongol pottery has a relief decoration under a cobalt-blue (sometimes turquoise-blue) glaze. This ware, consisting of large vases and tiles, can be dated to the late 13th and the early 14th century. Two cobalt-blue vases are in American collections: one is in the Horace Havemeyer Collection in the Metropolitan Museum, dated A.H. 681 (A.D. 1282/83); the other, in the Freer Gallery, Washington, D.C., is dated A.H. 683 (A.D. 1284/85). Both have a relief decoration of animals and flying geese in a seminaturalistic landscape.

Numerous dated lustered tiles, mihrabs, and vessels give a complete picture of the stylistic development from the second half of the 13th century to the end of the 14th. Considerable use was made of lustered tiles for the decoration of dwellings, public buildings, mosques, and tombs. Some tiles are star- or cross-shaped; others are rectangular and were used for mihrabs or decorative friezes. The star- or cross-shaped tiles are decorated with arabesques and palmette scrolls reserved on a luster ground with etched minute spirals. Tiles of another group are decorated with animals, birds, and figure subjects in conventionalized landscapes of trees and plants, painted in a rich gold luster, occasionally with touches of cobalt and turquoise blue.

Toward the end of the 13th century the naturalistic element started to invade the pattern of lusterware. Abstract motifs, such as scrolls and palmettes, began to be treated as growing plants. Figure subjects depicting scenes from daily life or legendary episodes continued to be popular on tiles and vessels.

In the Mongol period another ceramic technique, faïence mosaic, became popular in Persia. In this technique the design is composed of small units of various shapes and sizes cut from large slabs of earthenware glazed in solid colors. The pieces, which follow the contours of the design, are held together with plaster, poured from the rear, which penetrates all the crevices. The art of faïence mosaic began to be practiced under the Saljuks and is best known to us from 13th-century buildings of Konia in Asia Minor. Here the interior decoration, with prayer niches (mihrabs) of several mosques, was executed by Persian ceramists in faïence mosaic. In the 14th century this technique was fully developed. The Persian ceramists not only perfected the process but evolved new color schemes that were used for centuries.

The great development of faïence mosaic seems to have taken place in Isfahan, as a number of monuments indicate. An important monument is the tomb mosque of Baba Kasim, erected in 1340/41 by Sulaiman Abu'l Hasan Talut ad-Damghani. Not far from the tomb of Baba Kasim stands the Imami madrasa, dated A.H. 755 (A.D. 1354), which is richly decorated with geometric patterns and bands of inscription in faïence mosaic. The prayer niche, or mihrab, is now in the Metropolitan Museum.

Islamic pottery and tiles. Ceramic bird. Museum of Islamic Art, Cairo.

MAMLUK PERIOD

Contemporary with the Mongol period of Persia was the rule of Mamluks in Egypt and Syria. Pottery of the Mamluk period (13th–14th cent.) consists of vases and bowls from both Egypt and Syria, decorated with arabesques and inscriptions, often on a dotted background and arranged in bands or segments. A common type of Mamluk pottery of the 14th century consists of vessels made of red-brown clay, with a white slip covered with a yellowish, or sometimes green, transparent lead glaze. The decoration consists of inscriptions (sometimes with names), interlacings, and blazons of Mamluk officials, similar to those seen in metalwork and arabesques, and occasionally animals and human figures.

TIMURID PERIOD

There is relatively little Persian pottery of the Timurid period (15th cent.) in existence. Judging from representations of pottery in 15th-century miniatures, the Chinese influence was predominant. Some of the ceramics shown in miniatures were most probably true porcelains imported from China.

In the 15th century Persian potters not only continued the art of faïence mosaic but used it more frequently and over larger surfaces than in the 14th century. The decorative motifs of such mosaics consist of arabesques interlaced with floral scrolls bearing leaves, rosettes, and peonies, often within lobed medallions. A well-known 15th-century monument with splendid faïence mosaics is the Blue Mosque in Tabriz, built under Shah Jahan (r. 1437–67) of the Black Sheep Turkomans. Isfahan is particularly rich in monuments with 15th-century faïence mosaics. Other fine Timurid mosaics are in Samarqand in the mausoleum of Timur and in other 15th-century buildings.

SAFAVID PERIOD

The ceramic art of the Safavid period may be divided into two groups. One group has purely Persian decoration; the other imitates Chinese Ming porcelain. The Persian potters of the 16th century continued attempts to produce true porcelain, in imitation of Chinese ware, which was greatly admired by Shah Abbas I (r. 1587–1628), who imported great quantities of Chinese porcelain and even Chinese potters. Toward the end of the 16th century the potters achieved a semiporcelain, which, although not so hard as true porcelain, often closely approached the original ware. Sometimes the imitation was so well done that many Persian pieces have been mistaken for Chinese.

A group of white porcelains and semiporcelains, mostly of the 18th century and the beginning of the 19th, is often associated with Gombrun (Bandar Abbas), a port on the Persian Gulf. The Gombrun ware usually consists of deep bowls with pierced decoration covered with a transparent glaze.

Among the Safavid ceramics, those with luster decoration occupy a distinguished place. The art of luster painting was revived in the time of Shah Abbas by the potters of Isfahan and other places. Pear-shaped bottles with slender necks, bowls, vases, and small drinking cups were richly decorated with naturalistic landscapes, birds, and animals in luster of various colors.

The Safavid style of Persian ceramic art appears in all its splendor in large wall panels composed of square tiles.

Their use for wall decoration first became popular under Shah Abbas. Three panels of tiles are in the Metropolitan Museum; others are in the Victoria and Albert Museum and in the Louvre, Paris. They are supposed to have come from one of the pavilions that surrounded the garden on the Chahar Bagh promenade in Isfahan, from which ladies of the court watched the life of the street and various spectacles. The scenes are entirely pictorial in style and were copied from contemporary wall paintings created by the celebrated painter Riza-i-Abbasi. They represent garden feasts in which ladies of the court are attended by young men and women dressed in rich Safavid costumes or, occasionally, by men in Dutch costumes.

One type of Safavid pottery is classified as Kubatcha, since most of the examples were brought from a village of that name in the mountains of Daghestan, in the Caucasus. This type may be divided into two groups, one with painted black decoration under a blue or green glaze, the other with polychrome decoration under a transparent colorless glaze. The decoration of the polychrome group consists of Safavid landscapes with trees and plants, enlivened by the addition of human figures, animals, and birds. Kubatcha ware, like other Safavid ceramics, must be attributed to the late 16th and the 17th century. It was most probably made in the Persian province of Azerbaijan, where Tabriz was the most important artistic center.

TURKISH CERAMICS

The earliest known examples of the Turkish ceramic art of Asia Minor are known in architectural decoration and date from the 13th century. The mosques in Konia, the capital of the Saljuk empire, are embellished on both the exterior and the interior with bricks or with faïence mosaics, enameled in turquoise blue, cobalt blue, black, and white. The designs are purely geometric, consisting mainly of angular interlaced bands and inscriptions.

At the end of the 14th century, under the rule of the house of Uthman, the founder of the Ottoman empire, a new chapter in the art of Asia Minor began. Brussa, the early capital of the Ottomans, became an important ceramic center. The enameled bricks, or cut mosaics, that had been popular in the earlier period were superseded for the most part by tiles, usually rectangular but sometimes hexagonal in shape, decorated in polychrome enamels or in underglaze painting. Examples of 15th-century tile decoration occur in Brussa in the Green Mosque, completed in 1423, and in the Green Tomb of Sultan Mehmet I, built in 1421. The mihrab of the Green Mosque is decorated with arabesques and floral motifs derived from Persian art. That the mihrab was made by Persian artists is proved by an inscription on the niche: "Work of masters from Tabriz." The bright color scheme consists of green, yellow, and purple manganese.

The art of underglaze painting in blue and white, in imitation of Ming porcelain, was also known in Ottoman Turkey in the 15th century. Some of the finest examples of tilework with blue and white decoration are in the Mosque of Sultan Murad in Adrianople (Edirne), built in 1433. A group of bowls, dishes, vases, and mosque lamps, decorated with elegant floral scrolls, Chinese cloud bands, arabesques, and Kufic inscriptions, may be assigned to the late 15th century and the early 16th century. Excellent examples of this Ottoman pottery are in the British Museum, the Louvre, and the Museum of Turkish and Islamic Art, Istanbul.

The most important ceramic center of Asia Minor in the 16th and 17th centuries was Iznik (Nicaea), although other centers, among them, Kütahya and Istanbul, are known. The ceramic art of Iznik attained its highest development during the 16th century and in the first half of the 17th. Here some of the most beautiful Turkish pottery and tiles, both in black and white and in polychrome, were made. The Turkish potters had become thorough masters of the art of underglaze decoration. The polychrome ware shows the following colors: cobalt blue, turquoise blue, green, yellow, and a characteristic coral red, which was made from a clay, the Armenian bole, applied thickly to the surface of vessels or tiles. The decoration consists of Persian palmettes and new floral motifs that give a distinctive appearance to Turkish pottery and tiles. Among the floral motifs introduced by Turkish artists are carnations, tulips, hyacinths, roses, and plum trees, arranged in various compositions. Beautiful tile decoration may be seen in the Mosque of Rustam Pasha (1560), the harem of the old palace in Istanbul (1575), the Selimiye Mosque of Edirne (1575), and other buildings.

Among the Turkish ceramics of the 16th century is a group in which purple manganese is substituted for the color red. The designs on pottery of this type are in general similar to those of Iznik, but frequently a greater elegance of execution may be noticed. Examples in which purple manganese occurs have usually been assigned to the school of Damascus, but it can be now established that they were made in Iznik. That Turkish ceramics were also made in Syria is evident from excavated material found in Damascus.

Fine 17th-century tiles are in the Mosque of Sultan Ahmad (Ahmediye Mosque) in Istanbul. Iznik still held the leading place in the manufacture of tiles and pottery at that time. Under Sultan Ahmad I (r. 1603–17) there were 300 ceramic workshops in Iznik. Toward the end of the 17th century there was a gradual decline in the quality, design, and color of the Iznik ware.

To Kütahya, in Anatolia, are attributed 18th-century bowls, cups, coffeepots, and other dishes decorated with floral motifs and, occasionally, with figures. The design is usually crude, and among the vivid colors yellow is conspicuous.

BIBLIOGRAPHY. R. L. Hobson, *A Guide to the Islamic Pottery of the Near East* (British Museum), London, 1932; A. U. Pope, *A Survey of Persian Art*, vols. 2, 5, New York, 1938–39; A. Lane, *A Guide to the Collection of Tiles* (Victoria and Albert Museum), London, 1939; A. Lane, *Early Islamic Pottery*, London, 1947; A. Lane, *Later Islamic Pottery*, London, 1957.

MAURICE S. DIMAND

ISLAMIC TEXTILES.

ISLAMIC TEXTILES. In the early Muhammadan period (7th–8th cent.) the Near Eastern weavers continued to make textiles in the style and technique of the Coptic and Sassanian era. Gradually a true Muhammadan style, which spread over all the countries under Arab rule, developed.

ABBASID AND TULUNID PERIODS

The Copts were great craftsmen, and as such were extensively employed by the Arabs in the newly established textile manufactories, or *tiraz*. The term *tiraz* also applies to bands containing woven or embroidered inscriptions and to garments decorated in this way. The institution of *tiraz* factories, which existed in all the provinces, was of great importance in the official life of the Muhammadan rulers of the Umayyad and Abbasid dynasties (8th–9th cent.). These shops produced robes of honor with *tiraz* bands, which were presented to officials of high rank at least once a year.

The *tiraz* factories of Egypt under the Abbasid and Tulunid caliphs were famous for their linens and silks. Tinnis (Tennis), which had 5,000 looms, was renowned for several kinds of fabrics, such as *kasab*, a very fine linen used for turbans; *badana*, a fabric used for the garments of the caliphs; and *bukalimun*, a fabric with changing colors, used for saddlecloths and for covering litters. In Tuna, near Tinnis, fine linen cloth and *kiswas*, or coverings, were made for the Kaabah in Mecca. Dabik was famous for its silks, and in Damietta fine white linen cloths were woven. Other manufactories are known to have existed in Alexandria and in al-Fustat (Old Cairo). Several 10th-century linens of the al-Fustat looms are in museums. Arabic textiles were also made in Upper Egypt, for example, in al-Ashmunain and Bahnasa.

The majority of linen textiles with inscriptions, tapestry-woven in silk, are of the 10th century and often bear the names of al-Muktadir bi'llah and other caliphs. The Kufic writing of these textiles shows numerous decorative variations, some of the letters terminating in half palmettes.

FATIMID PERIOD

Magnificent textiles of Egypt and Syria, even surpassing those of the earlier Abbasid period, were produced in the Fatimid period (10th–12th cent.). The cloth made of linen and silk became extremely fine and was greatly admired by travelers. One source tells us that the texture of Cairene fabrics was so fine that a whole robe could be passed through a finger ring. In the arrangement of inscriptions and ornament the Fatimid weavers followed the scheme developed under the Abbasids. A fine example of luxurious Fatimid textile is a linen cloth in the Metropolitan Museum of Art, New York, decorated with horizontal bands, the central one with pairs of falcons, which together with palmettes form an intermittent scroll. The pattern is tapestry-woven in silk and gold threads of gilded goldbeater's skin. The style of the pattern is characteristic of the period of the caliph al-Mustansir (r. 1036–94). Such fine fabrics, decorated all over with gold tapestry, may be identified with garments called *badana*, which were made in Tinnis for the exclusive use of the caliphs. The Fatimid textiles of the 12th century followed the style of the 11th century. Often the decorative writing is ingeniously combined with arabesque motifs.

PAINTED AND PRINTED ABBASID AND FATIMID TEXTILES

Of great technical interest are linen textiles with inscriptions or decorations painted or stamped. Some of the inscriptions, painted in liquid gold, are probably identification marks of Egyptian weaving shops. Noteworthy also are several cotton textiles, dyed in the so-called *chiné*, or ikat, technique. One of the pieces, in the Museum of Islamic Art, Cairo, bears the name of a Rasulid prince of Yemen of the 10th century. These pieces, similar to cotton textiles with embroidered inscriptions, were made in the *tiraz* of San'a in Yemen.

The technique of stamping and printing patterns on textiles was developed in the Islamic period in Egypt, and it later spread to Europe, particularly to Germany. The Arabic weavers used wooden stamps for their printed textiles. An unusually fine linen fabric in the Metropolitan Museum has an allover pattern of lions with squares stamped in brown and gold. Here the weaver used six different stamps to print the design.

AYYUBID AND MAMLUK PERIODS

In the Ayyubid and Mamluk periods of Egypt, the tapestry technique inherited from the Fatimids was still practiced but to a lesser extent than earlier. The design of these textiles consists of peony palmettes and naturalistic leaves, which are similar in style to the ornament on Mamluk metalwork of the early 14th century. *See* ISLAMIC METALWORK (MAMLUK PERIOD).

SILK WEAVES FROM EGYPT AND SYRIA

The early Islamic woven textiles, in both wool and silk, continued at first in the style of East Christian and Sassanian weaves. Several silk weaves of the late 8th or early 9th century, in buff on a green ground, similar in style to the textiles found in Akhmim in Upper Egypt, may be attributed to Syrian looms, which existed in Damascus and in Antioch. Some silk weaves show an Islamic version of a Sassanian motif of a palmette tree. Both the angular outlines of the design and the arabesque scroll of the border are features of the early Islamic era.

Probably of the Fatimid period (11th cent.) is a woven silk fabric in the Fine Arts Museum, Brussels, decorated with rows of confronted birds separated by palmette devices and bearing on their wings Arabic inscriptions expressing good wishes. The coloring is unusual, as the fabric is divided into horizontal bands of blue, purple, yellow, and red without any relation to the design. In style this fabric recalls some of the lustered ceramics of the 11th or 12th century from al-Fustat; it may be similarly dated.

A number of silk fabrics in Chinese style from church treasuries, now in the Museum of Arts and Crafts, Berlin, and the Victoria and Albert Museum, London, bear the name and titles of Nasir ad-Din Muhammad ibn-Kalaun, the Mamluk sultan of Egypt and Syria who reigned intermittently from 1293 to 1340. The patterns of these fabrics were influenced by Chinese textiles, which were imported at that time to Near Eastern countries. The titles of Mamluk sultans of Egypt and Syria also occur on several brocades. A well-known piece in St. Mary's Church in Danzig is woven with flat strips of gilded leather on a black silk ground and has pairs of parrots and Chinese dragons inscribed with the title "an-Nasir." The inscription presumably refers to Nasir ad-Din Muhammad ibn-Kalaun. Other important brocades in the Chinese style are a chasuble and a cope in the same church and two dalmatics in Regensburg Cathedral bearing the name of the maker, "Master 'Abd al-'Aziz." These brocades have been attributed to the looms of China or Central Asia, but an Egyptian origin is not excluded.

EARLY IRANIAN TEXTILES

Persian woven silks of the early Islamic era are based on Sassanian tradition. To the period between the 7th and 9th centuries may be ascribed the sudarium of St. Victor and a fabric with a design of elephants, both in the treasury of the Cathedral of Sens. These silk fabrics, reminiscent in style and color scheme of Sassanian textiles, were probably made on the looms of western Persia.

A distinctive group of Persian silk textiles of the early Islamic era is characterized by angularly rendered animals and birds. The best-known specimens are the sudarium of St. Columba, which is ornamented with lions and is now in the Vatican, Rome; a similar stuff in the Cathedral of Nancy; and two fabrics in Sens, one with peacocks and another with horses. Similar Persian textiles were unearthed by Sir Aurel Stein in the caves of the Thousand Buddhas in Tun-huang, Chinese Turkestan. From literary sources we know that looms existed in Samarqand, and this group of textiles was probably woven there. A silk fabric from the church of St-Josse-sur-Mer, Pas-de-Calais, now in the Louvre, Paris, was woven in Khurasan, the chief centers of which were Merv (Marv) and Nishapur. It is decorated with large confronted elephants, bordered by rows of small camels and peacocks. The Kufic inscriptions give the name of Amir Mansur Bukhtagin of Khurasan, who died in 960, thus dating it to the 10th century.

SALJUK PERIOD

The invasion of Persia by the Turkish Saljuks in 1037 greatly changed the art of weaving in the Near East. That there was an important revival of arts and crafts under the Saljuks and their successors, who ruled over Persia, Mesopotamia, Syria, and Asia Minor, is evident from many silk weaves long known in various collections and some recently found in Persia, especially at Rayy, a famous weaving center. Although the influence of the Sassanian style may still be seen in the patterns of the early Saljuk pieces, it was gradually replaced by a style in which arabesque motifs of Islamic origin were combined with linear scrolls and palmette forms. Some of them were derived from textiles of the Buyid period (10th–11th cent.).

Saljuk textiles may be divided into several groups. Those of the early 11th century are still related in style to Persian textiles of the 8th to the 10th century. In the ripe Saljuk period, however, the design, hitherto more or less angularly treated, develops a quality characteristic of Saljuk art in general: the beautiful pattern with elegant and flowing outlines. This style may be seen in a number of pieces in European and American collections, most of which are of the 12th century, although a few are of the 13th. Also of this type are a green and white silk fabric with confronted griffins, in the Museum of Arts and Crafts, Berlin, and a red and green silk with lions, in St. Servatius Church, Maastricht. A black and white stuff with pairs of eagles, said to have come from Tabriz and now in the Museum of Arts and Crafts, Berlin, may be dated to the 13th century.

Literary evidence indicates that at an early period silk fabrics were woven in Baghdad. About ten textiles of the first half of the 10th century are inscribed with the name of the *tiraz* of Baghdad (Madinat as-Salam). Marco Polo, writing in the 13th century, mentions silk fabrics and gold brocades woven in Baghdad and Mosul. Silk fabrics were also manufactured in the Saljuk empire in Asia Minor. A 13th-century gold brocade in the Museum of Fine Arts, Lyons, is decorated with lions and inscriptions containing the name of Sultan Kai-Kubad (Keykubad) of Konia, who was either Kai-Kubad I (r. 1219–36) or Kai-Kubad II (r. 1249–57).

MONGOL AND TIMURID PERIODS

Very few Persian textiles can be assigned with certainty to the 14th or 15th century. The decoration of textiles of this period was strongly Chinese in character. Under the rule of the Mongols the demand for Chinese fabrics in Persia was so great that Chinese motifs were imitated by native weavers. Costumes of silk fabrics decorated in Chinese style are represented in Mongol and Timurid miniatures. They show dragons, phoenixes, *kilins*, and floral ornaments such as the peony and the lotus. Occasionally, these motifs are combined with purely Islamic ornaments, such as arabesques. The Metropolitan Museum possesses a rare silk brocade that may be assigned to the end of the 15th century. Here arabesques form an ogival diaper, each compartment containing floral scrolls with blossoms, naturalistic leaves, and peony palmettes in black and silver on an olive-green ground. The elegance of the design and the color scheme indicate a Timurid origin.

SAFAVID PERIOD

In the 16th century under the Safavids the golden era of Persian weaving began. Safavid silks may be divided into three groups: plain silk weaves, silk brocades, and silk velvets. Such fabrics were used for garments of princes and nobles, as well as for hangings and covers. The decoration consists of figure subjects, animals, birds, and floral motifs. The scenes are taken, for the most part, from the great Persian epics, such as the *Shah-nama* (Book of Kings), or from the romantic poems of Nizami; others depict Persian nobles hunting or enjoying the pleasures of life in their gardens.

One of the 16th-century silks in the Metropolitan Museum shows a Persian repeat design of a Persian youth with a bottle and a cup, standing in a rocky landscape among cypresses, cherry trees, animals, and birds. Also of the 16th century are velvets with either figures or small repeat patterns. To this group belong velvet panels (now in several American museums) from the interior decoration of a tent used by Kara Mustafa Pasha in 1683 at the second siege of Vienna. In the Armory of the Kremlin Museums, Moscow, there is a coat of silk brocade decorated with figure subjects and woven in polychrome silk on a blue background. Noteworthy silks and velvets of the 16th and 17th centuries are in Rosenborg Palace, Copenhagen. One is decorated with very large figures (about 20 in. high) of a prince and his attendant. These silk textiles were gifts of the Shah of Persia and were sent to Duke Frederick of Holstein-Gottorp in 1639.

Under Shah Abbas I the Great (r. 1587–1628), a noble patron of all the arts, the weaving of costly fabrics, brocades, and velvets continued to be practiced with great skill. In addition to the long-established looms of Yazd (Yezd) and Kashan, Shah Abbas founded other manufactories in Isfahan, where luxurious fabrics were woven. The names of several 16th- and 17th-century weavers such as Ghiyath, 'Abd Allah, ibn-Muhammad, Muizz ad-Din (son of Ghiyath), and Saifi-i-'Abbasi are known. The velvets and gold brocades made in the time of Shah Abbas are among the most sumptuous fabrics ever produced.

A masterpiece from the Persian looms of the Shah Abbas period is a large carpet of brocaded silk velvet in the Metropolitan Museum. It was formely in the possession of the royal house of Saxony, to which it had belonged since 1683, having been captured during the siege of Vienna. The design consists of two large, eight-pointed medallions and of segments of similar figures. The field, as well as the medallions, is richly ornamented with delicate flower and stem motifs. This velvet carpet was probably made at the Isfahan looms and may be assigned to about 1600. Other 17th-century brocades and velvets show seminaturalistic plants growing out of rocks, Chinese clouds, and butterflies in soft colors on a gold ground. Other brocades have a repeat pattern of birds on rose bushes.

New floral motifs, naturalistic in style, became popular in Persian textiles of the early 17th century. The decoration of many textiles consists of carnations, roses, and irises or wavy bands, woven in soft and delicate colors blending harmoniously with the gold or silver background. An integral part of the Persian costume of the Shah Abbas period and later was a richly decorated sash, the use of which spread from Persia to east Europe.

TURKISH TEXTILES

Under the patronage of the Ottoman sultans of Turkey, the weavers of Brussa developed a new, purely Turkish design in the second half of the 15th century. Brocades and velvets were used for garments of the sultans, many of which are preserved in the Istanbul museums. There are old labels that connect the garments with individual sultans, beginning with Mehmet II (r. 1451–81). The Turkish style was fully developed in the time of Sultan Bayazid II (r. 1481–1512).

The most characteristic pattern of Turkish textiles consists of naturalistic flowers such as carnations, tulips, hyacinths, roses, and sprays of plum blossoms. In addition, the Turkish weavers used palmettes of various types, some combined with pomegranates. These floral motifs are often

Islamic textiles. Brocade depicting a horseman leading a Mongolian captive, second half of the 16th century. Metropolitan Museum of Art, New York.

placed in ogival compartments, forming an allover diaper. The color scheme is usually limited to two or three colors, such as gold and red or red, blue, and gold. The ground is usually red but is sometimes blue, green, or purple. The brocades are similar in style to the velvets, although the former show a more elaborate design.

Embroideries were produced both in Asia Minor and in European Turkey. The embroideries of Asia Minor often recall Brussa velvets and brocades in their design, in which floral motifs, either stylized or naturalistic, are conspicuous. The early examples, which date from the 17th and 18th centuries, are embroidered in a darning stitch on linen or in couched work on silk.

A well-known group of Turkish embroideries consists of kerchiefs and towels, some of them used for ceremonial purposes only. Most of them date from the 19th century and are embroidered in a double darning stitch in silk and silver-gilt threads. Floral designs such as roses are the most popular ones, although motifs such as mosques and cypress trees were frequently used.

TEXTILES OF SPAIN AND SICILY

The Arab conquest of Spain in 711 introduced silk weaving of the Near East into Europe. Spanish textiles were mentioned in the papal inventories as early as the 9th century, and Idrisi (1099–1154), the Arab historian, recorded that there were 800 looms at Almería in Andalusia for the weaving of costly silk stuffs. Textiles were also woven in Murcia, Seville, Granada, and Málaga. In the Royal Academy of History, Madrid, is a fabric decorated with a tapestry-woven band in light blue, dark blue, and red, with octagons containing geometrically stylized animals, birds, and human figures. It is inscribed in Arabic with the name of Hisham II, caliph of Cordova (r. 976–1009). The design, which is undoubtedly of Egypto-Arabic origin, resembles some of the patterns on contemporary Hispano-Moresque ivory caskets.

An important group of Andalusian textiles of the 11th to the 12th century is characterized by a bold pattern of figures, birds, and animals. The best-known pieces are those with the representations of the legendary lion strangler and others with pairs of sphinxes. These pieces are preserved in the Episcopal Museum of Archaeology and Art, Vich, in the former State Museums (Applied Arts), Berlin, and in Cooper Union Museum, New York. They have a distinctive color scheme, being woven in red, green, and gold.

Another group of Hispano-Moresque textiles is identified with the help of a brocade in Berlin, which originally protected a document in the Cathedral of Salamanca, as belonging to the period of Ferdinand II, king of León (r. 1158–88). In this type of textile, which continued to be woven in the 13th century, pairs of griffins or birds appear in circular medallions, usually in red brown, cream white, and gold, sometimes in other colors. Other brocades of the 13th century are decorated with geometric patterns in which gold threads are profusely used. The cope of Don Felipe (d. 1274), now in the National Archaeological Museum, Madrid, is woven in tan and gold in a pattern of interlacing bands that form six-pointed stars. The 13th-century cope of St. Valerius in the Cathedral of Lérida is decorated with interlaced curved and straight lines within small squares.

Other 14th- and 15th-century textiles of Spain are decorated in the so-called Alhambra style and were probably products of Granada looms. The ornament consists of interlaced bands, polygons, inscriptions, and arabesques in vivid colors. Some of the fabrics bear an Arabic inscription reading "Glory to our Lord the Sultan." The Hispano-Moresque style did not lose favor until well into the 16th century, when Western patterns became prevalent.

Silk fabrics are known to have been woven in Sicily under Arabic rule in the 10th and 11th centuries, but no existing specimens can be attributed to the Sicilian looms of that period. Under the Normans, who perpetuated the customs and the arts of the Arabs, the art of weaving was highly developed. After the Oriental fashion the Norman kings in the 12th century established royal manufactories at Palermo that produced woven and embroidered silk fabrics of high quality. Magnificent dated examples in the Treasury of Vienna, such as the imperial mantle and alb, were made in Palermo. The former, dated A.H. 528 (A.D. 1134) and embroidered in gold with pearls on a red background, has a pattern of a camel being attacked by a lion, stylized in Oriental fashion. The alb was made under the Norman king William II in 1181 and shows a border of griffins and palmette trees in gold on a purple background. The brocade (still in Palermo) from the burial robe of the emperor Henry VI (d. 1197) is assigned to these manufactories.

INDIAN TEXTILES

Mughal textiles of India were under court control and show a mixture of Persian and Hindu motifs. Indian weavers also adopted many weaving techniques from Persia and, as in rug knotting, often surpassed their teachers. Mughal velvets are very rare and belong mostly to the period of Shah Jahan (r. 1628–58); the decoration consists mainly of naturalistic floral designs or of plants similar to those used in the rugs of the same period.

The weaving of silk brocades in India was highly developed in the Mughal period. Many centers of weaving are known, among the most famous being Lahore, Aurangabad in the Deccan, Chanderi in Gwalior, Benares, and Ahmedabad. Indian brocades have floral designs, rich color schemes, and a lavish use of gold. These brocades were made up into garments for men and women, including saris and sashes.

Embroidery was a popular art in India and was applied to cotton turbans, coats, sashes, and cushions. Among the famous Indian textiles are the Kashmir shawls, which usually date from the 18th century. Some of them are woven; others are embroidered. The characteristic design consists of dense floral patterns and cone-shaped motifs derived from Persian art.

Two methods of decorating fabrics, namely, block printing and resist dyeing, are of ancient Indian origin. In the Mughal period these techniques were brought to a high degree of perfection and were combined with painting. Painted and printed cottons, made mostly in Masulipatnam, are decorated with figure subjects or trees of life. Several cushion covers in the Metropolitan Museum are early examples of pintados; the men and women are dressed in Persian and Hindu costumes. According to inventory notes written on the back, they may be dated to about the middle of the 17th century.

BIBLIOGRAPHY. A. F. Kendrick, *Catalogue of Muhammadan Tex-*

tiles of the Medieval Period (Victoria and Albert Museum), London, 1924; N. A. Reath and E. B. Sachs, *Persian Textiles and Their Techniques from the 6th to the 18th Century*, New Haven, 1937; T. Oz, *Turkish Textiles and Velvets, XIV–XVI Centuries*, Ankara, 1950, *XVII–XIX Centuries*, Istanbul, 1951.

MAURICE S. DIMAND

ISOCEPHALY. Type of composition in which the natural proportions and perspective of the figures involved are distorted in order to produce a design having all the heads at the same height. It was used in classical Greece for decorative purposes, but in the Middle Ages the clarity afforded in reading figures assures a clearly symbolic rather than realistic narrative statement.

ISOLA BELLA. Island in Lake Maggiore, northern Italy, with the palatial private residence of the Borromeo family. It was first called Isola Isabella after the wife of Count Carlo Borromeo, who began revisions of the site in 1630. Crivelli, F. M. Richini, Biffi, Cagnola, and Carlo Fontana directed the work until 1671. The original monumental entrance on the water's edge is unfinished, but the great ballroom was finally completed in the 20th century by the present Prince Borromeo. The site is raised with terracing to 100 feet above the lake's level; unusually rich botanical varieties distinguish the garden, which rises to fantastic rockwork capped with terraces and statues. The palace, in the late baroque style with 18th-century and later revisions, has a pebble and rockwork basement and superbly decorated state chambers above.

BIBLIOGRAPHY. G. Masson, *Italian Villas and Palaces*, New York, 1959.

ISOMETRIC DRAWING. Type of axonometric projection in which a basic cube is so tilted to the plane of projection that all three of its axes are equally foreshortened. Such a view is obtained when the diagonal of the cube is perpendicular to the plane. Isometric projection foreshortens each axis about 81 percent of the actual length, although in application isometrics are generally drawn full length.

ISPAHAN, see ISFAHAN.

ISRAEL, NATIONAL MUSEUM OF, see JERUSALEM: ISRAEL NATIONAL MUSEUM.

ISRAELITE ART, see HEBREW ART.

ISRAELS, JOSEF. Dutch painter and graphic artist (b. Groningen, 1824; d. The Hague, 1911). He studied in Groningen and then went to Paris in 1845, when he became a student of Picot. Israëls's first aim was to be a history painter, but he soon left history for genre. In 1855 he went to a small fishing village for his health and there found the subjects for his future works: scenes from the lives of poor folk and fishermen, at times slightly sentimental, painted with a dark tonality and rough chiaroscuro derived from Rembrandt. Like Rembrandt, Israëls often painted pictures with Jewish subjects, for example, the brooding *A Son of the Chosen People* (1889; Amsterdam, Municipal Museum).

BIBLIOGRAPHY. M. Liebermann, *Jozef Israëls*, Berlin, 1901; M. Eisler, *Josef Israëls...*, London, 1924.

ISSOIRE: ABBEY OF SAINT-AUSTREMOINE. Twelfth-century Benedictine abbey in France. It is named for St. Stremonius, who introduced Christianity to Auvergne in the 3d century, and it is undoubtedly the finest example of the Auvergne style. The church is entirely in its original state except for the central tower and façade, rebuilt in the 19th century. In general the architectural style resembles that of Notre-Dame-du-Port at Clermont-Ferrand, though it has a second-story arcade pierced by occasional windows, which lightens the nave considerably. It was built shortly after Notre-Dame-du-Port, and seems to have been erected by the same builders. Especially noteworthy are the sculptures of the signs of the zodiac above the apse windows and the lozenge patterns on the exterior walls. On the columns of the choir and apse are fine narrative capitals, and those on the nave have interesting classical and mythological designs.

BIBLIOGRAPHY. P. Deschamps, *French Sculpture of the Romanesque Period...*, Florence, 1930?; K. J. Conant, *Carolingian and Romanesque Architecture, 800–1200*, Baltimore, 1959.

ISTANBUL, see CONSTANTINOPLE; ISLAMIC ARCHITECTURE (TURKISH ARCHITECTURE).

ISTANBUL: ARCHAEOLOGICAL MUSEUM. Turkish collection of classical antiquities situated in the Old Saray (Top Kapu Serai). It was installed in 1892 and was extended in later years. The Archaeological Museum houses among its architectural finds more than thirty plaques of the frieze from the Temple of Hekate (Lagina, Asia Minor; 2d–1st cent. B.C.), carved in relief with scenes of Gigantomachia and with some representations of undetermined subject matter; the frieze from the Temple of Artemis Leukophryene at Magnesia on the Meander (3d cent. B.C.); remains from the temple at Assos (Asia Minor; Doric, archaic; 6th cent. B.C.) and relief fragments from the architrave of the temple; and mosaics from Cos, including *Orpheus among the Animals* and Eros and marine centaurs.

The museum also contains a number of sarcophagi from Asia Minor. A white marble sarcophagus from Sidamara (1st half of 3d cent.) is in a perfect state of preservation. It is carved in relief on all four sides. The center of the main side is occupied by the figure of the deceased holding a book roll and surrounded on either side by two women and by the Dioscuri; the other sides have representations of hunting scenes and of sacrifice. The so-called sarcophagus of Alexander, of pentelic marble, was found in the royal necropolis at Sidon (end of 4th cent. B.C.); it was probably the sarcophagus of a prince. The sarcophagus of the "Mourning Women" from Sidon dates from the middle of the 4th century B.C. Also on view are the sarcophagus of the Satrap (so named because of the Oriental figure carved on all three sides), of Parian marble, which was found in Sidon; and the Lycian sarcophagus, so named because of its particular form, which reflects that of the tombs at Lycia. Its decoration is Greek, inspired by the Parthenon frieze. There are also a number of anthropomorphic sarcophagi from Syria. In addition, the museum houses an important collection of Cypriote antiquities (second only to that of the Metropolitan Museum of Art, New York) consisting of limestone statues and statuettes and terra cottas. There are terra-cotta statuettes from Priene and Myrina (3d–1st cent. B.C.); Clazomenaean sarcophagi of clay, from the Ionian school of the 6th century B.C.; jewelry from Troy, discovered by Schliemann; Mycenaean pottery; and Roman and Byzantine sculpture.

EVANTHIA SAPORITI

ITALIANIZERS. Northern European artists of the 16th and 17th centuries who studied in Italy and adopted certain aspects of the Italian style. Many slavishly imitated Italian models; others attempted to blend the style of Italy with that of their native traditions. Examples from the 16th century are Jan Gossaert and Bernard van Orley; from the 17th, Claes Berchem and Andries and Jan Both. *See* BERCHEM, CLAES PIETERSZ.; BOTH, ANDRIES DIRKSZ.; BOTH, JAN; GOSSAERT, JAN; ORLEY, BERNARD VAN.

ITALO-BYZANTINE STYLE. Relations between the peoples of the Italian peninsula and the Byzantine Empire, both direct and indirect, account for a body of medieval works of art that can be characterized as Italo-Byzantine in style. Parts of Italy were occupied by the Byzantines from the 6th through the 11th century. Influences upon Italy were considerable and many Eastern artists and monks fled the iconoclastic persecutions to settle in Italy. In addition, the presence of the Alpine barrier tended to preserve in Italy certain late-antique and Early Christian artistic modes from which the Byzantine style had in part originated.

Generally speaking, there were four centers of the style: Venice, Tuscany, Rome, and the deep south. In Venice the Cathedral of St. Mark, begun in the 11th century and derived from the Church of the Holy Apostles in Istanbul, is a synthesis of Byzantine and local inspiration; it was in turn the partial model for many churches in northern Italy and Aquitaine. Many of the carvings and mosaics of St. Mark's, of various periods, are in the Italo-Byzantine style. Both are rather prismatic and geometric in form, characterized by a typically Byzantine abstract quality. *See* ST. MARK'S, VENICE.

In Tuscany the forms of the Byzantine icon panels were prime elements in the paintings of the 11th through the 13th century. The major schools appeared in Siena, Lucca, and Pisa, which produced a quantity of painted crucifixes and altarpieces with figures evolved from the Byzantine canon of stylized ethereality. The genius of painters such as Duccio and Giotto, by the introduction of humanistic narrative and broader iconography, put an end to what had become a rather sterile craft. At their best, however, the products of the Tuscan schools magically balance an Italian sympathy with Byzantine sumptuousness and linear control.

In Rome ancient Romano-Hellenistic forms were intermingled with specifically Byzantine programs, as in the mosaics of SS. Cosmas and Damian (6th cent.) and S. Prassede (9th cent.) and in the early medieval wall paintings of S. Maria Antiqua. *See* SS. COSMAS AND DAMIAN, ROME; SANTA MARIA ANTIQUA, ROME; SANTA PRASSEDE, ROME.

The deep south, more directly connected with the Eastern Empire, received a number of provincial churches based upon Constantinopolitan prototypes (La Cattolica at Stilo; S. Andrea in Trani); sometimes these were sheathed with brilliant mosaics (La Martorana in Palermo). There is a considerable amount of parochial Byzantine wall painting in Apulia. *See* MARTORANA, LA, PALERMO; TRANI. *See also* CEFALU CATHEDRAL.

Interpretation of and reaction to the style was crucial to the development of 14th-century Italian painting, and there is a profound Italo-Byzantine element in the works of the great Venetian masters. (See illustration.)

BIBLIOGRAPHY. R. Byron and D. T. Rice, *The Birth of Western Painting*, New York, 1931; E. Sandberg-Vavalà, *Sienese Studies*, Florence, 1953; G. Francastel, *Italian Painting: Byzantine to Renaissance*, London, 1956; J. A. Hamilton, *Byzantine Architecture and Decoration*, 2d ed., London, 1956; O. Demus, *The Church of San Marco in Venice*, Washington, D.C., 1960.

WILLIAM L. MACDONALD

ITALY, MUSEUMS OF. See under the names of the following cities:

Agrigento. Municipal Archaeological Museum.

Ancona. Francesco Podesti Picture Gallery; National Museum of the Marches.

Arezzo. Medieval and Modern Picture Gallery and Museum.

Ascoli Piceno. Municipal Picture Gallery.

Bari. Provincial Picture Gallery.

Bergamo. Gallery of the Carrara Academy.

Bologna. Municipal Museum (Museo Civico); National Picture Gallery (Pinacoteca Nazionale).

Brescia. Museum of the Christian Era; Roman Museum; Tosio Martinengo Picture Gallery.

Ferrara. Municipal Picture Gallery; National Archaeological Museum.

Florence. Archaeological Museum; Cathedral Museum (Museo dell'Opera del Duomo); Gallery of the Academy; Museum of San Marco; National Museum (Bargello); Palazzo Vecchio (Palazzo della Signoria); Pitti Palace Museums; Uffizi Gallery.

Genoa. Gallery of the Palazzo Bianco.

Mantua. Gallery and Museum of the Ducal Palace.

Messina. National Museum.

Milan. Ambrosian Picture Gallery (Ambrosiana); Brera Picture Gallery; Museum of Ancient Art (Sforza Castle); Poldi-Pezzoli Museum.

Modena. Este Gallery and Museum.

Naples. National Archaeological Museum; National Museum and Gallery of Capodimonte; National Museum of St. Martin.

Orvieto. Cathedral Museum (Museo dell'Opera del Duomo).

Padua. Municipal Museum.

Palermo. National Archaeological Museum; National Gallery of Sicily.

Parma. National Gallery.

Pavia. Malaspina Picture Gallery.

Perugia. National Gallery of Umbria.

Pisa. Camposanto; National Museum of St. Matthew.

Ravenna. National Museum.

Rome. Barberini Palace (Galleria Nazionale d'Arte Antica); Capitoline Museums; Doria Pamphili Gallery; Lateran Museums; National Etruscan Museum of the Villa Giulia; National Gallery of Modern Art; National Museum of Rome (Terme Museum); Palazzo Venezia Museum; Pigorini Museum; Spada Gallery;

Vatican Museums; Villa Borghese Museum and Gallery.

Siena. Metropolitan Museum (Museo dell'Opera Metropolitana); National Picture Gallery (Pinacoteca); Palazzo Pubblico.

Turin. Egyptian Museum (Museo Egizio); Municipal Museum of Ancient Art (Palazzo Madama); Sabauda Gallery.

Urbino. National Gallery of the Marches.

Venice. Cà d'Oro; Correr Museum; Doge's Palace; Gallery of the Academy.

Verona. Castelvecchio Museum.

Vicenza. Municipal Museum.

ITCHO (Hanabusa Itcho). Japanese painter (1652–1724). Itchō studied poetry with Bashō and painting with Kanō Yasunobu, but later was expelled from Yasunobu's studio for being too independent. Because of Itchō's keen eye for genre subjects, his works assumed a satirical note, and he was sent into exile in 1698 for twelve years. His swift, light brushstrokes give the feeling of the gaiety and care-free atmosphere of the period.

BIBLIOGRAPHY. T. Akiyama, *Japanese Painting* [Geneva?], 1961.

ITHACA, N.Y.: ANDREW DICKSON WHITE MUSEUM OF ART, CORNELL UNIVERSITY. Established in 1953, the museum houses the university's collection of art. It includes painting from the 16th century to the present time, both European and American, and an outstanding collection of graphic art, with a large group of etchings and lithographs by Whistler.

I'TIMAD-UD-DAULA, TOMB OF, AGRA. Indian mausoleum erected in 1628 by Nur Jahan, daughter of I'timad-ud-Daula. She was the wife of the emperor Jahangir, for whom I'timad-ud-Daula had served as prime minister. Square in plan, the structure is a single story in height with low minarets at each corner, with the exception of a square tower rising above the tomb chamber. The exterior surfaces are brilliantly clad in *pietra-dura* work, in which lapis, onyx, jasper, topaz, and carnelian were inlaid in white marble. Screens of marble tracery fill all window openings.

BIBLIOGRAPHY. P. Brown, *Indian Architecture*, vol. 2: *Islamic Period*, 4th ed., Bombay, 1959.

ITSUKUSHIMA SHRINE. Japanese Shinto shrine near Hiroshima. The history of the shrine before the Fujiwara period is not certain, and it was extensively restored and enlarged in 1169. The general layout of the shrine is that of a formal Buddhist temple, except that at high tide the ground is inundated by sea water, and the buildings seem to float. The famous Noh stage projecting into the sea was built by Hideyoshi. Excellent examples of decorative arts of the Fujiwara period, such as a set of thirty-three sūtras donated by the Taira family, are found here. *See* HEIKE SUTRAS.

IVAN, *see* LIWAN.

IVANOV, ALEXANDER ANDREEVICH. Russian painter (1806–58). He was a pupil of his father, A. I. Ivanov,

at the St. Petersburg Academy. In 1831 he went to Rome, where he was to remain until shortly before his death. The Nazarenes, particularly Overbeck, appealing to his deeply religious nature, provided the major early influences on his work. Although Ivanov created luminous and richly naturalistic landscapes, he was mainly concerned with work on a monumental religious painting, *Christ's First Appearance to the People* (Leningrad, Russian Museum), over which he labored for twenty-five years and for which he produced innumerable sketches. The result is a curious mixture of classicism and naturalism. In later drawings Ivanov turned to traditional Russian Byzantine painting for inspiration.

BIBLIOGRAPHY. G. H. Hamilton, *The Art and Architecture of Russia*, Baltimore, 1954.

IVERNY, JACQUES. French painter (fl. 1411–38). Working in Avignon after the demise of the papal court, Iverny still shows the influence of the Sienese school in his decorative, aristocratic style. In addition to a signed triptych of the *Virgin Suckling the Child* in the Sabauda Gallery, Turin, the murals in the Castle of La Manta in Piedmont have sometimes been attributed to him.

IVES, JAMES MERRITT, *see* CURRIER AND IVES.

IVORY. Peculiar form of dentine or tooth, generally the tusk of an elephant or other large mammal, used in the arts interchangeably with bone, which is more brittle, and horn, which is softer. It is extremely durable and is affected mainly by severe dampness. From prehistoric times to the end of the 18th century ivory and its substitutes were used extensively for small sculpture and decoration. Carving and engraving are the two basic methods of working ivory, with painting or coloring often done in ancient and medieval times. Turning ivory on a lathe to achieve extravagant effects was introduced in the 17th century.

Some of the earliest ivories known date from the Magdalenian phase of the Upper Paleolithic age. These are a group of engraved and carved animal representations that reveal keen powers of observation and great craftsmanship (St-Germain-en-Laye, Museum of National Antiquities). Their realism contrasts with the stylization of the small female figures from the Aurignacian period. Evidently fertility symbols, the breasts and buttocks are exaggerated, as in the example from Lespugue, France, in Paris (Museum of Natural History).

Predynastic Egyptian figures in ivory are also small and stylized. Ivory was used for decoration in furniture by the Egyptians from early dynastic times on. There are footboards from Middle Kingdom beds richly inlaid with ivory decorated in floral and leaf patterns. In late dynastic times, after the fall of Amarna, the use of ivory became more extensive and the craftsmen showed great virtuosity in handling it. A painted ointment spoon with a lotus-leaf handle and an ointment box in the form of a grasshopper (both Brooklyn Museum) are clear evidence of this skill.

Although ivory was more rare in the Near East, there was no less artistry employed in its use there. Hittite ivories of the 14th century B.C. often repeat on a small scale the monumental sculpture of the time. In the 9th century B.C. Nineveh and Nimrud produced small ivory

Italo-Byzantine style. Lunette mosaic depicting Salome bringing the head of John the Baptist to King Herod. St. Mark's, Venice.

objects, or objects inlaid with ivory, as well as ivory architectural ornamentation in palace interiors. Although no longer extant, ivory furniture was mentioned in the account of the spoils Sennacherib received when he overthrew King Hezekiah.

Ancient Greek ivory sculpture is better known from archaic times than from the Golden Age and later. Literary descriptions, however, suggest that the Greek contribution in ivory was developed during the Golden Age, when the large-scale chryselephantine statues, such as Zeus at Olympia (435–430 B.C.) and Athena from the Parthenon (447–398 B.C.), were made. None of the large idols have survived, but from the descriptions it would appear that the surface of ivory was achieved through some process of combining tusks which has been lost.

Although very rare, examples from Hellenistic and Roman times are of fine quality. Evidence is to be found in such works as the *Tragic Actor* (Paris, Dutuit Collection).

The revival of interest in ivories coincides with a change to a less idealistic as well as less realistic style in the early Christian era. Particularly familiar are the consular diptychs, the covers for wax writing tablets, used from A.D. 330 to 500. In Byzantium the tradition of ivory sculpture was continued, and fine small-scale altarpieces were made along with boxes that had decorative plaques of mythological subjects. Examples decorated with Christian

iconography were replaced by secular work in the rich Roman tradition, such as the small casket with putti and foliate decoration (New York, Metropolitan Museum), stemming from the iconoclastic period. The climactic period of Byzantine ivory work comes in the 9th to 11th century with such examples as the famous Harbaville Triptych (Paris, Louvre).

In the West the revival of the arts during the reigns of Charlemagne (768–814) and the Ottos (936–1002) is particularly important because of the wealth of small-scale work of that period in ivory. The Lower Rhine and Cologne areas were centers of ivory carving in the 11th and 12th centuries, when the Romanesque style dominated, although rivals were active in England, France, and Italy. Oriental influences are discerned in decorative patterns, but classical influences are stronger in figures and in the general conception.

The Gothic style in ivories is not important until late in the 13th century. Large-scale replaced small-scale work. The production of Gothic ivories, centered in France, flourished through the 15th century. Besides delicate representations of the Virgin, delightful secular reliefs on combs, mirror cases, and jewel caskets are characteristic of the era. *Châtelaine de Vergi*, *Perceval*, *Le Chevalier au cygne*, *Tristan et Yseult*, and related tales were the subjects chosen to illustrate. Pastoral staves and related li-

Ivory. Rhenish reliquary with figures of the Magi, 12th century. Guelph Treasure, Museum of Arts and Crafts, Berlin.

turgical objects of the late 13th century round out the group. German and English examples of the time are generally less refined. Italian ivory sculpture of the 14th century has as its highlight the *Virgin and Child* by Giovanni Pisano (Pisa Cathedral) and numerically is best represented in the work of the Embriachi, a family of carvers remarkably active in northern Italy in the 14th century. Characteristic of the Embriachi are the small panels of bone joined together to form caskets, altarpieces, and other forms of relief sculpture. *See* EMBRIACHI.

Relatively little ivory sculpture was made in the Renaissance style. The few extant examples are of very high quality. In the 17th and 18th centuries there was a revival of interest in ivory, especially in Germany and Flanders. The influence of Rubens is apparent in the baroque compositions, in both freestanding groups and reliefs. Sculptors such as Adam Lenckhart (ca. 1610–61) did important work in ivory, and the tradition was carried into the 18th century by Leonard Baur (1681–1760) and David Le Marchand (1674–1726), who did portrait medallions along with sculpture in the round. Tankards with ivory bodies, decorated with classical reliefs in baroque compositions, were popular in Germany in the 17th century. Giovanni Bologna and Bernini were sources of inspiration for small sculpture of greater technical than artistic quality. With the concentration on technique and a dependence on earlier artists for design came the decline of ivory sculpture. Decorative work elaborately turned and made so that it would have shock appeal occupied 17th- and 18th-century ivory carvers. By the 19th century their work was out of fashion completely, and virtuoso pieces, curios rather than art, were imported from the Orient.

BIBLIOGRAPHY. A. M. Cust, *The Ivory Workers of the Middle Ages*, London, 1902; A. Maskell, *Ivories*, London, 1905; A. Gold-

schmidt, *Die Elfenbeinskulpturen*, 4 vols., Berlin, 1914–26; W. S. Smith, *Art and Architecture of Ancient Egypt*, Baltimore, 1958.

MARVIN D. SCHWARTZ

IVORY COAST. An outstanding center of Negro sculpture located in the Guinea coast region of West Africa. Major styles represented are those of the Guro, Baoule (Baule), Agni, and Senufo. Wood is the typical medium. Single and double figures, dance and initiation masks, loom pulleys, and some purely decorative smaller sculptures and reliefs are the principal forms.

While each of the tribal groups has its particular style or styles, there are many similarities of expression and technique throughout the Ivory Coast complex. Most figural works possess refinement of surface detail, marked thinness and elongation of the torso, and arms carved openly away from the sides, joining the trunk at midsection. The masks often have superposed human or animal figures.

See also AFRICA, PRIMITIVE ART OF (WEST AFRICA).

BIBLIOGRAPHY. M. E. Sadler, *Arts of West Africa*, Oxford, 1935; P. S. Wingert, *The Sculpture of Negro Africa*, New York, 1950; W. Fagg and E. Elisofon, *The Sculpture of Africa*, New York, 1958.

IVRIZ. Site at the head of a river in the Taurus Mountains in southern Turkey, where a magnificent rock relief was found. Its style is reminiscent of Hittite and Assyrian art. The carving shows King Urpalla (750 B.C.), a vassal of Assyria, standing before the weather god Tarhund in an attitude of gratitude, offering thanks for the god's agricultural gifts.

BIBLIOGRAPHY. L. Woolley, *The Art of the Middle East*, New York, 1961.

IWAN, *see* LIWAN.

IZQUIERDO, MARIA. Mexican painter (b. San Juan de los Lagos, Jalisco, 1906; d. Mexico City, 1955). The first woman painter of Mexico to be exhibited in the United States, Izquierdo studied at the Academy of San Carlos. During the late 1920s and early 1930s she worked with Rufino Tamayo. Because of this contact, presumably, her colors took on a brilliant indigenous character. At the same time she developed an artistic idiom that was purposely ingenuous and decorative, especially in her many circus themes. Beneath the naïveté, however, there exist more sophisticated elements such as cubism, Fauvism, and surrealism. A knowledgeable craftsman, Izquierdo experimented widely in techniques and materials.

BIBLIOGRAPHY. M. Helm, *Modern Mexican Painters*, New York, 1941.

IZUMO SHRINE. Japanese Shinto shrine in Shimane prefecture. It is one of the oldest Shinto shrines and was supposedly built in the prehistoric period. The shrine was reduced in size during the Kamakura period, and the original is believed to have been twice the height of the present structure, which dates from 1744. The present building preserves a primitive form of shrine architecture, especially in the arrangement of the entrance, which is placed off center.

BIBLIOGRAPHY. R. T. Paine and A. Soper, *The Art and Architecture of Japan*, Baltimore, 1955.

J

JACA CATHEDRAL. Spanish church, dedicated in 1063. At this time the three apses, the barrel-vaulted, nonprojecting transept, and the fine ribbed dome on squinches were complete. The Cathedral underwent further construction in the 11th and 12th centuries. The nave, with alternating supports, and the aisles have beautiful 16th-century star vaults. The excellence of its sculpture, particularly on the capitals and corbels of the two remaining apses and on the capitals of the interior, and the high quality of its architecture make Jaca one of the most important Romanesque monuments of Aragon, and indeed of all Spain. Because it was on the pilgrimage route to Santiago de Compostela, its influence was felt outside the province as well as locally.

BIBLIOGRAPHY. *Ars Hispaniae*, vol. 5: *Arquitectura y escultura románicas*, Madrid, 1948.

JACK OF DIAMONDS. Group of Russian artists under the influence of Cézanne, formed in the second decade of the 20th century. The group combined cubism with a form of exotic expressionism derived from native folk traditions of Russian Jewry to create the motifs and forms of their paintings. *See* LARIONOV, MICHAEL; MALEVICH, KASIMIR.

JACKSON, ALEXANDER YOUNG. Canadian painter (1882–   ). He studied in Chicago and in Paris and other European cities. From 1917 to 1919 he was an official Canadian War Records artist and later a "Group of Seven" member. He has lived principally in Toronto and is known for his landscapes of northern Ontario, rural Quebec, the Arctic, and the Rocky Mountains.

BIBLIOGRAPHY. A. Y. Jackson, *A Painter's Country: The Auto-biography of A. Y. Jackson*, Toronto, 1958.

JACKSON, JOHN. English painter (b. Lastingham, Yorkshire, 1778; d. London, 1831). He studied at the Royal Academy, to which he was elected in 1817, and went to Italy in 1819. His early drawings won him aristocratic patronage, and he soon acquired a reputation as a portrait painter and draftsman.

Jacobello del Fiore, *Justice*. Academy, Venice.

JACOBELLO DEL FIORE. Venetian painter (fl. 1394; d. 1439). He is the only one of an artist family known by works and was the dominant painter of his place and time, with many state commissions. Unoriginal, his Gothic elegance and more modern Giottesque masses change little from first to last dated works (1407–36). They are modified only in ornamental line, influenced by Gentile da Fabriano's visit, which becomes flamboyant and gorgeous with gold leaf in his *Justice* (Venice, Academy). Besides this, his most attractive works are small scenes of the lives of saints (Fermo Museum; Washington, D.C., National Gallery) whose dynamic flow is close to Pisanello.

BIBLIOGRAPHY. B. Berenson, *The Venetian Painters of the Renaissance*, 3d ed., New York, 1897; R. Van Marle, *The Development of the Italian Schools of Painting*, vol. 8, The Hague, 1927.

JACOBINS, CHURCH OF THE, TOULOUSE. Medieval church in southern France. It was a fortress-church of the Dominicans, who were established in Toulouse soon after the order had been founded in 1216 to stamp out the Albigensian heresy. Begun between 1260 and 1265 and completed by 1304, the church retains an extraordinary unity in plan and in aesthetic effect. The lengthy nave and the choir are divided longitudinally into two equal parts—one for the clergy, the other for the public—by lofty round columns, the easternmost of which, known as "the palm tree," gives rise to twenty-two ribs of the vault. Dominating the severe brick exterior is a fine octagonal tower. Also surviving are two galleries of the cloisters, the chapter house, and the 14th-century Chapel of St-Antonin, with interesting 14th- and 15th-century frescoes.

BIBLIOGRAPHY. P. Mesplé, *Les Jacobins de Toulouse*, Toulouse, 1954.

JACOB OF AMSTERDAM, *see* CORNELISZ., JACOB VAN OOSTSANEN.

JACOBSEN, ARNE. Danish architect and industrial designer (1902–   ). Trained as an architect, he has designed housing developments (at Klampenborg), gasoline stations, and a hotel in Copenhagen. During World War II he began designing fabrics and wallpapers that show the influence of William Morris, though his recent work in textile design is more subtle. Jacobsen's designs for flat-ware, chairs, desks, and numerous other interior fixtures are created for his own houses and for general distribution. His work is distinctively original in its simplicity and functional conception. In 1959 the first one-man exhibition held at the Royal Institute of British Architects was devoted to his work in design.

Much of his furniture is intended for industrial production with manufacturing techniques and materials specified. A three-legged chair, designed in 1952, of steel and laminated wood demonstrates how effective this total planning has been. An example of the elegant, yet comfortable, simplicity that characterizes these items is the "Egg," a swivel chair created in 1957 for the Danish manufacturer Fritz Hansen, and molded in upholstered plastic with an aluminum frame. It is in the Nordenfjeldske Museum of Decorative Art in Norway; other pieces are owned by the Museum of Decorative Art in Copenhagen.

BIBLIOGRAPHY. J. Barnett, "Jacobsen Exhibit at R.I.B.A.: Report from England," *Architectural Record*, CXXV, April, 1959; Landsforeningen Dansk Kunsthaandvaerk, *The Arts of Denmark*, Copenhagen, 1960.

ILSA KLOTZMAN

JACOBSEN, ROBERT. Danish sculptor (1912–   ). Born in Copenhagen, he has lived in Paris since 1947. Until about 1948 he worked in wood and stone. Iron constructions then superseded the earlier media. His style is strongly geometric and abstract. Jacobsen has exhibited at the Galerie Denise René and the Galerie de France in Paris, as well as in many European cities.

BIBLIOGRAPHY. L. Degand et al., *Témoignages pour l'art abstrait*, Paris, 1952.

JACOBSEN FURNITURE, see JACOBSEN, ARNE.

JACOBSZ., LAMBERT. Dutch painter of Biblical subjects (b. Amsterdam, ca. 1598; d. Leeuwarden, 1636). Jacobsz., who seems to have traveled to Italy, is said to have been a pupil of Rubens. In 1620 Jacobsz. married in Leeuwarden and became a citizen of that city the following year. He was also active as a Mennonite preacher. Most of his works are landscapes with Biblical subjects somewhat in the style of Pieter Lastman. Govert Flinck and Jacob Backer were his pupils.

BIBLIOGRAPHY. H. F. Wijnman, "Nieuwe Gegvens omtrent den Schilder Lambert Jacobsz.," *Oud-Holland*, XLVII, 1930.

JACOMART, see BACO, JAIME.

JACOMETREZO (Jacome de Trezzo) EL VIEJO, see TREZZO, JACOPO DA, THE ELDER.

JACOPINO DEL CONTE, see CONTE, JACOPINO DEL.

JACOPO, DON, see JACOPO DI FRANCESCO.

JACOPO, GHERARDO DI, see STARNINA, GHERARDO.

JACOPO DA BOLOGNA, see JACOPO DEGLI AVANZI.

JACOPO DA SANSEVERINO, see SALIMBENI DA SANSEVERINO, JACOPO AND LORENZO.

JACOPO DA VALENZA. Venetian painter (fl. 1488–1509). His signed Madonnas and other works date between 1488 and 1509. He first imitated Antonello da Messina and then turned to Alvise Vivarini's work of about 1485, using bright color and awkward form. His native Valenza may be in Piedmont, but it is probably the one in Sicily.

JACOPO DA VERONA. Italian painter (fl. late 14th cent.). According to an inscription of 1397, he was the painter of the impressive series of frescoes depicting scenes from the lives of Christ and the Virgin in the Oratory of S. Michele, Padua. Jacopo was in the tradition of Giotto and was probably a follower of Altichiero, as the vigorous naturalism, sturdy volumetric figures, and expansive space of these frescoes indicate. The illuminations for the *Bibbia istoriata padovana* (split between the British Museum, London, and the Library of the Academy of the Concordi, Rovigo) have also been attributed to him.

BIBLIOGRAPHY. C. Bettiol, *Jacopo da Verona in S. Michele . . .*, Padua, 1961; *Bibbia istoriata padovana della fine del Trecento . . .*, ed. G. Folena and G. L. Mellini, Venice, 1962.

JACOPO DEGLI AVANZI (Jacopo da Bologna). Italian painter of the school of Bologna (fl. ca. 1350–1400). He was a follower of Vitale da Bologna and worked with him on the frescoes at Mezzaratta. Many of Jacopo's paintings on panel are in the National Picture Gallery in Bologna.

BIBLIOGRAPHY. F. Filippini, "Jacopo Avanzi pittore bolognese del '300," *Reale deputazione di storia patria per le provincie di Romagna*, series 4, II, 1912.

JACOPO DEL CASENTINO. Italian painter of the Florentine school (ca. 1300–49/58). He was a follower of Giotto and adhered to the miniaturistic trend in Florentine painting. Jacopo's most important work is the *S. Miniato Altarpiece* in S. Miniato al Monte, Florence.

BIBLIOGRAPHY. R. Offner, *A Critical and Historical Corpus of Florentine Painting*, sec. 3, vol. 2, New York, 1930.

JACOPO DI CIONE, see CIONE, JACOPO DI.

JACOPO DI FRANCESCO (Don Jacopo). Italian calligrapher and miniature painter (b. Florence, ca. 1337; d. there, 1396). When he was eleven, he entered the Monastery of S. Maria degli Angeli in Florence, where there are numerous choir books decorated by him. Vasari considered him the best calligrapher in all of Europe.

JACOPO DI GASPARE, GIOVANNI BATTISTA DI, see ROSSO FIORENTINO.

JACOPO DI PAOLO. Italian painter (fl. 1390–1426). Possibly of a family from Reggio, Jacopo was one of the most active artists in Bologna, working in the tradition of Vitale da Bologna. His exaggerated linearity and gross treatment of human form and emotional expression may be seen in such a work as the *Crucifixion* (Bologna, National Picture Gallery).

JACQUE, CHARLES EMILE. French graphic artist and painter (b. Paris, 1813; d. there, 1894). Jacque was a well-known member of the Barbizon school, and his graphic works as well as his paintings are almost totally in the *paysage intime* tradition. His paintings, which are close

Charles Emile Jacque, a lithograph from *Les Malades et les Médecins*.

in style to Millet, were very popular in the 19th century. His best works, however, are in graphics: engraving, lithographs, woodcuts, and etchings. The etchings especially are skillfully rendered and subtle in their handling of light and texture, for example, the *L'Orage* series. More than 420 etchings have been cataloged, by far the largest number pastoral scenes.

JACQUES DE BESANCON. French illuminator (fl. 2d half of 15th cent.). A follower of Maître François, with whom he collaborated, Jacques de Besançon also emulated the style of Fouquet in traditional illuminations and in illuminated woodcuts for printed books.

JACQUET DE GRENOBLE, MATHIEU. French sculptor (d. 1610). He was probably the son of Antoine Jacquet, and was active at Fontainebleau under Henry II. Mathieu Jacquet, Guillaume Dupré, and Barthélemy Tremblay were the official portraitists of Henry IV. In 1597 Jacquet became court sculptor and in 1602, Guardian of Antiquities. His masterpiece is the *Belle Cheminée* at the Château of Fontainebleau. Heavily influenced by Fontainebleau school mannerism, his style is transitional to that of the 17th century.

BIBLIOGRAPHY. J. Coural, "Une Oeuvre inconnue de Mathieu Jacquet dit Grenoble," *La Revue des Arts*, VIII, 1958; E.-J. Ciprut, "Le Chef-d'oeuvre de Mathieu Jacquet de Grenoble: La 'Belle Cheminée' du Château de Fontainebleau," *Gazette des Beaux-Arts*, series 6, LIII, 1959.

JADE. Broad name given to a class of semiprecious mineral composed largely of silicate of aluminum or calcium with sodium or magnesium. Of the two major types, jadeite is harder and when polished is often translucent, whereas nephrite is slightly softer and more waxy in appearance, but both are true jade. Its hardness ranges between six and seven on the Mohr scale, which is equal to that of quartz, and in addition its peculiar interlocking crystalline structure makes it one of the toughest of all known minerals. Despite these characteristics jade is often elaborately carved by means of diamond drills, wire saws, and lapidary wheels containing such abrasives as garnet dust, quartz, and emery. The final polish is achieved on wood and leather wheels charged with ruby-dust paste. Deposits, often in the form of boulders, are found all over the world, but the principal sources are in upper Burma and in Turkestan; relatively little is found in China itself.

Although green and white are the best-known colors of jade, it occurs in almost every shade because of the presence of other elements in the mixture. The brilliant emerald-green shade known as Imperial is perhaps the most precious, especially in the West, but Oriental connoisseurs also prize the pure white, lavender, and yellow tones.

Prehistoric peoples in Europe and Central America, as well as in the Far East, used jade for axes and other utilitarian objects as well as for decorative purposes because of its strength and beauty. Since about 3000 B.C. jade has been the most valuable of gems in China. The Chinese word for jade, *yü*, also means the five cardinal virtues of man; and jade is considered to have both medical and magical powers. The word "jade" comes from the Spanish *ijada*, meaning "loin," reflecting the 16th-century notion that jade had the power to cure diseases of the kidney and spleen when placed near the affected organ. The word "nephrite" comes from the Greek word for kidney, as the mineral was thought to cure kidney diseases.

Oriental jade. The earliest-known jade objects date from the Yang-shao culture of China (ca. 3000–2200 B.C.) and are ritual disks about 5 inches in diameter with a hole in the center. Few other jade objects are known until the late Shang dynasty (ca. 1500–ca. 1027 B.C.), when ceremonial dagger blades and flat ax heads were made. During the Chou dynasty (ca. 1027–256 B.C.) jade carving developed as a fine art.

In later centuries expanding trade with Persia, India, Turkestan, and Japan caused foreign stylistic innovations to appear in Chinese carved jades. Some of the largest and most impressive pieces were produced during the Ming dynasty (A.D. 1368–1644). Stylistic affinities with bronze and ceramic work are apparent, and late jades show increasing European influence. Tiny tear bottles as well as great incense burners and vases were designed with a new intricacy and elaboration. During this period the famous Ming dragon motif was introduced and purely decorative forms reached their height.

The most ostentatious jades were produced during the Ch'ing dynasty (1644–1912). Technical perfection is unrivaled in the highly decorated pieces made before the 19th century. Among the most remarkable items are the great "Jade Mountains," which are the largest carved jades known. The biggest example, in the Forbidden City in Peking, is about 7 feet tall, weighs as many tons, and was made in 1778–88. It depicts a great mountain landscape filled with workmen of the emperor Yu, who, in 2205 B.C., kept flood waters from ruining the land. Smaller but still massive mountains exist, such as the piece in the Walker Art Center in Minneapolis. Other pieces made for the Ch'ing court include 6-foot screens composed of jade panels etched in gold and basins 70 inches wide. *See* CHINA: JADE.

Non-Oriental jade. Tools and weapons of jade have been found in the remains of prehistoric Swiss lake dwellers, and jade axes were used by the natives of New Zealand. In Central America and Mexico jade was used in greater abundance than any place outside the Orient for beads, pendants, axes, and statues. The Olmec and Aztec cultures used jade extensively, but the finest pieces come from the classical Mayan sites in Yucatán. One of the earliest dated objects found in the New World is the Leyden Plate (Leyden, Rijksmuseum voor Volkenkunde), discovered in Guatemala in 1864. About 8 inches high and of fine jade, it comes from the archaic Mayan culture and dates from about the 4th century A.D. Many early pre-Columbian jades preserve the shape of the original pebble or boulder, and are engraved rather than carved.

See also AMERICAS, ANCIENT, ART OF.

At times the term "jade" has been incorrectly but widely used to include Sassurite, green beryl, and some forms of serpentine and quartz, but an analysis of hardness, crystalline structure, and specific gravity will invariably differentiate these substances from jadeite and nephrite.

BIBLIOGRAPHY. U. Pope-Hennessy, *Early Chinese Jades*, London, 1923; S. C. Nott, *Chinese Jade throughout the Ages*, New York,

Jade. Aztec mask. National Museum of Anthropology, Mexico City. The Olmec and Aztec cultures used jade extensively.

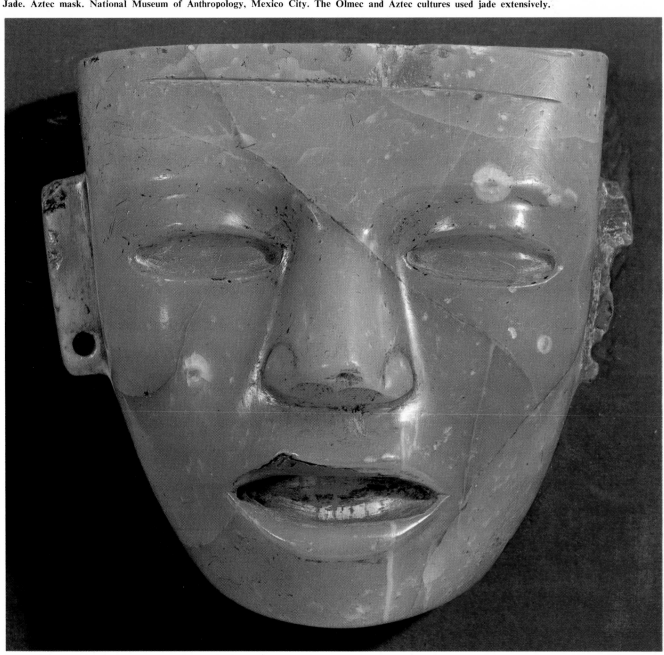

1937; P. Kelemen, *Medieval American Art*, New York, 1943; **B.** Laufer, *Jade...*, South Pasadena, Calif., 1946.

MARVIN D. SCHWARTZ

JAEN CATHEDRAL. Spanish Renaissance Cathedral. The Cathedrals of Jaén, Málaga, and Granada are the finest Renaissance monuments of Andalusia. A church was begun on the site in the late 15th century by Pedro López. It may have influenced the plan of the present structure, begun in 1540, whose elevation was fixed after a conference in 1548 attended by, among others, the architects Pedro Machuca and Andrés de Vandelvira (master of the works). The vast interior space, with aisles and nave of equal height, is roofed with domical vaults resting on compound Corinthian piers, each, as at Granada, bearing its section of entablature. The barrel-vaulted sacristy (1555–60) is Vandelvira's masterpiece. The twin-towered west façade (1667–88) was built from plans of Eufrasio López de Rojas and echoes Carlo Maderno's scheme for St. Peter's in Rome (begun 1607).

BIBLIOGRAPHY. *Ars Hispaniae*, vol. 11, Madrid, 1953; *Ars Hispaniae*, vol. 14, Madrid, 1957.

JAGANNATHA TEMPLE, PURI. Hindu temple built about A.D. 1150 in Purī, on the coast of Orissa State, India. It has become world-famous as the Juggernaut. Dedicated to one of the incarnations of Krishna, the temple occupies a site that may have originally been Buddhist. The Jagannātha is similar in structure to the great Liṅgarāja of Bhuvaneśvara in the same state.

BIBLIOGRAPHY. H. R. Zimmer, *The Art of Indian Asia*, 2 vols., New York, 1955; P. Brown, *Indian Architecture*, 4th ed., 2 vols., Bombay, 1959.

JAHANGIR PERIOD, *see* MUGHAL PAINTING OF INDIA (JAHANGIR PERIOD).

JAJAR KOHLAN, *see* TIMNA'.

JAKUCHU (Ito Jakucho). Japanese painter (d. 1800). First trained by a Kanō master, he later modified his style by incorporating the strong colors of Ming China and Kōrin, at the same time preserving an intense realism. Jakuchū was particularly fascinated by fowl, which he depicted in fresh and bold compositions with a keen understanding of their nature. *See* KORIN.

BIBLIOGRAPHY. R. T. Paine and A. Soper, *The Art and Architecture of Japan*, Baltimore, 1955.

JALOUSIE. Shutter with horizontal slats, fixed or adjustable. The jalousie is usually of wood, but the term is also applicable to units of metal or glass. Jalousies are used as screens and as protection against rain and sun while allowing the air to circulate.

JAMB. Side of an opening, as of a door or window. The reveal is the portion of the jamb between the frame and the outer surface of the wall. In wood construction the jamb is the part of the frame that forms the lining for the opening to receive the door.

JAMDET NASR. Site in Iraq on the Tigris River, southeast of Baghdad. It consists of three mounds; only Mound B was excavated in 1925–26 and 1928 by the Field Museum

Jamdet Nasr. Stone vessel. Chicago Natural History Museum.

(now the Chicago Natural History Museum) and Oxford University. The excavations produced material evidence of a new or protoliterate period in Mesopotamian history, which came to be known as the Jamdet Nasr period (3200–3000 B.C.) after this site. Remains of a large building were discovered on the eastern side of the mound. It is comparable to the Early Dynastic I or II (3000–2600 B.C.) Palace A at Kish and is therefore probably also a palace, although of the earlier, Jamdet Nasr period. Painted and unpainted pottery, seals and seal impressions of the Jamdet Nasr style, and tablets and stone vessels were found in this palace.

BIBLIOGRAPHY. S. Langdon, "Ausgrabungen in Babylonien seit 1918," *Der Alte Orient*, XXVI, 1928; E. Mackay, *Report on Excavations at Jemdet Nasr, Iraq* (Field Museum of Natural History, Chicago, Anthropology, Memoirs, vol. 1, no. 3), Chicago, 1931; D. B. Harden, "A Typological Examination of Sumerian Pottery from Jemdet Nasr and Kish," *Iraq*, I, April, 1934; H. Field and R. A. Martin, "Painted Pottery from Jemdet Nasr, Iraq," *American Journal of Archaeology*, XXXIX, July/September, 1935.

JAMES, HOMILIES OF. Byzantine illuminated manuscript, in the Vatican Library, Rome.

JAMES OF ST. GEORGE. Architect, probably from France, who was the great genius behind the design of Edward I's fortresses in North Wales. He was concerned with Flint, Rhuddlan, Aberystwyth, and Builth in the 1270s. In the next decade he created the inspired achievements of Conway, Caernarvon, and Denbigh. Harlech followed in 1283. *See* CAERNARVON CASTLE; CONWAY CASTLE; HARLECH CASTLE.

BIBLIOGRAPHY. J. Harvey, comp., *English Mediaeval Architects*, London, 1954.

JAMESONE, GEORGE. Scottish portrait painter (b. Aberdeen, 1588; d. Edinburgh, 1644). In 1612 he was apprenticed to John Anderson, an unknown Edinburgh painter. When Charles I visited Edinburgh in 1633, Jamesone painted his portrait; that same year he also traveled in Italy. The tradition that he studied with Rubens is generally discounted. Since his is the only identifiable name in early Scottish portraiture, many portraits of the period are attributed to him, usually on insufficient evidence. The few known portraits that survive are thinly painted in the style of Cornelius Johnson. Both the University collection and the Gallery in Edinburgh have examples of his work.

BIBLIOGRAPHY. E. K. Waterhouse, *Painting in Britain, 1530–1790*, Baltimore, 1953.

JAMES THE GREATER, ST. Apostle (1st cent.). Son of Zebedee and Salome, James, a fisherman like his brother John the Evangelist, was among the first to be called to follow Christ. James was present at the Transfiguration and at the Agony in the Garden, with Peter and John. James and Peter were leaders of the church in Jerusalem, where James was the first apostle to be martyred. James is said to have evangelized Spain and is its patron saint. His relics are at Santiago de Compostela. His attributes are a pilgrim's staff, hat, purse, and cockleshell and a sword. His feast is July 25. *See also* SAINTS IN ART.

JAMES THE LESS, ST. Apostle (1st cent.). Son of Alpheus and Mary Cleophas and brother of the apostle Jude Thaddeus, James was called "brother" of Jesus. He fasted until the Resurrection, when Christ gave him bread. James became the first bishop of Jerusalem. When thrown from the temple pinnacle, he was not hurt. He was condemned to death by the Sanhedrin, and his skull was broken by a fuller. His attribute is a fuller's club. His feast, formerly May 1, is now May 11. *See also* SAINTS IN ART.

JAMI MASJID (Jumma Musjid; Masjid-i-Jami). Great mosque, the principal mosque of a town. The Jami Masjid was usually approached by a colonnaded court, as in Jaunpur, Ahmedabad, and Bijapur, of the 15th and 16th centuries. *See* AHMEDABAD: JAMI MASJID; ARDABIL: MASJID-I-JAMI; BIJAPUR: JAMI MASJID; FATEHPUR SIKRI; JAMI MASJID, DELHI; JAUNPUR: JAMI MASJID; MASJID-I-JAMI, ISFAHAN; VARAMIN: FRIDAY MOSQUE.

JAMI MASJID, DELHI. Indian mosque situated in the heart of Old Delhi. One of the largest mosques in the world, featuring an open courtyard 400 feet on each side, it was built between 1644 and 1658. The building crowns a rocky outcrop; flights of steps lead to three portals which open into the courtyard. The sanctuary side of the courtyard displays two minarets and three domes of white marble, with the largest central dome rising to a height of 201 feet. Built of red sandstone and white marble, the vast structure is a most effective combination of monumental solidity and delicate decoration.

BIBLIOGRAPHY. R. C. Arora, *Delhi; The Imperial City*, New Delhi, 1953.

JAMNITZER (Gamitzer) FAMILY. German family of goldsmiths and engravers whose work marks the high point of Renaissance and mannerist goldsmithing in Nürnberg. Wenzel (b. Vienna, 1508; d. Nürnberg, 1585), probably the greatest German goldsmith, as well as an engraver, medalist, and maker of plaquettes and mathematical instruments, became a master goldsmith in the Nürnberg guild in 1534. His brother Albrecht, nephew Barthel, and sons Wenzel II, Abraham, and Hans II were part of his workshop. Wenzel's development from a Renaissance (e.g., silver gilt and enamel table ornament, before 1549; Amsterdam, Rijksmuseum) to a mannerist style (e.g., silver

Jamnitzer Family. Hans Jamnitzer, plaquette depicting Scylla and Minos. Rijksmuseum, Amsterdam.

gilt jewel casket set with diamonds, rubies, and semiprecious stones, ca. 1560; Munich, Residenz Treasury) was accompanied by an increasing use of rustic forms (e.g., nautilus ewer with silver gilt mounts, ca. 1570; Residenz Treasury). His most famous work is the *Merkel Centerpiece* (ca. 1549; Paris, Rothschild Collection). In addition to being court goldsmith to the emperors Rudolph II, Ferdinand I, and Prince Ferdinand of Tyrol, he was the author and engraver of the *Perspectiva literaria* (Nürnberg, 1557) and *Perspectiva corporum regularium* (Nürnberg, 1568). His son Hans II (b. Nürnberg, 1538; d. there, 1603) became a master goldsmith in 1563. Hans continued in Wenzel's rustic style, as is seen in a silver table bell with plants and reptiles cast from life (ca. 1560–70; Residenz Treasury). He has also been identified by Von Falke as the maker of a number of fine plaquettes marked "H. G." for Hans Gamitzer. These include a lead plaquette, *Minos Besieging Nisa* (1569; Rijksmuseum). Hans's son Christoph (b. Nürnberg, 1553; d. there, 1618) became a master goldsmith in Nürnberg in 1592. He is believed to have traveled in Italy on the basis of the designs in his *Neuw Groteszken Buch* (Nürnberg, 1610), which show his assimilation of, as well as his contribution of original elements to, the Italian grotesque tradition. His work as a mannerist goldsmith is exemplified by a silver gilt ewer made for Rudolph II (early 17th cent.; Vienna, Museum of Art History).

BIBLIOGRAPHY. M. Frankenberger, *Beiträge zur Geschichte Wenzel Jamnitzers und seine Familie* (Studien zur deutschen Kunstgeschichte, vol. 30), Strasbourg, 1901; M. Rosenberg, *Jamnitzer*, Frankfurt am Main, 1920; E. Kris and O. von Falke, "Beiträge zu den Werken Christoph und Hans Jamnitzers," *Jahrbuch der Preuszischen Kunstsammlungen*, XLVII, 1926; E. Kris, "Der Stil 'Rustique'," *Jahrbuch der Kunsthistorischen Sammlungen in Wien*, 1926; P. du Colombier, "Les Dix plus étonnants chefs-d'oeuvre de Wenzel Jamnitzer, le Benvenuto Cellini germanique," *Connaissance des Arts*, December, 1964.

CLARE VINCENT

JANE SEYMOUR, PORTRAIT OF. Oil painting by Holbein the Younger, in the Museum of Art History, Vienna. *See* HOLBEIN, HANS, THE YOUNGER.

JANET, *see* CLOUET, JEAN.

JANINET, JEAN FRANCOIS. French aquatint artist (b. Paris, 1752; d. there, 1814). He studied at the School of the Royal Academy but taught himself engraving. Contributing to the development of color printing by his use of an aquatint plate to superimpose colors, he achieved great popularity with prints after Boucher, Fragonard, Lavreince, Hubert Robert, and others.

BIBLIOGRAPHY. C. E. Russell, *French Colour-prints of the XVIIIth Century; The Art of Debocourt, Janinet and Descourtis,* London, 1927.

JANMOT, ANNE FRANCOIS LOUIS. French painter and poet (b. Lyons, 1814; d. there, 1892). He studied in Lyons and with Ingres and Flandrin in Paris. Janmot painted religious and symbolic works in a neoclassical style. He also painted portraits.

JANSENS, CORNELIUS, *see* JOHNSON, CORNELIUS.

JANSSENS, ABRAHAM. Flemish painter of allegorical, mythological, and religious subjects, and portraits (b. Antwerp, ca. 1575; d. there, 1631). In 1585 he was a pupil of Jan Snellinck. Janssens traveled in Italy (he was in Rome in 1598) and became a master in 1601.

He is an important representative of the Romanist trend, and his figure compositions are strongly influenced by Caravaggio, both in modeling and in the use of heavy shadows. Among Janssens' best-known productions are *Scaldis and Antwerpia* (1609; Antwerp, Fine Arts Museum) and the impressive *Crucifixion* (Valenciennes Museum), which is permeated with Italian reminiscences. In his later years he adopted the Rubensian style, without, however, attaining the great master's dynamism and vivacity of color. A series of Roman emperors (for example, *Nero*, 1618; Berlin, Schloss Grünewald) bears witness to Janssens' solid achievements in portraiture.

BIBLIOGRAPHY. G. Isario, *Caravage et le caravagisme européen,* Aix-en-Provence, 1941; H. Gerson and E. H. ter Kuile, *Art and Architecture in Belgium, 1600–1800,* Baltimore, 1960.

JANSSENS, HIERONYMUS (The Dancer). Flemish painter (1624–93). He was born in Antwerp and was a pupil of Christoffel Jacob van der Lamen. Janssens continued his master's style and painted interiors featuring fashionable society at dancing and musical parties (hence his nickname). His works are easily recognizable from the pastel hues of his palette and the stiff postures of the figures. In his small-size interior scenes, he occasionally comes close to Gonzales Coques.

BIBLIOGRAPHY. W. Bernt, *Die niederländischen Maler des 17. Jahrhunderts...,* vol. 2, Munich, 1948.

JANSSENS ELINGA, PIETER. Dutch-Flemish painter of interiors and still life (b. Bruges; d. before 1682). This artist is probably identical with the Pieter Janssens Elinga who was reported in Amsterdam as a musician from Bruges. In 1653 he was called a widower and therefore was probably older than Pieter de Hoogh (1629–after 1684),

who may have been his teacher. His interiors are extremely close to those of De Hoogh.

BIBLIOGRAPHY. C. Brière-Misme, "A Dutch Intimist, Pieter Janssens Elinga," *Gazette des Beaux-Arts,* XXXI, March–May, 1947, XXXII, November, 1947, XXXIII, June, 1948.

JANSSEN VAN KEULEN, CORNELIS, *see* JOHNSON, CORNELIUS.

JANUS. Italic and, later, Roman god of public and private gates and doorways. His busts, having one head but two faces set in opposite directions, were expected to guard both entrances and exits of a building from evildoers. Janus's head appears on Roman coins, and he was considered to be a patron of business ventures, since it was thought that his influence extended to fresh beginnings in human enterprise.

JAPAN. Throughout its history Japan often received artistic ideas and models from China. The periods of intensive borrowing were usually followed by equally energetic efforts to assimilate what was learned from the Chinese, and thus to create an art of its own out of the foreign prototypes. The reliance on China and its arts continued until the 19th century, when Europe set examples for the Japanese artists.

Jomon period (ca. 3500 B.C.–ca. 3d cent. B.C.). Some stone implements were discovered below the stratum containing Jōmon pottery pieces. However, the discussion of the art history of Japan can properly begin with the pottery of the Jōmon period. Jōmon pottery is characterized by a cord pattern (*jōmon*) pressed onto clay bodies of pottery wares and figurines. The Jōmon culture, which depended on a hunting and fishing economy, extended to almost all of the archipelago of Japan.

Yayoi period (ca. 3d cent. B.C.–ca. A.D. 3d cent.). A different type of pottery, called Yayoi pottery, made its first appearance about the 3d century B.C. It is characterized by a reddish body, thinner than the Jōmon pottery, and by the absence of a cord pattern. The forms are more regular, and it is fired at a higher temperature. It was named after the district in Tokyo where the first specimens of this pottery were discovered. The Yayoi culture was based on an advanced rice-growing agriculture.

Yayoi pottery was found together with such metal objects as *dōtaku* bells, mirrors, weapons, and horse trappings and objects made of glass and jade. Many of these objects are Chinese in origin. In fact, regular intercourse with Korea and China seems to have been established by the beginning of the Christian era. *See* GLASS.

Tomb period (ca. 3d cent.–552). Mounded tombs first appeared in the 3d century. Many of the larger tombs were constructed in a keyhole shape, wedge-shaped in front and circular in back. They were surrounded by moats, and clay images called *haniwa* were placed on or around these tombs. The *haniwa*, representing men, women, animals, and buildings, illustrate various aspects of Japanese life of this period. A large concentration of mounded tombs in the Yamato region (the present Kinki district) suggests that this area was the major power center of Japan. Numerous tribes were amalgamated under the leadership of the Yamato clan.

Asuka period (552–710). The period is named after the Asuka district, within which the imperial courts were moved from place to place on the death of each emperor. In 552 the Korean kingdom of Paekche (Japanese, Kudara) sent to the Japanese court an imperial message praising the virtue of Buddhism and advising the Japanese emperor to embrace its teachings. The message was accompanied by a bronze image of the Buddha, some volumes of Buddhist scriptures, and other presents. After a long period of political struggle between the supporters and opponents of the new faith, Buddhism was accepted by the court. Japanese Buddhism was further developed under the empress Suiko (593–628) and her regent, the crown prince Shōtoku (572–622), who were enthusiastic followers. The arts and sciences of China were brought into Japan with the Buddhist teachings and profoundly changed Japan's cultural life. (For correlation of Chinese, Indian, and Japanese Buddhist terminology, *see* BUDDHIST TERMS, CORRELATION OF.

Nara period (710–784). As Japan was closely drawn into the orbit of wealthy and powerful T'ang China, the Japanese felt a strong need for a permanent capital city that would equal the splendor of the Chinese capital of Ch'ang-an. In 710 the court moved from Asuka to Nara. The capital of Nara, which was modeled after Ch'ang-an, became the metropolis, the center of administration, the home of the arts, and the "Holy See" of Buddhism. T'ang China's influence was evident in every phase of Japanese life: in the planning of the city, in the administration of the country, in court life, and in literature and the arts. Following the Chinese example, histories of Japan were written for the first time: the *Kojiki* in 710 and the *Nihon Shoki* in 720. The first anthology of Japanese poetry, *Manyō-shū*, was also compiled in this period. *See* NARA.

In 741 the emperor Shōmu (701–756) issued an imperial edict that a Kokubunji (provincial monastery) and a Kokubunniji (provincial convent) should be built in each province. The Tōdaiji in Nara was to be the central temple governing these provincial establishments. In 752 the 53-foot-tall gilded bronze statue of Vairocana (Rushana) was dedicated in the Tōdaiji with unprecedented pomp and ceremony. The magnificant objects used in this ceremony and the treasures that once belonged to the emperor Shōmu were later donated to the Tōdaiji. They have been preserved ever since in this temple's warehouse, called the Shōsōin, which now belongs to the imperial household.

Heian period (794–1185). In 794 a new capital was established on the site of the present city of Kyoto. It was called Heian-kyō (Capital of Peace and Tranquillity), and it remained the capital of Japan until 1867. The city was built on the same lines as the Chinese capital of Ch'ang-an. The period from 794 to 897 is called the early Heian period, when the influence of the T'ang culture was still strong in every aspect of Japanese culture. However, the new doctrine of esoteric Buddhism (Mikkyō) was introduced from China, and there was a trend to build temples in the mountains away from the influence of city secular life. Saichō (called also Dengyō Daishi, 767–822) built the Enryakuji on Mt. Hiei and founded the Tendai sect after his return from China. Kūkai (known also as Kōbō Daishi, 773–835) studied in China in the early 9th century and founded the Shingon sect at the Kongōbuji on Mt.

Kōya. Saichō and Kūkai made a great contribution to the development of esoteric Buddhism and the arts connected with it. Buddhist statues with strange, frightening appearances and the mandara (Sanskrit, maṇḍala) paintings, showing the schematic relationship of countless deities, were produced for the service of the esoteric doctrine. *See* ENRYAKUJI; KYOTO; MIKKYO; SHINGON; TENDAI.

The period from 898 to 1185 is called the late Heian period. It is also known as the Fujiwara period, as the Fujiwara noblemen exercised uncontested power at the court. As the power of T'ang China was on the decline in the late 9th century, Japan felt it was no longer necessary to maintain official relationships with China. This was an extremely important era in the history of Japanese art. Chinese art no longer set examples for the Japanese artists, and the indigenous taste of the Japanese asserted itself more strongly. The Japanese created an art of their own by assimilating what they had learned from the Chinese. This was also the golden age of literature. Lady Murasaki's masterpiece, the *Tale of Genji*, was written about 1000, and it shows the maturity of the pure Japanese prose style.

The belief in the Western Paradise of the Amida Buddha, embraced by the Pure Land sect of Buddhism, became popular. Fujiwara courtiers were enthusiastic supporters of this sect, and their taste for superb elegance is reflected in the Hōōdō (Phoenix Hall) of the Byōdōin in Uji. Architects, garden designers, sculptors, painters, and lacquerers cooperated to create this masterpiece. The brilliant cultural metropolis of Kyoto was copied by the rulers of remote provinces throughout Japan, creating such cultural centers as Hiraizumi. The Fujiwara aristocracy lost its influence toward the end of this period. After a series of civil wars Minamoto Yoritomo emerged as the decisive victor. *See* HOODO OF BYODOIN.

Kamakura period (1185–1333). Yoritomo established himself in Kamakura, near Tokyo, and became the first of the shoguns who ruled Japan for the next 700 years. The vigorous spirit of the warrior leaders and their interest in the realistic portrayal of life and nature in a simple and direct manner are clearly reflected in the sculptures of the Unkei school, narrative scroll paintings (*emaki*), and portraiture. *See* KAMAKURA; UNKEI.

Zen Buddhism, which was introduced from China in the late 12th century, found enthusiastic followers among the Kamakura warriors. Its teachings, which emphasized self-discipline, quiet meditation, and a Spartan way of life, were congenial to the military men's psychology, and it quickly became the leading Buddhist doctrine. The arts of Sung and Yüan China were introduced with Zen Buddhism, and consequently monochrome landscape painting became the new vogue in the late Kamakura period. *See* ZEN.

Muromachi period (1336–1573). The Ashikaga family succeeded the Kamakura shoguns and established themselves in an area in Kyoto called Muromachi, for which the period is named. Under the reign of such art-conscious shoguns as Yoshimitsu (1358–1408) and Yoshimasa (1435–90), arts in the service of Zen Buddhism continued to flourish. The Kinkaku (Golden Pavilion) was built for Yoshimitsu and the Ginkaku (Silver Pavilion) for Yoshimasa. Monochrome landscape paintings in the Chinese manner were produced by Zen monk-painters, among whom Sesshū was the most important. The tea ceremony developed in this period, and its aesthetics still govern many aspects of Japanese life and arts. *See* GINKAKUJI; KINKAKUJI; SESSHU TOYO.

Momoyama period (1574–1614). There was a long confusing period of constant internecine warfare at the end of the Muromachi period followed by this brief interlude. Christianity was introduced in Japan during the Momoyama period. Contact with the Portuguese in the 16th century transformed many aspects of Japanese arts. Firearms of the West were introduced and created a profound change in the modes of warfare and fortification. Impressive castles and palaces with brilliantly decorated interiors characterize the heroic taste of the warlords.

Edo period (1615–1867). This period is named after the city of Edo (present-day Tokyo), where Tokugawa Ieyasu established himself as the first Tokugawa shogun. The Christians were severely persecuted in the 1630s. Japan not only banned Christianity and expelled Christian missionaries but it also closed its doors to the outside world. A long period of internal peace ensued, and Edo became the center of political, economic, and artistic activities. Religious art declined, but the arts for the common men, especially the wood-block prints called Ukiyo-e, became popular. Mass-produced pictures showing the women of the gay quarters and Kabuki actors epitomize the plebeian character of the arts. *See* TOKYO; UKIYO-E.

The Dutch and Chinese, who had limited access to Japan at the port of Nagasaki, brought books and some engravings, which aroused strong curiosity among Japanese scholars and artists. Western demands to open the Japanese ports were climaxed by the visit of the American Commodore Perry in 1853. After more than ten years of civil war, the imperial sovereignty was restored in 1867, and Japan opened her doors to the outside world.

Modern period (after 1868). After the imperial rule of Japan was restored and feudalism was abolished the Meiji government adopted a constitutional system. As Japan admitted the Western world, her arts and life underwent a profound change. There was a time at the beginning of the Meiji era (1868–1912) when all traditional arts were rejected. An American scholar, Ernest Fenollosa (1853–1908), working with Okakura Tenshin (known also as Okakura Kakuzō; 1862–1913), persuaded some Japanese artists and government officials to revitalize the traditional arts and to preserve the ancient art treasures.

The problems of the arts in 20th-century Japan are in general parallel to those in Europe and America. Painting, sculpture, and architecture after World War II reflect every stylistic change current in the West.

See also JAPAN: ARCHITECTURE, CERAMICS, GRAPHIC ARTS, LACQUERWARE, MUSEUMS, PAINTING, SCULPTURE, TEXTILES.

BIBLIOGRAPHY. K. Okakura, *The Ideals of the East, with Special Reference to the Art of Japan*, London, 1903; M. Anesaki, *Art, Life, and Nature in Japan*, Boston, 1933; D. T. Suzuki, *Essays in Zen Buddhism*, 2d series, London, 1950; G. Groot, *The Prehistory of Japan*, New York, 1951; R. Tsunoda, tr., *Japan in the Chinese Dynastic Histories* (Perkins Asiatic Monographs, no. 2), South Pasadena, Calif., 1951; D. Keene, *The Japanese Discovery of Europe: Honda Toshiaki and Other Discoverers, 1720–1798*, New York, 1954; H. Borton, *Japan's Modern Century*, New York, 1955; E. A. Burtt, ed., *The Teachings of the Compassionate Buddha*, New York, 1955; H. Webb, *An Introduction to Japan*, 2d ed., New York, 1957; R. T. Tsunoda et al., eds., *Sources of the Japanese Tradition* (Records of Civilization: Sources and Studies, 54), New York, 1958; E. O. Reischauer and J. K. F. Fairbank, *A History of East Asian Civilization*, 2 vols., Boston, 1960–65; G. B. Sansom, *Japan: A Short Cultural History*, rev. ed., New York, 1962; M. Anesaki, *History of Japanese Religion, with Special Reference to the Social and Moral Life of the Nation*, Rutland, Vt., 1963; Pacific Science Congress, 10th, Honolulu, 1961, *Japanese Culture: Its Development and Characteristics*, ed. R. J. Smith and R. K. Beardsley (Viking Fund Publications in Anthropology, no. 34), Chicago, 1963; J. Roggendorf, ed., *Studies in Japanese Culture*, Tokyo, 1963; E. O. Reischauer, *Japan, Past and Present*, 3d ed., rev., New York, 1964; S. Noma, *The Arts of Japan, Ancient and Medieval*, tr. and adapted by J. Rosenfield, Rutland, Vt., 1966.

MIYEKO MURASE

JAPAN: ARCHITECTURE. Japanese architecture, in its charming secular buildings as well as in its spectacular Buddhist temples, is a significant area in Japanese art. Its historic aesthetic value apart, Japanese architecture is of special interest to modern architects who have been strongly influenced by it in theory and in practice.

Prehistoric period (ca. 3500 B.C.–A.D. 552). Nothing is known about Japanese architecture before the Jōmon period (ca. 3500 B.C.–3d cent. B.C.). Simple, circular pit dwellings of modest dimensions from the Jōmon period are the first remains of the domestic architecture of Japan. In the Yayoi period (ca. 3d cent. B.C.–ca. A.D. 3d cent.), when a well-organized agricultural society emerged, pit dwellings became much larger, and they remained the most common house type. In the Tomb period (ca. 3d cent.–552) large imperial tombs consisting of earthen mounds surrounded by moats were built. Many of them are wedge-shaped in front and circular in back and are thus called "keyhole" tombs. Around the mounds were placed clay images called *haniwa*, among which were many models of houses. These *haniwa* houses and some Shinto shrines contain many architectural features now considered typically Japanese. The Shinto shrines in Ise and Izumo preserve the early architectural styles, although the present buildings date from later periods. They are characterized by unpainted wood, thatched or shingled roof, raised floor, asymmetrical plan, and adaptation of buildings to the natural environment. *See* IZUMO SHRINE.

Asuka period (552–710). Buddhism, which was introduced into Japan from Korea in 552, revolutionized Japanese architecture. The symmetrical layout of temple buildings on leveled ground, often covered with white sand, reflects the palatial building plan of China. Buildings stand on stone foundations, wood is brilliantly painted, colored tiles are used for roofs with golden finials at their tops, and eaves are supported underneath by an elaborate bracketing system. In contrast to the austere and small Shinto buildings, Buddhist temples are colorful and impressive in scale and style. The best examples of the Asuka Buddhist architecture are seen in Nara. They are the three-storied pagoda of the Hokkiji (706) and the pagoda, Kondō (Golden Hall), and Middle Gate of the Hōryūji, which were rebuilt immediately after the fire of 670. Although it is not a real temple, the Tamamushi Shrine of the Hōryūji has many architectural features that are characteristic of this period. *See* HORYUJI.

See also ASUKADERA.

Nara period (710–784). The newly established capital of Nara, known as Heijō-kyō, was the first planned capital city of Japan. Before the Nara period an imperial court was moved after each emperor died in order to avoid the pollution of death, in accordance with Shinto practice. As a result, imperial courts and capital cities in the pre-Nara periods were usually modest in size and appearance. The first planned capital of Nara was closely modeled after the Chinese capital Ch'ang-an, with the imperial palace at the northern end and with streets and avenues in gridiron arrangement. One important difference between Chinese and Japanese imperial cities was that the Japanese capital did not have walls surrounding the entire city or a large imperial hunting reserve, both of which were essential parts of a Chinese imperial city. *See* NARA.

Buddhist architecture of this period reflects a more complex and elaborate version of T'ang China's architecture. Temple buildings and compounds became larger. The structural weakness of Asuka architecture was eliminated by placing a more complex and functional bracket system at the four corners of the eaves. A perfect example of this new bracket system may be seen at the Eastern Pagoda of the Yakushiji (718) in Nara. Other architectural details also became massive and elaborate. *See* YAKUSHIJI, NARA.

The best example of the impressive temples of this period is the oft-destroyed and -reconstructed Golden Hall of the Tōdaiji in Nara, whose present structure dates from 1709. In the 8th century the temple was 11 bays wide, and it was tall enough to house a 53-foot-high bronze Buddha. A variety of the architectural styles prevalent in this period may be seen in buildings in Nara, such as the Golden Hall of the Tōshōdaiji (756–764), the octagonal Yumedono (Dream Hall) in the Hōryūji, the Hokkedō of the Tōdaiji (known also as the Sangatsudō; 733/746), the Shōsōin of the Tōdaiji (ca. 750), and the octagonal hall of the Eizanji (760–764). *See* TODAIJI, NARA; TOSHODAIJI; YUMEDONO.

Early Heian period (794–897). A new capital was begun at Nagaoka in 784 and continued for ten years. After this attempt proved unsuccessful the new capital was established in 794 in the present city of Kyoto. Called Heian-kyō (City of Peace and Tranquillity), it was laid out in the same manner as Nara. *See* KYOTO.

Esoteric Buddhism (Mikkyō) gave the greatest inspiration to the temples of this period. Temples were built on high mountains and not within the capital city itself. The Enryakuji of the Tendai sect was built on Mt. Hiei, at the northeastern corner of Kyoto; the Kongōbuji of the Shingon sect was erected on Mt. Kōya, near Osaka. Many esoteric temples of this period are considerably smaller than the temples of the Nara period. Buildings of the esoteric temples were laid out without regard for systematic or symmetrical relationships. They hug the hillside, or they are hidden in deep woods on mountains, thereby discouraging easy access by lay members of the Buddhist church. As exemplified by the Golden Hall and pagoda of Murōji (late 8th cent.), south of Nara, buildings of the esoteric temples are gracefully adapted to their natural settings. In this period the massiveness of Nara architecture gradually gave way to a more elegant and refined style, which suited the native taste. *See* ENRYAKUJI; MIKKYO; SHINGON; TENDAI.

Late Heian period (898–1185). A harmonious relationship between nature and buildings characterizes much of the late Heian architecture. The main hall of the Kiyomizudera in Kyoto and the Itsukushima Shrine in Miyajima are restorations from later periods, but they preserve the original layout and form of the buildings, which are in complete harmony with their natural environments. Buddhist influence on the Shinto architecture of this period is also evident in the Itsukushima Shrine, particularly in the use of bright colors on wood. The best examples of late Heian palace architecture are the Seiryō-den (emperor's living quarters) and Shishii-den (ceremonial hall) of the imperial palace in Kyoto. Native taste is preserved in the use of unpainted wood, shingled roof, and wooden floor. *See* ITSUKUSHIMA SHRINE; KIYOMIZUDERA.

Shinden-zukuri, a style of domestic architecture, was an expression of true Japanese taste. Unfortunately, not a single building in this style has survived. The Hōōdō (Phoenix Hall, 1052) of the Byōdōin in Uji was originally designed as a residential palace, and it contains some features of the *shinden* style of architecture. More traditional Buddhist architecture of this period may be seen in the pagoda of the Daigoji (952) in Kyoto and the main hall of the Jōruriji (ca. 1108) in Kyoto. The influence of the highly sophisticated metropolitan culture was felt far and wide. The Chūsonji and its subordinate buildings (ca. 1124) in Hiraizumi, in the northern part of Japan, were built by local members of the Fujiwara family, who wanted to reproduce the brilliant cultural metropolis of Kyoto. *See* HOODO OF BYODOIN; SHINDEN-ZUKURI.

Kamakura period (1185–1333). The two great temples of Nara, the Tōdaiji and the Kōfukuji, were destroyed in the civil war of 1180. The priest Chōgen (d. 1206), who supervised the reconstruction of both temples, introduced a new style of southern Chinese architecture. This style, known in Japan by the misleading name Tenjiku-yō (Indian style), was adopted for the Nandaimon (Great Southern Gate) of the Tōdaiji (1196–1203). Tenjiku-yō, however, failed to leave a lasting impact on Japanese soil. This was probably because the enormous quantity of wood required for Indian-style buildings was difficult to obtain; moreover, the style created a brutal effect by its sheer size and unadorned details. The Jōdo-dō (Amida Hall) of the Jodoji (1192) by Chōgen is one of the few buildings executed in the Indian style. *See* KOFUKUJI, NARA; NANDAIMON.

Zen (Chinese, Ch'an) Buddhism helped popularize another Chinese style. The first building constructed in Kara-yō (Chinese style) is the Kenchōji (1253) in Kamakura. The Shariden (Relic Hall, ca. 1285) of the Engakuji in Kamakura shows the purest form of this style. It is characterized by an earthen or stone floor, more decorative and complex brackets, and elaborately carved wooden members. The Kannon Hall of the Eihōji (ca. 1314) near Nagoya has many Kara-yō features, but they were modified to suit native Japanese taste. Other important buildings that preserve the more traditional features of Buddhist architecture are the Tahōtō of the Ishiyamadera (1194) near Kyoto, the main hall of the Rengeōin, popularly known as the Sanjūsangendō (Hall of Thirty-three Bays, 1266) of Kyoto, and the reconstructed buildings of the Kōfukuji. *See* KENCHOJI; RENGEOIN; TAHOTO OF ISHIYAMADERA; ZEN.

Muromachi period (1336–1573). Kara-yō continued to be popular in this period, and its characteristic features are seen in the Kaisandō (Founder's Hall) of the Eihōji

Japan, architecture. Buddhist temple of the Phoenix Hall (Hōōdō) of the Byōdōin, Uji, completed 1056.

(ca. 1352) in Gifu prefecture. Warriors' houses show a drastic change from the residential architecture of the preceding periods. The open and spacious rooms of the *shinden*-style houses were divided into smaller units. Some features found in the residences of Buddhist priests before this period were brought together in one room to form a *shoin*: an alcove (*tokonoma*), decorative shelves, and a bay window containing a reading desk. These features became the essential elements of the *shoin* style of residential architecture. The early stage of the development of this style may be seen in the Tōgudō of the Jishōji (1486) in Kyoto. Originally built as a villa for the Ashikaga shogun Yoshimasa, it was converted into a Buddhist temple after his death. The Ginkaku (Silver Pavilion) of the Jishōji, also known as the Kannon Hall, was constructed in 1489. The Kinkaku (Golden Pavilion) of the Rokuonji in Kyoto was built in 1398 as a villa for another Ashikaga shogun, Yoshimitsu; it was also converted into a Buddhist temple. The present structure was built after the temple was destroyed by fire in 1950. *See* GINKAKUJI; KINKAKUJI; SHOIN-ZUKURI.

Many important gardens were also built in this period. The history of gardens as an inseparable part of domestic architecture dates from the late Heian period. As the Hōōdō in Uji shows, nature was reproduced on a small scale as a garden and was incorporated into the building complex. Many Zen temples of the Muromachi period had such gardens, usually in front of the living quarters of abbots. A different type of garden, commonly known as

a "dry garden" because it utilized no water, also became popular in Zen temples. Dry gardens may reproduce nature, but more often they symbolically represent the world outlook and view of nature according to Zen. They developed with the encouragement of Zen masters such as Musō Soseki (1275–1351). He designed several sections of the gardens of the Saihōji and Daisenin in Kyoto, and they represent the ideal of the dry garden at its best. *See* DAISENIN GARDEN; SAIHOJI GARDEN.

See also RYOANJI GARDEN; TENRYUJI GARDEN.

Momoyama period (1573–1614). This period was a truly revolutionary one in architecture. Religious buildings of importance were no longer built. Instead, the man-centered secular architecture of castles and palaces set the trend. The introduction of firearms into Japan in the mid-16th century revolutionized warfare and fortifications. Azuchi Castle, which was built for Oda Nobunaga in 1576 but destroyed shortly after, heralded a new era in architecture. Castles were heavily fortified with thick walls and surrounding moats. They stood on stone foundations and had several turrets, magazines, and gateways. Elaborate gable designs decorated their multistoried buildings, which dominated the hilltops.

The early stage of the development of the keep (*tenshukaku*) may be seen at the Inuyama Castle (1601 and later) in Aichi prefecture, some parts of which date as far back as 1537. Its keep, which is composed of a tower standing over a *shoin* structure, is the oldest surviving example. Matsumoto Castle in Nagano prefecture was started in 1594, and its keep is the largest among the surviving examples. Himeji Castle (1608) of Hyōgo prefecture is the perfect and most beautiful example of castle architecture to be seen today. The interiors of these castles were decorated with brightly colored architectural sculptures and glittering gold-colored screen paintings. The Hiunkaku of the Nishi Honganji and Nijō Castle in Kyoto are but a few of the large number of Momoyama buildings illustrating the heroic taste of this period. The *shoin* style was perfected, and its best example may be seen in the guest chambers of the *Kōjōin* (1601) and the Kangakuin, both subtemples of the Onjōji near Kyoto. *See* HIMEJI CASTLE; HIUNKAKU, KYOTO; NIJO PALACE, KYOTO.

See also NAGOYA CASTLE.

A special form of architecture developed in connection with the cult of the tea ceremony. A simple, small *chashitsu* or *chaseki* (a room or a detached house designed for the tea ceremony) sharply contrasted with the grandeur and elegance that characterized castles and *shoin* buildings of this period. The rustic beauty of the *chaseki* is best seen in the Myōki-an (1573–91) of Kyoto, which set a standard for many later tea ceremony houses.

See also SAMBOIN GARDEN.

Edo period (1615–1867). The arts of wood carvers and builders are magnificently expressed at the mausoleum of Tōshōgū (1617 and later) in Nikkō, which was built for Ieyasu, the first Tokugawa shogun. Rich, colorful decorations epitomize the architectural taste of this period. Impressive castles continued to be constructed in the capitals of various provinces. With the elevation of living standards the domestic architecture of the people also became more refined and sumptuous. Many large gardens were built, the best examples of which may be seen at the Katsura Detached Palace and the Shugakuin Detached Palace. The Shugakuin garden represents a new type of garden, into which views of surrounding hills and mountains were introduced as an aesthetic element. *See* KATSURA PALACE; SHUGAKUIN PALACE GARDEN, KYOTO; TOSHOGU.

See also KOHOAN GARDEN.

Religious architecture declined in this period. Major efforts in this field were concentrated on the reconstruction of existing buildings. The main hall of the Kiyomizudera in Kyoto was rebuilt in 1633, the Kompon Chūdō of the Enryakuji at Mt. Hiei in 1640, and the Golden Hall of the Tōdaiji in 1709.

Modern period (after 1868). Modernization of the country brought a dramatic change in the architecture of Japan. New building materials, such as stone, brick, and reinforced concrete, were introduced in the construction of public buildings, which follow every stylistic change observed in the West. Domestic architecture, however, still retains many of its traditional features, especially in its openness, spaciousness, and flexible use of areas. Traditional features are often skillfully incorporated into modern houses built of new materials. The special qualities of Japanese domestic architecture particularly inspired some Western architects of the 20th century. In turn, a strong impact by such giants of the West as Frank Lloyd Wright and Le Corbusier is felt in many of the postwar buildings of Japan.

BIBLIOGRAPHY. T. Tamura, *Art of the Landscape Garden in Japan*, Tokyo, 1935; A. Soper, *The Evolution of Buddhist Architecture in Japan* (Princeton Monographs in Art and Archaeology, 22), London, 1942; Tokyo National Museum, *Pageant of Japanese Art*, vol. 6: *Architecture and Gardens*, Tokyo, 1952; J. Harada, *The Lesson of Japanese Architecture*, rev. ed., London, 1954; A. Akiyama, *Shinto and Its Architecture*, 2d ed., Tokyo, 1955; New York, Museum of Modern Art, *The Architecture of Japan* by A. Drexler, New York, 1955; R. T. Paine and A. Soper, *The Art and Architecture of Japan*, Baltimore, 1955; W. Blaser, *Japanese Temples and Tea-Houses*, New York, 1956; T. Yoshida, *The Japanese House and Garden*, New York, 1956; S. Horiguchi and Y. Kojiro, *Architectural Beauty in Japan*, 2d ed., Tokyo, 1957; T. Yoshida, *Gardens of Japan*, New York, 1957; B. Taut, *Houses and People of Japan*, 2d ed., Tokyo, 1958; J. B. Kirby, *From Castle to Teahouse, Japanese Architecture of the Momoyama Period*, Rutland, Vt., 1962; Kokusai Bunka Shinkōkai, *Tradition of Japanese Garden*, Tokyo, 1962; W. Alex, *Japanese Architecture*, New York, 1963; Y. Futagawa, *The Roots of Japanese Architecture*, New York, 1963; T. Ishimoto and K. Ishimoto, *The Japanese House: Its Interior and Exterior*, New York, 1963; National Commission for the Protection of Cultural Properties, ed., *Kokuhō (National Treasures of Japan)*, vol. 1: *From the Earliest Time to the End of the Nara Period*, Tokyo, 1963; A. L. Sadler, *A Short History of Japanese Architecture*, Rutland, Vt., 1963.

MIYEKO MURASE

JAPAN: CERAMICS. Pottery was first made in Japan during the Neolithic period, an era that extended from some time before 4500 B.C. until about 250 B.C. Deriving its name from the "rope pattern" upon which the decorations are based, this pottery is called Jōmon, a term also used to designate the entire period in all its aspects.

HISTORICAL DEVELOPMENT

Although different regions of the country were obviously not all at the same level of development at one time in the Jōmon period, it is usually divided into the following stages: ca. 3500–3000 B.C., ca. 3000–2000 B.C., ca. 2000–1000 B.C., and ca. 1000–250 B.C.

Jomon period. Examples of Jōmon pottery, showing marked regional characteristics, have been excavated from pit dwellings throughout Japan, and it is probable that there was a potter in each household. The potter's wheel was unknown, and vessels were built up in a coiling method with long strips of wet clay that were pressed into shape, smoothed out, and decorated.

The earliest Jōmon style, characterized by pointed bases, simple silhouettes, and rudimentary decoration, soon gave way to flat-based containers with more sophisticated decoration. During the middle Jōmon period (ca. 3000–2000 B.C.) the most outstanding examples of this type were produced. Freely modeled elements, including handles, were applied to the more imaginative and sculptural shapes, and the diagonal rope decoration was deeply impressed.

In addition to vessels, ceramic sculptures called *dogu* were made from the earliest time. The finest were also made during the middle period and, like the pots, tended to decline in vigor afterward. *See* JAPAN: SCULPTURE.

Yayoi period (ca. 3d cent. B.C.–ca. A.D. 3d cent.). While a neolithic civilization continued longer on the islands of Honshu and Hokkaido, the introduction of rice cultivation during the 3d century B.C. marked the beginning of the Bronze Age, which gradually spread northward from Kyushu, the island closest to the mainland. This era is known as the Yayoi period after a section of Tokyo where pottery of the era was first excavated in the 19th century.

Bronze weapons and mirrors were first imported from China and then produced in Japan. The experience gained in working metals undoubtedly influenced the firing techniques used in pottery making. Simple shallow kilns dug into the ground permitted a higher firing temperature and an adequate circulation of air, which resulted in the production of a red-bodied ware characteristic of the Yayoi period. (In early examples it is apparent that this firing technique was imperfectly controlled, and the brownish-black body color typical of Jōmon wares, the result of inadequate oxidation, is found.) Vigorous new shapes, which seem to indicate the use of a rudimentary potter's wheel, were introduced, with bulbous bodies, well-modeled necks, and flaring rims. In addition to incised and impressed comb and chevron patterns, painted slip decorations were used.

Tomb period (ca. 3d cent.–552). By the middle of the 3d century A.D. an organized communal structure, with fixed social levels and leaders, was well established, and the development of specific trade groups, comparable to European guilds, apparently took place. Pottery of the Yayoi type, called *haji*, continued to be made, though there was a marked decline in quality. The *haji-be*, or guild potters who made *haji*, also developed a new type of funerary ware called *haniwa*, unique to this period.

Burial customs became more elaborate, and the impressive funerary mounds built at that time have caused the period to be known as the Tomb period. The tumuli, or tomb mounds, were surrounded and sometimes covered by *haniwa*, or clay cylinders, made by the coiling method. The earliest *haniwa*, dating from the 3d century, are undecorated. In the 4th century they were often surmounted by models of houses and simple utensils, and by the 6th century a complete range of animal and human figures had appeared. Almost abstract in conception, these ornamental sculptures are exceptional in their clarity of expression and their great vitality.

Asuka period (552–710). With the rise of Buddhism, introduced from the mainland during the 6th century, the manufacture of *haniwa*, based on beliefs that were inconsistent with the new religious philosophy, declined. Meanwhile, the production of a new type of pottery, known as Sue ware, was developed and spread rapidly over the country. Derived from Korean wares of the later Three Kingdoms period and the Silla dynasty (ca. 400–935), Sue wares appear to have been made on a rapidly turned potter's wheel and fired in kilns, dug into the sides of hills, at temperatures equal to those used in the firing of stoneware. A carbon deposit, resulting from the presence of a reducing atmosphere, contributes toward making these wares imporous, a critical technical advance. In addition, many examples are partially covered with a natural ash glaze, at first accidental and then probably deliberate. Beautifully made in a wide variety of shapes, Sue wares continued to be made into the Heian period (794–1185), and more than 2,000 sites are known today.

Nara and Heian periods (710–1185). Lead-glazed wares were first made in the 8th century. Known as three-color Shōsōin ware, after the famous repository of the Tōdaiji in Nara, which houses all the known intact specimens, it was a frank imitation of Chinese wares of the T'ang dynasty (618–906). Beyond any aesthetic considerations, the importance of these wares lies in the fact that they were the first to be decorated with a true glazing technique not achieved through natural processes. Lead was used as a flux, and copper and iron oxides for color.

Kamakura period (1185–1333). The next step was the introduction of a true stoneware, which, in addition to its value as an imporous medium, could permit much greater flexibility in the use of a wide range of glazes than is possible with the lower-fired pottery. During the Kamakura period, a true, vitreous stoneware came into use. The ceramic industry was dominated by the Six Ancient Kilns of Tokonabe, Echizen, Shigaraki, Tamba, Bizen, and Seto. The wares of these kilns, with the exception of Seto, were unglazed, or only accidentally so, and utilitarian in nature. Though the Tokonabe works were probably the earliest and the most prolific, the Seto factory, best known for its ceremonial vessels with stamped, incised, and molded decorations, was the most important. The legendary founder of the kiln was Katō Shirōzaemōn Kagamasa, called Tōshiro, who studied ceramic techniques in China. *See* KATO SHIROZAEMON KAGAMASA.

Muromachi period (1336–1573). From the 13th century until the end of the Muromachi period the Seto factory, located in Aichi prefecture, Honshu, produced ceramics firmly based, both technically and aesthetically, on Chinese prototypes of the Sung dynasty (960–1279). Disregarding aesthetic considerations, probably its most important single contribution was the introduction of a high-fired iron glaze. Though not perfectly controlled (those of the Kamakura period tend to be irregular and to flake), these iron glazes vary in color from a deep brown (*temmoku*) to a blue-green (celadon), depending on how they are fired, and have a peculiar beauty. More important, however, the use of iron glazes permits greater flexibility in decorative techniques. Without them the remarkable accomplishments of the Momoyama period would hardly have been possible.

Momoyama period (1574–1614). The ceramic art of Japan probably reached its highest level of achievement during this brief period. The increasing popularity of Zen Buddhism resulted in a widened enthusiasm for the tea ceremony, and the ceramic industry devoted itself to producing appropriate implements. A new aesthetic concept emphasizing the beauty of natural forms was fundamental in Zen philosophy and strongly affected ceramic shapes. The uniformity of wheel-made pottery was regarded as artificial, and, even though the wheel continued to be used, molding became a more favored technique. Often, wheel-turned pieces were reshaped before being fired to avoid any sense of rigidity, or were thrown so rapidly that an asymmetric form resulted. The painted and slip decorations on these wares were equally affected by Zen philosophy and became free and unconventional in character.

Probably the most important factories during the Momoyama period were the Shino and Oribe kilns on Honshu and the Karatsu works in Hizen province on Kyushu. The former were founded by potters who had been driven from Seto by political unrest to the nearby district of Mino, where the kilns were established. In addition to the stoneware utensils with underglaze painted decoration in iron brown produced by the Shino potters, they made red and gray wares, characterized by carved designs inlaid with white slip in imitation of Korean wares of the Koryo dynasty (918–1392). The Oribe potters developed the use of a brilliant copper-green glaze, sometimes over molded decoration, and sometimes in conjunction with painting

in iron brown under a clear glaze. Black Oribe ware was also made.

The Karatsu factories that sprang up at this time on Kyushu were probably established by potters from Korea. Wheel-turned pottery, often asymmetric in shape, prevailed here. Decorations in iron brown under a finely crackled grayish glaze, usually thickly applied, are typical of the Karatsu wares.

Edo period (1615–1867). Though exceptionally fine examples of pottery and stoneware continued to be produced during the Edo period, the basic techniques had been established, and it was in the production of porcelain that the greatest advances were made.

PORCELAIN PRODUCTION

The early years of the 17th century found China in a state of social and political upheaval, a circumstance that had considerable effect on its long-established porcelain industry. For at least 500 years Chinese ceramics had been exported in quantity to the Near East, Southeast Asia, and Japan. Internal conditions now forced an end to this monopoly, and until the reign of K'ang Hsi (1662–1722), when prosperity and order were reestablished, China's position in the international market was negligible. During this period the manufacture of porcelain was perfected in Japan and stimulated by a ready market monopolized previously by the Dutch and Chinese.

According to records of the Dutch East India Company, which was permitted by Japan to establish a trading post at Hirado in 1609 (this "factory" was moved to Deshima, a part of Nagasaki, in 1641), Japanese porcelain dominated its market for thirty years after 1653. Then the great Chinese kilns at Ching-te Chen were reactivated, ending Japan's brief but impressive supremacy. However, Japanese porcelains had become so popular in the Western world that the Chinese found it expedient to copy them, and large quantities of Chinese "Imari" were shipped to Europe and America during the 18th century. Only after the decline of the export trade were truly refined porcelains produced in Japan. From earliest times pottery had commanded a position of enormous importance, both artistically and practically. But not until the 18th century was porcelain properly appreciated for its aesthetic as well as its utilitarian possibilities.

It was on Kyushu, southernmost of the Japanese islands and the one closest to the mainland, that the manufacture of porcelain began, early in the 17th century. The early kilns were probably supervised by Korean potters. The influence of Korean wares of the Yi dynasty (1392–1910) is readily apparent in the underglaze blue porcelains that predominated until the 1640s, when the use of polychromed overglaze enamel decoration was perfected. The Chinese wares of the Ming dynasty (1368–1644) were an equally important source of inspiration from an early period and played a considerable part in determining the decorative character of enameled "export" wares so familiar to Europeans. Even though the imagination of potter and foreigner alike was captured by the potentialities of the new enamel technique, substantial quantities of blue-and-white continued to be made for domestic use.

Japan, ceramics. Detail of Nabeshima porcelain dish decorated with fences and vine shoots, 18th century. National Museum, Tokyo.

These were, for the most part, inexpensive food containers, but they had great vigor and charm and have come to be much admired.

Before proceeding to a discussion of the "golden age" of Japan's porcelain industry, a brief digression into nomenclature seems advisable. With the exception of Kutani, located on the main island of Honshu, the leading porcelain manufactories were located in the district of Arita, an area some 15 miles square on Kyushu. These factories were numerous and small, rarely employing as many as ten people. Similar wares were produced by various kilns independently. As a result, a variety of wares, for lack of more specific identification, came to be called Imari, after a seaport city of Kyushu from which porcelains were exported to Honshu. Although Imari is probably the most generally recognized term in the West for Japanese porcelain, it is a misleading one, especially when applied to export wares shipped from Nagasaki. Instead, those enamel wares that cannot be assigned to a specific factory are referred to as Arita wares, a practice that is followed here.

To return to the evolution of Japanese porcelain, the contribution of Kakiemon I and the subsequent development of the kilns named after him must be considered first. Kakiemon I is traditionally recognized as the man who perfected the use of overglaze enamel polychrome decoration in the 1640s. It is legendary in Japan that after much research he developed "persimmon" enamel. The name Kakiemon is supposed to be derived from *kaki*, meaning "persimmon." The first Kakiemon wares were merely polychrome adaptations of the earlier Chinese-influenced underglaze blue wares, with the overglaze enamels thickly applied. Quite rapidly, however, Kakiemon I and his successors developed a style typically their own, characterized by delicate and naturalistic asymmetric designs sparingly applied to the surface; soft red and clear blue enamels predominated. *See* KAKI.

Early Kakiemon wares were sent to Europe, and when the demand for polychrome porcelains there became too great for the Kakiemon factories to satisfy, numerous kilns were established in the southern part of Arita, which quickly adopted Kakiemon's technique and adapted it to their own ends. These Arita wares, which so strongly influenced the early European porcelain industry, were more boldly decorated than the Kakiemon wares and relied heavily on the use of underglaze blue in combination with overglaze decoration. The enamels were thinner than those on Kakiemon wares, the rust-red that predominated often being so flatly applied that it appears to be an underglaze. Overglaze gold was added to the palette as a means of outlining the often blurred areas of blue. The designs, frequently based on peony, blossoming fruit, and chrysanthemum motifs, were more symmetrical than those of Kakiemon and usually covered a greater proportion of the surface.

A separate development in porcelain making was taking place in the 17th century at Kutani, on Honshu. The original Kutani kiln was established under noble patronage about 1650 by Goto Saijiro, who apparently learned the technique of overglaze enameling from the Kakiemons in Kyushu. Characterized by the use of thickly applied green and aubergine purple enamels, the early Kutani wares demonstrate greater freedom and strength in design and execution than are seen in the more delicate Kakiemon wares that influenced them. During the earliest years of Kutani manufacture the firing of the undecorated porcelain bodies was not properly controlled, causing warping, excessive bubbling, and cracking. The thickly applied enamels were often used to camouflage these defects, a process that required a fine degree of ingenuity.

Though the workmanship and aesthetic standards remained high as the kiln matured, the resemblance of Kutani wares to those of Arita increased and the kiln's products became less unique. It is likely, in fact, that many early-18th-century pieces attributed to this site were actually made at Arita in the Kutani style. In any case, it is known that production of the typical Kutani wares ceased around 1690 and that the factory was closed early in the next century. Except for a brief romantic revival under Yoshidaya early in the 19th century, the glory of Kutani was short-lived, and its products are much sought after.

As the 17th century drew to a close, the commerce in export wares was drastically curtailed and at the same time Japanese porcelains were reaching their highest level of perfection. This was partly due, of course, to experience. Better methods of washing the clays were employed and new deposits were discovered, leading to the production of a purer and whiter body. The use of enamels was perfectly controlled, and new colors were added to the palette. But technical perfection alone cannot explain the new vitality and magnificence and the creation of a new style. The cultural atmosphere of the Genroku era (1688–1703) was of equal importance, and it was a period when the fine arts flourished, new media of aesthetic expression were eagerly sought out, and porcelain was recognized as an ideal one. No effort or expense was spared in the production of fine wares for the aristocracy, and these were as highly regarded and carefully treasured as were paintings and sculpture.

The Kakiemon factory continued to flourish under Kakiemon VI (1690–1735) and achieved its greatest heights. Lobed, reeded, hexagonal, and octagonal shapes were frequently used, and the delicate designs characteristic of Kakiemon were beautifully adjusted to them. They were, in every sense, works of art rather than of craftsmanship.

While the firmly established Kakiemon kiln continued to prosper, new factories were founded, the most important of which was established by the Lord of Nabeshima at Okochi late in the 17th century. The products of this kiln were reserved exclusively for the use of the Nabeshima clan. The taste of the aristocracy determined the standards of the kiln, and its faithful adherence to these standards, both technically and artistically, is readily attested to by the surviving examples. The masterful use of underglaze blue and overglaze polychrome is unequaled in ceramic history.

By the end of the 18th century, despite a renewal of interest in the production of blue-and-white wares, the quality of Japanese porcelains had begun to decline. Excellent wares continued to be produced until the mid-19th century, but there was a marked loss of vitality. The art became more that of the copyist than of the creator.

Porcelain is still made in Japan, but the finest ceramic productions of today are in the medium of stoneware, which has always appealed more strongly to the Japanese imagination.

BIBLIOGRAPHY. S. Hayashiya, *Yakimono no bi (Artistic Development of Japanese Ceramics)*, Tokyo, 1960; R. A. Miller, *Japanese Ceramics*, Rutland, Vt., 1960; Y. Yashiro, ed., *Art Treasures of Japan*, vols. 1–2, Tokyo, 1960; Brooklyn Institute of Arts and Sciences, Museum, *Japanese Ceramics from the Collection of Captain and Mrs. Roger Gerry*, New York, 1961; F. Koyama and J. Figgess, *Two Thousand Years of Oriental Ceramics*, New York, 1961; Oakland (Calif.) Art Museum, *Japanese Ceramics from Ancient to Modern Times*, ed. F. Koyama, Oakland, 1961; M. Feddersen, *Japanese Decorative Art*, London, 1962; R. S. Jenyns, *Japanese Porcelain*, New York, 1965.

ROGER G. GERRY

JAPAN: GRAPHIC ARTS. One of the great contributions of Japanese culture lies in the field of the graphic arts. Owing to the considerably different development of Japanese society as compared to that of China, the reproductive media became more popular in Japan, especially from the 18th century.

Asuka to Momoyama period (552–1614). The printing technique of China was introduced in Japan along with Buddhism and all other forms of the high culture of China and Korea. Graphic arts, like all other arts of the early periods in Japan, served primarily as a handmaiden to the Buddhist religion. (For correlation of Chinese, Indian, and Japanese Buddhist terminology, *see* BUDDHIST TERMS, CORRELATION OF.)

The Japanese of the Nara period knew at least three different methods of printing designs on cloth. The imperial collection of the Shōsōin includes textiles decorated with designs dyed by a batik technique (*rōkechi*) that used carved seals, block printing (*kyōkechi*), and tie-dyeing (*kōkechi*). From this period, also, comes the oldest extant example of a block-printed Buddhist text of the Far East.

In 770 Empress Shōtoku (called also Empress Kōken) ordered a million copies of Buddhist charms to be printed and distributed to temples throughout the country, and many of these charms are extant. The custom of making a large number of copies of Buddhist charms or scriptures was based on the widespread belief that, as one made more copies of them, one gained more merits and the chance to be admitted to a Buddhist paradise increased. Printing offered an ideal solution to this desire for accumulating merits through multiple images or scriptures.

Although printed Buddhist images as a substitute for Buddhist paintings were not unknown in Japan, extant examples of this type are rare, and come only from the later periods. The oldest and commonest extant examples of printed pictures are the stamped images. Often no less than a thousand images of a Buddhist deity were repeated by worshipers who made it a daily or monthly duty to print a certain number. These stamped images are on the whole simple and often crude versions of the contemporary Buddhist paintings.

Knowledge of printing in Japan between 770 and the 12th century, however, is largely limited to literary references, as no work of this period has yet been discovered. Literary references to printed Buddhist sūtras, particularly of the Lotus Sūtra, begin to appear frequently from the early 11th century, but most extant examples of printed Buddhist sūtras or images date from about a century later.

Small printed images of Buddhist deities are most often

found inside Buddhist statues. One thousand stamped images (ca. 1108) of the Amida Buddha were found inside the Amida statue in the Jōruriji. Printed images of the Bishamon-ten or Tamon-ten (M. Ishida Collection), a god of happiness and war, were made in 1162 and placed inside a statue of the deity that was formerly in the Jōshinji. The number of examples of printed Buddhas suddenly increased at this time, and this tendency continued throughout the 13th, 14th, and 15th centuries.

From about the same time come the oldest printed pictures representing secular subject matter. The Lotus Sūtra and two other shorter sūtras were written on the faces of folding fans decorated with secular pictures. No fewer than 126 of these fans have been preserved in the Shitennōji alone, and more are in other collections. At least some outlines of the figures in these pictures were printed, and colors were filled in later by hand. The fan sūtras constitute a major landmark in the history of Japanese graphic arts, as they presage the development of the Ukiyo-e woodcuts of the Edo period.

Though printing techniques reached a high stage of development and many Buddhist sūtras were made with painted illustrations, there is no evidence before the 13th century that printed scriptures were made with printed illustrations. Even after the 13th century only a few—perhaps twenty in all—printed Buddhist scriptures have printed pictures, and with one or two exceptions they are all copies of Chinese works. It is also strange that, although the production of printed pictures and the illustrated narrative scrolls (emaki) reached a peak in the Kamakura period, it was not until the Muromachi period that printed pictures were used to illustrate narrative scrolls. Painted scrolls of the Yūzū Nembutsu Engi (All-permeating Invocation of Buddha) were first painted in 1314, and many copies and different versions were made thereafter. In 1390 blocks to make printed copies of this emaki were started, and many printed versions were made later, such as the Dai Nembutsu-ji version (1391) in Osaka. In the Muromachi period printed pictures were also used to illustrate popular novels and folktales published in book form.

Edo period (1615–1867). Woodcuts of the Edo period, known as Ukiyo-e (pictures of the floating world), represent the greatest and most brilliant achievement of Japanese printing, from both the technical and artistic point of view. However, all the technical requirements for the development of the Ukiyo-e prints in Edo (modern Tokyo) already existed in embryonic form in the Muromachi period. See UKIYO-E.

Publication of illustrated books of popular tales and novels, started in the Muromachi period, continued during the Momoyama period. Pictures in these books, however, were treated merely as an aid in understanding the text, which played the most important role. This relationship between text and picture was reversed by an early Edo painter, Hishikawa Moronobu (ca. 1618–94). Moronobu realized that the tremendous potentiality of printmaking might be a means to reproduce paintings in great quantity and at small cost. He began making printed illustrations for popular novels, but he gave primary importance to the pictures. He also published single-sheet prints, thus freeing pictures from dependence on text. These pictures by Mo-

ronobu, depicting scenes of the famous gay quarters of Yoshiwara, set the future course of the Ukiyo-e, which reached a rare artistic and technical level of sophistication after his time. See MORONOBU.

Moronobu's pictures had no colors, and only outlines were printed in black ink. Orange color was added, sometime between 1688 and 1704, and the resultant prints were called tan-e (orange pictures). Many of this type were produced by Torii Kiyonobu I (1664–1729) and Torii Kiyomasu I (fl. 1st half of 18th cent.), both of whom specialized in designing theater bills and signboards for the popular Kabuki theater. Another type of print, called urushi-e (lacquer pictures), was introduced between 1716 and 1736, shortly after tan-e made its appearance. Red, orange, yellow, and purple were added by hand to enrich the prints, and sometimes a shining lacquerlike effect of black lines was created by adding glue to the black ink. Many urushi-e were produced by Torii Kiyonobu II (1702–52), Okumura Masanobu (1686–1764), Okumura Toshinobu (early 18th cent.), and Nishimura Shigenaga (d. 1756). See KIYOMASU I; KIYONOBU I; KIYONOBU II; MASANOBU (OKUMURA MASANOBU); SHIGENAGA.

Yet even urushi-e did not satisfy the public's appetite for pretty pictures. From about 1748 benizuri-e (red-printed pictures) appeared to answer the growing public demand. For the first time in the history of printed pictures in Japan, colors were printed, not applied by hand. The printing of red and green in benizuri-e was a major development in the history of printmaking in Japan. Benizuri-e, printed on larger sheets of paper than were ever before used, often represented larger figures in free and relaxed poses, and these prints captured the popular imagination. Many benizuri-e were made by Ishikawa Toyonobu (1711–85) and Torii Kiyomitsu (1735–85). See KIYOMITSU; TOYONOBU.

Benizuri-e was only a step toward the final development of polychrome prints. The year 1765 was a revolutionary one in the history of Japanese woodblock prints. Suzuki Harunobu (1725–70) was commissioned to make designs for the calendar of that year, and he invented nishiki-e (polychrome prints, literally "brocade pictures"). In nishiki-e ten or even more colors may be printed by using different blocks for different colors. Nishiki-e revolutionized the techniques of cutting the block and printing the pictures. It also started a new trend among the designers of prints. Until this time artists who made prints were primarily painters. After the invention of nishiki-e, however, these painters came to consider the woodcut a means of artistic expression as challenging and satisfying as painting, and more and more of them gave up painting to devote themselves to printmaking. See HARUNOBU.

Soon after the publication of the calendar by Harunobu, his figures of romantic, doll-like young men and women were imitated by his contemporaries. Isoda Koryūsai (mid-18th cent.), Suzuki Harushige (known also as Shiba Kōkan, 1738–1818), and Komai Minobu (also called Komai Yoshinobu, fl. 1760s) produced prints of young beauties in the Harunobu manner. Harunobu's delicate style affected even those who specialized in more vigorous actor prints, such as Katsukawa Shunshō (1726–92) and Ippitsusai Bunchō (fl. mid-18th cent.). See BUNCHO (IPPITSUSAI BUNCHO); KOKAN; KORYUSAI; SHUNSHO.

Japan, graphic arts. Katsushika Hokusai, *Wave at Kanagawa*, 1823–29. Woodcut.

After Harunobu's death in 1770, however, Shunshō and others who had been under Harunobu's influence revolted against his dreamy, oversensitive figures, turning their attention to more robust and realistic female figures. This group of artists included Isoda Koryūsai, Kitao Shigemasa (1739–1820), and Torii Kiyonaga (1752–1815). A new type of healthy and mature-looking women was first depicted by Kiyonaga, who found many followers among his contemporaries. Kiyonaga often portrayed a group of women against a landscape or an architectural background, joining two or three sheets to accommodate his large and complex compositions. Kitagawa Utamaro (1753–1806) followed Kiyonaga's style as a young man, but about 1791 he changed completely. Utamaro represented only the large single torso of a woman against a neutral background, emphasizing the facial expression caught in a fleeting moment of her subtle mood. *See* KIYONAGA; SHIGEMASA; UTAMARO.

The last quarter of the 18th century was the golden age of Ukiyo-e, with Utamaro the leader of many artists, including Chōbunsai Eishi (1756–1829) and his pupils Chōkōsai Eishō, Chōkyōsai Eiri, and Ichirakutei Eisui. Kiyonaga's tradition was also continued, by Kubo Shumman (1757–1820), Kitao Masanobu (who as a novelist was called Santō Kyōden, 1761–1816), and Katsushika Shunchō (late 18th cent.). In May, 1794, Tōshūsai Sharaku appeared upon the scene like a comet, produced no fewer than 140 prints of actors and wrestlers, and, in February, 1795, disappeared just as suddenly. *See* EISHI; MASANOBU (KITAO MASANOBU); SHARAKU; SHUMMAN.

After the death of those masters in the late Edo period printmaking was monopolized by Katsushika Hokusai (1760–1849), Andō Hiroshige (1797–1858), and Utagawa Toyokuni I (1769–1825) and his followers, among whom Kunimasa (1773–1810), Kunisada (1786–1864), Kikukawa Eizan (1787–1867), Keisai Eisen (1790–1848), and Kuniyoshi (1797–1861) were particularly popular. *See* EISEN (KEISAI EISEN); HIROSHIGE; HOKUSAI; KUNISADA; KUNIYOSHI (UTAGAWA KUNIYOSHI); TOYOKUNI I.

Until Hokusai's time Ukiyo-e printmakers drew their subject matter from the women of the licensed quarters and from the actors of the Kabuki theater. Hokusai revolutionized the Ukiyo-e by turning his attention almost exclusively to landscape. Until his time landscape had been treated only as a background for figures, but Hokusai made it an independent theme in woodblock prints. Hokusai's landscape prints captured the enthusiasm of the public, which was beginning just at that time to enjoy, through the improved highway systems, easier and safer travel throughout the country. Both Hokusai and Hiroshige immortalized the beauty of the scenic spots of Japan in every kind of weather and season. Western knowledge of perspective and chiaroscuro was introduced to these painters and printmakers, and a stronger sense of reality enhanced their landscape prints. Shiba Kōkan (formerly called Suzuki Harushige) was a great influence in westernizing Japanese woodcuts to show scenes observed from a low point of view, correct perspective, and chiaroscuro in the European manner.

Modern period (after 1868). The death of Hiroshige signaled an end to the great creative period in the history of woodcuts in Japan. After the introduction of the modern technology of printing in the Meiji period (1868–1912), printing was used only for the practical purpose of reproduction. The arts of lithography and engraving were introduced by some European and American artists in the late 19th century, but not until the early 20th century was the knowledge of these Western printing methods used for artistic purposes. While the graphic arts were at a low ebb, a group of printmakers, led by Hiroshi Yoshida (1876–1950), Hasui Kawase (1883–1957), and Shinsui Itō (1898–   ), made an attempt to revive the Ukiyo-e of the Edo period. Their efforts were unsuccessful, but printing was finally undertaken again as a creative art, largely under the guidance of Kanae Yamamoto (1882–1946), who advocated a new concept of graphic art in which the printmaker was responsible for his work throughout the entire printmaking process. See YAMAMOTO, KANAE; YOSHIDA, HIROSHI.

In the Edo Ukiyo-e tradition, masters of woodcuts made only the designs for their prints, and the rest of the work was relegated to the woodblock carvers and to the printers. Yamamoto's idea found enthusiastic supporters among the young, Western-trained artists, such as Kazuma Oda (1882–1956), Hakutei Ishii (1882–1958), and Hanjirō Sakamoto (1882–   ). Their efforts to bring new ideas into the field of graphic art, particularly following the Western tradition of style and technique, were intensified in the 1920s. From that time until the present, Japanese graphic artists have been closely following every style change observed in the West. Among the important modern printmakers are Kōshiro Onchi (1891–1955), Shikō Munakata (1905–   ), Kiyoshi Saitō (1907–   ), and Jun-ichirō Sekino (1914–   ). See MUNAKATA, SHIKO; ONCHI, KOSHIRO; SAITO, KIYOSHI.

BIBLIOGRAPHY. W. von Seidlitz, *A History of Japanese Colour-Prints*, Philadelphia, 1910; B. Stewart, *Japanese Colour-Prints*, London, 1920; B. Stewart, *Subjects Portrayed in Japanese Colour-Prints*, London, 1922; L. Binyon and J. J. O'B. Sexton, *Japanese Colour Prints*, London, 1923; L. N. Brown, *Block Printing and Book Illustrations in Japan*, New York, 1924; P. N. Barnett, *Japanese Colour-Prints*, Sydney, Australia, 1936; L. V. Ledoux, *An Essay on Japanese Prints*, New York, 1938; J. R. Hillier, *Japanese Masters of the Colour Print*, London, 1954; J. A. Michener, *The Floating World*, New York, 1954; O. Statler, *Modern Japanese Prints: An Art Reborn*, Rutland, Vt., 1956; W. Boller, *Masterpieces of the Japanese Colour Woodcut*, Boston, 1957; L. Hájek, *The Osaka Woodcuts*, London, 1959; J. A. Michener, *Japanese Prints*, Rutland, Vt., 1959; S. Takahashi, *The Japanese Woodblock Prints through Two Hundred and Fifty Years*, Tokyo, 1961; R. D. Lane, *Masters of the Japanese Print*, Garden City, N.Y., 1962; M. Ishida, *Japanese Buddhist Prints*, New York, 1964; R. Penkoff, *Roots of the Ukiyo-e* (Ball State Monograph, no. 2), Muncie, Ind., 1964.

MIYEKO MURASE

JAPAN: LACQUERWARE.

Lacquer work has a considerable tradition in Japanese history, although here, as in other areas, China would appear to have precedence. Yet lacquer has its characteristic Japanese aspects and contributions.

Asuka period (552–710). The use of lacquer, a milky liquid extracted from the lacquer tree (*Rhus vernicifera*) and used for binding and decorative purposes, dates from ancient China. Excavations reveal that lacquer was also used in ancient Japan, toward the end of the Jōmon period (ca. 3500 B.C.–3d cent. B.C.). The Tamamushi Shrine (Tamamushi Zushi) in the Hōryūji shows that in the Asuka period lacquer designs were executed with a brush—a simple technique, but hard to control because lacquer is extremely sticky. Asuka artists used this material masterfully and were able to execute difficult designs with skill and ease. See TAMAMUSHI SHRINE.

Nara period (710–784). An 8th-century shrine, known as Lady Tachibana's Miniature Shrine, in the Hōryūji is decorated in lacquer. The figures of Buddhist deities are painted on the black-lacquered background. Their large, sensuous bodies are modeled in light and dark, and reflect a strong influence of T'ang Chinese painting. A large number of lacquerwares in the imperial storehouse of the Shōsōin of the Tōdaiji also show T'ang influence in design and technique. In the Nara period, various techniques of executing designs in lacquer were known to the Japanese. Three methods were commonly used: (1) *raden*, in which mother-of-pearl inlay was covered with lacquer; (2) *hyōmon*, or *heidatsū*, in which gold or silver cutout designs were pasted on the article, the lacquer applied, and the excess lacquer removed from the metal designs; and (3) *maki-e*, in which gold or silver dusts were sprinkled over designs executed in wet lacquer. Statues were made by the dry-lacquer method, which became an important technique of sculpture in this period.

Heian period (794–1185). Techniques and decorative motifs of the Nara period were still in use in the early Heian period, but from the 11th century on a truly Japanese taste began to influence the making of lacquerware. The *maki-e* technique became the most important method in the late 10th century. Designs executed in this method were often combined with shell inlays to create an elegant and fragile effect. Soft and exquisite color harmony was produced by mixing gold and silver powder, which was applied in delicately grading tones. Flowers and birds were still the most favored patterns, but Buddhist scenes and landscapes, as well as abstract designs, were made. Sūtra boxes and chests were the most common articles decorated in lacquer, the best examples of which date from the 12th century. A box in the custody of the National Museum of Tokyo shows a highly decorative treatment of wheels in waves. Other important 12th-century works are in the collections of the Itsukushima Shrine, in the Kongōbuji of Mt. Kōya, and of the Taimadera.

Kamakura period (1185–1333). Simplicity, dynamism, and realism characterize the lacquerware of this period. The new trend may be best illustrated by the large lotus flower designs on the shrine containing the *Taima Mandara*, in Taimadera. To create a powerful and realistic effect, *maki-e* designs were often raised in high relief by building up many coats of lacquer. A Chinese method of carving lacquerwares, known in Japan as *tsuishu*, was also introduced. This method, in which designs were carved through many layers of red or cinnabar lacquer, was skillfully imitated by Japanese craftsmen, and it developed into the powerful art of Kamakura-bori (Kamakura carving). See KAMAKURA-BORI.

Muromachi period (1336–1573). Japanese lacquerers learned new techniques and different shapes of wares from the imported Sung and Yüan lacquerwares. Sung and Yüan paintings were also brought to Japan in conjunction with Zen Buddhism. From these the Japanese learned new styles of design, some of which created an effect of ink painting. *Tsuishu* continued to be popular. *Chinkin*, in

Japan, lacquerware. Writing box, 15th century, Muromachi period. Lacquered wood. National Museum, Tokyo.

which paper-thin strips of gold were inlaid in finely engraved designs, was introduced from China in this period. A box with birds in a landscape (Tokyo National Museum) is an excellent example of a lacquer design executed in this fine technique. A new type of lacquerware called *negoro* appeared. No designs were made on *negoro* ware; it was appreciated solely for the strength, simplicity, and directness of the shape. Two families of *maki-e* makers became prominent, one headed by Igarashi Shinsai and the other by Kōami Michinaga (1410–78), both of whom served the Ashikaga shogun Yoshimasa. These two families continued to be active in this field in the succeeding periods.

Momoyama period (1574–1614). The Kōdaiji in Kyoto is known to have been dedicated by the wife of Hideyoshi after his death. Its interior was richly decorated with *maki-e* designs, some of which are attributed to Kōami Chōan (1569–1637), a descendant of Kōami Michinaga. This temple owns a sizable collection of magnificent lacquerwares that once belonged to Hideyoshi and his wife and represent the finest of the Momoyama craftsmanship. The style of the *maki-e* works represented by the Kōdaiji wares is known as the Kōdaiji *maki-e*. The designs of these wares reflect the dramatic and boldly decorative style of the contemporary screen paintings. Compositions are often divided into two sections by lightninglike zigzag lines, which create an abrupt transition between sections. Realistic flowers and birds are often combined with purely abstract and ornamental patterns. To heighten the drama and dynamism of designs, simpler techniques were used in decorating these wares.

Christian missionaries and Western traders introduced new motifs into Japan. The cross, vine, and other Western motifs were used to decorate articles made for the service of the Christian churches in Japan. The strange appearance and unusual costumes of the Europeans visiting Japan also served as subject matter for decorations on lacquerware.

Edo period (1615–1867). The rise of the merchant class, a higher living standard, and a period of relative peace helped produce a large quantity of elaborately decorated lacquerware. Lavish use of gold powder and fittings characterizes Edo works. There were three prominent schools of lacquerers active in Edo (modern Tokyo), the Kōami, Koma, and Kajikawa families. A fourth school, the Yamamoto family, worked in Kyoto. Not only professional lacquerers but also painters of high reputation decorated lacquerwares. A group of works is attributed to Kōetsu (1558–1637), a renowned art patron, calligrapher, and theoretician. Although the attribution may be doubtful, such works as a box for inkstone (Tokyo National Museum) at least reflect the aesthetic ideals of Kōetsu. They are also reminiscent of the style of paintings by Sōtatsu (fl. mid-17th cent.), who was Kōetsu's close associate. Kōrin (1658–1716), who was inspired by the arts of Kōetsu and Sōtatsu, made designs on many lacquerwares marked by great individuality and originality. One of the best examples of his lacquer designs is a box for inkstone with boldly abstract patterns of irises and a bridge (Tokyo National Museum). *See* KOETSU; KORIN; SOTATSU.

In the later Edo period, however, designs became overornate. Although there was often a display of brilliant technical versatility, lacquerwares lost the freshness and dynamism that characterized the works from the earlier periods. Minute details are overemphasized on such small objects as sword sheaths, *inrō* (medicine boxes), and *netsuke* (cord stoppers). More exciting developments occurred in local lacquer centers, which were established by feudal lords. Many of these centers still produce lacquer in modern Japan, for example, Aizu ware (Fukushima prefecture), Tsugaru ware (Aomori prefecture), Wakasa ware (Fukui prefecture), and Wajima ware (Ishikawa prefecture).

Modern period (after 1868). With the government's encouragement the lacquer industry continued to develop. New knowledge of Western technology enabled lacquerers to produce colors that had previously been unobtainable, particularly neutral tones and white. Rokkaku Shisui (1867–1950) made a particularly valuable contribution in this respect. Shibata Zeshin (1807–91), Agawa Shōmin (1847–92), and Kawanabe Itchō (1874–1955) are also among those who contributed to the renascence and development of the art of lacquer in modern Japan.

BIBLIOGRAPHY. London, Victoria and Albert Museum, Dept. of Woodwork, *Catalogue of Japanese Lacquer* (Victoria and Albert Museum, Publication, no. 159w), London, 1924–25; M. Kanda, ed., *Japanese Lacquer*, Tokyo, 1941; Tokyo National Museum, *Pageant of Japanese Art*, vol. 5: *Textiles and Lacquer*, Tokyo, 1954; M. H. Boyer, *Japanese Export Lacquers from the Seventeenth Century in the National Museum of Denmark* (Nationalmuseets skrifter, Større beretninger, 5), Copenhagen, 1959; U. A. Casal, *Japanese Art Lacquers* (Monumenta Nipponica Monographs, no. 18), Tokyo, 1961; National Commission for the Protection of Cultural Properties, ed., *Kokuhō (National Treasures of Japan)*, vol. 1: *From the Earliest Time to the End of the Nara Period*, Tokyo, 1963.

MIYEKO MURASE

JAPAN: MASKS, *see* BUGAKU MASK; GIGAKU MASK; NOH MASK.

JAPAN: MUSEUMS. See under the names of the following cities:

Atami. Art Museum.

Kyoto. National Museum.

Nara. National Museum.

Tenri. Museum.

Tokyo. National Museum; National Museum of Western Art; Nezu Art Museum.

JAPAN: PAINTING. Although Japanese painting, like all Japanese art, was strongly influenced by China, it has a long and distinguished history of its own.

(For correlation of Chinese, Indian, and Japanese Buddhist terminology *see* BUDDHIST TERMS, CORRELATION OF.)

Asuka period (552–710). The earliest, untutored stage of Japanese painting is characterized by simple, primitive paintings on tomb walls and drawings scratched on bronze bells. Although these works have a certain charm and tell us something about Japanese life at that time, they are not comparable to the highly developed art of contemporary China and Korea.

With the introduction of Buddhism from Korea in A.D. 552, a more developed art of painting was brought into Japan from the Asian continent. A growing demand for Buddhist paintings was met by Chinese and Korean immigrant artists until the Japanese themselves acquired skill. The paintings from the Tamamushi Shrine are the only major extant examples from the Asuka period. The slender, ethereal figures and the fantastic-shaped rocks show the influence of the stylized and abstract Chinese painting of the Northern Wei dynasty (386–535). Another significant evidence of the Northern Wei influence is a set of hand scrolls called the *Sūtras of the Past and Present Karma*, which was executed in the 8th-century Nara period. *See* TAMAMUSHI SHRINE.

Nara period (710–784). Japanese painters made a concerted effort to assimilate the Chinese art of the T'ang dynasty (618–906). The early Nara wall paintings in the Kondō of the Hōryūji (destroyed in 1949) were magnificent testimonials to the great achievement that Japanese artists made in a short period of time. The Buddhist deities represented on these walls reflected the material wealth and cultural splendor of the T'ang empire. In sharp contrast to the stylized, spiritualized figures of the Northern Wei dynasty, these deities were represented as corporeal beings with robust and supple bodies. Brushstrokes were firm and wiry, and strong shadings were used on bodies and draperies. *See* HORYUJI WALL PAINTINGS.

A small number of other extant paintings indicate that various styles of painting were practiced in this period. A more carefully executed, meticulous style is exemplified by the Kichijōten (Yakushiji) and painted decorations on the plectra for musical instruments in the Shōsōin collection. Another style, represented by a bodhisattva and a landscape in the same collection, both executed in ink on hemp cloth, shows the free yet controlled hand of the painter. *See* KICHIJOTEN IN YAKUSHIJI, NARA.

Early Heian period (794–897). Japanese Buddhists turned to the new esoteric Buddhist teaching, Mikkyō. Chinese paintings and drawings were brought into Japan by priest-students of the Mikkyō teaching, returning from China. These works served as models for Japanese artists working for esoteric Buddhist temples. Paintings such as the *Yellow Fudō* (Onjōji), for example, which represent deities with supernatural and fearsome countenances, were painted for the solemn, mysterious, and awe-inspiring ceremonies conducted at Mikkyō temples. The maṇḍala (Japanese, mandara), a diagram showing relationships among the Buddhist deities, was also important in the Mikkyō rites. The *Takao Mandara* (824–34; Jingoji) and the *Kojimadera Mandara* (Kojimadera) were made after T'ang models. They reveal powerful yet free brushstrokes, and deep shadings add sensuous beauty to spiritualized images of Mikkyō deities. *See* MANDARA IN KOJIMADERA, NARA; MIKKYO.

Late Heian period (898–1185). As the members of the Fujiwara family consolidated their political power, their aesthetic taste influenced the arts and literature. The *Fugen* (Tokyo National Museum) and the *Shaka* (12th cent.; Jingoji) are the best examples of sensitive and delicate Buddhist paintings that reflect a more purely Japanese sense of beauty. Paintings of Nirvāṇa (Kongōbuji) and the *Shaka's Reawakening* (12th cent.; Chōhōji) contain strong narrative elements which make these paintings less abstract than the esoteric paintings of the early Heian period. The teachings of Amidism (Jōdo sect) produced a specific type of Buddhist painting called Raigō-zu (pictures of the descent of Amida). The wall paintings in the Hōōdō of Byōdōin and a triptych at Mt. Kōya are the largest and best examples of the Raigō picture. *See* JODO.

Up to this time the subject matter of both religious and secular paintings was borrowed from Chinese history and literature. With the rise of a purely Japanese literature, however, secular paintings with Japanese subject matter gained popularity. These paintings, truly Japanese in style

Japan, painting. *Hunt at the Foot of Mt. Fuji*, detail from a decorated screen of eight panels, Edo period. Museum of Eastern Art, Venice.

and subject matter, are called Yamato-e (Japanese painting) in contrast to Kara-e (Chinese painting), which is modeled after Chinese prototypes. There are many examples of Yamato-e executed on screens (folding, sliding, and freestanding), in hand scrolls (*emaki* or *emaki-mono*), and in illustrated books. *See* KARA-E; YAMATO-E.

Only two Yamato-e screens of this period have survived: a landscape screen in the Tōji, called *Senzui Byōbu* (now in the collection of the National Museum of Kyoto), and the *Life of Prince Shōtoku* (1069; Tokyo National Museum) by Hata Chitei. The Tōji screen shows Chinese men, probably from a Chinese story; but the landscape setting is purely Japanese, with gentle, rolling hills and a large, calm body of water in the distance. The *Life of Prince Shōtoku* is a step closer to the pure Yamato-e, which illustrates a Japanese story in a Japanese setting.

The art of Yamato-e is illustrated best by the four great scroll paintings of the late Heian period: *Tale of Genji*, *Shigisan Engi*, *Ban Dainagon*, and *Animal Caricature*. The stories depicted in these narrative scrolls are purely Japanese, and the style of painting shows a highly successful adaptation of Chinese prototypes to Japanese taste. *See* ANIMAL CARICATURE SCROLLS; BAN DAINAGON SCROLLS; SHIGISAN ENGI SCROLLS; TALE OF GENJI SCROLL.

Kamakura period (1185–1333). A large number of scroll paintings were produced during this period, but many did not equal in quality the works of the late Heian period. A variety of subject matter was represented in the picture

scrolls, and historical, literary, and religious narratives continued to be illustrated.

A widespread cult of the founders of popular Buddhist sects gave rise to the *emaki* illustrating the lives of these priests. Some of the finest examples are the scrolls of *Kegon Engi* (13th cent.; Kōzanji), *Priest Hōnen* (14th cent.; Chionin), and *Life of Ippen*. Historical narratives mixed with fictitious and miraculous accounts also became popular subject matter, resulting in such great *emaki* as *Kibi's Adventure*. *See* IPPEN SCROLLS; KIBI'S ADVENTURE SCROLLS.

War narratives fascinated men of this period, and the military rulers encouraged the creation of a war literature and its illustration in picture scrolls. The finest example of this type of *emaki* is a set of three scrolls representing the Heiji Insurrection of 1159–60.

The down-to-earth and objective minds of the warriors of this period helped bring about a golden age of realistic portrait painting. This new trend toward realism is exemplified by the scrolls of the *Imperial Bodyguards* and Mitsunaga's *Annual Court Ceremonies and Festivals* (only a 17th-century copy remains, in the Tanaka Collection). Portraits of such military heroes as Yoritomo and Shigemori (late 12th cent.; Jingoji) show a more formal type of presentation, but the portrait of Priest Myōe (13th cent.; Kōzanji) is an unusual example of an informal portrait, showing the priest in meditation among the trees. Imaginary portraits of early literary figures were also painted in a realistic style. The scrolls of the *Thirty-six Poets* (13th cent.; formerly in the Satake Collection), for example, show the poets and poetesses from the Heian period as contemporary men and women of the Kamakura period. Fujiwara Takanobu and his son Nobuzane were the best-known portrait painters of the late Heian and Kamakura periods. Although their great talents are often highly praised in the literature of the period, it is difficult to find works which can be firmly attributed to them. *See* IMPERIAL BODYGUARDS SCROLL; NOBUZANE; TAKANOBU.

Toward the end of the 12th century, a new brush technique was introduced from the Northern Sung dynasty of China (960–1127), and it gradually replaced the art of Yamato-e. The *Twelve Devas* (1191; Tōji) by Takuma Shōga exemplifies the new technique, which is characterized by accentuated brushstrokes of varying width. The decline of Yamato-e was hastened by the rise of the Zen sect of Buddhism, which promoted ink paintings of landscapes of plants executed in free and spontaneous brushstrokes. Through their acquaintance with Zen Buddhism, the early ink painters, such as Kaō, Mokuan, and Ryōzen, were introduced to the ideals of Chinese ink painting. *See* KAO; MOKUAN REIEN; RYOZEN; SHOGA; ZEN.

Muromachi period (1336–1573). Zen monasteries were the center of cultural activities in this period. The first three important ink painters of Japan—Josetsu, Shūbun, and Sesshū—were all Zen priests who lived and worked in the Shōkokuji in Kyoto. Paintings such as *Catching a Catfish with a Gourd* by Josetsu were made for the practical purpose of teaching some of the complex Zen principles; others were executed as aids to meditation. Landscape paintings in ink were often accompanied by poems of the famous priest-poets, because paintings were regarded as illustrations of poems and, as such, subordinate to literature. Sesshū freed painting from its subordination to literature and brought the ink landscape painting closer to the Japanese people. He sought the subject matter for his paintings in the natural surroundings of his own country. His ideas of landscape painting found many followers, among whom Sesson, Shōkei, and Shūgetsu were the most important. *See* JOSETSU; SESSHU TOYO; SESSON; SHOKEI; SHUBUN; SHUGETSU TOKAN.

While the major contribution to the painting of this period was made by the ink painters, the Tosa family continued to paint in the Yamato-e tradition at the Painters' Bureau of the imperial court. Fresher and more exciting works were produced by Masanobu, the founder of the Kanō school, who created a new style by combining the bold, decorative quality of Yamato-e with the strong brushwork of ink painting. As the subject matter was simple and the style was broad, Kanō painting appealed greatly to the military leaders of the late Muromachi period. *See* KANO SCHOOL; MASANOBU (KANO MASANOBU); TOSA SCHOOL.

Momoyama period (1574–1614). Castles and palaces of impressive dimensions were built by the warrior heroes, and the interior walls, ceilings, and screens were decorated with sumptuous paintings. Eitoku established the tradition of mural painting, which was carried on by Chokuan, Sanraku, Sansetsu, Tōhaku, Tōgan, Yūshō, and others. Their paintings were large, and broad in style. Detail was sacrificed at times to produce ostentatious effects. The

sweeping lines and brilliant colors, shown against a glittering gold background, characterize the screen paintings of this period. *See* CHOKUAN; EITOKU; SANRAKU; TOGAN; TOHAKU; YUSHO.

In the late Momoyama period some artists turned to a more intimate aspect of folk life. A genre subject matter, as in the *Maple Viewing at Takao* (16th cent.; Tokyo National Museum) by Hideyori, was accepted even by the traditionalist Kanō artists. The life of the common man became in the Edo period an important subject for prints and paintings that are commonly called Ukiyo-e (pictures of the floating world). *See* HIDEYORI.

The advent of Christianity, which gained support after the first visit to Japan of Francis Xavier in 1549, introduced European religious paintings; they were copied by the Christianized Japanese painters. Most of these works were destroyed during the persecution that began in 1638. Two important examples of Christian paintings still extant are a portrait of Xavier (17th cent.; Kōbe Art Museum) and *Fifteen Mysteries of the Rosary* (17th cent.; Azuma Collection).

European genre scenes were copied on folding screens by the Japanese artists. Scenes of the Europeans' visit to Japan were also painted, in a traditional Japanese style. These paintings of Europeans, in either the Western or Japanese style, are generally called the pictures of *namban*, or southern barbarians, the name then commonly used for Westerners.

Edo period (1615–1867). The Kanō painters of the Edo period, except Tannyū, merely carried on the family tradition. The truly creative and original talents, such as Itchō and Morikage, were found among the painters who challenged the Kanō school and were in turn ostracized by it. *See* ITCHO; MORIKAGE; TANNYU.

Yamato-e ceased to develop, since its main exponents, the court painters of the Tosa and Sumiyoshi families, were capable only of preserving the family tradition. Only a group of 19th-century painters known as the Yamato-e Revivalists, who were influenced by the royalist movement, made a conscious effort to regain the past glory of Yamato-e. Its most important members were Tamechika, Totsugen, and Ukita Ikkei. The artists of the Sōtatsu-Kōrin school were the most successful in revitalizing Yamato-e, and they created a new and fresh style within the Yamato-e tradition. *See* SOTATSU-KORIN SCHOOL; SUMIYOSHI SCHOOL; TAMECHIKA; TOTSUGEN.

As the Tokugawa shoguns encouraged the study of Confucianism, Chinese literature and the arts regained influence. Scholar-painters, such as Gion Nankai, Sakiki Hyakusen, and Yanagizawa Kien, helped start Nanga. or the Southern school of painting. A favorite subject of Nanga painters was bizarre landscapes peopled with Chinese gentleman-scholars, and plants and flowers with philosophical overtones. The untrammeled style of Taiga's paintings epitomizes the Nanga works. Other important Nanga painters were Buson, Chikuden, Gyokudō, Mokubei, and Kazan. *See* BUSON; CHIKUDEN; GYOKUDO; KAZAN; MOKUBEI; NANGA SCHOOL; TAIGA.

Painters working outside the Kanō tradition, especially those of the Maruyama and Shijō schools, reacted against the academism of the Kanō school and strongly advocated direct study from nature. Genki, Gessen, Rosetsu, Soken, and Watanabe Nangaku were among the followers of Okyo, the founder of the Maruyama school. The Shijō school, founded by Goshun, produced Keibun, Toyohiko, Zeshin, and others. See GOSHUN; KEIBUN; MARUYAMA SCHOOL; OKYO; ROSETSU; SHIJO SCHOOL; TOYOHIKO.

The fourth and the most important group of Edo artists were the painters and printmakers of Ukiyo-e, who specialized in genre scenes. At first, scenes of streets, festivals, theaters, and gay quarters were depicted in paintings. To meet an increasing demand from less-wealthy patrons, however, pictures were executed in woodblock prints, which were less costly and more suitable for mass production. See UKIYO-E.

Some of the outstanding printmakers—Harunobu, Kiyonaga, Moronobu, Sharaku, and Utamaro—delighted in depicting beautiful women, actors of the Kabuki theaters, and courtesans of gay quarters in Kyoto and Edo (modern Tokyo). Hiroshige and Hokusai, the greatest of the later masters of print making, produced magnificent landscape prints inspired by native scenes. See HARUNOBU; HIROSHIGE; HOKUSAI; KIYONAGA; MORONOBU; SHARAKU; UTAMARO.

A fifth group of painters comprises those who were strongly influenced by Western painting. The Western style was introduced to Japan with the coming of Christianity and was further disseminated through the illustrated scientific books brought into the country by Dutch merchants. This group included Hirage Gennai (1726–79), Aōdō Denzen (1748–1822), Satake Shokuzan (1748–85), Kawahara Keiga (1786–1860), and Shiba Kōkan. These painters assiduously studied Dutch engravings and were particularly impressed by scientific perspective and chiaroscuro. Although they never constituted a dominant force in the Edo period, their knowledge of Western painting influenced a large number of artists still working in the traditional manner. It also prepared the way for the rise of the realistic painting of the Meiji period. See KOKAN.

Modern period (after 1868). After the fall of the Tokugawa shogunate in 1867, Japan began an intense effort to assimilate Western culture. Painters of the Meiji period (1868–1912) were divided into two large groups—one totally accepting the Western style and another attempting a revival of Japan's traditional art. The technique of oil painting was introduced into Japan by the English painter Charles Wirgman (1832–91) and the Italians Antonio Fontanesi (1818–82) and Edoardo Chiossone (1832–98). Many of their Japanese students who later traveled to France for further study helped fashion Japan's future course in oil painting. Significant artists of this group included Yamamoto Hōsui (1850–1906), Asai Chū (1856–1907), and Seiki Kuroda. See KURODA, SEIKI.

The collapse of the feudal system led to a momentary decline of the Kanō school and other painters working in the traditional style. The American philosopher Ernest Fenollosa (1853–1908) and his associate Okakura Tenshin (1862–1913) inspired the Kanō painters, especially Hōgai and Gahō, to follow an ideal of preserving and revitalizing traditional Japanese painting in the intensely Westernizing climate of the country. Their ideal was materialized in the works of later painters, such as Hishida Shunsō (1874–1911), Kanzan Shimomura, Taikan Yokoyama, and others, who brought new life into the tradition. A true marriage of Western and Japanese painting, however, remains a task to be accomplished by future generations of painters. See HASHIMOTO, GAHO; HOGAI; SHIMOMURA, KANZAN; YOKOYAMA, TAIKAN.

BIBLIOGRAPHY. M. Anesaki, Art, Life, and Nature in Japan, Boston, 1933; N. Tsuda, Ideals of Japanese Painting, Tokyo, 1940; Tokyo National Museum, Pageant of Japanese Art, vols. 1–2: Painting, Tokyo, 1952; R. T. Paine and A. Soper, The Art and Architecture of Japan, Baltimore, 1955; S. Hisamatsu, Zen to Bijutsu (Zen and Fine Arts), Kyoto, 1958; T. Nishimura, Namban Bijutsu: Christian Art in Japan, 1549–1639, Tokyo, 1958; Tōyō Bijutsu Kokusai Kenkyūkai, Index of Japanese Painters, Rutland, Vt., 1958; UNESCO, Japan: Ancient Buddhist Paintings (UNESCO World Art Series, 11), Greenwich, Conn., 1959; Y. Yashiro, ed., Art Treasures of Japan, vols. 1–2, Tokyo, 1960; T. Akiyama, Japanese Painting [Geneva?], 1961; J. McDowell and T. Mikami, The Art of Japanese Brush Painting, New York, 1961; J. E. H. C. Covell, Japanese Landscape Painting, New York, 1962; T. Hasumi, Zen in Japanese Art: A Way of Spiritual Experience, New York, 1962; S. Kikuchi, Japanese Arts, What & Where?, 2 vols., Tokyo, 1962; National Commission for the Protection of Cultural Properties, ed., Kokuhō (National Treasures of Japan), 6 vols., Tokyo, 1963–   ; UNESCO, Japanese Paintings from Buddhist Shrines and Temples, New York, 1963; S. E. Lee, A History of Far Eastern Art, Englewood Cliffs, N.J., 1964.

MIYEKO MURASE

JAPAN: PORCELAIN, see JAPAN: CERAMICS (PORCELAIN PRODUCTION).

JAPAN: SCULPTURE. Japanese sculpture may be classified into five main categories: prehistoric clay images, Buddhist statues, Shinto statues, architectural decorations, and secular sculpture of the modern period. Among these, Buddhist statues occupy the most important place in the history of Japanese sculpture.

(For correlation of Chinese, Indian, and Japanese Buddhist terminology see BUDDHIST TERMS, CORRELATION OF.)

Prehistoric period (ca. 3500 B.C.–A.D. 552). Two kinds of clay images were made: dogū, in the Jōmon period (ca. 3500–3d cent. B.C.), and haniwa, in the Tomb period (ca. A.D. 3d cent.–552). Dogū are small and usually have pronounced female characteristics. Their faces and dresses are decorated with either incised or raised cord patterns (jōmon), which also appear on the pottery. They were probably used in cult worship. Haniwa (clay cylinders) are funerary images. They were placed along the exterior of burial mounds, as if to guard the tombs. In this respect they are different from Chinese ming-ch'i, which were placed within burial chambers. In the earliest stage of their development haniwa were simple clay cylinders. Later, clay representations of men and women, domestic animals, and houses were mounted atop tall cylinders. Although simple in form and technique, these images vividly represent various aspects of the life of the early Japanese. They foreshadow the Japanese preference for simplicity of form and boldness of composition (qualities that were to survive throughout the history of Japanese sculpture) and reflect a deep understanding of the inherent nature of the materials used in making sculpture.

Asuka period (552–710). The introduction of Buddhism from Korea into Japan in 552 changed the aspect of the nation's sculpture. Buddhist deities became the sole subject matter, and bronze and wood replaced baked clay as materials. Korean and Chinese immigrant artists taught their Japanese colleagues the technique and iconography of Buddhist sculpture. The most prominent among the descendants of these immigrant artists was Tori Busshi, who made the great bronze Buddha of the Asukadera (Gangōji, 606) near Nara and the Shaka Triad in the

Kondō (Golden Hall) of the Hōryūji (623). The stern expression on their faces, their flat bodies, and the sharply delineated drapery folds reveal Tori's reliance on Chinese works of the Northern Wei dynasty. Many other works were executed in the Tori style: the Yakushi (Buddha of Healing) in the Kondō of the Hōryūji (608), the Yumedono Kannon in the Yumedono (Dream Hall) of the Hōryūji (7th cent.), a small Buddhist triad (628), also in the Hōryūji, and some other bronze statues. *See* TORI BUSSHI; YUMEDONO KANNON.

A group of 7th-century statues in wood show a sharp contrast to the works in the Tori style: the Kudara Kannon of the Hōryūji, the Kokūzō Bosatsu and the Yakushi in the Hōrinji near Nara, the Miroku Bosatsu in the Kōryūji in Kyoto, the so-called Chūgūji Miroku in the Chūgūji nunnery near the Hōryūji, and the Four Guardians (Shitennō) in the Kondō of the Hōryūji. These works have more rounded bodies, sweet and lyrical expressions on their faces, and softer drapery folds. These characteristics reflect the style of the sculpture of the Liang dynasty in southern China. *See* BOSATSU IN REVERIE IN CHUGUJI, NARA; KUDARA KANNON OF HORYUJI; MIROKU BOSATSU IN KORYUJI, KYOTO; SHITENNO IN GOLDEN HALL OF HORYUJI.

Nara period (710–784). The Japanese were greatly influenced by the arts of T'ang China. The capital city of Nara, established in 710, was closely modeled after T'ang China's capital, Ch'ang-an. Sculpture of the Nara period also shows a strong reliance on T'ang prototypes. In striking contrast to the formalized style of the Northern Wei sculpture, T'ang statues are dynamic and realistic. A large bronze head of Yakushi (678–685), which originally belonged to the Yamadadera and is now owned by the Kōfukuji in Nara, signals the turning point in the evolution of Japanese sculpture. Yakushi's head is large and his face plump; and nowhere is the ethereal remoteness of the Tori style or the sweet melancholy of the Kōryūji Miroku, both of which characterize Asuka sculpture, apparent.

This trend toward a strong and realistic representation of Buddhist deities reached new heights in the Shō Kannon and the Yakushi Triad in the Yakushiji (8th cent.). Strong, full modeling reveals the artist's deep understanding and appreciation of the human body. Similar characteristics are noted among works produced in the early 8th century, the most important being the Amida Triad in Lady Tachibana's miniature shrine in the Hōryūji, the pair of guardian figures (Niō) at the Middle Gate of the Hōryūji, and the Shaka in the Kanimanji in Kyoto.

Casting of the Great Rushana Buddha (Vairocana) of the Tōdaiji was the last and most ambitious large-scale sculptural undertaking in Japan's history. The completion of this statue, the largest ever made in Japan, in 752 signaled the end of the era when sculpture was made primarily in bronze.

Despite its fragile quality, unbaked clay became a favorite material for sculpture in the Nara period, because it was malleable, inexpensive, and easily obtainable. Clay was also well suited to the realistic modeling and the free representation of facial expressions and bodily movements that were the current sculptural ideals. However, unbaked clay statues were found to be too heavy and too fragile and were soon replaced by dry-lacquer sculptures.

The technique of making dry-lacquer statues was intro-duced from China. Two different methods were used during this period. One was to mix lacquer with wood shavings and then to apply the mixture to a wooden core to form the statue. The other method was more complicated. The clay model of a statue was made first, and then many thin layers of linen cloth, soaked in lacquer juice, were applied over it. Finally, after the lacquer had dried, the clay model was removed, and in its place a wooden armature was introduced. Dry-lacquer statues were lighter and more durable than clay statues, and many fine examples of such sculptures have survived. The most important examples are two portraits of priests, one of Ganjin (8th cent.) in the Tōshōdaiji in Nara and the other of Gyōshin (8th cent.) in the Hōryūji; the Ten Great Disciples and the Hosts of Eight Divisions (Hachibushū) in the Kōfukuji in Nara (ca. 734); and the Fukūkenjaku in the Sangatsudō of the Tōdaiji (8th cent.). *See* GANJIN IN TOSHODAIJI, NARA; HACHIBUSHU IN KOFUKUJI, NARA; TEN GREAT DISCIPLES IN KOFUKUJI, NARA.

Throughout the Asuka and Nara periods many Gigaku (ceremonial dance drama) masks were made in wood and dry lacquer. The 31 masks in the Hōryūji collection date from the early Nara period. The Shōsōin collection includes 164 masks, and the Tōdaiji owns 19, most of which were made in connection with the "eye-opening" ceremony of the Great Buddha of the Tōdaiji in 752. *See* GIGAKU MASK.

The Rushana Buddha (Vairocana) and other statues in the Tōshōdaiji in Nara were made during the last years of the Nara period. They represent a new tendency away from the naturalism of the earlier years of the Nara period. The bodies of these statues are massive, with their chests, stomachs, and thighs bulging out powerfully. However, the faces of these deities have a pronounced mystical and spiritual quality. With the exception of the Rushana Buddha, which is made of dry lacquer, all the statues in the Tōshōdaiji are made of wood. Each was carved primarily from a single block of wood, in a technique known as *ichiboku* (one-block-of-wood) carving.

Early Heian period (794–897). In the early Heian period wood virtually replaced all other materials of sculpture. It was the most easily obtainable material in Japan, and its pure and natural quality particularly appealed to the native taste.

The strong spirituality of the late Nara statues is equally apparent on those made for the temples of the Mikkyō (esoteric) sects. Many heads and arms were added to the esoteric deities to emphasize their superhuman powers. Fine examples of the esoteric deities are the Nyoirin Kannon of the Kanshinji in Osaka prefecture (ca. 840), the eleven-headed Kannon of the Hokkeji in Nara (9th cent.), the Godai (Five Great) Kokūzō Bosatsu of the Jingoji near Kyoto (ca. 850), and the statues in the Tōji in Kyoto, such as the Fudō (9th cent.), the Godai Myōō (834–48), and the Godai Bosatsu (ca. 840). Even the statues that were not made for the esoteric temples have a similar quality of power and mystery. Yakushi statues in the Jingoji (ca. 799) and the Shin Yakushiji (ca. 800) in Nara and the Shaka of the Murōji near Nara (9th–10th cent.) are good examples of these works. The drapery of the Murōji Shaka has characteristic *hompa* (rolling waves) folds, a series of rounded and pointed folds that are alternately carved in high and low relief, creating the impression of rolling waves. *See* Mikkyo; Nyoirin Kannon; Shaka in Muroji, Nara; Yakushi in Jingoji.

Before the early Heian period, the Shinto tradition did not include making statues of deities. Anthropomorphic representation of Shinto gods and goddesses began in the early Heian period and generally followed the development of style and technique observed in Buddhist sculpture. Portraits of Shinto deities in the Tōji (early 9th cent.) and the Matsuo Shrine (9th cent.), both in Kyoto, and those in the Yakushiji (ca. 890) have a serene beauty that is characteristic of the Shinto statues from this period. *See* Jingu Kogo in Yakushiji, Nara.

Late Heian period (898–1185). Buddhist sculpture gradually lost the fierce and massive quality that characterized early Heian works. The Amida Buddha in the Iwafunedera in Kyoto (946) is one of the earliest works to show a new trend toward a gentler and quieter expression. The Jōdo (Pure Land) sect, which was centered around the teaching of the Amida Buddha of the Western Paradise, gained popularity during this period. Sweetness, gentleness, and even cheerfulness characterize the faces of statues of the Amida Buddha, the most compassionate of all the Buddhas. *See* Jodo.

The spirit of the highly cultured court nobles of the late Heian period is best expressed in the elegant, gentle image of Jōchō's Amida (1053) and the Bosatsu in the Hōōdō (Phoenix Hall) of the Byōdōin at Uji. Jōchō's Amida established a standard for the Buddha image, and numerous Amida statues were made following this example. The Amida statue in the Hōkaiji (late 11th cent.) of Kyoto already shows a hint of mannered delicacy, which becomes even more apparent in other works executed in the same tradition. *See* Jocho.

Jōchō not only established a canon of Buddha statues; he also perfected the *yosegi* (joined-wood) technique of wood sculpture. In it, sections of statues first were carved and hollowed out separately and later were joined together. The *yosegi* technique was particularly effective in preventing statues from cracking, and facilitated the mass production of sculpture by a large group of artists and their assistants.

An assembled group of nine Amida Buddhas was popular in the iconography of the late Heian period. A set in the Jōruriji (ca. 1108) in Kyoto is a rare surviving example of this type. Other notable Amida Buddhas executed in the Jōchō style are in the Chūsonji (ca. 1124) in Hiraizumi, in the Sanzen-in (ca. 1148) and the Hōkongō-in (ca. 1171) in Kyoto, in the Fukiji (12th cent.) in Oita prefecture, and in the Zenkōji (12th cent.) in Yamanashi prefecture.

Kamakura period (1185–1333). Yoritomo established Japan's first military government (*bakufu*) in Kamakura, and this event brought about an important change in the arts of Japan. The two great temples in Nara, the Tōdaiji and the Kōfukuji, had been destroyed during the civil war of 1180, and Yoritomo soon ordered their reconstruction. The restoration of these temples provided a turning point in the history of Japanese sculpture. A large group of sculptors, led by Unkei and Kaikei, was employed for this great undertaking. Sculptors of the Unkei and Kaikei schools had lived in Nara and worked at the temples there

for generations, and consequently had been greatly influenced by the Nara ideals of sculpture. *See* Kaikei; Unkei.

Such works by Unkei as the Muchaku and Seshin (ca. 1208) in the Kōfukuji were inspired by the dynamism and naturalism of Nara sculpture. Other sculptors were also inspired by the works of the past. The Amida in the Kondō of the Hōryūji (1232) was made by Kōshō (fl. 1st half of 13th cent.), the fourth son of Unkei. It was modeled after the Yakushi Buddha, an Asuka work in the same temple. The Great Amida Buddha (ca. 1252) in Kamakura was inspired by the Great Buddha of the Tōdaiji, which dates from the Nara period. Although these works are revivalistic in nature, they are clearly distinguishable from their models. They show a greater degree of realism and intensity in facial expression and bodily movement than do their Nara prototypes. The sense of naturalism was strengthened by the use of inlaid eyes, which had been popular since the end of the late Heian period. *See* Amida Buddha, Great, of Kamakura; Kosho.

Fondness for the expression of power and movement is best exemplified by a pair of gigantic Niō (Guardians, 1203) at the Great Southern Gate of the Tōdaiji. They were completed in a little more than two months by Unkei and Kaikei, with the help of a large number of their assistants. *See* Nandaimon.

A strong sense of naturalism is manifest in the twenty-eight statues (before 1249) in the Myōhō-in in Kyoto (commonly known as Sanjū Sangen-dō, or the Hall of Thirty-three Bays) and a group of eight youthful figures (ca. 1197) in the Kongōbuji at Mt. Kōya. For the first time in the history of Japanese sculpture these statues were conceived in a truly three-dimensional space and were freed from the limitation set by the material. With their arms and legs positioned freely, these statues suggest an arrested moment of movement.

Many realistic portrait sculptures were produced in this period. The finest examples are the Uesugi Shigefusa in the Meigetsuin in Kamakura (13th cent.); the priest Chōgen (overseer of the Tōdaiji reconstruction) in the Shunjō-dō in Tōdaiji (ca. 1206); and Jōkei's imaginary portrait of Yuima (Vimalakirti) in the Kōfukuji (1196). *See* Jokei; Shigefusa in Meigetsuin, Kamakura.

Although Kamakura sculptures are extremely powerful and dynamic, they often lack the religious quality necessary for Buddhist sculptures. This lack was due to overemphasis on the naturalistic description of human bodies and their movements. In fact, the end of the Kamakura period signaled the end of the truly religious sculpture of Japan.

Muromachi period (1336–1573). The art of Buddhist sculpture, which began its decline toward the end of the Kamakura period, continued its downhill course. The only sculpture worthy of note in the Muromachi period is a group of portraits of Zen masters. As the Zen sect of Buddhism emphasized the need for portraits of the masters, the Kamakura tradition of realistic portraiture survived throughout this period. Masks used in the Noh drama achieved a higher artistic standard than religious sculpture. Before this period masks had usually been made by Bud-

Japan, sculpture. Statue of one of the "Twelve Divine Guardians," 13th century, Kamakura period. Detail. Wood. National Museum, Tokyo.

dhist sculptors working for temples, but in the Muromachi period Noh masks were made by artists who specialized in this genre. *See* Noh Mask; Zen.

Momoyama period (1574–1614). Religious sculpture almost totally disappeared in this period, and the sculptor's art survived only in the making of masks for the Noh drama, which reached the height of its refinement. Three families of Noh mask makers are especially worthy of note: Echizen-deme, Omi-izeki, and Ono-deme. A large number of sculptors were employed to decorate the interiors of palaces and castles with brilliantly colored ornamental carvings. Fine examples of these architectural decorations may be seen in the Shoin of the Nishi Hoganji, in Nijō Castle, and on the gate of the Daitokuji, all in Kyoto; and in the Hachiman Shrine in Sendai and in the Zuiganji in Matsushima (both 1607–09).

Edo period (1615–1867). The art of architectural decoration reached its height on the mausoleum of Tōshōgū in Nikkō, which was built for Ieyasu between 1634 and 1636. Small decorative carvings called *netsuke* (cord stoppers) characterize the carver's art of this period. They were made in many materials, such as wood, bone, ivory, bamboo, shell, and semiprecious stone. *See* Netsuke.

Modern period (after 1868). The adoption of Western sculptural concepts and techniques in the Meiji period (1868–1912) saved Japanese sculpture from total annihilation. Vincenzo Ragusa (1841–1928) of Italy introduced Western techniques and styles into Japan, and for the first time in its history sculpture was made purely for aesthetic purposes, free of religious functions. Plaster casts and stone carvings were made, and clay and metal were again used as important sculptural materials. Among the followers of the Western style of sculpture were Kōun Takamura (1852–1934), Fumio Asakura (1883–), and Kōtarō Takamura (1883–1956). Besides Western sculpture, traditional Buddhist statues were again produced. Kōun Takamura was one of the first modern sculptors who attempted to revitalize Buddhist sculpture with new form and spirit.

BIBLIOGRAPHY. L. Warner, *The Craft of the Japanese Sculptor*, New York, 1936; S. Noma, *Japanese Sculpture*, Tokyo, 1939; Bijutsu Shuppan Sha, ed., *Album of Japanese Sculpture*, Tokyo, 1952–53; Tokyo National Museum, *Pageant of Japanese Art*, vol. 3: *Sculpture*, Tokyo, 1952; R. T. Paine and A. Soper, *The Art and Architecture of Japan*, Baltimore, 1955; W. Watson, *Sculpture of Japan, from the Fifth to the Fifteenth Century*, London, 1959; E. D. Saunders, *Mudrā: A Study of Symbolic Gestures in Japanese Buddhist Sculpture*, New York, 1960; *Masterpieces of Japanese Sculpture*, introd., text and comment. by J. E. Kidder, Jr., Rutland, Vt., 1961; T. Kunō, *A Guide to Japanese Sculpture*, Tokyo, 1963; National Commission for the Protection of Cultural Properties, ed., *Kokuhō (National Treasures of Japan)*, 6 vols., Tokyo, 1963– ; J. E. Kidder, Jr., *Early Japanese Art, the Great Tombs and Treasures*, Princeton, 1964.   MIYEKO MURASE

JAPAN: TEXTILES. Because of the extremely humid climate, few ancient textile materials have survived in Japan. No textiles were discovered in the tombs of the prehistoric periods, and only a small number have survived even from such a late period as the Muromachi.

Asuka and Nara periods (552–784). The only exception to this general loss is the collection of 7th-century textiles in the Hōryūji and the early-8th-century materials in the Shōsōin imperial treasure house. Study of these materials reveals that highly developed Sui and T'ang Chinese techniques of weaving and dyeing and a wide range of Chinese designs were known to the Japanese in the Asuka and

Nara periods. These techniques and designs were often reproduced by Japanese artisans so skillfully, in fact, that it is quite difficult to determine the provenance of some materials.

Fragments of a once large piece of embroidery, known as the *Tenjukoku Mandara*, are owned by the Chūgūji nunnery near the Hōryūji. The mandara was made by a consort of Prince Shōtoku immediately after his death in 622. Although only a few fragments survive, it can still be seen that this embroidery depicted various scenes of the prince's life in the Buddhist paradise. Other textiles in the Hōryūji collection, now in the Tokyo National Museum, also date from the first half of the 7th century. There are other small pieces of silk embroidery in public and private collections in Japan. They represent Buddhist angels, and are done in highly developed embroidery technique. The unusual collection in the Shōsōin of the Tōdaiji includes thousands of fragments of textiles. Materials in this collection, now mostly in small pieces, were originally used at the "eye-opening" ceremony of the Great Buddha of the Tōdaiji in 752. The collection also includes materials that once belonged to the emperor Shōmu and were donated to this temple in 756.

These textiles show that a wide range of the Sui and T'ang techniques and patterns were known to the Japanese. Cotton, hemp, and silk were the most frequently used materials, with silk being the most valued. According to the weave of the silk, it is named *aya* (damask), *nishiki* (brocade), *ra* (silk gauze), and *tsuzure* (tapestry). For dye, vegetable materials were used; designs were made by batik (*rōkechi*, or *rōketsu* in modern Japanese), block printing (*kyōkechi* or *kyōketsu*), and tie-dyeing (*kōkechi* or *kōketsu*). Many textile designs of the Nara period can be traced not only to China but also to countries farther to the west, India and Sassanian Persia in particular. Knowledge of these designs clearly indicates Japan's position as the terminus of the Silk Road in relation to the arts of the greater East.

Two important 8th-century materials showing Buddhist scenes have survived. The *Taima Mandara*, owned by the Taimadera of Nara prefecture, was made in tapestry technique. Embroidery representing the scene of the Shaka's preaching was originally in the Kanshūji of Kyoto but is now in the Nara National Museum. The provenance of this embroidery is still questioned, but it was probably made in Japan in the middle of the 8th century. Particularly noteworthy is the close stylistic similarity of the figures in the *Taima Mandara* and the Kanshūji embroidery to the painted images of Buddhist deities that once decorated the walls of the Golden Hall of the Hōryūji.

Heian, Kamakura, and Muromachi periods (794–1573). The study of textiles from this long and important period is made difficult by a serious lack of existing materials. Few fragments have survived, and a better understanding of the Heian, Kamakura, and Muromachi textiles depends on the study of contemporary literature and painting.

A distinctly Japanese taste in the choice of quieter colors and delicate patterns began to appear in the early 10th-century costumes of the ladies and noblemen of the court. Otherwise, the techniques, materials, and designs established in the Nara period were used throughout these years, during which no spectacular achievements were made in the field of textiles. A slow decline of the textile art began in the Kamakura period, as the military leaders paid less attention to the finer details of life than did the court nobles of the preceding periods. New Chinese techniques and materials were brought to Japan in the Muromachi period. They influenced Japanese textiles only to the extent that they prepared the way for the brilliant flowering of the textile art in the Momoyama period. For example, *tsujiga-hana*, a new technique in which designs produced by tie-dyeing methods were combined with painted patterns, first appeared toward the end of the Muromachi period, but it was perfected in the Momoyama period.

Momoyama period (1574–1614). The most brilliant achievements in the field of textiles were made during this period. A type of kimono known as a *kosode* (a short-sleeved, one-piece dress) became the standard dress for all ages and classes, men and women alike. Standardization of dress made it inevitable that the originality and individuality of garments be marked by differences in material and design. Richly woven silk materials, already introduced from China in the Muromachi period, were successfully reproduced in Japan during the Momoyama period. Silk damask (*donsu*), satin (*shusu*), crepe (*chirimen*), and gold brocade (*kinran*), which introduces in the weave fine strips of gilded paper, were the most important materials.

The textile designs of this period reflect the style of contemporary screen painting. They are characterized by a love of display and extravagancy, particularly in the use of bold patterns and brilliant colors. Many splendid costumes were created for the Noh theater, which reached perfection in this period. In the Noh costumes delicate and realistic flowers or birds were often combined, or sharply contrasted, with strong abstract patterns in striking colors. Although the Momoyama period lasted less than a hundred years, textiles made the greatest stride known in Japan's past.

Edo period (1615–1867). The textile style and technique developed in the Momoyama period were perfected in the Edo period. The industry developed further with the help of rising commerce, a general affluence, and a long period of peace. Textiles may be characterized by an astonishingly wide range of designs, which were mostly executed by printing methods rather than by weaving. A new dyeing technique called *yūsen* was developed in the early 18th century. In this process complicated patterns can be dyed with ease by using thick paste to protect the painted areas. The *yūsen* silk fabrics are still the speciality of Kyoto.

Modern period (after 1868). Like all other arts of the modern period, textile art has been strongly influenced by Western science and technology, which were introduced into Japan in the late 19th century. Nishijin weavers of Kyoto, for example, quickly assimilated the Western technique of tapestry making and gained worldwide fame. Local centers of the textile industry, which were developed in the Edo period, are still active in modern Japan.

BIBLIOGRAPHY. H. C. Gunsalus, *Japanese Textiles*, New York, 1941; M. Ishida, *The Shōsōin: An Eighth Century Treasure House*, Osaka, 1954; Tokyo National Museum, *Pageant of Japanese Art*, vol. 5: *Textiles and Lacquer*, Tokyo, 1954; Nihon Sen'i Ishō Sentā, *Textile Designs of Japan*, 3 vols., Osaka, 1959–1961; National Commission for the Protection of Cultural Properties, ed., *K kuhō (National Treasures of Japan)*, 6 vols., Tokyo, 1963– ; Y. Tanaka *Nō Costumes of Japan*, Tokyo, n. d.

MIYEKO MURASE

JAPONAISERIE. French term for the infatuation with and imitation of Japanese decorative style in the fine or applied arts. The Japanese woodcut provided a new source of inspiration to such artists as Bresdin, Monet, Van Gogh, and Toulouse-Lautrec. A notable wave of *japonaiserie* was started in Europe by the Japanese exhibition in Paris in 1878; it had an important effect on the development of an independent style, Art Nouveau. See ART NOUVEAU.

JAPPELLI, GIUSEPPE. Italian architect (1783–1852). He worked in Padua. Trained as an engineer, he worked with Selva and visited England in 1836. He collaborated with A. Graenigo on the Caffè Pedrocchi (1816–31), one of the finest buildings of the Greek revival in Italy, and designed the Pedrocchino, the first example of the Gothic revival in Italy.

BIBLIOGRAPHY. N. Pevsner, "Pedrocchino and Some Allied Problems," *Architectural Review*, CXXII, 1957.

JAQUERIO, GIACOMO. Italian painter of Piedmont (fl. 1403–53). He was court painter to the Duke of Savoy and is known from signed frescoes at Ranverso (S. Antonio), which show fluid line and vehement power of form, somewhat akin to the artists around the Duke of Berry. Jaquerio also painted hunting frescoes at the castle of Mantua.

BIBLIOGRAPHY. A. Griseri, "Percorso di Giacomo Jaquerio," *Paragone*, XI, September, 1960.

JARDINIERE. Receptacle, usually in the form of an urn or vase, for plants, flowers, and other growing things. Its basic shape is the Greek krater. Essentially an antique invention, jardinieres became extremely important in interior decoration, and above all in garden ornamentation, of the baroque period. Many are elaborately shaped and richly decorated with reliefs.

JARVIS, JOHN WESLEY. American portrait painter (b. South Shields, England, 1780; d. New York City, 1840). He immigrated to Philadelphia in 1785 and was apprenticed (1796–1801) to the engraver E. Savage. He later painted portraits and miniatures with Joseph Wood in New York and executed a series of portraits of heroes of the War of 1812. Between 1814 and 1820 Sully and Inman were his assistants.

Jarvis was the foremost self-taught portrait painter in New York during the first quarter of the 19th century. The portrait *De Witt Clinton* (ca. 1810) reveals his approach to portraiture. Heads are strongly modeled, and the features are broadly and vigorously painted, with a concentration of expression around the eyes. His technique was hasty, but his colors are bold and clear, although sometimes inharmonious.

BIBLIOGRAPHY. H. E. Dickson, *John Wesley Jarvis, American Painter*, New York, 1949.

JASOKU (Soga Jasoku). Japanese painter (fl. late 15th cent.). Nothing is known of Jasoku's life except that he was closely associated with Ikkyū, a noted Zen priest and tea master in the Daitokuji in Kyoto. Jasoku founded the Soga school of painting. His works on screen panels in the Shinjuan of Kyoto, showing landscape, birds, and flowers, are done in strong lines and heavy shadows of dark tone contrasted with delicately shaded areas.

JATAKA. Buddhist term meaning "birth story." The Jātakas tell of the 550 former incarnations of Gautama Buddha.

JAUNPUR: ATALA MASJID. Indian mosque situated in a city near Benares, in eastern Uttar Pradesh. It was erected in 1408 by Shams ad-Din Ibrahim, a ruler of the Sharqi dynasty. The mosque plan is traditional, with a central courtyard surrounded by arcades, entrances on three sides, and the sanctuary area on the fourth. The lofty arched portal to the sanctuary has battered sides and leads into a rectangular hall covered by a single dome. This is a stone structure; its effect is massive, with the ornament roughly executed. The many openings and galleries serve to weaken the sense of architectural harmony.

BIBLIOGRAPHY. P. Brown, *Indian Architecture*, vol. 2: *Islamic Period*, 4th ed., Bombay, 1959.

JAUNPUR: JAMI MASJID. Indian mosque situated in a city near Benares, in eastern Uttar Pradesh. Erected about 1470 by Husein Shah, last ruler of the Sharqi dynasty, it is a larger version of the Atala Masjid in Jaunpur. Set on a high terrace, the great open courtyard, flanked by arcades in two stories, is entered by arched portals on three sides. On the fourth side of the courtyard a great arched façade leads to the sanctuary chamber and conceals the dome rising above the chamber. The construction in stone is vigorous but coarse in detail.

BIBLIOGRAPHY. P. Brown, *Indian Architecture*, vol. 2: *Islamic Period*, 4th ed., Bombay, 1959.

JAVA. Between the 7th and the 10th century, Javanese government and art were concentrated in central Java, following the influx of Hindu and Buddhist monks. During this period Buddhism reached its ascendancy under the Sailendras in the 8th century, although Hinduism coexisted with it. In northern central Java are to be found eight surviving temples, or candi (Jav., *caṇḍi*), on the plateau of Dieng, as well as the temples of Gedong Sanga. On the Kedu Plain, to the south, is the Barabudur (ca. 750–850), one of the great monuments of Buddhist art and architecture. Other Buddhist temples of the south are the Kalasan, Sari, and Sajiwan candis (8th cent.) on the Prambanam Plain and the Sewu and Plaosan candis (9th–10th cent.). There are also a number of Hindu candis on the Prambanam Plain, built in the late 9th or early 10th century. *See* BARABUDUR.

The 10th century saw a shift to eastern Java, where civilization flourished until the Muslim ascendancy of the 16th century. From this period, after the transfer of the capital by Siṇḍok (ca. 929–947), are the Gunung Gangsir (ca. 950) and the sepulchral bathing places at Djalatunda and Belahan (11th cent.). Javanese civilization reached its height in the 13th and 14th centuries as the state of Majapahit, which controlled much of Indonesia and the Malayan Peninsula. Monuments in the new Hindu capital of Singhasāri include the Singhasāri and Kidal candis. The great complex of temples at Panataran, begun in the

Java. Barabudur, central stūpa surrounded by latticed stūpas housing figures of Bodhisattva Vajrasana.

12th century, and a great many other temples were constructed at this time. Artistic activity in the 15th century went mostly into the building of Hindu mountain shrines, during the breakdown of the centralized state. In the 16th century the Muslims became the dominant force, and in the century that followed the Portuguese and then the Dutch gained their first foothold on the island. Many of the old forms were retained by the Muslims in their mosques and palaces. They also erected vast palaces of wood up to the 18th century. *See* INDONESIA.

BIBLIOGRAPHY. A. J. Bernet Kempers, *Ancient Indonesian Art*, Cambridge, Mass., 1959. DONALD GODDARD

JAWLENSKY, ALEXEY VON. Expressionist painter (b. Kuslovo, Russia, 1864; d. Wiesbaden, Germany, 1941). He went to school in Moscow and St. Petersburg. In 1896 he moved to Munich and studied with Anton Azbé. At that time, he met Wassily Kandinsky, Marianne von Werefkin, and David and Vladimir Burliuk, all fellow students. From 1902 on, he worked independently. He traveled in France and was influenced by Cézanne, Matisse, Hodler, and Van Gogh. In 1909 he joined the Neue Künstler Vereinigung in Munich. In 1912 he met Klee and Nolde and exhibited with them and with Feininger, Kandinsky, and other members of the Blaue Reiter group, but he did not become a member. In 1914 he moved to Switzerland. From 1917 to 1921 he painted a series of mystically Fauvist heads, his best-known works. In 1920 he had a retrospective exhibition at the Gurlitt Gallery in Berlin. He moved to Wiesbaden in 1921 and in 1924, along with

Feininger, Kandinsky, and Klee, formed Die Blauen Vier (The Blue Four) group which exhibited in Europe, the United States, and Mexico. From 1934 on he continued to paint small pictures of heads, but more abstractly.

In these last works, Jawlensky appears to have been influenced by cubism and, perhaps, by Dutch de Stijl! His first work, done in Russia, shows the influence of the realist Ilya Repin. During his expressionist period, he painted still lifes, figures, and landscapes in a manner that recalls Kandinsky. With a minimum of modulation, areas of color—fully saturated carmines, ultramarines, and emerald greens—are outlined by simplified, thickened contours and then juxtaposed for contrast. In his abstracted heads, Jawlensky reduces the features to straight, thick lines. A vertical close to the center of the picture plane represents a nose, while horizontals suggest eyes, eyebrows, and a mouth. The faces are shown close up. The lines are designed to resemble crosses, Russian icons, and the like, thus giving the work strong religious and mystical overtones. Jawlensky favored warm colors—siennas and vermilions—which are heightened in close contrast with deep, cool blues and greens and black. Jawlensky repeated a single theme many times in variation throughout his career.

BIBLIOGRAPHY. C. Weiler, *Alexej Jawlensky*, Cologne, 1959.

ROBERT REIFF

JEAN BOULOGNE (Giambologna), *see* BOLOGNA, GIOVANNI.

JEAN DE BEAUSSE, *see* TEXIER, JEAN.

JEAN DE BOULLOGNE, *see* VALENTIN, MOISE LE.

JEAN DE BRUGES, *see* HENNEQUIN, JAN.

JEAN DE CAMBRAI. French sculptor (b. Roupy-en-Picardie; d. Bourges, 1438). He worked first at Notre-Dame in Courtrai and at Cambrai and in 1387 entered the service of the Duc de Berry, for whom he collaborated with André Beauneveu. In 1397 Jean succeeded his master as First Sculptor to the Duke. He created most of the statues for the chapel of the palace at Bourges, directed the work at the château and chapel of Mehun-sur-Yèvre, and worked on the tomb of the Duke (Bourges Cathedral) from 1405 until the project was dropped in 1416, to be finished by Mosselman in 1453. In his effigy of the Duke, Jean's style is harder, more meticulously realistic, and less graceful than that of Beauneveu.

BIBLIOGRAPHY. M. Aubert, *La Sculpture française au moyen-âge*, Paris, 1946; T. Müller, *Sculpture in the Netherlands, Germany, France, and Spain, 1400–1500*, Baltimore, 1966.

JEAN DE CHARTRES. French sculptor (fl. Tours, 15th–16th cent.). A letter of Michel Colombe to Marguerite of Austria in 1511 mentions Jean de Chartres as serving some eighteen to twenty years as Colombe's pupil and collaborator. From 1493 to 1511 he was probably employed on the tomb of François II de Bretagne. Attributions to this proto-Renaissance sculptor in the Colombe tradition remain somewhat questionable.

BIBLIOGRAPHY. P. Pradel, "Le Sculpteur Jean de Chartres et son atelier," *Bulletin Monumental*, CIII, 1946; P. Pradel, *Michel Colombe, le dernier imagier gothique*, Paris, 1953.

JEAN DE LIEGE. Flemish sculptor (fl. 1361–82). Jean de Liège studied and collaborated with Jean de Huy. He became the favorite sculptor of Charles V of France, creating many works for him, including a sepulchral monument to hold the heart of the king at Rouen Cathedral, now destroyed. In his monument for the viscera of Charles IV and Jeanne d'Evreux in the Louvre, Paris, the stumpy proportions and blocked forms of the reclining effigies make it seem unlikely that he also created the imposing graceful statues of Charles V and Beatrix de Bourbon in the Louvre that are sometimes attributed to him.

JEANNERET, PIERRE, *see* LE CORBUSIER AND JEANNERET.

JEANNERET-GRIS, CHARLES-EDOUARD, *see* LE CORBUSIER.

JEAURAT, ETIENNE. French genre painter (b. Paris, 1699; d. Versailles, 1789). He accompanied his teacher, N. Vleughels, to Rome in 1724. He became a member of the French Royal Academy as a history painter in 1733 and then chancellor in 1767. Although he emulated Jean-Baptiste-Simon Chardin, his genre subjects (*Taking*

Alexey von Jawlensky, *The Princess*. Private collection, Cologne.

the Harlots to the Hospital; Paris, Perrault-Dabot Collection) possess a journalistic realism and humor akin to that of William Hogarth. At his death Jeurat was curator of the Crown Collections.

BIBLIOGRAPHY. S. Puychevrier, *Le Peintre Etienne Jeaurat*, Paris, 1862.

JEDBURGH ABBEY. Scottish Augustinian foundation of about 1138, which became an abbey about 1154. The west front, crossing, and parts eastward are 12th century. Additions are 13th century, and the north transept chapel is 15th century. Romanesque parts are best seen in the great central west door and in the vigorously decorated cloister door.

BIBLIOGRAPHY. Ministry of Works, *Ancient Monuments and Historic Buildings*, vol. 4, London, 1917-58.

JEFFERSON, THOMAS. American statesman and a leading figure in American architecture (b. Shadwell, Va., 1743; d. Monticello, Va., 1826). An amateur and a Palladian as well as a promoter of ancient Roman styles and Louis XVI classicism, Jefferson was influential in promulgating the new classic modes in American architecture. He considered Roman architecture appropriate for the new republic and based the Virginia State Capitol (1785-96) on the Maison Carrée, Nîmes, France. The Capitol is probably the first public building in the world derived from a classical temple. Jefferson's home, Monticello, near Charlottesville, Va. (1769-1806), is noted for its simple, monumental grandeur, and Bremo (1818), also in Virginia, reflects his classic conception of building. Helped by the suggestions of William Thornton and Benjamin H. Latrobe, Jefferson designed the University of Virginia (ca. 1816-42), whose Pantheon-like rotunda knits together the rows of pavilions. *See* MAISON CARREE, NIMES; MONTICELLO; VIRGINIA, UNIVERSITY OF; CHARLOTTESVILLE.

JEGHER, CHRISTOFFEL. Flemish maker of woodcuts (b. Antwerp, 1596; d. there, 1652/53). His fame rests on the nine woodcuts he made after designs by Rubens; these include the *Garden of Love* (in two sheets), *Hercules Fighting Envy*, the *Coronation of the Virgin*, the *Temptation of Christ*, and the *Rest on the Flight into Egypt* (one of his two chiaroscuro woodcuts). In them Rubens's monumental and dynamic compositions are translated with much more expressiveness than is managed by the engravers of Rubens's school. Rubens directly supervised the making of the woodcuts, retouching many of the proofs himself. The joint activity of the two artists dates from about 1632 to 1635/36. Jegher was employed as a book illustrator by the Plantin Press from 1625. The cutting of decorated initials, printers' marks, vignettes, and other illustrations in books constituted the major part of this work. From the mid-1630s he also printed his own works and later became a bookseller. The monogram "C.I." with a knife below, which always appears on his works, should not be confused with that of his son, Jan Christoffel, who signed his prints "I.C.I."

BIBLIOGRAPHY. T. F. X. van Lerius, *Biographies d'artistes anversois*, vol. 2, Antwerp, 1881; F. van den Wijngaert, *Inventaris der Rubeniaansche Prentkunst*, Antwerp, 1940; H. F. Bouchery and F. van den Wijngaert, *P. P. Rubens en het Plantijnsche Huis*, Antwerp, 1941; F. W. H. Hollstein, *Dutch and Flemish Etchings, Engravings, and Woodcuts, ca. 1450-1700*, vol. 9, Amsterdam, 1953.

CAROLINE KARPINSKI

Jehol, P'u-Tuo Tsung-chen Temple, built in the Tibetan style during the reign of Ch'ien-lung, 1767.

JEHAN LE HOME, *see* LOMME, JANIN.

JEHOL. Chinese region north of Peking, above the Great Wall of China. At one time it was referred to as the province of Jehol. The political definition of this area has varied; the People's Republic of China has eliminated Jehol entirely, partitioning the territory between the provinces of Hopei and Liaoning and the autonomous territory of Inner Mongolia.

The region is of importance in Chinese art history partly for the summer palaces built in the hills by the Manchu emperors. About 108 miles north of Peking, near the city of Ch'eng-teh in what is now Hopei Province, a series of temples and summer houses were erected between 1713 and 1780, mainly by Ch'ien-lung (r. 1736-96). The Tibetan style of several of the temples, particularly the P'u-ning and P'u-lo temples, reflects the renewed interest and contact with Tibet in the latter half of the 18th century.

BIBLIOGRAPHY. M. Igarashi, *Nekka koseki to Chibetto geijutsu* (Monuments of Jehol and Tibetan Art), Tokyo, 1943.

JELLETT, MAINIE. English painter (1897-1944). In 1920-21, she studied in Andre Lhote's studio, and after 1923 she came under the influence of Albert Gleizes. Her cubist work seems sometimes imbued with a futurist sense of velocity, as can be seen in *Let There Be Light* (1941). Her paintings are frequently religious in theme. In *Let There Be Light*, what is presumably the hand of God stretches forth from the top of the canvas. *Ninth Hour* (1943; Collection of Mrs. Rynne) is a cubist Crucifixion with attending saints. Yet her Connemara seascapes and landscapes are rendered in a far less avant-garde mode: in these works shaggy donkeys and ponies commonly run wild in the hill country.

BIBLIOGRAPHY. J. White, "The Art of Mainie Jellett," *The Studio*, CXXIX, June, 1945.

JEN JEN-FA. Chinese painter (1254-1327). His *tzu* was Tzu-ming and his *hao* Yüeh-shan. Jen Jen-fa served the Yüan dynasty government successfully in varied capacities. He was a talented engineer whose major contribution in this respect was a long work on water control, but his principal claim to a niche in the history of painting rests on his marvelous paintings of horses. Like most true scholar-officials, Jen Jen-fa was a master of calligraphy as well as painting, a man gifted in many areas. His horse paintings, for which he is certainly best known to the West, are in the direct tradition of Han Kan, Li Kung-lin, and Chao Meng-fu—stately tributes to the great importance of the horse to the Chinese. Among the very finest of Jen Jen-fa's is the hand scroll in the Cleveland Museum of Art. *See* Chao Meng-fu; Han Kan; Li Kung-lin.

BIBLIOGRAPHY. S. E. Lee and W. K. Ho, "Jên Jên-fa: Three Horses and Four Grooms," *Cleveland Museum of Art, Bulletin,* XLVIII, April, 1961.

JENNEY, WILLIAM LE BARON. American architect and engineer (1837–1907). Born in Fairhaven, Mass., he studied at Cambridge, Mass., and at the Ecole des Beaux-Arts, Paris, in the 1850s. Jenney became one of the founders of the Chicago school, and his commercial structures were among the first to reveal the new aesthetic, according to which large glass openings filled the bays between piers and spandrels, as in the First Leiter Building (1879). His Home Insurance Building (1883–85) is usually considered the first modern office building in which skeleton construction was used. Almost all its exterior walls are carried on the metal frame. In the notable Second Leiter Building (1889–90), the skeleton largely dictated the structure's appearance and became an architectonic means of expression. Many major architects of the Chicago school were trained in Jenney's office.

BIBLIOGRAPHY. C. W. Condit, *The Rise of the Skyscraper,* Chicago, 1952.

JENNYS, J. WILLIAM. American portrait painter (fl. New Milford, Conn., mid-1790s, and New York City, 1797–98). After 1800, Jennys painted portraits in the Connecticut Valley, central Massachusetts, Vermont, and New Hampshire (Portsmouth). His sitters, set in grayish ovals, are clearly delineated and rigidly posed.

BIBLIOGRAPHY. A. M. Dods, "Newly Discovered Portraits," *Art in America,* XXXIII, January, 1945.

JEN PAI-NIEN. Chinese painter (1840–95). Born in Chekiang Province, he moved to Shanghai and became a member of the White Lotus Society, an association of literati painters that was quite influential in the region. The works of Jen Pai-nien and other members of his family dominated *wen-jen,* or literati, painting during the later 19th century, and they were mainly responsible for carrying on in a vigorous way the great tradition of scholar painting in China. *See* Wen-jen-hua.

JENSEN, GEORG. Danish silversmith and designer (1866–1935). Born in Raadvad, Jensen apprenticed himself to a goldsmith at fourteen, and in 1904 set up his first workshop. In 1916, he founded the Georg Jensen Smithy and School, but today his fame rests as much with the Fifth Avenue furniture and housewares store in New York City that bears his name as with his silver and glass.

JENSEN-KLINT, PEDER VILHELM. Danish painter and architect (b. Skelskør, 1853; d. 1930). Trained as an engineer and painter before starting an architectural career, he worked in a 19th-century manner at the beginning of the 20th century. His best-known work is the bizarre

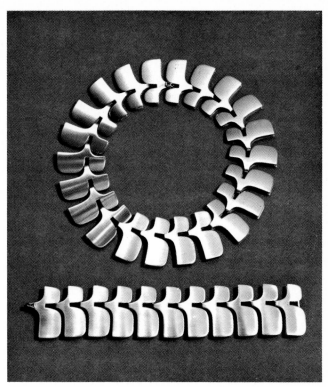

Georg Jensen. Necklace and bracelet designed by Dahlquist, 1965. Georg Jensen Silversmith Ltd., Copenhagen.

Grundvig Church in Copenhagen, designed in 1913 and built between 1921 and 1926.

JERABLUS, *see* Carchemish.

JEREMIAH. Old Testament prophet who is the purported author of the Book of Jeremiah. He proclaims that the Messiah (Jer. 23:5; 30:21) will be of the seed of David. Jeremiah's own life, during which he worked unceasingly for his people and received only their rejection, has been seen by Christian writers as a prototype of Christ's.

JERICHO. One of the earliest settlements in Palestine, already surrounded by two stone enclosures in the pre-pottery period (ca. 8000 B.C.). Jericho never showed urban layout or ordinances; it was destroyed and rebuilt several times during the Early Bronze Age (tower and ditch construction) and in the Middle Bronze Age when it had two cobbled streets with steps and a drain running down the slope. It was last destroyed about 1400 B.C.

Rooms or rectangular houses were built with plano-convex brick on stone foundations in Mesolithic times. In the Neolithic period the floors were plastered and burnished; a northern enclosure formed a sanctuary. In the Bronze Age, houses had an apsidal end, perhaps an influence from prehistoric Greece. One of the most interesting contributions of Jericho to art is the series of neolithic heads for ancestor worship which were modeled in clay around actual skulls with inlaid shells for the eyes. Some of the faces were of clay with shell eyes, painted hair, and characteristic flat features. A later vessel, modeled and painted into the features of a face, is also known.

BIBLIOGRAPHY. K. Kenyon, *Archaeology in the Holy Land*, New York, 1960. ALEXANDER M. BADAWY

JEROME, ST. Doctor of the Church (d. 419). Born in Stridon, he was baptized in Rome and studied there and in Antioch. Christ asked him in a dream whether he was Ciceronian or Christian. Jerome retired to the desert, was later ordained a priest in Antioch, and became secretary to Pope Damasus in Rome. He headed a religious community in Bethlehem and was the author of the Latin Vulgate translation of the Bible. In art, he is shown as a hermit or scholar with a tamed lion. His attributes are a cardinal's hat and a lion. His feast is September 30.

See also SAINTS IN ART.

JEROME DA FIESOLE, *see* GIROLAMO DA FIESOLE.

JERUSALEM. City in what was formerly Palestine. Because of the great importance of Jerusalem to Jews, Christians, and Muslims alike, generations of builders and artists have labored to beautify it. Many major monuments were destroyed in the numerous battles fought for its possession, and frequent changes of sovereignty and taste caused the drastic alteration of most of the remainder. In spite of war and demolition, the venerable city remains a museum of important works, however fragmentary, of Hebrew, Early Christian, early Muslim, and Crusader art.

The site was settled during the 3d millennium B.C., but Jerusalem did not become the chief city of the Hebrews until about 1000 B.C. During the following century King Solomon fortified the town, built a palace, and by about 950 had completed his famous Temple. Egyptian in plan and probably actually executed by Phoenician builders and artists, the Temple faced east and was divided into three major spaces, one being the Holy of Holies where the Ark of the Covenant was kept. *See* SOLOMON'S TEMPLE.

Solomon's Temple was destroyed in the Babylonian conquest of 587 B.C. Other temples were built on the site (about where the Dome of the Rock stands today) and were often reconstructed and repaired; the ultimate one, built by Herod Agrippa I, disappeared in the terrible sack of the city A.D. 70, though the future Roman emperor Titus tried to prevent its destruction. The Wailing Wall, a traditional shrine associated with the Temple, is Herodian in date in its lower courses; the upper blocks are probably Roman. The remains of the Antonia fortress, named in honor of Mark Antony, recall the power and policies of Herod in the 1st century B.C.

Jerusalem was not only renamed (Colonia Aelia Capitolina) but utterly transformed by Hadrian's officers after the revolt of Bar Kokhba, A.D. 132–135. The site of the Temple was plowed over, and a new town was laid out. Jews and Christians of Jewish birth were forbidden to enter the city. Only with the arrival in 326 of St. Helena, mother of the emperor Constantine, did Jerusalem become in any sense a Christian town. Having satisfied herself as to the location of Calvary and the Tomb, St. Helena caused these rocky sites to be cut back, and by her son's order the first buildings of the Holy Sepulchre were placed there. These consisted of an atrium, a five-aisled basilica culminating in a rounded shrine, an open court flanked by the mound of

Calvary, and a circular court around the Tomb, over which a domed rotunda (called the Rotunda of the Anastasis) was later placed. In the 11th century the site was badly damaged; in the 12th the Crusaders built a Western medieval church there. The Tomb itself has been many times damaged and reconstructed. *See* HOLY SEPULCHRE.

During the 4th century a round Church of the Ascension was built atop the Mount of Olives; the foundations may still be seen. There the instruments of the Passion were in early Christian times displayed to pilgrims, but in the Persian invasion and sack of 614 the works of Constantine and his successors perished as had those of King Solomon. In 638 the Muslims occupied the city, treating the occupants humanely, and turned their attention to the sacred rock where Solomon's Temple had once stood and from which the Prophet Muhammad had ascended into heaven.

There in 691 was erected the magnificent Dome of the Rock (Omar Mosque), the best-preserved and probably the finest of Jerusalem's major buildings. It has the additional value of giving some sense of the original effect of the Rotunda of the Anastasis at the Holy Sepulchre, for both are of the same size and general design. Near the Dome of the Rock are a number of smaller Muslim buildings dating from the 7th and 8th centuries. The Haram as-Sharif, the sacred Muslim enclosure, encompasses the Dome of the Rock, the Aqsa Mosque, and the Wailing Wall. *See* AQSA MOSQUE; DOME OF THE ROCK.

In 1099 the city was stormed and occupied by the Crusaders. This Latin occupation lasted less than a century, during which the Holy Sepulchre basilica was rebuilt and the Calvary chapels enclosed within it. Also dating from this period is the Church of St. Anne (1130s), a fine groin-vaulted church in the Provençal style; the Dome of the Ascension, on the summit of the Mount of Olives; and St. James, containing a ribbed dome in the Armenian fashion, as rebuilt from an 11th-century original.

Other important monuments and sites include the tomb of David, the Church of the Dormition, the Israel National Museum (incorporating the Bezalel National Art Museum, the Samuel Bronfman Biblical and Archaeological Museum, the Billy Rose Art Garden, and the Shrine of the Book), the Monastery of the Holy Cross, the Citadel, the Via Dolorosa, the Palestine Archaeological Museum, and, in the environs, the Monastery of St. Sabas. *See* JERUSALEM: ISRAEL NATIONAL MUSEUM; VIA DOLOROSA.

Jerusalem is not a city from which major stylistic principles have been exported, with the exception of the shrine form of the Anastasis rotunda. Rather it is a site to which artistic developments and ideas have been brought, and those by three or four clearly distinct societies. The result is a heterogeneous, almost miscellaneous ensemble, the value of which is to be found in the artistic expression given to the beliefs of such different faiths and peoples.

BIBLIOGRAPHY. H. Vincent and F. M. Abel, *Jérusalem: Recherches de topographie, d'archéologie et d'histoire*, 2 vols., Paris, 1912–26; J. W. Crowfoot, *Early Churches in Palestine*, London, 1941; L.-H. Vincent, *Jérusalem de l'Ancien Testament*, 2 vols., Paris, 1954–56; M. Join-Lambert, *Jérusalem, israélite. chrétienne, musulmane*, Paris, 1957; M. Avi-Yonah, *A Picture Story of the Holy City*, New York, 1961. WILLIAM L. MACDONALD

JERUSALEM: ISRAEL NATIONAL MUSEUM. Opened in 1965, this collection incorporates the Bezalel National

Jerusalem. Dome of the Rock (Omar Mosque), built in 691 on the site of Solomon's Temple.

Art Museum, the Samuel Bronfman Biblical and Archaeological Museum, the Billy Rose Art Garden, and the Shrine of the Book. The museum is housed in a complex of buildings on a hill. Most of the structures have been designed by the Israeli architects Alfred Mansfeld and Dora Gadd. The concrete buildings are basically a group of platforms with hyperbolic-parabolic roof shells; clerestory windows provide natural light.

The two main wings are the Bronfman Archaeological Museum and the Bezalel Art Museum. The first museum presents in depth a history of Palestine. The second museum, which is in the process of assembling a collection of paintings, has been actively advised by Willem Sandberg, former director of the Stedelijk Museum of Amsterdam, and by Sir Philip Hendy, former director of the National Gallery, London. Important gifts, particularly of modern art, have been received from donors throughout the world. The Bezalel Museum also contains a unique group of Judaic ceremonial objects as well as costumes and objects of Middle Eastern, North African, and Eastern European Jewish cultures.

The Art Garden, by the sculptor Isamu Noguchi, juts out from the hill in tilted arcs with an imaginative use of mazelike masonry areas. The Billy Rose Collection of sculpture includes works by Bourdelle, Maillol, Rodin, Zadkine, and Reder, among others. The Shrine of the Book, designed by Frederick Kiesler (in collaboration with Armond Bartos) for the shelter and display of the Dead Sea Scrolls, is boldly romantic in conception. Its poured-concrete ribbed dome is faced with white tiles and symbolically contrasts with a dark wall of basalt, representing the battle between the forces of light and darkness. Inside, a tunnel leads to the center of the dome, where the Scrolls are placed around a dramatically upward-shooting, bronze abstract form. (See illustration, p. 315.)

JESSE, TREE OF. Subject in Christian art in which the ancestors of Christ are represented as a genealogical tree whose roots are in Jesse. Jesse is shown reclining, with the branches of the tree ascending from his sides. This subject is frequently depicted on Gothic stained-glass windows and in the voussoirs of Gothic portals; both are exemplified at Chartres.

BIBLIOGRAPHY. A. Watson, *The Early Iconography of the Tree of Jesse*, London, 1934.

JESUIT STYLE. Architectural style of the Jesuit missions established among the Indians of eastern Bolivia, northeastern Argentina, Paraguay, and southern Brazil in the 17th and 18th centuries. Starting in 1609, thirty of these settlements were created among the Guarani Indians, and after 1675 another twenty-five were founded in eastern Bolivia. The earliest style, which carried into the 18th century, was characterized by structures with pitched wooden roofs supported on a perimeter of wooden columns and enclosed by an inner curtain wall of adobe or brick. A surviving example is the church of Yaguarón, near Asunción (1761–84). Later, with the success of the missions, vaulted stone buildings of European design were introduced. The complex of buildings at the Jesuit reduction of Trinidad, Paraguay (1725–67), designed by G. B. Primoli, epitomizes this phase. In the Asunción area wooden structures in the Jesuit style continued to be built even after the expulsion of the Jesuits from the Americas in 1767.

BIBLIOGRAPHY. J. Giuria, *La arquitectura en el Paraguay*, Buenos Aires, 1950; M. Buschiazzo, "La arquitectura de las misiones de Moxos y Chiquitos," *Anales del Instituto de arte Americano e investigaciones estéticas*, V, 1952.

JETTY, *see* OVERHANG.

JEU DE PAUME MUSEUM, PARIS, *see* PARIS: MUSEUMS (JEU DE PAUME).

JEWELRY, HISTORY OF. The designation "jewelry" may be applied to various eye-catching objects designed for personal adornment. Its techniques have often been those of the metalworker, who employs hammering, soldering, chasing, repoussé, welding, and engraving in the manufacture of jewelry. Important roles in the history of this branch of decorative art have also been played by the enameler, the gem cutter, and the maker of glass paste and other substitutes for precious stones. Although the basic function of necklaces, earrings, and bracelets is decoration of the person, certain items, such as amulets, are worn for magicoreligious purposes, while other pieces, such as crowns and chains, may designate rank or position. Quantities of jewelry have been found in ancient tombs, in caches, or as individual pieces lost by wearers. When few actual pieces remain, a natural result of frequent melting down of precious metals, it is possible to know what was worn in various periods from a study of paintings, sculpture, illustrated manuscripts, and descriptions given in old texts and inventories. *See* CHASING; REPOUSSAGE.

During prehistoric times, necklaces were made from polished pebbles, shells, carved bone and teeth, all requiring carefully drilled holes for thong suspension. With the invention of metallurgy, the Bronze Age jeweler was provided with bronze, silver, and, especially, gold. Amber and jet were also obtainable and highly prized. In ancient Egypt, the early dynasties depended on attractive stones such as turquoise and lapis lazuli, which were coated with vitreous glaze. By the 2d dynasty (ca. 3000 B.C.), faïence was developed to provide an inexpensive material for molded scarabs, for bracelets, and, especially, for the beads required to make up broad collars for both daily and funerary use. A peak in elegance and refinement of technique was reached in the 12th dynasty (ca. 2000–1788 B.C.), when semiprecious stones were cut into small slices to form cloisonné inlays in pectorals and bracelets. Beads of amethyst, carnelian, and gold were used to make necklaces of great beauty. By the 18th dynasty (ca. 1580–1090 B.C.) the wealth of the royal court was expressed in a lavish use of beaten gold for headdresses, collars, and seal rings. Although glass had been used in conjunction with semiprecious stones in wealthier times, it became even more popular for beads, inlay, and amulets during the late dynastic era, persisting in popularity into the Roman period.

The peoples of the ancient Near East were equally fond of jewelry. The Sumerian dynasty (ca. 3500 B.C.) produced the gold and lapis flower chaplet of Queen Shubad, as well as her choker of the same materials and her gold lunate earrings. During the time of the Babylonian and Assyrian ascendancies (ca. 1700–600 B.C.), kings wore gold necklaces richly ornamented with pendant figures bearing granulation, heavy pendant earrings, and armlets terminating in animal heads. The Achaemenian court of Iran (549–

History of jewelry. Etruscan gold necklace with rhomboidal meshes and Silenus heads, 6th–5th century B.C. National Archaeological Museum, Naples.

331 B.C.) continued to have jewelry made in the Assyrian tradition, with emphasis on stone inlay, a technique that later passed on to the Parthians (248 B.C.–A.D. 226). *See* GRANULATION.

The Greeks (7th–3d centuries B.C.) used few precious stones but were highly skilled in goldwork, especially embossing and filigree. Thin sheets of gold were the favored materials, as they had been in the Mycenaean civilization. The finely beaten gold was cut into pieces that were soldered to gold bases or worked into diadems bearing scenes in repoussé. Elaborate necklaces were made of plaited gold wire, often ending in tassels, rosettes, flowerets, and pendants in the form of vases or of mythological figures. Miniature works of sculpture in gold (cupids, amphorae, and so on) were suspended from both necklaces and individual earrings. Some earrings and bracelets were circlets terminated by animal heads (for example, gold dolphin-headed earrings, ca. 350 B.C.; London, Davis Collection). Other earrings had rosettes or embossed disks masking a pin at the ear with elaborate pendants. Pins, hairpins, and simple strings of gold beads were also worn. *See* EMBOSSING; FILIGREE.

The Etruscans wore similarly constructed ornate jewelry. They developed the art of filigree even further than the Greeks, and could ornament gold surfaces with almost microscopic grains of gold. Men and women alike wore great amounts of jewelry, and necklaces with a number of *bullae* (hollow pendants containing amulets) were almost universal. During the Hellenistic period, glass, agates, and other semiprecious stones were added for brighter color.

Under the Roman republic jewels were virtually banned except for signet rings. Later, under the empire, jewelry became large and bold. Roman women decked themselves with linked necklaces, diadems, large earrings (especially pearls), bracelets, stickpins, hairpins, and rings in a variety of styles unequaled until the 20th century. Bracelets were heavy gold circlets, bangles of twisted gold, or flexible bands (for example, the serpent bracelet; London, Victoria and Albert). The art of gem carving became highly developed (for example, the Gemma Augustea, ca. A.D. 10; Vienna, Museum of Art History).

During the migration period the fibula, or safety pin, became the leading piece of jewelry for both men and women. Many of the Gothic tribes, with a rich Black Sea–region tradition of jewelry making, were able to produce fibulae of various designs and also buckles, strap-end covers, bracelets, and earrings. Bronze, silver, gold, thin slices of garnet, and colored glass were all utilized. Celtic jewelry of the pre-Roman period is characterized by the torque (neck ring) and the highly skilled use of champlevé enamel as a decoration for bronze. Enamel continued into the Gallo-Roman period, a time when niello was introduced into Gaul by the Romans. Jewelry of the so-called barbarian tribes, who pushed into France, England, and Spain and who created pieces of fine craftsmanship in Scandinavia, is characterized by animal motifs and interest in band interlacery. *See* CHAMPLEVE ENAMEL; NIELLO.

The sophisticated cities of the Byzantine East witnessed an outpouring of luxurious gold jewelry, created in openwork or in beaten gold decorated with colorful enamel. Pearls and precious stones were also in use, as shown on mosaics that depict imperial personages wearing heavy crowns and infinitely rich collars. Belts and necklaces were also composed of gold coins, a practice imitated by the gold bracteates worn by Scandinavian chieftains.

By the Romanesque period (ca. 900–1100), jewelry had ceased to be included in burials, so that little of it remains. Sculptured royal figures are shown wearing crowns set with stones in filigreed cloisons. Their cloaks are fastened by centrally worn circular brooches, while their jeweled belts dangle against simple tunics. Actual techniques of this period may be studied on silver-gilt reliquaries, chalices, and book covers that were made in monastic workshops and preserved in church treasuries. These bear filigreed vine interlacery, champlevé enamel, and precious stones of cabochon cut. During the Gothic period hat badges of gold and enamel, designed with religious themes, were popular with wealthy courtiers.

Lowered necklines for 15th-century ladies made possible the wearing of necklaces of intricate gold wire set with pearls and gemstones. Increasing lavishness in jeweled headdresses and hair nets led to the 16th-century fashion of sewing jewels and pearls to clothing, as is shown in portraits of Queen Elizabeth I of England. Pearl chokers, earrings, and bracelets were also in great favor. The art of the goldsmithworker, who was also an enameler, culminated in figural pendants that could be hung from a gold chain or pinned to a bodice. In these, classical themes displaced religious subjects. Interest in intaglio-engraved gems and in cameo-cut profiles was revived, and Renaissance jewelry design for royal patrons was taken over by painters and sculptors, such as Holbein and Cellini. New cutting and polishing techniques for precious stones were developed, and published engravings made this knowledge and new designs widespread in Europe. *See* GOLDSMITH'S WORK.

In the East, India has always been a jewelry center, having practiced, for untold centuries, such techniques as filigree, enameling, and stone setting. Although the earliest surviving pieces go back only as far as the 18th century, they show high artistry, especially in the handling of silver. Necklaces often bear such minuscule elements as seed pearls and include naturalistic buds and flowers in their design. China, too, has produced jewelry of great intricacy, reaching a peak of refinement and delicacy in the ceremonial crowns of the 18th and 19th centuries. These included such elements as birds, flowers, and butterflies made of gold, seed pearls, coral, and jade, mounted on wire in the most fragile-appearing manner possible.

In the 17th century Europe saw a reduction in the types and quantity of jewelry worn, so that a single strand of pearls, a brooch, and a ring often sufficed for elegant ladies. The brilliant court entertainments of 18th-century Versailles ushered in a period of interest in the sparkle of diamonds mounted in silver. The marquise setting enhanced a centrally placed diamond by surrounding it with smaller ones. Men wore jeweled buttons, sword hilts, and shoe buckles and carried jeweled snuffboxes of blue enamel and gold. Often marcasite and "paste" stones substituted for real diamonds.

Portrait miniatures and Wedgwood plaques, worn as brooches or on necklaces, became popular during the late 18th and early 19th centuries, an era of strong classical revival. The comparative simplicity of this jewelry was rivaled by the showy extravagance of the "parure," a matched set of pieces (tiara, necklace, earrings, brooch, and so on) made of semiprecious stones. By mid-century, the Industrial Revolution had introduced mass-produced jewelry that utilized artificial gold, already known in England as "pinchbeck." For the wealthy Victorian, the discovery of new diamond mines brought about further elaborations in multifacet cutting, resulting in emphasis on rose and brilliant forms. Pear-shaped, square, and ovoid stones of great value came to be worn for their individual beauty, suspended on chains or set in platinum rings.

The 20th century has seen the creation of original pieces by Lalique, Fabergé, and other designers, which combine gold, enamel, precious stones, and pearls. Pins in an enormous variety of designs have enjoyed great popularity, but bead chokers, pearl strands, earrings, and jeweled watch bracelets have also vied for attention. Rhinestones and other synthetically produced gems have made possible jewelry that closely imitates expensive pieces in all but price. See LALIQUE.

BIBLIOGRAPHY. New York, Metropolitan Museum of Art, *Jewelry: The Art of the Goldsmith in Classical Times*, by C. Alexander, New York, 1928; F. W. Burgess, *Antique Jewelry and Trinkets*, New York, 1937; New York, Metropolitan Museum of Art, *Mediaeval Jewelry: A Picture Book*, text by J. J. Rorimer, 1944; E. B. Ricketson, "Barbarian Jewelry of the Merovingian Period," *New York, Metropolitan Museum of Art, Bulletin*, new series, V, 1947; E. D. S. Bradford, *Four Centuries of European Jewellery*, London, 1953; A. Darling, *Antique Jewelry*, Watkins Glen, N. Y., 1953; S. Oved, *The Book of Necklaces*, London, 1953.

EMMA N. PAPERT

JEWETT, WILLIAM. American portrait painter (b. East Haddam, Conn., 1789/90; d. Bergen, N.J., 1874). After a brief apprenticeship to a New London, Conn., coachmaker, Jewett moved to New York (1812), where he became a partner of Samuel Waldo. His works are academically strong and realistic.

BIBLIOGRAPHY. F. F. Sherman, "Samuel L. Waldo and William Jewett, Portrait Painters," *Art in America*, XVIII, February, 1930.

JEWISH ART. Art began to play an important role in Jewish religious life during the time of the Roman Empire. The gradual emergence of a religious art among the Jews arose, in large part, from the revolutionary changes that had been introduced into Judaism at an earlier period by the Pharisees, in response to the new needs and conditions stemming from a Hellenistic environment. Among these changes one must note the development of the synagogue, a building for prayer and devotion; the elevation of the scholar over the priest; and the replacement of sacrifices in a centralized Temple by a system of salvation that insisted that personal salvation in the world to come was dependent on the performance of authoritative religious acts in this world. (For the pre-Roman period, *see* HEBREW ART.)

Roman-Byzantine period. The most significant Jewish monument surviving from this period is the 3d-century synagogue of Dura Europos in Syria, excavated in 1932 by Yale University. On its walls, in three distinct tiers, were preserved some thirty paintings of Old Testament scenes. This is believed to be the first time in art that mural decoration with a unified iconographic conception based on the Bible is encountered. Moreover, the articulated cycle of themes on the walls of Dura, with its liturgical salvationary meanings, is a precursor of similar, well-

known cycles in medieval Christian art. It raises the question whether Jewish art served as a link between late pagan art and the emerging Christian art. Jewish art, it is evident, adapted the styles and conventions of pagan art to its own iconographic themes and may have transmitted them to Christian art. The Dura paintings also pose the questions whether the practice of mural decoration in synagogues was common among Jews of that period and whether the models for the synagogue paintings were rooted in manuscript illustrations, mosaics, or other mural paintings. *See* DURA EUROPOS.

The synagogue of Dura Europos is unique in that it is the only one of the period excavated to date that has a cycle of paintings on its walls. However, many other synagogues dating from the 3d to the 7th century have been unearthed, especially in the Galilee region of Israel. A typical one is the 6th-century synagogue of Beth Alpha in Galilee, which is modeled on the basilican plan. Its main prayer hall had a roof, and perhaps a women's gallery, supported by two rows of columns, which thus divided the hall into a nave and two aisles. The Torah shrine, which though portable in Dura had become stationary by this time, was placed within an apse. In keeping with a practice common in Palestinian synagogues of the 5th to the 7th century, the building contains a floor mosaic. Divided horizontally into three panels, the mosaic depicts the sacrifice of Isaac, the zodiac, and the Torah shrine surrounded by ceremonial appurtenances used in the synagogue. The mosaic was executed by two Jewish folk artists and is in an excellent state of preservation. *See* TORAH.

Emulating late pagan practices, Jews buried their dead in catacombs. Some catacomb complexes dating from the 2d to the 4th century have been discovered, mainly in Rome and in Israel. On the walls of such catacombs as those found at Villa Torlonia in Rome and Beth Shearim in Israel are depicted popular Jewish symbols of the period, such as the menorah, the lulab (palm branch), the etrog (citrus fruit), and the shofar (ram's horn), as well as pagan symbols. Sculptured sarcophagi with figural and animal decorations have also been discovered in these catacombs. *See* MENORAH.

Medieval Europe. Beginning with the 10th century Jews were invited into Germany. There, during the 11th and 12th centuries, their activities as merchants and moneylenders helped further the lavish building programs of feudal nobles and clergy in the flourishing town economies. In return for these services, the Jews were accorded special privileges and protection. They began to build synagogues in the 11th century in such important centers as Worms, where a small synagogue in typical Romanesque style stood until the Nazis destroyed it in 1938. It was a double-aisled, rectangular hall with six cross vaultings supported by two columns. Between the two columns stood the bimah, the reader's platform. *See* WORMS.

In the 13th and 14th centuries, synagogue buildings reflected the dominant Gothic style, as in Prague's Alt-Neuschul, which is still standing. Its exterior has a steeply rising roof with buttresses; in the interior, two tall pillars divide the hall into aisles and carry the Gothic vaulting. As at Worms, the bimah is placed between the pillars.

The Jews of Germany, especially during the 13th and 14th centuries, emulated their Christian neighbors by decorating their cherished religious books. In these manuscripts knights, gargoyles, and fantastic animals, drawn in a typically Gothic manner, covered the pages.

The manuscripts most frequently chosen for illumination were *Machzorim* (prayer books) of huge dimensions. They contain illustrations of such key moments in Jewish tradition as the sacrifice of Isaac—to accompany the liturgy for Rosh Hashanah (the New Year), when, according to tradition, God forgives Israel's sins because of the merit of Abraham; and the Revelation at Sinai—to accompany the liturgy for Shavuoth (the Feast of Pentecost), a holiday traditionally linked with the giving of the Law.

The feudal breakdown of Germany and the ensuing persecutions of the Jews, especially during the 14th and 15th centuries, had an impact on the art of the Jews. Manuscripts of this period generally lack the rich gold and silver illumination of the earlier books and contain illustrations that are often crude and naïve. A depiction that became very popular in these manuscripts was that of the coming of the Messiah, who, according to tradition, would relieve the Jewish people from the oppressive misery of their environment by ushering in an era of peace and plenty.

Persecutions and diminishing economic opportunities in the crumbling feudal system of medieval Christian Germany were curtailing the artistic participation of the Jews in that country. Christian Spain, however, which had emerged from its triumphant struggles against Muslim Spain, began to welcome Jewish participation in its economy during the 13th and 14th centuries. There, a select group of Jewish aristocrats, functioning in such key positions as tax farmers, bailiffs, counselors, and physicians, commissioned some of the finest illuminated Hebrew manuscripts produced in medieval Europe. Most popular were illuminated Haggadoth (read in the home during Passover), dating mainly from the 14th century, which, like some of the Christian Psalters, usually had an unrelated cycle of Biblical illustrations appended at the beginning. One such manuscript, the *Sarajevo Haggadah* (Sarajevo National Museum), includes sixty-five Biblical episodes, from the creation of the world to the death of Moses. Stylistically, these manuscripts, like such synagogues as the one built in Toledo for Samuel ha-Levi (El Tránsito, 1355–57), reflect the predominant styles of Christian works, which in Spain were Gothic, Italian, and Mudejar. Iconographically, however, many of the illustrations in the manuscripts are radically different from then-contemporary Christian Biblical illustrations and can be understood only in terms of Jewish sacred literature. *See* TRANSITO, EL, TOLEDO, SPAIN.

Sixteenth–eighteenth century Europe. Jewish art in Europe from the 16th to the 18th century, with the exception of Eastern Europe, was created mainly by non-Jews, while the few Jewish artists whose names have been recorded produced no noteworthy works. In Italy, especially in Venice, splendid baroque and rococo synagogues were built by such famous Christian architects as Baldassarre Longhena, who rebuilt in the 17th century the Scuola Spagnola in Venice's Ghetto Vecchio. In Amsterdam, the Dutch architect Elias Bouman built the Spanish-Portuguese synagogue. Simple but stately in design, it resembles neighboring Calvinist churches.

Eastern Europe, particularly Poland, contained the largest concentration of Jews in Europe during the 16th and 17th centuries and was one of the most important cultural and religious centers of Jewry. Jews functioned in Poland's feudal economy in such roles as merchants and managers of estates. Especially in the larger Polish towns, many synagogues were constructed by wealthy Jews. Fortresslike in appearance, with heavily buttressed walls, these stone synagogues often revealed an Italian influence, which was strong during that period.

A major change in the life of Polish Jewry occurred with the breakdown of Poland's feudal economy and the massacre of large numbers of Jews in the mid-17th century. Fleeing the major centers, many Jews relocated in Polish villages and towns, where they often turned to cultivating the land or to taking over the trades and crafts. In the villages, from the late 1600s to the 1800s, they built magnificent wooden synagogues, most of which survived until they were burned by the Nazis. Many of these synagogues boasted a multitiered hipped roof, which some writers have likened to a Chinese pagoda but which is more closely related to wooden church buildings in Eastern Europe. In the interior, the focus was on the bimah, which stood in the center of the room. Although serving no architectural function, the supports of the ornate bimah often reached to the ceiling, which was vaulted with tentlike structures and cupolas. The decorative effect of the elaborately carved bimoth, and the Torah shrines (which contain the sacred Scrolls of the Torah) on the eastern wall, was further heightened by polychromic paintings that, in some synagogues, covered every inch of wall space like richly woven fabrics.

In Eastern Europe, much attention was also lavished on ceremonial objects, which were created for both the synagogue and the home. Unlike the Jews of Western Europe, who were barred from joining the established guilds, Jewish craftsmen in Eastern Europe apparently had their own guilds. Among the objects they created were *Hanukkah menoroth* (to commemorate the Maccabean victory over the Syrians) in precious silver, with profuse floral and animal decoration and whimsical ornamentation, and spice boxes (for the *Havdalah* ceremony at the conclusion of the Sabbath) in the form of fanciful birds, trees, flowers, fish, and fruits.

Nineteenth and twentieth centuries. Prior to the 19th century, Jews were viewed as a religious entity and as a distinct community. Thus, their art was oriented, and perforce restricted, mainly to the interests of the medieval-type Jewish community. With the advent of the French Revolution, however, Jews were encouraged to accept, in addition to their religious loyalty, a national loyalty. This turn of events permitted Jews to develop fully their artistic talents as citizens, without restriction as to theme.

During the 19th and 20th centuries many Jews figured prominently in the development of modern art in the United States as well as in most major European countries and participated in such important artistic movements as impressionism, expressionism, and cubism. It must be emphasized, moreover, that while a painter of Jewish origin may derive inspiration from a Biblical or Hassidic idea, his painting belongs essentially to Western art (not Jewish art) and should be considered an integral part of the general history of 19th- and 20th-century art.

BIBLIOGRAPHY. J. Leveen, *The Hebrew Bible in Art*, London, 1944; F. Landsberger, *A History of Jewish Art*, Cincinnati, 1946; E. R. Goodenough, *Jewish Symbols in the Greco-Roman Period*, 12 vols., New York, 1953–66; C. H. Kraeling, *The Synagogue*, New Haven, 1956; M. and K. Piechotka, *Wooden Synagogues*, Warsaw, 1959; J. Gutmann, *Jewish Ceremonial Art*, New York, 1964; J. Gutmann, *Images of the Jewish Past: An Introduction to Medieval Hebrew Miniatures*, New York, 1965.

JOSEPH GUTMANN

JEWISH BRIDE, THE. Oil painting by Rembrandt, in the Rijksmuseum, Amsterdam. *See* REMBRANDT HARMENSZ. VAN RIJN.

JEWISH CEMETERY, THE. Oil painting by Ruisdael, in the State Art Collections (Picture Gallery), Dresden. *See* RUISDAEL, JACOB ISAACSZ. VAN.

JIGSAW PATTERN. Decorative motif consisting of a series of wavy lines which crisscross, beginning at right angles.

JINA. Sanskrit term meaning "conqueror." A jina is one who has subjugated the material and attained spiritual perfection, according to the Jains. He is also known as a Tīrthaṅkara.

JINGU KOGO IN YAKUSHIJI, NARA. Japanese wood sculpture (ca. 896). The famous empress Jingū (3d or 4th cent.), who led an expedition of conquest to Korea, is shown in this imaginary portrait as a Shinto goddess, since she had been deified after her death. Two other Shinto statues accompany her in the *Jingū Kōgō*. Her body is compact, and her white face sharply contrasts with the brilliant decorations on her dress.

BIBLIOGRAPHY. Tokyo National Museum, *Pageant of Japanese Art*, vol. 3: *Sculpture*, Tokyo, 1952; National Commission for the Protection of Cultural Properties, ed., *Kokuhō (National Treasures of Japan)*, vol. 2: *The Heian Period*, Tokyo, 1964.

JISHOJI, *see* GINKAKUJI.

JIZO, *see* KSHITIGARBHA.

JOAN OF ARC, ST. A patron saint of France (1412–31). A peasant born in Domrémy, Joan responded to "voices" and went to aid Charles VII, who was at war with England in Burgundy. Joining the army at Blois, she routed the English at Orléans and persuaded Charles to be crowned at Reims. Taken at Compiègne by Burgundians, she was sold to the English. Joan was tried as a heretic and a witch but was imprisoned when she recanted. After abjuring her retraction, she was burned alive as a relapsed heretic at Rouen. In art she is shown listening to voices, in armor, or at the stake. Her attributes are the lilies of France. Her feast is May 30.

See also SAINTS IN ART.

JOCHO. Japanese sculptor (d. 1057). A pupil of Kōshō, Jōchō was the first sculptor of Japan to be given a high priestly rank in recognition of his work. A large statue of the Amida Buddha of the Western Paradise in the Hōōdō (Phoenix Hall) of Byōdōin, Uji (1053), which became the model for numerous later statues of the Amida, is the only surviving example of his work. *See* KOSHO; UJI.

BIBLIOGRAPHY. R. T. Paine and A. Soper, *The Art and Architecture of Japan*, Baltimore, 1955.

Jōdo. Celestial musician on the wall behind the Amida Buddha, Phoenix Hall, Byōdōin, Uji.

JODE, PIETER DE, II. Flemish engraver (b. Antwerp, 1606; d. after 1674). Working exclusively as a reproductive printmaker, De Jode for the most part engraved portraits after Rubens, Jacob Jordaens, Gerard Seghers, Van Dyck, and others. His pedestrian style, deriving from Goltzius, lacks the latter's power and delicacy. In Paris in 1631–32, Mariette published his *St. Francis* after Federico Barocci. De Jode was in Brussels in 1667, and may have died in England.

BIBLIOGRAPHY. F. W. H. Hollstein, *Dutch and Flemish Etchings, Engravings and Woodcuts, ca. 1450–1700*, vol. 9, Amsterdam, 1953.

JODO. Japanese term for a Buddhist land of bliss presided over by a Buddha. More popularly, the word *jōdo* came to be associated with a branch of Buddhism that preaches the teachings of the Amitābha (Japanese, Amida) and the rebirth in his Western Paradise. Worship of the Amida, known as the Amidist or Jōdo (Pure Land) sect, was never organized into a separate school in India, but by the time it reached China in the 3d century, it had developed a number of traits that appealed to Chinese Buddhists. Genshin (also known as Eshin Sōzu, 942–1017) is often called the first Japanese patriarch of the Jōdo sect. The sect was established as an independent school in Japan under the leadership of Hōnen (also known as Genkū, 1133–1212), who maintained that the mere repetition of the Amida's name enabled men to be admitted to the Western Paradise.

The teaching of the Raigō concept (the joyous descent of the Amida and his bodhisattvas from heaven to take the dying to his Paradise) stimulated the creation of a number of important sculptures and paintings in China and Japan. The entire temple of the Phoenix Hall (Hōōdō) in Byōdōin, Uji, depicts the descent in both paintings and sculpture. A 12th-century painting at Mt. Kōya is another important example of Raigō art. *See* DESCENT OF AMIDA, REIHOKAN, MOUNT KOYA; HOODO OF BYODOIN.

BIBLIOGRAPHY. R. T. Paine and A. Soper, *The Art and Architecture of Japan*, Baltimore, 1955; G. B. Sansom, *A History of Japan*, 3 vols., Palo Alto, Calif., 1958; E. D. Saunders, *Buddhism in Japan*, Philadelphia, 1964; D. Seckel, *The Art of Buddhism*, London, 1964.

MIYEKO MURASE

JOEST, JAN. Netherlandish painter (d. 1519). Although his exact place of origin is uncertain, Joest in all probability came from the vicinity of Haarlem. He is known through two works: the wings of an altarpiece (1505–08) in the Church of St. Nicholas in Kalkar and an altarpiece in the Cathedral of Palencia, Spain, dated about the same time. These works display a painterly style and a greater interest in landscape and genre than in the religious aspects of the subjects.

JO-FEN YU-CHIEN, *see* YING YU-CHIEN.

JOHN, ST. Evangelist and apostle. The son of Zebedee and Salome and the brother of James the Greater, he was Christ's favorite. He preached in Judaea and Asia Minor. At Rome, under Domitian, he was plunged into boiling oil with no ill effects. Accused of magic, he was exiled to Patmos, where he wrote the Book of Revelation (the Apocalypse). At Ephesus, a priest of Diana gave him poison; he made the sign of the cross, drank, and was unaffected. He was carried to heaven as an old man. His attributes are an eagle, a chalice, a small dragon, and a book. His feast is December 27.
See also SAINTS IN ART.

JOHN, AUGUSTUS EDWIN, O.M. British portrait, figure, and landscape painter, draftsman, and etcher (1878–1961). Born in Tenby, Wales, John was one of four children, of whom Gwendolen became a considerable artist in her own right. John studied at the Slade School of Fine Art, London, with William Orpen and Ambrose McEvoy, from 1894 to 1898. In 1898 he won the Slade prize for *Moses and the Brazen Serpent.* His skill as a draftsman gained him a considerable reputation even while at the Slade, where one of his more influential teachers was Henry Tonks, an admirer of Degas. As a young painter, John was somewhat eclectic and borrowed from, among others, Watteau, Rembrandt, Goya, Puvis de Chavannes, and Daumier, but for some years after 1910 he adopted the brighter palette and broader treatment of postimpressionism.

Three years after leaving the Slade, he was appointed professor of painting at Liverpool University and held the post from 1901 to 1904. He became a member of the New English Art Club in 1903. By that time he had embarked upon his career as a portrait painter. He found much of his other subject matter among the underprivileged, for example, gypsies, tramps, and beggars, in whom he found an "absolute isolation" of character and greater inspiration than in his usual patrons.

On leaving Liverpool John spent some time following gypsy caravans in the company of John Sampson. He lived with the gypsies and learned their customs and language. His *Encampment on Dartmoor* (1906, private collection), notable for its fresh handling and colors, is one of the paintings executed during this period. In 1911 and until the outbreak of war, he went on painting trips with his friends Derwent Lees and J. D. Innes, traveling in his native Wales and in France. From Innes he derived a richer use of color and a romantic sense of landscape, resulting in a number of lyrical figure compositions. One was his large-scale work of 1911, *Lyric Phantasy;* another, *Galway* (1916). With the early death of Innes in 1914,

John began to lose this evocative pitch, and his major period of landscape painting ended.

John's later career was concerned primarily with portraits, of which he was a prolific producer. Early studies of members of his family, particularly those of his children Robin (1909) and David (1918), and oil portraits of George Bernard Shaw (ca. 1914) and Lady Ottoline Morrell (ca. 1926) are among his best and most skillfully composed. Many of the portraits, however, are of a more formal and sometimes stiff quality in spite of his loose, textured brushwork.

John was elected an associate of the Royal Academy of Arts in 1921 and was made full academician in 1928. He resigned in 1938, but was later reelected. He was a trustee of the Tate Gallery, London, from 1933 to 1940 and received the Order of Merit from King George VI in 1942.

BIBLIOGRAPHY. J. Rothenstein, *Augustus John,* London, 1944.
JOHN K. D. COOPER

JOHN, GWENDOLEN MARY. English painter (b. Haverfordwest, Pembrokeshire, 1876; d. Dieppe, France, 1939). Gwen John was the sister of Augustus John and a friend of Rodin and the poet Rilke. She studied at the Slade School of Fine Art in London and with Whistler in Paris. Like those of Whistler, her paintings—mostly portraits and interiors—are close-tone arrangements of simplified forms, but they are done with considerably more clarity and strength. In her haunting *Self-Portrait* (ca. 1900; London, Tate Gallery) these qualities approach severity. Her later works are less tightly painted but keep the same powerful economy. She rarely exhibited and preferred living in seclusion, mostly in Paris.

BIBLIOGRAPHY. J. Rothenstein, *Modern English Painters: Sickert to Smith,* London, 1952.

JOHN CHRYSOSTOM, ST. Father and Doctor of the Church and Patriarch of Constantinople (347–407). He studied law and theology at Antioch, and became a her-

Augustus John, *Lawrence of Arabia.* National Gallery, London.

mit, following Pachomius's rule. He then became a deacon and later a priest, winning renown in Antioch as the greatest Christian expositor (hence the name Chrysostom meaning golden tongued) and also as a liturgical reformer. As Patriarch of Constantinople in 398, he proposed to reform the city, but he incurred the anger of Empress Eudoxia and others and was exiled to Cucusus, then to Pityus, dying en route at Comana in Pontus. John Chrysostom is often shown dressed in a chasuble or cope with a pallium or an omophorion and usually without a miter. He often carries a book or a scroll rather than a specific attribute. His feast is January 27.

See also SAINTS IN ART.

JOHNS, JASPER. American painter (1930–   ). Born in Allendale, S.C., Johns attended the University of South Carolina and moved to New York in 1952. His paintings, exhibited at the Leo Castelli Gallery and now in international exhibitions and museums throughout the world, deny the emotional immediacy of abstract expressionism, creating an ambiguous and shielded relationship with the viewer. Starting in 1955 with a series in which the entire canvas is covered by the flat image of an American flag, he has since used such singular images as targets, words, and numbers, which create questions about experience by reducing it to a set of signs. This is most pointedly so of a painting such as *Device Circle* (1959; Connecticut, private collection), which presents the materials of the artist in a pseudogeometric, pseudo-ordered manner. Johns's paintings are raised to an iconic level by their exquisitely painted surfaces and their encaustic technique. His more recent works are freer in technique and often include real objects (*Fool's House*, 1962; New York, private collection). Johns is a leading figure in the "neo-Dadaist" trend in the United States and a forerunner of Pop Art.

BIBLIOGRAPHY. A. R. Solomon, *Jasper Johns*, New York, 1964.

DONALD GODDARD

JOHNSON (Jonson; Jansens), CORNELIUS (Cornelis Jonson van Ceulen; Cornelis Janssen van Keulen). English portrait painter (b. London, 1593; d. Utrecht, 1661). Johnson's parents were Flemish. In 1643, because of the Civil War, he left England for Holland, where he continued painting until his death. Until the arrival of Van Dyck in 1632, Johnson was probably England's most successful portraitist; certainly, he is the first native painter to whom a large body of work can be definitely ascribed. Johnson rarely attempted the full figure; he produced mainly bust portraits set in painted ovals, somewhat like enlarged miniatures. His technique was excellent, and he responded sensitively to the character of his sitters. There are portraits by him in many English private collections; in the National Gallery and the National Portrait Gallery, both London; in the Boston Museum of Fine Arts; and in the Metropolitan Museum, in New York.

BIBLIOGRAPHY. E. K. Waterhouse, *Painting in Britain, 1530-1790*, Baltimore, 1953.

JOHNSON, EASTMAN (Jonathan Eastman Johnson). American genre and portrait painter (b. Lovell, Maine, 1824; d. New York City, 1906). After working for a Boston lithographer, Johnson turned to portrait painting. From 1849 to 1860, he studied in Düsseldorf, Paris, London,

and The Hague. Upon returning home, he executed frontier themes and then rural genre scenes and landscapes of New England and Nantucket. His style is characterized by broad liquid brush strokes, heavy impasto, and dramatic light effects.

BIBLIOGRAPHY. J. I. H. Baur, *An American Genre Painter: Eastman Johnson, 1824-1906*, Brooklyn, N.Y., 1940.

JOHNSON, PHILIP CORTELYOU. American architect (1906–   ). Johnson was born in Cleveland. He studied architecture at Harvard, and he was director of the Museum of Modern Art's Department of Architecture and Design from 1932 to 1954. In 1932, he published the significant *International Style*, a pioneer work of architectural criticism, and organized the first International Exhibition of Modern Architecture (both with Henry-Russell Hitchcock), held at the Museum of Modern Art. He started in private practice in 1945, working in the meticulous classicism of Mies van der Rohe, and collaborated with Mies on the Seagram Building, built in New York City in 1958. Johnson has been very influential as an architect, writer, and lecturer.

BIBLIOGRAPHY. H.-R. Hitchcock, "Philip Johnson," *The Architectural Review*, CXVII, April, 1955.

JOHNSON, S. C., WAX COMPANY, ADMINISTRATION AND LABORATORY BUILDINGS, RACINE, WIS. Headquarters of the S. C. Johnson Wax Company designed by Frank Lloyd Wright. In the Administration Building (1936–39), Wright's aversion to "box" architecture receives radical expression through his use of the circle as the architectural motif.

The interior is a vast unified office (ca. 230 ft. square) roofed in glass. More than eighty hollow columns of reinforced concrete are distributed regularly about the room. Rising gracefully from small bronze shoes anchored in the concrete floor and gradually tapering outward as they ascend, they flare abruptly into large disks at the top. The columns and capitals, identical in shape, are of two sizes: the taller support the pyrex-glass tube ceiling; the shorter carry the balconies, which go all the way around the walls and contain offices. Not all the taller columns are needed to support the lightweight glass roof; the greater number are nonfunctional. For Wright, the elaboration of the plastic idea takes precedence over the principle of the structural economy of means.

The ceiling supplies the greater part of the light, which is diffused softly between the lily-pad capitals. Additional light of the same kind is provided by horizontal bands of pyrex glass tubing, one set in the exterior wall directly beneath the balconies and another, broader, band higher up on the wall, which curves to the roof. Echoing the circularity of the capitals are the round-backed chairs and round-ended desks, neatly arranged in rows on the floor space. This room has been compared to a grotto, lit from above and containing a forest of stalactites.

At the entrance side of the building, round-ended blocks containing the more important offices flow diagonally into the central area just described. These units are two stories higher than the rest of the building; the stories are demarcated by bands of glass tubing. Atop the middle of each block is a circular, two-step tower.

The circle theme is again seen in the treatment of the

S. C. Johnson Wax Company, Administration and Laboratory Buildings, Racine, Wis. An integrated building complex designed by Frank Lloyd Wright.

non-load-bearing exterior walls. These do not meet in sharp corners; they flow into one another through a 90° arc. In the same way, the traditional cornice has been replaced by curved glass tubing that rounds the walls into the roof. The walls themselves are built of red brick over a base of white stone trim; they are interrupted by the band of glass tubing at balcony level.

Integrated with the Administration Building is the fifteen-story laboratory tower (1946–49). It is constructed on a "tap-root" principle, with square floors alternating with round balconies, cantilevered like tree branches from a giant hollow core of concrete, whose foundation is deeply sunk. This central stack contains the elevator, stairs, and utility grooves. Leading into the last is a duct system cast in each of the hollow reinforced-concrete floors. The tower's non-load-bearing walls consist of bands of red brick at the floor endings, and between these bands, sheets of joined horizontal glass tubes. Thus a maximum of light enters the tower's superimposed two-story laboratories.

BIBLIOGRAPHY. I. McCallum, *Architecture USA*, New York, 1959; P. Blake, *The Master Builders*, New York, 1960; J. Joedicke, *A History of Modern Architecture*, New York, 1960; E. Kaufmann and B. Raeburn, eds., *Frank Lloyd Wright: Writings and Buildings*, New York, 1960; V. Scully, Jr., *Frank Lloyd Wright*, New York, 1960.

LEON JACOBSON

JOHNSTON, DAVID CLAYPOOLE. American genre painter and caricaturist (b. Philadelphia, 1799; d. Dorchester, Mass., 1865). Sometimes called the American Cruikshank, he opened a print studio, where he made caricatures of his fellow Philadelphians. After a brief career as an actor (1821–26), Johnston resumed his pictorial satires and lampoons in Boston.

BIBLIOGRAPHY. C. S. Brigham, *David Claypoole Johnston: The American Cruikshank*, Worcester, Mass., 1941.

JOHNSTON, HENRIETTA. American painter of portraits in pastel (fl. South Carolina, 1707–20). Her tombstone in St. Philip's Churchyard, Charleston, S.C., records that she was buried on March 9, 1728/29. Examples of her work are in the Gibbes Art Gallery, Charleston, and in the collection of the South Carolina Historical Society.

BIBLIOGRAPHY. E. Willis, "Henrietta Johnston, South Carolina Pastellist," *Antiquarian*, XI, September, 1928.

JOHN THE BAPTIST, ST. Prophet and martyr. Son of the priest Zacharias and Elizabeth, Mary's cousin, John lived as an ascetic in the Judaean desert, preached, and did penance. He recognized Jesus, who had John baptize Him, as the Messiah. John censured the marriage of Herod Antipas to a blood relative and was decapitated. He is shown as Jesus' playmate or as an ascetic in a camel hair tunic. His attributes are his own head on a dish, a nimbed lamb on a book, and a long cross with a scroll inscribed "Ecce agnus Dei" (Behold the Lamb of God). His feasts are June 24 (birth) and August 29 (beheading). *See also* SAINTS IN ART.

JOHN THE FEARLESS, TOMB OF. Late Gothic sculpture, by Jean de la Huerta and Antoine Le Moiturier, in the Museum of Fine Arts, Dijon.

JOIGNY, JUAN DE, *see* JUNI, JUAN DE.

JOINT. Bookbinding term for the hinge connecting the spine of a book to its covers. A French joint is one which has an additional leather hinge on the inside of the covers.

BIBLIOGRAPHY. E. Diehl, *Bookbinding: Its Background and Technique*, vol. 2, New York, 1946.

JOIST. Horizontally placed support, usually a timber, to which the boards of a floor or the laths of a ceiling are attached. Several ceiling joists are attached, in parallel rows a few feet apart, to the upright supports. Joists are commonly called beams.

JOIST, BAR. Light steel beam made largely of bars and resembling a truss. It is also called an open-web joist or a trussed joist.

JOKEI (Sumiyoshi Jokei). Japanese painter (1599–1670). A pupil of Tosa Mitsuyoshi, Jokei took the family name of Sumiyoshi in 1662 in order to restore the noted school of the Kamakura period. In 1626 he made a copy of Mitsunaga's *Annual Court Ceremonies Scrolls*, the originals of which were destroyed in 1653. *See* SUMIYOSHI SCHOOL.
BIBLIOGRAPHY. R. T. Paine and A. Soper, *The Art and Architecture of Japan*, Baltimore, 1955.

JOKHA, *see* UMMA.

JOLI, ANTONIO. Italian topographical painter and stage designer (b. Modena, ca. 1700; d. Naples, 1777). He studied with Pannini in Rome and worked in Modena and Venice before moving to London, where he became a scene painter for the King's Theater, Haymarket (1744–48). He may have painted the landscape panels for Heidegger's House at Richmond. About 1750 Joli went to Madrid and by 1762 he was living in Naples.
BIBLIOGRAPHY. E. Croft-Murray, "The Painted Hall in Heidegger's House at Richmond" (2 pts.), *The Burlington Magazine*, LXXVIII, April and May, 1941.

JOMON, *see* JAPAN: CERAMICS.

"JONATHAN B.," *see* BLACKBURN, JOSEPH.

JONES, DAVID. English painter, mainly in water color, engraver, and writer (1895–). Born in Brockley, Kent, he studied at the Camberwell Art School and the Westminster School of Art. His painting technique stems from the school of Paris, but the inspiration for his lyrical, sensitive landscapes comes from his study of Celtic myths and from legends and symbols of medieval Christianity. From 1922 to 1926 he worked with the sculptor Eric Gill, from whom he learned engraving on copper and wood. He has illustrated with engravings the morality play, *Chester Play of the Deluge* (1927), and *The Ancient Mariner* (1928). In 1937, he won the Hawthornden prize for literature with *In Parenthesis*, a poetic account of his experiences in World War I.
BIBLIOGRAPHY. H. Read, *Contemporary British Art*, London, 1951; J. Rothenstein, *Modern English Painters: Lewis to Moore*, London, 1956.

JONES, INIGO. English architect (b. London, 1573; d. 1652). Although little is known of his early life, it is established that he worked first as a painter and that by 1605 he was designing costumes and stage sets for the English court. Jones had been to Italy in 1601; he made a more extensive visit with the Earl of Arundel in 1613–14, inspecting Palladio's architecture around Vicenza and talking to Scamozzi, who had been one of Palladio's students. After his return, Jones became Surveyor General of the King's Works (1615) and introduced the Palladian style to England in direct opposition to the Jacobean tradition,

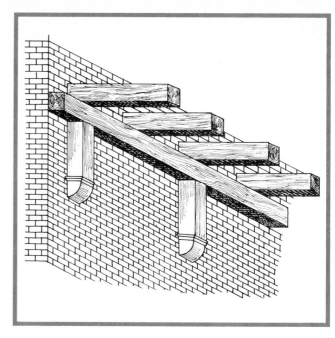

Joist. Support for floor boards and ceiling laths.

which was characterized by more informal ground plans and picturesque silhouettes.

Jones's earliest work was the Queen's House, Greenwich (1616), based on a Palladian villa scheme. The original plan called for two double-cube buildings (main rooms twice the height and width of lesser rooms), two stories in height, placed on each side of a public road and connected by second-floor bridges. There was a loggia on the park side, a rusticated basement, and above, a balustrade. *See* GREENWICH, QUEEN'S HOUSE.

His Banqueting Hall, London (1619–22), was designed as a freestanding block, enriched by pilasters, decorative swags, and doubled-end pilasters in the best Palladian tradition. The façade, solid and masculine as Jones intended, is characterized by a rather English linear simplicity of classic forms. The interior was designed on his principle of the double cube, with rooms rising two stories to a coffered ceiling.

His St. Paul's Covent Garden, London (1630), was the first modern Christian church in a classic style, its Roman Ionic portico anticipating the subsequent classic revival. Jones was also associated with the planning of Covent Garden, London's first formally planned square. In 1635 he made repairs to the old St. Paul's Cathedral, adding a giant Corinthian portico to the entrance which was based on a drawing by Palladio for the restoration of an ancient Roman temple; the portico clashed garishly with the medieval structure behind. *See* ST. PAUL'S CATHEDRAL, LONDON.

Jones's later works include Wilton, near Salisbury (1649), related in elevation and style to the Banqueting Hall, and possibly Chevening (1640), a brick, hip-roofed house, rectangular in shape and two rooms deep, of some influence in the development of the later Anglo-Dutch style. He was a master of detail rather than of handling masses. His designs for Whitehall Palace (ca. 1630; never erected), though unprecedented in England for their scope, reveal, by the poor interrelationship of parts, his inability to project buildings on a grand scale. Perhaps because Jones arbitrarily transplanted to England Palladio's classic order and restraint, his style was not immediately continued by his successors. His greatest influence was to come only in the following century, with the Palladian revival of Lord Burlington and his circle.

BIBLIOGRAPHY. J. Lee-Milne, *The Age of Inigo Jones*, London, 1953.

MATTHEW E. BAIGELL

JONES, JOE (Joseph John). American landscape painter, muralist, and lithographer (b. St. Louis, Mo., 1909; d. Morristown, N.J., 1963). Jones was a self-taught artist. His early works are social protest paintings, and for a time he was a regionalist, but his later landscapes are more lyrical in feeling. He did a mural for the ocean liner "Independence."

JONES, JOHN. English engraver (fl. ca. 1740–97). Jones used both stipple and mezzotint, although his reputation is based on the latter. His plates date from between 1783 and 1797. Most are of men and are copies after Romney, Reynolds, Gainsborough, and other English masters of the portrait.

BIBLIOGRAPHY. A. M. Hind, *A History of Engraving and Etching...*, 3d ed., rev., London, 1923 (repr. New York, 1963).

JONES, THOMAS DOW. American sculptor (b. Oneida County, N.Y., 1810; d. Columbus, Ohio, 1881). He worked in Cincinnati, Detroit, Boston, and New York City. Among his best-known works are portraits of Lincoln and Salmon P. Chase. Jones was also a medallionist.

BIBLIOGRAPHY. E. M. Clark, *Ohio Art and Artists*, Richmond, Va., 1932.

JONGH, CLAUDE DE. Dutch painter of landscapes and cityscapes (d. Utrecht, 1663). De Jongh was listed as a member of the Utrecht Guild of St. Luke in 1626 and was reported as a master in the same organization in 1633. He was in Haarlem for a while before 1630. De Jongh was also in London, where he painted views of the Thames and London Bridge (1650).

BIBLIOGRAPHY. J. Hayes, "Claude de Jongh," *The Burlington Magazine*, XCVIII, January, 1956.

JONGH, LUDOLF LEENDERTSZ. DE. Dutch genre and portrait painter (b. Overschie, 1616; d. Hillegersberg, 1679). De Jongh was the pupil of Cornelis Saftleven at Rotterdam, of Antonie Palamedes Stevens at Delft, and of Jan van Bijlert at Utrecht. He was active in France from 1635 to 1642. In 1642 he was back in Rotterdam, where he remained until 1665. He then returned to Hillegersberg, where he spent the rest of his life. Dirck Wijntrack was his brother-in-law. De Jongh collaborated with Joris van der Haagen.

BIBLIOGRAPHY. P. Haverkorn van Rijsewijk, "Ludolf (Leuff) de Jongh," *Oud-Holland*, XIV, 1896.

JONGHELINCK, JACQUES. Flemish sculptor (b. Antwerp, 1530; d. there, 1606). His training may have come from one of the Italian sculptors working in Antwerp. Commissioned by Philip II of Spain, he created the tomb of Charles the Bold (1558) in Notre-Dame, Bruges, modeled on Pieter de Breckere's tomb of Marie de Bourgogne in the same church. He also executed eight allegorical figures for the town hall of Antwerp, on the occasion of the entrance of Alexander Farnese, and figures for the Fontaine de la Teuillée in Brussels.

JONGKIND, JOHANN BARTHOLD. Dutch painter and etcher (b. Latrop, 1819; d. Côte-Saint-André, Isère, 1891). He studied with Andreas Schelfhout, a landscape painter, at the Academy of Art at The Hague. In 1845 Jongkind met Eugene Isabey, and his early work shows Isabey's influence. In fact, the next year Jongkind went to Paris on Schelfhout's advice to study with Isabey and also with

Inigo Jones, Queen's House, Greenwich, 1616, based on a Palladian villa scheme. The architect's earliest work.

François Picot. Jongkind was given a royal grant from the Dutch government. He exhibited at the Paris Salon in 1848 and again in 1852. He drew the attention of Charles Baudelaire and Emile Zola, both of whom wrote favorably of his work. He made friends with Corot, Daubigny, and Troyon. No doubt there was some influence of the Barbizon school on Jongkind, but his style owes much to the 17th-century Dutch masters. Unable to sell his work, he had to escape creditors by returning frequently to his native Holland. He specialized in scenes of the Normandy coast, having spent the summers from 1862 to 1866 at Le Havre, Sainte-Adresse, and Honfleur.

His style had matured by about 1860. He, like Constable and Corot, worked in two manners, one "official," one informal. His "official" paintings, destined for the Salon, were worked up from sketches in the studio. They are more consciously constructed and have more detail and finish than those of his other manner, represented best by his water colors, which are informal, spontaneous, and complete in themselves by modern standards. In these works Jongkind assumes importance as a precursor of impressionism along with Boudin. His empirical approach is a reaction to the idyllic eclecticism characteristic of Dutch painting of the first half of the 19th century. In his water colors Jongkind made a free drawing, usually with a pencil or crayon, and then built it up with washes, blots, and spots of water color. His line was often agitated and searching, reminiscent of Rembrandt's. His color tended to be naturalistic. He used the medium to exploit its transparency. He added notations in pencil on those drawings and water colors, which were considered by him to be preparatory. These paintings, expressive of an innocent eye, direct and instinctive, were the ones which Monet saw in 1862, when he met and admired Jongkind. This luminous, transitory technique also had much influence on Sisley and Pissarro.

Jongkind was a shy man who suffered from a persecution complex that led to excessive drinking and the suspension of his grant from the Dutch government. Like all the landscapists of his generation, he was a nomad. He traveled about France, Belgium, Switzerland, and Holland. As the finest Dutch paintings since the 17th century, his works were popularized in writings of the De Goncourt brothers.

BIBLIOGRAPHY. A. E. A. Moreau-Nélaton, *Jongkind, raconté par lui-même*, Paris, 1918; P. Signac, *Jongkind*, Paris, 1927; P. Colin, *...J. B. Jongkind*, Paris, 1931; G. Besson, *Johan-Barthold Jongkind*, Paris, 1948.

ROBERT REIFF

JONSON, CORNELIUS (Cornelis Jonson van Ceulen), *see* JOHNSON, CORNELIUS.

JONY, JUAN DE, *see* JUNI, JUAN DE.

JOOS VAN GHENT, *see* JUSTUS OF GHENT.

JOOS VAN WASSENHOVE, *see* JUSTUS OF GHENT.

JORDAENS, HANS (Jean), III ("Lange" Jordaens). Flemish painter of religious and gallery pictures (b. Antwerp, ca. 1595; d. there, 1643). He was a pupil of his father, Hans Jordaens II, and became a master in 1620. He is known mostly for religious scenes, such as *The Passage of the Jews through the Red Sea* (Berlin, former State Museums), which is signed and dated 1624. These scenes resemble the works of Frans Francken the Younger, but are further developed in a Rubensian manner. Jordaens's copies after *The Five Senses* by Jan Breughel I used to belong to the former Imperial Austrian collections but disappeared during the 18th century. Finally, the Museum of Art History in Vienna preserves his *Cabinet of an Amateur*, which faithfully reproduces Rubens's *Resurrection of Lazarus* and other paintings.

BIBLIOGRAPHY. S. Speth-Holterhoff, *Les Peintres flamands de cabinets d'amateurs au XVIe siècle*, Brussels, 1957.

JORDAENS, JACOB. Flemish painter of portraits and religious and mythological subjects (b. Antwerp, 1593; buried in Putte, 1678). He was apprenticed to Adam van Noort in 1607 and became a master in 1615 (as *Waterscilder*, or painter in tempera, although he was to paint mostly in oils). In 1616 he married Van Noort's daughter.

By 1621 Jordaens had already been nominated dean of the Guild of St. Luke. In 1635 he did some decorations under Rubens's guidance for the Joyous Entry of Cardinal Infant Ferdinand. Subsequently, Rubens called upon Jordaens for help in the execution of some large canvases (scenes from Ovid's *Metamorphoses*) destined for the Torre de la Parada, for which Rubens had done the sketches. After the great master's death, Jordaens was generally rated Flanders's first painter. The decorations at the Huis ten Bosch in The Hague stem from 1651–52, and in 1661–62 Jordaens received a commission for three large paintings for the Amsterdam City Hall. Although he became a Protestant about 1655, he continued to furnish altarpieces for Catholic churches.

Rubens and Van Dyck were the artists of the upper strata: portrait painters of kings, aristocracy, and intelligentsia, and providers of religious and mythological canvases for the same clientele. Jordaens, however, disdained the lofty in favor of matter-of-fact reality.

Jordaens's early style owes more to Van Dyck than to Rubens. The touch is broad, colorful, yet coarse, and the execution is exceedingly free. Early works are an amalgam of mannerist and evident Caravaggesque influences, as can be observed in the large nudes of *Daughters of Cecrops* (1617; Antwerp, Fine Arts Museum) or in the luxuriant *Allegory of Fertility* (Brussels, Fine Arts Museum). Candlelight effects and half figures cut off at the sides characterize his religious productions. Rubensian classicism becomes apparent in later works, fusing dramatic effects with decorative conceptions. *The Ferry at Antwerp* (Copenhagen, State Museum of Fine Arts) exemplifies this period. Late works are often weak and done with extensive studio help.

Works such as *The King Drinks!* (Brussels, Fine Arts Museum; variants elsewhere) and *Satyr and Peasant* (Brussels, Fine Arts Museum) are characteristic of his manner, style, and inventiveness. They typify Jordaens as the authorized interpreter, with Pieter Brueghel the Elder, of the Flemish temper and fancy.

BIBLIOGRAPHY. L. van Puyvelde, *Jordaens*, Brussels, 1953; R. A. d'Hulst, *De Tekeningen van Jakob Jordaens*, Brussels, 1956.

ERIK LARSEN

JORGAN TEPE, *see* NUZI.

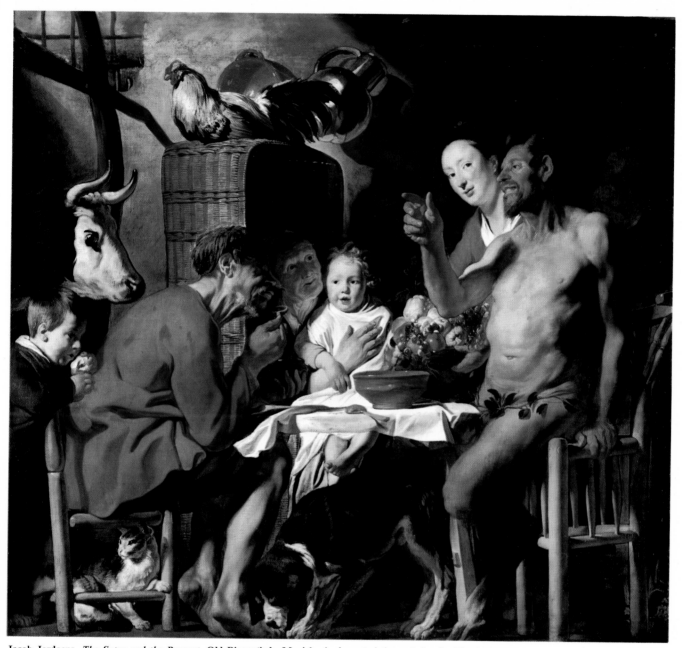

Jacob Jordaens, *The Satyr and the Peasant*. Old Pinacothek, Munich. A characteristic work by the Flemish painter.

JORGE INGLES. Spanish painter (fl. mid-15th cent.). As his name seems to indicate, this Castilian artist may have been of northern extraction. Franco-Flemish qualities are certainly present in his only known work, the retable of the writer and statesman the Marqués de Santillana, executed for the hospital church of Buitrago (1455), now in the collection of the Duque del Infantado, in Madrid. The two panels with kneeling portraits of the Marqués and his wife, which originally flanked a statue of the Virgin surrounded by twelve angels, derive from prototypes in Flemish painting in poses, settings, and rendering of detail and drapery, but show greater schematization of the sensitively drawn figures and faces and the lateral spatial setting.

BIBLIOGRAPHY. F. J. Sánchez Cantón, "Maestro Jorge Inglés, pintor y miniaturista del Marqués de Santillana," *Boletín de la Sociedad española de Excursiones,* 1917.

JORN, ASGER. Danish painter (1914–   ). After working briefly with Léger (1936) and collaborating with Le Corbusier at the Paris International Exposition (1937), Jorn has become one of the major expressionist painters of the period following World War II. Ensor and Klee provided strong early influences. Jorn has always been an advocate—in his painting and writing and as a member of such groups as the Imaginist Bauhaus, the Situationist International, and the Surindépendents—committed to art as an immediate, existentialist activity and opposed to a rational, constructivist approach. He was the principal figure in the activities of the influential CoBrA group (1948–51). Jorn's paintings, violently swirling patterns of raw-colored pigment with figurative elements emerging like phantoms, reflect the artist's desire to reach buried levels of human experience and reflect his attachment to Scandinavian myth and folk art. *See* Cobra Group.

BIBLIOGRAPHY. V. Schade, *Asger Jorn*, Copenhagen, 1965.

JOSEPH, ANTONIO. Haitian painter (1921–). Born in Barahona, Dominican Republic, Joseph fled to Haiti in 1938. In 1944 he became a student at the Centre d'Art in Port-au-Prince, where he was given seven exhibitions through the 1950s. He has traveled through the United States and has twice been awarded Guggenheim grants. Unlike most Haitian painters, Joseph makes use of a subtle colorism and shows the influence of European art, particularly cubism.

JOSEPH, JASMIN. Haitian sculptor and painter (1923–). A native of northern Haiti, Joseph was brought to the Centre d'Art in Port-au-Prince by the American sculptor Jason Seley in 1948. He does mostly religious sculptures, the most interesting of which are a series of terracotta windows in the Episcopal church at Port-au-Prince depicting the Stations of the Cross.

JOSEPH, ST. Spouse of the Virgin Mary and stepfather of Jesus. The son of Heli, of the line of David, Joseph was a carpenter who made yokes, plows, and even mouse traps. A pious old man of eighty when he married the youthful Mary, he can be represented in art as younger. His cult originated in the East and was promoted in the West in the 15th century by St. Bernardino of Siena, and later by SS. Theresa and Francis de Sales. His attributes are carpenters' tools, a flowering rod or dove on a rod (symbolizing his victory over Mary's suitors), a candle or a lantern (used Christmas night), and lilies. His feast is March 19. *See also* Saints in Art.

JOSEPH MASTER, *see* Reims: Cathedral.

JOSEPH OF ARIMATHEA, ST. Israelite "counselor" mentioned by Luke, and probably a member of the Sanhedrin. After Jesus' death, Joseph demanded the body from Pilate and then, aided by Nicodemus, took the body down from the cross, wrapped it in linen, and laid it in the sepulchre. The apocryphal *Gospel of Nicodemus* relates how he gathered Christ's blood in a chalice. Joseph founded a church at Lydda, Palestine (Israel), and is supposed also to have built a church in Glastonbury, England. His attributes are Christ's shroud, the crown of thorns, nails, pliers, and a jar of ointment. His feast is March 17. *See also* Saints in Art.

JOSEPHSON, ERNST. Swedish painter (1851–1906). After attending the Royal Academy Art School in Stockholm (1867–76), he traveled in the Netherlands, Italy, France, and Spain. From 1879 to 1887 he made his headquarters in Paris. Josephson was the leader of the Opponents (against the Royal Academy of Fine Arts). His early portraits and figure pieces are indebted to Rembrandt in their golden colors, expressive chiaroscuro, and sensuous surface. Later, influenced by Velázquez and Manet, he became interested in optical effects, but he retained his sensitive characterization in portraiture and his romantic sym-

bolism in such paintings as *The Water Sprite*. Josephson succumbed to schizophrenia in 1888 and was taken back to Sweden. Freed completely from aesthetic conventions, he created paintings and drawings of great expressiveness and purity, often anticipating Picasso, Kokoschka, and Matisse. He is best represented in the National Museum, Stockholm, and the Art Gallery, Göteborg.

BIBLIOGRAPHY. E. Blomberg, *Ernst Josephson, hans liv*, Stockholm, 1951; E. Blomberg, *Ernst Josephsons konst*, 2 vols., Stockholm, 1956–59; Portland Art Museum, *Paintings and Drawings by Ernest Josephson* (exhibition catalog), Portland, Ore., 1964.

JOSES FAMILY, *see* Dinanderie.

JOSETSU. Japanese priest and painter (fl. early 15th cent.). Josetsu worked in the Shōkokuji of Kyoto as the Ashikaga shogun's first official painter. *Catching a Catfish with a Gourd* (Kyoto, Taizōin), painted for Shogun Yoshimochi (1386–1428), illustrates the sort of "life questions" often posed for Zen priests to meditate on. The delicate lines and subtle ink wash in this work reflect the direct influence of Sung China's ink painting. *See* Zen.

BIBLIOGRAPHY. T. Akiyama, *Japanese Painting* [Geneva?], 1961.

JOSHUA. Old Testament prophet and successor of Moses. Joshua guided his people to the promised land, where he led the Battle of Jericho (Josh. 6:16–22). The scene representing the fall of Jericho first became popular in art during the Renaissance, although the entire story of Joshua's exploits had been depicted as early as the 4th century in the mosaic cycle at S. Maria Maggiore in Rome.

Ernst Josephson, *The Water Sprite*. National Museum, Stockholm.

Juan de Juanes (Juan Vicente Masip the Younger), *The Last Supper*. Prado, Madrid.

JOSHUA ROLL. Illuminated Byzantine manuscript, in the Vatican Library, Rome. *See* BYZANTINE ART AND ARCHITECTURE.

JOUARRE: CRYPT OF SAINT-EBREGISILE. Crypt of a French Merovingian abbey in the Ile-de-France, founded about 630 by Ado, brother of St. Ouen. It is noted for its sculpture. Marble capitals with foliate motifs show a high degree of skill. Three tombs of stone in the crypt are carved with figural and decorative motifs stylistically related to Celtic work in Ireland; they are among the rare examples of figurative work in Merovingian art.

BIBLIOGRAPHY. M. Aubert, *La Sculpture française au moyen-âge*, Paris, 1946.

JOURDAIN, FRANTZ. French architect (1847–1935). He worked in Paris. Jourdain built the main branch of the Samaritaine Department Store, a prominent specimen of Art Nouveau, which is distinguished for the straightforward design of its metal and glass structure.

JOUVENET, JEAN-BAPTISTE (Jean III). French history painter and decorator (b. Rouen, 1644; d. Paris, 1717). He was descended from an Italian family of painters. He studied with his father, Laurent Jouvenet II, in 1661 and with Charles Le Brun, with whom he worked on large decorative schemes at Versailles and Marly. In 1672 he won the Prix de Rome. He enlivened the Le Brun style with baroque expressiveness, without the influence of Ru-

bens, whose importance for Jouvenet is often overstressed. Strong naturalism in the physical types and still-life elements are seen in his ceilings of the Parlements of Rennes and Rouen, in the chapels at Versailles and the Invalides, and particularly in the *Miraculous Draught of the Fishes* (Paris, Louvre). He transmitted his style to his nephew, Jean Restout the Younger.

JUAN BAUTISTA DE TOLEDO, *see* TOLEDO, JUAN BAUTISTA DE.

JUAN DE BADAJOZ. Spanish architect (fl. 1499–1549). Juan de Badajoz was a late Gothic master who is credited with the design of the monumental lantern at the Cathedral of Orense (1499–1505) in which he combined Gothic and Mudejar forms. His source is believed to have been the no longer extant lantern of Burgos Cathedral. In 1549 he directed the vaulting of two walks in the cloister of S. Marcos at León.

BIBLIOGRAPHY. L. Torres Balbás, *Ars Hispaniae*, vol. 7: *Arquitectura gótica*, Madrid, 1952.

JUAN DE COLONIA, *see* HANS OF COLOGNE.

JUAN DE FLANDES, *see* FLANDES, JUAN DE.

JUANES, JUAN DE (Juan Vicente Masip the Younger). Spanish painter (ca. 1523–79). Juanes may have been born in Fuente la Higuera and probably worked with his father as a young man. He later became an extremely successful painter of religious and devotional works, many of which have been treated as objects of veneration in the strong climate of Spanish Catholicism. Popular themes in this vein are the Madonna and Christ the Saviour. In other works he developed the dynamic, closely knit figural compositions of his father within a milder context. The line is looser, poses are more mannered, and figures are more fluidly connected with an airy landscape, and in many of the figures the influence of Raphael's idealization may be seen. Notable among Juanes's works are the *Last Supper* and other paintings in S. Nicolás, Valencia; the *Last Supper* in the Prado, Madrid; *The Mystical Marriage of the Venerable Agnesto*, in the Provincial Museum of Fine Arts, Valencia; and scenes from the life of St. Stephen, in the Prado. In the last of these works the manneristic poses, expressions, and use of space are more pronounced.

BIBLIOGRAPHY. A. Igual Ubeda, *Juan de Juanes*, Barcelona, 1943.

DONALD GODDARD

JUANI, JUAN DE, see JUNI, JUAN DE.

JUAREZ, JOSE. Mexican painter (b. Mexico City, ca. 1615; d. there, ca. 1690). Chief pupil of the Spanish-born artist Sebastián López de Arteaga, José was the most important member of a dynasty which spanned four generations. He was the son of Luis and the grandfather of Nicolás and Juan Rodríguez Juárez. Stylistically the art of José Juárez falls into two categories. In one group brilliant colors and delicate modeling predominate, along with some indigenous motifs; in the other, somber hues, murky backgrounds, and dynamic presentations are most prominent. In both categories critics have discovered accents that sometimes recall Rubens or Rembrandt. Whatever his manner, José conformed closely to the baroque tradition in his painterly and dramatic technique.

BIBLIOGRAPHY. M. Toussaint, *Arte colonial en México*, 2d ed., Mexico City, 1962.

JUAREZ, JUAN RODRIGUEZ, see RODRIGUEZ JUAREZ, JUAN.

JUAREZ, LUIS. Spanish colonial painter in Mexico (fl. Mexico City, 1600–35). Luis Juárez was a disciple of Baltasar de Echave y Orio. *La oración del huerto* (Morelia Cathedral) shows his religious spirit as well as his limited dramatic resources. Numerous paintings survive in the Academy of S. Carlos, Mexico City, the Regional Museum of Anthropology and History, Guadalajara, and elsewhere. His son was José Juarez.

BIBLIOGRAPHY. M. Toussaint, *Arte colonial en México*, 2d ed., Mexico City, 1962.

JUBE, see ROOD LOFT.

JUDAS KISS, see BETRAYAL, THE.

JUDAS (Jude) THADDEUS, ST. Apostle and brother of James the Less. He is surnamed Thaddeus to distinguish him from Judas Iscariot. After the death of Jesus, he is supposed to have preached in Palestine, Syria, and Mesopotamia. The *Golden Legend* claims that he cured King Abgar of Edessa of leprosy by rubbing his face with a letter written by Christ. His attributes are a club, sword, hatchet, halberd, T-square (he was an architect), and processional cross with long shaft (showing he died not on but for the cross). His feast is October 28. *See* SIMON, ST. *See also* SAINTS IN ART.

JUDD, DONALD. American sculptor (1928–   ). Born in Excelsior Springs, Mo., Judd studied at the Art Students League in New York City, William and Mary College in Williamsburg, Va., and Columbia University. At first a painter, influenced by Barnett Newman, Mark Rothko, and others, Judd turned to sculpture in 1961. His works, although made up of simple geometric forms, are not so much concerned with geometric construction as with the qualities of forms under differing conditions of light, the materials used, transparency, repetition, openness, and so forth. The forms are manufactured, usually in plastics, plywood, and particularly galvanized iron.

JUDKINS, ELIZABETH. English graphic artist (fl. 1772–75). The few plates by her hand show finesse in both mezzotint and line engraving. Most plates are portraits of women after great English portraitists. The best is a half portrait of the actress Frances Abington (1772), after Reynolds. James Watson was probably her mentor.

BIBLIOGRAPHY. C. J. Davenport, *Mezzotints*, London, 1904.

JUEL, JENS. Danish painter (b. Balslev, 1745; d. Copenhagen, 1802). The most important Danish portrait painter of the 18th century, Juel began his career as a student of Johann Gehrmann in Hamburg. Between 1772 and 1780 he traveled throughout Europe, painting portraits of notable personages in Rome, Paris (*Portrait of J. F. Clemens*, 1776), Geneva (*Profile Portrait of Goethe*), and Hamburg (*Portrait of Klopstock*, 1779). Two years after his return to Copenhagen Juel was appointed court painter, and in 1784 he was made professor at the academy in Copenhagen. In addition to his famous portraits, Juel also painted still lifes, landscapes, and several genre paintings. His style represents a transition from the courtly elegance of the rococo to the more sedate Biedermeier style. In this he is similar to his German contemporary Anton Graff.

BIBLIOGRAPHY. K. J. Madsen, *Kunstens Historie i Danmark*, Copenhagen, 1901–07.

JUGENDSTIL, see ART NOUVEAU.

JUHL, FINN. Danish architect and designer (1912–   ). Born in Copenhagen and educated at the Royal Academy of Fine Arts there, he was an originator of the "Danish modern" style. He is known for the thoughtful detailing and highly sculptured forms of his own elegant furniture. Juhl also designs rugs, lighting, interiors, and houses.

JU-I. Chinese term referring to an S-curved scepter. Translated literally, *ju-i* means "as you like" and probably had reference to an object used in court ceremonies. The scepter appears in Buddhist iconography as a symbol of discussion or dialogue, usually held by Mañjuśrī in his famous debate with Vimalakīrti. The *ju-i* made of jade or other precious material, was reproduced often in China and was presented as a token of esteem.

JULES, MERVIN. American painter and graphic artist (1912–   ). Born in Baltimore, Md., he studied at the Maryland Institute of Fine and Applied Arts and with Thomas Hart Benton at the Art Students League in New York. Jules is most readily associated with expressionism and with the satirical social comment of his paintings and lithographs of the 1930s and 1940s. His recent work has become milder and more varied in content and more purely aesthetic in point of view.

JULIA BASILICA, ROME. Ancient public building in the Roman Forum. Erected by Julius Caesar in 54 B.C., it was rebuilt by Diocletian after a fire A.D. 283. The basilica consisted of a nave surrounded by a double aisle of arches resting on piers with transverse arches carrying quadripartite groined vaults. The nave was lighted by a clerestory. The exterior wall was articulated by engaged Doric columns with superimposed Ionic pilasters.

BIBLIOGRAPHY. W. J. Anderson, R. P. Spiers, and T. Ashby, *The Architecture of Greece and Rome*, vol. 2: *The Architecture of Ancient Rome*, London, 1927.

JULIAN THE HOSPITALER, ST. Legendary saint of the Middle Ages. A stag Julian hunted foretold he would murder his father and mother. He left home, entered the service of the king, who knighted him, and married. His parents, seeking him, were received by his wife and put in her bed. Returning home, Julian mistook them for his wife and a lover and murdered them. To expiate his crime, he ferried pilgrims, including Christ as a leper, and built a hospital. He is shown on horseback with a hawk. His attributes are a stag, a sword, an oar, and a boat. His feast is February 12. *See also* SAINTS IN ART.

JULII, MAUSOLEUM OF THE, SAINT-REMY, *see* SAINT-REMY, MONUMENT OF.

JULIOT (Julyot) FAMILY. French sculptors (fl. Troyes, 16th cent.). Jacques Juliot I (d. before 1562) executed the alabaster tomb of the Abbot of Montier-la-Celle and the retable for the Abbey of Larribour (Troyes, Fine Arts Museum), his most famous work. He did also an altar for St-Nizier, Troyes. His son, Jacques Juliot II, was active at Fontainebleau from 1540 to 1550, and did a retable for St-Urbain, Troyes. The grandson, Jacques Juliot III, has no preserved works. The Juliots share the characteristics of the *imagier* tradition at Troyes, with an increasing influence from the mannerism of Dominique Florentin (Domenico Ricoveri del Barbiere).

BIBLIOGRAPHY. R. Koechlin and J. J. Marquet de Vasselot, *La Sculpture à Troyes et dans la Champagne méridionale au seizième siècle*, Paris, 1900.

JULIUS CAESAR, FORUM OF, ROME. Roman forum begun in 51 B.C. on the north side of the Tabularium. It was dedicated by Caesar in 46 B.C. The first of the imperial forums, it was intended as a meeting place rather than as a market. It consisted of a rectangular court surrounded by a colonnade and a wall. The Temple of Venus Genetrix stood in the center of the court. *See* VENUS, TEMPLE OF, ROME.

BIBLIOGRAPHY. W. J. Anderson, R. P. Spiers, and T. Ashby, *The Architecture of Greece and Rome*, vol. 2: *The Architecture of Ancient Rome*, London, 1927.

JULYOT FAMILY, *see* JULIOT FAMILY.

JUMAID, *see* ISLAMIC PAINTING (JALAIRID SCHOOL).

JUMIEGES: ABBEY CHURCH OF NOTRE-DAME. French church originally founded by St. Philibert in 654. However, the present great ruin dates from 1037 to 1067; its intended dedication in 1066 was delayed by Duke William's war with England. Today the two great square towers of the west front, surmounted by octagons, still stand. The nave was divided into four wide bays, using an alternating system of massive compound piers and columnar supports. The triforium has handsome triple arches, and above are two clerestory windows. The capitals, of a simplified Corinthian design, were originally painted. Fine Caen limestone was used throughout to support wooden roofs. This church represents the full maturity of the Norman Romanesque style except for the solution of the vaulting problem.

BIBLIOGRAPHY. K. J. Conant, *Carolingian and Romanesque Architecture, 800–1200*, Baltimore, 1959.

JUMMA MUSJID, *see* JAMI MASJID.

JUNI (Joigny; Jony; Juani), JUAN DE. Spanish sculptor and architect (b. Joigny? France, ca. 1506; d. Spain, 1577). Working in Spain from 1533, he began in a High Renaissance style, changed by 1538 to mannerism, and later worked in a protobaroque style. He executed works in terra cotta, polychromed wood, and stone. However heavy the proportions, his figures are electric with emotion and galvanic in action, as in the *St. Matthew* (León, San Marcos Museum). Like his younger contemporary El Greco, he was even more extreme than the Spanish in the superreality of his mystical effects. A century before Borromini, he set walls in motion in a dramatic crescendo, as the main altarpiece in the Benavente Chapel, Medina del Rioseco (1557), shows.

BIBLIOGRAPHY. R. García Guereta, *El retablo de Juan de Juni de Nuestra Señora "La Antigua" de Valladolid*, Madrid, 1923; E. García Chico, *Juan de Juni*, Valladolid, 1949.

JUNIUS BASSUS SARCOPHAGUS. Early Christian sarcophagus with relief sculptures, in St. Peter's, Rome.

JUNKER, JOHANN. German sculptor (fl. 1598–1623). He was trained in Italy and was active in Würzburg and Mainz and at Aschaffenburg Castle. Junker's ecstatic, spiritualized figures and rich compositions of varicolored marbles herald the beginning of the baroque style in southern Germany. Notable are his altar for the castle chapel and the Altar of the Magdalen in the Stiftskirche, both in Aschaffenburg.

JUNO, *see* HERA.

JU PEON, *see* HSU PEI-HUNG.

JUPITER, *see* ZEUS.

JUPITER (Zeus), TEMPLE OF, *see* AKRAGAS; BAALBEK; POMPEII.

JUPITER ANXUR, TEMPLE OF, TERRACINA. Sanctuary built on a promontory above the Roman colony of Tarracina (Volscian Anxur; modern Terracina), south of Rome. It stood on an arcaded platform. The arcades, consisting of a series of gigantic arches, were placed in front of a concrete curtain wall that concealed a corridor of vaulted chambers. Some revolutionary elements, such as the use of concrete and of arches, were employed here. Various dates have been assigned to the temple, from the 3d century B.C. to 60 B.C.

BIBLIOGRAPHY. W. J. Anderson, J. P. Spiers, and T. Ashby, *The Architecture of Greece and Rome*, vol. 2: *The Architecture of Ancient Rome*, London, 1927; G. M. A. Hanfmann, *Roman Art*, Greenwich, Conn., 1964.

JUPITER CAPITOLINE, TEMPLE OF, ROME. Earliest and most magnificent of all ancient Roman temples, situated on the Capitoline hill. It was dedicated to Jupiter Optimus Maximus. Begun by Tarquin I, it was completed by his son in 509 B.C. The temple stood on an artificial platform. It was hexastyle, with a peristyle on each side and with three cellae. The original temple was decorated with sculpture in terra cotta which, according to Pliny's description, was executed by Vulca, an Etruscan artist from Veii. A clay quadriga crowned its pediment. The temple was burned in 83 B.C. and was reconstructed by Sulla, who embellished it with marble brought from Athens. Later the temple was burned and restored several times under various emperors. A representation of the temple as it was restored under Domitian is depicted on a relief from a lost Arch of Marcus Aurelius (Rome, Palazzo dei Conservatori).

BIBLIOGRAPHY. W. J. Anderson, R. P. Spiers, and T. Ashby, *The Architecture of Greece and Rome*, vol. 2: *The Architecture of Ancient Rome*, London, 1927; G. Lugli, *Roma antica: Il centro monumentale*, Rome, 1946.

JUPPE, LUDWIG. German sculptor and carver (b. Marburg, ca. 1465; fl. there until 1538). He studied in the Kalkar workshop of Master Arnold. His most important work is the tomb of Wilhelm II (1516; Marburg, Elisabethkirche). Juppe was the most important personality in Renaissance tomb sculpture in the region of the Middle Rhine.

BIBLIOGRAPHY. H. Neuber, "Ludwig Juppe von Marburg," *Beiträge zur Kunstgeschichte Hessens und des Rhein-Main-Gebietes*, IV, 1915.

JUPPIN, JEAN-BAPTISTE. Flemish landscape painter (b. Namur, 1675; d. there, 1729). After studying in Brussels, Juppin went to Italy (ca. 1710), stayed about a year at the academy in Rome, and traveled throughout the peninsula. Back in Flanders by 1717, he worked for churches in Liège and specifically for the episcopal palace and the city hall. His Italianate landscapes, reminiscent of those of J. F. van Bloemen, were settings for Biblical scenes; the figures were usually the work of Engelbert Eisen and Edmond Plumier. St. Martin and the Church of Amay in Liège house works by Juppin.

BIBLIOGRAPHY. J. Philippe, *La Peinture liègeoise au XVIIe siècle*, Brussels, 1945.

JUSTE, ANTONIO AND GIOVANNI I, *see* GIUSTI, ANTONIO AND GIOVANNI I.

JUSTUS OF GHENT (Joos van Ghent; Joos van Wassenhove). Flemish painter (1430/35–1476?). He was entered in the lists of the painters' guild at Antwerp in 1460, and is next recorded in 1464 as a free master at Ghent, where he was the first major painter to be listed after the death of Hubert van Eyck. Justus remained on the Ghent lists until 1465, and some time later went to Italy, where he was eventually employed by Federigo da Montefeltro, duke of Urbino (patron of Piero della Francesca). He remained in the Duke's employ from at least 1472 to 1475, after which our knowledge of Justus and his activities ceases.

Justus was possibly the teacher or mentor of Hugo van der Goes. They were, at least, close friends. When Hugo was admitted to the Ghent painters' guild in 1467, Justus was his guarantor. It is further known that Hugo lent money to Justus for his Italian trip.

The indigenous style of Ghent, without major practitioners for more than a generation, was *retardataire* in contrast with that of such centers as Bruges, Brussels, and Louvain. It is natural, therefore, that Justus's art should at first have been eclectic. His two known major pre-Italian works, an *Adoration of the Magi* (before 1465; New York, Metropolitan Museum) and a huge *Crucifixion* triptych (ca. 1465; Ghent, St. Bavon), are definitely influenced by Rogier van der Weyden, Dirk Bouts, and the Master of Flémalle. Justus, however, was not merely an uninspired imitator. Contrary to the prevalent practice of Flemish art, he was not overwhelmingly interested in realistic genre detail; instead he synthesized forms and motifs borrowed from his predecessors into a simple, rhythmic monumentality. His *Adoration of the Magi*, although related to the works of Rogier and Bouts, achieves a new spatial clarity and a simplification and enlargement of forms largely by diminishing the number and importance of unessential details. In the *Crucifixion* triptych, the Calvary panel repeats Flémallian and Eyckian motifs; but Justus brings to the composition a clearer and fuller integration of fore-middle-, and distant ground.

Dating from his Italian period are the *Communion of the Apostles* (Urbino, National Gallery) and a series of twenty-eight portrait panels of philosophers and poets done for a *studiolo* in Federigo's palace at Urbino. The panels are now divided between the Louvre, in Paris, and Urbino. The Italian works show an unresolved eclectic mixture of Flemish, Italian, and Spanish styles (a Spanish painter collaborated with Justus on the panels); yet they maintain the simple dignity and monumentality that had recommended this Flemish painter to one of the leading patrons of the Italian Renaissance.

BIBLIOGRAPHY. J. Lavalleye, *Juste de Gand, peintre de Frédéric de Montefeltre*, Louvain, 1936.

STANLEY FERBER

JUVARA, FILIPPO. Italian architect of the Piedmontese school (1678–1736). Juvara was born in Messina, where his father was a silversmith. From 1703/04 to 1714 he was in Rome, first as a pupil of the academic late baroque architect Carlo Fontana and after 1708 as an architect and stage designer for Cardinal Ottoboni. In 1714 Vittorio Amedeo II of Savoy, King of Sicily, appointed Juvara Frst Architect to the King at Turin. Juvara went on to become the leading internationally known architect of Europe. Between 1719 and 1720 he spent a year in

Justus of Ghent, *The Communion of the Apostles*, ca. 1472–75. National Gallery, Urbino.

Portugal on the planning of the convent palace of Mafra for John V (built by Ludovice); in 1720 he was in London and Paris; and in 1735 he went to Madrid to design the new Royal Palace (built with alterations after his death by G. B. Sacchetti) and the garden façade of S. Ildefonso near Segovia for Philip V.

Juvara's production in Turin was enormous. As a city planner he laid out whole new quarters of the city. He also worked as an interior decorator and a designer of furniture and applied art. In the city he built the Palazzo Birago della Valle (1716), the Palazzo Richa di Covasolo (1730), and the Palazzo d'Ormea (1730). For Vittorio Emanuele, in or near Turin, he built the Villa Venaria Reale (1714–26), the Palazzo Madama (1718–20), the Castello di Rivoli (1718–21), and the Castle of Stupinigi (begun in 1718). His basilical churches are S. Filippo Neri (1715), Sta Croce (begun in 1718), and the Chiesa del Carmine (1732–35; gutted during World War II; restored 1950–53). There are, finally, the two centralized churches: the Chapel of the Venaria Reale (1716–28) and the sanctuary of Superga (1715–27) on a hill some miles east of Turin. In the execution of his designs Juvara was assisted by painters, sculptors, and stucco workers from all parts of Italy.

His style is characterized less by a development of original ideas than by its variety and its brilliant restatements of the leading ideas of his time. The Palazzo Madama is modeled on Versailles, but the design is bolder and more effective. At Stupinigi, Juvara chose and expanded to an

Filippo Juvara, the Castle of Stupinigi, near Turin. The Italian star-shaped castle plan on an unprecedented scale.

unprecedented scale the Italian star-shaped castle plan. S. Filippo Neri reiterates the tradition of basilican churches exemplified by Palladio and Alberti. In the Chiesa del Carmine, Juvara made various innovations, including a skeleton of high pillars in place of a nave wall. At the Chapel of Venaria Reale the Greek cross of St. Peter's is combined with Palladian (as in Il Redentore, Venice) screening columns. Juvara's masterpiece, Superga, is the apogee of the development of the centralized church since the Renaissance. Its interior combines Borromini and Bernini; its verticality, skeletal structure, and scenic unification of spaces recall late baroque buildings in Austria and Switzerland. With Juvara, Italian architecture comes to a close and merges with the architecture of Europe.

BIBLIOGRAPHY. L. Rovere, V. Viale, and A. E. Brinckmann, *Filippo Juvara*, Milan, 1937; R. Wittkower, *Art and Architecture in Italy, 1600–1750*, Baltimore, 1958.

HELLMUT WOHL

JU WARE. Chinese designation for an imperial ceramic ware of the Sung dynasty. The name comes from Ju-chou, a district in Honan Province where the kiln site was first established during the building of the Imperial Palaces at the capital of K'ai-feng. The kiln site has not been identified as yet, although there have been a number of explorations in the ancient Ju-chou district by Japanese scholars. The ware was apparently made only during the period when the Sung court was at K'ai-feng, and the kiln site was probably destroyed in the Tatar invasions which forced the court to move south to Hang-chou in 1127.

The ware is distinguished by a finely textured body and a thick blue-gray to green-gray glaze marked by delicate crackle. The pottery forms in Ju ware are simple and of almost classic severity. These qualities, along with the subtlety of glaze texture and coloring, make this ware among the most desirable and eagerly sought after by collectors. Ju ware is also one of the rarest Chinese wares in existence.

BIBLIOGRAPHY. P. David, "A Commentary on Ju Ware," *Transactions of the Oriental Ceramic Society*, XIV, 1936–37; Oriental Ceramic Society, *Ju and Kuan Wares . . .* (exhibition catalog), London, 1952.

K

Kachina. Drawings of *kachinas* by a Pueblo Indian, ca. 1885. Private collection, Paris.

KAABAH, *see* KIBLEH.

KACHINA. Term used to refer to several hundred Pueblo Indian nature spirits and spirits of the dead. Dancers costumed as *kachinas* summon these supernatural beings from concealment. *Kachina* cults, which originated in prehistoric times, have remained powerful among the Zuñi and Hopi, and a tradition of colorful, exciting ceremonies, masks, and accessories still exists. *Kachina* dolls, or miniature figures, are commercially available and are also used to instruct Pueblo Indian children. *See* HOPI INDIANS; PUEBLO INDIANS; ZUNI INDIANS.

Kachina figurines and costumes comprise one of the most important extant artistic traditions extending back into American Indian prehistory. The art is a highly symbolical one involving both organic and geometric designs. The materials used include brightly painted soft wood, horsehide, cloth, and feathers.

See also NORTH AMERICAN INDIAN ART (SOUTHWEST).

BIBLIOGRAPHY. E. Earle and E. Kennard, *Hopi Kachinas*, New York, 1938; F. J. Dockstader, *The Kachina and the White Man* (Cranbrook Inst. of Science, Bull. 35), Bloomfield Hills, Mich., 1954.

KAEMPFER PRINTS. Series of twenty-nine Chinese prints purchased by a German doctor named Kaempfer while he was serving with the Dutch fleet at the Japanese port of Nagasaki. These famous and rare works were brought to Europe in 1692 and were eventually purchased by the Sloane family, which deposited them with the British Museum when that institution was founded in London. They have thus remained well preserved and are among the finest examples of early color printing in China. The precise identification of the artists of these prints is not known, although the name Ting Liang-hsien is connected with the series. The prints deal with birds, flowers, and insects, and they were in all probability used as greeting cards by the Chinese.

BIBLIOGRAPHY. W. Speiser, R. Goepper, and J. Fribourg, *Chinese Art: Painting, Calligraphy, Stone Rubbing, Wood Engraving*, New York, 1964.

KAENDLER (Kandler), JOHANN JOACHIM. German sculptor (b. Fischbach, Saxony, 1706; d. Meissen, 1775). A student of Benjamin Thomae, court sculptor of the Duke of Saxony, Kaendler was the model master of the Meissen porcelain factory from 1733 on. He worked on the famous Swan Service for Count Bruhl. During the height of his career (1742–63) he made the molds for the small groups and figures in the rococo style that influenced all porcelain production of the time.

BIBLIOGRAPHY. H. Gröger, *Johann Joachim Kaendler...*, Dresden, 1956.

KAHLO DE RIVERA, FRIDA. Mexican painter (b. Coyoacán, 1910; d. there, 1954). Her father was an important German-born photographer; her mother, Mexican. Frida was preparing herself for a medical career, but a serious accident when she was sixteen forced her into a lifelong round of operations and periods of recuperation. Her first prolonged hospitalization led to the therapy of painting. At eighteen she married Diego Rivera; this union lasted to her death, through separations, divorce, and remarriage. As teacher at the Esmeralda School she found many disciples, and her own work was widely exhibited in Mexico, New York, and Paris. Throughout her paintings runs a constant allusion to Diego Rivera, expressed in a highly personal form of symbolic realism (rather than surrealism), in which her portrait and his are used with various psychological links and references. Her life revolved about her family home at Coyoacán (now a museum), where a remarkable collection of folk art and costumes provided an exotic setting for her periods of melancholy illness and her theatrical, cultivated entertaining.

BIBLIOGRAPHY. M. Helm, *Modern Mexican Painters*, New York, 1941; B. S. Myers, *Mexican Painting in Our Time*, New York, 1956; R. Flores Guerrero, *Cinco pintores mexicanos*, Mexico City, 1957. JOSEPH A. BAIRD, JR.

KAHN, ALBERT. American architect (b. Rhaunen, Westphalia, 1869; d. Detroit, 1942). He immigrated to the United States in 1881. He is best known for his industrial buildings, whose precise cubic shapes anticipate Mies van der Rohe's work of the 1950s. Kahn's Ohio Steel Foundry Company Building (1939) at Lima, Ohio, has walls entirely of glass to give the maximum light. Among his large plants are the River Rouge Plant at Dearborn, Mich., and the Glenn L. Martin Assembly Plant at Baltimore, Md., where the Assembly Building has a clear span of 300 feet. Con-

Kahrie-Djami, Istanbul. Central-plan Byzantine edifice, 12th–14th century.

struction of the airplane begins at one end of a 450-foot run, and a railroad spur enters the plant for delivery and shipping purposes.

BIBLIOGRAPHY. T. F. Hamlin, *Forms and Functions of Twentieth-Century Architecture*, vol. 4, New York, 1952.

KAHN, LOUIS. American architect (1901–). Kahn was born in Saaremaa (Swedish, Oesel), U.S.S.R., and went to the United States in 1905. He received his architectural training at the University of Pennsylvania and has worked in Philadelphia since 1921 as a draftsman, architect, and city planner. He has had his own practice since 1934. Kahn's efforts as a planner culminated with his unrealized Philadelphia City Plan Project (1956–57). After teaching architecture at Yale University (1947–57), he went to the University of Pennsylvania in 1957.

Kahn at first adhered to the geometric purity of the International Style. His later work has developed toward pictorial boldness, with materials, forms, and structure strongly expressed and contrasted, as in the Yale University Art Gallery (1951–53). In the Richards Medical Research Building (1957–61) at the University of Pennsylvania the towers that contain stairs and exhaust and intake ducts for the laboratories feature prominently as volumetric entities. The Mill Creek Housing Project II (1959–62) in Philadelphia, where red brick and concrete are used, recalls Le Corbusier at the Maisons Jaoul (1952) in Neuilly. The monumental Indian Institute of Management, at Ahmedabad (completed 1966), has massive brickwork. A central education building is ringed with L-shaped fortress-like towers that serve as hostels. In 1966 work started on Kahn's new capital city for Dacca, East Pakistan.

BIBLIOGRAPHY. V. Scully, Jr., *Louis I. Kahn*, New York, 1962.
ABRAHAM A. DAVIDSON

KAHN, MAX. American color lithographer (1904–). Born in Russia, he studied at Bradley University, Peoria, Ill., and later, in Paris, he studied under Bourdelle, Despiau, and Friesz. He now teaches at the Art Institute of Chicago and at the University of Chicago. His color litho-

graphs are generally large and bold animal or human figure compositions.

KAHRIE-DJAMI (Church of the Chora), ISTANBUL. Centrally planned Byzantine church, built from the 12th through 14th century. It is sometimes known by its original name, the Church of St. Saviour in Chora, because of its location in the fields outside the old city walls of Constantinople.

A large, central square nave (bema) carries a dome on a drum, resting on pendentives. The east end terminates in a large apse flanked by two smaller apses. A narthex, at right angles to the axis established by the main apse, is at the west end. Such was the basic plan of the church prior to 1118. In 1331 the north aisle and an outer narthex were added. A full report on the architecture of Kahrie-Djami awaits the completion of the studies by the Byzantine Institute of America.

The interior is rich in marble revetments and mosaics. Best preserved are the mosaics in the nartharxes, done in the early 14th century under the patronage of Theodore Metochites, statesman and scholar. Depicting events from the life of the Virgin and the childhood of Christ, they are subtle and delicate in color, and display a rich use of decorative pattern, ornament, and narrative detail. Thus, built on the eve of the demise of the Byzantine Empire, Kahrie-Djami stands as a monument to a new flowering of Byzantine art.

BIBLIOGRAPHY. A. van Millingen, *Byzantine Churches in Constantinople*, London, 1912; A. Grabar, *Byzantine Painting*, Geneva, 1953.
STANLEY FERBER

KAI-DIBA DANCE SHIELDS, *see* OCEANIC ART (MELANESIA: TROBRIAND ISLANDS).

K'AI-FENG (Pien-ching). One of the two great cities of Honan Province, China. Known in the Northern Sung period (960–1126) as Pien-ching, it served as the capital and housed the imperial palaces. When the Sung emperors began its design they were faced with an existing T'ang city, and much energy was expended on enlarging and improving the capital precincts. The redesigning of the city was completed shortly before the Kin (Chin) Tatars sacked it in 1126, destroying most of the Northern Sung efforts. But literary accounts of Pien-ching leave little doubt that it was a dazzling city, fully the equal of the famous cities of Ch'ang-an and Lo-yang. Numerous towers dominated the city, with the temple of Hsiang-kuo-ssu serving as a major landmark. *See* CH'ANG-AN; LO-YANG.

Of the existing monuments in modern K'ai-feng that date to the period when the city enjoyed its greatest florescence, two pagodas deserve special mention: the T'ieh-t'a (Iron Pagoda) and the Fan-t'a (Fan Pagoda). The T'ieh-t'a, an octagonal brick structure thirteen stories high, dates from 1044. The Fan-t'a, which belonged to the Hsiang-kuo-ssu temple, was built in 977; later destroyed, it was rebuilt in 1384. Originally conceived as a hexagonal pagoda of nine stories, the Fan-t'a was truncated to three stories in the rebuilding; it remains one of the major extant

Ando Kaigetsudō, painting on paper. Collection of National Museums of Japan.

Kailāsa Temple, Ellora. Rock-cut Hindu sanctuary decorated with a profusion of figural sculpture, begun 757–783.

monuments of Sung architecture in K'ai-feng. *See* T'IEH-
T'A, K'AI-FENG.

BIBLIOGRAPHY. A. C. Soper, "Hsiang-kuo-ssu, an Imperial Temple of Northern Sung," *Journal of the American Oriental Society,* LXVIII, January, 1948; L. Sickman and A. Soper, *The Art and Architecture of China,* Baltimore, 1956.   MARTIE W. YOUNG

KAIGETSUDO, ANDO. Japanese painter (fl. early 18th cent.). He specialized in the portrayal of elegantly dressed courtesans. The tall, curvaceous and sensuous beauties are often shown full length in twisted poses. All that is known of Kaigetsudō's life is that in 1714 he was exiled because of his involvement in a love affair between a Kabuki actor and a maid-in-waiting of the shōgun.

Most of the paintings with the signature of Kaigetsudō can be attributed to him. However, his followers Anchi, Dohan, and others, who also used the name of Kaigetsudō, made many woodblock prints showing similar types of women of the pleasure quarters. Ando Kaigetsudō did not make prints. (See illustration.)

BIBLIOGRAPHY. L. V. Ledoux, *Japanese Prints of the Primitive Period in the Collection of Louis V. Ledoux,* New York, 1942.

KAIHO SCHOOL. School of Japanese painters. It was founded by Yūsetsu (1598–1677), the son of Yūshō. Yūsetsu chose the more decorative aspect of his father's art as his own style, and it became the trademark of this school. Although the school continued to be active in Kyoto throughout the Edo period, it did not produce many great artists, with the exception of Yūsetsu himself and his second son, Yūchiku (1654–1728). Other, less important members of this family were Yūsen, Yūzō, and Yūtoku. *See* YUSHO.

BIBLIOGRAPHY. T. Akiyama, *Japanese Painting* [Geneva?], 1961.

KAIKEI. Japanese sculptor (d. ca. 1240). He was trained by Kōkei, Unkei's father. While Unkei excelled in fierce, dynamic figures, Kaikei's forte was quiet, gentle figures of the Amida Buddha. The *Miroku* (1189; Boston, Museum of Fine Arts), one of his earliest works, already shows his tendency toward a sensitive, delicate style. *See* UNKEI.

BIBLIOGRAPHY. R. T. Paine and A. Soper, *The Art and Architecture of Japan*, Baltimore, 1955.

KAILASA. Mountain in the Himalayas, north of Mānasa Lake. In Hinduism, Kailāsa is the paradise of Siva; in Buddhism, Kuvera's abode.

KAILASANATHA TEMPLE, *see* KANCHIPURAM.

KAILASA TEMPLE, ELLORA. Rock-cut Hindu sanctuary begun by order of Krishna II, first king of the Rāṣṭrakūṭa dynasty of central India, between 757 and 783. It is carved from a block 267 feet long and 154 feet wide (the dimensions of its court), cut out and isolated from the side of a mountain. The Kailāsa temple consists of many separate units, all of which are decorated with a profusion of figural sculpture. Rising to a height of 95 feet and measuring about 100 by 150 feet at its base, the temple includes a main shrine, containing a Siva liṅgam, a pillared hall, and a smaller shrine for Nandi, Siva's bull vehicle. Cloisters have been cut into the cliff on the sides of the temple.

See also ELLORA; INDIA.

BIBLIOGRAPHY. B. Rowland, *The Art and Architecture of India*, 2d ed., Baltimore, 1959.

KAIRWAN (Qairawan): MOSQUE OF SIDI OKBA (Sidi Uqba). Umayyad mosque in Tunisia. Elements of two earlier mosques on this site were demolished in a complete rebuilding in 836, and a series of additions was made as late as the 13th century. Oriented toward Mecca, the huge, irregularly rectangular structure is about 395 feet long and 230 feet wide. Entrances lead into the open court, which is flanked by shallow halls on the long sides and, at the end, by a hall with seventeen aisles in sixteen bays in front of a mihrab decorated with luster tiles.

BIBLIOGRAPHY. K. A. C. Creswell, *A Short Account of Early Muslim Architecture*, Harmondsworth, 1958.

KAISANDO. Japanese Zen Buddhist temple in the Eihōji near Nagoya. The Kaisandō (memorial chapel of the monastery's founder) is dedicated to the founder of the Eihōji, Buttoku Zenshi. He was a pupil of the Zen national master Musō Soseki (1275–1351), who is believed to have founded the Kannon Hall within the same temple compound in 1314. The Kaisandō is often said to have been built in 1352, although the actual date might be slightly later. It is the oldest surviving example of a Japanese building type in which three separate buildings are combined to form one unit. At the rear is a sanctuary, to which is connected a forehall used for memorial services. Between them is a connecting passageway covered with a low roof. This type was later widely copied in Zen monasteries throughout Japan.

BIBLIOGRAPHY. R. T. Paine and A. Soper, *The Art and Architecture of Japan*, Baltimore, 1955.

KAISARIANI, MONASTERY CHURCH OF. Greek church in the Hymettus, near Athens. It is an early ex-

ample of a Byzantine domed cross-plan church. Dating from the late 10th century, the church is of a characteristically small size. Four equal arms cross, and at the crossing four columns support a slender octagonal drum upon which a small dome rests. The three aisles terminate in three apses, of which the central one is the largest. The narthex is barrel-vaulted and has a central dome resting upon an octagonal drum. The interior has rich fresco decoration throughout.

BIBLIOGRAPHY. O. Wulff, *Altchristliche und byzantinische Kunst*, 2 vols. in 1, Berlin, 1914.

KAISER-FRIEDRICH MUSEUM, BERLIN. The collections are now divided between East and West Berlin. *See* BERLIN: MUSEUMS (WEST BERLIN: FORMER STATE MUSEUMS, PICTURE GALLERY; EAST BERLIN: MUSEUM ISLAND).

KAIT BAY (Qayt Bay), TOMB OF. Mamluk tomb located in the area known as the Tombs of the Caliphs, to the east of Cairo, Egypt. It is one element of a complex that includes a mosque, a school, and a library. The portal of the freestanding structure is flanked by a single towering minaret, and a dome on a very high tambour rises over the tomb chamber. The elaborate interior decoration features marble mosaic work.

K'AI-YUAN-SSU, I-HSIEN. Temple situated on the border of Hopei Province, China. The K'ai-yüan-ssu is a building complex that dates from 1105. A richly deco-

Kairwan, Mosque of Sidi Okba. Umayyad mosque in Tunisia.

rated octagonal cupola rises from a square bay in the central hall, flanked on the east and west by two other chapels.

BIBLIOGRAPHY. L. Sickman and A. Soper, *The Art and Architecture of China*, Baltimore, 1956.

KAKEMONO. Vertical Japanese hanging scroll with painting or calligraphy, having two wooden rods. The upper rod is pierced so that the scroll can be hung on the wall; the lower rod is used to roll the scroll when it is not in use. Most *kakemono* also have decorative brocaded margins. Horizontal Japanese scrolls are known as *makimono*. See MAKIMONO.

BIBLIOGRAPHY. Tokyo National Museum, *Pageant of Japanese Art*, vols. 1-2: *Painting*, Tokyo, 1952.

KAKI. Japanese term meaning "persimmon [colored]." It is used in reference to the brown-colored Temmoku or Chien-ware class of Chinese ceramics. *See* TEMMOKU.

KAKIEMON, *see* JAPAN: CERAMICS (PORCELAIN PRODUCTION).

KAKUYU, *see* TOBA SOJO.

KALABSHA, TEMPLE OF. Situated in Egyptian Nubia about 40 miles south of Aswan, this important temple was built by Augustus on the ruins of a New Kingdom structure. In 1962–63 it was moved above the Aswan Dam waters. The second largest and most complete Greco-Roman temple in Nubia, it is in a near-perfect state of preservation. Although the painted inscriptions have suffered from being submerged nine months out of every year, the numerous Greek inscriptions of the 2d and 3d centuries of the Christian era and Egyptian texts can be read.

The walls of the main chamber bear bas-relief inscriptions and offering scenes describing the ceremonies held there in front of the double naos dedicated to two aspects of the god of the temple, the Nubian Mandulis, Isis, also worshiped there, is represented in large, Greco-Roman reliefs at the rear of the temple. The inner enclosure wall into which is built the traditional pylon encompasses an area about 235 feet long and about 116 feet wide.

KALAMIS, *see* CALAMIS.

KALASA. In Indian art, a rain vase, associated with the elixir of life. The *kalaśa* is also the finial at the top of a Hindu temple.

KALAT SEMAN: CONVENT OF ST. SIMEON STYLITES. East Christian convent church in north Syria, dating from the second half of the 5th century. Its cruciform plan is formed by four three-aisled columnar basilicas, which come together around a central octagonal courtyard containing the Column of St. Simeon Stylites (d. 459). The vaulting of the court has been debated: some believe it was domed; others considered it more likely to have had a pyramidal type of timber roof.

The eastern basilica terminates in an eastern apse and two flanking apsidioles. The entire structure is built of native hewn stone, typical of Syrian architecture, and is decorated with stone moldings and stringcourses, also typical of the architecture of this region. The church is considered by some to be a forerunner of the domed cross-plan structures of Byzantine architecture.

KALB LOUZEH, CHURCH OF. Early Christian 5th-century building in Syria. Kalb Louzeh exemplifies one type of East Christian basilican church. Specifically Syrian is the heavy, blocklike stone masonry, which was used rather than the prevalent Early Christian brick and rubble-fill construction.

The church is now in a ruined state; the remains show a semicircular stone-vaulted apse flanked by side chambers and two aisles separated from the nave by heavy, squat piers, spanned axially by low arches. Kalb Louzeh was towerless, and typically utilized continuous, simple stringcourses for decoration. Despite the excellent stonework and the vaulted apse, the church seems not to have been vaulted, for an interior console frieze appears to have been designed to support beams for a timber roof.

KALCKREUTH, LEOPOLD, GRAF VON. German painter (b. Düsseldorf, 1855; d. Eddelson-bei-Hittfeld, 1928). He studied under Schauss and Struys in Weimar (1875–78) and under Benczur, Piloty, and Diez in Munich. After his tenure as a professor at the academies in Weimar (1885–90) and Karlsruhe (1895–99) and as director of the Stuttgart Academy (1900–05), he settled near Hamburg. He exerted a great influence in these cities and was the first president of the Deutscher Künstlerbund (founded in 1903). His paintings are impressionistic in technique. They can be seen in various German museums; the Art Gallery in Hamburg has harbor views and many fine portraits. His open-air scenes of peasants, recalling Millet, are usually symbolic.

BIBLIOGRAPHY. K. Scheffler, *Talente*, Berlin, 1921.

KALF (Kalff), WILLEM. Dutch painter of genre, landscape, and still life (b. Rotterdam, 1619/22; d. Amsterdam, 1693). It is not certain who Kalf's teacher was; however, several early works, such as *Still Life* (1643; Cologne, Wallraf-Richartz Museum), show a close affinity with the works of François Rijckhals, who seems to have developed the Dutch *pronk* (show or ostentation) still life. Kalf was active in Paris between 1642 and 1646. In 1651 he married the diamond engraver, calligrapher, poet, and composer Cornelia Fluvier at Hoorn. The Dutch poet Joost van den Vondel composed a poem in honor of the marriage. From 1653 on, Kalf is recorded at Amsterdam. He also seems to have been an art dealer. Among Kalf's early works are several versions of his *Peasant Interior* (Göteborg, Art Gallery); although they contain still-life groupings, they present a direct contrast to the strong but extremely refined *pronk* still-life paintings for which he is best known (Amsterdam, Rijksmuseum; De Lutte, H. E. ten Cate Collection). He also did a few landscapes.

BIBLIOGRAPHY. H. E. van Gelder, *W. C. Heda, A. van Beyeren, W. Kalf*, Amsterdam, 1941; R. van Luttervelt, "Aanteekeningen over de Ontwikkeling van Willem Kalf," *Oud-Holland*, LX, 1943; I. Bergström, *Dutch Still-life Painting in the Seventeenth Century*, New York, 1956; J. Rosenberg, S. Slive, and E. H. ter Kuile, *Dutch Art and Architecture, 1600–1800*, Baltimore, 1966.

LEONARD J. SLATKES

Willem Kalf, *Still Life*. Rijksmuseum, Amsterdam.

KALI. Hindu goddess, the fierce and bloody consort of Siva and the terrible aspect of Devī. Kālī, whose name means "black," is represented with a black skin and a hideous countenance, dripping blood and encircled with snakes. She is draped with strings of skulls and human heads and resembles a fury rather than a goddess.

KALKAR, JAN STEPHAN OF, *see* CALCAR, JAN STEPHAN OF.

KALLIMACHUS, *see* CALLIMACHUS.

KAMA. Hindu god of love. Kāma is lord of the apsarases and, like Cupid, is armed with bow and arrows.

KAMAKURA. Japanese city in Kanagawa prefecture, south of Tokyo. A small fishing village before the late 12th century, it became the *de facto* capital of Japan in 1192, when Minamoto Yoritomo established Japan's first military government there. The city maintained its power as the political center of Japan until 1333, and gave its name to a period in Japan's history. Many temples and shrines were built there during the Kamakura period, but the city never attained the high cultural standard and prestige enjoyed by Kyoto. Among Kamakura's notable monuments are the Tsuruga-oka, Hachiman-gū, Engakuji, Kenchōji, and Zuisenji. Important museums of the city are the Kamakura Art Museum, Museum of Modern Art, and Gallery of the Tokiwayama Foundation. *See* JAPAN (KAMAKURA PERIOD); KENCHOJI.

BIBLIOGRAPHY. S. Kaneko, *Guide to Japanese Art*, Rutland, Vt., 1963.

KAMAKURA-BORI. Japanese lacquer process that imitates Chinese carved lacquer. The carving is done on wood rather than on solid lacquer; the wood is then covered with lacquer, usually a red base and black overlay. It was first used during the Kamakura period, reportedly by the artist Kōen.

KAMARES WARE. Type of pottery found in the sacred cave of Kamares, a neolithic site on the south slope of Mt. Ida, in Crete. It dates from the Middle Minoan period (2200–1580 B.C.). The term "Kamares style" denotes a fine polychrome pottery richly decorated with floral and geometric patterns and marine forms. The pottery includes the earliest examples of glazed ware of high artistic quality.

BIBLIOGRAPHY. S. Marinatos, *Crete and Mycenae*, New York, 1960.

KAMPMANN, HACK. Danish architect (b. Ebeltoft, 1856; d. Copenhagen, 1920). He is responsible for many notable buildings in Aarhus, such as the Custom House (1897), Theater (1898–1900), and City Library (1898–1902), typical of Scandinavian work at the end of the 19th century.

KANAOKA (Kose no Kanaoka). Japanese painter (fl. late 9th cent.). He was a superintendent of the imperial park and an imperial court painter. He is regarded as one of the first painters to present a purely Japanese subject matter, although his training was in the Chinese tradition. Literary sources describe his landscape painting as showing "mountains piled up in fifteen layers," implying that his landscape painting was still under the strong influence of the T'ang painting of China.

BIBLIOGRAPHY. T. Akiyama, *Japanese Painting* [Geneva?], 1961.

KANCHIPURAM (Conjeeveram). City on the east coast of the Deccan, in Madras State, India, 45 miles southwest of the city of Madras. It was the capital of the Pallava rulers from about A.D. 575–600, although it had been a

Kāñchīpuram. Kailāsanātha Temple, ca. 700.

center of intellectual life for many years earlier. The Chinese pilgrim Hsüan-tsang visited the city in 640 and was greatly impressed by its splendor. About 700 Rājasiṁhavarman built the Kailāsanātha temple, dedicated to Siva and his consort Pārvatī in their Himalayan garden of Kailāsa. Its shrine, covered by a śikhara (pyramidal tower), and its *maṇḍapa* (pillared hall for worshipers) are surrounded by a wall of cells topped by a parapet of cupolas. The pillars are supported by rampant lions, some of which carry riders. About ten years later the somewhat larger temple of Vaikuṇṭha Perumāl was built at Kāñchīpuram; it exhibits similar characteristics of Pallava architecture in their most mature form.

BIBLIOGRAPHY. P. Brown, *Indian Architecture*, 4th ed., 2 vols., Bombay, 1959.

KANDINSKY, WASSILY. Russian painter (b. Moscow, 1866; d. Neuilly-sur-Seine, 1944). Kandinsky was one of the greatest innovators in the history of modern art; moreover, his discovery of the possibilities of abstract or nonfigurative painting has amounted to one of the very few fundamental changes of imagery and form in any epoch. His revolutionary compositions of 1910–14 played a seminal role in the total concept of subsequent nonobjective art.

Kandinsky, whose father was a Russian merchant, lived with his parents in Rome and Florence during his early childhood. He attended Moscow University, taking an advanced degree in social sciences and law, and in 1889 accompanied a scientific mission to the region of Vologda, where he was deeply impressed by Russian folk art. He visited Paris later that year. In 1896, having determined to study painting, he went to Munich, studying first at Anton Azbé's school, then under Franz von Stuck at the Munich Academy of Fine Arts until 1900.

Kandinsky founded the avant-garde Phalanx group in 1901, and in 1902 opened his own art school. Between 1903 and 1907 he traveled extensively in the Near East, Holland, Italy, and Germany and exhibited with Die Brücke in Dresden. He headed the Neue Künstlervereinigung (New Artists Federation) in Munich in 1908–09. Out of this association emerged the illustrious Blaue Reiter group in 1911.

Kandinsky's painting underwent a remarkable, although logical, transformation between 1901 and 1908. He at first worked in an almost academically naturalistic manner, which he applied to portrait studies and landscape. Certain paintings of 1905–06 disclose an interest in Russian folkloristic and religious themes, but the semiabstract landscapes of 1908–09 developed out of the Western tradition of representation, not out of decorative sources. The *Street in Murnau* (1908) and *Bavarian Mountains* (1909) are close to French Fauvism in color and to a lesser extent in touch. His first completely abstract work, a water color of 1910 (usually titled *Composition I* or *Improvisation*), composed of freely brushed shapes of light blues, reds, and greens conjoined by inventive linear scratchings, clearly derives from the representational manner just preceding it at the same time as it is liberated from all imitative purposes.

Between 1910 and 1914 Kandinsky was incredibly productive. At times he worked totally abstractly, and again he returned to oils and water colors in which references were made to mountain landscapes or street scenes (*Autumn I*, 1911; *Improvisation*, 1912; *Small Pleasures*, 1913). Among the most compelling of Kandinsky's pre-World War I abstractions is *Black Lines* (1913; Munich, Thannhauser Gallery). He referred to the musical connotations of some of his abstractions.

At the outbreak of war in 1914 Kandinsky went to Switzerland, then to Russia. He was appointed a member of the Cultural Commissariat in 1918, and until 1921 he taught at the Moscow Academy of Fine Arts. He also established some twenty museums in various parts of Russia. He returned to Germany in 1921 and in 1922 was appointed professor in the Bauhaus at Weimar. As a teacher, Kandinsky was notably systematic, imaginative, and sympathetic.

After 1921 Kandinsky's abstractions, evidently following a trend that had begun after 1914 during his Russian sojourn, became increasingly geometric in form. The poetic fluidity of the 1910–14 *Improvisation* series was discarded in favor of a new, clean-edged discipline suggestive of the patterns of the architect's French curve and T square (*Improvisation 8*, 1923; *Black Relation*, 1924). Certain later compositions reveal a tendency to soften the precision of the new style, but Kandinsky's aesthetic remained geometrically conditioned until the end of his life.

He formed the Blaue Vier (Blue Four) in 1924 with his Bauhaus associates Paul Klee, Lyonel Feininger, and Alexey von Jawlensky. The group exhibited in Europe, the United States, and Mexico. Kandinsky moved with the Bauhaus to Dessau in 1925. He traveled extensively from 1929 to 1931, meeting James Ensor in Belgium and holding an important one-man show at the Galerie Zak in Paris. When the Bauhaus was closed by the Nazis in 1933, Kandinsky went to Neuilly-sur-Seine, a suburb of Paris, where he lived for the rest of his life. His works, like those of most German expressionists, were labeled "degenerate" by the Nazis in 1937.

Outstanding collections of Kandinsky's works are in the Municipal Gallery and Lenbach Gallery, Munich; the Guggenheim Museum, New York; and the Collection of Mme Nina Kandinsky, Neuilly-sur-Seine. Kandinsky's importance to modern painting was increased by his contributions as a theorist and writer on art. His most important written work, *Uber das Geistige in der Kunst . . .* (*Concerning the Spiritual in Art . . .*), 1912, was translated into many languages and exerted considerable influence on the modern movement. He was also personally instructive to many of his colleagues, especially Klee, Marc, Macke, Von Jawlensky, Gabriele Münter, and other of his Blaue Reiter associates.

See also EXPRESSIONISM.

BIBLIOGRAPHY. W. Kandinsky, *Uber das Geistige in der Kunst . . .*, Munich, 1912 (Eng. tr., F. Goeffing et al., *Concerning the Spiritual in Art . . .*, New York, 1947); W. Kandinsky and F. Marc, eds., *Der Blaue Reiter*, 2d ed., Munich, 1914; W. Kandinsky, *Punkt und Linie zu Fläche*, 2d ed., Munich, 1926; *Art d'Aujourd'hui*, no. 6, Paris, 1950; M. Bill et al., *Wassily Kandinsky*, Boston, 1951; W. Grohmann, *Wassily Kandinsky: Leben und Werk*, Cologne, 1958; M. Seuphor, *Ein Halbes Jahrhundert abstrakte Malerei . . .*, Munich, 1962.

JOHN C. GALLOWAY

Wassily Kandinsky, *Et Encore*, 1940. Museum of Fine Arts, Bern.

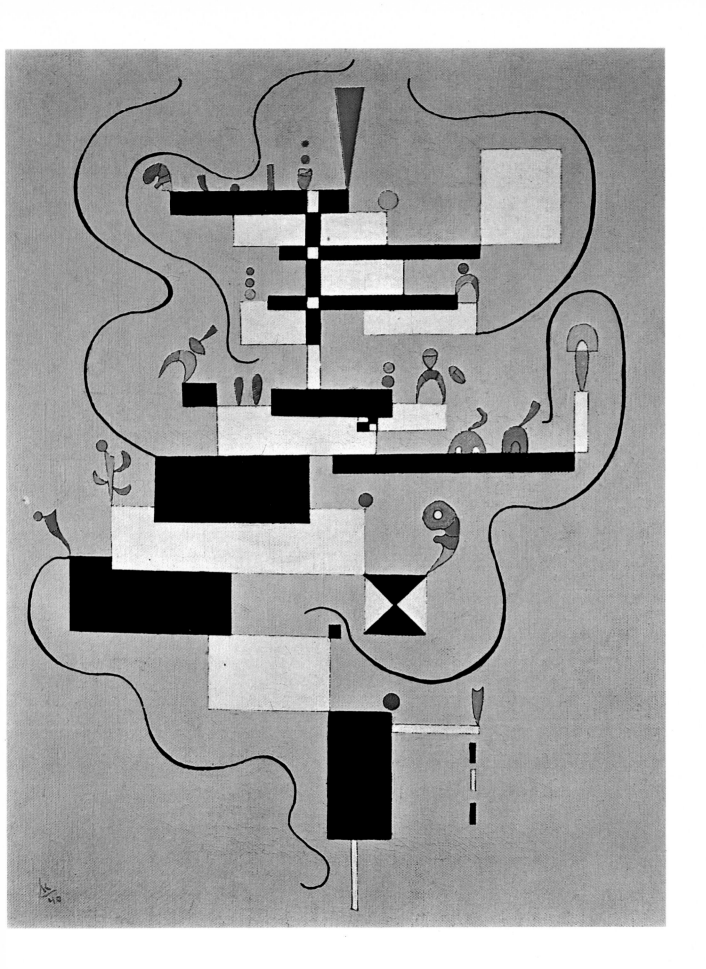

K'ang-hsi ware. Blue-and-white vase of the type exported to Europe in quantity. Victoria and Albert Museum, London.

KANDLER, JOHANN JOACHIM, *see* KAENDLER, JOHANN JOACHIM.

KANDY, *see* CEYLON.

KANE, PAUL. Canadian painter (1810–71). Born in Ireland, he immigrated in 1818 to Toronto. After working as an itinerant portraitist, he visited the Mediterranean. Kane crossed Canada under the auspices of the Hudson Bay Company (1846–48), making studies of Indian life. These

were later used as the basis for a series of romantic canvases.

BIBLIOGRAPHY. P. Kane, *Wanderings of an Artist among the Indians of North America . . .*, Toronto, 1925.

KANESH, *see* KULTEPE.

K'ANG-HSI WARE. Varied types of Chinese porcelain manufactured under the patronage of the Ch'ing emperor K'ang-hsi (r. 1662–1722). They are characterized by high technical perfection and the use of richly colored glazes, including powdered blue, *sang de boeuf* (deep red), clair de lune (pale blue), and peach bloom (apple green tinged with soft red). Popular blue-and-white wares were exported to Europe in great quantity. Bright enamels were widely used for overglaze painting.

See also BATAVIAN WARE.

BIBLIOGRAPHY. British Museum, Dept. of Oriental Antiquities and of Ethnography, *Handbook of the Pottery and Porcelain of the Far East*, by R. L. Hobson, 2d ed., London, 1937.

KANG HUI-AN (In-jae). Korean painter (1419–65). A famous landscapist of the early Yi period and a member of the Royal Academy, he excelled in poetry and calligraphy as well as in painting. He followed the styles of the Northern Sung masters Ma Yüan and Hsia Kuei. Kang Hui-an painted figures and birds with equal dexterity. He accepted no disciples and never exhibited his works to the public. One of his best-known paintings is *Sage in Meditation* (Seoul, National Museum), which shows the influence of Zen Buddhism. See HSIA KUEI; MA YUAN; ZEN.

BIBLIOGRAPHY. E. McCune, *The Arts of Korea*, Rutland, Vt., 1962.

KANGRA SCHOOL, *see* RAJPUT PAINTING OF INDIA.

KANISHKA RELIQUARY. Cylindrical bronze, covered and inscribed, from Shāh-jī-kī-Dherī, Gandhāra (Peshawar, Archaeological Museum). It is decorated with figures in relief. On the cover is a seated Buddha flanked by a standing Brahmā and Indra, all three haloed. Around the body are garland-bearing yakshas, a Buddha, and a royal figure. Before the bronze was cleaned, the inscription seemed to refer to Kanishka I, a Kushan emperor; afterward, to an unidentifiable monastery. According to style, the reliquary dates from the 2d century A.D.

BIBLIOGRAPHY. D. Barrett, "Gandhara Bronzes," *The Burlington Magazine*, CII, August, 1960.

KANNON (Kwannon), *see* AVALOKITESVARA.

KANNON IN HORYUJI, *see* KUDARA KANNON OF HORYUJI.

KANNON IN KANSHINJI, *see* NYOIRIN KANNON.

KANNON IN YUMEDONO, *see* YUMEDONO KANNON.

KANO SCHOOL. School of Japanese painters. It was founded in the Muromachi period (1336–1573) by Masanobu, who secured his family's position as the official painter of the shogunal government. The school exerted its influence over official taste throughout the Edo period, and even in the Meiji era. Masanobu's style, based on

Chinese ink painting with some modifications to suit Japanese taste, became the school's trademark. Eitoku (fl. 16th cent.) was the giant of the family, and he established a family tradition of monopolizing large commissions to decorate castles and palaces. In 1621 Tannyū and his brothers moved to Edo; hence they were called the Edo Kanō. Sanraku and other members of the school remained in Kyoto and came to be known as the Kyō Kanō. Sanraku's son Sansetsu (1589–1651) and his descendants formed a nucleus of the Kyō Kanō group, of which Sanraku's grandson Einō (1634–1700) is one of the better-known artists. *See* EITOKU; MASANOBU (KANO MASANOBU); SANRAKU; TANNYU.

The Edo Kanō further branched out to include several other groups. Among them four family dynasties—Hamachō, Kajibashi, Kobikichō, and Nakabashi—were the most powerful and were called the *oku-eshi* (painters who controlled the leading studios). There were twelve other family branches called the *omote-eshi* (painters of the official academy) and another group of independent Kanō artists known as the *machi-eshi* (city painters).

Not only the Tokugawa shogunal government patronized the Kanō painters; the local lords also followed the example set by the shoguns, and no other schools could rival the power of this family. But security and conventional training restricted their creative vitality, and often pupils, such as Morikage and Itchō, rebelled against the rigid code of the school and developed more interesting styles of their own. *See* ITCHO; MORIKAGE.

BIBLIOGRAPHY. R. T. Paine and A. Soper, *The Art and Architecture of Japan*, Baltimore, 1955; T. Akiyama, *Japanese Painting* [Geneva?], 1961.

MIYEKO MURASE

KANSAS CITY, MO.: WILLIAM ROCKHILL NELSON GALLERY OF ART AND MARY ATKINS MUSEUM OF FINE ARTS.

Founded by the journalist William Rockhill Nelson and established with funds from his estate, the museum is housed in a classical building that was completed in 1933.

Ancient art is well represented, particularly that of the Mesopotamian area. Highlighting this group are Sumerian figures, a bull capital from Persepolis, and a head of Hammurabi. There are also a number of Egyptian, Etruscan, Greek, and Roman works.

Major works in the collection of European paintings are Lorenzo Monaco's *Madonna of Humility*, Memling's *Madonna and Child Enthroned*, Petrus Christus's *Madonna and Child in a Gothic Room*, Poussin's *Triumph of Bacchus*, El Greco's *Portrait of a Trinitarian Monk*, and Caravaggio's *St. John the Baptist*. There are paintings by Lorenzo di Credi, Rembrandt, Titian, Tintoretto, Bronzino, Veronese, Velázquez, Georges de La Tour, Claude Lorraine, Chardin, Boucher, Gauguin, Cézanne, and more recent artists. In the area of American painting, the museum owns an important group of Binghams as well as works by Copley, Inness, West, Raphaelle Peale, and other 19th- and 20th-century artists. Medieval, Renaissance, and modern sculpture and European and American period rooms and decorative arts are also exhibited.

Most remarkable are the collections of Oriental art, which include the largest group of Indian bronzes in the United States. Of particularly high quality are the extensive groups of Chinese bronzes, paintings (for example, *Palace Ladies Tuning the Lute and Drinking Tea* attributed to Chou Fang, fl. late 8th cent.; *Twelve Views from a Thatched Cottage* attributed to Hsia Kuei, fl. early 13th cent.), sculpture, ceramics, and jades.

BIBLIOGRAPHY. *Handbook of the Collections in the William Rockhill Nelson Gallery of Art and Mary Atkins Museum of Fine Arts*, Kansas City, Mo., 1959. DONALD GODDARD

KANTHAROS (Cantharus). Greek vase type, consisting of a large cup with two long curving handles and often with a high stem or "foot." Although such cups are often portrayed in painting on other types of vases, few examples

Kanō school. Kanō Eitoku (attrib.), scroll depicting a scene from the legend of the hermit Ch'ao-fu. National Museum, Tokyo.

Kao K'o-kung, *Mountains in the Clouds*. Palace Collection, Formosa.

have survived, perhaps because they were made of metal that has since been reused.

BIBLIOGRAPHY. G. M. A. Richter and M. J. Milne, *Shapes and Names of Athenian Vases*, New York, 1935.

KAO. Japanese painter (fl. early 14th cent.). Kaō is often identified with another painter, Ryōzen. Nothing is known about his life. He was one of the earliest painters in Japan to learn the art of ink painting from Chinese works. He often painted Zen themes, in simple, uncluttered compositions, with strong and spontaneous brushstrokes. *See* RYO-ZEN.

KAO CH'I-P'EI. Chinese painter (1672–1732). His *tzu* was Wei-chih and his *hao* Ch'ieh-yüan. A native of Mukden, he had a brilliant official career during the reigns of K'ang-hsi and Yung-cheng and was a precocious and gifted painter of striking talent. In addition to painting in the traditional styles with a brush, Kao Ch'i-p'ei perfected the technique of finger painting, employing all parts of his hand—fingertips, sides, and fingernails. His finger paintings be-

came so popular that in his later years he devoted his life to mass-producing them for an ever-increasing audience. Some of his best works are in the album format and show a lively imagination combined with vigorous handling; other works, particularly the large-scale conservative paintings in the usual brush technique, seem keyed more closely to the mediocre taste of the Manchu court.

BIBLIOGRAPHY. J. Fontein, "Een album van Kao Ch'i-pei," *Bulletin van het Rijksmuseum*, III, 1956.

KAO K'O-KUNG. Chinese painter (1248–1310). His *tzu* was Yen-ching and his *hao* Fang-shan (or Fang-shan lao-jen). He is usually considered the first great Yüan-dynasty landscapist. He was a Central Asian by ancestry but received a classical Chinese education and had a brilliant official career under the Mongols. Yet Kao K'o-kung was respected by the new generation of recluse landscapists like Ni Tsan, and his paintings were celebrated for the poetic effects captured through the exploitation of mist. In some ways he is very reminiscent of Mi Fu in his handling of landscape, and like Mi Fu, Kao K'o-kung's painting *oeuvre* does not bulk large. Apparently he painted with enormous difficulty, and it was only in the company of friends and wine that Kao K'o-kung turned to the art of the brush. He took a house in Hang-chou and entered the circle of the literary elite. It was only after his death that his fame spread, and he became a celebrated exponent of the southern school of painting in the eyes of 17th-century critics. His paintings today are scarce, the better-known attributed examples being in the Sun Yat-sen Museum in Formosa. *See* MI FU; NI TSAN; NORTHERN AND SOUTHERN SCHOOLS OF CHINESE PAINTING.

BIBLIOGRAPHY. O. Sirén, *Chinese Painting, Leading Masters and Principles*, vol. 4, New York, 1958. MARTIE W. YOUNG

KAOLIN, *see* PORCELAIN.

KAO-TSUNG, TOMB OF. Chinese tomb of the T'ang dynasty, located near Hsien-yang in Shensi Province. This tomb of the emperor Kao-tsung (r. 650–683) is notable mainly for the gigantic stone sculptures that lined the "spirit road" (*shen-tao*) leading to the burial site. The finest of these somewhat crude images is a beautiful horse with stylized wings, a monumental stone piece that reflects much of the grandeur of T'ang realism in sculpture but at the same time combines aspects of the earlier linear style of the Han and Six Dynasties periods.

BIBLIOGRAPHY. O. Sirén, *Chinese Sculpture from the Fifth to the Fourteenth Centuries*, 4 vols., London, 1925.

KAO YANG, *see* TEN-BAMBOO STUDIO, ALBUM OF.

KAPILAVASTU (Kapilavatthu). Capital city of Kosala, the kingdom of Suddhodana, and birthplace of Gautama Buddha.

KAPKAP, *see* OCEANIC ART (MELANESIA: SOLOMON ISLANDS).

KAPROW, ALAN. American artist (1927–   ). Kaprow studied at the Hans Hofmann School in New York City

(1947–48) and with the composer John Cage (1956–58). Also trained in art history at Columbia University, he now teaches in that field. Kaprow's first one-man show of paintings and works in other media was given at the Hansa Gallery, New York, in 1952, but he is known primarily for his invention of the "happening." In this form of combined theater and art, first tried by Kaprow in 1958, a total environment is created for a series of actions that are carried out by participants according to a scenario.

KAPUP, CHRISTOPH. German sculptor (fl. late 16th cent.). A native of Nordhausen, he designed the chancel in the Cathedral of Magdeburg (1595/97), on which he was assisted by Sebastian Ertle. It presents a highly plastic, heavily decorative, but fluid late Renaissance style.

KARA-E. Japanese term (meaning Chinese picture) for a type of secular painting. The term was first used to designate all Chinese secular paintings that were imported from China. Kara-e also included paintings executed in Japan in the Chinese manner and representing Chinese stories with Chinese figures against Chinese backgrounds. The term made its first appearance in literature in the late 9th century, precisely at the moment when the term "Yamato-e" (Japanese picture) appeared for the first time, suggesting that the two were used as antonyms. The distinction between them was based more on subject matter than on any stylistic characteristic. From the late 9th century Yamato-e replaced Kara-e as a means of decorating the houses of the nobles, and Kara-e was used on screens especially designed for official and formal functions at the court.

A transitional stage from Kara-e to Yamato-e may be observed in the landscape screen Senzui Byōbu (late 12th cent.) in the Kyōō Gokoku-ji (also known as Tōji), Kyoto, in which a Chinese literary theme is represented against gentle, rolling hills reminiscent of the Kyoto area, and which may aptly be described as landscape painting in the Yamato-e manner. Although neither Yamato-e nor Kara-e at first had any stylistic implication, later, in the Kamakura period, the term "Kara-e" was used to distinguish monochrome painting in ink—whether of Chinese or Japanese origin—from polychrome pictures, which were then called Yamato-e. See YAMATO-E.

BIBLIOGRAPHY. A. Soper, "The Rise of Yamato-e," *Art Bulletin*, XXIV, December, 1942; K. Toda, "Japanese Screen Paintings of the Ninth and Tenth Centuries," *Ars Orientalis*, III, 1959.

MIYEKO MURASE

KARATEPE (Asitawad). Ancient provincial town in northern Cilicia, Turkey, famous for a bilingual inscription discovered in a small building known as the Country Palace. In Hittite and Phoenician script, the inscription was found among other reliefs of small artistic value, carved on slabs of uneven size. One such relief depicts birds of prey; another, showing a human figure surrounded by beasts, is reminiscent of Mesopotamian art. The carvings, although showing some originality, are a crude imitation of various foreign styles and symbolism, with Phoenician, Assyrian, and even Egyptian influences evident; some, however, portray conventional Hittite themes. The architecture of Karatepe was Hittite and probably evolved from Hurrian

Bernard Karfiol, *Seated Nude*, 1929. Museum of Modern Art, New York.

art. The building found there has stone foundations and large cut and polished orthostates, elaborately carved in relief.

BIBLIOGRAPHY. S. Lloyd, *The Art of the Ancient Near East*, London, 1961; L. Woolley, *The Art of the Middle East*, New York, 1961.

KARATSU, see JAPAN: CERAMICS.

KARA-YO, see JAPAN: ARCHITECTURE (KAMAKURA PERIOD; MUROMACHI PERIOD).

KARFIOL, BERNARD. American painter (b. Budapest, Hungary, 1886; d. New York City, 1952). He studied at the National Academy of Design in 1900 and the following year with Jean-Paul Laurens in Paris. Karfiol exhibited in the Armory Show of 1913. He first worked in a manner derived from the precubist Picasso, painting tense, elongated figures whose stylizations revealed an interest in archaic art. In the 1920s Cézanne's volumes and brushwork and Renoir's warm color became the chief sources for Karfiol's tender studies of children and for his nudes, for example, *Seated Nude* (1929; New York, Museum of Modern Art). His later figures are more academic in style.

BIBLIOGRAPHY. J. P. Slusser, *Bernard Karfiol* (American Artists Series), New York, 1931.

KARIES, NIKOLAUS. German architect (fl. 1558–90). He worked in Flensburg. He is responsible for additions to

Glücksberg Castle (1582–87), which are in a strong, severe, and simple style.

KARLE (Karli). Village near Bombay, India. The Hīnayāna phase of Buddhist architecture culminates in the great chaitya hall at Kārle. According to a recent study, the chaitya was carved from living rock in the third quarter of the 1st century A.D. An outstanding feature of the Kārle chaitya is the façade screen, which is carved out of rock rather than of wood, as in earlier cave temples. In front of the façade are two freestanding columns with lotiform capitals supporting a group of addorsed lions that show an Indianization of the Persepolitan column as seen in Maurya times. Graceful sculptural relief appears in the narthex in the form of *mithūnas* (loving or royal couples); the figures of the Buddha are later Mahāyāna additions. *See* HINAYANA; MAHAYANA.

BIBLIOGRAPHY. W. Spink, "On the Development of Early Buddhist Art in India," *Art Bulletin*, XL, June, 1958; P. Brown, *Indian Architecture*, vol. 1: *Buddhist and Hindu Periods*, 4th ed., Bombay, 1959; B. Rowland, *The Art and Architecture of India*, 2d ed., Baltimore, 1959.

KARLSBERG, *see* GYULAFEHERVAR CATHEDRAL.

KARLSRUHE: STATE ART GALLERY. German collection founded about 1800. It is housed in a gallery building that was erected in 1837–46. German paintings from the 15th to the 20th century are the main treasures; among the earlier works are Matthias Grünewald's *Crucifixion* and *Christ Carrying the Cross* from the *Tauberbischofsheimer Altar* and one of the many versions of Lucas Cranach the Elder's *Judgment of Paris.* Among the works of the romantic school and the later 19th century are paintings by C. D. Friedrich, Overbeck, Von Schwind, Böcklin, Feuerbach, and Leibl. Hans Thoma, who once was director of the academy and gallery in Karlsruhe, is especially well represented in the Hans Thoma Museum, which was added to the main building in 1908. Among 20th-century artists, members of the Blaue Reiter and Die Brücke groups are represented by excellent examples. Paintings by French 17th- and 18th-century artists as well as Dutch and Flemish masters of the 16th and 17th centuries supplement the treasures, as do works in the graphic arts from all European schools from the 15th to the 20th century.

BIBLIOGRAPHY. H. Jedding, *Keysers Führer durch Museen und Sammlungen*, Heidelberg, Munich, 1961.

LOTTE PULVERMACHER-EGERS

KARLSTEIN CASTLE. Czechoslovakian castle, built in 1348–65 near Prague by Mathieu d'Arras and Peter Parler. It is the most important of the castles founded by Emperor Charles IV, king of Bohemia.

The importance of Karlstein resides in its several chapels with their elaborate decoration and interesting paintings. The Chapel of St. Catherine, with walls in semiprecious stones and gilded plaster, contains important paintings, especially the fresco over the altar depicting the Emperor and his wife adoring the Virgin and Child. Closely connected in style, and revealing considerable Italian influence, are frescoes in the Chapel of the Virgin (ca. 1357) depicting scenes from the Apocalypse and from the life of Charles IV. Even more important is the Chapel of the

Holy Cross, consecrated in 1365, also adorned with semiprecious stones and heavily gilded. The upper parts of the walls are covered with half-length figures of saints in panels painted between 1357 and 1367 by Theodoric of Prague, documented as court painter to Charles. The creator of the second Bohemian style, with its soft, broadly painted forms, Theodoric fused Italian ideas learned from Tommaso da Modena, who was called to Prague by Charles, with the local Bohemian idiom. His influence is felt particularly in northern Germany in the works of Master Bertram. *See* THEODORIC OF PRAGUE.

BIBLIOGRAPHY. J. Neuwirth, *Mittelalterliche Wandgemälde und Tafelbilder der Burg Karlstein in Böhmen*, Prague, 1896; A. Stange, *Deutsche Malerei der Gotik*, vol. 2, Berlin, 1936; Prague, Universita Karlova, Ustav pro dějinyuměni, *Gothic Painting in Bohemia, 1350–1450*, by A. Matějček and J. Pešina, 4th ed., Prague, 1956.

EDWARD P. LAWSON

KARNAK. Arabic name (meaning fortified palace) of a modern village in Egypt given to the complex of ruins that was originally Northern Thebes. An avenue of sphinxes 1.86 miles long connected the Temple of Khons at Karnak to that of Amun at Luxor in Southern Thebes. The complex consists of several temples, three of which are enclosed, each within a girdle wall of brickwork.

The largest enclosure is that of the Great Temple of Amun, flanked on the south by that of his consort Mut and on the north by that of Mont, the original god of the district. The Great Temple of Amun is the largest cult temple in Egypt, under construction from the Middle Kingdom until the Kushite dynasty (2060 B.C.–7th cent. B.C.). It is enclosed within a temenos wall measuring about 1,542

Karlstein Castle, built 1348–65 by Mathieu d'Arras and Peter Parler.

by 2,037 feet. The temple proper has a rectangular outline (1,066 by 295–328 ft.) with an axis perpendicular to the east bank of the Nile. It is an excellent example of the growth of a temple by accretion, where the courtyards and pylons were added by successive Pharaohs. There are six pylons in the main part of the temple. It is connected on the south to the Temple of Mut by four courtyards and four pylons. *See also* SESOSTRIS I, STATION CHAPEL OF.

The great Hypostyle Hall at Karnak (ca. 338 by 170 ft.) is a stupendous architectural achievement. It has two rows of 12 large, open papyriform columns (ca. 69 ft. high) along the nave and 122 smaller bundle papyriform columns in both aisles. The sacred lake, used for religious festivals, has a rectangular plan and is provided with retaining walls. It is located south of the earliest part of the temple. In the northern corner of the enclosure is a colossal scarab set on a base, dedicated by Amenhotep III to the sun god Atum-Khepreʻ. Behind the ruins dating from the Middle Kingdom is the great Festival Hall built by Thutmose III for his jubilee. It is set transversely to the longitudinal axis of the Temple of Amun and has a unique hypostyle hall. In the three central aisles there are tent-pole columns tapering upward and topped with bell-shaped capitals. The two lateral aisles are lower and bordered by pillars. The hall served later as a Coptic church. Several of the other rooms of the temple contain some interesting elements, the most important being the Karnak Table (southwest corner), with a list of the Pharaohs and the

botanical room (center east) with reliefs representing Syrian plants and animals.

Beyond the four courtyards and pylons south of the Temple of Amun, an avenue of sphinxes leads to the gateway in the girdle wall of the Temple of Mut, enclosing also the temples of Amenhotep III (northwest) and Rameses II (southeast). Colonnades, freestanding and forming porches in front of the pylon, or in rows flanking the axial alley, or in porticoes along three sides of the courtyard, as well as numerous colossi of Amenhotep III and statues of the goddess Sekhmet, characterize the style. A horseshoe-shaped sacred lake surrounds the rear part of the structure on three sides.

The architecture at Karnak is on a colossal scale and is not marred by the deterioration of style that appears later in the Ramesside mortuary temples in Western Thebes. Extensive reliefs depicting historical scenes, covering the pylons and the external walls, characterize religious buildings dating from the Empire.

BIBLIOGRAPHY. G. Legrain, *Les Temples de Karnak*, Brussels, 1929; A. Varille and C. Robichon, *Rapports de fouilles à Karnak (Nord)*, Cairo, 4 vols., 1943–54; A. Schwaller de Lubicz, *The Temples of Karnak*, 2 vols., London, 1962.

ALEXANDER M. BADAWY

KARTTIKEYA. Hindu god of war and the planet Mars, son of Śiva and Pārvatī or Gaṅgā. Kārttikeya is also called Skanda, or Kumāra, the "youth."

KASAKOV, MATVEI FEODOROVICH. Russian architect (1733–1812). He worked in Moscow. One of the most gifted and influential architects of the neoclassical period in his country, he is responsible for the second palace at Tsaritsyn (now Stalingrad) and the new palace at the Kremlin, as well as for the Senate, which is the most classical of all his buildings. *See* KREMLIN, MOSCOW.

BIBLIOGRAPHY. G. H. Hamilton, *The Art and Architecture of Russia*, Baltimore, 1954.

KASCHAU CATHEDRAL, *see* KASSA CATHEDRAL.

KASCHAUER, JAKOB. Austrian painter and sculptor (fl. 15th cent.). First mentioned in 1429 while working in Vienna, he is believed to have been of Bohemian origin. His greatest work is the altar of the Freising Cathedral, which exists only in fragments in Munich and Stuttgart museums. It exhibits a style that is transitional between the decorative style of the first half of the 15th century and the naturalism of the mid-century.

BIBLIOGRAPHY. W. Pinder, *Die deutsche Plastik des 15. Jahrhunderts*, Munich, 1924.

KASHAN CERAMICS, *see* ISLAMIC POTTERY AND TILES (SALJUK PERIOD).

KASHMIR. Northwestern state of India, bordered on the west by Pakistan, on the north by China, and on the east by Tibet. It is in dispute between India and Pakistan, which controls some of its territory. The art of Kashmir reflects its position as a frontier region. During the reign of Lalitāditya (725–756) Kashmir reached its greatest size. Lalitāditya built many temples, including the great Sun Temple at Martand, which incorporated influences of late Roman and Syrian architecture as well as elements from

Karnak. Hypostyle Hall of Ramses II, 19th dynasty.

Indian art such as Gupta plinths, ceilings of intersecting squares, capped gables, and sharply slanted double-pyramid rooftops. He decorated the stūpa at Pandrethan with sculptures in the Chinese manner of the Wei dynasty. However, the artists of Kashmir invented the three-faced Vishnu image, depicting the god's royal, boar, and lion qualities at the same time, and Indian artists adopted this type.

After Lalitāditya, a succession of kingdoms struggled with one another, and Kashmir became unimportant until its conversion to Islam in the 16th century.

Gandhāran sculpture came to Kashmir as painted stucco in the 3d century A.D., spreading from there into Central Asia. It was made of stucco in Kashmir, since its usual material, phyllite, was not available there. The artistic production varied greatly in quality because of demands for quantities of decorative reliefs. New modes in stucco developed in Afghanistan, and this Hellenistic style dominated the cultural developments that followed in Kashmir. The Gandhāran impact did not fade away until the 10th century.

In all this artistic cross fertilization, the impact of Indian Gupta art was felt in the 6th and 7th centuries. Paradoxically, it was influential almost at the same time that Lalitāditya's capital of Parihasapura was started, with a giant Buddha figure (now lost) patterned after the great Buddha at Bāmiyān. The elegant dignity of the Gupta manner existed in the buildings, such as those at Martand. Walls suggest movement within themselves, with recesses for windows with perforated stone slabs that alternate with projections. Images in niches are crowned by monster faces. Heavy interiors are structured by vertical and horizontal friezes of figures. Yet in this array there is a sense of weakness undermining a once-strong vision, falling into self-consciousness and a concern for luxury.

Painting in the 10th and 11th centuries was influenced by the Pala paintings of Bengal; the illuminated manuscripts have bright colors and hard lines. In the 18th century the Kangra style was introduced. The miniature tempera paintings produced in Kashmir were made for the court in book form and reveal a manner of delicate grace in depicting the story of the Hindu god Krishna as a romantic tale as well as one of divine love. Mural painting, show-ing some Gupta influence, is known only from examples outside Kashmir in western Tibet. The remaining paintings in eastern Kashmir, or Ladakh, are completely religious Buddhist paintings done with the complexity and symmetry of Tibetan painting, filled with gods, demons, and Buddhas, striving for serenity within a field of excitement.

BIBLIOGRAPHY. H. Goetz, *India, Five Thousand Years of Indian Art*, New York, 1959.

JOHN BRZOSTOSKI

KASR AL-HAIR AL-GHARBI, see ISLAM (EVOLUTION OF STYLE).

KASR-IBN-WARDAN. East Christian mid-6th-century church and palace in Syria. A tall, domed, and centralized structure, the church is chiefly of interest as an example of the forms of the time of Justinian in which combinations of central and longitudinal axes were sought.

BIBLIOGRAPHY. H. C. Butler, *Early Christian Churches in Syria*, ed. and completed by E. B. Smith, Princeton, 1929.

KASSA (Kaschau, Kosice) CATHEDRAL. Hungarian cathedral of St. Elizabeth, now in Czechoslovakia, originally built in the middle of the 13th century with a single nave and a polygonal choir. This structure burned in the late 14th century. A new building was begun in the early 15th century, employing a French basilican plan with nave and two aisles, although this was changed to include two additional aisles during the restoration of 1877–96. The north portal has a sculptural program with a *Last Judgment* at the center.

BIBLIOGRAPHY. A. Hekler, *Ungarische Kunstgeschichte*, Berlin, 1937.

KASSEL: STATE PICTURE COLLECTIONS. Founded in 1779 as the Museum Fridericianum, the first public museum in Germany. The beginnings of the collection can be dated to the time that William IV was landgrave of Hesse (1567–92).

German paintings from the 16th century to 19th-century romanticism range from Dürer, Cranach, and Altdorfer to Tischbein and C. D. Friedrich. Paintings from the Dutch and Flemish schools include masterworks by Rembrandt (for example, three self-portraits; a portrait of his first wife, Saskia; *The Blessing of Jacob*; and *Landscape with Ruins*), seven works by Frans Hals, and thirteen canvases by Rubens. The Italian works range from the 16th to the 18th century, including two portraits by Titian. There are drawings and other graphic arts by Hessian artists of the 18th through the 20th century and also by such artists as Rubens and Watteau.

Furniture from the Renaissance to the Biedermeier period, ceramics, gold- and silverwork, and arms are outstanding. The so-called Astronomisch-physikalische Kabinett is a unique feature of the collections. It contains scientific instruments and apparatus from England, France, Germany, and Italy. Among these items are the Azimutalquadrant (navigational quadrant) executed by the astronomer-landgrave William IV and Tycho Brahe in 1575 and the steam cylinder (ca. 1705) by Denis Papin, the oldest of its kind in existence.

BIBLIOGRAPHY. H. Jedding, *Keysers Führer durch Museen und Sammlungen*, Heidelberg, Munich, 1961.

LOTTE PULVERMACHER-EGERS

Kashmir. Arantipoc Temple, 9th century.

KASSEL APOLLO. Roman copy of a statue of Apollo, generally known as Kassel from its principal replica in the State Picture Collections, Kassel. It is a copy of a well-known Greek work of the first half of the 5th century B.C. The god is represented standing and completely naked. The hair is elaborately carved, and heavy tresses fall down the neck.

KASSITE ART. The Kassites (ca. 1530–1180 B.C.) from western Iran firmly established themselves in southern Mesopotamia shortly after the sack of Babylon by the Hittites from Anatolia in 1595 B.C. From the 15th century on, the Kassite kings resided at the site of Dur Kurigalzu, the modern 'Aqar Qūf, approximately 20 miles west of Baghdad, where the remains of their immense ziggurat can still be seen. (This structure was thought by early Western travelers to be the Biblical Tower of Babel.)

The excavations at Dur Kurigalzu revealed a palace with courtyards surrounded by a number of rooms, some extremely long and narrow. In one area (H) the walls were preserved; they are covered with a fine mud plaster surface and decorated with paintings of geometric and floral designs and processions of male figures in long fringed garments and tall caps. The figures, standing at pavement level in the doorways, are outlined in red and have red flesh and black beards, hair, and shoes. Above them is a band of geometric ornament. A few terra-cotta works of human and animal sculpture, realistic but small, were also found in the palace. The paintings and sculptures date from the end of the Kassite dynasty.

At Warka, south of Dur Kurigalzu, a temple dedicated to Inanna was built by the Kassite king Karaindash (ca. 1440 B.C.). It is a simple building with a long cella, small anteroom, and two long side rooms. At the four corners are immense bastions. The outside niches contain male and female deities holding flowing vases. They are formed from molded mud bricks. The new technique of molding bricks, a form of mass production, continued to be popular through the Achaemenian period. Stone was so scarce in southern Mesopotamia that its use for extensive architectural decoration was impossible. Similar molded bricks with goddesses and bull men grasping sacred trees were used in this period at Susa in Iran.

The commonest stone sculptures are the boundary stones, or kudurru, carved with emblems of the gods or the image of the ruler. The cylinder seals at first follow the tradition of Old Babylonian seals and characteristically show a human figure and a lengthy prayer. Occasional filling motifs, such as dogs, flies, Maltese crosses, and rhombs, are also included. Later in this period, in the 14th and 13th centuries B.C., Assyrian influence prevails; animal figures and landscape details, mountains and elaborate sacred trees, are frequently represented. *See* BOUNDARY STONES; SEALS: STAMP AND CYLINDER.

BIBLIOGRAPHY. British Museum, Dept. of Egyptian and Assyrian Antiquities, *Babylonian Boundary-Stones and Memorial-Tablets in the British Museum*, ed. L. W. King, London, 1912; T. Baqir, "Excavations at 'Aqar Qūf, 1942–1943," *Iraq* (Supplement, 1944); T. Baqir, "Iraq Government Excavations at 'Aqar Qūf, Second Interim Report, 1943–1944," *Iraq* (Supplement, 1945); T. Baqir, "Iraq Gov-

Kassite art. One of the kudurru of Melishipad II. Louvre, Paris.

ernment Excavations at 'Aqar Qūf, Third Interim Report, 1944–45," *Iraq*, VIII, 1946; H. Frankfort, *The Art and Architecture of the Ancient Orient*, Baltimore, 1954.   PRUDENCE O. HARPER

KASUGA SHRINE, NARA. Japanese Shinto shrine. It was founded in the early 8th century by the Fujiwara family to house their four guardian gods. The main building existing today was built in 1863, but it still preserves the 8th-century form, as the shrine had been duplicated faithfully every twenty years. In contrast to other Shinto shrines, its architectural members in wood are painted bright red in the manner of Buddhist temples. The borrowing of Buddhist forms was encouraged by the fact that the shrine had always been closely connected with the nearby Buddhist temple of the Kōfukuji, which was also patronized by the Fujiwara family. *See* KOFUKUJI, NARA.

BIBLIOGRAPHY. R. T. Paine and A. Soper, *The Art and Architecture of Japan*, Baltimore, 1955.

KASYAPA (Chinese, Chia-yeh-po). One of the most famous disciples of the historical Buddha Sākyamuni. Kāśyapa is often depicted in painting and sculpture paired with Ananda in attendance on the Buddha. In China he is considered the first patriarch after the death of the master and is shown with a very wrinkled face to indicate his age and status. Both Ananda and Kāśyapa are encountered frequently in the first phase of Buddhist art in China, notably at such sites as Tun-huang. *See* ANANDA.

KATO SHIROZAEMON KAGAMASA (Toshiro). Japanese potter (fl. 13th cent.). Katō Shirōzaemōn Kagamasa visited China in 1223 to study ceramic techniques. Upon his return to Japan he settled near Seto, in Honshu, where he had found a supply of good clay. His pieces, consisting mainly of tea utensils, were of an excellent stoneware coated with a brown or reddish underglaze and then decorated by a poured overglaze of brilliant black.

BIBLIOGRAPHY. W. E. Cox, *The Book of Pottery and Porcelain*, vol. 1, New York, 1944.

KATSUKAWA SCHOOL. Eighteenth-century school of Japanese Ukiyo-e printmakers. It was founded by Shunshō,

Kasuga Shrine, Nara, founded in 768. One of the oldest existing Shinto shrines.

who revolutionized the portraits of actors. Shunshō had many talented pupils, among them such specialists in actor prints as Shunei (1762–1819) and Shunkō. Shunshō (fl. late 18th cent.) specialized in the portrayal of elegant women. *See* SHUNKO; SHUNSHO; UKIYO-E.

KATSUMOCHI (Iwasa Katsumochi), *see* MATABEI.

KATSURA PALACE. Japanese villa on the western outskirts of Kyoto. The villa seems to have originated as a small country house for Prince Tomohito (d. 1629), who was an adopted son of Hideyoshi. The Prince was granted this estate by a Tokugawa shogun sometime between 1615 and 1623, and construction of the villa started shortly afterward. More buildings were added and the garden was enlarged in 1642. Other improvements were made in 1658 and 1663. The main structure of the villa, made up of four staggered building blocks, faces a large garden, which includes artificial hills, pavilions, a pond, and bridges. The pond is in the center of the garden and is surrounded by teahouses and lanes from which changing views of the garden may be enjoyed. The Katsura garden is considered one of the finest examples of this type of garden.

BIBLIOGRAPHY. S. Horiguchi, *The Katsura Imperial Villa*, Tokyo, 1952; Y. Ishimoto, *Katsura*, New Haven, 1960; Kokusai Bunka Shinkōkai, *Tradition of Japanese Garden*, Tokyo, 1962.

KAUFFMANN, ANGELICA. Swiss painter (b. Chur, 1740; d. Rome, 1807). From childhood she traveled considerably, and on visits to Rome she became familiar with the neoclassic style as taught by Mengs, which formed her own manner of painting. Kauffmann went to London in 1766, became a founder-member of the Royal Academy of Arts, and lived in England until she settled in Rome in 1782. Although she painted a number of easel pictures, including portraits and mythologies, she is best known for decorative panels done for the interiors of houses designed by the Adam brothers. Her delicate if sometimes insipid manner changed little throughout her life. Her work may be seen at its best in a house such as 20 Portman Square, London (now the Courtauld Institute of Art).

BIBLIOGRAPHY. G. C. Williamson and Lady V. Manners, *Angelica Kauffmann*, London, 1924.

KAUFMANN, EDGAR, JR. American critic, writer, lecturer, and architect (1910–   ). Born in Pittsburgh, Pa., he studied painting in New York City, Venice, Florence, and London. He returned to the United States in 1933 and became an apprentice to Frank Lloyd Wright under a Taliesin fellowship (1934–35). Kaufmann was associated with the Museum of Modern Art in New York from 1940 to 1955; he was director of its Department of Industrial Design (1946–49) and director of Good Design (1950–55), a program of thrice-yearly exhibitions of good design in household furnishings, produced in cooperation with the Merchandise Mart of Chicago. He also wrote the museum's booklets *What is Modern Design?* (New York, 1950) and *What is Modern Interior Design?* (New York, 1953).

He has edited a number of important books on architectural history, including *Taliesin Drawings* (New York, 1952).

KAULBACH, WILHELM VON. German painter, illustrator, and muralist (b. Arolsen, Waldeck, 1805; d. Munich, 1874). His father, a goldsmith, was his first teacher. In 1822 Kaulbach went to the Düsseldorf Art Academy to study with Peter Cornelius. He assisted Cornelius with his murals at the University of Bonn, and when Cornelius went to Munich in 1825 to become director of the Bavarian Academy Kaulbach went with him. He was to continue to paint in the manner of his teacher, whose mural style derived from Italian High Renaissance art, notably late Raphael, from Dürer, and from late neoclassical sources. Kaulbach's pictures were composed almost entirely of human figures, with special emphasis on drawing and on balance and order in composition. The themes were classical or historical, heavy with moral and didactic significance.

In 1826 Kaulbach executed his first important work, a mural in the Odéon in Munich, *Apollo among the Muses.* This painting was well received and led to new commissions, including a series of murals for the palace of Duke Maximilian—scenes based on the writings of Goethe, Wieland, Klopstock, and Hermann. He made his first visit to Rome in 1835, and his second three years later. In 1837 he was appointed court painter by Ludwig I. That same year he painted one of his best-known works, *The Battle of the Huns,* which is characteristic of his grand manner. It shows a spacious area with figures of dying German soldiers having visions of heroes soaring upward toward some Christian Walhalla. The many figures, in stock, heroic poses, are aligned in the curves and diagonals of a compositional formula. All forms are defined with the same degree of overinsistence.

In 1841 Kaulbach illustrated *Reynard the Fox.* He later did the illustrations for the poetry of Klopstock, Goethe, Schiller, and Shakespeare. He succeeded Cornelius in the post of director of the Munich Academy in 1843 and held it until his death. From 1845 to about 1865 he was occupied with a series of six frescoes, illustrating different periods in history, for the vestibule of the great staircase of the Neues Museum in Berlin. A copy of one of these, *Crusaders before Jerusalem,* is in the Metropolitan Museum of Art in New York. These works became well known throughout Germany, as did other of Kaulbach's vast historical murals, through engravings made from them.

His son Hermann was a painter, and specialized in historical genre scenes. Anton Romako was Kaulbach's best-known student.

BIBLIOGRAPHY. H. Müller, *Wilhelm von Kaulbach*, Berlin, 1893; F. von Ostini, *Wilhelm von Kaulbach* (Künstler-Monographien, LXXXIV), Bielefeld, 1906; J. Dürck-Kaulbach, *Erinnerungen an Wilhelm von Kaulbach und sein Haus*, 3d ed., Munich, 1921.

ROBERT REIFF

Katsura Palace, Kyoto. The ko-shoin, a garden pavilion for study and contemplation.

Kazan Cathedral, Leningrad. The plan by A. N. Voronikhin was influenced by St. Peter's and Bernini's piazza in Rome.

KAUS, MAX. German painter and printmaker (1891–). Although self-taught, Kaus was influenced by Heckel and others. He has always resided and taught in his native Berlin but has visited Paris frequently. Portraits, flower studies, and landscapes and interiors with figures are his usual subjects. His paintings and water colors are to be found in museums in Berlin (Print Cabinet, former State Museums), Halle, Hannover, Cologne, Detroit, and Pittsburgh. Although basically expressionistic, Kaus's early style is softened by flowing lines and melting colors. After World War II his work became semiabstract.

BIBLIOGRAPHY. G. Händler, *German Painting in Our Time*, Berlin, 1956.

KAVALLA, *see* NEAPOLIS.

KAWAI, GYOKUDO. Japanese painter (1873–1957). Gyokudō Kawai first studied the Shijō school method in Kyoto, but he became dissatisfied with it and moved to Tokyo, where he studied the Kanō style under Gahō. Kawai later absorbed the naturalism of Western painting and is often credited with having perfected modern landscape painting in Japan. *See* HASHIMOTO, GAHO; KANO SCHOOL; SHIJO SCHOOL.

BIBLIOGRAPHY. N. Ueno, ed., *Japanese Arts and Crafts in the Meiji Era* (Centenary Culture Council Series, Japanese Culture in the Meiji Era, vol. 8), Tokyo, 1958.

KAY, WILLEM, *see* KEY, WILLEM.

KAYNOOT, *see* KEYNOOGH.

KAZ, NATHANIEL. American sculptor (1917–). He was born in New York City and studied under George Bridgman at the Art Students League. Kaz has taken several awards and prizes in competitions at the Detroit Institute of Arts, the Audubon Association, and elsewhere. His work is represented in the Brooklyn Museum, the Whitney Museum of American Art in New York, and the Museum of Modern Art in New York. *Cyrano* (1950; Whitney Museum of American Art), one of his best-known works, is a provocative combination of traditional figure pose and bent, twisted nonfigural extensions of body rhythms into space. It is distantly connected with, though it by no means resembles, futurist lines of vibration external to the principal form.

KAZAN (Watanabe Kazan). Japanese painter (1793–1841). Kazan was also a warrior and scholar. He studied painting with Bunchō but later was influenced by European painting, as shown in his realistic portrait paintings, particularly in the new manner of modeling in light and dark. He committed suicide after being arrested for his active participation in Dutch studies and for his opposition to the shogun's exclusion policy. *See* BUNCHO (TANI BUNCHO).

BIBLIOGRAPHY. R. T. Paine and A. Soper, *The Art and Architecture of Japan*, Baltimore, 1955.

KAZAN CATHEDRAL, LENINGRAD. Russian church designed for Czar Paul I (r. 1796–1801) by A. N. Voronikhin but begun and finished in the reign of his successor, Alexander I (r. 1801–11). Built in Italian Renaissance forms, it replaced an earlier church dedicated to the Virgin. The plan was influenced by St. Peter's in Rome and the

Charles Samuel Keene, *Sir John Everett Millais*. National Portrait Gallery, London.

Bernini piazza there. Since ritual orientation was obligatory, Voronikhin set his church on a Latin-cross plan parallel to the Nevski Prospekt and then devised two semicircular colonnades to flank the north and south transept entrances. A third, which was never finished, would have enclosed a large square opposite the west façade.

Even though Voronikhin adhered to the Corinthian order and even though the use of materials is luxurious throughout, the exuberant panoply of the southern baroque seems caught and frozen here. The building owes more to the neoclassicism of the Paris Academy, where the architect studied, than to 16th-century Rome.

BIBLIOGRAPHY. G. H. Hamilton, *The Art and Architecture of Russia*, Baltimore, 1954.

KEATING, GEORGE. Irish engraver and publisher (b. Ireland, 1762; d. London, 1842). Keating is known for competent prints in mezzotint, dotted manner, and aquatint. Most are portraits: for example, *Arthur O'Leary*, after John Murphy (1784), and *Kemble as Richard III*, after Stuart. Keating studied with William Dickinson.

BIBLIOGRAPHY. J. C. Smith, *British Mezzotinto Portraits*, 4 vols., London, 1883-84.

KEENE, CHARLES SAMUEL. English painter, caricaturist, illustrator, and etcher (b. London, 1823; d. there, 1891). He worked first for a lawyer, then for an architect. At nineteen he was apprenticed to a wood engraver for five years. Among his works of this period were the illustrations to an edition of *Robinson Crusoe*. He began to work for *Punch* about 1851, appearing with an unsigned drawing satirizing contemporary French politics,

and contributed steadily to *Punch* and other magazines thereafter. His first signed drawing for *Punch* was an initial in the issue of June 3, 1854.

Keene was an immensely gifted draftsman, admired by such different artists as Pissarro, Degas, Tonks, and Sickert (who made copies of his work). The now almost incomprehensible captions attached to his drawings do not detract from their aesthetic qualities. Keene concentrated mostly on the middle and lower classes. With the strictest economy of linear means, he fixed the forms of a number of English types (the drunkard, the London policeman, the provincial) and placed them in perfectly realized and consistent landscape and urban settings.

Although he worked in black-and-white, Keene's technique included such a wide variety of tones that some critics were led to speak of his "color." His primary means for producing atmospheric effects and the rendering of space was varying dilutions of black ink, but he also used rough paper and unorthodox tools for the same ends. His methods necessitated close cooperation with his engraver. The style of Keene's drawings went from an early relative tightness to a more broad treatment in the 1880s and 1890s in which suggestion was more important than actual delineation.

Keene produced few oils, but he often painted in water color, retaining, however, the style more proper to his drawings. He also made approximately thirty-four etchings of landscapes, portraits, and figures in interiors; they were not for sale, but were executed as drawing exercises and as part of his constant self-discipline in his art. Keene remained aloof from the sentimental tendencies of his time; he was content to draw his subjects as best he could and always carefully avoided pointing a moral. He nevertheless created works that are great art as well as invaluable records of 19th-century British life.

BIBLIOGRAPHY. G. S. Layard, *The Life and Letters of Charles Samuel Keene...*, London, 1893; C. S. Keene, *The Works of Charles Keene...*, London, 1897; C. S. Keene, *Charles Keene: The Artists' Artist...*, introd. L. Lindsay, London, 1934; D. Hudson, *Charles Keene*, London, 1947.

JEROME VIOLA

KEEP (Donjon). Large tower in a medieval castle. The word donjon is an archaic form of "dungeon." Usually the strongest part of a castle and occupied by its lord, the donjon was often completely separated from the other works. Early donjons were usually round, later 14th-century ones rectangular. With the changed nature of fortifications in the 14th-century, the donjon declined in importance.

In Norman castles the shell keep was built on a mound of earth and protected by a wall of masonry, which replaced earlier timber palisading. The rectangular keep, used contemporaneously with the shell keep and introduced from France, was generally four stories high. Standing in a bailey or court and surrounded by a high wall and moat, it was sometimes protected by a forebuilding and contained a large hall with a solar, or withdrawing room, above. The Tower of London (11th cent.) is a rectangular keep.

KEEPING ROOM. Main room in simple early Plymouth and Salem cottages of colonial New England. Entered from a small vestibule, the keeping room with its large vestibule was a combination living room, dining room, and kitchen. Also called the hall, it had medieval English precedents.

KEIBUN (Matsumura Keibun). Japanese painter (1779–1843). Keibun was the younger brother and pupil of Goshun. He excelled in delicate studies of flowers and birds, based on close observation of nature and arranged to form decorative patterns. His paintings were executed in subtle brushstrokes expressing gentle sentiment. *See* GOSHUN.

KEIJSER, THOMAS DE, *see* KEYSER, THOMAS DE.

KEIL, BERNARDO. Danish painter (b. Elsinore, 1624; d. Rome, 1687). After training in Copenhagen, he was a pupil of Rembrandt (ca. 1642–44) in Amsterdam. Active in Italy from 1651, Keil did large-scale genre subjects.
BIBLIOGRAPHY. R. Longhi, "Monsù Bernardo," *Critica d'arte*, III, 1938.

KEIRINCKX, ALEXANDER. Flemish landscape painter (b. Antwerp, 1600; d. Amsterdam, 1652). He left Antwerp about 1626 and by 1636 had settled in Amsterdam. His early works were influenced by Gillis van Coninxloo; they feature the typical Flemish convention of aerial perspective and are easily recognizable from the agitated shapes of the trees. After 1635–40 Keirinckx adopted the tenets of Dutch landscape art: a generally brown tonality, yellowish accents in the middle ground, and a light blue sky, the whole bathed in golden atmosphere. During his last years he moved toward a low horizon and ample skies, in imitation of Hercules Seghers, Jan van Goijen, and Jacob van Ruisdael. The figures are mostly from Cornelis van Poelenburgh, as in *The Forest* (The Hague, Mauritshuis Art Gallery).
BIBLIOGRAPHY. Y. Thiéry, *Le Paysage flamand au XVIIe siècle*, Brussels, 1953.

KEITH, WILLIAM. American landscape painter (b. Aberdeenshire, Scotland, 1839; d. Berkeley, Calif., 1911). He first settled in New York City, where he worked as an engraver for *Harper's*. After studying in Europe, he moved to California and became a landscape painter. His detailed views are characterized by dark foregrounds set against brilliant sunsets.
BIBLIOGRAPHY. F. Cornelius, *Keith, Old Master of California*, New York, 1942.

KELCHS, *see* KELS.

KELDERMANS, ROMBOUT. Flemish architect (d. 1531). He was the most important member of a family of architects active from the 14th to the 16th century. Keldermans went to Italy in 1487 and on his return served as architect of Charles V in Antwerp, Brussels, and Mechlin. His style is rooted in the Flamboyant Gothic tradition but moves toward a transition to the Renaissance manner.

KELLNER (Keller; Kelner), HANS. German goldsmith (fl. Nürnberg). Kellner's life span is not known, but he was a master in 1582, served as a witness in 1601, and the

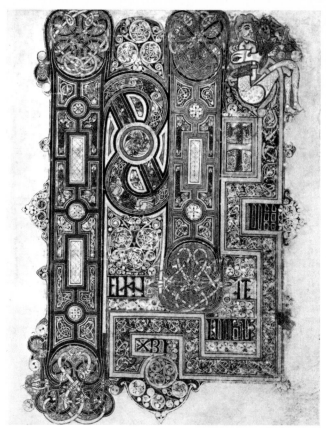

Book of Kells. Opening page of St. Mark's Gospel. Trinity College Library, Dublin.

city of Frankfurt purchased his work in 1617. Kellner worked in the elaborate protobaroque style and the neo-Gothic style of about 1600 to produce some of the finest work of his time.
BIBLIOGRAPHY. M. Rosenberg, *Die Goldschmiede Merkzeichen...*, 3d ed., vol. 3, Frankfurt am Main, 1925.

KELLS, BOOK OF. Hiberno-Saxon illuminated manuscript in the Trinity College Library, Dublin. *See* HIBERNO-SAXON ART.

KELLY, ELLSWORTH. American painter (1923–   ). Kelly studied at the Boston Museum School and lived in Paris between 1948 and 1954. He has executed sculptural decorations for the Transportation Building in Philadelphia (1957) and the New York State Pavilion at the New York World's Fair (1964–65). His paintings appeared at the São Paulo Bienal (1961) and received prizes at the Carnegie International (1962; 1964). Influenced primarily by Arp in his paintings of the 1950s, Kelly used a flat and smoothly but irregularly outlined shape of color on a neutral field, creating an expansive tension with the frame. His recent paintings have depended on luminous color alone to create space, sometimes with several canvases, each a different color, juxtaposed.

KELMSCOTT PRESS, *see* MORRIS, WILLIAM.

KELNER, HANS, *see* KELLNER, HANS.

Kenilworth Castle. Ruins of the castle, including remains of Norman construction, 1160–80.

KELS (Kelssen; Kelchs; Kelts), HANS, THE ELDER.

Austrian wood carver (b. Kaufbeuren, ca. 1480; d. there, 1559). He was the father of the Renaissance medalist Hans Kels the Younger and of Veit Kels. Kels the Elder remains a shadowy figure, and probably did not share in the production of the medals made by his son. In 1507 he was paid by Maximilian I for "a few figures," one of which has been tentatively identified with the *Maximilian* portrait relief (ca. 1506–07; Munich, Bavarian National Museum). The attributed *Triumph of Maximilian* (Paris, Louvre) is probably not his.

BIBLIOGRAPHY. G. Habich, *Die deutschen Schaumünzen des XVI Jahrhunderts*, vol. 2, pt. 1, Munich, 1932.

KELS (Kelssen; Kelchs; Kelts), HANS, THE YOUNGER.

Austrian medalist, sculptor, and wood carver (b. Kaufbeuren, ca. 1507/09; d. Augsburg, 1565/66). The second son of Hans Kels the Elder, he trained in his father's workshop. Kels the Younger went to Augsburg as late as 1541 and became a master as a sculptor. On the grounds of their highly developed Renaissance style, all the portrait medals, such as the wooden model for a medallion of Charles V and Ferdinand (1537; Hamburg, Museum of Industrial Arts), together with the gaming board (1537; Vienna, Museum of Art History) signed "Hans Kels zu Kaufbeirer," are now attributed to Kels the Younger rather than to Kels the Elder.

BIBLIOGRAPHY. G. Habich, *Die deutschen Schaumünzen des XVI Jahrhunderts*, vol. 1, pt. 1, and vol. 2, pt. 1, Munich, 1929–32.

KELSO ABBEY.

Late-12th-century Scottish church. Only the north and south transepts, crossing tower, fragments of the nave, and south choir aisle remain. The plan was unique, like a Latin cross reversed west-east, with the nave just a square vestibule. The upper story of the tower is of the 13th century.

BIBLIOGRAPHY. D. Macgibbon and T. Ross, *The Ecclesiastical Architecture of Scotland*, vol. I, Edinburgh, 1896.

KELSSEN (Kelts), *see* KELS.

KEMENY, ZOLTAN.

Hungarian-Swiss metal sculptor, painter, and architect (b. Hungary, 1908; d. Zurich, 1965). Zoltán Kemény immigrated to Paris in 1930 and worked as an architect, but after moving to Switzerland in 1942 he became known as a painter. By thickening paint with sand and plaster, he developed reliefs. He finally became a sculptor, working directly with metal in an abstract style, and in 1964 he received the grand prize in sculpture at the Venice Biennale.

KEMERYCK, COLYN VAN, *see* NOLE, JACOB DE.

KEMEYS, EDWARD.

American sculptor (b. Savannah, 1843; d. Georgetown, 1907). Kemeys studied in New York City and then in Paris. His chief works are of animals, for example, the enormous head of a buffalo for the St. Louis railroad station. Many of his bronze sculptures are at the National Gallery of Art in Washington, D.C.

KEMP, ROGER.

Australian painter (1910–   ). He was trained in Melbourne at the National Gallery classes. His art is associated with the contemporary Australian school of abstract painting. His low-toned architectonic panels are painted in prevailing colors of red and blue and achieve a majestic depth and resonance.

KEMPENEER, PIETER (Pedro de Kempener), *see* CAMPANA, PEDRO.

KENCHOJI.

Japanese Zen Buddhist temple in Kamakura. It was established in 1253 by a Sung Chinese missionary, Tao-lung (Japanese, Dōryū). The Kenchōji was the first true Zen monastery to be built in Japan, and was designed as a replica of a famous Ch'an (Zen) headquarters in Hang-chou, China. It served as a model for other Japanese Zen monasteries of later periods.

KENILWORTH CASTLE.

English castle, begun in the late 12th century. The remains of the keep, with a curtain wall enclosing an inner bailey, which must have been erected between about 1160 and 1180, constitute the earliest section. The keep is an impressive rectangle with square towers at the angles.

The present form of the castle was established at a later date, for a great hall and state apartments were added on the west and south by John of Gaunt from 1361. There were also extensive alterations by the Earl of Leicester from 1568, including "Leicester's Buildings" on the southeast. Mortimer's tower was the 13th-century entrance, but it was superseded when Leicester erected his gatehouse in traditional Tudor form. The outer baileys were surrounded by an elaborate network of meres (lakes or ponds).

BIBLIOGRAPHY. Ministry of Works, *Kenilworth Castle*, London, 1958.

John Frederick Kensett, *Lake George*. Metropolitan Museum of Art, New York (Bequest of Maria De Witt Jesup, 1915),

KENSETT, JOHN FREDERICK. American landscape painter (b. Cheshire, Conn., 1816; d. New York City, 1872). He studied engraving with his father and painting with his uncle in New York City and then went to Europe (1840–48), where he shared a studio with Champney in Paris and Thomas Hicks in Rome, and resided for several years in Germany and England. Returning to America, he opened a studio in New York and became a recognized member of the second generation of Hudson River school artists.

Trenton Falls, New York, illustrates his early manner of detailed observation of natural growth and classic purity of form and scale. Later his harmonious tones and architectonic compositions became impressionistic in treatment and possessed a wondrous spirit and felicity toward nature.

BIBLIOGRAPHY. C. E. Sears, *Highlights among the Hudson River Artists,* Boston, 1947.

KENSINGTON PALACE, LONDON. Royal palace enlarged for King William III from 1689 by Christopher Wren and the Office of Works. The King's Gallery was constructed after 1694 and the Orangery in 1705. Remodeling, based on designs by William Benson, took place about 1718. From 1722 many rooms, including the King's Staircase, were painted by William Kent, who finished the interior of Benson's Cupola Room.

KENT, ROCKWELL. American painter, illustrator, graphic artist, and writer (1882–   ). Born in Tarrytown Heights, N.Y., he studied with William Merritt Chase, Abbott Handerson Thayer, Robert Henri, and Kenneth Hayes Miller. Kent began, on the fringe of the Henri group, as a painter of darkly tonal landscapes, for example, *Road Roller, New Hampshire* (1909; Washington, D.C., Phillips Collection). The characteristics here evident, such as the strong, rhythmic design and the emphasis on simplified and expressive silhouetted shapes, were to be developed in Kent's large production of paintings, especially landscapes, the result of his wide travel and interest in the symbolic treatment of nature, and in his many book illustrations and prints.

BIBLIOGRAPHY. R. Kent, *Rockwell Kent* (American Artists, monograph 2), New York, 1946; R. Kent, *It's Me O Lord,* New York, 1955.

KENT, WILLIAM. English architect, painter, and landscape gardener (ca. 1685–1758). He studied in Rome, returning to England in 1719 as a history painter, in which capacity he executed ceilings at Kensington Palace in London about 1724. Patronized by Lord Burlington, for whom he did interiors at Chiswick House about 1727, he obtained the position of master carpenter of the Office of Works.

Kent was a Palladian who first expressed this style on a large scale at Kew Palace, Surrey, about 1730. Yet he was also an eclectic, and his "Jacobethan" at Esher Place, Surrey, anticipated Walpole's Gothic revival by thirty years. Holkham Hall, Norfolk, his best-known house, was begun in 1734. As a landscape designer he occupies an important position, having led the reaction against formality to create natural Claudian landscapes.

BIBLIOGRAPHY. M. Jourdain, *The Work of William Kent,* London, 1948.

KENZAN (Ogata Kenzan). Japanese potter (1664–1743). Kenzan was the younger brother of the painter Kōrin, with whom he sometimes collaborated. Both came under the influence of the lacquerer and potter Kōetsu, a family friend. Kenzan utilized a soft-fired, coarse-grained body, which was frequently square in shape. His painted decoration usually was executed in dark-brown iron oxide over a yellowish glaze, although he occasionally used colored enamels. Because of its calligraphic quality, his painting is simple and direct, and is sometimes, wrongly, considered impressionistic. Most of his pieces were designed for the tea ceremony. *See* KOETSU; KORIN.

BIBLIOGRAPHY. R. A. Miller, *Japanese Ceramics*, Rutland, Vt., 1960; M. Feddersen, *Japanese Decorative Art*, London, 1962.

KEPES, GYORGY. American designer, painter, educator, and author (1906–   ). Born in Selyp, Hungary, Kepes studied at the Royal Academy in Budapest (1924–28) and later joined the Bauhaus in Berlin (1931–34). He worked there, and later in London (1935–36), with the effects of light and shadow on photo-sensitized paper and on stage and exhibition design. In 1937 he went to the United States and became head of the light and color department of the Institute of Design in Chicago (1937–43). There he continued his film experiments, for example, *Photomontage* (1937). He has worked in advertising design and interior design. Since 1946 he has been professor of visual design at the Massachusetts Institute of Technology, and since 1960 the editor of *Visual Arts Today*.

BIBLIOGRAPHY. G. Kepes, *Language of Vision*, Chicago, 1944; G. Kepes, *The New Landscape in Art Science*, Chicago, 1956; Massachusetts Institute of Technology, The New Gallery, *Recent Paintings by Gyorgy Kepes*, Cambridge, Mass., 1959.

KEPHISODOTUS, *see* CEPHISODOTUS.

KERKOVIUS, IDA. German painter and designer of tapestry and fabrics (1879–   ). Born in Riga, Latvia, she studied at the Stuttgart Academy and from 1920 to 1923 with Klee and Kandinsky at the Bauhaus in Weimar. Many of her works of the 1920s, landscapes and still lifes, are solid compositions of highly simplified but still recognizable shapes. In the next decade her work became almost totally abstract, at times strongly reminiscent of Klee. Since the 1940s she has returned to the figure, expressionistically treated in imaginative or symbolic scenes, brightly colored and decorative. Her tapestries are usually abstract and decorative arrangements of playful shapes.

BIBLIOGRAPHY. K. Leonhard, *Die Malerin Ida Kerkovius*, Stuttgart 1954.

KERN, LEONHARD. German sculptor (b. Forchtenberg, 1588; d. Schwäbisch Hall, 1662). The effect of Kern's years in Italy (1609–14), where his studies included anatomy and architecture, is evident in his heavy, Michelangelesque reclining figures on the outer portals of the Nürnberg Town Hall, which personify the four empires. However, his known work comprises mostly small figures.

KERN, MICHAEL. German sculptor (b. Forchtenberg, 1580; d. there, 1649). After studying with Jacob Müller in Heilbronn, Kern executed many altars, tombs, portals, and other religious works in and around Würzburg. The German Renaissance tendency to attempt ascendant effects

with disparate and weighty elements is still evident in such works as the portal of the church in Dettelbach (1612–13).

KERNSTOCK, KAROLY. Hungarian painter (b. Budapest, 1873; d. there, 1940). He was a student of Hollósy in Munich and Bouguereau in Paris and of the Benczur Masters' School in Budapest. Taking up the banner of Hollósy, he became the leader of the realist group and painter of the workers' movement in Hungary.

KERSCHBAUMER, ANTON. German painter (b. Rosenheim am Inn, 1885; d. Berlin, 1931). He studied in Berlin and Munich. From an early impressionistic style, he moved toward highly colorful and charged landscapes influenced by Van Gogh, Cézanne, and Matisse.

KESSEL, FERDINAND VAN. Flemish painter (b. Antwerp, 1648; d. Breda, 1696). He was the eldest son and pupil of Jan van Kessel I and was active in Antwerp and Breda. Although Ferdinand is mainly known for religious, mythological, and animal scenes in the tradition of Jan Breughel I, he occasionally painted battle scenes. For King Jan Sobieski III of Poland he painted, among other works, *The Four Elements*, which was later destroyed by fire.

BIBLIOGRAPHY. F. J. van den Branden, *Geschiedenis der Antwerpsche Schilderschool*, Antwerp, 1883.

KESSEL, JAN VAN, I. Flemish painter (b. Antwerp, 1626; d. there, 1679). He was a pupil of his uncle Jan Breughel II. Kessel I painted still lifes and flowers in the manner of Jan Breughel I, and also often copied Jan Davidsz. de Heem and Daniel Seghers. Kessel I's small paintings of painstakingly executed insects, shells, and fish are especially noteworthy.

BIBLIOGRAPHY. F. J. van den Branden, *Geschiedenis der Antwerpsche Schilderschool*, Antwerp, 1883.

KESSEL, JAN VAN, II. Flemish painter (b. Antwerp, 1654; d. Madrid, 1708). He was the younger son and pupil of Jan van Kessel I and was active in Antwerp and Madrid. Kessel II executed many portraits. He was appointed court painter in Madrid in 1686. His best-known work is *Philip IV on Horseback* (Madrid, Prado).

BIBLIOGRAPHY. F. J. van den Branden, *Geschiedenis der Antwerpsche Schilderschool*, Antwerp, 1883.

William Kent, Holkham Hall, Norfolk, begun 1734.

Key Marco Indians. Wooden mask, Florida. Museum of the American Indian, New York.

KETEL, CORNELIS. Dutch portrait and history painter (b. Gouda, 1548; d. Amsterdam, 1616). He was a pupil of Antonie van Blockland van Montfoort at Delft in 1565, and spent several years in Paris and Fontainebleau. Ketel revisited Gouda for a short time in 1572 before going to England, where he was court painter. He returned to Amsterdam in 1581. His penetrating and skillfully composed group portraits are important for the development of this genre in Holland.

BIBLIOGRAPHY. A. B. de Vries, *Het Noord-Nederlandsch Portret in de tweede Helft van de 16e Eeuw*, Amsterdam 1934.

KEULEN, CORNELIS JANSSEN VAN, *see* JOHNSON, CORNELIUS.

KEUNINCK, KERSTIAEN DE. Flemish landscape painter (b. Kortrijk, ca. 1560; d. Antwerp, 1632/35). He became a master in Antwerp in 1580. He specialized in woodland compositions in the manner of Gillis van Coninxloo, with a dash of Lucas van Valckenborch and an imaginative twist that adds movement to the rhythmic in-

teraction of masses. Most of his compositions depict fantastic mountain valleys from which isolated old trees stand out. The figures (small Biblical or mythological scenes) generally occupy the foreground. The color scheme is fanciful, characterized by yellow accents set in opposition to an overall blue tonality. Although he was active until about 1632, the artist's style remained connected to that of the 16th-century landscape painters. An example is *Landscape with the Devil* (Berlin, former State Museums).

BIBLIOGRAPHY. Y. Thiéry, *Le Paysage flamand au XVIIe siècle*, Brussels, 1953.

KEY, ADRIAEN THOMASZOON. Flemish painter of portraits and religious subjects (fl. 2d half of 16th cent.). He was the nephew of Willem Key. Adriaen Key was inscribed as an apprentice in the Antwerp guild register in 1558 and ten years later he was received as a master. In 1580, 1582, and 1588 he registered apprentices in his workshop, and his name is mentioned in guild account books in 1588/89.

Some critics now hold that Key deserves better than the reputation that has hitherto accompanied his painted *oeuvre*. It is possible that he worked during his youth under the direction of his uncle, which would account for the flabbiness of his draftsmanship. Later he drew inspiration from the manner of Anthonis Mor and produced, especially in his portraits, remarkable works of monumental conception and solid technique. *Portrait of a Man* (1580; Brussels, Fine Arts Museum) is an eloquent example of Key's mature style.

BIBLIOGRAPHY. L. van Puyvelde, *La Peinture flamande au siècle de Bosch et Breughel*, Paris, 1962.
ERIK LARSEN

KEY (Kay), WILLEM. Flemish history and portrait painter (b. Breda, ca. 1520; d. Antwerp, 1568). A student of Pieter Coecke van Aelst in 1529, Key worked with Lambert Lombard in 1540 and joined the Antwerp guild in 1542. His portraits, much like those of Anthonis Mor, were highly regarded in his day. His religious works are in the tradition of Quentin Metsys.

BIBLIOGRAPHY. R. H. Wilenski, *Flemish Painters, 1430–1830*, 2 vols., New York, 1960.

KEY (Keyhold). In building, the key is the rough plaster that is forced between the laths of a wall to afford a ground for subsequent layers of smooth plaster or other covering. By extension, it is any rough cast plaster or mortar, or even roughened masonry, used as a holding ground for plaster. It also means the keystone of an arch. *See* KEYSTONE.

KEY MARCO INDIANS (Key Dwellers). A prehistoric group, evidently predecessors of the Calusa, the Key Marco Indians inhabited the southern Gulf Coast of Florida. Their culture was one of fishing and hunting, with supplemental agriculture. While they practiced pottery and weaving, their outstanding art was sculpture in wood. Their style, without peer in the pre-European sculpture of North America, is notable for its restrained, sometimes delicate naturalism. The principal site was excavated by Frank H. Cushing in the 1890s. A number of the sculptures disintegrated or split upon being retrieved from the mud deposit, and few pieces are in existence. Both the human figure and animal forms were represented and most of the sculptures were polychromed.

See also NORTH AMERICAN INDIAN ART (EASTERN UNITED STATES AND CANADA).

BIBLIOGRAPHY. F. H. Cushing, "Exploration of Ancient Key Dweller Remains on the Gulf of Florida," *American Philosophical Society, Proceedings,* XXXV, 1897.

KEYNOOGH (Kaynoot? Keynoogh van Mechelen?).

Flemish painter (ca. 1505–after 1570). Keynoogh, who was called "de Doove," meaning "the Deaf," was a student of Mathys Wellens de Cock, with whom he collaborated. Keynoogh's style was, according to van Mander, akin to Patinir's. No individual work is known, but he may have painted the figures in works of Cock, for example, *Landscape with Good Samaritan* (formerly Amsterdam, De Boer Collection) and *St. John on Patmos* (Berkenwoude, A. J. Rehorst Collection).

BIBLIOGRAPHY. G. J. Hoogewerff, "Matthijs Wellens de Cock et Hans Dooven Keynoogh," *Meddeelingen van het Nederlandsch historisch Instituut te Rome,* V, 1935; C. van Mander, *Dutch and Flemish Painters,* tr. with introd. by C. van de Wall, New York, 1936.

KEY PATTERN, *see* FRET.

KEYSER, HENDRIK DE.

Netherlandish architect and sculptor (b. Utrecht, 1565; d. Amsterdam, 1621). De Keyser, the head of a family of architects and sculptors in the late 16th and the early 17th century, was the first person in Amsterdam to introduce the architectural forms and styles of the late Italian Renaissance. He studied with Cornelis Bloemaert in Utrecht and later accompanied his son, Abraham Bloemaert, to Paris, remaining there until 1591 when he left to become chief engineer of the city of Amsterdam, a position arranged by Cornelis Bloemaert.

During his early years in Amsterdam De Keyser worked on many small objects, such as the wooden model of a figure for the *pokal* (goblet) of St. Martin (Haarlem, Frans Hals Museum). He began work on the Zuiderkerk (South Church) in 1606 (tower completed in 1614) and in 1607 executed a marble relief on the tower of the Spinnhaus. He visited London in 1607 to study various types of architecture suited to the function of a stock exchange. There he met the prominent English sculptor Nicholas Stone, who returned with him to Amsterdam, became his assistant for the ensuing six years, and married his daughter.

De Keyser's Amsterdam Exchange (1608–11; destroyed) was inspired by what he had seen in London. He constructed a triumphal arch for the entry of Elizabeth Stuart into Amsterdam in 1613. From 1614 until the time of his death he worked on the tomb of William I (William the Silent) in the Nieuwe Kerk (New Church), Delft—an immense project combining marble and bronze sculptural work. In 1618 he completed the stone façade of the Town Hall in Delft. His masterpiece is the Westerkerk (West Church) in Amsterdam (erected 1620–38).

BIBLIOGRAPHY. E. Neurdenburg, *Hendrick de Keyser,* Amsterdam [1929]; J. Rosenberg, S. Slive, and E. H. ter Kuile, *Dutch Art and Architecture, 1600–1800,* Baltimore, 1966.

PATRICIA C. FITZGERALD

KEYSER, NICAISE DE.

Belgian painter (b. Santvliet, 1813; d. Antwerp, 1887). He studied with Joseph Jacobs and Van Bree in Antwerp and traveled in Italy, France, and Germany. De Keyser first painted Biblical scenes, and later worked on dramatic historical and battle paintings.

KEYSER (Keijser), THOMAS DE.

Dutch history and portrait painter and architect (b. Amsterdam, 1596/97; d. there, 1667). He was the son and pupil of Hendrik de Keyser. Thomas is said to have studied with his father from 1616 to 1618. A portrait by Thomas, now lost, is said to have been dated 1616. In 1640 he became a member of the Amsterdam stonemasons' guild; he was also active as a stone merchant. In 1662 he was appointed stonemason of the city of Amsterdam. He painted very little after 1640.

De Keyser's earliest extant work is his 1619 *Anatomy Lesson of Dr. Sebastian Egbertsz.* (Amsterdam, Rijksmuseum, on loan from the city of Amsterdam), which was painted as the chimneypiece for the chamber of the Amsterdam surgeons' guild. He also painted civic guard group portraits such as *The Company of Captain Allart Cloeck and Lieutenant Lucas Jacobsz. Rotgans* (1632; Rijksmuseum, on loan from the city of Amsterdam). Because of the liveliness and expressiveness of his style he was one of the most popular portrait painters in Amsterdam until the arrival of Rembrandt in that city about 1632. De Keyser's style is basically conservative when compared with the innovations in portraiture established by artists such as Frans

Hendrik de Keyser, the Westerkerk (West Church), Amsterdam.

Thomas de Keyser, *The Company of Captain Allart Cloeck and Lieutenant Lucas Jacobsz. Rotgans.* Rijksmuseum, Amsterdam.

Hals and Rembrandt. He also painted a few religious and mythological subjects. As an architect De Keyser was responsible for the tower of the Amsterdam Town Hall, now the Royal Palace.

BIBLIOGRAPHY. J. O. Kronig, "Thomas Hendricksz. de Keyser," *Onze Kunst*, XVI, 1909; R. Oldenbourg, *Thomas de Keysers Tätigkeit als Maler*, Leipzig, 1911; J. Rosenberg, S. Slive, and E. H. ter Kuile, *Dutch Art and Architecture, 1600–1800*, Baltimore, 1966.

LEONARD J. SLATKES

KEYSTONE. Voussoir, usually a wedge-shaped block, at the crown of an arch. Keystones are often elaborated with ornament and with sculpture, as in the Arch of Titus, Rome. *See* VOUSSOIR.

KHADATU, *see* ARSLAN TASH.

KHAFAJE. Site some 9 miles east of Baghdad, Iraq, on

Keystone. Voussoir at the crown of an arch.

Khafaje. Limestone statues from the Early Dynastic period.

the Diyala River. Khafaje's history remains obscure, and its ancient name is still unknown. Excavations at Khafaje were conducted by the Iraq Expedition of the Oriental Institute of the University of Chicago from 1930 to 1937. The site consists of four unconnected mounds, A, B, C, and D. At Mound A, which was the most thoroughly examined, architectural remains of houses and five temples, dating from late protoliterate (3200–3000 B.C.) and Early Dynastic (3000–2340 B.C.) times, as well as a large building of the Isin-Larsa period (2017–1763 B.C.), were located in a comparatively small area. Mounds B, C, and D produced some pottery shards of the Old Babylonian period (1792–1595 B.C.).

The earliest Sin temple, dedicated to the moon god Sin, overlies a stratum of the middle of the protoliterate period. The temple's ten building levels, from the protoliterate through the Early Dynastic period, show a gradual expansion and change in architectural form, from an isolated temple to a unit that included utilitarian rooms. Sin Temples VI to X, dated to the Early Dynastic period, are built entirely of plano-convex bricks.

The Temple Oval, the largest temple in Khafaje, is so named because the outer and inner enclosure walls are built in a huge oval. This temple is also built of plano-convex bricks, and its three building levels are dated to the 2d and 3d Early Dynastic periods. The temple site, previously occupied by houses, is three-quarters of an acre wide and was excavated in antiquity down to virgin soil and filled with desert sand, probably for ritual purification. On top of this the temple foundations were laid. All these activities suggest a truly gigantic organization of labor. The rooms in the temple court were used as bakeries, workshops, and storerooms for seeds and agricultural implements.

In the temples mentioned above and the Nintu Temple many cylinder seals were found, as well as pottery including theriomorphic vessels, amulets, stone relief plaques, and stone and copper statues of the 2d and 3d Early Dynastic periods.

BIBLIOGRAPHY. H. Frankfort, et al., *Tell Asmar and Khafaje*, vol. 1–, Chicago, 1932–; H. Frankfort, *Sculpture of the Third Millennium B.C. from Tell Asmar and Khafājah*, Chicago, 1939; P. Delougaz and S. Lloyd, *Pre-Sargonid Temples in the Diyala Region*, Chicago, 1942; H. Frankfort, *More Sculpture from the Diyala Region*, Chicago, 1943; H. Frankfort, *Stratified Cylinder Seals from the Diyala Region*, Chicago, 1955. AYAKO IMAI

KHAJURAHO.

Village in northern Madhya Pradesh, India, renowned for a magnificent group of Hindu and Jain temples. Some twenty temples, out of an original group of about eighty-five, remain at Khajurāho, scattered over an area of about 1 square mile; they were built within a century, from about A.D. 950 to 1050, by the Chandella Rajputs, who ruled over the area from the 9th to the 13th century. Khajurāho at one time must have been a capital of the Chandellas or at least a great religious center; ruins of the ancient city cover an area of about 8 square miles. Prior to the time of the Chandellas the site apparently was Buddhist. A large image of Buddha was found, inscribed with characters of the 9th or 10th century; it is now in the outdoor museum at Khajurāho. The Chandella kings were Saivites but were tolerant, and there are Jain temples and temples dedicated to Vishnu as well as those of Siva.

Khajurāho. Kandariya Mohadevo Temple, Chandella dynasty.

All the remaining temples at Khajurāho, whether Saivite, Vaishnavite, or Jain, exhibit a common style, and there is little evidence of any evolutionary development during the relatively short period of their construction. Typically a temple of Khajurāho consists of three main parts: an entrance portico, an assembly hall, and the cella, or main shrine. There may be a vestibule to the cella, transepts, and a processional path around the cella. The parts are arranged in the form of a Latin cross, with the long axis running from east to west and a single entrance, generally at the east end. The temple is not enclosed with a wall, as is customary elsewhere, but stands high on a plinth of solid masonry. All the parts are integrated into a unified design. The richly carved exterior walls blend gradually into the tall multiple-domed roofs, which culminate in the graceful śikhara rising high above the cella.

In the body of the temple the mass of solid masonry is relieved by balconied window openings and, between the windows, a double or triple frieze of hundreds of human figures in a variety of poses. The interior columns and ceilings are elaborately carved. The sculptured figures of Khajurāho, which are almost fully in the round, are famous for their animated gestures and stylized beauty of form. Many of the poses are erotic in nature, probably representing a religious symbolism of the time.

See also INDIA (EVOLUTION OF TEMPLE AND CAVE ARCHITECTURE AND SCULPTURE).

BIBLIOGRAPHY. B. L. Dhama and S. C. Chandra, *Khajurāho*, Delhi, 1953; *Mārg*, X, June, 1957 (issue on Khajurāho); P. Brown, *Indian Architecture*, 4th ed., vol. 1: *Buddhist and Hindu Periods*, 4th ed., Bombay, 1959. CHARLES D. WEBER

KHANDAGIRI AND UDAYAGIRI, ORISSA. Hill sites near Bhuvaneshvar in Orissa, India, in which are carved Jain monasteries of the 1st and 2d centuries A.D. Each monument has cells arranged around three sides of an open court and several have façades decorated with religious and animal sculptures, including the Hāthī Gumphā, the Rānī Gumphā, and the Bāgh Gumphā.

KHARGIRD MADRASA, *see* SALJUK ARCHITECTURE (IRAN).

KHASI. Method of wall decoration popular in India and Persia. Walls are covered with glazed and painted tiles or with blocks of mortar made up of variously shaped and colored pieces in decorative patterns.

KHASNE (Khazneh), TOMB OF, PETRA, *see* PETRA.

KHEKER FRIEZE. In Egyptian art, the uppermost ornamental band of vertical elements imitating the bound tufts at the top of a partition made of plant stems. Already stylized and translated into stone in the 3d dynasty (funerary structures of Djeser at Saqqara), it was a common feature at the top of mural compositions and furniture. *Kheker* in Egyptian means "adorn."

BIBLIOGRAPHY. A. Badawy, *A History of Egyptian Architecture*, vol. 1, Giza, 1954.

KHMER ART. The Khmers, a people of mixed and unclear ancestry, developed a great civilization in the area of modern Cambodia, including at times parts of Thailand, Laos, and Vietnam. It lasted some thirteen centuries, with a cultural zenith at Angkor from the 9th to the 12th century. The art of the Khmers, like their religion and many of their other cultural institutions, was closely related to that of India. However, Khmer art is no mere provincial offshoot of Indian art; rather it is a local art, sparked into being and constantly stimulated by contacts with India. *See* CAMBODIA.

The few works of art remaining from the earliest periods—the time of the Fu-Nan state (1st century of our era–ca. 550) and its successor, the Chen-la state (ca. 550–802)—are often called early Khmer, pre-Khmer, Indo-Khmer, or pre-Angkorian. Stone carvings of Buddha, Vishnu, and Krishna of Fu-Nan are close to the Indian late Gupta style, but the sense of volume and aesthetic independence from the architectural setting are more profound. Chen-la sculpture, known best in gently swelling, rounded feminine figures and monumental, elegant figures of Vishnu and Hari-Hara, possesses a distinctive, native Khmer vitality. Early Khmer architecture, largely in ruinous condition, is distinguished by ornate, beautifully carved stone lintels.

The Angkor period saw the revitalization of the nation after the disintegration of Chen-la and a period of Javanese domination. It lasted until the final disintegration of the Khmer civilization in the 15th century, producing what is perhaps the greatest and most impressive series of architectural complexes in the history of mankind, reaching its culmination in the grandest monument of the Khmers, Angkor Vat.

Based in part on the concept of Devarāja, the divinity of the king who upon his death became identified with one of the major deities, Siva, or Vishnu, or even Bud-

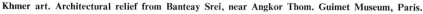

Khmer art. Architectural relief from Banteay Srei, near Angkor Thom. Guimet Museum, Paris.

dha, the Khmer temple became a physical symbol of the religious order of the universe. In the center of a walled enclosure, representing the world, stood the main shrine, representing Mt. Meru, the home of the gods. It was the residence of the chief deity of the temple, who dwelled there in the form of his image. Smaller shrines for accessory deities were arranged in geometric plan around the central shrine. The whole, a symbol of cosmic order, was square or rectangular and was oriented to the points of the compass, usually facing east. Sculptured scenes on the walls showed the exploits of the gods or worshipers paying homage. All elements, sculptural as well as architectural, were subordinated to the total expression of rhythmic proportion and absolute harmony. The miles of complex, calligraphic relief sculptures have a special refinement and grace that differentiate them from their Indian sources.

BIBLIOGRAPHY. G. de Coral Rémusat, *L'Art khmer, les grandes étapes de son évolution*, Paris, 1940; L. P. Briggs, "The Ancient Khmer Empire," *Transactions of the American Philosophical Society*, New Series, XLI, 1951; B. P. Groslier, *The Art of Indochina*, American ed., New York, 1962; G. Coedès, *Angkor*, tr. and ed. E. F. Gardiner, New York, 1963; M. Giteau, *Khmer Sculpture and the Angkor Civilization*, New York, 1966.   CHARLES D. WEBER

KHORSABAD (Dur Sharrukin).

Residential city of Sargon II (722–705 B.C.) of Assyria, northeast of Nineveh, Iraq. Built in the desert, it was left incomplete at Sargon's death.

Its enclosure wall is quadrangular (ca. 5,600 by 6,000 ft.) and oriented to the cardinal points of the compass at its corners. Buttresses appear at regular intervals on its external face and seven gateways protrude from both the inside and the outside of the wall, two on each side, except for the northwest wall, which has only one. Each gate consists of two towers flanking the entrance and two transverse rooms. Gypsum slabs set upright as orthostates lined the lower part of the wall.

Only the two groups of monumental buildings have left traces on their platforms; the private houses have disappeared, although the early excavators reported an orthogonal system of streets. A platform abuts the northwest wall and is surrounded by a buttressed wall forming a citadel. Of its two gateways, the main one opens onto a square flanked by two groups of administrative buildings. At the rear of this court is a broad ramp leading to a higher platform upon which the palace of Sargon was built, protruding boldly from the alignment of the city wall in order to control any attack made against that side. The citadel gates are similar to those of the city wall, with colossal, monolithic man-headed bulls guarding the entrance. *See* KHORSABAD: WINGED BULL; SARGON II, PALACE OF.

Connected to the south corner of the palace by a bridge, the Temple of Nabu, oriented differently, was accessible from the street that ran south of the square. It was set on a platform of baked brick in bitumen, accessible by means of a ramp and ornamented with a top row of terra-cotta pegs with glazed heads. The portal of the temple was flanked by two towers, and the second gate had pedestals of glazed brick. Near the south corner of the city enclosure was a second palace on a smaller platform, which also protruded from the external alignment. It featured a series of narrow, short or long halls with a *bit-hilani* (columned hall) and a wide but short entrance hall

Khorsabad. Winged bull with human face. Louvre, Paris.

containing two front pillars, typical of the Syrian palaces. The layout of the streets that led to the city gates conformed to a harmonic system, although the location of the gateways was dictated by the topography.

BIBLIOGRAPHY. G. Loud, *Khorsabad*, vol. 2, Chicago, 1938.
ALEXANDER M. BADAWY

KHORSABAD: WINGED BULL.

Human-headed, five-legged gate guardian of the palace of Sargon II (722–705 B.C.), now in the Louvre, Paris. Made of gypseous alabaster with encrustations of colored stones, it is 13 feet 10 inches high. Four such bulls in pairs usually guarded approaches to the palace. Another Khorsabad bull is now in the Oriental Institute of the University of Chicago.

BIBLIOGRAPHY. A. Parrot, *The Arts of Assyria*, New York, 1961.

KHWAJA RABI, SHRINE OF, *see* MESHED.

KIBI'S ADVENTURES SCROLL.

Japanese *emaki* (13th cent.). The scroll (Boston, Museum of Fine Arts) depicts various adventures of the 8th-century Japanese minister Kibi who defeated Chinese scholars in academic competitions. Some stylistic similarities with the Ban Dainagon scrolls are to be noted, but the Kibi scroll is probably from a slightly later date.

BIBLIOGRAPHY. *Nihon emakimono zenshū (Japanese Scroll Paintings)*, vol. 5: *Kokawa-dera engie-e, Kibi daijin nottōe*, Tokyo, 1962.

KIBLEH (Qibla). Indicator in a mosque that gives the direction toward which the faithful turn in prayer. The *kibleh*, in the mihrab, or niche, points to the Kaabah, or holy shrine, in the Great Mosque in Mecca.

KICHIJOTEN IN JORURIJI, NEAR NARA. Japanese wood sculpture (ca. 1212). Kichijōten or Kisshōten (Sanskrit, Mahāśri), the goddess of fecundity and the incarnation of feminine beauty, is represented as a noblewoman of the Fujiwara period. Her brilliantly colorful court costume sharply contrasts with the whiteness of her plump face. The statue bears a close resemblance to the Nara painting of the same deity, reflecting a general trend in Kamakura sculpture to seek inspiration from the arts of the T'ang past.

BIBLIOGRAPHY. Tokyo National Museum, *Pageant of Japanese Art*, vol. 3: *Sculpture*, Tokyo, 1952; *Masterpieces of Japanese Sculpture*, introd., text, and commentaries by J. E. Kidder, Jr., Tokyo, 1961.

KICHIJOTEN IN YAKUSHIJI, NARA. Japanese painting (8th cent.). It is painted in varied colors on hemp cloth. The goddess Kichijōten, or Kisshōten, is depicted in the form of a court lady in full regalia standing in quiet dignity. Her plump face and richly decorated costume are in the court fashion of T'ang China, and yet the delicacy and sensitivity in the representation of the elegant goddess reveal a native touch.

BIBLIOGRAPHY. T. Akiyama, *Japanese Painting* [Geneva?], 1961; National Commission for the Protection of Cultural Properties, ed., *Kokuhō (National Treasures of Japan)*, vol. 1: *From the Earliest Time to the End of the Nara Period*, Tokyo, 1963.

KICK, CORNELIS. Dutch still-life and portrait painter (b. Amsterdam, 1635; d. there, 1681). He was the son and pupil of Simon Kick. Little is known of Cornelis's activity as a portrait painter; however, his still-life paintings show him to be a follower of Jan Davidsz. de Heem. Elias van den Broeck is documented as a pupil of Kick in 1665. According to Houbraken, Jacob van Walscapelle also studied with Kick.

BIBLIOGRAPHY. A. P. A. Vorenkamp, *Bijdrage tot de Geschiedenis van het Hollandsch stilleven in de zeventiende eeuw*, Leyden, 1934.

KICK, SIMON. Dutch genre and portrait painter (b. Delft, 1603; d. Amsterdam, 1652). His father was a craftsman who imitated Oriental lacquer ware. Kick worked in the manner of such painters as Hendrick Pot, Dirck Hall, and Willem Duijster. Kick specialized in genre groups of soldiers and small portraits. Cornelis Kick was his son and pupil.

BIBLIOGRAPHY. A. Bredius and W. Bode, "Der Amsterdamer Genremaler Symon Kick," *Jahrbuch der Preussischen Kunstsammlungen*, X, 1889.

KIEL: ART GALLERY. German collection founded in 1857. The present building, erected in 1909, has a notable collection of paintings and drawings from the 17th to the 20th century, with emphasis on 19th- and 20th-century artists from the region, that is, Schleswig-Holstein, especially the northern German expressionists (eight paintings by Nolde, eleven by Rohlfs). Of the approximately 15,000 prints, 16th-, 18th-, and 20th-century German works predominate. Among the sculptures, works by Rodin, Barlach, Kolbe, and Lehmbruck are noteworthy.

BIBLIOGRAPHY. H. Jedding, *Keysers Führer durch Museen und Sammlungen*, Heidelberg, Munich, 1961.

KIENBUSCH, WILLIAM. American painter (1914–   ). He was born in New York City, where he now lives. In 1936 he graduated from Princeton University and studied with Eliot O'Hara, Mervin Jules, and Anton Refregier. He went to Maine after World War II and came under the influence of Marsden Hartley. In 1949 Kienbusch had his first one-man show in New York. He was given a retrospective at the Carnegie Institute and his work was included in the 1955 Whitney Museum of American Art show "The New Decade."

In his best-known pictures, he abstracts the Maine scene—its islands, buoys, pine trees, and sheds—seizing upon details and expanding them without losing the flavor of rural New England. In 1958 he went to Crete and painted the ruins of Cnossus and Phaistos in a similar manner.

BIBLIOGRAPHY. J. I. H. Baur, ed., *The New Decade*, New York, 1955.

KIENLE (Kienlein), HANS LUDWIG, THE ELDER. German goldsmith and mint master (b. Ulm, 1572; d. there, 1653). A silver cup and cover signed "Hanns Ludovig Kienle F. 16 Ulmae 26" (Stockholm, National Museum) is the oldest identified work by a member of this prominent family of goldsmiths in Ulm. The maker, Hans Ludwig the Elder, a master goldsmith in 1622 and mint master at Ulm in 1635, has been identified as the son of Marx (master in 1612), brother of Marx Ludwig (1583–1646), father of Johann Adam the Elder (1628–91), and uncle of Hans Ludwig the Younger (1623–70). Cups in the form of a silver stag with coral horns (Frankfurt am Main, Kunstgewerbe Museum) and of a gilded silver horse and rider (1630; Amsterdam, Rijksmuseum) are examples of Hans Ludwig's mannerist work. As mint master, he probably provided the model for the gold and silver Ulm ducats signed "H. L." (1635) and the gold ducat signed "HLK" (1639).

KIESLER, FREDERICK JOHN. Austrian-American architect and stage designer (b. Vienna, 1892; d. New York City, 1965). He studied with Adolf Loos (ca. 1910), was associated with de Stijl in the early 1920s, and in 1926 immigrated to the United States, where he was a scenic designer at the Juilliard School of Music, New York, and director of the Architectural Laboratory at Columbia University. Essentially an architectural experimenter, his most significant work, historically, was La Cité dans l'Espace (Paris Exhibition of 1925), a suspended Cartesian space grid constructed of rails and planes. His last major work (with Armond Bartos) was the poetically conceived Shrine of the Book, housing the Dead Sea Scrolls, in Jerusalem. *See* JERUSALEM: ISRAEL NATIONAL MUSEUM.

BIBLIOGRAPHY. R. Banham, *Theory and Design in the First Machine Age*, London, 1960.

KIEV. Capital of the Soviet Ukraine, founded before the 10th century. As one of the oldest cities in the Soviet Union, Kiev preserves evidence of Russia's earliest architectural development.

The major monument is Sta Sophia and its monastic complex, built under Yaroslav the Wise (r. 1019–54) and dedicated in 1037. A magnified variation of Basil I's Nea in Constantinople, Sta Sophia indicates the close dependence of early Russian upon Byzantine architecture. The interior is richly decorated with mosaics and frescoes of saints, martyrs, and the family of Yaroslav.

After centuries of warfare and devastation, the 18th century witnessed a reconstruction of the entire monastic complex. The material was brick and stucco, and the style was Russian baroque, with its typical gilded onion domes and bright coloring. *See* PETCHERSKAYA LAVRA.

KILIAN, LUKAS. German engraver (1579–1637). Most important member of an Augsburg family, he was the eldest son of Bartholomäus (1548–83). Lukas traveled in Italy from 1601 to 1604, an exposure that influenced his subject matter as well as his style. He made views, portraits, and designs, all handled with richly imaginative style. Most important are his fantastic morphological ornament designs, for example, *Grotesken für die Wand* (1607), although during his lifetime his portraits were more influential on 17th-century German and Dutch engravers.

BIBLIOGRAPHY. A. Hämmerle, *Die Augsburger Künstlerfamilie Kilian*, Augsburg, 1922.

KILKENNY CATHEDRAL. One of the largest Irish cathedrals, completed about 1275. The plan is cruciform with a central tower and, added later, a crossing vault of the 15th-century star type. Two notable parts of the Cathedral are the Lady Chapel, with its graceful lancet work, and the west doorway.

BIBLIOGRAPHY. H. G. Leask, *Irish Churches and Monastic Buildings*, vol. 2, Dundalk, 1958.

KILN. Oven planned for the firing of ceramic products. It can vary in size, design, capacity, fueling method, period of operation, and temperature attained. A traditional type is the periodic kiln, which is heated and cooled for each batch of ware. In open kilns clay containers or saggers protect the ware from smoke and flame. Muffle kilns surround the firing chamber with a wall that radiates heat and provides the lower temperatures needed to mature glaze or harden overglaze enamels.

BIBLIOGRAPHY. B. H. Leach, *A Potter's Book*, 4th ed., New York, 1949; W. B. Honey, *The Art of the Potter*, London, 1946.

KILPECK, CHURCH OF. English church built about the 1170s. Its plan is a square nave, square choir, and semicircular apse. It is remarkable for its amazing array of Norman sculpture and ornamentation of the chancel arch, south door, and corbel tables—all probably part of a local Herefordshire school.

BIBLIOGRAPHY. N. Pevsner, *Herefordshire*, Harmondsworth, 1963.

KIM HONG-DO (Tan-won). Korean painter (b. 1760). He was an extremely versatile artist who painted landscapes, figures, flowers, and birds. His brushstrokes are more delicate and smooth than those of Chong Son but firmer than those of Hyon-ja. Kim Hong-do's absorption in the artistic life so detached him from the world that he occasionally lacked even the minimum sustenance. Some representative works of the many that have survived are *Spring Journey*, *Lotus*, and *Sea Gulls and Waves*, all in the collection of Mr. Hyung-pil Chun, which show characteristic spiral lines; and *Cranes* and *Peasant in a Rice Field*, both in the collection of Mr. Jai-hyang Sohn. Also by Kim Hong-do is a monumental Buddhist painting on the back

Frederick John Kiesler, Shrine of the Book, Israel National Museum, Jerusalem.

wall of the main hall of the Yongjusa temple in Suwon, Korea. *See* AN KYON (HYON-DONG-JA); CHONG SON.

BIBLIOGRAPHY. E. McCune, *The Arts of Korea*, Rutland, Vt., 1962.

KIM MYONG-GUK (Yon-tan). Korean painter (fl. 1st half of 17th cent.). He excelled in landscape and figure painting, especially of Bodhidharma. His landscapes are characterized by their monumentality. In 1636 he accompanied a Korean official mission to Japan, where his painting was said to have been highly praised. Two of his famous surviving paintings are *God of Longevity* and *Dialogue between the Fisherman and the Woodcutter*, both in the collection of Mr. Hyung-pil Chun.

BIBLIOGRAPHY. E. McCune, *The Arts of Korea*, Rutland, Vt., 1962.

Kinetic sculpture. Gianni Colombo, *Great Pulsating Surface*. Schwarz Gallery, Milan.

KINETIC SCULPTURE. Sculpture incorporating some aspect of motion. Early examples were Duchamp's bicycle wheel of 1913, entitled *Mobile*; Gabo's *Kinetic Sculpture*, exhibited in 1922; Moholy-Nagy's light machine of 1930; and Calder's machine-propelled and later wind-driven mobiles, which appeared from 1932 on. More recently, kinetic sculpture has included movable works, in which the observer can rearrange the sculpture, sometimes to the extent of a complete redesign, as in Kobashi's *Plumbob IV* (1960; Princeton, N.J., P. J. Kelleher Collection), and machines in diverse forms, usually driven by electric motors, with gears, cams, cranks, and levers, as in Ultvedt's *Construction* of 1961 and Tinguely's *Water Sculpture* of 1960. Tinguely, among others, has introduced the element of sound: some of his machines pound at a rock-and-roll tempo. (See illustration.) *See* CALDER, ALEXANDER; DUCHAMP, MARCEL; GABO, NAUM; MOHOLY-NAGY, LASZLO; TINGUELY, JEAN.

BIBLIOGRAPHY. G. W. Ricky, "The Morphology of Movement: A Study of Kinetic Art," *Art Journal*, XXII, Summer, 1963.

KING, JOHN CROOKSHANKS. Scottish-American sculptor (b. Scotland, 1806; d. Boston, 1882). He went to the United States in 1829. He first worked as a machinist, then turned to sculpture in the 1830s. He worked principally as a marble portrait artist and lived mainly in Boston.

BIBLIOGRAPHY. A. T. Gardner, *Yankee Stonecutters*, New York, 1945.

KING, WILLIAM. American sculptor (1925–). Born in Jacksonville, Fla., he studied in New York City with Milton Hebald and John Hovannes and taught at the Brooklyn Museum School (1953–60). King has had a number of exhibitions and one-man shows at the Alan and Terry Dintenfass galleries in New York. He is known for the understated satire of single, elongated figures, such as that of a businessman.

KING DRINKS, THE. Oil painting by Jordaens, in the Fine Arts Museum, Antwerp. *See* JORDAENS, JACOB.

KINGMAN RIOFRIO, EDUARDO. Ecuadorian painter (1913–). Born in Loja, he was a pupil at the School of Fine Arts in Quito under Victor Mideros and collaborated with Camilo Egas in New York, producing paintings for the New York World's Fair of 1939. In 1947 he became director of the National Museum and of the National Artistic Patrimony of Ecuador. As a painter, illustrator, and printmaker, he has been deeply influenced by the Mexican muralists, and particularly by Diego Rivera.

KING'S CHAPEL, BOSTON. Designed by Peter Harrison (1749–58), the building was not completed until 1787, when the Ionic porch was added. (Its spire was never constructed.) Though derived from James Gibbs's churches, the scale, carving, and sense of space make this one of the finest American Georgian churches.

BIBLIOGRAPHY. H. S. Morrison, *Early American Architecture*, New York, 1952.

KING'S COLLEGE CHAPEL, ABERDEEN, *see* ABERDEEN: KING'S COLLEGE CHAPEL.

KING'S COLLEGE CHAPEL, CAMBRIDGE, ENGLAND. The chapel is the only portion of the design for King's College that was carried out; its first stone is said to have been laid by Henry VI himself on July 25, 1446. It has an extremely simple interior and plan but with masterfully executed decoration. There is no differentiation at all between nave and choir. The decoration is repetitive: the same window tracery is used twenty-four times, and the same paneled fan-vaulting motif is used throughout. It succeeds, however, in combining a practical, matter-of-fact spirit with a sense of mystery and an almost Oriental effusion of ornament.

BIBLIOGRAPHY. R. Willis and J. W. Clark, *The Architectural History of the University of Cambridge, and of the Colleges of Cambridge and Eton*, vol. 1, Cambridge, 1886; N. Pevsner, *An Outline of European Architecture*, 7th ed., Harmondsworth, 1963.

KINGSLEY, ELBRIDGE. American illustrator (b. Carthage, Ohio, 1841; d. Brooklyn, N.Y., 1915). Kingsley studied at Cooper Union, New York City. He worked in a softly shaded woodcut technique, mostly after Murphy, Tryon, and his own designs. *Century Magazine* commissioned him for a landscape series of original woodcuts. His works may be found in the New York Public Library and at Mount Holyoke College, South Hadley, Mass.

BIBLIOGRAPHY. *American Art Annual*, XIV, 1917.

KINKAKUJI. Japanese temple in Kyoto. It was originally built in 1397 as a grand Kitayama villa for the Ashikaga shogun Yoshimitsu. After Yoshimitsu's death it was converted into a Zen monastery called the Rokuonji, but it is more commonly known as the Kinkakuji (Temple of the Golden Pavilion). Most of the original buildings were either moved elsewhere or were destroyed by fire; the Kinkaku (Golden Pavilion) was the last remaining build-

Kinkakuji. An exact replica of the Golden Pavilion.

ing until 1950, when it too was razed by a fire set by a young priest. An exact replica of the original pavilion, three-storied and covered with gold leaf, now stands facing a pond in the garden, casting a brilliant golden image on the water.

BIBLIOGRAPHY. Tokyo National Museum, *Pageant of Japanese Art*, vol. 6: *Architecture and Gardens*, Tokyo, 1952; R. T. Paine and A. Soper, *The Art and Architecture of Japan*, Baltimore, 1955; Kokusai Bunka Shinkōkai, *Tradition of Japanese Garden*, Tokyo, 1962.

KINNARA. Mythical being with a human body and a horse's head, depicted in Buddhist and Hindu art. *Kinnaras* are celestial choristers and musicians, dwelling in the realm of Kuvera on Mt. Kailāsa.

KINRANDE. In Japanese ceramics, the use of gold with overglaze enamels to achieve a brocadelike pattern.

KINUTA. Japanese name for a shape often encountered in Chinese ceramics that resembles a mallet and is occasionally called a "paper beater." The vase is cylindrical with a flattened shoulder area, a narrow neck, and a flared flattened lip. The neck often has two handles in the shape of dragons or fish. The form is extensively encountered in the Lung-ch'üan celadons, and the term *kinuta* came to stand for this shape of ware with a blue-gray celadon glaze, so much so that the designation "*kinuta* glaze" is sometimes found. Strictly speaking, the term is a misnomer. *See* LUNG-CH'UAN.

KIOSK. Open pavilion; in Turkish architecture, a summerhouse usually supported on slender columns. More commonly, the term denotes a light structure of an ornamental character.

KIOWA INDIANS. A tribe of Plains Indians whose mobility and dependence upon horses led them, as it did other Plains groups, to confine artistic creativity to forms easily transported. Their principal art is painted animal hide, especially in the forms of war shields and containers. The designs on the shields were believed to contain magical powers.
See also NORTH AMERICAN INDIAN ART (PLAINS).

BIBLIOGRAPHY. O. B. Jacobson, *Kiowa Indian Art*, Nice, 1929; J. C. Ewers, *Plains Indian Painting*, Stanford, Calif., 1939.

KIPRENSKY, OREST ADAMOVICH. Russian painter (1773–1836). His self-portraits have a romantic cast, the sitter fixing his gaze on the spectator. He admired Gros and Géricault, but at the end of his life emulated the Italian mannerists and Raphael.

BIBLIOGRAPHY. G. H. Hamilton, *The Art and Architecture of Russia*, Baltimore, 1954.

KIRCHNER, ERNST LUDWIG. German expressionist painter and graphic artist and a leading figure in Die Brücke (b. Aschaffenburg, 1880; d. Davos, 1938). His first interests were in early German woodcut artists such as Dürer. In 1901, while in Dresden studying architecture, he began to paint in company with another architectural student, Fritz Bleyl, and in 1903–04 he attended art school. He then returned to architecture school, where he met Erich Heckel, who joined him and Bleyl in their pursuit

King's College Chapel, Cambridge, England. Fan vaulting.

of art; the three worked in a store converted into a studio. In 1904 Kirchner developed a neoimpressionist style and became influenced also by medieval German art and Japanese prints. At this time he saw African and Oceanic art in the Dresden Ethnological Museum, which proved significant in the development of his future primitivistic leanings and those of Die Brücke. *See* EXPRESSIONISM.

Kirchner's earliest drawings and graphics show a high degree of originality but also reveal strong Jugendstil elements and the influence of Edvard Munch's linear sweep and flat color areas. These sources, together with the flat, brilliant areas of Félix Vallotton, contributed to the decorative and two-dimensional character of Kirchner's early work.

In 1905, with the addition of Karl Schmidt-Rottluff, Die Brücke was organized; and in 1906 Emil Nolde, Max Pechstein, Cuno Amiet, and Axel Gallén-Kallela joined the group. During the summers of 1907 to 1909 on the Moritzburger Lakes they made studies of the nude in nature, and during the winters they worked in the studios of Heckel and Kirchner. As the influence of Van Gogh made itself increasingly felt in the group, Kirchner's color became more spatulated and expressively brilliant. Although they were under French influence, Kirchner and his circle, unlike the Fauvist painters, leaned toward an erotomania derived from Munch, with symbolic representations of men and women portrayed together in various circumstances. Never content with a "form for form's sake" presentation, Kirchner preferred to convert the form of visible nature into a symbol of life.

In 1910 Otto Müller was the final recruit to Die Brücke; and in that year Kirchner produced the group's annual subscribers' portfolio of graphic works. In 1911 they moved to Berlin, and Kirchner's drawings began to run in *Der Sturm*, Germany's leading avant-garde periodical. His works were included in two Blue Rider (Blaue Reiter) exhibitions of 1912, but his personal style was now clear.

The exciting life of the city added a psychological and dynamic quality to a whole new series of subjects that reveal Kirchner as perhaps the outstanding and typical figurative expressionist. In his nudes outdoors, nature is used as a mirror of the artist's soul; the figures emerge from their background in a state of nature, their emotions heightened by conflicting rather than complementary color, by brutalized forms, and by a tense, distorted space. Similarly, the city scenes of Kirchner and his friends (for example, his *Street Scene*, 1913; New York, Museum of Modern Art) have a philosophical intention in their portrayal of anonymous masklike faces moving aimlessly about the streets. Kirchner is more analytical in these themes than in the representations of nudes outdoors, which were more poetic and universal. But both types of subject convey his interpretive attitude, the basic expressionist quality of searching for some deeper value beyond the outward appearance, which he altered by distortions of form, color, and space. His infrequent portraits (for example, *Sick Woman*, 1912; Frankfurt am Main, private collection) are as probing and subjective as his other works.

In 1917 Kirchner settled in Switzerland near Davos, and the rest of his life was spent in a mountain retreat at Langmatt. Now the city philosopher became the poet of the mountains and peasants. His nervous, graphic Berlin style yielded to a more sculpturesque form and a new color quality, no longer stressing dissonances but emphasizing an enamellike brilliance that supports the new formal qualities. This quest for monumentality and serenity is far removed from the spirit of his earlier work. His figures convey the roughhewn feeling of some archaic period, the glorified, symbolic peasants disclosing another philosophical facet of his creativity.

BIBLIOGRAPHY. B. S. Myers, *The German Expressionists: A Generation in Revolt*, New York, 1957; W. Grohmann, *E. L. Kirchner*, Stuttgart, 1958 (Eng. tr., New York, 1961); Kunstverein für die Rheinlande und Westfalen, *Ernst Ludwig Kirchner* (exhibition catalog), Düsseldorf, 1960.   BERNARD S. MYERS

KIRK OF STEIL, see LADYKIRK, CHURCH OF.

KIRKSTALL ABBEY. English abbey whose accepted Cistercian plan was begun about 1152. The exterior is remarkably consistent, with little later alteration except heightening of the crossing tower between 1509 and 1528. The church was completed to the west portal by 1175. The interior has rib vaults to the chancel and nave aisles, based on the Durham prototypes of about 1095.

The monastic buildings follow the pattern of Fountains but, unlike that abbey, parts of the cloisters remain. The chapter house is of two periods: the west parts are late 12th century and the east parts date from about 1230. The infirmary and abbot's lodging are of the 13th century.

Ernst Ludwig Kirchner, The Artist and His Model. Kunsthalle, Hamburg.

South of the cloister is the 13th- and 15th-century refectory, and west of this the guest house and gatehouse.

BIBLIOGRAPHY. N. Pevsner, *Yorkshire, The West Riding*, Harmondsworth, 1959.

KIRKWALL: ST. MAGNUS'S CATHEDRAL. Norsefounded church in the Orkney Islands, Scotland. The choir with ambulatory, transepts, and aisled nave was erected in 1137–52 and lengthened east and west in the 13th century. As the bishopric was under authority of the Norwegian Metropolitan of Trondheim, Kirkwall is regarded as the great monument of the Orkney Norsemen.

BIBLIOGRAPHY. D. Macgibbon and T. Ross, *Ecclesiastical Architecture of Scotland*, vol. 1, Edinburgh, 1896.

KIRTTIMUKHA. Grotesque mask used in Buddhist art. The *kīrttimukha* is usually highly stylized and lacks the lower jaw. It appears at the top of the enframement of an opening, as on the chaitya-hall window of Cave XIX, Ajaṇṭā, and the niches flanking the Viśvakarmā chaitya hall at Ellora, both of the Gupta period; and on doorways and niches of early medieval Javanese monuments, such as at Barabudur.

KISFALUDI-STROBL, ZSIGMOND. Hungarian sculptor (1884–   ). Born in Alsórojk, he studied under Loránfi in Budapest and Brenck in Vienna as well as under Alajos Strobl and Telcs in Budapest. A traditional realist, he is represented in museums throughout Europe. His major work of the post–World War II period is a monument to the fallen Soviet soldier in Budapest.

KISH. Site in south Iraq, just east of Babylon. Henri de Genouillac first excavated Kish in 1911–12. Later, in fourteen seasons from 1923 to 1941, excavations were undertaken by the Field Museum (now the Chicago Natural History Museum) and Oxford University.

Kish consists of many mounds and is divided into two parts by the former bed of the Euphrates. In the western part, the main landmark is Tell Uhaimir with the remains of the Ziggurat of Unir-Kidur-Mah and the Temple of E-Mete-Ursag. These constructions were built and kept in repair by rulers of the 1st dynasty of Babylon and the Neo-Babylonian period. In the eastern part, Palace A and Cemetery A were discovered on the southern side of Tell Ingharra; they are the most important archaeological remains at Kish. The palace underlies the cemetery and consists of three groups, built of plano-convex bricks. Among the art objects from the palace, limestone and shell inlays are outstanding. Pottery and copper weapons and vessels were found in the cemetery. They can be correlated with objects of similar kinds from the Royal Cemetery at Ur (2425–2350 B.C.), from Susa, and from the 3d Early Dynastic and Akkad levels (2350–2180 B.C.) at Assur, Tepe Gawra, and Nuzi.

On the western side of Tell Ingharra, situated north of Palace A and Cemetery A, the Y city was excavated. Jamdet Nasr pottery was discovered at the lowest level. There was also evidence of buildings, but they were not traced. Over this Jamdet Nasr level lay three building levels of city walls and a street. They were all built of plano-convex bricks and are therefore to be dated to the Early Dynastic period (ca. 3000–2340 B.C.). From Y city and its

Kish. Pottery vessel from the palace there, Early Dynastic period. National Museum, Baghdad.

graves come copper stands of cult objects, daggers, a rein guide decorated with an onager, and clay figurines, including a group that represents a chariot scene. Building remains dated to the Akkad period were discovered northeast of Y city. These overlay the so-called red stratum, which yielded pottery, seals, and sculptures of the 3d Early Dynastic and Akkad periods.

In the central part of Tell Ingharra, the Temple of E-Hursag-Kalamma and two ziggurats were unearthed. The temple is dated to the Neo-Babylonian period (612–539 B.C.) from its foundation offerings, but curiously it was built of plano-convex bricks, which were otherwise used only in the Early Dynastic period. Besides the above-mentioned discoveries, there are in other parts of the site architectural and archaeological remains of the 1st dynasty of Babylon (ca. 1792–1595 B.C.), the Kassite dynasty (1530–1180 B.C.), the Neo-Babylonian period, and the Parthian and Sassanian periods (3d cent. B.C.–A.D. 7th cent.).

BIBLIOGRAPHY. H. de Genouillac, *Fouilles françaises d'El-'Akhymer: Premières recherches archéologiques à Kich*, vols. 1–2, Paris 1924–25; S. H. Langdon, *Excavations at Kish*, vols. 1, 3, 4, Paris, 1924–34; E. Mackay, *Report on the Excavation of the "A" Cemetery at Kish, Mesopotamia*, vol. 1, Chicago, 1925; "Excavations at Kish and Barghuthiat, 1933," *Iraq*, I, 1934.
AYAKO IMAI

KISLING, MOISE. French painter (b. Cracow, Poland, 1891; d. Sanary, France, 1953). At fifteen he won a competition that gained him entrance to the Cracow academy. His teacher, Joseph Pankiewicz, who had been to France and had met the impressionists and also Bonnard and Vuillard, inspired Kisling to go to Paris, where he arrived in 1910 and soon became a well-known figure in Montparnasse. He made a trip to Brittany; then, in 1911–12, he spent some time in Céret in the company of Braque, Picasso, Juan Gris, and the poet Max Jacob. During this period Kisling painted Cézanne-inspired landscapes, but the painter who most impressed him was Derain.

Kisling's painting was appreciated by only a few persons until 1919, when he exhibited at Druet's and his work was a great success. He began to free himself from all influences and soon acquired a very personal style. As he was gifted with a Slavic sense of color and a graphic elegance, he became a fashionable portrait painter. Kisling's painting betrays no struggle or anguish but is content to portray well-being and fashionable ease. His color is always warm and creates a joyous enthusiasm for life, which reflected his attitude.

His curves and distorted forms have much in common with Modigliani's art. Like Modigliani also, Kisling was above all interested in portraits and in the nude. He excelled in painting women, content to create a superficial record pleasing to the eye. As a minor representative of the school of Paris, he reflects the era between the two World Wars. In 1928–29 he visited Holland and two years later went to the United States, where his work was very popular. In 1946 he returned to Paris. During his last years he produced fewer paintings. Typical of his best work is *Portrait of a Boy* (1937), in which his brio and verve enhance the effect of brilliant color.

BIBLIOGRAPHY. G. Charensol, *Moïse Kisling*, Paris, 1948; B. Dorival, *Twentieth-Century French Painters*, 2 vols., New York, 1958; B. Dorival, *The School of Paris in the Musée d'Art Moderne*, London, 1960; R. Nacenta, *School of Paris*, London, 1960.
ARNOLD ROSIN

KISS, AUGUST KARL EDUARD. German sculptor (b. Paprotzan, 1802; d. Berlin, 1865). He studied at the Berlin Academy and with Rauch, F. Tieck, and Schinkel. Kiss produced statues and monuments of dramatic composition that exhibit great knowledge of human and animal anatomy.

KISS, THE. Marble sculpture by Rodin, in the Rodin Museum, Paris. *See* RODIN, AUGUSTE.

KISSHOTEN, *see* KICHIJOTEN.

KIVA. Hopi Indian ceremonial chamber. An underground structure, the early kiva was circular in plan; the rectangular chamber is assumed to be a later development. The kiva was reached from the roof by ladders and contained altars, masks, and other ceremonial apparatus. A small round hole in the floor, called the "sipapu," served to communicate with the underworld. The sipapu symbolized for Pueblo peoples the place from which their ancestral tribes first emerged and their final place of departure.

KIYOCHIKA (Kobayashi Kiyochika). Japanese print designer (1847–1915). Kiyochika first studied photography and later learned painting from Zeshin and oil painting from the English painter Charles Wirgman, who was staying in Japan. Fascinated by European etchings and lithographs, he sought to fuse Japanese and Western styles in his woodblock prints. Chiaroscuro and perspective in the European manner mark his prints.

BIBLIOGRAPHY. J. A. Michener, *Japanese Prints*, Rutland, Vt., 1959.

KIYOHIRO (Torii Kiyohiro). Japanese Ukiyo-e print designer (fl. mid-18th cent.). He was a pupil of Kiyomitsu. Most of Kiyohiro's actor prints are of the *benizuri-e* type

Moise Kisling, *Still Life with Pitcher*. Ghez Collection, Geneva. A painter influenced by Cézanne and Derain.

(two-color prints in red and green), and his portraits of youthful beauties, often partially nude, show the influence of Toyonobu. *See* KIYOMITSU; TOYONOBU; UKIYO-E.

BIBLIOGRAPHY. L. V. Ledoux, *Japanese Prints of the Primitive Period in the Collection of Louis V. Ledoux*, New York, 1942.

KIYOMASU I (Torii Kiyomasu I). Japanese Ukiyo-e print designer (fl. 1694–1716). He is believed to have been the eldest son of Kiyonobu I, from whom he learned the art of printmaking. Kiyomasu I specialized in the portrayal of beautiful women and actors, in which he perfected the distinctive Torii style. His figures are often more graceful than those of Kiyonobu, but it is difficult to distinguish between them. *See* KIYONOBU I; TORII SCHOOL; UKIYO-E.

BIBLIOGRAPHY. L. V. Ledoux, *Japanese Prints of the Primitive Period in the Collection of Louis V. Ledoux*, New York, 1942.

KIYOMASU II (Torii Kiyomasu II). Japanese Ukiyo-e print designer (1706–63). He was a pupil and son-in-law of Kiyonobu I and became the third leader of the Torii school. He excelled in hand-colored lacquer prints (*uru-*

shi-e), but his compositions are often awkward and lacking in freshness. *See* KIYONOBU I; TORII SCHOOL; UKIYO-E.

BIBLIOGRAPHY. L. V. Ledoux, *Japanese Prints of the Primitive Period in the Collection of Louis V. Ledoux*, New York, 1942.

KIYOMITSU (Torii Kiyomitsu). Japanese Ukiyo-e print designer (1735–85). Son of Kiyomasu II, he continued the Torii tradition in actor prints, and his work represents the final period of glory of his family's speciality. Kiyomitsu was a profile artist. In particular, his *benizuri-e* (red-and-green prints) portraying half-nude women, have freshness and dramatic grace. *See* KIYOMASU II; TORII SCHOOL; UKIYO-E.

BIBLIOGRAPHY. L. V. Ledoux, *Japanese Prints of the Primitive Period in the Collection of Louis V. Ledoux*, New York, 1942.

KIYOMIZU. Old pottery market near the Kiyomizu temple in Kyoto, one of a group of kilns in the vicinity of Kyoto that was strongly influenced by the work of Ninsei. Usually, overglaze enamels were used over a thick, drippy glaze. The name "Kiyomizu" usually implies that the piece was made in Kyoto in the style of Ninsei. Most specimens were made for use in the tea ceremony. *See* NINSEI.

BIBLIOGRAPHY. R. A. Miller, *Japanese Ceramics*, Rutland, Vt., 1960.

KIYOMIZUDERA. Japanese Buddhist temple in Kyoto. It was built in the early 9th century as a small private temple. The present main hall was reconstructed in 1633. It stands on a steep cliff, and its front, extending halfway over the cliff, forms a spacious stage supported by tall pillars. Two projections with independent roofs flank the stage, creating a complex and intricate roof profile over the entire building. The main hall is a good example of early Edo architecture.

BIBLIOGRAPHY. Tokyo National Museum, *Pageant of Japanese Art*, vol. 6: *Architecture and Gardens*, Tokyo, 1952.

KIYONAGA (Torii Kiyonaga). Japanese Ukiyo-e print-maker (1752–1815). The son of a bookseller, he studied with Kiyomitsu. Kiyonaga became the fourth leader of the Torii school and is often considered one of the greatest print designers who carried this art to its peak. He first specialized in actor prints, but later was influenced by the pictures of delicate women made by Koryūsai. His women are taller than those of the earlier Ukiyo-e masters and healthier and more voluptuous than those of Koryūsai. They are often depicted with stylish young men against a realistic background of Edo scenes, a type that later helped formulate the art of Utamaro. Kiyonaga's poetic and evocative style, combined with grandeur and solidness of draftsmanship, dominated the print field for more than twenty years. *See* KIYOMITSU; KORYUSAI; TORII SCHOOL; UKIYO-E; UTAMARO.

BIBLIOGRAPHY. C. Hirano, *Kiyonaga*, Cambridge, Mass., 1939; L. V. Ledoux, *Japanese Prints, Bunchō to Utamaro, in the Collection of Louis V. Ledoux*, New York, 1948; J. A. Michener, *Japanese Prints*, Rutland, Vt., 1959.

KIYONOBU I (Torii Kiyonobu I). Japanese Ukiyo-e print-maker (1664–1729). He studied painting with his father, Kiyomoto, but was strongly influenced by the works of Moronobu and the masters of the Kanō and Tosa schools. Kiyonobu I specialized in the portrayal of Kabuki actors

Kiyonaga, Ukiyo-e print of two women and a child.

in their most famous roles, and established a close tie with the theatrical world. Bold design and a dramatic concept combined with sweeping contour lines characterize his work, the best of which was done in hand-colored *tan-e* (reddish-orange prints). *See* KANO SCHOOL; MORONOBU; TOSA SCHOOL; UKIYO-E. *See also* KIYONOBU II.

BIBLIOGRAPHY. L. V. Ledoux, *Japanese Prints of the Primitive Period in the Collection of Louis V. Ledoux*, New York, 1942; J. A. Michener, *Japanese Prints*, Rutland, Vt., 1959.

KIYONOBU II (Torii Kiyonobu II). Japanese Ukiyo-e print designer (1702–52). He was the third son of Kiyonobu I and probably collaborated in the later work of his father, making it difficult to distinguish the works of these two artists. *Benizuri-e* (red-and-green prints) bearing the signature of Kiyonobu I are all by Kiyonobu II. *See* KIYONOBU I; UKIYO-E.

BIBLIOGRAPHY. L. V. Ledoux, *Japanese Prints of the Primitive Period in the Collection of Louis V. Ledoux*, New York, 1942.

KLAAUW, JACQUES, *see* GRIEF, JACQUES.

KLATTAU, LAURIN VON, *see* LAURIN VON KLATTAU.

KLEE, PAUL. Swiss-German painter (b. Münchenbuchsee, near Bern, 1879; d. Muralto-Locarno, 1940). Klee has been identified with surrealism, Dada, and nonobjective art. His painting, however, belongs, with allowance for a keenly personal aesthetic, to the development of abstract expressionism and his contribution to that history was a distinguished one.

In Bern Klee studied the violin. He chose the visual arts for a career, but his early training in music is clearly evident in his painting. His works often disclose elements affiliated with sound and the principles of musical composition.

Klee left Bern for Munich in 1898, first studying at Knirr's art school, then working under Franz von Stuck at the Munich Academy. He was confronted by a complex of *fin-de-siècle* sources: Jugendstil, impressionist and postimpressionist exhibitions, Böcklin's somber allegories, and the academy itself. Klee's protosurrealist graphic works of 1903–05 suggest additional influences as well: Goya, Redon, Ensor, and, in all probability, literary works of a macabre kind. He was also stimulated by the traditional art of Italy during a visit there in 1901 and by the Fauvist style (although he did not immediately respond to it), observed in Paris in 1905.

Given to deliberate rather than spontaneous assimilation of sources, he did not clearly divulge a fully mature method until 1914, after his association with the Blue Rider group in Munich in 1911–12 and his acquaintance with Delaunay and orphist cubism in 1912. According to Klee's own observation, it was the stimulation of the landscape of North Africa during a visit there with Macke in 1914 that led him to recognize color as his central inspiration. It is likely that this stimulus served as the catalyst for what he had assimilated from Kandinsky and other Blue Rider artists and from orphism, not only with respect to color but also in terms of a more rhythmic organization of forms.

Klee appears to have found his own way just before he entered the German army in 1914. He continued to

Paul Klee, *To Parnassus*, 1932. Oil on canvas. Museum of Fine Arts, Bern. A mosaiclike work.

paint from time to time throughout his war service, and his work was exhibited by the Dada Gallery in Zurich in 1917. His greatest development occurred after 1919 as he exploited both representational and abstract approaches. He sometimes created works of a poetically sensitive geometry, working during the same period on his unique, personally construed fantasies of plant and animal forms, usually whimsical allegories of creature and environment.

In 1920 Klee had a huge retrospective at the Goltz Gallery in Munich (his first major one-man show had been held at the Thannhauser Gallery, Munich, in 1911), and he was appointed to the faculty of the Bauhaus at Weimar. His intricate teaching theories were published in his *Pädagogisches Skizzenbuch* (*Pedagogical Sketchbook*) in 1925. He was represented in a number of exhibitions during his Bauhaus tenure, including one-man shows at the Kronprinz Gallery in Berlin (1923), the Société Anonyme in New York (1924), and the Galerie Vavin-Raspail in Paris (1925). His work was also shown at the first surrealist exhibition in Paris in 1925. Klee visited Egypt in 1927. He taught

at the Düsseldorf Academy of Art in 1931 and also traveled to Sicily that year.

When the Nazis closed the Bauhaus in 1933 Klee returned to Switzerland. He was given a retrospective in Bern, Lucerne, and Basel in 1935. Klee was seriously ill from a progressive skin and muscular disease during the late 1930s. The style of his painting, once characterized by his remarkably acute linear or fluid nuances, changed to a flat-patterned, broadly drawn, and simplified expression. His imagery, always deeply personal and still whimsical despite the ravages of his illness, was depicted in a bolder but more easily executed manner, sometimes with a single color drawn through with thickly brushed outlines.

It is possible to subdivide Klee's art into many styles, but four major periods may be defined to include the salient changes in his growth. His earliest significant landscape studies in pencil date from the 1890s (*Across the Elfenau*, 1897) and signify a searching, somewhat impressionist, and by all means talented approach. A second phase includes the pre-World War I etchings and engravings of grotesque themes (*Comedian*, 1904; *Hero with a Wing*, 1905) and brush-and-pen drawings, especially portrait studies and landscapes (*Self-Portrait*, or *Young Man at Rest*, 1911; Bern, Bürgi Collection).

Klee's unmistakably individual style emerges, however, in his smallish water colors dating especially from 1914 (an untitled abstraction, 1914; Bern, Klee Foundation) and in pictures in various media, including such combinations as water color, pen, and rubbed printer's ink (*The Twittering Machine*, 1922; New York, Museum of Modern Art), oil (*Dance-Play of the Red Skirts*, Bürgi Collection), and gouache (*Steamship and Sailing Boats at Sunset*, 1931; private collection), continuing through several linear, geometric, and mosaiclike substyles until about 1935. The fourth period comprises an increasingly simplified, flatly painted and broadly drawn series of gouaches and oils done between 1935 and 1940, typified by *Revolution of the Viaduct* (1937; Hamburg, Art Gallery) and *Locksmith* (1940; Basel, Public Art Collections). The latter is typical of his late style, and consists of a remarkably simple, thickly drawn black line through flat shapes of bright red.

Although his style and personally symbolic content are unique, Klee has been strongly influential for his liberation of the painterly imagination. He was one of the most original technicians and theorists among the earlier abstract expressionist artists of this century. His art inspired the Dadaists and surrealists even though he was not actually a member of either group.

BIBLIOGRAPHY. P. Klee, *Pädagogisches Skizzenbuch* (Bauhausbücher, 2), Munich, 1925 (Eng. tr., S. Peech, *Pedagogical Sketchbook*, New York, 1944); D. Cooper, *Paul Klee*, Harmondsworth, 1950; W. Grohmann, *Paul Klee*, New York, 1954; W. Haftmann, *The Mind and Work of Paul Klee*, New York, 1954; N. Hulton, *An Approach to Paul Klee*, New York, 1956; P. Klee, *The Thinking Eye*, London, 1961.   JOHN C. GALLOWAY

KLEIN, CESAR. German painter, graphic and applied artist, and teacher (b. Hamburg, 1876; d. Pansdorf, 1954). He studied in Düsseldorf and Berlin and was a leading member of the 1918 Novembergruppe. From an expressionist style Klein moved toward a mild surrealism, sometimes abstract and increasingly decorative. Much of his work, as both artist and teacher, was in murals and mosaics.

KLEIN, YVES. French painter (b. Nice, 1928; d. Paris, 1962). Klein traveled in England, Spain, and the Far East before settling in Paris in 1955. His first monochrome paintings appeared in 1950 and at about the same time he produced the first of his monotone symphonies, which he later used (1960) to accompany the creation of paintings composed of the impressions left by nude models covered with paint. For the lobby of the Opera House in Gelsenkirchen, Germany, he created two huge monochrome murals and two reliefs using sponges (1957–59). Klein was one of the founders of the New Realist group with Jean Tinguely, Pierre Restany, Daniel Spoerri, and others.

BIBLIOGRAPHY. The Jewish Museum, *Yves Klein* (exhibition catalog) New York, 1967.

KLEINHOLZ, FRANK. American painter and graphic artist (1901–   ). Born in New York City, he studied with Alexander Dobkin, Sol Wilson, and Yasuo Kuniyoshi. Originally a lawyer, he began to paint about 1939. His

Gustav Klimt, *Portrait of Margaret Stonborough-Wittgenstein*. New Gallery, Linz.

colorful paintings are of children, landscapes, and street scenes, in simplified design.

KLENZE, LEO VON. German architect (1784–1864). He worked in Munich. Klenze studied in Paris at the Ecole Polytechnique under Durand and was greatly influenced in his practice by French academic designs. He also visited Italy and England, where he absorbed the spirit of the classical ruins and the picturesque style.

His work, within the romantic-classical tradition, follows the trend from strict classicism to a more ornate Renaissance vocabulary. His first major work, the Munich Glyptothek (1816–30), illustrates the influence of Durand; his Walhalla, Regensburg (1831–42), follows Greek and Roman prototypes; and his Munich Ruhmeshalle (1843–53) turns to Hellenistic models. The Leningrad Hermitage Museum (1839–49) reflects the growing taste for elaboration, and his Pinakothek in Munich (1826–33) is the earliest monumental example of neo-High-Renaissance design.

KLERK, MICHEL DE. Dutch architect (b. Amsterdam, 1884; d. there, 1923). He worked in the office of P. J. H. Cuijpers (1898–1910) and was in private practice in Amsterdam from 1911. De Klerk was one of the principal figures in the Amsterdam school, which flourished from about 1910 through the 1920s as a foil for de Stijl. The Eigen Haand (1917–21) in Zaanstraat, Amsterdam, an exuberantly expressive group of flats, was his major work.

BIBLIOGRAPHY. P. Kramer, "De bouwwerken van M. de Klerk," *Wendingen*, VI, nos. 9, 10, 1924; G. A. Platz, *Die Baukunst der neuesten Zeit*, 2d ed., Berlin, 1930.

KLIMT, GUSTAV. Austrian painter (b. Baumgarten, near Vienna, 1862; d. Vienna, 1918). Klimt studied at the School of Applied Art in Vienna, where he was strongly influenced by Ferdinand Laufberger. With his brother Ernst and Franz Matsch, Klimt set up an atelier whose chief activity was the execution of decorative murals. Klimt's first commission came in 1883 for the murals in the Stadttheater and Kurhaus in Karlsbad. This was followed by the murals in the Steigenhaus in Vienna in 1886.

During this period and until the death of his brother in 1892, Klimt's personal style was not appreciably different from that of his contemporaries, but after a pause of six years, in 1898 Klimt began to strike out on his own. In that year he founded the Viennese Secession and emerged as the leading Austrian painter of Art Nouveau. In 1903 he reached the height of his popularity with the ceiling paintings for the University of Vienna.

In the same year he broke with the Secession, and he turned more to panel paintings (*The Kiss*, 1908; Vienna, Austrian Gallery of the 19th and 20th Centuries), which combined his previously highly decorative style with a more forceful linearism. During this late mature period his portraits were especially successful (*Frau Fritze Riedler*, 1906; Austrian Gallery of the 19th and 20th Centuries) and mark him as an important forerunner of expressionism.

BIBLIOGRAPHY. H. Bahr and P. Altenberg, *Das Werk von Gustav Klimt*, Leipzig, 1918.   JULIA M. EHRESMANN

KLINE, FRANZ. American painter (b. Wilkes-Barre, Pa., 1910; d. New York City, 1962). He attended Boston University and Heatherley's Art School, London (1937–38). His abstract style developed after World War II, at which

Max Klinger, *Head of Wilhelm Mundt*. Bronze. Kunsthalle, Mannheim.

Franz Kline, *New Year Wall Night*, 1960. Sidney Janis Gallery, New York.

time Kline, with Motherwell, Pollock, and other New York avant-gardists, held open discussions in Greenwich Village. His first one-man show was at the Egan Gallery, New York, in 1950. He was represented in "The New Decade" (1955) at the Whitney Museum of American Art, New York; in "Twelve Americans" (1956) and "The New American Painting" (1958) at the Museum of Modern Art, New York; and in the São Paulo and Venice international exhibitions (1957 and 1960).

Kline's action style, strongly personal and influential, is typified in such canvases as *New York* (1953; Buffalo, N.Y., Albright-Knox Art Gallery) and *Siegfried* (1958; Pittsburgh, Pa., Carnegie Institute). He formed powerful, skidding strokes of black in irregular grid patterns on white grounds, sometimes with half-suppressed edges of color appearing alongside the black forms.

BIBLIOGRAPHY. R. Goodnough, "Kline Paints a Picture," *Art News*, LI, 1952; New York, Museum of Modern Art, *12 Americans*, New York, 1956; L. Steinberg, "Kline's Pictures at the Sidney Janis Gallery," *Arts*, XXX, 1956.

KLINGER, MAX. German sculptor (b. Leipzig, 1857; d. near Nürnberg, 1920). He entered the School of Fine Arts in Karlsruhe (1874) and was a pupil of Gussow. When Gussow was named professor at the Academy in Berlin, Klinger moved there to continue his study and, in addition, to work in Böcklin's studio. Klinger traveled to Brussels and Austria, lived awhile in Paris and longer in Rome (1888–98), and finally settled in Leipzig. He was also a painter and an engraver.

In his sculpture he was influenced by Rodin and was reacting against the idealistic work of Hildebrand. He is best known for his sculpted head of Nietzsche (1902) and for the bronze head of the philosopher Wilhelm Wundt (1908; Mannheim), both forceful, realistic pieces.

BIBLIOGRAPHY. J. Selz, *Modern Sculpture: Origins and Evolution*, New York, 1963.

KLITGAARD, GEORGINA. American painter (1893–). Born in New York City, she studied at the National Academy of Design. She paints colorful, strongly composed, and loosely brushed landscapes of New York State.

KLITIAS, *see* CLEITIUS AND ERGOTIMOS.

KLOMP (Clomp), ALBERT JANSZ. Dutch landscape and animal painter (b. Amsterdam, ca. 1618; d. there, 1688). He painted landscapes with animals that recall the style of Paulus Potter, Adriaen van de Velde, and Karel Dujardin. Klomp appears to have developed late, perhaps in the 1660s.

BIBLIOGRAPHY. W. Bernt, *Die niederländischen Maler des 17. Jahrhunderts...*, vol. 2, Munich, 1948.

KLOSSOWSKI DE ROLA, *see* BALTHUS.

KLOSTERNEUBURG, MONASTERY OF. Reform Benedictine monastery near Vienna, Austria. Klosterneuburg had an active scriptorium in the late 12th and the 13th century. Stylistically related to the active Austrian school of manuscript illumination centered in Salzburg, the Klosterneuburg manuscripts show the late, almost unbroken continuation of the German Ottonian tradition.

KLUMB, HENRY. German-American architect (1905–). Born in Cologne, he was a graduate of the School of Architecture there (1926) and subsequently a pupil of Frank Lloyd Wright (1929–33). Klumb was planner-architect for the Los Angeles City Planning Commission in 1943–44 and director of planning for the Puerto Rico Housing Authority in 1945–46. He now maintains an office in San Juan, Puerto Rico.

KLUTH, KARL. German painter (1898–). Born in Halle an der Salle, he studied in Karlsruhe. Kluth paints landscapes, portraits, and figures in a style strongly influenced by Die Brücke expressionism and the later work of Edvard Munch.

KMIT, MICHAEL. Australian painter (1910–). He was born in the Ukraine and has achieved celebrity in Australia for his religious pictures, which are influenced by Byzantine icons and also by Chagall. He is the best known of an Australian group of émigré artists.

KNATHS, KARL. American painter (1891–). Born in Eau Claire, Wis., he studied at the Art Institute of Chicago. His early paintings were impressionistic. Most of his later subjects are taken from scenes and activities around Provincetown, where he settled about 1919. About 1930, with the adoption of a theoretical system of painting, Knaths's work became more abstract. The influence of cubism is dominant, either obviously, as in the still life

Sir Godfrey Kneller, *Portrait of Sir Richard Steele*, 1711. National Portrait Gallery, London.

Mexican Platter (1946; New York, Whitney Museum of American Art), or more subtly, in the linear framework of the forms, as in *Net Mender* (1957; Washington, D.C., Phillips Collection). Knaths's own lyrical approach to nature at times transcends his theories, as in *The Sun* (1950) and *Pine Timber* (1952; both Washington, D.C., Phillips Collection).

BIBLIOGRAPHY. P. Mocsanyi, *Karl Knaths*, Washington, D.C., 1957; L. Goodrich and J. I. H. Baur, *Four American Expressionists...*, New York, 1959.

KNEE BRACE. Diagonal member connecting a truss to a column to provide lateral rigidity.

KNELLER, SIR GODFREY. English portrait painter of German birth (b. Lübeck, 1646/49; d. London, 1723). He received his early artistic training in Holland, where he studied with Bol, and where he may possibly have come in contact with Rembrandt. Kneller also worked in Italy, where he met many of the leading artists of the day, including Maratta, G. B. Gaulli, and possibly Bernini. About 1674 he settled in England. He attracted the interest of the Duke of Monmouth, through whom he came to the attention of Charles II. Thereafter Kneller enjoyed wide reputation and extensive patronage for the rest of his life. He was the dominant painter in England during the last twenty years of the 17th century and during the first twenty years of the 18th.

Kneller's artistic personality took form in the early 1680s and did not undergo any major change later in his career. He was an uneven artist who frequently, under the pressure of many commissions, turned out careless work.

Nevertheless, he was capable of producing, at almost any point in his career, pictures of vitality and brilliance. His pigment at its best is applied with breadth, assurance, and a crispness that is 18th century in feeling. His color and composition do not have the richness and complexity of Lely, but he is a somewhat more penetrating student of character than the latter. Like most portrait painters of the period, Kneller retained a staff of assistants who executed the subsidiary parts of the picture (draperies, perukes, backgrounds, and so on); he himself normally painted only the face of the sitter and possibly touched up the remainder.

In addition to their artistic interest, Kneller's portraits also form an important historical record concerning the appearance of many of his distinguished contemporaries. He painted several series of portraits, including the *Hampton Court Beauties* (in the tradition of Lely's *Windsor Beauties*) and a group of admirals (Greenwich, National Maritime Museum). The best-known and the most distinguished of these series are of the forty-two members of the Kit Cat Club, a social club consisting primarily of prominent members of the Whig faction. These paintings (London, National Portrait Gallery) are of comparatively small size (36 by 28 in.) and show the head, shoulders, and usually one hand. The Kit Cat size, as it came to be known, subsequently remained a very popular one in British portraiture. With Kneller the long dominance of foreign-born artists in British painting came to an end; thereafter native artists commanded the scene.

BIBLIOGRAPHY. E. K. Waterhouse, *Painting in Britain, 1530–1790*, Baltimore, 1953. ROBERT R. WARK

KNIBBERGEN, FRANCOIS VAN. Dutch landscape painter (b. The Hague, 1597; d. after 1665). He was the pupil of Michiel van den Zande of Utrecht, and in 1614 spent some time in Italy with his teacher. Knibbergen was active in The Hague from 1629. In 1636 there was a sale of his paintings. His name does not appear after 1636, but there are dated works by him from the years 1653 and 1665. Knibbergen's landscapes show the influence of Jan van Goijen.

BIBLIOGRAPHY. W. Bernt, *Die niederländischen Maler des 17. Jahrhunderts...*, vol. 2, Munich, 1948.

KNIFEGRINDER, THE, *see* ARROTINO, L'.

G. W. Knobelsdorff, Chinese teahouse, Sans Souci, Potsdam, 1744.

KNIGHT, CHARLES. English draftsman and engraver (b. 1743; d. London, 1826). Knight's life is traceable only through his output, which continued even in his eighty-third year. He was in London in 1781, 1792, and 1826 and is known to have begun his career in a publishing house, engraving portraits for Harding's *Shakespeare Illustrated*, *Sharpe's Classics*, and similar works. Working under or perhaps simply in imitation of Bartolozzi, Knight developed a soft style that has classified him as a Bartolozzi follower. Once he had adopted this soft style, he employed the dotted print almost exclusively, as in the portrait *Miss Farren*, his most brilliant print. His plates were exceedingly popular in the 19th century, and some were sold under the names of other artists, particularly William Dickinson. The list of artists after whom he worked is long; most are English.

BIBLIOGRAPHY. A. M. Hind, *A Short History of Engraving and Etching*, 2d rev. ed., London, 1911.

KNIGHT, DAME LAURA. English painter and etcher (1877–1970). She studied at the Nottingham School of Art and began to exhibit at the Royal Academy in 1903. Since 1912 her work has been shown in many English and American galleries and museums. She was created a Dame of the British Empire in 1929. Her style, based on the old masters, is characterized by brilliant color and vigorous drawing, qualities appropriately effective in her many popular representations of circus and music hall scenes. Examples of her work are in the permanent collections of the Royal Academy, Tate Gallery, and Victoria and Albert Museum in London, and in many others.

BIBLIOGRAPHY. L. Knight, *Oil Paint and Grease Paint* (autobiography), London, 1936.

KNIGHT, DEATH, AND THE DEVIL. Engraving by Dürer. *See* DURER, ALBRECHT.

KNIJFF (Knyff), WOUTER. Dutch landscape painter (b. Wesel, ca. 1607; d. Bergen op Zoom? after 1693). Knijff lived in Haarlem from 1639, and it was probably there that he was influenced by the works of Jan van Goijen. Similar stylistic elements may have been transmitted by such Haarlem painters as Salomon van Ruysdael and Pieter Molijn. In 1640 Knijff entered the Guild of St. Luke in Haarlem. Pieter Joosten was his pupil.

BIBLIOGRAPHY. L. Preston, *Sea and River Painters of the Netherlands in the Seventeenth Century*, London, 1937.

KNOBELSDORFF, GEORG WENCESLAUS. German painter, architect, and landscape architect (1699–1753). He worked in Berlin and Potsdam. On his return from an Italian trip in 1736, he began his architectural career becoming architect to Frederick the Great. He strove consciously to achieve a national German style emphasizing solidity and classical principles. His first major work, the Berlin Opera House (1741–43), correct and sober, hails the new classical spirit. His later Potsdam work is less severe, possibly because of the festive character of the setting and the influence of his patron on the design. As landscape architect, he is responsible for the Berlin Tiergarten and the park at Sans Souci. *See* SANS SOUCI PALACE, POTSDAM.

BIBLIOGRAPHY. A. Streichhan, *Knobelsdorff und das Friderizianische Rokoko*, Burg bei Magdeburg, 1932.

KNOCKER. Hinged device attached to or near a door that, when struck against itself, produces a rap intended as a summons. The ornamented knocker has been in almost continual use since the 8th century (the lion-head knockers on Aachen Cathedral are notable examples) and was particularly elaborate in Renaissance and baroque architectural decoration.

KNOLL ASSOCIATES. Established in 1938 by Hans Knoll, this company is a major distributor of contemporary furniture and fabrics, with eleven showrooms throughout the United States. In 1943 Florence Knoll established the Knoll Planning Unit, where designs for furnishings, interiors, and advertisements materialize. Some notable designers who have created for Knoll are Mies van der Rohe, Saarinen, and Bertoia.

BIBLIOGRAPHY. O. Gueft, "Florence Knoll and the Avant Garde," *Interiors*, CXVI, July, 1957.

KNOOP, GITOU. French sculptor (1902–   ). Born in Russia, he has been a French citizen since 1933 and lives in New York City and Paris. He studied with Bourdelle. In the 1940s he developed a geometrically abstract, massive-formed style, influenced by Arp. Knoop has had one-man shows in Paris at the Galerie Pierre, the Galerie Schoeller, and the Salon des Réalités Nouvelles, and in New York at the Wildenstein Gallery and the Betty Parsons Gallery.

BIBLIOGRAPHY. *Salon des Réalités Nouvelles*, Rouen, 1947–

KNOSSOS, *see* CNOSSUS.

KNOTT, RALPH. English architect (1878–1929). He won the 1907 competition for the London County Hall, which was completed in 1922. It represents the national eclectic Palladian style, much respected at the time, but it is now seen as a manifestation of acceptance and respectability.

BIBLIOGRAPHY. "Ralph Knott" [Obituary], *Royal Institute of British Architects, Journal*, XXXVI, February 9, 1929.

KNYFF, WOUTER, *see* KNIJFF, WOUTER.

KOBELL, FERDINAND. German painter and etcher (b. Mannheim, 1740; d. Munich, 1799). He studied with Verschaffelt in Mannheim and for a short time with the etcher Wille in Paris. After serving for nearly twenty years at the court at Mannheim, Kobell was appointed director of the Bavarian State Picture Galleries (New Pinacothek) in Munich in 1793. He is chiefly known for his excellent landscapes, which on the one hand show strong ties with the great masters of traditional landscape painting—Claude Lorraine and Rembrandt—and on the other, an acute study of nature that paved the way for the realism of the mid-19th century. Among his most famous landscapes are the four views of Aschaffenburg (ca. 1786; Munich, Bavarian State Picture Galleries, New Pinacothek). He was the father of Wilhelm von Kobell.

BIBLIOGRAPHY. C. Glaser, *Die Graphik der Neuzeit*, Berlin, 1922; W. Lessing, *Wilhelm von Kobell*, Munich, 1923.

KOBELL, WILHELM VON. German painter and graphic artist (b. Mannheim, 1766; d. Munich, 1853). One of the most important members of the Munich school of romantic painters, he studied with his father, Ferdinand Kobell. Von Kobell was active chiefly in Munich from 1792. In 1808 he was made professor at the Academy. He is known chiefly as a painter of battle scenes, for example, *The Siege of Kosel* (1808; Munich, Bavarian State Picture Galleries, New Pinacothek) and *Encounter by Bar-sur-Aube* (1832; Berlin, former State Museums). He also painted landscapes that display an interest in atmospheric effects similar to that of Caspar David Friedrich, for example, *Rider at the Tegernsee* (1832; Berlin, former State Museums). Von Kobell's graphic works, chiefly military subjects, number some 134 prints.

BIBLIOGRAPHY. R. Oldenbourg, *Münchner Malerei, im 19. Jahrhundert*, Munich, 1922; W. Lessing, *Wilhelm von Kobell*, Munich, 1923; R. Hamann, *Die deutsche Malerei vom Rokoko bis zum Expressionismus*, Leipzig, 1925.

KOBENHAUPT (Kobenhaubt; Kopenhaupt), GEORG. German goldsmith (fl. 1540–72). A native of Würzburg, Kobenhaupt was admitted as a master in 1540 to the goldsmiths' guild at Strasbourg, where his mark is recorded on a guild plate in the Museum of Decorative Art. The influence of the French and German Renaissance can be seen in such works as the gilded silver *Rappolstein Cup* (ca. 1543; Munich, Residenz Treasury), embossed with scenes of silver mining, Roman battles, and allegorical figures. His work is last recorded in 1572.

BIBLIOGRAPHY. H. Thoma and H. Brunner, eds., *Schatzkammer der Residenz München* (catalog), Munich, 1964.

KOBKE, CHRISTEN SCHJELLERUP. Danish painter (b. Copenhagen, 1810; d. there, 1848). One of the leading Danish romantic painters, Købke began his artistic career as a student in the Copenhagen Academy in 1822. He later entered the studio of C. A. Lorentzen, an artist working in a variation of Greuze's style; he concluded his studies in the studio of C. W. Eckersberg. Købke first achieved fame in 1830, when one of his most acclaimed works, the *Interior of the Cathedral of Aarhus*, was bought by the Art Society of Copenhagen. Købke specialized in scenes of Denmark, especially landscapes, and in portraits.

BIBLIOGRAPHY. E. Hannover, *Maleren Christen Købke*, Copenhagen, 1893; M. Krohn, *Maleren Christen Købkes*, Copenhagen, 1917.

KOBORI ENSHU, *see* ENSHU.

KOCH, GAETANO. Italian architect (1849–1910). He worked in Rome. His best-known buildings are the two arcaded ones (1896–1902) in the Piazza della Repubblica (formerly Piazza dell'Esedra). The grand scale and dignified character of the buildings and their setting make the piazza an impressive addition to late-19th-century urban planning.

KOCH, JOSEPH ANTON. Tyrolean painter (1768–1839). Escaping from academic training at the Stuttgart Karlsschule, Koch went to Strasbourg (1791), Switzerland (1792–94), and finally Rome. There he developed a style of landscape painting that combined elements of the classical tradition derived from Poussin with a harder, more detailed characterization of actual sites (*Schmadribach Waterfall*, two versions: 1805, Leipzig, Museum of Fine

Arts; 1821, Munich, Bavarian State Picture Galleries), a romantic conception of nature, and quaintly archaistic accessory figures (*Bernese Oberland*, three versions, painted between 1815 and 1817: Dresden, State Art Collections; Innsbruck, Tyrolean Landesmuseum; Vienna, Austrian Baroque Museum). In his life and work he bridged the classicist and romantic eras, befriending Thorwaldsen and the Nazarenes, with whom he collaborated at the Casino of the Villa Giustiniani-Massimo in Rome (*Dante Frescoes*, 1825–28). His influence on younger romantics—Horny, Fohr, Richter, Fries, and Preller—was great.

BIBLIOGRAPHY. O. R. von Lutterotti, *Joseph Anton Koch*, Berlin, 1940.

KOCH, PYKE. Dutch painter (1901–   ). Born in Beek, he had little formal training but studied a great deal on his own. In the acerbic clarity and detail of his portraits, figures, and allegories, Koch may be linked with the expressionism of the New Objectivity.

KOCK, HIERONYMUS, *see* COCK, HIERONYMUS.

KODJA KALISSE, CHURCH OF. Anatolian church dating from the second half of the 5th century. Kodja Kalisse is one of the earliest extant examples of the domed basilica. Its three aisles are separated by piers with engaged columns. The side aisles terminate in nichelike apsidioles set into massive walls. An additional nave bay extends beyond the apsidioles and terminates in a semicircular apse. Preceding this area, two bays of the nave are vaulted by a large dome. With the exception of the aisle bays flanking the domed area, the bays of the nave and aisles are articulated by framing arches. The effect is almost that of a segregated crossing.

The church appears to have been part of a cloister, for the narthex is entered through a door at its side that is not axial with the nave. This door is richly sculptured with fine foliate relief forms and with angels holding a medallion. This type of domed basilica had significant influence on late Byzantine architecture and on the Romanesque architecture of southern France.

BIBLIOGRAPHY. O. Wulff, *Altchristliche und byzantinische Kunst*, 2 vols. in 1, Berlin, 1914.

KOECK VAN AELST, PIETER, *see* COECKE VAN AELST, PIETER.

KOEDIJCK (Koedyck), ISAAC. Dutch painter of genre and interior scenes (b. Amsterdam, 1616/18; d. there? 1668). It is possible that Koedijck was a pupil of Gerrit Dou in Leyden, for the influence of Dou upon his work is quite strong. Koedijck was active in Leyden and Amsterdam until 1651. After six years of financial difficulties he went to Batavia and later became court painter to the grand mogul Jahangir of Agra. Koedijck also worked, mostly as an informant and merchant, for the Dutch East India Company. He returned to Holland in 1659 and was active in Haarlem and Amsterdam.

BIBLIOGRAPHY. C. Hofstede de Groot, "Isack Koedijck," *Festschrift für Max J. Friedländer*, Leipzig, 1927.

KOENIGSFELDEN: ABBEY OF SS. CLARA AND FRANCIS. Secularized abbey in Switzerland. The double monastery was founded by Elizabeth, wife of King Albert I, in 1311 and long governed by her daughter Agnes, the widowed Queen of Hungary (d. 1364). It soon became the richest nunnery of the diocese of Constance. The church, a large basilica built strictly according to Franciscan rules, was completed in 1320–30. The polygonal apse contains eleven large stained-glass windows of the first half of the 14th century, which are among the best of the period. They represent the life of Christ, the apostles, and saints and were donated by the dukes Henry, Otto, and Albert VII of Austria and by Rudolf of Lorraine, among others. The St. Francis window, with its red background, is the most elegant example of the courtly series, which was created by a workshop from the Upper Rhine.

BIBLIOGRAPHY. M. Stettler, *Stained Glass of the Early Fourteenth Century from the Church of Koenigsfelden*, New York, 1949; E. Maurer, *Die Kunstdenkmäler des Kantons Aargau*, vol. 3, Basel, 1954.

KOERNER, HENRY. American painter (1915–   ). Born in Vienna, he studied at the Vienna Academy. He went to the United States in 1938. Koerner paints genre subjects with a sharp-focus, photographic naturalism reminiscent of Flemish painters. At times his symbolic themes are treated in a style influenced by the expressionism of Otto Dix and Max Beckmann. The socially satiric intention of Koerner's work can be seen in the panoramic *Vanity Fair* (1946; New York, Whitney Museum of American Art). More recently, he has done many covers for *Time*, in a loosely painted version of Cézanne's modeling.

See also MAGIC REALISM.

KOETSU (Hon Ami Koetsu). Japanese artist (1558–1637). Koetsu was adopted into a family of sword connoisseurs. A great art patron and a noted calligrapher, painter, and potter, he founded an artists' colony near Kyoto, where he inspired many artists. In numerous scrolls and albums he collaborated with Sōtatsu and produced superb calligraphy on sheets richly decorated by Sōtatsu. Koetsu's Raku ware teabowls are surpassingly fine; for example, his Fuji-san is one of the most famous Japanese teabowls. He also produced some fine masks for the traditional Noh drama. *See* NOH MASK; RAKU WARE; SOTATSU.

KOFTGARI (Koft; Koft work). Ornamental work of steel inlaid with gold. It is a technique of Indian damascene craftsmen.

KOFUKUJI, NARA. Japanese Buddhist temple. The monastery was originally founded as the Yamashinadera in 669 by a member of the Fujiwara clan, but later it was transferred to the Asuka area, and the temple came to be called the Umayazakadera. The site of the monastery was again changed, and the present location in Nara was chosen at the time of the transfer of the capital to this city in 710. The construction of the new temple at the present site was virtually finished by 746, and its name was changed to the Kōfukuji. The monastery enjoyed prestige and privileges for a long time as the family temple of the powerful Fujiwara clan. It was damaged by fire and during civil wars, the last major destruction taking place in 1327.

It differs from many other temples in that it has three Golden Halls (Buddha halls) and two octagonal structures, one of which is at the site usually allotted for a pagoda.

The Hokuendō (North Octagonal Chapel), reconstructed about 1210, and the Middle Golden Hall, rebuilt in the early 15th century, were among the first buildings to be completed (ca. 721) in the original construction of the Nara period. There are many excellent examples of Nara sculpture in the Kōfukuji, as well as works by Unkei and his school. *See* HACHIBUSHU IN KOFUKUJI, NARA; TEN GREAT DISCIPLES IN KOFUKUJI, NARA.

BIBLIOGRAPHY. R. T. Paine and A. Soper, *The Art and Architecture of Japan*, Baltimore, 1955; National Commission for the Protection of Cultural Properties, ed., *Kokuhō (National Treasures of Japan)*, vol. 4: *The Heian Period*, Tokyo, 1966.

MIYEKO MURASE

KOGURYO TOMBS: MURAL PAINTINGS. Wall paintings dating from the 4th to the 7th century, discovered in some forty tombs around the P'yongyang and Tungkon areas in Korea. They were executed on a lime-plaster base directly on the granite surface; in only one instance was the painting executed on marble. The technique is the same as that of the Six Dynasties period in China (386–589): the contours were drawn first, and then the colors were applied, bound with a mixture of sesame oil and lead oxide. The subject matter includes human and animal figures in procession, hunting scenes, and genre scenes.

KOHLAN, *see* TIMNA'.

KOHN, MISCH. American painter and printmaker (1916–   ). Born in Kokomo, Ind., he studied at the John Herron Art Institute in Indianapolis. He was in Mexico in 1943–44. Kohn was awarded Guggenheim fellowships (1952 and 1955) and a Tamarind fellowship in lithography (1960). He is best known for large wood engravings such as *Tiger* (1949), and more recently for equally large lift-ground aquatints such as *Lion* (1957).

BIBLIOGRAPHY. C. Zigrosser, *Misch Kohn*, New York, 1960.

KOHOAN GARDEN. Japanese garden of the Kohōan, a subtemple of the Daitokuji in Kyoto. A fire in 1793 destroyed much of the garden and the building, and the present one is a later restoration. Rocks, a stone bridge, and dwarfed pines are arranged on the earthen surface to represent, in miniature scale, the eight famous views around Lake Biwa near Kyoto. Its teahouse, known as the Bōsen, was built sometime between 1624 and 1644 by Kabori Enshū (1579–1647), a noted tea master, architect, and garden designer.

BIBLIOGRAPHY. Tokyo National Museum, *Pageant of Japanese Art*, vol. 6: *Architecture and Gardens*, Tokyo, 1952.

KOIMESIS CHURCH, NICAEA. Church in Nicaea (Iznik), Turkey, destroyed in the Greco-Turkish War of 1921–22. A provincial domed Byzantine structure of inscribed-cross plan, it was a possible prototype of the Macedonian-revival architectural style. The building was particularly noted for its fine 8th- or 9th-century mosaics.

KOJA RABI, SHRINE OF, *see* MESHED.

KOKAN (Shiba Kokan). Japanese printmaker (1738–1818). Kōkan also used the name Harushige Suzuki on his prints of beautiful women. He first studied with a painter of the Kanō school but later entered the studio of Harunobu, whose name he often falsified on his own prints after the master's death in 1770. Deeply influenced by "Dutch learning," Kōkan was the first Japanese artist to employ the technique of etching, showing shading and perspective in the European manner. *See* HARUNOBU; KANO SCHOOL.

BIBLIOGRAPHY. J. A. Michener, *Japanese Prints*, Rutland, Vt., 1959.

KOKEDERA GARDEN, *see* SAIHOJI GARDEN, KYOTO.

KOKOSCHKA, OSKAR. Austrian expressionist painter (1886–   ). Born in Pöchlarn on the Danube, he now lives in London and Switzerland. He studied at the Arts and Crafts School in Vienna from 1905 to 1908 on a scholarship. His strongest influences were Klimt, Hodler, and Munch, and his early graphic works (the illustrations for his own story, *The Dreaming Boys*, 1908) were conditioned by the Jugendstil and Secession manners then highly influential in Vienna and elsewhere among German-speaking artists. Kokoschka knew Schiele during this period.

Kokoschka was dismissed from the Arts and Crafts School because of the exoticism of his pictures and writings, but he was simultaneously taken up by the Viennese avant-garde. His two exhibitions at the Kunstschau in 1908 and 1909 and two of his plays of 1908, *Sphinx and Strawman* (produced again in the early 1920s by the Dadaists) and *Murderer, Hope of Women*, led to violent public opposition. In 1909 he began to travel; later, his trips were sponsored by dealers or collectors. He was active as a consultant to Herwarth Walden for *Der Sturm* between 1910 and 1914 in Berlin, during which time he exhibited at the Hagenbund show, the Cologne Sonderbund, and at a one-man show at Der Sturm gallery in 1912.

From 1908 to 1914 Kokoschka painted a series of the most remarkable portraits of this century, psychologically incisive and highly personal in technique: *Hans Tietze and Erica Tietze-Conrat* (New York, Museum of Modern Art), *Peter Altenberg*, *Frau Lotte Franzos*, *Ritter von Janikowsky*, all 1909; and *Count Verona*, *The Duchess of Rohan-Montesquieu*, and *Frau Dr. K.*, all 1910. Kokoschka was wounded in World War I and discharged in 1916 for

Kōfukuji, Nara. The Higashi-Kondō (left) and the Five-storied Pagoda (right) of the Buddhist temple.

Oskar Kokoschka, *View of Salzburg*. New Pinacothek and New State Picture Gallery, Munich.

extreme psychological instability. After treatment, he was appointed professor of art at the Dresden Academy in 1919 but left the position abruptly in 1924, traveling throughout Europe and in the Near East until 1931. This period yielded a series of powerful landscapes, "portraits of cities," including *Paris Opera* (1924; New York, private collection), *Tower Bridge* (1925–26; Minneapolis Institute of Arts), *Lyons* (1927; Washington, D.C., Phillips Collection), and *Dolce Bridge, Scotland* (1929; Los Angeles, private collection).

He settled in Vienna, where a large retrospective of his work was held in 1937. That same year his art was condemned as "degenerate" by the Nazis and he left Vienna. He lived in Britain during World War II, and produced many antiwar canvases on themes of destruction and despair (*What Are We Fighting For*, 1942–43, artist's collection). After the war Kokoschka visited the United States where he painted *Montana*—related to his cityscapes of the 1920s (1947; Zurich, Kunsthaus)—and Switzerland, where the Basel Art Gallery held a large one-man show. He was also represented in the 1947 Venice Biennale and had a major retrospective at the Tate Gallery, London, in 1962. Since 1948 he has lived mainly in Switzerland.

Kokoschka is one of the major expressionist artists of the time. Especially noteworthy are his remarkable portraits preceding World War I and the strong landscapes of the late 1920s.

BIBLIOGRAPHY. E. K. Hoffmann, *Kokoschka: His Life and Work*, London, 1947; O. Kokoschka, *Oskar Kokoschka, a Retrospective Exhibition*, introd. J. S. Plaut, Boston, 1948; H. M. Wingler, *Oskar Kokoschka . . .*, Salzburg, 1958; Arts Council, *Kokoschka* (catalog), introd. E. H. Gombrich, London, 1962.

JOHN C. GALLOWAY

KOLBE, GEORG. German sculptor (b. Waldheim, 1877; d. Berlin, 1947). Kolbe's first training and practice were in graphic arts and painting. His career was centered in Dresden, Munich, and Leipzig. His influences included Max Klinger, whose sculpture combined certain elements of neoclassicism with Rodinesque contrasts of high finish and unrefined areas of material. This paradox was to characterize much of Kolbe's expression following his conversion to sculpture in 1900, after travel to France and Rome in 1898. After 1903 Kolbe's activities were concentrated in Berlin. He visited Greece and Egypt in 1913, when he was already widely accepted professionally in Germany.

Kolbe's favored medium was bronze. He used it in a variety of busts, figures, and memorials dating from the first years of his career. Like Maillol, who with Klinger and Rodin formed the paradoxical sources of Kolbe's basic aesthetic, he preferred the nude figure, especially that of

Georg Kolbe, *Grief*, 1921. Bronze. Museum of Modern Art, New York.

the female, as a vehicle. Movement, sometimes implicitly violent but invariably arrested rather than outgoing, marks his style. Limbs may be strongly extruded from the body, as in *Grief* (1921; New York, Museum of Modern Art), but may incompletely express the indicated emotion of the total composition.

Quieter structuring is more nearly typical, however, as in *Assunta* (1921; Detroit Institute of Arts), a thinly formed female nude with upraised hands at the level of the breast, not yet completing the gesture of clasping. The surface is similar to that of *Grief* and other characteristic bronze works. It appears at first to have a highly polished finish, but it is actually a compromised texture, which in quality lies somewhere between a fully broken exterior, as in Rodin, and cubic, smoothly modeled volumes, as in Maillol. Kolbe's sentiment seldom denotes a maturity of interpretation; rather, it imparts to *Assunta* and related figures a curiously mannered gracefulness. He is invariably in full command of the structuring of his figures in the sheer technical sense. His capacity to synthesize anatomy, to reduce salient forms to simplified masses and planes, is eminently competent.

Kolbe is often grouped with artists of the expressionist movements in Germany, but such a classification is apt only in the most leniently applied sense, since his style fails to reflect the emotive values of expressionism. While Kolbe's aesthetic cannot be criticized as impersonal, it contrasted sufficiently with that of the incisive images of most of Germany's gifted artists to be exempt from official Nazi censure. Kolbe became extraordinarily popular and continued to work in Germany until after World War II. He was commissioned to do more than a dozen public monuments, some of them of large format.

Kolbe's stronger works include, in addition to those mentioned, a bust of Johann Sebastian Bach (1903; Leipzig Museum), *Seated Girl* (1907; private collection), *Portrait*

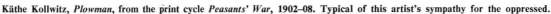

Käthe Kollwitz, *Plowman*, from the print cycle *Peasants' War*, 1902–08. Typical of this artist's sympathy for the oppressed.

of *W. R. Valentiner* (1920), and *Seated Figure* (1926; both New York, Museum of Modern Art).

BIBLIOGRAPHY. R. Binding, *Inhalt und Schönheit des Werkes von Georg Kolbe*, Berlin, 1933; W. Pinder, *Werke der letzten Jahre; mit Betrachtungen über Kolbes Plastik*, Berlin, 1937; E. Trier, *Moderne Plastik*, Frankfurt am Main, 1955.

JOHN C. GALLOWAY

KOLIN: ST. BARTHOLOMEW.

Church in Bohemia, in western Czechoslovakia. The dark 13th-century hall nave contrasts with the tall choir built by Peter Parler after a fire in 1349. This arrangement represents a simplification of the principles developed in the Cathedral of Prague and leads to the more ostentatious Cathedral of Kutná Hora.

BIBLIOGRAPHY. K. M. Swoboda, *Peter Parler*, Vienna, 1942.

KOLLWITZ, KATHE.

German graphic artist, painter, and sculptor (b. Königsberg, 1867; d. Moritzburg, 1945). Käthe Kollwitz (nee Schmidt) studied drawing with Rudolf Mauer at the age of thirteen; later she pursued art studies with Emile Neide, Stauffer-Bern, and Ludwig Heterich. Her early works were chiefly paintings, but she gradually found graphic arts more suitable to her vision, as she herself has said, "to express the suffering of man which never ends and now is immeasurably great."

In 1891 she married Karl Kollwitz and they moved to Berlin, where he practiced medicine in a poor suburb for workers. She continued with her art and gave her first public exhibition in 1893.

The milestones of her creative life are six great cycles of etchings, lithographs, and woodcuts. The first, *Weavers' Rebellion* (1895–98; three lithographs, three etchings), based on Hauptmann's play *Die Weber*, depicts the plight of indigent Silesian weavers. In 1899 she received an award for this work in the Dresden German Art Exhibition, and in 1900 a prize in London.

At the time of her second cycle, *Peasants' War* (1902–08; seven prints executed in complicated techniques), she was experimenting with the variety afforded by the graphic media. Again, the theme of revolt among the oppressed appears, but on a larger scale. For this she was awarded the Villa Romana prize, which entailed a year's residence in Florence. She sculptured the first version of her memorial for fallen volunteers in 1915; this was later destroyed. In 1925 she made a second version, which was set up in the soldiers' cemetery at Essen-Roggeveld near Dixmuide. It represents a grieving mother and father—portraits of herself and her husband. In 1919 she became the first woman professor elected to the Berlin Academy of Art.

The sequence *War* (1922–23; seven woodcuts) reflects the reactions of a wife and mother. Her fourth cycle, three woodcuts called *Proletariat*, appeared in 1925; this was one of her most powerful works. At the beginning of the Nazi regime in 1933 she lost her professorship in the Berlin Academy. From 1934 to 1935 she produced her last great cycle of seven lithographs, *Death*. Käthe Kollwitz spent the last three years of her life at Moritzburg Castle as a guest of the Prince of Saxony.

Her artistic vision remained virtually unchanged from the beginning: the plight of the poor and the downtrodden and the ubiquity of death—all seen with a woman's sympathy and expressed with ever simpler and bolder means.

BIBLIOGRAPHY. H. Kollwitz, ed., *Diary and Letters, Käthe Kollwitz*, Chicago, 1955; R. J. Fanning, *Käthe Kollwitz*, Karlsruhe, 1956.

FRANKLIN R.. DIDLAKE

KOLN, *see* COLOGNE.

KOM EL AHMAR, *see* HIERAKONPOLIS.

KONAK. Large Turkish mansion; also an official residence or government house. A konak used as a summerhouse is called a "yali" and is comparable to a villa.

KONARAK (Konarka).

Village in Orissa State, northeastern India. Konārak is the site of the Sūrya Deul, a Hindu sun temple conceived as the divine chariot of the Lord of the World. Built by Narasimhadeva of the Gaṅgā dynasty between 1238 and 1264, the temple is perhaps the most impressive single ruin of northern Indian art and one of the finest achievements of Indian temple architecture. The highest tower of the building, the śikhara which was to have covered the *garbhagriha* (holy of holies), fell while under construction. The extant building comprises the remains of the *maṇḍapa* (assembly hall for worshipers) and the *nat-mandir* (dance hall), reached by a flight of stairs. On a checkerboard background are placed musicians, dancers, and *mithūnas* (loving couples). Although the school of sculpture relates to Bhuvaneśvara and although the subjects are explicitly erotic, they do not appear to be connected with fertility and have therefore given rise to much spec-

Konārak. Sūrya, the sun god, at the base of the śikhara.

ulation. The most likely explanation may be that the sculptures depict the pleasures that may be expected to be at the disposal of the faithful in the world of the gods. *See also* INDIA.

BIBLIOGRAPHY. A. K. Coomaraswamy, *History of Indian and Indonesian Art*, New York, 1927; H. R. Zimmer, *The Art of Indian Asia*, 2 vols., New York, 1955.

JANET S. R. HILL

KONDANE. Cave site in Kolaba District, Maharashtra State, India. Situated at Kondāne are a chaitya hall and vihāra (Buddhist monastery) belonging to the Hīnayāna phase of Buddhist architecture. Kondāne is probably contemporary with Bhārhut (the early part of the Suṅga dynasty). Much of the interior of the chaitya has been destroyed, but it can be noted that upright beams on either side of the archway were carved partly of stone rather than of wood, as in earlier chaityas. A rare feature of the vihāra, to the left of the chaitya, is the pillared central hall. This pillared central hall also existed in the vihāra at Pitalkhorā. *See* HINAYANA.

BIBLIOGRAPHY. W. Spink, "On the Development of Early Buddhist Art, in India," *Art Bulletin*, XL, June, 1958; P. Brown, *Indian Architecture*, vol. 1: *Buddhist and Hindu Periods*, 4th ed., Bombay, 1959.

KONIG, LEO VON. German painter (b. Brunswick, 1871; d. Tutzing am Starnbergersee, 1944). König studied in Berlin and at the Académie Julian in Paris. He was primarily a painter of portraits in a strongly brushed, mildly expressionistic style.

BIBLIOGRAPHY. L. von König, *Gestalt und Seele: Das Werk des Malers Leo von König*, Leipzig, 1936.

KONIGSLUTTER CATHEDRAL. German 12th-century Romanesque Benedictine church. All that remains is the cloister, significant for its carved capitals and columns. Columns are ornamented with basket-weave, herringbone, and other decorative patterns, while the capitals are carved in beautiful foliate forms approaching naturalism but retaining some linear decorative ordering.

BIBLIOGRAPHY. J. Baum, *Malerei und Plastik des Mittelalters in Deutschland, Frankreich und Britannien*, Wildpark-Potsdam, 1930.

KONIJNENBURG, WILLEM A. VAN. Dutch painter (b. The Hague, 1868; d. there, 1943). He studied with D'Arnaud-Gerkens and then at the academy at The Hague. A prominent figure among Dutch painters after about 1895, when he changed over from the realism of The Hague school to symbolic themes and rigidly geometric principles of design, Konijnenburg subsequently published his theories in *Die aesthetische Idee* (The Hague, 1916). His work includes complex theological paintings, such as the *Triumph of St. Thomas Aquinas* (1924-38; Zwolle, Dominican Monastery), monumental designs for tapestries and stained-glass windows, and many portraits and secular works.

BIBLIOGRAPHY. G. Knuttel, *Willem van Konijnenburg*, Amsterdam, 1941.

KONINCK (Koning), PHILIPS (de). Dutch painter of genre, history, portraits, and landscape (b. Amsterdam, 1619; d. there, 1688). Koninck was a pupil of his elder brother Jacob Koninck at Rotterdam in 1639. According to A. Houbraken, Koninck was a pupil of Rembrandt at Amsterdam. While his training in Rembrandt's studio is not absolutely certain, his early works are clearly influenced by Rembrandt's style. In his own day Koninck's history paintings and portraits were highly praised by his friend the Dutch playwright and poet Joost van den Vondel. Today, however, Koninck is best known as a landscape painter.

Shortly after his move to Amsterdam, Koninck seems to have begun painting landscapes. In about 1651 he did his most Rembrandtesque landscape (Winterthur, Reinhart

Philips Koninck, *Landscape with Huts*. Rijksmuseum, Amsterdam. A characteristic panorama with fine cloud effects.

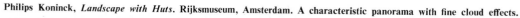

Konrad von Soest, *The Crucifixion*, central scene of the *Wildungen Altar*. Parish church, Wildungen.

Foundation). It would seem likely that Koninck had some contact with Rembrandt at this time, for his conception of landscape in turn seems to have influenced Rembrandt. It is also possible that the unique landscape painter Hercules Seghers had an influence on the style of Koninck's wide panoramic landscapes, with their grand scope and lighting and their fine cloud effects, such as *Farmhouses along a Road* (1655; Knowsley Hall, collection of the Earl of Derby).

BIBLIOGRAPHY. G. Falck, "Einige Bemerkungen über Philips Konincks Tätigkeit als Zeichner," *Festschrift für Max J. Friedländer*, Leipzig, 1927; H. Gerson, *Philips Koninck*, Berlin, 1936; W. Stechow, *Dutch Landscape Painting of the Seventeenth Century*, London, 1966.   LEONARD J. SLATKES

KONISTRA. Arena, or place covered with sand, in ancient Greek structures. At times the term is used to describe the orchestra and, by extension, the entire enclosure of a theater.

KONJIKIDO. Japanese Buddhist temple in the Chūsonji, Hiraizumi. The Chūsonji was built in 1105 by Kiyohira,

the founder of the Fujiwara clan of northern Japan. The monastery and its garden, together with other temple buildings around it that were founded by the later generations of the clan, were designed to reproduce the beauty and glory of the sophisticated metropolis of Kyoto. The Buddha Hall of the monastery, the Konjikidō (Gold-colored Hall, 1124), was once covered with gold leaf. This hall is the only building remaining after the fire of 1337.

Three platforms in the Konjikidō contain mummies of three generations of the Fujiwara clan, and on them stand three large groups of late Fujiwara and early Kamakura sculptures. The outer shell that encases this hall was built in 1288 as a protection against weather.

BIBLIOGRAPHY. Tokyo National Museum, *Pageant of Japanese Art*, vol. 6: *Architecture and Gardens*, Tokyo, 1952; National Commission for the Protection of Cultural Properties, ed., *Kokuhō (National Treasures of Japan)*, 6 vols., Tokyo, 1963–

KONRAD VON SOEST. German painter (fl. Westphalia, near Dortmund and Soest, ca. 1400–25). His name was derived from the inscription on his famous altar for the parish church of Wildungen. He worked in Dortmund, and his name is mentioned in the books of the Dortmund brotherhood between 1413 and 1422. Although nothing is known about his artistic training, it seems certain from his style that he must have traveled in France.

His most important works are the *Wildungen Altar* (1404; Wildungen, Parish church), the *Virgin Mary Altar* (ca. 1420; Dortmund, Marienkirche), two panels with SS. Ottilie and Dorothea (Münster, Landesmuseum of Art and Cultural History), a wing of an altar with SS. Reinold and Paul (Munich, Old Pinacothek), and a much-restored altar (Aachen, Cathedral). Of these the *Wildungen Altar* and the *Virgin Mary Altar* are by far the best preserved and are the principal sources for the study of his style.

The *Wildungen Altar* bears the inscription *Hoc opus completum per Conradum pictorem de Susato / Sub anno Domini MCCCC quarto* [?] *ipso die beati Egidii confessoris* on the frame of the outside of the wing. This inscription constitutes the oldest "signature" and date found on a northern European painting. The altar consists of thirteen representations from the life of Christ, with the Crucifixion in the center surrounded by smaller scenes, and four saints on the exterior of the wings. Certain stylistic traits such as love of ornamentation, delicacy of modeling, predisposition toward elegant elongated figures, and interest in landscape and animal painting draw this work into close affinity to the works of the Limbourg brothers and place Konrad von Soest within the tradition of the International Gothic style.

The Dortmund *Mary Altar* is a later work and exhibits a style that turns from the ornate prettiness of the *Wildungen Altar*. The figures lose their weightlessness and assume a more solid solemn dignity. A recently proposed reconstruction indicates that the general arrangement was also strengthened and enlarged.

Konrad von Soest was one of the leading artistic personalities of his time and, together with Master Francke, represented the strongest voice of the International Gothic style in German art.

BIBLIOGRAPHY. K. Steinbart, *Konrad von Soest*, Vienna, 1946; H. May, *Konrad von Soest. Der Dortmunder Marienaltar*, Dietz an der Lahn, 1948.

DONALD L. EHRESMANN

KONSTANZ: ROSGARTEN MUSEUM. German collection founded in 1870. The museum is housed in a former guild house dating from before 1324; there have been some later additions. It offers a fine survey of art and culture in the Lake Constance district, from prehistoric drawings (dating from the Magdalenian period) to 19th-century paintings. Among the manuscripts, a *Biblia pauperum* (southern Germany, ca. 1350) and a chronicle of the Council of Constance (1414–18) by Ulrich Richental (ca. 1460) deserve mention.

BIBLIOGRAPHY. H. Jedding, *Keysers Führer durch Museen und Sammlungen*, Heidelberg, Munich, 1961.

KOOL (Koolen; Cool; Coolen), WILLEM GILLISZ. Dutch painter of landscapes, beach scenes, and fish (b. Haarlem, 1608/09; d. there, 1666). From 1638 Kool is mentioned as a member of the Guild of St. Luke in Haarlem. He painted river and canal views in the style of Jan van Goijen. Because of a similar style and monogram Kool's

Korai. *Peplos Kore*, ca. 550 B.C. Acropolis Museum, Athens.

work is sometimes confused with that of Wouter Knijff.

BIBLIOGRAPHY. W. Bernt, *Die niederländischen Maler des 17. Jahrhunderts ...*, vol. 2, Munich, 1948.

KOPENHAUPT, GEORG, *see* KOBENHAUPT, GEORG.

KOPMAN, BENJAMIN. American painter, sculptor, and graphic artist (b. Vitebsk, Russia, 1887; d. Teaneck, N.J., 1965). Mostly self-taught, he painted landscapes, figures, and fantastic subjects in a controlled expressionistic style. He was influenced by Nolde, Chagall, and, especially in later paintings, Rouault.

BIBLIOGRAPHY. D. Ignatoff, *Kopman*, New York, 1930.

KORAI. Group of archaic Greek freestanding female statues varying in date between 575 and 480 B.C. The majority of the statues were found on the Acropolis in Athens (now in the Acropolis Museum), but some were found in Delphi, Delos, and Asia Minor. The figures are represented frontally; they stand erect, clad invariably in the Doric woolen peplos or the Ionic chiton and himation. Most of the statues carry attributes and were perhaps figures accompanying a female deity. Rich polychromy was used, and traces of color remain on the statues.

Characteristic of all the statues is the wide use of stylization in the folds of the drapery and the rendering of the hair. The stylistic development of the Korai statues is characterized by a striving toward fuller plasticity of the figure and toward a more successful coordination between the garment and the articulation of the limbs underneath it. Among well-known Korai statues are the *Berlin Goddess* (ca. 575 B.C.; Berlin, former State Museums,

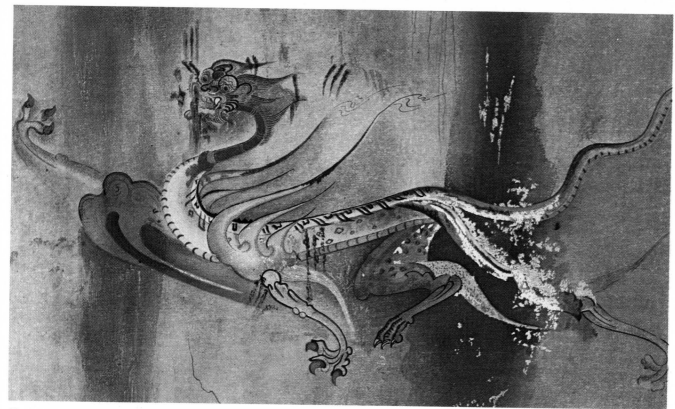

Korea. Dragon, wall painting in a tomb near P'yongyang, Koguryo period.

Greco-Roman Collection); the *Peplos Kore* (ca. 550 B.C.; Athens, Acropolis Museum); the *Antenor Kore* (ca. 530 B.C.; Acropolis Museum); and the *Euthydikos Kore* (ca. 480 B.C.; Acropolis Museum).

BIBLIOGRAPHY. H. Payne, *Archaic Marble Sculpture from the Acropolis*, London, 1936; G. M. A. Richter, *A Handbook of Greek Art*, London, 1959.

EVANTHIA SAPORITI

KORCULA CATHEDRAL, *see* CURZOLA CATHEDRAL.

KOREA. Korea, apart from its own cultural contribution—made under the strong influence of China—is also important for the role it played as a transmitter of Chinese art and general culture to Japan.

Colony of Lolang (108 B.C.–A.D. 313). One of four military colonies established in northwest Korea by the Chinese emperor Wu-ti in 108 B.C., Lolang lasted until A.D. 313, when it was taken over by the combined forces of the kingdoms of Koguryo and Paekche. The ancient capital of Lolang was discovered by a group of Japanese archaeologists in 1913 on the south bank of the Taedong River about 6 miles from P'yongyang. They located more than 10,000 tombs in the same general area, and 70 tombs have been excavated. The treasures, especially the lacquer ware and the silver and gold objects, found in these tombs are considered to be the most perfectly preserved remains of Han dynasty Chinese decorative art.

THREE KINGDOMS PERIOD

Between the second half of the 1st and the 4th century A.D. three centralized tribal groups emerged as three independent kingdoms: Koguryo in the north, Paekche in the southwest, and Silla in the southeast. The art of this period is characterized by the general assimilation of Chinese art and the gradual development of a Korean style. The earlier consolidation of political powers in Koguryo and its geographical proximity to China permitted this kingdom to be slightly ahead of the other two in accepting the cultural influence of China during the period of the Six Dynasties (386–589). Paekche received Chinese cultural influence through Koguryo, although some direct influence from China was felt through sea contact with southern China. The Silla kingdom received Chinese culture indirectly through Paekche and Koguryo. Buddhist iconography as manifested in Chinese art became the dominant theme in the art of the Three Kingdoms after the 4th century. (For correlation of Chinese, Indian, and Japanese Buddhist terminology, *see* BUDDHIST TERMS, CORRELATION OF.)

Koguryo (2d half of 1st cent.–668). After the fall of Lolang in 313, the Koguryo kingdom grew rapidly until it included all of northern Korea. The traditional dates for the kingdom of Koguryo (Chinese, Kao-chu-li) are 37 B.C. to A.D. 668. Modern scholars, however, prefer the second half of 1st century as the beginning date for this kingdom.

The art of Koguryo has been preserved principally in the tombs, many of which have wall paintings. These paintings furnish valuable materials for the study of such art not only of Korea but also of the entire Far East between the 4th and the 6th centuries. Judging from the structure of the tombs and the remains within them, the art and architecture of Koguryo was much more vigorous than that of Silla. Koguryo art influenced that of Silla and

Paekche, especially in the arrangement of tombs. Several hundred tombs have been uncovered in the vicinity of two old capitals, T'ungkou, near the Korea-Manchuria border in the southern tip of the Chinese province of Ki-ling, and P'yongyang, still the capital of North Korea. More than forty tombs with wall paintings have been excavated since World War II alone. The wall paintings from them may be dated between the 4th and the 7th centuries. *See* KOGURYO TOMBS, MURAL PAINTINGS.

These tombs are square, unlike the Chinese mound, and they are oriented toward the four points of the compass. They have polished stone walls, although some are plastered. The wall paintings range from the very naïve to the highly refined and may be ranked with the finest paintings in the Far East. The influence of Han art is seen principally in the portrayal of moving clouds, flying angels, and galloping animals; the paintings also portray genre scenes and stylized floral and geometric designs. Some of the more significant tombs near T'ungkou are the Tomb of the Dancers, Three-chambered Tomb, Tomb of the Four Spirits, Tomb of the Lotus, Tomb of the Concentric Circles, and Tomb Number 17 in Wukuaifen. Of the scores of tombs in the vicinity of Koguryo's southern capital at P'yongyang, the more significant tombs are the Great Tomb, Shinbari Tombs I and II, and Twin Pillar Tomb. Most of the murals of the southern tombs were executed after the removal of the capital to P'yongyang in 427.

Judging from the scattered remains of a green-glazed ware, Koguryo ceramics were apparently superior to those of neighboring kingdoms to the south.

Paekche (2d half of 3d cent.–663). Paekche is located in the southwest of the Korean peninsula. It acted as the recipient of continental artistic influence from Central Asia and China and as a bridge of learning for Japan. Unfortunately most of its artistic monuments have been destroyed.

The Hinayana Buddhist sect was first introduced and officially adopted in 384, and numerous temples were built throughout the kingdom. At Puyo, the site of the capital of Paekche, six temple sites were discovered in 1940. One of the significant extant monuments is a stone pagoda at the site of Chongim-sa temple in Puyo, which stands 28½ feet high. *See* HINAYANA.

Historical records reveal that Paekche first sent a group of image makers and temple architects to Japan in 577; a second group was sent in 588. The contribution of Paekchean architects may be seen in the celebrated Buddhist temple of the Hōryūji (607) near Nara, Japan. A fire in 670 destroyed all but the Golden Hall of the Hōryūji, but the temple was reconstructed shortly after on the same plan. *See* HORYUJI.

The wooden Kudara (Japanese for Paekche) Kannon in the Hōryūji is a testimony to the art of Paekchean sculptors. The celebrated Yumedono Kannon was considered the greatest monument of Korean art by its discoverer, Ernest Fenellosa. The openwork crown on the Kudara Kannon and the metal border on the Tamamushi Shrine in the Hōryūji are similar enough to the golden ornament discovered by Sekino to be considered a link between the art of Paekche and the metalwork on the art treasures in the Hōryūji. It is through the existing monuments at the Hōryūji, then, that the art of Paekche may be visualized.

See KUDARA KANNON; TAMAMUSHI SHRINE; YUMEDONO KANNON.

Silla (2d half of 4th cent.–668). Compared to that of the neighboring kingdoms, the cultural growth of Silla was delayed because of its geographical isolation from China, the main source of continental cultural influence in Korea. On the other hand, the geographical separation saved Silla from the advances of the Chinese army, although not from Japanese attacks by sea or from military advances of the neighboring Korean kingdoms.

A great number of tombs of this ancient kingdom have been unearthed in the 20th century and have yielded much of the treasures of Silla. In the Golden Crown tomb, for example, a gold crown with spangles and crescent jades and topped by a pointed cap was discovered along with many golden earrings. Another significant find in that tomb was a gold belt and a buckle. Since the hook, and not the buckle, was the customary fastener in China, the Silla gold belt seems to indicate non-Chinese origin. Typical earthenware found in these tombs includes cups, jars with crudely incised or stamped designs, and vases on tall stands. Most of these earthenware vessels were made for practical use.

In the vicinity of Kyungju, the ancient capital of Silla, two of the oldest architectural monuments in Korea still stand to attest the glory of this period. The first is an astronomical observatory 22 feet high in stone called Chum Sung Dae (Star-gazing Platform; mid-7th cent.). The second monument is a pagoda on the site of Pun-Hwangsa, dated 634, which is the oldest date given to any pagoda in Korea. *See* KYUNGJU.

Among the Buddhist representations in the 6th century the most popular deity was the bodhisattva Maitreya. The extant examples of the Maitreya vary in size and media from giant rock images to tiny metal figurines. The Maitreya of this period are customarily represented standing or in the pose of the Bodhisattva of Meditation, with the right leg crossed over the left knee and the right hand supporting the cheek.

UNIFICATION AND AFTER

United Silla period (668–918). With the help of a T'ang army Silla defeated Paekche and Koguryo and unified Korea in 668. This period was blessed with unprecedented peace and prosperity, and art flowered into full splendor. Many of the artistic remains of this period, however, were destroyed during the Japanese invasion (1592–98).

A considerable number of Buddhist temples were built under the influence of a powerful Buddhist sect, Hwaom, soon after unification. The minor arts of the period were dedicated principally to the embellishment of these temples and palaces. Of the great temples built during this time the most celebrated is the temple of Pulguksa and its cave shrine, called Sokkulam. It is located about 8 miles east of Kyungyu, the capital of Silla. Pulguksa is the oldest surviving temple in Korea. It was founded about 535 and repaired between 661 and 680; its reconstruction was completed in 752. Of the original structure of the Pulguksa an arched stone stairway, balustrade, stone pagodas, lanterns, and two bronze images remain. Although the foundations were made without mortar, the temple has survived the vicissitudes of time. *See* PULGUKSA TEMPLE.

Sokkulam is an artificial stone cave with an unroofed passage leading to a small rotunda with a domed roof. A massive Buddha statue sits on a pedestal in the center of the rotunda. Around the main Buddha figure there is a circumambulatory passage, which suggests a return to the ancient Indian temple plan. The granite-lined walls of both entrances to the cave and the walls of the rotunda are decorated with highly refined relief images of bodhisattvas, arhats, and guardian kings. The garments of these figures emphasize the thinness of the fabric and the fleshy body beneath, showing that the art of Gupta, especially that of the Ajaṇṭā Caves, had penetrated to Korea by this time. A group of Chinese sculptors is said to have collaborated in the carving of these figures. *See* AJANTA; SOKKULAM.

Pulguksa is also famous for two stone pagodas: the Tabotap (Sanskrit, Prabhutaratna) pagoda (535; repaired in 751) and the Sakyamuni pagoda (mid-8th cent.), known as the "pagoda that casts no shadow."

There are dozens of other pagodas from the United Silla period, but they conform to the general Silla type, with a base, boxlike stories, and truncated cornices. Of special interest is the pagoda from the Hwangboksa (706), which was built on a rear terrace as a repository for relics. A relic box with an inscribed date was discovered inside the second story of the pagoda. The box contained small images, a sarira box, glass beads, bronze bowls, gold strings, and other objects.

Unfortunately none of the secular buildings of this period has survived. The paintings likewise have been destroyed. One must turn to the paintings on the Tamamushi Shrine and to the wall paintings in the Golden Hall of the Hōryūji in Nara, Japan, to get a glimpse of the skill, style, medium, and subject matter of Korean paintings of this period. (The Nara works, lost in the fire of 1949, now exist only in reproduction.) *See* HORYUJI WALL PAINTINGS.

That the high quality of artistic achievement at this time permeated every medium of art is substantiated by the remains of molded, pressed, incised, or carved roof tiles, walls, and pavements. A small number of remaining bronze figures of Buddhist deities indicate Silla preference for the full-blown and fleshy representation of figures.

Koryo period (918–1392). After a bloodless rebellion in 918, an army officer, Wanggon, took control of the country. The Kingdom of Koryo was not formally established, however, until 935, when the rule of the last king of Silla ended. Wanggon's able leadership saved the country from five foreign invasions during his reign.

Buddhism reached its highest native development during this period. Numerous Buddhist temples were built under royal patronage, but very few have survived. The Pusoksa temple in the Yongju district in the northern Kyongsang Province may be singled out for the exceptional treasures it houses. Two of its wooden halls, Hall of Eternal Life and Founder's Hall, date from 1350 and represent the oldest surviving wooden structures in Korea. The Hall of Eternal Life contains a wooden Amitābha which is considered one of the finest specimens of Koryo sculpture. The paintings of bodhisattvas and guardians on the walls of the Founder's Hall represent the earliest wall paintings in Korea outside tombs. *See* PUSOKSA TEMPLE.

Numerous pagodas and stūpas survive from this period. Two important ones are a nine-storied octagonal pagoda in Wolchongsa in Kangwon Province and the stūpa (1017) of a court priest, Song Pup, which stands on the Kyongbok Palace grounds in Seoul. A pagoda that shows a strong influence of Indian art is the funerary pagoda of the monk Haerin, called Kyonmyo-t'ap, near Wonju in Kangwon Province. Another pagoda that shows the polygonal style of an Indian type is the twenty-one-sided marble one built by Chinese sculptors in the Pagoda Park of Seoul. Two important stone lanterns are the 6-foot lantern in the Silluksa temple (1379) and the 20-foot lantern in the Hwaomsa temple (14th cent.).

Ceramics from the Koryo period show remarkable elegance and subtlety of color and design. Koryo celadons, in particular, are known the world over as some of the most beautiful potteries ever made. The Koryo potters received their early inspiration and training in the production of high-fired porcelain wares from the Yüeh factories of Chekiang Province in southern China. Koryo soon developed a native style in pottery unmatched in elegance of form and natural grace. A significant contribution of Koryo potters was their use of underglaze copper oxide, which turned brilliant red when baked. The Chinese use of this technique does not seem to have started until a hundred years later. The golden age of the ceramic ware of this period was reached about the first quarter of the 12th century. After the Mongol invasion of 1231 the tendency toward an excessive decoration on pottery began to appear, and the creative ability of the Koryo potters was stifled to the point of sterility.

Yi period (1392–1910). The founder of the Yi dynasty, Yi Songge, known as King Yi T'ae-jo, took control of the country in 1392 and organized a strongly centralized Confucian state, modeled after Ming China. The new system of government produced a class of learned scholar-officials who were chosen through the newly instituted selective service examinations. The early Yi kings established well-defined relationships with both China and Japan. Annual trade and tribute missions were sent to China, and a set number of Japanese came each year to trade.

During the reign of King Sejong (1419–50) a Confucian college in Seoul and subsidiary colleges in the provinces were established. Sejong commissioned a group of scholars to develop the Korean alphabet especially for the benefit of women and children. The result was one of the simplest and most flexible alphabets in the world.

From the inception of the Yi period land was redistributed to the tenant farmers and was controlled by the central government through land taxation. The mining of gold was forbidden for fear of attracting foreign interests. In the long run such tight control and the destruction of budding commercialism produced economic stagnation and political factionalism.

Since the agrarian economy in Korea did not produce a wealthy middle class, there was no patronage of art by a middle class as there was in China and Japan. The only significant patron was the king. The early Yi kings, like the Ming emperors of China, founded an academy for the recruitment and encouragement of gifted artists. Most of the important artists belonged to the royal academy. The academy was not free from factionalism, however, and eventually various labels were attached to groups of painters. Soon there emerged two main groups of painters. The Northern school came to be identified with the traditionally Chinese style of painting, and the Southern school, by its gentleman-painter attitude and nationalistic elements.

Throughout the Yi period many painters worked in the traditional style, with bright colors and detailed forms in the T'ang style. Many other painters, however, attempted new creations with monochrome washes and small dots. During the 15th century landscape painting was most popular. The 16th-century painters imitated the decorative style of the Chinese painters, although the traditional style was still in vogue. Toward the 17th century a highly personalized style of ink painting, which was executed rapidly to maintain its spontaneity, became fashionable. The gentleman-painters in Korea resented the newly established Manchu dynasty in China and continued to follow the tradition of the Ming painters throughout the 18th century. By the 19th century the jagged and uneven calligraphic style of painting had come to be preferred to the smooth brush style. The Western style of oil painting became widespread in Korea. The majority of the painters, however, did their best work in the traditional Korean media. *See* AN KYON; CHONG SON; KANG HUI-AN; KIM HONG-DO; KIM MYONG-GUK; SHIN YUN-BOK; YI CHONG; YI IN-MUN; YI SANG-JWA.

In architecture, from the beginning of the Yi period, numerous secular buildings were constructed, and many towns and monastic establishments were rebuilt. Very few buildings from the early Yi period survive. After the transfer of the capital from Kaesung to Seoul in the beginning of the Yi period, a number of impressive palaces were built in Seoul. The Kyongbok Palace (1395; reconstructed in 1867) was built on the Chinese axial plan in the shape of a magic square or mandala. Farther to the east of the Kyongbok Palace is the Changdok Palace (1804), which represents the best construction of the later Yi period.

Hundreds of town gates were built during the Yi period. Dozens still stand, presenting a curious contrast to the modern parts of towns. Among the famous ones are the Great South Gate and the Kwangwha Gate of Seoul and the East Gate and the West Gate of Suwon. Hundreds of Confucian shrines and halls called *sowon* survive. The *sowon* served as clubs for the local literati as well as examination centers for men of letters.

The Yi kings systematically extolled Confucianism and suppressed Buddhism. As a result, most of the Buddhist temples in the vicinity of Seoul and Kaesung were abandoned in ruins. Some dozen temples in the remote hills managed to survive the pressure from the court and the Confucian scholar-officials. In these temples the tradition of Buddhist art and iconography was kept alive. The great majority of residences in Korea still consist of the small mud-and-stone house of one, two, or three wings, with straw-thatched or tiled roof, a courtyard, and a gate. These houses are usually fenced. The representative tomb of the Yi period is an earthen mound on a hillside.

During this period blue-and-white glazes and underglaze pottery with bold and splashy decorations became popular. The lustrous green-blue glazes of Koryo type were no longer produced.

See also KOREA: ARCHITECTURE; KOREA: CERAMICS; SEOUL: MUSEUMS.

BIBLIOGRAPHY. A. Eckhardt, *A History of Korean Art*, London, 1929; E. Keith and E. K. Robertson Scott, *Old Korea*, London, 1946; G. W. Hewes, *Archaeology of Korea: A Selected Bibliography* (Research Monographs on Korea, Series F, no. 1), Chicago, 1947; C. Osgood, *The Koreans and Their Culture*, New York, 1951; Ministry of Foreign Affairs, *Korean Arts*, 3 vols., Seoul, 1956–63; R. T. Paine, ed., *Masterpieces of Korean Art* (exhibition catalog), Boston, 1957; C. Kim and G. St. G. M. Gompertz, eds., *The Ceramic Art of Korea*, London, 1961; W. Forman and J. Bařinka, *The Art of Ancient Korea*, London, 1962; G. St. G. M. Gompertz, *Korean Celadon and Other Wares of the Koryŏ Period*, London, 1963; National Museum of Korea, *Selected Museum Exhibits, 1945–1965*, Seoul, 1965.

CORNELIUS CHANG

KOREA: ARCHITECTURE.

The architecture of Korea may be divided into five major periods: prehistoric, Three Kingdoms, United Silla, Koryo, and Yi.

Prehistoric period (to ca. 3d cent. A.D.). The prehistoric dwellings of Koreans were subterranean pits, either circular or square in shape. The many pit dwellings uncovered in northeastern Korea are circular, about 13 to 18 feet in diameter, with central fireplaces. In the northwest, however, square pits were predominant. A Chinese document of the period describes Korean houses as subterranean pits with mound-shaped roofs and entrances at their tops. What is now called *ondol*, a system that provides rows of smoke ducts beneath the mud of the floor, was already known in this early period.

Three Kingdoms period (ca. 2d half of 1st cent.–668). Since no buildings survive from the Koguryo period, what is known of its architecture has been gathered from pictorial representations of pavilions, houses, and room interiors on the walls of the Koguryo tombs. Judging from these tomb paintings, Koguryo architecture was very similar to the architecture of contemporary China, especially that of the Northern Wei dynasty (386–534), which is well represented in engravings on the walls of Chinese stone cave temples. *See* KOGURYO TOMBS: MURAL PAINTINGS.

Wooden architecture in Korea developed significantly with the spread of Buddhism, which became the national religion in each of the Three Kingdoms. Monumental temples in wood as well as stone pagodas were built in many parts of the land. According to T'ang historical documents, these temples were roofed with tiles, whereas the private residences were thatch-roofed.

See also KOREA (THREE KINGDOMS: KOGURYO; PAEKCHE; SILLA).

United Silla period (668–918). During the three centuries beginning in the mid-7th century, the art of Silla was greatly influenced by that of the T'ang dynasty in China (618–906). Korean art reached its height and set the basic pattern for later developments during this period. Many temple sites are located near Kyungju, the ancient capital of Silla. The temple of this period adhered to the so-called twin-pagoda plan, with two stone pagodas erected in front of a main hall facing south. Unfortunately, none of the Silla wooden structures survives to this day. Since Japanese Tempyō architecture is closely related to the contemporary Chinese architecture of the T'ang period, which served as the model for the architecture of the United Silla period, the surviving Japanese temples provide some insight into the Silla style. *See* KYUNGJU.

Koryo period (918–1392). During the latter part of this period a new style of architecture called *tien-chu* (literally, "Indian") was introduced from the Fukien area of China. The new style, which actually has no relationship to India itself, is characterized by column-head bracketing, uncoffered ceilings, and so on. Traditionally, the multibracket style had been used to support eaves beams between columns, and the ceilings had always been coffered.

Yi period (1392–1910). The capital was moved from Kaesung to Seoul shortly after the founding of the new dynasty. The column-head bracket system of the late Koryo period continued to be popular until about the beginning of the 16th century, when the multibracket system was revived. The great majority of Koryo and early Yi buildings were destroyed by the Japanese invaders under Hideyoshi's command toward the end of the 16th century. Subsequently, in the mid-Yi period, a considerable number of buildings were constructed in which a decorative tendency is clearly detectable both in the interiors and the exteriors.

In the later Yi-period architecture, the bracket system is reduced to the use of a simple block of wood carved in the shape of a bracket. During this period the oxtongue-shaped member that projects at the front end of the bracket arm becomes long and slim. In the architecture of the earlier Yi period, the oxtongues are short and thick. The Kyongbok Palace (1395), which was rebuilt in 1867, may be cited as a typical example of Yi architecture that shows all the major characteristics of the period.

BIBLIOGRAPHY. E. McCune, *The Arts of Korea*, Rutland, Vt., 1962; Ministry of Foreign Affairs, *Korean Arts*, vol. 3: *Architecture*, Seoul, 1963.   CORNELIUS CHANG

KOREA: CERAMICS.

The ceramic tradition of ancient Korea, like that of Japan and other Far Eastern areas, can be traced back as far as prehistoric times; in this instance, it can also be traced forward into the modern Yi period.

Three Kingdoms and United Silla periods (ca. 3d cent.–918). The pottery cultures of the Three Kingdoms (Silla, Paekche, Koguryo) and of United Silla form one continuous tradition. The first major development in the pottery culture of Silla took place sometime before the second half of the 4th century, when the development of the tunnel kiln transformed the soft reddish prehistoric wares into hard gray stoneware. From the 5th century onward numerous tumulus mounds of impressive dimensions were built around the capital city of Kyungju in North Kyungsang Province. In these tombs large quantities of pottery, sometimes more than 200 pieces in a single tomb, were buried. It is impossible to determine all the uses of the pottery during this period, but apparently some pieces were made specifically to be buried in tombs. The pottery used in everyday life was of two general types: one, a hard gray ware decorated, customarily, with lattice or geometric designs similar to the Scythian decorations on mirrors and horse fittings; the other, a soft reddish-brown earthenware that recalls the red neolithic pottery.

Two of the more interesting shards from the Silla period are from a pair of vessels in the form of mounted horsemen found in the Golden Bell Tomb. The commonest Silla pottery form, however, is the mounted cup, with or without a cover, dating from the 4th into the 7th century. Tens of thousands of these have been discovered in tombs. Most Silla pottery is unglazed, although a dull green glaze, reminiscent of the thick green glaze of the ware of the Han colony of Lolang, has also been found.

Silla gradually absorbed the other kingdoms that had existed on the peninsula: Kaya in the south, in 562; Paekche in the southwest, in 660; and Koguryo in the north, in 668. Unfortunately, most Paekche pottery was destroyed during the conquest and occupation by the Silla and the T'ang armies from 660 to 663. From the scanty evidence, it is known that it was decorated only slightly but with refinement.

The pottery of Koguryo was likewise underdecorated and was roughly made in comparison with the Silla wares. Some of the best pottery was made from the 4th to the 6th century in the southeast-coast kingdom of Kaya, which maintained close contact with Japan. Kaya pottery influenced the Yayoi and Sueki ware of Japan from the 5th through the 7th century.

Koryo period (918–1392). The early culture of Koryo shows little break with its predecessor. In the field of ceramics, however, a revolutionary height was reached by the Koryo potters.

The official kilns were founded at Kangjin, in South Cholla Province, and at Puan, in South Ch'ungch'ong Province. For centuries, until late in the period, the finest celadon wares were produced in these kilns. Mr. Honey of the Victoria and Albert Museum, London, wrote that some of this ware "... reaches heights hardly attained even by the Chinese." This is not to say, however, that the Chinese ceramics did not influence Koryo wares. An in-

Korea, ceramics. Celadon vase with black and white inlays, Koryo period, 12th century. Museum of Fine Arts, Boston.

scribed jar, dated 993 and made for a shrine commemorating the founder of the dynasty, for example, shows the influence of Chinese Yüeh ware in its primitive oxidized celadon glaze. The Sung traveler Hsü-ching, who visited Kaesung in 1123, noted that the numerous Khitan captives who were taken to Koryo after the fall of the Liao dynasty (between 1114 and 1124) contributed to the improvement in the style of ceramics as well as that of costumes. Furthermore, Sung wares have been found in Koryo tombs.

Some of the more significant technical innovations made by the Koryo ceramic designers involve their use of underglaze iron, underglaze slip white, gold-leaf, and marble clay decorations. Koryo potters also seem to have invented a technique of inlaying, the first datable example of which was found in the tomb of a Koryo noble who died in 1159.

The greatest triumph of Koryo potters remains, however, their halcyon glaze. Koryo poets have attributed to it "the radiance of jade . . . the crystal clarity of waters . . . as if the artist had borrowed the secret from heaven." The production of superior ceramic ware reached its highest refinement in the period from about 1100 to the first Mongol attack in 1219. During Mongol rule (1259–1354) the quality of Koryo ceramics deteriorated rapidly: the bright glazes darkened and browned, and design became elaborate and degenerate under the influence of the complicated Mongol-Persian designs. As governmental control over the kiln weakened, the potters introduced folk-art variations, bringing an end to the era of classic celadon wares.

Yi period (1392–1910). A Koryo general overthrew his masters and founded the Yi dynasty, moving the capital to Seoul. Since it was a relatively effortless and bloodless changeover, cultural continuity was substantially preserved. In the beginning of the new dynasty, a Koryo inlaid celadon technique known as *punch'ong* (Japanese, *mishima*) continued to predominate. It was produced in the vicinity of Kyungju, once capital of United Silla, during the 14th century.

Some thirty to forty local kilns were developed into official kilns in the Kwangju area, about 15 miles north of Seoul, in the beginning of the 15th century. The "official" wares produced at these kilns were the Korean version of Ming blue-and-white ware and were restricted largely to upper-middle-class use.

What appealed to the typical Yi taste was, however, the almost puritanical white ware of the period, which represented the Neo-Confucian ideal of conscious austerity. Much of the best of this ware was entirely undecorated.

From the end of the 16th century, however, the recurrent Japanese invasions bore heavily on the kilns. Japanese soldiers looted potteries and often took the potters to Japan, where they founded much of the modern ceramic tradition at Arita, Hagi, Naeshirogawa, and elsewhere. Many of the Korean kilns never recovered. From 1600 on, a variety of Japanese wares outstripped those of Korea. Since Korea's relations with the Ch'ing dynasty of China were cool, the official kilns at Ch'ing-tê-ch'en did not influence the Korean potters of this period.

Fortunately, many of the ancient tombs have yielded their contents to the world, and as a result, most of the ancient wares are known today. Ceramic production as an ancient and living tradition of Korea is now dead.

BIBLIOGRAPHY. Chōsen Sōtokufu, ed., *Chōsen Koseki Zufu* (Illustrated Korean Antiquities), 15 vols., Seoul, 1915–35; F. Koyama ed., *Sekai Tōji Zenshū* (Complete World Ceramics), vols. 13 and 14, Tokyo, 1955; G. Henderson, "Korean Ceramics: Problems and Sources of Information," *Far Eastern Ceramics Bulletin*, X, March-June, 1958; W. Kim, *Studies on Silla Pottery*, New York, 1958; G. St. G. M. Gompertz, *The Ceramic Art of Korea*, London, 1961; G. St. G. M. Gompertz, *Korean Celadon and Other Wares of the Koryŏ Period*, London, 1963.

CORNELIUS CHANG

KOREA, MUSEUMS OF, *see* SEOUL: MUSEUMS (National Museum of Korea; Toksu Palace Museum of Fine Arts).

KORIN (Ogata Korin). Japanese painter, calligrapher, and designer of pottery and lacquer ware (1658–1716). The son of a wealthy silk merchant of Kyoto, and a relative of Kōetsu, Kōrin grew up in the cultivated middle-class society of the capital. He was first trained in the Kanō school, but later he admired and followed Sōtatsu's works, some of which he copied. Kōrin led a life of pleasure and luxury until about 1697, when he became virtually bankrupt and decided to work as a professional painter. At first he made designs for the pottery wares of his younger brother, Kenzan, but from about 1701 he worked as a serious painter. He is the greatest artist of the decorative school of painting started by Kōetsu and Sōtatsu. Simplified composition, stressing decorative power in spacing and patterning of forms, and the use of dramatic color contrast made his paintings greatly admired both in Japan and in the West. *See* KANO SCHOOL; KENZAN; KOETSU; SOTATSU.

BIBLIOGRAPHY. D. Randall, *Kōrin*, New York, 1960; T. Akiyama, *Japanese Painting* [Geneva?], 1961.

KORVEY, *see* CORVEY.

KORWAR (Korovar), *see* MELANESIA; OCEANIC ART (MELANESIA: NEW GUINEA).

KORYUSAI (Isoda Koryusai). Japanese Ukiyo-e print designer (fl. mid-18th cent.). Koryūsai is believed to have been a pupil of Shigenaga. He admired and followed the style of his friend Harunobu, and in his early works he used the derivative name of Haruhiro. He is noted for his large pillar prints (average size about 5 by 11 in.). After the 1780s he ceased to make prints and devoted himself to painting. *See* HARUNOBU; SHIGENAGA; UKIYO-E.

BIBLIOGRAPHY. L. V. Ledoux, *Japanese Prints, Bunchō to Utamaro in the Collection of Louis V. Ledoux*, New York, 1948.

KOSHO. Japanese sculptor (fl. mid-13th cent.). The fourth son of Unkei, Kōshō cooperated with his father and brothers in the reconstruction of the Kōfukuji in Nara. His most important works are the Amida Buddha in the Golden Hall of the Hōryūji (1232), done in the Asuka manner, and a realistic portrait of the priest Kūya in the Rokuharamitsuji of Kyoto. *See* UNKEI.

BIBLIOGRAPHY. R. T. Paine and A. Soper, *The Art and Architecture of Japan*, Baltimore, 1955.

KOSICE CATHEDRAL, *see* KASSA CATHEDRAL.

Kōrin, *The God of Wind*. National Museum, Kyoto.

K'O-SSU. Chinese term referring to a silk tapestry containing a pictorial design. The characters employed by the Chinese for writing *k'o-ssu* have varied and may be translated as "cross silk," "woven-weft silk (or threads)," or "woven-weft colors." The modern writing of *k'o-ssu* in Chinese means "cut threads (or silk)" and refers to the fact that the individually colored weft threads, which are woven into the warp, terminate at the boundaries of each color section rather than continuing across the width of the cloth. The effect is similar to that of inlay: when examined closely, the small pinholelike spaces appearing between each area of color look like the slashes of a knife; thus the modern description of "cut" threads.

The development of *k'o-ssu* in China forms an independent and complex chapter in the history of textiles and has long fascinated Chinese collectors and some Western historians. The current belief is that *k'o-ssu* tapestry techniques were first effectively exploited during the Southern Sung period (1127-1279), although *k'o-ssu* may have been an invention of a Turkic people, the Uighurs, who had occupied China's western border from the 9th to the 11th century. *K'o-ssu* became popular during the Ming period (1368-1644), when the textile industry in general flourished in China, and again in the Ch'ing period during the reign of the emperor Ch'ien-lung. The technique was used to produce stunning pictorial effects, and copies of famous paintings with complicated compositions and minute details could be effectively reproduced in *k'o-ssu*. Among the best-known examples of the technique are the pair of tapestries in the National Palace Museum Collection, Sun Yat-sen Museum, near Taipei (Taiwan), attributed to Shen Tzu-fan of the Sung dynasty. One represents *Doves on a Flowering Peach Tree*, the other a landscape; both were exhibited in the 1935-36 exhibition at Burlington House in London and in the Chinese Art Treasures from the Palace Museum exhibition which toured the United States during 1961-62.

BIBLIOGRAPHY. B. Vuilleumier, *Symbolism of Chinese Imperial Ritual Robes*, London, 1939; S. Cammann, "Notes on the Origin of Chinese K'o-ssu Tapestry," *Artibus Asiae*, XI, 1948; J. P. Dubosc, "Contribution à l'étude des tapisseries d'époque Song," *Artibus Asiae*, XI, 1948.

MARTIE W. YOUNG

KOUROS TYPE. Type of standing youth in Greek sculpture. Also called the Apollo type, it represents a standing nude youth in a frontal position, with broad shoulders, a narrow waist, one leg slightly forward, and the weight of the body evenly distributed. The arms are parallel to the sides of the body, the fists usually clenched and touching the thighs. The hair, stylized, falls over the shoulders in ornamental geometric patterns. The face is enlivened by the so-called archaic smile. The type is predominant in Greek sculpture of the archaic period (615–485 B.C.); it was not confined to statues representing the god Apollo but was used for all male statues in the 6th century B.C. Some are known to be representations of victors in the games and were dedicated to the gods.

The Kouros type can be divided into two major categories: (1) the mainland Doric type, in which the statue is conceived as a compact geometric volume; and (2) its Ionic counterpart, which displays a flowing contour and roundness in form. The main impetus appears to have come from the eastern islands and the coast of Asia Minor,

which had close contacts with Egypt. This explains the derivation of the Kouros statues from Egyptian sculpture. The technique employed was that of carving rather than modeling, and the tools used by the artist were the chisel and the hammer. The statues were hewn out of rectangular blocks of marble; early examples retain the form of the block of stone from which they emerged.

Tentative dating has been attempted, and the Kouroi statues have been classified in various groups: (1) *Sounion (Sunium) group* (615–590 B.C.). The best example belonging to this group is the colossal statue of a youth found near the Temple of Poseidon in Sounion (Athens, National Archaeological Museum). To this group also belongs the Kouros in the Metropolitan Museum of Art, New York, which clearly displays the four separate planes of the rectangular block from which it was carved and shows the geometric architectonic interrelation of the various parts of the body. Grooves and ridges forming a linear pattern indicate anatomical details. (2) *Orchomenos-Thera group* (590–570 B.C.). The best example is the Kouros from Thera (Athens, National Archaeological Museum). Greater corporeal unity and rounder forms are attempted here. The archaic smile appears for the first time. (3) *Tenea-Volomandra group* (575–550 B.C.). This group is represented by the well-known *Tenea Kouros* (Munich, State Antiquities Collection). It is characterized by coordination of the masses of the body, interrelation of the four planes of the statue, and softer modeling. (4) *Melos group* (555–540 B.C.). The slender, graceful Kouros from Melos (Athens, National Archaeological Museum) shows a tendency toward a flowing contour, as well as smoothness and unity of the parts of the body. (5) *Anavysos-Ptoon 12 group* (540–520 B.C.). The group exhibits a more vigorous style and great liveliness. The various parts of the body are conceived in the round, and anatomical details are shown in modeling rather than in incised form. (6) *Ptoon 20 group* (520–485 B.C.). In this group there is an attempt at movement. The weight of the body shifts to the receding leg, and there is a break from rigid frontality. The best surviving example of a bronze Kouros, the *Piraeus Kouros* (Athens, National Archaeological Museum), belongs to this group. The main theme in the development of the Kouros in the 6th century is the evolution from stylization to naturalism. Naturalism is fully attained in the last Kouros of the series (Athens, National Archaeological Museum), inscribed on the base "ARISTODIKOS." The final stage in the development is reached here in a complete interrelation of the parts of the body and in a naturalistic rendering of the various anatomical details.

BIBLIOGRAPHY. E. Buschor, *Frühgriechische Jünglinge*, Munich, 1950; G. M. A. Richter and I. A. Richter, *Kouroi*, 2d ed., London, 1960.

EVANTHIA SAPORITI

KO WARE, *see* KUAN WARE.

KRAFFT, JOHANN AUGUST. German painter and etcher (b. Altona, 1798; d. Rome, 1829). He studied in Hamburg, Copenhagen, Dresden, and Munich. Krafft went to Rome in 1826 and became known for his genre paintings of Italian life and scenes with children.

KRAFT, ADAM. German sculptor (ca. 1455/60–1509). He rivaled Veit Stoss as the preeminent late Gothic sculptor in Nürnberg, where his activity is documented from 1490 to 1509. Nothing is known of his training. From 1490 to 1492 Kraft carved a relief triptych for Sebald Schreyer and Mathias Landauer on the outside of the choir of St. Sebald in Nürnberg; the reliefs, which depict the Passion and Resurrection of Christ are based on paintings that hung over the Schreyer-Landauer family tombs. The monument makes use of a stage-like box and several levels of relief to dramatically set the narrative in space.

Kraft's theatrical genius is given full expression in the great tabernacle in St. Lorenz (1493–96), a slender, graceful tower of Gothic architectural forms that reaches up to the vaults of the choir. The large, kneeling portraits of Kraft and his two assistants serve as atlantes at the base of the monument and each tier is a setting for reliefs and then freestanding scenes of the Passion of Christ, culminating in the Crucifixion.

The reliefs of Kraft's later years are less spectacular and more subdued: those for the Weigh House (1497) and for the Pergenstorffer (1498–99), Rebeck (1500), and Landauer (1503) families. The sandstone reliefs of the Stations of the Cross for the Cemetery of St. John (1505–08; Nürnberg, Germanic National Museum), achieve the drama of Kraft's earlier works but in slow, deliberate, agonizing rhythms.

BIBLIOGRAPHY. W. Schwemmer, *Adam Kraft*, Nürnberg, 1958.

DONALD GODDARD

KRAMER, PIETER LODEWIJK. Dutch architect (1881–   ). Born in Amsterdam, he studied in the studio of P. J. H. Cuijpers (1903–13). He designed several of the expressionistic apartments in Amsterdam and De Bijenkorf, a department store in The Hague (1926).

BIBLIOGRAPHY. G. A. Platz, *Die Baukunst der neuesten Zeit*, 2d ed., Berlin, 1930.

KRAMSKOI, IVAN NIKOLAYEVICH. Russian painter and graphic artist (b. Novaya Sotnya, 1837; d. St. Petersburg, 1887). Kramskoi studied at the St. Petersburg Academy, but resigned from that institution to become a leading member of the "Wanderers" group. He painted portraits and religious subjects in a naturalistic style. *See* WANDERERS, THE.

KRAN. Tribe living near the Dan in the Liberia–Ivory Coast border area. Their masks are among the most grotesquely spectacular of this region, embodying, like certain Ngere works, composite images of human and boarlike features. Some expert brass casting is done. The human figure seldom is carved in the round.

See also AFRICA, PRIMITIVE ART OF (WEST AFRICA: LIBERIA).

BIBLIOGRAPHY. E. Leuzinger, *Africa: The Art of the Negro Peoples*, New York, 1960.

Kouros type. Archaic figure of an idealized youthful athlete, ca. 600 B.C. Metropolitan Museum of Art, New York (Fletcher Fund, 1932).

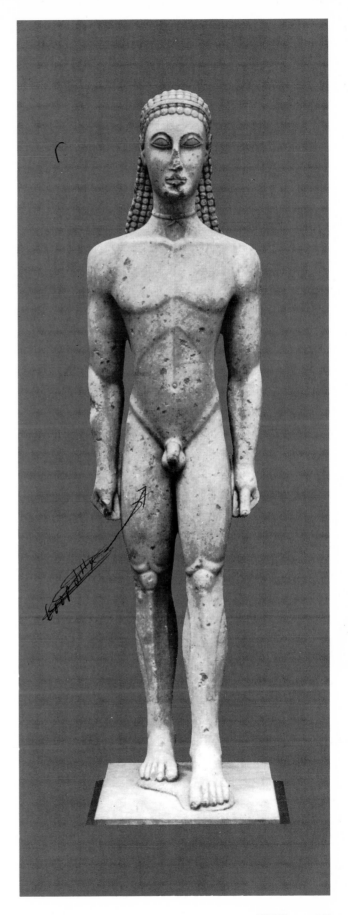

KRATER (Crater). Large pottery vessel with a mouth broad enough to allow a jug to be dipped within it. It was used for mixing wine with water in ancient Greece. Most examples were embellished with fine paintings, often of mythological subjects. Four distinct shapes enjoyed popularity from the 6th through the 4th century B.C.: column, volute, calyx, and bell.

BIBLIOGRAPHY. G. M. A. Richter and M. J. Milne, *Shapes and Names of Athenian Vases*, New York, 1935.

KREFELD: KAISER-WILHELM MUSEUM. German collection founded in 1897. It is still housed in the original building, which was enlarged in 1912. The museum specializes in paintings, from medieval times to the present, particularly by masters of German schools, notably expressionism. This collection is supplemented by a rich body of works by graphic artists, especially of the 19th and 20th centuries, and an outstanding collection of more than 3,000 posters, from 1900 to the present. Examples of sculpture go back as far as about 1100 (a Romanesque crucifix) and include fine Rhenish Madonnas (from ca. 1400) and pieces from the Italian Renaissance (by Donatello, Verrocchio, the Della Robbias, and so on), 19th-century works by Meunier and Rodin, and 20th-century works by Lehmbruck, Picasso, Calder, and others. The applied arts are represented by articles such as furniture from the late Middle Ages through 1900 and a glass and ceramics collection. There are also fine specimens of non-European art from the Near East, the South Seas, and Africa.

BIBLIOGRAPHY. H. Jedding, *Keysers Führer durch Museen und Sammlungen*, Heidelberg, Munich, 1961.

KREIS, WILHELM. German architect (b. Eltville, 1873; d. Honnef, 1955). Kreis studied in Brunswick, Karlsruhe, and Berlin and taught and worked in Düsseldorf and Dresden from 1926 on. Among his executed works are the tall Wilhelm Marx Haus, Düsseldorf (1924), and exhibition buildings in Düsseldorf (1926).

BIBLIOGRAPHY. G. A. Platz, *Die Baukunst der neuesten Zeit*, 2d ed., Berlin, 1930.

KREMLIN, MOSCOW. Walled inner city of the Russian capital, located on the Moskva River. The Kremlin is an impressive ensemble of palaces and churches of various periods. Its origins go back to a wooden citadel of the 11th to 12th centuries that stood on the site of the present Armory. Several times enlarged, the Kremlin was finally rebuilt in stone (1366–67). In the following decades the Cathedral of the Nativity of the Virgin was erected, and other churches were embellished with icons by such painters as Theophanes the Greek and Andrei Rublev.

In the 15th century, changes in architectural fashion and the discovery of new techniques of fortification made a thoroughgoing reconstruction desirable. Aristotele Fioravanti of Bologna was summoned to take charge of this work, and his Cathedral of the Assumption (1475–79), erected in a somewhat "modernized" form of the traditional Russian style, became Russia's mother church. Other buildings, including the Nikolskaya and Arsenal towers, are north Italian in inspiration. The Granovitaya Palata (faceted hall), built by Pietro Solario between 1487 and 1491, displays a splendid rusticated façade. *See also* USPENSKY CATHEDRAL, MOSCOW.

The Cathedral of the Archangel Michael (1505–09) served as the pantheon of the Russian czars. Towering over these buildings is the Ivan the Great Belfry (1505–08). The 17th century saw the construction of the Teremnoy (Belvedere) Palace, the Poteshny (Amusement) Palace, and the residence of the patriarch. When St. Petersburg became Russia's capital in 1713, the development of the Kremlin came to an abrupt halt. Between 1776 and 1788, however, Matvei Kazakov built the Senate, which is justly famed for its spacious state room surmounted by a coffered dome. The Kremlin suffered severe damage during Napoleon's occupation of Moscow and was restored between 1814 and 1835. The Armory (1844–51) houses a unique collection of metalwork and precious objects; the exhibits include arms and armor, regalia, gold and silver vessels, and ornate coaches.

Jutting out from the Kremlin wall into Red Square is the Tomb of Lenin, a massive, off-center stepped pyramid designed by A. V. Shchoussev in 1926. Within, the body of Lenin is displayed like a relic in melodramatic lighting.

The latest substantial addition to the Kremlin is the Palace of the Congresses of 1961, designed by M. V. Posokhin and others in a version of the International Style of the West.

BIBLIOGRAPHY. B. A. Rybakov, ed., *Treasures in the Kremlin*, London, 1962; N. N. Voronin, ed., *Palaces and Churches in the Kremlin*, London, 1966.

WAYNE DYNES

KREMSER-SCHMIDT, *see* SCHMIDT, MARTIN JOHANN.

Per Krohg, *Hjemkomsten*, 1923. Fresco. Maritime School, Oslo.

KRESILAS, see CRESILAS.

KRICKE, NORBERT. German sculptor (1922–   ). Born in Düsseldorf, he attended the Berlin Academy of Art. After World War II, in which he was a military flier, he traveled widely in Europe. He has had one-man exhibits in Munich, Paris, Wuppertal, and Freiburg im Breisgau. The artist's style is remarkably tense, reflecting his memories of auditory mechanical sensations connected with flying. He uses bunched compositions of metallic rods or wires, some knotted, some extended sheaflike in space. Kricke lives in Düsseldorf.

BIBLIOGRAPHY. Kaiser Wilhelm Museum, *Norbert Kricke*, Krefeld, 1962.

KRIEGHOFF, CORNELIUS. Canadian painter (b. Amsterdam, 1815; d. Chicago, 1872). He trained in Düsseldorf. In Canada from 1840 to 1868, he lived first in Montreal, and then in Quebec. Krieghoff was a prolific painter of French-Canadian *habitant* life.

BIBLIOGRAPHY. M. Barbeau, *Cornelius Krieghoff . . .*, Toronto, 1934.

KRIMMEL, JOHN LEWIS. American painter and miniaturist (b. Württemberg, Germany, 1787; d. Philadelphia, 1821). He went to the United States in 1810. Krimmel painted portraits and city genre scenes, for example, *The Fourth of July in Center Square, Philadelphia* (ca. 1810; Philadelphia, Pennsylvania Academy of Fine Arts).

KRISHNA (Krsna). Most celebrated hero of Indian mythology and most popular of all the Hindu deities. He is the eighth avatar of Vishnu, about whom, in the Bhāgavata Purāna, many stories are told concerning his mischievous pranks as a child, the follies of his boyhood, and the amours of his youth. In the Bhagavad Gītā, Krishna is the charioteer of the warrior Arjuna, who addresses him as the "supreme universal spirit." His principal wife was Rukmiṇī, but, being the divine lover, he had some 16,000 more and supposedly a total of 180,000 sons. Dark of skin, he is usually represented as deep blue in color, playing the flute for the cows and the *gopīs* (cowherd girls).

KRITIOS AND NESIOTES, see CRITIUS AND NESIOTES.

KRIVOKLAT (Purglitz) CASTLE. Czechoslovakian castle built in the late 13th century and rebuilt under Vladislav II in 1493–1522. It was later altered several times (1826–84, 1906–12, and 1925–38). Of its ancient portions, still preserved are the palace, the chapel, the fortress, and a cylindrical tower.

BIBLIOGRAPHY. Z. Wirth, *Burgen und Schlösser in böhmischen Ländern*, Prague, 1960.

KROHG, PER. Norwegian painter (1889–1965). From 1897 to 1930 he lived principally in Paris. He studied under his father, Christian Krohg, at the Académie Colarossi (1903–07), and with Matisse (1907–09). In 1930 he returned to Norway. Krohg taught at the State Art and Craft School from 1935 to 1946, when he was appointed professor at the State Art Academy, Oslo. A major figure in the renaissance of mural painting in Norway since World War I, Krohg executed several important commissions, including frescoes in the Maritime School and Town Hall, Oslo, and a mural in the Security Council chamber of the United Nations, New York. His style is decorative and expressive with large, flowing rhythms. In his easel paintings (landscape, genre, portraits) there is often a freer, shimmering movement of line and values and, at times, a monumental or decorative character related to the frescoes.

BIBLIOGRAPHY. P. Krohg, *24 farveplansjer etter malerier*, forord av J. H. Langaard, Oslo, 1947.

KROLL, LEON. American painter and lithographer (1884–   ). Born in New York City, he studied at the Art Students League and the National Academy there and in Paris with Jean-Paul Laurens. Kroll's early works are strongly brushed urban and industrial landscapes such as *The Bridge* (1910–11; Baltimore, Union Memorial Hospital), which are loosely related to the style of the New York realists. His later paintings are basically academic in style, despite the sense of plasticity and color derived from Cézanne and Renoir. Their subjects are mostly still lifes and the figure, such as *Nude in a Blue Chair* (1930; New York, Whitney Museum). Kroll has executed murals for the Justice Building, Washington, D.C. (1937), and the War Memorial in Worcester, Mass. (1938–41).

BIBLIOGRAPHY. L. Kroll, *Leon Kroll* (American Artists, monograph 17), New York, 1946.

KROLLER-MULLER MUSEUM, OTTERLO, see OTTERLO: KROLLER-MULLER MUSEUM.

KRONSTADT CATHEDRAL. Russian cathedral, named the Church of St. Andrew. It marks the apogee of Russian neoclassicism. The Cathedral is the work of Adrian Dmitrievich Zakharov (1761–1811), the architect responsible for the major building enterprises of imperial St. Petersburg.

BIBLIOGRAPHY. G. H. Hamilton, *The Art and Architecture of Russia*, Baltimore, 1954.

KRSNA, see KRISHNA.

KRUGER, FRANZ. German painter (b. Köthen, 1797; d. Berlin, 1857). An important representative of the Berlin Biedermeier style, Krüger is called "Pferde Krüger" (Horse Krüger) because of his many equestrian portraits and parade and festival scenes, such as *Parade auf dem Opernplatz* (1829), in the Hermitage, Leningrad. He was trained at the Berlin Academy (1812–14), where he was later a professor, and was also attached to the Prussian court as a painter.

BIBLIOGRAPHY. E. Waldmann, *Die Kunst des Realismus und des Impressionismus im 19. Jahrhundert*, Berlin, 1927.

KRUMPER, HANS. German sculptor and architect (b. Weilheim, ca. 1570; d. Munich, 1634). Krumper was a student of Hubert Gerhard in Munich and also traveled to Italy. From 1609 he was court painter in Munich. His most important works are bronze sculptures in the style of Romanizing Netherlandish artists such as Pieter de Witte and Federico Sustris. A typical example is his *Patrona Bavariae* (1616; Munich, Residenz Palace).

BIBLIOGRAPHY. N. Lieb, *Münchener Barockbaumeister*, Munich, 1941.

KRUYDER, HERMAN. Dutch painter (b. Lage Vuursche, 1881; d. Amsterdam, 1935). He studied in Haarlem. Kruyder moved from an early realistic style toward a decorative semireligious expressionism in paintings of landscapes, figures, and animals influenced by Constant Permeke.

KRZESZOW, ABBEY CHURCH OF, see GRUSSAU, ABBEY CHURCH OF.

KSHITIGARBHA (Ksitigarbha; Japanese, Jizo; Chinese, Ti-tsang). "Earth" bodhisattva (the name means "Matrix of the Earth"), who has vowed to save all creatures from hell during the interim between the passing of Gautama Buddha and the advent of Maitreya. His symbols are the *cintāmaṇi* (magic jewel) and *khakkhara* (alarm staff), the latter to warn insects in his path so that he may not step on them. *See* GAUTAMA; MAITREYA.

As Ti-tsang, the last of the major bodhisattvas to be added to the Buddhist religion, he is essentially a creation of the Chinese. Prominently worshiped in the Far East Ti-tsang, or Jizō, is viewed as the protector of children, the guardian of travelers, the guardian of the earth, and the compassionate bodhisattva who relieves those suffering in hell. He was well established in the Buddhist pantheon in China by the 7th century.

BIBLIOGRAPHY. M. W. De Visser, "The Bodhisattva Ti-tsang (Jizō) in China and Japan," *Ostasiatische Zeitschrift*, II, III, 1913-1915.

KU. Chinese term for one of the most distinctive forms of ancient bronze ritual vessels. The *ku* is shaped like a tall beaker, with a wide flaring lip resembling a trumpet and a slighter spreading foot. Just below the middle of the vessel is a pair of cruciform perforations that seems to have escaped satisfactory explanation, as have the precise origin and exact use of this beautifully shaped vessel.

KUANG. Chinese term for a class of ancient ceremonial bronze vessels shaped like the familiar gravy boat used in the West. There are variations of types within the overall class of *kuang*. Some types are lidded; others have ladles and are open. The foot is most frequently round or ovoid, although a number of squared *kuang* exist. There is no known pottery prototype for this particular class of vessel; its history is essentially seen in the bronzes. In the lidded varieties of the vessel, the shape assumes that of a zoomorph, which is made up of elements combined from owls, tigers, snakes, or bulls. The precise use of the *kuang* is a matter of speculation, although there is little doubt that they were employed as containers for liquids.

BIBLIOGRAPHY. W. Willets, *Chinese Art*, vol. 1, Harmondsworth, 1958.

KUANGTUNG WARE. Brown-bodied Chinese stoneware, usually with a blue-black glaze that is streaked. The name refers to the province of Kuangtung in southern China. Most of the kilns were located outside Canton.

KUAN-HSIU. Chinese Ch'an (Zen) painter (832–912). His family name was Chiang, Kuan-hsiu being the religious name by which he is best known in the history of art. He was born in Chin-hua, Chekiang Province. Quite early in his life he was placed in a Ch'an monastery, and even-

Alfred Kubin, *The Girl on the Hippopotamus.* **Drawing.**

tually he earned recognition for his poetry, painting, and teaching. His most striking contributions to Chinese painting history are the series of lohans that he painted on numerous occasions. *See* ARHAT; ZEN.

The best known of the extant attributed lohan paintings is the set in the Imperial Household Collection, Tokyo (formerly in the collection of Baron Takahashi), in which the sixteen lohans are depicted individually in a bizarre and grotesque manner bordering on caricature. The series has suffered from later retouching, but two of the paintings are well enough preserved to merit close attention. One is sometimes called a self-portrait of Kuan-hsiu himself; the other portrays a lohan seated on a strangely shaped rocky ledge. Altogether the set of lohans is a unique manifestation of Ch'an Buddhist painting at an early stage of development in China and can be seen as the precursor of the "shock-image" type of painting encountered in later Ch'an paintings of the Southern Sung period.

MARTIE W. YOUNG

KUAN TAO-SHENG. Chinese painter (1262–ca. 1325). The wife of the famous Chao Meng-fu, she came from Wu-hsing in Chekiang Province. She was at one time a pupil of Chao Meng-fu, and, like all members of the Chao family, she became known as a painter. The subjects that most interested her were bamboos and orchids. *See* CHAO MENG-FU.

KUAN T'UNG. Chinese painter (fl. 1st quarter of 10th cent.). Kuan T'ung, who was born in Ch'ang-an, is usually linked with Ching Hao as one of the great 10th-century landscape painters. Little is known of his life, and few of his paintings have survived, as is the case with Ching Hao. Among the better-known works attributed to Kuan T'ung is the large landscape *Waiting for the Ferry* in the National Palace Museum Collection, Sun Yat-sen Museum in Formosa. *See* CHING HAO.

KUAN WARE. Term widely encountered in discussions of Chinese ceramics, the character *kuan* meaning "imperial" or "official." The name, strictly speaking, is applied to wares produced at the imperial kilns in Hang-chou, the capital of the Southern Sung dynasty after 1127. Among the Kuan-ware kilns were those of Chiao-t'an. The kilns remained active after the fall of the Southern Sung dynasty. *See* CHIAO-T'AN.

In general, Kuan ware is distinguished by a thick opaque glaze that was applied in several layers and has a rather wide crackle. The color shades from grayish brown through gray to a beautiful blue lavender. The brown-gray pieces were once called Ko ware, *ko* meaning "elder brother," a reference to the elder Chang, who is credited with developing the ware. The term "Ko ware" is more or less obsolete and is hardly distinguishable from Kuan ware in general. Some sources also call ware produced by the Hang-chou imperial kilns "southern Kuan."

BIBLIOGRAPHY. Oriental Ceramic Society, *Ju and Kuan Wares...* (exhibition catalog), London, 1952.

KUAN-YIN, *see* AVALOKITESVARA.

KUBERA, *see* KUVERA.

KUBIN, ALFRED. Austrian expressionist graphic artist, illustrator, and painter (1877–1959). In his autobiography, *Sansara* (1913), Kubin described his early life as a series of vivid traumatic experiences with family unhappiness and school failure. He was born in Bohemia and attended the Industrial Art School at Salzburg; he then became apprenticed to an uncle who was a photographer in Klagenfurt. Kubin's stark grim linear distortions embody a fantastic world of visions of haunting immediacy. In his novel of 1909, *Die andere Seite*, Kubin wrote of his dream world that "here fantasies were simple reality."

Kubin arrived in Munich in 1898, when that city was in the midst of artistic ferment. His drawing *Crushing* (1903) shows a strange animal, half fish, half reptile, about to crush a tiny man situated at the edge of an abyss. Like this drawing, much of Kubin's work is underscored thematically by an imminent catastrophe. In spirit, Kubin is related somewhat to Ensor; in spite of the uniqueness of his work, he is indebted to artists who were popular around the turn of the century, notably Goya and Beardsley, and he had the greatest respect for the work of Max Klinger. *Mme la Décadence* (1900) shows the influence of Beardsley but the combination of elements is entirely Kubin's.

In 1903 Kubin exhibited with Kandinsky in the Phalanx; found his first patron, Hans von Weber of Munich, who financed his first portfolio; and completed his *War* series. In 1905 in Paris he met Redon and turned toward a more direct symbolism. In his pen drawing, *Night Encounter*, there is no direct threat of violence, but the shadowiness of the background and the dim light seem to presage some sinister turn of events. After 1905 Kubin began a fantastic biological series: in his pictures of mollusks and amoebas, he combined microscopic observation with dream images.

The many books Kubin illustrated seem to have been chosen for their macabre settings. Among these were Poe's *Goldbug* (1910) and *The Beating Heart* (1923), Wilde's *The Ballad of Reading Gaol* (1918), and Barbey d'Aurevilly's *Devil's Children* (1921). In spite of some apparent similarities to Klee, Kubin shows little of Klee's gentle humor but rather a satanic glee. Kubin's art is an imaginative and psychological experience that had considerable influence during the post-World War I era.

BIBLIOGRAPHY. L. W. Rochowanski, "Austrian Painters of Today," *The Studio*, CXXXVIII, July, 1949; B. S. Myers, *The German Expressionists: A Generation in Revolt*, New York, 1957; P. Selz, *German Expressionist Painting*, Berkeley, 1957.

ABRAHAM A. DAVIDSON

KUDARA KANNON OF HORYUJI. Japanese wood sculpture (7th cent.). According to an ancient legend, the statue was either made in Japan, by a Korean artist who had emigrated from Kudara (Japanese for Paekche, a Korean kingdom), or made in Korea and imported to Japan. Its slender, cylindrical body is extremely tall, and the shallow delicate carving of the drapery folds suggests a thin, clinging material. The weightless elegance of the body and the gentleness of expression enhance the character of the Kannon (Sanskrit, Avalokiteśvara), the most compassionate of the bodhisattvas.

BIBLIOGRAPHY. R. T. Paine and A. Soper, *The Art and Architecture of Japan*, Baltimore, 1955; *Masterpieces of Japanese Sculpture*, introd., text, and commentaries by J. E. Kidder, Jr., Rutland, Vt., 1961.

KUDON, *see* GAUTAMA.

KUDU. Architectural ornament used on Brahmanical temples of southern India from about the 8th century. Kudus derive from the ornate late form of the chaitya hall façade arch and serve as acroterial antefixes above the line of the cornice.

KUDURRU, *see* BOUNDARY STONES.

KUEI. Chinese term for a group of ancient bronze ritual vessels used as food containers. The *kuei* is usually deep and circular in shape with two or four vertical handles (occasionally no handles at all). There are many variants of the shape. In the middle Chou period (900–600 B.C.) the vessel was mounted on a massive rectangular base that was cast as one piece with the vessel itself; other examples from the same period stand on three small legs. The term *kuei* is a modern form of the character *chiu* found in the ancient inscriptions.

K'UEI DRAGON. Motif in the vocabulary of early Chinese ritual vessels. A form of dragon having one leg, the *k'uei* frequently appears in conjunction with the t'ao-t'ieh mask. It is mentioned in three pre-Han-dynasty texts (before 2d cent. B.C.) in association with myth and rainmaking. In the Sung dynasty (960–1279) the *k'uei* was identified with the motif that occurs so often on Shang bronzes, in which a dragonlike creature can be seen, usually in side view with one leg prominent. The *k'uei* is always shown with mouth agape in the bronze designs; when two *k'uei* dragons are butted together nose to nose, they form the essential features of the famous t'ao-t'ieh mask seen frontally. *See* T'AO-T'IEH.

Kufic. Inscription on the rim of a bowl, probably from Nishapur. Victoria and Albert Museum, London.

The *k'uei* appears as an ornamental motif in bronze design quite apart from the t'ao-t'ieh, however, and is frequently shown independently, with horns or beaks sometimes added. Next to the t'ao-t'ieh, the *k'uei* is the most common single motif in the design vocabulary of the early Chinese bronze casters, and, as in the case of the t'ao-t'ieh, the precise meaning of this creature is a matter of speculation.

BIBLIOGRAPHY. W. Watson, *Handbook to the Collections of Early Chinese Antiquities*, London, 1963; W. K. Ho, "Shang and Chou Bronzes," *Cleveland Museum of Art, Bulletin*, LI, September, 1964.

MARTIE W. YOUNG

KUFIC. Angular variety of Arabic lettering whose name is derived from Kufa, in Mesopotamia. It lends itself to carved inscriptions because of its geometric precision; thus it was reserved for Korans and other formal manuscripts. Types of Kufic include Abbasid (9th–10th cent.), which features short verticals and drawnout horizontals. From Iranian Kufic, which emphasized verticals, was evolved Saljuk (10th–12th cent.), a script whose verticals terminated in decorative arabesques and palmettes.

BIBLIOGRAPHY. M. S. Dimand, *A Handbook of Muhammadan Art*, 3d ed., New York, 1958.

KUHN, JUSTUS ENGELHARDT. American painter (fl. 1708–17; d. 1717). Kühn's portraits of children of wealthy Maryland landowners reveal, beneath overly lavish accessories and insistent detail, something of the power of design and the sense of pattern of the early limners. *Eleanor Darnall* (Baltimore, Maryland Historical Society) is a fine example of his work.

BIBLIOGRAPHY. J. H. Pleasants, *Justus Engelhardt Kühn*, Worcester, 1937.

KUHN, WALT. American painter (1880–1949). Kuhn was born in New York City. In 1899 he took a position as a cartoonist in San Francisco. He contributed to a number of publications in the East, such as the *New York Sun* and the old *Life*. He was thirty when he sold his first picture. Kuhn studied informally in Paris and visited Germany, Holland, and Spain. He taught at the New York School of Art in 1908–09 and at the Art Students League in 1926–27. An important adviser to the lawyer John Quinn in forming a collection, Kuhn also served in a similar capacity to Miss Lillie Bliss, many of whose acquisitions were bequeathed to the Museum of Modern Art in New York.

Kuhn was secretary to the Association of American Painters and Sculptors (1912), when Arthur B. Davies was president. Together, they were significant in organizing and presenting the Armory Show of 1913 in which such modern masters as Matisse, Picasso, Duchamp, Brancusi, and others were first presented to a large public. Kuhn was also included in the exhibition, and in 1938 he wrote a brochure on the show. As a consultant and designer for the Union Pacific Railroad, he designed the interiors of club cars and planned, in part, the Sun Valley resort in Idaho. In 1948 he produced his *State of Maine Follies*, a revue with circus acts, burlesque skits, and choruses for an open-air theater in Ogunquit, Maine.

Kuhn's earliest paintings recall those of Robert Henri and George Luks; that is, they develop from the Ashcan school tradition. A distinct change occurred after his intimate involvement with the Armory Show; his painting began to show the influence of Matisse, Derain, and Picasso of the Blue Period. In his mature work, for which he is best known, the role Cézanne played in the formation of his style is apparent.

Kuhn's best-known works are those of clowns and acrobats. They are rarely shown performing but appear isolated in a portrait situation, as if they were posing for the artist just prior to or after a performance. Kuhn is fond of showing them partially in costume with grease paint on. He never shows them as comic figures, nor does he

Walt Kuhn, *The Blue Clown*, 1931. Whitney Museum of American Art, New York.

sentimentalize them. He often places them in a strong overhead light and defines contours with bold, linear accents. *The Blue Clown* (1931; New York, Whitney Museum of American Art) is a typical painting. Kuhn also did a number of still lifes, favoring game or apples spilling from a basket. These pictures often recall the rugged realism of Courbet.

BIBLIOGRAPHY. P. Bird, *Fifty Paintings by Walt Kuhn*, New York, 1940; P. R. Adams, "Walt Kuhn," *College Art Journal*, IX, no. 1, 1949.   ROBERT REIFF

KU HUNG-CHUNG. Chinese painter (fl. Southern T'ang court, mid-10th cent.). Ku Hung-chung was a rival for figure-painting honors with Chou Wen-chü. He is famous for one particular painting called *The Night Entertainment of Han Hsi-tsai*, a work that has been preserved in several versions, one of which may well date to the time of Ku Hung-chung. This hand scroll, now in the Hui-hua-kuan in Peking, supposedly was a truthful piece of recording by Ku Hung-chung of the lavishly scaled entertainments enjoyed by Han Hsi-tsai, a man of great learning who was being considered for high office by the Emperor.

BIBLIOGRAPHY. L. Sickman and A. Soper, *The Art and Architecture of China*, Baltimore, 1956.

KU K'AI-CHIH. Chinese painter (ca. 345–405). A native of Kiangsu Province, Ku K'ai-chih was known by his *tzu* Ch'ang-k'ang but was more often referred to by his *hao* Hu-t'ou. Along with his contemporary, Lu T'an-wei, he is considered the greatest of the ancient masters. The earliest critic to mention him was Hsieh Ho, who did not accord him the first rank but rather reserved his praises for Lu T'an-wei; on the other hand, Chang Yen-yüan, the outstanding spokesman of the T'ang dynasty, considered Ku K'ai-chih the greater of the two early giants of painting. Subsequent critics have tended to agree with Chang Yen-yüan, and most traditional histories of Chinese painting begin their accounts with Ku K'ai-chih. *See* CHANG YEN-YUAN; HSIEH HO; LU T'AN-WEI.

The rather colorful life and career of Ku are recounted in a number of sources, including the official history of the Chin period. Many interesting stories which surround Ku must be accorded apocryphal status, but of his forceful personality there can be little doubt. His painting style, however, is less well preserved. The essay attributed to Ku K'ai-chih, entitled *On Painting the Cloud-terrace Mountain*, has been handed down probably in a corrupted and fragmentary form, since it is more an elaborate description of a Taoist painting than a statement of Ku's ideas concerning landscape painting.

The most famous of Ku K'ai-chih's attributed paintings is the hand scroll preserved in the British Museum, London, and usually titled in Western literature *Admonitions of the Instructress to the Court Ladies* (Nü-shih-chen in Chinese). A great deal has been written about the scroll, and its history in terms of previous collections is well recorded. Although the *Admonitions* scroll is not universally accepted as an original from Ku's hand, modern critical scholarship has not been able to do more than suggest that it is possibly a later copy, judging by details of shading in some portions of the scroll. But it is quite possible that the British Museum scroll represents something unique in Chinese painting history: an authentic document of the 4th century.

The *Admonitions* scroll is a didactic painting, consisting of illustrations to a moralizing text, and concerns the matter of how court ladies should deport themselves. The sermon is delivered by the court instructress, who appears in the final scene with scroll and brush in hand. The admonitions are given by means of short verses accompanying each of the seven scenes that make up the scroll. The style of the painting is one of remarkable delicacy and firmness of brush lines, quite different from the calligraphic strokes seen in the earlier Ross tiles in the Museum of Fine Arts, Boston. Ku K'ai-chih's figure proportions are cast in the same Six Dynasties style observed in Buddhist sculpture: wispy, attenuated forms that seem to float on the surface of the painting, contained by even boundary lines of unvarying thickness, with light washes of color against the silk ground. Subsequent repaintings have marred the scroll to a great extent, but enough is left to indicate a masterly hand at work.

The second attributed Ku K'ai-chih painting is the *Nymph of the Lo River* (Lo-shen t'u), version of which are in the Freer Gallery, Washington, D.C., and the National Palace Museum Collection, Sun Yat-sen Museum, in Taiwan (Formosa). The well-known Freer version is a later copy, and on this point there is virtual agreement, although the date of the copy is uncertain. The painting probably preserves some aspects of Ku's composition, and literary records confirm that Ku did execute such a scroll at one time in his career. The Freer scroll, therefore, is an interesting document even as a copy, preserving dimly,

Ku K'ai-chih, *Admonitions of the Instructress*, detail. Paint on silk. British Museum, London.

at least, another side of Ku K'ai-chih in terms of subject matter (the legendary tale) and in the landscape elements employed in this painting.

BIBLIOGRAPHY. E. Chavannes, "Note sur la peinture de Kou Kai-tcne conservée au British Museum," *T'oung Pao*, X, 1909; A. Waley, *An Introduction to the Study of Chinese Painting*, London, 1923; P. Pelliot, "Le plus ancien possesseur connu du 'Kou K'ai-tche' du British Museum," *T'oung Pao*, XXX, 1933; Ch'ên Shih-hsiang, *Biography of Ku K'ai-chih* (Institute of East Asiatic Studies, University of California, Chinese Dynastic Histories Translations, no. 2), Berkeley, 1953; M. Sullivan, "On Painting the Yün-t'ai-shan, a Reconsideration of the Essay Attributed to Ku K'ai-chih," *Artibus Asiae*, XVII, 1954; T. Pan, *Ku K'ai-chih (Chung-kuo ming-hua ts'ung-shu)*, Shanghai, 1958.   MARTIE W. YOUNG

KULMBACH, HANS SUSS VON (Hans Suess). German painter and draftsman for the graphic arts and glass painting (b. Kulmbach, 1480; d. Nürnberg, 1522). With the exception of Hans Baldung-Grien, Kulmbach was the most important of Dürer's students. He studied with Jacopo de' Barbari before joining Dürer's workshop early in the 16th century, and from 1514 to 1516 he worked in Cracow. Kulmbach later returned to Nürnberg, where he worked until his death.

The relationship between Dürer and Kulmbach was very close. Dürer frequently provided the designs for Kulmbach's more monumental works. Consequently, Kulmbach's style was strongly influenced by his master, and his best works were created in conjunction with him. Kulmbach's most important works are eight panels with the *Scenes from the Lives of St. Peter and St. Paul* (1511; Florence, Uffizi), *Adoration of the Magi* (1513; Berlin, former State Museums), the famous *Tucher Altar* (1514; Nürnberg, St. Sebaldkirche), the *St. Katherine Altar* (1516; Cracow, Marienkirche), the *Coronation of the Virgin*

Kültepe. Terra-cotta pitcher. Hittite Museum, Ankara.

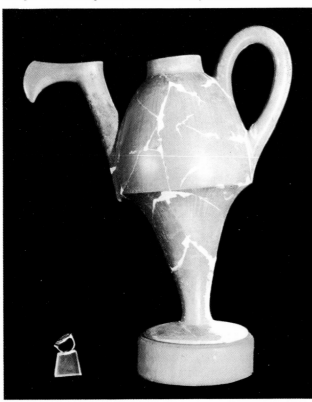

(Vienna, Academy of Fine Arts), and the *Johannes Altar* (Cracow, St. Florian). Notable portraits by his hand are in Munich, Vienna, Besançon, Mannheim, and Dublin museums.

Kulmbach's style is more delicate than that of Dürer; his figures are less plastic. His landscapes are more open, more like Italian park landscapes of the Venetian Renaissance painting than the wilderness landscapes of German 16th-century painting. Kulmbach's color is also more subdued, with delicate warm tones predominating. These stylistic features give his art an appearance that is more Italian than Düreresque. The source of Kulmbach's Italianism is at present inexplicable, for no documentary evidence exists which indicates an Italian trip. His early apprenticeship with Jacopo de' Barbari is only a partial explanation, since Kulmbach's later Italianisms differ from Barbari's style.

BIBLIOGRAPHY. F. Winkler, "Die Holzschnitte des Hans von Kulmbach," *Jahrbuch der preussischen Kunstsammlungen*, LXII, 1941; F. Winkler, *Hans von Kulmbach; Leben und Werk*, Kulmbach, 1959.   DONALD L. EHRESMANN

KULTEPE (Kanesh). Important ancient town in northeastern Anatolia, Turkey. The center of various successive cultures, it reached a high degree of civilization from about 2000 to 1700 B.C. Inhabited by the Hattians and colonized by the Assyrians, it was captured by Anittas, the Hittite king, in about 1850 B.C. A dagger bearing Anittas's name was found in a Kültepe palace, along with burnished clay rhytons with bulls' heads and a fragment of a basalt lion's head, proving the existence of sculpture there early in the 2d millennium B.C. In Karun, a suburban trading station of Kültepe, Assyrian business archives, consisting of thousands of clay tablets, were discovered. There was also remarkable polychrome pottery—red burnished clay vessels with dragons' heads for handles and geometric designs. The domestic buildings were of the megaron type —a large hall with four columns supporting the roof grouped around a central hearth.

BIBLIOGRAPHY. S. Lloyd, *The Art of the Ancient Near East*, London, 1961; L. Woolley, *The Art of the Middle East*, New York, 1961.

KUMP, ERNEST J. American architect (1911–   ). He was born in Bakersfield, California. Kump was a partner of C. H. Franklin in Fresno before establishing his own office in San Francisco (1942). His practice includes many educational and civic buildings in California.

BIBLIOGRAPHY. New York, Museum of Modern Art, *Built in U.S.A., 1932–1944*, ed. E. Mock, New York, 1944.

KUNDIKA. Type of water vessel that originated in India but became popular in Chinese ceramic production after the introduction of Buddhism. It is characterized by a globular body, a long neck ending in a tapering spout after a flared section, and a smaller spout on the shoulder of the vessel. The vessel was used by Buddhist monks and was called *pao-p'ing* by the Chinese.

KUNG HSIEN. Chinese painter (fl. Nanking, 2d half of 18th cent.). His *tzu* was Pan-ch'ien. Kung Hsien is usually considered the foremost painter of the "Eight Masters of Nanking." Although he was regarded by contemporaries as a somewhat strange and eccentric individual who

Kung Hsien, *Landscape*, detail of a handscroll. Ink on paper. Atkins Museum of Fine Arts, Kansas City, Mo.

chose to remain aloof from people, his dynamic personality seems to have influenced other painters; certainly his bold, rich, yet moody landscapes were stunning revelations of a private and new way of looking at the world. His famous remark, "There has been no one before me, and there will be no one after me," indicates his total independence and individualism. He cultivated a small garden outside Nanking and died in poverty, totally consistent to the end in his view of himself and others. His landscapes have a characteristic somber and ghostly tone, with deep tonalities of ink and leaden skies that are reminiscent of El Greco. People are never seen in his paintings; in this respect he seems to have an affinity with Ni Tsan, the Yüan painter whose technical approach was virtually the opposite of his. *See* NI TSAN.

BIBLIOGRAPHY. A. Lippe, "Kung Hsien and the Nanking School," *Oriental Art*, n.s., II, 1956, IV, 1958.

KUNG K'AI. Chinese painter (fl. 2d half of 13th cent.). His *tzu* was Sheng-yu. Born in Huai-yin, Kiangsu Province, Kung K'ai was active at the Kin (Chin) capital in Peking during the Southern Sung period, and he gained a measure of recognition for his horse paintings. He is equally well known, however, for his paintings of Chung K'uei, the giant demon queller of Chinese legend, and in certain respects Kung K'ai himself had some of the physical and psychological attributes of this demon-hero. One famous painting by Kung K'ai in the Freer Gallery, Washington, D.C., is devoted to the Chung K'uei legend. *See* CHUNG K'UEI, THE DEMON QUELLER.

KUNG-PI, *see* BLUE-AND-GREEN STYLE.

KUNISADA (Utagawa Kunisada; Toyokuni III). Japanese Ukiyo-e print designer (1786–1865). Kunisada was a pupil of Toyokuni I and became the third leader of the Utagawa school. His portraits of actors and women epitomize the general decline of grace and quality in Ukiyo-e prints and reflect the decadent atmosphere of the end of the Edo period. *See* TOYOKUNI I; UKIYO-E; UTAGAWA SCHOOL.

BIBLIOGRAPHY. J. A. Michener, *Japanese Prints*, Rutland, Vt., 1959.

KUNIYOSHI (Utagawa Kuniyoshi). Japanese Ukiyo-e printmaker (1797–1861). Kuniyoshi was a pupil of Toyokuni I. He is noted for prints of fierce warriors, historical subjects, and actors of the Kabuki theater. His landscape prints are unusual in that they show a successful fusion of native and European styles. *See* TOYOKUNI I; UKIYO-E.

BIBLIOGRAPHY. B. W. Robinson, *Kuniyoshi*, London, 1961.

KUNIYOSHI, YASUO. American painter (b. Okayama, Japan, 1893; d. New York City, 1953). After going to the United States in 1906, he was encouraged by a high-school teacher to study art. He went to the Los Angeles School of Art and Design and later studied with Kenneth Hayes Miller at the Art Students League in New York. His first one-man show was held in 1922 in New York at the Daniel Gallery. In 1925 and 1928 he went to Paris where he saw much modern painting and was influenced by it. In 1931 he returned to Japan for a visit, and in 1935 he went to Mexico on a Guggenheim grant. Kuniyoshi was

Yasuo Kuniyoshi, *Deliverance*. Pencil. Whitney Museum of American Art, New York.

the first president of Artists Equity and cofounder of the American Artists Congress. In 1948 he was given a large retrospective exhibition at the Whitney Museum of American Art in New York, and in 1952 he was represented at the Venice Biennale.

In the early 1920s, Kuniyoshi took Campendonk and Chagall as models. With whimsical slyness, he depicts mischievous boys, heavy-lidded cows, fantastic landscapes, and the like in a piquant, decorative manner. In the 1930s his painting is more lyrical and naturalistic. He limits himself largely to studies of languid, pensive women and to still lifes composed of such disparate elements as a rose, a dismembered hobbyhorse, a torn poster, binoculars, a vase, an old umbrella, and so on. Gradated tones suggest atmosphere. Contours are extended and textures exaggerated. Silvery grays, delicate tans, rusts, and olive greens are favored colors.

In his last period, his palette is extended and bright colors—frosty reds, saffron yellows, lilacs, acid greens, and sharp blues—are juxtaposed to lend a posterlike, bittersweet quality somewhat in the manner of Ben Shahn's contemporaneous work. Kuniyoshi's painting assumes an ominous, almost sinister cast. His still lifes are composed of crumpled paper, rent cloth, disjointed mannequins, and so on, shown against a brooding sky or desolate stretch of land. He painted carnival figures, not as symbols of entertainment but as mystical, foreboding creatures, assemblages of grinning masks and limbs dehumanized in cataleptic gestures. These creatures perform mechanically and without benefit of an audience.

BIBLIOGRAPHY. L. Goodrich, *Yasuo Kuniyoshi*, New York, 1948.
ROBERT REIFF

K'UN-TS'AN (Shih-ch'i). Chinese painter (ca. 1610–ca. 1693). He was a native of Wu-ling in Hunan Province.

Classified as one of the 17th-century "eccentric" painters of China, K'un-ts'an led the moderate life of a Buddhist priest, and "eccentricity" was far less evident in his behavior than was the case with many of his contemporaries with whom he was later linked. As a young man he entered the priesthood, and with the fall of the Ming house in 1644 he retreated to the hills to pursue the personal meditation that inspired him. This monk-painter devoted his paintings to the depiction of mountain landscapes.

His works show a remarkable stylistic homogeneity: dense, complex in detail, with a richness of surface that is almost sensuous in its visual effect. In many respects his paintings echo the qualities of the earlier 10th-century landscapes: heroic and grand in concept. In the special world he created through his landscapes K'un-ts'an found the answer to his most pressing question, "how to find peace in a world of suffering."

BIBLIOGRAPHY. V. Contag, *Zwei Meister chinesischer Landschaftsmalerei: Shih-t'ao und Shih-ch'i*, Baden-Baden, 1955.

KUO CHUNG-SHU. Chinese painter (fl. 2d half of 10th cent.). His *tzu* was Shu-hsien. Kuo Chung-shu held several government positions, but his reckless behavior and addiction to wine eventually resulted in his exile. He was a gifted and precocious scholar who excelled in the category of *chieh-hua*, architectural paintings. A number of small album leaves in American collections are still attributed to this master.

KUO HSI. Chinese painter (fl. 2d half of 11th cent.). Born at Wen-hsien in Honan Province, Kuo Hsi was called to the court and served in the Painting Academy. He became a prolific landscape painter and was unanimously praised by his contemporaries and by later critics as well. In some ways he was the last great voice of the monumental style in the Northern Sung period, the consolidator of tendencies explored by the 10th-century masters, particularly Li Ch'eng, the painter to whom Kuo Hsi was most indebted stylistically. *See* LI CH'ENG.

The most important painting attributed to Kuo Hsi is the magnificent *Early Spring* in the National Palace Museum Collection, Sun Yat-sen Museum, in Taiwan (Formosa), a work dated by inscription to the year 1072. A work of overpowering scale and dimensions, it captures the special qualities of northern China: a landscape that is harsh, barren, enshrouded by mist, and marked by convoluted, almost tortured mountain forms that emerge as organic and powerful structures. But beneath this vision of Kuo Hsi is the constant concern for verisimilitude, and in its details *Early Spring* shows Kuo Hsi's preoccupation with representation of the real world: carefully distinguished trees, people, and temples, delineated with clarity and force.

Kuo Hsi's total concern with capturing the sense of reality is revealed also in his famous essay *Shan-shui hsün* (Remarks on Landscapes), where he defines as the ideal the construction of a landscape painting that arouses the feeling "one is really there." Among the paintings in the United States attributed to Kuo Hsi note should be made of the partial hand scroll in the Freer Gallery, Washington, D.C., which depicts a mountain-river landscape. The scroll, although lacking the organic mountain masses of

Early Spring, is further evidence of Kuo Hsi's special concern with capturing the physical reality of the great rivers, valleys, and mountains of China.

BIBLIOGRAPHY. Kuo Hsi, *An Essay on Landscape Painting*, London, 1936; O. Sirén, *Chinese Painting, Leading Masters and Principles*, vol. 1, New York, 1956; A. Waley, *An Introduction to the Study of Chinese Painting*, reissue, New York, 1958.

MARTIE W. YOUNG

KUO SSU. Chinese painter (fl. 2d half of 11th cent.). The son of the famous Kuo Hsi, he entered the Painting Academy of Hui-tsung about 1100. He specialized in horses, but he is historically more important as the author of an essay entitled *Lin-ch'üan kao-chih* (Lofty Message of Forests and Streams) in which are contained the thoughts and perhaps the notes of his illustrious father. *See* KUO HSI.

BIBLIOGRAPHY. O. Sirén, *Chinese Painting, Leading Masters and Principles*, vol. 2, New York, 1956.

KUPKA, FRANK (Frantisek). Czechoslovakian painter (b. Opocno, Bohemia, 1871; d. near Paris, 1957). Kupka may be identified with orphist cubism and with the development of nonobjective, geometrical abstraction. He studied at the Prague School of Fine Arts in 1888. In 1891 he lived in Vienna and exhibited at the first Kunstverein; in 1895 he settled in Paris. At the turn of the century Kupka was a prolific illustrator of books, one of which was Elie Faure's *Song of Songs* transposition. He won a prize at the 1902 St. Louis International Exposition.

In 1906 he began a series of exploratory studies which in 1911 emerged as abstractions. His Salon d'Automne entries of 1910 revealed both Fauvist and cubist tendencies and are notable principally for their bright color. To some degree under the influence of Delaunay's orphism, Kupka in 1912 and 1913 exhibited abstract compositions (*Fugue in Red and Blue*; *Philosophical Architecture*) in which rectangles, turned in space so as to have the effect of trapezoids or parallelograms, were brilliantly painted in primary hues.

Kupka's painting received only moderate attention until the 1930s. He was honored by a retrospective at the Jeu de Paume Museum in Paris in 1936. A second comprehensive exhibition was given in Czechoslovakia in 1946, and a museum was founded there in his name. He was a leader of the Salon des Réalités Nouvelles in Paris and was made an officer of the Legion of Honor. An important one-man show was given at the Galerie Louis Carré, Paris, in 1951; and a retrospective was held posthumously at the National Museum of Modern Art, Paris, in 1958.

Additional key works by Kupka include *Black Accents* (1913; private collection), *Red and Blue Vertical Planes* (1913; Carré Gallery), *The Cathedral* (1913–14; private collection), and a series of *Architectural Studies* done in the 1920s. Certain of these compositions bear a distinct similarity to the later geometrical abstractions of Josef Albers and the Op Art of the 1960s.

Kupka is only presently being recognized as a major figure in the early history of nonobjective, geometrical painting. He is without question one of the earliest abstract painters and may have worked in geometrical forms even before Malevich did.

BIBLIOGRAPHY. B. Dorival, *Twentieth Century French Painters*,

Kuo Hsi, *Clearing Autumn Skies over Mountains and Valleys*. Freer Gallery, Washington, D.C.

2 vols., New York, 1958; R. Nacenta, *School of Paris*, London, 1960; J. Cassou and D. Fedit, *Kupka: Gouaches and Pastels*, New York, 1965; Vachtova, *Kupka*, New York, 1968.

JOHN C. GALLOWAY

KUPPER, C. E. M., *see* DOESBURG, THEO VAN.

KURODA, SEIKI. Japanese painter (1866–1924). Kuroda was born of a noble family in Kagoshima. He went to Paris to study law in 1884 but changed his mind and studied painting with Raphael Collin. The first Japanese painter to introduce impressionism in Japan, Kuroda made a great contribution in establishing a Western style of painting there.

BIBLIOGRAPHY. N. Ueno, *Japanese Arts and Crafts in the Meiji Era* (Centenary Culture Council Series, Japanese Culture in the Meiji Era, vol. 8), Tokyo, 1958.

KURSI. Mosque furniture; specifically, a lectern for the Koran, often in the form of a hexagonal-shaped table. The form probably originated with serving tables used in the homes of aristocratic families.

KURUMBA, *see* AFRICA, PRIMITIVE ART OF (WEST AFRICA: UPPER VOLTA).

KUSEIR 'AMRA, *see* QUSAYR 'AMRA.

Frank Kupka, *Contrepoints liés.* Carlo Belloli Collection, Milan-Basel. A work by one of the earliest abstract painters.

Kwakiutl Indians. Large movable raven mask. Museum of the American Indian, New York.

KUSEL, MELCHIOR. German engraver (b. Augsburg, 1626; d. there, 1683). Melchior was a younger brother of Matthäus Küsel. After studying in Frankfurt am Main with Matthäus Merian, he returned permanently to Augsburg in 1651. He made a large number of engravings in a highly "finished" style. His principal work is a series of 148 etchings of various sizes, mostly after designs of Wilhelm Bauer. Known as *Miniatures of the Emperor*, it depicts scenes from the life of Christ, seaports, and views of Italy.

BIBLIOGRAPHY. P. F. Gwinner, *Kunst und Künstler in Frankfurt am Main*, Frankfurt am Main, 1862.

KUTANI, see JAPAN: CERAMICS (PORCELAIN PRODUCTION).

KUTNA HORA (Kuttenberg): ST. BARBARA. Church in Bohemia, in western Czechoslovakia. The Cathedral of this historic city was begun in the late Gothic style by Peter Parler in the 1380s and continued by Benedikt Rejt (Ried) in the late 15th century. The nave and four side aisles are covered by a richly varied vaulting system. There are 15th-century frescoes and baroque altar paintings by I. J. Raab and P. Brandl.

BIBLIOGRAPHY. Z. Wirth, *Kutná Hora: La Ville et son art*, Prague, 1931.

KUVERA (Kubera; Vaisravana). One of the eight Buddhist Dharmapālas, or defenders of the law. Kuvera is the god of wealth, the custodian of jewels and precious metals, and the regent of the north. He is one of the Lokapālas, or guardians of Mount Sumeru, the center of the universe. His home is on Mount Kailāsa. Kuvera is attended by *yakshas* and *kinnaras*; his Sakti, or consort, is Vasudhārā. He may ride either a lion or a horse. He is represented with an older, bearded face having a fierce expression; he wears a five-lobed crown, floating scarves, and many jewels and holds a *nakula* (mongoose), which symbolizes his power over the nāgas as guardians of the earth's treasures.

KUYU, see AFRICA, PRIMITIVE ART OF (CENTRAL AFRICA: CONGO-BRAZZAVILLE).

KUYUNJIK, see NINEVEH, PALACES OF.

KUZE KANNON, see YUMEDONO KANNON.

KWAKIUTL INDIANS. Indian tribal group located principally on the eastern portion of Vancouver Island, British Columbia, and on the coast of the nearby mainland. Kwakiutl society, while resembling in general the rank-conscious systems prevalent in more northerly groups, placed less emphasis upon super-families of clans, with the result that the house chiefs, or supervisors of communal dwellings, had great authority.

Kwakiutl art was used as a prestigious symbol of wealth and rank. Some of the most astonishing of the Northwest Coast masks, house posts, and painted house fronts came from the Kwakiutl. The style is florid, bold both in imagery and in use of color, and often grotesque, though technically refined, in its interpretation of animal and human forms.

See also BRITISH COLUMBIAN INDIANS; NORTH AMERICAN INDIAN ART (NORTHWEST COAST).

BIBLIOGRAPHY. F. Boas, "The Social Organization and the Secret Societies of the Kwakiutl Indians" (U.S. National Museum, Report, 1895), Washington, D.C., 1897; F. J. Dockstader, *Indian Art in America*, Greenwich, Conn., 1961.

KWANNON (Kannon), see AVALOKITESVARA.

KWAN-YIN, see AVALOKITESVARA.

KWIDZYN CASTLE, see MARIENWERDER CASTLE.

KYLBERG, CARL. Swedish painter (1878–1952). Kylberg first studied architecture. Turning to painting, he worked mostly at Göteborg on the west coast of Sweden. His seascapes, usually of single sailboats against a becalmed sea or a rocky shore, have a serious, lonely character that derives largely from the architectonic simplification in horizontal bands and, above all, from the mysterious, glowing colors: intense yellow, orange, and smoldering red against blue, green or gray. Contour is dissolved, substance transcended, in this visionary world. While Kylberg sometimes painted specifically religious themes (*Peace on Earth*, 1939–40), his seascapes and still lifes also have a mystic quality. He often painted in Denmark. He is well represented at the Louisiana, Humlebaek, and in Copenhagen

Kylix. Wide, shallow drinking cup. Example above decorated with youths and maidens painted by Douris. Metropolitan Museum of Art, New York.

as well as at the Modern Museum, Stockholm, and the Art Gallery, Göteborg.

BIBLIOGRAPHY. J. de Laprade and Martin Strömberg, *Carl Kylberg*, Paris, 1948; G. Näsström, *Carl Kylberg*, Stockholm, 1952; C. Kylberg, *Ur ett livs dagbok*, Stockholm, 1962.

KYLIX (Cylix). Shallow, wide drinking cup having two handles and a high foot. It was used in ancient Greece for drinking wine. Since the broad inner surface offered a circular area for decoration, some of the best works of the Greek vase painters appear on kylixes, which reached their highest popularity from the late 6th to the early 5th century B.C.

BIBLIOGRAPHY. G. M. A. Richter and M. J. Milne, *Shapes and Names of Athenian Vases*, New York, 1935.

KYO. Japanese term for ceramics produced in and around Kyoto; in general, those decorated with overglaze enamels. The potter Ninsei was the dominant figure of the Kyoto school, of which the Kiyomizu wares were a part. *See* KIYOMIZU; NINSEI.

See also JAPAN: CERAMICS.

KYOM-JAE, *see* CHONG SON.

KYOTO. Modern capital city of Kyoto prefecture, in western Japan. Founded by the emperor Kammu in 794, the city was the national capital until 1868, when the seat of the modern government was transferred to Tokyo. Called Heian-kyō in ancient times, it was modeled after the Sui and T'ang Chinese capital of Ch'ang-an. Although the city suffered from many destructions, it remained the cultural center of Japan, even during the Kamakura and Edo periods, when it was deprived of political power. Kyoto escaped destruction during World War II, and its magnificent shrines, temples, gardens, and palaces reveal the history of the continuity and transformation of Japanese culture during the thousand years from the 9th to the 19th century. Among Kyoto's many monuments are the imperial palace, the imperial villas of Katsura and Shugakuin, Nijō Palace, the Heian Shrine, and the Daitokuji, Ginkakuji (or Jishōji), Kiyomizudera, and Ryōanji. *See* GINKAKUJI; JAPAN: HEIAN PERIOD; KATSURA PALACE; KIYOMIZUDERA; NIJO PALACE; RYOANJI GARDEN.

See also HIUNKAKU; KINKAKUJI; KYOTO: NATIONAL MUSEUM; NISHI HONGANJI; UJI.

BIBLIOGRAPHY. R. A. B. Ponsonby-Fane, *Kyoto, The Old Capital of Japan (794-1869)*, Kyoto, 1956; *Kyoto*, comp. by the City of Kyoto, Tokyo, 1962; G. Mosher, *Kyoto, a Contemplative Guide*, Rutland, Vt., 1964.

MIYEKO MURASE

KYOTO: NATIONAL MUSEUM. Japanese collection formerly known as the Kyoto Imperial Museum. It was opened to the public in 1897. The present name was adopted in 1952, when its administration was transferred to the national government. The new building, opened in 1966, houses a large and important collection of Japanese art, with special emphasis on sculpture, painting, calligraphy, and minor arts from the Heian and later periods. Many important art objects that belong to temples and shrines in the Kyoto area are on permanent loan for exhibits.

BIBLIOGRAPHY. S. Kaneko, *Guide to Japanese Art*, Rutland, Vt., 1963.

KYUNGJU. Old capital of the United Silla dynasty (668–918), in North Kyungsang Province, Korea. Nearby are the famous Pulguksa temple and a well-known rock-cut cave chapel called Sokkulam. These two structures house some of the most significant works of Korean sculpture. *See* PULGUKSA TEMPLE; SAKYAMUNI (GRANITE); SOKKULAM.

L

Laach, Abbey Church of Maria Laach. West front, completed end of 12th and beginning of 13th century.

LAACH: ABBEY CHURCH OF MARIA LAACH. German church on the Laachersee, part of a Benedictine abbey founded in 1093. The major building program took place between 1130 and 1156; the west front and exterior portions were not completed until the end of the 12th and the beginning of the 13th century.

The church, generally, follows the plan of St. Michael's, Hildesheim, but in a later, Lombard-influenced stage of development. It is completely groin-vaulted, and its interior is simple, almost austere, in design. This aspect places the church early in German Romanesque development. The exterior offers a rich silhouette of six towers, varied roof lines, and an effective decorative use of blind arcades and corbel-table friezes. The last-named elements indicate Lombard influence. The varied decorative exterior contrasts strongly with the earlier, simpler interior, showing the direction of German Romanesque architectural development.

LABARUM. Standard of Emperor Constantine I reported to have been designed to commemorate the vision he experienced at the Milvian Bridge battle. The labarum consists of a lance with a crossbar from which is suspended a purple banner. The whole is crowned by the Chi-Rho monogram. The labarum is essentially a combination of the Christian standard and the Roman military standard. *See* CHI-RHO MONOGRAM.

LABENWOLF, PANKRAZ. German sculptor and ceramic worker (b. Nürnberg, 1492; d. there, 1563). Possibly a student of Peter Vischer in Nürnberg, Labenwolf became a master in 1519 and established a well-known workshop there. His most notable works are the grave plaque of Graf W. von Zimmern (1554; Messkirch, Stadtkirche) and the Putti Fountain (1556; Nürnberg, Rathaus court).

BIBLIOGRAPHY. A. Feulner and T. Müller, *Geschichte der deutschen Plastik*, Munich, 1953.

LABILLE-GUIARD, ADELAIDE (Madame Vincent). Frenche portrait painter (b. Paris, 1749; d. there, 1803). She was a friend of Mme du Barry, a pupil of the miniaturist F.-E. Vincent, and an academician (1783). Her portraits in oil and pastel of royal ladies are more virile, bold,

and lifelike than those by Mme Vigée-Lebrun, though pictorially less appealing. Adélaïde Labille-Guiard's work was most fashionable during the French Revolution.

BIBLIOGRAPHY. L. Dumont-Wilden, *Le Portrait en France* (Bibliothèque de l'art du XVIIIe siècle), Brussels, 1909.

LABORS OF THE MONTHS. Personification of the months of the year by their characteristic occupations. These personifications appeared first in Early Christian floor mosaics and then in Carolingian manuscripts. They became very common in later medieval art, especially in the relief decorations of the great cathedrals, for example, the Cathedral of Amiens. The realistic treatment of these scenes reached its high point in the Netherlandish Books of Hours; the *Très riches heures du Duc de Berry*, by the Limbourg brothers, illustrates this development.

BIBLIOGRAPHY. J. C. Webster, *The Labors of the Months in Antique and Medieval Art to the End of the Twelfth Century*, Princeton, 1938.

LABROUSTE, HENRI. French architect (1801–75). He lived in Paris. A pupil of Vaudoyer and L. H. Lebas, Labrouste was awarded the Prix de Rome in 1824. He is best known for his Bibliothèque Ste-Geneviève, Paris (1843–

Henri Labrouste, Bibliothèque Ste-Geneviève, Paris, 1843–50.

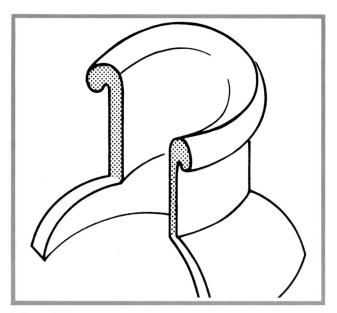

Labrum. Latin name given to the stone bathing basins used in the Roman baths.

Lacertine. Animal head post in the form of a serpent's head. Universitets Oldsaksamling, Oslo.

50), which combines exposed ironwork on the interior with an elegantly and originally detailed masonry exterior. His reading room in the Bibliothèque Nationale, Paris (1862–68), also used an advanced technique of exposed, ornamental metal structure. The emphasis on polychromy is related to his Roman archaeological studies and to the contemporary theories and work of Hittorff. Considered the leader of the rationalist (or Neo-Greek) style, Labrouste was dedicated to the teaching of its principles in his atelier, which he opened in 1830. *See* BIBLIOTHEQUE SAINTE-GENEVIEVE, PARIS.

BIBLIOGRAPHY. *Souvenirs D'Henri Labrouste: Notes recueillies et classées par ses enfants*, Paris, 1928.

LABRUM. Latin name, meaning "lip," given to the stone bathing basins used in the Roman baths. More generally, it refers to any vessel with a brim turned over like a lip.

LABYRINTH. Intricate maze, associated with the legendary structure built by Daedalus for King Minos of Crete to contain the Minotaur. The Minotaur was later slain by Theseus, who found his way out of the labyrinth, on Ariadne's advice, by means of a thread he strung along behind him. The term is assumed to derive from "labrys," the sacred double ax of the Cretans, and has been associated with the bull cult in Crete.

LACE. Textile decoration consisting of a pattern of openwork threads of linen, silk, or cotton. The youngest of the decorative textile crafts, lace first appeared in 16th-century Italy. At the outset two distinct techniques of lace-making were developed: needle-point lace and pillow lace, also known as bobbin lace.

The first step in creating needle-point lace is the drawing of a pattern on parchment that has been affixed to a piece of linen backing. Threads are laid along the major lines of the design on top of the parchment and secured with a few stitches through the parchment and linen. These threads form the skeleton on which the finer threads are woven to produce the lace meshwork. Each thread is woven by hand with a needle. The dense parts, which form the main design, are called *toilé*. Connecting the *toilé* areas are thin mesh areas called *réseaux* or simply single threads or ties known as brides. The finished lace is removed from the parchment pattern and linen backing by cutting the few stitches that initially connected the design to the backing.

Pillow lace also begins with a pattern on parchment or paper. This pattern is carefully pricked with holes along its outline. The pricked pattern is then fastened on a pillow with pins. Threads on bobbins are attached to the upper part of the pillow, and the laceworker proceeds by weaving the threads in braid fashion, working down and around the pins. The pins serve the same purpose as the skeleton threads in needle-point lace.

Soon after the invention of needle-point and pillow lace in Italy—probably in Venice—both forms of lace-making were introduced into Flanders and France. Designs were quickly spread from center to center by numerous pattern books. One such book was published by Alessandro Paganino in Venice in 1527, and another by Pierre Quinty in Cologne in the same year.

The provenance and dating of old lace is determined by the type of decoration and the technique employed. Venetian lacemakers of the 16th century excelled in the production of needle-point lace with closely spaced rose motifs woven to create a raised appearance. Milan produced a pillow lace with large heavy vine patterns during the 17th century. After 1700 Italy was eclipsed by France and Flanders in the production of lace. In general, France specialized in needle-point lace and Flanders in pillow lace. Both forms of lace, as produced in these countries, tended toward a clearer division between design and background and away from the tight high-relief lace of the earlier period.

The high point of lacemaking was reached in Flanders during the baroque era. Its chief centers were Brussels, Mechlin, and Valenciennes. The lace from each center can be identified by the type of mesh used. The 19th-century invention of the lacemaking machine has almost made handmade lace extinct.

BIBLIOGRAPHY. M. Dreger, *Entwicklungsgeschichte der Spitze*..., Vienna, 1910; M. Schuette, *Alte Spitzen*, 3d ed., Berlin, 1926.

DONALD L. EHRESMANN

LACERTINE ORNAMENT. Term (Lat. *lacerta*, lizard) used to describe a lizardlike or serpentine type of animal interlace often consisting of stylized creatures whose backward-turned heads bite the bodies of those following them. It was a particular forte of Celtic and Scandinavian art. See ANIMAL INTERLACE.

LACHAISE, GASTON. American sculptor (b. Paris, 1882; d. New York City, 1935). In 1895 he attended the Ecole Bernard Palissy, and in 1898 worked under Gabriel J. Thomas. Lachaise studied at the Ecole des Beaux-Arts until 1905. He went to the United States and worked for H. H. Kitson until 1912. In 1913 he became Paul Manship's assistant. Lachaise's first important work was *Standing Woman* (1912–27), and his first show was in 1918. From 1919 to 1925 he did portraits of contributors to *The Dial*. He made architectural reliefs for the Telephone Building, New York, in 1921, and for Rockefeller Center, New York, in 1931 and 1935. The Museum of Modern Art, New York, owns *Standing Woman* (1932), *Torso* (1934), and *Floating Figure* (1927). *Head* (1928) is in the Whitney Museum of American Art, New York; several works are in the Warburg and Chrysler collections and in the collection of Lachaise's widow. Lachaise gave a sophisticated form to robust sensuality.

BIBLIOGRAPHY. New York, Museum of Modern Art, *Gaston Lachaise*, 1935; Los Angeles County Museum, *Gaston Lachaise, 1882–1935: Sculpture and Drawings*, New York, 1964.

LA CHAPELLE, GEORGES DE. French painter (fl. Caen, 1638–48). He was born in Toulon. He traveled to the Levant and did a series of portraits of Turkish types, which were engraved by Charles Nicolas Cochin the Elder. La Chapelle took special pride in the exact rendering of embroidery, jewels, and topographical settings.

BIBLIOGRAPHY. L. Réau, *Histoire de l'expansion de l'art français moderne: Le Monde slave et l'Orient*, Paris, 1924.

LA CHARITE-SUR-LOIRE. French town near Nevers and site of an important Cluniac church. Related to the pilgrimage school, the church was built between about 1059 and 1107. Modeled primarily on Cluny II, it was enriched by triforium arches and polyfoil windows of Spanish and Moorish origin. About 1125 a large rebuilding program, designed to convert the church from the early Romanesque pattern of Cluny II to the High Romanesque of Cluny III, was undertaken. This change engendered an enlarged and imposing new façade with twin towers. Only the northern tower was completed, and the new five-portal façade (as in Burgos Cathedral, Spain) remained unfinished. The old apse echelon was replaced by an ambulatory with radiating chapels. La Charité, as it now stands, shows perfectly the transition from early to High Romanesque outside the influence of the new Gothic movement.

LACHTROPIUS (Lactorius; Lacterius), NICOLAES. Dutch painter of still life and flowers (fl. ca. 1650–1700). Little is known of the activity of Lachtropius, whose work, according to contemporary documents, met with little success in his own day. He was active in Amsterdam and in Alphen on the Rhine. A signed *Still Life* (1679; Vienna, formerly Figdor Collection) is in the style of Otto Marcellis van Schrieck.

BIBLIOGRAPHY. A. P. A. Vorenkamp, *Bijdrage tot de geschiedenis van het Hollandsch stilleven in de zeventiende eeuw*, Leyden, 1934.

LACONICUM. One of the rooms in Roman thermae used to induce perspiration by hot dry air. In the Thermae of Diocletian, Rome, the laconicum was a relatively small circular room between the tepidarium and the caldarium.

LACQUER. Term applied to the painting medium derived from the resin of the tree *Rhus vernicifera*. This tree is common in China and Japan, where lacquer is extensively used to decorate furniture, utensils, and so forth. The lacquer is applied in numerous layers, each of which takes more time to dry than the previous one. When dry, lacquer is so hard it can be carved; it is also extremely durable, being impervious to spirits and water.

LACTORIUS (Lacterius), NICOLAES, see LACHTROPIUS, NICOLAES.

LADBROOKE, ROBERT. English painter and lithographer (b. Norwich, 1770; d. there, 1842). Ladbrooke began as a printer. He was the friend and brother-in-law of the landscape painter John Crome, who greatly influenced Ladbrooke's own detailed and personal treatment of landscape.

La Charité-sur-Loire. Cluniac church, view of apse with radiating chapels.

With Crome, in 1803, he founded the Norwich Society of Artists, known as the Norwich school. A quarrel between the two friends divided the society into two factions, but they were subsequently reconciled. Besides his landscapes, Ladbrooke did an early series of crayon portraits and, late in his life, lithographs of the churches of Norfolk, which were published after his death.

BIBLIOGRAPHY. G. Holme, ed., *The Norwich School...*, London, 1920.

LADDER-BACK CHAIR. In English and American furniture the ladder-back consists of a series of curving horizontal splats between the back stiles. It is encountered first in 18th-century country furniture. Later it was used on Chippendale-style chairs with straight legs; the splats repeat the design of the top rail.

BIBLIOGRAPHY. W. Nutting, *Furniture Treasury...*, New York, 1954.

LADH KHAN TEMPLE, AIHOLE, *see* AIHOLE.

LADYKIRK, CHURCH OF (Kirk of Steil). Unusually complete Scottish building of 1500, in Ladykirk, County Berwick. It is cruciform, with a west tower and with apses in the transept ends as well as in the chancel. William Adam completed the tower in 1743.

BIBLIOGRAPHY. J. S. Coltart, *Scottish Church Architecture*, New York, 1936.

LAEMEN, CHRISTOFFEL, *see* LAMEN, CHRISTOFFEL JACOB VAN DER.

LAER, PIETER VAN (Bamboccio). Dutch genre painter (b. Haarlem, ca. 1592; d. there, 1642). His first teacher

Ladder-back chair. A pattern, ca. 1760. Victoria and Albert Museum, London.

Pieter van Laer, *The Blacksmith*. Engraving on copper.

is not known; after about 1626, while living in Rome in the parish of S. Maria del Popolo, Van Laer shared his quarters with various other painters, including Jan van der Camp. He joined the Netherlandish artists' association, the Bentvueghels (birds of a flock), in Rome, and, as was their custom, he received a nickname, Bamboccio (awkward simpleton or puppet), because of his physical deformity. He remained active in Rome until about 1639, when he was recorded back in Holland. He was a painter of Roman low life, market scenes, and other plebeian activities, and the term *bamboccianti* derived from his nickname was applied to the entire group of works in this genre right down to the 19th century. However, today we tend to reserve the word *bamboccianti* for Van Laer and his immediate followers, such as the Italian painter Michelangelo Cerquozzi and the Flemish artist Jan Miel. *See* BAMBOCCIANTI.

Van Laer's style is best exemplified by the *Cake Vendor* (Rome, National Gallery) with its sharp light effects suggesting the influence of the Italian painter Caravaggio. Van Laer also painted a sharply incisive self-portrait (Rome, Pallavicini Gallery), in profile, which disregards the formal portrait tradition in favor of the new *bamboccianti* aesthetic of realism.

BIBLIOGRAPHY. G. J. Hoogewerff, "Pieter van Laer en zijn Vrienden," *Oud-Holland*, XLIX, 1932, L, 1933; G. Briganti, "Pieter van Laer e Michel Cerquozzi," *Proporzione*, III, 1950; G. Briganti, *I bamboccianti* (exhibition catalog), Rome, 1950; J. Rosenberg. S. Slive, and E. H. ter Kuile, *Dutch Art and Architecture, 1600–1800*, Baltimore, 1966.

LEONARD J. SLATKES

LAERMANS, EUGENE. Belgian painter and engraver (b. Brussels, 1864; d. there, 1940). He studied at the Brussels Academy. Laermans was primarily a realistic figure painter whose subjects—workers, peasants, the poor, and so on—implied a sympathy with the lower social classes, for example, the crowd scene in *Un soir de grève* (1893; Brussels, Municipal Museum). The Laermans painting which perhaps best shows the peasants' longing for a better life was the important triptych *Les Emigrants* (1896; Antwerp, Fine Arts Museum). His work gradually became more simplified with greater stress on compact outlines, as in *Le Repos sur la colline* (1923; Brussels, Municipal Museum).

BIBLIOGRAPHY. G. Vanzype, *Eugène Laermans*, Brussels, 1908; P. Colin, *Eugène Laermans*, Brussels, 1929.

LAETHEM-SAINT-MARTIN SCHOOL. School of art of Laethem-Saint-Martin, a village on the Lys River near Ghent, Belgium, founded at the close of the 19th century when Valerius de Saedeleer settled there. The outstanding beauty of this part of Belgium soon attracted a number of Flemish artists who formed a group around De Saedeleer, the three most important being Gustave van de Woestijne, Albert Servaes, and the sculptor Georges Minne. Laethem already had an extremely gifted primitive painter named Van den Abeele, who had a realistic conception of nature. He was almost forty when he began to paint and was the animator of the first Laethem group. *See* WOESTIJNE, GUSTAVE VAN DE.

De Saedeleer, a great admirer of Brueghel and the Flemish primitives, especially excelled in the representation of snow seen through the dark branches of dead trees (*Winter Landscape with Farm*, 1907). He remained at Laethem from 1904 to 1908. *See* SAEDELEER, VALERIUS DE.

Servaes was first influenced by Minne. He combined Flemish realism with such personal power and originality that the clergy banned from the churches his religiously inspired works, including a *Stations of the Cross*, which created a scandal. He also executed large decorative panels, stained-glass designs, and drawings for the Orval Abbey. *See* SERVAES, ALBERT.

A few years later a second group of painters, including Albert Saverys, Constant Permeke, Gustave and Léon de Smet, Fritz van den Berghe, Edgar Gevaert, Humbert Malfait, Jules de Sutter, and Piet Lippens was formed at Laethem. Strongly opposed to impressionism, they painted villagers and peasant types with a kind of healthy expressionism that was completely Flemish in tradition. They sought to evoke a certain joyousness of life and expressed it in vigorous forms that not only were in contradiction to academic canons but also were attacked by the Royal Academy. *See* BERGHE, FRITZ VAN DEN.

Permeke is perhaps the foremost figure of the second Laethem group and is the best representative of Flemish expressionism. His rough, full forms, as in *The Fiancés* (1923), express his monumental vision of nature and man. *See* PERMEKE, CONSTANT.

Gustave de Smet became one of the most determined advocates of modern painting. His expressionism developed a strong personal note with its reddish colors and its simplification of design. Less vigorous and gifted than Permeke but more delicate and sensitive, De Smet represents the gracious and tender aspect of Flemish expressionism (for example, *La Loge*). *See* SMET, GUSTAVE DE.

Minne created emaciated, mystical sculptured figures with great purity of form to express meditation, melancholy, and sometimes suffering. He exerted an influence not only on the second Laethem-Saint-Martin group (*Mother and Child*, 1908) but on certain German sculptors, especially Lehmbruck. *See* MINNE, GEORGES.

Thanks to its original talents, the Laethem-Saint-Martin school made an indispensable contribution to modern European art, and its influence is still being felt.

BIBLIOGRAPHY. A. de Ridder, *La Jeune peinture belge*, Brussels, 1928; L. van Puyvelde, *Georges Minne*, Brussels, 1930; E. de Bruyne, *Servaes*, Brussels, 1932; G. Marlier, *L'Expressionnisme flamand, l'Amour de l'Art*, Paris, 1934; P. Haesaerts, *Permeke ou la volonté de grandeur*, Amsterdam, Antwerp, 1938; P. Haesaerts, *L'Ecole de Laethem-Saint-Martin*, Brussels, 1945.

ARNOLD ROSIN

LAFABRIQUE, NICOLAS. Flemish painter (b. Namur, 1649; d. Liège, 1733). Lafabrique painted genre and animal scenes and portraits. He traveled in France and Italy and finally settled in Liège. He adopted the style of Bertholet Flémalle and became a Poussinesque classicist.

BIBLIOGRAPHY. J. Helbig, *L'Art mosan depuis l'introduction du christianisme jusqu'à la fin du XVIIIᵉ siècle*, vol. 2, Brussels, 1911.

LA FARGE, JOHN. American painter, muralist, and stained-glass designer (b. New York City, 1835; d. Providence, R.I., 1910). He went to Paris in 1856, where he worked briefly with Couture and met many of the artists who were to influence his style: Puvis de Chavannes, Millais, and Rossetti. In 1859 he went to Newport, R.I., where he met William Morris Hunt, who decisively turned him toward painting.

In the 1860s La Farge was probably the most modern of all contemporary American painters in his intense realism of light and natural forms and the consequent restricted modeling and concern for flat pattern, as in *Self-portrait* (1859; New York, Metropolitan Museum). It is significant that La Farge independently became interested in the formal design of Japanese prints at about the same time they were discovered in Paris. The high points of La Farge's attempts at a thorough realism, concerning all details of composition, particularly the depiction of time of day and lighting, are the Newport landscapes *Paradise Valley* (ca. 1868; Boston, Mary Lathrop Collection) and *Bishop Berkeley's Rock* (1868; Metropolitan Museum).

Quite rapidly, however, La Farge's realism changed to an idealism both of subject and style. *The Muse of Painting* (1870; Metropolitan Museum) is a standard academic classical painting, although the feeling for decorative pattern is still strong. In 1876, at the invitation of H. H.

Laethem-Saint-Martin School. Constant Permeke, *The Stable*, 1933. National Museum of Modern Art, Paris.

John La Farge, *Bishop Berkeley's Rock, Newport.* **Metropolitan Museum of Art, New York (Gift of Frank Jewett Mather, Jr., 1949).**

Richardson, La Farge decorated the interior of Trinity Church, Boston. The success of these decorations, which were a strong influence on the next generation of American muralists, led to many famous commissions for La Farge, including wall paintings for St. Thomas's Church in New York City (destroyed) and the eclectic, Renaissance-based *Ascension* for the Church of the Ascension in New York City.

La Farge had meanwhile become interested in the then moribund art of stained glass. His experiments with the chromatic possibilities of opalescent glass allowed expression to his genuine gifts for color and pattern and were instrumental in the revival of the art. A good example of La Farge's glass work is *Red and White Peonies* (1886; Boston, Museum of Fine Arts), made for the London house of the painter Alma-Tadema.

In 1886 La Farge and his friend Henry Adams began travels in Japan and the South Seas. The water colors of scenes from these journeys are among the best works of his career. Among them are *The Siva Dance, Samoa* (ca. 1891; Boston, Museum of Fine Arts) and the highly imaginative *Rishi Calling up a Storm* (late 1880s; Cleveland Museum of Art).

BIBLIOGRAPHY. J. La Farge, *Considerations on Painting,* New York, 1895; R. Cortissoz, *John La Farge,* Boston, 1911.

JEROME VIOLA

LAFEVER, MINARD. American architect and writer (b. New Jersey, 1798; d. 1854). Almost entirely self-taught, he is best known for his many handbooks; because of these he has been called perhaps the greatest designer of architectural decoration of his time in the United States. He worked primarily in New York City.

LAFOSSE, CHARLES DE. French decorative painter (b. Paris, 1636; d. there, 1716). He was the son of a goldsmith. Following a sojourn in Italy (1658–63), he worked under Charles Le Brun at the Tuileries and Versailles (1670s). Later, Lafosse provided mythological paintings for the Trianon (began 1688) and painted the cupola of the Dôme of Les Invalides in Paris (begun 1692). He went to London twice (1689 and 1702; decorations for Mon-

tagu House). He became an academician in 1673, his reception piece being the *Rape of Proserpina* (Paris, Ecole des Beaux-Arts), and became chancellor in 1715. The influence of Correggio and Veronese made his mature style more baroque than it had been under Le Brun, his color lighter, and his brushstrokes more fluid. After 1680 Lafosse became the foremost French advocate of Rubens. His work anticipated rococo lightness, which he transmitted to Watteau through their common friendship with P. Crozat.

BIBLIOGRAPHY. A. Blunt, *Art and Architecture in France, 1500–1700,* Baltimore, 1954.

LAFRENSEN, NILS, *see* LAVREINCE NICOLAS.

LA FRESNAYE, ROGER DE. French cubist and realistic painter (b. Le Mans, 1885; d. Grasse, 1925). In 1903 he entered the Académie Julian, where he received traditional academic training. In 1908 he transferred to the Académie Ranson, sponsored by Maurice Denis and Paul Sérusier, whose art influenced La Fresnaye. He also came to know and admire Cézanne's painting. In 1910 La Fresnaye traveled extensively in Italy and Germany and then began his first cubist experiments. A year later he met Villon and Gleizes, and with them, Apollinaire, Léger, Metzinger, and others was active in founding the Section d'Or. It was in this period, prior to 1914 when he entered the infantry, that he produced all the work on which his reputation rests. He made a series of cubist drawings and water colors in 1917.

One of La Fresnaye's earliest cubist paintings is *Cuirassier* (1910; Paris, National Museum of Modern Art). He took the theme from Géricault; the color reflects his admiration for Cézanne; and the forms show the influence of Braque and Picasso. In *The Artillery* (1911–12; Chicago, Marx Collection) he suggests the marshaling of armed

Roger de la Fresnaye, *Cuirassier.* **National Museum of Modern Art, Paris.**

forces into action by repeating forms in parallel progressions and emphasizing diagonal rhythms. Figures are faceless and severely reduced and geometrized. It is possible that he saw a large exhibition of futurist art held in Paris in 1912. These military themes resulted from his preoccupation with illustrating Claudel's *Tête d'Or*.

Like other members of the Section d'Or, La Fresnaye may be compared to Picasso and Braque; however, he extended their use of color and suggested atmosphere and radiance. He favored figures in a landscape over still life and portrait situations. His innovations are to be found in *Conquest of the Air* (1913; New York, Museum of Modern Art). In this large canvas Roger and his brother are seen discussing sailing and flying. No airplanes are in evidence; a sailboat is marginal. The scene is given the quality of exhilaration and airiness as the crystalline blues circulate throughout the work. It lacks the rhythmic inventiveness and subtlety of Picasso and has a synthetic decorative quality characteristic of many of the lesser cubist artists. In his last work, La Fresnaye, like Lhote, turned to a figurative neoclassicism.

BIBLIOGRAPHY. R. Cogniat and W. George, *Oeuvres complètes de Roger de La Fresnaye*, Paris, 1950. ROBERT REIFF

LAGAE, JULES. Belgian sculptor (b. Rosselaers, 1862; d. Bruges, 1931). He studied with Van der Stappen at the Brussels Academy of Fine Arts, worked in the studios of J. M. T. Lambeaux and Julien Dillens, and won the Prix de Rome in 1888. Lagae did some monumental sculptures, but his most successful works are portrait and figure busts, such as the *Mother and Child* in the Fine Arts Museum, Brussels, in which the expression of delicate sentiment and the soft finish of the marble derive from his admiration for Florentine 15th-century sculpture.

LAGASH, *see* TELLOH.

LAGOOR, JOHAN (Jan de). Dutch landscape painter and etcher (fl. after 1643; d. after 1659). Little is known of Lagoor's activity. He entered the Haarlem Guild of St. Luke in 1645 and was a director in 1649. When he was declared insolvent in Amsterdam (December, 1659) an inventory of his possessions was made. The influence of the landscape style of Paulus Potter can be seen in his works.

BIBLIOGRAPHY. W. Bernt, *Die niederländischen Maler des 17. Jahrhunderts...*, vol. 2, Munich, 1948.

LAGRENEE, LOUIS-JEAN-FRANCOIS, THE ELDER. French history painter (b. Paris, 1725; d. there, 1805). A pupil of Charles André van Loo, he won the Prix de Rome in 1749. Lagrenée was court painter to Catherine of Russia in 1760, director of the Academy at St. Petersburg, director of the French Academy in Rome from 1781 to 1787, and curator of museums under the Empire. His intention, like that of Joseph-Marie Vien, is neoclassicizing. His figure style is indecisive, and the rounded forms and elongated eyes vapidly recall those of Boucher.

LA HIRE (La Hyre), LAURENT DE. French history and landscape painter, decorator, draftsman, and engraver (b. Paris, 1606; d. there, 1656). He was the son of Etienne de La Hire, a painter active in Poland, with whom he studied drawing, perspective, and architecture. Under G.

Laurent de la Hire, *St. Peter Curing the Sick*. Louvre, Paris.

Lallemand he was set to copying works by Primaticcio and Ambroise Dubois at Fontainebleau, the effect of which can be seen in the sharp perspective of La Hire's *Nicolas V before the Body of St. Francis* (1630; Paris, Louvre).

An undercurrent of naturalism implies an awareness of Caravaggio and Bolognese artists. Much more apparent in his early maturity (1635–37) is the effect of 16th-century Venetian artists, probably through Jacques Blanchard and the study of works by Titian and Veronese in the collection of the Duc de Liancourt. This is seen in *Conversion of St. Paul* (Paris, Church of St-Thomas-d'Aquin).

In his mature period (1638–48) the influence of Nicolas Poussin, who was in Paris from 1640 to 1642, is most evident. It is, however, the Venetian style of Poussin that is reflected in such works as *Mercury Giving the Infant Bacchus to the Nymphs* (1638; Leningrad, Hermitage). In 1648 he was one of the founders of the Royal Academy.

In his last phase (1648–56) two divergent trends reveal themselves: academic and free. In the first he adopts a cold classicism, melding the mature style of Poussin with that of Phillipe de Champaigne, as evidenced in *Allegory of Music* (1648; New York, Metropolitan Museum), one of seven life-size decorative paintings representing the seven liberal arts, executed for Gédéon Tallement. Here one sees not only sculpturesque hardness and archaeological correctness based upon classical humanism but also a lyrical grace. In the exaggerated length of the mandolin and the close, cutoff perspective one also detects vestiges of Fontainebleau mannerism. The combined clarity of motifs and the quiet isolation of the Muse, moreover, confirm La Hire as a contemporary of Georges de La Tour. The second aspect of La Hire's late period is more personal. In poor health, he painted small pictures, chiefly landscapes, *Paysage au Porcher* (1648; Berlin, formerly H. Voss Collection) and *Landscape with Bathers* (1653; Louvre). They strike a balance between classical generalization and Netherlandish realism that is typically French.

His paintings and drawings—in the museums of Arras, Besançon, Paris (Louvre), Montpellier, and Orléans—were also engraved by himself, C. Langlois, and F. Chaveau. La Hire's work typifies French 17th-century cultural standards of reason and good taste.

BIBLIOGRAPHY. G. Guillet de Saint George, in L. Dussieux, ed., *Mémoires inédits sur la vie et les ouvrages des membres de l'Académie royale de peinture et de sculpture*, 2 vols., Paris, 1854; L. Dimier, *Histoire de la peinture française du retour de Vouet à la mort de Lebrun, 1627 à 1690...*, vol. 1, Paris, 1926; A. Blunt, *Art and Architecture in France, 1500–1700*, Baltimore, 1954.

GEORGE V. GALLENKAMP

LAHORE. City in West Pakistan whose origin is lost in antiquity. Captured in 1022 by Mahmud of Ghazni, Lahore was the capital of the Ghaznavid province of the Punjab and as such a center of scholarship and letters. Qutb ad-Din Aibeg, first ruler of the sultanate of Delhi (1206–10), spent much time in Lahore, where his tomb may be seen. In 1524 the city fell to Zahir ad-Din Muhammad, known as Babur, the founder of the Mughal empire. Although overshadowed by Delhi, Lahore does display important monuments of the Mughal period, especially of the years between 1556 and 1707.

The emperor Akbar (r. 1556–1605) built a wall to enclose a new city and a fort within this area. Stretches of the massive walls remain, as do gateways, one called the Akbari Gate. Jahangir (r. 1605–28) was fond of Lahore; his works include the Pearl Mosque within the fort. Jahangir's tomb was erected on the outskirts of the city in 1637 by his son and successor, Shah Jahan (r. 1628–58). It is a square, arcaded structure with a minaret at each corner, but unlike most Mughal mausoleums it lacks a central dome. Wall surfaces of white marble are enlivened with colorful *pietra-dura* work. Shah Jahan was also responsible for a Hall of Audience within the fort and for the lovely Shalimar Gardens, some 5 miles north of the city. The gardens, covering 80 acres, feature airy pavilions overlooking a great pool with playing fountains.

Aurangzeb (r. 1658–1707) added to the structures within the fort, but his great contribution was the Badshahi Mosque, completed in 1674 on a site west of the fort. Modeled after the Jami Masjid at Delhi, it features the largest open courtyard of any mosque in the world. The vast central structure of red sandstone is crowned by three bulbous domes of white marble. Between the Badshahi Mosque and the fort is the Hazuri Garden, now the site of the tomb of the poet who conceived the state of Pakistan, Muhammad Iqbal. North of the garden is the pavilion and tomb of Ranjit Singh, who consolidated much of the Punjab into a Sikh kingdom between 1802 and his death in 1839. Other monuments of interest include the Mosque of Wazir Khan, built in 1634 and displaying wall surfaces covered with enameled tiles; the adjacent Golden Mosque of 1753; and, near the mausoleum of Jahangir,

Lalique. Brooch with pendant pearls.

the dilapidated tomb of his wife, Nur Jahan. In the newer parts of the city, public buildings erected in the 19th century, when Lahore was part of British India, feature the red sandstone and the decorative details common to the Mughal period. *See* BADSHAHI MOSQUE, LAHORE.

BIBLIOGRAPHY. D. N. Wilber, *Pakistan: Its People, Its Society, Its Culture*, New Haven, 1964.

DONALD N. WILBER

LA HYRE, LAURENT DE, *see* LA HIRE, LAURENT DE.

LAINBERGER, SIMON. German wood sculptor (fl. Nürnberg, ca. 1475–1500; d. ca. 1503). In 1494 he was called with Peter Vischer the Elder to Heidelberg by the elector palatine Philip. Lainberger's work there is unknown. His style was previously understood on the basis of two works, the *Crucifixion* group of the high altar in the Church of St. Georg in Nördlingen and the *Madonna from Dangolsheim* (Berlin, former State Museums). Today these works are attributed to two different artists, the Master of the Nördlingen High Altar and the Master of the Dangolsheim Madonna, leaving no ascertained works by Lainberger.

BIBLIOGRAPHY. A. Feulner and T. Müller, *Geschichte der deutschen Plastik*, Munich, 1953.

LAIRESSE, GERARD DE. Flemish painter of historical, allegorical, and mythological scenes (b. Liège, 1641; d. Amsterdam, 1711). He was a pupil of his father, Reynier de Lairesse, and of Bertholet Flémalle. Gerard's early paintings, strongly influenced by Nicolas Poussin, depict scenes done in the classicist manner, with strongly colored figures. After fleeing to Holland in 1664, the artist continued for a time in the academic tradition and became the head of an effective school. His late works are reminiscent of the style then prevalent at the court of Louis XIV. He was not only a strong artistic personality; his *Groot Schilderboeck*, written after he became blind (ca. 1690), had lasting impact for the theories of art it set forth. Among his numerous signed works, *Achilles Recognized by Ulysses* (The Hague, Mauritshuis Art Gallery) deserves special mention.

BIBLIOGRAPHY. R. Oldenbourg, *Die flämische Malerei des 17. Jahrhunderts*, 2d ed., Berlin, 1922; J. J. M. Timmers, *Gérard de Lairesse*, Amsterdam, 1942.

LA JOUE, JACQUES II DE. French painter and designer of ornament (b. Paris, 1687; d. there, 1761). La Joue painted landscapes, marinescapes, hunting pictures, and decorative scenes of fantastic architecture. He was privately engaged by such patrons as Mme de Pompadour. While his painterly style gave him an enthusiastic if short-lived following, his ornament designs were of more lasting importance.

BIBLIOGRAPHY. C. Gronkowski, "La Collection Dutuit au Petit Palais," *La Renaissance de l'Art Français et des Industries de Luxe*, IV, July, 1921.

LAKE DWELLINGS. Until World War II lake dwellings were thought to be structures built on piles sunk into a lake. In popular books they are attributed to one period, the Neolithic, and one country, Switzerland. Actually they occur in the Neolithic period, the Bronze Age, and even the Iron Age. They are found not only in Switzerland but in Italy, Austria, France, and parts of Germany. Recent Swiss excavations have thrown doubt on the classic theory of lake dwellings as pile dwellings built out over water. These excavations show that they were erected on solid ground along the shores of lakes. The piles or stacked platforms simply lifted the houses off the moist ground. The houses seem to have become lake dwellings only because of changes in lake levels.

BIBLIOGRAPHY. W. U. Guyan et al., *Das Pfahlbauproblem* (Monographien zur Ur- und Frühgeschichte der Schweiz, vol. 11), Basel, 1955.

LAKE SHORE DRIVE APARTMENTS, CHICAGO, *see* Mies van der Rohe, Ludwig.

LAKSHMI (Laksmi; Sri). Hindu goddess of fortune, wife of Vishnu and mother of Kāma. Like Aphrodite, she was born from the froth of the ocean. Although she is said to have four arms, Lakshmī is represented with but a single pair, befitting her identity as goddess of beauty. Clothed

Wifredo Lam, *The Jungle*, 1943. Museum of Modern Art, New York (Inter American Fund).

in little but strands of jewels, she stands in the easy *tribhanga* (three-bendings) pose, holding out her symbol of the lotus flower. Sri is also an honorific prefix to the names of gods, kings, heroes, and men and books that are highly esteemed.

LAL, *see* Mughal Painting of India (Akbar period).

LALAING, JACQUES DE. Belgian sculptor and painter (b. London, 1858; d. Brussels, 1917). The son of a Belgian diplomat, he studied at the Brussels Academy of Fine Arts with Portaels and Van Cluysenaar. As a painter of historical and genre scenes Lalaing won prizes at the salons of Paris and Brussels, but he is better known for his monumental sculptures, in which he was particularly adept at portraying the power of horses and other animals in movement. Examples of his work in this genre are *Combat of the Horsemen*, in the Fine Arts Museum, Brussels; an equestrian statue of Leopold I, in Ostend; and *The Tiger Fight*, in the Fine Arts Museum, Ghent.

LALANNE, MAXIME. French painter and etcher (b. Bordeaux, 1827; d. Nogent-sur-Marne, 1886). Lalanne's output is centered on landscapes and street scenes executed during his travels. He made his debut in the Paris Salon in 1852 with a crayon drawing. In 1863 he showed his first etchings, views of Paris streets. There followed 196 different etchings: views of Paris, Bordeaux, and London; French, Dutch, and Swiss landscapes. The style of his city views is dependent on Méryon; his landscapes are close to those of Huet. Lalanne's best etchings were produced in the 1860s, and his *oeuvre* includes some etchings after other masters. One of his main plates is *Rue des Marmousets, Paris* (1863).

BIBLIOGRAPHY. C. Glaser, *Die Graphik der Neuzeit*, Berlin, 1922.

LALIQUE. Type of fine decorative glass developed by the 19th-century French jeweler René Lalique. The decoration consists mainly of applied reliefs of figures, animals, flowers, and so on.

LALOUX, A. F. VICTOR. French architect (1856–1937). He worked in Paris. A pupil of J. André, Laloux is often considered the most accomplished French architect of his day. He is responsible for the Gare d'Orsay (1898–1900). His style, ingenious, impersonal, and highly eclectic, stands at the end of the classic tradition in French architecture.

BIBLIOGRAPHY. H. B. Cox, "Victor Laloux; the Man and his Work," *Architects' Journal*, LI, 1920.

LAM, WIFREDO. Cuban painter (1902–   ). Born in Sagua la Grande, Lam studied in Havana and Madrid. In 1938 he went to Paris, where his first exhibition attracted the attention and aid of Picasso and led to Lam's association with André Breton and the surrealists. At first his style was strongly influenced by Picasso. Rather than using orthodox surrealist techniques, Lam paints amalgams of organic and sexual forms and the magical fetishes of primitive societies, combining these elements into demonic and frightening figures, as in the closely packed *The Jungle* (1943; New York, Museum of Modern Art).

BIBLIOGRAPHY. L. Kirstein, *The Latin American Collection of the Museum of Modern Art*, New York, 1943.

LAMA, GIULIA. Italian painter (fl. Venice, 1st half of 18th cent.). Possibly a daughter of the painter Agostino Lama, she was a student and one of the few accomplished followers of Piazzetta. Her known works are *Old Man Praying* (Donà dalle Rose Collection), *Crucifixion* (Venice, S. Vitale), *Immaculate Conception* (church of Malamocco, near Venice), and a self-portrait (1725; Florence, Uffizi). For the most part she achieves theatrical effects by exaggerating the baroque lighting, gestures, and compositions of Piazzetta.

BIBLIOGRAPHY. M. Goering, "Giulia Lama," *Jahrbuch der Preussischen Kunstsammlungen*, LVI, no. 3, 1935.

LAMB, HENRY. British painter, chiefly of portraits and portrait groups (1885–1961). Born in Adelaide, Australia, and educated at Manchester, England, Lamb initially studied medicine. Then until 1911, when he settled in England, he studied painting and worked in France. During World War I he resumed his medical career. He was official war artist in both world wars. Lamb was elected full academician of the Royal Academy of Arts in 1950.

Although Lamb was an original member of the Camden Town Group of sixteen artists (founded in 1911), his career was not centered on its activities. His first successes were with paintings of his war experiences. He was strongly preoccupied with the study of form in his earliest works, which reveal a sense of firmness in modeling, warm color, and a judicious balance in composition.

Lamb is widely represented in English public collections, especially the Tate Gallery, London. His portrait of the writer Lytton Strachey (Tate) is one of the most distinguished and individual English portraits of this century.

BIBLIOGRAPHY. M. Chamot, *Modern Painting in England*, London, 1937; J. Rothenstein, *Modern English Painters: Sickert to Smith*, 2 vols., London, 1952.

LAMB, WILLIAM, *see* SHREVE, LAMB, AND HARMON.

LAMB, THE. A symbol for Christ and also the attribute of St. John the Baptist. St. John, who spoke of Christ as "the Lamb of God," is frequently depicted in a hair shirt, holding a cross staff in one hand and a little lamb in the other.

LAMBEAUX, JOSEPH MARIE THOMAS (Jef). Belgian sculptor (b. Antwerp, 1852; d. Brussels, 1908). He studied at the Academy of Fine Arts in Antwerp with Jean Geefs. In Lambeaux's work realistic, monumental figures appear within the context of themes of basic human activities and of a symbolic order.

LAMBERECHTS, FRANS. Belgian sculptor (1909–   ). Born in Brussels, he had practical study in carving as a traveling decorative mason and studied art at the Brussels Academy. Since the late 1930s he has worked in abstract, flowing stone forms suggesting Arp and Brancusi but sometimes with distant reference to the figure.

BIBLIOGRAPHY. Flouquet, "Frans Lamberechts," *La Maison*, 1957.

LAMBERT, GEORGE WASHINGTON. Australian painter, draftsman, and sculptor (b. Russia, 1873; d. 1930). He was a painter and draftsman in the classic manner. Lambert was a key figure in the development of Australian art. He transformed the insular activity by providing a more universal approach through the old masters, particularly the great Renaissance draftsmen.

LAMBERT HOTEL, PARIS, *see* LE VAU, LOUIS.

LAMBERT, ST. Bishop of Maastricht after about 670 (b. ca. 635; d. 700). He was reportedly killed by Pepin of Heristal, Mayor of the Palace, because Lambert had attacked his immorality. Lambert is represented in Flemish and German art as a bishop saint. His remains are venerated at Liège. *See also* SAINTS IN ART.

LAMBERTI, NICCOLO DI PIETRO (Il Pela; Niccolo d'Arezzo). Italian sculptor and architect (b. ca. 1370; d. Florence, 1451). A transitional artist of the early Renaissance, he carved a statue of St. Mark for the façade of Florence Cathedral (1408–15), now in the Cathedral Museum, and in 1416 was engaged with assistants on the sculptural decoration of the pinnacles of the façade of St. Mark's in Venice.

LAMBERTI, PIETRO DI NICCOLO. Italian sculptor (b. Florence, ca. 1393; d. Venice? 1435). He was the son of the sculptor Niccolò di Pietro Lamberti. In 1410 Pietro was engaged in work at Or San Michele in Florence, in 1415 he matriculated in the Stone and Wood Carvers' Guild there, and in 1416 he went to Venice, probably in the company of his father, whom he assisted on the façade sculpture of St. Mark's. Between 1430 and 1434 Pietro was in Verona. In Venice he collaborated with Giovanni di Martino from Fiesole to carve the tomb of Doge Tom-

Pietro di Niccolò Lamberti, *Judgment of Solomon*, capital, Doge's Palace, Venice.

maso Mocenigo (1423) in SS. Giovanni e Paolo, and in the following years he participated in the sculptural decoration of the Doge's Palace, being responsible probably for the capital of the *Judgment of Solomon*. He brought to the late Gothic in Venice a Florentine sense of vigorous form without appreciably affecting the course of Venetian sculpture.

BIBLIOGRAPHY. J. Pope-Hennessy, *Italian Gothic Sculpture*, London, 1955.

LAMBERTI, STEFANO. Italian architect and wood carver (b. Brescia, 1485; d. there, 1538). Lamberti was one of the chief wood carvers of the Italian Renaissance. His principal works, all in Brescia, are the door and decoration on the street floor of the Loggia, the frame of Romanino's *Madonna* (1508) in S. Francesco, and the organ case in the Old Cathedral.

BIBLIOGRAPHY. A. Ugoletti, *Brescia*, Bergamo, 1909.

LAMB OF GOD (Agnus Dei). One of the oldest Christian symbols, found in Early Christian catacombs. The Lamb is shown with either the resurrection banner of Christ or the chalice of the Last Supper, and always has a cross nimbus. The Adoration of the Lamb is the central panel of Van Eyck's *Ghent Altarpiece*. Small wax lambs were common devotional objects among late medieval pilgrims.

LAMEN (Laemen), CHRISTOFFEL JACOB VAN DER. Flemish painter (b. Antwerp, ca. 1615, or 1606; d. ca. 1651). He painted fashionable society at its amusements: banqueting, dancing, and gaming. His style is based on the genre scenes of Frans Francken the Younger, but some similarity to kindred Dutch artists (such as Antonie Palamedes Stevens) cannot be denied.

BIBLIOGRAPHY. W. Bernt, *Die niederländischen Maler des 17. Jahrhunderts...*, vol. 2, Munich, 1948.

LAMI, EUGENE-LOUIS. French painter and lithographer (b. Paris, 1800; d. there, 1890). He entered the studio of Horace Vernet in 1815, and in 1817 he transferred to Gros's studio, where he studied aquarelle painting with Bonington. Lami's first artistic success came with a series of lithographs, *Collection des uniformes des armées françaises*, published between 1822 and 1825. He then turned to painting battle scenes (*Capitulation at Antwerp*, 1837; Versailles Museum) which earned him considerable popularity. At Bonington's suggestion Lami traveled twice to England (1826 and 1848–52), where he further developed his water-color technique. It is chiefly for his fine water colors depicting scenes of contemporary Parisian society that Lami is remembered today. Like his German contemporary Adolf von Menzel, Lami combined a painterly technique with detailed realism to capture the elegant flair of 19th-century high-society life (*Banquet in Honor of the Queen of England in the Palace of Versailles*, 1855; Paris, Louvre).

BIBLIOGRAPHY. H. Béraldi, *Les Graveurs du XIXe siècle*, vol. 9, Paris, 1889; P. A. Lemoisne, *L'Oeuvre d'Eugène Lami (1800–1890)*, Paris, 1914.

LAMOUR, JEAN. French ironsmith (b. Nancy, 1698; d. there, 1771). He first worked in Metz about 1712 and later went to Paris. In 1738 he was employed in Nancy by Stanislas I Leszczyński, former king of Poland, for whom he made the balustrade in the Hôtel de Ville and

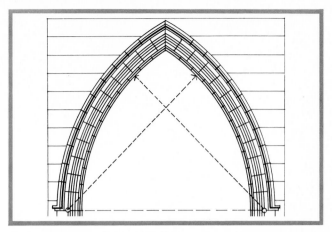

Lancet. Pointed or acute arch, its two arcs being drawn from centers on the springing outside the arch.

the great rococo grilles in the Place Stanislas (1751–55). Lamour published the designs in 1767 in the *Recueil des ouvrages de Serrurerie*.

BIBLIOGRAPHY. R. Chavancé, *Jean Lamour et la ferronnerie d'art*, Paris, 1942.

LAMP, JOHANN BAPTIST, *see* LAMPI, JOHANN BAPTIST, THE ELDER.

LAMP. Term applying to various objects designed to produce artificial light or heat. The lamp as a work of the minor arts was particularly important in the classical period, when lamps were often richly decorated with reliefs and painting. Both utilitarian and devotional, or funerary, lamps were decorated. Innumerable examples of funerary lamps have been found in Etruscan and Roman tombs.

LAMP BLACK. Type of black pigment made from the condensed soot of burning oil, tar, or resin. It is characteristically fine in texture and particularly suited to the production of ink. Chinese ink, for example, is made from this form of vegetable black. Most modern pigments, however, come from synthetic dyes.

BIBLIOGRAPHY. M. Doerner, *The Materials of the Artist...*, rev. ed., New York, 1949.

LAMPI (Lamp), JOHANN BAPTIST, THE ELDER. Tyrolese historical and portrait painter (b. Romeno, 1751; d. Vienna, 1830). He studied with his father and with Unterberger and Lorenzi. Lampi became a professor in the Vienna Academy (1786). His fashionable portraits depict the royal families of Poland and Russia and notables of Stockholm, Verona, and other cities.

LANCASTER, CASTLE OF. Fortress in Lancashire, England, erected partly on a former Roman site. The Norman keep was built by Roger of Poitou some time before 1102, and much of the rest of the building, including Adrian's Tower, was constructed in 1209. Twice it was damaged in battles; it was restored during the 14th century and again during the 18th century.

BIBLIOGRAPHY. W. Farrer and J. Brownbill, eds., *The Victoria History of the County of Lancaster*, 8 vols., London, 1906–14.

LANCET. Pointed or acute arch, its two arcs being drawn from centers on the springing outside the arch. As a sharp

Nicolas Lancret, *Summer*. Louvre, Paris. A decorative panel from the series of *The Seasons*.

arch, it is associated especially with the tall, narrow openings of English medieval architecture. The Gothic lancet window may be composed of many juxtaposed lancets.

LANCRET, NICOLAS. French genre painter, decorator, and illustrator (b. Paris, 1690; d. there, 1743). He learned engraving from his brother. At fifteen he was enrolled in the Royal Academy as a pupil of P. Dulin. He was expelled in 1708 but was readmitted the next year. Failing to win the Prix de Rome in 1711, he renounced history painting and sought training with Claude Gillot, through whom he met Watteau, who became his artistic idol though not his teacher. Lancret was received in the Academy as an associate in 1718, and as a member in 1719 as *peintre de fêtes galantes*, only two years after the initial use of this title for Watteau. His reception piece was *A Gallant Conversation* (London, Wallace Collection).

After 1732 Lancret did decorations for Fontainebleau, La Muette, Versailles (the dining room of the Petits Appartements and the Salon d'Apollon), and Trianon (a series, *Chasses des animaux*, of which *The Tiger Hunt* is in the Amiens Museum). His prestige as a chronicler of contemporary modes and mores was international, and eminent collectors—among them Frederick the Great, who possessed twenty-six of his works—vied for his production. In 1735

Lancret became councillor of the Academy and exhibited at the Salon. Frequenting the beau monde, he met actresses, singers, and dancers, including La Sallé and M.-A. de Cuppi (called La Camargo), whom he painted four times (Nantes; Potsdam; Leningrad; London, Wallace Collection). His masterpiece is twelve illustrations for the *Contes* of La Fontaine.

Lancret never achieved Watteau's poetic heights. He took his cue from the fashionable actuality of Watteau's *Enseigne de Gersaint* (Paris, Louvre) and brought it down to the level of polite genre. His work is never prosaic, however, for delicate sentiment and elegant manners are ever present. While Watteau imbued his work with plaintive repose, Lancret infused his with animated gaiety. Most of his works are decorative in purpose, conceived in series as overdoors or incorporated into paneling. Examples are *The Seasons* (Louvre); *The Hours of the Day* (London, National Gallery); *Déjeuner de jambon*, one of the four parts of the *Repas* series, the other three of which were by Jean-François de Troy (Chantilly, Condé Museum). His imitators were F. Octavien and B. de Bar. His works were engraved by J.-P. Lebas, C.-N. Cochin the Elder, N. de Larmessin, and others.

BIBLIOGRAPHY. G. Wildenstein, *Lancret...*, Paris, 1924.

GEORGE V. GALLENKAMP

LANDEVENNEC GOSPELS. Celtic illuminated manuscript, in the Public Library, New York.

LANDOWSKI, PAUL MAXIMILIEN. French sculptor (b. Paris, 1875; d. there, 1961). He studied with Barrias. Landowski was primarily a monumental sculptor. His sensitivity for linear decoration is apparent in his reliefs. He is best known for his huge statue of Christ overlooking Rio de Janeiro Harbor (dedicated 1931).

BIBLIOGRAPHY. R. Isay, *Paul Landowski*, Paris [1933?].

LANDSCAPE PAINTING. Picture whose principal subject is a stretch of countryside, usually with vistas reaching to the horizon. There are topographical landscapes, in which a real section of country is represented, as well as imaginary scenes. It may be a pure landscape (that is, having no figures) or a type in which figures may be introduced but play a secondary role.

In Asia landscape has been a major category of painting since the Six Dynasties (221–589) of China; as an expression of Taoist philosophy it attained its greatest heights during the Sung Dynasty (960–1279). In the West landscape as an independent subject did not appear until Hellenistic and Roman times (for example, *Odyssey Landscapes*, Rome, Vatican Museums). After the rediscovery of observed nature in the late Gothic and early Renaissance periods (for example, Ambrogio Lorenzetti, Jan Van Eyck), landscape did not achieve a respected position until the 17th century, particularly in Holland.

BIBLIOGRAPHY. M. J. Friedländer, *Landscape, Portrait, Still-life*, New York, 1962.

LANDSCAPE SCREEN IN TOJI, KYOTO. Japanese screen painting on silk (late 11th cent.). Now in the collection of the National Commission for the Protection of Cultural Properties, the six-fold screen was used at the initiation service in the Shingon (True Word) sect, although the subject matter of the painting is strictly secular. It represents a Chinese poet-scholar hermit seated in a small mountain hut and receiving visiting noblemen. The men are dressed in Chinese costumes, suggesting that the painting was copied from a Chinese model. Yet there is more of the native spirit in its representation of a landscape with gentle, rolling hills and a vast panorama of the distant sea, seen from a high point of view.

BIBLIOGRAPHY. T. Akiyama, *Japanese Painting* [Geneva?], 1961; National Commission for the Protection of Cultural Properties, ed., *Kokuhō (National Treasures of Japan)*, 6 vols., Tokyo, 1963–

LANDSCAPE WITH CYPRESSES. Oil painting by Van Gogh, in the Tate Gallery, London. *See* VAN GOGH, VINCENT WILLEM.

LANDSEER, SIR EDWIN HENRY. English animal painter (b. London, 1802; d. there, 1873). Landseer was something of a prodigy: he was drawing, etching, and painting before the age of twelve, was a pupil of Benjamin Robert Haydon in 1815, and in that year exhibited drawings at the Royal Academy of Arts. He entered the Royal Academy schools in 1816. His *Fighting Dogs Getting Wind* (1818) was purchased by Sir George Beaumont, and *Alpine Mastiffs Reanimating a Distressed Traveller* (1820) was the first of many of his pictures to win popularity through engraving. His brother Thomas was the chief

engraver of his work. Landseer was elected associate of the Royal Academy in 1826 and full academician in 1831. In 1850 he was knighted. He declined the presidency of the Royal Academy in 1865.

Landseer's immense reputation during his lifetime was based on a long series of subject pictures in which animals (in particular dogs, horses, and stags) are given human attributes. The titles best explain his approach: *The Highland Shepherd's Chief Mourner* (1837), *Dignity and Impudence* (1839), *The Monarch of the Glen* (1851). It is, however, now generally recognized that he must not be judged on these works alone. He was a splendid draftsman, and his drawings are among the finest of his time. His smaller oil sketches, particularly those made in the Highlands of Scotland, are highly accomplished, and some of his less well-known exhibition pieces, for example, *The Challenge* (1844; Duke of Northumberland Collection), are fine productions. His work belonged naturally to the literary-romantic mood of the 1820s, and in the sentimentality that increasingly pervaded it he yielded to mid-century tastes.

He was a favorite painter of Queen Victoria and the Prince Consort, and the royal collections contain a number of his works. The most vivid collection of his drawings belongs to the Duke of Abercorn. Landseer's work may be seen in London at the Tate Gallery and at the Victoria and Albert Museum. Landseer made the models for the lions at the corners of the Nelson Monument, Trafalgar Square, London, 1859.

BIBLIOGRAPHY. Royal Academy, *Catalogue, Landseer Exhibition*, London, 1961.

KENNETH J. GARLICK

Sir Edwin Henry Landseer, *Dignity and Impudence*. National Gallery, London.

LANDSHUT: HEILIG-GEIST-SPITALKIRCHE. German church built in the early 15th century. Perhaps the most important building by the architect Hans Stethaimer, it is noted for its exceptionally elegant proportions and richness of sculptural decoration, which compare favorably with the Parler-atelier churches of Kolín and Kutná Hora (Kuttenberg) in Bohemia.

BIBLIOGRAPHY. E. Hanfstaengl, *Hans Stethaimer*, Leipzig, 1911.

LANFRANCHI, FRANCESCO. Italian architect (fl. Turin, 2d half of 17th cent.). Roman, north Italian, and French elements are combined in his buildings. Among his works are the Palazzo di Città (1659–66) and S. Rocco (1667–91; the façade was constructed in 1890).

BIBLIOGRAPHY. G. Chevalley, *Gli architetti, l'architettura e la decorazione delle ville piemontesi del XVIII secolo*, Turin, 1912.

LANFRANCO, GIOVANNI. Italian painter (b. Parma, 1582; d. Rome, 1647). He worked with Agostino Carracci in Parma (1600–02) and then with Annibale Carracci in Rome, where he remained except for a return to Parma (1610–12) and a sojourn in Naples (1633–46). Although Lanfranco is considered a Carracci follower, his Parmesan background, in which Correggio and Schedoni figure, led

him in the painterly and lyrical direction seen in the *Magdalen* (ca. 1605; Naples, Capodimonte). This soon gave way to a more monumental style with a modified chiaroscuro in such works as the fresco of *Joseph Interpreting Dreams* (1614; Rome, Mattei Palace). His mature works, with their Correggiesque illusionism and dynamic action, helped bring the baroque to classical Rome in the 1620s and to Naples toward the middle of the century. Notable examples are the frescoes in the cupola of S. Andrea della Valle, Rome (1625–28), and those in the cupola of the Cappella di S. Gennaro in Naples Cathedral (1641–43).

BIBLIOGRAPHY. P. della Pergola, "Giovanni Lanfranco," *Il Vasari*, VI, 1933–34; L. Salerno, "The Early Work of Giovanni Lanfranco," *The Burlington Magazine*, XCIV, 1952; I. Toesca, "Note sul Lanfranco nella cappella Buongiovanni in Sant'Agostino di Roma," *Bollettino d'arte*, XLIV, 1959.

LANGEAIS, CASTLE OF. Fortified French castle in the Department of Indre-et-Loire. It was built in 1465 on the site of older fortresses by Jean Bourré, a minister of Louis XI. The forbidding entrance façade is marked by three great towers with battlements and conical roofs, joined together by a protected causeway designed for defense. The lower floors, however, have large windows, unsuitable for military purposes. These, as well as the pleasant court-

Giovanni Lanfranco, vault fresco of the Madonna and S. Carlo in Glory. S. Carlo ai Catinari, Rome.

yard wings, are evidence of growing interest in residential architecture in late-15th-century France.

BIBLIOGRAPHY. T. Cook, *Twenty-five Great Houses of France*, London, 1917; H. Guerlin, *Les Châteaux de Touraine*, Paris, 1929; F. Enaud, *Les Châteaux forts en France*, Paris, 1958.

LANGHANS, CARL GOTTHARD. German architect (1732–1808). He worked in Breslau and Berlin. He showed strong classical tendencies even before his trip to Italy in 1768–69. After moving to Berlin in 1788, he worked at Charlottenburg and Potsdam. His most important work is the neoclassic Brandenburg Gate (1789–93).

LANGRES CATHEDRAL. Gothic cathedral in northeastern France, probably begun after 1160. The nave was complete by 1196, its three-story elevation resembling that of Autun Cathedral. Despite its later rib vaults (and still later flying buttresses), Langres exhibits Romanesque heaviness.

BIBLIOGRAPHY. R. Branner, *Burgundian Gothic Architecture*, London, 1960.

LANG SHIH-NING, see CASTIGLIONE, GIUSEPPE.

LANGUEDOC, CHURCHES OF. Languedoc, in southwestern France, reached great cultural heights under the leadership of the counts of Toulouse during the 11th and 12th centuries. On the pilgrimage routes from Arles and Le Puy to Santiago de Compostela, Languedoc contained the most important pilgrimage churches: Ste-Foy, Conques; St-Martial, Limoges; St-Sernin, Toulouse. In addition, it had a number of interesting regional variants of the pilgrimage church, such as the abbey church of Beaulieu (ca. 1135) and St-Léonard (ca. 1150). *See* BEAULIEU-SUR-DORDOGNE, CHURCH OF; CONQUES: ABBEY CHURCH OF SAINTE-FOY; PILGRIMAGE; SAINT-SERNIN, TOULOUSE.

Perhaps the most important feature of Languedoc churches is their frequent and striking use of sculpture. The sculpture of the churches of Languedoc and of Burgundy represent the two most important schools of French Romanesque sculpture. In Languedoc the most significant examples are to be found in Moissac, St-Sernin, and Souillac. *See* MOISSAC: CHURCH AND CLOISTER; SOUILLAC, CHURCH OF.

LANG-YAO, see SANG DE BOEUF.

LANINO, BERNARDINO. Italian painter (ca. 1510–83). He was active in Vercelli. He was a pupil and close follower of Gaudenzio Ferrari in his early production. In works executed after a short visit to Milan, solidity and color merge remarkably well with Leonardesque shadow and caricature (frescoes, Milan, S. Nazaro).

BIBLIOGRAPHY. Vercelli, Museo Borgogna, *Mostra di Gaudenzio Ferrari*, Milan, 1956.

LANKES, JULIUS J. American wood engraver, illustrator, and author (1884–1960). Born in Buffalo, he studied at the Boston Museum of Fine Arts School under P. Hale and later collaborated with Charles Burchfield on woodcuts. Lankes taught at Wells College in Aurora, N.Y., and wrote *A Woodcut Manual* (1932) and other books. His woodcuts of the American scene have a silhouettelike quality.

BIBLIOGRAPHY. C. Zigrosser, *The Artists in America*, New York, 1942.

Lantern. A structural element most common in baroque architecture.

LANTANA, GIOVANNI BATTISTA. Italian architect of the school of Brescia (1581–1627). Lantana is recorded in 1603 as the designer of the new Cathedral of Brescia. It is one of several buildings of the period that combine the centralized plan of St. Peter's with a longitudinal axis, in this case an extended choir. *See* BRESCIA: CATHEDRAL.

BIBLIOGRAPHY. R. Wittkower, *Art and Architecture in Italy, 1600–1750*, Baltimore, 1958.

LANTERN. Any raised structure, usually in the form of a small tower with decorative arcades, mounted in the center of a dome or roof. Originally, the function of lanterns was to admit light and allow smoke to escape, but after the Renaissance most lanterns were decorative replicas of the larger centralized structures underneath. They are most common in baroque architecture.

LANTERN, BRONZE, IN TODAIJI, NARA. Japanese sculpture (8th cent.). The octagonal bronze lantern stands in front of the Great Buddha Hall of the Tōdaiji (the lighting of many lanterns was believed to be an act of penance for many sins). The eight perforated panels of its fire chamber are decorated with floral motifs and music-making bodhisattvas, executed in shallow relief. The bodhisattvas' feminine, fleshy bodies and full cheeks reflect the ideals of physical beauty in T'ang China.

BIBLIOGRAPHY. R. T. Paine and A. Soper, *The Art and Architecture of Japan*, Baltimore, 1955; National Commission for the Protection of Cultural Properties, ed., *Kokuhō (National Treasures of Japan)*, vol. 1: *From the Earliest Time to the End of the Nara Period*, Tokyo, 1963.

LANTERNE DES MORTS. Small stone structure, usually in the form of a small tower, built in the graveyard to hold a lamp that was illuminated in the evening for the dead. It was common in the 11th and 12th centuries, particularly in France.

LANTHORN. Term used to describe a lantern or cupola found in colonial Georgian houses and in early American post-Revolutionary architecture.

LAN YING. Chinese landscape painter (1585–after 1660). His *tzu* was Lan T'ien-shu. Born in Ch'ien-t'ang in Chekiang Province, he is traditionally considered the last painter of the Che school, and since this school of painting has suffered various fortunes at the hands of Chinese critics and collectors Lan Ying has been somewhat neglected in both Chinese and Western writings. He was a prolific artist, sometimes quite dazzling and brilliant. His landscapes were usually done in light colors, with a distinctive quality of personal touch that is most apparent in his figures. Many fine works by this artist are in American museums and private collections. *See* CHE SCHOOL.

BIBLIOGRAPHY. O. Sirén, *Chinese Painting, Leading Masters and Principles*, vol. 5, New York, 1958.

LANYON, PETER. English painter (1918–64). He was born in St. Ives, Cornwall, where he always lived. He studied under William Coldstream at the Euston Road School. After service in World War II he taught at the Bath Academy of Art, Corsham. His work received many international prizes and was widely exhibited. English landscape, especially the landscape of Cornwall, was the strongest influence on his paintings. The form was abstract, however, and thus gave new life to the English landscape tradition. The older generation of artists at St. Ives, especially Naum Gabo, Barbara Hepworth, and Ben Nicholson, were important in the formation of Lanyon's style, but it always remained very personal and revealed in color and design his deeply emotional response to landscape. Lanyon's later works showed a development in greater size and brighter colors.

LANZI, LOGGIA DEI, FLORENCE. Italian vaulted arcade facing the Piazza della Signoria. It was begun in 1376 by Benci di Cione and Simone di Francesco Talenti and was finished in 1391. Its three semicircular stone arches anticipate Renaissance architectural developments. The Loggia dei Lanzi now shelters sculptures by Cellini, Giovanni Bologna, and others. Its name is derived from its use as assembly hall and guardroom of the foot soldiers (*lanzi*) of Cosimo de' Medici the Younger.

BIBLIOGRAPHY. M. Kirchmayer, *L'architettura italiana*, 3d ed., 2 vols., Turin, 1958–60.

Lararium. Small, nichelike shrine for images of the *lares*.

LAOCOON. A Trojan priest who opposed bringing the Wooden Horse of the Greeks within the walls of Troy. In order to silence Laocoön, the gods sent two large serpents that strangled him and his two sons.

The myth is illustrated by the famous marble group discovered on the Esquiline in 1506 and now in the Vatican Museums. According to Pliny the Elder, it was the work of three Rhodian sculptors, Hagesander (Agesander or Agesandros), Polydorus, and Athenodorus (*Natural History*, XXXVI, 37). The statue has often been dated about 30 B.C. on the basis of epigraphical evidence relating to the sculptors' names, but its style suggests that it is a Pergamene work of the mid-2d century B.C.

The *Laocoön* is an outstanding example of the mastery of drama and pathos achieved by Hellenistic sculptors. Michelangelo and his contemporaries freely acknowledged its influence on their work. In the 1950s the original bent position of the right arm (known from the finds at Sperlonga) was substituted for the incorrect baroque restoration, which shows the arm reaching upward.

BIBLIOGRAPHY. M. Bieber, *Laocoön: The Influence of the Group since Its Discovery*, New York, 1942; G. M. A. Richter, *Three Critical Periods in Greek Sculpture*, Oxford, 1951.

JEROME J. POLLITT

LAON CATHEDRAL. French church begun between 1150 and 1155 and completed by 1205. It had an important influence on the Cathedral of Notre-Dame in Paris. The crossing lantern, the towers flanking the transepts, and the towers of the west front give Laon a most inspiring silhouette. The top story of the towers of the west front is decorated with magnificent oxen, commemorating the faithful beasts who hauled the stone to build the cathedral. The deeply set porches of the west front herald the transept porches of Chartres.

Most of the large sculptures were destroyed during the French Revolution and restored in the 19th century. However, much original and rich ornamentation still exists, dating mostly from the late 12th and the early 13th century.

BIBLIOGRAPHY. M. Aubert and S. Goubet, *Gothic Cathedrals of France and their Treasures*, London, 1959.

LAPIDARY. Pertaining to the art of cutting and polishing precious and semiprecious stones. It also refers to a type of medieval book, which was a supplement to the bestiary, containing allegorical interpretations of the Christian meaning of various gems.

LAPIS LAZULI. Dark blue, semiprecious stone used in jewelry and intarsia work, and in pulverized form, for the production of the pigment ultramarine. The most prized variety is nearly solid blue; lesser grades have flecks of white and yellow.

LAPITHAE (Lapiths). In Greek mythology, a tribe of Thessalians who waged a battle with the Centaurs at the wedding feast of the Lapith king Pirithous. The Centaurs triggered the struggle when they attacked the bride and other Lapith women in a drunken frenzy. The most famous representation of the battle, the pediment of the Temple of Zeus at Olympia, symbolizes the triumph of civilization over barbarism. *See* ZEUS, TEMPLE OF, OLYMPIA.

Nicolas de Largillière, *Louis XIV with His Family*, 1708. Wallace Collection, London.

LA PLANCHE, DE (Van den Planken), FAMILY. Important family of tapestry makers in Paris for three generations. The first, François, was invited from Oudenaarde, Flanders, by Henry IV in 1607 to work at the Gobelins manufactory in partnership with Marc and Hierosome de Comans. His son, Raphael, broke away to found an independent workshop in the Faubourg St-Germain in 1633, which was taken over by François's grandson, Sébastien François, in 1661, and liquidated in 1667. The tapestries have wide borders of High Renaissance motifs framing scenes in the French classical style, often after contemporary artists.

BIBLIOGRAPHY. H. Göbel, *Wandteppiche*, pt. 2, Leipzig, 1928.

LARARIUM. Small, nichelike shrine, usually near the hearth in a Roman house, in which the images of the *lares* (household gods) were kept. A lararium was found intact in the house of Menander at Pompeii.

LARDERA, BERTO. Italian sculptor (1911–   ). He was born in La Spezia. Lardera is mainly self-taught. He has had one-man exhibitions in New York City at the Knoedler Art Galleries, in Paris at the Galerie Denise René, in Milan at Il Milione, and elsewhere, and has been represented in international exhibitions since the 1940s. His style is abstract but based on figural shapes. He lives in Paris.

BIBLIOGRAPHY. M. C. Lacoste, "Lardera, découpeur d'espace," *L'Oeil*, XXXVII, 1958.

LARES. Class of benevolent gods in Roman mythology who were the protectors of the family and its household. There were also *lares* who protected public buildings and even the state itself (*lares communales*). In the home, their toga-clothed images were placed in the lararium between two *penates* (gods of the storeroom). They were given offerings of food at every meal and special offerings at festive occasions. *See* LARARIUM.

L'ARGENTA, *see* ALEOTTI, GIOVANNI BATTISTA.

LARGILLIERE (Largillierre), NICOLAS DE. French portrait painter (b. Paris, 1654; d. there, 1746). His family moved to Antwerp about 1657, and there, except for a sojourn in England (1665–67), the artist was raised. He was the pupil of Antoon Goubau from 1668 until 1672, when he was received as master in the Antwerp guild of painters. In 1674 Largillière moved to London as assistant to Sir Peter Lely, court portraitist, to whose works he added still-life, drapery, and landscape backgrounds, and restored master paintings in the collection of Charles II. In Paris in 1680 he worked first for Adam Frans van der Meulen and gained the protection of Charles Le Brun, head of the Royal Academy. There, as the result of his Flemish education, Largillière later distinguished himself as a partisan of the "Moderns," or Rubenists.

He began his career conservatively, however. *Pupil and Tutor* (1685; New York, formerly Mrs. F. Feder Collection) and *James II and Mary of Modena* (made during a trip to London, 1685; London, National Portrait Gallery) reflect the restrained Netherlandish idiom used by G. Soest, W. Wissing, and Sir Godfrey Kneller, which was favored in England at that time. Largillière became an associate of the Paris Royal Academy in 1683 and a member in 1686 as "painter of historiated portraits." His reception piece, *Portrait of C. Le Brun* (Paris, Louvre), was an innovation, the state portrait of an artist. In 1687 the city fathers of Paris commissioned a series of five *Echevin* portraits in which officials are represented at solemn civic occasions in buoyant baroque splendor. Only one of the series, *Ex-Voto to St. Genevieve* (1694; Paris, St-Etienne-du-Mont), remains. At the Academy he rose to chancellor in 1733 and became director from 1738 to 1742. Ill-health forced him to resign the directorship.

In 1699 he married the daughter of the landscape painter J.-B. Forest. He represented his wife, himself, and their daughter in a pastoral group (Louvre; preliminary study, Hartford, Wadsworth Atheneum). His glamorous presentation of sitters—modishly alluring for women, startlingly vivacious for men—made him favored over his rival but lifelong friend, Hyacinthe Rigaud, the more conservative court portraitist, by minor French and foreign nobility

(*Baroness de Pragins*, New York, Metropolitan Museum; *Jean Pupil de Craponne*, Grenoble Museum); by royal mistresses (*Allegory of Vertumnus and Pomona*, representing the Regent and Mme de Parabère, formerly Sauerbach Collection); and by actresses (*Mademoiselle Duclos*, Chantilly, Condé Museum). One of numerous exceptions is the group portrait *Louis XIV with His Family* (1708; London, Wallace Collection).

Largillière's works synthesize the vigor of Rubens and the elegance of Van Dyck with the traditional French psychological realism. The glittering, often mannered brilliance of his technique, opulently colored, fluid, and strongly impressionistic, especially in drawings, underlines his transitional importance between classical academicism and 18th-century virtuosity.

BIBLIOGRAPHY. G. Pascal, *Largillierre*, Paris, 1928.

GEORGE V. GALLENKAMP

LARIONOV, MICHAEL. Russian abstract painter (1881–1964). Born in Ternopol in the Ukraine, he studied at the Moscow Academy. He painted his first abstract painting in 1909, and published a rayonist manifesto in 1913. He was a friend of Malevich and a teacher of Tatlin, and was closely associated professionally with Natalie Gontcharova, whom he married. Larionov was the founder of Jack of Diamonds, a group promoting modern art in Moscow. Larionov and Gontcharova moved permanently to Paris and exhibited their rayonist art at Paul Guillaume's gallery. They stopped painting to design décor for the Diaghilev Russian ballet and continued to do so until Diaghilev's death in 1929. *See* GONTCHAROVA, NATALIE; JACK OF DIAMONDS; RAYONISM.

Combining pointillist luminous color and elements from cubism, Larionov reduced landscape elements to rays (hence the name "rayonism"), usually on the diagonal, in a manner suggesting lines of force, as did the Italian futurists.

BIBLIOGRAPHY. M. Seuphor, "Russia and the Avant-Garde," *Selective Eye*, New York, 1956–57.

LARISA, PALACE OF. Greek palace built on an archaic acropolis overlooking the Hermos River in Anatolia. It lies within the district of the great Ionic cities. The palace is characterized by a portico consisting of four columns with Aeolian capitals bearing an architrave and pediment. It has the earliest existing Greek peristyle court known, dating from about 450 B.C.

BIBLIOGRAPHY. *Larisa am Hermos*, vol. 1, ed., J. Boehlau and K. Schefold, Berlin, 1940.

LARKIN BUILDING, BUFFALO, N.Y., *see* WRIGHT, FRANK LLOYD.

LAROON, MARCELLUS, JR. English painter and draftsman (1679–1774). Laroon was active primarily during the second quarter of the 18th century. He is best known for his drawings, which are usually of groups of figures. These resemble conversation pieces in form, but do not appear to contain actual portraits. His rather busy but attractive draftsmanship is highly personal and cannot be readily confused with the work of his contemporaries. The paintings retain many of the same qualities as the drawings and have a sketchy appearance quite unlike the normal English mode of painting at the time.

BIBLIOGRAPHY. E. K. Waterhouse, *Painting in Britain, 1530–1790*, Baltimore, 1953; R. Raines, *Marcellus Laroon*, London, 1966.

Michael Larionov, *Rays*. Michael Larionov Collection, Paris.

LARSSON, CARL. Swedish painter (1853–1919). He lived in France in the 1870s and 1880s. He worked with the Swedish open-air painters in blond, fresh colors, diffused light, and limpid atmosphere. The style of his later work, murals as well as intimate family pictures, is linear, rhythmic, and decorative, influenced by Japanese prints and Swedish folk art.

BIBLIOGRAPHY. G. Nordensvan, *Carl Larsson*, 2 vols., Stockholm, 1920–21.

L'ART RUPESTRE. Inclusive French term for all paintings or incised drawings made by prehistoric and primitive peoples in caves or rock shelters.

LASANSKY, MAURICIO. American printmaker (1914–   ). He was born of Lithuanian parents in Buenos Aires, where he studied painting, sculpture, and engraving. In 1936 he became director of the Free Fine Arts School, Villa María Córdoba, Argentina. He went to the United States on a Guggenheim fellowship (1943–44) to study the Metropolitan Museum of Art's print collection and to work with Stanley William Hayter. Three subsequent Guggenheim fellowships have enabled Lasansky to study in Europe.

In 1945 he went as a visiting lecturer to the State University of Iowa, where he created a graphic arts department that has become an important graphics center. In 1967 he was designated the first Virgil M. Hancher Professor of Art at the University.

Lasansky has continued to direct perhaps the most influential print workshop in the United States. His students have won many of the major awards in printmaking. His own work is primarily in the intaglio medium. It is bold, colorful, and full of symbolism, expressing his belief that printmaking is a major art form.

BIBLIOGRAPHY. C. Zigrosser, *Mauricio Lasansky*, New York, 1960.
KNEELAND MC NULTY

LA SCALA OPERA HOUSE, MILAN. Opera house in northern Italy by Giuseppe Piermarini (1776–78). The façade is neoclassic, and the auditorium is famous for its acoustics. Bombed out in 1943, La Scala was reconstructed in 1946. It houses a museum and library of theater, music, and dance. The name of the opera house recalls an earlier occupant of its site, the Church of S. Maria della Scala, built in 1381 for Regina della Scala, wife of Bernabò Visconti.

BIBLIOGRAPHY. C. Gatti, *Il Teatro alla Scala rinnovato*, Milan, 1926.

LASCARIS, PIETRO. Italian sculptor (fl. Padua, Venice, and Ferrara; d. 1531). Lascaris may have been of Greek origin; nothing is known about his life or training. Only two works are ascertained to be by his hand: a half-figure of the Madonna in the lunette of Sta Maria dei Miracoli, Venice, and a marble statue of St. Justina in antique dress in S. Antonio, Padua.

BIBLIOGRAPHY. L. Planiscig, *Venezianische Bildhauer der Renaissance*, Vienna, 1921.

LASCAUX. Cave in the Department of the Dordogne, southwestern France. The prehistoric paintings and engravings of Lascaux were discovered on September 12, 1940, when five boys went to the rescue of their dog, which had fallen into a fissure eroded in the slope of a hill overlooking the town of Montignac. The boys literally fell into a passage that led into a great hall measuring 60 by 30 feet. Its ceiling was found to be covered by a vast painting dominated by four large black bulls, one of which is some 18 feet long. The other animals—horses, bovids, and bears—are smaller in scale.

Two passages lead out from the Great Hall of the Bulls. The smaller, called the Painted Gallery, which seems to have more consciously composed animal groups than the Great Hall, is important especially for a group of three red-and-black bovids and bistre-and-black horses decorating the vaulted ceiling. The wider Lateral Passage has only traces of paintings of horses and bovids, since here an air current seems to have damaged the paintings. In the passage are found engravings of animals, often superposed, sometimes covered by a maze of incised lines that makes their interpretation difficult.

The Lateral Passage leads into the Chamber of Engravings, whose walls are covered in some areas by overlapping engraved and painted figures and in others by animal forms made by engraving or painting or a combination of the two. The Chamber of Engravings gives access to the long narrow Main Gallery, about 27 yards long and 1–3¼ yards wide. Here the paintings are dominated by friezes of horses, although there are ibex and bison and the famous frieze of deer heads. The Main Gallery slopes downward rather steeply until it reaches the Chamber of Felines, which has not only an engraved group of felines but also other animal groups and lattice designs. The passage continues beyond this point, and there are further engravings and paintings. The Shaft of the Dead Man is adjacent to the Chamber of Engravings. Here, some 16 feet below the adjoining Apse, is a painting of a man between a rhinoceros and a wounded bison.

The vast complex of paintings at Lascaux is executed in a limited range of colors. Some of the animal forms are defined by outlining; others are filled in with a wash. The preservation of their brilliance is due in large measure

Marcellus Laroon, Jr., *Interior with Figures*. Tate Gallery, London.

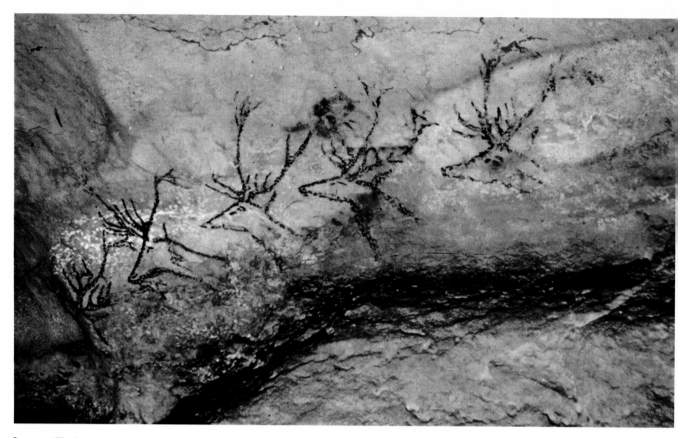

Lascaux. The famous frieze of deer heads in the Main Gallery, probably dating from the early Magdalenian period.

to a thin calcite film, which has been deposited over their surface since Paleolithic times. This sanctuary of hunting magic is usually dated to the middle Upper Paleolithic. Archaeologically this date rests upon the lamps, charcoal, and spears found in the Shaft of the Dead Man. The spear points seem to be Périgordian or early Magdalenian; the charcoal has a radiocarbon date of about 15,000 years ago. Stylistic analysis aided by the superposition of paintings and engravings suggests that there were at least three phases in the development of the art of Lascaux, but there is not enough difference between phases to indicate marked changes in culture. Most of the work must date to the second half of Breuil's Aurignacio-Périgordian age. A few paintings, such as those in black, might extend into the proto-Magdalenian.

BIBLIOGRAPHY. F. Windels, *The Lascaux Cave Paintings*, London, 1949; A. Leming, *Lascaux, Paintings and Engravings*, Harmondsworth, 1959. HOMER L. THOMAS

LAS HUELGAS, CONVENT OF. Convent for Cistercian nuns near Burgos, Spain, founded by Alfonso VIII in 1187. The church (1203–26), by Master Ricardo, has vaults of the Angevin type. The older Chapel of the Assumption is Mudejar. The 13th-century kings of Castile are buried in the church, and their well-preserved garments, jewelry, and arms are exhibited in the Museo de Ricas Telas.

BIBLIOGRAPHY. E. Lambert, *L'Art gothique en Espagne aux XIIe et XIIIe siècles*, Paris, 1931.

LA SONNETTE, JEAN MICHEL AND GEORGES DE, *see* SONNETTE, JEAN MICHEL AND GEORGES DE LA.

LASSAW, IBRAM. American sculptor (1913–   ). Born in Alexandria, Egypt, he went to the United States in 1921 and from the age of twelve studied sculpture. He attended the Clay Club, New York City, during 1928–32 and the Beaux-Arts Institute of Design in 1930–31. His first abstract work of 1931 made him a pioneer of abstract sculpture in America. In 1936 he was a founder of the American Abstract Artists group. He has participated in many national and international exhibitions, and his works have had frequent gallery showings in New York.

Working with Percival Goodman, Lassaw did several architectural commissions, including the *Pillar of Fire* at Temple Beth El, Providence, R.I. *Monoceros* (1952) is in the Museum of Modern Art, New York; *Profession* (1956) is in the Whitney Museum of American Art, New York; and *Theme and Variations, I* (1957) is in the Albright-Knox Art Gallery, Buffalo. Lassaw is important for his urban-inspired space cages of soldered metal and for his metaphorical imagery.

BIBLIOGRAPHY. I. Sandler, "Ibram Lassaw," in *Three American Sculptors*, New York, 1959.

LAST COMMUNION OF ST. JEROME. Oil painting by Domenichino, in the Vatican Museums, Rome. *See* DOMENICHINO.

LAST JUDGMENT, THE. Second Coming of Christ, in which, after the resurrection of the dead, He judges mankind. The *Homilies* of the 4th-century Church Father Ephräm of Syria, along with Biblical sources and popular egends, provide a literary basis for representation of the Last Judgment in art. As first fully depicted in Byzantine art, Christ is shown seated between Mary and St. John the Evangelist. He holds a sword in His right hand, a lily in His left. Below Him the newly resurrected are separated into groups of saved (on Christ's right) and damned (on His left). Representations of heaven and hell are sometimes shown on either side.

The Last Judgment scene was introduced in the West about 1000, the date of a wall painting of the Reichenau school at Oberzell. In the Romanesque and Gothic periods it was a popular subject for sculptural cycles on the main portal of churches. In Gothic art the damned and the saved are individualized, as are their corresponding rewards and torments; for example, the miser is hanged with the strings of his purse. The theme continued to be popular through the Renaissance from Fra Angelico to Michelangelo.

DONALD L. EHRESMANN

LAST JUDGMENT, THE. Fresco painting by Michelangelo, in the Sistine Chapel, the Vatican, Rome. *See* MICHELANGELO BUONARROTI.

LASTMAN, PIETER PIETERSZ. Dutch history painter (b. Amsterdam, 1583; d. there, 1633). He and his brother, who was also a painter, were the sons of Pieter Zeegersz.; they both used the surname Lastman. Pieter Lastman was a pupil of Gerrit Pietersz. Sweelinck. Lastman traveled to Rome, possibly as early as 1603 and certainly by 1604, where he was influenced by such artists as the German painter Adam Elsheimer, Caravaggio, and perhaps Jan Pijnas. However, Lastman's style does not seem to have been formed totally from the Caravaggesque side of Roman painting. Such paintings as the signed *Dispute between Orestes and Pylades* (1614; Amsterdam, Rijksmuseum), for example, indicate that Lastman also must have known the works of Annibale Carracci and his followers in Rome. This acquaintance is confirmed by Lastman's drawing style, which seems also to relate to the Carracci manner of drawing.

By 1607 Lastman was back in Amsterdam, where he remained for the rest of his life. He was one of the most important history painters in the Netherlands. As a teacher Lastman was particularly influential through his two famous pupils, Jan Lievens and Rembrandt. Lievens was his student about 1617, and Rembrandt spent approximately six months with Lastman about 1623. Lastman's influence was basic to the development of Rembrandt's early style.

BIBLIOGRAPHY. K. Freise, *Pieter Lastman, sein Leben und seine Kunst*, Leipzig, 1911; K. Bauch, "Entwurf und Komposition bei Pieter Lastman," *Münchener Jahrbuch der bildenden Kunst*, VI, 1955; K. Bauch, *Der frühe Rembrandt und seine Zeit*, Berlin, 1960.

LEONARD J. SLATKES

LAST SUPPER, THE. The meal Christ shared with His apostles on the night before His crucifixion. The Last Supper is not represented in Christian art until after the 6th

Pieter Pietersz. Lastman, *Dispute between Orestes and Pylades.* Rijksmuseum, Amsterdam.

century (Gospels of Rossano, Rossano Cathedral). In Byzantine art, the scene was based on the Matthew text, in which Judas grasps at the keys; in the West, its basis was John's text, in which Christ passes the loaf. Combinations of the two versions also exist. In Italy it was common for this scene to be represented on the walls of the refectory.

BIBLIOGRAPHY. M. Volberg, *L'Eucharistie dans l'art*, 2 vols., Paris, 1946.

LAST SUPPER, THE. Wall painting in mixed media by Leonardo, in Sta Maria delle Grazie, Milan. *See* LEONARDO DA VINCI.

LAT, *see* STAMBHA.

LATE-ANTIQUE STYLE. Pagan art of the late ancient world, from the second half of the 3d century to the first half of the 6th. Almost all the painting of the period is lost, except for the remarkable mummy portraits from the Fayoum in Egypt, but the earliest catacomb paintings belong to this style. Its principles are most apparent in sculpture, particularly in relief, where the Greco-Roman canon becomes schematized and stiffened, and sharp contrasts of light and shade are multiplied across intricately inflected surfaces, as in the *Ludovisi Battle Sarcophagus* (early 3d cent.; Rome, National Museum of Rome). Freestanding sculpture tends to become abstract, closed off from the world, and rather ethereal, as the portraits of Gallienus (ca. 250–270) and the Venice Tetrarchs (early 4th cent.; Venice, St. Mark's) show. Barbarian influences, subclassical forms, and the desperation of a world torn by strife all contributed to the formation of the style. *See* CATACOMB PAINTING; FAYOUM PORTRAITS.

BIBLIOGRAPHY. A. Riegl, *Spätrömische Kunstindustrie*, Vienna 1927; C. R. Morey, *Early Christian Art*, 2d ed., Princeton, 1953 E. Kitzinger, *Early Medieval Art in the British Museum*, 2d ed. London, 1955.

LATE MINOAN ART, *see* CRETE.

LA TENE PERIOD. Second phase of the Iron Age in Europe, following the Hallstatt period. It is characterized by the predominance and spread of the Celtic tribes. Named for the settlement of La Tène on the Lake of Neuchâtel in Switzerland, this culture arose in the 5th century B.C. among Celtic peoples of eastern France and western Germany. It possessed an art strongly influenced by the colonial Greeks of the western Mediterranean and expanded in the 5th and 4th centuries B.C. to dominate all of France and western and southern Germany. During the great Celtic migrations, it was carried into Britain and eastward into the Balkans and even southern Russia.

The period is marked by complex curvilinear ornament, incised pottery, inhumation, and the more frequent use of iron for tools and weapons, although bronze continued in use for decorative objects and was often ornamented with champlevé enamel. On the Continent, La Tène art lasted until the Roman conquest, but in Wales, Cornwall, Ireland, and Scotland it survived through the Roman period and was a factor in the formation of Dark Ages art.

See also OPPIDA.

BIBLIOGRAPHY. T. G. E. Powell, *The Celts*, New York, 1958.
HOMER L. THOMAS

LATERAN, THE, ROME. Italian palace, church, and baptistery. Though situated across the Tiber from Vatican City, the complex forms part of that state under the

Late-antique style. *Ludovisi Battle Sarcophagus*, early 3d century. National Museum of Rome.

La Tène Period. Black-surfaced jar with incised decoration, from Marson (Marne). Early La Tène culture. British Museum, London.

The Lateran, Rome. S. Giovanni in Laterano, façade by Alessandro Galilei. 1733–36.

Lateran Treaty of 1929. The Lateran Palace houses the Lateran Museums. *See* ROME: MUSEUMS (LATERAN MUSEUMS).

SAN GIOVANNI IN LATERANO

Church of the bishop of Rome, Constantine's first donation to his new faith. Shortly after his victory over Maxentius (313) the Emperor presented the Palace of the Laterani to the bishop of Rome as the site of the first major Christian church in that city. With minor additions and modifications, the church existed in its Early Christian form until fires in 1308 and 1361 almost destroyed it. The current edifice is largely the baroque structure as rebuilt by Francesco Borromini (1646–49).

Knowledge of the Constantinian basilica is based upon old drawings, paintings (a fresco in S. Martino al Monte in Rome), and archaeological investigation. These sources show that S. Giovanni was a five-aisled basilica with a single large semicircular eastern apse. There were no galleries, but a clerestory rose above the level of the side aisles. The church had an open-beamed timber roof. Nave and aisle columns, capped with antique Corinthian or Ionic capitals, carried arcades. A continuous arcade (no longer extant) at the end of the aisles served to create a segregated transept before the apse. S. Giovanni thus conformed to a type that has been called the Constantinian T basilica.

The baroque church by Borromini is built around the remains of the Early Christian church. This strange procedure was adopted because Pope Innocent X, who had commissioned the rebuilding, insisted that the early building be preserved. Borromini solved the problem by encasing alternate pairs of the original columns within monumental pierlike pilasters. Each of the colossal pier units is articulated by a deep niche containing sculpture. Thus, a subtle but rich alternating rhythm is established. The distinct stylistic personality of Borromini is displayed in the continuation of the nave arcade across the corners of the entrance wall, which transforms the rigid axiality of the early basilica into an enclosed space more typical of Borromini's own contributions to baroque architecture.

Although current research indicates that Borromini intended to vault the nave, he never completed this project, and the present ceiling is a heavy wooden coffered construction (1564–72) by Daniele da Volterra. The aisles, niches, and tabernacles are treated with contrasting light and dark marble to create a rich and complex coloristic harmony throughout the building.

The monumental façade of S. Giovanni (1733–36) was designed by Alessandro Galilei, whose project was chosen in a competition involving twenty-three architects. The use of the gigantic order stems from Maderno's design for the façade of St. Peter's, but Galilei's façade is more severe and stresses the rhythmic contrast between massive columns and open arcades.

BIBLIOGRAPHY. O. K. Wulff, *Altchristliche und byzantinische Kunst*, 2 vols. in 1, Berlin, 1914; R. Wittkower, *Art and Architecture in Italy, 1600–1750*, Baltimore, 1958; W. F. Volbach, *Early Christian Art*, New York, 1962. STANLEY FERBER

SAN GIOVANNI IN FONTE

The Lateran baptistery, octagonal in plan, retains more of its original Early Christian character than any other part of the complex in spite of subsequent restoration. The interior is divided into two concentric naves by a ring of eight porphyry columns carrying an architrave with an inscription from the reign of Sixtus III (5th cent.). Smaller columns that support the cupola rest on the architrave. A circular pool in the center of the pavement was used for baptism by immersion.

RAYMOND LIFCHEZ

LATHAM, RICHARD. American industrial designer (1920–   ). The son of an artist, he was born in Kansas City, Mo. He first studied engineering; then industrial design at the Art Institute of Chicago and abstract design under Mies van der Rohe. Latham's first industrial design

job was with Montgomery Ward. Later he became director of design for the Raymond Loewy office in Chicago, but left in 1955 to set up his present partnership: Latham, Tyler, Jensen, Inc. In 1960 he served as president of the American Society of Industrial Designers. His office now has branches in Long Beach, Calif., and in Denmark.

LATHEM-SAINT-MARTIN SCHOOL, *see* LAETHEM-SAINT-MARTIN SCHOOL.

LATIN AMERICAN ART, *see* AMERICAS, ANCIENT, ART OF; COLONIAL ART: LATIN AMERICA; MEXICO; PERU; SOUTH AMERICAN INDIAN ART, PRIMITIVE.

LA TOUR, GEORGES DE. French painter of religious and genre scenes (b. Vic-sur-Seille, 1593; d. Lunéville, 1652). This artist has recently regained the status he enjoyed just prior to the ascendency of the art of Versailles. His works had formerly been attributed to Velázquez, Zurbarán, Fray Juan Andres Ricci, and even to the 18th-century pastel portraitist Maurice-Quentin de La Tour.

Georges de La Tour was impelled by the monumental simplicity of visual reality. His personal communication, especially in his late religious works, was of a transcendental truth through the achievement of an ideal of absolute silence. Though his work is a product of numerous and complicated foreign influences, it remains truly French in respect to lucid structure, pictorial richness, and ultimate reserve. The explicit sources of his style and the chronology of his development remain problematic.

La Tour was of noble birth in Lorraine, which was an independent duchy until 1633. In 1620 he is recorded as a master painter in Lunéville, where he had opened a studio with apprentices. He remained in Lunéville with the possible exception of three lapses: (1) before 1618, when it is traditionally accepted, though not proved, that he studied in Italy, perhaps under Guido Reni; (2) 1621–22, when he may have gone to Italy or to Holland and there may have known Hendrick Terbrugghen and Gerrit van Honthorst; and (3) 1638–41, when the French occupation of Lorraine is believed to have made him elect, for at least part of this span of years, to share the exile of his patron, Duke Charles IV, in the Netherlands. However, in 1639 he is recorded as "Painter to the King" (Louis XIII), for whom he executed one of four known *St. Sebastian* works (Paris, Louvre version). After 1643 he did commissions for the Duc de La Ferté-Senecterre, the new governor of Lorraine. From 1644 to 1652 he was *peintre attitré de Lunéville.*

His art was initially manneristic in tendency. During his early maturity it became increasingly naturalistic in the revolutionary baroque manner of Caravaggio, although the influence must be assumed to be indirect, possibly through Honthorst and Terbrugghen.

The chronology of his art is most reasonable, at present, on the following basis:

Early years (before 1621). *The Cheat* (Paris, Landry Collection) is an exercise in a manner practiced in Nancy by Le Clerc in painting and by Callot in etching. It is primarily manneristic.

Georges de La Tour, detail of *The Magdalene with an Oil Lamp,* 1635–40. Louvre, Paris.

Early maturity (1621–25). *St. Jerome* (Stockholm, National Museum) reveals the first impact of Terbrugghen's style as seen in such a work as Terbrugghen's *Four Evangelists* (Deventer Stadhuis), dated 1621, when La Tour may have visited Utrecht. The application of realistic detail to a peculiar waxlike modeling evinces the Dutch preoccupation with rugged, picturesque, and descriptive qualities. Certain of the forms in *St. Jerome* suggest the artist's incipient interest in large generalized geometric shapes as a means of unifying the composition within a limited picture plane. *Fortune Teller* (New York, Metropolitan Museum) very probably belongs to this period, as the forms, like those of *St. Jerome,* are more plastically defined without the emphasis of spotlighting, which had made the motifs of *The Cheat* flat, as if cut out, and the details too dryly pronounced.

Transition (1625–ca. 1630). *Job and His Wife* (Epinal Museum) has suddenly become a night scene illuminated by an unshaded candle, though descriptive realism persists. This work leads into his fourth phase.

Maturity (1630–45). In this period the influence of Terbrugghen and Honthorst becomes positive. They were the real exponents of night lighting. One of La Tour's mature works is *Christ and St. Joseph in the Carpenter Shop* (ca. 1645; Louvre), in which the compositional motifs are magnificently balanced though dramatically opposed. They are plastically defined close to the picture plane and unified, at last, with conviction, by a single emphatic light source. A solemn quietude begins to infuse the whole, though there are vestiges of realism, such as Joseph's forehead and hands.

Last years (1645–52). His final style is seen in such works as the *Nativity* (Rennes Museum) and *St. Sebastian Being Ministered to by St. Irene* (Berlin, former State Museums). All but the most geometric ornamental detail vanishes, and the forms are reduced to their essentials. They are now softly modeled, suggesting monoliths of a fine coherent rock, just short of pure geometry. The eternal stillness of an isolated corner of a quarry, closely observed under torchlight or candlelight, is elicited. So cautiously do the forms dovetail that the work of Vermeer, who was twenty years old when La Tour died, is prophesied. In La Tour's late works an immutable grandeur and solemn simplicity reign, contrary to the pervasive exuberance of the baroque age.

His works are found in the museums of Berlin, Cleveland, Detroit, Epinal, Grenoble, Hartford, Kansas City, Le Mans, Nancy, Nantes, New York (Metropolitan Museum and Frick Collection), Paris (Louvre), Rouen, and Stockholm.

BIBLIOGRAPHY. P. Jamot, *Georges de la Tour,* Paris, 1942; F.-G. Pariset, *Georges de La Tour,* Paris, 1948; A. Blunt, "Georges de La Tour by F.-G. Pariset" (book review), *The Burlington Magazine,* XCII, 1950.

GEORGE V. GALLENKAMP

LA TOUR, MAURICE-QUENTIN DE. French portrait painter in pastel (b. St-Quentin, 1704; d. there, 1788). He went to Paris in 1723. The engraver N.-H. Tardieu sent him to work for J.-J. Spoëde and C. Dupouch, who taught painting at the Academy of St. Luke in Rome. La Tour went to Cambrai in 1724–25 to portray diplomats, and thence to London with the British plenipotentiary. Though

Maurice-Quentin de La Tour, *Maréchal de Saxe.* Musée Carnavalet, Paris.

he was largely self-taught, the counsel of J. Restout on his return to Paris constituted his first sound technical lessons. He profited by the vogue for pastel portraits and made pastels his medium for virile psychological portraiture. A Royal Academy associate in 1737, he exhibited at the Salon with consistent acclaim from 1737 to 1773, when he suffered a nervous breakdown. He was taken home to St-Quentin, where he was welcomed by the community. He had become an Academy member in 1746 (his diploma piece was *Portrait of Restout*; Paris, Louvre) and a coun-

Benjamin Henry Latrobe, *Cathedral of the Assumption*, Baltimore, Md.

cillor in 1751. In 1750 he was named "Painter to the King" by Louis XV.

In St-Quentin he founded a free school of drawing (1779). He established prizes for draftsmanship at the Academy of Science in Amiens (1783) and at the Academy of Painting in Paris (1776).

The Musée Lecuyer at St-Quentin contains a galaxy of his portraits of 18th-century personalities, their eyes sparkling with mischievous charm and intelligence. He is considered by some critics to have been the finest portrait draftsman between the Clouets and Degas. La Tour's masterpieces are frequently his "preparatory sketches," which are unspoiled by overworking and by experimentation with fixatives. With the exception of his life-size portraits *Duval de l'Epinoy* (1745; Lisbon, Gulbenkian Collection), *Président de Rieux* (1741; Paris, Wildenstein Collection), and *Mme de Pompadour* (1756; Louvre), décor is sacrificed for physiognomical focus. Other works are in French and American collections. Two in the Fogg Art Museum, Cambridge, Mass., are outstanding.

BIBLIOGRAPHY. P. A. Besnard, *La Tour: La Vie et l'oeuvre de l'artiste*... (catalog), by G. Wildenstein, Paris, 1928; E. L. and J. A. de Goncourt, *French XVIII Century Painters*, New York, 1948.

GEORGE V. GALLENKAMP

LA TRINITE, CAEN, *see* ABBAYE-AUX-DAMES, CAEN.

LATROBE, BENJAMIN HENRY. American architect and engineer (b. Fulneck, Eng., 1764; d. New Orleans, 1820). A student of Cockerell and Smeaton, Latrobe designed buildings in England, including Hammond Lodge, Sussex. He left for Norfolk, Va., in 1795. Latrobe was a romantic classicist, and much of his work retains respect for smooth wall surfaces and intelligent application of detail as well as for engineering considerations. His Bank of Pennsylvania in Philadelphia (1799–1801; destroyed), based on the Erechtheum in Athens, initiated the use of Greek-inspired detail in the United States. In Sedgeley (the Crammond home) in Philadelphia (1799; destroyed) and in the alternative design for the Baltimore Cathedral of the Assumption (1805), Gothic motifs were pioneered (although Latrobe's other plan, in neoclassic style, was the one chosen for the Cathedral). As surveyor of public buildings (1803–12 and 1815–17) he virtually completed the Senate and House chambers of the U.S. Capitol in Washington. Latrobe profoundly influenced the course of architecture in the United States, transforming it into a profession and setting high standards of excellence. *See* CAPITOL, THE, WASHINGTON, D.C.

BIBLIOGRAPHY. T. F. Hamlin, *Benjamin Henry Latrobe*, New York, 1955.

MATTHEW E. BAIGELL

LATTANZIO DA RIMINI. Venetian painter (fl. 1492–1505). He was a leading associate of Giovanni Bellini in the Ducal Palace. Lattanzio's chief surviving work, the *St. Martin Altarpiece* (1500; Brembana Cathedral, near Bergamo), reflects Cima in landscape and sharp light, though it is weak in the figures.

BIBLIOGRAPHY. G. Fiocco, "Piccoli Maestri," *Bollettino d'arte*, XVI, February, 1923.

LATTICE ORNAMENT. Type of architectural ornament consisting of an openwork screen. The openwork is formed by one set of parallel strips crossing another. The pattern

Francesco Laurana, portrait bust of Baptista Sforza, wife of Federigo da Montefeltro. National Museum, Florence.

produced by the crossings may be square, rectangular, or diamond-shaped.

LAUGHING CAVALIER, THE. Oil painting by Hals, in the Wallace Collection, London. *See* HALS, FRANS FRANSZ.

LAUNITZ, ROBERT EBERHARD SCHMIDT VON DER. American sculptor (b. Latvia, 1806; d. New York City, 1870). He studied under Thorwaldsen. Launitz came to the United States in 1828 and became a partner in Frazee's marble-cutting firm. He carved both decorative furnishings and portraits. Thomas Crawford and Truman Bartlett were his pupils.

BIBLIOGRAPHY. C. E. Clement and L. Hutton, *Artists of the Nineteenth Century and Their Works*, 5th ed., Boston, 1884.

LAURANA, FRANCESCO. Italian sculptor, medalist, and architect (b. Laurana, near Zadar, Dalmatia, ca. 1425; d. Avignon, 1502). Little is known about his early life. It is not known whether he was related to Luciano Laurana, who is believed to have been born in the same town in the same decade. This uncertainty has led to a debate over whether Francesco or Luciano is the Laurana mentioned in documents as a student of Brunelleschi in Florence. The first certain reference to Francesco Laurana is in 1458, when he is listed in the building records of the Castel Nuovo in Naples; it is believed that he worked on the triumphal gate of the Castel Nuovo, although this gate has also been attributed to Luciano.

Dated medals by Francesco show that he was active at the court of René I of Anjou from 1461 to 1466. For several years thereafter he was active in Sicily. In 1471 he made a marble Madonna for S. Maria della Neve in Palermo, which he signed "Franciscus Laurana me fecit." In 1474 Laurana was in Naples working on the decoration for the Chapel of St. Barbara in the Castel Nuovo. In 1477 he again worked for René of Anjou in Avignon and Marseilles. He finished the decoration for the Chapel of St-Lazare in the Cathedral of Marseilles in 1481 and in the same year completed a sculptured altar with the *Carrying of the Cross* commissioned by René of Anjou for the Church of the Colettines in Avignon (now in St-Didier). From 1483 until his death he worked chiefly in Marseilles.

Laurana was one of the most important Italian sculptors of the early Renaissance, especially since he was a chief agent for the spread of the Renaissance style to France. Before his first trip to France he worked with Agostino di Duccio and was strongly influenced by that Florentine sculptor. Laurana is believed to have worked with Agostino on the decoration of the Tempio Malatestiano in Rimini. While in Sicily he formed his personal style, a combination of French late Gothic with strong influences from Agostino. This style is best observed in the reliefs of the Church Fathers (ca. 1468) in the Mastrantonio Chapel of S. Francesco in Palermo and the statue of the Madonna (1474) in S. Sebastiano in Naples. The quality and originality of the work done during Laurana's second stay in France declined as a result of the employment of less competent French assistants.

Laurana is best known for his many marble portrait busts of women, which have been praised, particularly in past generations, for the delicacy with which femininity is captured. There are numerous Laurana busts in museums in Europe and the United States, many of which should be seen as shop works. The best and most famous example is the bust of Beatrice of Aragon in the Museum of Art History, Vienna, a variation of which is in the Metropolitan Museum of Art, New York. Other fine examples are found in the National Museum, Florence, the Louvre, Paris, and the former State Museums, Berlin.

BIBLIOGRAPHY. F. Burger, *Francesco Laurana*, Strasbourg, 1907; W. Rolfs, *Franz Laurana*, Berlin, 1907; J. Pope-Hennessy, *Italian Renaissance Sculpture*, London, 1958.

DONALD L. EHRESMANN

LAURANA, LUCIANO (Dellaurana). Dalmatian architect active in Italy (d. Pesaro, 1479). The architecture of this ambiguous figure is still a matter of considerable controversy. A group of castles executed in southern France for René of Anjou and the monumental gate of the Castel Nuovo in Naples have traditionally been attributed to him, but there is no documentary basis. The documents do indicate work of an unspecified nature in Mantua and Pesaro in 1465, perhaps having to do with fortifications.

A letter-patent of Federigo da Montefeltro dated June 10, 1468, names "Maestro Lutiano" as director and supervisor of the Ducal Palace in Urbino. By 1472 he was discharged from this post. The precise nature of his work in Urbino is not revealed by the documents, but it is probable that he was responsible for the opening phases of the project, which involved enlarging the preexisting parts of the palace and preparing the foundations and terrain for the construction of the new palace. This may imply a

Laurencin, *The Rehearsal*. National Museum of Modern Art, Paris.

certain amount of architectural planning. By 1476 he is documented in Pesaro at work on the Rocca Costanza. He was employed on fortifications and bridges for that city until his death.

See also LAURANA, FRANCESCO.

BIBLIOGRAPHY. A. Venturi, *Storia dell'arte italiana*, vol. 8, pt. 1, Milan, 1923; R. Papini, *Francesco di Giorgio, architetto*, vol. 1, Florence, 1946.   JOHN R. SPENCER

LAURENCIN, MARIE. French painter (b. Paris, 1885; d. there, 1956). Marie Laurencin attended the Lycée Lamartine until she was twenty. She received discouraging advice from her drawing teacher but attended drawing classes at a municipal night school. Later she met Clovis Sagot, a minor art dealer, who spoke to Picasso and Apollinaire about her; soon afterward Gertrude Stein bought one of her paintings. Although Laurencin took an active part in the feverish discussions that gave rise to cubism, she remained strangely uninfluenced by this movement. Her group portraits of Apollinaire and his friends have much simplicity, the bodies and faces are greatly stylized, and the color is applied in a flat, decorative manner.

Laurencin wrote poetry in her youth, and her paintings of graceful, large-eyed, slender-limbed girls have not only a poetic but above all a feminine appeal. She exhibited for the first time at the 22d Salon des Indépendants in 1906. Her art never changed its character. Throughout her career she sought the same dream of gentleness and serenity in the soft or sometimes pathetic faces of women and girls, as in *Portrait* (1913; Paris, Jean Paulham Collection) and *La Femme au chien* (1938; Dinard, private collection). She illustrated Poe's *The Raven* for Apollinaire, using red and black lines and dots; this was perhaps her sole attempt at nonfigurative work.

She was equally versatile in lithography and water color (for example, in illustrating André Gide's *La Tentative amoureuse* and *Alice au pays des merveilles*). In 1924 she

Henri Laurens, *The Siren*, 1944. National Museum of Modern Art, Paris.

designed the décor for Poulenc's *Les Biches* for the Ballets Russes and, in 1928, that for Musset's *A Quoi rêvent les jeunes filles* for the Comédie Française.

BIBLIOGRAPHY. B. Dorival, *Twentieth-Century French Painters*, 2 vols., New York, 1958; R. Shattuck, *The Banquet Years*, New York, 1958; H. Read, *A Concise History of Modern Painting*, London, 1959; B. Dorival, *The School of Paris in the Musée d'Art Moderne*, London, 1960.
ARNOLD ROSIN

LAURENS, HENRI. French sculptor, painter, and illustrator (b. Paris, 1885; d. there, 1954). Before meeting Braque and joining the cubists in 1911, he worked as a decorator in terra cotta, under the influence of Rodin. His first exhibit was in 1913. His polychromed sheet-iron construction of 1914 is one of the first abstract sculptures. By 1915 his art had evolved into shallow, often painted reliefs and constructions of cubist subject and form. Laurens was a member of the Section d'Or. It was not until the late 1920s that his style acquired the curvacious, sensuous notations by which he interpreted the feminine form. The National Museum of Modern Art, Paris, has his *Siren* (1944) and *The Great Musician* (1938); the Museum of Modern Art, New York, his *Head* (1918). Laurens's most important work was done as a cubist sculptor, with his demonstration that the structure and expressiveness of sculpture need not depend upon a description of the human model.

BIBLIOGRAPHY. H. Laurens, *Laurens*, by C. Goldscheider, Amsterdam, 1957.

LAURENT, ROBERT. American sculptor (1890–1970). He was born in Concarneau, France, worked as an apprentice art dealer in Paris in 1905, and was influenced by Gauguin and Picasso. In 1907 he took drawing lessons in Rome from Maurice Sterne. He became a carver of picture frames, and in 1910, when he came to New York City, he worked for leading American painters. His first sculptures, about 1913, were in a relief style, influenced by Lehmbruck.

Laurent began carving in the round in 1913 and joined with avant-garde artists in New York. His first exhibit was at the Daniel Gallery in 1916. He rose to prominence with his animal and figure sculptures of the 1920s and 1930s and with commissions such as the *Goose Girl* (1932) for Radio City Music Hall, New York. In later years he reverted to a classical mode. The Chicago Art Institute owns *Kneeling Woman* (1938), and the Brooklyn Museum has *Wave* (1925). His *Spanning the Continent* (1935) was done for Philadelphia's Fairmount Park. Before World War II Laurent was one of the pioneer American sculptors working in direct carving.

BIBLIOGRAPHY. Indiana University, *Laurent, Fifty Years of Sculpture*, text by H. R. Hope, Bloomington, 1961.
ALBERT ELSEN

LAURI, FILIPPO. Italian historical and mythological painter (b. Rome, 1623; d. there, 1694). He was a pupil of his brother Francesco and of Angelo Caroselli, whom he surpassed in talent. Lauri supplied the figures for paintings by Claude Lorraine, utilizing the style of Albani. His lively bacchanals and "fables," excellently drawn, were in great demand.

LAURIE, ROBERT. English engraver (b. London, 1740; d. there, 1804). He made engravings and mezzotints, was a print seller, and was credited with the invention of a device to aid in printing colors in mezzotint. He made portraits and various subjects after Rubens, Rembrandt, and Van Dyck, among others.

BIBLIOGRAPHY. A. M. Hind, *A Short History of Engraving and Etching*, 2d rev. ed., London, 1911.

LAURIN VON KLATTAU. Bohemian manuscript illuminator (fl. early 15th cent.). The leading illuminator of his time in Prague, he was a native of Klattau (Klatovy), in western Bohemia. He was responsible for a Missal for the Archbishop of Hasenburg (1403–11; Vienna, National Library) with richly decorated initials and border designs.

LAUSANNE: CANTONAL MUSEUM OF FINE ARTS. Swiss collection located in the canton of Vaud. It has occupied the Palais de Rumine since 1904. The museum owns a large collection of paintings, sculptures, drawings, and prints by Vaudois artists and a smaller group by other Swiss artists, including Anker and Hodler, from the 18th to the 20th century. Among the Dutch and French paintings of the 17th and 18th centuries are works by Mignon, Brouwer, Mignard, Largillière, and Rigaud. The 19th- and 20th-century collection has paintings by Corot, Courbet, Cézanne, Rousseau, Renoir, Degas, Bonnard, Vuillard, Matisse, Marquet, Vlaminck, and Utrillo and sculptures by Rodin, Bourdelle, Maillol, Despiau, and Milles. There is also a small collection of ancient Egyptian sculpture and Oriental art.

LAUSANNE: CATHEDRAL. Swiss cathedral (1175–1275) saved and restored by Viollet-le-Duc (1873–79). Remains of earlier 8th-, 9th-, and 11th-century structures have been discovered in excavations. The cruciform plan and three-story elevation show the influences of Langres Cathedral (choir), Laon Cathedral, and Notre-Dame in Dijon. The south portal is carved with excellent figures of apostles and prophets (ca. 1240). The richly decorated west portal was

Sir John Lavery, *The Tennis Party*. Art Gallery, Aberdeen. A work exhibited at the Royal Academy of Arts in 1886.

attached to the narthex between 1516 and 1535. The stalls (1250–70) and the polychromy of the south transept provide excellent examples of cathedral ornamentation and furnishings. In the south transept is the rose window mentioned by Villard de Honnecourt. Its glass (ca. 1230) depicts allegorical and astronomical subjects and shows influences from the Picardy region.

LAUTENSACK, HANNS SEBALD. German etcher, painter, and woodcut and medal designer (1524–after 1560). A native of Nürnberg, Lautensack produced many landscape etchings that follow the tradition of the Danube school. His view of Nürnberg, however, which was made with six plates, is straightforward reportage on the look of the city. His many etched portraits often have small landscapes in the background. Twice he represented himself in the foreground of Nürnberg, sketching and greeting friends. The subject of a so-called self-portrait has recently been identified as Ulrich Schwaiger(?). A print after a Giulio Romano battle subject is an anomaly in Lautensack's work. In 1560 he was living in Vienna, where he made two etchings and one woodcut for the commemoration of a festival, published under the title *Thurnier Buch*.

BIBLIOGRAPHY. A. Schmitt, *Hanns Lautensack*, Nürnberg, 1957.

LAUTREC, HENRI DE TOULOUSE, *see* TOULOUSE-LAUTREC, HENRI DE.

LAVABO. Large washbasin or trough frequently located in monastic cloisters. The term also denotes a room in a monastery containing a lavabo.

LAVARDIN: SAINT-GENEST. French basilica begun about 1040. A three-aisled structure of five bays, it has massive square nave pillars and is preceded by a low, sturdily built narthex. The central apse dates from 1080. In addition to its powerful Romanesque architecture, St-Genest boasts some impressive sculpture, in particular, an unusual pair of mid-11th-century capitals with crude representations of animals, a seated Virgin and Child, and

a St. Benedict(?). Remarkable early frescoes are extant, dating from the second half of the 12th century into the 15th. The *Baptism of Christ* (ca. 1150–75) is especially notable.

BIBLIOGRAPHY. R. Gamard, "Lavardin," in *Touraine Romane*, text by O. Aymard et al. [La-Pierre-qui-Vire (Yonne)], 1957.

LA VENTA CULTURE, *see* OLMEC ART.

LAVER, AUGUSTUS, *see* FULLER AND LAVER.

LAVERY, SIR JOHN. British portrait, genre, and landscape painter (1856–1941). Born in Belfast, he settled in Glasgow at seventeen and began a three-year apprenticeship to a painter-photographer. He worked mostly on touching up portrait photographs. In his spare time he attended classes at the Glasgow School of Art. Lavery began as an independent artist in 1879 after exhibiting an oil at the Glasgow Institute. Soon after, he went to London and attended Heatherley's School of Art. During this period he was particularly interested in painters such as Alfred Stevens and Lord Leighton, and for a time after 1881 studied at the Académie Julian in Paris under T. Robert-Fleury and Bouguereau, whose sentimental allegorical paintings Lavery had admired in England. He exhibited at the Paris Salon from 1883, and in the same year began to work at Grès-sur-Loing, an artists' colony south of the forest of Fontainebleau. There he painted plein-air landscapes in the manner of Bastien-Lepage and, to some extent, Manet. *The Tennis Party* (Aberdeen Art Gallery), which dates from this period, was exhibited at the Royal Academy of Arts in 1886.

On his return to Britain he began his long and successful career as a portrait painter. He received a commission from the Glasgow Corporation in 1888 to record Queen Victoria opening the Glasgow Exhibition of that year, and this very large painting, which took him two years to complete, and 250 related sketches and drawings were presented to the city in 1890.

Before settling permanently in London, Lavery was associated for a time with the Glasgow school, in particular with James Guthrie and Alexander Roche. He began also to live and work in Tangier, passing through Spain en route, where he was able to study Spanish painting. His portrait of R. B. Cunninghame Graham (Glasgow Art Gallery), which dates from this period, shows a strong indebtedness to Velázquez. Lavery became best known for his male portraits and, in later life, was given a large number of commissions by the Irish government.

While in London he met and became a close friend of Whistler, whose painting he much admired. In 1897 Whistler became president and Lavery vice-president of the new International Society of Sculptors, Painters and Gravers, formed as a rival of the Royal Academy, but with an emphasis on mounting exhibitions abroad.

Lavery was knighted in 1918, was made an associate of the Royal Academy in 1911, and a full academician in 1921. He is well represented in the galleries of Dublin, Belfast, and Glasgow. His autobiography, *The Life of a Painter*, was written in his eighty-fourth year.

BIBLIOGRAPHY. W. S. Sparrow, *John Lavery and his Work...*, London, 1911.

JOHN K. D. COOPER

LAVRA MONASTERY CHURCH. Church of one of the monasteries on Mt. Athos, Greece. The Lavra, or Grand Lavra, Monastery was founded at the end of the 10th century by a nobleman of Trebizond. Its church, or catholicon, completed in 1004, is a Byzantine cross-domed basilica whose nave and aisles are expressed by arcades on the façade. It contains frescoes by the Cretan painter Theophanos dated 1535.

BIBLIOGRAPHY. J. A. Hamilton, *Byzantine Architecture and Decoration*, 2d ed., London, 1956.

LAVREINCE, NICOLAS (Nils Lafrensen). Swedish painter (b. Stockholm, 1737; d. there, 1807). His father, a portrait painter, taught him miniature painting in gouache. Receiving additional training in Paris, he came to love Parisian life, and it was there—despite frequent sojourns in Stockholm—that he produced most of the work for which he became famous. In 1773 he was made a member of the Swedish Royal Academy and Painter to the King. He then settled in Paris until the Revolution, when he returned to Stockholm where he spent the rest of his life. His frivolous subjects from French upper-class life, executed with much attention to detail, were favored for engraving by Janinet, De Launay, Dequevauvillier, and others. Many of Lavreince's drawings have been overlooked owing to variations in the spelling of his signature.

BIBLIOGRAPHY. E. Bocher, *Les Gravures françaises du XVIIIe siècle*, vol. 1, Paris, 1875.

LAWRENCE, JACOB. American painter (1917–   ). He was born in Atlantic City, N.J., and now lives in Brooklyn. In the early 1930s he took free art lessons at a Harlem public library and then at a Works Project Administration school in New York, later receiving a scholarship for the American Artists School. He painted for eighteen months under the Federal Art Project. In 1940 he received the first of three grants from the Rosenwald Fund. He painted his *...and the Migrants Kept Coming* series then,

Nicolas Lavreince, *The Concert*. Veil-Ticard Collection. A scene from French upper-class life.

a set of sixty pictures, half purchased by the Museum of Modern Art, New York City, and half by the Phillips Collection, Washington, D.C.

Lawrence then did a set of twenty-six gouaches, the *Life in Harlem* series, the *Coast Guard* series, based on his experiences as a steward's mate and officer in the Coast Guard, and the *War* series. He showed his understanding of the mentally ill in the 1950 series on life in Hillside Hospital, *Sanitarium*. In 1955 he began a projected series of sixty tempera paintings entitled *Struggle: From the History of the American People*. In the late 1950s and early 1960s he depicted the struggle for desegregation in the South, and in 1964 he traveled to Nigeria, where he painted the local scene. In 1960–61 he was given a touring retrospective exhibition, which opened at the Whitney Museum of American Art in New York.

Lawrence reduces figures to flat pattern in a manner recalling Shahn, but without the latter's sophistication. He combines bright, often raw color with neutrals and sharp browns and black, giving his social themes a symbolic sense and relieving them of the taint of sentimentality. Lawrence is one of the leading American Negro painters of our time; his art remains a strong statement of the social problems and aspirations of Negroes in the North and South.

BIBLIOGRAPHY. R. Pearson, *The Modern Renaissance in American Art*, New York, 1954; American Federation of Arts, *Jacob Lawrence*, introd. A. B. Saarinen, New York, 1960.

ROBERT REIFF

LAWRENCE, SIR THOMAS. English portrait painter (b. Bristol, 1769; d. London, 1830). He was a prodigy whose talent was first noticed in the pencil profiles he made at the Bear Inn, Devizes, where his father was the landlord.

He executed pastel portraits at Bath from 1782 to 1787, when he settled in London and exhibited at the Royal Academy of Arts. He first exhibited an oil painting in 1788. Although he received some instruction at the Royal Academy schools, he was to all intents and purposes self-taught.

Lawrence's early career was phenomenally successful. He was commissioned in 1789 to paint a portrait of Queen Charlotte (London, National Gallery), which he exhibited at the Royal Academy exhibition of 1790 with *Miss Farren* (New York, Metropolitan Museum), and after this he had large numbers of sitters. He succeeded Sir Joshua Reynolds as Painter-in-Ordinary to the King and Painter to the Dilettante Society in 1792, and was elected associate of the Royal Academy in 1791 and full academician in 1794. Almost all the work he produced before 1800 shows a promise that he never quite fulfilled. These early portraits combine the academic and traditional manner of Reynolds with a new romantic brilliance, and a very few, for example, *William Lock* (1790; Boston, Museum of Fine Arts), are among the masterpieces of European portraiture of the time.

Lawrence was an artist of great ambition and of more intellectual power than is generally credited to him. He aspired to the grand manner, but recognized (though never fully admitting it) that his most serious effort of the

Sir Thomas Lawrence, *Portrait of George IV, King of England*. Vatican Museums, Rome.

kind, *Satan Summoning His Legions* (1797; London, Royal Academy), was not a success. He employed assistants at an early stage and from 1800 made increasing use of them. The quality of his portraiture is particularly uneven in the period from 1800 to 1815. He was knighted in 1815.

In 1818 Lawrence was sent to Europe by the Prince Regent to paint a series of portraits of the allied heads of state and military leaders. These are now in the Waterloo Chamber, Windsor Castle, and include two of his finest works, *Pope Pius VII* and *The Archduke Charles of Austria*. They have a sophistication that his earlier romantic portraits lack, but do not have the same vitality. They are, however, painted with a remarkable fluency and richness of color, which resulted from prolonged experiment and study of the old masters. Many of his later portraits, for example, *Lady Peel* (New York, Frick Collection) and *Master Lambton* (Earl of Durham Collection), were widely popularized in engravings. He succeeded Benjamin West as President of the Royal Academy in 1820.

Lawrence was a highly skillful draftsman and made a large number of portrait drawings. He was a great student of old master drawings, and his own collection was unrivaled.

BIBLIOGRAPHY. D. E. Williams, *Life and Correspondence of Sir Thomas Lawrence*, London, 1831; Sir W. Armstrong, *Lawrence*, London, 1913; K. Garlick, *Sir Thomas Lawrence*, London, 1954.

KENNETH J. GARLICK

LAWRENCE, KANS.: UNIVERSITY OF KANSAS MUSEUM OF ART. Founded in 1917 on the basis of the Thayer Collection, the museum is now housed in the Richardson-style Romanesque Spooner Hall, designed by William van Brunt. The collection contains some small pieces from ancient Egypt, Greece, and Rome, as well as Byzantine icons and medieval statuary, including a *Madonna and Child* by Riemenschneider. Works of sculpture and decorative art complement the survey of European painting of the 15th to the 18th century, which emphasizes Italian primitive works from the Kress Collection and German baroque works.

Some of the modern European painters and sculptors represented are Canova, Rossetti, Monet, Manet, Maillol, and Epstein. In American painting and sculpture, works by Rembrandt Peale, Cole, West, Sully, Homer, Remington, Inness, Bierstadt, Sargent, Benton, Curry, and Lipton are prominent. There are also examples of Indian, Chinese, and Japanese sculpture, painting, and ceramics.

BIBLIOGRAPHY. University of Kansas, *Handbook: The Museum of Art*, Lawrence, Kans., 1962.

LAWRENCE OF ROME, ST. Martyr (d. 258). He was brought from Aragon to Rome by Pope Sixtus II, who ordained him one of his seven deacons. After Emperor Philip was murdered by Decius(?), his son entrusted treasure (including Church possessions) to Sixtus, who was then martyred. Lawrence distributed these holdings among the poor. The emperor Valerian had him tortured and roasted on a grill. His attributes are a grill, purse, chalice with gold pieces, deacon's dalmatic, and processional cross. His feast is August 10. *See also* SAINTS IN ART.

LAWSON, CECIL GORDON. English painter and engraver (b. Wellington, Shropshire, 1851; d. London, 1882).

Some of his landscapes suggest impending disaster, others emanate tranquillity. *The Minister's Garden* (ca. 1878; Manchester, Whitworth Art Gallery) falls in the latter category. In the foreground are flowers, a rude wooden fence, and beehives; in the background is a great expanse of rolling country. Lawson was equally adept at depicting moorland, marsh, meadow, and woodland. He was especially skillful in his handling of lush greens and rich harmonies of blues. For the most part he was a pure landscape painter who very rarely introduced incident or explanatory accessory. Some of his work suggests his observation of Rubens.

BIBLIOGRAPHY. J. L. Caw, *Scottish Painting, Past and Present, 1620–1908*, Edinburgh, 1908.

LAWSON, ERNEST. American painter (b. San Francisco, 1873; d. New York City, 1939). He studied in Kansas City, New York, and Paris. Influenced by the French and American impressionists, Lawson created his own atmospheric paintings, using cool winter scenes along the Harlem and Hudson rivers as his preferred themes. He was a member of The Eight and, later, of the National Academy.

BIBLIOGRAPHY. E. Neuhaus, *History and Ideals of American Art*, Palo Alto, Calif., 1931; O. W. Larkin, *Art and Life in America*, rev. ed., New York, 1960.

LAYENS, MATHIEU DE. Flemish architect (d. 1483). Layens was municipal architect of Louvain, where he built the City Hall (1447–63), one of the richest examples, sculpturally and decoratively, of the Flamboyant Gothic style, and the Porte de Malines (1445/46; dismantled in 1807). He directed the work at the Church of St-Pierre and reconstructed its tower after it had burned (1458–64). *See* Louvain: Hotel de Ville; Louvain: Saint-Pierre.

LAY FIGURE. Life-size mechanical figure whose intricate joints can be made to assume and hold a given pose for an artist. The lay figure is more realistic than a mannequin and is sometimes used as a support for drapery. It appears not to have been in general use before the 19th century.

LAY-IN. In painting, the first step after the drawing; that is, the execution of the main masses of light and dark. Sometimes the laying-in is done in a neutral monochrome so as not to interfere with the subsequent application of color. It is also called underpainting. The Italian word for lay-in is *macchia*.

LAZARUS. Brother of Martha and Mary of Bethany (who is often confused with Mary Magdalen) and an intimate friend of Jesus, who raised him from the dead (John 11:1–44). The scene of the resurrection of Lazarus is often depicted in art (for example, 2d-cent. fresco, Rome, Calixtus Catacomb; 12th-cent. mosaic, Palermo, Cappella Palatina). Because of a confusion of legends, he is often identified with a later Lazarus, who was supposedly set adrift in the Mediterranean by the Jews and was carried to Marseilles, where he became archbishop. Thus he is sometimes portrayed with Martha and Mary Magdalen in a boat without sails or rudder, as in the left panel of the *Magdalen Altar* (1431; Tiefenbronn, Pfarrkirche), which was executed by Lukas Moser.

LAZO, AGUSTIN. Mexican painter (1900–   ). Born in Mexico City, he trained at the Mexican Academy, first under the "open-air" impressionist Ramos Martínez and then under Diego Rivera (1917). Lazo then studied in Europe. In the late 1920s he joined "The Contemporaries," a group of intellectuals that was opposed to "Mexicanism" and murals. Its members were dedicated to internationalism and easel painting.

Categorically surrealist, Lazo's art is compounded of interior visions linked by tenuous but palpable threads to external reality. He depicts his imaginative themes with coarse vibrant strokes that charge his delicate moods with an unexpected expressiveness. Lazo is also a playwright and stage designer.

BIBLIOGRAPHY. V. Stewart, *45 Contemporary Mexican Artists*, Stanford, Calif., 1951.

LAZZARINI, GREGORIO. Italian painter (1665–1730). Born in Venice, he studied in his youth with G. Forabosco. Lazzarini is best known as the head of an important school in Venice, one of whose greatest pupils was Tiepolo. Lazzarini's style, evident in numerous large compositions, replaced the prevalent mannerist trend in Venetian painting with the formal qualities of solidity and expressiveness of the baroque schools of Bologna and Florence. Although he was unusually capable of massing large numbers of active figures into coherent compositions intensified by rich colors, his work frequently displays the conventional and dispassionate approach of the academician.

BIBLIOGRAPHY. V. da Canal, *La vita di Gregorio Lazzarini*, Venice, 1809; C. Donzelli, *I pittori veneti del Settecento*, Florence, 1957.

LEACH, BERNARD. British potter, engraver, and author (1887–   ). Born in Hong Kong, he was educated in England at the Slade School of Art (1903) and the London School of Art (1908). Leach then went to Japan (1909), where he studied pottery making with a sixth-generation Kenzan. He returned to England (1920) with Shoji Hamada and founded the Leach Pottery at St. Ives, Cornwall. His work is a blend of Oriental and Occidental influences.

BIBLIOGRAPHY. Great Britain, Arts Council, *Bernard Leach*, London, 1961.

LEADS. Marks, frequently highly decorative, used in choral manuscripts to indicate that part of the canon in which the two halves of the choir alternate. Leads are also called *presa*.

LEAF AND DART. Pattern of conventionalized pointed leaves usually applied to the *cyma reversa*. An example is found in the shaft of the archaic Temple of Diana in Ephesus. The pattern is also called "heart and dart" and "leaf and tongue." *See* Cyma.

LEAL, FERNANDO. Mexican painter (1900–   ). Leal was born in Mexico City and is a product of the "open-air" schools. As critic, writer, and pioneer of printmaking, he helped initiate the mural renaissance at the National Preparatory School (1922). Folk and religious themes characterize his murals.

BIBLIOGRAPHY. A. Reed, *The Mexican Muralists*, New York, 1960.

LEANING TOWER, THE, *see* Bologna; Pisa.

LEATHER. Skin of an animal prepared through tanning or a similar process for use. From primeval times leather of all sorts has been used in the arts. Leatherwork reached its apex in French bookbinding of the 16th and 17th centuries. Leather is decorated by blind tooling, by the impression of a design with gold leaf, and by painting.

LEBAS, JEAN. French architect (fl. ca. 1472–92). Jean Lebas and his son constructed the tower and the turret of the Church of St-Michel at Bordeaux. The spire, which collapsed in 1768, was rebuilt in the 19th century.

LEBAS, LOUIS HIPPOLYTE. French architect (1782–1867). He worked in Paris. A pupil of Vaudoyer and Percier, Lebas designed Notre-Dame-de-Lorette following an Early Christian model that he interpreted in classical terms; it is considered a major monument of romantic classicism.

BIBLIOGRAPHY. L. Vaudoyer, *Notice historique sur la vie et les ouvrages de M. Le Bas*, Paris, 1869.

LEBDA, *see* LEPTIS MAGNA.

LEBES. Currency in the form of cups made of gold or another valuable metal that were used in Crete in the Early Minoan period. According to inscriptions found at Cnossus, lebes were made in denominations of 5, 10, 50, and 100. Lebes are examples of a transitional form of currency, standing between useful objects employed in barter and standardized currency.

LE BLON, JAKOB CHRISTOF. German painter and engraver (b. Frankfurt am Main, 1667; d. Paris, 1741). Experimenting in Amsterdam and London with color printing, he developed a three-color process by superimposing color plates (blue, red, and yellow, and sometimes a fourth tint) on the same composition. He described the process in *Coloritto; or, the Harmony of Colouring in Painting...*, published in 1730.

BIBLIOGRAPHY. F. W. H. Hollstein, *Dutch and Flemish Etchings, Engravings, and Woodcuts*, vol. 2, Amsterdam, n.d.

LE BRETON, GILLES. French master mason (16th cent.). He was responsible for major parts of the first building campaign of Francis I at Fontainebleau, for which he signed a contract in 1528. From the surviving Porte Dorée we can judge Le Breton's application of Italian Renaissance forms to the traditional French fortified castle gate, a combination of the imported with the indigenous that is definitive for French architecture of the 16th century.

BIBLIOGRAPHY. A. Blunt, *Art and Architecture in France, 1500–1700*, Baltimore, 1954.

LE BROCQUY, LOUIS. English painter (1916–   ). Born in Dublin, he is self-taught and works in a manner influenced by the expressionists and the younger painters of the school of Paris. He has exhibited in London since 1945 and participated in exhibitions at the Tate Gallery, the Arts Council, the Venice Biennale (1956), and the Arts Club of Chicago. He is also well known as a designer of textiles, tapestry, and packaging.

LE BRUN, CHARLES. French administrator of painting and the decorative arts; painter of religious, mythological, historical, and allegorical scenes, and portraits; draftsman and decorator (b. Paris, 1619; d. Montmorency, 1690). In the arts his supremacy paralleled the international prestige of France during the reign of Louis XIV and can be equated to the political success of Louis's First Minister, J. B. Colbert, who, as Surintendant des Bâtiments, was Le Brun's immediate superior. If Le Brun was not an imaginative artist, he did make French art the convincing vehicle of state propaganda.

He came from a family of artists, and was the son of a sculptor. He was apprenticed about the age of thirteen to F. Périer, decorator of Paris town houses, whose style reflected the Roman baroque tradition of the Carraccis and Giovanni Lanfranco. Chancellor Séguier became Le Brun's protector and placed him with Simon Vouet, the best-thought-of teacher of the time. Through Cardinal Richelieu, Le Brun became "Painter to the King" (Louis XIII) before he was nineteen. In 1642 he went to Rome with Poussin. He remained there until 1646, partially as Poussin's pupil, yet deriving a strong influence from the Roman baroque decorator Pietro da Cortona and even from the *tenebrosi* (*Death of Cato*, 1646; Paris, Louvre). Le Brun shrewdly discerned the future course of French painting as favoring the rational classicism of Poussin, and in 1644 he exhibited anonymously his enormously successful *Horatius Cocles Defending Rome* (London, Dulwich College Picture Gallery), a deliberate attempt to rival Poussin. On his return to Paris, he at once eclipsed the aged Vouet, having won the favor of Mazarin and of Anne of Austria, for whom he painted the *Crucifixion with Angels* (Louvre).

In 1648 he promulgated the organization of the Royal Academy of Painting and Sculpture, which became the official teaching organ of artists and the unifier of artistic doctrine. Though Le Brun was only one of the twelve original founders, the Academy's table of organization was geared to his ascendant authority and ultimately gave him dictatorship of all the arts, except architecture, in France. *See* ROYAL ACADEMY OF PAINTING AND SCULPTURE, FRANCE.

In 1649 Le Brun decorated the Hôtel de Lambert. In 1655 he was named Rector of the Academy and in 1658 Chancellor.

The most important year in his career was 1661. It began when Nicolas Fouquet, minister of finance, made him director of artworks at his Château of Vaux-le-Vicomte. The imposing grandeur of his works provoked the envy of the young king Louis XIV. Le Brun painted, in the king's presence, *Alexander and the Family of Darius* (Louvre), which later became a model for academic students. He decorated Colbert's Château of Sceaux, designed royal pageants, and decorated the Galerie d'Apollon in the Louvre. In 1662 he became First Painter to the King and was ennobled. In 1663 he became Chancellor for Life of the Academy, Keeper of the Royal Collections, and director of the royal Gobelins tapestry and furniture works (confirmed in 1667). In 1666 he organized the French Academy in Rome. In 1675 he was director of the Academy of St. Luke in Rome; in 1679 he became Rector for Life of the Paris Academy. *See* VAUX-LE-VICOMTE, CHATEAU OF.

From 1679 to 1684 Le Brun, while art director at Ver-

Charles Le Brun, *Chancellor Séguier*, 1661. Louvre, Paris. An equestrian portrait in the French classical style.

sailles, executed the paintings and decorative schemes of the Ambassadors' Staircase, the Salons of War and of Peace, and the Hall of Mirrors, composed of thirty compositions symbolizing glorious events in the King's career and inspired directly by Cortona's planetary chambers in the Pitti Palace, Florence. The gardens of Versailles, by André Le Nôtre, follow Le Brun's plan for the gardens at Vaux. Antoine Coysevox and numerous other sculptors followed his designs down to the last piece of garden sculpture. From 1661 until Colbert's death in 1683, when Le Brun assumed directorship of the Academy, no item of decoration for royal dwellings was created that had not been conceived by him and executed at his direction by an army of artisans at the Gobelins works; no official painting emerged without his sanction. Though the *style Louis XIV* was tediously uniform, the technical level of performance was high and the products were classically grandiose. *See* VERSAILLES: PALACE.

After the death of the Marquis de Louvois, Colbert's successor, in 1691 Le Brun, though maintained as First Painter, was superseded in the Academy by Pierre Mi-

gnard. In his last years he painted religious works (*The Life of Christ* series, Louvre, and elsewhere) in the late-17th-century ecclesiastical French baroque style. He died while working on a *Last Supper*.

Though the standards he set were both eclectic and academic, his real artistic preference was naturalism. This is apparent in *Hercules and the Horses of Diomedes* (1640; Nottingham, City Museum and Art Gallery), executed before he went to Italy, and it persists in almost all his mature works, in spite of his academic pronouncements favoring the "Ancients" over the "Moderns," or Rubenists. He takes the severe classicistic edge off Poussin in favor of baroque dramatic pictorialism and naturalism. The subjects are more pathetic than heroic. This predilection is more apparent in his lectures on the parallel between human and animal expression (taken from Descartes' *Traité des passions*, 1649) and the modes for representing the emotions. Though he attempted to be didactic, reducing all expression, human and artistic, to the formulas required by his own academic program, he remains truly French through his need for spontaneous communication.

In the domain of portraiture this characteristic is brilliantly apparent. The *Portrait of Jabach and His Family* (1647; Berlin, former State Museums) recalls the powerful realism of Van der Helst, but is more imposing. *Chancellor Séguier* (1661; Louvre) exemplifies the French classical style for an equestrian portrait. Its stateliness is suitable to the era, and the physiognomical realism is traditionally French. Nevertheless, through his dedication to academic standards Le Brun forfeited his ideal of overt naturalism in portraiture.

It is because of the concept of art promulgated by Louis XIV, Colbert, and Le Brun that Paris replaced Rome as the artistic capital of Europe. Le Brun's principal pupils were F. Verdier, R.-A. Houasse, R. Lefebvre, J. Vivien, C. de Lafosse, and C. Audran III. The translators of his tapestry cartoons (such as *History of Alexander*, 1660–62; *History of the King*, 1663; and *The Royal Dwellings*, after 1680), A. F. van der Meulen and A. Genoëls, are outstanding. Works other than those listed are in Berlin, Budapest, Florence, and Vienna, and numerous provincial museums in France.

BIBLIOGRAPHY. H. Jouin, *Charles Le Brun et les arts sous Louis XIV . . .*, Paris, 1889; A. Fontaine, *Les Doctrines d'art en France . . .*, Paris, 1909; P. Marcel, *Charles Le Brun*, Paris, 1909; A. Fontaine, *Académiciens d'autrefois . . .*, Paris, 1914; Versailles, Musée National, *Charles Le Brun, 1619–1690* (exhibition catalog), Paris, 1963.
GEORGE V. GALLENKAMP

LEBRUN, ELIZABETH, *see* VIGEE-LEBRUN, MADAME LOUISE-ELISABETH.

LEBRUN, NAPOLEON. American architect (1821–1901). He was born in Philadelphia and was trained by Thomas U. Walter. Lebrun's work encompasses the mid-19th-century revival styles as well as modern skyscrapers. Among his best-known buildings are the Academy of Music in Philadelphia (1852–57), whose interior is neobaroque, and the Metropolitan Life Building in New York, completed by his sons in 1909.

LEBRUN, RICO. American painter (b. Naples, 1900; d. California, 1964). Rico (real name Federico) went to the United States in 1924. Lebrun's remarkable drawings and paintings derive their visual excitement from the style of the Italian baroque painters. His subjects, however, are modern: the horrors of war, the fascination of slaughterhouses, and rusting farm machinery are all treated with great emotional intensity. Lebrun's sense of tradition and his strong concern for the sufferings of man in the 20th century led him to do an elaborate series of Crucifixion studies (1947–50). These culminated in the large triptych *Crucifixion* (1951; Syracuse University), where the pathos of Grünewald is married to the construction of Picasso's *Guernica*. He also executed a series of paintings based on the concentration camps of World War II.

BIBLIOGRAPHY. P. Selz, *New Images of Man*, New York, 1959; F. Lebrun, *Drawings*, Berkeley, 1961.

LECCE: CATHEDRAL. Remarkable late baroque structure, utilizing medieval foundations, in the region of Apulia, Italy. The first Cathedral was rebuilt in 1114 by Bishop Formoso, aided by a Norman count, Geoffredo II. The new Cathedral, begun in 1659–63, was finished in 1670 under Bishop Pappacoda, with G. Zimbalo (Lo Zingarello) as architect; elaboration of the interior continued into the 18th century. The west façade (1660) and north façade (later) show the development of Leccese variations on the Roman baroque, with strong mannerist survivals and revivals in ornamental details. The tower (1661–87) is stylistically related to the west façade, with its emphasis on flat patterns, rather than to the north façade, with its plastic definition of forms.

BIBLIOGRAPHY. G. Paladini, *Guida storica ed artistica della città di Lecce*, Lecce, 1952; R. Wittkower, *Art and Architecture of Italy, 1600–1750*, Baltimore, 1958.

LECCE: SANTA CROCE. Large Renaissance-baroque church in the region of Apulia, Italy. Built essentially between 1532 and 1689, it was begun by G. Riccardi da Lecce (Beli Liccardi) for the Celestine fathers. Later designers included F. A. Zimbalo, G. Zimbalo (Lo Zingarello), and C. Penna. The façade has dates of 1582 and 1607; work continued to 1697. With the suppression of the Celestines in 1807, Sta Croce was abandoned until 1828. Restoration was ordered in 1828 and 1833 after the despoliation of the interior (1812–13), and the building was transferred to an archconfraternity. Declared a national monument in 1906, it was a parish church again by 1915. The adjacent Celestine convent is now the prefecture of Lecce. The church presents a rich combination of styles: the façade has a rose window, gargoyle balconies, and lavishly carved late baroque details; the interior altarpieces have twisted columns and stucco adornment.

BIBLIOGRAPHY G. Paladini, *Guida storica ed artistica della città di Lecce*, Lecce, 1952; R. Wittkower, *Art and Architecture of Italy, 1600–1750*, Baltimore, 1958.

LECK, BART VAN DER. Dutch painter, graphic artist, and designer (b. Utrecht, 1876; d. Blaricum, 1958). He studied at the Amsterdam Academy. Van der Leck's early paintings were generally realistic, but with symbolic tendencies. About 1910 he became interested in social subjects, for example, *Leaving the Factory* (Rotterdam, Boymans-Van Beuningen Museum), which he painted with a strong emphasis on two-dimensional composition. By 1916 his figures had been rigorously stylized to flat, geometric forms organized entirely on the surface of the picture, for example, *The Tempest* (1916; Otterlo, Kröller-Müller Museum). In 1917, when he was in contact with Mondrian, Van der Leck joined the de Stijl movement and began to work in a nonobjective style, as in *Composition* (1917; Kröller-Müller Museum). After 1919 he returned to his earlier geometric treatment of figures, still retaining, however, his belief in the social utility of art.

BIBLIOGRAPHY. H. L. C. Jaffé, *De Stijl: 1917–1931*, Amsterdam, 1956.

LE CLERC, JEAN. French religious painter and etcher (b. Nancy, 1587/88; d. there, 1633). His formative years were spent in Rome and Venice with Adam Elsheimer and Carlo Saraceni. Le Clerc took back to Nancy· (ca. 1621) a Caravaggesque treatment of light and shadow that affected the art of Jacques Callot and Georges de La Tour, though his anatomical realism and vivacity of movement recall the nude studies by the brothers Antonio and Piero del Pollaiuolo.

BIBLIOGRAPHY. F.-G. Pariset, *Georges de La Tour*, Paris, 1948.

LECOMTE, FELIX. French sculptor (b. Paris, 1737; d. there, 1817). A student of Falconet and Vasse, Lecomte developed into an academic and prosaic classicist. In addition to aristocratic portraits and mythological works, he created the tomb of Stanislas I Leszczyński of Poland in the Church of Bons-Secours in Nancy (1774).

LE CORBUSIER (Charles-Edouard Jeanneret-Gris). Swiss-French architect, planner, sculptor, painter, and critic (b. La Chaux-de-Fonds, Switzerland, 1887; d. Cap Martin, France, 1965). He was trained as an engraver in the La Chaux-de-Fonds Art School (1900), and later traveled in Greece and the Balkans (1906–08) and worked in the studio of Auguste Perret (1908–09), an early pioneer in ferroconcrete, the material that became standard for Le Corbusier. He then traveled in Germany (1910–11) and also worked there in the office of Peter Behrens.

In 1920 Le Corbusier founded (with the poet Paul Dermée and the painter Amédée Ozenfant) the avant-garde magazine *L'Esprit Nouveau*, which helped to formulate new attitudes toward city planning, architecture, and many other cultural areas. Some of his articles were incorporated into his most important literary work, *Vers une architecture* (1923), a scorching polemic that called for the burial of the past and the birth of a new architecture based upon the logic of the machine and the necessities of the present. In 1922 Le Corbusier opened a studio at 35 rue de Sèvres, Paris, with his cousin and collaborator, Pierre Jeanneret, where many younger-generation architects worked, among them José Luis Sert and

Affonso Reidy. He was one of the initiators of C.I.A.M. (1928) and a moving force from its founding. *See* C.I.A.M.; LE CORBUSIER AND JEANNERET.

Some of Le Corbusier's earlier works are unexecuted projects that were seminal for his later executed pieces. The Domino project (1914–15) was a prefabricated, modular unit of ferroconcrete, while the Citrohan projects (1919–22) established many of his major architectural elements: the open plan, the cubic volume suspended on piers, and the usable roof enclosure.

During the 1920s he executed a number of designs for dwellings: the Vaucresson House (1922–23, near Paris), the Ozenfant House (1922–23, Paris), the La Roche House (1923, Paris), the Cook House (1926, Paris), the Garches House (1927), and housing at Pessac (1925) and at the Weissenhof Exhibition (1927, Stuttgart). All except the La Roche House have been drastically remodeled or have deteriorated. Le Corbusier's classic formulation of this period was the Savoye House (1929–30). *See* SAVOYE HOUSE, POISSY-SUR-SEINE; WEISSENHOF EXHIBITION.

Also during this decade Le Corbusier crystallized his basic attitude toward the city in projects for the reconstruction of Paris (1922–25) and in schemes for a vertically oriented city, consisting of cruciform skyscrapers surrounded by blocks of lower structures, all precisely organized in an open terrain. His book *Urbanisme* was published in 1925, and many planning schemes followed. Le Corbusier's most notable and prescient achievement of the first decade of his active career was the unexecuted design for the Palace of the League of Nations (1927), a

Le Corbusier, Unité d'Habitation, 1947–52. Marseilles. Ferroconcrete construction on massive piers.

work in size and complexity greater than the Bauhaus and prophetic of the best to come in subsequent decades.

During the next decade several important works were executed: the Centrosoyus in Moscow (1929–35), still in good condition; the Salvation Army Building, Paris (1929–33, remodeled); and the Swiss Pavilion at University City, Paris (1930–32), a ferroconcrete box dramatically elevated on sculptured piers, foreshadowing the Ministry of Health and Education in Rio de Janeiro (1937–42; with Lúcio Costa, Oscar Niemeyer, and others) and the Unité d'Habitation in Marseilles (1947–52). The Marseilles project is a residential community housing 1,600 people in a single architectural unit, the apartments ranging from singles to large family complexes. The structure contains shopping, recreational, and nursery facilities in a richly plastic ferroconcrete beehive supported on massive piers. *See* NIEMEYER, OSCAR.

Notre-Dame-du-Haut (1950–55), a pilgrimage chapel at Ronchamp, shocked the architectural world with its expressive sculptural quality and its personal forms, a drastic departure from the architect's earlier classical vocabulary. The building is one of the most impressive objects built by modern man. *See* RONCHAMP.

As one of his last projects, Le Corbusier (with Maxwell Fry, Jane Drew, and Pierre Jeanneret) was involved in the design of Chandigarh, capital of the state of Punjab in India, the culmination of the sculptural, architectural, and planning efforts of this artistic giant. *See* CHANDIGARH.

BIBLIOGRAPHY. *Le Corbusier* [*et P. Jeanneret*]: *Oeuvre complète*, ed. W. Boesiger et al., 7 vols., Zurich, 1937–65; S. Papadaki, ed., *Le Corbusier: Architect, Painter, Writer*, New York, 1948; F. Choay, *Le Corbusier*, New York, 1960; Le Corbusier, *Creation is a Patient Search*, New York, 1967; *Le Corbusier, 1910–1965*, ed. W. Boesiger and H. Girsberger, New York, 1967; Le Corbusier, *The Radiant City*, New York, 1967.

THEODORE M. BROWN

LE CORBUSIER AND JEANNERET. French architectural partnership of Le Corbusier (1887–1965) and his cousin Pierre Jeanneret (1896–   ). The team worked out of a studio in Paris, 35 rue de Sèvres, from 1922 to 1945. During these years Jeanneret, a quiet man who stayed in the background, contributed to the work of his flamboyant and famous cousin, and credit for Le Corbusier's work of this period should technically be shared with Jeanneret. Since 1945 Jeanneret has worked independently, but to date no serious attempt has been made to determine his contribution or to evaluate his work. *See* LE CORBUSIER.

LECTERN. Reading desk constructed of wood or metal and used since medieval times as a support for liturgical books. Many lecterns are intricately carved and painted. They are usually shaped like eagles or pelicans, whose outstretched wings form the table.

LECTIONARY. Liturgical book containing excerpts from scripture to be read at Mass. These excerpts, called pericopes, begin with the characteristic "Incipit" and "Explicit." Frequently the lectionary is separated into the Epistles and Evangeliary (Gospels), the former being read at the south side of the sanctuary, the latter, at the north side.

LECTIONARY OF LUXEUIL. Merovingian illuminated manuscript, in the National Library, Paris.

LECURT, *see* CORTE, JOSSE DE.

LECYTHOS, *see* LEKYTHOS.

LEDA. Wife of Tyndareos of Sparta. Leda was visited by Zeus in the form of a swan. Subsequently, she became the mother of two sons, Castor and Polydeuces (Pollux), known also as the Dioscuri, and of two daughters, Clytemnestra and Helen. In different versions of this Greek myth, Leda's children were thought to have been fathered by Zeus or by her husband. Leda's seduction is often depicted in Renaissance Italian painting.

BIBLIOGRAPHY. M. Grant, *Myths of the Greeks and Romans*, Cleveland, 1962.

LEDERER, HUGO. German sculptor (b. Znaim, Austria, 1871; d. Berlin, 1931). He studied in Dresden, Breslau, and Berlin. His early portraits and figure groups combined naturalism with baroque composition. Later he worked in a monumental, formally simplified manner, as in the Bismarck Monument in Hamburg (1901–06).

BIBLIOGRAPHY. H. Krey, *Hugo Lederer...*, Berlin, 1931.

LEDESMA, GABRIEL FERNANDEZ, *see* FERNANDEZ LEDESMA, GABRIEL.

LEDOUX, CLAUDE-NICHOLAS. French architect (1736–1806). He worked in Paris. At first an accomplished engraver, he entered Jacques François Blondel's school to study architecture. Ledoux's best-known works are the salt factory at Arc-et-Senans (1775–79) and the Paris toll houses (1784–89), which demonstrate his interest in pure geometric form and in an eclectic vocabulary. When political events made it impossible for him to remain active as an architect, he devoted himself to preparing a collection of his entire *oeuvre*, existing and projected, with commentary. His surviving works illustrate his break with the baroque tradition, and his projected schemes are related to the ideal fantasies of Boullée.

BIBLIOGRAPHY. G. Levallet-Haug, *Claude-Nicholas Ledoux*, Paris, 1934.

LEDUC, OZIAS. Canadian painter (1864–1955). Leduc lived as a recluse in rural Quebec. In his youth he assisted minor church decorators. On a visit to France in 1897 he was influenced by the minor impressionists. He was a muralist and painter of delicate oil landscapes, portraits, and trompe-l'oeil still life, which have inspired recent French-Canadian painters.

LEE, DORIS EMRICK. American painter and lithographer (1905–   ). Born in Aledo, Ill., she studied at the Kansas City Art Institute, with André Lhote in Paris, and with Arnold Blanch and Ernest Lawson. A painter of figures, landscapes, and portraits, she is best known for her rural genre subjects done in a primitivistic, semicaricatural style.

LEE, WESLEY DUKE. Brazilian painter (1931–   ). Born in São Paulo, Lee studied at the Museum of Modern Art there and at the Parsons School of Design in New York City. He worked in advertising (1955–57) and studied in Paris (1958). He has had one-man shows in São Paulo

(1961 and 1962), and he won the first prize for painting at the Tokyo Biennial in 1965.

BIBLIOGRAPHY. S. Catlin and T. Grieder, *Art of Latin America since Independence*, New Haven, 1966.

LEECH, JOHN. English draftsman and illustrator (b. London, 1817; d. there, 1864). A famous caricaturist, Leech became known through his *Etchings and Sketchings* (1835) and subsequently contributed more than 3,000 etched illustrations to *Punch* (1841–64). His best-known book illustrations are for Dickens's *Christmas Carol*.

BIBLIOGRAPHY. W. P. Frith, *John Leech: His Life and Work*, 2 vols., London, 1891.

LEEDS: CITY ART GALLERY. English museum built in 1888 and extended in 1925. It is strong in 19th- and 20th-century English painting, water colors, and sculpture. Some 17th-century Dutch, modern French, and Barbizon school paintings are exhibited as well as Leeds and Staffordshire pottery.

LEEMANS, ANTONIUS (Anthony). Dutch painter of still life and portraits (b. The Hague, ca. 1631; d. Amsterdam, before 1673). He was active in The Hague, Alkmaar, Amsterdam, Utrecht, and Dordrecht. Johannes Leemans, who painted in a similar manner, was probably his brother. Antonius seems to have also painted several group portraits.

BIBLIOGRAPHY. A. P. A. Vorenkamp, *Bijdrage tot de geschiedenis van het Hollandsch stilleven in de zeventiende eeuw*, Leyden, 1934.

LEEUW, PIETER VAN DER. Dutch landscape painter (b. Dordrecht, 1647; d. there, 1679). He was the pupil of his father, Bastiaan van der Leeuw. Pieter was one of the founders of the Guild of St. Luke at Dordrecht, and in 1678 he was a member of the board of governors. He painted landscapes with animals in the style of Adriaen van de Velde.

BIBLIOGRAPHY. W. Bernt, *Die niederländischen Maler des 17. Jahrhunderts...*, vol. 2, Munich, 1948.

LEEWAN, *see* LIWAN.

LE FAUCONNIER, HENRI. French painter (b. Hesdin, 1881; d. Paris, 1946). He went to Paris in 1901. About 1909 he became friendly with the group of painters associated with cubism, particularly Gleizes and Delaunay. Le Fauconnier's increasing dependence on cubism can be seen in the progression from the simplified geometric shapes and dull coloring of his basically decorative *Portrait of Jouve* (1909; Paris, National Museum of Modern Art) to the allegorical *L'Abondance* (1910–11; The Hague, Gemeentemuseum), in which, despite the fragmentation of the bodies, he manages not to lose the relatively firm outline of the figures. Le Fauconnier eventually arrived at a personal cubism with landscapes, still lifes, and figures treated in terms of ordered, overlapping planes.

BIBLIOGRAPHY. J. Romains, *Le Fauconnier*, Paris, 1921.

LEFEBVRE (Le Febure), CLAUDE. French portrait painter and etcher (b. Fontainebleau, 1632; d. Paris, 1675). He was the pupil of his father, Jean Lefebvre I, and of Eustache Le Sueur. Few of Lefebvre's works are known, except through engravings. He was influenced first by the simplicity and realism of Philippe de Champaigne, but later adopted the manner of Charles Le Brun. As a result, his paintings became structurally looser, conforming to the style of of-

Henri Le Fauconnier, *Portrait of the Poet Castiance*. Private collection.

ficial portraiture in the third quarter of the century. In 1664 he was made professor at the Royal Academy, and he exhibited nine portraits in the Salon of 1673. His activity took him to England. His chief work is the *Preceptor and His Pupil* (Paris, Louvre).

LEFEBVRE, GUILLAUME (Willame). Flemish copper and brass caster of Tournai (fl. 1431–76). He is first mentioned in 1431, when he executed four copper angels for the high altar of the Cathedral at Cambrai. His most significant work is the baptismal font of Notre-Dame (1446; Hal, St. Martin), consisting of the crowned St. John the Baptist, four Church Fathers, the twelve Apostles, saints, and donors. Lefebvre worked in a solid mid-15th-century idiom.

LEFEBVRE, JULES JOSEPH. French painter (b. Tournan, 1836; d. Paris, 1912). He studied with Léon Cogniet and at the Ecole des Beaux-Arts in Paris. Lefebvre won the Prix de Rome in 1861, and later won many other medals. He worked in the strictest academic style. He painted historical genre subjects but soon concentrated on the nude figure, almost exclusively female, in a long series of paintings with mythological titles and the traditional emphasis on accurate drawing. A combination of the two forms can be seen in the detailed *Lady Godiva* (1890; Amiens, Museum of Picardy). Lefebvre was also popular as a painter of society portraits.

LEFUEL, HECTOR MARTIN. French architect (1810–80). He worked in Paris. He was a pupil of J. N. Huyot.

Lefuel's main work is the design of the New Louvre, which he inherited from L. T. J. Visconti in 1853. Lefuel enriched the design, and provided one of the main Parisian examples of Second Empire architecture with its bold plasticity and creative eclecticism. *See* LOUVRE PALACE, PARIS.

BIBLIOGRAPHY. L. Hautecoeur, *Histoire de l'architecture classique in France*, vol. 7, Paris, 1957.

LEGARDA, BERNARDO. Spanish colonial sculptor in Ecuador (fl. 1st half of 18th cent.). Legarda, a mestizo, had a large studio in Quito, where he produced polychrome wood sculpture in the Sevillan style (for example, *Tota pulchra*; Quito, Monastery of S. Francisco). Unusual energy and dignity distinguish his work.

BIBLIOGRAPHY. P. Kelemen, *Baroque and Rococo in Latin America*, New York, 1951.

LEGENDA AUREA (Golden Legend). The collected accounts of the lives of the saints set down from written and oral records by the Dominican archbishop of Genoa, Jacobus de Voragine (1230–1298/99). The *Legenda aurea* became extremely popular in the late Middle Ages; its 177 chapters are today the art historian's principal source for the lives of the saints.

BIBLIOGRAPHY. G. Ryan and H. Ripperger, trs., *The Golden Legend of Jacobus de Voragine*, New York, 1941.

LEGER, FERNAND. French cubist painter (b. Argentan, 1881; d. Grif-sur-Yvette, 1955). Léger was one of the major contributors to the cubist style. He worked for architects in Caen and Paris from 1897 to 1902 and was in military service in 1902–03. Refused regular admission to the Ecole des Beaux-Arts, Léger studied there and at the Académie Julian as an independent, also visiting the Louvre and earning his living as a photographic retoucher. He lived in Montparnasse from 1905 until 1907, and before 1910 became acquainted with Matisse, Braque, Picasso, and the writers Max Jacob, Apollinaire, André Salmon, and Maurice Raynal. He met with the cubist circle at Jacques Villon's studio in 1910–11 and exhibited at the famous Section d'Or (Galerie de la Boétie) in 1912. He also gave a one-man show at Kahnweiler's gallery that year.

Always an independent-minded artist, Léger in 1913–14 extended his own variety of cubism to include powerfully modeled forms suggestive of mechanical movement (*Contrast of Forms* series). He exhibited in the 1913 Herbstsalon in Berlin (Der Sturm Gallery). From 1919 until the middle 1920s he was associated with the purist movement of Le Corbusier and Ozenfant, sharply clarifying his volumes and color and involving human and ma-

Fernand Léger, *The Tugboat*, 1920. Municipal Museum, Grenoble. A work by one of the major contributors to the cubist style.

Alphonse Legros, *Portrait of the Artist's Father*, 1857. Museum of Fine Arts, Tours.

Museum of Modern Art, and Paris, National Museum of Modern Art), *The City* (1919; Philadelphia Museum of Art), *La Danse aux clés* (1930; Paris, National Museum of Modern Art), *Butterflies and Flowers* (1937; Carré Gallery), and *The Great Parade* (1954; New York, Guggenheim Museum).

Léger was a central figure in the development of cubism, although he grew away from the movement and developed a strongly personal expression. The clarity of his modeling and his use of bright color, often depicting machine subjects or rhythms, are a distinctive phenomenon in modern art.

See also BIOT: FERNAND LEGER MUSEUM.

BIBLIOGRAPHY. K. Kuh, *Léger*, Urbana, Ill., 1953; P. Descargues, *Fernand Léger*, Paris, 1955; Paris, Musée des Arts Décoratifs, *Fernand Léger, 1881–1955*, Paris, 1956; R. Rosenblum, *Cubism and Twentieth Century Art*, New York, 1960.   JOHN C. GALLOWAY

LEGROS, ALPHONSE. French painter, graphic artist, and sculptor (b. Dijon, 1837; d. Watford, near London, 1911). His early studies were in Lyon under Jean-Baptiste Beuchot and in Paris at the Ecole des Beaux-Arts, which he left in 1855. In 1857 Legros made his debut in the Salon with a portrait of his father (Tours, Museum of Fine Arts). At this time he was part of Courbet's circle. In 1863 he moved to London, where he remained for the rest of his life. In London Legros worked in close association with Whistler, Rossetti, and Watts.

Today Legros is known mainly for his graphic works, through which he exercised considerable influence on later generations of English graphic artists, among them Shannon and Holroyd. Many of his graphics deal with fantastic and macabre themes, such as the series of etchings on death (*Death of the Vagabond*; *Death of St. Francis*), which exhibit a close study of Holbein and Baldung-Grien. His portraits, such as those of Watts and Kipling, were popular. Legros's major works of sculpture are two foun-

chine forms as coordinates within the same canvas (*The Mechanic*, 1920, Paris, Carré Gallery; *Three Women,* 1921, New York, Museum of Modern Art). He collaborated with Dudley Murphy in 1923 on the film *Ballet mécanique*, one of the earliest "art" movies, whose content centered on simple, mechanical objects. During the 1920s he knew the de Stijl group. He also conducted his own art school.

Léger visited the United States in 1931 and was stimulated by the environment of New York City. He traveled to Greece and again to New York during the 1930s, decorating Nelson Rockefeller's apartment and creating the décor for the Lifar ballet *David Triumphant* (1937). He also painted a mural on the theme of transportation at the Paris World's Fair that year. Léger lived in New York from 1940 to 1946, at which time his subjects were acrobats and cyclists. During this period his style grew more complex: the powerfully modeled volumes of much of his earlier work gave way to flat patterns of brilliant color upon which he chiefly used strong linear definitions. He was also active in lithography.

Following his return to France in 1946, Léger was active in decorating churches and public buildings (stained-glass windows for the church at Assy in 1948, for the Bastogne Memorial in 1950, and for the Church of Sacré-Coeur, Adincourt, in 1954; murals for the General Assembly Building of the United Nations, New York; and several important mosaics). He also created sets and costumes for the opera *Bolivar* by Milhaud (1950).

Other works by Léger include *Nudes in the Forest* (1910; Otterlo, Kröller-Müller Museum), *The Stairway* (1913; Zurich, Art Gallery; similar canvases in New York,

Wilhelm Lehmbruck, *Kneeling Woman*, 1911. Cast stone. Museum of Modern Art, New York (Mrs. John D. Rockefeller, Jr. Fund).

tains in the park of Welbeck Abbey. Among his students was William Strang.

BIBLIOGRAPHY. Grosvenor Galleries, *A Catalogue of Paintings, Drawings, Etchings and Lithographs by Professor Alphonse Legros*, London, 1922; M. Salaman, *Alphonse Legros*, London, 1926.

LEGROS, PIERRE I AND II. French sculptors of the 17th and 18th centuries. Pierre I (b. Chartres, 1629; d. Paris, 1714) was a pupil of Jacques Sarrazin and became a member of the Royal Academy in 1666 and professor in 1702. He is responsible for much of the work done at Versailles from 1670 to 1692.

Pierre II (b. Paris, 1666; d. Rome, 1719), his son, studied with his father and with Jean Lepautre, and lived in Rome from 1690 to 1695. Pierre II's works were done mainly for Roman churches and for the cloister of the Abbey of Montecassino. His most famous work is the altar *Religion Overthrows Heresy* (1695–99) in Il Gesù, Rome. From father to son, the style changes from French classicism to a slightly rococo aspect.

BIBLIOGRAPHY. P. d'Espezel, "Notes historiques sur l'oeuvre et la vie de Pierre II Le Gros," *Gazette des Beaux-Arts*, series 6, XII, 1934.

LEHMBRUCK, WILHELM. German sculptor, graphic artist, painter, and poet (b. Meiderich, 1881; d. Berlin, 1919). Before the age of fourteen he showed a love of carving in chalk and plaster. From 1895 to 1899 he attended the Düsseldorf School of Arts and Crafts. Between 1899 and 1901 he worked as a sculptor's assistant and then entered the Düsseldorf Art Academy, where he studied from 1901 to 1907. While there, he was a master pupil of Karl Janssen. Lehmbruck traveled to Italy in 1905 on prize money won by his sculpture. The Academy purchased his *Woman* in 1905. In 1907 his sculpture *Mother and Child*, which reflected his social consciousness, was successfully exhibited in Paris. He lived in Paris from 1910 until 1914 and was befriended during this time by Archipenko, Matisse, Brancusi, and Modigliani.

Lehmbruck's early style seems to have been formed before he saw the work of Maillol in 1910. His signature style of ascetic, spiritually lean, and angular figures rapidly emerged while in Paris, as can be seen in *Kneeling Woman* (1911) and *Rising Youth* (1913). The dramatic attenuation of his figures may have been the result of the influence of both Gothic sculpture and Picasso's Blue Period. Lehmbruck was consciously seeking a new style by which to interpret modern heroism. At the outbreak of World War I he went to Berlin, where he exhibited at the Secession in 1916 and suffered bitter criticism for his *Man Flung Down*. Like his *Seated Youth* of 1916–18, this sculpture was intended as a personal memorial to German youth killed in the war and to the death of his own hopes. In 1917–18 he had a studio in Zurich, and in 1918 was appointed to the Prussian Academy of Arts.

The most comprehensive collection of Lehmbruck's sculpture is owned by his wife and includes the *Bust of Mme L.* (1910), *Sitting Child* (1910), *The Temptation* (1911), and *Kneeling Woman* (1911; a cast is in New York, Museum of Modern Art). The Lehmbruck Museum, Duisburg, owns *Torso of a Young Girl* (1913–14) and *Rising Youth* (cast in New York, Museum of Modern Art), *Sitting Girl* (1913–14), *Man Flung Down* (1915–16), *Head of a Thinker* (1918), and *Praying Woman* (1918). The Folk-

Wilhelm Leibl, *Three Women in Church*. Art Gallery, Hamburg. A work from the artist's "Holbein" period.

wang Museum, Essen, owns *Standing Woman* (1910) and *Mother and Child* (1907). Lehmbruck created some of the last and rare images of pathos and heroism of spirit in modern sculpture in a deeply personal style that meaningfully extended the figure tradition from the medieval period into the 20th century. *See* DUISBURG: LEHMBRUCK MUSEUM.

BIBLIOGRAPHY. C. Giedion-Welcker, *Contemporary Sculpture*, New York, 1955; W. Lehmbruck, *Wilhelm Lehmbruck*, by W. Hofmann, New York, 1959.

ALBERT ELSEN

LEIBL, WILHELM. German painter of portraits and genre (b. Cologne, 1844; d. Würzburg, 1900). Son of the Cologne Cathedral music master, he studied at the Munich Academy between 1864 and 1869, under Anschütz, the genre painter Ramberg, and the history painter Piloty. He came into contact with Courbet in Munich in 1869 and on his advice visited Paris, until the outbreak of the war in 1870. Leibl returned to Munich, where he remained until 1873, and from then until his death lived in a succession of Bavarian villages, which provided him with genre subjects.

His paintings are marked by a realism that found favor with Courbet, whose own work provided a parallel to Leibl's development. Leibl's art, however, was firmly rooted in the great realist masters of the past, for example, *The Portrait of Frau Lorenz Gedon* (1868/69; Munich, Bavarian State Picture Galleries) and *Cocotte* (1869; Cologne, Wallraf-Richartz Museum), in which the influence of Hals is particularly apparent. Leibl's early works are marked by a looseness of handling and by a tonal treatment of light that is also related to the work of Vermeer, another artist whom he admired. He was impressed, too, by contemporary developments in Paris, for example, the work of Manet; this influence can be seen in such works as *The Painter Sattler with a Hound* (1870; Bavarian State Picture Galleries). Between 1870 and 1880 he entered his "Holbein" period, which is marked by a careful, precise realism and hard outline reminiscent of the 16th-century German master. This phase is typified by *Three Women in Church* (1881; Hamburg, Art Gallery) and, in his portraits, by the *Portrait of Gräfin Treuberg* (1878; Hamburg, Art Gallery).

His genre scenes, influenced by his interest in the Dutch masters, were developed concurrently with his portraiture and culminate in the more loosely handled *In the Kitchen* (1898; Stuttgart, State Gallery). His work in this manner could be compared with that of Bastien-Lepage or the British painters of the Newlyn school. His insistent realism, unlike that of Von Menzel, never degenerated into sentimentality, though his interest in color and light remained centered on tonal values and he never attempted the broken brushstroke of the impressionists.

BIBLIOGRAPHY. E. Waldmann, *Wilhelm Leibl: Eine Darstellung seiner Kunst*, Berlin, 1914; J. Mayr, *Wilhelm Leibl, sein Leben und Schaffen*, 4th ed., Berlin, 1935.

MALCOLM CORMACK

LEIGHTON, LORD FREDERIC. English painter and sculptor (1830–96). His career as an artist was decided at the age of fourteen when his talent was recognized by Hiram Powers, whom he met in Florence. Leighton studied in Florence, Frankfurt, Brussels, Paris, and Rome. He credited Steinle, his teacher at the Staedel Institut, Frankfurt, as his real master.

Leighton's first painting exhibited at the Royal Academy in 1855, *Cimabue's Madonna*, was an overwhelming success and was purchased by Queen Victoria. In 1878 he was elected president of the Academy. Among his many paintings of classical subjects are the murals *The Arts of War and Peace* (London, Victoria and Albert). Later in life he began his essays in sculpture. He was an eclectic (depending primarily on Greek and Italian High Renaissance sources) whose lack of individual vision was one of the factors that kept him from being a great artist.

LEIJSTER (Leyster), JUDITH JANSDR. Dutch painter of genre, some portraits, and still life (b. Haarlem, 1609; d. Heemstede, 1660). The surname Leijster is adopted from the name of her father's brewery at Haarlem, the Ley-ster(re), meaning "Lodestar." She must have received some early training in art, for by 1626/27 she was already listed as painting in Haarlem. In 1628 her parents were living at Vreeland, near Utrecht, and her early works show the impact of the Utrecht followers of Caravaggio. It has also been suggested that she studied with Hendrick Terbrugghen in Utrecht at this time.

About 1629 Leijster probably became a student of Frans Hals at Haarlem. She was probably the "Judith Jans(dr.)" who witnessed the baptism of one of Hals's children at Haarlem in 1631. In 1633 she was a member of the Haarlem painters' guild. She married the painter Jan Molenaer in 1636 at Heemstede. In 1637 the couple was living in Amsterdam, and they seem to have remained there until 1648, when they returned to Heemstede and the neighboring Haarlem.

Leijster's 1631 *The Rejected Offer* (The Hague, Mauritshuis Art Gallery) combines the influence of Frans Hals with Utrecht-like artificial light sources (of Gerrit van Honthorst, for example). In handling as well as in the treatment of the theme of venal love, this picture anticipates the works of Vermeer. There are no known works dated after 1652.

BIBLIOGRAPHY. C. Hofstede de Groot, "Judith Leyster," *Jahrbuch der preussischen Kunstsammlungen*, XIV, 1893; A. von Schneider, "Gerard Honthorst und Judith Leyster," *Oud-Holland*, XL, 1922; J. Harms, "Judith Leyster. Ihr Leben und ihr Werk," *Oud-Holland*, XLIV, 1927; E. Neurdenberg, "Judith Leyster," *Oud-Holland*, XLVI, 1929.

LEONARD J. SLATKES

LEINBERGER, HANS. German sculptor (b. Landshut, 1480/85; d. 1531/35). He was one of the leading figures in German Renaissance sculpture. Some of his important works are an altar in Moosburg (1511–14), a Madonna at St. Martin in Landshut, *St. James* in the Bavarian National Museum, Munich (ca. 1525), *St. George* in the Frauenkirche, Munich (ca. 1525), the high altar in Polling (1526–27), and a design for a bronze figure of Albert IV of Hapsburg for the tomb of Maximilian I at the Hofkirche (Court Church) in Innsbruck. Working in wood, Leinberger combined the intense emotional expression and realism of the late Gothic period with a sharply drawn and monumental conception of human form.

BIBLIOGRAPHY. C. T. Müller, *Hans Leinberger*, Berlin, 1938; G. Lill, *Hans Leinberger*, Munich, 1942.

LEINFELLNER, HEINZ. Austrian sculptor (1911–   ). Born in Steinbrück, he attended the Graz School of Arts and Crafts and then became a pupil of Anton Hanak at the Vienna Academy (1933–39). From 1947 to 1951 Leinfellner worked in Wotruba's studio. He traveled to Italy

Judith Jansdr. Leijster, *The Rejected Offer*, 1631. Mauritshuis, The Hague.

nd other Continental countries. His work has been shown n the Venice and São Paulo biennials. Although he be-ȝan as a cubist, he now creates figurative compositions ısing a variety of materials.

LEISTIKOW, WALTER. German painter, graphic artist, ɪnd decorative designer (b. Bromberg, 1865; d. Schlachten-ᵴee, 1908). He studied briefly at the Berlin Academy and ᴡith Eschlike and Gude. Leistikow is best known as a ɪandscape painter, particularly of the area around Berlin. His paintings are decorative in their careful adjustment of forms to the total surface of the canvas. Natural elements—trees, earth, clouds—are for the most part seen as flat, strongly silhouetted shapes. The scene, spatially constructed by vertical addition rather than perspective, often is some-what romantic in feeling. The decorative elements are na-turally more obvious in his tapestry designs.

BIBLIOGRAPHY. L. Corinth, *Das Leben Walter Leistikows*, Berlin, 1910.

LEI-WEN (Thunder Pattern). Chinese term for a type of decorative system employed on ritual bronzes of the Shang and Chou dynasties (ca. 1500–256 B.C.). *Lei-wen* can be translated literally as "thunder marks" and is usually re-ferred to in Western literature as the "thunder pattern," to describe the spiral designs that are used for background and borders and sometimes appear on the bodies of ani-mal forms in the early periods of bronze art in China. There are many variants to the spirals: rounded, squared, S-shaped, and sometimes with added hooks or quill-like projections.

LEKYTHOS (Lecythos). Pottery jug for oil or perfume that was also used as a funerary offering in ancient Greece. Featuring a single, earlike handle, it was characterized by a flaring mouth, a short neck, and an ovoid or globular body ending in a circular foot. The painted decoration applied to such jugs varies according to the period of production, with especially charming scenes appearing on black-figured examples of the mid-6th century B.C.

BIBLIOGRAPHY. G. M. A. Richter and M. J. Milne, *Shapes and Names of Athenian Vases*, New York, 1935.

LELIENBERGH, CORNELIS. Dutch painter of still life (b. before 1626; d. after 1676). A native of The Hague, Lelienbergh became a member of the Guild of St. Luke there in 1646 and three years later married the daughter of an art dealer in that city. In 1656 he was one of the founders of the painters' confraternity Pictura. He was liv-ing in Schlosse Maerspeug, Beamter, in 1666. Lelienbergh painted hunting still lifes with birds, hares, and so on, in the general style of Jan Weenix.

BIBLIOGRAPHY. A. P. A. Vorenkamp, *Bijdrage tot de geschiedenis van het Hollandsch stilleven in de zeventiende eeuw*, Leyden, 1934.

LE LIGET: CHAPEL OF ST. JOHN OF LIGET. French chapel founded by Henry II of England in expiation for the murder of Thomas à Becket. Soon after the foundation of the Carthusian monastery of Liget (1176–89) the order built nearby a small circular chapel covered with a cupola. The paintings on the interior (ca. 1197–1201) constitute one of the most interesting cycles of Romanesque frescoes in France. The cupola painting of Christ in Glory has disappeared, but on the walls, below a frieze of patriarchs

and prophets, six grand scenes remain: the *Nativity, Pre-sentation in the Temple, Descent from the Cross, Holy Women at the Tomb, Dormition of the Virgin,* and *Tree of Jesse.*

BIBLIOGRAPHY. M. Thibout, "La Chapelle Saint-Jean du Liget et ses peintures murales," *Congrès Archéologique de France, CVI*ᵉ *Session, Tours,* Paris, 1949.

LELLI, ERCOLE. Italian painter, sculptor, architect, and engraver (b. Bologna, 1702; d. there, 1766). He was an engraver of religious subjects. Of the paintings, the only ones known to be his are several works in the churches of Bologna and Piacenza. He was the director of the Academy in Bologna.

LE LORRAIN, see LORRAINE, CLAUDE.

LE LORRAIN, ROBERT. French sculptor (1666–1743). He studied with Antoine Coysevox and became a sculptor to the king and an instructor in the Royal Academy. Le Lorrain contributed to the development of the rococo style. Typical of his work are *Galatea* (1701; Kress Collection) and *Horses of Phoebus Apollo* (Paris, Hôtel de Soubise).

LE LOUP, JEAN. French architect (13th cent.). He was the second master of Reims Cathedral, succeeding Jean d'Orbais. Le Loup was master for sixteen years, probably between 1231 and 1247, and his work included alteration of the north transept façade, giving it three portals rather than one. See REIMS: CATHEDRAL.

BIBLIOGRAPHY. L. Demaison, *La Cathédrale de Reims*, 3d ed., Paris, 1954.

LELY, SIR PETER (Peter van der Faes). English por-trait painter of German birth (b. Soest, Westphalia, 1618; d. London, 1680). He was trained in Holland and became

Sir Peter Lely, *Countess of Shrewsbury*. National Portrait Gallery, London.

a member of the Haarlem guild in 1637. It is not known precisely when he went to England, but he was in London by 1647.

Lely's work gives ample evidence that he had studied Van Dyck. He also appears to have given some attention early in his career to painting subject pictures and enriching his portraits with symbols and allegorical references. He managed to avoid becoming seriously involved in the political upheavals of mid-17th-century England. By the early 1660s he was firmly established as the leading painter in England, a position he retained until his death. He was very successful financially, and was thus able to gather a distinguished collection of master paintings and drawings (some of them acquired at the sale of the collection of Charles I).

Lely is now remembered primarily as the portraitist of the court of Charles II. His series of the ladies of the court, known as the *Windsor Beauties* (Hampton Court), epitomizes the rather heavy, sensuous languor associated with the Restoration. More virile is the series depicting flag officers at the battle of Lowestoft, painted in the late 1660s on commission from the Duke of York. In these portraits, Lely closely approaches the manner of his Dutch contemporaries in forthright, vigorous presentation. During the 1670s Lely's portraits became more clearly dominated by mannerisms, his color more reserved, and his paint application less vigorous.

Most of Lely's best work is in England: Hampton Court; the National Maritime Museum, Greenwich; and the National Portrait Gallery, London.

BIBLIOGRAPHY. C. H. Collins Baker, *Lely and the Stuart Portrait Painters*, 2 vols., London, 1912; R. B. Beckett, *Peter Lely*, London, 1951; M. Whinney and .O. Millar, *English Art, 1625–1714*, Oxford, 1957.

ROBERT R. WARK

LEMAIRE, JEAN. French architectural and perspective painter (b. 1598; d. Gaillon, 1659). After twenty years in Rome he collaborated with Poussin on the decoration of the Long Gallery of the Louvre. His views, both real and imaginary, are conceived as stage settings, overlaid with classical architectural bric-a-brac.

BIBLIOGRAPHY. A. Blunt, "Jean Lemaire: Painter of Architectural Fantasies," *The Burlington Magazine*, LXXXIII, 1943.

LE MANS. Capital of the Sarthe Department in northwestern France. Two important churches dominate Le Mans: the Church of Notre-Dame-de-la-Couture (12th–14th cent.) and the Cathedral, dedicated to St. Julian, first bishop of Le Mans in the 3d century. The Cathedral, begun in the Romanesque period, was completed between the 13th and the 15th century. Although the Romanesque nave is decidedly severe, the choir and transepts are handsomely proportioned in the best Gothic tradition. There is much worthwhile sculpture to be seen on both these monuments. *See* NOTRE-DAME-DE-LA-COUTURE, LE MANS. *See also* STAINED GLASS.

The Church of St-Julien-du-Pré is Romanesque. There are several interesting Renaissance mansions. The museum contains some fine paintings and enamels. *See* LE MANS: FINE ARTS MUSEUM.

BIBLIOGRAPHY. M. Aubert and S. Goubet, *Gothic Cathedrals of France and Their Treasures*, London, 1959.

LE MANS: FINE ARTS MUSEUM. Notable among the paintings in this French collection are works by Valdé Leal, Georges de La Tour, Géricault, Delacroix, and Constable. The collection of gold- and silverwork is highlighted by the famous champlevé enamel plaque (ca. 1151–60) of Geoffrey Plantagenet.

BIBLIOGRAPHY. A. Le Feuvre and A. Alexandre, *Catalogue du Musée des Arts*, Le Mans, 1932.

LEMERCIER, JACQUES. French architect (b. ca. 1580–85; d. 1654). Trained as a French architect, he spent seven years in Rome, where he absorbed the Italian prebaroque academic style. His later work is a result of these two influences, and his importance to architecture lies in his introduction of the Italian idiom to France. His most important works are the extension of Lescot's wing of the Louvre, the Palais Royal, the château and town of Richelieu, and the Sorbonne chapel. He also completed François Mansart's Church of Val-de-Grâce by adding the dome, considered the most dramatic and impressive 17th-century dome in Paris. *See* LOUVRE PALACE, PARIS; SORBONNE UNIVERSITY AND CHURCH; VAL-DE-GRACE, PARIS.

LEMIEUX, JEAN-PAUL. Canadian painter (1904–   ) After studying in Montreal, he attended the Grande Chaumière and Colarossi Academies in Paris. He has taught in Quebec since 1937. His paintings are nostalgic landscapes and figure studies in oil.

BIBLIOGRAPHY. C. Picher and M. Cadieux, "Jean-Paul Lemieux...," *Canadian Art*, XVII, 1960.

LE MOINE, FRANCOIS, *see* LEMOYNE, FRANCOIS.

LE MOITURIER, ANTOINE (Maistre Anthoniet). French sculptor (b. Avignon, ca. 1425; d. Dijon, ca. 1497). He was a nephew and student of Jacques Morel. Le Moiturier completed the tomb of John the Fearless (1466–70; Dijon, Museum of Fine Arts), which had been started some years earlier at the Chartreuse de Champmol, Dijon, by Jean de la Huerta. Highly praised in his day, he may also have been responsible for the unique tomb of Philippe Pot (1477–83; Paris, Louvre). In this work the attendant mourners of earlier tombs are transformed into massive figures bearing the effigy of the deceased. The tomb continues the monumental Dijon tradition of Claus Sluter but in a softer and more restrained manner.

BIBLIOGRAPHY. T. Müller, *Sculpture in the Netherlands, Germany, France, and Spain, 1400–1500*, Baltimore, 1966.

LE MOT, FRANCOIS-FREDERIC. French sculptor (b. Lyons, 1772; d. Paris, 1827). A pupil of Dejoux, Le Mot went to Rome in 1790; he made his Salon debut in Paris in 1801 and became a member of the Institut de France in 1809. In 1822 he supervised engravers in the French Mint. In 1808 he executed the lead quadriga for Napoleon's Arc de Triomphe du Carrousel in Paris, and in 1818 he did an equestrian statue of Henry IV for the Place du Pont-Neuf in Paris to replace that of Giovanni Bologna and Pietro Tacca. Le Mot's style is vigorous and classicizing.

LEMOYNE (Le Moine), FRANCOIS. French decorative painter (b. Paris, 1688; d. there, 1737). He studied with R. L. Tournières and L. Galloche. Lemoyne traveled to

Jean-Baptiste Lemoyne, *Duc de la Vallière*. Versailles Museum.

Italy in 1711. He became a professor at the Royal Academy in 1733 and First Painter to the King in 1736. Lemoyne translated the Roman baroque decorative manner of Pietro da Cortona and G. A. Pellegrini into a diminutive waxen figure style, important in the transition to the *style rocaille*, or French rococo art (Paris, Saint-Sulpice; Versailles).

BIBLIOGRAPHY. L. Dimier, *Les Peintres français du XVIIIe siècle...*, vol. 1, Paris, 1928.

LEMOYNE, JEAN-BAPTISTE. French sculptor (1704–78). He studied with his father, Jean-Louis Lemoyne, and with Robert Le Lorrain. Lemoyne became a favorite sculptor at the court of Louis XV, and many of his important works were bronze portrait busts of that king, destroyed during the French Revolution. Most of Lemoyne's extant works are busts of prominent 18th-century figures. Typical are the *Duc de la Vallière* (Versailles Museum) and *Mlle Dangeville* (1761; Paris, Théâtre Français). He followed the French baroque style, but enlivened it with a playful, decorative handling of form that is essentially rococo and expressive of the elegance of the French court. He was a reputable teacher; among his students were J.-B. Pigalle, J. Caffieri, E.-M. Falconet, and J. A. Houdon.

BIBLIOGRAPHY. L. Réau, *Les Lemoyne*, Paris, 1927.

LE MUET, PIERRE. French architect (1590–1669). He worked in Paris. Best known for his book on French domestic architecture, he also wrote a commentary on Vignola and translated Palladio. His most important surviving work, the Hôtel Tubeuf, now part of the Bibliothèque Nationale, shows the mannerist features of the early years of the 17th century in France.

BIBLIOGRAPHY. L. Hautecoeur, *Histoire de l'architecture classique en France*, vol. 1, Paris, 1943.

LE NAIN BROTHERS. French painters of genre, religious scenes, and portraits: Antoine (ca. 1588–1648), Louis (ca. 1593–1648), and Mathieu (ca. 1607–77). They were born

at Laon and all probably died in Paris. The three brothers were original members of the Royal Academy. Because only fifteen signed and dated works exist (executed between 1641 and 1648), none of which specifies a Christian name, positive attribution to any one of the three remains problematic, in spite of vast scholarly research on the subject. Various instances of stylistic overlapping encourage belief in collaboration (*Venus at the Forge of Vulcan*, Reims Museum, and *Le Cortège du Bélier*, Paris, private collection), which is plausible because of their close association. Antoine is recorded as master painter to the Abbey of St-Germain-des-Prés, Paris, in 1629. Louis and Mathieu, who were still apprentices, arrived the next year. Mathieu is listed as master painter to the city of Paris in 1633. Though the origins of their styles are obscure, it is probable that they were jointly trained in their native town in the Netherlandish style prevailing there of Hendrick Avercamp and Adriaen Pietersz. van de Venne.

Antoine Le Nain is said to have excelled in miniatures and small portraits. Therefore, a series of small-scale paintings on copper, in which the figures are quietly posed without much compositional skill and painted in strong local tones, are attributed to him. Though *The Little Singers* (ca. 1645–48; Duke of Cervinara Collection) is considered by some as being beyond his capacities, and consequently a work of Louis, this late work, in which Antoine could have profited by his brothers' lessons, is his most accomplished one. What at first glance appears to be genre is ultimately family group portraiture; modest bourgeois and occasionally peasants (*A Woman and Five Children*, 1642; London, National Gallery) are stiffly posed with Sunday afternoon decorum, in varying and unrelated directions around a table or in front of their hearth (*Portraits in an Interior* and *Family Reunion*; both Paris, Louvre). Occasionally a nobleman posed for him (*Portrait of the Marquis de Troisvilles*, Rueil, Countess de Mont-Réal Collection).

Louis Le Nain's much more advanced style occasioned the initial interest in this family of artists. Eighteenth-century writers refer to him as "le Romain"; 17th-century writers classify him as a painter of bambocciades (low-life scenes) in imitation of Pieter van Laer (called Bamboccio), a Dutch painter active in Rome, whose monumentally simple compositions and cool, grayish palette are echoed in Louis's work. These appellations sanction the belief that between 1626 and 1630 Louis went to Rome, perhaps in the company of Van Laer. Such a trip would account for reflections in his work (*Peasant Family*, ca. 1645–48, Louvre; and perhaps *Le Cortège du Bélier*, unsigned, Paris, private collection) of the early style of Velázquez, who was in Rome in 1629–30. Louis's works are larger in scale than Antoine's, more subdued in color, and more fully modeled and imposing, though unbelabored compositionally. He painted peasant scenes (*Peasants at Supper* and *La Charrette*, both Louvre; *Peasants in a Landscape*, Hartford, Conn., Wadsworth Atheneum). In spite of aerial and atmospheric perspective, his figures, though authentically of the earth, seem to exist immutably as if paralyzed in a vacuum of stage props. The loneliness of open spaces is felt in a manner that suggests modern surrealism. Oc-

Le Nain brothers. Louis Le Nain, *Peasants at Supper*. Louvre, Paris. Attributions to any one of the brothers remains problematic.

casionally he tried his hand at religious subjects (*Adoration of the Shepherds*, Louvre).

His cool and quiet scenes, in which a glass of deep red wine may be presented in a family toast, differ essentially from the Dutch genre painters. His presentation is mute in its verisimilitude. His peasant life is crystalline in its essential dignity. In this respect he concurs with the spiritual quiet and classical reserve of Georges de La Tour. In a period when mannerism was the favored vein in court circles, this raises the question of patronage. In all probability Louis's clientele was the dedicated provincial magistracy, still soberly appreciative of their peasant origins.

Mathieu Le Nain's clientele was a more prosperous and urban middle class. Through the prestige of his older brothers, he had a successful career with municipal connections. A lieutenant in the Paris militia and a chevalier, probably of the Order of St-Michel, he liked to style himself the Seigneur de Jumelle, after the name of a farm he owned near Laon. His art, more assured than his brothers', reflects a somewhat pretentious nature. He takes pleasure in underlining social distinctions for the sake of opulent ef-

fect. In his masterpiece, *Corps de garde* (1643; Paris, Baroness de Berckheim Collection), officers are gathered at a table lit by a single candle, and a well-dressed Negro servant timidly peers past them at the observer.

Mathieu's figures are more lively than those of his brothers, but they do not swagger, for reserve is common to the Le Nains. Mathieu is inclined to sentimentality as well as to snobbishness, by-products of a socially evolved generation. His *Le Jardinier* (Deventer, Dr. van der Ven Collection) represents a humble young gardener offering flowers to his demure mistress. At this time in the 17th century the French and Dutch painters of realism succumbed to courtly attitudes, typical of Versailles, in contrast to the sober simplicity of the early century in both countries, and also, in Mathieu's case, to the naïve sincerity of his brothers, then long deceased.

Imitators of the Le Nains are Jean Michelin, Wallerant Vaillant, and Jacob van Loo. Works by the Le Nains are in Boston, Bristol, Hagerstown, Md., London (Victoria and Albert), New York (Metropolitan Museum), San Francisco

(California Palace of the Legion of Honor), and several French provincial museums.

BIBLIOGRAPHY. P. Fierens, *Les Le Nain*, Paris, 1933; V. Lazareff, *The Brothers Le Nain*, Moscow, 1936 (in Russian).

GEORGE V. GALLENKAMP

LENBACH, FRANZ VON. German painter (b. Schrobenhausen, Upper Bavaria, 1836; d. Munich, 1904). The most admired German portrait painter of the romantic period, Lenbach studied in Munich with Piloty. He traveled with Piloty to Italy in 1858, returning in 1860 to Weimar, where he met Begas and Böcklin. Accompanied by Böcklin, Lenbach traveled extensively in Italy, France, and Spain between 1863 and 1868, copying old masters for Count Schack.

Upon his return to Munich, Lenbach's personal style as a portraitist began to emerge. He was immediately successful. In 1878 he began a friendship with Prince von Bismarck, which led to his introduction to the highest circles of German society. In addition to the many portraits of Bismarck, Lenbach painted King Ludwig I of Bavaria (1868; Munich, Bavarian State Picture Galleries, New Pinacothek), Kaiser Wilhelm I (Leipzig, Museum), and Pope Leo XIII (1885; New Pinacothek). Lenbach's villa in Munich, built for him (1883–89) in the Italian Renaissance style by the architect Seidl, became the Lenbach Museum (now Municipal Gallery and Lenbach Gallery) in 1924.

Lenbach's style was eclectic. He employed a chiaroscuro technique derived from Rembrandt and Titian and a sense of color and painterly technique derived from Velázquez and Reynolds. But, as with these great portraitists, his fame rests on a very acute observation of the personality of his subjects.

BIBLIOGRAPHY. A. Rosenberg, *Lenbach* (Künstler-Monographien, XXXIV), Bielefeld, 1898; H. Kehrer, *Franz von Lenbach*, Berlin, 1937.

DONALD L. EHRESMANN

LENCKER, HANS, THE ELDER. German goldsmith and engraver (fl. 1549–85). He was a member of a Nürnberg family of goldsmiths and a brother of the goldsmith Elias Lencker (master in 1562). Hans the Elder is first recorded in Nürnberg in 1549 and as a master in 1550. His goldsmith work in the German Renaissance style includes two gilded silver pedestals with supports in the form of dolphins and bands of translucent-enameled hunting scenes (ca. 1580; Munich, Residenz Treasury). He is also the author of *Perspectiva Literaria* (Nürnberg, 1567) and *Perspectiva* (Nürnberg, 1571). In 1572 and again in 1576 Lencker was at the Dresden court of Prince Christian I as a teacher of perspective; after 1574 he also worked for the courts of Bavaria and Hesse.

BIBLIOGRAPHY. M. Rosenberg, "Hans Lencker," *Zeitschrift des Bayerischen Kunstgewerbe Vereins in München*, XLIII, 1894.

LENCKER (Lenkart; Lenker; Leucker; Leuckhardt), JOHANNES. German goldsmith (b. ca. 1573; d. Augsburg? 1637). He was perhaps a pupil of the Renaissance goldsmith C. Lencker, under whose artistic influence Johannes remained until his later years. He became a master in the Augsburg goldsmiths' guild in 1616. A number of Lencker's works in the mannerist style have been identified, including gilded silver mounts, for a boat-shaped agate cup, in the form of a Triton and Nereids and set with diamonds and rubies (ca. 1625–30; Munich, Residenz Treasury) and a gilded silver cup in the form of a Nereid riding a Triton (ca. 1600; Amsterdam, Rijksmuseum).

BIBLIOGRAPHY. O. von Falke, "Der Augsburger Goldschmied Johannes Lencker," *Pantheon*, I, 1928.

LENDINARA, CRISTOFORO DA. Italian wood intarsist (fl. 1449–91). He first worked with his brother Lorenzo, a pupil of Piero della Francesca. Cristoforo's major works, *The Evangelists* (Modena Cathedral) and city views (Lucca Gallery), show Piero's forms and perspective virtuosity.

BIBLIOGRAPHY. A. C. Quintavalle, *Cristoforo da Lendinara*, Parma, 1959.

L'ENFANT, PIERRE CHARLES. American architect, engineer, and urban planner (1754–1825). Born in France, he went to the United States and served as George Washington's military engineer, designing many forts. His first major architectural effort was the reconstruction of City Hall in New York City (1787; destroyed), in which he married French classicizing details to a structure monumental in scale. While he is known to have had some influence in liberating New York's architecture from its Georgian strictures, he was more famous for his Morris House in Philadelphia (1794; destroyed ca. 1800), a mansarded pile so ambitiously planned in both size and materials that it never was completed. His most significant work in the

Franz von Lenbach, *Portrait of Richard Wagner*. **Municipal Gallery and Lenbach Gallery, Munich.**

Pierre Charles L'Enfant. Washington, D.C., showing the radial street pattern and long, open vistas provided in his plan.

United States was his plan of 1790–93 for the new capital, Washington. L'Enfant derived its radial plan and long, unimpeded vistas from 17th-century French landscape architecture. *See* WASHINGTON, D.C.

LENIN, TOMB OF, MOSCOW, *see* KREMLIN, MOSCOW.

LENINGRAD (St. Petersburg; Petrograd). Russian city founded by Peter the Great in 1712 as a practical demonstration of his political and social concepts. A barren marsh was transformed into a flourishing metropolis. St. Petersburg served as the capital of Russia from 1712 until 1918. In 1914 the city was renamed Petrograd, and in 1924, Leningrad.

There is a variety of museums in Leningrad, including the Hermitage, one of the leading museums in the world, which owns masterpieces by such artists as Leonardo, Titian, Cranach, El Greco, Rubens, Rembrandt, and Van Dyck. The Russian Museum has an extensive collection of Russian art. *See* LENINGRAD: HERMITAGE MUSEUM.

Among Leningrad's older buildings are the first Summer Palace (1711–14) by Domenico Tressini, with allegorical scenes in relief in the panels between the first and second stories, and the so-called Twelve Colleges (1722–32), also by Tressini, a long row of twelve two-story pavilions embraced within a colossal order of pilasters resting on a basement. Tressini's Cathedral of SS. Peter and Paul (1714–25), the first ecclesiastical structure erected in St. Petersburg and the burial place of Russian czars from Peter the Great on, has been largely restored. The roof and dome, destroyed in 1756, were completely remodeled under Catherine the Great, and only the eastern façade, with its vigorous Corinthian pilasters, shows the original design.

In the Alexander Nevsky Lavra stands the Cathedral of the Trinity, designed by Tressini in 1715; the plan was revised by Tressini and Theodor Schwertfeger and the Cathedral was built by Schwertfeger (1720–32). It was rebuilt by I. Y. Starov (1776–90). A basilica of classical design, it is dominated by two blocky façade towers and a tall crossing dome.

Toward the middle of the 18th century a baroque flavor colored St. Petersburg's architecture, for example, B. F. Rastrelli's Stroganov Palace (1750–54), in which the upper stories are bound together by a giant order of coupled columns, the inner pairs supporting a curved, broken, and recessed pediment. Another example is Rastrelli's Winter Palace (1754–62), in which the façades are unusually extended. In the second half of the 18th century the architecture was characterized by clarity and simplicity, as can be seen in the Academy of Fine Arts (1765–72), designed by A. F. Kokorinov and J. B. M. Vallin de la Mothe. Neoclassic buildings were constructed in the late 18th and the early 19th century; fine examples are the Tauride Palace designed by Starov (1783–88) and the Cathedral of the Virgin of Kazan by A. N. Voronikhin (1801–11). In the early 19th century more monumental buildings appeared, such as Thomas de Thomon's Stock Exchange (1805–10), but by the end of the century a dry eclecticism had come to prevail. In the early 1900s a more forward looking, though still classicizing, architecture was represented by the German Embassy Building, designed by Peter Behrens. *See* KAZAN CATHEDRAL, LENINGRAD; WINTER PALACE. *See also* ST. ISAAC'S CATHEDRAL; TSARSKOE SELO, PALACE OF.

BIBLIOGRAPHY. G. H. Hamilton, *The Art and Architecture of Russia*, Baltimore, 1954; P. Descargues, *The Hermitage*, London, 1961.

ABRAHAM A. DAVIDSON

LENINGRAD: HERMITAGE MUSEUM. Peter the Great laid the foundations for the vast Russian collection of art works that would ultimately be housed in the Hermitage.

The first European paintings he bought included works by Rubens, Van Dyck, Rembrandt, Steen, Van Ostade, Wouwermans, and Brueghel. He also favored contemporary paintings glorifying his own achievements. He had classical works sent to Russia by his Roman ambassador and ordered the preservation of all Russian antiquities. During the reign of Peter's daughter, Elizabeth, the Winter Palace was built by B. F. Rastrelli (1754–62). This became the chief museum, to which other buildings were later added.

Catherine the Great continued Peter's policies in buying Western art. Diderot kept her advised of forthcoming sales in Paris. Galitzin acquired for her the Coblentz Collection of forty-six paintings and 6,000 drawings in Brussels in 1768; many of the drawings and five of the paintings were by Rubens. In 1769 Catherine bought the collection of the Count de Brühl in Dresden, which included paintings by Rubens, Bellotto, and Watteau. The Crozat Collection of some 400 pictures by Italian, Dutch, Flemish, and French masters was purchased in 1771. Soon afterward the Choiseul Collection of Flemish and Spanish works was obtained. In 1778 the Walpole Collection of some 200 French, Italian, Dutch, Flemish, and British works was purchased from England, in the face of considerable protest. In 1784 the Baudouin Collection of Dutch and Flemish paintings was added.

Catherine's son, Paul, continued to collect along the lines laid down by his predecessors. Alexander I acquired a number of important 19th-century collections as well as individual masterpieces. During his reign the work of Russian artists was represented more widely among the imperial paintings than formerly.

Under Nicholas I the Czar's private collection became a public one. The keynote of this period was a shift of interest from French art to German. The Hermitage underwent a thorough pruning, and about one-quarter of the pictures were sold, not entirely wisely. New exhibition rooms were built, problems of selection for display were scrupulously debated, and paintings were arranged by schools for the first time. After 1830 the newly discovered Scythian objects were added. Although Alexander II was less concerned with the Hermitage than were his forebears, one of the museum's most famous paintings, the Leonardo *Madonna Litta*, was acquired by him in 1856.

Between 1910 and 1932 the number of paintings in the Hermitage doubled, as Russian private collections were transferred to the public domain. When the demands of space became pressing, the collections were once more reorganized, and many pictures were shifted among the country's museums. In addition, a number of private and public sales were held, and hundreds of paintings, prints, drawings, and other objects of art went to foreign museums and collectors.

In the early years of the 20th century the collectors Sergei Shchukin and Ivan Morosov were particularly important in gathering a rich representation of impressionist, postimpressionist, Fauve, and cubist painting. These works were at one time in the Museum of Modern Western Art in Moscow, but in 1948 they were divided between the National Museum of Fine Arts in Moscow and the Hermitage. *See* MOSCOW: MUSEUMS (NATIONAL MUSEUM OF FINE ARTS).

FRANKLIN R. DIDLAKE

Present collections of the Hermitage. There are now more than 2 million objects in the Hermitage, including primitive and modern art of the U.S.S.R., ancient and modern European art, and Eastern art. The section on Russian culture ranges from the 9th to the 20th century and includes examples of Russian silver such as the reliquary of Alexander Nevsky. The rooms devoted to primitive culture contain objects from prehistory and the famous Scythian collection of objects found in the Ukrainian tumuli (combs, gold vases, breastplates) and in the burial mounds of the Siberian Altai Valley.

The ancient art section presents Greek, Hellenistic (from the Crimea), and Roman art (especially fine portraits). The Oriental area encompasses Caucasian works and Central Asian arts (Bactrian, of Tamerlane's period), together with Egyptian, Byzantine, Sassanian, Chinese, Indian, and Japanese art.

The department of Western European art fills over 100 rooms. The Italian school from the 13th to the 18th century is represented by Leonardo (the *Benois Madonna* and a product of his workshop, the *Madonna Litta*), Raphael (the *Conestabile Madonna* and the *Holy Family*), and Michelangelo (sculpture of the *Crouching Boy*) as well as by Simone Martini, Fra Angelico, Filippo Lippi, Perugino, Giorgione (*Judith*), Titian (eight works including *Pope Paul III*, *Danaë*, *Flight into Egypt*, and *St. Sebastian*), Veronese, Salvator Rosa, Tiepolo, and Canaletto.

The Spanish school includes Morales, Ribera, Zurbarán, Murillo, Velázquez (among others, the portrait of Count Olivares) and one work by El Greco (*SS. Peter and Paul*). In the Flemish school there are forty-one canvases by Rubens (including *Perseus and Andromeda* and *Landscape with a Rainbow*) and many others by Van Dyck (*Charles I*), Jordaens, Teniers, Snyders, and Jan Breughel I. The Dutch collection has examples from all areas of Dutch painting; it contains two portraits by Frans Hals and works by minor masters, as well as twenty-five paintings by Rembrandt (for example, *The Sacrifice of Abraham*, *Flora*, *Danaë*, *The Prodigal Son*, and *Old Man in Red*) and many of his etchings.

Early Flemish painters include Rogier van der Weyden, the Master of Flémalle, Lucas van Leyden, Pourbus the Elder, and Pieter Brueghel the Elder. The German school shows paintings by Lucas Cranach the Elder (*Venus and Love*) and Holbein (*Portrait of Erasmus*) and engravings by Dürer. English works include paintings by Reynolds and Gainsborough and engravings by Hogarth.

The French collection is unique, especially in the impressionist area. The earlier schools are represented by Clouet, Vouet, Louis Le Nain, Callot, Poussin (for example, *Tancred and Erminia*), Claude Lorraine—an entire room, including *Morning (Evening) at the Port*—Rigaud, Largillière, Watteau (including *Savoyard* and *Caprice*), Pater, Lancret, Boucher, Nattier, Van Loo, Chardin (*Grace before Meat*), Greuze, Fragonard, and Hubert Robert. French furniture, jewelry, tapestries, and sculptures by Houdon and Rodin are also exhibited. French painting of the 19th and the early 20th century is represented by Delacroix (*Lion Hunt in Morocco*), Barye, Daubigny, Rousseau, Corot, Millet, Daumier, and Fromentin; and from the impressionists onward, by Monet (*Poppy Field*, *The Thames*), Pissarro, Sisley, Renoir (*Lady in Black*), Degas (*Toilette*),

Cézanne (*Mont Ste-Victoire, The Smoker*), Van Gogh, Gauguin (a whole room, including a *Nativity* and *Tahitian Woman with Flowers*), Bonnard, Henri Rousseau, Derain, Van Dongen, Marquet, Toulouse-Lautrec, Matisse (an entire room, including *La Desserte* and *La Danse*), and Picasso (Blue and cubist periods, including *Absinthe Drinker, Woman with a Fan*, and *Portrait of Vollard*).

BERNARD S. MYERS

LENKART (Lenker), JOHANNES, see LENCKER, JOHANNES.

LE NOTRE, ANDRE. French landscape architect (1613–1700). Trained by his father, whom he succeeded as first gardener of the Tuileries (1637), Le Nôtre is considered the greatest exponent of the formal French garden plan. He is responsible for the original gardens and parks of most of the famous 17th-century châteaux in France, including those of Vaux-le-Vicomte (begun 1655) and Versailles (begun 1662). Inventive and systematic, he was able to produce infinite variations and dramatic effects within a regular rational scheme of strict axiality. Water effects, theatrical perspectives, labyrinths, and grottoes surprised and enchanted the visitor to his gardens. Le Nôtre was a consultant to the Kings of England, Holland, Denmark, and Sweden, and thus his influence was felt throughout Europe. *See* VAUX-LE-VICOMTE, CHATEAU OF; VERSAILLES: PALACE.

BIBLIOGRAPHY. J. Guiffrey, *André Le Nostre*, Paris, 1912; E. de Ganay, *André Le Nostre, 1613–1700*, Paris, 1962.

LENZ, PETER. German architect, sculptor, and painter (b. Haigerloch, 1832; d. Beuron, 1928). Lenz studied sculpture at the Munich academy (1850–58). Opposing the naturalism of his day, he devoted himself to the revival of religious art based on a geometric canon of human proportions and form derived primarily from ancient Egyptian art. His theories were put into practice in his designs for the St. Maur Chapel, near Beuron, and its fresco decorations (1868–71). In 1878 Lenz took vows as a Benedictine monk, taking the name Desiderius. With Gabriel Wüger he founded the Beuron school of art in 1894 and directed the decoration of the Abbey of Montecassino (tower frescoes, 1876–80 and 1885–93; crypt mosaics, 1898–1913). Although Lenz's theories led to a rather rigid and dogmatic art, they had an important influence on such artists as Jan Verkade, who worked at Beuron, and the symbolist painter Paul Sérusier.

BIBLIOGRAPHY. M. Dreesbach, "P. Desiderius Lenz von Beuron: Theorie und Werk," *Studien und Mitteilungen zur Geschichte des Benediktinerordens und seiner Zweige*, LXVIII, 1957.

LEOCHARES. Greek sculptor (fl. ca. 370–325 B.C.). He is known to have worked on the frieze of the Mausoleum of Halicarnassus and later to have executed commissions for Philip of Macedon and Alexander the Great. Among the Roman copies possibly reflecting his work, the most often mentioned are the *Zeus and Ganymede* and the *Apollo Belvedere*, both in the Vatican Museums.

BIBLIOGRAPHY. G. Richter, *The Sculpture and Sculptors of the Greeks*, rev. ed., New Haven, 1957.

LEON. Town situated on the left bank of the Bernesga River in Spain. It is the capital of the province of León

and the seat of a bishop. The name León goes back to "Legio Septima Gemina," the 7th legion of Augustus. After Roman rule it belonged to the Goths. It was taken by the Moors in the early 8th century and liberated in the 10th, though it was for a short time recaptured by the great Moorish general al-Mansur. Ordoño II, son of King Alfonso of Asturias, chose León as his capital. The crowns of León and Castile were joined by Ferdinand I of Castile in the 11th century.

The Cathedral of S. María la Regla (known as "the lantern") was begun on the site of some still-existing Roman ramparts in 1199 and building continued until the 16th century. It is splendidly decorated. The Church of S. Isidoro is a fine example of Spanish Romanesque. It was founded in the 10th century and rebuilt by Ferdinand I. It contains the Panteon de los Reyes (Pantheon of the kings and queens of León), which is decorated with Romanesque murals. León's other main monument is the Monastery of S. Marcos. It was originally constructed in the 12th century as a hospital and hostelry but was rebuilt by Juan de Badajoz in the Plateresque style (1513–49) to serve as the headquarters for the Order of St. James. *See* SAN ISIDORO.

HELLMUT WOHL

LEONARDESQUE. General term used to describe a style resembling that of Leonardo da Vinci. The main features are an extremely painterly, even smoky, technique and a love of the mysterious.

LEONARDI, LEONCILLO, see LEONCILLO.

LEONARDO, JUSEPE. Spanish painter (b. ca. 1600; d. Saragossa, 1656). Influenced by the Carduchos and by Caxés, Leonardo was a follower of Velázquez at the royal court in Madrid until his mental collapse in 1648. His large battle scenes and religious paintings, composed in brilliant colors and dynamic rhythms played out into deep space, are more obviously baroque than those of his famous mentor.

LEONARDO DA BESOZZO. Italian painter (fl. 1421–88). After working with his father, Michelino da Besozzo, at Milan Cathedral in 1421, Leonardo apparently spent most of the rest of his career in Naples. His fresco series in S. Giovanni a Carbonara probably dates from after 1433. As a court painter of King Alfonso I in 1454, he designed coats of arms and banners as well as frescoes for the "room of angels" in the Castel Nuovo (1458). He seems to have been active in Naples as late as 1488. The early fresco cycle, on which he was assisted by Perinetto da Benevento, depicts scenes from the lives of the Virgin and of the hermits of the Augustinian order. The northern Gothic linearity of his father's art is less pronounced and the figures are less elongated, although they have the courtly slightness of northern art. The anecdotal quality and playful use of architectural forms and space in the *Nativity of the Virgin* are indications of Leonardo's connection with the miniaturist traditions of Lombard art.

BIBLIOGRAPHY. R. van Marle, *The Development of the Italian Schools of Painting*, vol. 7, The Hague, 1926.

LEONARDO DA VINCI. Italian painter, sculptor, architect, engineer, and scientist of the Florentine school (b. Vinci, near Florence, Apr. 15, 1452; d. Amboise, May 2, 1519). Leonardo was the most original of the universal men of the Renaissance. His scientific investigations, preserved in his *Notebooks*, were, like his art, part of a quest for understanding the principles that underlie the processes of nature. The most significant fact about Leonardo's achievement is this unity of his scientific and artistic work.

Leonardo da Vinci was the illegitimate son of the notary Ser Piero da Vinci, in whose house he grew up. At the age of fifteen he was apprenticed to Andrea del Verrocchio, the most respected master in Florence at that time. Leonardo completed his apprenticeship and was registered in the painters' guild in 1472, but he remained in Verrocchio's studio until 1476. Although his training had been chiefly in painting and sculpture, he was also beginning to work as an inventor and festival designer. Leonardo's earliest extant works are from this period: the angel's head and the distant landscape in Verrocchio's *Baptism of Christ* (ca. 1473) and the drawing of a *Landscape* (1473; Florence, Uffizi). Also from this period are four pictures that are at least in part from Leonardo's hand: the *Annunciation* (Uffizi), *Annunciation* (Paris, Louvre), *Madonna with the Vase* (Munich, Bavarian State Picture Galleries, Old Pinacothek), and *Dreyfus Madonna* (Washington, D.C., National Gallery).

Leonardo set up his own studio about 1477/78. A number of works painted during the next five years have survived: the unfinished *St. Jerome* (ca. 1480; Rome, Vatican Museums); *Benois Madonna*, begun in 1478 but only completed after 1500 with the help of an assistant (Leningrad, Hermitage); the portrait *Ginevra de' Benci* (Washington, D.C., National Gallery); and the *Adoration of the Magi*, begun in 1481 for the Monastery of S. Donato a Scopeto near Florence, but not carried past the underpainting when Leonardo left for Milan in 1482 (Uffizi). He was summoned to Milan by Duke Lodovico Sforza (Il Moro) as the result of a petition in which he offered his services chiefly as a civil and military engineer, and he remained in his service until the Duke was exiled by the French in 1499.

Of the many and varied commissions that Leonardo executed in Milan, only a few remain: the *Madonna of the Rocks*, begun in 1483 (Louvre; the version in London, National Gallery, is a later copy); the fresco of the *Last Supper* in the refectory of S. Maria delle Grazie (1495–97); the fresco decoration in the Sala delle Asse of the Sforza Castle (1498); the *Portrait of a Musician* (Milan, Ambrosian Picture Gallery); the portrait of one of Duke Lodovico's mistresses, Cecilia Gallerani (known as the *Lady with the Ermine*; Cracow, Czartoryski Museum); and the *Madonna Litta*, which is, however, a product of Leonardo's workshop (Hermitage). Among many drawings of uncompleted Milanese projects the most important are those of a monumental equestrian bronze statue of Francesco Sforza. A life-size clay model of the horse from that statue was shown in 1493 at the wedding of Emperor Maximilian to Bianca Maria Sforza, but neither the figure of the rider nor the casting of the whole work was ever completed. Leonardo's architectural projects of these years—none of which was built—are also documented only in drawings (including studies for various types of centralized, domed churches) and notes. In addition to these activities Leonardo worked as a designer and director of court festivals, such as pageants, tournaments, and theater productions.

In Milan Leonardo began his first systematic scientific studies, based on practical experience, in anatomy, botany, mathematics, physics, and mechanics, and wrote most of his *Treatise on Painting*. He also collaborated with the mathematician Luca Pacioli, for whose work on proportions he drew the schemes of stereometric and geometric figures. With the fall of the Duke in 1499 Leonardo left Milan and, by way of Mantua and Venice (where he made a plan of defenses against the Turks), returned to Florence in April, 1500.

In that year he began the painting *St. Anne with the Madonna and Child* (completed in 1507, Louvre; cartoon in London, National Gallery). In 1502 he entered the service of Cesare Borgia, the general in command of the papal forces, as chief inspector of fortifications and military engineer. Leonardo's maps and city plans, which anticipate the development of modern cartography, were made during his travels in this capacity. In 1503 he was once again in Florence, working as a military engineer in the war against Pisa and developing a scheme for diverting the Arno River so as to deprive Pisa of her means of access. In the same year Leonardo was commissioned to paint a mural in the council chamber of the Palazzo della Signoria of a famous episode from the history of Florence. He chose the Battle of Anghiari (1441)—specifically, the battle for the enemy standard. The cartoon had been completed and the fresco begun when Leonardo left Florence in 1506. The unfinished mural was already deteriorating because of an artificial drying process and was later painted over. The cartoon of the central portion of the composition has survived in Rubens's splendid copy.

During these years Leonardo also painted the *Mona Lisa* (Louvre) and worked on a few pictures that are known only from copies, such as the *Leda*. His chief interest was his scientific investigations. He carried out dissections, made exhaustive studies of the flight of birds (documented in his treatise on this subject), and began to organize his notes with a view to preparing a comprehensive exposition of the mechanical forces in nature.

In June, 1506, Leonardo returned to Milan. He remained there as artistic advisor to the French governor, Charles d'Amboise, until 1513, with the exception of a stay in Florence during the winter of 1507–08. In Milan Leonardo drew up plans for a residential palace for the governor. He also designed projects for the tomb of Prince Gian Giacomo Trivulzio in the form of an equestrian monument. But Leonardo's most important work during the second Milanese period was his anatomical studies, which became the focus of his artistic gifts, and his researches in inorganic nature—geology, geophysics, and hydrology.

In 1513 Leonardo went to Rome, where he had a studio in the Belvedere of the Vatican. Virtually nothing of his activity there is known, except for the entries and drawings on anatomy, mathematics, and mechanics that fill his notebooks. Leonardo's last painting, *St. John the Baptist* (Louvre), dates from this time. In 1517 he left Rome to become *premier peintre, architecte, et mechanicien* to Francis I

at his court at Amboise. No paintings from these last years have come down to us. Leonardo designed decorations and costumes for court festivals and continued his scientific work. The drawings of the *Visions of the End of the World* (often called the *Deluge*; Windsor Castle, Royal Library), with their all-engulfing formations of spirals, were probably done at this time. Leonardo died at Amboise.

In painting Leonardo was the founder of the classic style of the High Renaissance. Working in an oil medium, he extended the range of values to include the whole scale of dark to light by means of subtle, fluid gradations—the technique known as chiaroscuro. The space of his pictures and many of his drawings seems to be filled with light and atmosphere so that the edges of figures and objects are slightly blurred. In this way Leonardo reduced the detailed definition of form of the 15th-century style and achieved, at the same time, a far greater sense of organic life.

Leonardo's compositions are simple and grand; they are not based on the alignment of a number of planes in linear perspective, as in 15th-century compositions, but on forms radiating outward from the center or spiraling around an inner core. The most characteristic example of this new compositional concept is the *contrapposto* posture of figures, which became one of the hallmarks of the classic style. Leonardo's influence was particularly strong in the Milanese school, but beyond this, it reshaped, as that of few individuals has, the whole course of painting in Europe.

BIBLIOGRAPHY. E. Verga, *Bibliografia vinciana*, 2 vols., Bologna, 1931; E. MacCurdy, ed., *The Notebooks of Leonardo da Vinci*, 2 vols., London, 1938; J. P. Richter, ed., *The Literary Works of Leonardo da Vinci*, 2d ed., 2 vols., London, 1939; A. E. Popham, *The Drawings of Leonardo da Vinci*, 2d ed., London, 1949; K. Clark, *Leonardo da Vinci*, 2d ed., Cambridge, 1952; L. H. Heydenreich, *Leonardo da Vinci*, 2 vols., New York, 1954.

HELLMUT WOHL

LEONARDO DI SER GIOVANNI.

Florentine goldsmith (fl. 2d half of 14th cent.). A student of Francesco di Niccolò, Leonardo executed with him the left wing of the *S. Jacopo Altar* of Pistoia Cathedral. The right wing of the altar, which depicts the life of St. James, was done by Leonardo alone. In 1366 he was commissioned, along with Betto di Geri, to execute a silver altar frontal (*dossale*) for the Baptistery in Florence. The Florence *dossale*, like the altar in Pistoia, reveals the strong influence of Andrea Pisano.

BIBLIOGRAPHY. O. H. Giglioli, *Pistoia nelle sue opere d'arte*, Florence, 1904; A. Venturi, *Storia dell'arte italiana*, vol. 4, Milan, 1906.

LEONARD OF LIMOGES, ST.

Monk (6th cent.). He was born of a noble Frankish family near Orléans, according to an 11th-century source, and spent his youth at the court of King Clovis. Educated and won to the monastic life by St. Remi, St. Leonard founded the monastery of Noblac near Limoges on land given him by an unidentified king because he had saved the life of the queen in childbirth. The king gave him the privilege to free prisoners. His attributes are prisoner's chains, monk's robe, and deacon's dalmatic. His feast is November 6.

See also SAINTS IN ART.

LEONCILLO (Leoncillo Leonardi).

Italian sculptor (1915–). Born in Spoleto, Leoncillo studied at the Academy of Art in Perugia and then directed a ceramics workshop in Umbertide. Since 1942 he has been living in Rome, where he teaches ceramics at the Academy of Fine Arts. His early work was expressionistic, but his recent work is more geometric and abstract.

BIBLIOGRAPHY. M. Seuphor, *The Sculpture of This Century*, New York, 1960.

LEONI, LEONE.

Italian sculptor, goldsmith, and medalist (b. Menaggio, 1509; d. Milan, 1590). From 1542 to 1545 and from 1550 to 1590 he was the master moneyer of Milan. In 1516 he collaborated on Mantuan décor for the marriage of Francesco Gonzaga and Eleanor of Austria. In the service of Charles V, he signed his medals (1537–61) "sculptor of Caesar." Leoni was the most important medalist in 16th-century Italy. His statue of *Charles V Trampling Fraud* (1549–64; Madrid, Prado) was the first nude heroic statue since antiquity. His style is that of manneristic slickness with attention to all details. He was the father of Pompeo Leoni.

BIBLIOGRAPHY. E. Plon, *Leoni ... et Pompeo Leoni ...*, Paris, 1887; A. Venturi, *Storia dell'arte italiana*, vol. 10, pt. 3, Milan, 1937.

LEONI, POMPEO.

Italian sculptor and medalist (b. ca. 1533; d. Madrid, 1608). He was the son and pupil of

Pompeo Leoni, *Countess of Lerma*, for the mortuary monument in St. Paul, Valladolid. Provincial Museum, Valladolid.

Leonardo da Vinci, *Ginevra de' Benci*. National Gallery, Washington, D.C.

Leonid, *Shrimp Fishermen*, 1937. Museum of Modern Art, New York (Gift of James Thrall Soby).

Leone Leoni. About 1556 Pompeo went to Spain to implement his father's work, although often he would supply the casting that his father would chisel, gild, and assemble. In 1570 Pompeo executed a colossal statue for the décor of the wedding of Philip II and Anne of Austria. From 1579 to 1591 he was intermittently at work on his masterpiece, the main altar of the church at the Escorial, including some fifteen statues of saints and twelve statues of apostles, of gilded and enameled bronze. From 1576 to 1587 he executed the tomb of the Inquisitor Don Fernando de Valdés. He worked on the Hapsburg tomb statues flanking the main altar at the Escorial from 1593 to 1598. His medals are weak imitations of his father's, and his reputation lies in his figural statues.

BIBLIOGRAPHY. E. Plon, *Leoni . . . et Pompeo Leoni . . .*, Paris, 1887; A. Venturi, *Storia dell'arte italiana*, vol. 10, pt. 3, Milan, 1937; B. G. Proske, *Pompeo Leoni*, New York, 1951.

LEONID (Leonid Berman). Russian-American painter (1896–   ). The brother of the painter Eugène Berman, Leonid was born in St. Petersburg. He went to Paris in 1919 and studied at the Académie Ranson. He exhibited in Paris with the neoromantic group in 1926, and his early work was influenced by the dark, moody atmosphere of neoromanticism. By 1930 he had found his characteristic subjects, the coasts and harbors of Europe (later the northeastern United States as well), which he painted with rich color and a strongly poetic feeling for the deep spaces of sky, shore, and sea bathed in sunlight and atmosphere, for example, *Mussel Gatherers at High Tide* (1937; New York, Museum of Modern Art).

BIBLIOGRAPHY. J. T. Soby, *After Picasso*, Hartford, 1935.

LEONTOPOLIS, *see* YAHUDIYAH.

LEOPARDI, ALESSANDRO. Italian goldsmith, bronze caster, architect, and sculptor (fl. 1482–1522/23). He is first mentioned in 1482 in Venice. Listed at various times as a mint master in the service of the Venetian Republic, he gained particular fame for the casting and finishing of the bronze equestrian monument of Bartolommeo Colleoni (1490–95) in the Campo SS. Giovanni e Paolo, Venice, modeled by Andrea del Verrocchio and signed by Leopardi, who in consequence was credited with the entire monument. To Leopardi are due the design of the base of the monument; probably the design as well as the casting of the signed bronze pedestals of three flagstaffs (1505–

Nicolas-Bernard Lépicié, *Fanchon Rising*. Formerly Wildenstein Collection, now Museum of Saint-Omer, France.

7), richly decorated in the manner of Riccio, in the Piazza . Marco, Venice; and the project (1522) for S. Giustina, Padua.

LEPAUTRE, ANTOINE. French architect (1621–81). He worked in Paris. His most famous building is the Hôtel de Beauvais (1652–55), remarkable for its ingenious arrangement on an irregular site. His published engravings of bold and fantastic projects for country and town houses show him to be the most baroque of French 17th-century architects.

BIBLIOGRAPHY. L. Hautecoeur, *Histoire de l'architecture classique n France*, vol. 2, Paris, 1948.

LEPAUTRE, JEAN. French architect and ornamental engraver (b. Paris, 1617; d. there, 1682). Prominent in the creation of ornament designs for the French baroque Louis XIV style, Lepautre drew heavily from the Italian baroque, which he had studied in Italy. His inventiveness embraced all aspects of church and residential decoration, which were codified by Jombert in *Oeuvres d'architecture de Jean Lepautre* (1751).

BIBLIOGRAPHY. P. Jessen, *Der Ornamentstich*, Berlin, 1920.

LEPCIS MAGNA, *see* LEPTIS MAGNA.

LEPERE, AUGUSTE-LOUIS. French painter, graphic artist, and illustrator (b. Paris, 1849; d. Domme, 1918). He was the son of the sculptor François Lepère. In 1862 Auguste Lepère entered the atelier of the engraver Burn Smeeton, to whom he owes the general character of his style. He made original woodcuts—excellent architecture pages—and also made reproductions of Constable, Watelin, Leclerc, Daumier, and Doré. Lepère illustrated magazines (*La Revue Illustrée*) and books (*Le Journal*, by Clovis Hugues; *Paysages parisiens*, by E. Goudeau). His few known paintings were in the Luxembourg Museum, Paris.

BIBLIOGRAPHY. Clément-Janin, "Quelques graveurs de Paris," *La Renaissance de l'Art Français et des Industries de Luxe*, III, October, 1920.

LEPICIE, BERNARD-FRANCOIS. French engraver and writer on art (b. Paris, 1698; d. there, 1755). He was a pupil of Duchange and Mariette. Best known for his engravings after the works of other artists, Lépicié worked in England for a while making copies of the Raphael cartoons at Hampton Court. In 1740 he became an academician, and between 1737 and 1748 he exhibited both paintings and engravings in the Salons. Works by such contemporary artists as De Largillière, Rigaud, and particularly Chardin provided the basis for Lépicié's *oeuvre*, although he also made engravings after Rembrandt, Raphael, Teniers, and other older masters. As secretary and historiographer to the Royal Academy, Lépicié compiled a *catalogue raisonné* of the king's collection and wrote *Vues des premiers peintres du roy depuis Lebrun*. He was the father of Nicolas-Bernard Lépicié.

LEPICIE, NICOLAS-BERNARD. French painter of history, genre, and portraits (b. Paris, 1735; d. there, 1784). He studied with his father, Bernard Lépicié, an engraver, and later with Charles van Loo, who had no influence on his art. Lépicié exhibited in the Salons of 1764 and 1767 and became a member of the Royal Academy as a history painter in 1769, Painter to the King, and a professor in

1777. *Fanchon Rising* (Museum of Saint-Omer) reflects the artistic sensibility of Chardin in the delicate handling of light and color, particularly evident in his portraits and genre scenes of women and children. Lépicié specialized in intimate bourgeois subjects. A.-C.-H. Vernet was his foremost pupil.

BIBLIOGRAPHY. P. Gaston-Dreyfus and F. Ingersoll-Smouse, *Catalogue raisonné de l'oeuvre peint et dessiné de Nicolas-Bernard Lépicié (1735-1784)*, Paris, 1923.

LE PRINCE, JEAN-BAPTISTE. French painter and etcher (b. Metz, 1734; d. St-Denis-du-Port, 1781). Le Prince, whose greatest accomplishment was the discovery of an etching aquatint process, was sought after as a skilled practitioner of rococo decorative painting and etching during his lifetime. After studying with Boucher and Vien, Le Prince went to Italy in 1754. His early fame is attested to by a commission in 1757 from the Russian czar to decorate the ceilings of the palace in St. Petersburg. In 1763 he returned to Paris and two years later was made a member of the Royal Academy. His most popular works were and are rococo-style etched genre scenes, particularly from Russian folk life, for example, *The Oven* (1770), *Russian Dance*, and *The Traveler*. Le Prince is represented in many French museums by paintings and graphic works.

BIBLIOGRAPHY. L. Réau, "L'Exotisme russe dans l'oeuvre de J.-B. Le Prince," *Gazette des Beaux Arts*, LXIII, 1921.

Leptis Magna. Villa of the Nile, personification of the Nile.

Les Eyzies. Venus of Laussel, Upper Paleolithic period.

LEPTIS MAGNA (Lepcis Magna; Lebda). Ancient city in western Libya. It has imposing ruins of buildings erected under Roman imperial patronage. To the 1st century belong the Forum Vetus and its basilica; a market and a theater, the gifts of a wealthy citizen; temples dedicated to Roma and Augustus, to Liber Pater, to Magna Mater, and to Ceres; and a structure called the Calcidium whose function is as yet unknown.

The introduction of marble from the East in place of local stone worked a fundamental change in the architecture. The Baths of Hadrian (A.D. 127), which have a palaestra and a portico, reveal sophisticated planning and taste. The balanced arrangement within the area of the great Severan Forum, of the basilica, and of the temple is a superb example of Roman imperial monumentalization. Much of this latter work dates from the time of Septimius Severus (r. 193–211), who was born in Leptis.

Unquestionably, however, there is conspicuous evidence of Near Eastern influences in the sculptured decoration of the basilica. Similar Eastern influence is noted in another Severan monument, the quadrifrons arch.

Other important ruins include the harbor with its temple and lighthouse, a monumental street, a large circus with the site of an amphitheater, two nymphaea, the beautifully preserved Hunting Baths, several churches, and what may be a synagogue. The Archaeological Museum in Tripoli contains numerous smaller finds. (See illustration.)

BIBLIOGRAPHY. J. B. Ward Perkins, "Severan Art and Architecture at Leptis Magna," *Journal of Roman Studies,* XXXVIII, 1948; J. B. Ward Perkins, J. M. C. Toynbee, and R. Fraser, *The Hunting Baths at Lepcis Magna,* Oxford, 1949; J. B. Ward Perkins, "The Arch of Septimius Severus at Lepcis Magna," *Archaeology,* IV, 1951; K. D. Mathews and A. W. Cook, *Cities in the Sand,* Philadelphia, 1957; G. C. Picard, "Influences étrangères et originalité dans l'art de l'Afrique romaine sous les Antonins et les Sévères," *Antike Kunst,* V, 1, 1962.   BLUMA L. TRELL

LE PUY CATHEDRAL. One of the important Romanesque churches of the pilgrimage route in France, dating from the late 11th and the early 12th century. The Cathedral is built of native black and red granite, and the striking color striations of its ashlar courses point to strong Moorish influences.

The Cathedral has a simple cruciform plan but is especially interesting for the disposition of its elements and its decorative motifs. The east end terminates in a beautifully proportioned, staged tower that dominates the building. The crossing is capped by an octagonal vaulted lantern; the older portion of the nave (two bays) is covered with octagonal domical vaults that rest on squinches. The newer part of the nave, built out over the slope of the hilltop site, terminate in an impressive open porch. The Moorish elements (from Spain) are seen in the frequent use of cusped arches around portals and windows.

LERAMBERT, HENRI. French painter (d. 1609). Listed as "peintre ordinaire du Roy" and "peintre pour les tapisseries," Lerambert worked at Fontainebleau (1568–70) as well as in Paris. A collection of drawings and cartoons for tapestries attributed to Lerambert and preserved in the Cabinet des Etampes show him to be one of the French mannerists. A *Coriolanus* and an *Artemisia* series are attributed to him.

LERCH, NICOLAUS, *see* GERHARD, NIKOLAUS, FROM LEYDEN.

LERIDA CATHEDRAL. Spanish Cathedral, partially destroyed in 1717 and used as a military citadel until 1948. The Old Cathedral (Seo Antigua) is a handsome monument of part Romanesque and part Gothic design. Begun by Pedro of Aragon in 1203, it was consecrated in 1278. The octagon over the crossing is essentially Romanesque, and the single campanile on the west front dates from the early 15th century. The Gothic cloister, which serves as an atrium, has exceptionally fine tracery. The doorway leading from the cloister into the nave is Romanesque in style and very delicately carved; both interlacing arches and zigzag designs are used. A large number of fine sculptures have been found in the fortifications, which were built in 1717 from stones removed from the Old Cathedral.

BIBLIOGRAPHY. G. E. Street, *Some Account of Gothic Architecture in Spain,* London, 1914.

LE ROMAIN, *see* MIGNARD, PIERRE.

LE ROUX, ROLAND (Roullant). French sculptor (d. Rouen, 1527). The pupil of his uncle, Jacques Le Roux, Roland succeeded him as head executant of work on the Rouen Cathedral, where he did some 261 statues and constructed the grand portal (1509–30). Roland Le Roux was the architect of the Bureau of Finances (1510) and of the Palace of Justice, and worked on the tomb of Cardinal Georges d'Amboise (1520–25). He is one of the significant figures of the Proto-Renaissance style in France. *See* ROUEN.

BIBLIOGRAPHY. M. Vachon, *La Renaissance française,* Paris, 1910

LE ROY, PIERRE FRANCOIS. Belgian sculptor (b. Namur, 1739; d. Brussels, 1812). He studied with Laurent Delvaux in Nivelles, at the Royal Academy in Paris, and with Bridan, with whom he also collaborated and traveled to Italy. Upon his return to Belgium Le Roy worked for Prince Charles of Lorraine, the Viennese court, and churches and convents in his native country. Much of his work, particularly the portraits and allegorical figures, is harshly classical. His religious figures are more baroque in their emphasis on dynamic movement and expression.

BIBLIOGRAPHY. M. Devigne, *Laurent Delvaux et ses élèves*, Brussels, 1928.

LESCAZE, WILLIAM, *see* HOWE AND LESCAZE.

LESCOT, PIERRE. French architect (b. 1515; d. Paris, 1578). He was a leading architect of his time. Essentially decorative in his approach, he collaborated in all his major works with the sculptor Jean Goujon. The Louvre Pavilion of Henry II, commissioned in 1546, is his major surviving monument. His Hôtel de Carnavalet in Paris, the only remaining town house of this phase of French architecture, has been largely rebuilt. *See* GOUJON, JEAN; LOUVRE PALACE, PARIS; PARIS: MUSEUMS (CARNAVALET MUSEUM).

BIBLIOGRAPHY. A. Blunt, *Art and Architecture in France, 1500–1700*, Baltimore, 1954.

LESENE. Pilaster without a base or capital, often called "pilaster strip." Lesenes are found on Anglo-Saxon and early Romanesque churches. They may have functioned as bonding courses in the rubble walls of the Anglo-Saxon structures, where they shored up long expanses of wall and prevented plaster from cracking and spreading. They are believed to have been merely decorative in Romanesque structures. *See* PILASTER.

LES EYZIES. Village situated on the Beune River, a tributary of the Vézère, in the Department of the Dordogne, southwestern France. Les Eyzies lies in the heart of one of the richest regions for the archaeology of the Paleolithic period. Within the village itself there are two caves important for Upper Paleolithic finds. The type site for the Magdalenian period, La Madeleine, lies only a short distance away, as does the famous site of Cro-Magnon, important for the skeletal finds of Cro-Magnon man. Nearby are the two famous sites of Laugerie-Basse, significant for its Magdalenian sequence, and Laugerie-Haute, with its classic sequence of Mousterian, Aurignacian, Solutrean, and Magdalenian. Other caverns of the region of Les Eyzies include Font-de-Gaume, La Mouthe, and Cap Blanc, important for their paintings. *See* MADELEINE, GROTTE DE LA.

LESLIE, CHARLES ROBERT. English-American portrait and narrative painter (b. London, 1794; d. there, 1859). His parents were American, and the family returned to Philadelphia in 1799. Leslie later received instruction in painting from Thomas Sully. He returned to England in 1811, was admitted as a student at the Royal Academy schools, and remained in London with the exception of a short period as a teacher at West Point Academy (1833). He was a skillful painter of fairly small-scale costume pieces that were mostly illustrations to humorous scenes from Shakespeare, Cervantes, Molière, and other familiar writers. In 1838 he was commissioned to paint the large *Queen Victoria Receiving the Sacrament at Her Coronation* (Buckingham Palace). He formed friendships with Washington Irving, Constable, Landseer, and Washington Allston, and was a frequent guest of Lord Egremont at Petworth. His *Memoirs of John Constable* (1843) and *Autobiographical Recollections* (ed. Tom Taylor, 1865) are valuable source books.

Charles Robert Leslie, *Queen Victoria Receiving the Sacrament at Her Coronation*. Buckingham Palace, London.

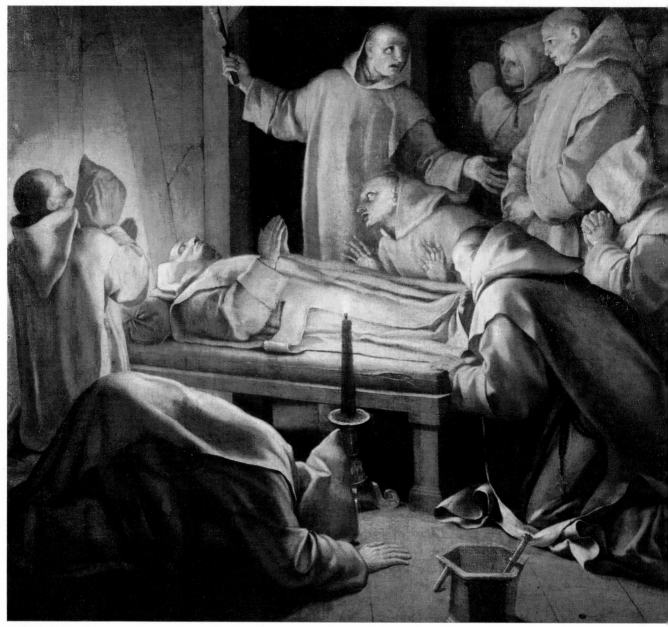

Eustache Le Sueur, *The Death of St. Bruno*, from the *Life of St. Bruno* series, 1648–50. Louvre, Paris.

LESSER PROPYLON, ELEUSIS. Monumental north gate to the sanctuary of Eleusis, Greece. It was built by Appius Claudius Pulcher about 50 B.C. Constructed of Pentelic marble, it consisted of a paved forecourt that was flanked by two walls lined with Ionic columns carrying an entablature and by a broad doorway; its roof was supported on the inside by two caryatids and on the outside by two Corinthian columns with hexagonal abaci that supported a mixed Doric-Ionic entablature decorated with emblems of Demeter.

BIBLIOGRAPHY. E. Mylonas, *Eleusis and the Eleusinian Mysteries*, Princeton, 1961.

LESSING, KARL FRIEDRICH. German painter and engraver (b. Breslau, 1808; d. Karlsruhe, 1880). Lessing studied in Berlin and Düsseldorf. He painted landscapes and dramatic historical and religious scenes in a realistic style.

LE SUEUR, EUSTACHE. French painter of religious and mythological scenes and portraits (b. Paris, 1616; d. there, 1655). He was the son of a wood carver. Though he never went to Rome, he enjoyed throughout the 18th century in France a prestige almost equal to that of Poussin. He was one of the twelve founders of the Royal Academy in 1648, and became its rector. His development has four phases.

Youth (1637–45). About the age of sixteen he entered the studio of Simon Vouet. By 1637 he had developed sufficiently to assume a commission made to his master for a series of tapestry cartoons (*The Dream of Poliphilis*) of which three survive. The firmer modeling and more rigid design of his work of the early 1640s show him to be more classical than his master (*Presentation of the Virgin*, 1640–45; Leningrad, Hermitage). During this time he functioned independently as a portraitist (*Portrait of Presumed M. Albert*, Guéret, Municipal Museum), though the influence of Jacques Blanchard is apparent.

Early maturity (1646–49). His first major commission was for decorative works in the Cabinet de l'Amour of the Hôtel Lambert (1646–47). These panels, illustrating the story of Cupid, manifest a classical calm more assured than that of Vouet. This no doubt reflects the digested influence of Poussin. Poussin's drawing for a *Holy Family* (Berkshire, Windsor Castle) was apparently the basis for three painted variations by Le Sueur (Chantilly, Condé Museum; London, National Gallery; Pavlovsk). In the Cabinet des Muses of the Hôtel Lambert (1647–49) the joint influence of Poussin and particularly Raphael, whom Le Sueur knew only through drawings and engravings, is obvious. The *Three Muses* panel (Paris, Louvre) reflects the easy grandeur of form typical of Raphael; the composition also especially indicates Le Sueur's knowledge of the *Parnassus* in the Stanza della Segnatura in the Vatican, Rome. Black-and-white chalk drawings on gray paper (*The Muse Erato* and *Study of a Man Standing*, both Paris, Ecole des Beaux-Arts) confirm this source.

Mature style (1648–50). Le Sueur's mature style is demonstrated in the *Life of St. Bruno* series, which was executed for the Charterhouse of Paris and is now in the Louvre, except for *St. Bruno Praying*, a separate commission, which is in Berlin (former State Museums). In these his personal style, perhaps best qualified as a French reflection of the international baroque style, appears. Its elements include a genuine affinity with Carthusian introspection (as in the works of Zurbarán), Poussin's statuesque stability, and Raphael's simple grandeur. This synchronization of styles also makes summary use of Carracci interior chiaroscuro.

Last years (1650–55). His last years demonstrate a submergence of individuality into the style of Raphael's tapestry cartoons. *St. Paul at Ephesus* (1649; Louvre) introduces a whole series of borrowings, and only the *Mass of St. Martin* sustains his mature conviction. Le Sueur's career served as an example to academic students in the future: the study of the antique, Raphael, and Poussin. Other works are found at Grenoble, La Rochelle, Le Mans, Marseilles, Nantes, Rouen, and Tours.

BIBLIOGRAPHY. G. Rouchès, *Eustache Le Sueur*, Paris, 1923.

GEORGE V. GALLENKAMP

LE SUEUR, HUBERT. French sculptor (fl. 1610–51). Le Sueur was born in France, where he was *Sculpteur du Roi* by 1610 and was noted as a bronze caster. But he is known almost exclusively for the works he executed in England between about 1626 and 1643. In numerous tomb monuments, such as those of Sir Thomas Richardson (1635) and Lady Cottington (ca. 1634) in Westminster Abbey, he introduced complicated allegorical ensembles. He also introduced the portrait bust on a pedestal to England. He did many such busts of Charles I as well as an equestrian monument of that king at Charing Cross, London (ca. 1633), in a slick, almost schematic style.

BIBLIOGRAPHY. M. Whinney, *Sculpture in Britain, 1530–1830*, Baltimore, 1964.

LESUEUR, JACQUES-PHILIPPE. French sculptor (b. Paris, 1757; d. there, 1830). Lesueur won the Prix de Rome in 1780 and received most of the honors of the Academy throughout his life. He executed the *Peace of Pressburg* for the Arc de Triomphe du Carrousel and other official commissions, as well as portraits and mythological works.

LESUEUR, JEAN BAPTISTE. French architect (1794–1883). He worked in Paris. A pupil of Percier and Fontaine, Lesueur added a pronounced Italianate flavor to his classical training. Such designs as the Vincennes parish church, in the early Italian Renaissance style, illustrate the growing tendency toward elaboration of his earlier classic style.

BIBLIOGRAPHY. L. Hautecoeur, *Histoire de l'architecture classique en France*, vol. 6, Paris, 1955.

LESYNGHAM, ROBERT. English architect (fl. 2d half of 14th cent.). He was associated with building works at Gloucester and Exeter Cathedrals. He probably designed the Exeter cloisters (1377–78), including the upper part of the west front, the screen, and the east window (1389–90). The style suggests his responsibility for the earlier Gloucester cloisters.

LE TAVERNIER, JEAN, I. Flemish illuminator (d. after 1477). He resided in Oudenaarde, was recorded in Tournai, and worked for Philip the Good (1450–60). Influenced by Van der Weyden, he often worked in grisaille.

BIBLIOGRAPHY. F. Winkler, *Die flämische Buchmalerei des XV. und XVI. Jahrhunderts*, Leipzig, 1925.

LETELLIER, GUILLAUME. French architect (d. 1484). Letellier directed the building of the Church of Notre-Dame at Caudebec-en-Caux from 1453 on. He designed the nave, the choir with ambulatory and chapels, and the Chapel of the Virgin, all in the Flamboyant style.

LETHABY, WILLIAM RICHARD. English architect (1857–1931). He was a pioneer in the teaching of industrial design. His architectural works are few (for example, Avon Tyrrell in Hampshire, 1891). As the first principal of the Central School of Arts and Crafts (1896), he made it one of the best-organized contemporary art schools.

BIBLIOGRAPHY. R. Blomfield, "W. R. Lethaby, an Impression and a Tribute," *Royal Institute of British Architects, Journal*, XXXIX, February 20, 1932.

LETI, *see* OCEANIC ART (INDONESIA).

LETTERINI (Litterini), BARTOLOMMEO. Italian religious and historical painter (b. Venice, 1699; d. there, 1745). He was a pupil and follower of his father, Agostino, and one of the more successful imitators of Titian. Bartolommeo excelled especially in rendering Madonnas with great sensitivity, sweetness, and sentiment.

LEU, HANS, THE YOUNGER. Swiss painter (ca. 1490–1531). Leu was trained in the late Gothic tradition by his father, Hans Leu the Elder, and broadened his outlook during his travels through Germany (1507–13), where he became acquainted with Nikolaus Manuel-Deutsch, Hans Baldung-Grien, and Albrecht Dürer. Although Leu was

Emanuel Leutze, *Washington Crossing the Delaware*. Art Gallery, Bremen. A widely popular painting from American history.

the leading painter of his time in Zurich, few of his works remain. The influence of the Danube school is evident in the romantic landscape settings of such paintings as *St. Jerome in the Wilderness* (1515) and *Orpheus and the Animals* (1519), both in the Public Art Collections, Basel.

LEUCKER (Leuckhardt), JOHANNES, *see* LENCKER, JOHANNES.

LEUFERT, GERD. Venezuelan painter (1914–   ). Born in Latvia, Leufert studied in Madrid, in New York City, and at the University of Iowa. His work is hard-edge geometric abstraction with limited color (for example, *VB/AM 15*, 1959–61; Caracas, Museum of Fine Arts). His paintings are owned by the Museum of Modern Art in New York, the Art Museum in Basel, and other museums.

BIBLIOGRAPHY. Museo de Bellas Artes, *Pintura venezolana 1661–1961*, Caracas, 1961.

LEUTSCHAU: CATHEDRAL OF ST. JAMES, *see* LOCSE: CATHEDRAL OF ST. JAMES.

LEUTZE, EMANUEL. American painter (b. Gmünd, Germany, 1816; d. Washington, D.C., 1868). Leutze went to the United States as a child and began the study of painting in Philadelphia. He entered the Düsseldorf Academy in 1841 and remained in Düsseldorf until about 1859, painting statically posed, detailed scenes from American history that had wide success in the United States. The most famous of these is probably his *Washington Crossing the Delaware* (1851; Bremen, Art Gallery). He also painted romantic landscapes such as *The Hohenstaufen, Württem-*

berg (New York, Century Association), and, commissioned in 1860, the decoration for the southwest staircase of the Capitol in Washington, D.C., *Westward the Course of Empire Takes Its Way*.

BIBLIOGRAPHY. A. H. Hutton, *Portrait of Patriotism...*, Philadelphia, 1959.

LEUX (Luycx) VON LEUXENSTEIN, FRANS, THE ELDER. Flemish painter of portraits and religious subjects (b. Antwerp, 1604; d. Vienna, 1668). He was a pupil of Remakel Sina and became a master in 1620. By 1638 he had become painter to Ferdinand III at Prague, and he later became painter to Leopold I at the Viennese court (1658). Leux von Leuxenstein belongs to the Van Dyck following, although his drawing became flat and his palette less vivid as soon as he left Antwerp. He is, in fact, generally considered a weak parallel to Justus Susterman in Florence. *Christ Appearing to the Holy Women* (Vaduz, Liechtenstein Collection) shows his use of Rubensian types in somber tonalities. Portraits from his brush are to be found in museums in Prague, Vienna, Stockholm, Madrid, and elsewhere.

BIBLIOGRAPHY. R. Oldenbourg, *Die flämische Malerei des 17. Jahrhunderts*, 2d ed., Berlin, 1922.

LEVASSEUR, JEAN-CHARLES. French engraver (b. Abbeville, 1734; d. Paris, 1816). He studied with Philippe Lefèvre in Abbeville and with Jacques-Firmin Beauvarlet and Jean Daulle in Paris. Levasseur was an active reproduction engraver, mainly in line engraving. He is usually classed among the many rococo, or Watteau, engravers.

BIBLIOGRAPHY. H. Cohen, *Guide de l'amateur de livres à gravures du 18e siècle*, 6th ed., Paris, 1912.

LE VAU, LOUIS. French architect (b. Paris, 1612; d. 1670). Le Vau was probably trained by his father, a master mason. Between 1639 and 1648, he designed a number of residences on the Ile St-Louis in Paris, including the Hôtel Lambert, with its rooms arranged around a court and lavishly decorated with stuccoes, paintings, and sculpture. A similar coordination of the arts occurred at the Château of Vaux-le-Vicomte, with Le Vau designing the architecture (1657–61), Le Nôtre the gardens, and Le Brun the interior decoration. In 1654 Le Vau was made First Architect to the King, but only in 1661 was he actively employed by Louis XIV. His buildings of the period include the Collège des Quatre Nations, Paris (from 1661), and parts of the Louvre (1661–63). From 1664 Le Vau found less favor at the royal court. Colbert rejected his design for the East Front of the Louvre (1664), but Le Vau later collaborated with Perrault and Le Brun on the present East Front (1667–70). Le Vau's last work was the classically geometric garden façade at Versailles (begun 1669), which was later covered up and extended by Jules-Hardouin Mansart's additions to the palace. *See* Louvre Palace, Paris; Quatre Nations, College des, Paris; Vaux-le-Vicomte, Chateau of; Versailles: Palace.

BIBLIOGRAPHY. L. Hautecoeur, *Histoire de l'architecture classique en France*, vol. 2, Paris, 1948; A. Blunt, *Art and Architecture in France, 1500–1700*, Baltimore, 1954.

LEVER HOUSE, NEW YORK. The most influential American office building of the mid-20th century, located in New York City at Park Avenue between 53d and 54th Streets. It was built for Lever Brothers in 1952 by Gordon Bunshaft of Skidmore, Owings, and Merrill, and planned for sole occupancy by the Lever Brothers firm. The building faces on an entire block of Park Avenue.

Lever House composes into a tower over a platform, which together provide 131,000 square feet of office space. The platform is a two-story structure covering the entire site except for an open, landscaped patio and a 10-foot setback on the Park Avenue side. The twenty-one-story rectangular tower, which rises over the platform at its 54th Street end, occupies only one-fourth of the site area.

The ground floor of the two-story platform is completely open on the Park Avenue (east) and 53d Street (south) sides. It is marked out by square, regularly spaced columns, sheathed in stainless steel, which support the second floor and permit free access from street to patio. On the 54th Street (north) side is a glass-enclosed lobby with stainless-steel trim. Adjoining it are service areas, including a loading platform and a ramp leading down to a garage. On the west side are an auditorium and a display kitchen. The second floor follows the outline of the ground floor; and the roof is a landscaped terrace.

The tower, beginning at the third floor, is set back 40 feet from the 54th Street side of the platform. The third floor, containing a kitchen, cafeteria, and dining area, is recessed at its narrow, Park Avenue end. The other twenty stories of the tower overhang it in a block and seem to float over the two-story platform. Each of the tower stories measures 53 by 180 feet and is given over to offices.

The building's steel frame is set back from the ends of the floors, so that the tower exterior is an uninterrupted curtain of greenish-blue, heat-resistant glass and darker blue spandrels. Contrasting with this background of color are the sill, mullions, and heads, sheathed in stainless steel.

BIBLIOGRAPHY. "Glass-Walled Skyscraper," *Engineering News-Record*, CXLVIII, May 1, 1952; "Lever House Complete," *Architectural Forum*, XCVI, 1952; L. Mumford, *From the Ground Up*, New York, 1956.

LEON JACOBSON

LEVI, JULIAN EDWIN. American painter (1900–   ). Born in New York City, he studied at the Pennsylvania Academy of Fine Arts with Henry McCarter and Arthur Carles. After returning from travel in 1927, his paintings, especially still lifes, were influenced by cubist abstraction. In the 1930s, however, he turned to what became his characteristic subjects, seashore and fishing scenes, for example, *Fisherman's Family* (1939; New York, Metropolitan Museum). The isolation of the figures and objects in these paintings at times suggest surrealism, but more often the mood of poignant loneliness is closer to the neoromanticism of Berman and Bérard.

LEVINE, JACK. American painter (1915–   ). Born in Boston, he studied art at the Boston Museum School. He

Jack Levine, *The Passing Scene*. Museum of Modern Art, New York.

became a pupil and protégé of Denman Ross at Harvard (1929), and during the 1930s contributed to the Federal Art Project.

He is an expressionist who paints Biblical and social themes. *The Feast of Pure Reason* (1937; New York, Museum of Modern Art) dramatically reveals his biting satire and mordant humor. His manner recalls El Greco's spiritualized lighting, Soutine's rich colors and distorted forms, and Daumier's trenchant caricatures. He has received wide recognition in the United States and abroad, including an honorary one-man show at the 1960 Interamerican Biennial Exhibition in Mexico City.

BIBLIOGRAPHY. F. S. Wight, *Jack Levine*, Boston, 1952.

LEVITAN, ISAAC ILYITCH. Russian painter (b. Kibarty, 1861; d. Moscow, 1900). In 1889 he visited France, where he was influenced by Corot and the Barbizon school. Idyllic scenes and soft color made him Russia's most famous landscape painter.

LEVITSKY, DMITRI. Russian painter (b. Kiev, 1735/37; d. St. Petersburg, 1822). The most famous Russian portraitist of his time, Levitsky was strongly influenced by the manners and customs shown in French rococo painting, for example, *Princess Davydov and Mlle Rzhevski* (1776; Moscow, Tretyakov Gallery). His later portraits were more simplified in forms and composition.

LEVOCA: CATHEDRAL OF ST. JAMES, *see* LOCSE: CATHEDRAL OF ST. JAMES.

LEVY, RUDOLF. German painter (b. Stettin, 1875; d. 1944). He studied in Munich from 1897 to 1903 and spent the next eleven years in Paris, where he was strongly influenced by the Fauves, Matisse in particular, and by postimpressionism. His subjects were mostly still lifes and landscapes of the south of France. Although he often used a strong, solid outline in his still lifes, the modulation from one color area to another, sometimes sharp, sometimes subtle, and the general placement remind one of Cézanne. The Matisse influence can be seen in the graceful linearity of his compositions.

Wyndham Lewis, *Ezra Pound*. Tate Gallery, London.

LEWANDOWSKI, EDMUND. American painter (1914–). He was born in Milwaukee, Wis., and studied there. Associated with the precisionists, he paints landscapes and industrial and machine subjects such as *Ore Freighter* (1948; Minneapolis, Walker Art Center).

BIBLIOGRAPHY. Walker Art Center, *The Precisionist View in American Art*, Minneapolis, 1960.

LEWIS, FREDERICK CHRISTIAN. English engraver and landscape painter (b. London, 1779; d. Enfield, 1856). He received instruction from Joseph Stadler, a German engraver. Primarily a reproduction master, Lewis made many stipple engravings as engraver to George IV and Victoria. Many of Lawrence's portraits were Lewis's subjects. Among his works are *Recollections of Eminent Masters* and a number of water-color and oil landscapes.

BIBLIOGRAPHY. T. M. Rees, *Welsh Painters, Engravers, Sculptors (1527–1911)*, Carnarvon, n.d.

LEWIS, JOHN FREDERICK. English painter (b. London, 1805; d. 1876). He was the son of Frederick Christian Lewis. John Lewis grew up with Landseer and like him painted animal pictures. In 1824 he was employed by George IV to paint sporting subjects at Windsor. He went to Spain in 1832 and on his return published a folio volume, *Lewis's Spanish Sketches*. He then worked almost entirely in water color and was interested only in landscape and local scenes. He spent nearly ten years in the East and developed a very minute and brilliantly colored style that recalls that of the Pre-Raphaelites. His subjects were taken from Eastern life and scenery, which continued to fascinate him after his return to England in 1851. In the 1850s he again took up oil painting, but still employed the extremely detailed method and brilliant color of his water-color technique. He was one of the first English artists to feel the lure of the East, and his best known works are of Eastern subjects.

BIBLIOGRAPHY. J. L. Roget, *A History of the "Old Water-Colour" Society*, 2 vols., London, 1891.

LEWIS, WYNDHAM. British painter (1884–1957). Born in Nova Scotia, Lewis studied at the Slade School and traveled widely in Europe. Returning to England in 1909, he threw himself into the battle for modern art with explosive force. He was a member of the Camden Town Group and the London Group, and worked in the Omega Workshop before a quarrel with Roger Fry. His close connections with the avant-garde and the influences of cubism and futurism led to the development of vorticism, with which Lewis's name is most associated. He did not confine his activities to painting, for he wrote several satirical novels and produced works of criticism. He also produced a series of incisive pencil portrait drawings. Lewis's paintings clearly show his fascination with the technical and mechanical developments of the 20th century. *See* VORTICISM.

BIBLIOGRAPHY. W. Lewis, *Wyndham Lewis, the Artist, from "Blast" to Burlington House*, London, 1939; C. Handley-Read, ed., *The Art of Wyndham Lewis*, London, 1951.

LEYDEN, LUCAS VAN. Dutch painter and engraver (b. Leyden, ca. 1489/94? d. there, 1533). According to Karel van Mander, who is one of the major sources of knowledge

Lucas van Leyden, *Sermon in Church*. Rijksmuseum, Amsterdam.

of Lucas, the boy learned the rudiments of painting from his father, Hughe (Hugo) Jacobsz., an otherwise unknown artist. Later Lucas became the pupil of Cornelis Engebrechtsz., in whose studio he studied glass staining and, apparently, engraving. It is as an engraver that he is best known today. His earliest engraving, *Mahomet and the Monk Sergius*, is dated 1508. It is, in part, because of this accomplished print that Van Mander's date of 1494 as the year of Lucas's birth has been questioned and his birth has been placed instead about 1489. Yet his reputation as an infant prodigy had been established early in the 16th century and cannot be dismissed lightly.

In his early engravings Lucas shows the influence of such early Netherlandish printmakers as the Master of the Gardens of Love, the Master of the Banderols, and the Monogrammist FVB, as well as the influence of the engravings of Albrecht Dürer. In this regard, Dürer's *St. Eustace* (1501) and *Adam and Eve* (1504) seem to have been especially influential.

Among Lucas's finest engravings of the first decade of the 16th century are *The Raising of Lazarus* (1508) and the famous series of nine prints known as *The Circular Passion* (1509). From the second decade there are his *Milkmaid* (1510), one of the earliest genre engravings, and his largest engraving, the *Ecce Homo* (1510), which had an influence on Rembrandt's well-known etching of the same subject.

During a stay in Antwerp (1521–22) Lucas met the other great printmaker of his time, Dürer. The meeting was a friendly one, as we know from an excerpt in Dürer's diary. Immediately afterward, Dürer's influence is again dominant in Lucas's engravings. Apparently he also came in contact with Jan Gossaert or Jan van Scorel, for his works exhibit an increasing concern with the Renaissance style of Italy, especially as it had been interpreted by those two artists. Another source for the new Romanism evinced in his late works may have been the engravings of Marcantonio Raimondi.

Much less is known about the origins of Lucas's painting style. The earliest known signed and dated work is a *St. Anthony* (1511; Brussels, Fine Arts Museum). In his mature works, such as *The Virgin and Child with the Magdalen and Donor* (Munich, Bavarian State Picture Galleries, Old Pinacothek), signed with the L monogram found on his engravings and dated 1522, Lucas shows his adherence to the Romanism exemplified in the works of Gossaert.

BIBLIOGRAPHY. M. J. Friedländer, *Die altniederländische Malerei*, vol. 10, Berlin, 1932; F. W. H. Hollstein, *Dutch and Flemish Etchings, Engravings and Woodcuts...*, vol. 10: *L'Admirable Lucas van Leyden*, Amsterdam, 195?.

NORMAN W. CANEDY

LEYDEN, NICOLAUS VON, *see* GERHARD, NIKOLAUS, FROM LEYDEN.

LEYDEN: HOOGLANDSCHE KERK. The Church of St. Pancras in Leyden, Netherlands, is a spacious late Gothic structure built during the 15th century on the site of an earlier fabric. Its adjoining tower goes back to the older foundation (ca. 1300). The present church was begun in 1366, the nave was started in 1377, and the choir was founded in 1381. Work continued until the 16th century.

The plan is a cross basilica with a nave and two aisles, and aisles flanking the transept. The north transept has elaborate pinnacles on the exterior. The interior of the nave is covered with a wooden barrel vault.

BIBLIOGRAPHY. F. A. J. Vermeulen, *Handboek tot de Geschiedenis der Nederlandsche Bouwkunst*, vol. 1, The Hague, 1923.

LEYS, HENRI. Belgian painter and etcher (b. Antwerp, 1815; d. there, 1869). He studied at the Antwerp Academy with Gustav Wappers and also with Ferdinand de Braekeleer. Leys went to Paris in 1840. He was early impressed by Delacroix's rich coloring, but applied it to finely drawn history scenes. After a period of historical genre subjects, he was influenced, about 1845, by the earlier Dutch masters of genre and interiors, particularly Ter Borch and Metsu. By the middle 1850s Leys had returned to detailed history paintings. The mural decorations in the Town Hall of Antwerp occupied him from 1863 until his death.

BIBLIOGRAPHY. P. Colin, *La Peinture belge depuis 1830*, Brussels, 1930; G. Vanzype, *Leys et son école*, Brussels, 1949.

LEYSTER, JUDITH JANSDR., *see* LEIJSTER, JUDITH JANSDR.

LEYTENS (Lytens), GIJSBRECHT. Flemish painter (baptized 1586; d. before 1656). Leytens was a pupil of Jacob Vrolyck and became a master in Antwerp in 1617. He is known solely from *Landscape with Waterfall* (Brunswick, Herzog-Anton-Ulrich Museum), which shows him to be a follower of Josse de Momper's late style. The proposed identification of Leytens with the Master of the Winter Landscapes remains problematical. *See* MASTER OF THE WINTER LANDSCAPES.

BIBLIOGRAPHY. Y. Thiéry, *Le Paysage flamand au XVIIe siècle*, Brussels, 1953.

LHERMITTE, LEON-AUGUSTIN. French painter and etcher (b. Mont-Saint-Père, 1844; d. Paris, 1925). A student

André Lhote, *Rugby*, 1917. National Museum of Modern Art, Paris. Cubist work tempered by traditional painting.

of Horace Lecoq de Boisbaudran, Lhermitte debuted in the Salon of 1864 with a charcoal drawing, *Marne River by Alfort*. He traveled to England in 1871–72, and in 1880 he won *hors concours* at the Salon. Lhermitte was at the height of his popularity in 1900, when he won first prize at the world exhibition in Paris. Throughout his career he concentrated on scenes of peasant life (*Death of the Wood-cutter*, 1893, Amiens, Museum of Fine Arts; *The Harvest*, 1874, Carcassonne Museum; *The Vintage*, 1884, New York, Metropolitan Museum) and religious paintings (*Christ among the Poor*, 1892, Boston, Museum of Fine Arts). He worked in a realistic style similar to Courbet's, which he tried to adapt to a more romantic interpretation of subject matter. In his late works he shows some aware-ness of impressionism.

BIBLIOGRAPHY. R. Walker, "Léon A. Lhermitte," *Art Journal*, 886; F. Henriet, *Les Eaux-fortes de Léon Lhermitte*, Paris, 1905.

LHOTE, ANDRE. French painter and critic (b. Bordeaux, 1885; d. Paris, 1962). Lhote first worked with a sculptor-decorator, then learned painting himself, and exhibited at the Salon des Indépendants beginning in 1906 and at the Salon d'Automne in 1907. He was immediately appreciated by the critics and poets. As an important art critic, Lhote not only contributed to the *Nouvelle revue française* until 1940 but, in his *Treatise on Landscape*, *Treatise on the Figure*, *Writings on Art*, and *Egyptian Painting in the Valley of Kings*, raised major questions, analyzing the aims of art from the earliest times to the present and explaining matters of technique. He exercised a lasting influence on the young French generation by his writings and his ex-ample and, above all, by his role as a teacher: in 1922 he founded a school and freely gave advice to all who came to him. He had participated in cubist activities yet had not lost himself in the movement. His acknowledged cult of Cézanne and his great admiration for Picasso did not prevent him from developing his own style.

Liang K'ai, *The Sixth Patriarch Cuts a Bamboo*. Ink on paper. National Museum, Tokyo.

Lhote's canvases are generally pleasing in color and design, reflecting his desire to reconcile traditional paint-ing with cubism. A typical example is *Rugby* (1917; Paris, National Museum of Modern Art). The figures and objects are geometrically transcribed and the planes clearly brought out through contour and color, with emphasis on move-ment and intelligibility of style. Like his idol Cézanne, Lhote attempted the absolute, trying to put everything into his pictures: form, light, space, color, intelligence and sen-sibility, energy and stability. Right up to his death his pri-mary interest was in theory, proving in his pictures that space could be expressed without perspective while preserv-ing the characteristic flat surface appearance. In addition to his numerous exhibitions, Lhote received several mural commissions (Palais de la Découverte, Paris, 1937) and illustrated the works of Cocteau, Claudel, Blaise Cendrars, Jules Romains, and others.

BIBLIOGRAPHY. B. Dorival, *Twentieth-Century French Painters*, 2 vols., New York, 1958; H. Read, *A Concise History of Modern Painting*, London, 1959; B. Dorival, *The School of Paris in the Musée d'Art Moderne*, London, 1960; R. Nacenta, *School of Paris*, London, 1960.

ARNOLD ROSIN

LI AN-CHUNG. Chinese academy painter (fl. 12th cent.). He was active at both the Northern and the Southern Sung courts. Very little is known of him through Chinese sources, but he has always been highly praised by Japanese collectors for his special bird-and-flower paintings in the manner of Hui-tsung. *See* HUI-TSUNG.

BIBLIOGRAPHY. J. F. Cahill, *Chinese Paintings, 11th–14th Centuries*, New York, 1960.

LIANG K'AI. Chinese painter (ca. 1140–ca. 1210). He was a pupil of Chia Shih-ku and began his career as a painter in the Northern Sung Academy at K'ai-feng. Later he became a Ch'an (Zen) Buddhist convert at the Liu-t'ung Temple near Hang-chou. As is the case with so many of the Ch'an painters, very little information concerning Liang K'ai is relayed in standard Chinese sources. His reasons for leaving the academy are not clear, but there is no doubt of his connection with the first real expressions of Ch'an painting in the Sung period. *See* ZEN.

Of the twenty or so paintings that can be safely attri-buted to Liang K'ai, most are in Japanese collections and seem to fall into two distinct styles. The first group, rep-resented by the famous *Sākyamuni Leaving His Mountain Retreat* in the National Museum, Tokyo, and by a number of pure landscapes, comprises paintings executed by Liang K'ai while a member of the academy. Although these paintings have all the elements of Southern Sung academic works, the cold and remote air that pervades them and the selection of rather unattractive motifs mark Liang K'ai as being a rather unique academician. The second stylistic group of Liang K'ai paintings is devoted to appropriate Ch'an subject matter and exploits the abbreviated, explo-sive brushwork that is one of the features of the Ch'an Southern Sung style.

BIBLIOGRAPHY. W. Speiser, "Liang K'ai," *Ostasiatische Zeitschrift*, XXVII, 1941; S. Shimada and Y. Yonezawa, *Painting of the Sung and Yüan Dynasties*, Tokyo, 1952; Bijitsu Kenkyū-sho, *Liang K'ai*, Kyoto, 1957.

MARTIE W. YOUNG

LIAO-YANG TOMB (Pei-yuan Tomb). Chinese tomb in the southern Manchurian city of Liao-yang, near Port Ar-

Liberale da Verona, *Adoration of the Shepherds*, central panel. Cathedral, Verona.

thur, discovered by Japanese archaeologists. A stone tomb with mural paintings on the inner walls, it had apparently been looted in ancient times, but the paintings are well enough preserved to offer some evidence for the state of painting reached by the Han dynasty (206 B.C.–A.D. 221). Details of construction and comparison with other finds in the region have made the Han date of the tomb fairly secure. The walls are devoted to familiar Han subject matter: processions of chariots, performances of acrobats, ghosts of ancestors. The style of these tomb paintings foreshadows later 4th-century tombs found in Korea and is indicative of the widespread nature of Han civilization in the 1st and 2d centuries of our era.

BIBLIOGRAPHY. W. Fairbank and M. Kitano, "Han Mural Paintings in the Pei-yüan Tomb at Liao-yang, South Manchuria," *Artibus Asiae*, XVII, 1954.

LIAUTAUD, GEORGES. Haitian sculptor (1899–   ). Born in Croix-des-Bouquets, where he has maintained a blacksmith's shop for many years, Liautaud is Haiti's leading sculptor. Most of his works are flat figures or symbols cut out of steel gasoline drums and based on careful drawings; they draw on voodoo and Christian symbolism and have the appearance of spiritual entities. Liautaud's work has been shown at the Centre d'Art in Port-au-Prince and the São Paulo Bienal as well as in the United States and Europe.

LIBERAL ARTS, THE SEVEN. The term was first used in late Roman times to designate the studies needed for philosophy. The arts themselves were originated as part of Greek education. They included grammar, rhetoric, logic, arithmetic, geometry, music, and astronomy, although others were often substituted in ancient and medieval times. Painting was added to the list by Leonardo in his *Paragone*. The Liberal Arts are often personified in painting and sculpture.

LIBERALE DA VERONA. Italian painter and miniaturis (ca. 1445–1526/29). After working in Verona, he spen 1467–76 and perhaps longer around Siena, where many music manuscripts with his miniatures survive (Chius Cathedral and especially Siena, Piccolomini Library). H worked with Girolamo da Cremona. By 1488 Liberale wa in Verona again, where the better young artists became hi pupils.

His late works include *St. Sebastian* (versions in Berlin former State Museums, and Milan, Brera), the *Berlin Altar piece* (1489; former State Museums), and, in Verona, the *Adoration of the Shepherds* (Cathedral), damaged frescoes and numerous smaller works (Castelvecchio Museum) Inevitably influenced by Mantegna in sharp line and shin ing color, he is close to Girolamo in sinuous movement.

BIBLIOGRAPHY. Liberale da Verona, *Miniature di Liberale da Ve rona dai corali per il Duomo di Siena*, text by E. Carli, Milan 1953.

LIBERGIER, HUGUES. French architect (d. 1263). H was master of St-Nicaise in Reims (begun in 1231), on of the finest Rayonnant Gothic buildings. He was burie at St-Nicaise, but his tombstone is now in Reims Cathedral He is shown on the tombstone with a rule, compass, an square.

BIBLIOGRAPHY. E. Panofsky, *Gothic Architecture and Scholasticism* Latrobe, Pa., 1951.

LIBERI, PIETRO. Italian painter (b. Padua, 1614; d Venice, 1687). Liberi studied with Varotari and spent hi early career as a soldier, merchant, and slave in Tunis He traveled widely in Europe, studied in Florence and Rome (particularly the work of Pietro da Cortona), and became a court painter in Germany, where he is reported to have become wealthy by making counterfeit jewels. Set tling in Venice in 1659, he had a palace built for himsel on the Grand Canal (Moro-Lin Palace) and founded a school for painters. Among his many large and sumptuous works are a ceiling fresco in the sacristy of S. Antonio in Padua and altarpieces in S. Maria della Salute and the Gesuiti in Venice. The first-mentioned work presents a confusion of intertwined nudes and stylized shapes and shows the influence of Pietro da Cortona. In mythologica works Liberi continued the Venetian tradition of sensuali ty in a formularized baroque manner.

BIBLIOGRAPHY. S. de Kunert, "Notizie e documenti su Pietro Li beri," *Rivista d'arte*, XIII, 1931.

LIBERIA, *see* AFRICA, PRIMITIVE ART OF (WEST AFRICA).

LIBERTY LEADING THE PEOPLE (La Barricade). Oil painting by Delacroix, in the Louvre, Paris. See DELA-CROIX, EUGENE.

LIBER VITAE OF NEWMINSTER, *see* NEWMINSTER REGISTER OF.

LIBRI, FRANCESCO DAI. Italian painter and miniaturist of Verona (1452–1514). His miniatures are influenced by Mantegna (signed *Adoration of the Magi*, New York, Pierpont Morgan Library). Altarpieces attributed to him, mainly in the Castelvecchio Museum in Verona, resemble the works of Liberale da Verona.

LIBRI, GIROLAMO DAI. Italian painter of Verona (1474–1555). He was the son of Francesco dai Libri. After early work as a miniaturist Girolamo painted almost exclusively large altarpieces which show little development. Their dry color and sharp line suggest the late Mantegna. Their exceptional quality lies in the importance given to landscape, which penetrates the area of the figures with large luminous forms. *Adoration with the Rabbit* (1515), *Madonna of the Umbrella Tree* (1530), and *Madonna of the Oak* (all Verona, Castelvecchio Museum) are notable.

BIBLIOGRAPHY. *Capolavori della pittura veronese* (catalog), ed. A. Avena, Verona, 1947.

LIBRI CAROLINI (Caroline Books). Treatise in four books (ca. 790–792), reported to have been the work of Charlemagne. It attacks Byzantine iconoclasm for prohibiting images as well as what was considered excessive de-

Girolamo dai Libri, *Madonna of the Oak*, Castelvecchio Museum, Verona.

Li Ch'eng, *Buddhist Temples after Rain*. William Rockhill Nelson Gallery of Art, Kansas City.

votion to images after their restoration (Second Council of Nicea, 787). The work is clearly that of a skilled theologian, possibly Alcuin of York, although recent studies attribute it to Theodulf of Orléans. Charlemagne, irritated by the aloof Byzantine attitude toward his claims to becoming emperor, instigated it. The original manuscript, lacking the preface and book 4, is preserved in the Vatican Library; the early Caroline minuscule is that of the Palace school. *See* MINUSCULE; PALACE SCHOOL.

LI CHAO-TAO, *see* LI SSU-HSUN.

LI CHEN. Chinese painter (fl. 2d half of 8th cent.). He is virtually unrecorded in Chinese sources, and his chief fame rests on the fact that Kōbō Daishi, the founder of the Shingon sect of Buddhism in Japan, brought back with him some of Li Chen's paintings when he returned after his visit to China in 804. The paintings, representing the five patriarchs of Shingon (in Chinese, Chen-yen) Buddhism, are preserved at the Tojiji in Kyoto. *See* SHINGON.

LI CH'ENG. Chinese landscape painter (fl. ca. 960–990). He was born in Ch'ang-an, but his family moved to Ying-ch'iu in Shantung Province shortly after the establishment of the Sung empire. He was trained in the classics and Confucianism, and his life was devoted to the cultivated pursuits of the true scholar. With Ching Hao and Kuan T'ung, Li Ch'eng forms the great triumvirate of Five Dynasties–early Sung landscape masters. He became especially famous for his use of the "crab-claw" stroke in his depiction of blasted, wintry pine trees. Li Ch'eng was apparently not a prolific painter, and his works were scarce by the next generation, according to the famous connoisseur Mi Fu. Among the handful of attributed Li Ch'eng paintings in existence today is a fine work in the William Rockhill Nelson Gallery of Art, Kansas City, entitled *Buddhist Temples after Rain. See* CHING HAO; KUAN T'UNG.

BIBLIOGRAPHY. O. Sirén, *Chinese Painting, Leading Masters and Principles*, vol. 1, New York, 1956.

LICHFIELD CATHEDRAL. Cathedral in Lichfield, England, built during the 13th and 14th centuries. One of the major secondary monuments of English Gothic architecture, the present building replaced a 12th-century Anglo-Norman cathedral, which had an ambulatory and apse. The nave (ca. 1250–80), one of the great works of the early Decorated style, is related to the nave of Westminster Abbey, except for the unusual clerestory windows, which have a curved, triangular design. Of special interest, in addition to the elongated octagonal chapter house dating from about 1240–50, are the Lady Chapel and the *chevet*, begun about 1320, in the late Decorated style. Lichfield preserves its full complement of three towers and spires, although the crossing spire is a 17th-century copy of the 14th-century original. The west façade, impressive at a distance, is an unfortunate Victorian restoration.

BIBLIOGRAPHY. H. Batsford and C. Fry, *The Cathedrals of England*, 10th ed., London, 1960.

LICH GATE. Roofed gateway to a churchyard in which the coffin was placed before burial. The first portion of the burial service was often read at the lich gate.

LI CHIAI, *see* YING-TSAO FA SHIH.

LICHTENSTEIN, ROY. American painter (1923–   ). A native of New York City, he studied at the Art Students League there under Reginald Marsh after attending Ohio State University. One of the leading practitioners of Pop Art, he has monumentalized comic-strip sequences and photoreproduction techniques, such as Benday dots, in a deadpan manner. *See* POP ART.

LICINIO, BERNARDINO. Venetian painter (1489–ca. 1560). He is most interesting for his portraits, especially large family groups. Influenced by Palma and Cariani, they are dry and literal, but unusual documents. Those in Hampton Court (1524) and Alnwick Castle in England, the Borghese Gallery in Rome, and the Hermitage in Leningrad are notable.

BIBLIOGRAPHY. B. Berenson, *The Venetian Painters of the Renaissance*, 3d ed., New York, 1897.

LIE, JONAS. American painter (b. Moss, Norway, 1880; d. New York City, 1940). He went to the United States in 1893 and studied in New York at the National Academy, the Art Students League, and Cooper Union. He traveled in Europe in 1906, and his experience of the paintings of Monet led him to his characteristic loosely painted version of impressionism. Lie's paintings of the construction of the Panama Canal, for example, *The Conquerers: Culebra Cut, Panama Canal* (1913; New York, Metropolitan Museum), brought him his first success. Among his popular subjects were city scenes, bridges, New England coast scenes, and colorful landscapes such as *Sapphire and Amethyst* (1930; Minneapolis Institute of Fine Arts). Elected an academician in 1925, Lie was president of the National Academy from 1934 to 1939.

LIEBERMANN, MAX. German impressionist painter and graphic artist (b. Berlin, 1847; d. there, 1935). He studied with Steffeck from 1866 to 1868 and the next four years at the Weimar Kunstschule. The first picture Liebermann

Lichfield Cathedral. A monument of English Gothic architecture.

Max Liebermann, *Portrait of Prof. Sauerbruch*. Art Gallery, Hamburg.

exhibited was *Women Plucking Geese* (1872; formerly National Gallery in Berlin). The work is derived from the realism of Wilhelm Leibl and the early Thoma. The theme is in the genre tradition, but goes further, to suggest that the work of these peasants is demeaning; it shows the unrelieved dreariness of the low-ceilinged room and the resigned manner of the laborers.

He went to France in 1873 and for a period of five years stayed mostly in Paris, where he met Mihály von Munkácsy. In 1873 Liebermann went to Barbizon on a painting excursion and became acquainted with Millet, whose art strongly influenced him. He also got to know Corot, Constant Troyon, and Daubigny. Contact with these artists not only strengthened Liebermann's conviction in pursuing proletarian themes but also inspired him to lighten his palette. In Holland he saw the art of Josef Israëls, which served even more to reinforce the effect the Barbizon school artists had on him.

Liebermann returned to Munich in 1878 and exhibited *Christ in the Temple*. It caused a furor because the clergy found it irreverent and too coarsely realistic. He stayed in Munich until 1884, then left to live in Berlin for the remainder of his life. Liebermann went counter to the established order of the academy in Germany with his relentless realism. In 1887 he painted one of his finest and best-known works, *The Flax Spinners* (Berlin, National Gallery). In it he shows workers involved in monotonous labor. Without resorting to sentimentality or propagandistic fervor, Liebermann points up the evils of the Industrial Revolution, which he believed dehumanized the peasant by making him little more than an extension of a machine.

He became absorbed in impressionism, the then radical movement drifting from France to Germany. It led him to alter his style in the early 1890s. He loosened his brushstroke, giving a slashing, virtuoso quality to his work. He further lightened his tonality and extended the range of his palette. In *Polo Players* (1902; Hamburg, Art Gallery) the influence of Degas can be detected. In 1898 Liebermann became a member of the Berlin Academy and later its president. Despite this, he was not won over to academism. On the contrary, Liebermann, with Slevogt and Corinth, took a positive stand against the established order with the Secession, of which Liebermann became president in 1899. His late work suffers in comparison with that of the French impressionists. His reputation today depends largely on his sober paintings of the life of depressed humble folk done in the 1880s.

BIBLIOGRAPHY. M. Liebermann, *Max Liebermann als Schriftsteller*, Berlin, 1922; K. Scheffler, *Max Liebermann*, 4th ed., Munich, 1923.

ROBERT REIFF

LIEBES, DOROTHY. American textile designer (1899–). Born in California, she designs both handwoven and machine-made textiles, often using unorthodox materials in her colorful fabrics. She was director of the Arts and Skills Division of the Red Cross during World War II, and designed textiles for the United States theater at the World's Fair in Brussels (1958).

BIBLIOGRAPHY. E. McCausland, "Dorothy Liebes, Designer for Mass Production," *Magazine of Art*, XL, April, 1947.

LIEBFRAUENKIRCHE (Frauenkirche), DRESDEN. Baroque church (destroyed in 1945). In 1722 the Dresden authorities commissioned Georg Bähr to design a large church. As executed, the church represented a triumphant compromise between Bähr's design and one by the architect Knöffel. A tall and massive structure of stone, centrally planned and galleried internally to permit the maximum audience participation, it was one of the greatest monuments of Protestant baroque church architecture.

BIBLIOGRAPHY. W. Lange, *Die Frauenkirche zu Dresden*, Berlin, 1955.

LIECHTENSTEIN GALLERY, VIENNA, *see* VIENNA: MUSEUMS.

LIEDET (Lyedet), LOYSET. Flemish miniaturist (fl. ca. 1460–78). A native of Hesdin, he was apparently apprenticed to Simon Marmion. Liedet had a flourishing atelier after about 1460 in Bruges, where he is last recorded in 1478.

BIBLIOGRAPHY. L. M. J. Delaissé, *La Miniature flamande à l'époque de Philippe le Bon*, Milan, 1956.

LIEGE, JEAN DE, *see* JEAN DE LIEGE.

LIEGE. City in Belgium about 50 miles east of Brussels. It is noted for having been a main center of Mosan art, the indigenous art of the Meuse River valley.

Starting in the late 10th century and continuing through the 11th century, a school of ivory carving was extremely active in Liège. In the 12th and 13th centuries the city reached the peak of its artistic importance with a noted school of bronze work. Among the very few names of this period known to us to be active in the media of metalwork, both Godefroy de Claire and Renier of Huy worked in Liège. The Church of St-Barthélemy in Liège still possesses the magnificent bronze baptismal font made by Renier (ca. 1107–18). See GODEFROY DE CLAIRE; MOSAN ART; OTTONIAN ART; RENIER OF HUY.

Mosan art, which appears to have been centered in Liège, is now looked upon as one of the important contributory sources in the growth of a monumental Romanesque style.

See also LIEGE: FINE ARTS MUSEUM; ST. PAUL'S CATHEDRAL, LIEGE.

BIBLIOGRAPHY. H. Swarzenski, *Monuments of Romanesque Art...*, Chicago, 1954.

LIEGE: FINE ARTS MUSEUM. Belgian collection devoted to French and Belgian painting dating from the 17th to the 20th century, with emphasis on the later period. Included are works by Ingres, Gauguin, Monet, Pissarro, Ensor, Picasso, Chagall, Utrillo, Daubigny, and Corot.

LIENAU, DETLEF. American architect (b. Schleswig-Holstein, 1818; d. 1887). After studying in Munich, and with Henri Labrouste in Paris, Lienau went to the United States (1848). His Shiff House in New York City (1850) probably introduced the Second Empire style to the country. He formed a link between the classicist styles of the early and late 19th century.

LIEN-HUA-SHOU, *see* PADMAPANI.

LIERNE. Short intermediate rib in Gothic vaulting. The lierne does not mark a change of direction or an intersec-

ion of vaulting surfaces. Rather, lying on the surface which contains it and not rising from the impost or springing or defining a ridge, the lierne essentially is a subdividing member, as in the Cathedrals of Canterbury and Gloucester. *See also* TIERCERON.

LIEVENS (Lievensz.), JAN. Dutch history, genre, portrait, and landscape painter and graphic artist (b. Leyden, 1607; d. Amsterdam, 1674). He was the son of Lieven Hendricx, an embroiderer from Ghent. Lievens became a pupil of Joris van Schooten at the age of eight, and two years later he went to Amsterdam to study with Pieter Lastman (1617–19). Shortly afterward he returned to his native Leyden, where in the later 1620s he was closely associated with Rembrandt. In 1626/27 Lievens painted a *Portrait of Constantijn Huygens* (Douai, Municipal Museum); Huygens gave early support to both Lievens and Rembrandt.

Lievens seems to have had an extremely close working relationship with Rembrandt, and there are several works, such as the *Portrait of a Child* (Amsterdam, Rijksmuseum), which are signed "Lievens retouched by Rembrandt" (*Rembrandt geretucee . . . Lieve . . .*). As early as 1632 contemporary documents show that it was often difficult to separate the early works of the two men: a painting of *Simeon in the Temple*, probably the painting by Rembrandt (The Hague, Mauritshuis Art Gallery), was listed as either "Rembrandt or Jan Lievens" in a 1632 inventory. A number of early Lievens compositions are clearly related to works by Rembrandt. For example, Lievens's *Raising of Lazarus* (1631; Brighton, Art Gallery and Museum) is clearly based on a Rembrandt painting of the same subject. During this period Lievens seems also to have been influenced by the Utrecht followers of Caravaggio in such artificially lighted compositions as the *Boy Blowing on a Burning Coal* (Warsaw, National Museum).

Dutch sources indicate that Lievens went to England in 1631. He was still in Leyden in 1632, however, and there is no firm evidence that he was ever in England. By 1635 he had settled in Antwerp and entered the painters' guild in that city. In 1638 he married the daughter of the sculptor Andries Colyns de Nole. In Antwerp he was friendly with Adriaen Brouwer and Jan Davidsz. de Heem. Lievens became a citizen of Antwerp in 1640. In 1644, however, he was in Amsterdam, possibly living with the painter Jan Molenaer, and seems to have remained there until 1653.

Lievens was active at The Hague from 1654 to 1658 and was one of the founders of the painters' confraternity Pictura. He possibly returned to Amsterdam in 1659 but at least seems to have maintained his contact with that city, for in 1656 he painted a large *Quintus Fabius Maximus and His Son* for the Amsterdam Town Hall, possibly replacing a Rembrandt of the same subject. In 1664 he painted a large allegorical representation, *War*, for the chamber of the provincial assembly of Holland at The Hague, which is still *in situ*.

BIBLIOGRAPHY. H. Schneider, *Jan Lievens: Sein Leben und seine Werke*, Haarlem, 1932; K. E. Simon, "Beiträge zur Malerei des Rembrandtkreises: I. Lievens und Ter Brugghen," *Zeitschrift für*

Jan Lievens, *Portrait of a Child.* **Rijksmuseum, Amsterdam.**

Kunstgeschichte, V, 1936; K. Bauch, "Rembrandt und Lievens," *Wallraf Richartz Jahrbuch*, XI, 1939; K. Bauch, *Der frühe Rembrandt und seine Zeit*, Berlin, 1960; N. Maclaren, *National Gallery Catalogues: The Dutch School*, London, 1960; J. Rosenberg, S. Slive, and E. H. ter Kuile, *Dutch Art and Architecture, 1600–1800*, Baltimore, 1966.

LEONARD J. SLATKES

LIGHT AND SHADOW, *see* CHIAROSCURO.

LIGHTHOUSE. Usually, a functional tower to support a guiding light for ships. But monumental types, some of them ancient, although no longer extant, are known. *See also* PHAROS.

LIGOZZI, JACOPO. Italian painter and draftsman (b. Verona, ca. 1547; d. Florence, 1626). Little is known of his training, but his development shows the influence of Paolo Veronese's early works. By 1575 Ligozzi was in Florence. His religious subjects are representative of much of the Florentine painting of the Counter Reformation. Such works as *The Discovery of the Holy Cross* (Florence, Sta Croce) show indebtedness to Alessandro Allori. Although Ligozzi's paintings are mainly undistinguished, his drawings of plants, animals, and birds (Florence, Uffizi) are the finest of their kind and time.

BIBLIOGRAPHY. A. Venturi, *Storia dell'arte italiana*, vol. 9, pt. 7, Milan, 1934; M. Bacci and A. Forlani, *Mostra di disegni di Jacopo Ligozzi . . .*, Florence, 1961.

LI JIH-HUA. Chinese painter, critic, and connoisseur (fl. late 16th–early 17th cent.). Li Jih-hua was a native of Chia-hsing in Chekiang Province. Although a number of signed and dated works by this painter have been preserved, primarily in Japanese collections, he is best known for his writings, particularly for a diary he kept of the paintings he saw daily between the years 1589 and 1616. These notes give invaluable insights into the nature of collecting and critical attitudes toward the art of painting in the late Ming dynasty.

LI K'AN. Chinese painter of bamboos (1245–1320). Born near modern Peking, Li K'an was known also by his *tzu* Chung-pin and his *hao* Hsi-chai tao-jen. He had a brilliant official career and is cited often in the various chronicles of the Yüan dynasty, but his principal contribution to Chinese culture was in the field of bamboo painting. He is well known for a treatise he wrote on this special branch of painting (*Chu-p'u*) as well as for actual exercises in this difficult subject matter. The William Rockhill Nelson Gallery of Art, Kansas City, possesses a remarkably fine section of a hand scroll by Li K'an representing clumps of bamboo stalks.

BIBLIOGRAPHY. E. A. Prinz zur Lippe-Biesterfeld, "Li K'an und seine ausführliche Beschreibung des Bambus Beiträge zu Bambusmalerei der Yüan-zeit," *Ostasiatische Zeitschrift*, XXVIII, 1942–43.

LI KUNG-LIN (Li Lung-mien). Chinese painter (ca. 1045–1106). The son of a wealthy family, he was born in Shuch'eng, Anhui Province. His *tzu* was Po-shih, but he is best known to Western collectors by his *hao*, Lung-mien. This pen name was taken in 1100, when he left government service in the city of K'ai-feng and retired to the Lung-mien Hills south of his home town. Li Kung-lin was

Li Kung-lin, *Imaginary Voyage into the Hsiao-hsiang Region*. National Museum, Tokyo.

a noted Confucian scholar, a close friend of Su Shih and Mi Fu, and an instrumental figure in the early *wen-jen-hua* movement. He was acknowledged as the leading painter of his day, a superb master of the brush in every respect. His reputation among Western observers was gained at first on the basis of his horse paintings. Chinese literary sources do attest to a considerable number of horses painted by Li Kung-lin throughout his career, but his principal preoccupation was with Buddhist and Confucian subjects. *See* MI FU; SU SHIH; WEN-JEN-HUA.

In his painting style Li Kung-lin followed an orthodox linear manner that was based on T'ang conventions but was far more realistic in terms of observation. The technical dexterity present in his work and his particular choice of the fine-line *pai-miao* style set him apart from other early *wen-jen* painters. On the other hand, his revival of earlier T'ang modes seemed to fit in with the whole spirit of antiquarianism that was part of the *wen-jen* movement, and for this reason, if none other, Li Kung-lin was greatly admired by his colleagues. Li Kung-lin was a noted collector of antiquities, as was Mi Fu, and was deeply immersed in the sense of history while retaining his visual awareness of the world around him. *See* PAI-MIAO.

BIBLIOGRAPHY. A. E. Meyer, *Chinese Painting as Reflected in the Thought and Art of Li Lung-mien*, New York, 1923; O. Sirén, *Chinese Painting, Leading Masters and Principles*, vol. 2, New York, 1956; Chou Wu, *Li Kung-lin* (Chung-kuo hua-chia ts'ung-shu, vol. 12), Shanghai, 1958; J. F. Cahill, *Chinese Paintings, 11th-14th Centuries*, New York, 1960.
MARTIE W. YOUNG

LILIO, ANDREA (Andrea d'Ancona nella Marca). Italian religious painter (b. Ancona, 1555; d. Ascoli, 1610). He worked in Rome for Pope Sixtus V on the Vatican Library, the Lateran Palace, and other commissions. For the next pope, Clement VIII, he decorated churches and convents with elaborate ornamental multifigured frescoes.

LI LIU-FANG. Chinese painter (1575–1629). He was known by his *tzu* Ch'ang-heng. A native of Hsieh-hsien, Anhui Province, he spent most of his life in Chia-ting near Shanghai. Li Liu-fang is classified among the "Nine Friends in Painting" and included among the "Four Masters of Chia-ting." Not a particularly gifted painter, he gained his reputation for the low-keyed and intimate studies of older masters that he produced in some numbers.

BIBLIOGRAPHY. K. Tomita and K. M. Ch'iu, "An Album of Six Chinese Paintings Dated 1618, by Li Liu-fang," *Boston Museum of Fine Arts, Bulletin*, XLVIII, June, 1950.

LILLE: FINE ARTS MUSEUM. One of the richest provincial collections in France. It is particularly strong in paintings by Flemish and Dutch artists, such as Dirk Bouts, Rubens, Van Dyck, Jordaens, Ostade, Van Goijen, De Witte, and Hals. There are Spanish paintings by Goya and Ribera, together with some Italian and German works, notably Holbein's *Woman and Child*. French paintings include David's *Belisarius*, Courbet's *After Dinner at Ornans*, and a number of impressionist landscapes. The collection of drawings boasts some specimens from the hand of Michelangelo. Also displayed are ivories, enamels, gold- and silverwork, ceramics, and coins.

BIBLIOGRAPHY. F. Benoit, *La Peinture au Musée de Lille*, Paris, 1909.

LI LUNG-MIEN, *see* LI KUNG-LIN.

LIMA: CATHEDRAL OF LA ASUNCION. Peruvian church begun in 1540 and subsequently redesigned by the Spanish architect Francisco Becerra in 1582 and 1598. A principal edifice of 16th-century Spanish colonial building, it is an aisleless structure with Mudejar ceilings of geometric pattern in wood, approached by large walled courtyards where the Indians once gathered for religious instruction. The Cathedral is rectangular in plan and of the hall-church type in elevation.

Earthquake damage in 1606 and 1609 required the replacement of the groin vaults with rib vaults (1613–22); they were finally rebuilt along with much of the rest of the building in wood and plaster after the earthquake of 1746. Despite many changes and repairs, the interior reflects the austere Vignolan *estilo desornamentado* (ornamentless style) of Spain before 1585.

BIBLIOGRAPHY. G. Kubler and M. Soria, *Art and Architecture in Spain and Portugal and Their American Dominions, 1500–1800*, Baltimore, 1959.

LIMA: MUSEUM OF ART. Peruvian collection started privately in 1954. The restoration of the building, which was donated by the city of Lima, was financed by the Peruvian and French governments. Experts from UNESCO helped with the architecture and the organization of the museum. Exhibits range from ancient Nazca ceramics to modern abstract paintings. The collections represent sixteen pre-Columbian cultures and the Quito school of colonial painting as well as European trends. There are also furniture, silverware, and jewelry from the 17th through the 19th century.

LIMA: SAN FRANCISCO. Peruvian monastery church first constructed in the 16th century but rebuilt (1657–74) after the earthquake of 1656. Designed by the Portuguese architect Constantino de Vasconcelos, with the help of Manuel de Escobar and others, the church presents a façade of two massive, rusticated towers framing the narrow and gracefully vertical central portal. Divided into three aisles, the interior has a vaulted ceiling and dome decorated with Moorish motifs. The attached cloister makes ingenious and harmonious use of a two-story arcade, with an alternating system of arches and ovals adjusting the upper story to the larger, straighforward procession of arches in the lower story.

BIBLIOGRAPHY. B. Gento Sanz, *San Francisco de Lima*, Lima, 1945.

LIMBOURG BROTHERS. The most noted Franco-Flemish illuminators of their time (fl. before 1399–ca. 1439). They worked primarily for the great patron of arts, Jean, duc de Berry.

The brothers have been identified as Paul (Pol), Hermann, and John (Jehanequin) Malouel. Coming from Guelders, in the Lowlands, they were apprenticed before 1399 to a goldsmith in Paris, where their training and early attachment to the court of Burgundy thoroughly acquainted them with the leading art trends of the day. Their early works, such as the *Heures d'Ailly* (ca. 1403; M. de Rothschild Collection) for the Duc de Berry, show the influence of the Boucicaut Master, of Jacquemart de Hesdin, and of Melchior Broederlam. Most important was Hesdin, whose Italianate qualities appear in the Limbourgs' works. The brothers, not daring innovators at this stage, were effectively able to synthesize the various experimental developments of their contemporaries. To this synthesis they brought a finesse of line and execution and an attention to details that clearly indicate their early goldsmith training.

The major work of the Limbourgs is the *Très riches heures du Duc de Berry* (Chantilly, Musée Condé). Started in 1413 and not finished at the time of the Duke's death in 1416, it was finally completed by Jean Colombe. This manuscript is perhaps the epitome of late medieval illumination. It is composed, as are most Books of Hours, of a Calendar, Hours of the Virgin, and other liturgical el-

Limbourg brothers, illumination, from the *Très riches heures du Duc de Berry*. Musée Condé, Chantilly.

ements. The Calendar presents a scene of appropriate labors for each month. Each scene is set against a background of one of the Duke's castles, done with such detail and individualization as to make them identifiable. The labors are depicted with an eye for local color and picturesqueness, representing what might be called the first true genre painting in the North.

Among the other illustrations of the *Très riches heures* is a unique illumination of the "Zodiacal Man," which indicates the persistence of the medieval notion of the determining nature of the zodiac on the various parts of the human body. Other of the major illuminations show the Limbourgs' knowledge of and indebtedness to Italian art. The *Presentation of Christ* is an almost exact translation of Taddeo Gaddi's *Presentation of the Virgin* (Florence, Sta Croce, Baroncelli Chapel). In like manner, the figure of Adam in the *Fall of Man and Expulsion from Paradise* seems an almost direct copy of Brunelleschi's Isaac, from his famous "competition panel" of 1401 (Florence, National Museum). These and numerous other such cases make it seem a certainty that one of the brothers visited Italy and was especially influenced by Florentine art.

The great contribution of the Limbourgs is their consolidation of the many rapid advances of the illuminator's art. It was from this solid basis that the art of the first generation of Flemish panel painters developed.

BIBLIOGRAPHY. P. Durrieu, *La Miniature flamande au temps de la cour de Bourgogne*, Brussels, 1921.

STANLEY FERBER

Limburg an der Lahn. Cathedral of St. George, 13th century.

LIMBURG AN DER LAHN: CATHEDRAL OF ST. GEORGE.

German 13th-century cathedral. It rises dramatically and picturesquely above a precipitous cliff overlooking the Lahn River. Beneath it are clusters of ancient water mills and half-timbered 15th-century houses. The present Cathedral, originally an abbey church, was built on the site of the Basilica of St. George Martyr, which was dedicated in 909, and which itself had been erected, according to legend, on the site of the Roman fort of Drusus. The Cathedral was dedicated in 1235.

The exterior displays the characteristic grandeur of the German Romanesque and is crowned by seven towers symbolizing the seven sacraments. The great tower over the crossing, symbolizing the Last Supper, was considered of special significance to the faithful.

The interior, dating from the 13th century, reflects the influence of Gothic forms, strongly resembling the Cathedral of Laon. Though it is a characteristic three-aisle church, the elevation is of four stories. The main triforium is deeply recessed, and the gallery is divided by a triple pointed arcade, the center arch of which is heavily stilted. The upper triforium is a shallow arcade consisting of four arches to each bay. Single windows that pierce the clerestory are today unfortunately filled with poor glass, since the original windows were removed in the 18th and 19th centuries. A great deal of bad restoration was done at Limburg at that time, and a considerable number of important 13th-century wall paintings were lost. However, in 1935 careful restoration revealed a number of original works, including the 13th-century paintings of the four elements, the four rivers of Paradise, and the archangels Michael and Gabriel, as well as the especially fine scene of Samson uprooting a tree.

A fine 13th-century monument to the founder, Conrad Kurzbold, Salic count of the Niederlangaus, who died in 948, is in the Cathedral. The sculptor created an idealized image that represented the concept of 13th-century chivalry. It is a youthful ascetic interpretation, sober and noble.

BIBLIOGRAPHY. E. von Niebelschütz, *Der Dom zu Limburg*, 2d ed., Munich, 1950.

ALDEN F. MEGREW

LIMNING. Obsolete term for the art of painting miniature portraits such as those first done by Holbein and others in the 16th century. Miniatures were particularly popular in 17th-century England; about 1600 Nicholas Hilliard wrote a treatise called *The Arte of Limning*, which was finally published in 1912. By transference, the term was also applied to early portrait painting in the American colonies.

LIMOGES, *see* LIMOUSIN.

LIMOGES: CATHEDRAL OF SAINT-ETIENNE. French Gothic cathedral. The most interesting part is the 13th-century choir, which was probably built from designs by Jean Deschamps, who was also the architect of Notre-Dame-du-Port at Clermont-Ferrand. The remainder of the Cathedral dates largely from the 14th and 16th centuries. Above the entrance is a 16th-century rood loft containing six bas-reliefs of the Labors of Hercules.

LIMOUSIN. Former province and center of a regional French school of architecture, painting, and sculpture, in a vast plateau covering most of the western portion of the Massif Central in France. Limoges was its capital and chief city. Limousin became an important center of art during the Middle Ages.

The Romanesque monastic church of St-Martial at Limoges, of the pilgrimage type with tribunes, or galleries, over the nave, transept, and choir aisles, was destroyed during the Revolution. The abbey of St-Martial was renowned for its illuminated manuscripts. The Cathedral, begun in 1273, perhaps by Jean Deschamps, is the most important Gothic monument of the city. *See* LIMOGES: CATHEDRAL OF SAINT-ETIENNE.

Limoges is perhaps best known for its enamels, executed from the 12th century on, for the most part in the champlevé technique, in which the design is gouged out of the metal plaque and the liquid enamel poured into the resultant hollow. The Municipal Museum and the Musée National Adrien-Dubouché boast important collections of Limousin enamels. In the 15th and 16th centuries Limousin artists used a different technique, which involved painting with enamel directly onto the copper plaque. *See* ENAMEL. *See also* PENICAUD FAMILY; REYMOND FAMILY.

BIBLIOGRAPHY. M. M. S. Gauthier, *Emaux limousins champlevés des XIIe, XIIIe et XIVe siècles*, Paris, 1950.

JOHN B. CAMERON

LIN, see CHINA: PAINTING (COPIES).

LINARD, JACQUES. French still-life painter (b. Paris? ca. 1600; d. Paris, 1645). Almost nothing is known of this painter, whose still lifes rank with the best done in France during the reign of Louis XIII, notably those of Louise Moillon and Lubin Baugin. In 1631 Linard held the title *peintre et valet de chambre ordinaire du roi.* His works successfully combine realism and poetry and feature fruits and flowers on the edge of a table.

BIBLIOGRAPHY. M. Faré, *La Nature morte en France*, Geneva, 1962.

LINCLUDEN COLLEGIATE CHURCH. Fourteenth-century church within a 12th-century Benedictine nunnery, both of which are in ruins, in southwestern Scotland. The church contains one of the oldest surviving rood screens in Scotland and the tomb of the Princess Countess of Douglas.

BIBLIOGRAPHY. J. S. Coltart, *Scottish Church Architecture*, New York, 1936.

LINCOLN, ALEXANDER OF, *see* ALEXANDER OF LINCOLN.

LINCOLN, NEBR.: SHELDON MEMORIAL ART GALLERY. Museum located at the University of Nebraska. It is housed in a building designed by Philip Johnson and completed in 1963. Its rectangular travertine walls, broken only on two sides by six flat-arched doorways, conceal a functional, two-story interior containing a small auditorium and fourteen galleries for exhibiting the university's modest but discriminating collection, which consists mainly of modern American painting and sculpture (since 1920), with some European examples.

Among the artists represented are Barlach (*Standing Woman with Folded Arms*), Beckmann, Bellows, Blume (*The White Factory*), Brancusi, Calder, Callahan, Corinth, Crawford, Davis (*Arch Hotel*), De Kooning, Demuth (*Backdrop of East Lynne*), Edwin Dickinson (*Girl on Tennis Court*), Eakins (*Portrait of Mrs. Samuel Murray*), Eilshemius, Feininger (*City Moon*), Glackens, Graves (*Eagle of the Inner Eye*), Hartley (*Mount Katahdin, Autumn, No. 1*), Hepworth, Hofmann, Homer (*Fly Fishing, Saranac Lake*), Hopper, Kirchner, Lachaise (*Portrait of John Marin*), Levine (*Pensionnaire*), Marin (*Pertaining to Nassau Street, New York*), Marini (*Horseman*), Miró, Moore, Morandi, Motherwell, O'Keeffe (*New York, Night*), Rattner, Rodin (*Portrait of Charles Baudelaire*), Ryder, Sheeler, Siqueiros, Sloan (*Portrait of Robert Henri*), Stamos, Stella, and Zorach.

BIBLIOGRAPHY. E. Spaeth, *American Art Museums and Galleries*, New York, 1960.

JOHN D. MORSE

LINCOLN CATHEDRAL. One of the finest Gothic buildings in Great Britain. The Cathedral at Lincoln replaced an 11th-century cathedral that had been damaged in an earthquake in 1185. Begun in 1192 under Bishop St. Hugh, the present building incorporated some earlier work, especially in the wide (175 ft.) west-façade screen. The odd *chevet* vaults date from 1210; the complex nave vaults (by 1233) are the antithesis of contemporary French vaults (such as those of the Amiens Cathedral nave). The plan includes two transepts, inspired by Canterbury, and terminates to the east in the celebrated Angel Choir (1256–ca. 1280), the perfection of the English Decorated style.

Lincoln Cathedral. The Angel Choir, 1256–ca. 1280, and cloister.

The chapter house (ca. 1220) is the earliest example of the polygonal plan used on a large scale. The sculptured angels are related to the Anglo-French style of Westminster.

BIBLIOGRAPHY. G. Webb, *Architecture in Britain: The Middle Ages*, Baltimore, 1956.

LINCOLN MEMORIAL, WASHINGTON, D.C., *see* BACON, HENRY.

LINDAU (Ashburnham) GOSPELS. Carolingian illuminated manuscript with gold upper and lower covers, in the Pierpont Morgan Library, New York. *See* CAROLINGIAN ART AND ARCHITECTURE (IVORIES AND METALWORK); HIBERNO-SAXON ART.

LINDISFARNE. Island sometimes known as the Holy Island, located off the northwest coast of England. Famous for the monastery founded there in 635 by St. Aidan of Iona, Lindisfarne became a hub of culture and learning. It was the center of Northumbrian art during the 7th and 8th centuries, its most notable productions being illuminated manuscripts. *See* NORTHUMBRIAN ART.

The most famous of its manuscripts is the Lindisfarne Gospels (late 7th cent.; London, British Museum). The work shows the fusion of late-antique models (probably derived from copies) and "traditional" Barbarian decorative motifs. Figural representation is highly stylized; Barbarian motifs are introduced, especially in the rich carpet pages. One sees the visually dynamic intermixture of spirals, lozenge shapes, interlace, and lacertine that characterize so much of the Barbarian style. *See* BARBARIAN STYLE.

See also HIBERNO-SAXON ART.

BIBLIOGRAPHY. N. Pevsner, *The Buildings of England*, vol. 15: *Northumberland*, Harmondsworth, 1957.

LINDNER, RICHARD. German-American painter (1901–   ). Born in Hamburg, Lindner studied at the School of Fine and Applied Arts, Nürnberg, and the Academy of Fine Arts, Munich. Leaving Nazi Germany in 1933, he settled in Paris and in 1941 went to the United States, where he has lived since. Following a period as a successful illustrator for *Fortune, Vogue, Harper's Bazaar*, and other magazines, Lindner has turned exclusively to painting since 1952. The mechanistic eroticism of Lindner's inflated figures reflects both the satiric approach of German art in the 1920s and the "pop" culture of the United States.

BIBLIOGRAPHY. William and Noma Copley Foundation, *Lindner* [London, 1960?].

LINDSAY, NORMAN. Australian etcher, pen draftsman, illustrator, and novelist (1879–   ). His erotic illustrations, done in the Jugendstil manner, scandalized his generation. His first novel, *Red Heap*, was banned in Australia. He is the most unconventional and best-known member of a family of active artists.

LINE AND WASH. Type of drawing in which the outline, usually in ink, is shaded with tones produced by water color or ink diluted with water. Known since antiquity,

Johannes Lingelbach, **Peasants Loading a Hay Cart, 1664. National Gallery, London.**

line and wash drawings were particularly popular during the baroque period. The many fine wash drawings by Tiepolo exemplify the technique.

LINECUT. Method of graphic reproduction similar to woodcut, but executed in metal and used in modern book production. The effect is that of a line drawing; no intermediary tones are produced. Modern linecuts are made photomechanically.

LINE ENGRAVING, *see* ENGRAVING.

LINE OF BEAUTY. Term used by William Hogarth in his treatise, *The Analysis of Beauty* (1753), to describe the essential characteristic of all great art. It is the abstract basis of painting and literally the line that carries the eye of the observer through the work. The idea derives from the 16th-century mannerist theory of Lomazzo, who writes of a serpentine line that expresses the inner vision of the artist, but Hogarth, unlike Lomazzo, claims to find it in nature first. The line of beauty used in three dimensions Hogarth terms the line of grace. Although much parodied, this idea was taken up with great enthusiasm by the neoclassicists, particularly the writer Winckelmann and the painter Mengs.

LINGAM. Phallus, Hindu symbol under which Siva is universally worshiped. The lingam is represented as a cone or column, often with the figure of the god superimposed or enclosed, revealed through an elliptical opening.

LINGARAJA TEMPLE, *see* BHUVANESVARA.

LINGELBACH, JOHANNES. Dutch painter of landscape and genre (b. Frankfurt am Main, 1622; d. Amsterdam, 1674). Lingelbach seems to have been brought to Amsterdam while still quite young. It is not known who his master was, but his work broadly fits into the tradition of Pieter van Laer. In 1642 Lingelbach traveled to France, where he spent two years before continuing on to Italy. He arrived in Rome in 1644 and spent a number of years there. In 1650 he returned to Amsterdam via Germany.

The major influences found in Lingelbach's work are all from members of the Dutch Italianate landscape tradition. The influence of Van Laer is still felt in Lingelbach's 1664 *Folk Scene on the Piazza del Popolo at Rome* (Vienna, Picture Gallery of Academy of Fine Arts). However, such works as the *Entrance Ramp to the Capitoline Hill in Rome* (Amsterdam, Rijksmuseum) are conceived in a manner that recalls the harbor scenes of Jan Baptist Weenix. Another important influence on Lingelbach's works is the work of Philips Wouwermans (*Peasants Loading a Hay Cart*, 1664; London, National Gallery). Lingelbach seems to have collaborated with a number of artists, painting the figures for Jan Hackaert, Philips Koninck, Frederick de Moucheron, and others.

BIBLIOGRAPHY. A. Busiri Vici, "Fantasie romane di Johannes Lingelbach," *Studi Romani*, VII, January–February, 1959; N. Maclaren, *National Gallery Catalogues: The Dutch School*, London, 1960; M. E. Houtzager et al., *Nederlandse 17e eeuwse Italianiserende Landschapschilders*, Utrecht, 1965.

LEONARD J. SLATKES

LINING. Restoration technique in which an old, damaged canvas backing a painting is strengthened by the addition of a new, stronger piece of canvas. It is also known as relining.

LINKOPING CATHEDRAL. Swedish cathedral begun in 1150 in the Romanesque style. The north portal dates from that period. It was completed in the 15th century in the Gothic style. The decorative blind arcades of the north and south inner walls show the transition from the Romanesque to the Gothic pointed, trefoil arches. The Gothic hall nave is of the late 13th and the early 14th century. The three high chapels behind the chancel, completed in 1498, and the choir by Master Gerlach of Cologne are late Gothic.

BIBLIOGRAPHY. A. Hahr, *Architecture in Sweden*, Stockholm, 1938.

LINNELL, JOHN. English portrait and landscape painter (b. London, 1792; d. Redhill, 1882). He studied at the Royal Academy schools and also under the water-color painter John Varley. He first exhibited at the Royal Academy in 1807. In 1818 he met William Blake, whom he admired, and in 1822 was responsible for introducing Blake to Samuel Palmer. Palmer later married Linnell's daughter. Linnell painted penetrating and delicate small-scale portraits, but from about 1847 concentrated on landscapes. He brought into conventional landscape painting something of Palmer's romanticism and an unusual richness of color.

BIBLIOGRAPHY. A. T. Story, *The Life of John Linnell*, London, 1892.

LINOLEUM CUT. A relief print process. Analogous in spirit and effect to the woodcut, the linoleum cut is rel-

Linoleum cut. Bruno Binosi, *Composition*. Private collection, Milan.

atively easier to handle, and its special textures often give a heavy, rich tone to the print. Although artists and collectors alike have not favored the linoleum cut, its potentialities for contemporary visual expression are shown in the examples by Picasso.

An unmounted piece of battleship linoleum, preferably white or off-white in color, is scraped to remove the manufacturer's finish. The artist cuts into the linoleum with a knife, defining edges and removing lines and areas that should appear as whites in the final print. Equal proportions of artist's black oil paint and black printer's ink are used in inking.

BIBLIOGRAPHY. J. Heller, *Printmaking Today*, New York, 1958.

LINT, HENDRIK FRANS VAN (Studio). Flemish painter (b. Antwerp, 1684; d. Rome, 1763). He was a disciple of Pieter van Bredael. Van Lint settled in Rome early in life. While his first works were done in the manner of Theobold Michau and Cornelis Huysmans, he soon took to painting Italian *vedute* (views) in the style of Gaspare Vanvitelli.

BIBLIOGRAPHY. H. Gerson and E. H. ter Kuile, *Art and Architecture in Belgium, 1600–1800*, Baltimore, 1960.

LINT, PIETER VAN. Flemish painter (1609–90). A native of Antwerp, Van Lint painted religious and mythological compositions and portraits. He became a master in 1633 and worked first in the impasto technique and chiaroscuro palette of the Flemish Caravaggists. He later changed to a Rubensian color scheme and a form language that drew inspiration from Anthony van Dyck. Van Lint had numerous pupils.

BIBLIOGRAPHY. R. Oldenbourg, *Die flämische Malerei des 17. Jahrhunderts*, 2d ed., Berlin, 1922; R. H. Wilenski, *Flemish Painters, 1430–1830*, vol. 1, London, 1960.

LINTEL. Horizontal member spanning an opening and supporting a load. Lintels are most often built of stone or brick masonry and steel. The lintel bearing on posts, called post-and-lintel construction, is one of the simplest and earliest forms of construction and constitutes the basic structural system of Egyptian and ancient Greek architecture.

LIN T'ING-KUEI. Chinese painter (fl. 12th cent.). Lin T'ing-kuei was active in the region of Ning-p'o, Chekiang Province. He is not recorded in any of the standard biographical sources for Chinese painters and is known principally for the part he played in producing the set of 100 paintings devoted to lohans, which he executed with Chou Chi-ch'ang. *See* ARHAT; CHOU CHI-CH'ANG.

BIBLIOGRAPHY. Wen Fong, "The Lohans and a Bridge to Heaven," *Freer Gallery of Art, Occasional Papers*, III, 1958.

LINTON, WILLIAM J. American wood engraver and author (1812–97). Born in London, he studied under G. W. Bonner and J. O. Smith. Linton went to the United States in 1866 and later taught at Cooper Union in New York City. He illustrated and published many books and pamphlets with wood engravings and is the author of *The History of Wood Engraving in America* (1880 and 1882).

LINTOTT, EDWARD BARNARD. English portrait painter, landscapist, and water-colorist (b. London, 1875; d.

1951). He received a conservative education at the Académie Julian in Paris under Laurens and Constant, and also studied at the Ecole des Beaux-Arts. Lintott was acting librarian at the Royal Academy of Arts from 1915 and art adviser to the *London Times* from 1924. Later he moved to the United States. His portraits of notable American and British sitters are marked by good design, harmonious color, and faithful likeness, although they show little psychological insight.

LINZ: NEW GALLERY (Neue Galerie der Stadt Linz). Austrian museum devoted primarily to 19th- and 20th-century painting, sculpture, drawings, and prints from the German-speaking countries. The German painters Max Liebermann and Lovis Corinth are particularly well represented. Other paintings of interest are by the Swiss Böcklin; the Germans Friedrich, Feuerbach, Thoma, Trübner, Slevogt, Nolde, Hofer, Modersohn-Becker, Müller, Pechstein, and Nay; the Austrians Makart, Romako, Klimt, Schiele, and Kokoschka; and the Hungarian Munkácsy.

BIBLIOGRAPHY. Neue Galerie der Stadt Linz, Wolfgang Gurlitt Museum, *Katalog der Schaussammlung*, Linz, 1959.

LION. From the beginning of Western history the lion has been a symbol in every culture that was aware of its existence. In Egypt and the ancient Near East the lion was an important symbol of the power and nobility of the ruler, for example, the Lion Gates at the Palace of Sargon II at Khorsabad. In Christian art the lion is sometimes the symbol for Christ. This symbolism originated in a legend concerning lion cubs who were born dead but who came to life three days later when their father breathed upon them. The lion also symbolizes St. Mark and is the attribute of St. Jerome.

LION GATE, MYCENAE. Well-preserved Mycenaean gate (ca. 1250 B.C.), known since antiquity. It was never buried. The gate (ca. 9½ ft. wide and ca. 10 ft. high) consists of four large monoliths of stone, forming the two jambs, the lintel, and the threshold. The wall above the lintel forms an empty triangle, the "relieving triangle." A limestone slab is placed there, blocking the void of the triangle. The slab presents in relief two heraldic lions separated by a downward tapering central column that is raised on top of two altars and carries a capital with entablature. This column has been interpreted by some scholars as the cult image of the protecting deity of the city. The relief is the earliest-known piece of monumental sculpture from the Greek mainland. It reveals an advanced technique in modeling. The heads of the lions, which were carved separately of different material, are now missing.

BIBLIOGRAPHY. W. B. Dinsmoor, *The Architecture of Ancient Greece*, 3d ed., London, 1950; G. E. Mylonas, *Ancient Mycenae*, Princeton, 1957.

LIONNI, LEO. American graphic artist (1910–   ). Born in Amsterdam, he earned a Ph.D. in economics at the University of Genoa. He became active in painting, advertising, and design in Milan, at the same time writing on art, architecture, and films. He went to the United States in 1939 and soon had such clients as N. W. Ayer and Son and the Container Corporation of America. But Lionni is most famous as art director of *Fortune*, where

Jean-Etienne Liotard, *Lady Taking Chocolate*. State Art Collections, Picture Gallery, Dresden.

he has set a top standard of graphic excellence and sophistication. Lionni has served as head of the Graphic Design Department at the Parsons School of Design, as president of the American Institute of Graphic Arts, and as co-editor of *Print* magazine.

LIOTARD, JEAN-ETIENNE. Swiss painter of portraits and landscapes, pastelist, miniaturist, and engraver (b. Geneva, 1702; d. there, 1789). After serving an apprenticeship with D. Gardelle and J. Petitot in Geneva, he went to Paris with his twin brother, Jean-Michel Liotard, and they worked with the engravers J.-B. Massé and B. Audran II respectively. After engraving Watteau's *Sick Cat* with much finesse and briefly studying with François Lemoyne, Liotard launched into a spectacular career as a fashionable portraitist in pastel, but was forced by competition to travel for a living. From 1736 to 1738 he traveled to Naples in the suite of the ambassador, De Puisieux, and subsequently to Rome, where he met Sir William Ponsonby, later Lord Bessborough. Sir William took him through the islands of the eastern Mediterranean to Constantinople (1738–43). There he did portraits for the French consul, the Comte de Bonnéval (called "Achmed Pacha"), and his circle. Lio-

tard's affectation of beard and Levantine dress earned him the nickname, the "Turkish Painter."

He did portraits of the ruler of Jassy in Moldavia on his way to Vienna (1743–45), where he was acclaimed by the court of Maria Teresa. From 1745 to 1748 he was in Venice and Geneva, and from 1748 to 1753 in Paris. He exhibited at the 1753 Salon. In England (1753–55) he portrayed the Prince of Wales and strongly influenced Francis Cotes. In Holland (1753, intermittently to 1770) he portrayed the Dutch court and became an amateur dealer in Dutch old master paintings. After a final sojourn in England (1772–74), where he exhibited at the Royal Academy on two occasions, he retired to Geneva.

Though some of his portraits have been characterized as dry, belabored, and gingerbread-colored, as psychological studies they partake of the quasi-scientific rage of the age for the revelation of personality. His celebrated portrait *Mme de L'Epinay* (1760; Geneva Museum of Art and History) reveals a near-clinical interest in psychopathy. *François Tronchin* (1757; Bessinges, Tronchin Collection) is suggestive of Mme Tussaud's wax effigies. Occult compositions, such as the *Portrait of the Countess of Coventry in Greek Dress* (1754; Amsterdam, Rijksmuseum), anticipate the chance views of later artists. The *Lady Taking Chocolate* (versions in Dresden, State Art Collections, Picture Gallery, and Bessborough Collection) remains charming in the salutary 18th-century vein. The complexity of his personality reflects the encyclopedic interests and romantic sentiments of the time. His pastel self-portraits (1749, with beard; 1775, as an old man; both Geneva Museum of Art and History) reveal a fascination with self-analysis and photographic realism. His works are found in Amsterdam, Carcassonne, Dresden, Geneva, London (Victoria and Albert), Paris, and Vienna.

BIBLIOGRAPHY. E. Humbert et al., *La Vie et les oeuvres de J. E. Liotard, 1702–1789...*, Amsterdam, 1897; F. Fosca, *Liotard (1702–1789)*, Paris, 1928.

GEORGE V. GALLENKAMP

LIPCHITZ, JACQUES. Lithuanian-American sculptor (1891–). He was born in Druskieniki, left school in Vilna in 1909, and went to Paris with the intention of becoming a sculptor. He became a student at the Ecole des Beaux-Arts, at first in the studio of Jean Antoine Injalbert. In 1910 he shifted to a direct carving class and became a pupil of Raoul Verlet at the Académie Julian. Lipchitz attended an evening sketching class in Montparnasse and studied primitive, archaic, ancient, and Gothic art in the Louvre. He began his own art collection about 1910.

In 1913 he met Picasso through Diego Rivera. His work at that time, as seen in *Woman and Gazelles*, was moving in a direction different from that of cubism. By 1914 his *Sailor With a Guitar* (Philadelphia Museum of Art), made in Madrid after a summer in Mallorca, showed the beginning of his sympathy with the cubists. This affinity became stronger even before the formation of a close friendship with Juan Gris in 1916. His *Bather* (1915) and brilliant *Man with a Guitar* (1916; New York, Guggenheim Museum) rank with the finest cubist sculptures. The human form has been remade into an imaginative schematic idea, a notational system of incomplete and interlocking forms such as we find in the work of Picasso and Braque during that time. Lipchitz's polychromed reliefs of 1918 seem to be developments of the still lifes painted by Picasso. His themes, which include the bather, seated man, and Pierrot, attest to the view that one of the revolutions in modern sculpture first occurred in form rather than in content.

Lipchitz's first one-man exhibition took place in 1920 at the Leonce Rosenberg Gallery in Paris. It was at about this time that his reputation began to increase. He received a commission for five reliefs from Dr. Albert C. Barnes. These reliefs were installed on the exterior of the Barnes Foundation in Merion, Pa., in 1922. That same year Lipchitz joined the Esprit Nouveau group, which included Ozenfant and Le Corbusier and which was concerned with the unification of art and architecture. By now his style had broadened and matured to the extent that he could return to portraiture, and in 1922 he did a striking head of his first wife. His cubist works now oscillated between rigid vertical forms and increasingly curved, faceted volumes.

With *Bather* (1923–25; owned by the artist), which is more than 6 feet in height, Lipchitz increased the scale of his work. He has continued to create very large, medium-size, and small works throughout his career. In 1925 his experiments with small cardboard shapes cast in the lost-wax process led to his "transparents," such as *Pierrot with Clarinet* (1926) and *Acrobats on a Ball* (1926; Baroness Gougaud Collection). In these works he frequently opened up the interiors of his sculptures. In 1927 Lipchitz was commissioned by Vicomte Charles de Noailles to do his first large-scale group composition, *La Joie de Vivre*, and it was set up in the Vicomte's garden at Hyères. In 1960 Lipchitz reworked this monumental sculpture slightly and exhibited it at the Whitney Museum of American Art, New York.

Between 1926 and 1930 he worked on one of his most important sculptures, *Figure*, originally intended for a private garden and now in the New York Museum of Modern Art sculpture garden. *Figure* is one of the most imaginative human metaphors in modern sculpture; its chainlike form is a powerful image of internal tension. By contrast, in 1928 Lipchitz made the more relaxed *Reclining Woman with Guitar* for the garden of Mme de Mandrot at Le Pradet, Toulon. In the same garden he placed his *Song of the Vowels* in 1931 (now in Zurich, Art Gallery). In 1930 Lipchitz had his first retrospective at the Galerie de la Renaissance in Paris, but it was not until 1935 that he had his first major exhibition in the United States, at the Brummer Gallery in New York.

The early 1930s saw Lipchitz working in different modes and often reworking themes from his earlier period in such works as *Mother and Child* (1922–30; artist's collection) and the moving *Return of the Prodigal* (1931), in which the artist images his feelings of "thirst" for the love of the family. By this time his forms had acquired a more sensuous volume, and the cubist skeletal armature had been fleshed out. From cubism, however, as well as from his contact with fantastic painting, he had enriched the meaning of his work through free association and through a personal development of the compound image. Good examples of this evocative type of multiple imagery can be seen in the *Harpists* (1930) and *Benediction* (1942; both

Jacques Lipchitz, *Mother and Child II*, 1941–45. Museum of Modern Art, New York (Mrs. Simon Guggenheim Fund).

B. J. Reis Collection). In the early 1930s Lipchitz also began his series of botanical metaphors, which were sometimes erotic evocations of birth and growth such as *Chimène* (1930) and *Spring* (1942; Reis Collection).

In 1936–37, during the Paris World's Fair, an entire gallery was given over to the exhibition of his work, including the prize-winning *Prometheus* sculpture. The Prometheus theme was an important one for Lipchitz, and he reworked it for the Ministry of Education and Health Building in Rio de Janeiro in 1943-44. It was his statement of man's triumph over the forces that plague him and signaled his renewed interest in the modern reinterpretation of older myths. Also in the 1940s he undertook his *Sacrifice* series, a personal commentary on man's spiritual history and rise from human or blood offering to the humane worship of the Virgin. The series includes *Prayer* (1943; Ingersoll Collection).

In 1941 Lipchitz went to live in the United States. During a visit to France in 1946 he was commissioned by Father Couturier to make a baptismal font for the Church of Notre-Dame-de-Toute-Grâce, Assy. Completed in 1954, it is probably the finest religious sculpture in modern art. Casts of the work, known also as the *Virgin of the Inverted Heart*, are in New Harmony, Ind., in the shrine designed by Philip Johnson, and in the monastery on the isle of Iona. Other important commissions include the *Birth of the Muses* for Mrs. John D. Rockefeller III (1944–50) and a version of the *Prometheus* for Fairmount Park in Philadelphia.

In 1952 fire destroyed his New York City studio as

well as important works of art and working models. With funds obtained in part from portrait commissions he built a new studio near his home at Hastings-on-the-Hudson, N.Y., where he now lives and works. In 1959 Lipchitz exhibited a series of small lost-wax cast automatics, a series that was devoted to exploring "the limits of the possible" and recall his earlier work with the transparents. Having pioneered in cubism, surrealism, the return to myths, and spontaneous sculpture, Lipchitz then chose to rework some of his earlier cubist pieces. He has given to sculpture great dramatic scope and depth as well as a seriousness and excitement that rivals those qualities in the best of modern painting.

BIBLIOGRAPHY. New York, Museum of Modern Art, *The Sculpture of Jacques Lipchitz*, by H. R. Hope, New York, 1954; A. M. Hammacher, *Jacques Lipchitz, His Sculpture*, New York [1961?].
ALBERT ELSEN

LIPPI, FILIPPINO. Italian painter (b. Prato, 1457; d. Florence, 1504). He was the son of the painter Filippo Lippi. Filippino's work can be roughly divided into three periods. The early work is so close to Botticelli that it has been attributed to the "Amico di Sandro." From about 1485 Filippino's style developed independently but was still somewhat derivative in character. By the 1490s he had evolved a mature style that was to influence Piero di Cosimo and the Florentine mannerists of the 16th century.

Filippino's first appearance in the documents does not occur until 1466, when he accompanied his father to Spoleto. In 1472 he is documented as being in the shop of Botticelli. While the major painters were working at the Vatican in 1481–83, he remained in Florence to complete the decoration of the Brancacci Chapel, which had been started by Masolino and Masaccio. From 1488 to 1493 Filippino was in Rome painting the Caraffa Chapel in S. Maria sopra Minerva. Returning to Florence in 1493, he remained there until his death.

The early phase of Filippino's career is characterized by a sweetness and delicacy derived from Fra Filippo and Botticelli. The *Esther* series of about 1478, the *Adoration of the Magi* (ca. 1475–80; London, National Gallery), and the *Adoration* (ca. 1480; Leningrad, Hermitage) are all close to Botticelli in style. Although they are still somewhat derivative, the Brancacci frescoes and the roundels for S. Gimignano (1483–84) conclude this period in a rather personal vein.

The *Apparition of the Virgin to St. Bernard* (1486; Florence, Badia) ushers in what might be called a mature style and it also prepares the way for the late works. Of great importance for an understanding of Filippino's style at this moment are the frescoes of the Caraffa Chapel and the altarpiece for Tanai di Nerli (ca. 1488) in Sto Spirito, Florence.

The late works have a nervous and agitated quality that seems to prefigure Florentine mannerism. The signed and dated *Adoration of the Magi* (1496; Florence, Uffizi) is far more manneristic than the panel destined for the monks of S. Donato a Scopeto, which Leonardo had left unfinished in 1481. The frescoes in the Strozzi Chapel of S. Maria Novella (1500–02) emphasize the horror, tensions, and ambiguities that also characterize the art of the following historical period. In these and other later works

Filippino is truly a unique artist with much to offer succeeding generations.

BIBLIOGRAPHY. A. Scharf, *Filippino Lippi*, Vienna, 1950; L. Berti and U. Baldini, *Filippino Lippi*, Florence, 1957.
JOHN R. SPENCER

LIPPI, FRA FILIPPO. Italian painter (b. Florence, ca. 1406; d. Spoleto, 1469). One of the major innovators of the Renaissance, he made the more difficult aspects of Masaccio's art acceptable and determined the direction of a great part of Florentine painting.

In accordance with the custom of the time Lippi's impoverished parents placed him in a monastery. He took his vows at S. Maria del Carmine in Florence in 1421, is listed in the monastic rolls as a painter in 1430, and is last mentioned in Carmelite documents in 1432. Documented in Padua in 1434, he was certainly back in Florence by 1436 and resided there for the remainder of his life. In 1452 he received the commission to decorate the choir of the Cathedral of Prato and apparently took up temporary residence in that city, for he was appointed chaplain to the nuns of S. Margherita in 1456. In 1460 he signed the Prato frescoes, although final payment was not made until 1464. Through the good offices of Cosimo de' Medici, Pope Pius II released Fra Filippo and the nun Lucrezia Buti from their vows in 1461 and permitted them to marry. In 1466 Lippi and his shop accepted the commission to fresco the choir of the Cathedral of Spoleto.

On the basis of his early work Lippi has traditionally been identified as a student of Masaccio, although recent criticism has tended to see the influence of the Italian 14th century as well. His earliest known work, *The Confirmation of the Carmelite Order*, is generally dated 1432. This detached fresco, now in the Forte di Belvedere in Florence, which originally flanked Masaccio's lost *Sagra* in the Carmine cloister, reflects in the massiveness of its figures

Filippino Lippi, *The Apparition of the Virgin to St. Bernard.* Badia, Florence.

Fra Filippo Lippi, *Coronation of the Virgin*, detail. Uffizi, Florence.

some aspects of Masaccio's art. The *Madonna and Child of Corneto Tarquinia* (1437; Rome, National Gallery) also recalls Masaccio in the bulk of its figures, but it is already stamped with Lippi's personal style. From this same period (1432–37) come two other controversial paintings attributed to Lippi: a fresco in Empoli and a *Madonna of Humility* (Milan, Sforza Castle).

On his return to Florence Lippi executed three works, which were to establish his reputation. Of these the *Barbadori Altarpiece* (ca. 1437; Paris, Louvre) indicates clearly his command of the Florentine concepts of space and of the sculptural treatment of the figure. To this he added his own understanding of color, which he used both to heighten and to modify geometric spatial constructions. In the *Coronation of the Virgin* (ca. 1441–47; Florence, Uffizi) the spatial and coloristic inventions of the earlier altarpiece are developed in a richer and more complex manner. It also shows the influence of Fra Angelico, although a confrontation of the Coronations done by the two men at about the same date reveals more strikingly the differences rather than the similarities. It is the *Annunciation* (ca. 1438), still in the Medici Church of S. Lorenzo, that best indicates Lippi's early Florentine style. Here he shows himself the master of the new perspective techniques and of a composition that probably had its origins in Masaccio. His Madonna derives from Donatello's *Cavalcanti Altarpiece*. These disparate influences are combined in a wholly original composition that makes use of color to control the too rapid recession of the orthogonals. The frame of the painting is used to outline the architecture of the room and to separate the observer from the action, a compositional innovation that remained popular to the end of the century.

Lippi came decidedly under the influence of Fra Angelico during the 1440s. His *Madonna and Saints* (ca. 1442–45; Uffizi) for the Medici Chapel of the Novitiate in Sta Croce is strongly reminiscent of Fra Angelico's *Bosco ai Frati Altarpiece*. The *Adoration of the Magi* roundel (ca. 1445–47; Washington, D.C., National Gallery) has always been considered a collaborative effort. The *Annunciation* (ca. 1443–47; Munich, Old Pinacothek), however, is partly a reprise of the S. Lorenzo *Annunciation* and partly an exhibition of the decorative qualities that were to find such strong expression in Botticelli and in a group of minor masters close to Lippi.

In the 1450s his work took on a strongly personal flavor. The frescoes in Prato combine the rationality of perspective construction in the scenes at the lower levels with the mystic irrationality of pietism in the intermediate levels. His *Life of the Virgin* roundel (ca. 1452; Florence, Pitti Palace) contains this duality in one painting; the ambiguities of spatial relationships and of figure proportion indicate the stylistic problems that confronted the artist. The signed *Adoration of the Child* (ca. 1459; Berlin, former State Museums), painted for the private chapel of the Medici, and the *Camaldoli Adoration* (ca. 1463; Uffizi) indicate the mystic and pietistic quality that dominated Florentine art at this date. In the seated *Madonna and Child* (1465; Uffizi), if we are to recognize, as tradition has it, the portrait of his wife in the Madonna and of their young son,

Filippino, in the angel, then this is surely one of the most personal and lyrical works of Lippi.

The last works, the frescoes at Spoleto, were probably designed by Lippi, but records of his sickness at this time and the frescoes themselves indicate that much of the execution was accomplished by his shop. It is, in fact, the members of the shop who complicate many of the attributions to Lippi. The Master of the Castello Nativity, Botticelli, and Fra Diamante, to name only the most important, were all profoundly influenced by his style.

Fra Filippo Lippi remains an artist of considerable stature and one of extreme importance for an understanding of the development of Renaissance painting in Florence. He bridged the stylistic gap between Masaccio and his contemporaries, adopted and questioned the innovations of Fra Angelico, and, more important, contributed innovations of his own that were to shape the style of Botticelli, Filippino Lippi, and a host of lesser artists.

BIBLIOGRAPHY. R. Oertel, *Fra Filippo Lippi*, Vienna, 1942; M. Pittaluga, *Filippo Lippi*, Florence, 1949.

JOHN R. SPENCER

LIPPI, GIOVANNI DI BARTOLOMMEO, *see* NANNI DI BACCIO BIGIO.

LIPPI, LORENZO. Italian painter (b. Florence, 1606; d. there, 1665). A student of Matteo Rosselli, Lippi followed in the conservative tradition of his master, Allori, Cigoli, and other Florentine artists. The influence of Caravaggio and other artists is evident in such pictures as the *Martyrdom of St. Andrew* (Florence, S. Agata), but Lippi normally followed the older style in stressing the discreteness and grace of individual forms.

LIPPINCOTT, J. GORDON. American industrial designer (1909–). He was born in New York City and educated at Swarthmore College and Columbia University. Lippincott was director of product development in Pratt Institute's Department of Industrial Design and operated as an independent designer before joining Walter Margulies to form one of the largest industrial design firms in the nation. Especially known for its corporate identity programs and package design, Lippincott and Margulies is organized along the lines of an advertising agency and has adopted much of the philosophy of the advertising world.

BIBLIOGRAPHY. J. G. Lippincott, *Design for Business*, Chicago, 1947.

LIPPO DALMASIO DE' SCANNABECCHI (Dalmasio Scannabecchi). Italian painter (ca. 1352–before 1421). A son of the Bolognese painter Dalmasio, Lippo is first recorded in 1373 and lived mostly in Pistoia between 1377 and 1389. He was probably a student of Simone dei Crocifissi, whose compositional patterns, square faces, and coarse workmanship he imitated in his earliest dated work, the *Coronation of the Virgin* (1394), in the National Picture Gallery, Bologna. Subsequently Lippo created many Madonnas in a refined and smoothly executed style. Characteristic is the *Madonna* (1397) in the Misericordia Church, Bologna, with its luminous aureole, sweet expressions, and gracefully sweeping draperies. More monumental are the triptych with the *Enthroned Madonna* in the College of

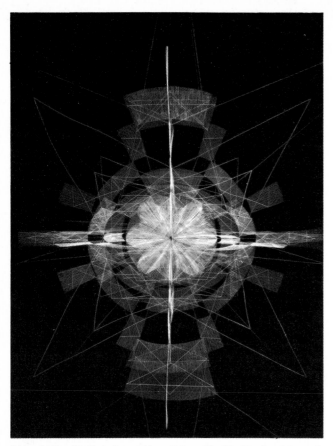

Richard Lippold, *Variation within a Sphere, No. 10: The Sun.* Metropolitan Museum of Art, New York (Fletcher Fund, 1956).

Seymour Lipton, *Sorcerer*, 1957. Whitney Museum of American Art, New York.

Sta Croce, Bologna, and the fresco of the *Madonna with St. Benedict and Pope St. Sixtus* in the lunette over the entrance to S. Procolo, Bologna.

BIBLIOGRAPHY. R. van Marle, *The Development of the Italian Schools of Painting*, vol. 4, The Hague, 1924.

LIPPOLD, RICHARD. American sculptor (1915–   ). He was born in Milwaukee. His early training was as an industrial designer at the Art Institute of Chicago, and he also studied at the University of Chicago in 1933–34. He worked as a designer until 1941, although he had his first sculpture show in 1938. He decided on sculpture rather than music as a career in the early 1940s.

Lippold is a self-taught sculptor, but his design background is manifest in his thin wire symmetrical constructs (altar sculpture, 1961; Portsmouth, R.I., St. Gregory the Great) and in the impeccable craftsmanship of his elegant space cages. He has taught at the Layton School of Art, Milwaukee (1940–41), at the University of Michigan (1944), at Goddard College (1945–47), and since the early 1950s, at Hunter College. The Museum of Modern Art, New York, owns his *Variation No. 7* and *Full Moon* (1949–50), and the Metropolitan Museum of Art, New York, commissioned *Sun* (1953–56). Lippold's cool, inflexible armatures convey a lyrical feeling for nature and sculpture.

BIBLIOGRAPHY. New York, Museum of Modern Art, *15 Americans*, ed. D. C. Miller, New York, 1952.

ALBERT ELSEN

LIPPO MEMMI, *see* MEMMI, LIPPO.

LIPPO VANNI, *see* VANNI, LIPPO.

LIPTON, SEYMOUR. American sculptor (1903–   ). He was born in New York City, where he lives and works. He was interested as a young man in drawing, in copying old masters, and in work with tools and machines. He attended the City College of New York in 1922–23, and received a degree in dentistry from Columbia University, which he had attended from 1923 to 1927. During those years he read on art and aesthetics and in 1926 became interested in modern art, after seeing the work of Matisse and the cubists. He made small carvings in ivory and gold, principally jewelry, about 1928. Before 1930 he made a 2-foot-high clay statue, *Leonardo da Vinci Holding a Bird*. He first took up sculpture seriously in 1932, but did not attach himself to a teacher. Much of his training came from visits to the Whitney Museum of American Art, the Metropolitan Museum of Art, and the Museum of Modern Art, as well as the former Bucholz-Valentin Gallery.

During the 1930s he did mostly wood carving that suggested the influence of Barlach and Henry Moore and used socially conscious themes, for example, *Lynching* (1935) and *The Dispossessed* (1937). He first exhibited in a group show at the John Reed Club, New York, in 1933–34 and had his first one-man show at the A.C.A. Gallery in 1938. Between 1939 and 1941 he began to open up his forms and to seek a means by which to interpret man's internal life and the powerful dark forces that lie beneath the surface of nature. During the 1940s Lipton evolved a personal metaphoral style that produced some of modern sculpture's most ferocious imagery, such as the *Moloch* series (in lead) of 1948. These are brutal images, often of fantastic mythological hybrids or mutants from biology, endowed with hook or horn—all projections of the sculptor's pessimism about the powers motivating life.

In 1948 he had his first exhibition at the Betty Parsons Gallery, and was recognized as a leading American sculptor. Although he had taught sculpture at the New School in 1938–43 and at Cooper Union in 1943–44, it was not until 1954 that Lipton devoted full time to sculpture. The 1950s saw his signature style develop in bronze and nickel silver on sheet steel and Monel metal. He created a series of strongly designed and dramatic ideographs based on biology, history, and older art. His important architectural commissions included work for a Tulsa synagogue (1953) and for the IBM plant at Yorktown Heights, N.Y. (1960).

His work has been in many national and international exhibitions, notably the 1958 Venice Biennale, and is included in leading American collections. The Museum of Modern Art in New York owns *Sanctuary* (1953), Nelson Rockefeller owns *Cloak* (1951) and *Storm Bird* (1955), the Albright-Knox Art Gallery, Buffalo, has *Sea King* (1955), the Whitney Museum of American Art, New York, has *Sorcerer* (1957), Inland Steel owns *Hero* (1957), the Metropolitan Museum, New York, has *Pioneer* (1958), and the Yale Art Gallery, New Haven, has *Jungle Bloom* (1951) and *Sentinel* (1951). A modeling constructivist, Lipton has enriched modern sculpture with a viable physiology for the human form, rich poetical symbolism, and a style that uniquely holds in tension elements of disparate qualities.

BIBLIOGRAPHY. M. Seuphor, *The Sculpture of this Century*, New York, 1960; A. Elsen, "Seymour Lipton, Odyssey of the Unquiet Metaphor," *Art International*, V, February, 1961.

ALBERT ELSEN

LIRA, PEDRO. Chilean painter (b. Santiago, 1845; d. there, 1912). Lira studied law and painting in Chile, then completed his art studies in Paris (1873–82). In Santiago he helped organize the National Museum of Fine Arts and taught in the School of Fine Arts, which he directed after 1892. The style of his early work is academic romanticism (for example, *The Love Letter*, ca. 1892; Santiago, National Museum of Fine Arts), that of his later work, a tentative impressionism.

BIBLIOGRAPHY. A. R. Romera, *Historia de la pintura chilena*, Santiago, 1960.

LISBOA, ANTONIO FRANCISCO, see ALEIJADINHO.

LISBON. Capital city of Portugal, situated on the Atlantic coast between hills to the north and the great estuary of the Tagus River to the south. Much of the center of town was destroyed in the earthquake of 1755. The Ethnological Museum houses the most important collection in Portugal of national antiquities, especially of the prehistoric, Iberian, Roman, and medieval periods. The National Museum of Antiquities contains important collections. *See* LISBON: MUSEUMS.

The most important monuments of Lisbon date from the Manueline period: S. Maria de Belém, begun in 1502, and its cloister, finished about 1517; and the 16th-century

Tower of Belém by Francisco d'Arruda. S. Vicente de Fora, built by the Italian architect F. Terzi, was begun in 1582 on the plan of the Gesù in Rome. Terzi also designed S. Roque (ca. 1570; façade reconstructed after 1755 earthquake). *See* BELEM: MONASTERY OF ST. JEROME.

See also CINTRA, PALACE OF.

BIBLIOGRAPHY. E. Lambert, *L'Art en Espagne et au Portugal*, Paris, 1945.

LISBON: MUSEUMS. Important public art collections in Lisbon, Portugal, are located in the museums listed below.

Calouste Gulbenkian Foundation. The very varied collections include tapestries, manuscripts, ceramics, European paintings of the 15th–19th century (notably works by Gainsborough, Rubens, Rembrandt, Corot, Degas, and Manet), Egyptian sculpture, and examples of Islamic minor arts.

BIBLIOGRAPHY. *Pinturas da Colecção da Fundação Calouste Gulbenkian*, Lisbon, 1961.

National Museum of Antiquities. The extensive holdings of the Portuguese school of the 15th and 16th centuries are dominated by the great altarpiece painted by Nuno Gonçalves about 1460. The collection of foreign paintings includes works by Memling (*Virgin and Child*), Bosch (*Temptation of St. Anthony*), Anthonis Mor (*Portrait*), Dürer (*St. Jerome*), Holbein (*Virgin with Saints*), Pieter de Hoogh (*Conversation*), and Francisco Zurbarán (works painted for the monastery of S. Vicente de Fora). The gold- and silverwork collection includes the remarkable ostensory of Belém of 1506 and a number of fine 18th-century French pieces. The museum also displays Chinese and European ceramics and tapestries and other textiles.

LI SHAN. Chinese painter (fl. ca. 1715–55). A native of Hsin-hua in Yang-chou, he is numbered among the "Eight Eccentrics of Yang-chou" and studied painting under Kao Ch'i-p'ei. Li Shan is best known for his flower-and-bird paintings, as well as for his bamboos. His calligraphy was praised by contemporary Chinese as being in the ancient manner. *See* KAO CH'I-P'EI; YANG-CHOU, EIGHT ECCENTRICS OF.

BIBLIOGRAPHY. Ku Lin-wên, ed., *Yang-chou pa-chia shih-liao*, Shanghai, 1962.

LISHT. Site in Middle Egypt near the fortified city of Itj-tawy, built by Amenemhat I, founder of the 12th dynasty, as his capital. Both he and his successor, Senusert I, erected their pyramids there, surrounded by the small pyramids of the royal family and, outside the enclosure, by the mastabas of the officials. The pyramid temple of Senusert I copied that of Pepi II. The inner enclosure wall of the pyramid was of limestone carved at intervals with a colossal panel (*serekh*) representing the palace façade and enclosing the royal name, surmounted by the royal falcon.

BIBLIOGRAPHY. J. Gautier and G. Jéquier, *Mémoire sur les fouilles de Licht*, Cairo, 1902.

LISIEUX: CATHEDRAL OF SAINT-PIERRE. French church begun between 1160 and 1170 by Bishop Arnoul. He was responsible for the completion of the nave and a good part of the choir before he retired in 1182. The influence of both Laon and Paris is apparent in the nave. Norman influence is strong in the sculptural ornament.

LISMER, ARTHUR. Canadian painter (1885–   ). Lismer was born in England and since 1911 has lived in Canada. He is a leading educator in the field of children's art. His paintings are landscapes, mostly of the Canadian north, and he was a "Group of Seven" member.

BIBLIOGRAPHY. J. A. B. McLeish, *September Gale: A Study of Arthur Lismer of the Group of Seven*, Toronto, 1955.

LISS (Lys), JOHANN. German painter of peasant and gallant scenes and of religious and mythological compositions (b. Oldenburg, Holstein, ca. 1593/97; d. Venice, 1629/30). It is not known with whom Liss served his apprenticeship, but he arrived in Amsterdam in 1616 and spent the years from 1616 to 1619 there, in Haarlem, and in Antwerp. Afterward he spent some time in Paris, and by 1621 had arrived in Venice. He traveled to Rome in 1622, became a member of the Schilderbent and received the nickname "Pan." By 1622–23 he was back in Venice, where he made his home until his death.

Liss was influenced in his early works by the Netherlanders, such as Frans Hals, Dirck Hals, and Willem Buijtenwegh. In Rome he fell under the spell of Caravaggio and his followers. In Venice he drew inspiration from Titian, Veronese, and Tintoretto, and became an outstanding colorist.

He is the originator of the Venetian *Sittenbild* (genre picture), but his main importance lies in the inventiveness of his compositions, coupled with an almost modern palette and a broad technique. Although he often repeated himself, his canvases were to exercise a decisive impact in both Italy and the Netherlands. His most extensive composition is *The Banquet* (Kassel, Gallery).

BIBLIOGRAPHY. K. Steinbart, *Johann Liss*, Vienna, 1946.

ERIK LARSEN

LISSANDRINO, see MAGNASCO, ALESSANDRO.

LISSE, DIRCK VAN DER. Dutch landscape painter (d. The Hague, 1669). Born in Breda, he was a pupil of Cornelis van Poelenburgh at Utrecht. In 1639 Van der Lisse married in The Hague and joined the Guild of St. Luke five years later. He was one of the founders of the painters' confraternity Pictura in 1656. He was burgomaster of The Hague in 1660. His landscapes with figures follow the style of Van Poelenburgh.

BIBLIOGRAPHY. W. Bernt, *Die niederländischen Maler des 17. Jahrhunderts...*, vol. 2, Munich, 1948.

LISSITZKY, LAZAR (El). Russian painter and graphic and exhibition designer (b. Smolensk province, 1890; d. Moscow, 1941). Lissitzky studied at the school of engineering and architecture in Darmstadt, Germany, and traveled (1909–14) throughout Europe. After returning to Russia,

Johann Liss, *The Banquet*. Art Gallery, Kassel. The artist's most extensive composition.

he became an architect's apprentice (1915) and an illustrator of Jewish children's books in Vitebsk (1917), along with Chagall and other artists. Under the revolutionary government, Lissitzky became a professor at the Vitebsk School of Art (1918), directed by Chagall. In 1919 he came into contact with Malevich and the suprematist movement, executed the first of a series of abstract paintings known as *Prouns*, and designed posters for the Soviet government combining abstract shapes and typography.

During the 1920s Lissitzky became one of the most influential typographical and exhibition designers in Europe. Working in the Soviet Union, he had continual contact with the constructivist, Bauhaus, and de Stijl movements, starting with his participation in the constructivist conference at Düsseldorf in 1922. His book designs, such as those for editions of Mayakovsky's poetry, combine suprematist and constructivist principles. In planning exhibitions in the Soviet Union and Europe, he related individual works to an overall design, culminating in the vast photomontage for the Soviet section of the International Press Exhibition in Cologne (1930).

BIBLIOGRAPHY. H. Richter, *El Lissitzky*, Cologne, 1958.

DONALD GODDARD

LI SSU-HSUN. Chinese painter (651–716). He was the eldest member of a family that included a number of painters of note in Chinese history. Li Ssu-hsün was well received in the T'ang court, and when the emperor Hsüan-tsung (r. 713–756) ascended the throne, Li was given the title of general of the Palace Guard. He is sometimes referred to in later Chinese literature as the Elder (or Greater) General Li to distinguish him from his son Li Chao-tao, the Younger (or Smaller) General Li, who was also a painter. In the case of both men, however, our knowledge of their painting styles is based on early Chinese literary accounts rather than on existing examples that can with some certainty be attributed to them. The two men are associated with the development of the coloristic, meticulous style of landscape called ch'ing-lü (blue-and-green style). The most famous early example of this style, sometimes attributed to Li Chao-tao, is the painting in the Sun Yat-sen Museum, Formosa, variously titled *Travelers in the Mountains* and *Ming-huang's Journey to Shu*. See BLUE-AND-GREEN STYLE.

BIBLIOGRAPHY. Li Lin-ts'an, "A Study of the Masterpiece 'T'ang Ming-hung's Journey to Shu,'" *Ars Orientalis*, IV, 1961.

MARTIE W. YOUNG

LI T'ANG. Chinese painter (fl. ca. 1050–after 1130). Although he is one of the major figures in Sung painting history, very little is known of his personal life. A native of San-ch'eng, Honan Province, he began his painting career in K'ai-feng under the academy of Hui-tsung, and, although he held no official position, he apparently was a highly regarded painter. When the academy was reorganized under Kao-tsung (r. 1127–62), during the early years of the Southern Sung, Li T'ang was made its first director, given the title of Ch'eng-chung-lang, or "patriotic officer." Although he served the southern court only briefly in his new capacity, he is regarded as the key painter in the transition from the Northern Sung monumental style of landscape painting to the more romantic and intimate paintings that seem to typify most of the Southern Sung efforts in landscape.

There are very few extant paintings by Li T'ang, and of the few there are some apparent questions of authenticity. The only dated painting bearing Li T'ang's signature is the large hanging scroll representing mountains and pine trees in the Sun Yat-sen Museum, Formosa. The date of 1124 that appears on this painting seems to agree with its style, for the work can be related to other Northern Sung landscapes. Another pair of landscapes in the Kōtōin of Daitokuji, Kyoto, have signatures of Li T'ang but no date. The signatures were discovered with the aid of infrared photography. The style of these two landscapes, all that remains from what was probably a set of four paintings depicting the seasons, is strikingly different from the Sun Yat-sen Museum dated work of 1124. The landscape is seen in a much more fragmentary manner, greatly reduced in scale from the monumental grandeur of the Northern Sung landscapes. There are also significant differences in handling, with broad washes used to depict rocks and a marked absence of the labored surface seen in the painting of 1124. Such differences point clearly to the later Southern Sung style, and if the Kōtōin paintings can be accepted as authentic works of Li T'ang there can be little doubt that the later styles of Ma Yüan and Hsia Kuei owe their inspiration to this great master who straddled the Northern and Southern Sung. See HSIA KUEI; MA YUAN.

BIBLIOGRAPHY. S. Shimada, "On the Landscape Paintings in the Kōtō-in Temple, Kyoto," *Bijitsu Kenkyū*, IV, 1951; R. Edwards, "The Landscape Art of Li T'ang," *Archives of the Chinese Art Society of America*, XII, 1958.

MARTIE W. YOUNG

LITERARY ART. Very general term applicable to any art derived from or dependent on a written source. Therefore, the most complete literary art is essentially a narrative, illustrative art, such as that which accompanies a written source. Most romantic art is basically literary art, as, for example, Blake's illustrations for the *Divine Comedy*.

LITERATI PAINTING, see WEN-JEN-HUA.

LITHOGRAPHY. Method of graphic reproduction developed at the close of the 18th century. It is a planographic (surface) process that obtains prints from a stone or metal plate on which an image has been drawn with greasy substances, making use of the natural antipathy between grease and water. A variety of effects may be achieved, ranging from deep rich areas of solid black to thin sketchy gray lines. Lithography allows great freedom of expression and consequently became a favorite medium during the impressionist period, for example, of Toulouse-Lautrec.

Though there are some printmakers who prefer to make lithographs on grained zinc or aluminum plates, the majority still prefer the traditional blue-gray block of Bavarian limestone, a delightful surface on which to work, despite its awkwardness and bulk. The first problem may involve removal of a previous drawing from the stone, which is often reused. This is accomplished by graining or grinding the stone with carborundum, until the "ghost," or previous image, is gone.

The stone may be drawn upon with lithographic crayons or pencils, tusche, rubbing ink, asphaltum, and even soap, separately or in combination. White on black effects may be obtained with razor blades, lithographic needles, and similar tools. The drawing is etched with a syrupy solution of gum arabic and nitric acid. Before printing, the stone is washed with water, and it is kept moist on the lithographic press. Finally, it is rolled with lithographic ink and run through the press.

BIBLIOGRAPHY. A. A. Dehn and L. Barrett, *How to Draw and Print Lithographs*, New York, 1950; J. Heller, *Printmaking Today*, New York, 1958.

JULES HELLER

LITHOTINT TECHNIQUE. A planographic (surface) process, essentially a wash drawing technique, that is a variation on the lithograph. A lithographic stone is grained with carborundum. By the use of soft brushes and several mixtures of tusche and water, a wash drawing is made on the freshly grained stone. When the drawing is dry and all corrections have been made, the stone is etched with a solution of nitric acid, gum arabic, and water. The procedure then is the same as in lithography. Lithotint is an experimental printing technique demanding great skill. *See* LITHOGRAPHY.

BIBLIOGRAPHY. J. Heller, *Printmaking Today*, New York, 1958.

LI TI. Chinese painter (fl. 12th cent.). He began his career in the Painting Academy at K'ai-feng in the Northern Sung period and later became an official in the Southern Sung Academy at Hang-chou. Li Ti is best known for his paintings of buffalo and herd boys, and a number of works of this category in the United States are attributed to him.

Lithography. Honoré Daumier, *The Night-bird.*

LI TRIPOD. Cooking vessel of distinctive shape that was widely distributed in the northern Chinese provinces of Honan and Shantung during Neolithic times. It consisted of a substantial body and three hollow bulbous legs. This very functional form of vessel, referred to by the modern Chinese character *li*, or "tripod," occurred also in the bronze ritual vessels of Shang times and later, and was undoubtedly the earliest type of bronze vessel made in China.

BIBLIOGRAPHY. H. Creel, *The Birth of China*, London, 1936.

LI TSAI. Chinese painter (fl. mid-15th cent.). He is not well recorded in Chinese literary sources. Li Tsai was a classicist who modeled himself on earlier Northern Sung landscape masters such as Kuo Hsi. He is best known for the influence he had on the great Japanese painter Sesshū, who, on his visit to China in 1468, found that Li Tsai was one of the most famous painters of his day. *See* KUO HSI; SESSHU TOYO.

LI-TS'UN, *see* AN CH'I.

LITTERINI, BARTOLOMMEO, *see* LETTERINI, BARTOLOMMEO.

LITTLE MASTERS. Group of 16th-century German graphic artists who excelled in the production of small-format engravings. The group designation is merely formal, for the artists had little in common stylistically and worked in different centers: Altdorfer in Regensburg; the Behams in Nürnberg; Binck in Cologne; and Aldegrever in Westphalia. The German term is *Kleinmeister*. *See* ALDEGREVER, HEINRICH; ALTDORFER, ALBRECHT; BEHAM, BARTHEL; BEHAM, HANS SEBALD; BINCK, JACOB.

BIBLIOGRAPHY. H. W. Singer, *Die Kleinmeister*, Bielefeld, Leipzig, 1908.

LITTLE METROPOLITAN CHURCH (Panagia Gorgopiko), ATHENS. Thirteenth-century Greek church. Sometimes known as the "smallest cathedral in the world," it measures 25 by 38 feet. Completed about 1250, it has an inscribed Greek-cross plan (four equal crossarms within a square plan) with the quincunx (five-domed) vaulting system of mid-Byzantine architecture. A peculiar Greek variation of this theme is the tying of the chancel and east bays to the aisles by continuous barrel vaults.

The exterior employs an extremely decorative style of masonry. Hewn stone is outlined by brick, and frequently pieces of carved antique marble take the place of the hewn stone. The effect is one of a rich masonry "tapestry."

LITURGY. Term encompassing all aspects of the arrangement of public worship in the church. Its essence is the coordination of music, texts, and visual symbolism to form a ritual. The changes in the growth of Christian liturgy have profoundly affected the visual arts, which, particularly in the Middle Ages, were almost a creation of the liturgy.

LIU SUNG-NIEN. Chinese painter (fl. early 13th cent.). Liu Sung-nien was active in the Southern Sung painting academy during the reign of the emperor Ming-tsung (1195–1224). Along with Ma Yüan and Hsia Kuei he is considered a member of the triumvirate of painters who ed the Southern Sung academy in formulating its distinctive style. His landscapes with scholars seem more influenced by the style of an older master such as Chao Po-chü, but the lyric mood of his works is quite in keeping with the spirit of the Southern Sung. *See* CHAO PO-CHU; HSIA KUEI; MA YUAN.

BIBLIOGRAPHY. L. Sickman and A. Soper, *The Art and Architecture of China*, Baltimore, 1956.

LIUTHARD GROUP, *see* CAROLINGIAN ART AND ARCHITECTURE (IVORIES AND METALWORK).

LIVERPOOL: ST. GEORGE'S HALL, *see* ST. GEORGE'S HALL, LIVERPOOL.

LIVERPOOL: WALKER ART GALLERY. English collection founded by Sir Andrew Barclay Walker in 1877. It features early Italian and Flemish paintings and a comprehensive survey of English painting from Holbein to the present, with particular emphasis on the Pre-Raphaelites and 19th- and 20th-century academic painting.

LIVIA, HOUSE OF, ROME. Private house of Livia, wife of Emperor Augustus, situated on the Palatine hill. Built in the second half of the 1st century B.C., it was purchased by Augustus from the Hortensii family. It consists of an atrium, a triclinium, the so-called tablinum, and living quarters. The house is decorated with mural paintings of mythological scenes, which are among the finest examples of Augustan painting.
See also PERSPECTIVE.

LIVRO DE COMO SE FAZEN AS CORES. Portuguese treatise on the art of manuscript illumination, probably dating from after the 13th century. It exists in a Portuguese text, written in Hebrew characters by Abraham ben Juda ibn Hayyim, which forms part of MS. De Rossi 945 in the Palatina Library, Parma.

LIWAN (Leewan; Ivan; Iwan). Raised part of a room, especially that of a reception room of a Muslim house. The term also refers to a chamber or hall opening on a court, an open recessed arcade or porch, or a gallery in a Muslim mosque.

LJUBLJANA: NATIONAL MUSEUM OF LJUBLJANA. Yugoslavian museum, important for its collections of prehistoric art, for example, the famous bronze situla from Vace. The museum offers a survey of the development of Slovenian sculpture and painting from Romanesque times through impressionism.

LLANDAFF CATHEDRAL. Welsh Romanesque church with the impressive arch to the Lady Chapel and the nave's south door dating from about 1170. The nave is Early English from about 1190, and the west front dates from about 1220. The most notable feature is the new parabolic arch across the nave with Sir Jacob Epstein's *Majestas.*

LLANOS, FERNANDO DE LOS. Spanish painter (d. after 1525). He was born in La Mancha. With his countryman Fernando Yáñez de la Almedina, Llanos studied under Leonardo da Vinci in Florence and may have been his Spanish assistant on the *Battle of Anghiari* fresco. Back in Valencia, Llanos collaborated on several works with Yáñez, including the twelve monumental paintings for the doors of the high altar in the Cathedral that depict scenes from the life of the Virgin (1507–10). The stronger sections of this work are generally attributed to Yáñez, the more accomplished artist. Subsequently settling in Murcia, Llanos continued to produce paintings in imitation of Leonardo.

BIBLIOGRAPHY. C. R. Post, *A History of Spanish Painting*, vol. 11, Cambridge, Mass., 1953.

LOCAL COLOR, *see* COLOR, LOCAL.

LOCHES: SAINT-OURS. French church dating to before 1168. It is a medieval oddity. Both the east and the west ends culminate in spired towers, and the two bays of the aisleless nave are covered by hollow octagonal spires. The style is certainly related to that of Périgord. Beneath the west tower, which serves as a narthex, is a handsomely sculptured doorway.

LOCHHEAD, KENNETH. Canadian painter (1926–   ). He studied in Kingston, Ontario, and at the Pennsylvania Academy and the Barnes Foundation in Philadelphia, and now directs the Regina College of Art. Formerly he painted surrealistic oils, but since a recent European trip he has turned to monochromatic abstraction in tempera.

BIBLIOGRAPHY. Ottawa, National Gallery of Canada, *Catalogue of Paintings and Sculpture*, ed. R. H. Hubbard, vol. 3: *Canadian School*, Ottawa, 1960.

LOCHNER, STEPHAN. German painter (b. Meersburg am Bodensee, ca. 1410; d. Cologne, 1451). The leading master of the Cologne school of painting during the first half of the 15th century, Lochner has enjoyed considerable popularity, especially in the 19th century. His early life is almost completely unknown, and it is only from the 1430s on that a clear idea of his art is discernible. From that time on he was active at Cologne, where he became an important citizen, was influential in the city government, and received numerous commissions from the most important patrician families. The *Altar of the Patron Saints* was painted shortly before his election to the city council in 1447. Dedicated to the city patrons, the altar was given by Lochner to the chapel of the Town Hall and moved to the Cathedral after the French Revolution.

Lochner's work presents problems when an attempt is made to group the paintings according to a progressive evolution of style. Typical of this problematic aspect of Lochner's work is the *Last Judgment Altar* (center panel, Cologne, Wallraf-Richartz Museum; inner wings, Frankfurt am Main, Städel Art Institute; outer wings, Munich, Old Pinacothek). Produced originally for the Church of St. Lawrence in Cologne, this altarpiece is strongly influenced by Netherlandish painting. Some authorities see this work as an early one, possibly a result of studies in the Netherlands. Other authorities see it as a late work, representing an archaizing phase. Works that can be dated with certainty are the *Crucifixion with the Virgin, St. John, and Four Saints* (Nürnberg, Germanic National Museum), dated 1435–40 on heraldic evidence; *Virgin with the Violet* (Cologne, Archiepiscopal Diocesan Museum), dated 1433 or

shortly before; and *Presentation in the Temple* (Darmstadt, Hessian Landesmuseum), dated 1447.

In general, Lochner's style represents a fusion of the lyricism and delicacy of the older Cologne tradition and the realism of early Netherlandish painting. But he adds a uniquely personal sense of rhythm, which results in a masterful control of composition far in advance of his time. This is vividly portrayed in the famous *Altar of the Patron Saints*. The composition is strongly rhythmical, yet in detail the realism of the Netherlandish school is expertly employed.

See also WEICHER STIL.

BIBLIOGRAPHY. H. Reiners, *Die Kölner Malerschule*, Munich-Gladbach, 1925; W. Bombe, *Stephan Lochner*, Berlin, 1937; O. H. Förster, *Stefan Lochner, ein Maler zu Köln*, 3d ed., Bonn, 1952.

DONALD L. EHRESMANN

LOCK, ADAM. English architect (d. ca. 1229). Although not responsible for the west front of Wells Cathedral, which was begun after 1230, he may have been the master of Wells and the designer of its unified plan before 1215.

BIBLIOGRAPHY. J. H. Harvey, comp., *English Mediaeval Architects*, London, 1954.

LOCRI EPIZEPHYRII. Greek colony on the Calabrian coast of southern Italy. An Ionic temple was erected about 450 B.C. in Locri, at a site called Maraza, on the foundations of a primitive temple. This temple had a different orientation from that of its predecessor. It was peripteral and had a cella with distyle porch in antis and an opisthodomos. The façade had six columns; the rear, seven. The pediments were crowned by marble acroteria representing male figures riding seahorses. The carving on the necking of the capitals, consisting of a lotus and palmette border, shows great refinement in its execution. This temple is of great interest because it presents an early example of Ionic influence in the West. Locri is also known to us for its great number of clay *pinakes* (tablets).

BIBLIOGRAPHY. W. B. Dinsmoor, *The Architecture of Ancient Greece*, 3d ed., London, 1950.

LOCSE (Leutschau; Levoca): CATHEDRAL OF ST. JAMES. Gothic hall church of the early 14th century, with three naves, in eastern Czechoslovakia. Seven of the Cathedral's altars are particularly fine examples of Slovak Gothic, with some elements that foreshadow Renaissance style. The 14th-century bronze baptismal font and the Gothic frescoes (ca. 1420) that reflect the influence of the Bohemian school are also noteworthy.

BIBLIOGRAPHY. A. Hekler, *Ungarische Kunstgeschichte*, Berlin, 1937.

LOCULUS. Recess or cell, as in ancient tombs; also a burial niche in a catacomb. Loculi in Roman *coemeteria* as well as in Early Christian tombs contained corpses and were sometimes sealed with a slab bearing the name of the deceased, as in the tomb of the Gens Cornelia, Rome.

LODI, GIOVANNI DI DOMENICO DA, *see* BATTAGIO, GIOVANNI DI DOMENICO.

Stefan Lochner, *The Presentation in the Temple*. Hessian Landesmuseum, Darmstadt.

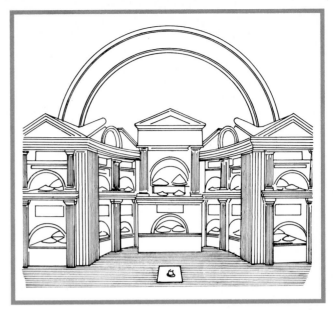

Loculus. Drawing of Pomponius Hilas's columbarium at Porta Latina, Rome.

LOEWY, RAYMOND. American industrial designer (1893–   ). Since the early 1930s the name "Loewy" has been synonymous with industrial design in America. Probably more than any other man, Loewy has put the profession (as well as himself) before the public eye.

After educating himself in his native Paris as an engineer, Loewy started a career as a fashion illustrator for a number of American periodicals. His earliest work also involved revamping window displays for such New York stores as Saks Fifth Avenue and Macy's. It was not until 1927 that Loewy launched his own industrial design organization, in New York, making it one of the earliest in the country. Having designed for Westinghouse Electric, Gestetner, Ltd., and Hupmobile, Loewy had solidly established himself by 1932 as a leader in the new movement to bring functional design to the products of industry. But the first inkling of the myth-making, magic quality that the public came to associate with him, and that later surrounded his name, was not apparent until 1934. In that Depression year Loewy redesigned the Coldspot refrigerator for Sears, Roebuck and Company, and the product's sales jump (from 60,000 units before his work to 275,000 units afterward) was attributed largely to his design.

Among Loewy's significant long-range programs have been cars for Studebaker, locomotives and stations for the Pennsylvania Railroad, buses for Greyhound, and farm equipment for International Harvester. His work ranges from graphic design in packaging, through marketing studies for supermarkets, to product, interior, and architectural design.

BIBLIOGRAPHY. R. Loewy, *The Locomotive*, London, 1937; R. Loewy, *Never Leave Well Enough Alone*, New York, 1950.

ANN FEREBEE

LOGEION. Literally, a "speaking place." In the Hellenistic theater the logeion was a narrow platform above the proscenium from which some actors spoke. The Roman logeion was the lower stage in front of the proscenium on which the actors appeared.

LOGGIA. Roofed structure open on one or more sides. The term is also associated with a porch or gallery, as distinguished from an ambulatory or covered passageway. Loggias were especially popular during the Italian Renaissance; examples are in the Doge's Palace, Venice, and the Palazzo del Consiglio, Verona. *See also* BIGALLO, LOGGIA DEL, FLORENCE; LANZI, LOGGIA DEI, FLORENCE.

LOHAN, *see* ARHAT.

LOKAPALA (Japanese, Shi tenno; Chinese, T'ien-wang). Buddhist world guardian. He is one of the four regents who preside over the four cardinal points and are believed to dwell on Mt. Sumeru (Kailāsa) at the gates of the paradise of Sakra (Indra), the protector of Buddhism. The Indian versions of the Lokāpalas, associated with the four quarters, are Kuvera, north; Virūḍhaka, south; Dhṛtarāṣṭra, east; and Virūpākṣa, west.

LOKESVARA. Indochinese Buddhist form of Avalokiteśvara. Lokeśvara, or Lord of the World, is represented with one to sixteen heads and with one to sixteen pairs of arms. His four faces crown each of the fifty-one towers of the Bayon in Angkor Thom, Cambodia.

LOMAS RISHI (Rsi) CAVE. Jain monument cut into the living rock of the Barābar Hills in Bihar State, India. It

Loggia. Roofed structure open on one or more sides.

was probably executed about 250 B.C. during the reign of Emperor Aśoka (Maurya period). Both in the domical interior and in the highly polished carving of the exterior portal, it is a reflection in durable stone of perished wooden structures with thatched roofs and overhanging eaves. The arch over the portal comprises four registers: over the doorway, a plain band; next, elephants approaching stūpas (Jain and Buddhist reliquary mounds); then another plain band; and finally a register that exactly reproduces latticework. The portal's ogival frame duplicates a form natural to architecture in bamboo and other pliable wood. This structure as a whole is probably the prototype of the rock-cut chaitya hall.

See also INDIA.

BIBLIOGRAPHY. P. Brown, *Indian Architecture*, 4th ed., 2 vols., Bombay, 1959; B. Rowland, *The Art and Architecture of India*, 2d ed., Baltimore, 1959.

LOMAZZO, GIOVANNI PAOLO. Italian painter, writer on art, and poet (b. Milan, 1538; d. there, 1600). A pupil of Gaudenzio Ferrari, Lomazzo painted many frescoes and altars in Milanese churches—grandiose compositions stuffed with rhetorical Leonardesque figures, on a substratum of Ferrari's continuous linear treatment and rather pedestrian detail. His *Trattato dell'arte della pittura* (Milan, 1584) is the most extensive and elaborate mannerist treatise on painting; its arguments are recast in mystico-cum-architectonic, though briefer, form in his *Idea del tempio della pittura* (Milan, 1590).

BIBLIOGRAPHY. A. Venturi, *Storia dell'arte italiana*, vol. 9, pt. 7, Milan, 1934; J. Schlosser, *La letteratura artistica...*, 3d ed., Florence, 1964 (for art theory).

LOMBARD, LAMBERT. Flemish painter (b. Liège, ca. 1506; d. there, 1566/67). He was said to have been a pupil of one Jean Denense, of Jan Gossaert, and of Aerdt de Beer in Antwerp. Lombard had returned by 1535 to Liège, which was to be the principal center of his activity. From a trip to Italy in 1537/38 he returned with books of drawings after antique statues and reliefs, and his studio became the center for the Romanization of such 16th-century Flemish artists as Frans Floris, Willem Key, and Hubert Goltzius. It is remarkable that Lombard's antiquarian interest extended to Italian and Netherlandish painting of the 14th and 15th centuries. In most of the paintings traditionally attributed to him tensions are set up between the sharp, marmoreal figures of the foreground and the complex, atmospheric backgrounds indigenous to Netherlandish painting. Lombard also did some designs for stained glass.

BIBLIOGRAPHY. M. J. Friedländer, *Die altniederländische Malerei*, vol. 13, Leyden, 1936.

LOMBARDI, ALFONSO. Italian sculptor (b. Ferrara, 1497; d. Bologna, 1537). In his prolific output Lombardi handled most of the types and materials of Renaissance sculpture, creating tombs, religious sculpture, classical figures, and portraits in marble, bronze, and terra cotta. In his *Pietà* at Bologna Cathedral the emotional agitation of the work of his Bolognese predecessors, Mazzoni and Niccolò dell'Arca, is given a more monumental form. The intense spirituality of Spanish realism is rivaled in his glazed terra-cotta figures of saints executed for the Ferrara Cathedral.

Pietro Lombardo, detail of the monument to Doge Pietro Mocenigo. SS. Giovanni e Paolo, Venice.

LOMBARDI, ANTONIO, *see* LOMBARDO, ANTONIO.

LOMBARDI, PIETRO, *see* LOMBARDO, PIETRO.

LOMBARDI, TULLIO, *see* LOMBARDO, TULLIO.

LOMBARDINO, *see* LOMBARDO, CRISTOFORO.

LOMBARDO (Lombardi), ANTONIO. Italian sculptor (ca. 1458–ca. 1516). He lived primarily in Venice and followed his father, Pietro Lombardo, in the use of classical prototypes for his statues and reliefs. Antonio's works, as in St. Mark's, Venice, and in Padua, have a quiet vitality; he turned to decorative carving in later life. Three of Antonio's sons, Aurelio, Girolamo (da Ferrara), and Lodovico (da Ferrara), also worked as sculptors.

See also LOMBARDO, PIETRO.

BIBLIOGRAPHY. J. Pope-Hennessy, *Italian Renaissance Sculpture*, London, 1958.

LOMBARDO, CRISTOFORO (Il Gobbo; Lombardino). Italian sculptor and architect (fl. Lombardy, 1st half of 16th cent.). In 1510 he was active on the Cathedral of Milan, and in 1515 he finished the tomb of Lancino Curzio in Milan, which had been begun by Agostino Busti in 1513. Lombardo is mentioned in 1538 as the architect of the Church of S. Maria presso S. Celso, Milan, for which he also executed the decoration of the court portal on the street front. In 1543 he carved a statue of St. Catherine, now in the south transept of the Cathedral of Milan.

BIBLIOGRAPHY. U. Nebbia, *La scultura nel duomo di Milano*, Milan, 1908.

LOMBARDO (Lombardi; Solari), PIETRO. Italian sculptor and architect (b. Carona, Lombardy, probably 1435; d. Venice, 1515). He is mentioned for the first time in 1464, when he was engaged on the monument of Antonio Roselli in S. Antonio, Padua, completed in 1467. Soon afterward he was in Venice, where he carved the tomb of Doge Pasquale Malipiero (d. 1462) in SS. Giovanni e Paolo; carried out the reconstruction of S. Giobbe, from about 1470; and designed and executed the tombs of Doge Niccolò Marcello (d. 1474) and Doge Pietro Mocenigo (d. 1476) in SS. Giovanni e Paolo. The last, mentioned as complete in 1481, was carved with the assistance of his sons Tullio and Antonio, who often worked with him, and won the artist great fame in Venice. *See* SS. GIOVANNI E PAOLO, VENICE.

During the next two decades Lombardo was employed either as designer or as executing artist, and generally with the help of his sons, on a series of important projects in Venice and elsewhere in northern Italy. These include the tombs of Lodovico Foscarini (d. 1480), destroyed (formerly in S. Maria dei Frari); Dante, adjoining the Church of S. Francesco at Ravenna (1482); Jacopo Marcello (d. 1484), in S. Maria dei Frari; Bishop Giovanni Zanetti (d. 1484 or shortly after), in the Cathedral at Treviso; and Senator Onigo (d. 1490), in S. Niccolò at Treviso; also the building and decoration of S. Maria dei Miracoli (1481–89) and the decoration of the Scuola di S. Giovanni Evangelista (1480s) and the Scuola Grande di S. Marco (1488–90). In 1495 Lombardo undertook the construction of a chapel in the Ducal Palace at Mantua, and after the flight of Antonio Rizzo from Venice in 1498 he was appointed to serve as protomagister of the Doge's Palace. The Vendramin Palace on the Grand Canal (1481–1509) has also been attributed to Lombardo. *See* VENDRAMIN PALACE, VENICE.

See also VENICE.

His role in the family workshop after 1500 is generally subordinate to that of his sons. In 1501 he supervised the construction of the Cappella del SS. Sacramento in the Cathedral of Treviso, which was designed by his son Antonio; in 1507 he acted in a similar capacity at S. Salvatore, Venice, which was built by his son Tullio; and in 1509 he presented with Antonio a model for the rebuilding of the Scuola Grande della Misericordia.

Pietro Lombardo was the most important of the Lombard sculptors who worked in Venice during the 15th century, and successfully led the way to the full Venetian Renaissance. As a youth he absorbed a knowledge of the tomb sculpture of Bernardo Rossellino and Desiderio da

Settignano in Florence, and he brought with him to Venice a keen appreciation of the antique. While generally less secure in the balancing of figures and architecture than the Florentines, he nevertheless achieved a sense of order and movement in his monumental projects, and in his figurative work conveyed considerable intensity of feeling in spite of a certain constraint and hardness.

See also LOMBARDO, ANTONIO; LOMBARDO, TULLIO.

BIBLIOGRAPHY. A. Venturi, *Storia dell'arte italiana*, vol. 6, Milan, 1908; L. Planiscig, *Venezianische Bildhauer der Renaissance*, Vienna, 1921; G. Mariacher, "Pietro Lombardo a Venezia," *Arte veneta*, IX, 1955; J. Pope-Hennessy, *Italian Renaissance Sculpture*, London, 1958; C. Seymour, *Sculpture in Italy, 1400–1500*, Baltimore, 1966.

DARIO A. COVI

LOMBARDO, SANTE. Italian architect (ca. 1504–ca. 1560). He worked mainly in Venice. He was the son of the sculptor Tullio Lombardo. Sante was important in making the transition from decorative to constructive qualities in architecture. His work on the façade of the Scuola di S. Rocco, Venice, executed for the confraternity of St. Roch, utilizes an effective combination of composition and detail.

LOMBARDO, TOMMASO (Tommaso da Lugano). Italian sculptor (fl. Venice, ca. 1550). A student and follower of Sansovino, Lombardo assisted him on the bronze tribune reliefs in St. Mark's (1537–44). Lombardo also carved a Madonna after Sansovino's design for the main portal of St. Mark's. A signed work by his hand is the *Madonna*

Tullio Lombardo, *The Coronation of the Virgin.* S. Giovanni Crisostomo, Venice.

with St. John the Baptist in the Cappella Melio of S. Sebastiano in Venice, where he also did a statue of St. Jerome for the Church of the Holy Saviour.

BIBLIOGRAPHY. L. Planiscig, *Venezianische Bildhauer der Renaissance*, Vienna, 1921.

LOMBARDO (Lombardi; Solari), TULLIO. Italian sculptor (ca. 1455–1532). He began working in the studio of his father, Pietro Lombardo, about 1475, and was responsible for most of the figure sculptures on the Vendramin monument, which was completed in the mid-1490s for SS. Giovanni e Paolo, Venice. His later relief of the Coronation of the Virgin at S. Giovanni Crisostomo, Venice, maintained the classical approach of the Vendramin monument. Within this approach Tullio's sculpture exhibits his feeling for the sensuous human form. His reliefs (ca. 1520) in S. Antonio, Padua, demonstrate an advanced sense of movement and style. Tullio was regarded by some of his contemporaries as the greatest Venetian marble sculptor of his time and occupied a position as a humanist sculptor, similar to that of Andrea Briosco, in Padua. Tullio's son Sante worked as an architect. *See* LOMBARDO, PIETRO; LOMBARDO, SANTE.

BIBLIOGRAPHY. J. Pope-Hennessy, *Italian Renaissance Sculpture*, London, 1958.

LOMBARD SCHOOL (Painting). The Lombard school of painting first achieved importance during the late 14th and early 15th century, when painters such as Giovannino de' Grassi, Michelino da Besozzo, Belbello da Pavia, and Bonifacio Bembo were important in the development of the International Gothic style. At that time the chief centers of the Lombard school were at Milan, Cremona, and Mantua. *See* BELBELLO DA PAVIA; BEMBO, BONIFACIO; GIOVANNINO DE' GRASSI; MICHELINO DA BESOZZO.

See also INTERNATIONAL GOTHIC PAINTING.

In the latter part of the 15th century local schools arose in Milan and Brescia, which were greatly influenced by Leonardo and Venetian painting. These schools continued to flourish into the 16th century until they were eclipsed by the Lombard mannerism of painters such as Giovanni Paolo Lomazzo. A notable Lombard baroque master was Giovanni Crespi. *See* CRESPI, GIOVANNI BATTISTA; LOMAZZO, GIOVANNI PAOLO. *See also* BRESCIAN SCHOOL; MILANESE SCHOOL.

BIBLIOGRAPHY. W. Suida, "Neue Studien zur Geschichte der lombardischen Malerei des XV. Jahrhunderts," *Repertorium für Kunstwissenschaft*, XXV, 1902.

LOMBARD STYLE (Architecture). Certain ornamental features of Romanesque architecture, which seem to have originated in Lombardy, distinguish the Lombard style, or "the first Romanesque." After 800, distinct decorative and nonstructural elements appear in such Lombard churches as S. Vincenzo in Prato, Milan (ca. 815), and S. Pietro at Agliate, near Milan (ca. 875): arched corbel tables, arched recesses high under the eaves, and the frequent use of pilaster strips. They became the hallmarks of the Lombard style. Lombard masons, who achieved excellent structural as well as decorative results in their stonework, traveled widely and carried the Lombard style with them. Most notably, the exported style appears in Normandy and Germany.

See also BOBBIO, ABBEY OF; MAGISTRI COMACINI.

Some question has arisen regarding the spread of Lombard-style motifs. From their very name it is generally assumed that Lombardy was their place of origin, and all manifestations of these motifs presuppose Lombard influence. There is some evidence, however, that their origin may have been otherwise. Although one such motif, the exterior dwarf gallery, is found on the 9th-century apse of Sant'Ambrogio, Milan, it is also seen on the 9th-century abbey church of Hersfeld, Germany, and on the 10th-century church at Spiez, Switzerland. The motif can thus be seen as prevalent in Europe during the 9th and 10th centuries. (A possible prototype for this motif appears on the late-3d-century Roman city gate of Trier, Germany.) See HERSFELD ABBEY; SANT'AMBROGIO, MILAN. See also CREMONA CATHEDRAL.

The question, then, is where such forms developed and how they spread during Romanesque times. The *premier roman*, an archaistic "folk architecture," had crudely continued Roman construction and forms in an unbroken tradition through the Carolingian and Ottonian periods. One center of the *premier roman* was the Upper Rhine and the Alpine valleys, and from the evidence it is possible to conclude that influences moved both north and south from this germinal area. Once the style had spread and been adopted, there was continual interchange, but the first major Romanesque impetus moved north from Lombardy. Art historians have indicated the role of the above-mentioned traveling bands of expert Lombard masons in transmitting these forms.

See also ROMANESQUE ART AND ARCHITECTURE.

STANLEY FERBER

LOMI, ARTEMISIA, see GENTILESCHI, ARTEMISIA.

LOMI, ORAZIO, see GENTILESCHI, ORAZIO.

LOMME, JANIN (Jehan le Home). Flemish sculptor of Tournai (fl. early 15th cent.). Working in Spain, he created many tombs for members of the family of the King of Navarre after 1411. They are to be found in the Cathedrals of Pamplona and Tudela. The tomb of Charles the Noble and his wife (1416–20) in Pamplona Cathedral, with its reclining effigies and heavily draped mourners, is related to those of Philip the Bold and John the Fearless in Dijon, where Lomme lived between 1405 and 1410.

BIBLIOGRAPHY. D. Roggen, "Jehan Lomme en Klaas Sluter," *Gentse Bijdragen tot de Kunstgeschiedenis*, XIII, 1951.

LONDON. Capital of England. London is located on the tidal estuary of the Thames River, which favored its development as a maritime power, an industrial and mercantile giant, and capital of a far-flung empire. The oldest known relics are those of the Romans, now mostly built over. A fragment of the Roman city wall, built of rubble with brick stringcourses, is visible at the southeast angle of the Tower moat, and excavations have brought to light the extent and course of the wall that girdled the city. Roman coins and sculpture have been dredged from the river near the Tower of London. It appears that London Bridge was built on the site of the Roman bridge, and the Tower was built on the site of the Roman fortress protecting the port and the bridge. See TOWER OF LONDON.

Earliest of the Norman monuments in London is the

Lombard style. Façade of S. Ambrogio, Milan.

White Tower, built by William the Conqueror in 1078. Within its massive walls is St. John's Chapel, a small but perfect example of Norman ecclesiastical architecture. The White Tower now houses a museum of arms, armor, and instruments of torture. The next oldest Norman building is St. Bartholomew's, which belonged to a priory founded in 1123. The Norman Church of All-Hallows-by-the-Tower, rich in antiquarian interest, was seriously damaged in World War II and has been restored. See ST. JOHN'S CHAPEL, TOWER OF LONDON.

The "Temple Church," formally the Church of St. Mary the Virgin, consecrated in 1185, was one of the round churches of the Knights Templars in England. Restored in the 19th century, and again after war damage in 1941, it stands in the green quadrangle of the two Inns of Court of the Temple, recalling the Crusaders who once held this property. Its circular nave is late Norman, its chancel Early English. See TEMPLE CHURCH.

Much more ambitious in scale is Southwark Cathedral, on the south bank of the Thames, which was begun in 1207 as the church of the Augustinian Priory of St. Mary of the Ferry, long called "St. Mary Overie." It is mainly Early English, and was restored in the 19th century. Not far from Southwark is Lambeth Palace, the London residence of the Archbishop of Canterbury. The gateway dating from 1499 and the 15th-century tower of the adjoining parish church of St. Mary are the oldest authentic remnants here. See SOUTHWARK CATHEDRAL.

London's chief medieval relics are on the north bank of the river, in the City of Westminster, which grew up around the historic Benedictine abbey. William the Conqueror had himself crowned in the abbey church just after the Battle of Hastings, and it has since remained the coronation church of English monarchs. The church as seen today, chiefly Early English in style, was begun in 1245, when Henry III was moved to participate in the great wave of Gothic cathedral building that was transforming Europe. See WESTMINSTER ABBEY.

Also in Westminster is St. Margaret's Church, a 15th-century Perpendicular structure with a fine stained-glass window at the east end. An unusual example of secular public building of the 14th–15th century is the Guildhall. St. James's Palace, badly damaged by fire in the early 19th century, has a gateway and other fragments of Tudor construction that were spared. *See* ST. JAMES'S PALACE.

A few Elizabethan houses are still to be seen in London. There are some in Holborn, overshadowed by Victorian buildings and the towering structures that replaced houses bombed out in World War II. The Elizabethan half-timbered house wall above the Early English gateway leading to the Norman Church of St. Bartholomew the Great in Smithfield is another good example.

The style of Inigo Jones, with its Palladian echoes, introduced Italian Renaissance developments into London's architecture, both secular and ecclesiastical, in the first half of the 17th century. Jones's Banqueting Hall, Whitehall, built between 1619 and 1622, with its ceiling painted by Rubens between 1630 and 1635, stands out in its classical restraint amid the grandiose public buildings, mostly 18th century, that surround it. *See* WHITEHALL PALACE.

See also ASHBURNHAM HOUSE.

Following Jones came England's greatest architect, Sir Christopher Wren, whose most acclaimed work is the great domed St. Paul's Cathedral, under construction from 1675 to 1710, which looms over London at the top of Ludgate Hill. It replaced the medieval cathedral destroyed in the fire of 1666. Many of Wren's delightful small churches, with ingeniously varied steeples that were a hallmark of his style, were damaged or destroyed in World War II. With them went the fine ornamental woodwork by Grinling Gibbons and other distinguished craftsmen that was an essential feature of Wren's interiors. Wren also designed that inescapable landmark, The Monument, a 202-foot-tall column that commemorates the fire, and notable secular buildings, including part of Kensington Palace, which now houses the London Museum, and Marlborough House in Pall Mall, built about 1710 for the Duke of Marlborough. *See* KENSINGTON PALACE; ST. PAUL'S CATHEDRAL.

The Church of St. Martin-in-the-Fields, a model of Georgian reticence and dignity that had so many modest echoes in New England, was designed by James Gibbs and completed in 1726. Boodle's Club, built in 1765 on St. James's Street, is a splendid example of Georgian secular architecture, and brick row houses of the period are also still to be seen. *See* ST. MARTIN-IN-THE-FIELDS.

Among London's varied 18th-century survivals is the quiet residential street of Queen Anne's Gate, Westminster (1702–14). There are a few 18th-century houses in colorful Shepherd's Market, off Piccadilly, which was built up about 1735. Exemplifying the period's more grandiose aspirations is the long façade of Somerset House (1776–86), fronting on the river, the masterpiece of Sir William Chambers. Still another aspect of 18th-century London is presented by the dignified building (1773–77) by the Adam brothers in Portman Square, now the home of the Warburg and Courtauld Institutes. Apsley House, at Hyde Park Corner, a brick building by the Adam brothers, built between 1771 and 1778 and enlarged and refaced with stone in 1820, is open to the public as the Wellington Museum (paintings, sculpture, decorative arts, and memorabilia).

Of all great cities one of the least arranged and most accidental in its growth, London owes its most notable

planned areas to the Regency period and the architec John Nash. His grand plan encompassed Carlton Hous Terrace, completed in 1831, facing the Mall, with S James's Park beyond; Buckingham Palace, rebuilt at th end of the broad, tree-lined Mall from 1824 to 1837 afte Nash's designs (but later altered), and facing its spaciou esplanade, later considerably obstructed by the huge al too-Victorian memorial to the Queen; Regent Street, wit the steepled Tempietto of Nash's All Souls' Church (1822 25) at its north end; and Regent's Park (1812), with th dignified terraces that Nash designed to surround it.

Regent's Park, with its ornamental waters and brillian flower beds, its Zoological and Botanical Gardens, is bu one of the generous open spaces that make London, de spite its size and congestion, a green and lovely place Others are Kensington Gardens, Hyde Park, Green Park and St. James's Park.

The Victorian complex of public buildings in Kensing ton includes Albert Hall, Commonwealth Institute, Scienc Museum, Natural History Museum, and Victoria and A bert Museum. A. W. N. Pugin played an influential part i the Gothic revival. He designed the ornamental feature of the Houses of Parliament, a generally successful imita tion of the English Perpendicular style, built between 183 and 1860 after plans by Sir Charles Barry and his so Edward, which provided the impetus for Victorian Gothi building in London. The Law Courts of 1878 show th extremes to which this trend could go. *See* PARLIAMENT HOUSES OF.

The neoclassic British Museum, with its vast Ionic po tico, was built between 1823 and 1855 after designs b Sir Robert Smirke. The National Gallery, by William Wi kins (1832–38), faces the handsome expanse of Trafalga Square, laid out in 1829 by Sir Charles Barry. Also neo classic in style is the Tate Gallery, overlooking the Tham in Millbank. (For all museums, *see* LONDON: MUSEUMS

Modern concrete and steel structures, some emphasiz ing verticality, have transformed the skyline of Londo since the end of World War II. Two examples of mode height bring us back to the Thames, that central fact the city: the Royal Festival Hall, designed by R. H. Ma thew and J. L. Martin, completed in 1951, and Waterlo Bridge, designed by Sir Giles Gilbert Scott, opened in 195

In addition to the aforementioned art collections ther are others of considerable importance: the National Po trait Gallery; the Wallace Collection; the Percival Davi Foundation of Chinese Art, with a renowned collectio of porcelains and library; Kenwood House, a collection art and furnishings in a beautiful 18th-century mansio situated on the open reaches of Hampstead Heath; S John Soane's Museum; the Courtauld Institute Galleries i Woburn Square; the Queen's Gallery, in Buckingham Pa ace; and Burlington House, home of the Royal Academ where exhibitions are held. *See* ROYAL ACADEMY OF ART ENGLAND.

See also ST. BRIDE'S FLEET STREET; ST. MARY-LE-BOW ST. MARY-LE-STRAND; ST. STEPHEN WALBROOK.

BIBLIOGRAPHY. J. Stow, *A Survey of London*, 1st ed., Londo 1598, 6th ed., 2 vols., London, 1754–55; S. E. Rasmussen, *Londo The Unique City*, London, 1937; P. Abercombie, *Greater Londo Plan, 1944*, London, 1945; N. Pevsner, *The Buildings of Englan* vols. 6, 12, Harmondsworth, 1952, 1957; Town Planning Institu *Report on Planning in the London Region*, London, 1956; K. Clar *The Gothic Revival*, 3d ed., New York, 1962. MADLYN KA

LONDON: MUSEUMS. Important public art collections in London, England, are located in the museums listed below.

British Museum. The museum was begun in 1753 with the collection of Sir Hans Sloane and the Harleian and Cottonian manuscripts. This nucleus went on display in 1759 at Montagu House. A new wing was added about 1805 to house a number of additions, including Sir William Hamilton's Greek vases (acquired in 1772), Egyptian antiquities (acquired in 1802), and the Townley Marbles (acquired in 1805). With the arrival of the Phigaleian Marbles (1815) and the Elgin Marbles (1816) and with the acquisition of King George III's library (1823), it was necessary to build a new museum.

Building began in 1823 to the designs of Robert Smirke. First came the King's Library on the East Wing, then the West Wing (1833–38), and finally the demolition of Montagu House and the erection in 1842–47 of the south front with its columnar porch and its pediment sculptures by Westmacott. Finds from excavations at Nineveh and Halicarnassus and continued additions to the library required further extensions. These were executed by Sidney Smirke in 1852–57. The circular domed reading room, designed by the chief librarian, Sir Anthony Pinazzi, was opened in 1857. Later enlargements include the White Wing at the southeast angle (1884) and the King Edward VII Galleries on the north, designed by Sir John Burnet in 1914.

The building is an imposing structure in a formal Greek revival style. The contents are even more impressive in their unparalleled wealth and variety. The highlight of the large collection of Greek and Roman sculpture is the Elgin Marbles, named after Thomas Bruce, 7th Earl Elgin, who sold them to the British government. The marbles include the Parthenon pediment groups, metopes, and frieze, as well as sculptures from the Erechtheum and other Greek buildings. The Phigaleian Marbles are from the Temple of Apollo Epikourios at Bassae, near Phigaleia. Also of special interest are the remains of the Mausoleum of Halicarnassus (353–351 B.C.).

The most famous piece in the collection of Egyptian sculpture is the Rosetta Stone. Other Egyptian rooms display jewelry, models, and implements. The collections of antique vases, Greek and Roman bronzes, and glass are noteworthy, particularly the Portland Vase of the early Roman period.

The art of ancient Mesopotamia is represented by examples from the earliest period (ca. 3000–2000 B.C.), such as an inlaid panel from Ur and a copper relief from Al-'Ubaid; the Babylonian period; and the Assyrian period, for example, reliefs from the palace of Assurbanipal.

The Sutton Hoo Treasure, the richest ever found in Britain, from a 7th-century ship burial excavated in 1939, includes the remains of the earliest-known north European harp and a wealth of splendid gold objects and ornaments. The primitive arts of Africa and the South Pacific are represented in quantity as well as quality. There are fine bindings in the King's Library and a large collection of autographs and manuscripts.

BIBLIOGRAPHY. N. Pevsner, *Buildings of England*, vol. 6: *London, Except the Cities of London and Westminster*, Harmondsworth, 1952; *Guide to the British Museum*, London, 1961.

JOHN HARRIS

Courtauld Institute of Art. Museum established in 1931 as a department of the University of London. It was the first center within the British Commonwealth devoted to systematic study and research in the history of art, and the first university department in Great Britain to grant degrees in this discipline. Samuel Courtauld donated the lease of Home House, Portman Square, to house the institute. This gift has preserved the town house built and decorated by Robert Adam in 1773–77 for the Countess of Home. Courtauld also established a trust (Home House Society) to care for and house his private collection of late-19th-century French paintings. Other private collections later bequeathed to the institute include Italian Renaissance paintings given by Viscount Lee of Fareham, the Roger Fry Collection, and old master drawings left by the late Sir Robert and Lady Witt.

Among the celebrated pictures in the Courtauld Collection are Manet's *Bar at the Folies-Bergère* and Renoir's *La Loge*. Cézanne is represented by a particularly fine version of *The Card Players*, the landscape *Lac d'Annecy*, the *Still Life with a Plaster Cupid*, and *Man with a Pipe*. There is also one of Gauguin's Tahitian figures, *Nevermore*, as well as the Van Gogh *Self-Portrait with a Bandaged Ear* and a brilliant *Sunflowers*.

BIBLIOGRAPHY. D. Cooper, *The Courtauld Collection*, London, 1954.

ALLAN MC NAB

Dulwich College Picture Gallery. Located in the London suburb of Dulwich, this collection of European paintings was opened in 1814. It is housed in a building by Sir John Soane. The gallery is strong in Dutch and Flemish works; some of the artists represented are Aelbert Cuijp, Rembrandt, Raphael, Poussin, Watteau, Murillo, Reynolds, and Gainsborough. Seven works by Poussin, including *The Triumph of David* and *Rinaldo and Armida*, are the highlights of the collection.

London Museum. This museum was opened to the public in 1912, and the collection was moved to Kensington Palace in 1956. The exhibits of tools, costumes, books, games, maps, topographical displays, and other documentary evidences are arranged chronologically to illustrate the history of the site and city of London from the Stone Age to the present.

National Gallery. England's national museum, located at Trafalgar Square, was founded in 1824 when Parliament voted money for the purchase and exhibition of thirty-eight paintings from the collection of Julius Angerstein. By 1855 a consistent policy of acquisition had been established, and today the museum is considered one of the finest in Europe.

The quality of the collection can be seen by citing a small selection of the most famous examples of its Italian paintings. Northern Italy is represented by Pisanello's *Vision of St. Eustace*, Antonello da Messina's *St. Jerome in His Study*, both Giovanni Bellini's and Mantegna's similar versions of *Agony in the Garden*, and such 16th-century examples as Titian's *Bacchus and Ariadne*, Tintoretto's *St. George and the Dragon*, and Veronese's *Family of Darius before Alexander*. Early Renaissance works include Masaccio's *Madonna and Child Enthroned* (from the *Pisa Altar*), part of Uccello's *Battle of San Romano*, Botticelli's *Mars and Venus*, Piero della Francesca's *Baptism of Christ*, and Antonio del Pollaiuolo's *Martyrdom of St. Sebastian*.

Works by Raphael, Leonardo (one of the versions of the *Madonna of the Rocks*), and Correggio form a background to mannerism, exemplified by Parmigianino's *Vision of St. Jerome*, Sebastiano del Piombo's *Raising of Lazarus*, and Bronzino's *Cupid, Venus, Folly, and Time*. The 17th-century collection, built around a nucleus of Annibale Carracci's paintings, includes such names as Caravaggio, Reni, Guercino, and Domenichino, while the 18th century centers on the Venetians Tiepolo and Guardi.

The French school, covered from the 15th through the 19th century, includes six Poussins (among them the *Adoration of the Golden Calf* and two *Bacchanals*), numerous Claude Lorraine landscapes, fragments of Manet's *The Execution of Maximilian*, and Renoir's *Les Parapluies*. Among the more notable paintings of the Flemish, Dutch, and German schools are Van Eyck's *The Arnolfini Marriage*, Holbein's *The Ambassadors*, Rembrandt's *Woman Bathing*, *Self-Portrait*, and the monumental *Portrait of a Man on Horseback*, and Rubens's *Château Steen*. Spain is represented by such works as El Greco's *Agony in the Garden*, Velázquez's *Rokeby Venus*, and Murillo's *St. John and the Lamb*.

BIBLIOGRAPHY. All the following books have the title *National Gallery Catalogues*: N. Maclaren, *Spanish School*, London, 1952; M. Davies, *Early Netherlandish School*, 2d rev. ed., London, 1955; M. Levey, *The Eighteenth-Century Italian Schools*, London, 1956; M. Davies, *French School*, 2d rev. ed., London, 1957; *Summary Catalogue*, London, 1958; M. Davies, *The British School*, 2d rev. ed., London, 1959; C. Gould, *The Sixteenth-Century Venetian School*, London, 1959; M. Levey, *The German School*, London, 1959; N. Maclaren, *The Dutch School*, London, 1960; M. Davies, *The Earlier Italian Schools*, 2d rev. ed., London, 1961; C. Gould, *The Sixteenth-Century Italian Schools, Excluding the Venetian*, London, 1962.

STEPHEN E. OSTROW

National Portrait Gallery. Founded in 1856 and opened in 1859, the collection is now housed in a building designed by Ewan Christian (1890–96), next to the National Gallery. It includes more than 4,000 portraits of British royalty, statesmen, poets, writers, artists, and other historical figures of the last four centuries, arranged in chronological order. Some of the artists whose works are included are Honthorst, Lely, Kneller, Rubens, Van Dyck, Clouet, Coello, Copley, Dobson, Gainsborough, Hogarth, Reynolds, Romney, and Stuart.

Queen's Gallery. Established in 1962 in a wing of Buckingham Palace to accommodate changing exhibits of works from the royal collections of fine arts, porcelain, silver, furniture, tapestry, and armor.

Sir John Soane's Museum. Collection housed in the residence of the architect Sir John Soane in Lincoln's Inn Fields, London. It was designed in 1812 by Soane in his austere, neoclassic style. After his death in 1837 the building and its contents were made into a museum for "the promotion of the study of Architecture and the Applied Arts." Soane's breadth of interest is illustrated by the many Roman sculpture fragments and casts, ancient Egyptian sarcophagus in the domed room, and Gothic fragments and casts kept in the medieval-styled Monk's Yard, Cloister, and Tomb. In the picture room are two series of paintings by Hogarth, *The Rake's Progress* and the *Election*, as well as paintings by Watteau, Canaletto, and Turner. Included in the important collection of 20,000 architectural drawings are many by Wren, Chambers, Adam, and Dance, and the Elizabethan plans of Thorpe.

BIBLIOGRAPHY. A. T. Bolton, *Sir John Soane's Museum: Description of the House and Museum*, 11th ed., Oxford, 1930.

Tate Gallery. The museum, which owes its name and origin to Sir Henry Tate, who presented his collection of paintings to the nation in 1889, was designed by Sidney R. J. Smith in 1897 and extended in 1899 and 1910. It comprises the National Collections of British Painting of the 18th to the 20th century and modern European painting and sculpture. The collection of Turner's paintings, drawings, and water colors is the largest in the world. Of special interest are the fine series of Blake water colors, including the illustrations for Dante's *Divine Comedy*, and the many works by Burne-Jones, D. G. Rossetti, and other Pre-Raphaelites. Among the French impressionist and postimpressionist paintings are Seurat's *Une Baignade* and other important canvases by Manet, Renoir, Cézanne, Degas, Toulouse-Lautrec, and Bonnard. The gallery's sculpture collection, a representative survey, is especially strong in the works of Alfred Stevens.

BIBLIOGRAPHY. R. Alley, *Tate Gallery Catalogues: The Foreign Paintings, Drawings and Sculpture*, London, 1959; M. Chamot, D. Farr, and M. Butlin, *Tate Gallery Catalogues: The Modern British Paintings, Drawings and Sculpture*, London, 1964.

Victoria and Albert Museum. In 1857 the museum moved to its present site, joining the aggregate South Kensington Museum as part of Prince Albert's scheme for a cultural center. In 1899 Queen Victoria laid the foundation stone for a new building, which was designed by Sir Aston Webb. Containing works of fine and applied arts of all styles, periods, and countries, it is one of the world's major museums. Among its most important collections are Italian and Gothic sculpture, medieval ivories, Oriental pottery and porcelain, Italian majolica, English pottery, medieval and Renaissance jewelry, textiles, furniture, engravings, drawings, and paintings, notably the famous Raphael tapestry cartoons. It has recently added a Costume Court. The museum includes the National Art Library and administers Ham House and Osterley Park.

BIBLIOGRAPHY. Victoria and Albert Museum, *Guide*, rev. ed., London, 1954.

Long and short work. Type of corner construction employed in Anglo-Saxon churches.

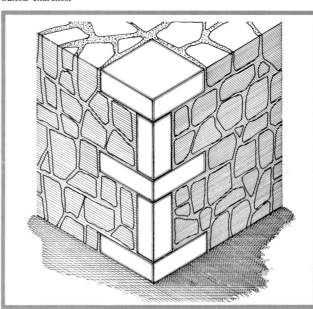

Wallace Collection. Formed by generations of the Seymour-Conway family, earls and marquesses of Hertford, the collection was inherited by Sir Richard Wallace, son of the fourth marquess, and was bequeathed to the nation by Lady Wallace in 1898. It stands in a house that was built about 1776 by the Duke of Manchester and was greatly altered by Sir Richard Wallace and later by the nation. The collection is notably rich in arms and armor and in French furniture of the Louis XIV to Louis XVI period. Among the paintings are important works by Bronzino, Guardi, Boucher, Poussin, Bonington, Reynolds, Rembrandt, Rubens, and particularly Watteau and Fragonard, plus a fine selection of Dutch and Flemish 17th-century works. The Italian majolica, Sèvres porcelain, and sculpture collections are also noteworthy.

BIBLIOGRAPHY. Wallace Collection, *A General Guide to the Wallace Collection*, London, 1958.

LONDON GROUP, THE. Group of English artists, founded in 1913, composed of a union of earlier groups, such as the Camden Town Group and the vorticists. Its formation was a reaction to Roger Fry's exhibition of postimpressionism. Harold Gilman was the first president; the group is still in existence. *See* CAMDEN TOWN GROUP; GILMAN, HAROLD; VORTICISM.

LONG AND SHORT WORK. Type of corner construction employed in Anglo-Saxon churches. Long and short slabs of stone are placed at right angles to one another (that is, vertically and horizontally) at the corners and groins of exterior walls.

BIBLIOGRAPHY. D. T. Rice, *English Art, 871-1100*, Oxford, 1952.

LONGFORD CASTLE. English castle built for Thomas Gorges about 1580. It is in triangular form with circular towers at the angles. The entrance front has a screen of superimposed arcades and pilasters. It was extensively remodeled about 1740 after designs by Roger Morris and was enlarged by D. A. Alexander from 1802.

LONGHENA, BALDASSARE. Italian architect of the Venetian school (1598-1682). Longhena was the only 17th-century Venetian architect important enough to rival his Roman contemporaries. His major work is S. Maria della Salute (begun in 1631 and under construction for more than twenty years). He also designed the Cathedral at Chioggia (1624-47), S. Maria agli Scalzi in Venice (begun 1656), the small Chiesa dell'Ospedaletto in Venice (1670-78), and many Venetian palaces. His high baroque style, rich in the use of sculpture and luminous effects, is seen to great advantage in the Palazzo Pesaro and the Palazzo Rezzonico.

The plan of S. Maria della Salute is an octagon surrounded by an ambulatory and surmounted by a dome. It is followed by a chancel terminated at the sides by semicircular apses and surmounted by a second, smaller dome. The interior is a series of carefully controlled vistas integrated by means of optical and scenographic devices. The same principles of design prevail on the exterior, whose most distinctive feature is the pairs of decorative spirals that serve as buttresses for the dome. *See* SANTA MARIA DELLA SALUTE, VENICE.

BIBLIOGRAPHY. R. Wittkower, *Art and Architecture in Italy, 1600-1750*, Baltimore, 1958.

LONGHI (Falca), ALESSANDRO. Italian painter (b. Venice, 1733; d. there, 1813). The son of the genre painter Pietro Longhi, Alessandro at first studied with his father, then became the pupil of the obscure Giuseppe Nogari. Although he was the leading society portraitist of his time, he has been considered merely facile in his character studies. It has been contended, however, that in his handling of paint he harked back to the great 16th-century Venetians.

Alessandro commonly portrayed senators, prelates, and leading artists and writers. For the most part his character study is not penetrating; the facial features are usually pleasingly generalized. The sitter is often bedecked in the full regalia of his office. The attorney Niccolò Erizzo is shown in his handsome trial robes before the base of a great column (ca. 1766; Verona). But in the portrait of the writer Carlo Goldoni (Venice, Correr Museum), the sitter stands somewhat less formally, has an animated expression, and, holding a book, gestures invitingly toward the observer. The image is built up through a creamy impasto. Also, in *Teresa Barbarigo* (1778; Venice, Collection of Donà delle Rose) the paint is handled with admirable freshness. In 1780 the Venetian naval official Jacopo was pictured in his gold-embroidered red robes (Correr Museum), painted in sumptuous color. Among the group portraits is *Members of the Pisani Family* (ca. 1760; Venice, Collection of Bentivoglio d'Aragona).

Alessandro was also an engraver. In 1762 he published biographies of a group of important contemporary Venetian artists, and illustrated each with a portrait engraving. His paintings for churches are few.

BIBLIOGRAPHY. V. Moschini, "Per lo studio di Alessandro Longhi," *L'Arte*, III, March, 1932; E. Arslan, "Di Alessandro e di Pietro Longhi," *Emporium*, XCVIII, August, 1943; R. Wittkower, *Art and Architecture in Italy, 1600-1750*, Baltimore, 1958; M. Levey, *Painting in XVIII Century Venice*, London, 1959.

ABRAHAM A. DAVIDSON

Baldassare Longhena, the high-baroque Palazzo Rezzonico, on the Grand Canal, Venice.

Pietro Longhi, *The Toilette*. Palazzo Rezzonico, Venice. A work by a painter of Venetian domestic scenes.

LONGHI, LUCA. Italian painter, the leading artist of Ravenna in the 16th century (1507-80). He executed many altarpieces in Ravenna in a routine late mannerist style flavored with archaism in the Francia tradition. He also produced some rather stiff but strong portraits.

BIBLIOGRAPHY. Ravenna, Accademia di belle arti, Galleria, *La galleria dell'Accademia di Ravenna*, ed. A. Martini, Venice, 1959.

LONGHI, MARTINO (Il Giovane). Italian architect (b. Rome, 1602; d. Viggiù, 1657). He was the son of Onorio Longhi and the grandson of Martino "Il Vecchio" Longhi.

His most notable work is the façade of SS. Vincenzo ed Anastasio, across from the Trevi Fountain in Rome (1646-50), where he used massed columns. He continued work on S. Carlo al Corso, and at least began the Church and façade of S. Antonio de' Portoghesi (1638 on).

BIBLIOGRAPHY. R. Wittkower, *Art and Architecture in Italy, 1600-1750*, Baltimore, 1958.

LONGHI (Lunghi; Longo), MARTINO (Il Vecchio). Italian architect (b. Viggiù; d. Rome, 1591). He followed Vignola in his treatment of wall surfaces. The Church of

S. Girolamo degli Schiavoni (1588–89) and the Altemps Chapel of S. Maria in Trastevere, both in Rome, show his elaborately paneled façade architecture at its most characteristic. He was the father of Onorio Longhi.

BIBLIOGRAPHY. H. Hibbard, *The Architecture of the Palazzo Borghese*, Rome, 1962.

LONGHI, ONORIO. Italian architect (1569–1619). The son of Martino "Il Vecchio" Longhi, he was particularly active as a designer of altars. A friend of Caravaggio, he was exiled from Rome in 1606 as the result of a quarrel and went to Milan. He returned to Rome to begin construction of the Lombard church, S. Carlo al Corso (1612), which was finished long after his death.

BIBLIOGRAPHY. G. Baglione, *Le vite de' pittori, scultori ed architetti...*, Rome, 1642.

LONGHI (Falca), PIETRO. Italian painter (b. Venice, 1702; d. there, 1785). After an apprenticeship with Antonio Balestra, Longhi began his career as a figure painter but proved to be far from successful. In Bologna Giuseppe Maria Crespi taught him the possibilities of genre with scenes of low life that did not always stop short of the sick and the sordid. Longhi tempered these extremes and produced such charming works as *A Peasant Girl* (Bassano, Museo Civico). Returning to Venice in 1732, he began to paint the subjects associated with his name today—Venetian public and domestic scenes. His early efforts were clumsy, and even later his works betrayed defects of composition, but the large sums he earned indicate his popularity at the time. He was the father of Alessandro Longhi.

BIBLIOGRAPHY. M. Levey, *Painting in XVIII Century Venice*, London, 1959.

LONGHOUSE. Iroquois communal dwelling, built of upright poles bound by horizontal ones and roofed with pole rafters in gable form. Such dwellings, rectangular in plan and sometimes 100 feet long by about 16 feet wide, contained raised bunks in which the occupants slept.

LONGINUS OF JERUSALEM, ST. Identified with the centurion assigned by Pilate to stand guard with soldiers at the Crucifixion. Longinus recognized the divinity of Christ after a drop of Christ's blood ran down the lance curing his eye malady. He left the army, lived as a monk at Caesarea, and was beheaded at the order of Pilate. He is often confused with another Longinus, the Roman soldier who pierced Christ's side with a lance (in Greek, *longke*) to be sure He was dead. His attribute is a lance. His feast is March 15.

See also SAINTS IN ART.

LONGLEAT HOUSE. English house built about 1557. John Thynne, its owner, had superintended the building of Somerset House between 1547 and 1552 for the Protector Somerset. One of the most influential buildings of its time, Somerset was almost certainly reflected in the extension to Longleat. A fire occurred in 1567 and a new house was finished by 1573 although the top story was not added until after 1580. The designer (certainly of the later stages) of this second house was Robert Smythson.

His total responsibility is undecided. In any case Longleat stands unrivaled as the perfect Renaissance house of its time in Europe.

BIBLIOGRAPHY. C. Hussey, "Longleat, Wiltshire," 4 parts, *Country Life*, CV, April 8, 15, 22, 29, 1949.

LONGO, MARTINO, *see* LONGHI, MARTINO (IL VECCHIO).

LONGUEIL, JOSEPH DE. French engraver (b. Givet, 1730; d. Paris, 1792). He received instruction at Lille and later studied under Lebas and Johann Georg Wille. Longueil worked primarily as a book illustrator, with most of his illustrations made in collaboration with Charles Eisen. Panhard attributes 507 etchings to Longueil: vignettes, as in *Henriade* by Voltaire, and various single sheets, most of them genre or narrative works. Longueil was one of the better French vignettists of the 18th century.

BIBLIOGRAPHY. F. Panhard, *Joseph de Longueil, sa vie—son oeuvre*, Paris, 1880.

LOON, THEODORE VAN. Flemish painter of religious subjects (ca. 1581–1667). He was active in Brussels but twice journeyed to Italy, where he stayed from 1602 to 1608 and in 1628–29. Theodore van Loon was one of the chief exponents of Caravaggism in the southern Low Countries; he drew inspiration mainly from Borgianni and attained results that can best be likened to Domenichino's and Reni's youthful styles.

BIBLIOGRAPHY. R. Oldenbourg, *Die flämische Malerei des 17. Jahrhunderts*, 2d ed., Berlin, 1922.

LOOS, ADOLF. Austrian architect and critic (1870–1933). Born in Brünn, he worked principally around Vienna, though he spent several years of the 1890s in the United States. Loos returned to Austria in 1897 to become, in the first decade of the 20th century, one of the most articulate leaders of the international revolt against Art Nouveau. He was a powerful spokesman for a new architecture based upon pure, undecorated form and the rational manipulation of materials and spaces. Among his more important works, all in Vienna, are the Steiner and

Longleat House. One of England's influential Renaissance buildings.

Scheu Houses (1910; 1912) and the Goldman and Salatsch Building (1910), austere cubic compositions, evolved from their inner activities. The best extant example of his work is the interior of the Kärtner Bar in Vienna (1907). Of as great importance as his architectural works to the development of contemporary architecture are his many polemical essays, including *Ins Leere gesprochen* (1897–1900) and *Ornament und Verbrechen* (1908).

BIBLIOGRAPHY. L. Münz, *Adolf Loos*, Milan, 1956; R. Banham, *Theory and Design in the First Machine Age*, London, 1960.

LOOTEN, JAN. Dutch landscape painter (b. Amsterdam, ca. 1618; d. London, ca. 1680). Looten was reported in Amsterdam in 1659 and soon afterward traveled to England. He was living in London in April, 1669, when Samuel Pepys visited him. According to Houbraken, Jan Griffier was Looten's pupil in England. Looten was apparently patronized by James II. His landscapes follow the tradition of Jacob van Ruisdael and possibly Meindert Hobbema. Contemporary Flemish landscape painting also seems to have influenced him.

BIBLIOGRAPHY. W. Bernt, *Die niederländischen Maler des 17. Jahrhunderts...*, vol. 2, Munich, 1948.

LOPEZ DE ARTEAGA, SEBASTIAN. Spanish colonial painter in Mexico (b. Seville, 1610; d. Mexico City, ca. 1656). Sebastián López de Arteaga was trained in Seville and went to Mexico before 1643. His rare paintings are tenebrist and naturalistic (for example, *The Incredulity of St. Thomas*; Mexico City, National Museum of History). A *Crucifixion* and a *Betrothal of the Virgin* (both in the National Museum of History) are among the best of his works.

BIBLIOGRAPHY. M. Toussaint, *Arte colonial en México*, 2d ed., Mexico City, 1962.

LOPEZ Y PORTANA, VICENTE. Spanish painter (b. Valencia, 1772; d. Madrid, 1850). López was associated with academies throughout his career. Trained in the Valencia Academy and under Maella in the Academy of S. Fernando in Madrid, he was made director of the Valencia Academy (1801), painter to Charles IV (1802), First Painter to the Court under Ferdinand VII (1814), director of the academies (1817), and conservator of the Prado, Madrid. He executed allegorical frescoes in the Palace of the Orient, Madrid (1828); many religious paintings in a vigorous, superficial late baroque style; and traditional devotional images of the Virgin. But he was used most frequently as a portraitist by the court and excelled in rendering richly ornamented costumes on his pleasantly smiling subjects. His one attempt at character study, in the *Portrait of Goya* (1826) in the Prado, is almost a caricature of the great artist's serious mien.

BIBLIOGRAPHY. M. de Lozoya, *Vicente López*, Barcelona, 1943.

LO P'ING. Chinese painter (1733–99). His *tzu* was Liang-feng. A native of Yang-chou in Kiangsu Province, he was a pupil of Chin Nung and was included among the "Eight Eccentrics of Yang-chou." He was probably the most popular of the Yang-chou painters, a popularity that can be traced in part to the special subject of ghosts which Lo

P'ing was fond of depicting. Like many of the Yang-chou eccentrics, he is well represented in Japanese collections. *See* CHIN NUNG; YANG-CHOU, EIGHT ECCENTRICS OF.

BIBLIOGRAPHY. J. Cahill, "A Rejected Portrait by Lo P'ing: A Pictorial Footnote to Waley's '*Yüan Mei*,'" *Asia Major...*, n.s., VII, 1959.

LOREDAN PALACE, VENICE. Italian palace, originally a Gothic building belonging to the Mocenigo family. It was bought by the Loredan family in 1536, when it was completely rebuilt, with Renaissance forms and characteristics, by Antonio Scarpagnino. The palace is the present home of the Istituto Veneto di Scienza, Lettere ed Arti (founded in 1810).

BIBLIOGRAPHY. G. Lorenzetti, *Venice and Its Lagoon*, Rome, 1961.

LORENESE, CARLO, *see* MELLIN, CHARLES.

LORENZETTI, AMBROGIO. Italian painter of the Sienese school (fl. 1319–47). Ambrogio Lorenzetti, one of the most original artists of the 14th century, was the brother of the painter Pietro Lorenzetti. His first known picture is a *Madonna and Child* of about 1317 in the Brera Picture Gallery in Milan, and his earliest dated work is a *Madonna and Child* of 1319 from Sant'Angelo a Vico l'Abate, near Florence, now in the Uffizi Gallery in Florence. In 1327 Ambrogio is registered in the Florentine painters' guild; the frescoes in the chapter house of S. Agostino, which he painted at that time, have been lost.

From Florence he went to Massa Marittima to paint the large altarpiece of the *Maestà* (ca. 1330) for the Cathedral. The first major statement of his mature style, it shows the Madonna and Child on a throne built on a series of platforms on which are seated the three theological virtues, with saints and angels crowded closely together at either side. About 1332 Ambrogio painted the four panels with scenes from the life of St. Nicholas that are now in the Uffizi.

Ambrogio's most extensive and famous works are the frescoes in the Sala della Pace of the Palazzo Pubblico in Siena (1338–39). Covering the upper zones of all four walls of the room, they consist of two large allegories, *Good Government* and *Bad Government*, and four compositions showing the effects of good and bad government in the country and the city. They are notable for their forcefulness of characterization, their boldness and inventiveness in realistic portrayal, and their experimental method of depicting space as a continuously receding panorama. In 1340 Ambrogio painted a *Madonna and Child*, now virtually effaced, in the loggia of the Palazzo Pubblico and, at about the same time, executed the panel known as the *Madonna del Latte* in the Seminary of S. Francesco in Siena. The *Presentation in the Temple* (1342; Uffizi) is one of the most significant compositions of the 14th century, and the *Annunciation* (1344; Siena, Pinacoteca) is the first example of what Panofsky has called the "interior by implication." Of Ambrogio's frescoes in S. Francesco, only the badly damaged compositions *Franciscan Martyrdom* and *Boniface VIII Receiving St. Louis as a Novice* have survived.

Ambrogio initiated a new trend in Sienese painting, moving away from the tradition of Duccio toward the

Ambrogio Lorenzetti, *Good Government*, detail, 1338–39. Sala della Pace, Palazzo Pubblico, Siena.

premises of Giotto. His innovations in the organization of compositions and of spatial schemes anticipated many of the formulations of the Renaissance. He had many pupils and followers who perpetuated his manner in Siena.

BIBLIOGRAPHY. G. Sinibaldi, *I Lorenzetti*, Siena, 1933; E. Carli, *Ambrogio Lorenzetti*, Ivrea, 1954; G. Rowley, *Ambrogio Lorenzetti*, 2 vols., Princeton, 1958.

HELLMUT WOHL

LORENZETTI, PIETRO. Italian painter of the Sienese school (fl. 1320–44). Pietro was the brother of the painter Ambrogio Lorenzetti. Although his style is distinct and separate from Ambrogio's, the brothers share a common adherence to the monumental and sober art of Giotto rather than to the followers of Duccio.

Pietro's first dated work is the polyptych *Madonna and Child with Saints* of 1320 on the high altar of S. Maria della Pieve in Arezzo. In 1329 he painted an altarpiece for the Carmelite monks at S. Ansano a Dofana, which is still in its original location with the exception of four of its predella panels which are in the Pinacoteca in Siena. Several works may be assigned to the years between these two dates, among them a *Virgin and Child Enthroned*,

in the Johnson Collection, Philadelphia Museum of Art, a *Madonna and Child* in the Cathedral at Cortona, and several frescoes in the Lower Church of S. Francesco at Assisi: the *Madonna and Child between SS. Francis and John the Evangelist, Christ's Death and Resurrection*, and the *Stigmatization of St. Francis*. There are also frescoes of the *Passion of Christ* in the Lower Church that are by followers of Pietro.

His next dated works are three pinnacles showing St. Bartholomew, St. Cecilia, and St. John the Baptist (1332; Siena, Pinacoteca) and a large *Madonna and Child* (1340; Florence, Uffizi). The latter shows the monumental, severe manner that Pietro evolved in his later works. Pictures that may be assigned to the 1330s are the diptych of the *Madonna and Child* and *Christ as the Man of Sorrows* in the Lindenau Museum in Altenburg, the *St. Lucy* now in the sacristy of S. Lucia de' Magnoli in Florence, the *St. Catherine* in the Metropolitan Museum of Art in New York, *SS. Peter and John the Baptist* in the Vatican, and the *Crucifixion* fresco in S. Francesco in Siena.

Pietro's last dated, and in some respects most remarkable, work is the *Nativity of the Virgin* triptych of 1342

LORENZETTI, PIETRO 465

Pietro Lorenzetti, *The Deposition*, ca. 1320–29. Fresco. Lower Church of S. Francesco, Assisi.

in the Opera del Duomo in Siena. The room in which the birth takes place is represented as a three-dimensional stage whose dimensions are identical with those of the two sections of the frame of the triptych that contain them, an illusionistic formulation which foreshadows the works of Mantegna (*S. Zeno Altarpiece*, Verona, S. Zeno) more than a century later. Pietro had many assistants and followers, though his influence was not so great as that of his brother.

BIBLIOGRAPHY. E. T. De Wald, *Pietro Lorenzetti*, Cambridge, Mass., 1930; G. Sinibaldi, *I Lorenzetti*, Siena, 1933.

HELLMUT WOHL

LORENZETTI, UGOLINO. Anonymous Italian painter (14th-cent. Sienese school). The name of this painter was created by Bernard Berenson to indicate the combined influences of Ugolino da Siena and Pietro Lorenzetti apparent in the group of paintings attributed to him, of which the *Nativity* in the Fogg Art Museum, Cambridge, Mass., is undoubtedly the masterpiece. His style generally progresses from the thin hard outlines and features of Ugolino's work to the broader and more stable forms of Pietro Lorenzetti, while retaining, as well, a love of graceful detail reminiscent of the art of Duccio.

BIBLIOGRAPHY. B. Berenson, "Ugolino Lorenzetti," *Art in America*, V, October, 1917, VI, December, 1917.

LORENZETTO (Lorenzo de Ludovico di Guglielmo Lotti). Italian sculptor and architect (b. Florence, 1490; d.

Rome, 1541). Lorenzetto was a follower of Michelangelo. He worked on the monument to Cardinal Forteguerra, which Verrocchio had begun, in Pistoia Cathedral. He later worked with Raphael on the erection of the Chigi Chapel, S. Maria del Popolo, Rome, and did Raphael's tomb at the Pantheon. Afterward Lorenzetto became chief of works at St. Peter's, Rome.

LORENZI, BATTISTA DI DOMENICO (Battista Giovanni del Cavaliere). Italian sculptor (b. Settignano, 1527/28; d. Pisa, 1594). A pupil of Bandinelli, he was one of three young sculptors commissioned to execute the Michelangelo monument in Sta Croce, Florence, an undistinguished work designed by Vasari (begun 1564). Lorenzi seems to have been regarded as the most promising of the three artists selected and was chosen to execute one of the three statues as well as the decoration of the frame. His statue, representing Painting, was originally intended to portray Sculpture; its thematic metamorphosis leaves it somewhat ambivalent in character. Stylistically, the piece is representative of an unimaginative, if capable, adherence to the dogmas of the Florentine Academy. Lorenzi had also been active earlier as one of the secondary artists decorating Michelangelo's catafalque for funeral ceremonies at Florence, and he later produced statues of saints for the cathedral in Pisa.

BIBLIOGRAPHY. J. Pope-Hennessy, *Italian High Renaissance and Baroque Sculpture*, London, 1963.

LORENZI, FRANCESCO. Italian painter (b. Mazzurega, 1723; d. Verona, 1787). Lorenzi studied with Matteo Brida in Verona and Giovanni Battista Tiepolo in Venice, where he created a number of altarpieces in his early years. Working on frescoes and paintings throughout northern Italy, he remained a close imitator of Tiepolo. He also produced engravings, pastel portraits, and genre scenes.

LORENZI, STOLDO (Stoldo di Gino). Italian sculptor (b. Settignano, 1534; d. Pisa, 1583). Strongly influenced by Tribolo and Giovanni Bologna, Lorenzi produced an *Angel with Candelabra* for the Pisa Cathedral and completed some work begun there by Francesco Mosca. He also made a bronze *Galatea* in a serpentine pose for the Studiolo in the Palazzo Vecchio, Florence (1570), and statues of Adam and Eve for the façade of Santa Maria presso San Celso in Milan (1575).

LORENZO, FIORENZO DI, *see* FIORENZO DI LORENZO.

LORENZO D'ALESSANDRO (Lorenzo da Sanseverino the Younger). Marchigian painter (b. Sanseverino; d. there, 1503). He is recorded from 1462 on. His artistic development is debated. The earliest dated painting extant is the triptych of 1481 in SS. Pietro e Paolo at Corridonia (Pausola). It marks, roughly, the turning point in Lorenzo's career. Works thought to be earlier than about 1481 reflect the International style of the Salimbeni and the more progressive styles of Antonio da Fabriano and Girolamo di Giovanni da Camerino. Beginning even somewhat before 1481, and increasingly thereafter, Lorenzo's art fell under the influence of Carlo Crivelli, Matteo da Gualdo, and Niccolò di Liberatore da Foligno (Alunno)—three artists of similar tendency. That Lorenzo combined all this within a personal style justifies his place as the most important native painter active in the Marches in the later 1400s.

BIBLIOGRAPHY. L. Serra, ... *L'arte nelle Marche* ..., 2 vols., Pesaro, 1929–34; P. Zampetti, ed., *Carlo Crivelli e crivelleschi*, Venice, 1961.

LORENZO DA SANSEVERINO, *see* SALIMBENI DA SANSEVERINO, JACOPO AND LORENZO.

LORENZO DA VITERBO. Italian painter (ca. 1437–76). He was the leading artist of Viterbo in the 15th century. Documents indicate the presence of Lorenzo in Rome in 1462, when Melozzo da Forlì, Piero della Francesca, and Benozzo Gozzoli were there. His one major work, the frescoes in the Mazzatosta Chapel of S. Maria della Verità in Viterbo, completed in 1469, is a compendium of the influences of these artists as well as of Andrea del Castagno.

The vault frescoes are divided into quadrants. Each of these has a frontal figure of an evangelist seated between two theologians, filling out the arc, and a half-length figure of a prophet and symbol of the evangelist at the apex. The silhouetting of these figures against a starry sky is characteristic of the rather simplified motives of Lorenzo's style. In the *Annunciation* of the right-wall lunette, of which only the angel remains, Lorenzo attempted to imitate the mathematical order of Piero, but the regular rhythm of the background pilasters denies Piero's complexity of relationships and emphasizes the flatness of the profiled angel.

Battista di Domenico Lorenzi, allegorical figure representing painting, on Michelangelo's catafalque in Sta Croce, Florence.

Lorenzo da Viterbo, vault frescoes with evangelists and prophets. Mazzatosta Chapel, S. Maria della Verità, Viterbo.

Lower on the right wall, in the *Nativity*, Lorenzo adopted the narrative style of Benozzo Gozzoli, who had worked in Viterbo in 1453. On the wall over the altar the *Madonna in a Mandorla* is a hieratic vision with statically arranged groups of angels on either side of the central image. The kneeling apostles of the *Assumption* below combine Melozzo's compact, incisive outlines with Castagno's harsh modeling. The *Presentation of the Virgin* in the left-wall lunette and the *Marriage of the Virgin* below this develop the spatial influence of Piero further.

BIBLIOGRAPHY. F. Zeri, "Una pala d'altare di Lorenzo da Viterbo," *Bollettino d'arte*, XXXVIII, 1953.   DONALD GODDARD

LORENZO DI BARTOLO (Di Bartoluccio; Di Bartolo Michele), *see* GHIBERTI, LORENZO.

LORENZO DI CREDI, *see* CREDI, LORENZO DI.

LORENZO DI NICCOLO GERINI.
Italian painter of the Florentine school (fl. 1392–1411). Lorenzo was the son of Niccolò di Pietro Gerini and, presumably, his pupil. He was later influenced by Spinello Aretino and Lorenzo Monaco. In 1392 Lorenzo was working with his father in Prato for Francesco Datini. His first independent work is a signed triptych, *St. Bartholomew and Scenes from His Life* (1401; San Gimignano Museum). In 1402 he painted the high altar for S. Marco in Florence (now in S. Domenico in Cortona) and a polyptych, the *Madonna and Child*, in the church at Terrenzano. Lorenzo matriculated in the Florentine painters' guild in 1408, and in the Company of St. Luke in 1410. He is last mentioned in 1411 in connection with works no longer extant in the Church of S. Pier Maggiore. Lorenzo's *oeuvre* includes a virtually ruined *Coronation of the Virgin with Saints* (1408) in the Medici Chapel in Sta Croce and many other altarpieces attributed to him in Florence and elsewhere. He was a competent, often pleasing exponent of the late Giottesque style.

BIBLIOGRAPHY. O. Sirén, "Lorenzo di Niccolo," *The Burlington Magazine*, XXXVI, 1920; R. van Marle, *The Development of the Italian Schools of Painting*, vol. 3, The Hague, 1924; R. Offner, "Mostra del tesoro di Firenze sacra," *The Burlington Magazine*, LXIII, October, 1933.   HELLMUT WOHL

Lorenzo di Niccolò Gerini, *Coronation of the Virgin with Saints*. Medici Chapel, Sta Croce, Florence.

LORENZO DI PIETRO (Vecchietta).
Italian painter, sculptor, silversmith, architect, and military engineer (b. Castiglione d'Orcia, ca. 1412; d. 1480). He is responsible for, among other works, the bronze effigy (1467) of Mariano Sozzini in the National Museum (Bargello), Florence; the bronze tabernacle (1467–72) on the high altar of Siena Cathedral; and a bronze figure (1476) of the Risen Christ in S. Maria della Scala, Siena. Strongly influenced by Donatello, these works show a new orientation in Sienese sculpture.

LORENZO MAITANI, *see* MAITANI, LORENZO.

LORENZO MONACO (Piero di Giovanni).
Italian painter and miniaturist of the Florentine school (1370/71–1425). A Sienese by birth, Piero acquired the name Lorenzo Monaco (Lorenzo the Monk) when he entered the Camaldolese Order at S. Maria degli Angeli in Florence as a novice in 1391. His first dated works are of 1404—*Christ as Man of Sorrows with Mary and St. John* in the Gallery of the Academy in Florence and a triptych, *Madonna and Child*, in the Diocesan Museum in Empoli—and are executed in the refined, calligraphic manner of the International Gothic. Lorenzo's earliest works, however, such as the *Madonna and Child* in the Fitzwilliam Museum in Cambridge, England, are in the Giottesque tradition and possess, more than those of his Florentine contemporaries, great consonance in the treatment of form.

With his adoption of the International style Lorenzo's pictures become delicate and patterned, as in the *Madonna of Humility* (Copenhagen, State Museum of Fine Arts), the diptych *Christ on the Mount of Olives* (Paris, Louvre), the *Three Marys at the Tomb* (1408; Louvre), and the *Madonna and Child* (1408; Turin, Municipal Museum of Ancient Art). From 1406 to 1411 Lorenzo worked on a large polyptych, *Madonna and Child*, for the monastery of Monte Oliveto (now in Florence, Uffizi), and in 1413 he completed the altarpiece of the *Coronation of the Virgin* for S. Maria degli Angeli (Uffizi) with scenes from the legend of St. Benedict in the predella. These works show increasing clarity of form, on both a large and a small scale, and sophistication in the use of color and light. There are many documents of Lorenzo's activity as a miniaturist between 1409 and 1413, but it has proved difficult to assign any specific illuminations to him.

During the last decade of his life Lorenzo's style was characterized by rigorous control of design and a tendency toward the creation of fantastic and visionary realms, as in the *Adoration of the Magi* in the Uffizi, the predella panels with the *Miracle of St. Nicholas* and the *Legend of St. Onophrius* in the Academy, Florence, and the drawings of the *Visitation* and the *Journey of the Magi* in the former State Museums, Berlin. Lorenzo achieves a monumental sense of form in the frescoes of the *Life of the Virgin* in the Bartolini Chapel in S. Trinità, Florence. The *Annunciation Altarpiece* in this chapel shows the influence of the naturalistic and rationalistic art of the Renaissance in its method of illumination and scheme of perspective. There are many other works by Lorenzo in Florence and elsewhere. He had several pupils and followers, many of whom acted as his assistants. Lorenzo Monaco's art is

Lorenzo Monaco, *Annunciation with SS. Catherine, Anthony, Proculus, and Francis.* Academy, Florence.

one of the high points of the decorative tendency in Florentine painting.

BIBLIOGRAPHY. O. Sirén, *Don Lorenzo Monaco*, Strasbourg, 1905; R. van Marle, *The Development of the Italian Schools of Painting*, vol. 9, The Hague, 1927; G. Pudelko, "The Stylistic Development of Lorenzo Monaco," *The Burlington Magazine*, LXXIII, 1938 and LXXIV, 1939.

HELLMUT WOHL

LORENZO VENEZIANO. Venetian painter (fl. 1356–72/79). Although he was doubtless a pupil of Paolo Veneziano, Lorenzo's chief importance lies in his revolutionary break with the still essentially Byzantine tradition of his master and his growing allegiance (promoted by Bolognese and other mainland influences) to a more realistic, Gothic style.

BIBLIOGRAPHY. R. Pallucchini, *La pittura veneziana del Trecento*, Bologna, 1955.

LORJOU, BERNARD. French painter (1908–   ). A native of Blois, Lorjou acquired his artistic education on his own. His earliest painting was a portrait of his parents; he was then fourteen years old. A trip to Spain (1931) aroused his enthusiasm for El Greco, Velázquez, and Goya. After World War II he contributed to the renaissance of a realistic and popular movement in painting. He exhibited at the Salon d'Automne and at the Salon des Indépendants and, in 1954, at the Galerie Charpentier. In 1948 Lorjou shared the Prix de la Critique with Bernard Buffet, and he became one of France's foremost exponents of the latest version of expressionism. His colorful and often crude forms, the paint thickly and purely applied, are evidence of his indebtedness to Van Gogh, Soutine, and James Ensor. Lorjou's painting as a counterforce to geometrical abstraction has exercised a certain influence on young French painters.

BIBLIOGRAPHY. B. Dorival, *Twentieth-Century French Painters*, 2 vols., New York, 1958.

LORME, ANTONIE DE (Antonie Delorme). Dutch-Flemish architectural painter (b. Tournai; d. Rotterdam, 1673). De Lorme is documented in Rotterdam in 1627 when he witnessed a document for his master, the architectural painter Jan van Vucht. His early work consists mainly of views of fantastic and imaginary churches. In the 1650s this style was replaced by a more realistic manner.

BIBLIOGRAPHY. H. Jantzen, *Das niederländische Architekturbild*, Leipzig, 1910.

LORRAINE (Gellee or Gelee), CLAUDE (Le Lorrain). French landscape painter, draftsman, and etcher (b. Chamagne, near Nancy, 1600; d. Rome, 1682). Though the French refer to him as "Le Lorrain" and the English as "Claude Lorraine," his real name is Claude Gellée (Gelée). Orphaned about the age of twelve, he went to Freiburg-im-Breisgau to live with a brother who taught him engraving, and from there to Rome with a relative, a dealer in lace. There he found employment as a pastry cook in the house of the landscape painter A. Tassi, from whom, as an apprentice, he soon learned the rudiments of painting. About 1623 Claude studied briefly under the Fleming G. Wals, in Naples. He was permanently affected by the sights in and around the Gulf of Naples, from Pozzuoli to Sorrento, from Capri to Ischia. In 1625 he went from Rome to Loreto and Venice, through the Tyrol and Bavaria, sketching all the way. He then went to Nancy where, for a time as an assistant, he filled in architectural backgrounds in the ceiling paintings (now destroyed) of Claude Deruet in the Carmelite church. By 1627 he was back in Rome, and there is no indication that he ever again left.

Commissions from the French ambassador Béthune, Cardinals Crescenzio and Bentivoglio, and Urban VIII indicate that before 1640 his career was successfully launched. A measure of his prestige is the *Liber veritatis* (London, British Museum), a compendium of 200 detailed drawings, later engraved. He was obliged to make the drawings to record his paintings as a guarantee against imitation and forgery. After an uneventful but highly productive life, he died a respected member of the foreign colony of artists.

He and Nicolas Poussin were the most distinguished exponents of the classical baroque style favored by the French after the formation of academic precepts in the mid-century. Claude, however, did not rank high in academic circles; his style, less formal and more poetic, was never cited as the official standard of that day. He found his

Claude Lorraine, *Embarkation of St. Ursula*. National Gallery, London. A work of this artist's mature years.

inspiration in the deserted Roman Forum and the surrounding countryside, on the sites of ancient villas, amidst vast panoramas often stretching to infinity. To Claude's admirers his landscapes were the visual counterpart of the works of the 1st-century Roman poet Vergil. They were the vehicle for expression of a sentiment inspired by the beauty of the natural world, accompanied by the charm of its human relationships, though never in the spirit of the *fête champêtre*. He deemphasized the role of man in nature and sometimes, it is believed, permitted others to paint the figures in his works. In his last work, *Ascanius and the Stag* (1682; Oxford, Ashmolean Museum), the hunters are so attenuated and so neutrally clad that they become spectral denizens of a dream world, in which only the vestige of a topographical site, the coastline of Sorrento and Capri, floats distantly in clouds of mist, an anchor between the real and the visionary.

The chronology of Claude's style demonstrates an evolution from the prosaic to the poetic.

Early years (1627–40). While somewhat influenced by Domenichino, Claude's landscape style in his early years is primarily rooted in the late mannerism of the northerners established in Rome. In *Mill* (1631; Boston, Museum of Fine Arts), the composition reflects that of Paul Bril, with artificially demarcated planes, arranged one behind another like theatrical backdrops, starting with an inevitable tree; the foreground is filled with genre incidents. A convincing bucolic mood pervades, however, as a result of an enveloping atmosphere borrowed from Adam Elsheimer. At this time Claude did topographical scenes (*Siege of La Rochelle*, 1631; *Campo Vaccino*, before 1636; both Paris, Louvre), suggesting the influence of J. Callot's figure style and A. Tassi's compositions.

Mature years (1640–60). In his mature years Claude mastered all types of landscapes, manifest in the vast variety of his drawings. These include everything from prosaic notations of landscape details to spontaneously executed value studies, some nearly Chinese in their immaterial suggestiveness of characteristic effects. Some combine all these aspects, factual and conceptual, and result in a startling impressionism. In one of the views of Tivoli, as a result of suspending crimson wash over warm bister, the town floats above dematerialized rocky hills. Some of his drawings are preparatory to painting and many are highly finished. These prove that he manipulated his trees, in the process of composing, much as Poussin did his human figures, like miniature models on a stage set. But Claude, unlike Poussin, was uninterested in subject matter. His preoccupation was expressive content, avoiding specific theme, which resulted in the near personification of the various phases of the day. After modern cleaning, the previous conclusion that all his effects were golden sunsets has been exploded. Claude chose serene and typical light effects. He used light to impose unity as well as to elicit imagination in infinitely varied ways. Even with ships and buildings against a setting sun (*Embarkation of St. Ursula*, 1641; London, National Gallery), he diluted silhouette by vaporous atmosphere.

He wandered everywhere sketching the Roman campagna with the eyes of a poet; pictorial, not monumental,

consideration motivated his choice of subject, and his drawings are loosely composed and often meld many views. His perspective is intuitive, and its quality of conviction is derived from the subtle gradation of tones (*Ermini and the Shepherds*, 1666; Holkham, Earl of Leicester Collection) rather than from the scientifically linear perspective· of Poussin. Only occasionally did he accede somewhat to Poussin's formal means of simple cubical forms rising solidly from a horizontal plane (*Apollo Guarding the Herds of Admetus*, 1654; Earl of Leicester Collection). Even in such cases, branches wave in moving air and the light permeates their feathery leaves. Poussin's scenes seem rock-hewn, like antique high relief, while with Claude everything is evanescent. His choice of antique motifs was romantically gauged by their picturesqueness, always in ruins, whether classical or Gothic, and rarely archaeologically sound.

Late years (1660–82). Claude's late years manifest the intensification of his occasional bold tendencies of the past. *Perseus and the Medusa* (1674; Earl of Leicester Collection) is strongly asymmetrical; the jagged contour of the rock arch is audaciously opposed to a towering, diaphanous tree, and tiny ephemeral figures dart about in silvery moonlight that pours over the milky surface of the sea. If Poussin is the last phase in the rational treatment of landscape, Claude might be said to be the first in a long history of pictorialism leading to the 19th-century romantics and impressionists.

Claude's works are found in Berlin, Boston, Brussels, Dresden, Leningrad, London (National Gallery), Madrid, Munich, New York (Metropolitan Museum and Frick Collection), Philadelphia, Rome (Doria Pamphili Gallery), and many other places.

BIBLIOGRAPHY. W. F. Friedländer, ... *Claude Lorrain*, Berlin, 1921; A. Blum, *L'Oeuvre graphique du XVIIe siècle: Les Eaux fortes de Claude Gellée dit Lorrain*, Paris, 1922; A. M. Hind, *Catalogue of the Drawings of Claude Lorrain* ..., London, 1926; P. Courthion, *Claude Gellée, dit Le Lorrain* ..., Paris, 1932; M. Röthlisberger, *Claude Lorrain: The Paintings*, New Haven, 1961.

GEORGE V. GALLENKAMP

LORRAINE. Region in northern France around the upper Meuse and Moselle Rivers. Throughout the Middle Ages Lorraine was part of the Holy Roman Empire, and cultural ties were generally closer with the lower Meuse and Rhine Valley regions than with France. The crafts flourished there in the later Middle Ages; the great metalworker Nicolas de Verdun was from Lorraine. However, French Gothic architecture appears in the Cathedrals of Toul and Metz. In the 17th and 18th centuries, when Lorraine had become an integral part of the French state, the elegant and sober architecture of French classicism spread throughout the region; the townscape of Nancy represents a noteworthy achievement of this phase. At the end of the 19th century Lorraine became a center of Art Nouveau craftwork. *See* ART NOUVEAU; METZ CATHEDRAL; NANCY; NICOLAS DE VERDUN.

LORSCH: GATEHOUSE. German *Tornhalle* near Worms, one of the few extant examples of Carolingian architecture. A cloister was founded there by Pepin the Short in 762. No documentation exists, but the gatehouse itself probably dates from about 800. No adequate explanation

Lorsch Gospels. An illuminated page of this Carolingian manuscript. Vatican Library, Rome.

has been found for its function, although it is thought to have been based on the gatehouse of Old St. Peter's, Rome.

LORSCH GOSPELS. Carolingian illuminated manuscript, in the Vatican Library, Rome.

LOS ANGELES, CALIF.: LOS ANGELES COUNTY ART MUSEUM. General art collection established in 1911. It has displays of Egyptian, Oriental, and classical works, including glass and textiles; Gothic and Renaissance painting and sculpture; stained glass and tapestries; English and French painting, sculpture, and decorative art; and American art from the 18th century to the present. With the building of new galleries this museum has acquired a substantial number of examples of modern European art, especially in the French and German area.

The variety of painters represented includes Petrus Christus (*Portrait of a Man*), Hans Holbein the Younger (*Portrait of a Young Woman*), Boucher, Fragonard, Greuze, and Sir Thomas Lawrence (*Portrait of Arthur Atherly*). From the 19th and 20th centuries there are Degas (*Two Sisters*), Cézanne (*Still Life with Cherries and Peaches*), Gauguin, Matisse, Modigliani (*Portrait of Jean Cocteau*),

Picasso (*Courtesan with Jeweled Collar*), Rouault (*Samson Turning the Millstone*), Nolde, Beckmann, and Stuart Davis (*Premiere*). The contemporary artists include Pollock, Rothko, Guston, and Motherwell.

LOSCHI, JACOPO D'ILARIO. Italian religious and historical painter (b. Parma, 1459; d. Carpi, 1504). He produced many competent works for the churches of Parma, Modena, and Carpi, among them frescoes done with his father-in-law, B. Grossi, and a *Virgin and Child* for the Servi at Carpi (lost since 1707), which became famous for the miracles connected with it.

LOST-WAX PROCESS, *see* CAST AND CASTING.

LOTHAIR, CROSS OF. Carolingian metalwork, in the Treasury, Cathedral of Aachen, Germany.

LOTHAIR, GOSPELS OF. Carolingian illuminated manuscript, in the National Library, Paris. *See* TOURS SCHOOL.

LOTTI, LORENZO DE LUDOVICO DI GUGLIELMO, *see* LORENZETTO.

LOTTO, LORENZO. Venetian painter, one of the great masters of the High Renaissance (ca. 1480–1556). He worked mainly in small towns near Venice, painting many altarpieces and portraits, but he always felt restless and unappreciated. His chief stops were 1503, Treviso; 1506, Recanati; 1508, Treviso; 1509, Rome; 1512, Recanati and nearby; 1513–26, Bergamo with some side trips; 1527, Venice; 1531, Jesi; 1532, Treviso; 1535, Jesi; 1538, Ancona; 1540–42, Venice; 1542–45, Treviso; 1545, Venice; 1549–52, Ancona; and 1552–56, Loreto. Except for Rome, Venice, Treviso, and Bergamo, these cities are in the Marches.

Lotto is generally considered a pupil of Alvise Vivarini, and this is confirmed by a Madonna (Verona, Castelvecchio Museum) signed "Alvise" but identical with Lotto's first Madonnas and perhaps painted by him in the shop. It already shows his known style, making suggestions of an early phase dubious, except perhaps to include the *Pages by a Tomb* (Treviso, S. Niccolò), unusual because they are frescoes.

Lotto's chief early paintings are the *Madonna with St. Peter Martyr* (1503; Naples, Capodimonte), *Bishop Bernardo de' Rossi* (1505; Capodimonte) and the allegorical cover of that portrait (Washington, D.C., National Gallery), *The Assumption* (1506; Asolo Cathedral), *St. Jerome* (1506; Paris, Louvre), and the *Recanati Polyptych* (1508; Recanati, Civic Museum). These works already show his intense color and strained poses and expressions; surfaces are hard and gleaming. The patterns are maintained but the tone is softened in pictures done after his visit to Rome: *Entombment of Christ* (Jesi, Pinacoteca Comunale) and the portrait of the Torre brothers (1515; London, National Gallery).

Lorenzo Lotto, *The Mystical Marriage of St. Catherine*. Gallery of the Carrara Academy, Bergamo, Italy.

The altarpieces of the Bergamo period develop a wild flutter of forms (1516, S. Bartolommeo; 1521, S. Bernardino and Sto Spirito), as do smaller works such as *Susanna and the Elders* (1517; Florence, Contini Bonacossi Collection). This quality, along with woolly textures and night light, suggests interest in German painters. The swooning dance of *Christ Taking Leave of His Mother* (1521; Berlin, former State Museums), the *Bridal Couple with Cupid* (1523; Madrid, Prado), and the *Mystical Marriage of St. Catherine* (1523; Bergamo, Gallery) represent Lotto at his peak.

Lotto never relinquished solid modeling in favor of Venetian atmospheric unity, though the agitated figures sometimes seem attacked by the air. But his many portraits done in Venice develop a dusky tone and restrained design. After executing large fresco cycles with engaging rural naturalism (1524, Trescore; 1525, Bergamo, S. Michele) he created variations on the haunted movement of his earlier work, with softer light, in *The Annunciation* (Recanati), *Chastity* (Rome, Pallavicini Collection), *Lucretia* (London, National Gallery), and the *St. Lucy Altarpiece* (1532; Jesi, Pinacoteca Comunale), his masterpieces of the 1530s.

The last works are more formal and pious though still intricate, for example, the *Madonna of the Rosary* (1539; Cingoli, S. Domenico), *St. Antoninus of Florence Giving Alms* (1542; Venice, SS. Giovanni e Paolo), and a pair of portraits (1544; Milan, Brera). Lotto had no influence; he developed a side issue in the history of painting but is one of its great individuals.

BIBLIOGRAPHY. Venice, Palazzo Ducale, *Mostra di Lorenzo Lotto* (catalog), ed. P. Zampetti, Venice 1953; B. Berenson, *Lorenzo Lotto*, complete ed., New York, 1956.

CREIGHTON GILBERT

LOTUS. Sweet-smelling pink and blue flower that grew freely in ancient Egypt and India. The lotus was a symbol of nascent life and became a typical element of decorative art in friezes, ceilings, and jewelry. In Egyptian architecture of the Old Kingdom and the Middle Kingdom, the lotiform column had a capital imitating either a bud or an open umbel (cluster), usually topping a bundle shaft.

In India, the lotus was one of the symbols of the Buddha himself, and was used during the early years of the development of Buddhism, before anthropomorphic representations of the Buddha were admissable. *See* LOTUS SUTRA.

LOTUS SUTRA (Miao-fa-lien hua-ching). Basic text for Mahāyāna Buddhism in China, known also by its Sanskrit title *Saddharmapundarika*. The Lotus Sūtra was instrumental in determining much of the iconography of early Chinese Buddhist sculpture and painting. *See* MAHAYANA.

The *Saddharmapundarika* originated in India sometime around the 1st century A.D., but the earliest known translation into Chinese dates from 406. Well over 1,000 copies of this translation (executed by the priest Kumarajiva) were found in the great sealed library of Tun-huang alone, testifying to the popularity and enormous influence this one text must have had over the period of the 5th through the 8th century in China. *See* TUN-HUANG.

The doctrine expounded by the Lotus Sūtra was central to the concept of Mahāyāna; the eternal nature of the Buddha and his appearance in various sequences of time and manifestations were firmly established, and extolled throughout the text was the idea that those who heard the preaching of a Buddha could attain the final enlightenment. Salvation thus became intertwined with the notions of rebirth into paradise, where access to the preaching of Buddha could be gained. Two major scenes drawn from the Lotus Sūtra appear often in early Chinese Buddhist art: the Buddha preaching the Lotus Sūtra on the Vulture Peak and the dialogue between Sākyamuni and Prabhūtaratna. *See* PRABHUTARATNA; SAKYAMUNI.

BIBLIOGRAPHY. W. E. Soothill, *The Lotus of the Wonderful Law,* Oxford, 1930; J. L. Davidson, *The Lotus Sūtra in Chinese Art*, New Haven, Conn., 1954.

MARTIE W. YOUNG

LOUIS (Bernstein), MORRIS. American painter (b. Baltimore, 1912; d. Washington, D.C., 1962). Louis studied at the Maryland Institute of Fine and Applied Art (1929–33) and worked under the Federal Arts Project during the 1930s. Until he was introduced in New York City to Helen Frankenthaler's method of staining the canvas with thinned paints, Louis created abstract paintings and collages in the cubist tradition. The new technique freed him from traditional drawing and enabled him to use color, in a series of evolving images, to create its own tensions and organic relationships out of an original impulse.

BIBLIOGRAPHY. Boston, Museum of Fine Arts, *Morris Louis, 1912–1962*, Boston, 1967.

LOUIS, ST. (Louis IX of France). French king and crusader (b. Poissy, 1214; d. Tunis, 1270). He became king of France in 1226, with his mother, Blanche of Castille,

Lotus Sūtra. Example on the fan-shaped page of a copybook, 12th century. Color and ink on paper. National Museum, Tokyo.

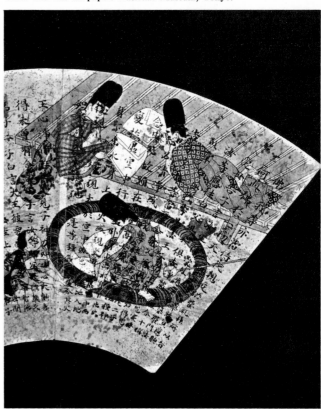

Philippe-Jacques Loutherbourg, *Lake Scene in Cumberland, Evening.* Tate Gallery, London.

as regent. Pious and generous, he ruled justly and wisely. He led a crusade in 1248, and was taken prisoner at Damietta; on his second crusade in 1270, he died of the plague. In art, he is shown doing good works, such as nursing the sick. His attributes are a royal costume embroidered with the lily, a crown, a scepter, the crown of thorns, three nails from the Crucifixion, and a model of Ste-Chapelle. His feast is August 25.

See also SAINTS IN ART.

LOUIS, SERAPHINE, *see* SERAPHINE.

LOUIS, VICTOR. French architect (1735–1807/10). He worked in Paris and Bordeaux. Associated with the traditional baroque style, Louis designed mainly theaters. His best-known works are the Théâtre Français in Paris (1786–90) and the Grand-Théâtre de Bordeaux (1773–76), which contain technical improvements on the Paris Opéra.

BIBLIOGRAPHY. C. Marionneau, *Victor Louis*, Bordeaux, 1881.

LOUIS OF TOULOUSE, ST. Bishop (1274–97). Second son of Charles II of Naples and great nephew of St. Louis of France, he was also related to St. Elizabeth of Hungary. He renounced the crown to his brother Robert and joined a Franciscan order in 1296. At the command of Pope Boniface VIII, he became bishop of Toulouse, but died after six months' rule. He was noted for austerity and charity. He is shown wearing the Franciscan habit, a cope

decorated with lilies, and a miter and holding a staff. His feast is August 19.

See also SAINTS IN ART.

LOUIS XIII, LOUIS XIV, LOUIS XV, LOUIS XVI STYLES, *see* FURNITURE.

LOUTHERBOURG, PHILIPPE-JACQUES. French painter of landscapes, sea pieces, battle scenes, idylls, architectural views with genre scenes, and portraits; stage designer; draftsman; and engraver (b. Strasbourg, 1740; d. Chiswick, London, 1812). He was the son of an engraver and miniaturist, originally from Basel. He moved with his family to Paris in 1755 and became a pupil first of C. A. Van Loo, then of the Tischbeins, and finally of F.-J. Casanova. Loutherbourg's adaptation of Casanova's style, in which the romantic landscape and battle-scene traditions are coalesced, led to sensational success of his first exhibition at the Salon of 1763. Loutherbourg was admitted to the Royal Academy as an associate that year and was made a member in 1768. During a trip to Provence, Dandré-Bardon helped him to gain admission to the Academy of Marseilles.

In 1771 he settled in London, where he was stage designer for the Drury Lane Theatre under David Garrick and R. B. Sheridan. He created spectacular stage machinery, among which an Eidophusikon was much admired by Sir Joshua Reynolds. In 1780 he became a member of the Royal Academy, where he regularly exhibited romantic landscapes (*View of a Landscape in Cumberland under a Menacing Sky*, London, National Gallery). These landscapes were to influence Gainsborough and Turner. He also painted naval battle scenes (*Defeat of the French Fleet at Brest*, 1794; location unknown). He became official painter to the British Army and Navy, and illustrated an edition of Shakespeare. In 1807 he was made official painter to the Duke of Gloucester (*The Meeting at the Races*, formerly Collection of the Duke of Gloucester). The artists R. Cosway, B. West, Turner, and J. Farington, as well as members of the British royal family, were among his friends. Loutherbourg's influence on English landscape painting and subsequently on French impressionism has never been fully investigated.

The largest collection of his works is to be found in the Strasbourg Museum of Fine Arts.

BIBLIOGRAPHY. G. Levallet-Haug, "Philippe-Jacques Loutherbourg," *Archives alsaciennes d'histoire de l'art*, XVI, 1948; J. Seznec and J. Adhémar, *Diderot salons*, Oxford, Eng., vol. 1, 1957; vol. 2, 1960.

GEORGE V. GALLENKAMP

LOUVAIN: HOTEL DE VILLE. Gothic civil building erected (1448–59) in Louvain, Belgium, by Mathieu de Layens. It symbolizes the commercial importance of 15th-century Louvain. The elaborately decorated façade of the Hôtel de Ville, complete with angle turrets and spires, compares favorably with those of the town halls of Brussels and Bruges.

LOUVAIN: SAINT-MICHEL. Belgian church designed by the Jesuit Hesius in 1650. It is conservative, even medieval, in plan. The interior is, however, tastefully decorated, and the façade is one of the finest, most exuberant Belgian manifestations of the baroque.

BIBLIOGRAPHY. H. Gerson and E. ter Kuile, *Art and Architecture in Belgium, 1600–1800*, Baltimore, 1960.

LOUVAIN: SAINT-PIERRE. Flemish late Gothic church (1425–79). A Flamboyant structure, mainly the work of Sulpice van Orst, it was largely dependent for its design on French developments. Its great feature is an attractive, homogeneous choir. The ribs of the quadripartite vaulting continue their lines without interruption to the pavement level, enclosing an elegant clerestory and triforium levels with lacelike traceries. Of no less importance are the wooden Calvary group of Flemish workmanship, the hexagonal tabernacle of the second quarter of the 15th century by Mathieu de Layens, and the two triptychs by Dirk Bouts.

BIBLIOGRAPHY. S. Brigode, *Les Eglises gothiques de Belgique*, 2d ed., Brussels, 1947.

LOUVAIN SCHOOL. Flemish school of painting whose most important artist was Dirk Bouts. The school, which flourished in Louvain during the second and third quarters of the 15th century, was particularly influential in the development of landscape painting. *See* BOUTS, DIRK.

LOUVER. Lantern or turret in medieval roofs used to circulate air and admit light. The term is also applied to inclined slats arranged to keep out rain but admit light and air.

Louvain, St-Pierre. View of its late Gothic choir.

LOUVRE PALACE, PARIS. Royal palace of the kings of France, now occupied by the Louvre Museum and the Ministry of Finance. *See* PARIS: MUSEUMS (LOUVRE).

The history of the Louvre begins with a fortress—a large cylindrical keep surrounded by turreted walls—built at the end of the 13th century by King Philip Augustus on the right bank of the Seine to protect Paris against the English. In the 14th century Charles V employed Raymond du Temple to transform the fortress into something like a fortified palace; during the 15th century, however, the monarchy developed a preference for the Loire Valley, and the Louvre received little attention.

During the later part of his reign Francis I brought the court back to Paris. In 1527 he ordered the demolition of the Louvre's keep, the Tour de Paris. In 1546 he commissioned Lescot to pull down the west wing of the castle and to replace it with a new wing. Lescot built his wing in a mature Renaissance style in which Italian classicism is fused with recognizably French elements. He employed the sculptor Goujon to carve reliefs for the exterior and the gallery supported by caryatids in the *salle* on the ground floor. At the south end of his wing he built a higher pavilion, the Pavillon du Roi. In 1564 Catherine de Médicis commissioned Philibert De l'Orme to build the Tuileries Palace some distance to the west of the Louvre and outside the city walls. To link the two palaces, the Petite Galerie was built, running south from the Pavillon du Roi; it was continued westward by the Grande Galerie, which reached the Tuileries at the Pavillon de Flore. This project was not completed until after the Wars of Religion and the accession of Henry IV. *See* TUILERIES PALACE.

The 17th century saw the completion, after a good deal of designing and redesigning, of the Cour Carrée, the enlarged courtyard, four times the original area, created by new wings. Between 1624 and 1654 Lemercier built the Pavillon de l'Horloge at the north end of Lescot's wing (with sculpture by Sarrazin) and repeated Lescot's design on the other side of the pavilion to establish the double-length wing. He also continued this work on the north side of the court. In 1640 Richelieu persuaded Poussin to come

Louvre Palace, Paris. Former royal palace completed during the 19th century.

to Paris from Rome to plan the decoration of the Grande Galerie. Poussin made designs that influenced French decoration for some decades, but he completed only part of the work and returned to Rome after eighteen months. Poussin's decorations have been destroyed and the Grande Galerie remained unused for a long time; its lower stories were used to lodge court artists and to house the royal printing works. Some minor improvements were made to fit the palace for the residence of the young Louis XIV after the troubles of the Fronde (1648–53). A fire in the Petite Galerie (1661) led to the creation of the Galerie d'Apollon, richly decorated in 1663 by Le Brun and his assistants with paintings and stucco relief sculpture. Le Vau at the same time continued the construction of the Cour Carrée, including on the south side an imposing domed centerpiece intended to echo the Collège des Quatre-Nations he was building across the river. The Louvre dome was subsequently removed.

In 1664 Colbert was appointed Superintendent of Buildings. The Louvre still lacked an impressive main façade to the east, and Colbert, hoping to tie Louis XIV to Paris, strove to educe a sufficiently splendid plan. He sought projects from a number of architects and received designs from Bernini, among others. In 1665 Bernini came to Paris to complete his designs, which involved remodeling the whole court, and to be present when the king laid the foundation stone of the new building. Hardly had he left for Rome when work was stopped and the whole matter reconsidered. In 1667 a three-man committee was formed to draw up an alternative project: the architect Le Vau, the painter Le Brun, and Claude Perrault, a physician and amateur of architecture. One of their two designs was accepted by the king, and by 1670 the colonnaded east front of the Louvre was more or less complete; once again there had been a highly successful and original adaptation of Italian elements to French taste.

Nevertheless, Louis XIV transferred his court to Versailles. In his absence the French academies established themselves in the Louvre. In 1725 the Academy of Painting and Sculpture held an exhibition in one of the larger rooms, the Salon Carré; exhibitions held there every year from 1737 to 1848 thus became known under the title the Salon. The Tuileries Palace in the 18th century took over the Louvre's function of royal residence in Paris, and little was done to complete the Louvre beyond a certain amount of tidying up by Jacques-Ange Gabriel.

During the French Revolution the Louvre was turned into a museum; it opened in 1793 with an exhibition of paintings in the Grande Galerie. Napoleon's campaigns brought a flood of works of art to Paris; they were accommodated in the new museum. In 1806 Napoleon turned out the academies and resident artists and ordered the completion of the Cour Carrée. He employed Percier and Fontaine to arrange the toplighting of the Grande Galerie and to insert some optical breaks in its uncomfortable length. The same architects also began to build a corresponding east-west wing to be attached to the Tuileries at the north end and to run along the newly formed rue de Rivoli. Having cleared the houses still standing around the old Place du Carrousel between the Louvre and the Tuileries, they erected the elegant Arc de Triomphe du Carrousel (1806–08) as a gateway to the latter.

The last phase of the building history of the Louvre began in 1848. First Duban, then Visconti, and finally Lefuel completed the long north wing and formed the Place Napoléon III between the Carrousel area and the Cour Carrée by inserting wings with smaller courts in the angle of the Petite Galerie and the Grande Galerie and in the corresponding position on the north side. In 1849 Delacroix did some ceiling decorations in the Galerie d'Apollon to complete the work begun by Le Brun.

The destruction by fire of the Tuileries in 1871 left a big gap in the gigantic composition that had been achieved with so much effort. Lefuel rebuilt some portions so as to leave the long north and south wings complete, but no attempt was made to rebuild the palace itself.

BIBLIOGRAPHY. L. Hautecoeur, *Histoire du Louvre: Le Château, le palais, le musée*, Paris, 1928; G. Bazin, *Le Louvre*, Grenoble, 1933; A. Blunt, *Art and Architecture in France, 1500–1700*, Baltimore, 1953.

NORBERT LYNTON

LOVERA, JUAN. Venezuelan painter (b. Caracas, 1778; d. there, 1841). Lovera was trained in Caracas and had his own studio by 1799. He was in the Army of Independence (1814–20) and then painted scenes of independence and portraits in Caracas. Clear color and expressive line mark his style.

BIBLIOGRAPHY. E. Planchart, *La pintura en Venezuela*, Caracas, 1956.

LOW, DAVID. English cartoonist (1881–1963). Low was born in Dunedin, New Zealand. He went to London in 1919, where he became political cartoonist for the *Star*, the *Evening Standard* (1927), the *Daily Herald* (1950), and *The Manchester Guardian* (1953). Among the most notable cartoon characters Low created are the T U C Horse and Colonel Blimp. Sharply satirical, Low often concentrated upon specific personalities such as Sir Winston Churchill.

LOWEN: MONASTERY CHURCH, see HESIUS, WILHELM.

LOWER CONGO, see Africa, Primitive Art of (Central Africa: Congo-Leopoldville).

LOWESTOFT WARE. Soft-paste porcelains, mostly table- and tea-ware, produced at Lowestoft, Suffolk, between 1757 and about 1802. Underglaze blue and enamels were most frequently used. Patterns and motifs are usually Chinese-derived. The name has been mistakenly used in connection with Chinese ware produced for European consumption.

LOW RELIEF, see Bas-Relief.

LO-YANG. Chinese city situated in the province of Honan. This great city, at various times a capital, has played a most important role in China's long history. The alluvial plain of the Yellow River has, from earliest times, been the center of Chinese civilization, and in the region of Lo-yang there exist many monuments testifying to its importance. In the present city there are only a few isolated monuments left. A few miles south of Lo-yang, however, can be found the great temple series of Lung-men. *See* Lung-men.

　See also China: Architecture (Historical periods).
　BIBLIOGRAPHY. W. C. White, *Tombs of Old Lo-Yang*, Shanghai, 1934.

LOZENGE. Geometrical diamond-shaped figure whose opposing angles are equal. Lozenges, arranged in horizontal bands, were used as sculptured moldings in Romanesque buildings, and lozenge-patterned metal plates were applied to roofs and cupolas as a means of protection and decoration. The design was also a favorite in heraldic coats of arms, where an entire field might be composed of lozenges and thus termed "lozengy."

LOZOWICK, LOUIS. American graphic artist (1892–). Lozowick was born in Russia. He studied in Paris and Berlin and attended Ohio State University, in Columbus, and the National Academy of Design, in New York City. Industrial complexes, buildings, and bridges in New York provided themes for his early work, which emphasizes strongly simplified structural lines and modeling, sometimes with cubistic overtones. His later work is more textural and romantic. Lozowick is also the author of *Modern Russian Art* (1925).

LUBECK. City in northern Germany, located on an arm of the Baltic Sea between Holstein and Mecklenburg. Lübeck was founded in 1143 by the counts of Holstein and became a free imperial city in 1226. During the period of its artistic greatness in the 14th and 15th centuries it was the leader of the powerful Hanseatic League of north German trading cities. In this period its influence stretched to all parts of Scandinavia, the Baltic coast of Russia, and even England. Shifts in trading routes and political difficulties with its neighbors brought a gradual decline of Lübeck's power in northern Europe during the 16th and 17th centuries.

　Testifying to Lübeck's importance as a major center of Gothic architecture in north-central Europe is the Marien-

kirche (Church of St. Mary), built between 1251 and 1310, one of the finest creations of German Gothic brick architecture. A flourishing school of painting, whose guiding spirit was Master Francke, existed in Lübeck in the late 14th and early 15th centuries. This school spread throughout the Hanseatic League and extended its influence to Scandinavia and to England. During the 15th century Lübeck led northern Germany in sculpture. The leading figures in Lübeck sculpture were Johannes Jungen in the early 15th century and Bernt Notke in the late 15th and early 16th centuries. Notke's style was especially influential in Scandinavia. *See* Master Francke; Notke, Bernt; St. Mary, Lubeck.

　In addition to the famous Marienkirche, Lübeck possesses many important architectural monuments from the 14th and 15th centuries. The Cathedral, erected in the 12th century, received an impressive hall choir in the early 14th century. It contains the Triumphal Cross by Bernt Notke (1477). The Lübeck Rathaus was begun in the 13th century and built and expanded throughout the 14th and 15th centuries and is today one of the finest examples of its kind in northern Germany. The Old City, now greatly restored after extensive damage in World War II, once contained an array of patrician houses of the late Gothic and Renaissance periods. *See* Lubeck: Rathaus.

　The former St. Annen Monastery has a museum of Lübeck art and is particularly noted for its fine historical interiors and collections of minor arts. *See* Lubeck: Sankt Annen Museum.

　See also Lubeck Bible.

　BIBLIOGRAPHY. A. Goldschmidt, *Lübecker Malerei und Plastik bis 1530*, Lübeck, 1889; *Die Bau- und Kunstdenkmäler der freien Hansestadt Lübeck*, vols. 2–4, 1906–28; M. Hasse, *Lübeck*, Munich, 1963.

　　　　　　　　　　　　　　　　DONALD L. EHRESMANN

LUBECK: RATHAUS. German late Gothic brick town hall. Dating from the 13th to the 15th century, the Lü-

Luca di Tommé, polyptych of the *Madonna and Child with St. Anne.* Pinacoteca, Siena.

beck Rathaus consists of two rectangular buildings adjoining at right angles. It is noted for its huge gables and excellent Renaissance entrance hall facing the marketplace. In 1594 a fine Renaissance-style staircase was added to the side facing the Breitestrasse.

BIBLIOGRAPHY. K. Gruber, *Das deutsche Rathaus*, Munich, 1943.

LUBECK: SANKT ANNEN MUSEUM. German collection founded in 1800 and housed in the former St. Annen Monastery (1502–15). It is dedicated mainly to the art and cultural history of Lübeck. Among the paintings, Memling's *Altarpiece of the Greverade Family* (1491) is outstanding. Lübeck sculptures from the 13th to the 16th century, together with pieces of furniture and textiles, constitute fine examples of the art of this region of northern Germany.

BIBLIOGRAPHY. H. Jedding, *Keysers Führer durch Museen und Sammlungen*, Heidelberg, Munich, 1961.

LUBECK BIBLE. Important incunabular Bible printed by Stephen Arndes in Lübeck in 1494. The text is a translation into the dialect of Niedersachsen (Lower Saxony); the illustrations, many of which were later hand-colored, show a strong Italian influence.

BIBLIOGRAPHY. K. Schottenloher, *Das alte Buch*, Berlin, 1919.

LUBETKIN, BERTHOLD. English architect (1901–   ). Born in the Caucasus, he first worked in Paris in Perret's atelier in 1927, at which time he designed, with Ginsberg, 25 Avenue de Versailles. He left for England about 1930, and took part in the formation of the Tecton group. Zoo commissions followed, e.g., the Regent's Park gorilla house (1933) and the penguin pool (1934), the latter a sculptural essay in reinforced concrete. Using this material Lubetkin is at his best, as may be seen in functional plastic terms at Dudley Zoo and at a bungalow at Whipsnade (both 1937).

His first big jobs were the Highgate Hill flats in two

David Lucas, mezzotint engraving after Martin. Municipal Print Collection "Bertarelli," Milan.

phases (1934 and 1937), each of which set the idioms for his plastic surface values. The phase culminated in a transitional building, the Finsbury Health Center (1938). In postwar work, Spa Green (1951) and Priory Green (1951) show an inward-looking style—a concept negating the prime importance of the façade.

BIBLIOGRAPHY. R. F. Jordan, "Lubetkin," *The Architectural Review*, CVIII, July, 1955.

LUC, FRERE (Claude Francois). French painter (b. Amiens, 1614; d. Paris, 1685). Frère Luc studied under Simon Vouet and worked with Poussin. On a visit to Canada in 1670–71, he executed numerous religious paintings and some portraits that influenced greatly the development of early Canadian painting.

BIBLIOGRAPHY. G. Morisset,... *La Vie et l'oeuvre du Frère Luc*, Quebec, 1944.

LUCA DI TOMME. Italian painter of the Sienese school (b. 1330? d. after 1389). An eclectic follower of the Lorenzettis, Simone Martini, and Lippo Memmi, Luca was one of the busiest and most respected painters of the late 14th century in Siena. He, Bartolo di Fredi, and Andrea Vanni were the leading masters of the city.

He is first mentioned in 1355 as a member of the painters' guild. In 1373, 1375, and 1379 he was a member of the city government, and in 1388 and 1389, a member of the committee for the Cathedral. In 1366 Luca painted a *Crucifixion* now in the museum at Pisa. A polyptych with the *Madonna and Child with St. Anne* of 1367 is in the Pinacoteca at Siena, and a *Madonna and Child* polyptych dated 1370 is in the gallery at Rieti. No other works by Luca are documented. The questions of their stylistic character and date are by no means solved, though a great many pictures have been attributed to the master. One of the most charming is the *Assumption of the Virgin* in the Yale University Art Gallery, which shows Luca's debt to Pietro Lorenzetti in the facial types and his great gifts as a colorist in the pale blue, violet, and rose angels carrying the gold and white Madonna upward in a dark and light blue mandorla. Other works by Luca are in the Pinacoteca in Siena, the Fitzwilliam Museum in Cambridge, England, and elsewhere.

BIBLIOGRAPHY. R. van Marle, *The Development of the Italian Schools of Painting*, vol. 2, The Hague, 1924.

HELLMUT WOHL

LUCA FA PRESTO, *see* GIORDANO, LUCA.

LUCARNE. Term for any of a variety of roof or dormer windows.

LUCAS, DAVID. English mezzotint engraver (1802–81). He was discovered by Samuel William Reynolds, who admired the young man's draftsmanship and apprenticed him for seven years until 1827. A series of twenty mezzotinted plates after John Constable, entitled *English Landscape* (1833), is his principal achievement. The purpose of this undertaking, accomplished at Constable's expense, was to acquaint the public with the artist's work, much as the *Liber studiorum* had done for Turner. Although the prints are close to the original designs, Constable made many changes while the engravings were in progress. For this set Lucas worked on steel plates, without etching, using only the scraper, roulette, and drypoint. Lucas also engraved larger plates in mezzotint after Constable, such as *Rainbow (Salisbury Cathedral)*, and did work after James Duffield Harding and others.

BIBLIOGRAPHY. A. Shirley, *The Published Mezzotints of David Lucas after John Constable, R.A.*, Oxford, 1930.

LUCAS VAN LEYDEN, *see* LEYDEN, LUCAS VAN.

LUCAS Y PADILLA, EUGENIO. Spanish painter (b. Alcalá de Henares, 1824; d. Madrid, 1870). Although he acquired some training at the Academy of S. Fernando in Madrid, Lucas was mostly self-taught as a copyist of Velázquez and Goya. He achieved some success and renown in Europe, despite his remaining outside official channels. An ardent admirer of Goya, Lucas painted scenes of the bullfight, the Inquisition, battles, the Spanish countryside, and *majas*, as well as of the revolution of 1854, with which he was in sympathy. Many of these were later passed off as originals by the master. Most of Lucas's works are generalized imitations of Goya, usually in terms of a panoramic conception in which the sketchiness and loose drawing of Lucas's style conceal transitions made more boldly and forms drawn more concretely by Goya.

BIBLIOGRAPHY. E. Du G. Trapier, *Eugenio Lucas y Padilla*, New York, 1940.

LUCCA. City in Tuscany, central Italy, originally settled by the Romans. Much of its medieval character has been preserved. Although subject to many overlords, Lucca retained its democratic (after 1628, oligarchic) independence

Eugenio Lucas y Padilla, *Majas at the Balcony*. Museum of Modern Art, Madrid.

until 1805. The Cathedral was begun in 1040, but of that period only the apse and campanile remain; the nave and transept were built in the 14th-century Gothic style. The west façade (1204) shows the typical Pisan arrangement of three arches with three rows of open galleries above. The *Volto Santo*, a wood crucifix that is a highly cherished relic of Pisa and the Middle Ages, is contained within the Cathedral. The Church of St. Michael, built entirely in marble, has an even more splendid façade (12th–13th cent.) in a similar design. Several secular buildings are noteworthy, such as the old Ducal Palace by Ammanati (1578) and the early Renaissance Palazzo Pretorio. *See* LUCCHESE SCHOOL; SAN FREDIANO, LUCCA.

LUCCHESE SCHOOL. Outside Pisa, the most important painters of the 12th and first three-quarters of the 13th century in Tuscany were those in Lucca. Their typical works are monumental crucifixes, painted panels with the figure of Christ encircled by scenes from His life. The earliest dated example (1138), in the Sarzana Cathedral, has rigid and blocky Romanesque forms. The leading painters of the 13th century, Berlinghiero Berlinghieri and his sons Bonaventura, Barone, and Marco, introduced the linear grace, formal stylization and chiaroscuro of Byzantine art and seem to have had a strong influence on the development of Florentine art until the emergence of Cimabue. *See* BERLINGHIERI, BERLINGHIERO; BERLINGHIERI, BONAVENTURA.

BIBLIOGRAPHY. E. T. DeWald, *Italian Painting, 1200–1600*, New York, 1962.

LUCE, MAXIMILIEN. French painter and lithographer (b. Paris, 1858; d. there, 1941). He was apprenticed to a wood engraver and studied with C.-A.-E. Duran at the Ecole des Beaux-Arts. Luce's first exhibition, at the 1887 Salon des Indépendants, was of paintings of proletarian subjects; he was associated with anarchist causes. At about the same time he was influenced by divisionism through his friendship with Pissarro and Signac. Luce's divisionist paintings were mostly industrial landscapes, for example, *View of Montmartre* (1887; Otterlo, Kröller-Müller Museum). After the late 1890s he dropped the use of the divisionist technique and moved toward landscapes treated in broad areas of color.

BIBLIOGRAPHY. A. Tabarant, *Maximilien Luce*, Paris, 1928.

LUCERNARIUM, *see* LUMINARIUM.

LUCERNE: ART MUSEUM. Swiss collection housed, along with the Congress Hall and Restaurant, in a building designed by Arnim Meili (1933) in the International style. It consists primarily of paintings by artists from central Switzerland from the 15th through the 20th century. Works by Corinth, Pechstein, Dufy, Vlaminck, and Soutine highlight the small collection of European 20th-century paintings.

BIBLIOGRAPHY. A. Reinle, "Das Luzerner Kunstmuseum," *Luzern im Wandel der Zeiten*, XI, 1958.

LU CHI. Chinese court painter (fl. late 15th cent.). He was known for his large-scaled, decorative, and apparently pleasing paintings of birds and flowers. A technically accomplished painter, Lü Chi is abundantly represented in various public and private collections, and his best works reveal some of the decorative qualities that made him popular at the court.

BIBLIOGRAPHY. O. Sirén, *Chinese Painting, Leading Masters and Principles*, vol. 4, New York, 1958.

LU CHIH. Chinese landscape and flower painter (1495–1576). Lu Chih was active in Su-chou during the period when the region was at its height as a center of *wen-jen* painting. Skilled in calligraphy and poetry as well as painting and steeped in Confucian studies, he was the epitome of the well-rounded scholar-gentlemen. His landscapes are marked by a decided poetic flavor, careful understatements that are refined to an extreme. His particular model among ancient masters was the Yüan painter Ni Tsan, and much of Ni Tsan's sparing use of the brush and crystalline clarity is readily visible in most of Lu Chih's paintings. Among the scholar painters of the Ming period Lu Chih is well represented in American collections, with first-rate examples of his work in the William Rockhill Nelson Gallery of Art, Kansas City, the Art Institute of Chicago, the Freer Gallery, Washington, D.C., and the Museum of Fine Arts, Boston. *See* NI TSAN; WEN-JEN-HUA.

BIBLIOGRAPHY. K. Tomita and K. M. Chiu, "Shih Hu (Stone Lake), a Chinese Scroll Painting by Lu Chih," *Boston Museum of Fine Arts, Bulletin*, XLIX, June, 1951.

LUCIANI, SEBASTIANO, *see* SEBASTIANO DEL PIOMBO.

LUCIDEL, *see* NEUFCHATEL, NICOLAS.

LUCINA CRYPT, ROME. Burial place of Pope Cornelius (d. 235) within the Catacomb of Callixtus. It is one of the oldest sections of the renowned cemetery and is best known for its paintings. *See* CATACOMB PAINTING.

BIBLIOGRAPHY. P. Styger, "L'origine delle cripte di Lucina," *Rendiconti della Pontificia Accademia Romana di Archeologia*, III, 1924–25.

LUCIONI, LUIGI. American painter and graphic artist (1900–). Born in Malnate, Italy, he went to the United States in 1911. He studied in New York City at Cooper Union and the National Academy. Lucioni paints naturalistic, finely detailed landscapes, still lifes, interiors, and portraits.

LUCKX, KERSTIAEN, *see* LUYCKS, CHRISTIAAN.

LUCY OF SYRACUSE, ST. Virgin and martyr of Diocletian's period. She made a pilgrimage with her mother to the tomb of St. Agatha at Catania, and, upon her mother's cure, gave her fortune to the poor. Lucy's fiancé, furious, denounced her as a Christian. When she was ordered to a brothel, a yoke of oxen could not budge her; when she was ordered to be burned, flames failed to harm her; finally, she was stabbed in the throat. Her attributes are a sword, eyes on a dish, and a lamp (symbol of light, *lux*, from which her name is derived). Her feast is December 13.

See also SAINTS IN ART.

LUDICK, LODEWIJK (Loedewijck) VAN. Dutch landscape painter (b. Amsterdam, 1629; d. there, before 1697). Little is known of his career. He painted landscapes in the Italianate manner of Jan Both. Van Ludick is some-

Ludovisi Throne. Front panel with Aphrodite rising from the sea. National Museum of Rome.

times confused with his father, a merchant and connoisseur of paintings, who was a friend of Rembrandt and served as an expert at the time of Rembrandt's insolvency.

BIBLIOGRAPHY. W. Bernt, *Die niederländischen Maler des 17. Jahrhunderts...*, vol. 2, Munich, 1948.

LUDIUS. Roman painter (fl. 1st cent. B.C.). He lived in the time of the emperor Augustus and was mentioned by Pliny in his *Natural History* (XXXV, 16). Ludius specialized in painting wall decorations in villas. He is primarily known for his landscape and architectural representations and for themes pertaining to fishing, hunting, and so on. His wall paintings belong to the second Pompeian style.

LUDOVICE, JOAO FREDERICO (Johann Friedrich Ludwig). Portuguese architect (1670–1752). Born in Germany, João Ludovice worked first as a goldsmith in Rome (1697–1701) and Lisbon (1701–11). Under King John V he became the leading architect of Portugal, designing the palace-monastery at Mafra (1717–30), a monumental enterprise consisting of palace, cloister and church, and barracks. His Romanizing late baroque style may also be seen in the apse of Evora Cathedral (1716) and perhaps in the library of the University of Coimbra (1717–23). *See* MAFRA, PALACE OF.

BIBLIOGRAPHY. G. Kubler and M. Soria, *Art and Architecture in Spain and Portugal and Their American Dominions, 1500–1800*, Baltimore, 1959.

LUDOVISI THRONE. Marble monument discovered in the Ludovisi Gardens, now in the National Museum of Rome. It consists of three parts: a main front panel and two shorter side panels whose upper edges slope downward; the ensemble resembles a throne. All three panels have relief representations alluding perhaps to the birth of Aphrodite. The front panel represents the goddess rising from the sea, assisted by two female figures which frame her in a symmetrical composition. The drapery of these figures consists of several parallel vertical folds that obscure the body underneath. The side panels depict a nude girl playing a flute and a draped female figure pouring incense on a candelabrum. Both figures are seated on cushions. They are perhaps votaries of the goddess. Stylistically, the monument belongs to the early classical period (ca. 470–465 B.C.). A counterpart to this work is in the Museum of Fine Arts, Boston.

BIBLIOGRAPHY. A. W. Lawrence, *Classical Sculpture*, London, 1929.

LUDWIG, JOHANN FRIEDRICH, *see* LUDOVICE, JOAO FREDERICO.

LUDWIGSBURG PORCELAIN. German porcelain produced from 1756 to 1824. Begun as a private venture, it was taken over by the Duke of Württemberg in 1758. The porcelain is a smoky brownish or grayish paste. The rococo style, influenced by Frankenthal at first, dominated until 1775. The local court sculptors provided models after the 1760s. Between 1816 and 1824 French workmen were active there.

BIBLIOGRAPHY. H. Christ, *Ludwigsburger Porzellanfiguren*, Stuttgart, 1921.

LUGANO, TOMMASO DA, *see* LOMBARDO, TOMMASO.

LUGANO-CASTAGNOLA: THYSSEN-BORNEMISZA MUSEUM. Swiss collection formed in the 1920s by Baron Thyssen-Bornemisza. The collection was first shown at the Munich Pinacothek in 1930; since 1937 it has been installed in a new museum at the Villa Favorita in Lugano-Castagnola. More than 400 paintings dating from the 14th to the 18th century are on view, while the more recently acquired paintings of the 19th and 20th centuries are kept in private apartments of the villa.

A chronological survey of Italian painting is highlighted by a work of Bernardo Daddi, Gentile Bellini's *Annunciation*, Ghirlandajo's *Portrait of Giovanna Tornabuoni*, Fra Filippo Lippi's *Enthroned Madonna*, Carpaccio's *Portrait of a Young Knight*, Fra Bartolommeo's *Landscape with the Holy Family and St. John the Baptist*, Sebastiano del Piombo's *Portrait of Cardinal Carondelet*, Titian's *Portrait of Doge Francesco Venier*, Tintoretto's *Lucretia and Tarquinius*, Caravaggio's *St. Catherine of Alexandria*, Tiepolo's *Death of Hyacinth*, Canaletto's *Piazza S. Marco*, and Venetian views by Guardi.

The principal Flemish works are Van Eyck's *Annunciation*, Daret's *Nativity*, Van der Weyden's *Portrait of a Nobleman*, the Master of St. Gudule's *Seven Acts of Charity*, Memling's *Portrait of a Young Man*, Gerard David's *Crucifixion*, Gossaert's *Adam and Eve*, Joos van Cleve's *Self-Portrait*, Rubens's *Mary and Jesus Visited by St. John the Baptist*, and Van Dyck's *Portrait of Jacques Le Roy*.

Of interest in the German collection are Pacher's *Mystic Marriage of St. Catherine*, Dürer's *Jesus and the Scribes*, Altdorfer's *Portrait of a Woman*, Cranach's *Fountain Nymph*, Baldung-Grien's *Portrait of a Young Princess*, Huber's *Adoration of the Magi*, Holbein's *Portrait of Henry VIII*, and portraits by Bruyn and Beham.

Dutch 17th-century paintings include Rembrandt's *Tobias and His Wife*, Hals's *Family Portrait*, Ruisdael's *Winter Storm* and other landscapes, Maes's *Naughty Drummer*, a Kalf still life, and works by Bosschaert, Steen, Koninck, and Hobbema.

Prominent among the Spanish paintings are Juanes's *Joan the Mad*, El Greco's *Annunciation*, Velázquez's *Portrait of Queen Mary Anne of Spain*, a Zurbarán *Still Life*, Murillo's *St. Justa of Seville*, and Goya's *Portrait of Ferdinand VII*.

There are also interesting paintings of the French school by Chardin, Fragonard, Robert, Pater, and Lancret.

BIBLIOGRAPHY. E. Redslob, *Meisterwerke der Malerei aus der Sammlung Thyssen-Bornemisza*, Berlin, 1958.

DONALD GODDARD

LUGO CATHEDRAL. Romanesque church in northwestern Spain built between 1129 and 1177. The Cathedral was strongly influenced by Santiago de Compostela. Lugo has stylistic features that suggest the turn toward Gothic architecture. The galleries are mostly groin-vaulted, but where barrel vaulting is still employed it is given a sharp angle, almost effecting a pointed-arch form. *See* SANTIAGO DE COMPOSTELA.

LUIKEN, JAN, *see* LUYKEN, JAN.

LUINI, BERNARDINO. Milanese painter (ca. 1480/90–1532). He has left many works in Milan and in small nearby cities, including fresco cycles and many Madonnas. He stems from the Lombard tradition of tonal painting, especially Bergognone, and is confirmed in it by his interest in Leonardo; but his composition and modeling are traditional.

Luini's charming Madonnas have become anthology

Ludwigsburg porcelain. Pastoral scene. Folkwang Museum, Essen.

Bernardino Luini, *Madonna and Child with St. John.* Gallery of the Carrara Academy, Bergamo, Italy.

George Benjamin Luks, *Hester Street*, 1905. Brooklyn Museum. A typical subject of the Ashcan school.

pieces (*Madonna with Rose Hedge, Madonna with Kerchief*; both Milan, Brera); his most unusual works are frescoes, especially those with secular elements. Those from Villa Pelucca (*Story of Moses, Story of Pan*, and other myths; most in the Brera) and from Casa Rabia (*Story of Europa*, Berlin, former State Museums; *Story of Procris*, Washington, D.C., National Gallery), both about 1520, are followed in 1525 by the vivacious Christ cycle at Saronno (S. Maria dei Miracoli).

BIBLIOGRAPHY. A. Ottino della Chiesa, *Bernardino Luini*, Novara, 1956.

LUKE, ST. Evangelist who wrote his Gospel and the Acts of the Apostles. An Antioch physician, he was converted by St. Paul and went with him on his second and third missionary journeys to Asia Minor, Greece, and Jerusalem. St. Luke also accompanied St. Paul from Caesarea to Rome. After St. Paul's death St. Luke went to Achaia, where he was made bishop, and to Boeotia. According to tradition, he was crucified in Patras with St. Andrew. Late tradition says that St. Luke painted the Virgin, and he is represented in art with a painting. His attribute is an ox, usually winged. His feast is October 18.

See also SAINTS IN ART.

LUKS, GEORGE BENJAMIN. American painter (b. Williamsport, Pa., 1867; d. New York City, 1933). He studied at the Pennsylvania Academy of Fine Arts and in Düs-

seldorf, Munich, Berlin, London, and Paris. On his return to the United States he worked as a newspaper artist in Philadelphia, where he met Henri, Sloan, Glackens, and Shinn. In 1895 Luks was sent by the *Philadelphia Bulletin* to cover the fighting in Cuba. The next year he was in New York drawing illustrations, caricatures, and comic strips for the *World*. In 1907 the rejection of Luks's paintings by the National Academy led to Henri's withdrawal from the exhibition and to the formation of The Eight, which had its first and only showing at the Macbeth Gallery in 1908. Luks later taught at the Art Students League and at his own school.

His loose spontaneous brushwork and earthy subjects were in keeping with the flamboyance of his personality. The major influences on his style were the Munich school, Hals, and Henri. Luks painted the coal-mining towns of Pennsylvania, but his most important paintings were of scenes and figures of New York City's East Side, typical Ashcan subjects, which stressed a sort of heroic vigor rather than sordid poverty. The vitality and excitement of a crowded shopping street is vividly caught in *Hester Street* (1905; Brooklyn Museum), but in other paintings sympathy for the subject barely covers a strong sentimentality, as in *The Little Madonna* (1907; Andover, Mass., Philipps Academy, Addison Gallery of American Art) or the enchanting smiles of the little girls in *The Spielers* (1905; Addison Gallery). Luks was always overly dependent upon is powerful, almost virtuoso brushwork, which, at his best, he used in scenes of simple composition or strong action, for example, *The Wrestlers* (1905; Boston, Museum f Fine Arts).

After his Ashcan phase he painted many portraits; one f the most successful is the roguish *Otis Skinner as 'ol. Bridau* (1919; Washington, D.C., Phillips Collection). Luks's strong sensitivity to the qualities of pigment was ot always accompanied by a sense of pictorial construction r of true feeling for the subject. The remedy of conscious nd deliberate composition did not always lead to the usion of subject and setting, although in works such as he full-figure, genre portrait *Mrs. Gamely* (1930; New 'ork, Whitney Museum of American Art) the subject is rmly set into the picture space.

BIBLIOGRAPHY. E. L. Cary, *George Luks* (American Artists Series), lew York, 1931.   JEROME VIOLA

UMIA. Quasi-art form developed in the 1920s. It involves the moving and blending of colored lights in an ttempt to create "mobile" form. It is sometimes called color music" and the "art of light."

LUMINARIUM (Lucernarium). Air and light shaft in the orm of a chimney found in catacombs around Rome. Above the ground the luminarium appears as a round or riangular form.

LUMINISTS. Obsolete term for impressionist painters, particularly Monet and Pissarro, who were much interested n investigating the effects of light in their paintings. Seurat ttempted to reduce luminism to a fixed law of the spectrum y his pointillism. *See* IMPRESSIONISM; MONET, CLAUDE-)SCAR; PISSARRO, CAMILLE; POINTILLISM; SEURAT, JEORGES.

LUNCHEON OF THE BOATING PARTY. Oil painting by Renoir, in the Phillips Collection, Washington, D.C. *ee* RENOIR, PIERRE-AUGUSTE.

LUNCHEON ON THE GRASS, *see* DEJEUNER SUR L'HERBE.

LUND CATHEDRAL. Romanesque cathedral in Sweden, begun in 1080 with the crypt. Built by Canute the Holy, it was altered and enlarged after 1103, when Lund became the metropolitan of all Scandinavia. The revisions of 1103–46 were directed after 1120 by one Donatus, possibly an Italian; the style of the work of that period is definitely Rhine-Lombard, especially in the capital sculpture and in the blind arcading and gallery on the exterior of the apse. The four double bays of the nave may have been originally groin-vaulted, but the vault was rebuilt after 1234 and drastically restored in the 19th century. Despite this and the modernized 13th-century west towers, Lund remains one of the most impressive medieval architectural monuments in Scandinavia.

BIBLIOGRAPHY. T. Paulsson, *Scandinavian Architecture*, London, 1958.

LUNDBERG, GUSTAF. Swedish pastel portraitist (b. Stockholm, 1695; d. there, 1786). He studied painting under D. von Krafft in Stockholm, and in Paris after 1717 he studied with Rigaud, Largillière, P. J. Cazes, and De Troy. Lundberg was received into the Royal Academy in 1742 with portraits of Boucher and Natoire. He also painted Maria Leszczyńska. He returned to Stockholm in 1745, and was appointed court portraitist; in 1776 he became the director of the Stockholm Academy. His portrait of G. Taraval (Paris, Institut Tessin) shows Carriera's influence, which Lundberg fused in his art with the styles of Largillière and Nattier. More than 500 of his pastel portraits are known.

BIBLIOGRAPHY. O. Levertin, *G. Lundberg, en studie*, Stockholm, 1902.

LUNDENS, GERRIT. Dutch painter of genre, interiors, portraits, and miniatures (b. Amsterdam, 1622; d. there? shortly after 1683). Little is known of his early career. His works are generally in the manner of Metsu and Brakenburg. Lundens is best known for a small copy of Rem-

luminarium. Air and light shaft in the form of a chimney, found in Roman catacombs.

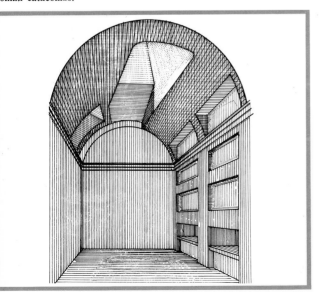

Lund Cathedral. One of Scandinavia's most impressive medieval churches.

LUNDENS, GERRIT   485

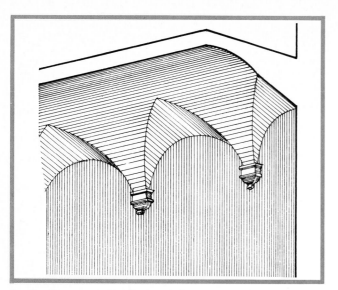

Lunette. Upper part of wall where it intersects a vault.

brandt's *Night Watch* (London, National Gallery); it shows the original size of the painting, which was later cut down. This attribution, however, has been questioned.

BIBLIOGRAPHY. N. MacLaren, *National Gallery Catalogues: The Dutch School*, London, 1960.

LUNEBURG: THE SAND. Street in the old city of Lüneburg, Germany. It contains several well-preserved residences of the 15th and 16th centuries. The houses are noted for their stepped gables richly decorated with friezes and for their intricately carved window frames and doorframes. The 16th-century houses have terra-cotta decoration instead of the *Taustein* (incrusted stone) decoration of the 15th century.

BIBLIOGRAPHY. J. Matthaei, *Lüneburg*, Munich, 1950.

LUNEBURG CATHEDRAL: GOLDEN PANELS. Two sets of movable altar wings from Lüneburg Cathedral, Germany (Hannover, Lower Saxony Landesmuseum). Dating from 1418, they originally covered the shrine of the high altar of the Cathedral. The paintings representing the Crucifixion, the Brazen Serpent, and the thirty-six scenes from the life of the Virgin are Westphalian and relate to the work of Konrad von Soest.

BIBLIOGRAPHY. H. von Einem, *Die Plastik der Lüneburger goldenen Tafel*, Hildesheim, 1929; A. Stange, *Deutsche Malerei der Gothik*, vol. 3, Berlin, 1938.

LUNENSCHLOSS, ANTON CLEMENS. German painter (b. Düsseldorf, ca. 1680/90; d. there, 1762). He studied in Antwerp with G. van Opstal and traveled to Italy in 1705-07. From 1720 on Lünenschloss was active in Würzburg. Among his works are the high altar in Würzburg Cathedral (1726) and the ceiling painting in the Würzburg Residenz and the monastery at Eberbach.

BIBLIOGRAPHY. G. Dehio, *Handbuch der deutschen Kunstdenkmäler*, vol. 1, Berlin, 1905.

LUNETTE. Upper part of wall where it intersects a vault, generally semicircular and often occupied by a window.

LUNG-CH'UAN WARE. Designation for a type of celadon produced in southern China. It is named after the

town in southwest Chekiang Province where the ware first were produced in the Sung dynasty. Lung-ch'üan eventually became the most famous of all the celadon wares and in the Western world the ware gave rise to the designation celadon, a reference to the special gray-green or gray-blue color of the glaze. The ware was exported in tremendous quantities throughout the world, to the West, to Africa, and to other areas of the Far East. *See* CELADON.

The body of Lung-ch'üan ware is gray-white in color but it turns to a characteristic reddish brown where it is exposed to fire without glaze. This particular characteristic of the clay led to the use of contrasting colors of reddish brown and gray-green in the decoration of the ware; by leaving the molded designs of fishes or dragons bare of glaze, the potters were able to achieve striking visual effects. Another special design effect in Lung-ch'üan ware was produced by dropping ferric oxide on the celadon glaze, a procedure that resulted in dark brown splashes. This "spotted celadon," wrongly termed "buckwheat celadon" in some Western literature, was called *tobi seiji* (literally, "flying celadon") in Japan, where it was highly admired and much sought after by Japanese collectors. Ultimately, the name Lung-ch'üan came to designate the type and style of ware rather than referring solely to the kiln site, for it was manufactured at many sites in Chekiang Province.

BIBLIOGRAPHY. G. Gompertz, *Chinese Celadon Wares*, London, 1958.

MARTIE W. YOUNG

LUNGHI, MARTINO, *see* LONGHI, MARTINO (IL VECCHIO).

LUNG-HSING-SSU, CHENG-TING. Chinese temples in the city of Cheng-ting, Hopei Province. The Lung-hsing-ssu exist on a site founded in 971. The three-story hall called the Fo-hsiang-ko is now in a ruined state but is notable for a colossal bronze figure of Kuan-yin around which the original building was erected. The Mo-ni-tien may antedate the Fo-hsiang-ko, although Japanese scholars place the date of this square hall at about 1050. The Mo-ni-tien is a relatively rare type among Buddhist structures in China: each of its four sides contains a projecting vestibule crowned by a hip-and-gable roof.

BIBLIOGRAPHY. L. Sickman and A. Soper, *The Art and Architecture of China*, Baltimore, 1956.

LUNG-MEN. Limestone caves, well known in Chinese sculptural history, situated on the steep banks of a river 15 miles south of Lo-yang in Honan Province. Work was begun at this location when the Wei rulers moved their capital to Lo-yang in 494 and continued during the T'ang dynasty. Some forty caves in all are in existence on both banks of the river, but many are in poor condition. The oldest of the Six Dynasties caves is the Ku-yang cave, begun shortly before the actual transfer of the capital. The numerous figures of Bodhisattvas seated in the cross-ankle pose seem to carry on directly the last stage of the Yunkang style.

The Pin-yang cave (Cave 3) is generally acknowledged to be the finest of the Northern Wei period. The cave was probably completed by 523 and thus typifies the fully developed Six Dynasties style. The main image consists of large Buddha, seated cross-legged at the back wall, flanked y disciples and Bodhisattvas. The great *mandorla* that rames the image is executed in low relief and gives the ffect of flickering flames dancing toward the ceiling. The elief carvings on the walls of the Pin-yang cave are in he full Chinese linear tradition, gracefully elongated forms eing beautifully disposed in an intricate composition. A ection of a donor panel from the Pin-yang cave can be een at the William Rockhill Nelson Gallery of Art in Kansas City.

Of the T'ang dynasty caves at Lung-men, Cave 6, known s the Feng-hsien temple, contains one of the most impres-ive of all T'ang Buddhist images. The central figure is of Vairocana, the universal Buddha, whose worship had only ecently been introduced into China. The Feng-hsien temple vas begun in 670 and completed in 675. The figure of Vairocana, measuring 50 feet overall, is flanked by two lisciples, two Lokapālas in full armor, and two muscular guardians. The figures are all full-bodied forms, the elon-gation of the Six Dynasties style now being replaced by a new concept of physical presence. The influence of the Gupta style of India is detectable in the solid and fleshy culptures produced at the Feng-hsien complex, and the ransition to the full T'ang style seen at T'ien-lung-shan s well under way. *See* LOKAPALA; T'IEN-LUNG-SHAN; VAI-ROCANA.

Lung-ch'üan ware. Celadon ware wine jar and cover, with light bluish-green glaze. Sung dynasty, 12th century (?).

Activity at Lung-men was apparently sporadic after the mid-8th century, and the period of greatest work under the T'ang emperors seems to have been confined to the latter half of the 7th century. In many respects the colossal Vairocana at Lung-men is the last successful large-scaled Buddha image in China.

BIBLIOGRAPHY. E. Chavannes, *Mission archéologique dans la Chine septentrionale*, vol. 1, Paris, 1909; D. Tokiwa and T. Sekino, *Shina Bukkyō Shiseki* (Monuments of Buddhism in China), II, Tokyo, 1926–38; S. Mizuno and T. Nagahiro, *Ryūmon Sekkutsu no Ken-kyū: A Study of the Buddhist Cave Temples at Lung-Mên, Honan*, Tokyo, 1941.

MARTIE W. YOUNG

LUPTON, THOMAS GOFF. English engraver and min-iature painter (b. London, 1791; d. 1873). He served his apprenticeship with George Clint, beginning in 1805. Lup-ton invented a soft steel plate for mezzotint but today is remembered for his competent portrait plates, mostly after Sir Thomas Lawrence, Sir Martin Shee, and Thomas Phil-lips. Plates of various subjects are attributed to Lupton.

BIBLIOGRAPHY. C. J. Davenport, *Mezzotints*, London, 1904.

LURCAT, ANDRE. French architect (1892–   ). Born in Bruyères-en-Vosges, he studied in Nancy and in Paris, which became his headquarters. Lurçat was one of the architects working in the 1920s and 1930s in the Inter-national style whose work is related to Le Corbusier's. Among Lurçat's projects are the Guggenbuhl House in Paris (1927), the Froriep-de-Salis House in Boulogne-sur-Seine (1927), and a school at Villejuif (1931–33).

BIBLIOGRAPHY. A. Lurçat, *Projets et réalisations*, Paris, 1929.

LURCAT, JEAN. French painter and tapestry designer (1892–1966). A native of Bruyères-en-Vosges, he studied for a short time at the Ecole des Beaux-Arts and at the Académie Colarossi (1912). He founded *Les Feuilles de Mai*, a review that included works by Bourdelle, Rilke, and Ilya Ehrenburg, and associated himself with Lafitte, executing a large fresco for the Académie des Sciences in Marseilles. In 1917 Lurçat exhibited for the first time at the Galerie Tanner in Zurich and executed his first tapestries, *Filles vertes* and *Soirée dans Grenade* (1917). The postwar period was marked by travel in Italy and the execution of his third and fourth tapestries, *Pêcheurs* and *Piscine* (1920).

Lurçat settled in Paris, participated in the Salon des Indépendants, designed the décor and costumes for Re-misov's *Celui qui reçoit les gifles*, and joined a group of painters, poets, and writers that included Max Jacob, Louis Marcoussis, and Paul Baudry. In 1922 Lurçat had his first exhibition in Paris, executed his fifth tapestry, *Le cirque*, and painted a large decoration for Edmond Bernheim. Two years later he paid a visit to North Africa and Greece, which resulted in his large tapestry *Les Arabes*. In 1930 he executed a large tapestry *L'Eté*. In 1934 he collaborated with the American Ballet Company, New York, and exhib-ited oil paintings and gouaches at the Moscow Museum of Modern Art (now a part of the National Museum of Fine Arts).

Lurçat began to concentrate on tapestry and in 1936 was commissioned by the Gobelins firm to execute *Les Illusions d'Icare*, which was offered by the French nation to the Queen of the Netherlands. A second tapestry, *Fo-*

Jean Lurçat, *Le Jardin des Coqs*. Aubusson tapestry. National Museum of Modern Art, Paris.

rêts, was commissioned in 1937. In 1939 Lurçat settled in Aubusson to supervise four large tapestries entitled *Les Quatre saisons*. From this period also date *Jardin des coqs* (Paris, National Museum of Modern Art) and *Le Poète*. In 1947 he published *Le Travail dans la tapisserie du moyen âge* and *Le Bestiaire de la tapisserie du moyen âge*. Lurçat worked in gouache, lithography, and ceramics, all marked by his strong decorative style in which color is always given a prominent place and is never sacrificed to composition.

He designed more than 1,000 tapestries and was France's foremost contemporary tapestry artist. His work and writings have influenced two generations.

BIBLIOGRAPHY. P. Soupault, *Jean Lurçat*, Paris, 1928; V. Salet, *La Tapisserie française du moyen-âge à nos jours*, Paris, 1946; A. Séné, *Aubusson et l'avenir*, Paris, 1951; J. Marcenac, *L'Exemple de Jean Lurçat*, Zurich, 1952; C. Roy, *Jean Lurçat*, Geneva, 1956.

ARNOLD ROSIN

LURISTAN. Province in the Zagros Mountains of western Iran, famous for the bronzes excavated there. The plethora of graves and bronze objects found in Luristan may be attributed to the great and frequent migrations of Indo-European nomad tribes from southern Russia, from the Caucasus, and from Central Asia into southern Iran that took place from the second half of the 2d millennium onward.

Between 400 and 500 cemeteries have been discovered, each containing about 200 graves. Pottery and glass, a few stone objects, and a vast quantity of ornamental bronzes were found; these are objects used by nomads, but were obviously the work of indigenous Iranian craftsmen. Char-

iot and harness fittings, rein rings, bits, and ornaments, weapons, and various types of charms and amulets have also been excavated. The execution is artistic and elegant, with many Iranian characteristics and also evidences of Mesopotamian and other influences.

Many tombs were found some distance away from the villages or towns of the time. It can be surmised from this that the nomad tribesmen of Luristan buried their dead far from the inhabited sites. No remains of human habitation have been discovered near the tombs.

Prominent among the nomad tribes of Luristan were the Cimmerians, who came from the Caucasus in the early 8th century B.C. These nomads also had religious centers where they congregated at certain times, and temples and shrines with votive objects have been found.

The Luristan bronzes often display openwork. They are usually decorated with the figure of a god, probably Sraosha, god of justice, fighting with two beasts. The figure, obviously of Mesopotamian influence, has two heads facing in opposite directions, with enormous eyes and projecting ears, and both arms outstretched, strangling the monsters. A wide girdle encircles the waist, from which hang two cocks' heads. The legs and rumps of both monster form the god's lower limbs.

All the art of Luristan is basically symbolic, and the human figure, depicted in the abstract, is usually shown in an attitude of prayer, with both arms raised and the palms of the hands turned forward. The nose is abnormally prominent, the eye sockets inlaid. Men and women are usually naked, except for their weapons and jewelry. With their vivid imagination and artistic talent the Luristan artists also created fantastic animals, polychrome jewelry and gold ornaments inset with semiprecious stones. Sometimes the artists showed unusual realism, as in a small bronze head of a nomad and in a horse engraved on a seal (both, Teheran Museum).

BIBLIOGRAPHY. S. Lloyd, *The Art of the Ancient Near East*, London, 1961; R. Ghirshman, *The Arts of Ancient Iran: From its Origins to the Time of Alexander the Great*, New York, 1964; A. Godard, *The Arts of Iran*, New York, 1965.

LUCILLE VASSARDAKI

LUST, ANTONI DE. Dutch painter of flower and fruit pieces (fl. mid-17th cent.). Little is known of De Lust's activity. He is reported in Leeuwarden in 1659. He may also have worked in Lyons and possibly in Paris.

BIBLIOGRAPHY. A. P. A. Vorenkamp, *Bijdrage tot de geschiedenis van het Hollandsch stilleven in de zeventiende eeuw*, Leyden, 1934.

LUSTER, *see* TILES, LUSTERED.

LUSTERWARE. Pottery that exhibits a metallic, pearly or iridescent sheen produced by applying a finely ground metal or metallic oxide to the glazed surface. Frequently dissolved in resinous oil, the powdered metal is mixed with an adhesive and spread as a thin film by painting, spraying, or stamping. A low temperature firing, between 600 and 800°C, fuses the luster to the glaze. Gold produces purple and ruby shades, silver yields pale yellow, and copper gives reds and browns. Lead, manganese, and nickel can also be used. *See also* ISLAMIC POTTERY AND TILES (UMAYYAD AND ABBASID PERIODS).

BIBLIOGRAPHY. C. W. Parmalee, *Ceramic Glazes*, Chicago, 1948; D. Rhodes, *Clay and Glazes for the Potter*, New York, 1957.

LUSTIG, ALVIN. American graphic designer (1915–55). Born in Denver, he attended Los Angeles City College, and at eighteen was art director of his first magazine, *Westways*. A refusal to be limited to a single medium characterized his life, and he moved from graphic design to the design of chairs, exhibits, interiors, fabrics, and houses. Lustig was preoccupied with formal elements in his graphic design; combining letter forms with geometric patterns, he exploited their relation to each other and to the page itself.

Between 1934 and 1936 Lustig attended the Art Center School, studied briefly with Frank Lloyd Wright, and traveled. For the next four years he operated his own typography and printing business. By 1940 he had completely given it up to design for such clients as *Arts and Architecture* magazine, New Directions books, and the National Broadcasting Company. In 1944 he became visual research director for *Look* magazine, but he continued to do freelance work for such clients as Knoll Associates.

He returned to Los Angeles in 1946, and turned increasingly to architectural, furniture, and fabric design. In 1951, with an appointment from Yale University as visiting critic in design, he moved east again and continued both graphic and three-dimensional design activities. Throughout his professional life Lustig maintained an interest in teaching, and taught at various universities and art schools.

A comprehensive exhibition of Lustig's work was prepared by the New York Museum of Modern Art in 1955. His work is also owned by the Metropolitan Museum of Art, the Stockholm National Museum, and the Victoria and Albert Museum. His work has received many awards for excellence of design.

BIBLIOGRAPHY. A. Lustig, *The Collected Writings of Alvin Lustig*, New Haven, 1959.

ANN FEREBEE

LU T'AN-WEI. Chinese painter (fl. 2d half of 5th cent.). He was highly praised in the early literature on painting. Hsieh Ho, for example, in his classification of the great masters placed him above the celebrated Ku K'ai-chih. Lu T'an-wei was famed for his use of the "one-stroke" method, or painting with a continuous line. No painting by him has survived, and any discussion of his skill is largely conjectural.

LUTERI, GIOVANNI, *see* DOSSO.

LUTFULLAH MOSQUE (Masjid-i-Sadr; Masjid-i-Shaikh Lutfullah), ISFAHAN. Safavid mosque on the eastern side of the Maidan-i-Shah in Isfahan, Iran. Erected between 1603 and 1609, it was first called the Masjid-i-Sadr and later became known as the Masjid-i-Shaikh Lutfullah. The mosque consists of a single square chamber crowned by a dome; splendid exterior and interior faïence decoration make it a masterpiece of its period.

BIBLIOGRAPHY. A. U. Pope, ed., *A Survey of Persian Art*, vol. 2, New York, 1939.

LUTTICHUIJS, ISAAK. Dutch-English portrait painter (b. London, 1616; d. Amsterdam, 1673). Luttichuijs probably studied in Amsterdam, where he was reported in 1638. His older brother Simon was also a painter.

BIBLIOGRAPHY. W. R. Valentiner, "Isaac Luttichuys: A Little Known Dutch Portrait Painter," *Art Quarterly*, I, 1938.

LUTYENS, SIR EDWIN. English architect (1869–1944). The fluidity and immense vocabulary of his designs place him in the line of the great Renaissance artists. He was, as well, a craftsman and a humanist. The urban plan for New Delhi, India, begun in 1912, and his Liverpool Roman Catholic Cathedral designs of 1929 are his best-known works.

BIBLIOGRAPHY. C. Hussey, *The Life of Sir Edwin Lutyens*, London, New York, 1950.

LUTZELBERGER, HANS. Swiss maker of woodcuts (fl. 1522–ca. 1538). He was active in Basel. Although it is likely that he worked for other woodcut designers, Lützelberger is famous for his collaboration with Hans Holbein the Younger, especially on the series popularly called *The Dance of Death*. His great skill and delicacy enabled him to cut in Holbein's miniature scale.

BIBLIOGRAPHY. E. His, "Hans Lützelberger," *Gazette des Beaux-Arts*, 2d ser. IV, December, 1871.

LUX, GWEN. American sculptor (1910–   ). A native of Chicago, Gwen Lux was a student at the Maryland Institute of Arts and the Boston Museum School and of Ivan Meštrović in Paris. She first worked in Europe. Among several public commissions in the United States awarded her during the early thirties was the muscular, expressionistic statue *Eve* for the Radio City Music Hall in New York City, which caused a great uproar. Since then she has been known primarily as an architectural sculptor, in which capacity she has collaborated with Ed-

Luristan. Bronze ornament. Faroughi Collection, Teheran.

ward Durrell Stone, Victor Gruen, Eero Saarinen, and other leading architects. Working in a wide variety of materials, including stainless steel and reinforced concrete, she has created monumental works for such structures as the McGraw-Hill Building in Chicago, the Northland Shopping Center in Detroit, the General Motors Research Plant in Warren, Mich., the U.S.S. "United States," and the Aviation High School in Long Island City. Like her smaller works, these range from the figurative tending toward linear abstraction to complete or symbolic abstraction.

LUXEMBOURG PALACE, PARIS. Royal residence built from 1621 to 1627 by the architect Salomon de Brosse for Marie de Médicis, widow of Henri IV and queen regent for her son, Louis XIII. Constructed on the left bank of the Seine, it is an Italianate building of symmetry and heavy elegance, influenced by the Queen's girlhood home, the Pitti Palace in Florence. Italian forms of exterior decoration can be seen in light, all-over surface rustication, ringed columns, Tuscan capitals, and window bosses. Each of the three stories is clearly delineated by stringcourses, which contrast with the vertical accents of pilasters flanking the windows.

The plan is traditionally French in its basic form, which is the imposing *corps-de-logis* with its high pitched roof, approached through an enclosed courtyard. Balustrades mark the beginning of the roofline, and symmetrical chimneys complete the ornament. An important feature is the one-story gallery that screens the court along the street. The central clock tower offers an imposing entrance to the court. Two pavilions, three stories high, flank the gallery. From these, narrow two-story wings stretch back across the court to connect with the palace; they are lower in roofline and subordinate to the main section. Located in these wings are galleries, which have been used for museum or library purposes. The west gallery was originally decorated by Rubens with allegorical scenes from the life of Marie de Médicis (now in Paris, Louvre).

The palace proper formed an elongated H in plan, with its four corner pavilions containing separate dwelling *appartements*. The central area was occupied by a stairwell, the front by audience chambers, and the rear by a chapel. The Queen occupied the palace from 1625 to 1631. It was a royal residence until the French Revolution, and then served as a political prison.

After 1800 the building became the official seat of government under the Consulate, and the architect Chalgrin was engaged to modify its structure in order to provide a vast assembly room. He built a hemicycle-shaped room facing a tribune placed against the rear façade, demolishing, for this purpose, the chapel and stairwell. He eliminated some of the walls to install a fashionable neoclassic vestibule with massive Doric columns on the ground floor, which runs straight through to the gardens. The Escalier d'Honneur was installed in part of the former Rubens Gallery, and new entrances for this approach and for the museum in the east wing were provided from the courtyard. Under Napoleon I the first floor room east of the hemicycle was used as a throne room.

After the restoration of the monarchy the palace was used by the Chambre des Pairs, or Senate. From 1814 to 1830 the only change was the redecoration of one of the east rooms on the ground floor. Gilded *boiserie* fragments, saved after Chalgrin's modernization, were used to create the Salle du Livre d'Or. Under Louis Philippe, in order to enlarge the great assembly room, or Salle des Séances, Alphonse de Gisors constructed a new building across the rear of the older one, repeating the same basic arrangement. The cross room between the new end pavilions became the library, where the cupola and pendentives were decorated by Delacroix (1840–45). During the same reign the old hemicycle area on the first floor front was used to form three rooms facing the court. In 1852 Louis Napoleon had the three rooms made into a single, lavishly decorated Throne Room, now the Salle des Conférences. Since that time the building has been used for senatorial and governmental functions and is now the seat of the Council of the Republic.

BIBLIOGRAPHY. A. Hustin, *Le Palais du Luxembourg*, Paris, 1904; G. Hirschfeld, *Le Palais du Luxembourg*, Paris, 1931; A. Blunt, *Art and Architecture in France, 1500–1700*, Baltimore, 1954.

EMMA N. PAPERT

LUXEUIL. Town in the Department of the Haute-Saône, in eastern France. It is the site of a monastery founded by the Irish missionary St. Columban about 590. In the 7th and the early 8th century Luxeuil was one of the most important centers for the diffusion of monastic learning. A score of manuscripts written in the distinctive Luxeuil script survives; this group includes the most significant examples of Merovingian illumination.

LUXOR. Modern town in Egypt after which the ruins of southern Thebes are named. Its ancient name, Ipet-resyt, derives from that of Ta-ipet (Thebes), which was also known as *nywt*, "The City" par excellence. The ancient city has not been excavated since it lies beneath the modern structures.

Only one temple is extant, that of Amun, which was flooded in ancient times during high water. Instead of being laid out at right angles to the bank of the Nile, its plan is parallel to it, oriented north to the Great Temple of Amun at Karnak. The temple proper was built by Amenhotep III to Amun, his consort Mut, and their son Khons. Two rows of tall papyriform columns with open capitals flank the axial alley leading to the temple, a treatment characteristic of Amenhotep III's buildings and also found in the Great Temple of Amun at Karnak. On three sides of the courtyard there runs a portico with bud papyriform columns two rows deep, and on the fourth side is an open hypostyle hall before a sanctuary remodeled by Alexander the Great for the sacred boat.

Besides the usual scenes in low relief showing the rituals performed in the various rooms, special mention should be made of the scenes of the theogamy of Queen Mutemuye and Amun and the consequent birth of Amenhotep III, as seen in the room east of the third hypostyle hall. In the second hypostyle hall, transformed into a chapel by the Copts (4th cent.), remarkable murals of saints cover the Egyptian reliefs. A wall was erected on either side of the processional colonnade and carved by Tutankhamen with realistic scenes, influenced by the Amarna style, of the sacred procession from Karnak to Luxor and back.

About a century later Rameses II, wishing to connect

Luxor. Temple of Amun, built by Amenhotep III, portico with double row of bud papyriform columns.

Luxor to Karnak, added a pylon to the front of the processional colonnade and a courtyard surrounded by a portico with bud papyriform columns two rows deep, at the end of which was another pylon. The whole scheme was set on an axis out of line with that of the temple, but oriented toward Karnak and corresponding to the axis of the avenue of sphinxes. An earlier small chapel of Thutmosis III was incorporated into the columned portico. Colossi of Rameses II (one of his favorite architectural elements) were at the front of both pylons. Two obelisks were erected in slightly asymmetrical positions to compensate in perspective for their different heights. A representation of the pylon featuring the tall flagstaffs is carved in the southwest corner of the portico.

Among the architectural characteristics at Luxor are, first, the use of the stylobate upon which the rear structure rests, marked on the external façades by a cavetto cornice; and second, the variety in style of the columns of the bud papyriform type (Middle Kingdom monolithic columns with triangular stems reused by Rameses II), the open papyriform type (Amenhotep III), the bundle shaft of round stems (Amenhotep III), and the single round shaft (Rameses II). There is also considerable variety in the styles of mural relief (Amenhotep III, Tutankhamen, and Rameses II).

BIBLIOGRAPHY. A. M. Blackman, *Luxor and Its Temples*, London, 1923; A. Schwaller de Lubicz, *Le Temple de l'homme*, 3 vols., Lyons, 1958.   ALEXANDER M. BADAWY

LUYCKS (Luykx; Luycks; Luckx), CHRISTIAAN (Kerstiaen). Flemish painter of still life and flower pieces (b. Antwerp, 1623; d. after 1653). His breakfast pictures show Dutch influence; in his flower paintings and garlands he followed in the footsteps of Daniel Seghers. Luyckx was mentioned in 1646 as being in the service of "His Royal Majesty of Spain."

BIBLIOGRAPHY. F. J. van den Branden, *Geschiedenis der Antwerpsche Schilderschool*, Antwerp, 1883.

LUYCX, FRANS, *see* LEUX VON LEUXENSTEIN, FRANS, THE ELDER.

LUYKEN (Luiken), JAN. Dutch draftsman, graphic artist, painter, writer, and poet (b. Amsterdam, 1649; d. there, 1712). He received his first training from an obscure artist named Martinus Zaagmolen. It is possible that Luyken learned etching from Cornelis Decker, as he collaborated with Decker on the illustrations for Luyken's first book, *Schat der Zielen* (1678). Luyken executed three of the illustrations himself, and the rest are mainly by Decker after Luyken's drawings. In 1699 Luyken was recorded in Haarlem, and four years later he was in Schelinkhout. Although he is known to have executed paintings, his work in this medium is practically unknown. He is best known for his numerous drawings and some 3,300 etchings. Many of these etchings are illustrations for books he himself wrote. His son Caspar was also a draftsman and graphic artist.

BIBLIOGRAPHY. J. G. van Gelder, *Prenten en Tekningen*, Amsterdam, 1958.

LUYNES, CHATEAU OF. French castle in the Department of Indre-et-Loire. Its grim appearance results from its thick walls and circular, turreted towers, built of rough stone at various dates. Known as Maillé, its original structures were erected in the 11th century on Gallo-Roman foundations. It was rebuilt after 1465, when more pleasant residential quarters were constructed in the courtyard, in imitation of those of Louis XII at Plessis-les-Tours. A combination of brick and stone was employed.

BIBLIOGRAPHY. J. Aufort and H. Colas, *Les Châteaux de la Loire*, Bordeaux, 1947; E. de Ganay, *Châteaux de France*, vol. 2, Paris, 1949.

LUZARCHES, ROBERT DE. French Gothic architect (13th cent.). He was the first master of the nave of Amiens Cathedral, begun in 1220. In the cathedral labyrinth, he is called a "master." He was one of the geniuses of French medieval architecture. *See* AMIENS: CATHEDRAL.

BIBLIOGRAPHY. M. Aubert, "La Construction au Moyen Age," *Bulletin Monumental*, CXIX, 1961.

LUZZI, LORENZO (Pietro), *see* MORTO DA FELTRE.

LYCEUM. Originally, the gymnasium or place of learning of ancient Athens located on the right bank of the Ilissus River. It had a temple surrounded by shaded walks and was famous as the school at which Aristotle taught. It was destroyed by fire in 200 B.C. Lyceum is now a general term used to denote any place where interested laymen gather for educational purposes.

LYCIA. Ancient kingdom on the southwest coast of Asia Minor, allied with the Hittites from 1297 to 1230 B.C. Nothing is known regarding Lycia's civilization during the 2d millennium B.C.; the oldest discovered documents date from the 6th century B.C., when Lycia was coming under Greek influence. In 546 B.C. Lycia's capital, Xanthus, was besieged by the Medes. The city fell, and Cyrus's general Harpagus became Lycia's governor. After Alexander's conquest of Persia, Lycia became part of the Seleucid empire, until taken over by the Romans.

No pottery has been found in Lycia, but many funerary monuments, reliefs, sarcophagi, and sculptured, house-shaped rock tombs with bases and pitched or flat roofs, usually supported by pillars, have been discovered. Two 4th-century rock tombs at Limyra are of Greek inspiration. At Xanthus many 5th- and 4th-century funerary monuments, reliefs, and friezes have been discovered; the most important is the Harpy Tomb (London, British Museum), adorned with beautiful marble bas-reliefs of Harpies carrying away the souls of the dead. These motifs are Persian, but the execution is Greek. From Xanthus comes one of the oldest examples of Lycian architecture, the Lion Tomb (540 B.C.; British Museum), with archaic Greek reliefs depicting the exploits of its dead prince; two sculptured lions guarded the tomb. The next oldest reliefs (525 B.C.; Istanbul, Archaeological Museum) come from a pillar tomb at Isinda (Belenkli); they also depict a dead prince's exploits, and are of Ionic influence. One Xanthus relief has sphinxes with archaic profiles. A decorative frieze shows lions, panthers, cocks, and hens, and another has chariots and horsemen of Persian influence.

The Lycian sculptors were remarkably skilled, and their reliefs are beautifully executed. The famous Nereid tomb-sarcophagus (British Museum) from Sidon is Lycian, influenced by Greek architecture. It is shaped like an Ionian temple; the rich ornamental sculptures depict the buried ruler as a Greco-Lycian prince seated amid his family. The Heroön of Trysa (Vienna, Museum of Art History) is lavishly decorated with bulls' protomas in relief, under which men and women sit. In a Xanthus pillar tomb a stele bears a long inscription in Lycian script, with twelve lines in Greek in its center, proclaiming that it stood in the city's agora and that the Harpy Tomb connected with the Temenos of the Twelve Gods. Nearby, other remains of buildings and monuments were found, and farther on Roman votive inscriptions and remnants of a forum. The famous house-shaped sarcophagus (ca. 400 B.C.; Istanbul, Archaeological Museum) from Sidon is decorated with reliefs. In Arsa, the ancient Arsada, tombs of the "Gothic" sarcophagus type were found, one with a human head carved on each side. A broken relief shows a Greek inscription and a woman wearing an Ionian chiton; another depicts a horseman wearing a short pleated tunic; others have coiled snakes and vases.

BIBLIOGRAPHY. F. J. Tritsch, "The Harpy Tomb at Xanthus," *The Journal of Hellenic Studies*, LXII, 1942; F. J. Tritsch, "False Doors on Tombs," *The Journal of Hellenic Studies*, LXIII, 1943; G. E. Bean, "Notes and Inscriptions from Lycia," *The Journal of Hellenic Studies*, LXVIII, 1948; R. Ghirshman, *The Arts of Ancient Iran: From Its Origins to the Time of Alexander the Great*, New York, 1964.

LUCILLE VASSARDAKI

LYDIA. Wealthy ancient kingdom in western Asia Minor, north of the Meander River. It was a flourishing center of commerce in the 1st millennium B.C.

In the beginning of the 7th century B.C., under King Alyattes (680 B.C.), the Lydians drove out the Cimmerians, who had conquered Phrygia, and took over the former Phrygian territory, which earlier had belonged to the Hittites and was rich in iron, gold, and silver. Later, Lydia was threatened by the Scythians, who swept down from southern Russia and devastated Anatolia (614 B.C.), and by the Medes, who under King Cyaxares crushed the Scythians and attacked Lydia (610 B.C.). Under Croesus (ca. 560–546 B.C.) Lydia regained her independence and became the supreme power in Asia Minor, taking over the

Lycia. Heroön of Trysa, detail. Museum of Art History, Vienna.

entire Anatolian Plateau, including central and eastern Syria, with its metal ores of the Lake Van district, west of the Halys River, and the Greek colonies on the Ionian coast.

During Croesus's reign Lydia developed the first monetary system. It spread quickly through Asia Minor, was adopted by Darius in Persia, and helped expand commercial relations throughout the then-known world, bringing great economic prosperity. Lydia evolved a great civilization, borrowing freely from various cultures—Hittite, Urartian, Assyrian, Akkadian, Phrygian, Persian, Ionian, Greek, and Roman. The center was its great capital Sardis, on the Paktolos River.

Purple sandstone, found in the area, was used for construction. The walls of ruined buildings have revetments with decorative colored terra-cotta tiles mounted in relief. The discoveries include exquisitely carved inlaid wooden furniture, carved polychrome tiles, gold plaques with Assyrian motifs, pottery of various types and periods, large urns with inscriptions in ink of the 1st century B.C., statues and gold figurines, stone and terra-cotta sarcophagi, marble stelae, gold, silver, bronze, and glass jewelry, cylinder seals, libation bowls, and coins in electrum, gold, and silver.

The great marble Temple of Artemis on Sardis's acropolis, built over an older temple, was destroyed by earthquakes and landslides, but excavations have unearthed two complete columns, several broken ones, carved bases, capitals, and portals; a lion's-head waterspout; engraved marble tiles; inscriptions on monolithic plinths; and carved friezes. Marble blocks with inscriptions in Greek or in Lydian and bilingual Greco-Lydian or in Lydo-Aramaic were discovered. A colossal marble head, believed to belong to a statue of Cybele, was also found.

A vast Lydian necropolis was discovered north of Sardis and smaller tumuli of various periods in the Paktolos Valley, as well as funerary limestone stelae with Lydian inscriptions giving the names of the deceased and one stele with five inscriptions in Lydian poetry. In 546 Croesus was defeated by Cyrus the Great, and Lydia became a Persian satrapy, passing finally to the Romans.

BIBLIOGRAPHY. E. Littman, ed., *Lydian Inscriptions*, 2 vols. (American Society for the Excavation of Sardis, vol. 6), Leyden, 1916-24; H. C. Butler, *The Excavations* (American Society for the Excavation of Sardis, vol. 1), Leyden, 1922; H. C. Butler, *The Temple* of *Artemis* (American Society for the Excavation of Sardis, vol. 2), Leyden, 1925; R. Ghirshman, *Iran: From the Earliest Times to the Islamic Conquest*, Harmondsworth, 1954; L. Woolley, *The Art of the Middle East*, New York, 1961.   LUCILLE VASSARDAKI

LYEDET, LOYSET, *see* LIEDET, LOYSET.

LYNEN, AMEDEE ERNEST. Belgian painter, engraver, and illustrator (b. Brussels, 1852; d. there, 1938). He studied at the Brussels Academy and with Paul Lauters. Lynen did genre paintings and many book illustrations, stressing the picturesque in both media.

LYONS (Lyon). City in east-central France. Preeminent for centuries in the manufacture of silk fabrics, Lyons boasts a historical museum of textiles, one of France's richest art museums, the Guimet Museum with Oriental art, and a museum of decorative arts. The Cathedral combines diverse Romanesque and Gothic elements, and the nearby former choristers' school has remnants of a rare early Romanesque cloister. The Church of St-Martin-d'Ainay, consecrated in 1107, is considered the oldest monument in Lyons and is noted for the consistency of its Romanesque style. The 12th-century portal of the former Church of St-Pierre is also a fine example of Romanesque architectural detail. There are many interesting residences of the 15th and 16th centuries. The Town Hall, built by Simon Maupin in 1646–55 (later alterations), has a richly decorated interior. A relic of the days when Lyons was the capital of the Gauls is the Roman theater on the Hill of Fourvière. *See* LYONS: CATHEDRAL; LYONS: MUSEUMS.

BIBLIOGRAPHY. Société Française d'Archéologie, *Lyon, Mâcon (Congrès Archéologiques)*, Paris, 1935.

LYONS: CATHEDRAL. Church in east-central France. Elements of Romanesque and successive styles of Gothic architecture in the Cathedral of St-Jean give evidence of construction spanning many centuries. Though much of the early sculpture has been damaged or destroyed, there remain 350 masterly bas-reliefs on the façade, executed about 1310, which are of iconographic and aesthetic interest. The former choristers' school adjacent to the Cathedral has remains of an 11th-century cloister.

BIBLIOGRAPHY. L. Bégule, *La Cathédrale de Lyon*, Paris, 1913?

LYONS: MUSEUMS. Important public art collections in Lyons, France, are located in the museums listed below.

Fine Arts Museum. The collection offers an extraordinarily wide-ranging coverage of the major branches and schools of European art. Notable among the sculptures are an Attic 6th-century B.C. kore, a Romanesque Madonna in wood, Nino Pisano's *Annunciation*, and Rodin's *Walking Man*. The paintings include such diverse works as Perugino's *Ascension*, Tintoretto's *Danaë*, El Greco's *Espolio*, Delacroix's *Odalisque*, and Géricault's *Madwoman*. A separate room is devoted to the paintings of the school of Lyons. There are various *objets d'art* from the Middle Ages and the Renaissance, as well as a large collection of Islamic decorative arts.

BIBLIOGRAPHY. R. Jullian, ed., *Catalogue*, Lyons, 1945-

Guimet Museum. Much of the collection formed by Emile Guimet in 1879 was transferred in 1888 to Paris, where it is now part of the Guimet Museum there. What remained in Lyons became the basis of a museum that is noted for its collections of ancient Egyptian and Near Eastern, Persian, Indian, Chinese, and Japanese art. *See* PARIS: MUSEUMS (GUIMET MUSEUM).

Textile Museum. Founded in 1856, the museum occupies the second floor of the Stock Exchange, designed in the Renaissance revival style by Dardel and built in 1855–60. Both its massive façades have pavilions with pointed roofs. It contains a unique historical collection of textiles.

LYRE. Musical instrument similar to a small harp. It was used in the ancient world as an accompaniment for songs or recitations. Known as a *kithara*, the hollow sound box at its base supported two outcurving arms resembling animal horns. The horns were joined close to their upper termini by a crosspiece from which gut strings were stretched vertically to a small bridge set just below the hole in the box. The left hand stopped the strings while the right struck them with a plectrum.

LYS, JOHANN, *see* LISS, JOHANN.

LYSICRATES, CHORAGIC MONUMENT OF, ATHENS. Small-scale circular building situated in the Street of the Tripods in Athens, Greece. The monument was erected to support a bronze tripod won by Lysicrates in 334 B.C. when he provided a chorus in the theater. It is 54 feet

Choragic Monument of Lysicrates, Athens. Erected 334 B.C.

high and consists of a square base of limestone that has on its upper part two circular steps of blue marble, above which rises a cylindrical structure of white Pentelic marble (7 feet in diameter). The cylinder has six engaged Corinthian columns that support an entablature decorated with a sculptured frieze depicting the story of Dionysos and the pirates. In this building we find the earliest example of external Corinthian columns. A convex roof over the cylinder consists of one block of marble; its upper surface is carved in imitation of bronze scale tiles. In the center of the roof rises the acanthus foliage that carried the tripod. This monument can be described as "baroque" in its elaborate ornamentation and in its complete freedom from convention.

Lysippus, *Farnese Heracles*. National Museum, Naples.

BIBLIOGRAPHY. W. B. Dinsmoor, *The Architecture of Ancient Greece*, 3d ed., London, 1950; A. W. Lawrence, *Greek Architecture*, Baltimore, 1957.

LYSIPPUS. Greek sculptor from Sicyon (fl. 2d half of 4th cent. B.C.). His innovations in proportion, composition, and naturalistic detail established a stylistic type that became the model for much of later Hellenistic sculpture.

The numerous references to him in ancient literature attest his fame, but it is from passages in Pliny's *Natural History* (XXXIV, 62–65) that we derive our specific knowledge of his style. We are told that he worked out a new canon of proportions for his figures, decreasing the size of the head in proportion to the body and substituting slenderer, more tightly knit bodily proportions for the block-like proportions (*quadratas staturas*) of his predecessors.

Pliny quotes Lysippus as having said that, while other sculptors portrayed men as they were, he, Lysippus, portrayed them as they appeared. This probably refers to his interest in the multiplicity of aspect achieved through torsion (which is characteristic of some of the works attributed to him), although it may simply refer to the quality of naturalism in his work. Whereas most earlier Greek statues were intended to be seen from one particular viewpoint, usually the front, and were confined to a flat plane, Lysippus allowed limbs to project into space and employed a twisted central axis in his figures. As a result of this composition, every viewpoint was accommodated by a subtle adjustment of surface planes.

One of Lysippus's most renowned works was the *Apoxyomenos* (*Youth Scraping Himself* or *The Scraper*). A Roman copy in the Vatican Museums, Rome, is generally taken to be a reproduction of this work. Although the copy is too insensitive to allow us to judge surface detail, it does have the compositional and proportional innovations mentioned above and is one of our best guides to the style of Lysippus.

Another work, the *Agias*, one of a group of Thessalian kings set up at Delphi, may be an early, less revolutionary work, possibly even an original by his hand. The inscription on the base of the *Agias* is duplicated on another base from Pharsalus that is signed by Lysippus. The marble work at Delphi may thus be a contemporary copy, by Lysippus or an assistant, of his original bronze in Pharsalus.

Lysippus was made court sculptor by Alexander the Great, and his famous portraits created a type of heroic ruler portrait that was used for many centuries. It is likely that Lysippus made several portraits of Alexander, and many of the famous portraits preserved today in copies—for example, the Azara herm in the Louvre, Paris, and the colossal head from Pergamon—must reflect the type he created.

Among the copies associated with the work of Lysippus, the *Farnese Heracles* type, the *Heracles Epitrapezios* type, and the "Eros-with-a-bow" type are well-grounded attributions, and several others have merit.

BIBLIOGRAPHY. M. Collignon, *Lysippe*, Paris, 1904; A. Maviglia, *L'attività artistica di Lisippo ricostruita su nuova base*, Rome, 1914; F. P. Johnson, *Lysippos*, Durham, N.C., 1927.

JEROME J. POLLITT

LYTENS, GIJSBRECHT, *see* LEYTENS, GIJSBRECHT.

M

MAAS, DIRK, *see* MAES, DIRK.

MAAS, GODFRIED, *see* MAES, GODFRIED.

MAASTRICHT CATHEDRAL. Dutch cathedral dedicated to St. Servatius and founded by St. Monulphus about 560. The building was reconstructed beginning in the 11th century in the Romanesque style, of which the choir and apses, completed in about 1225, are notable examples of the mature phase. A vast narthex, the most ancient part of the Cathedral, precedes the nave.

BIBLIOGRAPHY. E. O. M. van Nispen tot Sevenaer, *Uit de bouwgeschiedenis der Sint Servaaskerk te Maastricht*, Maastricht, 1933.

MABE, MANABU. Brazilian painter (1924–   ). Born in Kumamoto, Japan, Mabe was trained in Brazil, his home since the age of ten. He is considered one of Brazil's major informalist abstract painters. He won first prize at the São Paulo Bienal in 1959, the Fiat Prize at the Venice Biennale in 1960, and first prize at the Biennial of Young Artists in Paris in 1961.

BIBLIOGRAPHY. L. de Almeida Cunha, *Brasil* (Art in Latin America Today, vol. 1), Washington, D.C., 1960.

MABUSE, *see* GOSSAERT, JAN.

MacARDELL, JAMES. English engraver (b. Dublin, 1729; d. London, 1765). He was apprenticed to James Brooks after arriving in London in 1746. MacArdell is regarded as one of the most skilled mezzotinters and is known through his many portraits of well-known persons after eminent painters of his time. He also treated historical subjects after Van Dyck, Murillo, and Rembrandt.

BIBLIOGRAPHY. C. Davenport, *Mezzotints*, London, 1904.

McBEY, JAMES. Scottish-American engraver (b. Newburgh, Scotland, 1883; d. Tangier, Morocco, 1959). A bank employee and self-taught etcher, he produced his first plate in 1902. He visited Holland in 1910 and Spain in 1911. He then devoted his work to English scenery. During World War I he made sketches of the Western Front, and in 1917 was appointed Official Artist in Egypt, from which came the material for his war subjects and his Palestine sets. In 1926 and 1930 he published his Venetian sets and after that time etched only occasionally. After several visits to the United States, he became a citizen. His plates were executed like sketches; *Dawn: Camel Patrol Setting Out* was one of the most sought after.

BIBLIOGRAPHY. M. Hardie, *Etchings and Dry Points, from 1902 to 1924, by James McBey*, London, 1925.

MACCHIAIOLI. Group of Italian painters, working in Florence between 1850 and 1860, who were opposed to the current academic style. The movement remained active until about 1880. The name Macchiaioli derives from the use of spots (*macchie*) of color in their paintings. Their purpose, like that of the Barbizon school and the impressionists in France, was to return to nature in the open air and to render light and color in a direct manner, but their technique and analysis of color were more conservative than those of the French. Styles varied from an almost photographic realism to a more impressionistic manner in the work of the chief members of the group: Giovanni Fattori, Silvestro Lega, and Telemaco Signorini. *See* FATTORI, GIOVANNI.

BIBLIOGRAPHY. M. Giardelli, *I Macchiaioli e l'epoca loro*, Milan, 1958.

MACCIO, ROMULO. Argentine painter (1931–   ). Born in Buenos Aires, Rómulo Macció was apprenticed at fourteen in a publicity agency and later worked in graphic design and theatrical décor. He is self-taught as a painter. Macció has exhibited widely since 1956 (for example, at the Guggenheim International in New York in 1964). He won First International Prize at the Di Tella Institute, Buenos Aires, in 1963. He is a member of the New Figurative group.

BIBLIOGRAPHY. T. Grieder, "Argentina's New Figurative Art," *Art Journal*, XXIV, Fall, 1964.

MacCOLL, DUGALD SUTHERLAND. British painter, critic, and art gallery director (b. Glasgow, 1859; d. 1948). MacColl attended University College, London, and Lin-

Stanton Macdonald-Wright, *Embarkation*, **1962. Museum of Modern Art, New York (Gift of Mr and Mrs. Walter Nelson Pharr)**

Macchiaioli. Giovanni Fattori, *The Italian Battlefield after the Battle of Magenta*, detail. Gallery of Modern Art, Florence.

coln College, Oxford, where he won the Newdigate prize for poetry. He traveled extensively in Europe (1887–89) to acquire knowledge of great works of art. On his return he studied art under Frederick Brown. His work was exhibited at the New English Art Club and other galleries. He was art critic for the *Spectator* (1890–96), and then worked for the *Saturday Review*. He was active as critic, painter, and lecturer. In 1902 he published an authoritative book, *Nineteenth Century Art*, which rated the impressionists highly.

While editor of the *Architectural Review* (1901–05) MacColl attacked the handling of the Chantrey Bequest, stating that only works from the Royal Academy of Arts were bought and that many of these were mediocre. As a result the policy of the Chantrey Bequest administrators was broadened. In 1906 MacColl became keeper of the Tate Gallery, London, and instituted many reforms, buying more advanced pictures whenever he could. In 1911 he became keeper of the Wallace Collection, London, rehanging and recataloging the entire collection.

In the 1920s MacColl worked for the *Saturday Review* and later for the *Weekend Review*. He engaged in many controversies, writing books and articles constantly. In 1940 his collected *Poems* were published, and in 1945 his biography of Philip Wilson Steer won the James Tait Black Memorial prize. He was an honorary member of many societies. MacColl did much to reform art galleries and the arts in general and was influential in gaining acceptance for artists working in an advanced style. He was one of the founders of the Contemporary Art Society.

BIBLIOGRAPHY. D. S. MacColl, *Confessions of a Keeper*, London, 1931.

RICHARD L. ORMOND

McCULLOCH, ALAN McLEOD. Australian art critic, draftsman, painter, and writer (1907–   ). Born in Melbourne, he has traveled widely throughout the world and has developed an expressionistic painting style. He is art critic for the Melbourne *Herald* and has been a leader in many progressive activities to benefit Australian art.

MacDONALD, JAMES EDWARD HERVEY. Canadian painter (b. England, 1873; d. Toronto, 1932). He lived in Toronto from 1887 to his death. He studied art there and in London and worked as a graphic designer. From about 1907 he painted landscapes in Canada and the West Indies and was a Group of Seven member. MacDonald also published some poetry.

BIBLIOGRAPHY. E. R. Hunter, *J. E. H. MacDonald*, Toronto, 1940.

MACDONALD-WRIGHT, STANTON. American painter, writer, and teacher (1890–   ). He was born in Charlottesville, Va. In 1907 he went to France and studied in Paris at the Ecole des Beaux-Arts, the Académie Julian, and the Sorbonne. His early works show the influence of various painters, at first Rembrandt and Hals, then the landscape treatment of the Barbizon school, and, lastly, impressionism. He began to experiment with the theories of color and aesthetic expression of Helmholtz, Chevreul, and Rood, and, with the American painter Morgan Russell, founded the synchromist movement in 1912. Much of the rationale and technique of synchromism was derived from the orphism of Delaunay, although both Macdonald-Wright and Russell denied this origin and kept up a steady barrage of propaganda against their French rivals. *See* ORPHISM.

Synchromism, at first simply the application of new color theories to the traditional subjects of landscape, figure, and still life, evolved into a completely abstract style, using such basic shapes as the circle and the triangle. Macdonald-Wright's synchromist paintings were based on color used not, as by the impressionists, as a vehicle for the depiction of light but as a builder of form; the ultimate source for this was obviously Cézanne. With the help of elaborately constructed charts of the spatial and three-dimensional effects of color, Macdonald-Wright attempted to paint "pure," nonrepresentational, nonanecdotal compositions, organized solely according to internal aesthetic laws, which would affect the viewer without recourse to the forms of external reality in a manner analogous to that of music. The shifting planes and advancing and receding colors of the style can be seen in his *"Conception." Synchromy* (1915) and *"Oriental." Synchromy in Blue-Green* (1918; both New York, Whitney Museum of American Art).

Macdonald-Wright returned to representational painting about 1920 and afterward taught at the University of California at Los Angeles. He has also done realistic murals, such as the decorations for the Santa Monica, Calif., Public Library (1935).

BIBLIOGRAPHY. W. H. Wright, *Modern Painting*, New York, 1915; A. C. Ritchie, *Abstract Painting and Sculpture in America*, New York, 1951; S. Macdonald-Wright, *The Art of Stanton Macdonald-Wright, a Retrospective Exhibition . . .*, Washington, D.C., 1967.

JEROME VIOLA

MacDURNAN GOSPELS. Hiberno-Saxon illuminated manuscript, in the Library of Lambeth Palace, London.

MACEDONIAN STYLE. Term characterizing works produced during the mid-Byzantine period (9th–11th cent.). Great originality and inventiveness are displayed in architecture, as in Basil I's Nea, Constantinople. In painting, the works are marked by a renewed consciousness of classical motifs, as in the Paris Psalter (Paris, National Library). *See* NEA, CONSTANTINOPLE.

McEVOY, AMBROSE. English painter (b. Crudwell, Wiltshire, 1878; d. London, 1927). McEvoy studied at the Slade School. His early interior scenes are close-toned Whistlerian depictions of mood, and landscapes of the same period are similar in their wispy representations of atmosphere. *The Earring* (1911; London, National Gallery) shows the delicacy of subject and treatment to be found in all his subsequent figure paintings and in his many popular portraits, such as *Lieut. R. D. Sanford, R.N., V.C.* (1918; London, Imperial War Museum). For these portraits he used a loose, fluid brushstroke and bright, but carefully controlled, color.

BIBLIOGRAPHY. A. McEvoy, *The Work of Ambrose McEvoy*, London, 1923; R. M. Y. Gleadowe, *Ambrose McEvoy*, London, 1924.

McFARLAND, DONALD. American industrial designer (1920–). McFarland was born in Valley City, N. Dak. As president of the American Society of Industrial Designers (1958–59) he consolidated the reputation of his profession and won new prestige for industrial designers who work as staff members of major corporations rather than as independents. As manager of industrial design for General Electric's Radio Receiver Division, he influenced the appearance of some of the most widely produced consumer goods in America today. He is now president of the Long Beach, Calif., branch of Latham, Tyler, Jensen, Inc.

McFEE, HENRY LEE. American painter (b. St. Louis, Mo., 1886; d. Claremont, Calif., 1953). He studied in St. Louis and Pittsburgh and with Birge Harrison in Woodstock, N.Y. McFee was first interested in the rendering of volumes in space by the Florentine Renaissance painters. From about 1919 to 1924 he painted still lifes and landscapes under the influence of cubism and Cézanne. These compositions were large-planed with unusual attention paid to surface texture. His later paintings, mostly still lifes and figures, show the same concern for formal structure in a more realistic style.

BIBLIOGRAPHY. V. Barker, *Henry McFee* (American Artists Series), New York, 1931.

McGUINESS, NORA. Irish painter, theatrical designer, and illustrator (1905–). Nora McGuiness was born in Londonderry and studied at the Dublin College of Art, the Chelsea Polytechnic, and with André Lhote in Paris. She designed costumes and masks for the Abbey Theater, including masks for Yeats's *The Jealousy of Emir*. Her book illustrations, for example, those for Sterne's *Sentimental Journey* and Coleridge's *Christabel*, are influenced by the drawings of Aubrey Beardsley. Her paintings are richly colored and intimate treatments of scenes of Dublin life, sometimes atmospheric, with a special stress on old buildings. She exhibited at the 1950 Venice Biennale.

MACHADO DE CASTRO, JOAQUIM (Mathedo de Castro). Portuguese sculptor (b. Coimbra, 1731; d. Lisbon, 1822). He was the leading pupil of Alessandro Giusti, who had come from Rome in 1751 to found Portugal's first school of sculpture. Machado de Castro was Giusti's assistant from 1756 to 1770, and his style shows the baroque energy of that master combined with the use of stylish attitudes derived from his earlier master, Almeida. Machado de Castro's masterpiece is the equestrian statue of Joseph I

(1772) in Lisbon, the monumental composition of which is executed with an attention to minute and delicate detail. The many sketches in clay for this work are among his best works, and show his insistence on modeling directly from life. He founded the Casa da Escultura das Obras Publicas in Lisbon, was in charge of all royal sculptures, and helped to direct the Academy for the Drawing of the Nude.

BIBLIOGRAPHY. G. Kubler and M. Soria, *Art and Architecture in Spain and Portugal and Their American Dominions, 1500–1800*, Baltimore, 1959.

MACHIAVELLI, ZANOBI. Italian painter of the Florentine school (1418–79). He was a pupil and an assistant of Benozzo Gozzoli, though his style was mainly formed through the influence of Fra Filippo Lippi and Pesellino. Machiavelli is first recorded in 1464, when the Badia in Fiesole owed him payments for three paintings (now lost). In 1470 he is documented in Florence and in 1475/76 in Pisa. He signed pictures that are now in the former State Museums in Berlin (a *St. James* of 1473), the Museum of Fine Arts in Dijon (a *Coronation of the Virgin*, also of 1473), the National Gallery of Ireland in Dublin, and the National Museum of St. Matthew in Pisa (both *Sacre Conversazioni*). Attributed works are in the National Gallery in London, the Yale University Art Gallery in New Haven, Conn., and the Walters Art Gallery in Baltimore, Md. Machiavelli's style is an elaboration of the formulations of the major artists of the previous generation and is typical, in this regard, of the minor masters of Florence in the third quarter of the 15th century.

BIBLIOGRAPHY. M. Salmi, "Zanobi Machiavelli e il 'Compagno di Pesellino,'" *Rivista d'arte*, IX, 1916–18; B. Berenson, "Zanobi Macchiavelli," *The Burlington Magazine*, XLII, December, 1950; B. Berenson, *Essays in Appreciation*, New York, 1958.

MACHICOLATION (Machicoulis). Overhanging parapet with openings in the soffit through which, in medieval

Zanobi Machiavelli, *Coronation of the Virgin*, 1473. Museum of Fine Arts, Dijon.

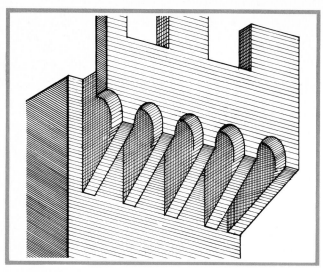

Machicolation. A defensive feature of medieval fortresses.

fortresses, stones, hot pitch, and missiles were dropped on attackers below.

MACHU PICCHU. Spectacular Inca city discovered by Hiram Bingham in 1911, located on a narrow ridge in the Andes northwest of Cuzco, Peru. It was surrounded on three sides by the Urubamba River 2,000 feet below, shielded on the remaining side by walls and check points on the only Inca highway entrance, and further guarded by lookouts on Huayna Picchu Mountain. It long remained safe from invaders. The precision of stonework and the efficiency of water use and of agricultural terraces indicate intensive occupancy. Excavation of numerous female skeletons has contributed to the theory that this was a sacred city with a cult of virgin priestesses. Machu Picchu may have been an outpost on the one practical western entrance

Machu Picchu. Ruins of the Inca city on a narrow ridge in the Andes.

to the tropical richness of the upper Amazon, into which the Urubamba drained.

BIBLIOGRAPHY. H. Bingham, . . . *Machu Picchu, A Citadel of the Incas*, New Haven, 1930; W. C. Bennett, *Ancient Arts of the Andes*, New York, 1954; J. A. Mason, *The Ancient Civilizations of Peru*, Harmondsworth, 1957.

McINTIRE, SAMUEL. American builder and carver (b. Salem, Mass., 1757; d. 1811). McIntire's work includes a number of important Salem buildings in which he adapted Palladian design to the neoclassic taste. He made sofas, chairs, tables, and chests with a basket of fruit or flowers as his signature. McIntire's efforts in sculpture are also significant.

BIBLIOGRAPHY. S. F. Kimball, *Mr. Samuel McIntire*, Portland, Me., 1940.

MacIVER, LOREN. American painter (1909–). Born in New York City, she attended the Art Students League at the age of ten and continued her studies privately. From 1936 to 1939 she worked with the Federal Art Project. She had her first one-man show in 1939, and many of her works are in public and private collections. Summers at Cape Cod and winters at Key West have provided some subjects for her art, but most of her paintings are of simple aspects of city life, stressing the poetic content of a prosaic group of details, such as children's chalk marks for hopscotch or a streaming window, wet with rain. She is a refined colorist, introspective and gently symbolic in the definition of an imaginative, idyllic world half seen, half remembered. An occasional portraitist, she is at her best in images of children and circus clowns, whose attitudes of whimsy and pathos are close to her heart.

BIBLIOGRAPHY. J. T. Soby, *Contemporary Painters*, 2d ed., New York, 1948; F. S. Wight, *American Painting in Our Century*, New York, 1949; J. I. H. Baur, *Loren MacIver* [and] I. Rice Pereira, New York, 1953.

MACKE, AUGUST. German expressionist painter (b. Meschede, Sauerland, 1887; d. France, 1914). He studied at the Düsseldorf Academy in 1904 and afterward traveled widely in France, Italy, and England. In 1911 he was associated with the Neue Künstlervereinigung in Munich and later, as a founder-member, with the Blaue Reiter. Paul Klee and Macke made a trip to Tunisia in April, 1914.

Macke synthesized cubist structure with the orphist color of Delaunay. His art is indebted to Seurat and often has futurist characteristics. His featureless figures with their tubelike limbs appear somber, muffled, and restricted, whether they exist as women looking in shop windows or as nudes in a jungle. His beautiful water colors of Tunisia, composed of interlocking prisms of radiant color, influenced Klee.

BIBLIOGRAPHY. G. Vriesen, *August Macke*, 2d ed., Stuttgart, 1957.

MACKE, HELMUT. German painter (b. Krefeld, 1891; d. Lake Constance, Hemmenhofen, 1936). A cousin of the painter August Macke, he studied in Krefeld from 1906 to 1908 with Thorn-Prikker. From 1910 to 1911 Macke was associated with the Blaue Reiter in Munich. His expressionist paintings were influenced by contemporary French art, particularly the work of Chagall and Matisse.

MACKENSEN, FRITZ. German painter, sculptor, and etcher (b. Greene, 1866; d. Bremen, 1953). He studied at

August Macke, *Portrait of Franz Marc*. Former State Museums (National Gallery), Berlin.

Charles Rennie Mackintosh, Glasgow School of Art, 1897–99. The architect's masterpiece.

the Düsseldorf Academy and in Munich and Karlsruhe. In 1889 he and Otto Modersohn founded the Worpswede art colony near Bremen. Mackensen painted farmers, laborers, and fishermen with a realism influenced by Courbet but with far greater sentimentality. His Worpswede paintings were mostly dark, with a worked and textured surface. His later paintings tightened somewhat in style, expecially in the treatment of figures, although he retained a looseness in landscapes.

BIBLIOGRAPHY. R. M. Rilke, *Worpswede...* (Künstler-Monographien, 64), 2d ed., Bielefeld, Germany, 1905; H. Wohltman, *Worpswede...*, Stade, Germany, 1955.

McKENSIE, VOORHEES, AND GMELIN, *see* NEW YORK TELEPHONE COMPANY BUILDING, NEW YORK.

McKIM, CHARLES FOLLEN, *see* MCKIM, MEAD AND WHITE.

McKIM, MEAD AND WHITE. American architectural firm of Charles Follen McKim (1847–1909), William Rutherford Mead (1846–1928), and Stanford White (1853–1906). Perhaps the most popular firm of its period, it was formed in 1879 and terminated by White's death in 1906. Maintaining high standards despite the amount of work it handled, the firm led in the academic reaction after 1880 with such works as the Villard Houses, New York City (1883–85), in Italian High Renaissance dress; the classically styled Pennsylvania Station (1906–10; destroyed) and Morgan Library (1905–06), both in New York City; but most

particularly in its influence on the designs for the Chicago World's Columbian Exposition of 1893. McKim also designed the Agricultural Building and the New York State Building for the Exposition, introducing eastern Beaux-Arts classicism to the Middle West. Equally adept in the programmatic colonial revival style, which it helped initiate with the Taylor House in Newport, R.I. (1885–86), the firm also designed more informal structures in that short-lived vogue, the Shingle style, including the Bell House (1881–82) and Low House (1887), both in Newport, R.I.

See also CHICAGO; PENNSYLVANIA STATION, NEW YORK; WHITE, STANFORD.

BIBLIOGRAPHY. McKim, Mead & White, *A Monograph of the Work of McKim, Mead & White, 1879–1915*, 4 vols., New York, 1914–15.

MATTHEW E. BAIGELL

MACKINTOSH, CHARLES RENNIE. Scottish architect (1868–1928). His first important work, the Cranston tearoom, Buchanan Street, Glasgow (1897–98; destroyed), influenced the style of the Viennese Sezession. His masterpiece is the Glasgow School of Art (1897–99). Its library wing (1907–08) is a synthesis of traditional Scottish forms with a functional expressionism, and links his style directly with the international modern movement. In the Cranston tearoom, Sauchiehall Street, Glasgow (1904, destroyed), Mackintosh was further involved in the spatial conceptions of his time and has been shown to be one of the few forerunners of Le Corbusier.

As an originator, Mackintosh was a supreme but lone

exponent in the Glasgow renaissance. He represented the final link with the European modern movement before the insipid revival of the Georgian idiom.

BIBLIOGRAPHY. T. Howarth, *Charles Rennie Mackintosh and the Modern Movement*, London, 1952.

MACLISE, DANIEL. Irish painter (b. Cork, 1811; d. 1870). He studied in Cork before going to London to attend the Royal Academy schools, where he was a brilliant pupil. He first made a name for himself in a series of eighty-four caricatures of literary figures for *Fraser's Magazine*. Always at home in the literary world, he had closer connections there than with his fellow artists. Literary themes provided him with the subject matter for his paintings, whose dramatic qualities and clear colors gave them a popular appeal. Public rather than private commissions brought out the really grand style of Maclise. His greatest works were the mural paintings for the rebuilt House of Commons—battle scenes of Wellington, Blücher, and Nelson, admirably suited to the artist's dramatic invention. Maclise was made a Royal Academician in 1840.

BIBLIOGRAPHY. W. J. O'Driscoll, *A Memoir of Daniel Maclise*, London, 1871.

MacMONNIES, FREDERICK WILLIAM. American sculptor (1863–1937). He studied with Saint-Gaudens and in Paris with Falguière and Mercié. Among MacMonnies's best-known works are *Nathan Hale* (1889; New York, City Hall Park), *Battle Memorial* (Princeton, N.J.), and *Pan of Rohallion* (Buffalo, Fine Arts Academy). His *Columbian Fountain*, designed especially for the Chicago World's Columbian Exposition of 1893, likewise followed the pictorial character of the so-called Second Empire style so popular in France in the late 19th century. MacMonnies also designed coins and medals. His contribution was marked by prodigious technical facility and the charm of diffused surface treatment; but none of his public monuments actually asserts independence of vision, and many are simply lacking in depth.

BIBLIOGRAPHY. W. H. Gerdts, *A Survey of American Sculpture*, Newark, N.J., 1962.

MacNEIL, HERMON A. American sculptor (1866–1947). MacNeil was born in Chelsea, Mass. He was a member of the National Sculpture Society and (from 1906) of the National Academy of Design and was an instructor at the Art Institute of Chicago. His murals were shown at international expositions in Chicago, Paris, St. Louis, and Buffalo. Equestrian groups were important in MacNeil's work, as were American Indian themes in general. The *McKinley Memorial* (Columbus, Ohio) and *General Washington* (New York) are characteristic of his eclectic style, which combines various late-19th-century European and European-derived American kinds of realism.

MACRINO D'ALBA (Gian Giacomo d'Alladio). Italian painter of Piedmont (1494–1508). He is known from few documents but numerous signed works, all of which are altarpieces, except for one portrait. While other Piedmontese painters of his time turned to northern Gothic forms, he looked to Italy; his works have a bland symmetry suggesting a least common denominator of late-15th-century forms. His art shows a preference for the Ferrarese and Umbrian schools in the age of Costa, Francia, and Il Pinturicchio.

BIBLIOGRAPHY. Turin, Mostra d'arte a Palazzo Carignano, 2d 1939, *Gotico e rinascimento in Piemonte* (catalog), Turin, 1939.

McSORLEY'S BAR. Oil painting by Sloan, in the Institute of Arts, Detroit. See SLOAN, JOHN.

McTAGGART, WILLIAM. Scottish painter (b. Aros, 1835; d. Broomieknowe, 1910). He studied at the Trustees' Academy in Edinburgh. McTaggart began with detailed, somewhat sentimental figure paintings, which often included children, for example, *Dora* (1869; Edinburgh, Royal Scottish Academy). By the middle 1870s, when his main purpose became the rendering of atmospheric effects, he had independently evolved an impressionistic technique, derived in part from Turner, using broken color and depicting swirling natural forces. He still used anecdotal subjects, but his best paintings, such as *The Storm* (1883; Kirkcaldy,

Villa Madama, Rome. Semicircular courtyard façade, designed by Raphael.

La Madeleine, Paris. Façade by Pierre Vignon.

Museum and Art Gallery), concentrated on the depiction of water and wind.

BIBLIOGRAPHY. J. L. Caw, *William McTaggart...*, Glasgow, 1917.

McWILLIAM, F. E. British sculptor (1909–   ). Born in Northern Ireland, he studied at the Slade School, London, and in Paris. He has had international exhibitions in Paris, London, Holland, and Antwerp. McWilliam's style is abstract, with some reference to the figure. He lives in London and in Ireland.

MADAMA, PALAZZO, TURIN, *see* TURIN: MUSEUMS (MUNICIPAL MUSEUM OF ANCIENT ART).

MADAMA, VILLA, ROME. Italian villa on Monte Mario, Rome. Though never completed, the Villa Madama remains a monument to Raphael's audacity as an architect. On terraces cut into the slope of Monte Mario a series of walled gardens on a central axis was created, at the top of which is a building with apsed and niched rooms about a circular courtyard. The semicircular façade with pilasters that was to form a part of the enclosure of the courtyard recalls Bramante at his most classical. It has been called a bold attempt to emulate the grandeur of Roman baths.

The monumental loggia, which was decorated in 1520 by Giulio Romano and Giovanni da Udine with some aid from Baldassare Peruzzi, also reflects ancient Roman models, such as the interiors of Nero's Golden House, as they were adapted for the decorative style of the Loggie of the Vatican under Raphael's direction.

BIBLIOGRAPHY. T. Hofmann, *Raffael in seiner Bedeutung als Architekt*, Zittau, 1908–11.

MADAME CHARPENTIER AND HER CHILDREN. Oil painting by Renoir, in the Metropolitan Museum of Art, New York. *See* RENOIR, PIERRE-AUGUSTE.

MADAME RECAMIER. Oil painting by David, in the Louvre Museum, Paris. *See* DAVID, JACQUES-LOUIS.

MADELEINE, GROTTE DE LA. Type site of the Magdalenian culture, located near Les Eyzies in the Department of the Dordogne, southwestern France. This grotto, really a rock shelter, has no mural art. It is important only for the Magdalenian period, and its habitation layers have yielded many fine examples of engraved and carved spear throwers and figures of animals. It is one of the richest of the Upper Paleolithic stations for portable art.

MADELEINE, LA (Church of Ste-Marie-Madeleine), PARIS. French church. Ange-Jacques Gabriel's concept of the Place de la Concorde demanded some architectural feature at the end of the Rue Royale. In 1764 Contant d'Ivry designed and began a church on a Latin-cross plan, but three years later Couture removed what little had been built to make way for his own design. In 1806 Napoleon commanded Pierre Vignon to transform the incomplete church into a *temple de la Gloire*, dedicated to the victories of the French Army. Still incomplete in 1814, the peripteral Corinthian temple was transformed by Vignon into a church, and it was opened as such in 1842. Rude,

Carlo Maderno, façade of S. Susanna, Rome, 1597–1603.

Barye, and others provided sculptural decorations and monuments.

BIBLIOGRAPHY. M. Dumolin and G. Outardel, *Les Eglises de France*, vol. 5: *Paris et la Seine*, Paris, 1936.

MADER-I-SHAH MADRASA, ISFAHAN. Safavid madrasa, or religious school, situated on the Chahar Bagh avenue in Isfahan. It was named after a "mother of the Shah" of Iran, who ordered its construction in 1706. The madrasa displays the familiar Safavid mosque plan, with a brilliant, faïence-clad dome rising high above the structure.

BIBLIOGRAPHY. A. U. Pope, ed., *A Survey of Persian Art*, vol. 2, New York, 1939.

MADERNO, CARLO. Italian architect (b. Capolago, 1556; d. Rome, 1629). He began his career in association with his relatives Domenico and Giovanni Fontana. Maderno's design for the façade (1597–1603) of S. Susanna, Rome, confirmed his position as the great architect of his generation and the early baroque. Under the Borghese pope, Paul V, he built the controversial nave and façade of St. Peter's, Rome. The novel use of columnar elements in his façades serves to build to a central climax. The Mattei di Giove Palace (1598–1611) shows Maderno's traditional ties but incorporates a novel stairway. He was active in villa design (Aldobrandini and Torlonia Villas, Frascati) and also completed many buildings begun by others, including S. Giovanni dei Fiorentini and S. Andrea della Valle. For S. Andrea he provided a façade (now largely the work of Carlo Rainaldi) and a dome that is based on, and second in size only to, that of St. Peter. He was the uncle and teacher of Francesco Borromini. *See* St. Peter's (New), Rome.

BIBLIOGRAPHY. N. Caflisch, *Carlo Maderno*, Munich, 1934.

MADERNO, STEFANO. Italian sculptor (b. Bissone, 1576; d. 1636). He was a member of the Fontana-Maderno-Castello clan, active in Rome. The high point of his otherwise mediocre career is the recumbent statue of the martyred *St. Cecilia* (1600; Rome, S. Cecilia in Trastevere), whose simple, moving qualities seem to inaugurate the baroque age.

BIBLIOGRAPHY. R. Wittkower, *Art and Architecture in Italy, 1600–1750*, Baltimore, 1958.

MADINAT AZ-ZAHRA, *see* Umayyad Architecture (Spain).

MADONNA. Art history has inherited the general use of the word Madonna (old Italian for "My Lady") to mean Mother of God, that is, the representation of Mary with the infant Christ. The Madonna is found as early as the 2d century in Early Christian art (Maria-Orans in catacomb painting) and, beginning in the 6th century, became a very popular and multifarious image in Byzantine art. *See* Blacherniotissa Madonna; Eleousa Madonna; Hodegetria Madonna.

Western medieval art adopted the Madonna representation from Byzantium. In Romanesque art the enthroned Madonna is the principal type; in the Gothic period it is the standing Madonna with the Child on her arm; and in the late Middle Ages other types, such as the Madonna in the Rose Arbor and the *Schutzmantelmadonna*, were added.

MADONNA DEL GRANDUCA. Oil painting by Raphael, in the Pitti Palace, Florence. *See* Raphael.

MADONNA DI FOLIGNO. Oil painting by Raphael, in the Vatican Museums, Rome. *See* Raphael.

MADONNA OF CHANCELLOR ROLIN. Tempera and oil painting by Jan Van Eyck, in the Louvre Museum, Paris. *See* Van Eyck, Jan.

MADONNA OF THE CHAIR. Oil painting by Raphael, in the Pitti Palace, Florence. *See* Raphael.

MADONNA OF THE CHERRIES. Oil painting by Titian, in the Museum of Art History, Vienna. *See* Titian.

MADONNA OF THE HARPIES. Oil painting by Andrea del Sarto, in the Uffizi Gallery, Florence. *See* Sarto, Andrea del.

MADONNA OF THE PESARO FAMILY. Oil painting by Titian, in S. Maria dei Frari, Venice. *See* Titian.

MADONNA OF THE ROCKS. Oil painting by Leonardo, in the Louvre Museum, Paris; second version in the National Gallery, London. *See* Leonardo da Vinci.

MADONNA OF VLADIMIR. Tempera panel by an unknown Russian artist, in the Historical Museum, Moscow.

MADONNA WITH THE LONG NECK. Oil painting by Parmigianino, in the Pitti Palace, Florence. *See* Parmigianino.

MADRASA (Medrese). Islamic college of theology, often built as an adjunct to an important mosque. It provides lecture halls, a library, and sleeping quarters. Each madrasa usually consists of an open quadrangle bordered by vaulted cloisters. These are attached to two-story buildings that have flat, beamed roofs, supported by columns. Many madrasas were established from the 11th through the 13th century.

MADRAZO Y AGUDO, JOSE DE. Spanish painter (b. Santander, 1781; d. Madrid, 1859). He studied briefly in Madrid and then in Paris under David, whose neoclassic style he adopted. In Rome Madrazo painted classical themes and became a member of the Academy of St. Luke. After painting the portraits of King Charles IV and María Luisa of Spain on their visit to Rome, he was made Painter to the Chamber in 1816. He returned to Spain in 1818, and became director of the Academy of S. Fernando in Madrid, where he introduced classical teaching methods, and created several large allegorical paintings as well as many portraits. With his appointment as director of the Prado in 1838, the Madrazo family became entrenched for many years in the official control of Spanish art.

See also Madrazo y Kuntz, Federico de.

MADRAZO Y KUNTZ, FEDERICO DE. Spanish painter (b. Rome, 1815; d. Madrid, 1894). He was the son of José de Madrazo y Agudo. Federico worked in Paris under Ingres, whose portrait, now at the Hispanic Society of America in New York, he painted in 1833. After he had worked for King Louis Philippe of France, Queen Isabella II of Spain made him Painter to the Chamber. Following in his father's footsteps, Federico was director of the Academy of S. Fernando in Madrid several times, as well as director of the Prado. In Spain he produced mostly stiff, aristocratic portraits. Portraits of himself and his family are looser, more casual, and less dependent on the adaptation of Ingres's style.

BIBLIOGRAPHY. M. Madrazo, *Federico de Madrazo*, Madrid, 1921.

MADRID. Capital of Spain, situated at the foot of the Guadarrama mountains on the high plateau of Castile. The recorded history of the city begins in the 10th century, when it was called Magerit. It was liberated from the Moors by Alfonso VI in 1083 and was accorded statutory rights (*fueros*). It was the site of the coronation of Henry III as king of Castile in 1390. During the 15th century its Alcázar was used as a residence and fortified by his successors. In 1561 Philip II chose Madrid as the capital of Spain, and it developed in accordance with its importance as a capital city. The period of its greatest architectural expansion was the late 19th and early 20th centuries, although many of the new buildings were revivalistic rather than forward-looking.

The early history of Madrid has left little more than

the 14th-century Mudejar tower of the church of San Pedro and the Plateresque Capilla del Obispo (1520), the oldest church in the city. Under the patronage of Philip III (r. 1598–1621) Madrid became a center of an architectural tradition that continued until the end of the 18th century. Its first important program was the Plaza Mayor, a rectangular space surrounded on four sides by arcaded town-houses drawn into a common façade. It was begun in 1619 by Gómez de Mora as an arena for festivals, tournaments, and bullfights. One of the best 17th-century examples of Madrid architecture is the Ayuntamiento (Town Hall) in the Plaza de la Villa. The exterior of the Jesuit church of San Isidro el Real (1626–61) belongs to the same tradition of severe, planimetric designs, but it has an elaborate, curvilinear baroque interior. An opulent and ornamental Baroque style also occurs in the portal of the 18th-century Municipal Museum (the former Hospice).

Madrid's major 18th-century buildings are designed according to the more strict, official classic taste. The tone is set by the Royal Palace (completed 1764), designed by G. B. Sacchetti and incorporating certain elements of a much more elaborate plan commissioned from Filippo Juvara in 1735. (Drawings for part of the work, once ascribed to Ventura Rodríguez, are now believed to have been misattributed.) It occupies the site of the ancient Alcázar, former residence of the kings of Castile. The later 18th century in Madrid is represented by the colossal neoclassic church of San Francisco Grande (built between 1776 and 1785 on plans by Cabezas and Sabatini), one of the largest domed structures in Europe, and the Prado, begun as a Natural Science Museum in 1785 for Charles III by Juan de Villanueva. The chapel of San Antonio de la Florida (1792–98) is undistinguished architecturally but contains the superlative frescoes by Goya on the interior of its cupola.

The neoclassic tradition was continued in the 19th century, along with a revival of Mudejar and Renaissance styles. Modern conceptions of functionalism appeared in the 20th century with the University City and several skyscrapers, including the Telephone Exchange.

See also MADRID: MUSEUMS; SAN FERNANDO, ACADEMY OF.

BIBLIOGRAPHY. P. Guinard, *Madrid*, Paris, 1935.

HELLMUT WOHL

MADRID: MUSEUMS. Important public art collections in Madrid, Spain, are located in the museums listed below.

Lazaro Galdiano Museum. Collection presented to the state in 1949 by Lázaro Galdiano. The museum displays various exhibits of sculpture, gold- and silverwork, glass, enamels, and paintings (works by Claudio Coello, Berruguete, Tiepolo, and Goya).

BIBLIOGRAPHY. J. Camón Aznar, *Guía abreviada del Museo Lázaro Galdiano*, Madrid, 1951.

National Archaeological Museum. Contains archaeological material from prehistory to the end of the Middle Ages collected from all parts of Spain. The Iberian sculptures present a remarkable fusion of Greek naturalistic motifs with an indigenous sense of abstract design. A group of pictorial mosaics highlights the Roman section. The Visigothic crowns from the Guarrazar Treasure are among the finest extant examples of medieval jewelry. Moorish art is represented by richly carved doorways and ceilings, as well as by many objects of the minor arts. The mu-

seum's archaeological collections proper are supplemented by baroque furnishings from the palaces of the Spanish kings.

BIBLIOGRAPHY. J. M. de Navascués, introd., *Guía del Museo Arqueológico Nacional*, Madrid, 1965.

Prado Museum. One of the world's greatest art museums, preeminent in Spanish paintings and unsurpassed in those of the Flemish and Venetian schools. Crowning its collection of Spanish works from all periods are virtually all of Velázquez's most important canvases and Goya's incomparable late frescoes, as well as many of his drawings and major easel paintings. The Prado is rich in paintings by Hieronymus Bosch, Patinir, and Titian. It displays masterpieces by Tintoretto, Veronese, Rubens, and Van Dyck in extraordinary numbers as well as paintings of the highest quality by the Master of Flémalle, Rogier van der Weyden, Pieter Brueghel the Elder, Raphael, Mantegna, Dürer, and Cranach. The works of El Greco, recently reinstalled, now compose the most complete representation of this master.

The museum is housed in an imposing neoclassic building designed by Juan de Villanueva. Construction was begun in 1785, and it became the home of the Royal Museum of Art, which was established by Ferdinand VII and opened to the public in 1819. The Royal Art Gallery became the property of the nation in 1868.

Spanish monarchs had begun to acquire works of art before the middle of the 15th century, and the royal collections provided the bulk of the Prado's collections. Charles V bought works by Memling, Bosch, and Jacopo Bassano as well as many by Titian, his favored portraitist. His son Philip II was also a connoisseur and added a number of Titians and other Venetian paintings. Velázquez, court painter to Philip IV, acquired Italian works for the Escorial, most of which later became part of the Prado collections. The Bourbons added numerous fine paintings by Italian and French 17th- and 18th-century masters. Among important later accessions were the Fernández-Durán bequest (1930), which included more than 3,000 drawings, and the fourteen "black works" of Goya, frescoes he had painted in his seventy-sixth year to decorate the walls of his country villa.

Medals from the collection of Pablo Bosch, furniture, tapestries, and the jewelry collection known as the "Dauphin's Treasure" are other noteworthy exhibits in the Prado. The museum's most famous piece of sculpture is the Greco-Iberian *Lady of Elche*.

BIBLIOGRAPHY. E. Harris, *The Prado*, New York, 1940; Museo del Prado, *Catálogo de los cuadros*, Madrid, 1949; F. J. Sánchez Cantón, *The Prado*, New York, 1959.

MADLYN KAHR

Royal Academy Museum of Fine Arts of San Fernando. Collection of paintings, sculpture, and drawings. Most of the great masters of Spanish painting, and many of the minor masters, are represented, including Claudio Coello, Ribera, Murillo, Velázquez, Tristán, Alonso Cano, Ricci, and Carreño. Of particular importance are works by Zurbarán and Goya, including the latter's *Self-Portrait at 69*, *Village Bullfight*, *Scenes of the Inquisition*, and *Procession of Flagellants*. Foreign artists include Rubens, Tiepolo, Maratta, Magnasco, Fragonard, and Mengs.

Royal Palace. Erected between 1738 and 1764, the palace was the chief seat of the Spanish kings until the abdication of Alfonso XIII in 1931. The interior decoration of the palace is notable for the splendid ceiling paintings (especially Tiepolo's vast *Glory of the Spanish Monarchy* in the throne room) and for the collection of more than 2,500 tapestries, mostly Flemish and Spanish. A wing of the palace is devoted to the Armería, which contains a collection of arms and armor begun by Charles V. The Carriage Museum occupies a separate building in the adjacent Campo del Moro Park.

BIBLIOGRAPHY. F. Niño Mas, *Illustrated Guide to the Royal Palace of Madrid*, 2d rev. ed., Madrid, 1952.

MADURA (Madurai). City in southern Madras State, India. Originally the capital of the Pāṇḍyas, it was taken over by the Chola kings in the middle of the 10th century A.D. Under the Cholas many important bronze statues and statuettes were produced. In the 14th century much of Madura was destroyed by the invading Muslims; the buildings now extant date largely from after 1565 and were produced under the princes of the Nāyyak dynasty, who established their capital here. The palace of King Tirumala (r. 1623–59) is one of the finest adaptations of the Hindu arch to European structural uses.

The outstanding building at Madura, which represents the final chapter of southern Indian architecture, is the Great Temple (17th–18th cent.), dedicated to Śiva and to his consort under her south Indian name of Mīnākshī (the Fish-eyed One). Owing to the enlargement of the Hindu ritual, the sanctuary is surrounded by a large courtyard to accommodate the great crowds who witnessed holy processions. The walls surrounding the temple complex are surmounted by huge rectangular towers (gopuras), which constitute the most imposing feature of the style.

BIBLIOGRAPHY. H. R. Zimmer, *The Art of Indian Asia*, 2 vols., New York, 1955; P. Brown, *Indian Architecture*, 4th ed., 2 vols., Bombay, 1959.

JANET S. R. HILL

MAECK, PHILIPPE. Belgian-Brazilian painter (1927–). Influenced by cubism and by Paul Klee, Maeck has used increasingly brilliant and typically tropical colors over his abstract patterns since moving to Brazil.

MAELLA, MARIANO SALVADOR DE. Spanish painter (b. Valencia, 1739; d. Madrid, 1819). Maella received his training at the Academy of S. Fernando in Madrid and the Academy of St. Luke in Rome. As a court artist he progressed to the post of director of the S. Fernando Academy in 1795. He produced ceiling frescoes for the palaces at Madrid and Aranjuez, the Cathedral of Toledo, and other places in the prevalent late baroque style, as well as many court portraits, which are generally more admired.

MAENADS. Legendary Asian women who, with bands of reveling satyrs and Seilenoi, formed the train of Dionysos, or Bacchus, god of wine. They are sometimes called Bacchantes. In actuality, they were participants in the orgiastic and even murderous rites of the Dionysiac cult. Classical reliefs, perhaps following a prototype of Kallimachos, represent them as diaphanously robed maidens, leaning upon the thyrsus, a cone-tipped staff twined with ivy.

BIBLIOGRAPHY. G. M. A. Richter, *A Handbook of Greek Art*, London, 1959.

Nicolaes Maes, *Card Players*. National Gallery, London.

MAES (Maesse; Maessen), BARENT, *see* FABRITIUS, BARENT.

MAES (Maas), DIRK. Dutch painter of animals, especially horses, and graphic artist (b. Haarlem, 1659; d. there, 1717). He received his training with Hendrik Mommers and Claes Berchem at Haarlem and was a cousin of the Haarlem painter Jan Maes. In 1678 Dirk Maes was a member of the Haarlem painters' guild, and in 1697 was recorded as a member of the artists' organization at The Hague. He worked for Willem III, whom he followed to England about 1700. Maes was a friend of Johan van Huchtenburgh, whose style he emulated in his paintings of horse battles, riding schools, and horse markets (many in Haarlem, Frans Hals Museum).

BIBLIOGRAPHY. W. Martin, *De Hollandsche schilderkunst in de zeventiende eeuw*, 2d ed., 2 vols., Amsterdam, 1942.

MAES (Maas), GODFRIED. Flemish painter (1649–1700). Born in Antwerp, he was a disciple of Pieter van Lint, and a painter of religious subjects and of portraits. Maes became a master in 1672. He belonged to the group of late successors of Rubens, whom he interprets with a pronounced Italian accent.

BIBLIOGRAPHY. F. J. van den Branden, *Geschiedenis der Antwerpsche Schilderschool*, Antwerp, 1883.

MAES, NICOLAES. Dutch painter of genre, history, and portraits (b. Dordrecht, 1634; d. Amsterdam, 1693). He first studied drawing with a mediocre master at Dordrecht. About 1650 he went to Amsterdam and studied painting with Rembrandt. Maes was back in Dordrecht by 1654 and remained there until 1673, when he established permanent residence in Amsterdam. He seems to have made a trip to Antwerp to see the work of Rubens, Van Dyck, and others, and is said to have met Jacob Jordaens. Various dates in the 1660s have been suggested for this journey. This would seem correct in the light of Maes's change of style toward a more Flemish, courtly manner of portrait painting. However, it is difficult to determine whether his change of style is the result of his journey or the reason for it.

Of the few works executed by Maes before he returned to Dordrecht about 1654, the most interesting is the large *Christ Blessing Children* (London, National Gallery), a painting that shows the impact of Rembrandt's style. Rembrandt's influence can still be seen in *Young Girl Leaning on a Window Sill* (Amsterdam, Rijksmuseum), a painting that must date from about the same time as the London picture. By 1655 Maes seems to have been working in an individual manner with such genre interiors as *Interior with a Sleeping Maid and Her Mistress: "The Idle Servant"* (1655; London, National Gallery). This picture and others that are related to it have an uncertain relationship to the works of such artists as Pieter de Hoogh and Carel Fabritius. Maes continued to paint similar genre works until about 1659. However, as early as 1656 he seems to have turned to portrait painting, and after 1660 he apparently limited himself to portraits in the more courtly manner, such as *Portrait of a Man* (Hannover, Lower Saxony Landesmuseum).

BIBLIOGRAPHY. W. R. Valentiner, "Early Drawings by Nicolaes Maes," *The Burlington Magazine*, XLIII, 1923; W. R. Valentiner, *Nicolaes Maes*, Stuttgart, 1924; N. Maclaren, *National Gallery Catalogues: The Dutch School*, London, 1960; J. Rosenberg, S. Slive, and E. H. ter Kuile, *Dutch Art and Architecture, 1600–1800*, Baltimore, 1966.

LEONARD J. SLATKES

MAESTA, *see* MAJESTAS.

MAESTRO JACOPO. Italian majolica painter (fl. 1508–25). One of the earliest and finest majolica painters at Cafaggiolo, near Florence, a factory that was most probably at one time under the patronage of the Medicis. The works of Jacopo, whose identity has not yet been satisfactorily established, are characterized by a predilection for motifs after Dürer and a fondness for the use of a brilliant yellow that shades gradually into green in the foreground.

BIBLIOGRAPHY. W. Honey, *European Ceramic Art . . .*, 2 vols., London, 1949–52.

MAFAI, MARIO. Italian painter (b. Rome, 1902; d. there, 1965). With Scipione, Mafai was a founder about 1930 of the influential and neoromantic Roman school. The delicate, almost tentative treatment of his paintings matches their subjects: dried flowers, melancholy landscapes and street scenes, decay.

BIBLIOGRAPHY. J. T. Soby and A. H. Barr, Jr., *Twentieth Century Italian Art*, New York, 1949.

MA FEN. Chinese painter (fl. during Northern Sung dynasty, 960–1127). The earliest-known member of the famous Ma family of painters, he was active in the academy. He is recorded in literary sources as having executed a number of long hand scrolls bearing such titles as the *Hundred Horses* and *Hundred Sheep*. His only surviving work is the extremely fine but somewhat controversial hand

scroll of the *Hundred Wild Geese* in the Honolulu Academy of Arts.

See also MA YUAN.

BIBLIOGRAPHY. E. C. Schenck, "The Hundred Wild Geese," *Honolulu Academy of Arts Annual Bulletin*, I, 1939.

MAFFEI, FRANCESCO. Italian painter (b. Vicenza, early 1600s; d. Padua, 1660). Although he first studied with the mannerist Alessandro Maganza, as the *Death of S. Gaetano* (ca. 1620; Vicenza, S. Stefano) indicates, Maffei's mature style was formed in Venice from 1638 under Veronese's influence in such works as the *Adoration of the Magi* (ca. 1640; Vicenza, Cathedral). He thereafter worked in Vicenza, Brescia, Rovigo, and finally Padua (1657). He worked in a rapid and nervous painterly technique, and tended to combine Tintoretto's "fantastic" luminosity with Veronesque colors, as shown in the *Miracles of Perugia and Foligno* (1656; Vicenza, Oratory of St. Nicholas). Maffei thus continued the tradition established by Feti, Liss, and Strozzi. Such late works as the *Rest on the Flight into Egypt* (Vicenza, Zitelle) approximate the style of the Venetian rococo.

BIBLIOGRAPHY. N. Ivanoff, *Francesco Maffei*, Padua, 1947; Vicenza, *Mostra di Francesco Maffei* (catalog), ed. N. Ivanoff, Venice, 1956.

MAFFEO DA VERONA, *see* VERONA, MAFFEO.

MAFFIOLI, ALBERTINO (Alberto da Carrara). Italian sculptor and architect (fl. 2d half of 15th cent.). Born in Carrara, he worked primarily at the certosa there, and for the lavatory of the monks he executed a lavabo (1489) that shows a delicacy of execution and a freedom of composition in the main relief. He also worked on the façade of the Cathedral of Cremona.

MAFRA, PALACE OF. Portuguese royal residence, built (1717–70) for King John V (1706–50) in the Estremadura region. It combined the functions of a royal palace and monastery church, and was conceived in a manner reminiscent of the great palace and monastery of El Escorial in Spain. The enormous complex was planned by the architect J. F. Ludovice (Ludwig) in the Italian manner; between 1719 and 1720 Filippo Juvara contributed designs. The palace represents a high point of Portuguese baroque architecture. Although the façade is rather barren, the church interior and library are richly ornamented.

BIBLIOGRAPHY. W. C. Watson, *Portuguese Architecture*, London, 1908; L. Reis Santos, *Monuments of Portugal*, Lisbon, 1951.

MAGANZA, GIOVANNI BATTISTA. Italian painter and poet (b. Calaone, 1510; d. Vicenza, 1586). He spent most of his life in Vicenza, where he was associated with the circle of Trissino and Palladio. Probably a disciple of Titian, whom he knew, Maganza was highly praised as a portraitist by his contemporaries. His paintings and frescoes for the churches of Vicenza are in a wooden mannerist style.

MAGDALEN COLLEGE, *see* OXFORD.

MAGDALENIAN CULTURE. Paleolithic culture that evolved out of the Aurignacio-Périgordian, or Gravettian, in southwestern France and northern Spain during the final stage of the Upper Paleolithic epoch. The development of this culture, which is named for the type site of La Madeleine in the Department of the Dordogne, took place as the Ice Age was coming to an end, at a time when renewed warmth was bringing a return of forests; this was eventually to drive out the herds of large game and to destroy the hunting basis of paleolithic culture. Artistically the Magdalenian was characterized by increasingly naturalistic engravings, polychrome painting, monumental relief sculpture, and an endless variety of bone, horn, ivory, and antler carvings, which display the same naturalism of style that is found in the engravings and paintings. *See* MADELEINE, GROTTE DE LA.

See also ALTAMIRA, CAVES OF.

MAGDALEN MASTER. Italian painter of the Florentine school (fl. ca. 1250–75). The basis for the reconstruction of this master's work is an altarpiece with superimposed scenes from the Magdalen's life on either side of the central figure, in the Gallery of the Academy in Florence. It is painted in the linear, flat style that had been formulated in Florence during the 13th century, and is only superficially related to Byzantine examples. Among other works by this anonymous painter are an altar frontal in the Yale University Art Gallery in New Haven, Conn., a small triptych in the Blumenthal Collection in New York, the splendid altar frontal in the Museum of Decorative Art in Paris, a *Madonna and Child* in S. Donato ai Torri in Compiobbi, and a *St. Luke* in the Uffizi Gallery in Florence.

BIBLIOGRAPHY. O. Sirén, *Toskanische Maler des XIII. Jahrhunderts*, Berlin, 1922; R. Offner, *Italian Primitives at Yale University*, New Haven, 1927.

MAGDEBURG CATHEDRAL. German Cathedral, also called the Church of SS. Maurice and Catherine. Erected after 1208 on the site of an earlier Benedictine abbey church, it was the earliest attempt at the Gothic style in Germany. The polygonal choir, the two east towers, and the two east bays of the nave were erected from 1208 to 1230. The French style can be seen in the choir with its two-storied ambulatory and series of chapels. The architectural details, however, are basically German. The nave dates from 1363 and the west towers from 1310 to 1520. The outside portal of the north transept has figures of the Wise and Foolish Virgins (ca. 1300) related to those of Strasbourg Cathedral. In the interior are a notable late Gothic choir screen (1445) and the tomb of Archbishop Ernest by Peter Vischer the Elder (1495).

BIBLIOGRAPHY. R. Hamman and F. Rosenfeld, *Der Magdeburger Dom*, Berlin, 1910; H. Giesau, *Der Dom zu Magdeburg*, 2d ed., Burg bei Magdeburg, 1940.

MAGENTA, GIOVANNI. Italian architect (1565–1635). He worked in Bologna in the early baroque style. He designed S. Pietro (1599); his plans were executed with some changes. Magenta's design for S. Salvatore (executed 1605–23) reflects his study of Roman thermae. S. Paolo (begun 1611) is an imaginative variant on Vignola's Gesù in Rome. Magenta became the General of the Barnabite order in 1612.

BIBLIOGRAPHY. R. Wittkower, *Art and Architecture in Italy, 1600–1750*, Baltimore, 1958.

MAGGIOTTO, DOMENICO FEDELI. Italian painter (b. Venice, 1713; d. there, 1794). He was a follower of Piaz-

zetta and one of the founders of the Venice Academy, for which he painted an allegory in 1755. In Maggiotto's great output of religious and historical paintings he followed the style changes of the time from the theatricality of Piazzetta to a flaccid but restless form of neoclassicism. His portraits and genre paintings, however, are vigorous and immediate. He was the father of Francesco Maggiotto.

BIBLIOGRAPHY. R. Pallucchini, "Domenico Fedeli detto il Maggiotto," *Rivista di Venezia*, XI, 1932.

MAGGIOTTO, FRANCESCO. Italian painter (1750–1805). Born in Venice, he was the son of the painter Domenico Fedeli Maggiotto, from whom he received his first training. Francesco won the first prize in painting at the Venice Academy at the age of thirteen. In general, he continued the style of his father, a close follower of Piazzetta. In such works as the *Wedding at Cana* (Padua, Oratorio delle Dimesse) Francesco reveals his neoclassical approach in the conventionality of his composition and the heaviness of his form and color. Working in a period of transition in Venetian art, Maggiotto had an eclectic style, combining elements from such diverse styles as those of Piazzetta, Tiepolo, Pittoni, and Pietro Longhi. Thus, while he is best known for his academic paintings with monumental figures executed in the grand manner, he also produced numerous genre pieces in the style of Longhi. The latter, however, he reduced to stiff moral allegories.

BIBLIOGRAPHY. C. Donzelli, *I pittori veneti del Settecento*, Florence, 1957; R. Pallucchini, *La pittura veneziana del Settecento*, Venice, 1960.

MAGIC REALISM (Magischer Realismus). A meticulously rendered, naturalistic style of painting that usually car-

Magdalenian culture. Bison, from La Madeleine. Antler carving. Museum of National Antiquities, Saint-Germain-en-Laye.

ries an intensity of mood. Although the tendency has existed since the German New Objectivity period of the 1920s, magic realism itself may be identified as a native American surrealism. The juxtaposition of objects does not feature dislocations as extreme as those in the surrealist work of, for example, Dali; but an incongruous and often a haunting effect is produced. The realistic element overrides the magical in most of this painting, and visual facts are usually reproduced in clinical detail. The technique is hard and linear and encompasses through its crystalline clarity a detachment and lack of sensuousness that has been noticeable in American painting since the days of the early limners and was continued in the works of Copley and Winslow Homer.

Such contemporary Americans as Henry Koerner, Andrew Wyeth, and Ben Shahn have worked in a magic-realist style; their careful craftsmanship is often the vehicle for a poignant fantasy. *See* SHAHN, BEN.

Koerner's *Monkey Bars* (1947; Mr. and Mrs. Robert Sherry Collection) shows children playing on the steel bars of a piece of playground equipment while two young men sit dejectedly within the bars, which form an imprisoning cage. The size discrepancies add to the eeriness of the scene. *See* KOERNER, HENRY.

Andrew Wyeth's *Christina's World* (1948; New York, Museum of Modern Art) presents a poignant scene with what seems to be clinical detachment. Each fact has been recorded with uncanny precision: a crippled girl, with great difficulty, is crawling up a hill toward distant barns. The artist, however, has taken a low viewing point and has thereby exaggerated the distance between the girl and

Magdeburg Cathedral. The earliest attempt at the Gothic style in Germany, erected ca. 1208–1520.

the far-off buildings, so that the observer senses the girl's terrible effort. The effect is heightened by the elimination of irrelevant factors: between the girl and the buildings stretches only the vacant field. *See* WYETH, ANDREW NEWELL.

The classification of magic realism is at best indistinct. Unlike European surrealism, magic realism has never harbored a group. But the recognition of such a general style on the part of art historians identifies the strands in 20th-century American painting that are analogous to but separate from European surrealism.

BIBLIOGRAPHY. S. Hunter, *Modern American Painting and Sculpture*, New York, 1959.

ABRAHAM A. DAVIDSON

MAGILP, *see* MEGILP.

MAGISTRI COMACINI. A charter of the Lombard king Rotharis, dated 643, refers to the *magistri comacini*. The context makes clear that there was a group, or more likely a guild, of master builders associated with the revival of stone masonry in and around Milan. The word *comacini* has raised numerous questions. Literally translated "from or of Como," it would place the active guild in that city. However, there is no evidence of such a workshop in Como. Alternately, the word may be a variation of the Italian *macina*, translated as "frame" or "scaffold," making the guild "masters of the scaffold." In either case Lombardy, in conjunction with the *magistri comacini*, developed a masonry style and technique that has aptly been related to the *premier roman* (pre-Romanesque).

Using both Roman brick and dressed stone, these masters evolved a skillful, solid stone and brick masonry with interesting and effective decorative patterns. The techniques and forms were gradually dispersed northward, across the Alps, along the Rhine, and eventually as far north as Sweden. Thus, many trace the revival of stone building technique in the Romanesque period to the beginnings made by the *magistri comacini*.

See also LOMBARD STYLE.

BIBLIOGRAPHY. J. Puig y Cadafalch, *La géographie et les origines du premier art roman*, Paris, 1936.

STANLEY FERBER

MAGNA MATER. Latin term for the "Great Mother," an ancient earth and fertility goddess. Her worship under various titles and names was practiced in Asia Minor, Crete, and other areas on the Mediterranean Sea. Sometimes her rites were connected with a divine lover who was killed and ritually revived, and her priests in Galatia were emasculated. She was called Kybele (Cybele) in Anatolia, Rhea or Mountain Mother of the Gods in Greece, and Ops in Rome. As Kybele, she was depicted as a mature woman seated in a chariot drawn by lions.

MAGNASCO, ALESSANDRO (Lissandrino). Italian painter (b. Genoa, 1667; d. there, 1749). After the death of his father, Stefano Magnasco, from whom he had learned the rudiments of painting, Alessandro Magnasco went to Milan (ca. 1680–82), where he studied with the Venetian Filippo Abbiati. Magnasco remained in Milan until 1703, at which time he returned to Genoa, only to begin a period of wandering in Tuscany and Emilia, with frequent visits back to Lombardy. By 1711 he had resettled in Milan,

Alessandro Magnasco, *The Baptism of Christ*. National Gallery, Washington, D.C. (Samuel H. Kress Collection, 1953).

remaining there until 1735, when he returned for good to Genoa.

While it is possible to name artists who form a background for his painterly style (Giordano, Maffei, and Mazzoni, for example) and for his wide range of subject matter (Salvator Rosa, Callot, and Cerquozzi), the individuality of Magnasco's vision belies such citations. Even in an early work, *Teaching the Raven* (ca. 1690–1700; Florence, Uffizi), the unreality of his figures, diffused as they are by rapid, sketchy brushstrokes and bleached out by an unnatural light, goes beyond the descriptive power of the words "genre" and "painterly." In his maturity these effects are intensified to a point where the surface of the painting, with its frantic linear highlights, thick impasto, and sketchiness, all but obliterates the "genre fantasy" he is portraying (*Marriage Banquet of Gypsies*, ca 1730–40; Paris, Louvre).

His range of subject matter is enormous and includes soldiers, gypsies, robbers, and fisherman, usually placed among ruins or in a landscape (*Soldiers at Play*, Boston, Museum of Fine Arts; *Seashore with Smugglers*, New York, Metropolitan Museum; *The Gypsies' Meal*, Uffizi),

as well as religious themes (*Landscape with Wandering Monks*, Milan, Brera; *Baptism of Christ*, Washington, D.C., National Gallery), all partaking of those stylistic qualities that have led to the label "phantasmagoria." The problem of interpretation, brought up by the seeming interchangeability of a gypsy and a monk, a fisherman and Christ, has further complications. Although the flickering light and activated surface give a painting such as *S. Carlo Borromeo Receiving Oblates* (Milan, Poldi-Pezzoli) an air of intense mysticism, the same stylistic ingredients can be seen in the *Inquisition Scene* (Vienna, Museum of Art History), which has a Daumier-like sense of caricature and criticism.

Magnasco was too individualistic and enigmatic to have followers, but his sketchy, painterly style did have invigorating effects on Venetian 18th-century painting, although the passionate intensity of his canvases remained unmatched.

BIBLIOGRAPHY. A. Magnasco, *Alessandro Magnasco*, by B. Geiger, Berlin, 1914; A. Magnasco, *Mostra del Magnasco* (catalog), ed. A. Morassi, 2d ed., Bergamo, 1949.

STEPHEN E. OSTROW

MAGNASCO, STEFANO. Italian painter (1635–after 1681?). He is associated with Valerio Castello in Genoa. Magnasco may have studied with Castello between 1655 and 1659. Magnasco then went to Rome, but his precise activity there is unknown. Essentially, his style remains but a weak reflection of the intensely dramatic and fiery manner of Castello. He was the father of Alessandro Magnasco.

MAGNELLI, ALBERTO. Italian painter (1888–   ). One of Italy's leading abstract painters, he was born in Florence and has been most influenced by Léger. He was associated in 1913 with the futurists, and his art is related to constructivism. Magnelli avoids any suggestion of personal expression in an effort to invest his painting with geometric abstraction.

BIBLIOGRAPHY. H. Read, *A Concise History of Modern Painting*, London, 1959.

MAGNI (Magno), CESARE. Italian painter (fl. ca. 1530–50). A follower of Cesare da Sesto, he attempted to imitate the style of Leonardo da Vinci in works now to be found in Milan, Saronno, Vigevano, and other Lombard cities.

MAGRITTE, RENE. Belgian painter (1898–1967). Born in Lessines, he studied at the Brussels Academy from 1916 to 1918. His earliest work was influenced by cubism and futurism. Magritte was a leader of the Belgian surrealists and was active in the Paris group of surrealists in the late 1920s. Throughout his career he used many of the devices of orthodox surrealism, but in a personal manner, refined and philosophical, disquieting but rarely as immediately shocking as others of the movement. He also avoided their automatic techniques and painted in an essentially realistic style.

His early surrealist pictures are governed by the incongruous juxtaposition of unrelated objects. *La Statue volante* (1927; London, private collection), for example, contains, among other things, a classical statue and bits of plumbing. The effect is of a Chirico-like melancholy. In some works painted several years later the incongruity of the assemblage is heightened by shifts in scale. From the late 1920s until about 1940 Magritte painted pictures that seem more like metaphysical problems in visual form than surrealist projections of the unconscious. His variation on the device of the double image, in which a part of the picture simultaneously functions in two separate contexts, occurs in a series of pictures, for example, *La Belle captive* (1931; Brussels, private collection), which depict a painted canvas on an easel set against a window or in a field. The painted canvas continues without a break the view of the landscape that would ordinarily be hidden by it. A related use of this device in found in *The Eye* (ca. 1935; New York, Museum of Modern Art), which is a close-up of an eye with a cloud-filled blue sky where the iris should be.

From 1940 to about 1946 Magritte painted gentle fantasy pictures in an impressionistic technique. After 1946 he again painted what appear to be metaphysical or philosophical problems, with brighter, more effective color than previously and more puzzling subject matter. *L'Empire des lumières* (1954; Museum of Modern Art) shows a tree-lined street at night, with a street light shining through the darkness, although there is broad daylight above the roofs. Magritte's paintings lie within and without surrealism at the same time. They quietly insist that there is a poetry of the intellect as well as a poetry of the unconscious.

BIBLIOGRAPHY. P. Nougé, *René Magritte...*, Brussels, 1943; R. Magritte, *Magritte...* with an introductory essay by L. Scutenaire, Antwerp, 1948; R. Magritte, *René Magritte* (exhibition catalog), Brussels, 1954; J. T. Soby, ed., *René Magritte*, New York, 1965.
JEROME VIOLA

MAGRO, DEL, *see* GIRALDI, GUGLIELMO.

MAHABALAPURAM, *see* MAMALLAPURAM.

MAHABODHI TEMPLE, *see* BODHGAYA.

MAHADEVA. Sanskrit term meaning "Great God." Mahādeva is a name for the Hindu god Siva.

MAHADEVI. Sanskrit term meaning "Great Goddess." Mahādevī is one of the names of Devī, the Hindu god Siva's consort.

MAHAL. Muslim palace.

René Magritte, *Le Thérapeute* (*The Healer*). Private collection, New York.

Ma Ho-chih, scroll with odes from the *Shih-ching*, detail. Museum of Fine Arts, Boston.

MAHAVIRA. Twenty-fourth, or last, of the Jain Tīrthaṅkaras. He lived in India (modern north Bihar) during the 6th century B.C. Mahāvīra (the name means "great hero") was the founder of Jainism in the sense that Gautama Buddha was the founder of Buddhism.

MAHAYANA. Northern school of Buddhism popular throughout Nepal, Tibet, China, Korea, and Japan but also having some acceptance in Indochina and Java. The Mahāyāna (Great Vehicle) differs from the Hīnayāna in having an expanded pantheon and in the Bodhisattva ideal that salvation may be obtained through the transfer of merit and not by one's efforts alone. *See* BODHISATTVA; LOTUS SUTRA. *See also* HINAYANA; VAJRAYANA.

MA HO-CHIH. Chinese painter (fl. late 12th cent.). A native of Ch'ien-t'ang in Chekiang Province, he was a prominent official but was not recorded as an academy painter. He is known for his illustrations to the classical odes from the *Shih-ching*; according to tradition, the emperor Kao-tsung practiced calligraphy by copying the text of the odes and instructed Ma Ho-chih to accompany each section with an illustration. Thus Ma Ho-chih is connected with a number of scrolls dealing with this subject, of which the section in the Museum of Fine Arts, Boston, is probably the best. But Ma Ho-chih's painting style, particularly his manner of painting trees with a flowing brush, was quite distinctive, and later painters would occasionally make a bow to him in this respect.

BIBLIOGRAPHY. K. Tomita and A. K. Chiu, "A Scroll of Six Odes from Mao Shih," *Boston, Museum of Fine Arts, Bulletin*, L, October, 1952.

MAHOMETAN. Variant form of Muhammadan. *See* Islamic articles.

MA-HSIA SCHOOL. In Chinese painting history, the works of Ma Yüan and Hsia Kuei, the two leading masters of the Southern Sung Academy in the 13th century. When the term "Ma-Hsia school" came into common usage is not clear, but it was a distinct concept certainly by the time of Tung Ch'i-ch'ang in the 17th century, when the two names carried with them special connotations. In Western writing the Ma-Hsia school usually refers to most of the products of the Southern Sung Academy in the landscape category and to specific elements of their style. *See* HSIA KUEI; MA YUAN.

BIBLIOGRAPHY. S. Shimada and Y. Yonezawa, *Painting of the Sung and Yüan Dynasties*, Tokyo, 1952; J. Cahill, *Chinese Paintings, 11th–14th Centuries*, New York, 1960.

MAHU, CORNELIS. Flemish painter (1613–89). Born in Antwerp, he painted still lifes in the manner of the Haarlem school, drawing inspiration principally from Willem Claesz. Heda. Mahu's relatively rare productions are known for their warm and blond hues; his breakfast paintings lack skillful composition and tend toward a juxtaposition of paraphernalia.

BIBLIOGRAPHY. F. J. van den Branden, *Geschiedenis der Antwerpsche Schilderschool*, Antwerp, 1883.

MAIANO, BENEDETTO DA. Italian sculptor and architect (ca. 1442-97). He matriculated in the Stone and Wood Carvers' Guild of Florence in 1473 and throughout most of his life worked in close association with his architect brother Giuliano. Characteristic examples of his work are the marble bust of Pietro Mellini (1474) in the National Museum, Florence; the *Altar of St. Fina* (completed in 1475) in the Collegiata, San Gimignano; and the *Altar of the Annunciation* (1480s) at Monte Oliveto, Naples. Benedetto da Maiano continued the Florentine decorator-

Benedetto da Maiano, marble bust of Pietro Mellini. National Museum, Florence.

sculptors' tradition of delicate carving and exquisite detail, but failed to attain the consummate mastery of a Desiderio da Settignano or an Antonio Rossellino, from whom he can claim artistic descent. In his last statues, a *Virgin and Child* and a *St. Sebastian* in the Oratory of the Misericordia, Florence, he anticipates High Renaissance aims of plastic concentration and mobility.

Benedetto's major work as an architect is the massive, heavily rusticated Strozzi Palace in Florence (begun 1489), which was later completed by Il Cronaca. He also built the loggia of S. Maria delle Grazie in Arezzo. *See* STROZZI PALACE, FLORENCE.

BIBLIOGRAPHY. L. Dussler, *Benedetto da Majano*, Munich, 1924; J. Pope-Hennessy, *Italian Renaissance Sculpture*, London, 1958.

MAIANO, GIOVANNI DA. Italian sculptor (1438–78). He was active in the workshop of his brothers Giuliano and Benedetto da Maiano, and probably carved the antependium of the *Pietà* beneath the tabernacle of the Madonna dell'Ulivo (Prato Cathedral). The tabernacle had originally been designed by Benedetto for the brothers' own chapel, which was to have been constructed near Prato.

MAIANO, GIULIANO DA. Italian architect, sculptor, and intarsia worker (b. Maiano, 1432; d. Naples, 1490). He collaborated with his brothers Benedetto da Maiano and Giovanni da Maiano in the leading Florentine intarsia workshop during the 1460s, when they made several panels for the New Sacristy of the Cathedral. But Giuliano was active primarily as an architect, working sometimes with his brother Benedetto. In such works as the Pazzi (Quaratesi) Palace in Florence (1459–69), the cloister of the Benedictine Abbey in Arezzo (1470), and Faenza Cathedral (1476–86), he closely followed the example of Brunelleschi, adopting also the more monumental forms and rhythms of Alberti. He also worked for the Duke of Calabria between 1485 and 1490 in Naples, where he designed the Porta Capuana, among other works. *See* QUARATESI PALACE, FLORENCE.

BIBLIOGRAPHY. L. Cendali, *Giuliano e Benedetto da Maiano*, Florence, 1926.

MAIDAN-I-SHAH, ISFAHAN. Focal feature of the extensive construction undertaken in Isfahan by Shah Abbas the Great of Iran. Laid out in 1611, with a length of 560 yards and a width of 175 yards, the Maidan-i-Shah, or Imperial Square, was surrounded by arcades in two stories and gave access to several great monuments of this period.

See also MASJID-I-SHAH, ISFAHAN; ROYAL BAZAAR, ISFAHAN.

BIBLIOGRAPHY. A. U. Pope, ed., *A Survey of Persian Art*, vol. 2, New York, 1939.

MAIDS OF HONOR (Las Meninas). Oil painting by Velázquez, in the Prado Museum, Madrid. *See* VELAZQUEZ, DIEGO RODRIGUEZ DE SILVA Y.

MAILLART, ROBERT. Swiss engineer (1872–1940). He was born in Bern and studied structural engineering at the Federal Institute of Technology, Zurich (1890–94). Maillart was one of the few creative engineers of our century. He spent his life working on the development of

Aristide Maillol, *Night*, 1902. Bronze. Estate of Maurice Wertheim.

reinforced concrete forms, pioneering mushroom column construction and warped slabs for bridges and buildings.

BIBLIOGRAPHY. M. Bill, *Robert Maillart*, 2d ed., Zurich, 1955.

MAILLOL, ARISTIDE. French sculptor, tapestry maker, painter, and draftsman (b. Banyuls-sur-Mer, 1861; d. near there, 1944). His gift for drawing appeared while he was in college in Perpignan. Between 1880 and 1886 he published in Banyuls a small magazine with his own illustrations. He decided to become a painter after copying works in the Perpignan museum. In 1887 he was in Paris and entered the Ecole des Beaux-Arts as a painting student of Gérôme and Cabanel. Two years later he met Bourdelle and saw Gauguin's work. Also in 1889 he began to make tapestries after study in the Cluny museum.

In 1890, encouraged by Gauguin, he left the Ecole to work on his own. In 1893 he exhibited a tapestry at the National Society Salon. His early work resembled that of the Nabis and of his friend Maurice Denis. In 1896 he started to carve sculpture in wood, after having made woodcuts in 1894. By 1898 he was working in terra cotta and enamel. His decision to become a sculptor was influenced by the impairment of his sight, which was caused by tapestry work.

In 1900 Vollard cast some of Maillol's terra cottas in bronze and in 1902 gave Maillol his first show, which was also admired by Rodin. That same year he began work on his first major sculpture, *Mediterranean*, for which his wife posed. By 1905 he received important commissions, for which he did *Action in Chains* and *Desire*. With these

Mainz Cathedral. The western apse of the mainly Romanesque church.

MAINARDI, SEBASTIANO (Sebastiano di Bartolo). Italian painter (b. San Gimignano, ca. 1460; d. Florence? 1513). He was the pupil, assistant, and brother-in-law of Domenico Ghirlandajo, but his role in Ghirlandajo's prosperous Florentine studio remains to be clarified. Whether he assisted Ghirlandajo on the frescoes in the Collegiata, San Gimignano (1474/75), is open to question. It is certain, however, that Mainardi helped with the decoration of the choir in the Cathedral of Pisa in 1493/94. While numerous Ghirlandajesque paintings bear an attribution to Mainardi, there are no signed works dated before 1500 that could help to identify his early and mature styles. The frescoes in the Chapel of S. Bartolo in S. Agostino, San Gimignano, which earlier bore the artist's initials and the date 1500, seem to support the contention that Mainardi's art became progressively weaker after the death of Ghirlandajo in 1494.

MAINERI, GIANFRANCESCO. Italian painter of Ferrara (fl. 1489–1505). He is known from documents of lost works and from several identical paintings of the Madonna (two signed) and of Christ bearing the Cross. These show a rich but dead imitation of Roberti.

MAINO (Mayno), JUAN BAUTISTA. Spanish painter (b. Pastrana, near Toledo, 1578; d. Madrid, 1649). He occupies an important place in the history of painting in Madrid before the time of Velázquez. Maino studied in Italy, where he is said to have been a student and friend of Annibale Carracci and Guido Reni. While something of Carracci may be detected in his early works, other influences are also felt, notably that of Savoldo, as in the frescoes of S. Pedro Mártir in Toledo.

Maino entered a Dominican monastery in Toledo in 1613. After 1615 he was made drawing master to Prince Philip; later, during Philip's reign, he remained as court painter, though without an official title. Maino worked with Velázquez at Buen Retiro, for which he painted his major work, *The Recapture of Bahía* (1635), a painting wholly Spanish in character and marked by the style of Velázquez.

Among other important works by Maino are the *Adoration of the Kings* in Madrid (Prado) and a portrait of Philip IV in armor (New York, Metropolitan Museum). His naturalism, as much a parallel development as a derivation from Caravaggio, is somewhat akin to that of Orazio Gentileschi. Dynamic in composition, Maino's works show a sober use of chiaroscuro and smooth brushwork.

BIBLIOGRAPHY. E. Harris, "Aportaciones para el estudio de Juan Bautista Maino," *Revista española de Arte*, XII, 1935; J. López-Rey, "Portrait of Philip IV by Juan Bautista Maino," *Art Bulletin*, XLV, 1963.

PHILIPPE DE MONTEBELLO

MAINZ: CATHEDRAL. German church originally founded during the reign of Emperor Otto II (973–83). The Cathedral was the major church foundation of his reign. Begun in 978 under the aegis of Archbishop Willigis, it burned in 1009, on the day of its dedication. It was rebuilt in a series of campaigns under the archbishops Eskenbald, Aribo, and Bardo. Further rebuilding and alteration took place between 1060 and 1137 and, again, from 1181 and 1239. Additions in the Gothic and Romanesque revival

early works Maillol's style was established; it underwent little change in the next forty years. His style had been formed before a trip to Greece in 1906, and his work thereafter showed no substantial influence from this contact with ancient art.

In 1907 he did a bust of Renoir and a statue of an adolescent male, *Young Cyclist*, both of which are rare in his *oeuvre*, for he favored the ripely mature feminine body above all. After 1910 Maillol's fame was international, and commissions from public and private sources were numerous. He occasionally did illustrations, such as woodcuts for Virgil's *Eclogues* (1912–13) and lithographs for Verhaeren's *Belle Chair* (1931). His first show in the United States was in 1925 at the Albright-Knox Art Gallery, Buffalo. He resumed painting in 1939.

The New York Museum of Modern Art owns *Desire* (1904), *Ile de France* (1910), *Chained Action* (1906), *Seated Figure* (1930), and *The River* (1939–43). His *Mediterranean* is in the Stephen Clark Collection. As an alternative to Rodin's style, Maillol championed emotional and formal restraint, clear and untroubled surfaces, and weighted volumes. Thus his figures serve as reminders of idyllic calm in a time of turbulence.

BIBLIOGRAPHY. J. Rewald, *Maillol*, London, New York, 1939; B. Dorival, *Maillol*, Paris, 1955.

ALBERT ELSEN

MAILLY, SIMON DE, see CHALONS, SIMON DE.

styles were made later, but the building still retains its Romanesque strength and grandeur.

The first church of Willigis (978–1009) shows an interesting carry-over of the Carolingian T-basilica revival. As in Fulda and earlier in Old St. Peter's, Rome, Mainz had a continuous transept and a single apse at the west end. A low western crossing tower was duplicated at the east end, which had dwarf transepts extending only to the side aisles. A long nave with a clerestory and two aisles connected the eastern and western masses, giving the whole a rather symmetrical, primarily horizontal silhouette. However, there was a simple compartmentalization of masses suggestive of later Romanesque developments. The first rebuilding, brought to completion under Archbishop Bardo in 1036, saw the addition of a western apse, making Mainz a "double-ender" like Fulda. Eastern stair towers rising to the height of the crossing tower were added at this time, and the western apse underwent a change. Excavations have not totally clarified the nature of this change. It is believed that the apse was replaced by a large square chancel, starting beyond the west transept, and that three semicircular apses were affixed to it in a trefoil plan.

The alterations of the late 11th and 12th centuries gave Mainz its truly Romanesque appearance. The Lombard motifs that had traveled down the Rhine and reached as far north as Sweden made themselves felt here. Blind arcades, corbel-table friezes, and pilaster strips were added to the exterior, giving the church its highly articulated, plastic wall surface. Engaged columns were added to the nave piers, and a system of groin vaulting with diaphragm arches (again Lombard) was introduced. The crossing towers were altered at the end of the 12th or the beginning of the 13th century. The early towers were square unarticulated masses. The later towers are octagonal, richly articulated by corbel tables and open galleries. The tower treatment probably derives directly from the Cathedral of Speyer, remodeled slightly earlier, and originated with Lombard building, as in Milan.

The building retains most of its Romanesque character, despite the pseudo-Gothic alterations of the west tower. This is due in no small part to the warmth of the native red sandstone that was used in the early construction.

BIBLIOGRAPHY. P. Metz, *Der Dom zu Mainz*, Cologne, 1927.

STANLEY FERBER

MAINZ: MUSEUM OF ANTIQUITIES AND PICTURE GALLERY.
German museum founded in 1814 and housed in the former royal stables (mid-18th cent.). The museum contains archaeological material from prehistoric and historic times of the region around Mainz. These works include early idols and stone and bronze implements and weapons, jewelry, and finds from Roman times. The picture collection has fine examples of European painting from the 14th to the 19th century, with the accent on painting from the Middle Rhine. Medieval and baroque sculpture from the Mainz region, together with drawings and works of applied arts (ivory, furniture, glass, textiles), are also exhibited. The museum has a collection of porcelain tableware and figures from the Höchst factory, which was most active in the 18th century.

BIBLIOGRAPHY. H. Jedding, *Keysers Führer durch Museen und Sammlungen*, Heidelberg, Munich, 1961.

MAIOLICA, *see* MAJOLICA.

MAISON, RUDOLF. German sculptor (b. Regensburg, 1854; d. Munich, 1904). Maison studied in Regensburg and Munich. A highly imaginative sculptor, he produced small polychrome figures and groups of type and genre subjects as well as monumental statues with neobaroque compositions.

MAISON CARREE, NIMES. Temple in southern France built during the time of Augustus (16 B.C.). The date of the Maison Carrée is fixed by traces of inscriptions on the front frieze of the architrave. The best preserved of all Roman temples, it is Corinthian, hexastyle, prostyle, pseudoperipteral, raised on a podium 11 feet high with a flight of nineteen steps. It has a portico three columns deep. The external walls of the cella have engaged Corinthian columns.

The temple, built of local limestone, is of small scale and measures 44 by 86 feet. A narrow frieze on the architrave has a Roman scroll carved in relief. A masterpiece of architectural achievement, the temple preserves in the purity of its plan and in the symmetry of its proportions the classicizing trends of the Augustan period.

BIBLIOGRAPHY. W. J. Anderson, R. P. Spiers, and T. Ashby, *The Architecture of Greece and Rome*, vol. 2: *The Architecture of Ancient Rome*, London, 1927; D. S. Robertson, *A Handbook of Greek and Roman Architecture*, 2d ed., Cambridge, 1959.

MAISONS-LAFFITTE, CHATEAU OF. French château situated on the left bank of the Seine, 11 miles west of Paris. It was built between 1642 and 1646 by François Mansart for René de Longueil, who allowed his architect an unusually free hand. In return the patron received an original masterpiece, the most complete embodiment of the architect's genius. The freestanding block has short arms projecting forward at either end, tall French roofs in separate sections breaking the monolithic quality of the lower stories, and a cool elegance of classical detail of which only Mansart was capable. The decoration of the interior, too,

Maison Carrée, Nîmes. A Roman temple built during the reign of the emperor Augustus.

Château of Maisons-Laffitte, near Paris. Vestibule by François Mansart.

is from Mansart's hand, particularly the hall and staircase, which also have sculptures by Sarrazin.

BIBLIOGRAPHY. A. Blunt, *François Mansart and the Origins of French Classical Architecture*, London, 1941.

MAISUR, *see* MYSORE.

MAITANI, LORENZO. Italian architect and sculptor (b. probably Siena, ca. 1275; d. Orvieto, 1330). Little is known of his early training, but he was associated with Ramo di Paganello, who may have influenced his style.

Maitani gained fame as an architect while working on the Cathedral of Siena, and in 1308 he was called to Orvieto in connection with the building of the cathedral there. His creative and technical abilities impressed the authorities of Orvieto, and he was appointed *capomastro* of the cathedral in 1310. He held this position until his death. During his stay at Orvieto various other projects engaged his attention, mainly in Perugia (1317 and 1319–21) and in Siena, where he assisted with the building of the New Cathedral (1322). He also contributed to projects at Montefalco (1323) and at Castiglione del Lago (1325).

Maitani's most important contribution to 14th-century art is the design of the Orvieto Cathedral façade. The influence of Giovanni Pisano's Siena Cathedral façade is apparent here. Also, certain of Giovanni's sculptures for the Siena façade appear to have inspired Maitani. Giovanni's *Symbols of the Evangelists* at Siena are echoed in those of Maitani at Orvieto, yet important differences of style should be noted. Giovanni carved his figures in compact, closed compositions; Maitani's *Virgin and Child Enthroned with Angels* exemplifies a greater freedom of movement. Although the Virgin and Child are of marble and somewhat static, the bronze angels are striding figures, reaching freely into space in poetical, lifelike gestures. Although the motif of the angels is similar to that used by Giovanni at Siena,

the thin-bodied and tightly pulled linear effects are more reminiscent of northern Gothic examples.

Four relief sculptures on the faces of the pilasters flanking the doorways suggest the work of several sculptors in addition to Maitani. Two of the panels may be assigned to Maitani: the *Scenes from Genesis* and the *Last Judgment*. The other two, *Scenes from the Life of Christ* and the *Prophecies and Redemption*, were probably done by other artists under the supervision of Maitani. Both the *Genesis* and *Last Judgment*, which are on the two outside pilasters, are unified by means of a vine ascending from the bottom of the composition; it branches out and symmetrically divides the spaces into vignettes of figures. The vine is cut in crisp, fluent detail and suggests French Gothic antecedents. Maitani is thought to have influenced the work of Andrea Pisano, who became the leading sculptor of Tuscany during the second quarter of the 14th century.

BIBLIOGRAPHY. J. Pope-Hennessy, *Italian Gothic Sculpture*, London, 1955.
BEN P. WATKINS

MAITRE FRANCOIS. French miniaturist (fl. late 15th cent.). His harsh style is far removed from that of Jean Fouquet, who may have been his father. Maître François's illustrations for the *City of God* of St. Augustine (ca. 1473; Paris, National Library) present him as a decorator unconcerned with refinement and atmosphere.

BIBLIOGRAPHY. J. Porcher, *Medieval French Miniatures*, New York, 1959.

MAITRES POPULAIRES. French term for artists who work at painting as a hobby or on off hours. It is equivalent to "Sunday painters" in English.

MAITREYA (Chinese, Mi-lo; Japanese, Miroku). Future, or fifth, Buddha, the successor to Gautama Buddha, who is to appear 4,500 years after him. Maitreya is one of the most widely depicted deities in China and Japan. His symbols are the *kalaśa* (vase with elixir of life) and the *cakra* (Wheel of the Law). His symbolic hand positions (mudrās) are *dharmacakra* or *vara* and *vitarka*. Maitreya dwells in the Tushita paradise as a Bodhisattva, awaiting the time when he can descend to earth. In Chinese Buddhist art he is often depicted in the cross-ankle seated pose. *See* DHARMACAKRA; VARA; VITARKA.

MAITREYA (stone). Buddhist statue (2d half of 10th cent.), located at Nonsan, Korea. This is the largest free-standing stone statue in Korea (60 ft. high). It has a long oval face and is covered by a slab, resembling a mortarboard hat, with little pendant bells.

BIBLIOGRAPHY. E. McCune, *The Arts of Korea*, Rutland, Vt., 1962.

MAITREYA OF NATIONAL MUSEUM, SEOUL. Gilded bronze Buddhist statue (6th–7th cent.) supposedly from the Andong area of Korea, now in the National Museum, Seoul. It is one of the two largest surviving bronze statues of Maitreya (height, $31^{11}/_{16}$ in.) from the period, the other being in the Toksu Palace Museum of Fine Arts, Seoul. Although the statue is cast in bronze quite skillfully, the formal, incised lines of the drapery resemble those of stone sculptures. The diadem is decorated with crescent-shaped finials. The scarf, which covers both shoulders, flares out over the upper arms. The Maitreya sits on a rectangular support with openings at the base in a pose of contemplation with the right elbow resting on the right knee and the right leg bent to rest on the left knee.

BIBLIOGRAPHY. R. T. Paine, ed., *Masterpieces of Korean Art*, Boston, 1957.

MAITREYA OF TOKSU PALACE, SEOUL. Gilded bronze Korean Buddhist statue (early 7th cent.), in the Toksu Palace Museum of Fine Arts, Seoul. This is one of the two largest Maitreya statues in bronze (height, 35¾ in.) from the period, the other being in the National Museum, Seoul. The diadem on this statue is thinner and the design simpler. The thin, clinging drapery reveals a well-rounded body; the soft modeling and the simple contour lines convey a sense of quiet dignity. A Maitreya, carved in wood, in the Kōryūji in Japan is so close in style to this statue that both are considered by some scholars to have come from the same workshop, despite the difference in medium. *See* MIROKU BOSATSU IN KORYUJI, KYOTO.

BIBLIOGRAPHY. R. T. Paine, ed., *Masterpieces of Korean Art*, Boston, 1957.

MAJA, NUDE. Oil painting by Goya, in the Prado Museum, Madrid. *See* GOYA Y LUCIENTES, FRANCISCO JOSE.

MAJANO, *see* MAIANO.

MAJESTAS (Maesta). Representation of Christ in Majesty in a mandorla surrounded by the four evangelical symbols.

The Majestas is also the depiction of the Madonna and Child enthroned surrounded by angels. Duccio's *Maestà* in the Museo dell'Opera del Duomo, Siena, is a good example. *See* CHRIST IN MAJESTY; DUCCIO DI BUONINSEGNA.

MAJOLICA (Maiolica). Generally defined today as a tin-glaze earthenware painted in "maiolica" colors: blue, green, manganese purple, yellow, and orange. More specifically it refers to certain Italian ceramics of the 14th to the 18th century. Originally the term was applied to the lustered wares of Valencia that were shipped to Italy from Majorca, and it is a corruption of that name. As early as 1454, however, potters referred to "maiolica" and meant a tin-glaze ware.

The process of making majolica was rather special. After the clay was shaped, either on the wheel or in a mold, it was fired. The ware, then a buff color, was next dipped in glaze, a composition of lead, tin, and silicate of potash. When the glaze dried, decoration was painted on and the piece fired a second time. The glaze was fixed on the body and whitened in this second firing, during which the painted-on pigments fused into the glaze. With majolica painting, a sure hand was required. The colors were absorbed as they came into contact with the unfired glaze, so that no retouching was possible. A contemporary account exists in the 16th-century treatise by Cipriano

Lorenzo Maitani, *God Creating the Animals*, façade of Orvieto Cathedral, early 14th century.

Piccolpasso in the Victoria and Albert Museum, London.

The history of majolica can be started at the end of the 14th century with what has been mistakenly called *mezza maiolica* by collectors. Actually it is true majolica, and the early examples have designs in green and manganese purple painted on a white ground. Traditional forms of medieval origin were commonly used. The early decoration followed Islamic models, since Islamic pottery was known and admired in 14th-century Italy. Although the largest finds have been at Orvieto, Florence was very likely the center of early majolica production.

Toward the middle of the 15th century two developments can be noted: blue and yellow were added to the Florentine potter's palette; and a group of wares, mainly drug jars, painted in dark purple and blackish impasto blue made their appearance. Most common are those with round bellies, flat bases, short flaring necks, and strap handles. Decoration consists of an overall leaf (often called "oak-leaf") design surrounding on each side a heraldic device, or a bust of a man or woman. After 1475 the blue lightened in tone. Technical competence rapidly increased and more designs were used in the second half of the 15th century. Hispano-Moresque influence from the wares of Valencia is found in many of the colorful late-15th-century wares. The Florentine decorator replaced the Valencian luster with purple. The drug jar, called albarello, was introduced then. *See* ALBARELLO.

Designs showing human figures began to appear in the second half of the 15th century when Florence was seriously rivaled by Faenza. Faventine wares are distinguished by a powerful color scheme. A brilliant glaze is painted over with rich dark blues, a deep purple, orange, or tawny brown, and, less frequently, with pale lemon, yellow and green, or greenish turquoise. Among the decorative borders are several that suggest movement through swirling arrangements of leaf patterns. Another favored decorative device was a diaper pattern of peacock feathers later used at Cafaggiolo. Wall plaques and pavements were made at the Faventine potteries. Religious and profane subjects were rendered in the Renaissance style by 1480.

In majolica the use of classical antiquity for inspiration in ornament did not become really important until after 1500 when the so-called fine period began. This period, lasting until 1530, was marked by subtle refinements, such as the decoration of the backs of plates and cups and the development of painting to such distinction that the ware was simply a vehicle for it. In many instances the picture occupied the whole area of a plate or bowl. Faenza had competition from the Medici pottery at Cafaggiolo (founded in 1506), Castel Durante, Urbino, Siena, and Deruta, a town near Perugia where a distinctive color scheme was developed. Deruta potters were the first to learn the secret of luster, although Gubbio, a 16th-century center of majolica painting, with Maestro Giorgio (Giorgio Andreoli) as the chief artist, improved upon luster and developed a distinctive shimmering ruby color. Potters from Urbino, Castel Durante, and other places sent painted work to Gubbio for luster to be added. *See* GUBBIO WARE.

The use of engravings as models for pictures on majolica was introduced at this time with the emergence of the narrative (*istoriato*) style. It was at its best in Castel Du-

rante and Urbino. Nicola Pellipario is the most renowned painter of *istoriato* majolica. Often basing his work on engravings or woodcuts, he went far beyond them in rendering stylish figures of great vitality and grace. Nicola worked at Castel Durante first and then Urbino. The style was carried on by many imitators in Urbino, Pesaro, and Venice, as well as in France. A change from the *istoriato* was introduced at Urbino in the workshop of Nicola's grandson, Orazio, who had adopted the family name of Fontana. Arabesques in the style of ancient Roman painting, as Raphael had employed them at the Farnesina in Rome, were used on white grounds. At the same time, Venetian potters developed a distinctive style of blue-and-white design. Eastern motifs were combined with those of classical antiquity in delightfully inventive designs. *See* FONTANA, ORAZIO; PELLIPARIO, NICOLA.

See also PALISSY, BERNARD; SAINT-PORCHAIRE.

About 1550, large forms—vases, wine coolers, and fountains with relief ornament—in shapes based on metalwork were introduced, as well as figures more amusing than aesthetically satisfying. One other reaction to the *istoriato* after 1550 was begun in the workshop of Virgiliotto Calamelli. Fewer colors were used, and the manner of painting was less naturalistic. Simple white pieces came into vogue in shapes also based on metalwork. The 17th century was a period of eclecticism in which earlier styles were revived and more popular pieces were produced. Potteries in Abruzzi and Sicily repeated early central Italian models in a cooler pale palette. The revivals continued into the 18th century in work that was lighter in body. Grad-

Majolica. Serving plate, 18th century, from the Antonibon Factory at Nove. Flangini Collection, Verona.

ually the majolica potteries began to produce faïence, more characteristic of their own age, and majolica was no longer made. *See* FAIENCE.

BIBLIOGRAPHY. B. Rackham, *Italian Maiolica*, London, 1952; G. Liverani, *Five Centuries of Italian Majolica*, New York, 1960.

MARVIN D. SCHWARTZ

MAJUSCULE. Paleographic term for all upper-case letters, whether capitals or uncials, as distinguished from the minuscule, or lower-case, letters.

MAKARA. Fabulous sea animal appearing in Hindu art. It represents the sign Capricornus in the Hindu zodiac. The *makara* is depicted with the head and forelegs of an antelope and the body and tail of a fish; there is also some resemblance to a crocodile or a dolphin. It is the vehicle of Varuṇa. *See* VARUNA.

MAKART, HANS. Austrian painter (b. Salzburg, 1840; d. Vienna, 1884). He studied briefly at the Vienna Academy, was a pupil of Piloty in Munich, and traveled in Europe and Egypt. Makart was a very successful creator of vast historical and allegorical paintings and decorations. He used a rich coloring, derived from the Venetian painters, and the sort of ample and sensuous figures and dramatic compositions found in Rubens. His large-scale use of these elements can be seen in *The Entry of Charles V into Antwerp* (1878; Hamburg, Art Gallery).

BIBLIOGRAPHY. E. Pirchan, *Hans Makart...*, Vienna, 1942.

MAKIMONO (Emaki; Emakimono). Japanese term for horizontal scroll painting. This type of painting was imported from China. The oldest Japanese example is the *Ingakyo Sūtra Scrolls* (8th cent.), in which the illustrations run above the text. A subsequent technique involved alternating a portion of text with an expanse of painting. A further refinement, occurring in the Heian romances such as the *Tale of Genji* (12th cent.), was the use of so fluid a calligraphy that the pictorial narrative remained virtually unbroken. Greater continuity was achieved in the *Shigisan Engi Scrolls* and *Animal Caricature Scrolls* of the Heian period, and in the *Ban Dainagon Scrolls* this art reached the peak of its expressive power. *See* ANIMAL CARICATURE SCROLLS; BAN DAINAGON SCROLLS; SHIGISAN ENGI SCROLLS; TALE OF GENJI SCROLL.

BIBLIOGRAPHY. R. T. Paine and A. Soper, *The Art and Architecture of Japan*, Baltimore, 1955; Y. Yashiro, *2,000 Years of Japanese Art*, New York, 1958.

MAKONDE, *see* AFRICA, PRIMITIVE ART OF (SOUTH-CENTRAL AND EAST AFRICA: TANGANYIKA).

MAKRON. Attic vase painter (fl. ca. 500–480 B.C.). He was the foremost artist in the workshop of the potter Hieron. Makron's work is characterized by a facile but sometimes careless draftsmanship applied to large, flowing rhythmical compositions; these qualities are best illustrated by his picture of a group of maenads on a cup in Berlin.

BIBLIOGRAPHY. G. M. A. Richter, *Attic Red-Figured Vases: A Survey*, New Haven, 1958.

MAKSOORAH, *see* MAQSURA.

MA KUNG-HSIEN. Chinese academy painter (fl. mid-12th cent.). The son of Ma Hsing-tsu and the third-genera-tion representative of the famous Ma family, he was active in the Southern Sung period in the Shao-hsing era (1131–62). One painting kept in the Nanzenji, Kyoto, bears his signature and shows a design that anticipates the work of his nephew Ma Yüan. *See* MA YUAN.

BIBLIOGRAPHY. O. Sirén, *Chinese Painting, Leading Masters and Principles*, vol. 2, New York, 1956.

MALAGA CATHEDRAL. Spanish church originally conceived of as a Gothic design by Enriques Egas. The present Renaissance structure was begun in 1528 and is stylistically related to the Cathedral of Granada. The work had numerous distinguished architects before it was left unfinished in 1783—in the 16th century, Diego de Siloe, Diego de Vergara, Andrés de Vandelviva, and Fernán Ruiz; in the 17th century, Díaz de Palacios; and in the 18th century, José Bada. The Cathedral of Málaga is built entirely of white limestone and occupies the site of a Moorish mosque, which was consecrated for the Christian faith in 1487.

BIBLIOGRAPHY. C. Sarthou Carreres, *Catedrales de España*, Madrid, 1946; J. H. Harvey, *The Cathedrals of Spain*, London, 1957.

MALANGGAN (Malagan), *see* NEW IRELAND; OCEANIC ART (MELANESIA: NEW IRELAND).

MALBONE, EDWARD GREENE. American painter and miniaturist (b. Newport, R.I., 1777; d. Savannah, Ga., 1807). He studied in Newport and with Samuel King in Boston. About 1794 Malbone established himself in Providence (he later worked in Boston, New York, Philadelphia, and Charleston) and soon became America's most important and popular portrait miniaturist, a position achieved by technical skill, lively color, and a sure instinct for the pleasing likeness. In 1801 he accompanied his friend Washington Allston to London. Malbone's much praised miniature, *The Hours* (Providence, Athenaeum), dates from this trip. On his return in the same year he settled in Charleston.

BIBLIOGRAPHY. R. P. Tolman, *The Life and Works of Edward Greene Malbone*, New York, 1958.

MALBORK, *see* MARIENBURG: CASTLE OF THE TEUTONIC KNIGHTS.

MALDARELLI, ORONZIO. American sculptor (1892–   ). Born in Naples, he came to America as a child but revisited Europe in the early 1930s. He studied at Cooper Union and the Beaux-Arts Design Institute in New York City. Maldarelli's art reflects a curious combination of influences from the sculpture of Elie Nadelman and Maillol and from Art Nouveau, with none of these aesthetics actually prevailing. His forms, as in *Gemini* (Philadelphia, Fairmount Park Association) and *Caress* (1944; New York, Whitney Museum), suggest a stylized adaptation of Maillol's more relaxed handling of the figure. Maldarelli has designed engravings for glassware made by the Steuben glass company. At his best, this artist reveals an understanding of anatomy and movement of the human figure, especially the female nude, even when the product may appear to be stylized or postured.

BIBLIOGRAPHY. A. C. Ritchie, *Sculpture of the 20th Century*, New York, 1952.

MALER, VALENTINE. Bohemian medalist, mint modeler and goldsmith (b. Iglau, Moravia, ca. 1540; d. Nürnberg, 1603). Active mainly in Nürnberg, where he became a master and married the daughter of Wenzel Jamnitzer (1569), Maler is also known to have worked in Saxony (1573–75) and possibily in Silesia. He is primarily known as the maker of more than 200 cast or struck mannerist portrait medals, many from wax models. Many of his medals are in the Bavarian National Museum, Munich, for example, the *Portrait of the Bishop of Würzburg* (1575).

BIBLIOGRAPHY. H. Habich, *Die deutschen Schaumünzen des XVI. Jahrhunderts*, vol. 2, pt. 1, Munich, 1932.

MALERISCH. German term, meaning "painterly," used to describe both the technique of painting and the other arts, such as sculpture and the graphic arts, where the emphasis is on values of light and shade as opposed to line. *Malerisch* also describes the general aspect of a work of art in the sense of the word "picturesque."

MALESKIRCHER, GABRIEL. German painter (fl. Upper Bavaria, ca. 1440-60). Previously he was identified as the master of the high altar of the cloister church of Tegernsee (panels now in Nürnberg, German National Museum).

Kasimir Malevich, *An Englishman in Moscow*, 1914. Municipal Museum, Amsterdam.

This identification was recently disproved and Mäleskircher is now without any attributable works.

BIBLIOGRAPHY. K. Oettinger, "Die Blütezeit der Münchner gotischen Malerei. II. Die Nachfolge des Worcester-Meisters," *Zeitschrift des Deutschen Vereins für Kunstwissenschaft*, VIII, 1941.

MALEVICH, KASIMIR. Russian painter (b. Kiev, 1878; d. Leningrad, 1935). Known as the founder of suprematism, Malevich was probably the first painter to produce purely geometric compositions. He studied at the Kiev School of Art and then at the Moscow Academy of Fine Arts (1900–04). His style came under French Fauvist influence about 1910, when he was active in the Jack of Diamonds group in Moscow. In 1911 he was represented in major exhibitions there and in St. Petersburg. He visited Paris in 1912 and was directly inspired by cubism. The *Scissors Grinder* (1912; New Haven, Yale University Art Gallery) and *Woman with Water Pails* (1912; New York, Museum of Modern Art) disclose his debt to the styles of various cubist painters and, perhaps less obviously, to futurism. The clarity of modeling and edges in these and related works suggests a personal effort to attain a purer, less sensuous technique than the still highly textural handling of most analytic cubist canvases.

Between 1912 and 1915 Malevich formulated his suprematist style, in which, as he stated in his book *Die gegenstandslose Welt* (*The Non-objective World*; 1927), he sought to free art from all pragmatic associations of subject. His *Suprematist Elements: Two Squares* (ca. 1913; New York, Museum of Modern Art) may be one of the first severely geometric abstractions in the history of modern art. Malevich at times reverted, however, to his special variety of cubism, as in *An Englishman in Moscow* (1914; Amsterdam, Municipal Museum).

Suprematism may or may not have been anticipated, insofar as its abstract concept is concerned, by Larionov's rayonist works, the first of which evidently appeared in 1910 or 1911. The utilization of only rectangles and squares, however, is Malevich's own development. *See* SUPREMATISM.

Between 1914 and 1918 he proceeded from black-on-black or white-on-white forms to red rectangles or squares on white grounds and more complex combinations such as trapezoids and partly curved shapes of yellow, violet, green, red, and black (*Suprematist Composition*, 1915–16, Leningrad). In such key works of suprematism of 1914–15 as *Eight Red Rectangles* (Amsterdam, Municipal Museum) Malevich achieved remarkable variety with great economy by subtly making slightly trapezoidal forms rather than precise rectangles, by establishing a diagonal movement rather than the indicated horizontal-vertical arrangement, and by delicately blurring the pristine edges of his shapes. An especially restrained work is his *White on White* (before 1918; New York, Museum of Modern Art).

In addition to showing with the Jack of Diamonds group after 1910, Malevich exhibited with the Blue Rider in Munich in 1912 and at the important suprematist show in Moscow in 1919, where Rodchenko hung his *Black on Black*. Malevich lived in Leningrad after 1921. As the probable founder of purely geometric painting, he was a pioneer of 20th-century abstraction.

BIBLIOGRAPHY. K. Malevich, *Die gegenstandslose Welt* (Bauhausbücher II), Munich, 1927 (Eng. tr., H. Dearstyne, The Non-objective

World, Chicago, 1959); E. Winter, "The Lost Leadership of Kasimir Malevich," *Art News*, LVII, December, 1958; R. Rosenblum, *Cubism and Twentieth-Century Art*, New York, 1960; C. Gray, *The Great Russian Experiment: Russian Art, 1863–1922*, New York, 1962.

JOHN C. GALLOWAY

MALFATTI, ANITA. Brazilian painter (1896–   ). Anita Malfatti studied in her native city of São Paulo and in Dresden, Berlin, and New York City (with Homer Boss at the Art Students League). She presented the first modern art exhibit by a Brazilian (1917; São Paulo) and exhibited in Modern Art Week (1922; São Paulo). She uses a Fauve-expressionist style (for example, *Mario Andrade*, 1922; São Paulo, Andrade Family Collection).

BIBLIOGRAPHY. P. M. de Almeida, *De Anita ao Museu*, São Paulo, 1961.

MALHY, SIMON DE, *see* CHALONS, SIMON DE.

MALI, *see* AFRICA, PRIMITIVE ART OF (WEST AFRICA).

MA LIN. Chinese painter (fl. mid-13th cent.). The son of the famous Ma Yüan and considered the last member of a great family of painters, Ma Lin was active in the Southern Sung Academy. His reputation has suffered somewhat from the accusation that his father often signed his more prominent name to landscapes actually painted by Ma Lin himself. A number of misattributed Ma Lins in Japanese collections further cloud the view of his real achievements, but in a number of works, such as *Sunset Landscape* (Tokyo, Nezu Collection) and *Listening to Wind in the Pines* (Formosa, Sun Yat-sen Museum), his wide-ranging abilities are clearly demonstrated and indicate that perhaps he should be reappraised as a worthy successor to the Ma Yüan style.

BIBLIOGRAPHY. J. Cahill, *Chinese Painting, 11th–14th Centuries*, New York, 1960.

MALINES: CATHEDRAL OF SAINT-ROMBAUT, *see* MECHLIN: CATHEDRAL OF ST. ROMBAUT.

MALINKE, *see* AFRICA, PRIMITIVE ART OF (WEST AFRICA: MALI).

MALLE BOBBE. Oil painting by Hals, in the former State Museums, Berlin. *See* HALS, FRANS FRANSZ.

MALLES VENOSTA (Mals): SAN BENEDETTO. Parish church near Bolzano in northern Italy. It was founded by the nearby monastery of Münster (Müstair) in Switzerland between 805 and 881 and was built before the end of the 9th century. The undivided boxlike interior is covered by a flat wooden ceiling. The straight east wall is supported by three horseshoe arches on stucco capitals. The east wall and part of the north wall have fragments of frescoes representing saints and two donor portraits. One is a nobleman; the other, a priest, who is holding a model of the church, is one of the finest Carolingian portraits extant.

BIBLIOGRAPHY. J. Garber, "Die karolingische St. Benediktkirche in Mals," *Zeitschrift des Ferdinandeums für Tirol und Vorarlberg*, Innsbruck, 1915.

MALLET-STEVENS, ROBERT. French architect (1886–1945). Born in Paris, he worked in his native city during the 1920s and 1930s in the austere, geometric form of the International Style. Among his buildings are the Alfa-Romeo Garage (Paris, 1925) and the Reifenberg and Martel houses (both Paris, 1927), in the manner of Le Corbusier.

BIBLIOGRAPHY. G. A. Platz, *Die Baukunst der neuesten Zeit*, 2d ed., Berlin, 1930.

MALLIA. Important Minoan town on the northern coast of Crete, noted for its palace (Middle Minoan I–III) and cemetery (Early Minoan I). Remnants of pottery and of hieroglyphic inscriptions from Mallia indicate the existence of an early culture. The name Mallia probably derives from *omala* or *omalia* (smooth) and was suggested by the level fields in the vicinity. *See* CRETE (PALACES: MALLIA).

BIBLIOGRAPHY. R. W. Hutchinson, *Prehistoric Crete*, Baltimore, 1962.

MALMAISON, CHATEAU OF. Seventeenth-century French country house in the western environs of Paris. Malmaison was acquired in 1799 by Napoleon Bonaparte, who had it enlarged and embellished by the architects Percier and Fontaine and the landscape designer Louis-Martin Berthault. The building was the residence of the empress Josephine, who left her personal stamp throughout. After a series of vicissitudes Malmaison was presented

Château of Malmaison, western environs of Paris. The bedroom of the empress Josephine.

to the French state in 1902 to serve as a museum of the art of the Napoleonic period. The collections include paintings, furniture, gold- and silverwork, porcelains, musical instruments, and Josephine's personal mementos.

BIBLIOGRAPHY. J. Bourguignon, *Malmaison*, Paris, 1937; J. Billiet, *Malmaison, Les appartements de Joséphine*, Paris, 1951.

MALMESBURY ABBEY. The church of this English Benedictine abbey was begun about 1145. The Romanesque monastic buildings on the north, the crossing with transepts and presbytery, and the east parts with ambulatory and Lady Chapel no longer exist. The nine-bay nave has an elevation of arcade, four-part gallery arches, and a later clerestory. It has cylinder piers with pointed arches and ribbed vaults over the aisles, but the Norman timber nave was replaced by a 14th-century one.

Malmesbury was created by a school of West Country masons working about 1160. The great south portal (ca. 1170–80) is of exuberant richness, with orders carved with figure subjects in shallow relief, and a series of apostles in the tympanum.

BIBLIOGRAPHY. A. W. Clapham, *English Romanesque Architecture after the Conquest*, Oxford, 1934.

MALMO: ST. PETER'S. Swedish church erected in the first half of the 14th century and restored in 1890. The nave and two aisles are continuous with the choir and ambulatory so that the transept is expressed only on the exterior, as in French High Gothic churches. St. Peter's belongs to a group of Hanseatic late Gothic structures found on both sides of the Baltic Sea.

BIBLIOGRAPHY. E. Lundberg, *Byggnadskonsten i Sverige under Medeltiden, 1000–1400*, Stockholm, 1940.

MALO, VINCENT. Flemish painter (b. Cambrai, ca. 1600; d. Rome or Genoa, 1650 or 1656 or 1670). He belonged to the Rubens circle and was a pupil of David Teniers the Elder. Malo painted genre scenes in the Italianate manner, landscapes, and religious subjects in a Rubensian style. Some of his works were retouched by Anthony van Dyck.

BIBLIOGRAPHY. R. Oldenbourg, *Die flämische Malerei des 17. Jahrhunderts*, 2d ed., Berlin, 1922.

MALOSSO, IL, *see* TROTTI, GIOVAN-BATTISTA.

MALOUEL, JEAN. Franco-Flemish painter (fl. 1396–1415). He is one of the few known representatives of the Paris school of panel painting of about 1400. He was from Guelders, and an uncle of the Limbourg brothers, whom he probably assisted in getting royal patronage. Malouel was in the service of Queen Isabeau in Paris until 1397; then he joined Philip the Bold, duke of Burgundy. Documents indicate that he was extremely active; although little of his work has survived, it is known that he received a commission in 1398 to do five large panels for the chapel of the Chartreuse de Champmol, Dijon, and that from 1401 to 1403 he was also to polychrome the *Well of Moses* at the Chartreuse. He died before completing the panels and Henri Bellechose was appointed to succeed him in the task.

Only two works, both in the Louvre Museum, Paris, can with any certainty be ascribed to Malouel. The earlier is a *Pietà*, one of the earliest known tondo panels. It depicts the Trinity with St. John, Mary, and angels, and God the Father holding the broken body of Christ in *pietà* fashion. The painting is subtle and delicate, with the linear and coloristic qualities of 14th-century Sienese painting. The reasons for ascribing it to Malouel are the appearance of the arms of France and Burgundy on the back and the stylistical resemblances it bears to the second panel, which is better documented.

This second panel, the *Martyrdom of St. Denis*, seems to be identified in documents mentioning a commission of 1398 for which one panel was to represent a life of St. Denis. The commission was completed on Malouel's death by Henri Bellechose. This panel clearly shows the work of two different hands, and, further, it has the arms of France and Burgundy on the back. The work of one of the artists involved, the more *retardataire*, shows great similarities to the aforementioned tondo. Depicted in narrative sequence are St. Denis in prison, St. Denis approaching the block, and the beheading of the saint. Hierarchically placed is a Crucifixion supported by God the Father, in a traditional Trinity arrangement. Against a background entirely in gold the brilliant blue, embroidered robes gleam. The rather Oriental splendor and Italo-Byzantine feeling of the whole is enhanced by the green modeling in the figure of the Crucified (as in Sienese painting) and the ornamental, Orientalizing inscriptions on the borders of the robes. Linear delicacy and the anatomical treatment of the body of Christ clearly relate this panel to the earlier tondo.

Malouel's importance is as a representative of the influential Paris school, which helped lay the foundations for the great developments in panel painting during the next generation.

BIBLIOGRAPHY. G. Bazin, *L'Ecole franco-flamande, XIV–XV siècles*, Geneva, 1941. STANLEY FERBER

Malmesbury Abbey. The church of this Benedictine abbey, begun 1145.

Jean Malouel, *Pietà*. Louvre, Paris. One of the earliest known tondo panels.

MALQATA. Arabic name of a site in Western Thebes where Amenhotep III (1405–1370 B.C.) built an extensive group of four palaces and had a large artificial lake excavated for his queen, Tiy. There is no formal layout. Brick was used for the walls, wood for columns and ceilings, and stone sparingly for column bases, doorways, and floors in bathrooms.

The largest palace of this Pharaoh (328 by ca. 197 ft.) is oriented north and south and has no monumental entrance, but it is accessible from the Middle Palace by a broad corridor. It consists of two ceremonial columned halls at the north end, each with a throne dais on the south wall, and a transverse lobby flanked by two storerooms that separate this part from the harem. Here a central columned hall, flanked by two rows of four contiguous suites, precedes the throne room and residence of the Pharaoh. The floors are painted with representations of ponds, birds, and plants, and the walls are covered with formal decorations of dadoes with false-door paneling, bands of rosettes topped with dancing Bes figures, and panels with animals springing about in a lively fashion. The ceilings are painted with a row of flying vultures within a frame of rosettes and spirals.

BIBLIOGRAPHY. Robb de P. Tytus, *A Preliminary Report on the Re-excavation of the Palace of Amenhotep III*, New York, 1903; W. S. Smith, *The Art and Architecture of Ancient Egypt*, Baltimore, 1958.   ALEXANDER M. BADAWY

MALRAUX, ANDRE. French art critic and novelist (1901–   ). Born in Paris, he first studied Far Eastern art and before the age of thirty was a recognized authority in this field. After World War II his first essays on the psychology of art began to appear: *The Voices of Silence* and *The Metamorphosis of the Gods*. Their intellectual power and literary brilliance perfectly link Malraux's theory of art to the heroic themes of his novels. They offer an all-encompassing view of art as an expression of man's attitude to life and death. That all art is a sequence of metamorphoses directly tied to man's varying reactions to "his portion of destiny" is a recurring theme. Earlier, in *The Psychology of Art*, he attempted an estimate of art beyond time and space. *Saturn* (1950) is a study of Goya; *Vermeer de Delft* (1952), an appraisal of the great Dutch master. *Le musée imaginaire de la sculpture* (*The Museum Without Walls*, 1952–54) is Malraux's inquiry into sculptured forms as world-forms, linked to his first love, archaeology. In 1954 he published *Des Bas-reliefs aux grottes sacrées*. The great influence of Malraux as an intellectual force received recognition in his appointment as Minister of Culture in the De Gaulle government. In this capacity he has reorganized French museums and has undertaken the restoration of historical buildings and other monuments.

BIBLIOGRAPHY. W. M. Frohock, *André Malraux and the Tragic Imagination*, Stanford, Calif., 1952; G. Picon, *Malraux par lui-même*, Paris, 1953; E. Gannon, S. J., *The Honor of Being a Man: The World of André Malraux*, Chicago, 1957; G. H. Hartman, *Malraux*, London, 1960.   ARNOLD ROSIN

MALS: SAN BENEDETTO, *see* MALLES VENOSTA: SAN BENEDETTO.

MALTA. Island country of the Mediterranean Sea. Steppingstone for many migratory and colonizing peoples, the Maltese Islands are rich in the art of many periods. The prehistoric megalithic temples and underground sanctuaries, which may date from the 3d and 2d millenniums B.C., are sophisticated in plan and construction. There are medieval constructions (St. Gregory) and Renaissance churches (St. John) that show an interweaving of northern and Mediterranean influences. The baroque style is much in evidence (Zeitun Church; Notabile Cathedral). In Musta the Church of the Rotunda is a notable example of 19th-century construction in masonry, with its Pantheon-sized domical vault of local stone.

BIBLIOGRAPHY. E. Sammut, *Art in Malta*, Malta, 1953; J. D. Evans, *Malta*, London, 1959.

MALTON, THOMAS, JR. English architectural and topographical draftsman (1748–1804). For a time he was a scene painter at Covent Garden. He was a more picturesque artist than either his father, Thomas, Sr. (1726–1801), or his brother James (ca. 1766–1803). Much of his work, including views of London and Bath, was engraved,

and his drawing of figures was particularly noteworthy. J. M. W. Turner studied under Malton.

BIBLIOGRAPHY. I. Williams, *Early English Watercolours*, London, 1952.

MALVITO, TOMMASO. Italian sculptor (fl. Como, Naples, late 15th cent.). Malvito was in Marseilles, France, from 1474 to 1483, where he assisted Francesco Laurana in the creation of sculptures for the Chapel of St-Lazare (1476–81; Marseilles Cathedral). There are many monuments from his stay in Naples (1484–1508), including the antependium of S. Giovanni a Carbonara and the tomb of Mariano d'Alagno and Caterina Orsini (1506–07). Malvito worked in a decorative, late-15th-century style.

BIBLIOGRAPHY. A. Muñoz, "Studi sulla scultura napoletana del Rinascimento: I—Tommaso Malvito da Como e suo figlio Gian Tommaso," *Bollettino d'arte*, III, 1909 (2 articles).

MAMALLAPURAM (Mahabalapuram). Village in Madras State, India, about 32 miles south of the city of Madras. A port for the capital of the Pallava dynasty during the 7th century, Māmallapuram is the site of seven monolithic temples called rathas, each quarried out of one huge boulder, the largest about 30 feet high. Each reproduces a different type of religious building prevalent at the time. The wood prototypes are faithfully preserved in the stone carvings to represent the common southern type of temple, with the pyramidal śikhara made up of strongly molded courses culminating in the solid *stūpikā* finial. One ratha shows a barrel roof with a chaitya gable at each end. Another represents an apsidal temple of the type better known through Buddhist chaitya halls. Still another imitates a small thatch-roofed hut. Although such a hut apparently was a vestige of the primitive dwelling, it is indicated that the thatch was secured by ornamental metal corners.

There are a number of cave temples at the site. These are generally shallow rectangular halls with shrines cut into their backs. The sculpture on the cave temples, as on the

Mamallapuram. Monolithic temples, Pallava dynasty, 7th century.

rathas, generally follows the graceful and sensuous style of Amarāvatī. However, there is a definite local style, seen primarily in the cult figures, which are frontal and have extremely wide shoulders and wide hips, exaggerated by scarves at the sides. This form of the Pallava tradition was to extend into the Chola dynasty, as late as the 10th century. A third style has affinities with Ceylon, from which it may derive. This can be seen in the most important cave, the Mahīshasura *maṇḍapa*, where some of the figures give the impression of emerging from the rock background as if the stone were treated in a repoussé technique. The various sculptural styles are combined on a huge cliff completely covered with sculptured figures depicting the legend of the Descent of the Ganges. Life-size figures of worshipers, ascetics, animals (including elephants), and deities in their imagined scale cover the huge boulder. Originally a cistern at the top held water that could be emptied through a channel in the middle of the composition, dramatizing the falling waters of the Ganges. An unfinished version of the same subject exists on another cliff nearby.

Toward the end of the 7th century the structural temple known as the Shore Temple was built. Actually, the Shore Temple is composed of two separate Saivite temples. The śikharas of these, although southern in form, rise more vertically than most examples of this type and form the prototype for the towering śikhara of the Rājorājeśvara at Tanjore, built about the year 1000.

BIBLIOGRAPHY. A. Rea, *Pallava Architecture* (Archaeological Survey of India, no. 11), Madras, 1909; A. Longhurst, *Pallava Architecture*, 3 pts. (Memoirs of the Archaeological Survey of India, no. 17), Simla, 1924–30; P. Brown, *Indian Architecture*, vol. 1: *Buddhist and Hindu Periods*, 4th ed., Bombay, 1959.

J. LEROY DAVIDSON

MAMBUNDA, *see* AFRICA, PRIMITIVE ART OF (SOUTH-CENTRAL AND EAST AFRICA: RHODESIA).

Mamluk architecture. Tombs of the Caliphs, east of Cairo.

MAMERTINE PRISON, ROME. Ancient prison, situated between the Temple of Concord and the Curia, at the foot of the Capitoline hill. In part it is as old as any structure in the city. In Roman times it was called the Carcer. The name Custodia Mamertini was given to it in the Middle Ages. The prison consists of two parts: (1) the lower and more ancient part, in the form of a circular chamber with walls built of blocks of tufa (this room was known in classical times as the Tullianum); and (2) an upper trapezoidal room with a barrel-vaulted roof and a square opening in the center that served as an entrance. In republican times many famous victims were executed there, and their bodies were thrown out on the Scalae Gemoniae.

MAMLUK ARCHITECTURE (Egypt and Syria). Egypt and Syria were ruled by Mamluk dynasties from 1252 until the capture of Cairo by an Ottoman force in 1517. In 1707 a less powerful Mamluk dynasty was restored in Egypt, to fall a century later before the armies of Napoleon. Powerful sultans ruled at Cairo, and it is their monuments that have remained so imposing down to the present. In addition, several of the sultans erected their mausoleums east of the city, and most of these monuments included within the same complex a mosque, a madrasa, and quarters for attendants. Syria, finally wrested from the Crusaders at the beginning of this period, remained a backwater, and few imposing new structures were erected. *See* CAIRO.

Bibars (Baybars), the first great sultan of this long line, bore a name that meant panther, and figures of this beast usually appear on works built during his reign, including the imposing bridge of Abu-Munagga near Cairo, with its frieze of panthers. His madrasa (1261–65) was almost completely destroyed in the 19th century. In 1266 he ordered the erection of a mosque; rectangular in plan, it has four great liwans opening onto its open court. The fabric is baked brick, enlivened with inscription bands in an archaic Arabic script called Kufic, done in plaster, and with carving in low relief on areas of dressed stone; the decoration was inspired, in part, by the earlier al-Azhar.

In 1284 Sultan Qalaun (Kalaun), the "duck," had work begun on a group of buildings, which included a hospital, or *maristan*, a mosque, and his tomb. Little remains of the hospital, which was a complete university of medicine, but the other structures have survived in fairly good condition. The tomb, including a minaret and a restored dome over the central chamber, bridges the gap between the earlier Fatimid structures and the full development of the Mamluk period. Part of the change is that the structure is turned in upon itself; not meant to be seen as a whole from any distance, it displays high, fortresslike walls.

Qalaun's son, an-Nasir Muhammad, who reigned intermittently from 1293 to 1340, was a very active builder. Most of his structures have vanished, but the fine minaret of his tomb, decorated with arcades in carved plaster and stalactite balconies, remains. The use of archaistic features, such as the crenelations of the Mosque of ibn-Tulun, continued in the structures of Qalaun and an-Nasir Muhammad. In 1339 a courtier of the latter sultan, Altunbegha al-Mardany, built a mosque that has details reminiscent of the Mosque of ibn-Tulun and the unusual feature of an elaborate *mushrabiya* across the face of the liwan. The mausoleum of Toghay, a wife of an-Nasir Muhammad, displays a wide band of faïence mosaic, clearly inspired by Iranian examples, around the base of its soaring dome.

Sultan Hasan, a son of an-Nasir Muhammad, whose reign from 1347 to 1360 was troubled and interrupted, was responsible for the construction of the mosque-madrasa that bears his name; it is one of the most renowned Muslim monuments of Cairo. Surrounding streets crowded the complex into an irregular outline. Its minaret is the tallest in Cairo, rising some 285 feet. The sheer, plain exterior walls conceal the interior with its standard four-liwan, or cruciform, plan. The same areas of fine, undecorated masonry prevail on the interior, but there are a few surfaces covered with rich decoration, including a Kufic inscription on the sanctuary liwan and a marble mihrab and mimbar. This monument, like many others of the period, was lit by elegant lamps of enameled glass.

In 1347 a son-in-law of an-Nasir Muhammad, the emir Aqsunqur, built a mosque that featured octagonal piers, rather than the usual columns, and displayed a splendid mihrab and a mimbar, both done in contrasting marbles. Its round minaret, with three stalactite balconies, is one of the finest in Cairo. Today the structure is often called the Blue Mosque, from the facing of blue, green, and white faïence tiles that cover one of the walls of the sanctuary. These tiles are of Turkish manufacture and date from the 17th century.

The so-called Hall of Bibars, one of the finest examples of domestic architecture of this period, was erected in 1353 as an element of a now vanished palace. The pierced dome and the stalactite corbels are examples of great refinement of detail.

In 1388 Sultan Barquq erected a cruciform-plan mosque-madrasa, adjacent to that of an-Nasir Muhammad, that is very reminiscent of the mosque-madrasa of Sultan Hasan. The decoration, in courses of marble of contrasting colors around the entrance portal and in the marble paving of the court, is much more exuberant than that of its prototype structure. Barquq's mausoleum (1400–10), erected by one of his sons, lies east of Cairo in an area known as the Tombs of the Caliphs. The rectangular structure surrounds an open court that is flanked by the rooms of a madrasa and a monastery. Two domes, built of stone rather than of brick, rise over the graves of Barquq and members of his family. In plan form, structural features, and decoration in a variety of materials, this structure is one of the most representative of the period. *See* CALIPHS, TOMBS OF THE; SULTAN BARQUQ, MOSQUE OF, CAIRO.

Of the mosque-madrasa of Sultan al-Muayyed (1416–22), adjacent to the earlier Bab Zuweila, only the eastern section survives, including a chevron-patterned dome above the tomb chamber. The mausoleum of Bars Bay, one of the Tombs of the Caliphs, was completed in 1432 and includes a mosque and the ruins of a monastery. The elaborate interlace pattern executed in stonework on the surface of the dome approaches the height of decorative richness in the series of such domes.

Kait Bay was a most active patron of architecture. At the area of the Tombs of the Caliphs his own structure was completed in 1474 and includes the mausoleum, mosque, madrasa, and library. Above the tomb chamber the dome rises sharply upon an unusually high zone of

transition. Exterior and interior details show attenuation and refinement. *See* KAIT BAY, TOMB OF.

Few new structures of great size and magnificence were undertaken by the Mamluks in Syria. The Crusader castles were taken over intact, Christian churches and cathedrals were turned into mosques, additions were made to the greater mosques of earlier periods, and lesser structures were erected by the lieutenants of the sultans. In Damascus the Zahiriya madrasa was built in 1279 to serve as the tomb of Sultan Bibars. It features a fine stalactite portal and interior surfaces covered with gold-ground mosaics. Kait Bay ordered the erection of the minaret at the southwestern corner of the Great Mosque of Damascus, and the structure is indistinguishable in style from those erected at Cairo itself. Caravansaries, public baths, and khans (city storehouses of wholesale merchants) were erected throughout Syria. *See* DAMASCUS.

Mamluk architecture was not represented by numerous vast structures but by multipurpose monuments serving religious requirements, with each part of these buildings of comparatively small scale. Technical skill was at its height. In construction it was displayed in fine masonry, in stalactite vaults, and in the attenuation of forms. In decoration it appeared in delicate tracery in stone and in carved plaster and brilliant mosaics, but each such element was confined within clearly marked boundaries or spread over surfaces separate from others. It was a period of high style, with productions different from those of other regions of the Muslim world.

DONALD N. WILBER

MAMLUK GLASSWARE, METALWORK, POTTERY, TEXTILES,
see ISLAMIC GLASS AND CRYSTAL (AYYUBID AND MAMLUK PERIODS); ISLAMIC METALWORK (MAMLUK PERIOD); ISLAMIC POTTERY AND TILES (MAMLUK PERIOD); ISLAMIC TEXTILES (AYYUBID AND MAMLUK PERIODS).

MAN, CORNELIS DE. Dutch painter of portraits, genre, and interior scenes (b. Delft, 1621; d. there, 1706). In 1642 De Man was inscribed as a member of the Delft Guild of St. Luke, and shortly afterward he left on a journey abroad. He spent nine years traveling in Paris, Florence, Venice, and Rome. He was reported back in Delft in 1654. De Man painted interiors in the manner of Pieter de Hoogh, Emanuel de Witte, and Johannes Vermeer.

BIBLIOGRAPHY. C. Brière-Misme, "Un Emule de Vermeer et Pieter de Hoogh: Cornelis de Man," *Oud-Holland*, LII, 1935.

MANAIGO, SILVESTRO. Italian painter (b. Venice, 1670; d. there, 1734). A student of Gregorio Lazzarini, Manaigo for the most part painted religious works in the somber and massive style of his master in the transitional period between the Venetian baroque and rococo.

MANARA, *see* MINARET.

MANASARA SILPASASTRA. Gupta Indian treatise on architecture. The Mānasāra Silpaśāstra was handed down from the gods to a class of rishis (inspired poets or sages) called Mānasāra.

MANASSIA. Monastic site overlooking the Resava River in central Serbia, Yugoslavia. Construction of the monastery was begun in 1407 and completed in 1418 by the despot Stefan Lazarević. Although Manassia was a center of book production, a cycle of mural paintings of the Morava period constitutes its chief claim to fame. Only one-third of the original paintings survive, but they are probably the most remarkable achievement of this period of Serbian art. The iconography and style of these paintings, many of which are concerned with the miracles and parables of Christ, depend on the Paleologan art of Constantinople. The Manassia paintings show close affinities with the Italo-Greek art of the Adriatic, which derives from the same source. Similarly, the architecture of the church is Byzantine, with details modified by Italian influence.

MAN AT THE CROSSROADS. Fresco painting by Rivera, in the Palace of Fine Arts, Mexico City. *See* RIVERA, DIEGO.

MANAURE, MATEO. Venezuelan painter and etcher (1926–). Born in Uracoa, he studied from 1941 to 1947 in Caracas. His early works are expressionistic figure paintings, but more recent ones are hard-edge, nonobjective compositions.

MANCADAM, JACOBUS SIBRAND. Dutch painter of landscapes and allegories (b. Friesland, ca. 1602; d. Leeuwarden, 1680). Little is known of Mancadam's training. He may have been born in Groningen. In 1634 and 1637/38 he was burgomaster of Franeker. He was reported as a citizen of Leeuwarden in 1645. His earlier works are landscapes, seemingly from nature, but he later was influenced by the Italianate style of such masters as Willem van Nieulandt and Bartholomeus Breenberg.
BIBLIOGRAPHY. M. E. Houtzager et al., *Nederlandse 17e Eeuwse Italianiserende Landschapschilders*, Utrecht, 1965.

MANCHESTER, ENGLAND: WHITWORTH ART GALLERY. Collection founded in 1889. Early Italian, Flemish, and German engravings and woodcuts complement an important collection of English water colors. The large textile collection includes Coptic weavings, Spanish and Italian ecclesiastical vestments, and English embroideries.

MANCHESTER, N.H.: CURRIER GALLERY OF ART. This museum has a distinguished collection of American art, ranging from the early primitives through the 18th, 19th, and 20th centuries, with works by Copley, Stuart, Sargent, Henri, Homer, Sheeler, and Wyeth. American furniture and silver are included in the decorative arts display. The gallery owns a fine Gothic tapestry, *The Visit of the Gypsies*, part of a series woven at Tournai about 1500. Two others in the series are in the Corcoran Gallery in Washington, D.C. The Currier has a small but select collection of European paintings, with landscapes by Ruisdael, Corot, Constable, and Monet.
BIBLIOGRAPHY. S. L. Faison, *A Guide to the Art Museums of New England*, New York, 1958.

MANCINI, DOMENICO. Venetian painter (fl. 1511). He is known from a signed triptych (Lendinara Cathedral) of which only the central Madonna is preserved. It is of sophisticated Giorgionesque style though literally borrowing motifs from Giovanni Bellini and Palma. Besides many problematic attributions of Giorgionesque works, it is debated whether he painted the portrait (1512; Leningrad, Hermitage) signed "Domenico" and the *Guitarist* (formerly Motta di Livenza, Scarpa Collection), signed "Mancin."
BIBLIOGRAPHY. J. Wilde, "Die Probleme um Domenico Mancini," *Jahrbuch der Kunsthistorischen Sammlungen in Wien*, VII, 1933.

MANDALA (Mandara). Hindu or Buddhist painting having a symbolic geometric arrangement of deities. In Vajrayāna Buddhism the *maṇḍala* (Sanskrit, meaning "circle") is a representation of the spiritual plan of the universe and may be used as the basic design of a monument (for example, the Barabudur temple complex in Java) or be painted on cloth, on temple walls, or on pavements with colored powder. *See* VAJRAYANA.

MANDALA, DEER, *see* DEER MANDALA.

MANDAPA. Open cult hall before the sanctuary in an Indo-Aryan-style Hindu temple.

MANDARA, *see* MANDALA.

MANDARA IN KOJIMADERA, NARA. Japanese silk painting (10th cent.). It consists of two paintings, the *Diamond Mandara* and the *Womb Mandara*, executed in gold and silver on purplish-blue silk. Mandara (mandala) pictures are the painted representation of the esoteric Buddhist doctrines. The *Diamond Mandara* has gods arranged in concentric circles, and the *Womb Mandara* shows them placed in squares. Firm yet supple outlines give the figures plasticity and strength.
BIBLIOGRAPHY. T. Akiyama, *Japanese Painting*, [Geneva?] 1961; National Commission for the Protection of Cultural Properties, ed., *Kokuhō (National Treasures of Japan)*, vol. 2: *The Heian Period*, Tokyo, 1964.

MANDER, KAREL VAN. Flemish painter, poet, and biographer (b. Meulebeke, near Coutrai, 1548; d. Amsterdam, 1604). After his apprenticeship he was associated with Lucas de Heere of Ghent and by 1569 was established in Meulebeke as an independent master. In 1573 Van Mander began ten years of travel, returning by 1583 to Haarlem, where he founded the Academy. He moved to Amsterdam in 1604.

His mature paintings, such as *The Martyrdom of St. Catherine* (1582/83; Coutrai, St. Martin), reflect the northern mannerist qualities of De Heere and Bartholomeus Spranger. Van Mander's late works, on the other hand, evince a return to the Flemish landscape tradition, as in the monogrammed and dated *The Preaching of St. John the Baptist* (1597; Hannover, Lower Saxony Landesmuseum). Like Vasari, Van Mander is better known today as a writer than as a painter. His *Schilderboek* (*Book of Painters*, 1st ed., 1604; 2d ed., 1618) is our chief source of information for the lives of northern artists.
BIBLIOGRAPHY. L. van Puyvelde, "Considérations sur les maniéristes flamands," *Revue Belge d'Archéologie et d'Histoire de l'Art*, XXIX, 1960.

MANDILION. A kind of loose-fitting frock with hanging sleeves worn by Roman soldiers. According to legend the image of Christ's face was miraculously transferred to a piece of linen carried by St. Veronica; King Abgar of

Manesse Manuscript. Wolfram von Eschenbach, miniature of the Minnesänger. University Library, Heidelberg, Germany.

Alfred Manessier, *Offering to the Earth*, 1961–62. Private collection, Paris.

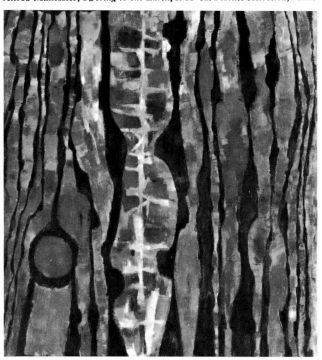

Edessa is also reported to have received a similar image of Christ on a piece of linen. These images are known as mandilions.

MANDORLA. Almond-shaped glory surrounding the figure of Christ in representations of the Majesty and the Ascension; it sometimes also surrounds the figure of Mary in the Assumption of the Virgin. It is found for the first time in Early Christian art surrounding the image of the Good Shepherd on sarcophagi. The mandorla is sometimes known as *Vesica piscis* (Latin for fish bladder) because of its shape.

MANESCARDI (Menescardi), GIUSTINO. Italian painter (ca. 1720–76?). Born in Milan, he was trained in the circle of Gaetano Zompini but was obviously more deeply influenced by the work of Giovanni Battista Tiepolo. Manescardi's mature works, such as *Moses Overturning the Crown of Pharaoh* (Washington, D.C., National Gallery), reveal solidity of design lightened by the vivacious action of the figures and by sparkling luminous color. Later, his style became dryer and more academic, losing the fresh originality of his early works.

BIBLIOGRAPHY. R. Pallucchini, *Storia della pittura veneziana*, vol. 1: *La pittura veneziana del Settecento*, Venice, 1960.

MANESSE MANUSCRIPT (Manessische Handschrift). Gothic illuminated manuscript, in the University Library, Heidelberg, Germany.

MANESSIER, ALFRED. French abstract painter (1911–   ). He was born at St-Ouen and has lived in Paris since 1941. In 1935, after studying architecture at the Ecole des Beaux-Arts, he turned to painting and studied with Bissière. Religious themes dominate Manessier's work after 1943. He designed stained-glass windows for churches at Breseux in Doubs and at Basel and Arles and the mosaic marquee of the Chapel of Ste-Thérèse at Hem, France (1958). His art has affinities with that of Bazaine, Estève, and Le Moal, with whom he has often exhibited. In 1955 Manessier won the Carnegie award at Pittsburgh.

In his paintings, shapes are loosely joined in patterns that recall panes of colored glass or mosaic. Although religious and nature themes are more often implied by the title of a picture than by its explicit representation, spiritual and mystical values are expressed by the illusion of light and the immediacy of the color.

BIBLIOGRAPHY. J. Cayrol, *Manessier*, Paris, 1955; B. Dorival, "Alfred Manessier, Religious Artisan," *The Selective Eye*, New York, 1956–57.

MANET, EDOUARD. French painter (b. Paris, 1832; d. there, 1883). Manet came from an aristocratic family, and his father was chief of personnel at the Ministry of Justice. Manet attended the Collège Rollin in Paris. His uncle, Edmond-Edouard Fournier, a knowledgeable art collector, interested the boy in painting and took him and a school chum, Antonin Proust, to the Louvre. On completion of his studies Manet announced that he wanted to become an artist, although his father wanted him to follow the law. As an alternative, he joined the Navy and in 1848 he went

Edouard Manet, *The Balcony*, detail. Louvre, Paris.

to sea. He failed his examinations for the Naval Training School a year later, and his father allowed him to study art.

He became a student of the academician Thomas Couture, as did Proust. Manet found Couture's approach sterile and resisted it. He copied at the Louvre, but it was not until 1856 that he left Couture. Manet had no desire to offend or resist the established art world as exemplified by the Academy, but on his own he found what he needed in the museums. In 1856 he traveled in Holland, Germany, Austria, and Italy to visit art collections. The following year Manet copied Delacroix's 1819 *Barque of Dante*, in the Louvre, and he and Proust visited Delacroix to pay their respects.

Manet submitted his *Absinthe Drinker* (Copenhagen, Ny Carlsberg Glyptothek) to the Salon in 1859, only to have it rejected; it shows an obvious debt to Velázquez, whom he admired and whose art he had copied. Two years later, however, he received an honorable mention for his *Spanish Guitar Player* (New York, Metropolitan Museum). In 1860, he became friends with Baudelaire and the following year with Degas. Manet's *Le Déjeuner sur l'herbe* (Louvre) was rejected for the 1863 Salon but was given a public viewing at the Salon des Refusés. It provoked hostility from the public and the press. Many objected to the combination of nude women and fully clothed men in contemporary dress; others found it harsh in color and careless and coarse in conception. Manet had based his painting on two early-15th-century works, Marcantonio Raimondi's engraving of a Raphael and Giorgione's *Concert champêtre*. By reducing the gradation of tones and showing the figures in a brilliant light, he created the effect of form devoid of nuance, stripped to the essentials, and of character almost brutally direct and impersonal. Color was acid, chalky, and posterish. Manet was concerned with the properties peculiar to painting and seemed detached from the subject matter.

His *Olympia* (Louvre), exhibited at the 1865 Salon, inspired further venom and outrage from the press and the public. Manet based his work on Titian's *Urbino Venus*. Manet's nude appears brazen, challenging, even proud as she looks directly at the beholder. Manet's enveloping light gives the whole a visual ruggedness and an unpremeditated quality as if viewed in a flash of intense light. The hard contour line, two-dimensional form, and solid-color areas are reminiscent of Japanese prints, which were then in vogue.

By suppressing values foreign to painting, by offering no extrapictorial message, Manet is said to have inaugurated modern painting. Though he was not opposed to representation, Manet freed art of the tyranny of subject matter. Manet had no program; he seems to have been a revolutionary in spite of himself. He had his champions, too, such as Baudelaire and Zola, whose portrait he painted (1868).

By 1865 Manet was the unofficial leader of the avant-garde painters. They would meet at the Café Guerbois. Manet's friend Proust was among them, as was the cadre of the impressionist group, Bazille, Nadar, Whistler, Renoir, Degas, Monet, and Cézanne. In 1867 Manet exhibited fifty of his pictures at the World's Fair in Paris, erecting a wooden structure for the occasion. In 1867 he painted the first version of *The Execution of Maximilian* (Mannheim, Municipal Art Gallery), a work inspired by a contemporary event but expressing no sense of outrage or passion. Instead, Manet quite characteristically stressed pictorial values at the expense of narrative.

At the outbreak of the Franco-Prussian War in 1870 Manet remained in Paris and served on the General Staff until January, 1871, when the French surrendered. That same year he sold a number of his paintings to the dealer Paul Durand-Ruel. He painted a number of seascapes in oil and water color in 1873. In 1874 the first impressionist exhibition was presented in Nadar's studio. Manet did not contribute to this show nor to any of the subsequent ones, but with the encouragement of Berthe Morisot he began to paint in a manner close to the impressionists and worked alongside Monet at Argenteuil. Manet's palette became lighter, his choice of color more varied. He abandoned studio situations for the most part and painted typical impressionist subjects: light-filled landscapes, the movement of a theater crowd, informal views of women at their toilettes. He painted several still lifes, usually of such gourmet foods as asparagus, oysters, and lemons, as well as flower pieces.

The *Bar at the Folies-Bergère* (London, Courtauld Institute), one of the finest of Manet's late pictures, was well received when shown at the Salon. Although the chief forms remain tactile, it is a phantasmagoria of light and glitter. Surrounding the girl behind the counter in a galaxy of pure sensation, Manet reduces forms to spots and patches of tone. He approaches abstraction because he stresses pattern. Manet's work was given an extensive showing in 1884, the year after his death. In 1890 *Olympia* was purchased by public subscription and presented to the Louvre, which accepted it seventeen years later.

BIBLIOGRAPHY. A. E. A. Moreau-Nélaton, *Manet, raconté par lui-même*, Paris, 1926; G. H. Hamilton, *Manet and His Critics*, New Haven, 1954; G. Bataille, *Manet*, New York, 1955; P. Courthion, ed., *Edouard Manet*, New York, 1962.   ROBERT REIFF

MANETTI, RUTILIO. Italian painter (b. Siena, 1571; d. there, 1639). Manetti first adopted the devotional manner of his master, Francesco Vanni, and of Barocci. The *Death of the Blessed Antonio Patrizi* (1616) in S. Agostino, Monticiano, marks the change to a Caravaggesque style, and thereafter his religious and genre paintings, including many of musicians, are conceived in shallow foreground planes and use a quixotic chiaroscuro.

MANFREDI, BARTOLOMMEO. Italian painter (b. Ostiano, near Mantua, ca. 1580; d. Rome, ca. 1620/21). Little is known of Manfredi's life. He apparently went to Rome early in his life (ca. 1600) and, after an apprenticeship with Cristoforo Roncalli, fell under the influence of Caravaggio (ca. 1610).

Unlike the other *Caravaggisti*, Manfredi followed the master's style throughout his brief career, aping his early manner and accentuating the coarser, genre elements (compare Manfredi's *Fortune Teller* in the Pitti Palace, Florence, with the more refined versions by Caravaggio in the Louvre, Paris, and the Capitoline Museum, Rome). In favoring such subjects as *Bacchus and a Drinker* (Rome, Barberini Palace) and *The Card Players* (Caen, Museum), he furthered derogatory opinion of "Caravaggesque realism," especially since many of his works were taken for Caravaggio originals. Even in mythological subjects, a sense of coarseness and brutality dominates, as in *Mars, Venus, and Cupid* (Chicago, Art Institute), where the god of war is portrayed as a hardened common soldier and the cupid writhes in agony. When turning to religious themes, Manfredi often completely obliterates the action in a wealth of genre motifs, for example, *The Denial of St. Peter* (Braunschweig, Herzog-Anton-Ulrich Museum), where one cannot single out the main characters.

Manfredi is, at best, an imitator. Although he incorporated Caravaggio's trademarks (chiaroscuro, realism, and genre themes) into his own paintings, he was unable to achieve either the dramatic focus or mystical overtones that distinguish the work of the master. But Manfredi influenced the development of 17th-century painting. He achieved great popularity in the second decade—his works were collected by the Duke of Tuscany, while he in turn was held in high esteem by the Florentine Academy—thus helping to spread Caravaggism in a relatively pure form. Furthermore, early sources state that the second generation of *Caravaggisti* who came to Rome from northern Europe tended to become Manfredi's, rather than Caravaggio's, followers.

BIBLIOGRAPHY. G. Isarlo, *Caravage et le caravagisme européen*, Aix-en-Provence, 1941; R. Longhi, "Ultimi studi sul Caravaggio e la sua cerchia," *Proporzioni*, vol. 1, Milan, 1943; Milan, Palazzo Reale, *Mostra del Caravaggio e dei caravaggeschi* (catalog), Florence, 2d ed., 1951.

STEPHEN E. OSTROW

MANGBETU, see AFRICA, PRIMITIVE ART OF (CENTRAL AFRICA: CONGO-LEOPOLDVILLE).

MANGLARD, ADRIEN. French painter of landscape and sea pieces and etcher (b. Lyons, 1695; d. Rome, 1760). He was a pupil of A. van der Cabel in Rome and studied the styles of Salvator Rosa and Claude Lorraine. In 1736 he was a member of the Royal Academy in Paris, associated with the Academy of St. Luke in Rome. His art represents the transition from Claude to Claude-Joseph Vernet, Manglard's foremost pupil.

MANI. Sanskrit term meaning "jewel", symbol for the law of the Buddha. The *mani* is shown rounded and pointed at the top.

MANIERA. Stylistic term applied to the work of some Italian late-16th-century painters who derived from mannerism. Originating in Rome, the mode spread to the north. It translated mannerist intellectuality into a decorative aestheticism with distortion used formalistically. Leading practitioners were Il Cavaliere d'Arpino, Niccolò dell'Abbate, Pomarancio, Primaticcio, and the Zuccaris. *See* ABBATE, NICCOLO DELL'; ARPINO, IL CAVALIERE D'; POMARANCIO (NICCOLO CIRCIGNANI); PRIMATICCIO, FRANCESCO; ZUCCARI, FEDERICO; ZUCCARI, TADDEO.

BIBLIOGRAPHY. J. Shearman, "Maniera as an Aesthetic Ideal," *Studies in Western Art*, vol. 2: *The Renaissance and Mannerism*, Princeton, 1963; C. H. Smyth, *Mannerism and Maniera*, Locust Valley, N.Y., 1964.

MANIERA GRECA. Italian term meaning "in the Greek manner," used to describe the prevailing style of Italian painting in the 13th century before Giottesque innovations.

The style, which was influenced primarily by Byzantine painting, was characterized by a freedom in the treatment of space and figural proportions, a highly developed sense of the decorative aspects of drapery, and a vibrant, and at times unrealistic, color sense.

BIBLIOGRAPHY. E. B. Garrison, *Italian Romanesque Panel Painting*, Florence, 1949.

MANIERE CRIBLEE ("Dotted Print" Technique). Relief process deriving from techniques used by goldsmiths in the 15th century. *Manière criblée* consists of printing from a metal plate or wood block scored with dots or unevenly shaped depressions. The image or design is defined as a series of white dots on a black ground; the plate or block is printed as a woodcut or relief print, and only the surface receives the ink.

After the transfer of the drawing to the plate or block, various punches are driven by a hammer to indent the surface; or, a special graver or burin is used to create a series of dots that clarify the artist's drawing. Proofs are struck off from time to time as "visual" progress reports, and when the printmaker is satisfied with his plate or block, an edition is printed in a manner similar to that of the woodcut.

BIBLIOGRAPHY. M. Geisberg, *Die Anfänge des Kupferstiches*, 2d ed., Leipzig, 1924; J. Heller, *Printmaking Today*, New York, 1958.

MANJUSRI (Chinese, Wen-shu; Japanese, Monju). Major Bodhisattva widely worshiped in the Far East. Mañjuśrī is considered the guardian of the sacred doctrines of the Mahāyāna sect. Often shown riding a lion, he emphasizes wisdom and is usually referred to as the Bodhisattva of Wisdom. He is more widely worshiped in China than in India, and by the 8th century he was believed by most Indians to be Chinese in origin. One of the four sacred mountains of China, the Wu-t'ai Shan in Shansi Province, is dedicated to Mañjuśrī.

MANMODA. Small unfinished chaitya hall at Junnār, Maharashtra State, India. It belongs to the Hīnayāna phase of Buddhist architecture. Mānmoda differs from earlier chaityas in that it has no porticoes or wooden vestibules. Over the sun window is a lunette carved with symbolic designs. *See* HINAYANA.

BIBLIOGRAPHY. P. Brown, *Indian Architecture*, vol. 1: *Buddhist and Hindu Periods*, 4th ed., Bombay, 1959.

MANNERISM. Style that developed in Italy (ca. 1520-80) as a reaction against the classicism of the High Renaissance. Mannerism rebelled against the rational disciplines of High Renaissance art, and expressed a new emotionalism and a complex intellectual aestheticism. It manifested itself in the ambiguous projection of space, a distortion of movement and proportion, and a linear sinuosity. In painting and sculpture the natural proportions of the human figure were subordinated to the overall rhythms of a composition, and in architecture the structural elements were used for aesthetic effect regardless of their functions.

The origins of mannerism may be traced to Michelangelo and Dürer. It emerged clearly (ca. 1520) in Florence with Pontormo and Rosso Fiorentino and in Rome (1524) with Parmigianino. The style later spread to northern Italy and to Fontainebleau in France, influencing many northern artists. Among the second generation of mannerists were Bronzino, Salviati, and Vasari. Its influence appears in numerous artists, including El Greco and Tintoretto. *See* Bronzino, Agnolo; Parmigianino; Pontormo; Rosso Fiorentino; Salviati, Francesco; Vasari, Giorgio.

See also Furniture (Mannerism).

BIBLIOGRAPHY. W. Friedländer, *Mannerism and Anti-Mannerism in Italian Painting*, New York, 1957.   BERNARD S. MYERS

MANNHEIM: MUNICIPAL ART GALLERY. German museum founded in 1909. It is one of the best medium-size collections of 19th- and 20th-century art in Germany. Among the artists of the romantic school and of the later 19th century, C. D. Friedrich, Böcklin, Feuerbach, H. von Marées, Thoma, and Trübner are represented, as are all the leading expressionists of the 20th century (Baumeister, Beckmann, Corinth, Max Ernst, Feininger, George Grosz, Heckel, Kirchner, Kokoschka, Modersohn-Becker, Rohlfs, Schlemmer, F. Winter, and others). French painters, from Géricault and Delacroix, Courbet, Corot, and Daumier to the impressionists and their followers, Manet, Monet, Renoir, Pissarro, Utrillo, and Vlaminck, are also included. In this group Manet's *Execution of Maximilian* (1867) is world famous. Water colors, drawings, and prints supplement the work of these and other contemporary artists. There are also sculptures by Arp, Barlach, Kolbe, Lehmbruck, Archipenko, Maillol, Marini, Moore, and Rodin. In the modern applied arts collection, Jean Lurçat's tapestry *L'Homme et les fables* is especially outstanding.

BIBLIOGRAPHY. H. Jedding, *Keysers Führer durch Museen und Sammlungen*, Heidelberg, Munich, 1961.

MANNI, GIANNICOLA DI PAOLO. Italian religious and historical painter (b. Perugia, ca. 1460; d. there, 1544). He was a co-pupil with Raphael and Lo Spagna under Perugino. As a mature artist, he faithfully followed and occasionally worked with Perugino. Later he attempted to imitate Andrea del Sarto.

MANNO DI BANDINO. Italian goldsmith and sculptor (fl. Siena and Bologna, 1st quarter of 14th cent.). His chief works are a copper gilt statue of Pope Boniface VIII (1301) and a silver reliquary of St. Florian (1312), both in S. Stefano in Bologna.

François Mansart, the Gaston d'Orléans wing of the château at Blois, 1635-38.

MANNO DI SEBASTIANO SBARRI, *see* Sbarri, Manno di Bastiano.

MANNOZZI, GIOVANNI (Giovanni da San Giovanni). Italian painter (b. San Giovanni Valdarno, 1592; d. Florence, 1636). A student of Matteo Rosselli, Mannozzi worked primarily in fresco at palaces and churches in Florence and Rome. His early works, such as the frescoes at the Convent of the Ognissanti in Florence (1616–19), are simply composed with the figures near the picture plane. A manneristic tendency to exaggerate figure proportions and gestures and a more complicated disposition of space characterize the frescoes in SS. Quattro Coronati in Rome (1623). In the frescoes at the Palazzo Pallavicini-Rospigliosi in Rome (1627) and the Sala degli Argenti of the Palazzo Pitti in Florence (1635), a greater fluidity and baroque involvement of figures are combined with the always present brittleness and timid use of space.

BIBLIOGRAPHY. O. H. Giglioli, *Giovanni da San Giovanni*, Florence, 1949.

MANOELINE GOTHIC, *see* Manueline Style.

MAN OF SORROWS. Devotional image, popular in the late Middle Ages, representing Christ upright, suffering from the wounds inflicted at the cross. A type common in 13th-century Italian and French art is the Christ of St. Gregory's Mass. It shows the dead Christ emerging from a sarcophagus, wearing the crown of thorns and carrying the reed scepter, sometimes supported by angels or by the Marys and St. John.

MAN RAY, *see* Ray, Man.

MANSARD. Roof type named for the 17th-century French architect François Mansart. A mansard set on a rectangular plan slopes steeply on each side, the slope being broken at the upper part of the roof where it becomes less steep to form the top hipped section. The steep lower roof section made it possible to utilize more fully the space underneath the roof. The mansard is also called a "curb roof."

MANSART, FRANCOIS. French architect (b. Paris, 1598; d. there, 1666). He was a pupil of Germain Gaultier and worked under Salomon de Brosse. The most classical and genuinely French architect of his time, Mansart demonstrates a clarity and precision of plan and elevation, correct use of the orders, and emphasis on the flat surface of the wall in works such as the Gaston d'Orléans wing of the château at Blois (1635–38), the château of Maisons-Laffitte (1642–46), near Paris, and the Church of the Val-de-Grâce, Paris (1645–46; completed by Lemercier).

During his later years he was neglected as an architect. His projects of the years after 1650, however, such as those for the Bourbon Chapel at St-Denis (1665) and the Louvre façade (1664), show a new richness, freedom, and monumentality of design, related to contemporary French baroque currents. *See* Maisons-Laffitte, Chateau of; Val-de-Grace, Paris.

See also Mansard.

BIBLIOGRAPHY. A. Blunt, *François Mansart*, London, 1941.

MANSART, JULES-HARDOUIN. French architect (1646–1708). He worked in Paris. Reputed to have received his first training from his great-uncle, François Mansart, he began receiving royal commissions in his late twenties. His early domestic architecture reveals an affinity to Le Vau in planning and elevation, but also foreshadows the rococo style in its ingenuity and inventiveness of planning, its emphasis on comfort, and its stress on the horizontal. In 1678 Mansart was put in charge of the vast extension of the Palace of Versailles, as well as the stables (1679–86), the orangery (1681–86), the Grand Trianon (1687), and the chapel (1689–1703). *See* VERSAILLES: PALACE.

His design for Marly, begun in 1697 (destroyed), was based on a new planning principle involving a series of small pavilions grouped around a central building and intimately related to their surroundings. In 1699 he was appointed Surintendant des Bâtiments (Superintendent of Buildings) and from then until his death he controlled all the public works in Paris and was responsible for two public squares, the Place Vendôme and the Place des Victoires, both planned as settings for statues of the king. He also designed, in his last years, the chapel for Les Invalides, bold and unclassical in conception and influential for later European architectural developments. *See* INVALIDES, LES, PARIS.

Mansart's many different projects indicate that he relied on assistants, most notably Lassurance (Pierre Cailleteau) and Pierre Le Pautre. However, Mansart's responsibility for the architectural side of his designs is generally accepted, since his planning talents and his gift for dramatic setting were in evidence from his first works. His meteoric career was founded on his sense of grandeur and display as well as on a considerable knowledge of the practical side of architecture. His taste, coinciding with that of his patrons, was for the lavish and effective rather than for excellence of quality or perfection. His influence was felt not only through his works but also in his teaching, since many of the architects of the younger generation, both French and foreign, passed through his workshop.

BIBLIOGRAPHY. S. F. Kimball, *The Creation of the Rococo*, Philadelphia, 1943; L. Hautecoeur, *Histoire de l'architecture classique en France*, vol. 2, Paris, 1948; A. Blunt, *Art and Architecture in France, 1500–1700*, Baltimore, 1954; P. Bourget and G. Cattaui, *Jules Hardouin Mansart*, Paris, 1960. DORA WIEBENSON

MANSHIP, PAUL HOWARD. American sculptor (1885–1966). Manship's art is associated with an attempt to carry over into recent times an extension of neoclassicism. From his 1916 *Dancer and Gazelles* in bronze (Toledo Museum of Art) to *Personification of the Elements* (New York, Western Union Building) and later public commissions, Manship revealed the development of an archaizing, prettifying tendency. His leadership in the National Sculpture Society served to influence popular taste toward a traditional approach.

MANSO, LEO. American painter and book illustrator (1914–   ). He studied at the Educational Alliance and the National Academy in his native New York City. Manso paints semiabstract landscapes, stressing the effects of light upon his subjects.

MANSUETI, GIOVANNI. Venetian painter (fl. 1485–1527). A pupil of Gentile Bellini, he did two paintings in a series on the miracles of the Cross for the Confraternity (Scuola) of S. Giovanni Evangelista (1494 and later; now Venice, Gallery of the Academy); Gentile did three of this series. His style closely imitates that of Gentile in richness of incident, but is sharply linear and airless, with an awkward effect. He also painted three similar scenes, perhaps toward the end of his life, for the Scuola di S. Marco (two in Venice, Academy; one in Milan, Brera). A third cycle, which was done for S. Maria dei Crociferi, is known through one surviving scene (1499; Vaduz, Liechtenstein Collection). His other works are routine altarpieces with standing saints.

BIBLIOGRAPHY. Venice, Gallerie dell'Accademia, *Gallerie dell'Accademia di Venezia* (catalog), by S. Moschini Marconi, vol. 1, Rome, 1955.

MANSUR. Mughal (Mogul) painter (fl. 17th cent.). He specialized in animal, bird, and flower paintings in a detailed, carefully executed manner. Mansur was attached to the court of Emperor Jahangir (r. 1605–27), who described him as unique in his generation in drawing and conferred upon him the title Nadir-ul-Asar (Wonder of the Age). There is a flower painting with Mansur's name on it in the Habibganj Library, Aligarh District, Uttar Pradesh, India, and there are bird paintings attributed to him in the Baron M. Rothschild Collection, Paris.

See also MUGHAL PAINTING OF INDIA.

MANTEGAZZA, CRISTOFORO AND ANTONIO. Italian sculptors and goldsmiths, brothers from Milan: Cristoforo (d. 1482); Antonio (d. 1489?). Cristoforo's name appears for the first time in 1464, Antonio's in 1473. Both were engaged on the construction of the façade of the Certosa of Pavia until their respective deaths, although the contribution of each has not been established satisfactorily. Quite likely Cristoforo carved, between 1465 and 1470, the reliefs of Biblical scenes on the upper part of the façade; and Antonio may have been responsible, after the death of his brother, for other sculptures on the façade and for such reliefs as the *Lamentation over the Dead Christ* in the Capitolo dei Fratelli. The reliefs are characterized by brittleness and nervousness, with slender figures and a multifaceted treatment of drapery folds.

BIBLIOGRAPHY. E. Arslan, "Sui Mantegazza," *Bollettino d'arte*, XXXV, 1950; J. Pope-Hennessy, *Italian Renaissance Sculpture*, London, 1958.

Cristoforo and Antonio Mantegazza, reliefs of the Flight into Egypt and a prophet, façade of the Certosa of Pavia.

MANTEGNA, ANDREA. Northern Italian painter (1431–1506). Son of a village carpenter, he was brought to Padua and apprenticed to Francesco Squarcione, with whom he stayed six years. He learned little from his master's painting, but more perhaps from his archaeological fragments and modern drawings, and certainly much more from Donatello's presence in the city.

Certified an independent master in 1448, Mantegna signed a lost altarpiece with the words, "by his own hand at age seventeen." In the same year he shared the fresco commission for the Ovetari Chapel in the Church of the Eremitani, Padua; after the two other painters died, he finished most of it, by 1453. The chief parts are scenes of the lives of SS. James and Christopher. At first, sharp, dry lines of great intensity portray scenes with perspective and archaeological interest, but very soon a more luminous, flexible image develops for which these lines provide only the taut framework. (These works were almost entirely destroyed by bombing in 1944.)

Mantegna's next great work is the altarpiece (1456–59) in S. Zeno, Verona. The richly carpentered frame assumes a triptych form with classical columns. On this frame hangs a painted space that is continuous through all three parts as if it were behind them; it extends backward to a porch and then to the sky. Eight saints, four on each side of the Madonna, are informally posed in depth. The old symmetrical altarpiece had formerly been given a naturalistic spatial treatment, but with isolated, static figures; Mantegna's figures and structure relate in a double rhythm. Here, northern Italy takes precedence over Florence in modernity. Mantegna's major source was Donatello's group of statues for the high altar at the Scuola del Santo in Padua. The S. Zeno predella scenes include the *Crucifixion* (Paris, Louvre), where the fixed linear structure sets up a space that flows downward and out from the picture. This anti-Florentine spatial idea is developed from Jacopo Bellini, whose daughter married Mantegna in 1453.

In 1459, after some hesitation, Mantegna moved to Mantua as court painter to the Gonzaga family; he remained there the rest of his life. He served three marquises, became a patriarch, and, though his salary was unreliable, could devote himself to work that interested him. The larger works of the first Mantuan decade are lost. Small ones include *Cardinal Mezzarotta* (Berlin, former State Museums), a revolutionary portrait design, with the head weighted to the side; *St. George* (Venice, Academy); and *Adoration of the Magi* (Florence, Uffizi), where an enamel gleam shows vigorous action in brilliant light. *St. Sebastian* (Louvre), one of three paintings of this theme, and the *Dead Christ* (Milan, Brera), which was influenced by Andrea del Castagno, show another of his inventions in spatially modernizing formal compositions. In each painting the main figure is central and rigid, but other figures emerge at the corners, transforming a timeless image into an event without violating its traditional form.

Portraits, action, and space are remarkable in the frescoes (finished in 1474) running around a room called the Camera degli Sposi in the Castello di San Giorgio (Castello di Corte), adjoining the Ducal Palace, Mantua. They prob-

Andrea Mantegna, *Judith and Holofernes*. National Gallery, Washington, D.C. (Widener Collection, 1942).

ably record the return to court of the Marquis's son. With sharply characterized heads, the frescoes move in a narrow frieze that seems to flow into the observer's space. The effect is a highly charged one, for the observers were the same persons portrayed. The source is tapestries, the chief secular, flattish covering for palace walls, but there are dramatic changes. The ceiling shows classicistic gray medallions of Roman emperors, and in the center is the famous illusionary ceiling, painted as a view into the sky, edged with a railing from which figures look down into the room. A tour de force of perspective and lighting from within the painting, this ceiling is the ancestor of the baroque ceiling with its expertness and shock value.

The largest late works are the *Triumphs of Caesar* (1486–89; Hampton Court Palace), a series of ten monochrome canvases, in a poor state of preservation. They have shallow space and display a classicism as dry as in the artist's earliest works. Mantegna interrupted work on them by a visit to Rome (1489) where he painted a chapel (destroyed) for the pope. He had made earlier, brief visits to Florence (1466), where he probably painted the moving portrait of Carlo de' Medici (Uffizi), Cosimo's illegitimate half-Negro son; and to Pisa (1467), where his advice probably influenced Benozzo Gozzoli's frescoes.

Many of Mantegna's ideas appear in engravings, successfully exploiting his sharp line. They seem to have been made to facilitate copying. Seven are traditionally considered by his own hand, even though their technical skill is strange in him. But those signed by imitators are all weaker. The seven may have been made under supervision, probably all after 1490.

For the third marquis, Mantegna painted the *Madonna of Victory* (1495; Louvre). It has a new counterpoint on the old altarpiece structure; the Madonna and donor lean toward each other, producing a diagonal accent later exploited by Correggio.

The learned and extravagant young marchioness Isabella d'Este invented complex allegories for her painters, many of whom declined the work or produced awkward results. She had more success with Mantegna, who painted for her (from 1496) the so-called *Parnassus* (Mars and Venus with Orpheus and nymphs), *Minerva Expelling the Vices*, and *Comus*, unfinished at his death (all Louvre). Details of their themes are disputed, but small figures are developed in a rich world in a new way to evoke the dynamics of psychologically meaningful action.

Mantegna's was the basic influence throughout northern Italy for fifty years. He had weak followers who were interested in archaeology or enamel colors, but he also stimulated the space and light of Vincenzo Foppa and especially of Giovanni Bellini.

BIBLIOGRAPHY. P. Kristeller, *Andrea Mantegna*, London, 1901; A. Mantegna, *Mantegna, Paintings, Drawings, Engravings*, complete ed. by E. Tietze-Conrat, London, 1955; G. Fiocco, *L'arte di Andrea Mantegna*, new ed., Venice, 1959; A. Mantegna, *All the Paintings of Mantegna*, by R. Cipriani, 2 vols., New York, 1964.
CREIGHTON GILBERT

MANTES: COLLEGIAL OF NOTRE-DAME. Gothic church in Mantes, France, built between about 1170/1175 and about 1250; the radiating chapels were added after 1285. A key example of the revival of the three-storied elevation in the late 12th century, it was partly inspired by Notre-Dame Cathedral in Paris (the original plan included flying buttresses).

BIBLIOGRAPHY. J. Bony, "La Collégiale de Mantes," *Congrès Archéologique de France, CIVe Session, Paris-Mantes*, Paris, 1947.

MANTOVANO, *see* RINALDO MANTOVANO.

MANTRA. Buddhist and Hindu incantation. It is that portion of the Vedas which consists of hymns, as distinct from the Brāhmaṇas.

MANTUA (Mantova). City in north-central Italy, surrounded on three sides by the Mincio River. Mantua was important as a cultural center under the Gonzagas (1328–1707). Medieval buildings include the rotunda of S. Lorenzo (11th cent.) and two civic structures, the Palazzo della Ragione and the Palazzo del Broletto (both 13th cent.). Leon Battista Alberti, the humanist architect of the early Renaissance, designed the churches of S. Sebastiano (a unique central-plan building begun in 1460) and S. Andrea (grandiose and influential; begun in 1472). *See* SANT'ANDREA, MANTUA.

In the 16th century Giulio Romano erected the Palazzo del Te, a masterpiece of mannerist architecture, and rebuilt the Cathedral. The Ducal Palace (13th–18th cent.) preserves a number of frescoed rooms (including the Camera degli Sposi, in the adjoining Castello di S. Giorgio, decorated by Andrea Mantegna ca. 1471–74) and houses an extensive painting gallery as well as archaeological and sculptural collections. *See* MANTUA: GALLERY AND MUSEUM OF THE DUCAL PALACE.

BIBLIOGRAPHY. Italy, Direzione generale per le antichità e belle arti, *Inventario degli oggetti d'arte d'Italia*, vol. 6: *Provincia di Mantova*, Rome, 1935; V. Restori, *Mantova e dintorni*, Mantua, 1937; Mantua, Galleria e museo di Palazzo Ducale, *La galleria di Mantova, Palazzo Ducale*, by L. Ozzòla, 2d ed., Cremona, 1948.

MANTUA: GALLERY AND MUSEUM OF THE DUCAL PALACE. Italian collection housed in the Ducal Palace, the chief seat of the Gonzaga family. The building was begun in the 13th century and has been enlarged several times. Its vast series of apartments includes the gallery of paintings (works by Pisanello, D. Moroni, Foppa, Tintoretto, Rubens, and others), the archaeological museum (Greek and Roman sculpture), the medieval and modern museum (sculpture of the 13th–18th cent.), and other collections. Outstanding among the decorated rooms is the Camera degli Sposi in the adjoining Castello di S. Giorgio (Castello di Corte), with the illusionistic frescoes that are Mantegna's masterpiece (ca. 1471–74). There are also apartments decorated by Giulio Romano and Primaticcio. The Gabinetti Isabelliani contain fine gilded ceilings of the 15th century.

BIBLIOGRAPHY. L. Ozzòla, *Il Museo d'arte medievale e moderna del Palazzo Ducale di Mantova*, Mantua, 1950.

MANUEL-DEUTSCH, NIKOLAUS. Swiss painter and designer of woodcuts (b. Bern, ca. 1484; d. there, 1530). His early life is undocumented, but it appears that he was living in his native Bern, possibly studying with a glass painter. It has also been proposed on the basis of stylistic similarities that he may have studied with Hans Fries or the so-called Nelken Meister of Bern. His art also attests to a close familiarity with Dürer's art and that of the Augsburg school of the Burgkmairs as well as with the Upper

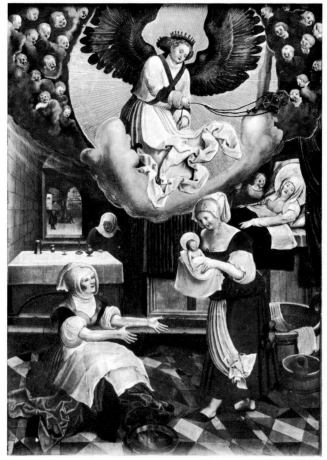

Nikolaus Manuel-Deutsch, *The Birth of the Virgin,* panel from the *Mary Altar,* 1515. Art Museum, Bern.

Rhenish art of Baldung-Grien and Grünewald. In 1528, he became a member of the lower council of the city of Bern and began publicly to advocate the introduction of the Reformation into Bern. He produced woodcuts and poems as propaganda for the cause of the Reformation and as attacks against Catholicism.

Manuel-Deutsch's major painted works are the panels of the *Mary Altar*, made for the Dominican cloister of Bern about 1515, the most important of which depicts the *Birth of the Virgin* on one side and *St. Luke Painting the Virgin* on the other (now Bern, Art Museum) and the *Beheading of St. John the Baptist* and the *Temptation of St. Anthony* (1520; both Basel, Public Art Collections). Another important work preserved only in drawings and copies was the great wall painting, the *Dance of Death* (1515–20; Bern, Dominican cloister). His most important woodcut series is that depicting the *Wise and Foolish Virgins*.

The style in his early works shows a close affinity to Hans Fries, especially in coloration. His later style draws closer to the Düreresque Upper Rhenish school as represented by the works of Hans Baldung-Grien. Particularly Swiss is the peculiar spatial restriction of the figures into a narrow area close to the picture frame combined with a most forceful animation achieved through gesture and intricate body movements. Figures which have strangely masklike faces and are clad in elaborate, frequently fantastic costumes are a hallmark of Manuel-Deutsch's art.

BIBLIOGRAPHY. B. Haendcke, *Nikolaus Manuel-Deutsch als Künstler*, Frauenfeld, 1889; J. Gantner and A. Reinle, *Kunstgeschichte der Schweiz...*, vol. 3, Frauenfeld, 1956.   DONALD L. EHRESMANN

MANUELINE STYLE. Portuguese architectural style in vogue during the reign of King Manuel I (1495–1521). An amalgam of Islamic, Flamboyant Gothic, and even Renaissance elements, this style, characterized by luxuriousness of decoration, is nevertheless unique. The great portal of the rotunda of Batalha Abbey, by Mateus Fernandes, and the nave of the abbey church of Tomar, by the Arrudas brothers, Diogo and Francisco, are typical examples of the Manueline style at its best. *See* BATALHA, CHURCH OF THE MONASTERY; FERNANDES, MATEUS; TOMAR.

See also BELEM: MONASTERY OF ST. JEROME; CASTILHO, JOAO DE.

BIBLIOGRAPHY. R. dos Santos, *O estilo manuelino*, Lisbon, 1952 (summaries in French and English); G. Kubler and M. Soria, *Art and Architecture in Spain and Portugal and their American Dominions, 1500–1800*, Baltimore, 1959.

MANUSCRIPTS, ILLUMINATED, *see* ILLUMINATIONS.

MANUSCRIPT WRITING (Paleography). The scientific study of writing, called paleography, is an invaluable aid in the dating and placing of manuscripts. As a specific discipline, paleography did not develop until the 17th and 18th centuries. The great early work in the field was by the Benedictine archaeologist and historian Jean Mabillon (1632–1707). He studied writing in connection with his *Acta sanctorum benedictorum*. In 1681 he published his *De diplomatica libri...*, in which he established various national scripts and distinguished diplomatic or charter script from literary (private or book) script. In addition, he recognized two distinct types of script: majuscule and minuscule. In 1708 De Montfaucon, another Benedictine and a pupil of Mabillon, did for Greek script what Mabillon had done for Latin. His *Palaeographia graeca* used

Manueline style. Mateus Fernandes, detail of the great portal of the rotunda of Batalha Abbey.

the term "paleography" for the first time. Later research has shown that local and national variations of Latin script were actually derived from, rather than merely influenced by, Roman sources.

Strictly speaking, paleography refers only to writing on manuscripts, not stone inscriptions (a separate study called epigraphy). For the purposes of this article, however, evidence will be drawn from any valid source; and the discussion will deal with the two major Western scripts, Greek and Latin. In the vocabulary of this science, letters may be majuscule, those that fall entirely within an upper and lower line, a two-line scheme; or minuscule, those that fall within a four-line scheme. In the latter, the body of the letter falls within the two center lines; the top line accommodates the "ascender," as in "b," and the bottom line, the "descender," as in "p." Letters may be unattached (*scriptura distincta*) or cursive (connected as in modern handwriting). Uncial is a form of rounded majuscule script, and half-uncial is an uncial script with minuscule tendencies.

Any discussion of Greek script is limited by the paucity of extant examples of Greek writing. In the pre-Christian period the earliest Greek manuscripts are papyri of the 4th century, of Egyptian origin. Taken in conjunction with other Greek manuscripts of later date, and from different parts of the Greek world (for instance, the Avroman and Dura parchments and the Herculaneum papyri), there is a surprising consistency and uniformity of writing style. Greek writing utilized, for the most part, uncials for literary works and a cursive script for documents. Generally, the development was from angular majuscules (the style of stone incision) to uncials (the style of pen on parchment or papyrus). The earliest examples of a well-formed, consistent cursive Greek script do not appear before the mid-3d century B.C.; then it is extremely sophisticated and attractive. This handsome cursive style, known as the "Chancery type" (because extant examples came from the chancelleries of the Hellenistic bureaucracies), gradually became less legible as writing emphasized speed.

The development of Latin script can be traced in greater detail, owing to the many extant examples. Starting with epigraphic evidence, as in a Hadrianic marble plaque of the 2d century of our era, we have an elegantly carved, carefully proportioned square capital (*capitalis quadrata*), characterized by the use of thick and thin lines. Words are separated by stops (dots) rather than spaces, and abbreviations are used. This script was in use through the 4th century, as seen in such manuscripts as the Vatican Vergil and the Vergil of St. Gall. By the 5th century *capitalis quadrata* had lost most of its character and tended to become taller and narrower, showing less variation in the thickness of its lines and a reduction of its horizontal elements. This new script, known as *capitalis rustica*, is exemplified in the Vergilius Romanus (Rome, Vatican Library).

Concurrently, there existed a type of cursive, the "older Roman cursive," derived in part from Greek uncials and in part from *capitalis quadrata*. It was not a true cursive, for the letters were not linked, and it degenerated into the highly illegible "younger Roman cursive" that formed the basis for most of the subsequent minor national scripts: Merovingian, Visigothic, Coptic, and Old Italian.

It even was an influence in the development of the Irish half-uncial. Latin uncials appear in a 4th-century palimpsest manuscript of Cicero (Vatican Library). It is an irregular majuscule, one that suggests minuscule possibilities. The 7th- or 8th-century Codex Amiatinus (Florence, Laurentian Library), probably of Hiberno-Saxon origin, uses a similar uncial script, but somewhat rounder and with clearer spacing. The Hiberno-Saxon uncial, an extremely legible majuscule script with minuscule suggestions, developed (ca. 750) into a half-uncial that combined uncial characteristics with those of a minuscule script, and reached its perfection in the Book of Kells (ca. 800; Dublin, Trinity College Library). The perfection of a hand-written script must be credited to the British Isles. This "insular script" had two branches: the rounded half-uncials of the Anglo-Saxon tradition, as in the Lindisfarne Gospels (8th cent.; Trinity College Library); and the square or pointed half-uncials of the Hiberno-Saxon tradition, as in the magnificent Book of Kells.

The English and Irish monks who came to the Continent brought their highly legible script with them. Charlemagne, seeking to recover writing from the depths of illegibility to which it had sunk within his empire, asked the Englishman Alcuin of York to undertake the task of script reformation. Faced with the numerous illegible national scripts then prevalent on the Continent, Alcuin designed a new script, based on the insular half-uncial. He developed the "Caroline minuscule," a true, consistent and extremely legible minuscule script, from the beautiful scripts of the Hiberno-Saxon school, and it suited Charlemagne's reform

Giacomo Manzù, *Portrait of a Lady*, 1946. Bronze. Museum of Modern Art, New York.

needs. The scriptorium at Tours, under the aegis of Alcuin, took the lead in the reform and produced outstanding examples of the new script in the famous Tours bibles: one in Zurich (ca. 800), one in London (ca. 830), and the first Bible of Charles the Bald (ca. 845–50; Paris, National Library). *See* TOURS SCHOOL.

The Caroline minuscule changed gradually from the 9th through the 12th century, becoming darker, heavier, and more angular. By the mid-13th century the script had become the so-called Gothic-Caroline minuscule; and by the mid-14th century, modified by excessively developed triangular serifs and heavy, dark, angular letters, it was a fully achieved Gothic minuscule—the script from which Gutenberg designed his first type faces.

In 15th-century Italy, however, the Renaissance humanists, in their return to classical antiquity, undertook the search for a new script. The "classical" script they "discovered" was the Caroline minuscule of the 11th century. Thus the Italian "humanistic script" of this period goes back, as do modern type faces, to the Caroline minuscule, probably the most important script ever devised in Europe.

The point at which manuscript writing ends, namely, the onset of printing, obviously also marks the end of paleography as a scientific study of that art.

BIBLIOGRAPHY. E. M. Thompson, *An Introduction to Greek and Latin Paleography*, Oxford, 1912; E. A. Lowe, *Codices latines antiquorum*, 6 vols., Oxford, 1934–53.   STANLEY FERBER

MANUSI. Sanskrit term meaning "man". Manuṣi is a Buddha or Bodhisattva who has taken human form.

MAN WITH THE GOLDEN HELMET. Oil painting by Rembrandt, in the former State Museums, Berlin. *See* REMBRANDT HARMENSZ. VAN RIJN.

MANZU, GIACOMO. Italian sculptor and draftsman (1908–   ). He was born in Bergamo and was apprenticed to a carver and gilder in 1919. Later he was an assistant to a stucco worker. While performing military service in Verona in 1928, he attended the art academy there. Although mainly self-taught, Manzù was impressed by Donatello, Rodin, Rosso, and Maillol, as well as by ancient sculpture. He made trips to Paris in 1933 and 1936. In 1941 he was named professor of sculpture at the Turin Albertina Academy. He contributed to international exhibitions from 1931. A series of Crucifixion reliefs done between 1939 and 1943 were censured by both the Fascists and the Church. His relief *Cardinal and Deposition* (1941–42) is in the R. Gualino Collection, and *Portrait of a Lady* (1946) belongs to Mrs. A. Lampugnani, of Milan. The subjects interpreted in his subtle, naturalistic style range from passive seated women and cardinals in quiet revery to images of brutal execution. In 1949 he executed reliefs for the fifth bronze door of St. Peter's, Rome, and in 1956 he was commissioned to do the central portal of Salzburg Cathedral. He has also worked in etching and lithography.

BIBLIOGRAPHY. A. C. Ritchie, *The New Decade*, New York, 1955; M. Seuphor, *The Sculpture of This Century*, New York, 1960.

MANZUOLI, TOMMASO D'ANTONIO (Maso da San Friano). Italian painter (b. Florence, ca. 1532; d. there,

1571). A follower of Pier Francesco di Jacopo di Domenico or Carlo Portelli, he painted mythological and religious scenes in the Tuscan mannerist style. His *Daedalus and Icarus* and *Diamond Mine* in the *studiolo* in the Palazzo Vecchio, Florence, show the strong influence of Rosso Fiorentino.

MAO I. Chinese painter (fl. late 12th cent.). The son of Mao Sung, he was active in the Southern Sung Academy. He gained his reputation chiefly for his small-scaled intimate paintings of birds and animals (particularly cats and dogs), and the minor chord in which he performed is indicative of academy ideals of the time. Most of Mao I's best works are preserved in Japanese collections today.

BIBLIOGRAPHY. J. Cahill, *Chinese Painting, 11th–14th Centuries,* New York, 1960.

MAORI ART. Art created by a warlike Polynesian people inhabiting New Zealand. Maori design, one of the most intricate expressions of the primitive world, was extended to both religious and secular objects ranging from small containers to great seagoing canoes, door panels, and ceremonial figures in relief. The worship of ancestors and pride in tribal rank, along with the related tradition of bravery in warfare, lay behind the production of typical Maori sculpture and architecture.

The Maori style is unmistakable for its lavish use of the spiral, double-spiral, and related curvilinear motifs on the surface of wooden human and mythical relief figures. Also unique are the fierce, snarling expressions of the human face with its emerging tongue, and the extensive practice of perforating areas within the field of wooden relief panels or posts. Skillfully inlaid passages of shell and a darkish-red, monochromatic stain appear in much Maori carving.

Special houses were decorated with large sculptured panels, often portraying chiefs flanked by heraldic *manaia,* or composite human-animal legendary images. Such friezes are richly patterned and punctured through the plank background. The human figure is thickset, the head being enormous in proportion. Superposition of forms is common. The continuous spiral motif connects one major shape with the next.

A complex system of *tapus* (taboos) accompanied the creation of Maori art. None but master designers, or tohunga, were permitted to undertake the completion of sacred reliefs, figures, or decorated canoes; and the special enclosure in which artists worked, as well as the wood itself and the sculptors' tools, were venerated. It was believed that the knowledge of artistic techniques originated with Maori gods in the remote past. Accordingly, the sculptor, though his art was considered but one of many community services, occupied an honored position. Tribal chiefs appeared at the dedication of great houses and at the launching of decorated canoes. The latter ceremony often involved human sacrifice.

Maori art characteristically appears in the medium of carved wood, but a secondary tradition existed in which ornaments and heitiki figures were carved in bone or jadeite. The technical virtuosity of the Maori and their intricate, sometimes spectacular use of spiral designs in monumental relief works is without peer in the world of primitive art. A splendid and characteristic example of

Maori Art. Wood-carved panel on the interior of the Tamatekapua Meeting House at Ohinemutu, Rotorua, New Zealand.

Maori art is the sarcophagus of the chief Waata Tarani in the Louvre Museum, Paris.

See also OCEANIC ART (POLYNESIA: NEW ZEALAND).

BIBLIOGRAPHY. W. P. Rowe, "The Origin of the Spiral in Maori Art," *Journal of the Polynesian Society,* XLVII, September, 1938; W. O. Oldman, *Skilled Handiwork of the Maori, Being the Oldman Collection of Maori Artifacts,* 2d ed. (Memoirs of the Polynesian Society, vol. 14), Wellington, 1946; P. S. Wingert, *Art of the South Pacific Islands,* New York, 1953; H. B. Chipp, "Formal and Symbolic Factors in the Art Styles of Primitive Cultures," *Journal of Aesthetics and Art Criticism,* XIX, Winter, 1960.

JOHN C. GALLOWAY

Maqsura. Example in the Taj Mahal, Agra.

MAO SUNG. Chinese painter (fl. early 12th cent.). A native of K'un-shan in Kiangsu Province, he was active in the academy under Hui-tsung and also in the early years of the Southern Sung period. He is recorded as a painter of monkeys, and the Manjūin in Kyoto has a well-known painting which bears a rather long-standing attribution to this artist. He was the father of Mao I.

BIBLIOGRAPHY. J. Cahill, *Chinese Paintings, 11th–14th Centuries,* New York, 1960.

MAQSURA (Maksoorah). Screen or partition in a mosque; by extension, the space enclosed by the screen. The term maqsura also denotes the prayer room of a mosque or the enclosed space around a tomb. In addition, it is sometimes applied to the central hall of a mosque.

MARA. Buddhist spirit of evil. Mara is the tempter of the Buddha under the Bodhi Tree before his Great Enlightenment.

MARAGLIANO, ANTON MARIA. Italian sculptor (b. Genoa, 1664; d. there, 1739). A pupil of the painter Domenico Piola, Maragliano studied in Genoa and there produced many works for churches. The *Madonna of Carmel* (S. Feda) is considered his chief work. He specialized in woodcarving that expresses a rococo flair for grace and color.

BIBLIOGRAPHY. R. Wittkower, *Art and Architecture in Italy, 1600–1750,* Baltimore, 1958.

MARATTA (Maratti), CARLO. Italian painter (b. Camerano, 1625; d. Rome, 1713). He began painting at the age of eleven, under the guidance of his half-brother Bernabò, who took him to Rome, where he worked in the studio of Andrea Sacchi until Sacchi's death in 1661. Maratta remained in Rome except for two trips to the Marches (before 1650 and ca. 1672) and one to Anagni (1659).

Although exposed to Sacchi's high baroque classicism from his youth, Maratta went through a long stylistic metamorphosis before arriving at a style that might be considered a continuation of his master's. His early works reflect the diversified influences of his Roman background; for example, the *Madonna and Saints* (Camerano, parish church) shows traces of Reni, Albani, and Titian. He soon assimilated Sacchi's linearism, structural organization, and monumental dignity, only to use them as a base on which to graft the stylistic tendencies of Lanfranco and Cortona; compare, for example, Maratta's *Adoration of the Magi* (1650; Rome, S. Giuseppe dei Falegnami), the *Nativity* fresco (1653–55; Rome, Chapel of S. Giuseppe in S. Isidoro), and the *Nativity* fresco (1657; Rome, Quirinal Palace). By the 1660s, however, Maratta finally achieved a style recognizably based on Sacchi, with clearly drawn, solid figures, balanced composition, a sense of dignity, and concentration on the legibility of the poses (and hence of the emotions) of the individual protagonists (*Immaculate Conception,* 1664; Siena, S. Agostino). The remainder of his development consists in the accentuation of this form of classicism, as may be seen in the *Immaculate Conception* (1686; Rome, S. Maria del Popolo), the *Baptism of Christ* (1697; Rome, S. Maria degli Angeli), and the *Baptism of Christ* (1710; Naples, Certosa di S. Martino).

Maratta, as an individual, reflects the complexities of Roman painting in the 17th century. Although he was working at a time when Sacchi's classicism dominated the Roman scene, the examples of Bolognese classicism and the baroque of Lanfranco and Cortona were sufficiently potent to influence painters of a later generation. However, the consolidation of the theoretical position of classicism, achieved by Bellori in the 1660s, and Maratta's eventual arrival at a pure classical style, in conjunction with his success in Rome during the last third of the century, led to the creation of "the Grand Manner," which then passed to France, to become immortalized in the grandiose projects of Louis XIV.

BIBLIOGRAPHY. A. Mezzetti, "Contributi a Carlo Maratti," *Rivista dell'Istituto Nazionale d'Archeologia e Storia dell'Arte,* n.s. IV, 1955.

STEPHEN E. OSTROW

MARBLE. Crystalline metamorphic rock composed of limestone (mainly calcium carbonate), which has been geologically compressed by heat and pressure. Its color, which can vary from pure white to black and many colors in between, is determined by mineral components. Since marble can be highly polished, it has been used for many centuries as an architectural facing and has always been popular as a material for the sculptor.

Parian marble is a white, granular stone from the Island of Paros in the Cyclades. It was favored by Attic and Aegean sculptors and architects of ancient Greece up to the middle of the 5th century B.C., when Pentelic marble came into use. A famous work in Parian marble is the pedimental sculptures of the Temple of Zeus at Olympia.

Pentelic marble, a crystalline, often grayish stone, was quarried at Mount Pentelicus between Athens and Marathon. It was used in many monuments of the classical period in Greek art, including the Parthenon.

A number of Carrara marbles are quarried near Carrara, Massa, and Seravezza in Italy, ranging from pure white to veined varieties. They were favored by Italian Renaissance sculptors, particularly Michelangelo. *See also* MARBLE, PURBECK; NAXOS MARBLE.

EMMA N. PAPERT

Carlo Maratta, *Baptism of Christ*, 1697. S. Maria degli Angeli, Rome.

MARBLE, PURBECK. English limestone, dark gray or gray-brown in color, having a white pattern made by the presence of fossil snails. It has been quarried since the Roman period in the area near Corfe Castle and appears architecturally in medieval cathedrals of England and northern France. Since it can be highly polished, it became popular as a medium for effigy figure sculpture during the 13th century.

MARBLED POTTERY. Type of pottery produced in China from the T'ang dynasty onward. The marbling was caused by the use of two or more different-colored clays, which were kneaded together and coated with clear or transparent glaze so that the colors showed through after firing.

MARBURG: CHURCH OF ST. ELIZABETH. First pure Gothic structure in Germany. The cornerstone was laid in 1235; in 1249 the bones of St. Elizabeth were transferred to the new church, which soon became a great pil-grimage shrine. The transept was refinished in 1257, and total consecration took place in 1283. The architects employed both local and French traditions: choir and transept reveal the triapsidal concept of the Cologne school, and the classical basilica plan is a French idea. The decoration of the interior is among the richest in Germany and includes a stone high altar of 1290, the shrine of St. Elizabeth (1235–49), and numerous tomb monuments.

BIBLIOGRAPHY. R. Hamann, *Die Elisabethkirche zu Marburg*, Burg bei Magdeburg, 1938.

MARC, FRANZ. German expressionist painter (b. Munich, 1880; d. Verdun, 1916). Marc received his first art training in 1900 at the Munich Academy. In 1903 he spent six months in Paris, at which time he saw his first impressionist pictures. From 1903 to 1907 he made many meticulous studies of animals and their anatomy. From 1907 to 1910 he earned his living teaching human anatomy.

Marc's earliest pictures are moody, lonely landscapes, which, with their flat areas and flowing contours, reveal the influence of Jugendstil. Only after 1909 did his art assume its well-known characteristics. It was then he saw the art of Kandinsky, Von Jawlensky, Macke, and Münter, and abandoned his academic approach. Like them, he sought to express the spirit of creation and expose the mystery of a primordial nature through abstraction, which he equated with spiritualization.

He first joined the Neue Künstlervereinigung, and in 1911–12 he became a founder-member of the Blue Rider. With Kandinsky he coedited its first publication, *The Blue Rider Almanac*, and helped organize its first exhibition. That same year he went to Paris with Macke and met Delaunay. Once he became a soldier he stopped painting; but he did keep a notebook, in which the sketches suggest that his art was moving toward complete abstraction.

His attitude toward art and life was that of a pantheistic

Marburg, Church of St. Elizabeth. First pure Gothic structure in Germany.

mystic. In a work such as *Blue Horses* (1911; Minneapolis, Walker Art Center), Marc used color symbolically. Blue, for him, signified the masculine principle, robust and spiritual; yellow was feminine, gentle, serene, and sensual. Green represented a reconciliation of these opposites. Though Marc theorized on color use, he never appeared to be bound by such notions. Rather, he used color instinctively. In his *Blue Horses* the horses seem withdrawn and demure. They pull their heads in and close their eyes. The undulating rhythms and soft contours of their enclosed forms are echoed in the shapes of the hills and clouds, trees and foliage. In his later works, deer, horses, and other such animals, which flee from danger rather than fight, are shown enmeshed and merged with their environment, usually a crystalline forest. The prismatic forms and refracted colors found in his pictures of about 1912 reflect the influence of Delaunay and possibly of the futurist Severini.

BIBLIOGRAPHY. K. Lankheit, *Franz Marc*, Berlin, 1950.

ROBERT REIFF

MARCANTONIO RAIMONDI, see RAIMONDI, MARCANTONIO.

MARCA-RELLI, CONRAD. American painter (1913–   ). He studied briefly at Cooper Union and privately in New York City. His barren cityscapes of the 1930s and 1940s show the influence of Italian art, particularly that of De Chirico. After experimenting with an abstract-expressionist approach in the early 1950s, he created the style that continues to typify his work, using cutout shapes of canvas in overall, overlapping patterns of figurative abstraction. Marca-Relli received an award from the Chicago Art Institute in 1954; his work appeared in the Venice Biennale of 1955 and the São Paulo Bienal of 1959.

BIBLIOGRAPHY. New York, Whitney Museum of American Art, *Marca-Relli*, by W. C. Agee, New York, 1967.

MARCELLUS, THEATER OF, ROME. Roman theater dedicated by Augustus in 13 or 11 B.C. to the memory of his nephew and son-in-law, Marcus Claudius Marcellus. Circular in shape, the theater originally consisted of three stories of open arcades. The walls between the arcades on the first story were decorated with engaged Doric columns with a Doric entablature; those of the second story had Ionic columns. Finally, the third story probably had engaged Corinthian pilasters. The greatest part of the building was constructed of travertine; the inside was covered with stucco and marble. Part of the interior masonry was of *opus reticulatum*. The building was partly destroyed in the 4th century A.D. Only the lower two stories of the original structure remain; the two top stories were added by Peruzzi in 1535.

BIBLIOGRAPHY. S. B. Platner, *The Topography and Monuments of Ancient Rome*, Boston, 1904; W. J. Anderson, R. P. Spiers, and T. Ashby, *The Architecture of Greece and Rome*, vol. 2: *The Architecture of Ancient Rome*, London, 1927.

MARCHAND, ANDRE. French painter (1907–   ). Born in Aix-en-Provence, he took evening courses there and later went to Paris, where he met Gruber. His influences ranged from Egyptian and primitive art to Cézanne. Marchand

Franz Marc, Cat under the Tree, 1910. Wagner Collection, Hannover.

exhibited at the Salon d'Automne (1930) and the Salon des Indépendants (1931) and with the Forces Nouvelles group without becoming a member. In 1937 he was awarded the Prix Paul Guillaume. He soon reacted against cubism and, turning to traditional perspective and light and shade, achieved a style which by its elegance and refinement recalls Chinese art (*Les Inconnus*, 1938; Paris, National Museum of Modern Art). Like Piero della Francesca, he prefers drawing to color, his figures having an immobile, classical quality. His later work, such as *La Lumière de l'oiseau* (1955; Paris, National Museum of Modern Art) is more abstract and lyrical.

BIBLIOGRAPHY. B. Dorival, *Twentieth-Century French Painters*, 2 vols., New York, 1958; H. Read, *A Concise History of Modern Painting*, London, 1959.

MARCHES, THE. Formerly, the section of Italy that encompassed the Papal States between Rome and the kingdom of Naples. Currently, the Adriatic coastlands centering in Ancona are known as the Marches.

The name derives from the various "mark" or "march" territories that were set up as buffer areas to defend and delineate the borders of the Carolingian empire. Hence, the parts of Italy with this name indicate where Carolingian hegemony conflicted with that of Byzantium or Islam.

Such marches in the 9th century were the Spanish March, just south of the Pyrenees and including Barcelona; the March of Friuli, at the head of the Adriatic, forming the separation from Byzantine Dalmatia; and the Pannonian March, demarcating areas of Carolingian and Slavic interest.

Where art survives in any of these areas of frequent strife, it is usually marked by a mixture and crossing of influences, giving rise to extremely interesting but atypical forms.

MARCHESI, GIROLAMO (Girolamo da Cotignola). Italian painter (b. Cotignola, 1471/81; d. Rome, ca. 1540). Active in Bologna, Naples, Rome, and throughout Romagna, Marchesi was an eclectic and mannered painter influenced by Bernardino and Francesco Zaganelli (probably his teachers), Palmezzano, Francia, and Raphael.

BIBLIOGRAPHY. R. Buscaroli, *La pittura romagnola del Quattrocento*, Faenza, 1931.

MARCHI (Marchis, Marchj, Marchy), AGOSTINO DE'. Member of a northern Italian family of wood carvers and intarsia artists (b. Crema; fl. Bologna). Between 1468 and 1477 he worked in intarsia on the choir stalls in S. Petronio, Bologna, now partially restored; in 1474 he worked on the Paschal candlestick; and in 1476 on the choir gallery and the organ case.

MARCILLAT, GUGLIELMO DI PIETRO DE. French-Italian painter and stained glass designer (b. Le Châtre, ca. 1470; d. Arezzo, 1529). In 1506 Pope Julius II called Marcillat and other French artists to Rome to design stained-glass windows for the Vatican Palace. Marcillat remained there until 1515, designing also two windows for S. Maria del Popolo depicting scenes from the life of the Virgin. In Cortona he executed frescoes for the Palazzo Passerini as well as windows for the Cathedral (one now in the Victoria and Albert Museum, London). Marcillat's major works, however, were done for the Cathedral of Arezzo: a series of stained-glass windows and frescoes in the vaults of the nave.

Although he worked in the French medieval tradition of stained-glass techniques, Marcillat was stylistically indebted to Michelangelo, Raphael, and other Italian High Renaissance masters. He ingeniously used the natural illusionism of glass to enhance the perspective illusionism of Renaissance painting. Vasari, who was a pupil of Marcillat, wrote of his master with high praise.

BIBLIOGRAPHY. G. Mancini, *Guglielmo de Marcillat*, Florence, 1909.

MARCKS, GERHARD. German sculptor (1889–). Born in Berlin, Marcks worked as an assistant with Richard Scheibe beginning in 1907. He taught at the Berlin School for Arts and Crafts for a year, at the Bauhaus in Weimar between 1920 and 1925, and then at a crafts school near Halle. His position was terminated when the Nazis came into power. Following World War II, Marcks was professor of art in Hamburg at the Academy of Fine Arts. He executed a number of public commissions in Cologne, Hamburg, Lübeck, and Mannheim and has been represented in several important exhibitions abroad. His style is representational with expressionist undertones, generally like that of Georg Kolbe but with additional attention to movement and distortion. His bronze *Runners* (1924; New York, Museum of Modern Art) is characteristic.

BIBLIOGRAPHY. H. Schaefer-Simmern, *Sculpture in Europe Today*, Berkeley, 1955.

MARCO DA SIENA (Marco dal Pino). Italian painter (b. Siena, ca. 1525; d. Naples, ca. 1587). His teachers were Beccafumi and Peruzzi. In Rome after 1549 he assisted Daniele da Volterra at Trinità dei Monti and the Vatican and Perino del Vaga at the Castel Sant'Angelo, becoming a Michelangelesque mannerist. Settling in Naples after 1566, he established a school and wrote tracts on architecture and Neapolitan painters.

MARCO DELL'AVOGARO. Italian miniaturist (fl. second half 15th cent.). He worked in Ferrara for the Dukes of Este from 1449 until 1476. Marco executed *Tito Livio* (Livy), 10 books illustrating events of the first decade of Rome, for Lionello d'Este (Modena, Este Library), and collaborated on the illumination of the Bible commissioned in 1455 by Duke Borso d'Este (Este Library).

MARCO D'OGGIONO (Oggione). Milanese painter (ca. 1475–1530). He was a pupil and close imitator of Leonardo da Vinci, and was locally much admired in his time. His many works are all consistent, with heavy forms, strained motion, and deep, almost grimy, shadow. Details of hair and garments are intricate. Besides altarpieces, his chief work is the fresco cycle *The Death of the Virgin* from S. Maria della Pace (Milan, Brera).

BIBLIOGRAPHY. W. Suida, *Leonardo und sein Kreis*, Munich, 1929.

MARCONI, ROCCO. Venetian hack painter (fl. 1504; d. 1529). A contemporary of the young Titian, he repeatedly

Gerhard Marcks, *Freya*. Bronze. Museum of Modern Art, New York (Gift of Curt Valentin).

Louis Marcoussis, *Still Life with Checkerboard*, 1912. National Museum of Modern Art, Paris.

painted on the theme of Christ and the Adulteress (signed versions are in Venice, Gallery of the Academy, and New York, Kress Foundation; there are about ten others). These were done in half-length, with hot colors and swarming figures.

BIBLIOGRAPHY. B. Berenson, *Italian Pictures of the Renaissance: Venetian School*, rev. ed., 2 vols., London, 1957.

MARCOUSSIS (Markous), LOUIS. Polish-French painter (b. Warsaw, 1878; d. Cusset, France, 1941). He went to Paris in 1903 and studied under Jules Lefebvre. His art was influenced by impressionism until 1907, when he turned to cubism. He participated in the Section d'Or group. After World War I his work was strongly influenced by cubism yet was closer to reality. His interest in pure forms, heightened by his poetical temperament, earned him an important place among the cubists with such works as *The Frequenter* (1920; Venice, Peggy Guggenheim Collection). Marcoussis was also an excellent engraver. *La Table devant le balcon* (1936) was included in the exhibition of Fifty Years of Modern Art at the Brussels Universal and International Exposition of 1958.

BIBLIOGRAPHY. A. H. Barr, Jr., *Cubism and Abstract Art*, New York, 1936; Exposition universelle et internationale de Bruxelles, *50 ans d'art moderne*, Brussels, 1958.

MARCUS AURELIUS, ARCH OF, ROME. Lost Roman arch, erected in A.D. 176 to commemorate Marcus Aurelius Antoninus's victories in the Sarmatian and German wars. This arch had presumably carried on its top the bronze equestrian statue of the Emperor, now in the Piazza del Campidoglio. *See* MARCUS AURELIUS, EQUESTRIAN STATUE OF, ROME.

It has been suggested that eleven rectangular relief panels had originally formed part of the decoration of this arch. Eight of these panels were reused on the attic of the Arch of Constantine (A.D. 312). The Emperor's face was recut to represent that of Constantine. The three remaining reliefs of the series are now in the Palazzo dei Conservatori, Rome. These relief panels had representations of the Emperor's triumphal entry into the city and of the Emperor sacrificing, addressing the army, receiving Dacian captives, and dispensing charity. The style of the carving adheres to the traditional forms of Roman state art. The figures are skillfully organized within their environment. They occupy the lower part of the relief, while buildings and landscapes are in the upper part of the panel. Some late features characteristic of the Antonine period were also employed. Among them are the wide use of drill holes for black-and-white effects, and a certain disproportion in the scale of the figures.

EVANTHIA SAPORITI

MARCUS AURELIUS, COLUMN OF, ROME. Monument erected in A.D. 193 to commemorate Marcus Aurelius Antoninus's victories over the Marcomanni and the Sarmatians (172–175). The column, in the Piazza Colonna, is 96½ feet high and has a diameter of almost 4 feet. The column consisted of a pedestal (now lost), a shaft composed of twenty-six rings of Luna marble, and a Doric capital, which originally was surmounted by a statue of the Emperor but was replaced with a bronze statue of St. Paul. The interior of the shaft contains a spiral staircase; the exterior is decorated with a continuous spiral frieze carved in relief and depicting episodes of the Emperor's campaigns. Often called the Antonine Column, it is a direct imitation of Trajan's Column in design and dimensions but differs from the latter in both style and technique. The use of high relief and sharp undercutting for the outlines of the figures creates a disturbing effect in the play of black and white.

BIBLIOGRAPHY. C. Caprino et al., *La Colonna di Marco Aurelio*, Rome, 1955; D. E. Strong, *Roman Imperial Sculpture*, London, 1961.

MARCUS AURELIUS, EQUESTRIAN STATUE OF, ROME. Bronze statue of the emperor Marcus Aurelius Antoninus (r. A.D. 161–180) in the Piazza del Campidoglio. The Emperor is represented on horseback, without his regalia, as the bringer of peace. According to a 12th-century pilgrims' guide, there was another small figure under the raised leg of the horse, that of a captive. The statue was known until the 10th century as *Caballus Constantini*. In 1538 it was transferred from the piazza of St. John Lateran to its present site.

BIBLIOGRAPHY. L. Curtius and A. Nawrath, *Das Antike Rom*, Vienna, 1944.

MARCUS VITRUVIUS POLLIO, *see* VITRUVIUS.

MAREES, HANS VON. German painter (b. Elberfeld, 1837; d. Rome, 1887). For three years, beginning in 1853, Marées studied with Steffeck in Berlin, and then he went to Munich to study at the Academy. He remained in Munich until 1869. In his first paintings, Marées specialized in small-scale Romantic genre scenes with forms clearly defined, using cool, subtle coloring. Themes involving soldiers on a highway, gypsies, and horses, as exemplified in *Resting Cuirassiers* (1861–62; Berlin, former State Museums), appealed to him. His work was to gain in freedom and suppleness with continuing facility and confidence.

The Artist with his Friend Lenbach and *The Bath of Diana* (both 1863; Munich, Bavarian State Picture Galleries) have an assurance and lyricism which anticipate his later style. He went to Italy in 1864 with the artist Lenbach and spent the rest of his life there except for a period from 1869 to 1873, when he lived in Berlin and Dresden. While in Italy, he and Lenbach were encouraged with commissions from the patron of the arts Graf Schack. Marées painted Roman landscapes, family group portraits, portraits of his father and of the aesthetician Conrad Fiedler, and a double portrait of Hildebrand and Grant.

His only mural cycle was done for the Zoological Station, Naples (1872–73). The scholar Anton Dohrn had established an international zoological research institute and commissioned Marées to decorate a large hall and library with frescoes, *The Ages of Man* and *The Golden Age*. Marées believed that man would return "to his true uninhibited state" after undergoing a period of inner purification. In his frescoes, he envisioned this earthly paradise-to-be. He shows nude men and women stripped to their natural state. They move like pagan somnambulists through idyllic orange groves. Theirs is a timeless world without stress or conflict, a primordial community governed by instinct and impulse. Marées has rejected all neobaroque formulas and returned to the bas-relief of the ancients and the figure compositions of Pompeii, of Piero della Francesca, Mantegna, and Giorgione. The influence

Hans von Marées, *Silent Waiting*, detail of the fresco series *The Ages of Man*, 1872–73. Zoological Station, Naples.

of Courbet is significant. Marées favors earthy, naturalistic color and simplified forms and brushwork. In excluding any obvious display of pictorial skills, Marées denies artifice to obtain qualities of naïveté and frankness.

Marées, like Gauguin, hoped to shrug off the weight of civilization by leaving his homeland. In Italy, he hoped for a personal disclosure of primitive truths in an ancient land. Though his aims were similar to Gauguin's in many respects, Marées lacked Gauguin's sophistication, imagination, and originality. In his late work Marées continued to develop the trend of his Neapolitan period. The same arcadian, pantheistic paradise and dreamy beings appear in his triptych *The Hesperides* (1884–85; Munich, Bavarian State Picture Galleries). Marées lived in Florence and finally in Rome. Such diverse painters as Arnold Böcklin and Max Beckmann derived from Marées some of their feeling for philosophical meaning and monumental composition.

BIBLIOGRAPHY. A. J. Meier-Graefe, *Hans von Marées: Sein Leben und sein Werk*, 3 vols., Munich, 1909-10; K. Fiedler, *Hans von Marées*, Munich, 1947; H. von Marées, *Die Fresken in Neapel...*, Munich, 1958.

ROBERT REIFF

MARESCALCHI, PIETRO DEI (Spada). Italian painter of Feltre (ca. 1520–89). As a brilliant, sketchy colorist, he plays a significant role in Venetian painting of the late Renaissance. Much influenced by Bassano, but looser and more impressionist, his work is also more eclectic, being affected in later years by Greco and Veronese. Though provincial and eclectic, Marescalchi is weaker yet even more modern than the latter two painters, and has been rightly compared to Domenico Feti.

Along with signed altarpieces in country churches, his most remarkable works are the *Assumption* (Feltre Cathedral); *Portrait of Dr. Dal Pozzo Aged 102* (1561; Feltre, Gallery); *Banquet of Herod* (1576; Bonn, Regional Museum); *Pietà* (Bassanello church); and *St. Peter Freed from Prison* (Villabruna church).

BIBLIOGRAPHY. G. Fiocco, "Pietro de' Marescalchi detto lo Spada," *Belvedere*, VII, 1929.

MARESCALCO, IL, *see* BUONCONSIGLIO, GIOVANNI.

MARGARET OF ANTIOCH, ST. Virgin and martyr of Diocletian's period. The daughter of a pagan priest of Antioch in Pisidia (Turkey), she was converted by a nurse who had her watch sheep. Governor Olybrius desired her, but she refused his advances and his command to worship pagan idols. He threw her into a dungeon. There the devil in the form of a dragon tried to devour her but vanished at the sign of the cross. Margaret was tortured and beheaded. Her attributes are a dragon and a cross. Her feast is July 20.

See also SAINTS IN ART.

MARGARITONE D'AREZZO. Italian painter of the school of Arezzo (fl. ca. 1250–75). He is believed to be identical with the painter Margaritone di Magnano who is mentioned as a witness in a contract involving the Convento S. Michele in Arezzo in 1262. Nothing else is known about Margaritone.

The number of his signed works is unusually large for a 13th-century painter: (1) An altar frontal from S. Margherita in Arezzo, signed "Margarit de Aritio me fecit," in the National Gallery in London, representing the Madonna and Child seated frontally in a mandorla with the symbols of the four Evangelists in the corners and four narrative scenes at the sides. (2) A *Madonna and Child with the Archangel Gabriel and Three Saints* in Montelungo, in which the halo and head of the Madonna project at an angle from the panel, a motif not uncommon during the 13th century; an inscription of 1636 dates the panel at 1250. (3) A *Madonna and Child* surrounded by four small figures of saints in the Lehman Collection in New York. (4) An altar frontal in S. Maria delle Vertighe, near Arezzo, with the Madonna and Child flanked by four narrative scenes and wings containing figures of the three Magi and three saints; from the inscription it emerges that Margaritone was here restoring an older panel, repainting the Madonna, and adding the wings.

Margaritone also signed six panels of a *St. Francis* showing the saint standing, hooded, holding a book in his left hand, and raising his right to show the sign of the stigmata. These are in the Medieval and Modern Picture Gallery and Museum at Arezzo, the church at Ganghereto, the National Picture Gallery in Siena, the Vatican Museums (Picture Gallery), S. Francesco in Castiglion Fiorentino (in which the saint is holding the cross in his right hand), and the museum in Montepulciano. A seventh *St. Francis*, not signed and cut down but close to Margaritone's style, is in S. Francesco a Ripa in Rome.

All the works, which are in poor condition and in part overpainted, reveal a provincial artist working with set formulations—secondhand reflections of Florentine, Sienese, and Byzantine elements—that show little variation or development. Vasari's biography of Margaritone also describes him as a sculptor and architect, but his activities in these fields have not been verified.

BIBLIOGRAPHY. A. del Vita, *Letture Vasariane*, vol. 1, Arezzo, 1910; R. van Marle, *The Development of the Italian Schools of Painting*, vol. 1, The Hague, 1923; L. Dami, "Opere ignote di Margarito d'Arezzo e lo sviluppo del suo stile," *Dedalo*, V, February, 1925; Florence, Mostra giottesca, 1937, *Pittura italiana del duecento e trecento* (catalog), Florence, 1943.

HELLMUT WOHL

MARI: WALL PAINTINGS. Only fragments remain of the wall paintings of the Mesopotamian palace of the kings of Mari, which was built by Zimrilim and was later destroyed by Hammurabi of Babylon in 1763 B.C. The fragments show traditional and narrative scenes known from cylinder seals and steles. There are also some original compositions, and in this group are mythological scenes, military scenes, and scenes of offering. One of the offering scenes consists of two registers. In the upper register is a figure dressed in a fringed shawl; in the lower are subsidiary figures wearing similar costumes and, in addition, wearing the felt caps still used in Syria and northern Iraq. These figures lead sacrificial bulls with gilt and silvered horn tips and with crescent pendants tied to their horns.

BIBLIOGRAPHY. H. Frankfort, *The Art and Architecture of the Ancient Orient*, 2d ed., Baltimore, 1959.

MARIA (Maria Martins). Brazilian sculptor (1900–   ). She was born in Campanha, Brazil. She studied piano and painting in Paris before turning to sculpture, and worked in ceramics in Japan during the 1930s. Her first exhibition was in Washington, D.C., in 1940. She has had one-man shows in Paris and New York City, and she was also represented in Paris at the Surrealist International of 1947. She works almost exclusively in bronze. The style is surrealist and semiabstract, as in *Eternal Insomnia of Earth* (1956). Her works in American collections include the over-life-size *Christ* (1941) in wood and *The Impossible* (1946) in bronze, both at the Museum of Modern Art in New York. She lives in Rio de Janeiro.

BIBLIOGRAPHY. M. Seuphor, *The Sculpture of This Century*, New York, 1960.

MARIA LAACH, ABBEY CHURCH OF, *see* LAACH: ABBEY CHURCH OF MARIA LAACH.

MARIANI, CAMILLO. Italian sculptor (b. Vicenza, 1565? d. Rome, 1611). He studied with a disciple of Alessandro Vittoria and presumably arrived in Rome in the 1590s. There he executed his masterpieces, eight stucco figures of saints in S. Bernardo alle Terme (1600), a church whose architecture has also been attributed to him. His work, Venetian in style, shows an insight into personality and a strength which distinguishes him from his contemporaries, linking his art with that of the "reforming" painters of the period. He was the teacher of Francesco Mochi.

BIBLIOGRAPHY. R. Wittkower, *Art and Architecture in Italy, 1600–1750*, Baltimore, 1958.

MARIANO, AGNOLO DI COSIMO DI, *see* BRONZINO, AGNOLO.

Margaritone d'Arezzo, *St. Francis*, detail. Panel. Medieval and Modern Picture Gallery, Arezzo, Italy.

MARIB. Ancient city in Yemen, in southern Arabia. It owed its prosperity to Mesopotamian trade. A huge dam, dating from the 1st millennium B.C. has been discovered, as well as a Temple of the Moon and a great number of statues and reliefs, mostly of Sabaean art, which flourished between 350 and 50 B.C. and was greatly influenced by Hellenistic art.

BIBLIOGRAPHY. L. Woolley, *The Art of the Middle East*, New York, 1961.

MARIE DE MEDICIS, LIFE OF. Series of oil paintings by Rubens, in the Louvre, Paris. *See* RUBENS, PETER PAUL.

MARIENBURG (Malbork): CASTLE OF THE TEU-TONIC KNIGHTS. East Prussian castle founded shortly before 1280 for twelve brothers of the order. It is the equal of the Palace of the Popes in Avignon in architectural interest. The entire complex has massive walls in the brick style (*Backsteingotik*) of construction employed along the Baltic coast, an architectural leitmotiv of the order. The nucleus and oldest part of the ensemble is the so-called Hochschloss, which was largely reconstructed during the 14th century. The Mittelschloss, begun in 1309, contains the palace of the Grand Master and is artistically the most important part of the complex; the most spectacular rooms are the Remter, or great halls. Especially notable are the winter and the summer Remter, the Grand Remter, and the chapter house built in the course of the 14th century, all containing magnificent late Gothic stellar vaults, perhaps influenced by English examples. From 1380 to 1398 the Rhenish master Nikolaus Fellenstein worked in the Mittelschloss.

BIBLIOGRAPHY. G. Dehio and E. Gall, *Handbuch der deutschen Kunstdenkmäler: Deutschordensland Preussen*, ed. B. Schmid and G. Tiemann, Tübingen, 1952; K. H. Clasen, *Deutsche Gewölbe der Spätgotik*, Berlin, 1958.

MARIENWERDER (Kwidzyn) CASTLE. German castle formerly in East Prussia and since 1945 in Poland. Built by the Teutonic Order, it dates from the 14th century. Its original shape was that of a square cloister with high fortified walls, which typified all the buildings of the Teutonic Order in this area. Unique, however, is the so-called *Dansker* (or Danish type) resembling a fortified bridge extending at right angles from the cloister complex.

BIBLIOGRAPHY. A. Winnig, *Der deutsche Ritterorden und seine Burgen*, Königstein im Taunus, 1956.

MARIESCHI, JACOPO DI PAOLO. Italian scenic painter (b. Venice, 1711; d. there, 1791). He was taught the principles of design and perspective by his father, Michele Marieschi, and by Gasparo Diziani. Imitating the style of Canaletto, he rendered views of Venice and architectural subjects.

MARIESCHI, MICHELE (Michiel) GIOVANNI. Italian painter and printmaker (b. Venice, 1710; d. there, 1743). The son of a wood carver and minor painter, Marieschi was possibly trained under Gasparo Diziani, who aided him in obtaining employment at the court of Saxony. Marieschi returned to Italy by 1735. In 1741, he published a series of twenty-one views (in etching) of Venice. Early landscapes were *capricci*; the view paintings probably date

John Marin, *The Mountain*. L. E. Stern Collection, New York.

after his return from Germany (he was influenced by Canaletto and Carlevarijs but influenced Guardi).

BIBLIOGRAPHY. M. Levey, *National Gallery Catalogues: The Eighteenth-Century Italian Schools*, London, 1956.

MARIETTE, PIERRE JEAN. French publisher, collector, dealer, and amateur printmaker (b. Paris, 1694; d. there, 1774). Surpassing his family tradition in print publishing, he became an astute connoisseur who amassed an enormous collection of prints and drawings. He also wrote the *Abecedario*, which contains the biographies of artists and represents the fruit of sixty years of scrupulous scholarship.

BIBLIOGRAPHY. L. T. Clément de Ris, *Les Amateurs d'autrefois*, Paris, 1877.

MARILLIER, CLEMENT-PIERRE. French engraver and draftsman (b. Dijon, 1740; d. Melun, 1808). He studied painting under Noel Hallé in Paris. Primarily a book illustrator, Marillier made vignettes for books by Dorat, Abbé Prevost, Voltaire, and Sauvigny. He illustrated travel books from his own designs.

BIBLIOGRAPHY. D. Guilmard, *Les Maîtres ornemanistes, dessinateurs, peintres, architectes, sculpteurs et graveurs*, 2 vols., Paris, 1880–81.

MARIN, JOHN. American painter (b. Rutherford, N.J., 1870; d. Cape Split, Me., 1953). Marin belonged to the first generation of avant-garde 20th-century painters in the United States and developed a keenly individual style, semiabstract and generally expressionistic but always based upon penetrating study of natural forms and their apparent rhythms.

Marin first worked as an architect's draftsman and opened his own office in 1893. At the age of twenty-nine he took up painting, studying at the Pennsylvania Academy of Fine Arts from 1899 to 1901 and with Frank Dumond at the Art Students League in New York City in 1904. Marin traveled in Europe, residing mainly in Paris, from 1905 to 1909. He worked in various ateliers learning engraving and etching and made studies of architectural monuments.

He had his first one-man show at Alfred Stieglitz's "291," or Little Gallery, in 1909. Another was held there in 1910, and the following year he showed several works at the Salon d'Automne in Paris. Marin was also represented in the 1913 Armory Show in New York; his water colors of

Manhattan themes anticipated his future staccato, shorthand fragmentations of landscape. The *Seaside Interpretation* (1914; Columbus Gallery of Fine Arts), *Camden Mountain across the Bay* (1922; New York, Museum of Modern Art), and *Maine Islands* (1922; Washington, D.C., Phillips Collection) show the development of a sturdy, imaginative expression. Marin's oil paintings, such as *Tunk Mountains* (1945; Phillips Collection) and *Sea Piece with a Boat* (1951; New York, Downtown Gallery), convey much the same spirited verve as do his water colors.

After his affiliation with Stieglitz's gallery about 1910, Marin showed at the Daniels Gallery and at the Museum of Modern Art (retrospective, 1936). He was given a large one-man exhibition at the Venice Biennale in 1950, the first time such recognition was accorded an American. He is represented in most major American collections. Marin is a forceful and outstanding water-colorist and a strong contributor to early modern painting in the United States.

BIBLIOGRAPHY. V. Barker, "The Water Colors of John Marin," *Arts*, 1924; Boston, Institute of Contemporary Art, *John Marin: A Retrospective Exhibition*, Boston, 1947; M. W. Brown, *American Painting from the Armory Show to the Depression*, Princeton, 1955; *John Marin: Tributes by William Carlos Williams, Duncan Phillips* [and] *Dorothy Norman*, Berkeley, 1956.

JOHN C. GALLOWAY

MARINALI, ORAZIO (Il Vecchio Marinali). Italian wood sculptor (b. Bassano, 1643; d. Vicenza, 1720). Marinali studied in Venice and then in Rome, returning to Venice by 1675. He often collaborated with his brothers Angelo Marinali and Francesco Marinali the Younger and was the teacher and father-in-law of Giacomo Cassetti. Among his works are ten angels with instruments of the Passion (Vicenza Cathedral). He also worked extensively for S. Maria di Monte Berico in Vicenza. Marinali worked in a classicizing baroque idiom with rather sharp and dry forms.

BIBLIOGRAPHY. A. E. Brinckmann, *Barockskulptur*, 2 vols., Berlin, 1919.

MARINE PAINTER. Painter who specializes in the production of seascapes, that is, paintings whose principal subject matter is an expanse of sea, with or without ships and other nautical objects. Marine painting first appeared in the Low Countries in the mid-17th century in the work of such masters as Simon de Vlieger and Willem van de Velde the Elder.

BIBLIOGRAPHY. E. K. Chatterton, *Old Sea Paintings*, London, 1928.

MARINETTI, ANTONIO (Il Chiozzotto). Italian history, religious, and genre painter (b. Chioggia, ca. 1710; d. Venice, 1796). He was a pupil and follower of Piazzetta. Though none of his works are known to be extant, a number of them are given favorable mention in old guides.

MARINETTI, EMILIO FILIPPO TOMMASO. Italian poet and writer (1876–1944). He was the chief spokesman of the futurist movement in Italy. Marinetti became editor of the magazine *Poesia* in 1905 and issued the first futurist manifesto in 1909, the year he met the painters Boccioni, Carrà, and Russolo. A year later they, with Balla and Severini, signed the futurist manifesto of painting, which called for the destruction of tradition and the emergence of a new art appropriate to the dynamism of the machine age. Marinetti later became a Fascist adherent.

MARINI, MARINO. Italian sculptor, painter, graphic artist, and draftsman (1901–   ). He was born in Pistoia. He was a student at the Academy of Fine Arts in Florence, where he studied sculpture and painting under Trentacosta, and was possibly influenced by the work of Medardo Rosso. Marini made several visits to Paris between 1919 and 1938. In 1928 he visited Greece and studied sculpture in Paris. From 1929 until 1940 he taught in Monza at the Villa Reale School of Art. Marini lived in Switzerland from 1942 to 1946. In 1950 he went to the United States and exhibited at the Curt Valentin Gallery. During the 1950s he exhibited internationally, and his work entered many of the leading art museums and finest private collections.

Throughout his career he continued to paint, draw, and make prints. His enthusiasm for color led to its introduction into his sculptures, notably in the equestrian series, *Cavalier in the Form of a Triangle* (1951; Baroness Lambert Collection). His preferred media for sculpture are plaster, wood, and cast metal; he rarely uses stone. His contribution to modern sculpture lies in part in his portraits, such as *Curt Valentin* (1954; New York, Museum of Modern Art), *Igor Stravinsky* (1950; San Francisco Museum of Fine Arts), and his self-portraits. These portraits recall late Roman heads and sculpture technique, but they have a unique modernity in the frankness of psychological exploration and in surface handling. Their plastic and spiritual individuality, unself-consciousness, and unheroicized truthfulness make them important developments

Marino Marini, *Horse and Rider*, 1957. Bronze. Peggy Guggenheim Collection, Venice.

beyond Rodin's work. Marini's sculptures of women favor static, sensually swollen forms with movement created by the surface excavations of the sculptor. Typical of these works are *Standing Nude* (1945; Antwerp, Fine Arts Museum) and *Dancer* (1949; J. T. Soby Collection).

His most distinguished series, that of the horse and rider groups, was inspired by the Han dynasty tomb horse and was begun in 1936 (for example, *Cavalier*, 1936, Milan, E. Jesi Collection). Ironically, the funereal inspiration is transformed into life-seeking images of man and beast. His variations on the motif have lead to erotic formations of both horse and rider (*Cavalier*, 1951, London, Hanover Gallery). The theme was used by Marini to project his feelings of despair over the tragedies of the war. Not unlike Picasso, he has focused upon the horse alone as a dramatic subject, as in *Great Horse* (1951; Nelson Rockefeller Collection). Marini's art testifies to the vigor and depth of the figural tradition in modern sculpture.

BIBLIOGRAPHY. M. Marini, *Marino Marini, Sculptor*, [by] U. Apollonio, 2d ed. rev., Milan, 1953; M. Marini, *Marino Marini* [by] E. Langui, New York, 1959.

ALBERT ELSEN

MARIOLATRY. Term applied to the heretical worship of the Blessed Virgin Mary as the possessor of unique divine honors. The practice appears to be an ancient one; the earliest record of it is St. Epiphanius's 4th-century condemnation of the Collyridian sect. The term is also used pejoratively by Protestant writers to criticize what they consider to be the excessive devotion to the Virgin in the Roman Catholic Church.

MARIOTTO ALBERTINELLI, *see* ALBERTINELLI, MARIOTTO.

MARIOTTO DI NARDO. Italian painter of the Florentine school (b. before 1394; d. after 1424). Mariotto was a prolific painter of frescoes and altarpieces in and around Florence. He was a follower of Jacopo di Cione and is stylistically related to, though weaker than, Niccolò di Pietro Gerini and Lorenzo Monaco.

MARIS, JACOB. Dutch painter (b. The Hague, 1837; d. Carlsbad, 1899). The brother of Matthew and Willem Maris, he studied at the academies of The Hague, Antwerp, and Paris. Influenced by the atmospheric effects of Corot and the Barbizon school, he painted genre, figures, and, especially, tonal studies of Dutch landscape subjects, for example, *Harbor Scene* (ca. 1885; Amsterdam, Rijksmuseum).

MARIS, MATTHEW. Dutch painter and graphic artist (b. The Hague, 1839; d. London, 1917). The brother of Jacob and Willem Maris, he studied in The Hague, Antwerp, and Paris. In his sometimes dreamy landscapes and figures, Maris was influenced by French symbolist painters and the British Pre-Raphaelites.

MARIS, WILLEM. Dutch painter (b. The Hague, 1844; d. there, 1910). He was the brother of Jacob and Matthew Maris, with whom he studied. Willem Maris painted landscapes and animal subjects with Corot-derived attention to the tonal rendering of light.

MARISOL (Marisol Escobar). American sculptor (1930–). Born in Paris of Venezuelan parents, Marisol has lived since 1950 in New York City, where she studied at the Art Students League and the Hans Hofmann School. The immobility of her genre-like groups of figures, which are composed of blocks of wood and plaster with features and details drawn onto them, expresses a fatalistic humor or melancholy.

MARK, ST. Evangelist who was converted after the Ascension. He accompanied Barnabas and Paul on the first missionary journey. He was the favorite disciple of Peter, under whose influence he wrote his Gospel. Peter sent him to Alexandria, where he became its first bishop. He was accused of practicing magic, arrested, dragged around city, and clubbed to death. Venetians stole his body in the 9th century, making their city a center of his cult. His attribute is a winged lion. His feast is April 25.

See also SAINTS IN ART.

MARKELIUS, SVEN. Swedish architect (1889–). Born in Stockholm, he studied at the Technical Academy and at the Academy of Fine Arts there. His work before World War II, influenced by Le Corbusier, includes apartments, offices, the concert hall at Hälsingborg (1932), and the Swedish pavilion at the New York World's Fair (1939). As head of town planning in Stockholm since 1953, he has been in charge of creating and developing Vällingby, the satellite city near the capital.

MARKO MONASTERY, SKOPLJE. Yugoslavian monastery named after Marko, the son of its founder Uvkašin and a heroic figure in Serbian legend. The monastery church is a cross-in-square structure of the 14th century whose east and west arms terminate in pointed gables, showing the influence of Greek Byzantine buildings of the period. *See also* SERBIAN PAINTING.

BIBLIOGRAPHY. G. Millet, *L'Ancien art serbe: Les Eglises*, Paris, 1919; J. A. Hamilton, *Byzantine Architecture and Decoration*, 2d ed., London, 1956.

MARKOUS, LOUIS, *see* MARCOUSSIS, LOUIS.

MARKS (Emblems), CHINESE. Chinese symbols painted, stamped, or engraved on pottery and porcelain. Many are ancient rebuses or Taoist and Buddhist symbols which convey wishes for felicity and long life. Others are studio marks and hallmarks or words of praise. Dates are indicated by six calligraphic characters in a double circle, giving the dynasty (sometimes omitted), the emperor's title, and the cyclical period. These indications are not always reliable since earlier reigns were sometimes substituted for the true period of manufacture.

BIBLIOGRAPHY. J. F. Blacker, *Chats on Oriental China*, New York, 1908; W. B. Honey, *The Ceramic Art of China and Other Countries of the Far East*, London, 1945.

MARKSMEN'S GUILD PIECES. Type of group portrait (Dutch, *Doelenstück*) popular in Holland during the second half of the 16th century and the early 17th century showing members of a local marksmen guild. This type of portrait was developed particularly by Frans Hals and Bartholomeus van der Helst. Rembrandt's *Night Watch* is such a marksmen's guild piece.

MARLOW, WILLIAM. English landscape painter (1740–1813). He studied at St. Martin's Lane Academy, London, and also under the marine painter Samuel Scott. He visited France and Italy (1765–68), thanks to the patronage of the Duchess of Northumberland. His work was exhibited at the Royal Academy of Arts from 1788 to 1796 and in 1807.

His English and Italian landscapes show more than mere topographical exactitude and exhibit pleasing color; they are sometimes almost romantic, though his compositions avoid the picturesque. His handling of trees is always lacking in vitality. Marlow was successful financially and after 1785 painted only for his own amusement. He is represented fairly generally in collections of English painting.

BIBLIOGRAPHY. E. K. Waterhouse, *Painting in Britain, 1530–1790*, Baltimore, 1953.

MARLY, HORSES OF, *see* COUSTOU, NICOLAS AND GUILLAUME.

MARMION, SIMON. Northern French painter and illuminator (b. Amiens, ca. 1420; d. Valenciennes, 1489). His most celebrated work is the *St. Bertin Altarpiece* (finished 1459; panels in London, National Gallery, and Berlin, former State Museums). M. J. Friedländer, who reconstructed his *oeuvre*, attributes to him the *St. Jerome as Cardinal* in the Johnson Collection, Philadelphia Museum of Art. Praised by Lemaire as the "prince d'enluminure," Marmion is credited with numerous illuminations that bear a similarity to the St. Bertin panels.

BIBLIOGRAPHY. G. Ring, *A Century of French Painting, 1400–1500*, London, 1949.

MARMITTA, FRANCESCO. Italian illuminator, miniaturist, and gem cutter (d. 1505). He was born in Parma. His identity as illuminator of the Petrarch manuscript in the Landesbibliothek, Kassel, has been established. The attribution originally made by Toesca has recently been supported by Pouncey, who dates the manuscript between 1485 and 1490 on the basis of its reliance on Lorenzo Costa's style of the mid 1480s. Other attributions made to Marmitta are the Durazzo Book of Hours (Genoa, Berio Library) and the Missal of Cardinal Domenico della Rovere (Turin, Municipal Museum of Ancient Art), both of which must date from about the turn of the 15th century.

BIBLIOGRAPHY. A. E. Popham and P. Pouncey, *Italian Drawings . . . in the British Museum*, London, 1950.

MAROCHETTI, BARON CARLO. Italian sculptor (b. Turin, 1805; d. Paris, 1867). Marochetti studied with Bosio and at the Ecole des Beaux-Arts in Paris, where he spent most of his life. After contributing to the frieze of the Arc de Triomphe de l'Etoile, he created many public monuments in a colossal romantic style, including an equestrian statue of Emmanuel Philibert, duke of Savoy, in Turin (1836) and a statue of Richard the Lion-Hearted in front of the Houses of Parliament in London (1860).

MARONE (Maroni), ROBERTO (Fra Raffaello da Brescia). Italian wood carver and intarsia specialist (b. Brescia, 1479; d. Rome, 1539). A monk of the Olivetan order, Fra Raffaello studied sculpture and woodworking with Giovanni Bologna. He is famous for intarsia decorations for church projects in Brescia, Verona, and Bologna in the Renaissance style.

BIBLIOGRAPHY. E. Molinier, *Histoire générale des arts appliqués . . .*, vol. 2, Paris, 1897.

MARQUESAS ISLANDS. Island group in eastern Polynesia, northwest of Easter Island. Sculpture is the principal art and includes figurines and over-life-size figures in volcanic stone as well as finely carved ceremonial clubs in heavy, densely grained wood. The style in stone and wood is related to and, in general concept, is suggestive of the Maori sculpture of New Zealand.

Forms are massive and boldly conceived, though executed with great care. The human face is stolid in expression. The eyes are enclosed by flat circular or elliptical bands which almost suggest spectacles. The mouth is similarly framed and has a slightly protruding tongue. Characteristic forms in wood are heads and staffs of clubs which contain repetitive motifs of the human face and footpieces of stilts which are also given human configuration.

See also OCEANIC ART (POLYNESIA).

BIBLIOGRAPHY. W. C. Handy, *L'Art des Iles Marquises*, Paris, 1938; W. O. Oldman, *The Oldman Collection of Polynesian Artifacts* (Memoirs of the Polynesian Society, vol. 15), New Plymouth, New Zealand, 1943; P. S. Wingert, *Art of the South Pacific Islands*, New York, 1953.

MARQUET, ALBERT. French Fauve painter (b. Bordeaux, 1875; d. Paris, 1947). In 1890 he went to Paris, where he attended first the Ecole des Arts Décoratifs and then the Ecole des Beaux-Arts. There he was originally a student of Cormon and later, in 1897, he joined the class of Gustave Moreau. Rouault and Matisse were fellow students. Marquet copied in the Louvre and showed a preference for Corot, Chardin, and Claude Lorraine. By 1899 he began to paint in a pre-Fauve style. He and Matisse, a lifelong friend, frequently painted together. Marquet exhibited at the Salon des Indépendants in 1901 and yearly thereafter for a decade. He had his first one-man show in 1907. One year later he entered the Académie Ranson, but this experience seemed to have had no appreciable effect on his style. By 1910 he began to travel extensively, painting wherever he went. He lived in Marseilles (1915–19) and in Algiers (1940–45).

By 1900 Marquet had developed a manner of painting and a repertory of subjects that he kept without considerable change throughout his career. His most characteristic pictures are panoramic views of the quays along the Seine in Paris and the ports of the world with their docks, cranes, tugboats, and ships at anchor. Marquet presents them as if from above, from a hotel room on a top floor. Marquet has in effect transposed late Monets, such as his *Thames* series, replacing the vibrating surfaces with unmodulated, light-reflecting planes derived from Matisse and, ultimately, from Gauguin and the Japanese print.

Marquet sought harmony through firm contours and accurate gradation of tone based on a careful study of atmosphere and light-and-shade relationships. Detail is repressed or reduced to a kind of shorthand. He abstracted to gain breadth of conception without sacrificing the particular essence of the scene at a certain time of day. He was fond of the neutral tones caused by a morning haze or an overcast sky. His art occasionally has a synthetic or calculated character. Marquet made several preliminary

Albert Marquet, *The Three Ships,* 1916. Private collection, Montreux, Switzerland.

studies for each picture. In 1925 he painted a number of water colors. He has also painted portraits and a few nudes with the same urbane, civilized understatement that characterizes his landscapes and marine paintings and that makes him the least "wild" of the Fauves.

BIBLIOGRAPHY. F. Jourdain, *Marquet,* Paris, 1959.

ROBERT REIFF

MARQUETRY. Term for the kind of intarsia employed on wood, especially on furniture. *See* INTARSIA.

MARQUISE. That part of an edifice which projects from the façade, unsupported by columns or posts, at a point between the first and second stories over the main entrance. A common element of theater architecture, it is also known as the marquee.

MARRIAGE A LA MODE. Series of oil paintings by Hogarth, in the National Gallery, London; also engraved version. *See* HOGARTH, WILLIAM.

MARS, *see* ARES.

MARS BORGHESE, *see* ALCAMENES.

MARSEILLAISE, LA, ARC DE TRIOMPHE DE L'E-TOILE, PARIS, *see* RUDE, FRANCOIS.

MARSEILLES: FINE ARTS MUSEUM. The Second Empire Palais de Longchamp houses pictures from the Flemish, Italian, and French schools. Of especial interest are the rooms devoted to the work of Pierre Puget and Honoré Daumier.

MARSEUS VAN SCHRIECK, OTTO, *see* SCHRIECK, OTTO MARCELLIS VAN.

MARSH, REGINALD. American genre painter and etcher (b. Paris, 1898; d. New York City, 1954). His family went to America when he was two. Both of his parents were painters. He attended Yale, where he was art editor of the *Record* and drew cartoons. Upon graduation he became staff artist for *Vanity Fair* and then for the *New York Daily News.* He took night classes with Sloan, Luks, and Miller at the Art Students League, and was influenced by his father's friend Boardman Robinson. In 1925 and again in 1928 Marsh went to Paris, where he copied Delacroix and Rubens at the Louvre. He painted murals for the Post

Office Building in Washington, D.C., and for the Customs House in New York City. He also made several etchings.

Marsh was attracted by the vitality of city life and the activities of the ordinary people, especially at play. His thinly painted pictures with their baroque compositions and vigorous line, featuring crowds sporting at Coney Island, powdery-white burlesque queens, and drifters along the Bowery, grew out of the liberal realist tradition of Hogarth, Daumier, and the Ashcan school.

BIBLIOGRAPHY. New York, Whitney Museum of American Art, *Reginald Marsh* (catalog), by L. Goodrich, New York, 1955.

MARSHALL, BENJAMIN. English sporting painter (1767–1835). He was one of the more distinguished of the great throng of British artists in the early 19th century who devoted themselves primarily to animal painting, particularly of horses. From 1812 until his death he lived at Newmarket, where his subjects were always close at hand. His best work was done before 1819, when a serious coaching accident permanently impaired his abilities. Marshall's touch is crisp and vigorous, but his modeling is rather tight and his color dry. His work is widely scattered, mostly in private collections. Two of his finest paintings, *Sam with Sam Chifney Jr. Up* and *Sailor with Mr. Thomas Thornhill*, are in the Henry E. Huntington Art Gallery, San Marino, Calif.

BIBLIOGRAPHY. W. Shaw Sparrow, *Stubbs and Ben Marshall*, London, 1929.

MARSHALL, WILLIAM. English engraver (fl. 1589–1649). Marshall, who worked mostly from his own designs, made line-engraved frontispieces and ornaments for book publishers between 1589 and 1649. In spite of his stiff style, Marshall's portraits are of special interest for the men they portray, Shakespeare and Ben Jonson among them.

BIBLIOGRAPHY. S. Colvin, *Early Engraving and Engravers in England, 1595–1645*, London, 1905.

MARSHALL FIELD WAREHOUSE, CHICAGO. One of H. H. Richardson's crowning achievements, this seven-story warehouse (1885–87; demolished 1930) created an influential commercial style of simple directness, organized fenestration, and rhythmic articulation. The structure was conservative, however, using massive weight-bearing granite and sandstone walls. Their solidity was somewhat mitigated by the vertical accents of the piers and mullions. The ground floor openings were low and wide; the middle stories were organized into a superimposed sequence of arches. The cornice, though large, did not project. The building was a definitive statement of Richardson's use of an arcaded front. Compared to the Cheney Building in Hartford (1875–76), its formal organization and freedom from archaeological detailing boldly revealed the new commercial aesthetic. *See* RICHARDSON, HENRY HOBSON.

BIBLIOGRAPHY. C. W. Condit, *The Rise of the Skyscraper*, Chicago, 1952.

MARS ULTOR, TEMPLE OF, ROME. Ancient temple in the Forum Augustus. It was constructed by the emperor Augustus in 14 B.C. The temple was octastyle and peripteral. The columns were of Luna marble with Corinthian capitals decorated with winged horses in their volutes, and the cella walls were lined with Luna marble. Six detached

Marquetry. Example of intarsia decoration by Giuseppe Maggiolini, 1790. Modern Art Gallery, Milan.

Reginald Marsh, *Negroes on Rockaway Beach*, 1934. Whitney Museum of American Art, New York.

columns raised on a dado stood in the interior. The ceiling of the peristyle was coffered. Three columns still stand.

BIBLIOGRAPHY. W. J. Anderson, R. P. Spiers, and T. Ashby, *The Architecture of Greece and Rome*, vol. 2: *The Architecture of Ancient Rome*, London, 1927.

MARSYAS. In Greek mythology, a satyr who picked up the flute invented but discarded by Athena, and became so skilled in playing it that he challenged Apollo to a contest. Apollo won and had Marsyas flayed alive for his impertinence. The *Marsyas* of Myron is the best-known representation of him in art. *See* MYRON.

MARSYAS AND THE MUSES, *see* PRAXITELES.

MARTHA OF BETHANY, ST. Sister of Mary and Lazarus, who provided a repast for Christ while Mary conversed with him. St. Ambrose says Christ cured Martha of the issue of blood. After Christ's Ascension, she went with Lazarus and Mary to Marseilles. She preached gospel at Tarascon, where she overpowered a dragon with holy

Homer Martin, *Harp of the Winds: a View on the Seine*. Metropolitan Museum of Art, New York.

water. Her attributes are a dragon, an aspergillum for holy water, a cooking ladle, and keys. Her feast is July 29.

See also SAINTS IN ART.

MARTIN, FLETCHER. American painter and graphic artist (1904–   ). Martin was born in Palisades, Colo., and was self-taught. His early paintings were of stylized figures in strong action. His later work, also realistic, tends toward overall abstract patterns.

BIBLIOGRAPHY. B. Ebersole, *Fletcher Martin*, Gainesville, Fla., 1954.

MARTIN, HENRI JEAN GUILLAUME. French painter (b. Toulouse, 1860; d. Paris, 1943). He studied with Jean-Paul Laurens in Paris, and went to Italy in 1885. The Italian trip changed Martin from a classicist to a painter of landscape and pastoral subjects in a rough-textured neoimpressionist style, at times with allegorical content. He did several wall decorations, among which are murals for the Capitol in Toulouse and the villa of Edmond Rostand at Cambo. The Toulouse decorations, a triptych of harvest and rural scenes, is particularly effective in its depiction of light, its placement of figures, and its spaciousness of composition, which is reminiscent of Puvis de Chavannes.

MARTIN, HOMER DODGE. American landscape painter (b. Albany, N.Y., 1836; d. St. Paul, Minn., 1897). He studied with William Hart at the National Academy of Design and then opened a studio in New York City. He was made an academician (1875) and became a founder of the Society of American Artists (1878). His early manner of landscape painting echoes the romantic, detailed panoramas of the Hudson River artists. It was not until he made a trip to France (1881–86) that he fell under the influence of the Barbizon school and Whistler. *St. Lawrence River at Gananoque, Ontario* (1893) reveals his later style in which he creates intimate views and painterly effects of color, tone, and pigment. His memory scenes, poetic and introspective, foreshadow the American impressionists.

BIBLIOGRAPHY. F. J. Mather, *Homer Martin, Poet in Landscape*, New York, 1912.

MARTIN, JOHN. English painter and engraver (b. Haydon, Northumberland, 1789; d. Douglas, Isle of Man, 1854). He began as a coach and china painter, and this experience influenced his handling of oils in later life. He went to London in 1806. Martin painted landscapes and Biblical and historical subjects. They all stress "sublime" effects with storm-rent skies and huge architectural and mountain settings whose scale completely dwarfs the tiny human figures. Although popular in his time, many of Martin's paintings are now untraceable and are known only through his mezzotint engravings. Their titles indicate his ambition: *Joshua Commanding the Sun to Stand Still* (1816), *Belshazzar's Feast* (1820), *The Fall of Nineveh* (1828), and *The Last Judgment* (1851).

BIBLIOGRAPHY. T. Balston, *John Martin 1789-1854: His Life and Works*, London, 1947.

MARTIN, KENNETH. English sculptor (1905–   ). Born in Sheffield, he studied at the Sheffield School of Art and at the Royal College in London. He was first a landscape painter and then turned to sculpture, developing a non-figural style about 1950. Typically he works in delicately aligned wire forms with interspersed flat geometrical shapes of metal, often using mobile suspension. His works have been shown in many recent major English exhibitions.

BIBLIOGRAPHY. L. Alloway, *Nine Abstract Artists*, London, 1954.

MARTIN, SIR LESLIE. English architect (1908–   ). Since 1934 he has been head of the Hull School of Architecture, specializing in architectural training. His Northwick School shows advanced ideas of standardization of parts. He was in partnership with Robert Matthew in designing the Royal Festival Hall (1947–51) and was appointed architect to the London County Council in 1953.

Arturo Martini, *Pope Pius II, Francesco and Bianca Maria Sforza, and the Foundation of the Hospital, in 1456*. Ospedale Maggiore, Milan.

MARTIN, MARY. English sculptor (1907–   ). Born in Folkestone, she studied at the Goldsmith Art School in the 1920s and married the sculptor Kenneth Martin in 1930. Her painting and sculpture developed strongly in the 1940s. After 1950 she specialized in making reliefs and severely abstract, vertical sculptures akin to Vantongerloo's of the late 1920s. Her interest in the relationship of sculpture to architecture is expressed in her art; she has also written about the subject.

BIBLIOGRAPHY. L. Alloway, *Nine Abstract Artists*, London, 1954.

MARTIN, VICENTE. Uruguayan painter (1911–   ). Born in Montevideo, he studied with Laborde, Prevosti, and Torres García. An abstractionist at first, Martin later turned to figurative painting. Distinctive of his style are roughly outlined and textured still lifes.

MARTIN-DIDIER-PAPE, see DIDIER, MARTIN.

MARTINEZ, ALFONSO. Spanish architect (fl. ca. 1386–1402). Martínez was the architect in charge of the building of the old Cathedral of Seville and the supposed author of the plans for the new Cathedral, founded in 1402.

MARTINEZ, ALONSO. Spanish sculptor (d. 1668). His work, in the tradition of the Seville school, has art historical importance as the bridge between the placid, classical realism of Montañés and the Berninesque style of Roldán. Famous in his day, he is now rated as second rank. A typical work is the *Immaculate Conception* (after 1655; Seville Cathedral).

BIBLIOGRAPHY. F. Jiménez-Placer, *Historia del arte español*, vol. 2, Barcelona, 1955.

MARTINEZ DE HOYOS, RICARDO. Mexican painter (1918–   ). Born in Mexico City, Martínez, holder of a law degree and a self-taught painter, has demonstrated versatility by forays into stage décor, book illustration, and teaching. In his painting he creates a primitive race of naked forms, reminiscent in their brooding monumentality of Aztec statuary (for example, *Childbirth*, 1959; New York, Contemporary Arts Gallery). Mostly recumbent, like the Chac-Mool of pre-Columbian sculpture, his Titans are bathed in primordial mist.

Figure studies, often defined in monochromatic harmonies, predominated before 1950. Since then Martínez has given increasing importance to landscape, interpreted in a lyrical mood somewhat different from that of his figures. He was chosen to represent Mexico in the São Paulo Bienal of 1963.

BIBLIOGRAPHY. B. S. Myers, *Mexican Painting in Our Time*, New York, 1956.

MARTINI, ARTURO. Italian sculptor (b. Treviso, 1889; d. Milan, 1947). After learning ceramics at an early age, Martini studied sculpture in Treviso and at the Venice Academy. He exhibited first in Paris (1911) and became a member of the Valori Plastici group in Rome after World War I. In addition to numerous terra cottas, drawings, and paintings, Martini executed a number of public monuments, including the *Italian Pioneers of America* (1927–28) in Worcester, Mass. His work has had a profound effect on subsequent Italian sculpture, particularly in those qualities that draw inspiration from the archaisms of ancient Etruscan and Roman sculpture.

BIBLIOGRAPHY. C. G. Argan, *Martini*, London, 1959.

MARTINI, SIMONE, see SIMONE MARTINI.

MARTINO, GIOVANNI DI. Italian sculptor (fl. Fiesole and Venice, 15th cent.). Martino was active in 1423 with Niccolò di Pietro on the tomb of Doge Tommaso Mocenigo (Venice, SS. Giovanni e Paolo), and eleven pillars on the west side of the lower Hall of Columns of the Doge's Palace in Venice are attributed to him. He worked in a Gothic idiom with the addition of realism in the vein of Donatello.

MARTINO DA UDINE, see PELLEGRINO DA SAN DANIELE.

MARTINO DI BARTOLOMMEO DI BIAGIO. Italian painter (fl. from 1389; d. after 1434). A student of Jacopo di Mino, Martino worked in Pisa from 1396 to 1405 and thereafter in Siena, where he created many frescoes and altarpieces. Common among these are repetitive versions of Madonnas and saints that are essentially imitative of the works of Taddeo di Bartolo.

MARTIN OF TOLEDO. Spanish architect (fl. 1227–34). Martin is recorded as master of the works at the Cathedral of Toledo in 1227 and 1234. He is believed to have made its original plans and to have begun the building.

BIBLIOGRAPHY. L. Torres Balbás, *Ars Hispaniae*, vol. 7: *Arquitectura gótica*, Madrid, 1952.

MARTIN OF TOURS, ST. Missionary among Gauls and founder of Western monachism (b. Hungary, ca. 315). He became catechumen and served in the Roman army in Italy and in Gaul. He divided his cloak with a beggar at Amiens; that night Christ appeared to him in a dream revealing He had been the beggar. Martin was baptized and founded a monastery in Ligugé, near Poitiers; later, as Bishop of Tours, he established the abbey of Marmoutiers near Tours. His feast is November 11.

See also SAINTS IN ART.

MARTINS, ALDEMIR. Brazilian draftsman (1922–   ). Born in Ingázeira, Ceará State, Martins expresses the harsh folk life of Brazil's northeast in stylized drawings, oils, and murals. He is best known for drawings, such as *Cangaceiro* (1960). His work has been shown since 1942 and has been awarded many prizes (for example, the gold medal at the National Salon of Modern Art in Rio de Janeiro in 1956).

MARTINS, MARIA, see MARIA.

MARTORANA, LA, PALERMO. Sicilian mid-12th-century church. The Church of S. Maria dell'Ammiraglio, known as La Martorana, was built and endowed by George of Antioch, a prominent figure at the court of King Roger II. The original form of the church was of a cross inscribed in a square, the central portion being a domed pavilion upon pendentives and columns. In the dome and upon neighboring vaults are mosaics of very high quality. The central, highest composition depicts a seated Christ Pantocrator (All-Ruler) surrounded by archangels who adore Him. Below them appear prophets and Evangelists; the Virgin in the apse has been lost. La Martorana is the most purely Byzantine of Western churches.

BIBLIOGRAPHY. O. Demus, *The Mosaics of Norman Sicily*, London, 1950.

MARTORELL, BERNARDO. Hispano-Flemish painter (d. ca. 1452). Little is known about Martorell, who appears to have been active primarily in Barcelona. From his extant work and those pieces attributed to him, it is certain that he worked or studied in Flanders, probably after painting his earliest recorded works in Barcelona. He is recorded as having been commissioned to do an altarpiece for the Shoemakers' Guild of Barcelona in 1437 and another for the Pedralbes Cloister, Barcelona, in 1439. It is not known whether the altarpieces now extant in those places are actually Martorell's.

A *St. George and the Dragon* (Chicago Art Institute) attributed to Martorell may be dated about 1440. It is derived from a miniature of the same subject in the *Book of Hours* of the Boucicault Master of about 1410. However, the stylistic qualities of Martorell's panel copy of the manuscript miniature suggest an intermediary step; another panel copy of the miniature by a Flemish master of the quality of Van Eyck may have existed. Such a hypothesis is tenuous, but it does serve to relate Martorell to his time and to establish his importance in Spanish painting. Martorell was, to the best of our knowledge, the first Spanish painter to carry the Flemish style to his homeland, and thus to become the founder of the Hispano-Flemish school of painting.

This working hypothesis is more fully substantiated by

La Martorana, Palermo. Mid-12th-century Byzantine church.

the single totally authenticated Martorell work. A miniature in the State Archives of Barcelona, dated 1448, it shows the same stylistic qualities as the Chicago *St. George*, only with a greater assimilation and fuller development of the Flemish manner. Other works, of debatable attribution, are altarpieces in Barcelona, Manresa, and Chicago. However, it is difficult to tell whether these are from Martorell's hand or are early Spanish workshop essays in the Flemish manner.

Martorell's importance rests not on the intrinsic value of any of his known or attributed works but rather on his historical position as the first Spanish painter in whom Flemish influence can be recognized.

BIBLIOGRAPHY. G. Richert, *Mittelalterliche Malerei in Spanien*, Berlin, 1925. STANLEY FERBER

MARTSEN, JAN (Jacob?), THE YOUNGER. Dutch painter and engraver of landscapes, cavalry battles, and horses (b. Haarlem, ca. 1609; d. after 1647). Martsen's first name is not completely certain, as the name Jacob appears on some of his engravings. He was influenced by the work of his uncle Esaias van de Velde. Martsen is known to have collaborated with Michiel Mierevelt on equestrian portraits of Prince Maurits and Fredrick Hendrick, with Martsen painting the horses.

BIBLIOGRAPHY. W. Bernt, *Die niederländischen Maler des 17. Jahrhunderts...*, vol. 2, Munich, 1948.

MARUYAMA SCHOOL. School of Japanese painters founded by Okyo. He trained many able painters, including Gessen (1721–1809), Goshun, Komai Genki (1747–79), Rosetsu, Watanabe Nangaku (1767–1813), and Yamaguchi Soken (1759–1818). Okyo's descendants, such as Ozui (1766–1829) and Oritsu (1817–75), although they were not important artists, also preserved the school's naturalistic style of painting. The Maruyama school continued to be popular until the end of the Edo period because its works were easy to understand. In the Meiji period its successors revitalized the school's art by introducing a Western style of painting that remains an influential force in modern Kyoto. *See* GOSHUN; OKYO; ROSETSU.

BIBLIOGRAPHY. T. Akiyama, *Japanese Painting*, [Geneva?], 1961.

MARV (Merv; Mary): MAUSOLEUM OF SULTAN SANJAR. Saljuk monument in the center of the Iranian city of Marv, now in the Turkmen S.S.R. This two-storied mausoleum of Sultan Sanjar (r. 1117–57) is built of brick and is magnificently decorated. Its double dome, arches, vaults, and galleries are adorned with decorated bricks, rich stucco patterns painted in blue. An inscription encircles the dome chamber, which has niche galleries faced with blue tiles.

BIBLIOGRAPHY. A. U. Pope, ed., *A Survey of Persian Art*, vol. 2, New York, 1939.

MARVILLE, JEAN DE, *see* DIJON; SLUTER, CLAUS.

MARX, ROBERTO BURLE. Brazilian landscape architect and painter (1909–   ). Burle Marx was educated in Berlin (1928–29) and in his native Rio de Janeiro. Botanical interests combined with art training led him to create a personal garden designed for visual effect. Lúcio Costa commissioned a garden (1933), which led to many important commissions (for example, Rio de Janeiro, Flamengo

Bernardo Martorell, *St. George and the Dragon*. Chicago Art Institute.

Gardens, 1963). He collaborated with Portinari on murals in the Ministry of Education in Rio de Janeiro (1937).

BIBLIOGRAPHY. P. M. Bardi, *The Tropical Gardens of Burle Marx*, Amsterdam, Rio de Janeiro, 1964.

MARY: MAUSOLEUM OF SULTAN SANJAR, *see* MARV: MAUSOLEUM OF SULTAN SANJAR.

MARY MAGDALEN, ST.
Holy woman from Magdala on the Sea of Galilee. With other women she served the material needs of Christ and his disciples after He had freed her from the possession of devils. She witnessed the Crucifixion and was the first to see the empty tomb and the resurrected Christ (the scene known as *Noli me tangere* in art). She has been wrongly identified with the penitent woman and with Mary of Bethany since Tertullian and thus often appears as these women in art. Her attribute is the jar of ointment with which she sought to anoint Christ after His death. Her feast is July 22.

See also SAINTS IN ART.

MARY OF BETHANY, ST.
Sister of Martha and Lazarus, often confused with St. Mary Magdalen. In the story of Christ's visit to the house of Mary and Martha (Luke 10:38–42) in Bethany, near Jerusalem, Mary's desire to be a disciple is contrasted with Martha's attention to the needs of hospitality. Mary later anointed Christ and was the only one to be visited with the knowledge of His death and salvation before it happened. In Renaissance and baroque painting she appears in the popular scene of Christ in the House of Mary and Martha.

See also SAINTS IN ART.

MARYS AT THE TOMB.
Scene described in Mark 16:1–7 in which the three holy women Mary Magdalen, Mary, mother of James, and Mary Salome visit the tomb of Christ to anoint His body. They find the tomb open and hear an angel declare Christ's resurrection. The scene is found in art since the 4th century in place of actual Resurrection scenes, which did not appear until the 12th century.

MARZAL DE SAX, ANDRES.
Spanish painter (fl. 1394–1410). Of Germanic origin, Marzal de Sax worked in Valencia with Pedro Nicoláu in the angular, linear manner of the late Gothic. In default of external evidence he has generally been assigned the more expressionistic and violent portions of works attributed to both of them; these portions are in accordance with the stylistic trends of late Gothic German art.

St. Mary Magdalen. Sculpture by Donatello, detail. Baptistery, Florence.

MARZIALE, MARCO. Venetian painter, active also in Cremona (fl. 1492–1507). He is known from signed and dated works, especially repetitions of the Supper at Emmaus and of the Circumcision. Dry in surface and elaborate in ornament, his paintings reflect the influence of Gentile Bellini and Vittore Carpaccio more than that of Albrecht Dürer, as is sometimes suggested.

BIBLIOGRAPHY. B. Geiger, "Marco Marziale und der sogenannte nordische Einfluss in seinen Bildern," *Jahrbuch der Königlich-preussischen Kunstsammlung*, XXXIII, 1912.

MASACCIO (Sculptor), *see* MASO DI BARTOLOMMEO.

MASACCIO (Tommaso Cassai). Florentine painter (b. San Giovanni Valdarno, 1401; d. Rome, 1428). Although he is often identified as Tommaso di Giovanni di Simone Guidi, his real name was Tommaso Cassai. The first great painter of the Italian Renaissance, he was perhaps apprenticed in the town of his birth to a distant cousin, Mariotto di Cristofano. Work by his younger brother Giovanni, a painter of no significance, has recently been rediscovered. Masaccio's father died when he was five; his mother remarried and was widowed again. He was a resident of Florence and joined the painters' guild on Jan. 7, 1422, and the Company of St. Luke in 1424.

Four certain works by him survive. The first is the *Madonna with St. Anne* (ca. 1423; Florence, Uffizi), a panel done in collaboration with Masolino. The second is the fresco of the *Trinity with Donors* (Florence, S. Maria Novella). There have been several recent discoveries about this fresco: the lowest section, showing a skeleton, was found under whitewash; its date, 1425 (previously considered 1427–28); and the identity of the donor, the *gonfaloniere* (city government chairman for a brief term) Lenzi. The third is the altarpiece for S. Maria del Carmine in Pisa, commissioned on Feb. 19, 1426, and paid for in installments. Donatello was witness to parts of this agreement, which ended on Dec. 26, 1426. Masaccio agreed to do no other work until it was finished. It was later dismantled, and only scattered parts have been recovered: the central Madonna (London, National Gallery); the five predella panels and four small saints from the frame (Berlin, former State Museums); the Crucifixion from the top center (Naples, Capodimonte), recently cleaned and showing slight changes; and the St. Paul (Pisa, National Museum of St. Matthew) and St. Andrew (Vienna, Lanckoronoski Collection) from the top sides. The fourth work is the frescoes in the Brancacci Chapel of S. Maria del Carmine, Florence, depicting the life of St. Peter, with the Adam and Eve story at the entrance, executed in collaboration with Masolino, probably in 1427. Masolino had done all the upper part before he left Italy in 1425; he returned in 1427 when both painters probably were active. Masaccio went to Rome in 1428, also leaving the chapel unfinished, and died there. Of several lost works, the chief ones were in S. Maria del Carmine in Pisa: a *St. Paul* and a *Consecration*.

The *Madonna with St. Anne* was considered entirely Masaccio's until recently. It is now agreed the surrounding angels are mainly by Masolino. The Christ Child is

Masaccio, *The Crucifixion.* Capodimonte, Naples.

fully typical of Masaccio, sculpturally plastic, with organic flesh texture and strongly lighted. The Anne is much discussed but was probably done by Masolino. The Madonna, usually considered the work of Masaccio, is as solid as the Child but rigid in pose; she may well represent drawing by Masolino and final painting by Masaccio. It is often suggested that the work was ordered from Masolino but left unfinished when he went on one of his trips.

The fresco of the *Trinity with Donors* is the first painting to use systematic perspective; it is derived from Donatello's use of it in relief sculpture. The complex space system has also been credited to the influence of Brunelleschi. The work is iconographically unique, blending the standard Trinity and Crucifixion images, with Christ as part of both. This Trinity type with Christ crucified is often extended by saints, but never by Mary and John, who here transform the work from icon to narrative. The space system has iconographic purpose: its lines group the figures in a diagram—dead body, live donors, Crucifixion, Trinity, that is, from pure matter to pure spirit. The theme is repentance in the face of death. Only Christ overlaps the lines, confirming the purposefulness. The work is a medieval religious concept, shown in a very modern spatial design, as in Jan van Eyck's symbolic genre.

The Pisa altarpiece develops space, mass, and light with great power. The central predella panel of the *Adoration of the Magi*, simple and structurally clear, suggests a criticism of Gentile da Fabriano's ornamental version of the subject in 1423. Masaccio was praised for unadorned purity by his first commentators.

Of six scenes by him in the Brancacci Chapel, three frescoes are on each of two levels. The famous *Expulsion* uses concentrated mass, simple movement, and facial expression underlined by strong shadow to give the two figures tremendous emotional expressiveness. They mark a return to Giotto's approach, modified by new complexity in perspective and anatomical drawing.

The even more famous *Tribute Money* is a rare theme; it was probably propaganda for the honest payment of the progressive income tax (introduced in 1427 to pay for the war provoked by the Duke of Milan's attack). The balance of figures and space creates a clear, broad, exact harmony, realizing the Renaissance ideal of man at the center of an orderly, comprehensible environment, neither dominating the other. The reduction of accurate observation to mathematical measurements creates the cultural climate for modern science. This is the largest of the frescoes.

St. Peter Baptizing has a similar semicircular design of figures. The shivering man is a virtuoso example of modeling with light and gesture to evoke human feeling. The three lower scenes have a fresher, more light-saturated brushstroke and more complex space. Peter and John, who are healing cripples by their shadow, are in a diagonal space and exploit movement in time for dramatic force. As the saints move forward, the cripples move back in a series from sick to cured; as they cross, the miracle occurs. A shadow as a miraculous agency was no doubt delightful to Masaccio. The *Distribution of Funds* (another theme of morality in public finance) uses a W-shaped space for two groups, an idea of Giotto. The *Healing of the Pagan King's Son* was left unfinished; the king is apparently a portrait of the enemy, the Duke of Milan. *St.*

Kano Masanobu, *Chou Mao-shu Admiring Lotus Flowers*. Ink and light color on paper. National Museum, Tokyo.

Peter Enthroned is still more complex in space (the main figure being above and behind others), and is the most swift and impressionist in luminous modeling.

Masaccio was not influenced by any painter except Giotto, who was admired by all but had not been the starting point for new developments. He was certainly affected by the great generation of older sculptors (all born between 1375 and 1385), not so much by Ghiberti as by the Roman classicist Nanni d'Antonio di Banco and the great Donatello. Brunelleschi affected him not only as the inventor of perspective (after Brunelleschi a universal device) but also more widely, as his famous early sculpture of Isaac indicates in its Giottesque concentration of mass and drama; it is closer to Masaccio than any other work.

Masaccio's frescoes were immediately influential on young artists, especially in modeling and space. Masolino modified his style from Gothic grace toward simplicity and weight in his part of the Brancacci Chapel. Two projects of Masolino, which were done in Rome about 1428, are often thought to contain small contributions by Masaccio's hand; these are the S. Clemente frescoes and the S. Maria Maggiore altarpiece (the Masacciesque sections are in London, National Gallery). In 1960 an altarpiece was discovered that is of special interest for its date, 1422, and location, very near San Giovanni Valdarno. It is very like the St. Anne, but inferior. Though claimed to be an early Masaccio, it may be the first example of his influence on other artists there. But it is closer to his own work than is the "early Masaccio" Madonna (Washington, D.C., National Gallery). Most other older attributions are now usually assigned to his influence.

BIBLIOGRAPHY. U. Procacci, *The Complete Paintings of Masaccio*, New York, 1962; L. Berti, *Masaccio*, Milan, 1964; C. Gilbert, *Masaccio*, New York, 1969.   CREIGHTON GILBERT

MASANOBU (Kano Masanobu). Japanese painter (1434–1530). Although not a Zen priest, Masanobu was an official painter to the shoguns and the first lay painter to work in an ink medium, which he learned from either Shūbun or Sōtan. In decorating the large interiors of temples, he modified the Shūbun style of ink painting, so that forms are clearly delineated, composition is balanced, and brushstrokes are sharply defined. *See* SHUBUN; SOTAN.

BIBLIOGRAPHY. R. T. Paine and A. Soper, *The Art and Architecture of Japan*, Baltimore, 1955.

MASANOBU (Kitao Masanobu). Japanese Ukiyo-e print designer (1761–1816). Masanobu was the most precocious of Shigemasa's several brilliant pupils but later became more famous as a novelist under the name of Santō Kyōden. His prints of elegant women show more stylistic affinity to those of Kiyonaga than to those of his teacher. *See* KIYONAGA; SHIGEMASA; UKIYO-E.

BIBLIOGRAPHY. J. A. Michener, *Japanese Prints*, Rutland, Vt., 1959.

MASANOBU (Okumura Masanobu). Japanese Ukiyo-e printmaker (1686–1764). Masanobu admired and followed the style of Kiyonaga. Often working as his own publisher, he could exercise great control over the final result of his designs. He was a versatile artist and experimented with different types of prints; he is credited with the invention of *uki-e* (perspective pictures) and was an accomplished painter. Refinement, sensitivity, and lyricism, combined with wit and verve, characterize his work and typify the mood of the affluent middle-class society in 18th-century Edo. *See* KIYONAGA; UKIYO-E.

BIBLIOGRAPHY. L. V. Ledoux, *Japanese Prints of the Primitive Period in the Collection of Louis V. Ledoux*, New York, 1942; J. A. Michener, *Japanese Prints*, Rutland, Vt., 1959.

MASCARINO (Mascherino), OTTAVIANO. Italian architect and painter (1536–1606). Of Bolognese origin, he worked in Rome. In such works as the Quirinal Palace (begun 1583) he followed the style of Vignola, but in his masterpiece, the nave of S. Salvatore in Lauro (1592–98), the articulation with coupled columns shows the influence of Pellegrino Tibaldi.

BIBLIOGRAPHY. V. Golzio, "Note su Ottaviano Mascherino architetto in Roma," *Dedalo*, X, 1929.

MASCHERINI, MARCELLO. Italian sculptor (1906–). Born in Udine, he studied in Trieste, where he now lives. He works figurally, mainly in bronze, using themes of dancers and bathers. Certain of these suggest the style of Elie Nadelman in their extreme elegance. He has exhibited widely in Europe.

BIBLIOGRAPHY. Städtische Galerie, *Marcello Mascherini*, Munich, 1957.

MASCHERINO, OTTAVIANO, *see* MASCARINO, OTTAVIANO.

MASEGNE, JACOBELLO AND PIERPAOLO DALLE. Italian sculptors, brothers: Pierpaolo (d. probably 1403) and Jacobello (d. 1409). Apparently trained in Venice and influenced there by Tuscan and German 14th-century sculpture, they espoused a style of late Venetian Gothic realism. First mentioned in 1383, they worked together until 1399, executing the monument of Giovanni da Legnano (d. 1383) in S. Domenico, Bologna, fragmentarily preserved in the Municipal Museum; the marble *Altar of S. Francesco*, Bologna (1388–92); and statues for the iconostasis of St. Mark's, Venice (1394). In 1399 they collaborated on the decoration of Milan Cathedral.

Jacobello was engaged independently by Francesco Gonzaga to work on the façade of Mantua Cathedral in 1396. Gian Galeazzo Visconti employed him in the Castello at Pavia in 1399. Pierpaolo executed independent work at Mantua and Venice, and is responsible for the *Virgin and Child with Saints* above the monument of Antonio Venier (d. 1400) in SS. Giovanni e Paolo, Venice.

BIBLIOGRAPHY. J. Pope-Hennessy, *Italian Gothic Sculpture*, London, 1955.

MASEGNE, PAOLO DI JACOBELLO DALLE. Italian sculptor (fl. late 14th cent.–early 15th cent.). Member of a northern Italian family of sculptors, exponents of late Venetian Gothic, he is the author of the tombs of Giacomo Cavalli (d. 1386) in SS. Giovanni e Paolo, Venice, and Prendiparte Pico (d. 1394), formerly in S. Francesco della Mirandola, now in the Municipal Museum, Modena.

MASEREEL, FRANS. Belgian printmaker, illustrator, theatrical designer, and painter (1889–). Born in Blankenberghe, he trained under Jean Delvin at the Ghent Academy and attained prominence for his social and political satire in Geneva (1916–21), where he did expressionistic black-and-white drawings and woodcuts for periodicals, books, and his own "novel in pictures," *Mon livre d'heures*. Masereel has lived in Paris (1921–45) and in Nice (since 1949) and has traveled extensively. His work, which verged toward the extremes of expressionism in the 1920s, excels in economy of means and projection of fantasy.

BIBLIOGRAPHY. S. Zweig et al., *Frans Masereel*, 2d ed., Dresden, 1961.

MASHHAD, *see* MESHED.

MASHONA, *see* AFRICA, PRIMITIVE ART OF (SOUTH-CENTRAL AND EAST AFRICA: RHODESIA).

MASIP, JUAN VICENTE, THE ELDER. Spanish painter (b. ca. 1495; d. Valencia? ca. 1550). Paintings now assigned to this artist were once ascribed to an early phase in the work of his son Juan de Juanes. His only authenticated work is the great altarpiece in the Cathedral of Segorbe (completed 1531–35), dedicated to the Virgin and depicting scenes from her life and those in which she took part. The massive figure style, facial types, and tightly organized compositions in the panels of this work suggest a connection with northern Italian painting, particularly with Pordenone, which has led some scholars to assume Masip's presence in Italy during his formative years. The setting of figure groups against a high horizon continues the practice of Spanish painting and is reminiscent of Flemish painting, as is the pervasive use of interlocking diagonals in creating a compositional web. Other works ascribed to Masip include the *Baptism of Christ* (1535) and the *Christ Crowned with Thorns* in Valencia Cathedral, the *Adoration of the Shepherds* in the Archaeological Museum, Valladolid, and paintings of the two St. Johns in the Colegiata, Gandía.

BIBLIOGRAPHY. C. R. Post, *A History of Spanish Painting*, vol. 11, Cambridge, Mass., 1953.

MASIP, JUAN VICENTE, THE YOUNGER, *see* JUANES, JUAN DE.

MASJID, *see* MOSQUE.

MASJID-I-JAMI, *see* JAMI MASJID; JAMI MASJID, DELHI; MASJID-I-JAMI, ISFAHAN.

See also AHMEDABAD: JAMI MASJID; ARDABIL: MASJID-I-JAMI; BIJAPUR: JAMI MASJID; FATEHPUR SIKRI; JAUNPUR: JAMI MASJID; VARAMIN: FRIDAY MOSQUE.

MASJID-I-JAMI, ISFAHAN. So-called Friday or congregational mosque, the largest in Iran. The ensemble reflects the entire history of Islamic architecture in the country.

Frans Masereel, *Carrefour*, black-and-white drawing. Fine Arts Museum, Brussels.

Maso di Banco, *Madonna and Child with Saints*, five panels from an altarpiece. Sto Spirito, Florence.

Around a vast open court are prayer halls, dome chambers, and other structures of the Saljuk, Mongol, Timurid, and Safavid periods.

See also SALJUK ARCHITECTURE (IRAN).

BIBLIOGRAPHY. A. U. Pope, ed., *A Survey of Persian Art*, vol. 2, New York, 1939.

MASJID-I-SADR, ISFAHAN, *see* LUTFULLAH MOSQUE, ISFAHAN.

MASJID-I-SHAH, ISFAHAN. Safavid mosque situated at the southern end of the Maidan-i-Shah in Isfahan. In 1612 Shah Abbas the Great of Iran ordered work begun on his "imperial mosque." Completed in 1637, it has a monumental portal which leads into an open court surrounded by arcaded halls. It features a great square chamber, crowned by a faïence-clad dome.

BIBLIOGRAPHY. A. U. Pope, ed., *A Survey of Persian Art*, vol. 2, New York, 1939.

MASJID-I-SHAIKH LUTFULLAH, ISFAHAN, *see* LUTFULLAH MOSQUE, ISFAHAN.

MASKS. In primitive cultures and since ancient times, masks have been the primary equipment in conveying symbolic identity. In ancient Greece, masks were used in the theater to signify characters in almost the same way as they are used in the classical Japanese theater. Wax death masks also originated with the Greeks. Masks found their widest use in the 18th-century rococo period, when they were a part of fanciful court games. *See* BUGAKU MASK; GIGAKU MASK; NOH MASK.

MASO DA SAN FRIANO, *see* MANZUOLI, TOMMASO D'ANTONIO.

MASO DI BANCO. Italian painter of the Florentine school (fl. ca. 1325–50). Maso was the most gifted and able pupil of Giotto, whose style he carried on with greater effectiveness and intelligence than any of his contemporaries. In the 15th century Ghiberti singled out Maso's works for particular praise and description.

Several painters with the name Maso are recorded in 14th-century Florence. Maso di Banco is most probably identical with Maso pittore filio olim Banchi, who is mentioned in connection with the Bardi family in a document of 1341. One of the members of this family had provided in his will (1336) for the foundation of a chapel bearing the Bardi name in Sta Croce, and the fresco decorations of this chapel, the Bardi di Vernio Chapel, are the main works of Maso. They represent five episodes from the legend of St. Sylvester. The best preserved and most impressive are *St. Sylvester Resurrecting an Ox* and *St. Sylvester Resurrecting the Two Magi Killed by a Dragon*. They possess great purity of design and beauty of color. Figures and architectural settings are defined with a view to expressing their stereometric, cylindrical, and cubic character in a way that anticipates the monumental style of Masaccio and Piero della Francesca in the 15th century. Other works attributed to Maso di Banco are a damaged fresco of the *Coronation of the Virgin* (Sta Croce museum); four panels (a *Madonna and Child with Saints*) from a polyptych (Berlin, former State Museums, Koenigsberg (?); New York, Metropolitan Museum); and five considerably damaged panels of an altarpiece in Sto Spirito in Florence.

Maso's style assimilated elements from Siena as well as from Florence. The elegance and suaveness of his contours suggest the inspiration of Simone Martini, and the emotional climate of his figures recalls the eloquence of Ambrogio Lorenzetti. In his color Maso may also have relied on Sienese examples, though similar coloristic sophistications were closer at hand in the art of Bernardo Daddi. In adopting such influences Maso's style always remained severe and monumental, but by enriching and extending the monumental style of Giotto in this way he became the most distinguished master of his day in Florence.

BIBLIOGRAPHY. W. Suida, "Studien zur Trecentomalerei," *Repertorium für Kunstwissenschaft*, XXVII, 1904; O. Sirén, *Giottino*, Leipzig, 1908; R. Offner, "Four Panels, a Fresco, and a Problem," *The Burlington Magazine*, LIV, May, 1929; J. White, *Art and Architecture in Italy, 1250–1400*, Baltimore, 1966.

HELLMUT WOHL

MASO DI BARTOLOMMEO (Masaccio). Italian sculptor (1406–57). Born in Capannole, he was an assistant of Donatello in the execution of the outdoor pulpit of Prato

Cathedral. In 1446 he participated there in the bronze work of the Chapel of the Cintola and was commissioned with Michelozzo and Luca della Robbia to make the bronze doors of the north sacristy of Florence Cathedral.

MASO FINIGUERRA, see FINIGUERRA, MASO.

MASOLINO (Tommaso di Cristoforo Fini). Italian painter (b. Panicale, 1383; d. Florence, 1447 or 1440). The documentary notices of his life are brief. He joined the painters' guild of Florence in 1423. In 1424 he was paid for a fresco in Empoli and in 1425 for minor work in Florence. In 1427 he was said to be "still in Hungary" probably working for Pippo Spano. (According to some accounts, he returned in that year to work with Masaccio in the Brancacci Chapel.) In 1432 he was paid for a fresco in S. Fortunato, Todi. See MASACCIO.

Difficult problems of attribution arise because of the lack of documents, the shortness of his career, and the variety of styles visible in his work. He apparently began quite close to the International Gothic, fell under the influence of his associate Masaccio, and finally drifted back to a variant of the International style.

His earliest dated work is a *Madonna* (1423; Bremen, Art Gallery). The *Madonna of Humility* (Munich, Old Pinacothek) must come from the same date. Both exhibit the tender color and flowing line of the late Gothic style. The frescoes in S. Stefano and the Collegiata in Empoli (1424–25) also betray influences from late-14th-century painting in Florence and from the International style of Gentile da Fabriano. Sometime about 1425 Masolino began the decoration of the Brancacci Chapel in S. Maria del Carmine, Florence. His frescoes in the vaults were destroyed by fire in 1771, but the *Temptation of Adam and Eve*, the *Preaching of St. Peter*, and the *Resuscitation of Tabitha* remain. The first fresco is still strongly related to the International style, but the last of the group indicates the impact of Masaccio's treatment of light and space. The *Madonna di Novoli* and a *St. Julian* from this period have also been attributed to him. The *Annunciation* diptych and the *Goldman Annunciation* (both Washington, D.C., National Gallery) date from about 1430 and are related stylistically to the Todi fresco of 1432.

Of Masolino's late works the frescoes in S. Clemente, Rome, the altarpiece for S. Maria Maggiore, Rome (Naples, Capodimonte; London, National Gallery; Philadelphia Museum of Art), and the frescoes at Castiglione Olona pose difficult problems. The two Roman works must have been started during Masaccio's lifetime (prior to 1428) and completed shortly after by Masolino. The frescoes in the Collegiata at Castiglione Olona may have been begun rather early (ca. 1425, according to some authors), but the frescoes in the Baptistery at Castiglione Olona must date from 1435. In these later works the ill-digested adoption of Masaccio's precepts results in a mannered exaggeration of space and figure and a return to something near the International style.

BIBLIOGRAPHY. M. Salmi, *Masaccio*, 2d ed., Milan, 1948; K. Clark, "An Early Quattrocento Triptych from Santa Maria Maggiore, Rome," *The Burlington Magazine*, XCII, 1951; U. Procacci, "Sulla cronologia delle opere di Masaccio e di Masolino tra il 1425 e 1428," *Rivista d'arte*, XXVII, 1953.

JOHN R. SPENCER

MASON LIMNER. American portrait painter (fl. Boston, 1670). This anonymous painter takes his name from the subjects of two of his portraits, both executed in 1670—*Alice Mason* (Quincy, Mass., Adams Memorial Society) and the group portrait *David, Joanna, and Abigail Mason* (private collection). These works are naïve though delightful costume pieces whose flatness and concern for pattern and line mark them as part of the Elizabethan tradition. Although similar to the portraits of the Gibbs children done by the Freake Master, the Mason paintings were done with smaller brushstrokes and appear to be the work of a different artist. As both groups were painted in 1670, one could not be an earlier and the other a more developed style of the same artist. See FREAKE MASTER.

BIBLIOGRAPHY. L. Dresser, *Seventeenth-Century Painting in New England*, Worcester, 1935.

MASONRY. That which is built by a mason, especially of brick or stone. Masonry is generally classified according to the shape of the masonry units and the assembly of such units to form a wall. Rubble is relatively unshaped by a mason; rough, or ordinary rubble, is unsquared stone or fieldstone, laid without coursing, as in the cyclopean masonry of Aegean construction. Random rubble is roughly shaped, its joints fitted together but laid without regular coursing; coursed rubble consists of roughly shaped stones on an approximately level bed. Squared stone is roughly squared and is known as block-in-course or hammer-dressed ashlar when squared with a hammer and laid in regular courses. In ashlar, stones are

Masolino, *The Presentation of the Head of John the Baptist at the Banquet of Herod and Herodias*, detail. Baptistery, Castiglione Olona, Italy.

Cyclopean masonry. Rough stone construction with pebble-and clay-filled joints.

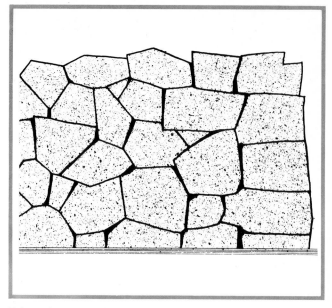

Polygonal masonry. Construction of irregular stones, sometimes rough-hewn as in Mycenae.

most accurately shaped to fit together. Descriptive of masonry in such structures as Greek temples and Renaissance palaces, ashlar is also called cut stone. *See* COURSE; MASONRY, CYCLOPEAN.

When masonry is laid without forming courses, it is random; it is polygonal or mosaic or cobweb rubble when the stones fitted together are irregular without parallel edges. In broken-range masonry, courses are continuous for only short lengths. Quarry face (as it comes from the quarry) is one of the various masonry faces. Split-face masonry is formed by splitting rock; masonry that is weatherworn or cut away with a broad chisel is known as rock or pitch-face masonry. Seam-face masonry is due to a natural seam or resembles one. Masonry is pointed when dressed with a pointing chisel until the surface is approximately flat but rough from the depressions left by the chisel. Masonry may be hammered, that is, having a rough and flat face marked by the hammer used in dressing it. Peen-hammered and bush-hammered masonry get their names from the types of hammer used. *See* MASONRY, POLYGONAL.

Distinctive stone faces are the congelated, which resembles congealed lime drippings, as in baroque work; vermiculated, when the masonry is given random curved grooves recalling worm markings; and rusticated, or rustic, with beveled edges or recessed joints. The diamond-faceted 16th-century Palazzo dei Diamanti, Verona, is an example of rusticated masonry. (The term rustic masonry is applied also to the use of uncut stones to give a rustic or rural look.)

Brick masonry is distinguished according to the type of unit and bond. *See* BRICK.

For aspects of Roman practice, *see* OPUS.

See also MASON'S MARKS.

MILTON F. KIRCHMAN

MASONRY, CYCLOPEAN. Walls constructed of large, rough stones, piled one on the other, are found in Aegean

construction and were used also by the early Greeks in building cities. The original fortification walls in Mycenae were cyclopean. The walls at Tiryns were built of massive stones, the joints being filled with smaller stones and yellow clay. Later generations believed the walls to be the work of a race of giants known as the Cyclopes. In Etruscan masonry, cyclopean walls were sometimes constructed without mortar. The term Pelasgic is sometimes applied to such construction following the lead of Herodotus, who indiscriminately referred to all aboriginal Greeks as Pelasgians, a northern tribe mentioned by Homer.

MASONRY, POLYGONAL. Masonry constructed of irregular stones usually having more than four sides and not meeting at right angles. The stones were often rough-hewn, as in the polygonal masonry in Mycenae.

MASON'S MARKS. Marks of workmanship incised by stone masons on architecture, especially in the Middle Ages. They first appeared in the 12th century, mainly in the form of composite initials about 10 centimeters high. In the 14th century they became smaller, measuring only 2 centimeters, and no longer represented letters, but, instead, various complex combinations of intersecting curved and straight lines. Their form was regulated by the masons' guilds.

MASS. The inclusive term for the entire Catholic ritual of the Eucharist, or Last Supper, the central act of public worship in the Christian church. The Mass consists of the Ordinary, or unchanging, parts and the Proper, or variable, parts. The former contains the Kyrie, Gloria, Credo, Sanctus and Benedictus, and the Agnus Dei; the latter, the Introit, Gradual, Alleluia or Tract, Offertory, and Communion.

Throughout the centuries artists have executed major works in various media in the area of liturgical art in the form of liturgical vessels, vestments, and books used in the celebration of the Mass and in the design of the church building itself (which is always related to some degree to ritual function, though less in the Renaissance than in the Romanesque and baroque periods) and its furnishing and decorations.

BIBLIOGRAPHY. J. A. Jungmann, *The Mass of the Roman Rite*, tr. F. A. Brunner, 2 vols., New York, 1951-55.

MASSACRE AT SCIO. Oil painting by Delacroix, in the Louvre Museum, Paris. *See* DELACROIX, EUGENE.

MASSACRE OF THE INNOCENTS. Episode in the life of Christ which follows the Adoration of the Magi (Matt. 2:16–18). In art, two separate scenes are usually shown: Herod, seated, giving the command; and the actual massacre of the children in the presence of their mothers. These very unpleasant aspects account for its relatively infrequent occurrence in art, although the episode has been represented since Early Christian times, for example, in the 5th-century mosaics in S. Maria Maggiore, Rome.

MASSIM, *see* OCEANIC ART (MELANESIA: TROBRIAND ISLANDS).

MASSIMO, CAVALIERE, *see* STANZIONE, MASSIMO.

MASSIO, GENTILE DI NICCOLO DI GIOVANNI DI, *see* GENTILE DA FABRIANO.

MASSON, ANDRE. French painter (1896–   ). Born in Balagny, he studied in Brussels and at the Ecole des Beaux-Arts, Paris, under Baudoin. From 1918 until the early 1920s he was influenced by the cubists, especially Juan Gris. Masson held a one-man exhibit at the Galerie

André Masson, *L'Enlèvement*, 1931. National Museum of Modern Art, Paris.

Simon in 1924, mainly of still lifes and landscapes with figures. At that time he met Ernst, Breton, and Miró and became a member of the surrealist group. He then came under the influence of Kafka and psychological literature and the painting of William Blake, turning to such themes as erotic dream fantasies and the metamorphosis of nature. Masson has been active as an illustrator since the 1920s, making drawings for *Justine* and other works by De Sade, his own *Bestiaire*, and books by André Malraux and Georges Bataille. He was represented in the 1936 International Surrealist Exhibition in London, in a two-man exhibition with Giacometti at the Basel Art Gallery, and in many other shows. Masson lived in the United States from 1941 to 1946. During that period he was especially active in printmaking.

Paintings such as *The Constellations* (1925; Paris, Galerie Furstenberg) indicate his cubist discipline (conditioned by Dada). *The Villagers* (1927; Paris, private collection) shows him close to Miró in both concept and technique, although Masson's touch is lighter and his forms more linear; his *Iroquois Landscape* (1943), painted during his sojourn in America, relates to the surrealist-abstract manner of Matta. A fully characteristic work is the *Summer Frolic* (1934; Paris, private collection), with its transcendental insect forms charging in a lively surface of pale greens, reds, and tans. Masson is distinguished for his imaginative formal treatment of a personalized order of surrealist imagery.

BIBLIOGRAPHY. A. Breton, ... *Le Surréalisme et la peinture* ..., 2d ed., New York, 1945; M. Jean, *The History of Surrealist Painting*, New York, 1960; O. Hahn, *Masson*, New York, 1965.

JOHN C. GALLOWAY

MASSON, ANTOINE. French engraver (b. Loury, near Paris, 1636; d. Paris, 1700). Trained as an armorer, he settled early in Paris and took up engraving and painting. His prints were especially celebrated for their delicacy. Masson was largely a copyist, as in *Christ with Disciples at Emmaus*, after Titian; some life-size portrait heads are interesting but are not his best works.

BIBLIOGRAPHY. A. Hayden, *Chats on Old Prints*, New York, 1906.

MASSON, HENRI. Canadian painter (1907–   ). Born in Namur, Belgium, he went to Canada about 1921. He had some formal study in Brussels and Ottawa but was mostly self-taught. Masson paints sketchily realistic figures, landscapes, and urban genre scenes.

MASSYS, *see* METSYS.

MASTABA. Ancient Egyptian tomb resembling a truncated pyramid. Assumed to have derived from the practice of piling heaps of stone to form a mound over mummy holes, the mastaba is usually rectangular in plan, with sides sloping about 75 degrees and a comparatively low, flat top. It consists of three elements: an outer chamber in which offerings were made to the *ka* of the deceased; an inner chamber, or serdab, with statues of deceased members of the family; and a chamber reached by an underground shaft and containing the sarcophagus. The mastaba of Thi, Saqqara, is a well-preserved example from the 5th dynasty.

MASTELLETTA (Giovanni Andrea Donducci). Italian painter (1575–1655). Born in Bologna, he studied there with the Carraccis and remained in the city except for a brief trip to Rome (between 1610 and 1613) and possibly to Venice (before 1615). His unorthodox style, characterized by insubstantial figures glowing in a darkened landscape (*Adoration of the Magi*, Parma, National Gallery), is singular in Carracci-dominated Bologna.

BIBLIOGRAPHY. M. Marangoni, *Arte barocca*, new ed., Florence, 1953; Bologna, Palazzo dell'archiginnasio, *Maestri della pittura del Seicento emiliano*, 3d Biennale d'arte antica (catalog), ed. F. Arcangeli et al., Bologna, 1959.

MASTER ALFONSO. Spanish painter. He is the artist mentioned by a 19th-century traveler as having been commissioned to do the retable for the monastic church of San Cugat del Vallés in 1473, now in the Museum of Catalonian Art, Barcelona, which has since been documented as a later work by Anye Bru. Master Alfonso has also been identified with Alfonso de Córdoba, who painted the vaults in the Royal Chapel of the Constable in Barcelona. *See* BRU, ANYE.

MASTER ARNOLD. German wood carver (fl. Kalkar, 1483–93). He was one of the most prominent members of the prolific Kalkar school. His major work, the middle shrine of the *Mary Altar* in the Nikolaikirche in Kalkar, contains nine reliefs of scenes from the life of Mary.

BIBLIOGRAPHY. E. Lüthgen, *Die niederrheinische Plastik*, Strasbourg, 1917.

MASTER ARNT (Arnt von Dorenwerth). Dutch wood carver (fl. Kalkar, ca. 1470–90; d. there, 1491/92). Together with other members of the famous Kalkar school of wood carvers, he worked on the altars of the Nikolaikirche in Kalkar.

MASTER BERTRAM (Meister Bertram von Minden). German painter and sculptor (b. Minden, ca. 1345; fl. Hamburg, until 1415). Very little is known concerning his artistic training or personal life beyond brief references to the commissioning of his major works. He is mentioned in the Hamburg Chronicle in the period from 1367 to 1387 as receiving payment for a picture of the Virgin for the Milderntor and a picture of angels that was placed over the Stadthaus (1367), for the erection of a statue of Mary in front of the Lübecker Tor (1377), for the completion of the *Grabow Altar* (1379), and for a painting on wood of St. Christopher and the Christ Child (1387). Of his personal life we know only that he was married in 1390 and undertook a pilgrimage to Rome the same year.

Two large winged altars, the *Grabow Altar* and the *Buxtehude Altar* (both, Hamburg, Art Gallery), are attributed to Master Bertram. The *Grabow Altar*, finished in 1379, is unanimously attributed to his hand, but scholarly opinion is divided over the attribution of the *Buxtehude Altar*. Some scholars see it as the work of an assistant in close collaboration with the master. Two additional altars, the *Passions Altar* (Hannover, Lower Saxony Landesmuseum) and the *Harvestehude Altar* (Hamburg, Art Gallery), are ascribed to Bertram's workshop.

The *Grabow Altar* is mentioned in the Hamburg Chronicle of 1383 as having been made for the high altar of

Master Bertram, *Grabow Altar*, detail. Art Gallery, Hamburg.

St. Peter's Church in Hamburg. Given to the city of Grabow in 1731, the altar consists of twenty-four panels depicting the history of creation, the patriarchs, and the childhood of Christ. When fully open the altar displays a Crucifixion with a large number of carved figures surrounded by two rows of single figures of saints, prophets, apostles, and martyrs. The carved works are also by Master Bertram.

Master Bertram's style is exceptionally naturalistic for German painting of the late 14th century. His figures are convincingly plastic and move in a surprisingly real space. But even more outstanding is his portrayal of human types and emotions that in its realism possesses the forceful directness of folk art. A close relationship with Bohemian painting is evident in the modeling of the figures, in the expressive use of landscape, and in the interest in animals. His art is considered one of the principal influences on the work of Master Francke.

BIBLIOGRAPHY. A. Lichtwark, *Meister Bertram*, Hamburg, 1905; A. Dorner, *Meister Bertram von Minden*, Berlin, 1937.
DONALD L. EHRESMANN

MASTER D. S. Swiss painter and graphic artist (fl. 1503–15). A leading designer for and probably also a craftsman of the woodcut, Master D. S. may have been born in

Basel. He was especially influential on Urs Graf. The origin of Master D. S. appears to be the Augsburg school or the Schongauer circle. He left a considerable number of illustrations, mostly for sacred texts. His paintings are less certain of attribution.

BIBLIOGRAPHY. H. Wescher-Kauert, "Ein Bildnis des Meister D. S.," *Pantheon*, X, 1932.

MASTER E. S. German engraver and goldsmith (b. ca. 1430; fl. Lake Constance area, until 1468). He is the most important German engraver of the period from 1451 or 1452, when he made his earliest prints, to 1468. His monogram appears only in the last years of his life (1466 and 1467). It is estimated that he made about 500 prints, of which 317 are known, more than one-third of them in unique impressions. Many are of miniature size. From two sets of playing cards, which must have had 48 or 52 pieces each, 42 of one and 15 of the other are extant. Among the engravings of Israel van Meckenem are copies after Master E. S. of about 38 prints the originals of which have been lost.

Master E. S. introduced subjects that had never before appeared in engraving: an alphabet composed of grotesque, fantastic, humorous figures of humans and animals; a greeting card for the New Year; a large design for a monstrance; and eleven plates of *Ars moriendi* (*The Art of Dying Well*), which were bound together with text in Latin or German. In addition to being prolific, he was pictorially inventive, producing eight different sets of Apostles, six Annunciations, twenty Madonnas, and five Nativities.

His style shows the conventions of a late Gothic artist: dainty, affected figures, tastefully draped cloth, and goldsmith's punches used on flowers and for ornamental stars. At the same time he was affected by the wave of Netherlandish, particularly Eyckian, influence in Germany. More than any of his predecessors in engraving, he paid attention to the structure and solidity of the human body; his people are more portraitlike, his animals closer to nature. His subjects are lighted from either left or right, and are often strongly shaded. Previous engravers had shadowed with tiny, light strokes, which vanished with the pressure of comparatively few printings. Master E. S. used short but deep wedge-shaped lines and transparent cross-hatching in the half tones.

Although he was endlessly copied by his contemporaries, his influence was superseded by that of his great follower, Martin Schongauer, who structured his art on the advances of Master E. S.

BIBLIOGRAPHY. M. Lehrs, *Geschichte und kritischer Katalog des deutschen, niederländischen und französischen Kupferstichs im XV. Jahrhundert*, vol. 2, Vienna, 1910; M. Geisberg, "The Master E. S.," *Print-Collector's Quarterly*, IX, 1922. CAROLINE KARPINSKI

MASTER F. R. (F. L. R.). Italian majolica painter (fl. ca. 1520–40). In 1933 a group of twenty pieces of Italian Renaissance majolica were identified as the work of a single majolica painter. Some had been painted at Faenza, the majority at Urbino. They are variously signed "F. R.," "F. L. R.," and with the Greek letter "psi"; some are unsigned. Examples are a fragment of a majolica plate, *Venus and Cupid*, signed "F. L. R." (Florence, National Museum), and a majolica plate, *Hercules and Omphale*, unsigned but dated 1522 (London, Victoria and Albert). Later, Ballardini equated the painter F. R. with Francesco Xanto Avelli da

Rovigo. Rackham continues to hold that Master F. R. has a separate artistic identity, that he first worked at Faenza, that he moved about 1528 to Urbino where he probably came into contact with Xanto about 1530, perhaps as a painter in the same *bottega*, and that he probably influenced Xanto's later pictorial style. *See* XANTO AVELLI DA ROVIGO, FRANCESCO.

BIBLIOGRAPHY. B. Rackham, "Xanto and 'F. R.': An Insoluble Problem?" *Faenza*, XLIII, 1957.

MASTER F. V. B. Flemish printmaker and publisher (fl. Bruges, ca. 1480–99). An old tradition ascribes the name Franz von Becholt to him. Basing his engraving technique on that of Martin Schongauer, nine of whose prints he copied, Master F. V. B. achieved a fine and regular line and a brilliant use of light and shade that are hardly inferior to his model. Although he derived technical solutions for rendering form from Master E. S., Master F. V. B.'s meticulous observation of natural details is reminiscent of Dirk Bouts and other Bruges masters. One of Master F. V. B.'s engravings, the *Madonna with a Flower*, is in fact based on a painting by Memling. Like the majority of 15th-century northern engravers, he produced ornament prints intended for patterns and decoration. Probably after Master F. V. B. died Israel van Meckenem retouched several of his plates, effaced the original monogram, and substituted his own.

BIBLIOGRAPHY. A. von Bartsch, *Le Peintre-graveur*, new ed., vol. 6, Würzburg, 1920; M. Lehrs, "The Master F V B," *Print-Collector's Quarterly*, X, 1923.

Master E. S., plate from *Ars moriendi*. Engraving. Albertina, Vienna.